INSTRUCTOR'S RESO

EDWARDS
&PENNEY
FIFTH EDITION
CALCULUS
WITH ANALYTIC GEOMETRY

PRENTICE HALL, UPPER SADDLE RIVER, NJ 07458

Supplement Editor: Audra Walsh
Special Projects Manager: Barbara A. Murray
Production Editor: Barbara A. Till
Supplement Cover Manager: Paul Gourhan
Supplement Cover Designer: Liz Nemeth
Manufacturing Buyer: Alan Fischer

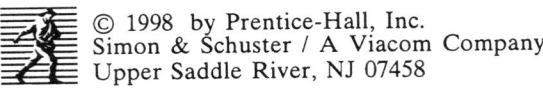

© 1998 by Prentice-Hall, Inc.
Simon & Schuster / A Viacom Company
Upper Saddle River, NJ 07458

All rights reserved. No part of this book may be
reproduced, in any form or by any means,
without permission in writing from the publisher

Printed in the United States of America

10 9 8 7 6 5 4 3 2 1

ISBN 0-13-757741-9

Prentice-Hall International (UK) Limited, *London*
Prentice-Hall of Australia Pty. Limited, *Sydney*
Prentice-Hall Canada, Inc., *London*
Prentice-Hall Hispanoamericana, S.A., *Mexico*
Prentice-Hall of India Private Limited, *New Delhi*
Prentice-Hall of Japan, Inc., *Tokyo*
Simon & Schuster Asia Pte. Ltd., *Singapore*
Editora Prentice-Hall do Brazil, Ltda., *Rio de Janeiro*

Contents

Chapter 1: Functions and Graphs 1

Chapter 2: Prelude to Calculus 18

Chapter 3: The Derivative 36

Chapter 4: Additional Applications of the Derivative 97

Chapter 5: The Integral 140

Chapter 6: Applications of the Integral 167

Chapter 7: Exponential and Logarithmic Functions 193

Chapter 8: Further Calculus of Transcendental Functions 221

Chapter 9: Techniques of Integration 241

Chapter 10: Polar Coordinates and Plane Curves 297

Chapter 11: Infinite Series 335

Chapter 12: Vectors, Curves, and Surfaces in Space 368

Chapter 13: Partial Differentiation 397

Chapter 14: Multiple Integrals 433

Chapter 15: Vector Calculus 458

Appendices 476

Preface

This manual contains solutions to problems in Chapters 1 through 15 of *Calculus with Analytic Geometry*, 5th edition (1998), by C. Henry Edwards and David E. Penney. Because the answers to most odd-numbered problems are given in the *Answer* section of the text, odd-numbered solutions are omitted from this manual whenever the answer alone to such a problem is sufficient. When a solution is long but not difficult, only the outline of a solution may appear. When a suggestion alone is sufficient, we often give only a suggestion, or in a few cases an alternative solution. Rarely, if an answer would spoil the problem for the solver (as in Miscellaneous Problem 117 of Chapter 9), none is given.

Many calculus problems can be solved by more than one method. We generally use the most natural method, but in rare instances offer a "clever" method in its place, but only when its educational value justifies such a substitution. In particular, in working these problems we used only those techniques developed in earlier sections (with rare exceptions, and then only when the alternative method is accessible and useful to the reader).

We gratefully acknowledge the encouragement, advice, and assistance of our colleagues and students in helping us to correct errors in previous editions of this manual. Special thanks go to Nancy and Mary Toscano of Toscano Document Engineers (Somerville, MA), whose staff checked the worked-out examples, answers to odd-numbered problems, and solutions to most of the problems in this manual. We also checked most solutions with *Mathematica*. Will Kazez and Ted Shifrin helped us with TeX and Adobe Illustrator, the two programs used to prepare the final version of this manual. Most of all, we thank Carol W. Penney for typesetting the text of all solutions manuals.

C. Henry Edwards (hedwards@math.uga.edu)

David E. Penney (dpenney@math.uga.edu)

The University of Georgia, Athens

August 1997

Typeset by $\mathcal{AMS}$-TeX

Chapter 1: Functions and Graphs
Section 1.1

1. (a) $f(-a) = -1/a$
   (b) $f(a^{-1}) = a$
   (c) $f(\sqrt{a}) = 1/\sqrt{a}$
   (d) $f(a^2) = 1/(a^2)$

2. (a) $f(-a) = a^2 + 5$
   (b) $f(a^{-1}) = a^{-2} + 5$
   (c) $f(\sqrt{a}) = a + 5$
   (d) $f(a^2) = a^4 + 5$

3. (a) $f(-a) = \dfrac{1}{a^2+5}$
   (b) $f(a^{-1}) = \dfrac{a^2}{1+5a^2}$
   (c) $f(\sqrt{a}) = \dfrac{1}{a+5}$
   (d) $f(a^2) = \dfrac{1}{a^4+5}$

4. (a) $f(-a) = \sqrt{1+a^2+a^4}$
   (b) $f(a^{-1}) = \sqrt{1+a^{-2}+a^{-4}}$
   (c) $f(\sqrt{a}) = \sqrt{1+a+a^2}$
   (d) $f(a^2) = \sqrt{1+a^4+a^8}$

5. $g(a) = 5$: $3a + 4 = 5$; $3a = 1$; $a = \frac{1}{3}$

6. $g(a) = 5$: $\dfrac{1}{2a-1} = 5$; $2a - 1 = \frac{1}{5}$; $2a = \frac{6}{5}$; $a = \frac{3}{5}$

7. $\sqrt{a^2 + 16} = 5$; $a^2 = 9$; $a = \pm 3$

8. $a^3 - 3 = 5$; $a^3 = 8$; $a = 2$

9. $\sqrt[3]{a+25} = 5$; $a + 25 = 125$; $a = 100$

10. $2a^2 - a + 4 = 5$; $2a^2 - a - 1 = 0$; $(2a+1)(a-1) = 0$; $a = 1$ or $a = -\frac{1}{2}$

11. $f(a+h) - f(a) = 3(a+h) - 2 - (3a - 2) = 3h$

12. $f(a+h) - f(a) = 1 - 2(a+h) - (1 - 2a) = -2h$

13. $f(a+h) - f(a) = (a+h)^2 - a^2 = 2ah + h^2$

14. $f(a+h) - f(a) = (a+h)^2 + 2(a+h) - (a^2 + 2a) = 2ah + h^2 + 2h$

15. $f(a+h) - f(a) = \dfrac{1}{a+h} - \dfrac{1}{a} = \dfrac{a-(a+h)}{a(a+h)} = -\dfrac{h}{a(a+h)}$

16. $f(a+h) - f(a) = \dfrac{2}{a+h+1} - \dfrac{2}{a+1} = -\dfrac{2h}{(a+h+1)(a+1)}$

17. $f(x) = 1$ if $x > 0$; $f(0) = 0$; $f(x) = -1$ if $x < 0$. Thus the range of f is the three-element set $\{-1, 0, 1\}$.

18. $f(n/3) = n$ for every integer n, so f takes on all integral values. Because f can assume only integral values, its range is the set Z of all integers.

19. Because the exponent takes on all integral values, odd and even, the range of f is the two-element set $\{-1, 1\}$.

20. $\{32, 55, 78, 101, 124, 147, 170, 193, 216, 239, 262, 285\}$

21. The set R of all real numbers

22. The set R of all real numbers

23. The set R of all real numbers

24. The set $[0, \infty)$ of all nonnegative real numbers, because $\sqrt{t}$ is defined only for $t \geq 0$.

25. The domain of f consists of those numbers x for which $3x - 5 \geq 0$: The interval $[\frac{5}{3}, \infty)$.

26. The set R of all real numbers, because $\sqrt[3]{x}$ is defined for all real values of x.

27. $1 - 2t \geq 0$; $t \leq \frac{1}{2}$

28. The set of all real numbers other than -2; in interval notation, $(-\infty, -2) \cup (-2, \infty)$.

29. The set of all real numbers other than 3.

30. We require $3 - t \geq 0$ and $3 - t \neq 0$, thus $t < 3$.

31. The set $\mathbb{R}$ of all real numbers, because $x^2 + 9 \geq 0$ for all real x.

32. We require $4 - z^2 > 0$, and thus that $-2 < z < 2$. Answer: the interval $(-2, 2)$.

33. We require $x \geq 0$ and $4 - \sqrt{x} \geq 0$. The latter implies $x \leq 16$, so the domain of f is the interval $[0, 16]$.

34. We require $\dfrac{x+1}{x-1} \geq 0$ and that $x \neq 1$. The former condition holds when numerator and denominator have the same sign, which implies $x > 1$ or $x \leq -1$. Thus the domain of f consists of those numbers x such that $x \leq -1$ together with those numbers x such that $x > 1$.

35. The domain of g consists of the set of all real numbers other than zero.

36. If a square has perimeter P then each of its edges has length $P/4$, so the area of the square is:
$$A(P) = \tfrac{1}{16}P^2, \qquad P \geq 0 \quad (\text{or } P > 0).$$

37. The radius of the circle is $r = \sqrt{A/\pi}$ and its circumference is $C = 2\pi r$. Therefore
$$C(A) = 2\sqrt{\pi A}, \qquad A \geq 0 \quad (\text{or } A > 0).$$

38. The radius of the sphere is $r = \sqrt{S/(4\pi)}$ and its volume is
$$V = \tfrac{4}{3}\pi r^3, \quad \text{so} \quad V(S) = \tfrac{1}{6}S\sqrt{S/\pi}, \qquad S \geq 0 \quad (\text{or } S > 0).$$

39. $C(F) = \tfrac{5}{9}(F - 32)$, $F > -459.67$.

40. If the rectangle has base x and height y, then $2x + 2y = 100$, so $y = 50 - x$.

41. A diagonal of the rectangle has length 4. If the rectangle has base x and height y, then $x^2 + y^2 = 16$ by the Pythagorean theorem, so $y = \sqrt{16 - x^2}$. All that remains is to substitute into the formula $A = xy$ to obtain $A(x) = x\sqrt{16 - x^2}$, $0 \leq x \leq 4$ (or $0 < x < 4$).

42. If x new wells are drilled, there will be $20 + x$ wells in all, each producing $200 - 5x$ barrels of oil per day. Hence the total daily production p of the oil field will be $p(x) = (20 + x)(200 - 5x)$, with domain consisting of all integers x in the range $0 \leq x \leq 40$.

43. Denote the height of the box by y and note that $x^2 y = 324$. The cost C of the box is the sum of the cost $(2x^2)$ of its base, four times the cost (xy) of one of its sides, and the cost (x^2) of its top. Thus $C = 3x^2 + 4xy$, and so
$$C(x) = 3x^2 + \dfrac{1296}{x}, \qquad x > 0.$$

44. If the rectangle has base of length y, then $2x + 2y = 36$, so that $y = 18 - x$ is the radius of the base of the generated cylinder. The height of the cylinder is x, so its volume is given by
$$V(x) = \pi(18 - x)^2 x, \qquad 0 \leq x \leq 18 \quad (\text{or } 0 < x < 18).$$

45. If the cylinder has height h, then $\pi r^2 h = 1000$. The total surface area of the cylinder is $2\pi r^2 + 2\pi rh$, so
$$A(r) = 2\pi r^2 + \dfrac{2000}{r}, \qquad r > 0.$$

46. If the box has height y, then $2x^2 + 4xy = 600$. Because the volume V is $V = x^2 y$, it follows that
$$V(x) = \tfrac{1}{2}x\left(300 - x^2\right), \qquad 0 < x \leq \sqrt{300} \quad \left(\text{or } 0 < x < \sqrt{300}\right).$$

47. The height of the box is x and its base is a square with edge length $50 - 2x$, so its volume is given by
$$V(x) = x(50 - 2x)^2, \qquad 0 \leq x \leq 25 \qquad (\text{or } 0 < x < 25).$$

48. $A(x) = x(50 - x)$, $0 \leq x \leq 50$. Here is a table of a few values of the function A at some special numbers in its domain:

x	0	5	10	15	20	25	30	35	40	45	50
A	0	225	400	525	600	625	600	525	400	225	0

It appears that when $x = 25$ (so the rectangle is a square), the rectangle has maximum area 625.

49. Recall that the total daily production of the oil field is $p(x) = (20 + x)(200 - 5x)$ if x new wells are drilled (where x is an integer satisfying $0 \leq x \leq 40$). Here is a table of *all* the values of the function p:

x	0	1	2	3	4	5	6	7
p	4000	4095	4180	4255	4320	4375	4420	4455

x	8	9	10	11	12	13	14	15
p	4480	4495	4500	4495	4480	4455	4420	4375

x	16	17	18	19	20	21	22	23
p	4320	4255	4180	4095	4000	3895	3780	3655

x	24	25	26	27	28	29	30	31
p	3520	3375	3220	3055	2880	2695	2500	2295

x	32	33	34	35	36	37	38	39
p	2080	1855	1620	1375	1120	855	580	295

and, finally, $p(40) = 0$. Answer: Drill ten new wells.

50. The surface area A of the box of Example 5 was
$$A(x) = 2x^2 + 500/x, \qquad 0 < x < \infty.$$

The restrictions x, $y \geq 1$ imply that $1 \leq x \leq \sqrt{125}$. A small number of values of A, rounded to three places, are in the following table.

x	1	2	3	4	5	6	7	8	9	10	11
A	502	258	185	157	150	155	169	191	218	250	287

It appears that A is minimized when $x = y = 5$.

52. ROUND(x) = FLOOR$\left(x + \frac{1}{2}\right)$. The range of ROUND$(kx)$ is the set of all integers if k is nonzero; it is $\{0\}$ if $k = 0$.

53. The range of $g(x) = \frac{1}{10}$ROUND$(10x)$ is the set of integral multiples of $\frac{1}{10}$.

54. ROUND2$(x) = \frac{1}{100}$ROUND$(100x)$.

55. ROUND4$(x) = \frac{1}{10000}$ROUND$(10000x)$.

56. CHOP4$(x) = \frac{1}{10000}$FLOOR$(10000x)$.

57.

x	0.0	0.2	0.4	0.6	0.8	1.0
y	1.0	0.44	−0.04	−0.44	−0.76	−1.0

The sign change occurs between $x = 0.2$ and $x = 0.4$.

x	0.20	0.25	0.30	0.35	0.40
y	0.44	0.3125	0.19	0.0725	−0.04

The sign change occurs between $x = 0.35$ and $x = 0.40$.

x	0.35	0.36	0.37	0.38	0.39	0.40
y	0.0725	0.0496	0.0269	0.0044	−0.0179	−0.04

From this point on, the data for y will be rounded.

x	0.380	0.382	0.384	0.386	0.388	0.390
y	0.0044	−0.0001	−0.0045	−0.0090	−0.0135	−0.0179

Answer (rounded to two places): 0.38. The quadratic formula yields the two roots $\frac{1}{2}\left(3 \pm \sqrt{5}\right)$; the smaller of these is approximately 0.3819660112501051517955.

58. 2.62 **59.** 1.24 **60.** −3.24 **61.** 0.72 **62.** 2.78
63. 3.21 **64.** 7.79 **65.** 1.62 **66.** −9.28

Section 1.2

1. $y = \frac{3}{2}x$ or $3x = 2y$.
2. $x = 7$ 3. $y = -5$
4. The points $(2, 0)$ and $(0, -3)$ lie on L, so the slope of L is $\frac{3}{2}$. An equation of L is $2y = 3x - 6$.
5. The slope of L is 2, so an equation of L is $y - 3 = 2(x - 5)$.
6. $2y + 7 = x$
7. The slope of L is -1; an equation is $y - 2 = 4 - x$.
8. $y = 6x + 7$.
9. The slope of L is -2; equation: $y - 5 = -2(x - 1)$.
10. The *other* line has slope $-\frac{1}{2}$, so L has slope 2 and therefore equation $y - 4 = 2(x + 2)$.
11. $x^2 - 4x + 4 + y^2 = 4$: $(x-2)^2 + (y-0)^2 = 2^2$. Center $(2, 0)$, radius 2.
12. $x^2 + y^2 + 6y + 9 = 9$: $(x-0)^2 + (y+3)^2 = 3^2$. Center $(0, -3)$, radius 3.
13. $(x+1)^2 + (y+1)^2 = 2^2$.
14. $x^2 + 10x + 25 + y^2 - 20y + 100 = 25$: $(x+5)^2 + (y-10)^2 = 5^2$. Center $(-5, 10)$, radius 5.
15. $x^2 + y^2 + x - y = \frac{1}{2}$: $x^2 + x + \frac{1}{4} + y^2 - y + \frac{1}{4} = 1$; $(x + \frac{1}{2})^2 + (y - \frac{1}{2})^2 = 1$.
16. $x^2 + y^2 - \frac{2}{3}x - \frac{4}{3}y = \frac{11}{9}$: $x^2 - \frac{2}{3}x + \frac{1}{9} + y^2 - \frac{4}{3}y + \frac{4}{9} = \frac{16}{9}$; $(x - \frac{1}{3})^2 + (y - \frac{2}{3})^2 = (\frac{4}{3})^2$. Center $(\frac{1}{3}, \frac{2}{3})$, radius $\frac{4}{3}$.
17. $y = (x - 3)^2$: Opens upward, vertex at $(3, 0)$.
18. $y - 16 = -x^2$: Opens downward, vertex at $(0, 16)$.
19. $y - 3 = (x + 1)^2$: Opens upward, vertex at $(-1, 3)$.
20. $2y = x^2 - 4x + 4 + 4$: $y - 2 = \frac{1}{2}(x - 2)^2$. Opens upward, vertex at $(2, 2)$.
21. $y = 5(x^2 + 4x + 4) + 3 = 5(x + 2)^2 + 3$: Opens upward, vertex at $(-2, 3)$.
22. $y = -(x^2 - x) = -(x^2 - x + \frac{1}{4}) + \frac{1}{4}$: $y - \frac{1}{4} = -(x - \frac{1}{2})^2$. Opens downward, vertex at $(\frac{1}{2}, \frac{1}{4})$.

23. $x^2 - 6x + 9 + y^2 + 8y + 16 = 25$: $(x-3)^2 + (y+4)^2 = 5^5$. Circle, center $(3, -4)$, radius 5.
24. $(x-1)^2 + (y+1)^2 = 0$: The graph consists of the single point $(1, -1)$.
25. $(x+1)^2 + (y+3)^2 = -10$: There are no points on the graph.
26. $x^2 + y^2 - x + 3y + 2.5 = 0$: $x^2 - x + 0.25 + y^2 + 3y + 2.25 = 0$: $(x - 0.5)^2 + (y + 1.5)^2 = 0$. The graph consists of the single point $(0.5, -1.5)$.

27. The graph is shown below.

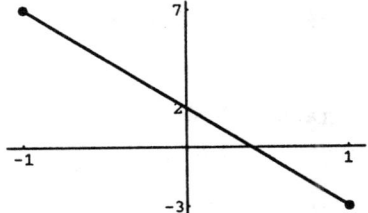

28. The graph is shown below.

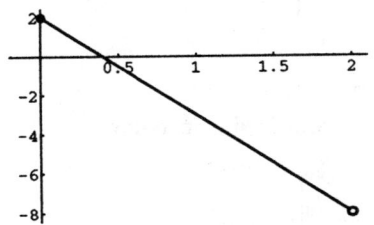

29. The graph is shown below.

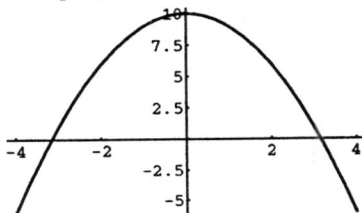

30. The graph is shown below.

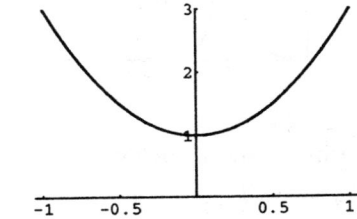

31. The graph is shown below.

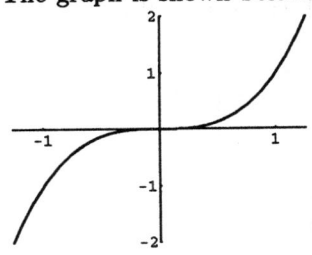

32. The graph is shown below.

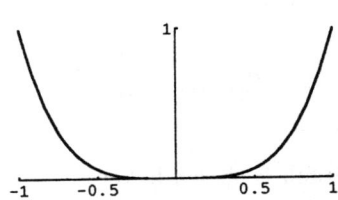

33. The graph is shown below.

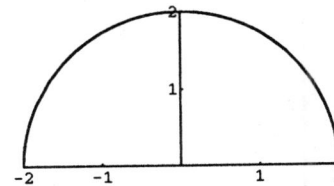

34. The graph is shown below.

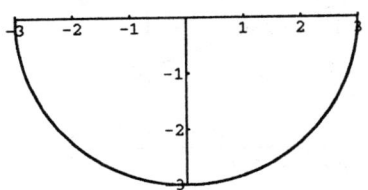

35. The domain of f consists of those numbers x such that $|x| \geq 3$. The graph is shown below.

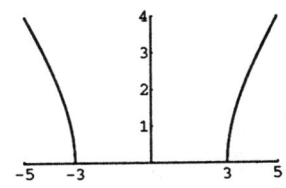

36. The graph is shown below.

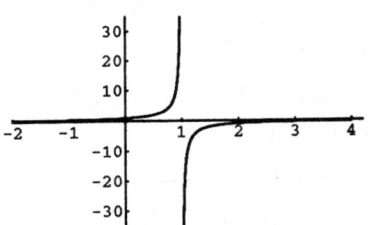

Section 1.2 Graphs of Equations and Functions

37. The graph is shown below.

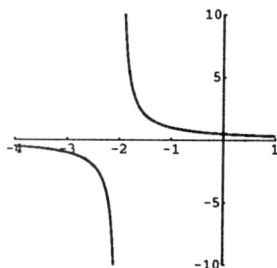

38. The graph is shown below.

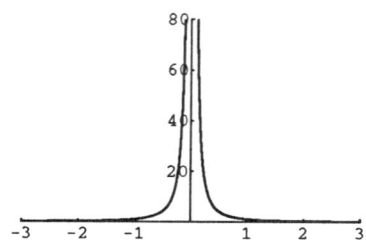

39. The graph is shown below.

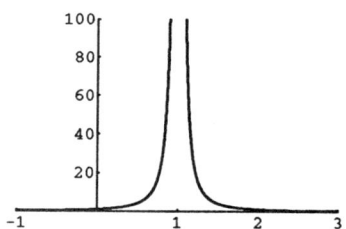

40. The graph is shown below.

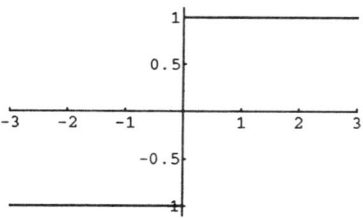

41. The graph is shown below.

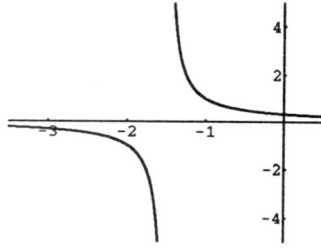

42. The graph is shown below.

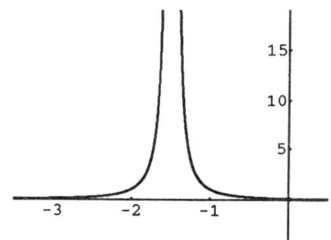

43. The graph is shown below.

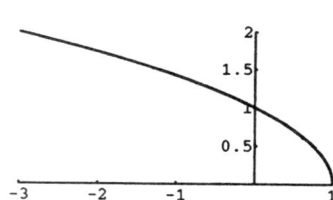

44. The graph is shown below.

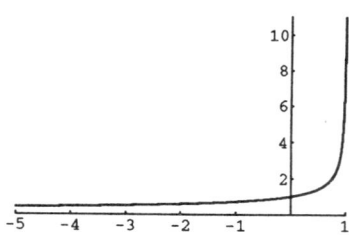

45. The graph is shown below.

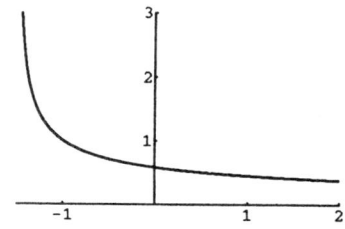

46. The graph is shown below.

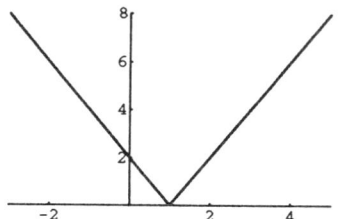

6   **Section 1.2 Graphs of Equations and Functions**

47. The graph is shown below.

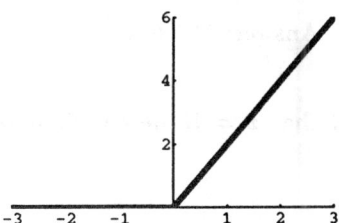

48. The graph is shown below.

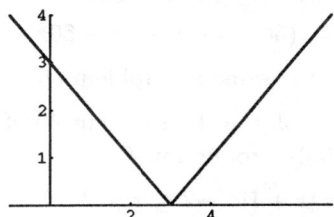

49. The graph is shown below.

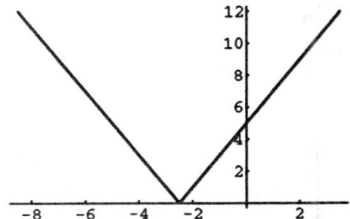

50. The graph is shown below.

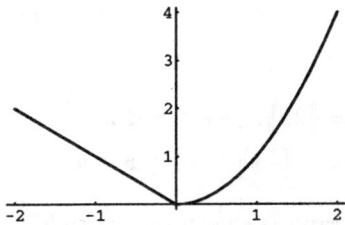

51. The graph is shown below.

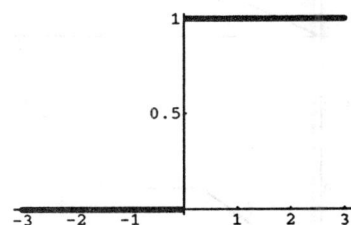

52. The graph is shown below.

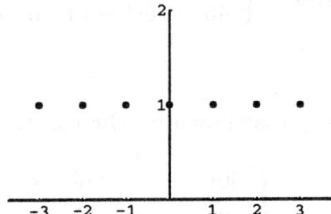

53. The graph is shown below.

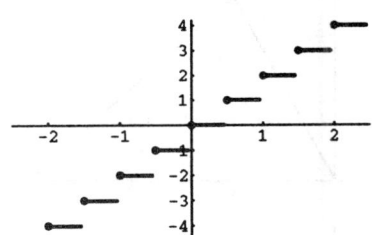

54. The graph is shown below.

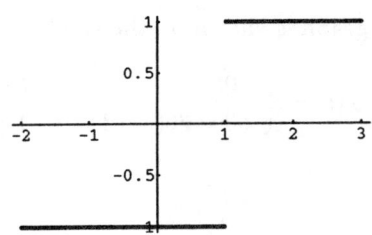

55. The graph is shown below.

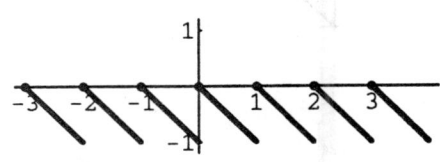

56. The graph is shown below.

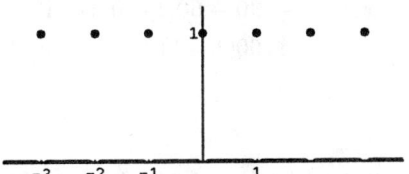

57. $y = 2(x^2 - 3x) + 7 = 2(x^2 - 3x + 2.25) + 2.5 = 2(x - 1.5)^2 + 2.5$, so the vertex is at the point $(1.5, 2.5)$.

58. $(2.5, -1.5)$ **59.** $(2.25, 1.75)$ **60.** $(3.2, -2.2)$ **61.** $(2.25, 8.5)$

62. $(-3.4, 4.8)$ **63.** $\left(-\frac{4}{3}, \frac{25}{3}\right)$ **64.** $\left(\frac{17}{9}, \frac{37}{9}\right)$

Section 1.2 Graphs of Equations and Functions   7

65. $y = -16(t^2 - 6t) = -16(t^2 - 6t + 9) + 144 = -16(t-3)^2 + 144$. Answer: 144 feet.

66. $A(x) = x(50 - x) = -(x^2 - 50x + 625) + 625 = 625 - (x - 25)^2$. Answer: 625 ft^2.

67. This is the same as Problem 66.

68. See the solution to Problem 49 of Section 1.1. There we found that $x = 10$ new wells maximizes total daily production P.

69. $f(x) = |x + 1|, \ -2 \leq x \leq 2$.

70. The function is given by:
$$f(x) = \begin{cases} 2x + 6 & \text{if } -3 \leq x < -2; \\ 2 & \text{if } -2 \leq x < 2; \\ \frac{1}{3}(10 - 2x) & \text{if } 2 \leq x \leq 5. \end{cases}$$

71. $f(x) = [\![2x]\!], \ -1 \leq x < 2$.

72. $f(x) = -[\![\frac{1}{2}x]\!], \ -4 \leq x < 4$.

73. The graph is shown on the right.
$$x(t) = \begin{cases} 45t & \text{if } t < 1; \\ 45 + 75(t - 1) & \text{if } 1 \leq t. \end{cases}$$

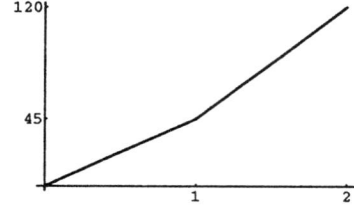

74. The graph is shown on the right.
$$x(t) = \begin{cases} 60t & \text{if } t < 1; \\ 60 & \text{if } 1 \leq t < 1.5; \\ 60(t - 0.5) & \text{if } 1.5 \leq t. \end{cases}$$

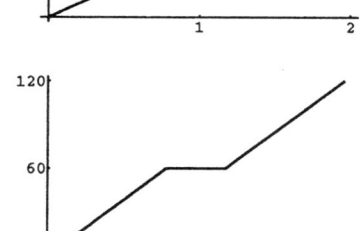

75. The graph is shown on the right.
$$x(t) = \begin{cases} 60t & \text{if } t < 1; \\ 60 - 30(t - 1) & \text{if } 1 \leq t. \end{cases}$$

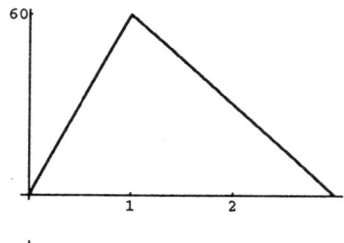

76. The graph is shown on the right.
$$x(t) = \begin{cases} 60t & \text{if } t < 0.5; \\ 30 - 60(t - 0.5) & \text{if } 0.5 \leq t < 1; \\ 60(t - 1) & \text{if } 1 \leq t. \end{cases}$$

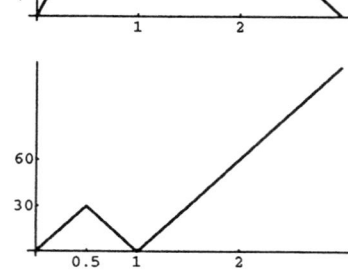

77. $C(p) = 0.03p + 0.68$. It costs $0.68 to set up the press and $0.03 for each page printed. The graph is shown on the right.

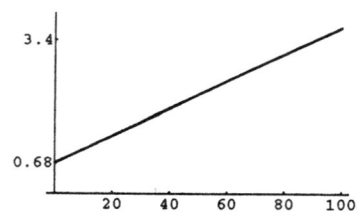

78. $C(x) = 27 + 0.35x$. $C(175) = 88.25$, so the cost for day 3 was $88.25. The slope represents 35 cents per mile. The y-intercept represents the base charge of 27 dollars per day. The graph is shown on the right.

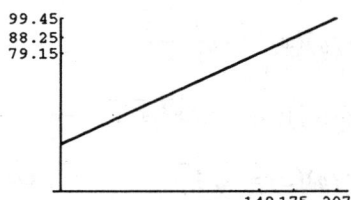

79. The graph is shown on the right.
$$C(x) = \begin{cases} 8 & \text{if } 0 < x \leq 8; \\ 8 - 0.8[\![-(x-8)]\!] & \text{if } 8 < x \leq 16. \end{cases}$$

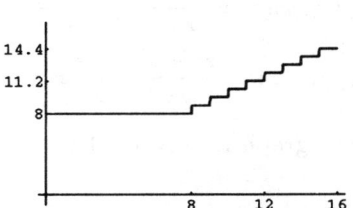

80. The graph is shown on the right.
$$C(x) = \begin{cases} 3 & \text{if } 0 < x \leq 2; \\ 3 - 0.5[\![-2(x-2)]\!] & \text{if } 2 < x \leq 10; \\ 11 - 0.5[\![-(x-10)]\!] & \text{if } 10 < x \leq 20. \end{cases}$$

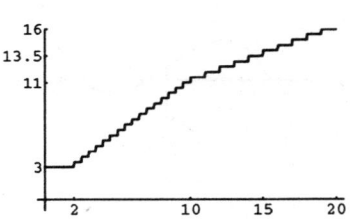

81. $V(p) = 1.667/p$. Volumes are $V(0.5) = 3.334$ and $V(5) = 0.3334$. The graph is shown on the right.

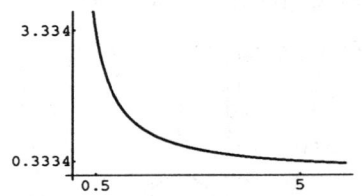

82. $T(t) = 61.25 + 17.85\cos(2\pi t/365)$. Average temperatures: $T(91) = 61.0$ on October 15 and $T(273) = 61.3$ on April 15. The graph is shown on the right.

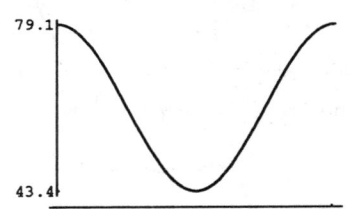

Section 1.3

1. $(f+g)(x) = x^2 + 3x - 2$, $(f \cdot g)(x) = x^3 + 3x^2 - x - 3$, and $(f/g)(x) = \dfrac{x+1}{x^2 + 2x - 3}$. The first two have domain the set $\mathbb{R}$ of all real numbers. The third has domain consisting of the set of all real numbers other than 1 and -3.

2. $(f+g)(x) = \dfrac{1}{x-1} + \dfrac{1}{2x+1}$, $x \neq 1, -\tfrac{1}{2}$; $(f \cdot g)(x) = \dfrac{1}{(x-1)(2x+1)}$, same domain; $(f/g)(x) = \dfrac{2x+1}{x-1}$, same domain.

3. $(f+g)(x) = \sqrt{x} + \sqrt{x-2}$, domain $x \geq 2$; $(f \cdot g)(x) = \sqrt{x^2 - 2x}$, same domain; $(f/g)(x) = \sqrt{\dfrac{x}{x-2}}$, $x > 2$.

4. $(f+g)(x) = \sqrt{x+1} + \sqrt{5-x}$, $-1 \leq x \leq 5$; $(f \cdot g)(x) = \sqrt{5 + 4x - x^2}$, same domain.

$(f/g)(x) = \sqrt{\dfrac{x+1}{5-x}}, \quad -1 \le x < 5.$

5. $(f+g)(x) = \sqrt{x^2+1} + \dfrac{1}{\sqrt{4-x^2}}, \quad -2 < x < 2;\quad (f \cdot g)(x) = \dfrac{\sqrt{x^2+1}}{\sqrt{4-x^2}},$ same domain; $(f/g)(x) = \sqrt{4+3x^2-x^4},$ same domain.

6. $(f+g)(x) = \dfrac{x-1}{x-2} + \dfrac{x+1}{x+2}, \quad x \ne \pm 2;\quad (f \cdot g)(x) = \dfrac{x^2-1}{x^2-4},$ same domain; $(f/g)(x) = \dfrac{x^2+x-2}{x^2-x-2}, \quad x \ne -2, -1, 2.$

7. The graph is shown below.

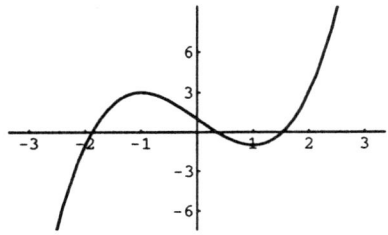

8. The graph is shown below.

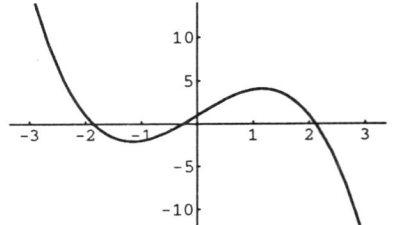

9. The graph is shown below.

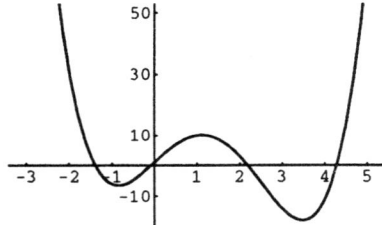

10. The graph is shown below.

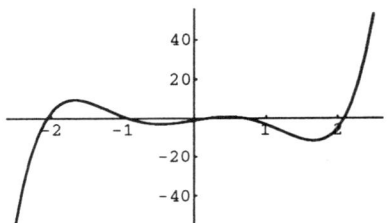

11. The graph is shown below.

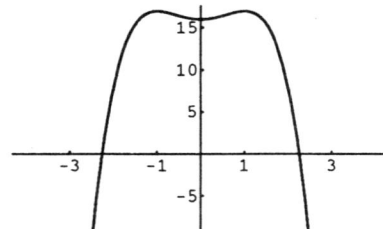

12. The graph is shown below.

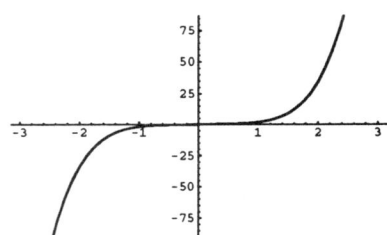

13. The graph is shown below.

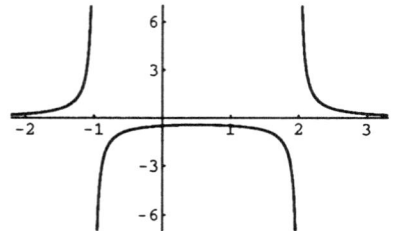

14. The graph is shown below.

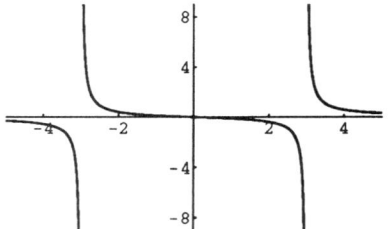

15. The graph is shown below.

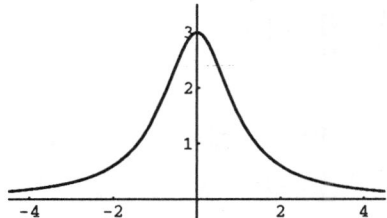

16. The graph is shown below.

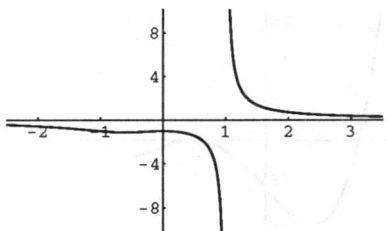

17. The graph is shown below.

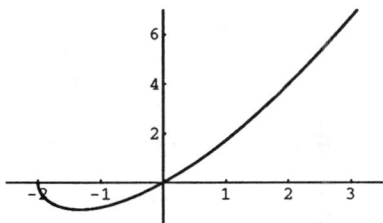

18. The graph is shown below.

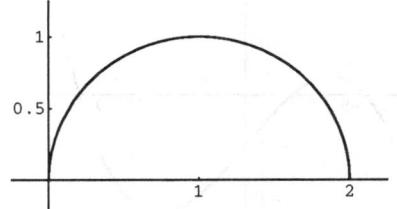

19. The graph is shown below.

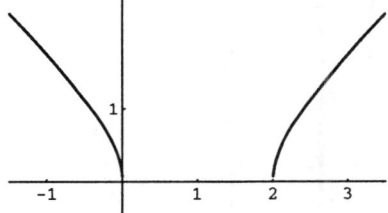

20. The graph is shown below.

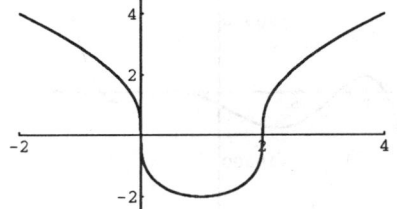

21. The graph is shown below.

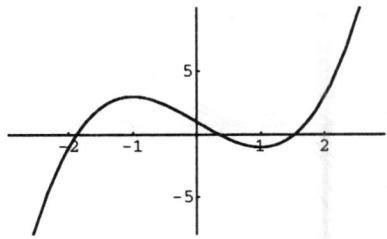

22. The graph is shown below.

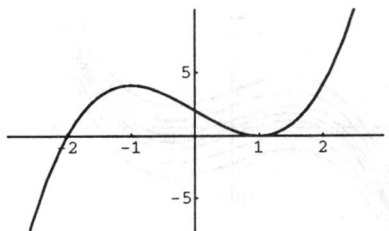

23. The graph is shown below.

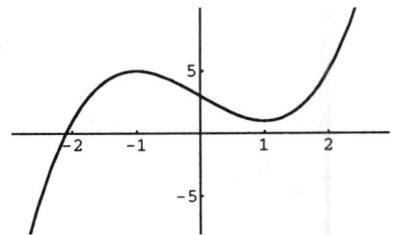

24. The graph is shown below.

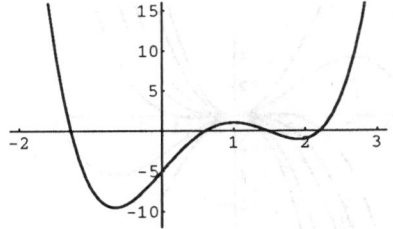

Section 1.3 A Brief Catalog of Functions, Part 1

25. The graph is shown below.

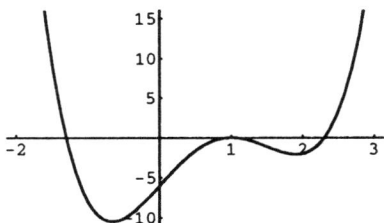

26. The graph is shown below.

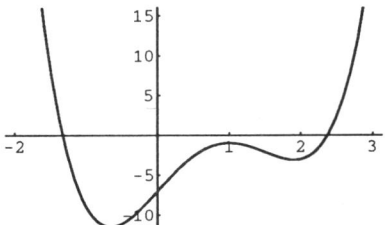

27. The graph is shown below.

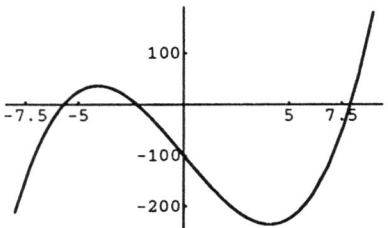

28. The graph is shown below.

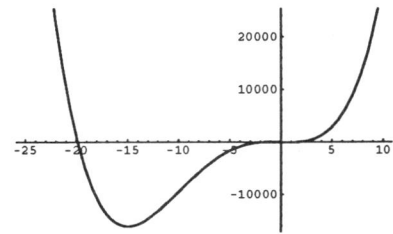

29. The graph is shown below.

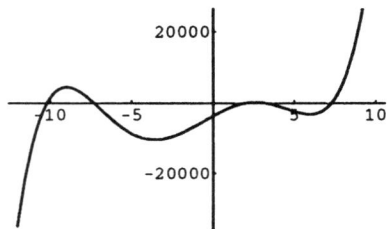

30. The graph is shown below.

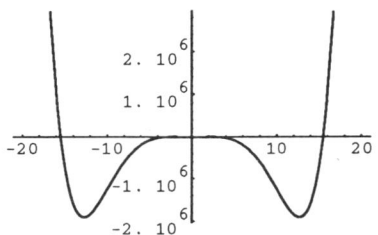

31. Graphs are shown below.

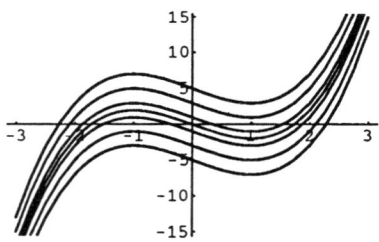

32. Graphs are shown below.

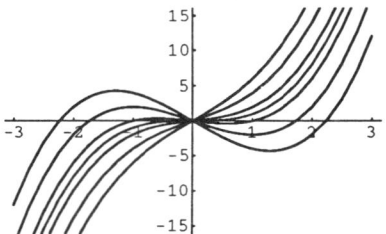

33. Graphs are shown below.

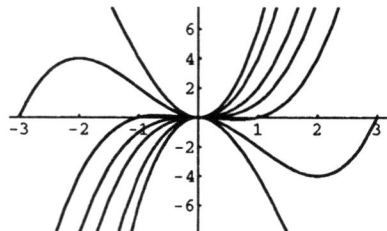

34. Graphs are shown below.

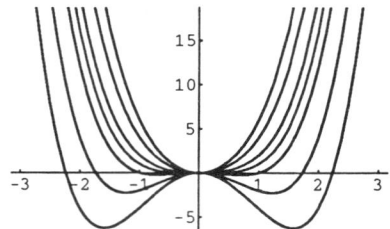

35. Graphs are shown below.

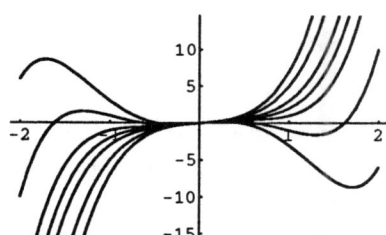

36. Graphs are shown below.

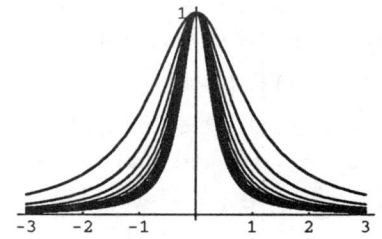

37. Graphs are shown below.

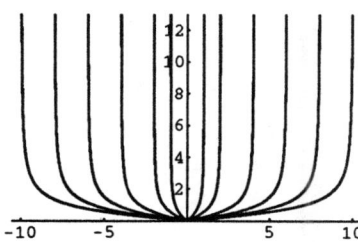

38. The length of the airfoil is approximately 1.0089; the width is appproximately 0.200057.

Section 1.4

1. Fig. 1.4.29 **2.** Fig. 1.4.33 **3.** Fig. 1.4.27 **4.** Fig. 1.4.32
5. Fig. 1.4.35 **6.** Fig. 1.4.28 **7.** Fig. 1.4.31 **8.** Fig. 1.4.36
9. Fig. 1.4.34 **10.** Fig. 1.4.30

11. $f(g(x)) = 1 - (2x+3)^2 = -4x^2 - 12x - 8;\quad g(f(x)) = 2(1-x^2) + 3 = -2x^2 + 5.$

12. $f(g(x)) = -17;\quad g(f(x)) = 17.$

14. $f(g(x)) = \left(\dfrac{1}{x^2+1}\right)^2 + 1;\quad g(f(x)) = \dfrac{1}{(x^2+1)^2 + 1}.$

16. $f(g(x)) = \sqrt{\cos x};\quad g(f(x)) = \cos\sqrt{x}.$

17. $f(g(x)) = \sin(g(x)) = \sin(x^3) = \sin x^3;\quad g(f(x)) = g(\sin x) = (\sin x)^3 = \sin^3 x.$ The graphs of $f(g)$ and $g(f)$ are shown next. Which is which?

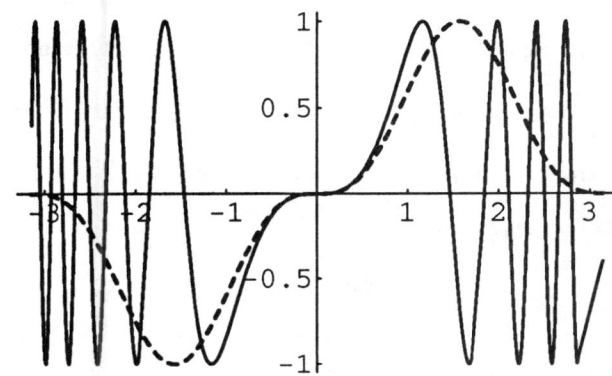

18. $f(g(x)) = \sin(\cos x),\quad g(f(x)) = \cos(\sin x).$

20. $f(g(x)) = 1 - \sin^2 x = \cos^2 x$; $g(f(x)) = \sin(1-x^2)$.
22. $k = 3$, $g(x) = 4 - x$
23. $h(x) = (2x - x^2)^{1/2}$: $k = 1/2$, $g(x) = 2x - x^2$
24. $k = 17$, $g(x) = 1 + x^4$
26. $h(x) = (4x - 6)^{4/3} = [(4x-6)^4]^{1/3} = [(4x-6)^{1/3}]^4$, so here are three correct answers (and there are others): $k = 4/3$ and $g(x) = 4x - 6$; $k = 1/3$ and $g(x) = (4x-6)^4$; $k = 4$ and $g(x) = (4x-6)^{1/3}$.
28. $k = -1$, $g(x) = 1 + x^2$ would seem to be the most natural answer.
29. $k = 1/2$ and $g(x) = \dfrac{1}{\sqrt{x+10}}$; $k = -1/2$ and $g(x) = x + 10$.
30. $k = 3$ and $g(x) = \dfrac{1}{1 + x + x^2}$; $k = -3$ and $g(x) = 1 + x + x^2$.

31.	one	32.	three	33.	one	34.	three	35.	five
36.	one	37.	three	38.	two	39.	six	40.	six
41.	3.32193 months	42.	14.275 years	43.	27.005 years	44.	276.92 years		
45.	98.15 years	46.	-0.7666	47.	4.84891	48.	$-0.9053, 1.132, 31.364$		

Chapter 1 Miscellaneous

1. $x \geq 4$ 2. $x \neq 2$ 3. $x \neq \pm 3$ 4. The set $\mathbb{R}$ of all real numbers
5. $x \geq 0$ 6. $x \neq 0, 2$ 7. $x \leq \frac{2}{3}$ 8. $-3 < x < 3$
9. $\mathbb{R}$ 10. $[2, 4]$
11. $100 \leq 800/p \leq 200$; $1 \leq 8/p \leq 2$; $p \leq 8 \leq 2p$ (because $p > 0$); $4 \leq p \leq 8$.
12. $70 \leq 32 + \frac{9}{5}C \leq 90$: $38 \leq \frac{9}{5}C \leq 58$; $\frac{190}{9} \leq C \leq \frac{290}{9}$. In approximate terms, $21.1 \leq C \leq 32.2$.
13. First, $R = E/I = 100/I$, so $25 < 100/I < 50$; $\frac{1}{50} < I/100 < \frac{1}{25}$; $2 < I < 4$.
14. Here, $\dfrac{L}{32} = \dfrac{T^2}{4\pi^2}$, but because $3 < L < 4$, $\dfrac{3}{32} < \dfrac{T^2}{4\pi^2} < \dfrac{4}{32}$; $\dfrac{12\pi^2}{32} < T^2 < \dfrac{16\pi^2}{32}$. But $T > 0$, and therefore $\dfrac{\pi}{4}\sqrt{6} < T < \dfrac{\pi}{2}\sqrt{2}$.
15. If the cube has edge length x, then $V = x^3$ and $S = 6x^2$. The latter implies that $x = (S/6)^{1/2}$, and thus that $V(S) = (S/6)^{3/2}$, $0 < S < \infty$.
16. If the cylinder has radius and height x, then its volume is $V = \pi x^3$ and its total surface area is $S = 2\pi x^2 + 2\pi x^2 = 4\pi x^2$; but $x = (V/\pi)^{1/3}$, so $S = S(V) = 4\pi(V/\pi)^{2/3}$, $0 < V < \infty$.
17. Let x denote the length of each of the three (equal) sides of the triangle. Draw an altitude of the triangle and apply the Pythagorean theorem to find that the altitude has length $h = \dfrac{\sqrt{3}}{2}x$. Thus the area of the triangle is $A = \frac{1}{2}xh = \dfrac{\sqrt{3}}{4}x^2$. But $x = \frac{1}{3}P$, so $A = A(P) = \dfrac{\sqrt{3}}{36}P^2$, $0 < P < \infty$.
18. If r is the radius of the circle, then its circumference is $2\pi r = 100 - x$, so $r = \dfrac{100 - x}{2\pi}$. The total area is $A = (x/4)^2 + \pi r^2$, so $A(x) = \frac{1}{16}x^2 + \dfrac{(100-x)^2}{4\pi}$, $0 < x < 100$.
19. $y - 5 = 2(x + 3)$ 20. $y + 1 = -3(x - 4)$
21. $2y = x - 10$ 22. $2y = 3x - 12$
23. Rewrite $y - 2x = 10$ in the slope-intercept form $y = 2x + 10$. This line has slope 2; because L is perpendicular to it, L has slope $-1/2$.

24. The segment has slope 2 and midpoint $(2, -3)$, so L has slope $-1/2$ and equation $y+3 = -\frac{1}{2}(x-2)$.

25. Fig. 1.MP.6   **26.** Fig. 1.MP.9   **27.** Fig. 1.MP.4   **28.** Fig. 1.MP.11

29. Fig. 1.MP.3   **30.** Fig. 1.MP.10   **31.** Fig. 1.MP.7   **32.** Fig. 1.MP.2

33. Fig. 1.MP.8   **34.** Fig. 1.MP.5

35. The graph is shown below.

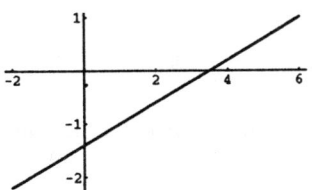

36. The graph is shown below.

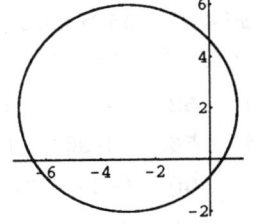

37. The graph is shown below.

38. The graph is shown below.

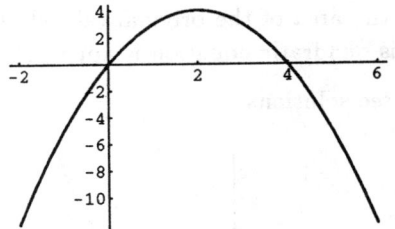

39. The graph is shown below.

40. The graph is shown below.

41. The graph is shown below.

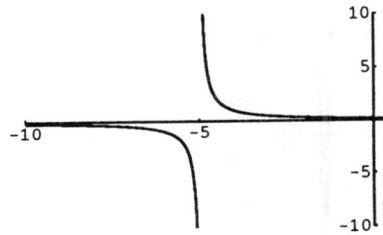

42. The graph is shown below.

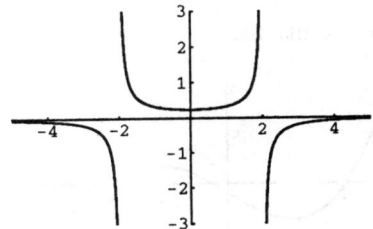

Chapter 1 Miscellaneous

43. The graph is shown below.

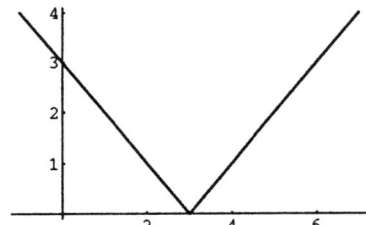

44. The graph is shown below.

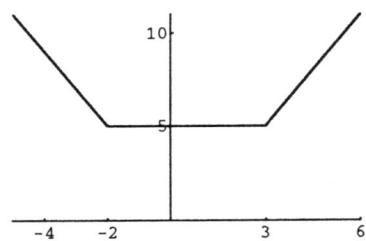

45. $|a+b+c| = |(a+b)+c| \leq |a+b|+|c| \leq |a|+|b|+|c|$.

46. $|a| = |(a-b)+b| \leq |a-b|+|b|$. Therefore $|a|-|b| \leq |a-b|$.

47. If $x-3 > 0$ and $x+2 > 0$, then $x > 3$ and $x > -2$, so $x > 3$. If $x-3 < 0$ and $x+2 < 0$, then $x < 3$ and $x < -2$, so $x < -2$. Answer: $(\infty, -2) \cup (3, \infty)$.

48. $(x-1)(x-2) < 0$: $x-1$ and $x-2$ have opposite signs, so either $x < 1$ and $x > 2$ (which leads to *no* values of x) or $x > 1$ and $x < 2$. Answer: $(1,2)$.

49. $(x-4)(x+2) > 0$: Either $x > 4$ and $x > -2$ (so that $x > 4$) or $x < 4$ and $x < -2$ (so that $x < -2$). Answer: $(-\infty, -2) \cup (4, \infty)$.

50. $2x \geq 15 - x^2$: $x^2 + 2x - 15 \geq 0$, so $(x-3)(x+5) \geq 0$. Now $x+5 > x-3$, so $x-3 \geq 0$ or $x+5 \leq 0$. Thus $x \geq 3$ or $x \leq -5$. Answer: $(-\infty, -5] \cup [3, \infty)$.

51. -1.140, 6.140 **52.** -0.872 4.205 **53.** 1.191, 2.309 **54.** -5.972, 1.172

55. -5.021, 0.896 **56.** -9.962, 1.740 **57.** $(5/2, 3/4)$ **58.** $(5/3, 8/3)$

59. $(7/4, -5/4)$ **60.** $(-12/5, 31/5)$ **61.** $(-33/16, 31/32)$ **62.** $(-37/9, 35/9)$

63. The small rectangle has dimensions $10 - 4x$ by $7 - 2x$; $(7)(10) - (10-4x)(7-2x) = 20$, which leads to the quadratic equation $8x^2 - 48x + 20 = 0$. One solution of this equation is approximately 5.5495, which must be rejected; it is too large. The value of x is the other solution: $x \approx 0.4505$.

64. After shrinking, the tablecloth has dimensions $60 - x$ by $35 - x$. The area of this rectangle is 93% of the area of the original tablecloth, so $(60-x)(35-x) = (0.93)(35)(60)$. The larger solution of this quadratic equation is approximately 93.43, which we reject as too large. Answer: $x \approx 1.573$.

65. Three solutions.

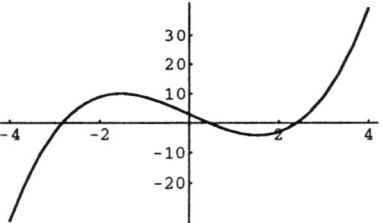

66. Two solutions.

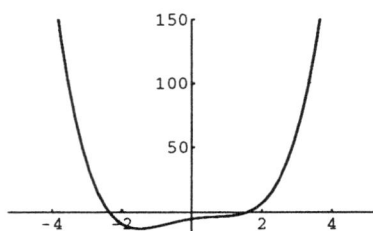

67. Three solutions.

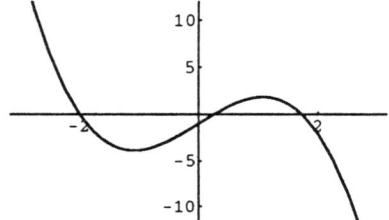

68. Two solutions.

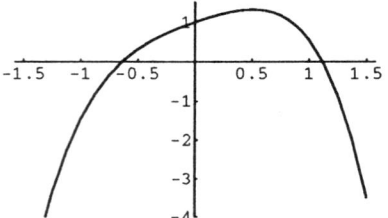

69. Three solutions.

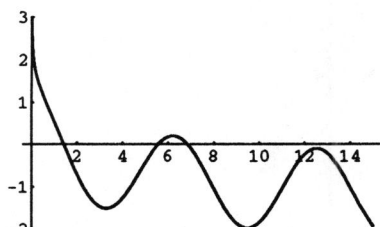

70. One solution.

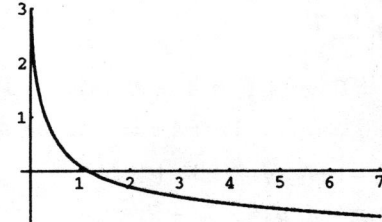

Chapter 2: Prelude to Calculus
Section 2.1

1. $f(x) = 0 \cdot x^2 + 0 \cdot x + 5$, so $m(a) = 0 \cdot 2 \cdot a + 0 \equiv 0$; $y \equiv 5$.
2. Take $a = 0$, $b = 1$, and $c = 0$. Then $m(a) \equiv 1$; $y = x$.
4. $m(a) = -4a$; $y = -8x + 9$.
6. $m(a) \equiv -3$; $y = -3x + 7$.
7. Take $a = 2$, $b = -3$, and $c = 4$. Then $m(a) = 4a - 3$.
8. $m(a) = -3 - 2a$; $y = -7x + 9$.
10. $f(x) = 15x - 3x^2$, so $m(a) = 15 - 6a$; $y = 3x + 12$.
12. $f(x) = -9x^2 - 12x$, so $m(a) = -18a - 12$; $y = -48x + 36$.
13. $f(x) = 4x^2 + 1$, so $m(a) = 8a$; $y = 16x - 15$.
14. $f(x) = 24x$, so $m(a) \equiv 24$; $y = 24x$.
16. $m(a) = 10 - 2a$; horizontal tangent at $(5, 25)$.
18. $m(a) = 2a + 1$; horizontal tangent at $(-\frac{1}{2}, -\frac{9}{4})$.
19. $y = x - \dfrac{x^2}{100} = x - \frac{1}{100}x^2$, so $m(a) = 1 - \frac{1}{50}a$; thus there is a horizontal tangent at $(50, 25)$.
20. $y = 100x - x^2$, so $m(a) = 100 - 2a$. Now $m(x) = 0$ when $x = 50$, and when $x = 50$, $y = 2500$. So there is a horizontal tangent at $(50, 2500)$.
21. $y = x^2 - 2x - 15$, so $m(a) = 2a - 2$. Here, $m(x) = 0$ when $x = 1$, and when $x = 1$, $y = -16$. So there is a horizontal tangent at $(1, -16)$.
22. $y = x^2 - 10x + 25$, so $m(a) = 2a - 10$. Thus $m(x) = 0$ when $x = 5$, and when $x = 5$, $y = 0$. So there is a horizontal tangent at $(5, 0)$.
23. $m(a) = 70 - 2a$; horizontal tangent at $(35, 1225)$.
24. $y = 100 - 20x + x^2$, so $m(x) = -20 + 2x$. There is a horizontal tangent at $(10, 0)$.
25. $m(x) = 2x$; the slope at P is -4; $y = -4x - 4$; $4y = x + 18$.
26. $m(x) = -1 - 4x$. The slope at P is 3, so an equation for the tangent line there is $y - 4 = 3(x + 1)$, and an equation for the normal line there is $y - 4 = -\frac{1}{3}(x + 1)$.
27. $m(x) = 4x + 3$, so the slope at P is 11.
28. The tangent line in question has slope $2x_0$, and thus has equation $y - y_0 = 2x_0(x - x_0)$. Now $y_0 = (x_0)^2$, so this equation may be simplified to $y = 2x_0 x - (x_0)^2$. The line with this equation meets the x-axis when $y = 0$, so that $2x_0 x = (x_0)^2$. If $x_0 \ne 0$, this implies that $x = x_0/2$, and so—whether or not $x_0 = 0$—the tangent line meets the x-axis at $(x_0/2, 0)$.
29. $y'(t) = 96 - 32t$; $m(t) = 0$ when $t = 3$. Therefore the maximum height attained by the ball is $y(3) = 144$ (ft).
30. The graph of $A(x) = x(50 - x) = 50x - x^2$ is a parabola opening downward. Since $m(x) = 50 - 2x$, the tangent line to the graph is horizontal at the point $(25, 625)$. The maximum possible area of the rectangle is 625.
31. If the two positive numbers are x and $50 - x$, then their product is $P(x) = x(50 - x)$, $0 < x < 50$. As in problem 30, the maximum possible value of P is $P(25) = 625$.
32. The projectile hits the ground when $y = 0$, which occurs when $x - (x/25)^2 = 0$: $x = 0$ or $x = 625$. Therefore the projectile travels a horizontal distance of 625 feet. Its maximum height is attained when $m(x) = 0$; that is, when $1 - \dfrac{2x}{625} = 0$: $x = 312.5$, and so $y_{\max} = 156.25$ (ft).

18   Section 2.1 Tangent Lines and Slope Predictors

33. If (a, a^2) is the point of tangency of the *other* line, then that line has slope $2a$ (because $m(x) = 2x$) and also has slope $(a^2 - 0)/(a - 3)$ (from the two-point formula for slope). Thus
$$2a = \frac{a^2}{a-3}; \quad 2a^2 - 6a = a^2; \quad a^2 = 6a.$$
So $a = 0$ or $a = 6$. We already know about $a = 0$; it yields the x-axis as the known tangent line. Thus $a = 6$. So the *other* line has slope $2a = 12$ and therefore equation $y = 12(x - 3)$.

34. Let (a, b) denote the point where one of the two lines is tangent to the parabola. Then $b = 4a - a^2$, and the slope of the tangent line there is $4 - 2a$. As in the solution of Problem 33, we then have
$$4 - 2a = \frac{4a - a^2 - 5}{a - 2}.$$
The two solutions of this equation are $a = 1$ and $a = 3$. Thus one tangent line has slope 2 and the other has slope -2; their equations are $y - 5 = 2(x - 2)$ and $y - 5 = -2(x - 2)$ respectively.

35. Suppose that (a, a^2) is the point on the graph of $y = x^2$ closest to $(3, 0)$. Let L be the line segment from $(3, 0)$ to (a, a^2). Under the plausible assumption that L is normal to the tangent line at (a, a^2), we infer that the slope m of L is $-\dfrac{1}{2a}$ because the slope of the tangent line is $2a$. Because we can also compute m by using the two points known to lie on it, we find that
$$m = -\frac{1}{2a} = \frac{a^2 - 0}{a - 3}.$$
This leads to the equation $0 = 2a^3 + a - 3 = (a-1)(2a^2 + 2a + 3)$, which has $a = 1$ as its only real solution. Intuitively, it's clear that there *is* a point on the graph nearest $(3, 0)$, so we have found it: That point is $(1, 1)$.

Alternatively, if (x, x^2) is an arbitrary point on the given parabola, then the distance from (x, x^2) to $(3, 0)$ is the square root of $f(x) = (x^2 - 0)^2 + (x - 3)^2 = x^4 + x^2 - 6x + 9$. A positive quantity is minimized when its square is minimized, so we minimize the distance from (x, x^2) to $(3, 0)$ by minimizing $f(x)$. But $m(x) = 4x^3 + 2x - 6 = 2(x - 1)(2x^2 + 2x + 3)$, and (as before) the equation $m(x) = 0$ has only one real solution, $x = 1$. Again appealing to intuition for the existence of a point on the parabola nearest to $(3, 0)$, we see that it can only be the point $(1, 1)$.

36. -2 **37.** 12 **38.** 3 **39.** 0.5 **40.** 0.25 **41.** -1 **42.** -4

Section 2.2

1. $\lim\limits_{x \to 3} (3x^2 + 7x - 12) = 3 \left(\lim\limits_{x \to 3} x\right)^2 + 7 \left(\lim\limits_{x \to 3} x\right) - \lim\limits_{x \to 3} 12 = 3 \cdot 3^2 + 7 \cdot 3 - 12 = 36.$

2. $\lim\limits_{x \to -2} (x^3 - 3x^2 + 5) = \lim\limits_{x \to -2} x^3 - 3 \lim\limits_{x \to -2} x^2 + \lim\limits_{x \to -2} 5 = -15.$

3. $\lim\limits_{x \to 1} (x^2 - 1)(x^7 + 7x - 4) = \lim\limits_{x \to 1} (x^2 - 1) \cdot \lim\limits_{x \to 1} (x^7 + 7x - 4) = 0 \cdot 4 = 0.$

4. $\lim\limits_{x \to -2} (x^3 - 3x + 3)(x^2 + 2x + 5) = \lim\limits_{x \to -2} (x^3 - 3x + 3) \cdot \lim\limits_{x \to -2} (x^2 + 2x + 5) = 1 \cdot 5 = 5.$

5. $\lim\limits_{x \to 1} \dfrac{x+1}{x^2 + x + 1} = \dfrac{\lim\limits_{x \to 1}(x+1)}{\lim\limits_{x \to 1}(x^2 + x + 1)} = \dfrac{2}{3}.$

6. $\lim\limits_{t \to -2} \dfrac{t+2}{t^2 + 4} = \dfrac{\lim\limits_{t \to -2}(t+2)}{\lim\limits_{t \to -2}(t^2 + 4)} = \dfrac{0}{8} = 0.$

7. $\lim\limits_{x \to 3} \dfrac{(x^2 + 1)^3}{(x^3 - 25)^3} = \dfrac{\lim\limits_{x \to 3}(x^2+1)^3}{\lim\limits_{x \to 3}(x^3 - 25)^3} = \dfrac{\left(\lim\limits_{x \to 3}(x^2+1)\right)^3}{\left(\lim\limits_{x \to 3}(x^3 - 25)\right)^3} = \dfrac{10^3}{2^3} = \dfrac{1000}{8} = 125.$

8. $\lim_{z \to -1} \dfrac{(3z^2 + 2z + 1)^{10}}{(z^3 + 5)^5} = \dfrac{\lim_{z \to -1} (3z^2 + 2z + 1)^{10}}{\lim_{z \to -1} (z^3 + 5)^5} = \dfrac{\left(\lim_{z \to -1} (3z^2 + 2z + 1)\right)^{10}}{\left(\lim_{z \to -1} (z^3 + 5)\right)^5} = \dfrac{2^{10}}{4^5} = 1.$

9. $\lim_{x \to 1} \sqrt{4x + 5} = \sqrt{\lim_{x \to 1} (4x + 5)} = \sqrt{9} = 3.$

10. $\lim_{y \to 4} \sqrt{27 - \sqrt{y}} = \sqrt{\lim_{y \to 4} (27 - \sqrt{y})} = \sqrt{\sqrt{25}} = 5.$

11. $\lim_{x \to 3} (x^2 - 1)^{3/2} = \left(\lim_{x \to 3} (x^2 - 1)\right)^{3/2} = 8^{3/2} = 16\sqrt{2}.$

12. $\lim_{t \to -4} \sqrt{\dfrac{t + 8}{25 - t^2}} = \dfrac{\sqrt{\lim_{t \to -4} (t + 8)}}{\sqrt{\lim_{t \to -4} (25 - t^2)}} = \dfrac{\sqrt{4}}{\sqrt{9}} = \tfrac{2}{3}.$

13. $\lim_{z \to 8} \dfrac{z^{2/3}}{z - \sqrt{2z}} = \dfrac{\lim_{z \to 8} z^{2/3}}{\lim_{z \to 8} (z - \sqrt{2z})} = \tfrac{4}{4} = 1.$

14. $\lim_{t \to 2} \sqrt[3]{3t^3 + 4t - 5} = \sqrt[3]{\lim_{t \to 2} (3t^3 + 4t - 5)} = 3.$

15. $\lim_{w \to 0} \sqrt{(w - 2)^4} = \sqrt{\lim_{w \to 0} (w - 2)^4} = \sqrt{(-2)^4} = 4.$

16. $\lim_{t \to -4} \sqrt[3]{(t + 1)^6} = \sqrt[3]{\lim_{t \to -4} (t + 1)^6} = 9.$

17. $\lim_{x \to -2} \sqrt[3]{\dfrac{x + 2}{(x - 2)^2}} = \sqrt[3]{\lim_{x \to -2} \dfrac{(x + 2)}{(x - 2)^2}} = 0.$

18. $\lim_{y \to 5} \left(\dfrac{2y^2 + 2y + 4}{6y - 3}\right)^{1/3} = \left(\tfrac{64}{27}\right)^{1/3} = \tfrac{4}{3}.$

19. $\lim_{x \to -1} \dfrac{x + 1}{x^2 - x - 2} = \lim_{x \to -1} \dfrac{x + 1}{(x + 1)(x - 2)} = \lim_{x \to -1} \dfrac{1}{x - 2} = -\tfrac{1}{3}.$

20. $\lim_{t \to 3} \dfrac{t^2 - 9}{t - 3} = \lim_{t \to 3} \dfrac{(t - 3)(t + 3)}{t - 3} = \lim_{t \to 3} (t + 3) = 6.$

21. $\lim_{x \to 1} \dfrac{x^2 + x - 2}{x^2 - 4x + 3} = \lim_{x \to 1} \dfrac{(x + 2)(x - 1)}{(x - 3)(x - 1)} = \lim_{x \to 1} \dfrac{x + 2}{x - 3} = -\tfrac{3}{2}.$

22. $\lim_{y \to -1/2} \dfrac{4y^2 - 1}{4y^2 + 8y + 3} = \lim_{y \to -1/2} \dfrac{(2y - 1)(2y + 1)}{(2y + 3)(2y + 1)} = \lim_{y \to -1/2} \dfrac{2y - 1}{2y + 3} = -\tfrac{2}{2} = -1.$

23. $\lim_{t \to -3} \dfrac{t^2 + 6t + 9}{t^2 - 9} = \lim_{t \to -3} \dfrac{(t + 3)(t + 3)}{(t + 3)(t - 3)} = \lim_{t \to -3} \dfrac{t + 3}{t - 3} = 0.$

24. $\lim_{x \to 2} \dfrac{x^2 - 4}{3x^2 - 2x - 8} = \lim_{x \to 2} \dfrac{(x - 2)(x + 2)}{(x - 2)(3x + 4)} = \lim_{x \to 2} \dfrac{x + 2}{3x + 4} = \tfrac{2}{5}.$

25. $\lim_{z \to -2} \dfrac{(z + 2)^2}{z^4 - 16} = \lim_{z \to -2} \dfrac{(z + 2)(z + 2)}{(z + 2)(z - 2)(z^2 + 4)} = \lim_{z \to -2} \dfrac{z + 2}{(z - 2)(z^2 + 4)} = 0.$

26. $\lim_{t \to 3} \dfrac{t^3 - 9t}{t^2 - 9} = \lim_{t \to 3} \dfrac{t(t^2 - 9)}{t^2 - 9} = 3.$

27. $\lim_{x \to 1} \dfrac{x^3 - 1}{x^4 - 1} = \lim_{x \to 1} \dfrac{(x - 1)(x^2 + x + 1)}{(x - 1)(x + 1)(x^2 + 1)} = \lim_{x \to 1} \dfrac{x^2 + x + 1}{(x + 1)(x^2 + 1)} = \tfrac{3}{4}.$

28. $\lim_{y\to -3}\dfrac{y^3+27}{y^2-9}=\lim_{y\to -3}\dfrac{(y+3)(y^2-3y+9)}{(y+3)(y-3)}=\lim_{y\to -3}\dfrac{y^2-3y+9}{y-3}=-\dfrac{27}{6}=-\dfrac{9}{2}.$

29. $\lim_{x\to 3}\dfrac{\frac{1}{x}-\frac{1}{3}}{x-3}=\lim_{x\to 3}\left(\dfrac{3-x}{3x}\right)\left(\dfrac{1}{x-3}\right)=\lim_{x\to 3}\dfrac{-1}{3x}=-\dfrac{1}{9}.$

30. $\lim_{t\to 0}\dfrac{\frac{1}{2+t}-\frac{1}{2}}{t}=\lim_{t\to 0}\left(\dfrac{2-(2+t)}{2(2+t)}\right)\left(\dfrac{1}{t}\right)=\lim_{t\to 0}\left(\dfrac{2-2-t}{2(2+t)}\right)\left(\dfrac{1}{t}\right)=\lim_{t\to 0}\dfrac{-1}{2(2+t)}=-\dfrac{1}{4}.$

31. $\lim_{x\to 4}\dfrac{x-4}{\sqrt{x}-2}=\lim_{x\to 4}\dfrac{(\sqrt{x}-2)(\sqrt{x}+2)}{\sqrt{x}-2}=\lim_{x\to 4}\sqrt{x}+2=4.$

32. $\lim_{x\to 9}\dfrac{3-\sqrt{x}}{9-x}=\lim_{x\to 9}\dfrac{3-\sqrt{x}}{(3-\sqrt{x})(3+\sqrt{x})}=\lim_{x\to 9}\dfrac{1}{3+\sqrt{x}}=\dfrac{1}{6}.$

33. $\lim_{t\to 0}\dfrac{\sqrt{t+4}-2}{t}=\lim_{t\to 0}\left(\dfrac{\sqrt{t+4}-2}{t}\right)\cdot\left(\dfrac{\sqrt{t+4}+2}{\sqrt{t+4}+2}\right)$
$=\lim_{t\to 0}\dfrac{t+4-4}{t(\sqrt{t+4}+2)}$
$=\lim_{t\to 0}\dfrac{t}{t(\sqrt{t+4}+2)}=\lim_{t\to 0}\dfrac{1}{\sqrt{t+4}+2}=\dfrac{1}{4}.$

34. $\lim_{h\to 0}\dfrac{1}{h}\left(\dfrac{1}{\sqrt{9+h}}-\dfrac{1}{3}\right)=\lim_{h\to 0}\dfrac{3-\sqrt{9+h}}{3h\sqrt{9+h}}$
$=\lim_{h\to 0}\left(\dfrac{3-\sqrt{9+h}}{3h\sqrt{9+h}}\right)\cdot\left(\dfrac{3+\sqrt{9+h}}{3+\sqrt{9+h}}\right)$
$=\dfrac{9-(9+h)}{3h\sqrt{9+h}\,(3+\sqrt{9+h})}=\lim_{h\to 0}\dfrac{-1}{3\sqrt{9+h}\,(3+\sqrt{9+h})}=-\dfrac{1}{54}.$

35. $\lim_{x\to 4}\dfrac{x^2-16}{2-\sqrt{x}}=\lim_{x\to 4}\dfrac{(x+4)(\sqrt{x}-2)(\sqrt{x}+2)}{2-\sqrt{x}}=\lim_{x\to 4}\left[-(x+4)(\sqrt{x}+2)\right]=-32.$

36. $\lim_{x\to 0}\dfrac{\sqrt{1+x}-\sqrt{1-x}}{x}=\lim_{x\to 0}\left(\dfrac{\sqrt{1+x}-\sqrt{1-x}}{x}\right)\cdot\left(\dfrac{\sqrt{1+x}+\sqrt{1-x}}{\sqrt{1+x}+\sqrt{1-x}}\right)$
$=\lim_{x\to 0}\dfrac{(1+x)-(1-x)}{x(\sqrt{1+x}+\sqrt{1-x})}$
$=\lim_{x\to 0}\dfrac{2}{(\sqrt{1+x}+\sqrt{1-x})}=1.$

37. $\dfrac{f(x+h)-f(x)}{h}=\dfrac{(x+h)^3-x^3}{h}=\dfrac{x^3+3x^2h+3xh^2+h^3-x^3}{h}=3x^2+3xh+h^2\to 3x^2$ as $h\to 0$.
When $x=2$, $y=f(2)=x^3=8$ and the slope of the tangent line to this curve at $x=2$ is $3x^2=12$, so an equation of this tangent line is $y=12x-16$.

38. $\dfrac{f(x+h)-f(x)}{h}=\dfrac{\left(\frac{1}{x+h}\right)-\left(\frac{1}{x}\right)}{h}=\dfrac{x-(x+h)}{hx(x+h)}=\dfrac{-1}{x(x+h)}\to -\dfrac{1}{x^2}$ as $h\to 0$. When $x=2$, $y=f(2)=\frac{1}{2}$ and the slope of the line tangent to this curve at $x=2$ is $-\frac{1}{4}$, so an equation of this tangent line is $y-\frac{1}{2}=-\frac{1}{4}(x-2)$, or $y=-\frac{1}{4}(x-4)$.

39. $\dfrac{f(x+h)-f(x)}{h}=\dfrac{\frac{1}{(x+h)^2}-\frac{1}{x^2}}{h}=\dfrac{x^2-(x+h)^2}{hx^2(x+h)^2}=\dfrac{-2x-h}{x^2(x+h)^2}\to -\dfrac{2}{x^3}$ as $h\to 0$. When $x=2$, $y=f(2)=\frac{1}{4}$ and the slope of the line tangent to this curve at $x=2$ is $-\frac{1}{4}$, so an equation of this tangent line is $y-\frac{1}{4}=-\frac{1}{4}(x-2)$, or $y=-\frac{1}{4}(x-3)$.

40. $\dfrac{f(x+h)-f(x)}{h} = \dfrac{\left(\dfrac{1}{x+h+1}\right)-\left(\dfrac{1}{x+1}\right)}{h} = \dfrac{x+1-x-h-1}{h(x+1)(x+h+1)} = \dfrac{-1}{(x+1)(x+h+1)}.$

This approaches $-\dfrac{1}{(x+1)^2}$ as h approaches 0. When $x=2$, $y=f(2)=\tfrac{1}{3}$ and the slope of the line tangent to this curve at $x=2$ is $-\tfrac{1}{9}$, so an equation of this tangent line is $y-\tfrac{1}{3} = -\tfrac{1}{9}(x-2)$, or $y = -\tfrac{1}{9}(x-5)$.

41. $\dfrac{f(x+h)-f(x)}{h} = \dfrac{\left(\dfrac{2}{x+h-1}\right)-\left(\dfrac{2}{x-1}\right)}{h} = \dfrac{2(x-1-x-h+1)}{h(x-1)(x+h-1)} = \dfrac{-2}{(x-1)(x+h-1)}.$

This approaches $\dfrac{-2}{(x-1)^2}$ as h approaches 0. When $x=2$, $y=f(2)=2$ and the slope of the line tangent to this curve at $x=2$ is -2, so an equation of this tangent line is $y-2 = -2(x-2)$, or $y = -2(x-3)$.

42. $\dfrac{f(x+h)-f(x)}{h} = \dfrac{\left(\dfrac{x+h}{x+h-1}\right)-\left(\dfrac{x}{x-1}\right)}{h} = \dfrac{(x-1)(x+h)-x^2-xh+x}{h(x-1)(x+h-1)}$

$= \dfrac{-1}{(x-1)(x+h-1)} \to \dfrac{-1}{(x-1)^2}$ as $h \to 0$.

When $x=2$, $y=f(2)=2$ and the slope of the line tangent to this curve at $x=2$ is -1, so an equation of this tangent line is $y-2 = -1(x-2)$, or $y = -x+4$.

43. $\dfrac{f(x+h)-f(x)}{h} = \dfrac{\left(\dfrac{1}{\sqrt{x+h+2}}\right)-\left(\dfrac{1}{\sqrt{x+2}}\right)}{h}$

$= \left(\dfrac{\sqrt{x+2}-\sqrt{x+h+2}}{h\sqrt{x+2}\sqrt{x+h+2}}\right)\cdot\left(\dfrac{\sqrt{x+2}+\sqrt{x+h+2}}{\sqrt{x+2}+\sqrt{x+h+2}}\right)$

$= \dfrac{-h}{h\sqrt{x+2}\sqrt{x+h+2}\left(\sqrt{x+2}+\sqrt{x+h+2}\right)} \to \dfrac{-1}{(x+2)\left(2\sqrt{x+2}\right)}$ as $h \to 0$.

When $x=2$, $y=f(2)=\tfrac{1}{2}$ and the slope of the line tangent to this curve at $x=2$ is $\tfrac{-1}{16}$, so an equation of this tangent line is $y-\tfrac{1}{2} = -\tfrac{1}{16}(x-2)$, or $y = \tfrac{-1}{16}(x-10)$.

44. $\dfrac{f(x+h)-f(x)}{h} = \dfrac{(x+h)^2 + \dfrac{3}{x+h} - x^2 - \dfrac{3}{x}}{h}$

$= (2x+h) + \dfrac{-3}{x(x+h)} \to 2x - \dfrac{3}{x^2}$ as $h \to 0$.

When $x=2$, $y=f(2)=\tfrac{11}{2}$ and the slope of the line tangent to this curve at $x=2$ is $\tfrac{13}{4}$, so an equation of this tangent line is $y-\tfrac{11}{2} = \tfrac{13}{4}(x-2)$.

45. $\dfrac{f(x+h)-f(x)}{h} = \dfrac{\sqrt{2(x+h)+5}-\sqrt{2x+5}}{h}$

$= \left(\dfrac{\sqrt{2(x+h)+5}-\sqrt{2x+5}}{h}\right)\cdot\left(\dfrac{\sqrt{2(x+h)+5}+\sqrt{2x+5}}{\sqrt{2(x+h)+5}+\sqrt{2x+5}}\right)$

$= \dfrac{2}{\sqrt{2(x+h)+5}+\sqrt{2x+5}} \to \dfrac{1}{\sqrt{2x+5}}$ as $h \to 0$.

When $x=2$, $y=f(2)=3$ and the slope of the line tangent to this curve at $x=2$ is $\tfrac{1}{3}$, so an equation of this tangent line is $y-3 = \tfrac{1}{3}(x-2)$, or $y = \tfrac{1}{3}(x+7)$.

46. $$\frac{f(x+h)-f(x)}{h} = \frac{\left(\frac{(x+h)^2}{x+h+1}\right) - \left(\frac{x^2}{x+1}\right)}{h} = \frac{(x+1)(x+h)^2 - (x+h+1)(x^2)}{h(x+1)(x+h+1)}$$
$$= \frac{x^2 + xh + 2x + h}{(x+1)(x+h+1)} \to \frac{x^2 + 2x}{(x+1)^2} \text{ as } h \to 0.$$

When $x = 2$, $y = f(2) = \frac{4}{3}$ and the slope of the line tangent to this curve at $x = 2$ is $\frac{8}{9}$, so an equation of this tangent line is $y - \frac{4}{3} = \frac{8}{9}(x-2)$, or $9y = 8x - 4$.

47.
x	10^{-2}	10^{-4}	10^{-6}	10^{-8}	10^{-10}
$f(x)$	2.01	2.001	2.	2.	2.

x	-10^{-2}	-10^{-4}	-10^{-6}	-10^{-8}	-10^{-10}
$f(x)$	1.99	1.9999	2.	2.	2.

The limit appears to be 2.

48.
x	10^{-2}	10^{-4}	10^{-6}	10^{-8}	10^{-10}
$f(x)$	4.0604	4.0006	4.00001	4.	4.

x	-10^{-2}	-10^{-4}	-10^{-6}	-10^{-8}	-10^{-10}
$f(x)$	3.9404	3.9994	3.99999	4.	4.

The limit appears to be 4.

49.
x	10^{-2}	10^{-4}	10^{-6}	10^{-8}	10^{-10}
$f(x)$	0.16662	0.166666	0.166667	0.166667	0.166667

x	-10^{-2}	-10^{-4}	-10^{-6}	-10^{-8}	-10^{-10}
$f(x)$	0.166713	0.166667	0.166667	0.166667	0.166667

The limit appears to be $\frac{1}{6}$.

50.
x	$4+10^{-2}$	$4+10^{-4}$	$4+10^{-6}$	$4+10^{-8}$	$4+10^{-10}$
$f(x)$	3.00187	3.00002	3.	3.	3.

x	$4-10^{-2}$	$4-10^{-4}$	$4-10^{-6}$	$4-10^{-8}$	$4-10^{-10}$
$f(x)$	2.99812	2.99998	3.	3.	3.

The limit appears to be 3.

51.
x	10^{-2}	10^{-4}	10^{-6}	10^{-8}	10^{-10}
$f(x)$	-0.37128	-0.374963	-0.375	-0.375	-0.375

x	-10^{-2}	-10^{-4}	-10^{-6}	-10^{-8}	-10^{-10}
$f(x)$	-0.378781	-0.375038	-0.375	-0.375	-0.375

The limit appears to be $-\frac{3}{8}$.

52.
x	10^{-2}	10^{-4}	10^{-6}	10^{-8}	10^{-10}
$f(x)$	-0.222225	-0.222222	-0.222222	-0.222225	-0.222222

x	-10^{-2}	-10^{-4}	-10^{-6}	-10^{-8}	-10^{-10}
$f(x)$	-0.222225	-0.222222	-0.222222	-0.222222	-0.222222

Limit: $-\frac{2}{9}$.

53.

x	10^{-2}	10^{-4}	10^{-6}	10^{-8}	10^{-10}
$f(x)$	0.999983	1.	1.	1.	1.

x	-10^{-2}	-10^{-4}	-10^{-6}	-10^{-8}	-10^{-10}
$f(x)$	0.999983	1.	1.	1.	1.

The limit appears to be 1.

54.

x	10^{-2}	10^{-4}	10^{-6}	10^{-8}	10^{-10}
$f(x)$	0.49996	0.5	0.5	0.499817	0

x	-10^{-2}	-10^{-4}	-10^{-6}	-10^{-8}	-10^{-10}
$f(x)$	0.499996	0.5	0.5	0.499817	0

Beware of round-off errors. The limit is 0.5.

55.

x	10^{-2}	10^{-3}	10^{-4}	10^{-5}	10^{-6}
$f(x)$	0.166666	0.166667	0.166667	0.166667	0.166667

x	-10^{-2}	-10^{-3}	-10^{-4}	-10^{-5}	-10^{-6}
$f(x)$	0.166666	0.166667	0.166667	0.166667	0.166667

The limit appears to be $\frac{1}{6}$.

56.

x	10^{-2}	10^{-4}	10^{-6}	10^{-8}	10^{-10}
$f(x)$	1.04723	1.00092	1.00001	1.	1.

x	-10^{-2}	-10^{-4}	-10^{-6}	-10^{-8}	-10^{-10}
$f(x)$	.954898	.999079	.999986	1.	1.

The limit appears to be 1.

57.

x	2^{-1}	2^{-5}	2^{-10}	2^{-15}	2^{-20}
$(1+x)^{1/x}$	2.25	2.67699	2.71696	2.71824	2.71828

x	-2^{-1}	-2^{-5}	-2^{-10}	-2^{-15}	-2^{-20}
$(1+x)^{1/x}$	4.	2.76210	2.71961	2.71832	2.71828

59. $\lim_{x \to 0} \dfrac{x - \tan x}{x^3} = -\frac{1}{3}$. Answer: -0.3333.

60. $\lim_{x \to 0} \dfrac{\sin 2x}{\tan 5x} = \frac{2}{5}$.

61. $\sin\left(\dfrac{\pi}{2^{-n}}\right) = \sin\left(2\pi \cdot 2^{(n-1)}\right) = 0$ for every positive integer n. Therefore $\lim_{x \to 0} \sin\left(\dfrac{\pi}{x}\right)$, if it were to exist, would be 0. Notice however that $\sin\left(3^n \cdot \dfrac{\pi}{2}\right)$ alternates between $+1$ and -1 for $n = 1, 2, 3, \ldots$. Therefore $\lim_{x \to 0} \sin\left(\dfrac{\pi}{x}\right)$ does not exist.

62. This limit is 10^{-5}.

Section 2.3

1. $\theta \cdot \dfrac{\theta}{\sin \theta} \to 0 \cdot 1 = 0$ as $\theta \to 0$.

2. $\dfrac{\sin \theta}{\theta} \cdot \dfrac{\sin \theta}{\theta} \to 1 \cdot 1 = 1$ as $\theta \to 0$.

3. Multiply numerator and denominator by $1 + \cos \theta$.

4. $\dfrac{\tan\theta}{\theta} = \dfrac{\sin\theta}{\theta\cos\theta} \to 1$ as $\theta \to 0$.

5. Divide each term in numerator and denominator by x. Then it's clear that the denominator is approaching zero whereas the numerator is not, so the limit does not exist. Because the numerator is positive and the denominator is approaching zero through negative values, the answer $-\infty$ is also correct.

6. As $\theta \to 0$, so does $\omega = \theta^2$, and $\dfrac{\sin 2\omega}{\omega} = \dfrac{2\sin\omega\cos\omega}{\omega} \to 2$.

7. Let $z = 5x$. Then $z \to 0$ as $x \to 0$, and $\dfrac{\sin 5x}{x} = \dfrac{5\sin z}{z} \to 5$.

8. $\dfrac{\sin 2x}{x\cos 3x} = \dfrac{2\sin x\cos x}{x\cos 3x} = \dfrac{2\cos x}{\cos 3x} \cdot \dfrac{\sin x}{x} \to 2$ as $x \to 0$.

9. This limit does not exist, but $\lim_{x\to 0^+} \dfrac{\sin x}{\sqrt{x}} = 0$.

10. Replace $1 - \cos 2x$ with $1 - (\cos^2 x - \sin^2 x) = 2\sin^2 x$ to see that the limit is zero.

11. Replace x with $3z$ and let $z \to 0$.

12. Use the fact that $\lim_{x\to 0} \dfrac{\sin 3x}{x} = 3$ to obtain the limit 9.

13. Multiply numerator and denominator by $1 + \cos x$.

14. $\lim_{x\to 0} \dfrac{\tan 3x}{\tan 5x} = \lim_{x\to 0} \dfrac{3}{5} \cdot \dfrac{\tan 3x}{3x} \cdot \dfrac{5x}{\tan 5x} = \dfrac{3}{5}$.

15. Replace $\sec x \csc x$ with $\dfrac{1}{\sin x \cos x}$.

16. $\lim_{\theta\to 0} \dfrac{\sin 2\theta}{\theta} = \lim_{\theta\to 0} \dfrac{2\sin\theta\cos\theta}{\theta} = 2\cdot 1\cdot 1 = 2$.

17. Multiply numerator and denominator by $1 + \cos\theta$.

18. $\lim_{\theta\to 0} \dfrac{\sin\theta}{\theta} \cdot \sin\theta = 1 \cdot 0 = 0$.

19. $\lim_{z\to 0} \dfrac{\tan z}{\sin 2z} = \lim_{z\to 0} \dfrac{\sin z}{2\sin z \cos^2 z} = \dfrac{1}{2}$.

20. $\lim_{x\to 0} \dfrac{\tan 2x}{3x} = \lim_{x\to 0} \dfrac{2}{3} \cdot \dfrac{\tan 2x}{2x} = \dfrac{2}{3}$ (with the aid of Problem 4).

21. $\lim_{x\to 0} x\cot 3x = \lim_{x\to 0} \dfrac{3x}{\sin 3x} \cdot \dfrac{\cos 3x}{3} = 1 \cdot \dfrac{1}{3} = \dfrac{1}{3}$.

22. $\lim_{x\to 0} \dfrac{x - \tan x}{\sin x} = \lim_{x\to 0} \dfrac{\left(\dfrac{x}{x} - \dfrac{\tan x}{x}\right)}{\left(\dfrac{\sin x}{x}\right)} = \dfrac{1-1}{1} = 0$.

23. $\lim_{x\to 0} \dfrac{1}{x}\sin\dfrac{x}{2} = \lim_{x\to 0} \dfrac{1}{2} \cdot \dfrac{\left(\sin\dfrac{x}{2}\right)}{\left(\dfrac{x}{2}\right)} = \dfrac{1}{2}$, so the answer is $\dfrac{1}{4}$.

24. $\lim_{x\to 0} \dfrac{\sin 2x}{\sin 5x} = \lim_{x\to 0} \dfrac{2}{5} \cdot \dfrac{\sin 2x}{2x} \cdot \dfrac{5x}{\sin 5x} = \dfrac{2}{5} \cdot 1 \cdot 1 = \dfrac{2}{5}$.

25. $\lim_{x\to 0} x^2 \cos 10x = 0$.

26. $-1 \leq \sin\dfrac{1}{x^2} \leq 1$ for all $x \neq 0$, so $-x^2 \leq x^2\sin\dfrac{1}{x^2} \leq x^2$ for all $x \neq 0$. Now let $x \to 0$ to obtain the limit zero.

27. Proceed almost exactly as in Problem 26 to obtain the limit zero.

28. Because $-1 \leq \sin\dfrac{1}{x} \leq 1$ for all $x \neq 0$, $-|\sqrt[3]{x}| \leq \sqrt[3]{x}\sin\dfrac{1}{x} \leq |\sqrt[3]{x}|$ for all $x \neq 0$. Now let $x \to 0$ to

Section 2.3 More About Limits

obtain the limit zero.

29. $3 - 0 = 3$ **30.** $4 + 3 \cdot 0 = 4$

31. If $x < 1$, then $x - 1 < 0$, so the limit does not exist.

32. If $x < 4$, then $4 - x > 0$, so the limit is zero.

33. $\sqrt{4-4} = 0$. **34.** If $x > 3$ then $9 - x^2 < 0$, so the limit does not exist.

35. $\sqrt{5 \cdot (5-5)} = 0$ **36.** $2 \cdot \sqrt{4-4} = 0$.

37. $\dfrac{4x}{x-4} \to +\infty$ as $x \to 4^+$, so the limit does not exist. In such a case it is also correct to write
$$\lim_{x \to 4^+} \sqrt{\dfrac{4x}{x-4}} = +\infty.$$

38. $6 - x - x^2 = (3+x)(2-x)$, so $3 + x > 0$ and $2 - x > 0$ for $x > -3$. Thus $\lim\limits_{x \to -3^+} \sqrt{6 - x - x^2} = 0$.

39. If $x < 5$, then $x - 5 < 0$, so $\dfrac{x-5}{|x-5|} = -1$. Therefore the limit is -1.

40. If $0 > x > -4$, then $16 - x^2 > 0$, so $\dfrac{16 - x^2}{\sqrt{16 - x^2}} = \sqrt{16 - x^2} \to 0$ as $x \to -4^+$.

41. If $x > 3$, then $x^2 - 6x + 9 = (x-3)^2 > 0$ and $x - 3 > 0$, so $\dfrac{\sqrt{x^2 - 6x + 9}}{x - 3} = \dfrac{|x-3|}{x-3} = \dfrac{x-3}{x-3} \to 1$ as $x \to 3^+$.

42. $\dfrac{x-2}{x^2 - 5x + 6} = \dfrac{x-2}{(x-2)(x-3)} = \dfrac{1}{x-3} \to -1$ as $x \to 2^+$.

43. If $x > 2$ then $x - 2 > 0$, so $\dfrac{2-x}{|x-2|} = -1$. Therefore the limit is also -1.

44. If $x < 7$ then $x - 7 < 0$, so $\dfrac{7-x}{|x-7|} = 1$. So the limit is 1.

45. $\dfrac{1-x^2}{1-x} = \dfrac{(1+x)(1-x)}{1-x} = 1 + x$, so the limit is 2.

46. If $x < 0$ then $x - |x| = 2x$, so the limit is $1/2$.

47. $\sqrt{(5-x)^2} = |5-x| = x - 5$ for $x > 5$; the limit is -1.

48. $\sqrt{(4+x)^2} = |4+x| = -(4+x)$ because if $x < -4$ then $4 + x < 0$. So the limit is -1.

49. $f(x) \to +\infty$ as $x \to 1^+$, $f(x) \to -\infty$ as $x \to 1^-$.

50. $f(x) \to +\infty$ as $x \to 3^-$, $f(x) \to -\infty$ as $x \to 3^+$.

51. If x is near -1 then $x - 1$ is near -2. So $f(x) \to +\infty$ as $x \to -1^-$, $f(x) \to -\infty$ as $x \to -1^+$.

52. If x is near 5 then $2x - 5$ is near 5. So $f(x) \to +\infty$ as $x \to 5^-$, $f(x) \to -\infty$ as $x \to 5^+$.

53. If x is near -2 then $1 - x^2$ is near -3. Hence $f(x) \to +\infty$ as $x \to -2^-$, whereas $f(x) \to -\infty$ as $x \to -2^+$.

54. $(x-5)^2 > 0$ for all $x \neq 5$, so $f(x) \to +\infty$ as $x \to 5$.

55. If $x > 1$ then $f(x) = \dfrac{1}{x-1}$; if $x < 1$ then $f(x) = \dfrac{1}{1-x}$. Therefore $f(x) \to +\infty$ as $x \to 1$.

56. The numerator $x + 1$ of $f(x)$ is near -2 for x near -3, while the denominator $(x+3)^2$ is positive for all $x \neq -3$. So $f(x) \to -\infty$ as $x \to -3$.

57. $\dfrac{x-2}{4-x^2} = -\dfrac{x-2}{(x-2)(x+2)} = \dfrac{-1}{x+2}$ for $|x| \neq 2$. So $f(x) \to -\infty$ as $x \to -2^+$, $f(x) \to +\infty$ as $x \to -2^-$, and $f(x) \to -1/4$ as $x \to 2$.

58. $\dfrac{x-1}{x^2 - 3x + 2} = \dfrac{x-1}{(x-1)(x-2)} = \dfrac{1}{x-2}$ for $x \neq 1$, $x \neq 2$. So $f(x) \to -1$ as $x \to 1$, $f(x) \to +\infty$ as $x \to 2^+$, and $f(x) \to -\infty$ as $x \to 2^-$.

59. $\lim\limits_{x \to 2^+} \dfrac{x^2 - 4}{|x - 2|} = 4$ and $\lim\limits_{x \to 2^-} \dfrac{x^2 - 4}{|x - 2|} = -4$.
The two-sided limit does not exist. The graph is shown on the right.

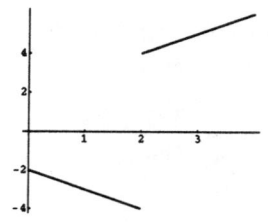

60. Because each of $\lim\limits_{x \to 2^+} \dfrac{x^4 - 8x + 16}{|x - 2|} = +\infty$ and $\lim\limits_{x \to 2^-} \dfrac{x^4 - 8x + 16}{|x - 2|} = +\infty$, the two-sided limit also fails to exist. The graph is shown on the right.

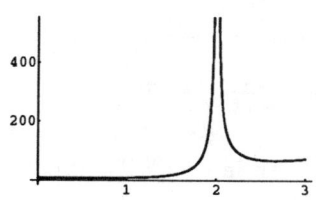

61. If x is an even integer then $f(x) = 3$, if x is an odd integer then $f(x) = 1$, and $\lim\limits_{x \to a} f(x) = 2$ for all real number values of a.

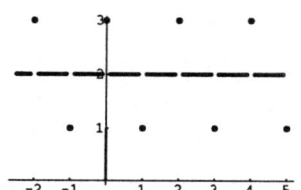

62. If n is any integer then $f(x) \to n$ as $x \to n$. Note: $\lim\limits_{x \to a} f(x) = a$ for all real number values of a.

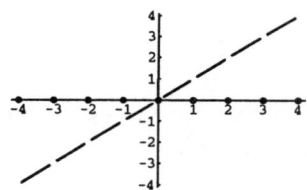

63. For any integer n, $\lim\limits_{x \to n^-} f(x) = 10n - 1$ and $\lim\limits_{x \to n^+} f(x) = 10n$.
Note: $\lim\limits_{x \to a} f(x)$ exists if and only if $10a$ is not an integer. The graph is shown on the right.

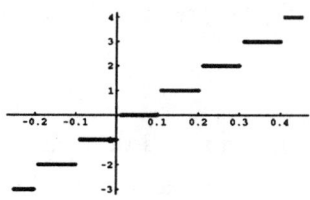

64. If n is any odd integer $\lim\limits_{x \to n^-} f(x) = 1$ and $\lim\limits_{x \to n^+} f(x) = -1$; if n is any even integer $\lim\limits_{x \to n^-} f(x) = -1$ and $\lim\limits_{x \to n^+} f(x) = 1$.
Note: $\lim\limits_{x \to a} f(x)$ exists if and only if a is not an integer. The graph is shown on the right.

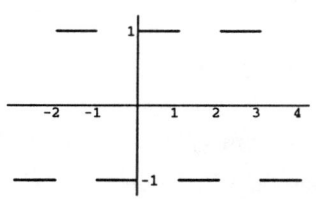

Section 2.3 More About Limits

65. If n is any integer, then $\lim_{x \to n^-} f(x) = \tfrac{1}{2}$ and $\lim_{x \to n^+} f(x) = -\tfrac{1}{2}$.
    Note: $\lim_{x \to a} f(x)$ exists if and only if a is not an integer. The graph is shown on the right.

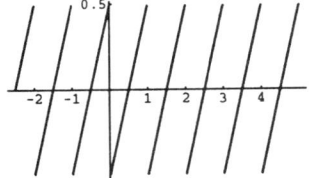

66. If n is an even integer, $\lim_{x \to n^-} f(x) = \dfrac{n}{2} - 1$ and $\lim_{x \to n^+} f(x) = \dfrac{n}{2}$.
    Note: $\lim_{x \to a} f(x)$ exists if and only if a is not an even integer. The graph is shown on the right.

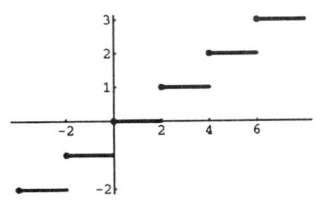

67. If n is any integer, $\lim_{x \to n^-} f(x) = -1$ and $\lim_{x \to n^+} f(x) = -1$.
    Note: $\lim_{x \to a} f(x) = -1$ at every real value of a. The graph is shown on the right.

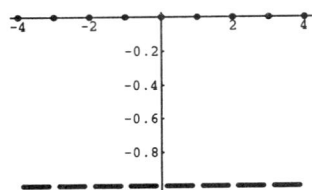

68. If n is a positive integer, $\lim_{x \to n^-} f(x) = \dfrac{n-1}{n}$ and $\lim_{x \to n^+} f(x) = 1$. For any integer $n < 0$, $\lim_{x \to n^-} f(x) = \dfrac{n+1}{n}$ and $\lim_{x \to n^+} f(x) = 1$. Also, $\lim_{x \to 0^-} f(x) = \infty$ and $\lim_{x \to 0^+} f(x) = 0$.
    Note: $\lim_{x \to a} f(x)$ if and only if a is not an integer. The graph is shown on the right.

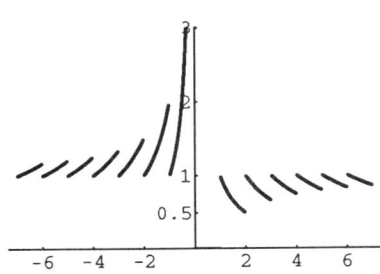

69. The graph shows that $\lim_{x \to a} g(x)$ exists if and only if a is not an integral multiple of $\tfrac{1}{10}$. The graph is shown on the right.

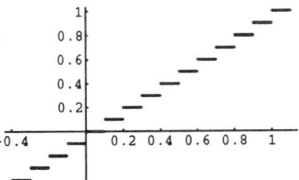

70. Let $f(x) = \text{sgn}(x)$ and $g(x) = -\text{sgn}(x)$.

72. Since $\lim_{x \to 0^-} f(x) = 1$ and $\lim_{x \to 0^+} f(x) = 0$, then $\lim_{x \to 0} f(x)$ does not exist. The graph is shown on the right.

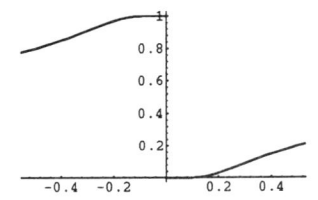

28   Section 2.3 More About Limits

73. $\lim\limits_{x \to 0} f(x) = 1$. The graph is shown on the right.

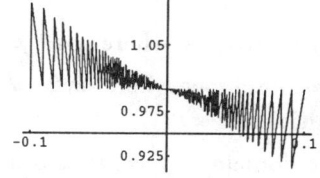

74. $\lim\limits_{x \to 0} f(x) = 0$. The graph is shown on the right.

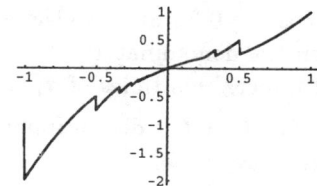

Section 2.4

4. $\lim\limits_{x \to a} g(x) = \dfrac{\lim_{x \to a} x^3}{\lim_{x \to a} x^2 + 2\lim_{x \to a} x + 5} = \dfrac{(\lim_{x \to a} x)^3}{(\lim_{x \to a} x)^2 + 2\lim_{x \to a} x + 5} = \dfrac{a^3}{a^2 + 2a + 5} = g(a)$.
   Therefore $\lim\limits_{x \to a} g(x)$ exists and is equal to $g(a)$ at every real value of a, and so g is continuous at every real number.

15. The cube root of every real number exists and is unique, so the domain of f is the set of all real numbers. By an argument similar to that in Example 10, f is continuous on the set $\mathbb{R}$ of all real numbers as well.

16. The domain is the set of all real numbers other than zero. The function g is continuous on its domain (it is not continuous at $x = 0$ because it is not defined there).

17. f is continuous for $x \ne -3$.

18. f is continuous for $t \ne 5$.

19. f is continuous on its domain $\mathbb{R}$ (the denominator is never zero).

20. g is continuous on its domain, $z \ne \pm 1$.

21. f is continuous for $x \ne 5$.

22. h is continuous on $\mathbb{R}$ (the denominator is never zero).

23. f is continuous on its domain, $x \ne 2$.

24. Because $t^4 \ge 0$ for all t, $t^4 + 4 > 0$ for all t, so $(t^4 + 4)^{1/4}$ exists for all t. By Theorem 2 and the limit laws, f is continuous on $\mathbb{R}$.

25. Every real number has a [unique] cube root, so by Theorem 2 and the limit laws f is continuous on its domain, $x \ne 1$.

26. F is continuous on $\mathbb{R}$.

27. The function f is continuous on its domain, the set of all real numbers other than 0 and 1.

28. f is continuous on its domain, the interval $[-3, 3]$.

29. f is continuous on its domain, the interval $(-2, 2)$.

30. We require that $1 - x^2$ and $4 - x^2$ have the same sign and for $4 - x^2$ to be nonzero. If $x^2 \le 1$ and $x^2 \le 4$, then $x^2 \le 1$, so $-1 \le x \le 1$. If $x^2 \ge 1$ and $x^2 \ge 4$, then $x^2 \ge 4$; but $x^2 \ne 4$, so $x > 2$ or $x < -2$. Thus the domain of f is the union of the three intervals $(-\infty, -2)$, $[-1, 1]$, and $(2, +\infty)$, and f is continuous there.

31. f is continuous on its domain, the set of all real numbers other than zero.

32. g is continuous where $\cos\theta \ne 0$; that is, it is continuous if θ is not an odd integral multiple of $\pi/2$.

33. f is continuous where $\sin 2x \ne 0$; that is, it is continuous at every real number other than the integral multiples of $\pi/2$.

34. The domain of f consists of those values of x for which $\sin x \ge 0$. So its domain is the union of all intervals of the form $[n\pi, (n+1)\pi]$ where n is an even integer. It is continuous on its domain.

35. f is continuous everywhere.

36. $1 + \cos u \ge 0$ for all u, so there is no difficulty with regard to the square root. But $G(u)$ is undefined when the denominator is zero, so the domain of G consists of those real numbers u other than the odd integral multiples of π; G is continuous on its domain.

37. The function f is discontinuous at $x = -3$, and cannot be made continuous there because it has no limit there.

38. f has a non-removable discontinuity at $t = \pm 1$.

39. $f(x) = \dfrac{x-2}{x^2-4} = \dfrac{x-2}{(x+2)(x-2)} = \dfrac{1}{x+2}$ provided $x \ne 2$. It is clear that f is discontinuous at 2 and at -2, cannot be made continuous at -2 because it has no limit there, but can be made continous at $x = 2$ simply by defining $f(2)$ to be $1/4$, the limit of $f(x)$ as $x \to 2$.

40. $G(u) = \dfrac{u+1}{u^2-u-6} = \dfrac{u+1}{(u-3)(u+2)}$, so G has no limit at either $u = 3$ or $u = -2$. Therefore it is not continuous at either point nor can it be made continuous at either point.

41. f is discontinuous at $x = \pm 1$ because of the zero denominator. There is no limit at either point, so f cannot be made continuous at either point.

42. If $x > 1$, then $h(x) = \dfrac{1}{(x-1)^2}$, so h is discontinuous at $x = 1$ and cannot be made continuous there.

43. Because $f(x) \to 1$ as $x \to 17^+$ whereas $f(x) \to -1$ as $x \to 17^-$, f has no limit at $x = 17$ and cannot be made continuous there.

44. $g(x) = \dfrac{(x+2)(x+3)}{x+2} = x+3$ provided that $x \ne -2$. So $x = -2$ is the only discontinuity of g. If we define $g(-2)$ to be 1, the limit of g as $x \to -2$, then g will be continuous at -2 as well.

45. The function f is discontinuous at $x = 0$ because it is not defined there. If we define $f(0)$ to be 0, then f will be continuous at $x = 0$ because its limit at $x = 0$ will be its value there.

46. The function f is not continuous at $x = 1$ because it is not defined there. If we define $f(1)$ to be 2, then f will become continuous at $x = 1$ as well because its limit at $x = 1$ will be equal to its value there.

47. The function f is not continuous at $x = 0$ because it is not defined there. If we define $f(0) = 1$, then f will become continuous at $x = 0$ as well because its limit at $x = 0$ will be equal to its value there.

48. The function f is not continuous at $x = 0$ because it is not defined there. If we define $f(0) = 0$, then f will become continuous at $x = 0$ as well because its limit at $x = 0$ will be equal to its value there.

49. If f is continuous at $x = 0$ then $f(0) = c = \lim_{x \to 0^+} f(x) = 4 - 0^2$, and so $c = 4$.

50. If f is continuous at $x = 3$ then $f(3) = 6 + c = \lim_{x \to 3^+} f(x) = 2c - 3$, and so $c = 9$.

51. If f is continuous at $x = 0$ then $f(0) = c^2 = \lim_{x \to 3^+} f(x) = 2c^2$, and so $c = 0$.

52. If f is continuous at $x = \pi$ then $f(\pi) = c^3 - \pi^3 = \lim_{x \to 3^+} f(x) = c \sin \pi = 0$, and so $c = \pi$.

53. Let $f(x) = x^2 - 5$. Then $f(2) = -1 < 0$ and $f(3) = 4 > 0$. Because $f(x)$ is a polynomial, f is continuous for all x. Therefore $f(x) = 0$ for some x in $(2, 3)$. (The actual value of x is $\sqrt{5} \approx 2.236068$.)

54. Let $f(x) = x^3 + x + 1$. Because $f(x)$ is a polynomial, f is continuous for all x. So f is continuous on $[-1, 0]$. Moreover, $f(-1) = -1 < 0 < 1 = f(0)$. Therefore $f(x) = 0$ for some number x in $[-1, 0]$.

(The value of x is approximately -0.6823278.)

55. Let $f(x) = x^3 - 3x^2 + 1$. Then f is continuous on $[0, 1]$ because $f(x)$ is a polynomial. Moreover, $f(0) = 1 > 0 > -1 = f(1)$. Therefore $f(x) = 0$ for some number x in $[0, 1]$ ($x \approx 0.6527$).

56. Let $f(x) = x^3 - 5$. Then f is continuous, $f(1) = -4$, and $f(2) = 3$. So $f(x) = 0$ for some x, $1 < x < 2$ (the actual value of x is approximately 1.709976).

57. Let $f(x) = x^4 + 2x - 1$. Then f is continuous on $[0, 1]$, $f(0) = -1$, and $f(1) = 2$. Therefore $f(x) = 0$ for some x in $[0, 1]$ (approximately 0.4746266).

58. Let $f(x) = x^5 - 5x^3 + 3$. Then f is continuous on $[-3, -2]$, because $f(x)$ is a polynomial. Moreover, $f(-3) = -105 < 0$ and $f(-2) = 11 > 0$. Therefore $f(x) = 0$ for some number x in $[-3, -2]$. (The value of that number x is approximately -2.291164).

59. Given: $f(x) = x^3 - 4x + 1$. Values of $f(x)$:

x	-3	-2	-1	0	1	2	3
$f(x)$	-14	1	4	1	-2	1	16

So $f(x_i) = 0$ for x_1 in $(-3, -2)$, x_2 in $(0, 1)$, and x_3 in $(1, 2)$. Because these intervals do not overlap, the equation $f(x) = 0$ has at least three real solutions.

60. Given: $f(x) = x^3 - 3x^2 + 1$. Values of $f(x)$:

x	-3	-2	-1	0	1	2	3
$f(x)$	-53	-19	-3	1	-1	-3	1

So $f(x_i) = 0$ for x_1 in $(-1, 0)$, x_2 in $(0, 1)$, and x_3 in $(2, 3)$. Because these intervals do not overlap, the equation $f(x) = 0$ has at least three real solutions.

61. S is discontinuous at the end of each year; that is, at each integral value of t. The graph is shown on the right.

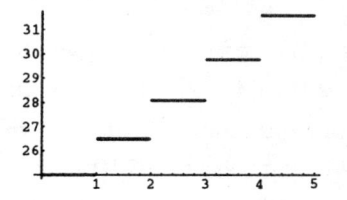

62. $S_2(t) = 25(1.015)^{[t]}$. This salary function is discontinuous at the end of each three-month period. You will accumulate more money with three-month raises than with annual raises; the total salary received by the end of the first five years with annual raises would be $140,930$ but with quarterly raises it would be $144,520$. Graphs of both functions are shown on the right.

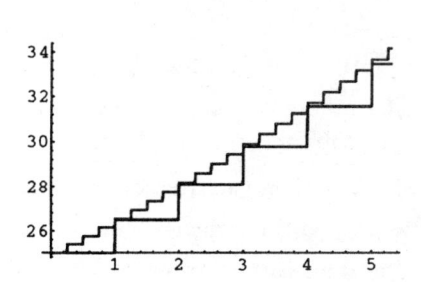

68. This function is discontinuous at each integer.

71. Apply the intermediate value theorem to $g(x) = x - \cos x$. Then $g(0) = -1 < 0 < \pi/2 = g(\pi/2)$. Because g is continuous, $g(c) = 0$ for some number c in $(0, \pi/2)$. The solution is approximately 0.7390851.

72. Apply the intermediate value theorem to the function $f(x) = x + 5\cos x$. Then $f(-\pi) < 0 < f(0)$ and $f(0) = 5 > 0 > f(\pi)$ and $f(\pi) < 0 < f(2\pi)$. Because f is continuous, $f(c) = 0$ for some number c in $(-\pi, 0)$, another in $(0, \pi)$, and a third in $(\pi, 2\pi)$. The three solutions are approximately -1.30644, 1.97738, and 3.83747.

Chapter 2 Miscellaneous

1. $0^2 - 3 \cdot 0 + 4 = 4$
2. $3 - (-1) + (-1)^3 = 3$
3. $(4-4)^{10} = 0$
4. $(1+1-1)^{17} = 1$
5. $\dfrac{1+4}{1-4} = -\dfrac{5}{3}$
6. $\dfrac{6}{9-3-3} = 2$
7. $\dfrac{x^2-1}{1-x} = -(x+1) \to -2$ as $x \to 1$.
8. $\dfrac{x+2}{x^2+x-2} = \dfrac{1}{x-1} \to -\dfrac{1}{3}$ as $x \to -2$.
9. $\dfrac{t^2+6t+9}{9-t^2} = \dfrac{t+3}{3-t} \to 0$ as $t \to -3$.
10. $\dfrac{4-x^2}{3+x} \to \dfrac{4}{3}$ as $x \to 0$.
11. $(9-1)^{2/3} = 4$
12. $\sqrt{9/4} = 3/2$.
13. $16^{3/4} = 8$
14. $\dfrac{(x^2+1)(x+1)(x-1)}{(x+3)(x-1)} = \dfrac{(x^2+1)(x+1)}{x+3} \to 1$ as $x \to 1$.
15. Multiply numerator and denominator by $\sqrt{x+2}+3$.
16. $x - \sqrt{x^2-1} = \dfrac{x^2-(x^2-1)}{x+\sqrt{x^2-1}} = \dfrac{1}{x+\sqrt{x^2-1}} \to 1$ as $x \to 1^+$.
17. Multiply numerator and denominator by $\dfrac{1}{\sqrt{13+x}} + \dfrac{1}{3}$.
18. For $x > 1$, $|1-x| = x-1$, so the fraction and its limit are equal to -1.
19. $\sqrt{(2-x)^2} = |2-x| = x-2$ for $x > 2$, so the fraction and its limit are equal to -1.
20. If $x < -2$ then $x+2 < 0$, so $|x+2| = -(x+2)$. Thus the fraction and its limit are equal to -1.
21. Because $x > 4$, $|x-4| = x-4$.
22. If $x < 3$ then $x^2 - 9 < 0$, so the limit does not exist.
23. If $x > 2$ then $4 - x^2 < 0$, so the limit does not exist.
24. The numerator approaches -3 while the denominator approaches zero through positive values, so the limit is $-\infty$. (It is also correct to say that the limit does not exist.)
25. The numerator approaches 4 while the denominator approaches zero through positive values. Therefore the limit is $+\infty$.
26. For $x < 1$, $x - 1 < 0$. So the numerator approaches 1 while the denominator approaches zero through negative values. Thus the limit is $-\infty$.
27. The numerator approaches 3 while the denominator approaches zero through positive values, and thus the limit is $+\infty$.
28. If $x \neq 1$ then the fraction is equal to $\dfrac{1}{x-1}$, and its denominator approaches zero through negative values, so the limit is $-\infty$.
29. The numerator approaches 2 while the denominator approaches zero through negative values; the limit is $-\infty$.
30. $\dfrac{(5+x)(5-x)}{(5-x)^2} = \dfrac{5+x}{5-x} \to -\infty$ as $x \to 5^+$.
31. $\dfrac{\sin 3x}{x} = \dfrac{3 \sin 3x}{3x} \to 3$ as $x \to 0$.
32. $\dfrac{\tan 5x}{x} = \dfrac{5}{\cos 5x} \cdot \dfrac{\sin 5x}{5x} \to \dfrac{5}{1} \cdot 1 = 5$ as $x \to 0$.
33. $\lim\limits_{x \to 0} \dfrac{\sin 3x}{\sin 2x} = \lim\limits_{x \to 0} \dfrac{3}{2} \cdot \dfrac{\sin 3x}{3x} \cdot \dfrac{2x}{\sin 2x} = \dfrac{3}{2} \cdot 1 \cdot 1 = \dfrac{3}{2}$.
34. $\lim\limits_{x \to 0} \dfrac{\tan 2x}{\tan 3x} = \lim\limits_{x \to 0} \dfrac{2}{3} \cdot \dfrac{\sin 2x}{2x} \cdot \dfrac{3x}{\sin 3x} \cdot \dfrac{\cos 3x}{\cos 2x} = \dfrac{2}{3}$.

35. $\lim\limits_{x \to 0^+} \dfrac{\sqrt{x}}{\sin \sqrt{x}} \cdot \sqrt{x} = 1 \cdot 0 = 0.$

36. $\lim\limits_{x \to 0} \dfrac{1 - \cos^2 3x}{2x(1 + \cos 3x)} = \lim\limits_{x \to 0} \dfrac{3}{2} \cdot \dfrac{\sin 3x}{3x} \cdot \dfrac{\sin 3x}{1 + \cos 3x} = \dfrac{3}{2} \cdot 1 \cdot \dfrac{0}{1} = 0.$

37. $\lim\limits_{x \to 0} \dfrac{1 - \cos 3x}{2x^2} = \lim\limits_{x \to 0} \dfrac{1 - \cos^2 3x}{2x^2(1 + \cos 3x)} = \lim\limits_{x \to 0} \dfrac{9}{2(1 + \cos 3x)} \cdot \dfrac{\sin 3x}{3x} \cdot \dfrac{\sin 3x}{3x} = \dfrac{9}{4}.$

38. $\lim\limits_{x \to 0} (x \cos x) \cdot \dfrac{x}{\sin x} \cdot \dfrac{x}{\sin x} = 0 \cdot 1 \cdot 1 \cdot 1 = 0.$

39. $\lim\limits_{x \to 0} \dfrac{\sec 2x \tan 2x}{x} = \lim\limits_{x \to 0} \dfrac{\sin 2x}{2x} \cdot \dfrac{2}{\cos^2 2x} = 2.$

40. $\lim\limits_{x \to 0} x^2 \cot^2 3x = \lim\limits_{x \to 0} \dfrac{3x}{\sin 3x} \cdot \dfrac{3x}{\sin 3x} \cdot \dfrac{\cos^2 3x}{9} = \dfrac{1}{9}.$

41. $f'(x) = 4x$; the slope of the tangent line at $(1, 5)$ is $f'(1) = 4$; an equation of the line is $y - 5 = 4(x - 1)$.

42. $f'(x) = 1 - 10x;$ $\quad f'(1) = -9;$ $\quad f(1) = -4;$ $\quad y + 4 = -9(x - 1).$

43. $f'(x) = 6x + 4;$ $\quad f'(1) = 10:$ $\quad f(1) = 2;$ $\quad y - 2 = 10(x - 1).$

44. $f'(x) = -2 - 6x;$ $\quad f'(1) = -8:$ $\quad f(1) = -4;$ $\quad y + 4 = -8(x - 1).$

45. $f'(x) = 4x - 3;$ $\quad f'(1) = 1:$ $\quad f(1) = 0;$ $\quad y = x - 1.$

46. $f(x) = \tfrac{1}{3}x - \tfrac{1}{16}x^2$, so $f'(x) = \tfrac{1}{3} - \tfrac{1}{8}x$. Then $f(1) = \tfrac{13}{48}$ and $f'(1) = \tfrac{5}{24}$, so one equation of the line is $y - \tfrac{13}{48} = \tfrac{5}{24}(x - 1).$

47. $f'(x) = \lim\limits_{h \to 0} \dfrac{2(x+h)^2 + 3(x+h) - 2x^2 - 3x}{h}$
    $= \lim\limits_{h \to 0} \dfrac{2x^2 + 4xh + 2h^2 + 3x + 3h - 2x^2 - 3x}{h}$
    $= \lim\limits_{h \to 0} \dfrac{4xh + 2h^2 + 3h}{h} = \lim\limits_{h \to 0} (4x + 2h + 3) = 4x + 3.$

48. $f'(x) = \lim\limits_{h \to 0} \dfrac{(x+h) - (x+h)^3 - x + x^3}{h}$
    $= \lim\limits_{h \to 0} \dfrac{x + h - x^3 - 3x^2h - 3xh^2 - h^3 - x + x^3}{h}$
    $= \lim\limits_{h \to 0} \dfrac{h - 3x^2h - 3xh^2 - h^3}{h}$
    $= \lim\limits_{h \to 0} (1 - 3x^2 - 3xh - h^2) = 1 - 3x^2.$

49. $f'(x) = \lim\limits_{h \to 0} \dfrac{\dfrac{1}{3 - x - h} - \dfrac{1}{3 - x}}{h}$
    $= \lim\limits_{h \to 0} \dfrac{3 - x - 3 + x + h}{h(3 - x - h)(3 - x)}$
    $= \lim\limits_{h \to 0} \dfrac{1}{(3 - x - h)(3 - x)} = \dfrac{1}{(3 - x)^2}.$

50. $f'(x) = \lim\limits_{h \to 0} \dfrac{\dfrac{1}{2x + 2h + 1} - \dfrac{1}{2x + 1}}{h}$
    $= \lim\limits_{h \to 0} \dfrac{2x + 1 - 2x - 2h - 1}{h(2x + 2h + 1)(2x + 1)}$
    $= \lim\limits_{h \to 0} \dfrac{-2}{(2x + 2h + 1)(2x + 1)} = -\dfrac{2}{(2x + 1)^2}.$

51. $f(x+h) - f(x) = h + \dfrac{x+h-x}{x(x+h)}.$

52. $f'(x) = \lim\limits_{h \to 0} \dfrac{\dfrac{x+h}{x+h+1} - \dfrac{x}{x+1}}{h}$
$= \lim\limits_{h \to 0} \dfrac{x^2 + xh + x + h - x^2 - xh - x}{h(x+h+1)(x+1)} = \lim\limits_{h \to 0} \dfrac{1}{(x+h+1)(x+1)} = \dfrac{1}{(x+1)^2}.$

53. $f'(x) = \lim\limits_{h \to 0} \dfrac{\dfrac{x+h+1}{x+h-1} - \dfrac{x+1}{x-1}}{h}$
$= \lim\limits_{h \to 0} \dfrac{x^2 + xh + x - x - h - 1 - x^2 - xh + x - x - h + 1}{h(x+h-1)(x-1)}$
$= \lim\limits_{h \to 0} \dfrac{-2}{(x+h-1)(x-1)} = -\dfrac{2}{(x-1)^2}.$

54. If $x > -3/2$, then $f(x) = 3 + 5x - x^2$, so $f'(x) = 5 - 2x$. If $x < -3/2$, then $f(x) = -3 + x - x^2$, so $f'(x) = 1 - 2x$. But the left-hand limit of $\dfrac{f(x+h) - f(x)}{h}$ at $x = -3/2$ is 4 whereas the right-hand limit there is 8, so $f'(-3/2)$ does not exist; f is continuous at $-3/2$ but its graph has a corner point at $(-3/2, -6.75)$. The graph of f is shown below; the part of the graph near the corner point is magnified in the graph on the right.

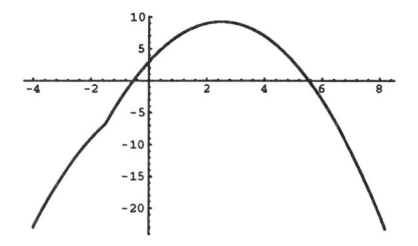

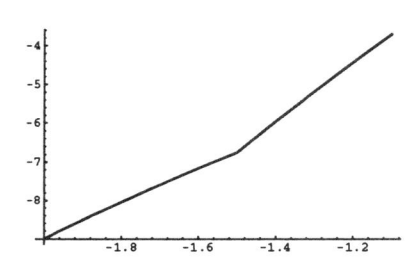

55. The slope of a line tangent to $y = x^2$ at (a, a^2) is $2a$. If such a line passes through $(3, 4)$, then the two-point slope formula yields $2a = (a^2 - 4)/(a - 3)$. It is now easy to solve to obtain the two values $a = 3 \pm \sqrt{5}$.

56. The given line has equation $y = -x - 3$, so its slope is -1. The radius of the circle from its center $(2, 3)$ to the point (a, b) of tangency is perpendicular to that line, so has slope 1. So the radius lies on the line $y - 3 = x - 2$; that is, $y = x + 1$. We solve $y = x + 1$ and $y = -x - 3$ simultaneously to find the point of tangency (a, b) to be $(-2, -1)$. The distance from the center of the circle to this point is $4\sqrt{2}$. Therefore an equation of the circle is $(x - 2)^2 + (y - 3)^2 = 32$.

57. Every rational function is continuous wherever its denominator is nonzero. Here, $f(x) = \dfrac{1}{1+x}$ provided that $x \neq -1$, and cannot be made continuous at $x = -1$. But $f(1) = 1/2$ makes f continuous at $x = 1$.

58. Every rational function is continuous wherever its denominator is nonzero. Here the denominator of $f(x)$ is zero when $x = 2$, and f cannot be made continuous there.

59. Every rational function is continuous wherever its denominator is nonzero. This function $f(x)$ is $f(x) = \dfrac{(x-1)(x+2)}{(x-1)(x+3)} = \dfrac{x+2}{x+3}$ provided that $x \neq -1$. If we define $f(1)$ to be $3/4$, then f will be continuous at $x = 1$, but f cannot be made continuous at $x = -3$ because f has no limit there.

60. $f(x) = 1$ if $x^2 > 1$, whereas $f(x) = -1$ if $x^2 < 1$. So f is discontinuous at ± 1, and cannot be made continuous at either point because its left-hand and right-hand limits are different at $x = -1$ and at $x = 1$.

61. Let $f(x) = x^5 + x - 1$. Then $f(0) = -1 < 0 < 1 = f(1)$. Because $f(x)$ is a polynomial, it is continuous on $[0,1]$, so f has the intermediate value property there. Hence there exists a number c in $(0,1)$ such that $f(c) = 0$. Thus $c^5 + c - 1 = 0$, and so the equation $x^5 + x - 1 = 0$ has a solution. (The value of c is approximately 0.754877666.)

62. Let $f(x) = x^5 - 4x^2 + 1$. Here are some values of $f(x)$:

x	-1	0	1	2
$f(x)$	-4	1	-2	17

Because $f(x)$ is a polynomial, it is continuous everywhere. Therefore $f(x_1) = 0$ for some number x_1 in $(-1, 0)$, $f(x_2) = 0$ for some number x_2 in $(0, 1)$, and $f(x_3) = 0$ for some number x_3 in $(1, 2)$. The numbers x_1, x_2, and x_3 are distinct because they lie in nonoverlapping intervals. Therefore the equation $x^5 - 4x^2 + 1 = 0$ has at least three real solutions. The actual values are $x_1 \approx 0.50842209$, $x_2 \approx 1.52864292$, and $x_3 \approx -0.49268877$.

63. Let $g(x) = x - \cos x$. Then $g(0) = -1 < 0 < \pi/2 = g(\pi/2)$. Because g is continuous, $g(c) = 0$ for some number c in $(0, \pi/2)$.

64. Let $h(x) = x + \tan x$. Then $h(\pi) = \pi > 0$ and $\lim_{x \to (\pi/2)^+} h(x) = -\infty$. The latter fact implies that $h(r) < 0$ for some number r slightly larger than $\pi/2$. Because h is continuous on the interval $[r, \pi]$, h has the intermediate value property there, so $h(c) = 0$ for some number c between r and π, and thus between $\pi/2$ and π.

65. Suppose that a straight line through $(12, \frac{15}{2})$ is normal to the graph of $f(x) = x^2$ at the point (a, a^2). Then $(a^2 - \frac{15}{2})/(a - 12) = -1/(2a)$. This equation has the three solution $a = -2, -1$, and 3. So there are three such lines, with slopes $\frac{1}{4}$, $\frac{1}{2}$, and $-\frac{1}{6}$, respectively.

66. Let $(0, c)$ be the center of such a circle, r its radius, and (a, a^2) a point in the first quadrant where the too-big circle and the parabola are tangent. The idea is to solve for a in terms of c and (possibly) r, then to impose the condition that there is *exactly one* solution for a! This means that the circle just reaches to the bottom of the parabola and not beyond. The condition we impose must be "minimal" in some sense yet to be determined. Solving for a, we find that $a = \pm \dfrac{\sqrt{-1 + 2c}}{\sqrt{2}}$. There will be exactly one solution when $c = \frac{1}{2}$, and in this case the radius of the circle—because it touches the parabola only at $(0, 0)$—will also be $r = \frac{1}{2}$. Answer: $\frac{1}{2}$.

Chapter 3: The Derivative
Section 3.1

1. $f'(x) = 4$ $(a = 0, b = 4, c = -5)$ 2. $g'(t) = -32t$

4. $f'(x) = -49$ 6. $\dfrac{dx}{dt} = 16 - 200t$

8. $\dfrac{dv}{dy} = 500 - 10y$ 10. $\dfrac{du}{dt} = 14t + 13$

11. $f'(x) = \lim\limits_{h \to 0} \dfrac{2(x+h) - 1 - (2x - 1)}{h} = \lim\limits_{h \to 0} \dfrac{2h}{h} = 2.$

12. $f'(x) = \lim\limits_{h \to 0} \dfrac{2 - 3(x+h) - (2 - 3x)}{h} = \lim\limits_{h \to 0} \dfrac{-3h}{h} = -3.$

13. $f'(x) = \lim\limits_{h \to 0} \dfrac{(x+h)^2 + 5 - x^2 - 5}{h} = \lim\limits_{h \to 0} \dfrac{2xh + h^2}{h} = \lim\limits_{h \to 0} (2x + h) = 2x.$

14. $f'(x) = \lim\limits_{h \to 0} \dfrac{3 - 2(x+h)^2 - 3 + 2x^2}{h} = \lim\limits_{h \to 0} \dfrac{-4xh - 2h^2}{h} = \lim\limits_{h \to 0} (-4x - 2h) = -4x.$

15. $f'(x) = \lim\limits_{h \to 0} \dfrac{\dfrac{1}{2(x+h)+1} - \dfrac{1}{2x+1}}{h} = \lim\limits_{h \to 0} \dfrac{2x + 1 - 2x - 2h - 1}{h(2x + 2h + 1)(2x + 1)}$

$\quad = \lim\limits_{h \to 0} \dfrac{-2}{(2x+1)(2x+2h+1)} = \dfrac{-2}{(2x+1)^2}.$

16. $f'(x) = \lim\limits_{h \to 0} \dfrac{\dfrac{1}{3-x-h} - \dfrac{1}{3-x}}{h} = \lim\limits_{h \to 0} \dfrac{3 - x - 3 + x + h}{h(3 - x - h)(3 - x)}$

$\quad = \lim\limits_{h \to 0} \dfrac{1}{(3-x-h)(3-x)} = \dfrac{1}{(3-x)^2}.$

17. $f'(x) = \lim\limits_{h \to 0} \dfrac{\sqrt{2x+2h+1} - \sqrt{2x+1}}{h} = \lim\limits_{h \to 0} \dfrac{2x + 2h + 1 - 2x - 1}{h\left(\sqrt{2x+2h+1} + \sqrt{2x+1}\right)}$

$\quad = \lim\limits_{h \to 0} \dfrac{2}{\sqrt{2x+2h+1} + \sqrt{2x+1}} = \dfrac{1}{\sqrt{2x+1}}.$

18. $f'(x) = \lim\limits_{h \to 0} \dfrac{\dfrac{1}{\sqrt{x+h+1}} - \dfrac{1}{\sqrt{x+1}}}{h} = \lim\limits_{h \to 0} \dfrac{\sqrt{x+1} - \sqrt{x+h+1}}{h\sqrt{x+h+1}\sqrt{x+1}}$

$\quad = \lim\limits_{h \to 0} \dfrac{x + 1 - x - h - 1}{h\sqrt{x+h+1}\sqrt{x+1}\left(\sqrt{x+1} + \sqrt{x+h+1}\right)}$

$\quad = \lim\limits_{h \to 0} \dfrac{-1}{\sqrt{x+h+1}\sqrt{x+1}\left(\sqrt{x+1} + \sqrt{x+h+1}\right)} = \dfrac{-1}{(x+1)2\sqrt{x+1}} = -\dfrac{1}{2(x+1)^{3/2}}.$

19. $f'(x) = \lim\limits_{h \to 0} \dfrac{\dfrac{x+h}{1-2x-2h} - \dfrac{x}{1-2x}}{h} = \lim\limits_{h \to 0} \dfrac{(x+h)(1-2x) - x(1 - 2x - 2h)}{h(1 - 2x - 2h)(1 - 2x)}$

$\quad = \lim\limits_{h \to 0} \dfrac{1}{(1-2x-2h)(1-2x)} = \dfrac{1}{(1-2x)^2}.$

20. $f'(x) = \lim\limits_{h \to 0} \dfrac{\dfrac{x+h+1}{x+h-1} - \dfrac{x+1}{x-1}}{h} = \lim\limits_{h \to 0} \dfrac{(x+h+1)(x-1) - (x+h-1)(x+1)}{h(x+h-1)(x-1)}$

$\quad = \lim\limits_{h \to 0} \dfrac{-2}{(x+h-1)(x-1)} = -\dfrac{2}{(x-1)^2}.$

21. $\dfrac{dx}{dt} = -32t$; $\dfrac{dx}{dt} = 0$ when $t = 0$; $x(0) = 100$

22. $\dfrac{dx}{dt} = -32t + 160$; $\dfrac{dx}{dt} = 0$ when $t = 5$; $x(5) = 425$

23. $\dfrac{dx}{dt} = -32t + 80$; $\dfrac{dx}{dt} = 0$ when $t = 2.5$; $x(2.5) = 99$

24. $\dfrac{dx}{dt} = 200t$; $\dfrac{dx}{dt} = 0$ when $t = 0$; $x(0) = 50$

25. $\dfrac{dx}{dt} = -20 - 10t$; $\dfrac{dx}{dt} = 0$ when $t = -2$; $x(-2) = 120$

26. $\dfrac{dy}{dt} = -32t + 160$; $\dfrac{dy}{dt} = 0$ when $t = 5$; $y(5) = 400$ (ft)

27. $\dfrac{dy}{dt} = -32t + 64$; $\dfrac{dy}{dt} = 0$ when $t = 2$; $y(2) = 64$ (ft)

28. $\dfrac{dy}{dt} = -32t + 128$; $\dfrac{dy}{dt} = 0$ when $t = 4$; $y(4) = 281$ (ft)

29. $\dfrac{dy}{dt} = -32t + 96$; $\dfrac{dy}{dt} = 0$ when $t = 3$; $y(3) = 194$ (ft)

30. Matches (c).
31. Matches (e).
32. Matches (b).
33. Matches (f).
34. Matches (a).
35. Matches (d).

36. The rate of change of C with respect to F is $dC/dF = \frac{5}{9}$. Because $F = 32 + \frac{9}{5}C$, the rate of change of F with respect to C is $dF/dC = \frac{9}{5}$.

37. Let r denote the radius of the circle. Then $A = \pi r^2$ and $C = 2\pi r$, so $r = \dfrac{C}{2\pi}$. Thus $A = \dfrac{1}{4\pi}C^2$, so the rate of change of A with respect to C is $dA/dC = \dfrac{C}{2\pi}$.

38. Let r denote the radius of the circular ripple in feet at time t (seconds). Then $r = 5t$, and the area within the ripple at time t is $A = \pi r^2 = 25\pi t^2$. The rate at which this area is increasing at time t is $dA/dt = 50\pi t$, so at time $t = 10$ the area is increasing at the rate of $(50\pi)(10) = 500\pi$ ft^2/s.

39. The velocity of the car (in feet per second) at time t (seconds) is $v(t) = x'(t) = 100 - 10t$. The car comes to a stop when $v(t) = 0$; that is, when $t = 10$. At that time the car has traveled a distance $x(10) = 500$ (ft). So the car skids for 10 seconds and skids a distance of 500 ft.

40. Because $V(t) = 10 - \frac{1}{5}t + \frac{1}{1000}t^2$, $V'(t) = -\frac{1}{5} + \frac{1}{500}t$ and the rate at which the water is leaking out one minute later ($t = 60$) is $V(60) = -\frac{2}{25}$ (gal/s) or—if you prefer— -4.8 gal/min. The average rate of change of V from $t = 0$ until $t = 100$ is $\dfrac{V(100) - V(0)}{100 - 0} = \dfrac{0 - 10}{100} = -\dfrac{1}{10}$. The instantaneous rate of change of V will have this value when $V'(t) = -\frac{1}{10}$, which we easily solve for $t = 50$.

41. First, $P(t) = 100 + 30t + 4t^2$. The initial population is 100, so doubling occurs when $P(t) = 200$; that is, when $4t^2 + 30t - 100 = 0$. The quadratic formula yields $t = 2.5$ as the only positive solution of this equation, so the population will take two and one-half months to double. Because $P'(t) = 30 + 8t$, the rate of growth of the population when $P = 200$ will be $P'(2.5) = 50$ (chipmunks per month).

42. In our construction, the tangent line at 1985 passes through the points $(1970, 258)$ and $(1980, 425)$, and so has slope 16.7; this yields a rate of growth of approximately 16.7 thousand per year in 1975. Note that the method is not exact.

43. On our graph, the tangent line at the point $(20, 810)$ has slope $m_1 \approx 0.6$ and the tangent line at $(40, 2686)$ has slope $m_2 \approx 0.9$. A line of slope 1 on our graph corresponds to a velocity of 125 ft/s (because the line through $(0, 0)$ and $(10, 1250)$ has slope 1), and thus we estimate the velocity of the car at time $t = 20$ to be about $(0.6)(125) = 75$ ft/s, and at time $t = 40$ it is traveling at

about $(0.9)(125) = 112.5$ ft/s. The method is crude; the answer in the back of the textbook is quite different simply because it was obtained by someone else.

44. With volume V and edge x, the volume of the cube is given by $V(x) = x^3$. Now $\dfrac{dV}{dx} = 3x^2$, which is indeed half the total surface area $6x^2$ of the cube.

45. With volume V and radius r, the volume of the sphere is $V(r) = \frac{4}{3}\pi r^3$. Then $\dfrac{dV}{dr} = 4\pi r^2$, and this is indeed the surface area of the sphere.

46. A right circular cylinder of radius r and height h has volume $V = \pi r^2 h$ and total surface area S obtained by adding the areas of its top, bottom, and curved side: $S = 2\pi r^2 + 2\pi rh$. We are given $h = 2r$, so $V(r) = 2\pi r^3$ and $S(r) = 6\pi r^2$. Also $dV/dr = 6\pi r^2 = S(r)$, so the rate of change of volume with respect to radius is indeed equal to total surface area.

47. We must compute dV/dt when $t = 30$; $V(r) = \frac{4}{3}\pi r^3$ is the volume of the balloon when its radius is r. We are given $r = \dfrac{60-t}{12}$, and thus
$$V(t) = \frac{4}{3}\pi \left(\frac{60-t}{12}\right)^3 = \frac{\pi}{1296}(216000 - 10800t + 180t^2 - t^3).$$
Therefore
$$\frac{dV}{dt} = \frac{\pi}{1296}(-10800 + 360t - 3t^2),$$
and so $V'(t) = -\dfrac{25\pi}{12}$ in.^{3}/s; that is, air is leaking out at approximately 6.545 in.^{3}/s.

48. From $V(p) = \dfrac{1.68}{p}$ we derive $V'(p) = -\dfrac{1.68}{p^2}$. The rate of change of V with respect to p when $p = 2$ (atm) is then $V'(2) = -0.42$ (liters/atm).

49. Let $V(t)$ denote the volume (in cm^3) of the snowball at time t (in hours), and let $r(t)$ denote its radius then. From the data given in the problem, $r = 12 - t$. The volume of the snowball is
$$V = \frac{4}{3}\pi r^3 = \frac{4}{3}\pi(12-t)^3 = \frac{4}{3}\pi\left(1728 - 432t + 36t^2 - t^3\right),$$
so its instantaneous rate of change is
$$V'(t) = \frac{4}{3}\pi\left(-432 + 72t - 3t^2\right).$$
Hence its rate of change of volume when $t = 6$ is $V'(6) = -144\pi$ cm^3/h. Its average rate of change of volume from $t = 3$ to $t = 9$ in cm^3/h is
$$\frac{V(9) - V(3)}{9 - 3} = \frac{36\pi - 972\pi}{6} = -156\pi \text{ (cm}^3\text{/h)}.$$

50. The velocity of the ball at time t is $\dfrac{dy}{dt} = -32t + 96$, which is zero when $t = 3$. So the maximum height of the ball is $y(3) = 256$ (ft). It hits the ground when $y(t) = 0$; that is, when $-16t^2 + 96t + 112 = 0$. The only positive solution of this equation is $t = 7$, so the impact speed of the ball is $|y'(7)| = 128$ (ft/s).

51. The spaceship hits the ground when $25t^2 - 100t + 100 = 0$, which has solution $t = 2$. The velocity of the spaceship at time t is $y'(t) = 50t - 100$, so the speed of the spaceship at impact is (fortunately) zero.

52. Because $P(t) = 100 + 4t + \frac{3}{10}t^2$, we have $P'(t) = 4 + \frac{3}{5}t$. The year 1986 corresponds to $t = 6$, so the rate of change of P then was $P'(6) = 7.6$ (thousands per year). The average rate of change of P from 1983 ($t = 3$) to 1988 ($t = 8$) was
$$\frac{P(8) - P(3)}{8 - 3} = \frac{151.2 - 114.7}{5} = 7.3 \text{ (thousands per year)}.$$

Section 3.2

1. $f'(x) = 6x - 1$
2. $g'(t) = -6t - 8t^3$
4. $g'(x) = (2x^2 - 1)(3x^2) + (4x)(x^3 + 2) = 10x^4 - 3x^2 + 8x$
5. If you write $h(x) = (x+1)(x+1)(x+1)$, you find that
$h'(x) = (x+1)(x+1) + (x+1)(x+1) + (x+1)(x+1) = 3(x+1)^2$.
If you write $h(x) = x^3 + 3x^2 + 3x + 1$, you find that $h'(x) = 3x^2 + 6x + 3 = 3(x+1)^2$.
6. $g(t) = (4t - 7)^2 = 16t^2 - 56t + 49$: $g'(t) = 32t - 56$.
7. $f(y) = 4y^3 - y$: $f'(y) = 12y^2 - 1$.
8. $f(x) = 4x^4 - x^{-2}$: $f'(x) = 16x^3 + 2x^{-3} = 16x^3 + \dfrac{2}{x^3}$.
10. $f'(t) = \dfrac{0 - (1)(-2t)}{(4 - t^2)^2} = \dfrac{2t}{(4 - t^2)^2}$
12. $f(x) = \dfrac{x}{x-2}$, so $f'(x) = \dfrac{(x-2) - x}{(x-2)^2} = \dfrac{-2}{(x-2)^2}$.
13. By first multiplying the two factors of $g(t)$:

$$g'(t) = 5t^4 + 4t^3 + 3t^2 + 4t.$$

By applying the product rule:

$$g'(t) = (t^2 + 1)(3t^2 + 2t) + (t^3 + t^2 + 1)(2t).$$

Of course both answers are the same.

14. As in Problem 13, there are two techniques; either way, $f'(x) = 238x^6 - 252x^3 + 12x^2 + 18$.
15. Write $g(z) = \tfrac{1}{2}z^{-1} - \tfrac{1}{3}z^{-2}$.
16. $f(x) = 2x - 3 + 4x^{-1} - 5x^{-2}$, so $f'(x) = 2 - \dfrac{4}{x^2} + \dfrac{10}{x^3} = \dfrac{2x^3 - 4x + 10}{x^3}$.
17. First write $g(y) = 6y^5 + 12y^4 + 16y^3 - 4y^2 - 6y$.
18. $f'(x) = \dfrac{(2x)(x^2 + 4) - (2x)(x^2 - 4)}{(x^2 + 4)^2} = \dfrac{16x}{(x^2 + 4)^2}$.
20. $u'(x) = \dfrac{-2(x+2)}{(x+2)^4} = -\dfrac{2}{(x+2)^3}$
22. $h'(x) = \dfrac{(2x - 5)(6x^2 + 2x - 3) - (2)(2x^3 + x^2 - 3x + 17)}{(2x - 5)^2} = \dfrac{8x^3 - 28x^2 - 10x - 19}{(2x - 5)^2}$
23. $g'(x) = \dfrac{(x^3 + 7x - 5)(3) - (3x)(3x^2 + 7)}{(x^3 + 7x - 5)^2} = \dfrac{3x^3 + 21x - 15 - 9x^3 - 21x}{(x^3 + 7x - 5)^2} = -\dfrac{6x^3 + 15}{(x^3 + 7x - 5)^2}$
24. First rewrite the function in the form $f(t) = \dfrac{t^2}{(t^2 + 1)^2}$.

Then $f'(t) = \dfrac{2t(t^2 + 1)^2 - 2t^2(t^2 + 1)(2t)}{(t^2 + 1)^4} = \dfrac{2t(1 - t^2)}{(t^3 + 1)^3}$.

25. First rewrite the function in the form $g(x) = \dfrac{x^3 - 2x^2}{2x - 3}$.

Then $g'(x) = \dfrac{(2x - 3)(3x^2 - 4x) - (2)(x^3 - 2x^2)}{(2x - 3)^2} = \dfrac{4x^3 - 13x^2 + 12x}{(2x - 3)^2}$.

26. First simplify: $f(x) = \dfrac{x^5 + x^3 - 1}{x^6 + x^4 + 1}$. Then

$$f'(x) = \dfrac{(x^6 + x^4 + 1)(5x^4 + 3x^2) - (x^5 + x^3 - 1)(6x^5 + 4x^3)}{(x^6 + x^4 + 1)^2}$$

$$= -\dfrac{x^2(x^8 + 2x^6 + x^4 - 6x^3 - 5x^2 - 4x - 3)}{(x^6 + x^4 + 1)^2}.$$

28. $\dfrac{dx}{dt} = -3t^{-2} + 8t^{-3}$

30. $u = \tfrac{2}{5}x^{-1} - \tfrac{3}{5} + \tfrac{2}{5}x^2$, so $\dfrac{du}{dx} = -\tfrac{2}{5}x^{-2} + \tfrac{4}{5}x$.

32. $f'(z) = \dfrac{-(1)(z^2 + 2z + 2 + 2z^2 + 2z)}{z^2(z^2 + 2z + 2)^2} = -\dfrac{3z^2 + 4z + 2}{z^2(z^2 + 2z + 2)^2}$

34. $u = \dfrac{t^2}{t^2 - 4}$ for $t \neq 0$. So $\dfrac{du}{dt} = \dfrac{(t^2 - 4)(2t) - (t^2)(2t)}{(t^2 - 4)^2} = -\dfrac{8t}{(t^2 - 4)^2}$.

36. $w = 2z^5 - \tfrac{3}{4}z^{-2}$, so $\dfrac{dw}{dz} = 10z^4 + \tfrac{3}{2}z^{-3}$.

37. $y = \dfrac{10x^6}{15x^5 - 4}$ for $x \neq 0$.

38. $\dfrac{dz}{dt} = \dfrac{-(4)(4t^3 - 12)}{(t^4 - tx^2 + 9)^2} = -\dfrac{16t}{(t^2 - 3)^3}$

40. $h(w) = w^{-1} + 10w^{-2}$, so $h'(w) = -w^{-2} - 20w^{-3}$.

41. $\dfrac{dy}{dx} = 3x^2$; the slope at P is 12.

42. $\dfrac{dy}{dx} = 6x$; the slope at P is 6. An equation of the tangent line is $y + 1 = 6(x - 1)$. Answer: $6x - y = 7$.

43. $\dfrac{dy}{dx} = -(x - 1)^2$; the slope at P is -1. An equation of the tangent line is $y - 1 = -(x - 2)$.

44. $\dfrac{dy}{dx} = 2 + x^{-2}$, so the slope at P is 6. An equation of the tangent line is $y + 1 = 6(x - 0.5)$; the answer is $6x - y = 4$.

45. $\dfrac{dy}{dx} = 3x^2 + 6x - 4$; the slope at P is 5.

46. $y = \dfrac{x^2}{x - 1}$ for $x \neq 0$, so

$$\dfrac{dy}{dx} = \dfrac{(x - 1)(2x) - x^2}{(x - 1)^2} = \dfrac{x^2 - 2x}{(x - 1)^2}.$$

The slope at P is zero; the line has equation $y = 4$.

47. Write $y = 3x^{-2} - 4x^{-3}$, so that $\dfrac{dy}{dx} = -6x^{-3} + 12x^{-4}$; the slope at P is 18.

48. $\dfrac{dy}{dx} = \dfrac{(3x - 2)(3) - (3)(3x - 2)}{(3x + 2)^2} = \dfrac{12}{(3x + 2)^2}$, so the slope at P is $\tfrac{3}{16}$. Answer: $3x - 16y = -2$.

49. $\dfrac{dy}{dx} = \dfrac{3x^2 + 6x}{(x^2 + x + 1)^2}$

50. $\dfrac{dy}{dx} = \dfrac{-(6)(-2x)}{(1 - x^2)^2} = \dfrac{12x}{(1 - x^2)^2}$; the slope at P is $\tfrac{8}{3}$.

51. $V = V_0(1 + \alpha T + \beta T^2 + \gamma T^3)$ where $\alpha \approx -0.06427 \times 10^{-3}$, $\beta \approx 8.5053 \times 10^{-6}$, and $\gamma \approx -6.79 \times 10^{-8}$. Now $dV/dt = V_0(\alpha + 2\beta T + 3\gamma T^2)$; $V = V_0 = 1000$ when $T = 0$. Because $V'(0) = \alpha V_0 < 0$, the

40   Section 3.2 Basic Differentiation Rules

water contracts when it is first heated. The rate of change of volume then is $V'(0) \approx -0.06427$ cm^3 per °C.

52. $W = \dfrac{2 \times 10^9}{R^2} = (2 \times 10^9)R^{-2}$, so $\dfrac{dW}{dR} = -\dfrac{4 \times 10^9}{R^3}$; when $R = 3960$, $\dfrac{dW}{dR} = -\dfrac{62500}{970299}$ lb/mi. Thus W decreases initially at about 1.03 oz/mi.

53. Draw a cross section of the tank through its axis of symmetry. Let r denote the radius of the (circular) water surface when the height of water in the tank is h. Draw a typical radius, label it r, and label the height h. From similar triangles in your figure, deduce that $h/r = 800/160 = 5$, so $r = h/5$. The volume of water in a cone of height h and radius r is $V = \frac{1}{3}\pi r^2 h$, so in this case we have $V = V(h) = \dfrac{\pi}{75}h^3$. The rate of change of V with respect to h is $dV/dh = \dfrac{\pi}{25}h^2$, and therefore when $h = 600$, we have $V'(600) = 14400\pi$; that is, approximately 45,239 cm^3 per cm.

54. $dy/dx = 3x^2 + 2x + 1$; the slope of the tangent line at $(1,3)$ is $y'(1) = 6$. The equation of the tangent line at $(1,3)$ is $y - 3 = 6(x-1)$; that is, $y = 6x - 3$. The intercepts of the line are $(0,-3)$ and $(1/2, 0)$.

55. The slope of the tangent line can be computed using dy/dx at $x = a$ and also by using the two points known to lie on the line. We thereby find that $3a^2 = \dfrac{a^3 - 5}{a - 1}$. This leads to the equation $(a+1)(2a^2 - 5a + 5) = 0$. The quadratic factor has negative discriminant, so the only real solution of the cubic equation is $a = -1$. The point of tangency is $(-1, -1)$, the slope there is 3, and the equation of the line in question is $y = 3x + 2$.

56. Let (a, a^3) be a point of tangency. The tangent line therefore has slope $3a^2$ and, because it passes through $(2, 8)$, we have
$$3a^2 = \dfrac{a^3 - 8}{a - 2}.$$
This leads to the equation $2a^2 - 2a - 4 = 0$, so that $a = -1$ or $a = 2$. Although $a = 2$ does not sstisfy the equation displayed here, this is only a technicality; it does yield the line tangent at $(2, 8)$ with slope 12. The solution $a = -1$ gives the line tangent at $(-1, 1)$ with slope 3. The two lines have equations $y - 8 = 12(x - 2)$ and $y + 1 = 3(x + 1)$; that is, $y = 12x - 16$ and $y = 3x + 2$.

57. Suppose that some line is tangent at both (a, a^2) and (b, b^2). Use the derivative to show that $a = b$.

58. Let $(a, 1/a)$ be a point of tangency. The slope of the tangent there is $-1/a^2$, so $-1/a^2 = -2$. Thus there are two possible values for a: $\pm\frac{1}{2}\sqrt{2}$. These lead to the equations of the two lines: $y = -2x + 2\sqrt{2}$ and $y = -2x - 2\sqrt{2}$.

59. Given $y = x^n$, we have $\dfrac{dy}{dx} = nx^{n-1}$. The line tangent to $y = x^n$ at $P(x_0, y_0)$ has slope that we compute in two ways and then equate:
$$\dfrac{y - (x_0)^n}{x - x_0} = n(x_0)^{n-1}.$$
To find the x-intercept of this line, substitute $y = 0$ into this equation; it follows that the x-intercept is $x = \dfrac{n-1}{n}x_0$.

60. Because $dy/dx = 5x^4 + 2 \geq 2 > 0$ for all x, the curve has no horizontal tangent line. The minimal slope occurs when dy/dx is minimal, and this occurs when $x = 0$. So the smallest slope that a line tangent to this graph can have is 2.

61. $D_x[f(x)]^3 = f'(x)f(x)f(x) + f(x)f'(x)f(x) + f(x)f(x)f'(x) = 3[f(x)]^2 f'(x)$.

64. With $f(x) = x^2 + x + 1$ and $n = 100$, we obtain $D_x(x^2 + x + 1)^{100} = 100(x^2 + x + 1)^{99}(2x + 1)$.

65. Apply the result of Problem 63 with $f(x) = x^3 - 17x + 35$ and $n = 17$.

Section 3.2 Basic Differentiation Rules 41

66. We begin with $f(x) = ax^3 + bx^2 + cx + d$. Then $f'(x) = 3ax^2 + 2bx + c$. The conditions in the problem require that (simultaneously)

$$1 = f(0) = d, \qquad 0 = f(1) = a + b + c + d,$$
$$0 = f'(0) = c, \quad \text{and} \quad 0 = f'(1) = 3a + 2b + c.$$

These equations have solution $a = 2$, $b = -3$, $c = 0$, and $d = 1$. Therefore $f(x) = 2x^3 - 3x^2 + 1$.

67. When $n = 0$, $\dfrac{dy}{dx} = -\dfrac{2x}{(1+x^2)^2}$; when $n = 2$, $\dfrac{dy}{dx} = \dfrac{2x}{(1+x^2)^2}$. In both cases there is only one horizontal tangent, at the point where $x = 0$.

68. When $n = 1$, $\dfrac{dy}{dx} = \dfrac{1-x^2}{(1+x^2)^2}$, so there are horizontal tangents where $x = \pm 1$.

69. If $n \geq 3$, then $\dfrac{dy}{dx} = \dfrac{x^{n-1}[(n-2)x^2 + n]}{(x^2+1)^2}$: if $n \geq 3$, then the derivative can be zero only when $x = 0$.

70. $f'(x) = 1$ when $x = \pm 1$.

71. $D_x f'(x) = 0$ when $x = 0, \pm\sqrt{3}$.

Section 3.3

1. $dy/dx = 5(3x+4)^4(3) = 15(3x+4)^4$
2. $dy/dx = -15(2-5x)^2$
4. $y = (2x+1)^{-3}$: $dy/dx = -6(2x+1)^{-4}$
6. $dy/dx = 24x^2(7-2x^3)^{-5}$
7. $dy/dx = -4(2-x)^3(3+x)^7 + 7(2-x)^4(3+x)^6$
8. $dy/dx = 5(x+x^2)^4(1+2x)(1+x^3)^2 + 6x^2(x+x^2)^5(1+x^3)$
10. $dy/dx = \dfrac{-6x(4+5x+6x^2)(1-x^2)^2 - 2(5+12x)(1-x^2)^3}{(4+5x+6x^2)^3}$.

A common factor of $4 + 5x + 6x^2$ was cancelled from both terms in the numerator and from the denominator.

12. $dy/dx = -5\bigl(x + (x+x^2)^{-3}\bigr)^{-6}\bigl(1 - 3(x+x^2)^{-4}(1+2x)\bigr)$
13. $dy/dx = 3(u+1)^2 du/dx = -\dfrac{6}{x^3}\left(\dfrac{1}{x^2}+1\right)^2$
14. $dy/dx = \dfrac{1-6x}{3(1+2x)^3}$
16. $dy/dx = \dfrac{-15}{(3x-2)^6}$
18. $dy/dx = \dfrac{1}{(2x+1)^2}$
19. $dy/dx = -\dfrac{2(x^3-1)^2(x^3+1)^2(5x^6-14)}{x^{29}}$. This is the result of considerable simplification of the initial result, which was $dy/dx = -4x^{-5}(x^{-2}-x^{-8})^3 + 3x^{-4}(8x^{-9}-2x^{-3})(x^{-2}-x^{-8})^2$.
20. $dy/dx = \dfrac{x^2(6x^4 - x^3 - 2x - 24)}{(-2x^5 - x + 4)^5}$. Again, this is the result of simplification of the initial result, which was $dy/dx = \dfrac{-8(1+2x^{-2})(x-2x^{-1})}{(2x+1-4x^{-1})^5} + \dfrac{1+2x^{-2}}{(2x+1-4x^{-1})^4}$.
22. $f'(x) = -\dfrac{15x^2}{(5x^3+2)^2}$

24. $f'(x) = 3(x^2 - 4x + 1)^2(2x - 4)$

26. $f'(x) = \dfrac{(x^2 + x + 1)^6(10x^2 + 17x + 3)}{(x+1)^5}$, upon simplification of
$f'(x) = \dfrac{7(2x+1)(x+1)(x^2+x+1)^6 - 4(x^2+x+1)^7}{(x+1)^5}$.

28. $h'(z) = 6z^3(z^2 + 4)^2 + 2z(z^2 + 4)^3$

30. $g'(t) = 2\left(t^2 + 1 + \dfrac{1}{t}\right)\left(2t - \dfrac{1}{t^2}\right)$

31. $f'(u) = 8u(u+1)^3(u^2+1)^3 + 3(u+1)^2(u^2+1)^4$

32. $g'(w) = (w+4)^5(2w-3) + 5(w+4)^4(w^2 - 3w + 4)$

34. $p'(t) = \dfrac{4(t^{-2} + 2t^{-3} + 3t^{-4})}{(t^{-1} + t^{-2} + t^{-3})^5} = \dfrac{4t^{11}(t^2 + 2t + 3)}{(t^2 + t + 1)^5}$

36. $g'(x) = 30[1 + 4(2x + 3x^2)(x^2 + x^3)^3][x + (x^2 + x^3)^4]^4 \cdot [1 + (x + (x^2 + x^3)^4)^5]^5$.
When $g'(x)$ is expanded completely (written in polynomial form), it has degree 359 and the term with largest coefficient is $74313942135996360069651059069038417440x^{287}$.

38. $dy/dx \equiv 1$

40. $dy/dx = -3(1-x)^2$

42. $dy/dx = -\dfrac{2}{(x+1)^3}$

43. $dy/dx = -\dfrac{2x}{(x^2+1)^2}$

44. $dy/dx = 4x(x^2 + 1)$

45. $f'(x) = 3x^2 \cos x^3$

46. $g'(t) = 3\sin^2 t \cos t$

48. $k'(u) = \cos u \cos(1 + \sin u)$

49. $r(t) = 2t$ and $a(t) = \pi(2t)^2$ and $a'(t) = 8\pi t$. When $r = 10$, $t = 5$, and at that time the rate of change of area with respect to time is $a'(5) = 40\pi$.

50. If the circle has area A and radius r, then $A = \pi r^2$, so that $r = \sqrt{A/\pi}$. If t denotes time in seconds, then the rate of change of the radius of the circle is

$$\frac{dr}{dt} = \frac{dr}{dA} \cdot \frac{dA}{dt} = \frac{1}{2\sqrt{\pi A}} \cdot \frac{dA}{dt}.$$

We are given the values $A = 75\pi$ and $dA/dt = -2\pi$; when we substitute these values into the last expression above, we find that $\dfrac{dr}{dt} = -\dfrac{1}{15}\sqrt{3}$.

51. Let A denote the area of the square and x the length of each edge. Then $A = x^2$, so $dA/dx = 2x$. If t denotes time (in seconds), then

$$\frac{dA}{dt} = \frac{dA}{dx} \cdot \frac{dx}{dt} = 2x\frac{dx}{dt}.$$

All that remains is to substitute the given data $x = 10$ and $dx/dt = -2$.

52. Let x denote the length of each side of the triangle. Then its altitude is $\frac{1}{2}x\sqrt{3}$, and so its area is $A = \frac{1}{4}x^2\sqrt{3}$. Therefore the rate of change of its area with respect to time t (in seconds) is

$$\frac{dA}{dt} = \frac{1}{2}x\sqrt{3}\frac{dx}{dt}.$$

We are given $x = 10$ and $dx/dt = 2$, so at that point the area is increasing at $10\sqrt{3}$ in.²/s.

53. The volume of the block is $V = x^3$ where x is the length of each edge. So $\dfrac{dV}{dt} = 3x^2\dfrac{dx}{dt}$. We are given $dx/dt = -2$, so when $x = 10$ the volume of the block is decreasing at 600 in.³/h.

54. By the chain rule, $f'(y) = h'(g(y)) \cdot g'(y)$; $f'(-1) = h'(g(-1)) \cdot g'(-1) = h'(2) \cdot g'(-1) = -1 \cdot 7 = -7$.

55. $G'(t) = f'(h(t)) \cdot h'(t)$. Now $h(1) = 4$, $h'(1) = -6$, and $f'(4) = 3$, so $G'(1) = 3 \cdot (-6) = -18$.

56. The derivative of $f(f(f(x)))$ is the product of the three expressions $f'(f(f(x)))$, $f'(f(x))$, and $f'(x)$. When $x = 0$, $f(x) = 0$ and $f'(x) = 1$. Thus when $x = 0$, each of the three expressions has value 1, so the answer is 1.

57. The volume of the balloon is given by $V = \frac{4}{3}\pi r^3$, so
$$\frac{dV}{dt} = \frac{dV}{dr} \cdot \frac{dr}{dt} = 4\pi r^2 \frac{dr}{dt}.$$
Answer: When $r = 10$, $dV/dt = 4\pi \cdot 10^2 \cdot 1 = 400\pi$ (approximately 1256.64) cm^3/s.

58. Let V denote the volume of the balloon and r its radius at time t (in seconds). We are given $dV/dt = 200\pi$. Now
$$\frac{dV}{dt} = \frac{dV}{dr} \cdot \frac{dr}{dt} = 4\pi r^2 \frac{dr}{dt}.$$
When $r = 5$, we have $200\pi = 4\pi \cdot 25 \cdot (dr/dt)$, so $dr/dt = 2$. Answer: When $r = 5$ (cm), the radius of the balloon is increasing at 2 cm/s.

59. Given: $\frac{dr}{dt} = -3$. Now $\frac{dV}{dt} = -300\pi = 4\pi r^2 \cdot \left(\frac{dr}{dt}\right)$. So $4\pi r^2 = 100\pi$, and therefore $r = 5$ (cm).

60. Let x denote the radius of the hailstone and let V denote its volume. Then
$$V = \frac{4}{3}\pi x^3, \text{ and so } \frac{dV}{dt} = 4\pi x^2 \frac{dx}{dt}.$$
When $x = 2$, $dV/dt = -0.1$, and therefore $-\frac{1}{10} = 4\pi \cdot 2^2 \cdot dx/dt$. So $dx/dt = -\frac{1}{160\pi}$. Answer: At the time in question, the radius of the hailstone is decreasing at $\frac{1}{160\pi}$ cm/s —that is, at about 0.002 cm/s.

61. Let V denote the volume of the snowball and A its surface area at time t (in hours). Then
$$dV/dt = kA \text{ and } A = cV^{2/3}$$
(the latter because A is proportional to r^2, whereas V is proportional to r^3). Therefore
$$dV/dt = \alpha V^{2/3} \text{ and thus } dt/dV = \beta V^{-2/3}$$
(α and β are constants). From the last equation we may conclude that $t = \gamma V^{1/3} + \delta$ for some constants γ and δ, so that $V = V(t) = (Pt+Q)^3$ for some constants P and Q. From the information $500 = V(0) = Q^3$ and $250 = V(1) = (P+Q)^3$, we find that $Q = 5\sqrt[3]{4}$ and that $P = -5 \cdot (\sqrt[3]{4} - \sqrt[3]{2})$. Now $V(t) = 0$ when $PT + Q = 0$; it turns out that
$$T = \frac{\sqrt[3]{2}}{\sqrt[3]{2} - 1} \approx 4.8473.$$
Therefore the snowball finishes melting at about 2:50:50 P.M. on the same day.

62. Let V denote the volume of the block, x the length of each of its edges. Then $V = x^3$. In 8 hours x decreases from 20 to 8, and dx/dt is steady, so t hours after 8 A.M. we have
$$x = 20 - \frac{3}{2}t.$$
Also
$$\frac{dV}{dt} = \frac{dV}{dx} \cdot \frac{dx}{dt} = 3x^2 \cdot \left(-\frac{3}{2}\right) = -\frac{9}{2}\left(20 - \frac{3}{2}t\right)^2.$$
At 12 noon we have $t = 4$, so at noon $dV/dt = -\frac{9}{2}(20 - 6)^2 = -882$: The volume is decreasing at 882 in.^{3}/h then.

63. $\frac{du}{dx} = \frac{du}{dw} \cdot \frac{dw}{dx}$. But substitute $\frac{du}{dw} = \frac{du}{dv} \cdot \frac{dv}{dw}$.

Section 3.4

1. $f(x) = 4x^{5/2} + 2x^{-1/2}$, so $f'(x) = 10x^{3/2} - x^{-3/2}$.
2. $g'(t) = 12t^{1/3} + t^{-4/3}$
3. $f(x) = (2x+1)^{1/2}$, so $f'(x) = (2x+1)^{-1/2}$
4. $h(z) = (7 - 6z)^{-1/3}$, so $h'(z) = 2(7 - 6z)^{-4/3}$.
5. $f(x) = 6x^{-1/2} - x^{3/2}$, so $f'(x) = -3x^{-3/2} - \frac{3}{2}x^{1/2}$.
6. $\phi'(u) = -\frac{14}{3}u^{-5/3} + \frac{2}{3}u^{-2/3} - 10u^{7/3}$
7. $f'(x) = \frac{3}{2}(2x+3)^{1/2} \cdot 2 = 3(2x+3)^{1/2}$
8. $g'(x) = 4(3x+4)^{1/3}$
9. $f'(x) = 6x(3 - 2x^2)^{-5/2}$
10. $f'(y) = -\frac{2}{3}(4 - 3y^3)^{-5/3} \cdot (-9y^2) = 6y^2(4 - 3y^3)^{-5/3}$
11. $f'(x) = \dfrac{3x^2}{2\sqrt{x^3+1}}$
12. $g(z) = (z^4 + 3)^{-2}$, so $g'(z) = -8z^3(z^4+3)^{-3}$.
13. $f(x) = (2x^2 + 1)^{1/2}$, so $f'(x) = 2x(2x^2 + 1)^{-1/2}$.
14. $f'(t) = \dfrac{\sqrt{1+t^4} - 2t^4(1+t^4)^{-1/2}}{1+t^4} = \dfrac{1 - t^4}{(1+t^4)^{3/2}}$
15. $f'(t) = 3t^2(2t^3)^{-1/2} = \frac{3}{2}\sqrt{2t}$
16. $g(t) = (3t^5)^{-1/2}$, so $g'(t) = -\frac{1}{2}(3t^5)^{-3/2} \cdot 15t^4$.
18. $g'(z) = 97(3z^2 - 4)^{96} \cdot 6z = 582z(3z^2 - 4)^{96}$
19. $g(x) = (x - 2x^3)^{-4/3}$, so $g'(x) = -\frac{4}{3}(x - 2x^3)^{-7/3}(1 - 6x^2)$.
20. $f'(t) = 5\left(t^2 + (1+t)^4\right)^4 \left(2t + 4(1+t)^3\right)$
21. $f'(x) = (1-x^2)^{1/2} - x^2(1-x^2)^{-1/2} = (1-2x^2)(1-x^2)^{-1/2}$
22. $g(x) = \left(\dfrac{2x+1}{x-1}\right)^{1/2}$, so $g'(x) = \dfrac{1}{2}\left(\dfrac{2x+1}{x-1}\right)^{-1/2} \cdot \dfrac{(x-1)\cdot 2 - (2x+1)\cdot 1}{(x-1)^2} = \dfrac{-3}{2(x-1)^2}\sqrt{\dfrac{x-1}{2x+1}}$.
23. $f'(t) = \dfrac{1}{2}\left(\dfrac{t^2+1}{t^2-1}\right)^{-1/2} \cdot \dfrac{(t^2-1)(2t) - (2t)(t^2+1)}{(t^2-1)^2}$

    $= \dfrac{1}{2}\left(\dfrac{t^2-1}{t^2+1}\right)^{1/2} \cdot \dfrac{-4t}{(t^2-1)^2} = -\dfrac{2t}{(t^2+1)^{1/2}(t^2-1)^{3/2}}$
24. $h'(y) = 17\left(\dfrac{y+1}{y-1}\right)^{16} \cdot \dfrac{(y-1)-(y+1)}{(y-1)^2} = -\dfrac{34(y+1)^{16}}{(y-1)^{18}}$
25. $f'(x) = 3\left(x - \dfrac{1}{x}\right)^2 \cdot \left(1 + \dfrac{1}{x^2}\right)$
26. $g'(z) = \dfrac{2z(1+z^2)^{1/2} - \frac{1}{2}z^2(1+z^2)^{-1/2}(2z)}{1+z^2} = \dfrac{2z(1+z^2) - z^3}{(1+z^2)^{3/2}} = \dfrac{z^3 + 2z}{(1+z^2)^{3/2}}$
27. $f'(v) = \dfrac{\frac{1}{2}v(v+1)^{-1/2} - (v+1)^{1/2}}{v^2} = \dfrac{v - 2(v+1)}{2v^2\sqrt{v+1}} = -\dfrac{v+2}{2v^2\sqrt{v+1}}$
28. $h'(x) = \dfrac{5}{3}\left(\dfrac{x}{1+x^2}\right)^{2/3} \cdot \dfrac{1-x^2}{(1+x^2)^2}$
29. $f(x) = (1-x^2)^{1/3}$, so $f'(x) = \frac{1}{3}(1-x^2)^{-2/3}(-2x)$.
30. $g(x) = (x + x^{1/2})^{1/2}$: $g'(x) = \frac{1}{2}(x + x^{1/2})^{-1/2}\left(1 + \frac{1}{2}x^{-1/2}\right)$, which simplifies to $g'(x) = \dfrac{1 + 2\sqrt{x}}{4\sqrt{x^2 + x}}$.

31. $f'(x) = (3-4x)^{1/2} - 2x(3-4x)^{-1/2} = 3(1-2x)(3-4x)^{-1/2}$

32. $g(t) = t^{-2}[t - (1+t^2)^{1/2}]$, so $g'(t) = -2t^{-3}[t - (1+t^2)^{1/2}] + t^{-2}[1 - t(1+t^2)^{-1/2}]$.

33. $f'(x) = \frac{2}{3}(1-x^2)(2x+4)^{-2/3} - 2x(2x+4)^{1/3} = \frac{4}{3}(4+2x)^{1/3}(2 - 6x - 5x^2)$

34. $f'(x) = -\frac{1}{2}(1-x)^{-1/2}(2-x)^{1/3} - \frac{1}{3}(1-x)^{1/2}(2-x)^{-2/3}$

36. $f'(x) = (1+2x+3x^2)^{10} + 10x(1+2x+3x^2)^9(2+6x)$

37. $f'(x) = \dfrac{2(3x+4)^5 - 15(3x+4)^4(2x-1)}{(3x+4)^{10}}$, which can be simplified to $f'(x) = \dfrac{23 - 24x}{(3x+4)^6}$.

38. $h'(z) = 4(z-1)^3(z+1)^6 + 6(z-1)^4(z+1)^5$, which can be simplified to $h'(z) = 2(z-1)^3(z+1)^5(5z-1)$

39. $f'(x) = \dfrac{(3x+4)^{1/3}(2x+1)^{-1/2} - (3x+4)^{-2/3}(2x+1)^{1/2}}{(3x+4)^{2/3}}$
$= \dfrac{(3x+4) - (2x+1)}{(3x+4)^{4/3}(2x+1)^{1/2}} = \dfrac{x+3}{(3x+4)^{4/3}(2x+1)^{1/2}}.$

40. $f'(x) = -5(1-3x^4)^4(12x^3)(4-x)^{1/3} - \frac{1}{3}(1-3x^4)^5(4-x)^{-2/3}$

41. $h(y) = \dfrac{(1+y)^{1/2} + (1-y)^{1/2}}{y^{5/3}}$, so
$h'(y) = \dfrac{\frac{1}{2}y^{5/3}[(1+y)^{-1/2} - (1-y)^{-1/2}] - \frac{5}{3}y^{2/3}[(1+y)^{1/2} + (1-y)^{1/2}]}{y^{10/3}}$
$= \dfrac{(7y-10)\sqrt{1+y} - (7y+10)\sqrt{1-y}}{6y^{8/3}\sqrt{1-y^2}}.$

42. $f'(x) = -\dfrac{1}{6x^{2/3}\sqrt{1 - x^{1/3}}}$

43. $g'(t) = \frac{1}{2}[t + (t + t^{1/2})^{1/2}]^{-1/2}[1 + \frac{1}{2}(t + t^{1/2})^{-1/2}(1 + \frac{1}{2}t^{-1/2})] = \dfrac{1 + \dfrac{1 + \dfrac{1}{2\sqrt{t}}}{2\sqrt{t + \sqrt{t}}}}{2\sqrt{t + \sqrt{t + \sqrt{t}}}}$

44. $f'(x) = \dfrac{x^4}{(1+x^2)^2\sqrt{1 - \dfrac{1}{1+x^2}}} + 3x^2\sqrt{1 - \dfrac{1}{1+x^2}}.$

45. $\dfrac{dy}{dx} = \dfrac{2}{3x^{1/3}}$, so $\dfrac{dy}{dx}$ is never zero: No horizontal tangents. There is a vertical tangent at $(0,0)$.

46. $\dfrac{dy}{dx} = \dfrac{4 - 2x^2}{\sqrt{4 - x^2}}$, so there are horizontal tangents at $(\sqrt{2}, 2)$ and $(-\sqrt{2}, -2)$. There are vertical tangents at $(2,0)$ and $(-2,0)$.

47. $\dfrac{dy}{dx} = \dfrac{1 - 3x}{2\sqrt{x}}$, so there is a horizontal tangent where $x = \frac{1}{3}$ and $y = \frac{2}{9}\sqrt{3}$. There is a vertical tangent at $(0,0)$.

48. $\dfrac{dy}{dx} = \dfrac{x}{(9-x^2)^{3/2}}$, so there is a horizontal tangent at $(0, \frac{1}{3})$. There are no vertical tangents because $y(x)$ is undefined at $x = \pm 3$.

49. $\dfrac{dy}{dx} = \dfrac{1}{(1-x^2)^{3/2}}$, so there are no horizontal tangents. There are no vertical tangents because $y(x)$ is undefined at $x = \pm 1$.

50. $\dfrac{dy}{dx} = \dfrac{x(2x^2 - 5)}{\sqrt{x^4 - 5x^2 + 4}}$; there is a horizontal tangent at $(0, 2)$ and vertical tangents at $(\pm 1, 0)$ and $(\pm 2, 0)$.

51. When $x = 4$, $y = f(4) = 4$ and $f'(4) = \frac{1}{2}$. The equation of the tangent line is $y - 4 = \frac{1}{2}(x - 4)$, or $2y - x = 4$.

52. When $x = 8$, $y = f(8) = 6$ and $f'(8) = \frac{1}{4}$. The equation of the tangent line is $y - 6 = \frac{1}{4}(x - 8)$, or $4y - x = 16$.

53. When $x = -1$, $y = f(-1) = 3$ and $f'(-1) = -2$. The equation of the tangent line is $y - 3 = -2(x+1)$, or $y + 2x = 1$.

54. When $x = \frac{3}{4}$, $y = f(\frac{3}{4}) = 1$ and $f'(\frac{3}{4}) = -2$. The equation of the tangent line is $y - 1 = -2(x - \frac{3}{4})$, or $2y = 5 - 4x$.

55. When $x = 0$, $y = f(0) = 0$ and $f'(0) = 2$. The equation of the tangent line is $y = 2x$.

56. When $x = 4$, $y = f(4) = -6$ and $f'(4) = -\frac{11}{4}$. The equation of the tangent line is $y + 6 = -\frac{11}{4}(x-4)$, or $4y = -11x + 20$.

57. Matches (d).
58. Matches (f).
59. Matches (b).
60. Matches (a).
61. Matches (e).
62. Matches (c).

63. $L = \dfrac{P^2 g}{4\pi^2}$, so $\dfrac{dL}{dP} = \dfrac{Pg}{2\pi^2}$, and hence $\dfrac{dP}{dL} = \dfrac{2\pi^2}{Pg}$. Given $g = 32$ and $P = 2$, we find the value of the latter to be $\pi^2/32 \approx 0.308$ (seconds per foot).

64. $dV/dS = \frac{1}{4}\sqrt{S/\pi}$, and $S = 400\pi$ when the radius of the sphere is 10, so the answer is 5 (in appropriate units).

65. Whether $y = +\sqrt{1-x^2}$ or $y = -\sqrt{1-x^2}$, it follows easily that $dy/dx = -x/y$. The slope of the tangent is -2 when $x = 2y$, so from the equation $x^2 + y^2 = 1$ we see that $x^2 = 4/5$.

66. Using some of the results in the preceding solution, we find that the slope of the tangent is 3 when $x = -3y$, so that $y^2 = \frac{1}{10}$. So the two points of tangency are $(-3/\sqrt{10}, 1/\sqrt{10})$ and $(3/\sqrt{10}, -1/\sqrt{10})$.

67. The line tangent to the parabola $y = x^2$ at the point $Q(a, a^2)$ has slope $2a$, so the normal to the parabola at Q has slope $-1/(2a)$. The normal also passes through $P(18, 0)$, so we can find its slope another way—by using the two-point formula. Thus

$$-\frac{1}{2a} = \frac{a^2 - 0}{a - 18};$$

$$18 - a = 2a^3;$$

$$2a^3 + a - 18 = 0.$$

By inspection, $a = 2$ is a solution. Thus $a - 2$ is a factor of the cubic, so

$$2a^3 + a - 18 = (a - 2)(2a^2 + 4a + 9).$$

The quadratic factor has negative discriminant, so $a = 2$ is the only real solution of $2a^3 + a - 18 = 0$. Therefore the normal line has slope $-1/4$ and equation $x + 4y = 18$.

68. Let $Q(a, a^2)$ be a point on the parabola $y = -x^2$ at which some line through $P(3, 10)$ is normal to the parabola. Then, as in the solution to Problem 55, we find that

$$\frac{a^2 - 10}{a - 3} = -\frac{1}{2a}.$$

This yields the cubic equation $2a^3 - 19a - 3 = 0$, and after a little computation we find one of its small integral roots to be $r = -3$. So $a + 3$ is a factor of the cubic; the other factor is $2a^2 - 6a - 1$, which is zero when $a = \dfrac{3 \pm \sqrt{11}}{2}$. The equations of the three lines are, with each of these three values of a, $y - 10 = -\dfrac{1}{2a}(x - 3)$.

69. If a line through $P(0, 5/2)$ is normal to $y = x^{2/3}$ at $Q(a, a^{2/3})$, then it has slope $(-3/2)a^{1/3}$. As in the two previous solutions, we find that

$$\frac{a^{2/3} - \frac{5}{2}}{a} = -\frac{3}{2}a^{1/3},$$

which yields $3a^{4/3} + 2a^{2/3} - 5 = 0$. Put $u = a^{2/3}$; we obtain $3u^2 + 2u - 5 = 0$, so that $(3u+5)(u-1) = 0$. Because $u = a^{2/3} > 0$, $u = 1$ is the only solution, so $a = 1$ and $a = -1$ yield the two possibilities for the point P and thereby the equations of the two lines.

71. Equation (3) is an *identity*, and if two functions have identical graphs on an interval, then their derivatives will also be identically equal to each other on that interval. There is no point in differentiating both sides of an algebraic *equation*.

Section 3.5

1. Maximum value 2 at $x = -1$ because f is a decreasing function; no minimum value because $(1, 0)$ is not on the graph.

2. Minimum value -1 at $x = -1$ because f is an increasing function; no maximum value because $(1, 3)$ is not on the graph.

3. Minimum value 0 at $x = 0$; no maximum value because $(-1, 1)$ and $(1, 1)$ are not on the graph of f.

4. No maximum value because $\lim_{x \to 0^+} f(x) = +\infty$. Minimum value 1 at $x = 1$ because f is a decreasing function.

5. Minimum value 0 at $x = 2$, maximum value 2 at $x = 4$.

6. The graph of f is a parabola opening downward with its vertex at $(0, 3)$, so the maximum value of f is 5 at $x = 0$. There is no minimum at $(-1, 4)$ because $f(1.5) = 2.75 < 4$. There is no minimum at $(-2, 1)$ because that point is not on the graph of f.

7. The graph of f is increasing, so f has a minimum at $(-1, 0)$ and a maximum at $(1, 2)$.

8. The maximum of $f(x)$ occurs where its denominator is minimal—that is, when $x = 0$. But f has no minimum because $f(x) \to 0^+$ as $x \to \pm\infty$.

9. Maximum $-1/6$ at $x = 3$, minimum $-1/2$ at $x = 2$.

10. Minimum 4 at $x = 1/2$, no maximum because $f(x) \to +\infty$ as $x \to 1^-$ and as $x \to 0^+$.

11. Because $f'(x) \equiv 3$ is never zero, the only candidates for extrema are the two endpoints -2 and 3. Now $f(-2) = -8$ and $f(3) = 7$, so the minimum value of f is -8 and its maximum value is 7.

12. Because $g'(x) \equiv -3 \neq 0$, the only candidates for extrema are the two endpoints -1 and 5. Minimum: $g(5) = -11$. Maximum: $g(-1) = 7$.

13. Because $h'(x) = -2x$ is never zero on the domain $[1, 3]$ of h, the extrema can occur only at the endpoints of the domain. And $h(3) = -5 < 3 = h(1)$, so the minimum value of h is -5 and its maximum value is 3.

14. $f'(x) = 2x$; $f'(x) = 0$ when $x = 0$. The minimum value of f is $f(0) = 3$; its maximum is $f(5) = 28$.

15. $g'(x) = 2x - 2$; $g'(1) = 0$. $g(-1) = 4$, $g(1) = 0$ (minimum), and $g(4) = 9$ (maximum).

16. $h'(x) = 2x + 4$; $h'(x) = 0$ when $x = -2$. $h(-3) = 4$, $h(-2) = 3$ (minimum), and $h(0) = 7$ (maximum).

17. $f'(x) = 3x^2 - 3$; $f'(x) = 0$ when $x = \pm 1$. And $f(-2) = -2 = f(1)$ is the minimum, $f(-1) = 2$ is neither, and $f(4) = 52$ is the maximum.

18. $g'(x) = 6x^2 - 18x + 12 = 6(x-1)(x-2)$, so $g'(x) = 0$ when $x = 1$ and when $x = 2$. So $g(0) = 0$ is the minimum value of g, $g(1) = 5$ and $g(2) = 4$ are neither maxima nor minima, and $g(4) = 32$ is the maximum value of g.

19. $h'(x) = 1 - \dfrac{4}{x^2}$; $h'(x) = 0$ when $x = \pm 2$, but -2 is not in the domain of h. The minimum is $h(2) = 4$ and the maximum value of h is $h(1) = h(4) = 5$.

20. $f'(x) = 2x - \dfrac{16}{x^2}$; $f'(x) = 0$ when $x^3 = 8$—that is, when $x = 2$. $f(1) = 17$ (maximum), $f(2) = 12$ (minimum), and $f(3) = 43/3$, (neither).

21. $f'(x) \equiv -2$; $f(-1) = 5$ (maximum), $f(1) = 1$ (minimum).

22. $f'(x) = 2x - 4$; $f'(x) = 0$ when $x = 2$. $f(0) = 3$ (maximum) and $f(2) = -1$ (minimum).

23. $f'(x) = -12 - 18x$; $f'(x) = 0$ when $x = -2/3$. $f(-1) = 8$, $f(-2/3) = 9$ (maximum), and $f(1) = -16$ (minimum).

24. $f'(x) = 4x - 4$; $f'(x) = 0$ when $x = 1$. $f(1) = 5$ (minimum) and $f(0) = f(2) = 7$ (maximum).

25. $f'(x) = 3x^2 - 6x - 9 = 3(x+1)(x-3)$; $f'(x) = 0$ when $x = -1$ and when $x = 3$. $f(-2) = 3$, $f(-1) = 10$ (maximum), $f(3) = -22$ (minimum), and $f(4) = -15$.

26. $f(x) = 3x^2 + 1 > 0$ for all x. $f(-1) = -2$ (minimum) and $f(2) = 10$ (maximum).

27. $f'(x) = 15x^4 - 15x^2 = 15x^2(x+1)(x-1)$; $f'(x) = 0$ when $x = -1$, $x = 0$, or $x = 1$. $f(-2) = -56$ (minimum), $f(-1) = 2$, $f(0) = 0$, $f(1) = -2$, and $f(2) = 56$ (maximum).

28. $f'(x) = -2$ for $1 < x < 3/2$, $f'(x) = 2$ for $3/2 < x < 2$; $f'(3/2)$ does not exist. $f(1) = 1 = f(2)$ (maximum) and $f(3/2) = 0$ (minimum).

29. $f'(7/3)$ does not exist and $f'(x)$ is never zero. $f(1) = 9$, $f(7/3) = 5$ (minimum), and $f(5) = 13$ (maximum).

30. $f(x) = -2x$ for $-2 \leq x < -1$, $f(x) = 2$ for $-1 \leq x \leq 1$, and $f(x) = 2x$ for $1 < x \leq 2$. So $f'(x) = -2$ for x in $(-2, -1)$, $f'(x) = 0$ for x in $(-1, 1)$, and $f'(x) = 2$ for x in $(1, 2)$; $f'(-1)$ and $f'(1)$ do not exist. $f(-2) = 4 = f(2)$ (maximum) and $f(x) = 2$ (minimum) for each x in $[-1, 1]$.

31. $f'(x) = 150x^2 - 210x + 72 = 6(5x-3)(5x-4)$; $f'(x) = 0$ when $x = 3/5$ and when $x = 4/5$. $f(0) = 0$ (minimum), $f(3/5) = 16.2$, $f(4/5) = 16$, and $f(1) = 17$ (maximum).

32. $f'(x) = 2 - \dfrac{1}{2x^2}$; there are no points in the domain of f at which $f'(x) = 0$. $f(1) = 2.5$ (minimum) and $f(4) = 8.125$ (maximum).

33. $f'(x) = \dfrac{1}{(x+1)^2}$ is never zero and exists for all x in $[0,3]$. $f(0) = 0$ (minimum) and $f(3) = 3/4$ (maximum).

34. $f'(x) = \dfrac{1-x^2}{(1+x^2)^2}$; $f'(x)$ always exists and $f'(x) = 0$ when $x = 1$ (and when $x = -1$, but the latter is not in the domain of f). $f(0) = 0$ (minimum), $f(1) = 1/2$ (maximum), and $f(3) = 0.3$.

35. $f'(x) = \dfrac{(x+1)(x-3)}{(x^2+3)^3}$; $f'(x)$ always exists and $f'(x) = 0$ when $x = -1$ and when $x = 3$. $f(-2) = 3/7$, $f(-1) = 1/2$ (maximum), $f(3) = -1/6$ (minimum), and $f(5) = -1/7$.

36. $f'(x) = -\tfrac{1}{3}x^{-2/3}$ is never zero and $f'(0)$ does not exist. $f(-1) = 3$ (maximum), $f(0) = 2$, and $f(8) = 0$ (minimum).

37. $f'(x) = \dfrac{1-2x^2}{(1-x^2)^{1/2}}$; $f'(x) = 0$ when $x = \pm\sqrt{2}/2$; $f'(x)$ does not exist when $x = \pm 1$ (the endpoints of the domain of f). $f(-1) = 0$, $f(-\sqrt{2}/2) = -1/2$ (minimum), $f(\sqrt{2}/2) = 1/2$ (maximum), and $f(1) = 0$.

38. $f'(x) = \dfrac{4-2x^2}{(4-x^2)^{1/2}}$; $f'(x) = 0$ when $x = \sqrt{2}$ ($-\sqrt{2}$ is not in the domain of f). $f(0) = 0 = f(2)$

(minimum) and $f(\sqrt{2}) = 2$ (maximum).

39. $f'(x) = \dfrac{6-4x}{3(2-x)^{2/3}}$; $f'(2)$ does not exist and $f'(x) = 0$ when $x = 3/2$. Note that f is continuous everywhere, even at the point $x = 2$. $f(1) = 1$, $f(3/2) \approx 1.19$ (maximum), $f(0) = 0$, and $f(3) = -3$ (minimum).

40. $f'(x) = \dfrac{1-3x}{2\sqrt{x}}$; $f'(x) = 0$ when $x = 1/3$, and $f'(0)$ does not exist. $f(0) = 0$, $f(1/3) = 2\sqrt{3}/9$ (maximum), and $f(4) = -6$ (minimum).

41. If $A \neq 0$, then $f'(x) \equiv A$ is never zero, but because f is continuous it must have global extrema. Therefore they occur at the endpoints. If $A = 0$, then f is a constant function, and its maximum and minimum value B occurs at every point of the interval, including the two endpoints.

42. The hypotheses imply that f has no critical points in (a,b), but f must have global extrema. Therefore they occur at the endpoints.

43. $f'(x) = 0$ if x is not an integer; $f'(x)$ does not exist if x is an integer.

46. Every real number that is an integer or half an odd integer is a critical point of f; f' does not exist at each such real number.

47. (c)   48. (f)   49. (d)   50. (b)   51. (a)   52. (e)

Section 3.6

1. With $x > 0$, $y > 0$, and $x + y = 50$, we are to maximize the product $P = xy$.

$$P = P(x) = x(50-x) = 50x - x^2, \qquad 0 < x < 50$$

($x < 50$ because $y > 0$.) The product is not maximal if we let $x = 0$ or $x = 50$, so we adjoin the endpoints to the domain of P; thus the continuous function $P(x) = 50x - x^2$ has a global maximum on the closed interval $[0, 50]$, and the maximum does *not* occur at either endpoint. Because f is differentiable, the maximum must occur at a point where $P'(x) = 0$: $50 - 2x = 0$, and so $x = 25$. Because this is the only critical point of P, it follows that $x = 25$ maximizes $P(x)$. When $x = 25$, $y = 50 - 25 = 25$, so the two positive real numbers with sum 50 and maximum possible product are 25 and 25.

2. If two parallel sides of the rectangle both have length x and the other two sides both have length y, then we are to maximize the area $A = xy$ given that $2x + 2y = 200$. So

$$A = A(x) = x(100 - x), \qquad 0 \leq x \leq 100.$$

Clearly the maximum value of A occurs at a critical point of A in the interval $(0, 100)$. But $A'(x) = 100 - 2x$, so $x = 50$ is the location of the maximum. When $x = 50$, also $y = 50$, so the rectangle of maximal area is a square of area $50^2 = 2500$ ft^2.

3. If the coordinates of the "fourth vertex" are (x, y), then $y = 100 - 2x$ and the area of the rectangle is $A = xy$. So we are to maximize

$$A(x) = x(100 - 2x) \qquad 0 \leq x \leq 50.$$

By the usual argument the solution occurs where $A'(x) = 0$, thus where $x = 25$, $y = 50$, and the maximum area is 1250.

4. If the side of the pen parallel to the wall has length x and the two perpendicular sides both have length y, then we are to maximize area $A = xy$ given $x + 2y = 600$. Thus

$$A = A(y) = y(600 - 2y), \qquad 0 \leq y \leq 300.$$

Adjoining the endpoints to the domain is allowed because the maximum we seek occurs at neither endpoint. Therefore the maximum occurs at an interior critical point. We have $A'(y) = 600 - 4y$, so the only critical point of A is $y = 150$. Then $y = 150$, we have $x = 300$, so the maximum possible area that can be enclosed is 45,000 m^2.

5. If x is the length of each edge of the base of the box and y denotes the height of the box, then its volume is given by $V = x^2 y$. Its total surface area is the sum of the area x^2 of its bottom and four times the area xy of each of its vertical sides, so $x^2 + 4xy = 300$. Now it is easy to write V as a function of x alone, with domain $1 \le x \le 10\sqrt{3}$; note that the maximum does not occur when $x = 10\sqrt{3}$, but the value of V must be checked at $x = 1$ as well as at any interior critical points.

6. Let $f(x) = x - x^2$, $0 \le x \le 1$. Then $f(x) = 0$ at the endpoints of its domain, so the maximum value of $f(x)$ must occur at an interior critical point. But $f'(x) = 1 - 2x$, so the only critical point of f is $x = 1/2$, which must yield a maximum because f is continous on $[0, 1]$. So the maximum value of $x - x^2$ for $0 \le x \le 1$ is $1/4$.

7. If the two numbers are x and y, then we are to minimize $S = x^2 + y^2$ given $x > 0$, $y > 0$, and $x + y = 48$. So $S(x) = x^2 + (48 - x)^2$, $0 \le x \le 48$. Here we adjoin the endpoints to the domain to ensure the existence of a maximum, but we must test the values of S at these endpoints because it is not immediately clear that neither $S(0)$ nor $S(48)$ yields the maximum value of S. Now $S'(x) = 2x - 2(48 - x)$; the only interior critical point of S is $x = 24$, and when $x = 24$, $y = 24$ as well. Now $S(0) = (48)^2 = 2304 = S(48) > 1152 = S(24)$, so the answer is 1152.

8. Let x be the length of the side around which the rectangle is rotated and let y be the length of each perpendicular side. Then $2x + 2y = 36$. The radius of the cylinder is y and its height is x, so its volume is $V = \pi y^2 x$. So
$$V = V(y) = \pi y^2 (18 - y) = \pi (18 y^2 - y^3),$$
with natural domain $0 < y < 18$. We adjoin the endpoints to the domain because neither $y = 0$ nor $y = 18$ maximizes $V(y)$, and deduce the existence of a global maximum at an interior critical point. Now
$$V'(y) = \pi(36y - 3y^2) = 3\pi y(12 - y),$$
So $V'(y) = 0$ when $y = 0$ and when $y = 12$. The former value of y *minimizes* $V(y)$, so the maximum possible volume of the cylinder is $V(12) = 864\pi$.

9. Let x and y be the two numbers. Then $x + y = 10$, $x \ge 0$, and $y \ge 0$. We are to minimize the sum of their cubes,
$$S = x^3 + y^3 : \qquad S(x) = x^3 + (10 - x)^3, \qquad 0 \le x \le 10.$$
Now $S'(x) = 3x^2 - 3(10 - x)^2$, so the values of x to be tested are $x = 0$, $x = 5$, and $x = 10$. At the endpoints, $S = 1000$; when $x = 5$, $S = 250$ (the minimum).

10. Draw a cross section of the cylindrical log—a circle of radius r. Inscribe in this circle a cross section of the beam—a rectangle of width w and height h. Draw a diagonal of the rectangle; the Pythagorean theorem yields $x^2 + h^2 = 4r^2$. The strength S of the beam is given by $S = kwh^2$ where k is a positive constant. Because $h^2 = 4r^2 - w^2$, we have
$$S = S(w) = kw(4r^2 - w^2) = k(4wr^2 - w^3)$$
with natural domain $0 < w < 2r$. We adjoin the endpoints to this domain; this is permissible because $S = 0$ at each, and so is not maximal. Next, $S'(w) = k(4r^2 - 3w^2)$; $S'(w) = 0$ when $3w^2 = 4r^2$, and the corresponding (positive) value of w yields the maximum of S (we know that $S(w)$ must have a maximum on $[0, 2r]$ because of the continuity of S on this interval, and we also know that the maximum does not occur at either endpoint, so there is only one possible location for the maximum). At maximum, $h^2 = 4r^2 - w^2 = 3w^2 - w^2$, so $h = w\sqrt{2}$ describes the shape of the beam of greatest strength.

11. Let x denote the length of each of the internal dividers and of the two sides parallel to them; let y denote the length of each of the other two sides. The total length of all the fencing is $4x + 2y = 600$ and the area of the corral is $A = xy$. Hence

$$A = A(x) = 300x - 2x^2, \quad 0 \le x \le 150.$$

Now $A'(x) = 0$ only when $x = 75$, so the maximum area of the corral is $A(75) = 11250$ yd^2.

12. Let r denote the radius of the cylinder and h its height. We are to maximize volume $V = \pi r^2 h$ given the constraint that the total surface area is 150π:

$$2\pi r^2 + 2\pi r h = 150\pi,$$

so that $h = \dfrac{75 - r^2}{r}$. Thus

$$V = V(r) = \pi r(75 - r^2) = \pi(75r - r^3), \quad 0 < r < \sqrt{75}.$$

We may adjoin both endpoints to this domain without creating a spurious maximum, so we use $[0, 5\sqrt{3}]$ as the domain of V. Next, $V'(r) = \pi(75 - 3r^2)$. Hence $V'(r)$ always exists, and its only zero in the domain of V occurs when $r = 5$ (and $h = 10$). Now V is zero at the two endpoints of its domain, so $V(5) = 250\pi$ is the maximum volume of such a cylinder.

13. If the rectangle has sides x and y, then $x^2 + y^2 = 16^2$ by the Pythagorean theorem. The area of the rectangle is then

$$A(x) = 2\sqrt{256 - x^2}, \quad 0 \le x \le 16.$$

A positive quantity is maximized exactly when its square is maximized, so in place of A we maximize

$$f(x) = (A(x))^2 = 256x^2 - x^4.$$

The only solutions of $f'(x) = 0$ in the domain of A are $x = 0$ and $x = 8\sqrt{2}$; the former minimizes $A(x)$ and the latter yields its maximum value, 128.

14. If the far side of the rectangle has length $2x$ (this leads to simpler arithmetic than length x), and the sides perpendicular to the far side have length y, then by the Pythagorean theorem, $x^2 + y^2 = L^2$. The area of the rectangle is $A = 2xy$, so we maximize

$$A(x) = 2x\sqrt{L^2 - x^2}, \quad 0 \le x \le L$$

by maximizing

$$f(x) = (A(x))^2 = 4(L^2 x^2 - x^4).$$

Now $f'(x) = 4(2L^2 x - 4x^3) = 8x(L^2 - 2x^2)$ is zero when $x = 0$ (rejected; $A(0) = 0$) and when $x = L\sqrt{2}/2$. By the usual argument, the latter maximizes $f(x)$ and thus $A(x)$. The answer is the value of $A(x)$ at the latter point, which can be simplified to L^2.

15. $V'(T) = -0.06426 + (0.0170086)T - (0.0002037)T^2$. The equation $V'(T) = 0$ is quadratic with the two (approximate) solutions 79.532 and 3.967. The formula for $V(T)$ is valid only in the range $0 \le T \le 30$, so we reject the first solution. Finally, $V(0) = 999.87$, $V(30) \approx 1003.763$, and $V(3.967) \approx 999.71$. Thus the volume is minimized when $T \approx 3.967$, and therefore water has its greatest density at about $3.967°$C.

16. Let $P(x, 0)$ be the lower right-hand corner point of the rectangle. The rectangle then has base $2x$, height $4 - x^2$, and thus area

$$A(x) = 2x(4 - x^2) = 8x - 2x^3, \quad 0 \le x \le 2.$$

Now $A'(x) = 8 - 6x^2$; $A'(x) = 0$ when $x = 2\sqrt{3}/3$. Because $A(0) = 0$, $A(2) = 0$, and $A(2\sqrt{3}/3) \geq 0$, the maximum possible area is $32\sqrt{3}/9$.

17. Let x denote the length of each edge of the base and let y denote the height of the box. We are to maximize its volume $V = x^2 y$ given the constraint $2x^2 + 4xy = 600$. Solve the latter for y to write

$$V(x) = 150x - \frac{1}{2}x^3, \qquad 1 \leq x \leq 10\sqrt{3}.$$

The solution of $V'(x) = 0$ in the domain of V is $x = 10$. Because $V(10) = 1000 > V(1) = 149.5 > V(10\sqrt{3}) = 0$, this shows that $x = 10$ maximizes V and that the maximum value of V is 1000 cm^3.

18. Let x denote the radius of the cylinder and y its height. Then its total surface area is $\pi x^2 + 2\pi xy = 300\pi$, so $x^2 + 2xy = 300$. We are to maximize its volume $V = \pi x^2 y$, but $y = \dfrac{300 - x^2}{2x}$, so

$$V = V(x) = \frac{\pi}{2}(300x - x^3), \qquad 0 \leq x \leq 10\sqrt{3}.$$

It is then easy to show that $x = 10$ maximizes $V(x)$, that $y = x = 10$ as well, and thus that the maximum possible volume of the can is 1000π in.^{3}

19. Let x be the length of the edge of each of the twelve small squares. Then each of the three cross-shaped pieces will form boxes with base length $1 - 2x$ and height x, so each of the three will have volume $x(1 - 2x)^2$. Both of the two cubical boxes will have edge x and thus volume x^3. So the total volume of all five boxes will be

$$V(x) = 3x(1 - 2x)^2 + 2x^3 = 14x^3 - 12x^2 + 3x, \qquad 0 \leq x \leq \frac{1}{2}.$$

Now $V'(x) = 42x^2 - 24x + 3$; $V'(x) = 0$ when $14x^2 - 8x - 1 = 0$. The quadratic formula gives the two solutions $\dfrac{4 \pm \sqrt{2}}{14}$. These are approximately 0.3867 and 0.1847, and both lie in the domain of V. Now $V(0) = 0$, $V(0.1847) \approx 0.2329$, $V(0.3867) \approx 0.1752$, and $V(0.5) = 0.25$. Therefore, to maximize V, one must cut each of the three large squares into four smaller squares of side length $\frac{1}{2}$ each and form the resulting twelve squares into two cubes. At maximum volume there will be only two boxes, not five.

20. Let x be the length of each edge of the square base of the box and let h denote its height. Then its volume is $V = x^2 h$. The total cost of the box is \$144, hence

$$4xh + x^2 + 2x^2 = 144; \quad h = \frac{144 - 3x^2}{4x}.$$

Therefore

$$V = V(x) = \frac{x}{4}(144 - 3x^2) = 36x - \frac{3}{4}x^2.$$

The natural domain of V is the open interval $(0, 4\sqrt{3})$, but we may adjoin the endpoints as usual to obtain a closed interval. Also

$$V'(x) = 36 - \frac{9}{4}x^2,$$

so $V'(x)$ always exists and is zero only at $x = 4$ (reject the other root $x = -4$). Now $V(x) = 0$ at the endpoints of its domain, so $V(4) = 96$ (ft^3) is the maximum volume of such a box. The dimensions of the largest box are 4 ft square on the base and 6 ft high.

21. Let x denote the edge length of one square and y that of the other. Then $4x + 4y = 80$, so $y = 20 - x$. The total area of the two squares is $A = x^2 + y^2$, so

$$A = A(x) = x^2 + (20 - x)^2 = 2x^2 - 40x + 400,$$

Section 3.6 Applied Maximum-Minimum Problems

with domain $(0, 20)$; adjoin the endpoints as usual. Then $A'(x) = 4x - 40$, which always exists and which vanishes when $x = 10$. Now $A(0) = 400 = A(20)$, whereas $A(10) = 200$. So to minimize the total area of the two squares, make two equal squares. To maximize it, make only one square.

22. Let r be the radius of the circle and x the edge of the square. We are to maximize total area $A = \pi r^2 + x^2$ given the side condition $2\pi r + 4x = 100$. From the last equation we infer that

$$x = \frac{100 - 2\pi r}{4} = \frac{50 - \pi r}{2}.$$

So

$$A = A(r) = \pi r^2 + \frac{1}{4}(50 - \pi r)^2 = (\pi + \frac{1}{4}\pi^2)r - 25\pi r + 625$$

for $0 \leq r \leq 50/\pi$ (because $x \geq 0$). Now

$$A'(r) = 2(\pi + \frac{1}{4}\pi^2)r - 25\pi;$$

$$A'(r) = 0 \text{ when } r = \frac{25}{2 + \frac{\pi}{2}} = \frac{50}{\pi + 4};$$

that is, when $r \approx 7$. Finally, $A(0) = 625$,

$$A\left(\frac{50}{\pi}\right) \approx 795.77 \quad \text{and} \quad A\left(\frac{50}{\pi + 4}\right) \approx 350.06$$

Results: For minimum area, use a circle of radius $50/(\pi + 4) \approx 7.00124$ (cm) and a square of edge length $100/(\pi + 4)$ (cm). For maximum area, bend all the wire into a circle of radius $50/\pi$.

23. Let x be the length of each segment of fence perpendicular to the wall and let y be the length of each segment parallel to the wall.

    Case 1: The internal fence is perpendicular to the wall. Then $y = 600 - 3x$ an the enclosure will have area $A(x) = 600x - 3x^2$, $0 \leq x \leq 200$. Then $A'(x) = 0$ when $x = 100$; $A(100) = 30{,}000$ (m^2) is the maximum in Case 1.

    Case 2: The internal fence is parallel to the wall. Then $y = 300 - x$, and the area of the enclosure is given by $A(x) = 300x - x^2$, $0 \leq x \leq 300$. Then $A'(x) = 0$ when $x = 150$; $A(150) = 22{,}500$ (m^2) is the maximum in Case 2.

    Answer: The maximum possible area of the enclosure is 30,000 m^2. The divider must be perpendicular to the wall and of length 100 m. The side parallel to the wall is to have length 300 m.

24. See Fig. 3.6.22 of the text. Suppose that the pen measures x (horizontal) by y (vertical). Then it has area $A = xy$.

    Case 1: $x \geq 10$, $y \geq 5$. Then

    $$x + (x - 10) + y + (y - 5) = 85, \text{ so } x + y = 50.$$

    Therefore
    $$A = A(x) = x(50 - x) = 50x - x^2, \qquad 10 \leq x \leq 45.$$

    Then $A'(x) = 0$ when $x = 25$; $A(25) = 625$. Note that $A(10) = 400$ and that $A(45) = 225$.

    Case 2: $0 \leq x \leq 10$, $y \geq 5$. Then

    $$x + y + (y - 5) = 85, \text{ so } x + 2y = 90.$$

Therefore
$$A = A(x) = x\frac{90-x}{2} = \frac{1}{2}(90x - x^2), \qquad 0 \le x \le 10.$$

In this case, $A'(x) = 0$ when $x = 45$, but 45 doesn't lie in the domain of A. Note that $A(0) = 0$ and that $A(10) = 400$.

Case 3: $x \ge 10$, $0 \le y \le 5$. Then
$$x + (x - 10) + y = 85, \text{ so } 2x + y = 95.$$

Therefore
$$A = A(x) = x(95 - 2x) = 95x - 2x^2, \qquad 45 \le x \le 47.5.$$

In this case $A'(x) = 0$ when $x = 23.75$, not in the domain of A. Note that $A(45) = 225$ and that $A(47.5) = 0$.

Conclusion: The area of the pen is maximized when the pen is square, 25 m on each side (the maximum from Case 1).

25. Let the dimensions of the box be x by x by y. We are to maximize $V = x^2 y$ subject to some conditions on x and y. According to the poster on the wall of the Bogart, Georgia, Post Office, the *length* of the box is the larger of x and y, and the *girth* is measured around the box in a plane perpendicular to its length.

Case 1: $x < y$. Then the length is y, the girth is $4x$, and the mailing constraint is $4x + y \le 100$. It is clear that we take $4x + y = 100$ to maximize V, so that
$$V = V(x) = x^2(100 - 4x) = 100x^2 - 4x^3, \qquad 0 \le x \le 25.$$

Then $V'(x) = 4x(50 - 3x)$; $V'(x) =$ for $x = 0$ and for $x = 50/3$. But $V(0) = 0$, $V(25) = 0$, and $V(50/3) = 250{,}000/27 \approx 9259$ (in.^{3}). The latter is the maximum in Case 1.

Case 2: $x \ge y$. Then the length is x and the girth is $2x + y$, though you may get some argument from a postal worker who may insist that it's $4x$. So $3x + 2y = 100$, and thus
$$V = V(x) = x^2 \left(\frac{100 - 3x}{2}\right) = 50x^2 - \frac{3}{2}x^3, \qquad 0 \le x \le 100/3.$$

Then $V'(x) = 100x - \frac{9}{2}x^2$; $V'(x) = 0$ when $x = 0$ and when $x = 200/9$. But $V(0) = 0$, $V(100/3) = 0$, and $V(200/9) = 2{,}000{,}000/243 \approx 8230$ (in.^{3}).

Case 3: You lose the argument in Case 2. Then the box has length x and girth $4x$, so $5x = 100$; thus $x = 20$. To maximize the total volume, no calculus is needed—let $y = x$. Then the box of maximum volume will have volume $20^3 = 8000$ (in.^{3}).

Answer: The maximum is $\dfrac{250{,}000}{27}$ in.^{3}.

26. In this problem the girth of the package is its circumference; no one would interpret "girth" in any other way. So suppose that the package has length x and radius r. Then it has volume $V = \pi r^2 x$ where $x + 2\pi r = 100$. We seek to maximize
$$V = V(r) = \pi r^2(100 - 2\pi r) = \pi(100 r^2 - 2\pi r^3), \qquad 0 \le r \le 50/\pi.$$

Now
$$V'(r) = \pi(200r - 6\pi r^2) = 2\pi r(100 - 3\pi r);$$

Section 3.6 Applied Maximum-Minimum Problems

$V'(r) = 0$ when $r = 0$ and when $r = \dfrac{100}{3\pi}$. But $V(0) = 0$, $V\left(\dfrac{50}{\pi}\right) = 0$, and $V\left(\dfrac{100}{3\pi}\right) = \dfrac{1{,}000{,}000}{27\pi} \approx$ 11789 (in.^{3}), obviously the maximum of V.

27. Suppose that n presses are used, $1 \leq n \leq 8$. The total cost of the poster run would then be

$$C(n) = 5n + (10 + 6n)\left(\dfrac{50000}{3600n}\right) = 5n + \dfrac{125}{9}\left(\dfrac{10}{n} + 6\right)$$

dollars. Temporarily assume that n can take on every real number value between 1 and 8. Then

$$C'(n) = 5 - \dfrac{125}{9} \cdot \dfrac{10}{n^2};$$

$C'(n) = 0$ when $n = \dfrac{5}{3}\sqrt{10} \approx 5.27$ presses. But an integral number of presses must be used, so the actual number that will minimize the cost is either 5 or 6, unless the minimum occurs at one of the two endpoints. The values in question are $C(1) \approx 227.2$, $C(5) \approx 136.1$, $C(6) \approx 136.5$, and $C(8) \approx 140.7$. So to minimize cost and therefore maximize profit, five presses should be used.

28. Let x denote the number of workers hired. Each worker will pick $900/x$ bushels; each worker will spend $180/x$ hours picking beans. The supervisor cost will be $1800/x$ dollars, and the cost per worker will be $8 + 900/x$ dollars. Thus the total cost will be

$$C(x) = 8x + 900 + \dfrac{1800}{x}, \quad 1 \leq x.$$

It is clear that large values of x make $C(x)$ large, so the global minimum of $C(x)$ occurs either at $x = 1$ or where $C'(x) = 0$. Assume for the moment that x can take on all real number values in $[1, \infty)$, not merely integral values, so that C' is defined. Then

$$C'(x) = 8 - \dfrac{1800}{x^2}; \quad C'(x) = 0 \text{ when } x^2 = 225.$$

Thus $C'(15) = 0$. Now $C(1) = 2708$ and $C(15) = 1140$, so fifteen workers should be hired; the cost to pick each bushel will be approximately \$1.27.

29. We are to minimize the total cost C over a ten-year period. This cost is the sum of the initial cost and ten times the annual cost:

$$C(x) = 150x + 10\left(\dfrac{1000}{2+x}\right), \quad 0 \leq x \leq 10.$$

$$C'(x) = 150 - \dfrac{10000}{(2+x)^2}; \quad C'(x) = 0 \text{ when } 150 = \dfrac{10000}{(2+x)^2},$$

so that $(2+x)^2 = \dfrac{200}{3}$. One of the resulting values of x is negative, so we reject it. The other is $x = -2 + \sqrt{200/3} \approx 6.165$ (in.). The problem itself suggests that x must be an integer, so we check $x = 6$ and $x = 7$ along with the endpoints of the domain of C. In dollars, $C(0) = 5000$, $C(6) \approx 2150$, $C(7) \approx 2161$, and $C(10) \approx 2333$. Result: Install six inches of insulation. The annual savings over the situation with no insulation at all then will be one-tenth of $5000 - 2150$, about \$285 per year.

30. We assume that each one-cent increase in price reduces sales by 50 burritos per night. Let x be the amount, in cents, by which the price is increased. The resulting profit is

$$P(x) = (50 + x)(5000 - 5x) - 25(5000 - 50x) - 100{,}000$$
$$= (25 + x)(5000 - 50x) - 100{,}000$$
$$= 25000 + 3750x - 50x^2, \quad -50 \leq x.$$

Because $P(x) < 0$ for large values of x and for $x = -50$, P will be maximized where $P'(x) = 0$:

$$P'(x) = 3750 - 100x; \quad P'(x) = 0 \text{ when } x = 37.5.$$

Now $P(37) = 953$, $P(37.5) \approx 953.13$, and $P(38) = 953$. Therefore profit is maximized when the selling price is either 87¢ or 88¢, and the maximum profit will be \$953.

31. Let x be the number of five-cent fare increases. The resulting revenue will be

$$R(x) = (150 + 5x)(600 - 4x), \quad -15 \leq x \leq 15$$

(the revenue is the product of the price and the number of passengers). Now

$$R(x) = 90000 - 3000x - 200x^2;$$

$$R'(x) = -3000 - 400x; \quad R'(x) = 0 \text{ when } x = -7.5.$$

Because the fare must be an integral number of cents, we check $R(-7) = 1012 = R(-8)$ (dollars). Answer: The fare should be either \$1.10 or \$1.15; this is a reduction of 40 or 35 cents, respectively, and each results in the maximum possible revenue of \$1012 per day.

32. The figure to the right shows a central cross section of the sphere and inscribed cylinder. The radius of the cylinder is r and its height is h; the radius of the sphere is R. From the Pythagorean theorem we see that $4r^2 + h^2 = 4R^2$. The volume of the cylinder is $V = \pi r^2 h$, and therefore we find that

$$V = V(h) = \pi(R^2 - \frac{1}{4}h^2)h$$

$$= \frac{\pi}{4}(4R^2 h - h^3), \quad 0 \leq h \leq 2R.$$

Then

$$V'(h) = \frac{\pi}{4}(4R^2 - 3h^2),$$

so $V(h) = 0$ when $3h^2 = 4R^2$, so that $h = \frac{2}{3}R\sqrt{3}$. This value of h maximizes V because $V(0) = 0$ and $V(2R) = 0$. The corresponding value of r is $\frac{1}{3}R\sqrt{6}$, so the ratio of the height of the cylinder to its radius is $h/r = \sqrt{2}$. The volume of the maximal cylinder is $\frac{4}{9}\pi R^3 \sqrt{3}$ and the volume of the sphere is $\frac{4}{3}\pi R^3$; the ratio of the volume of the sphere to that of the maximal inscribed cylinder is thus $\sqrt{3}$.

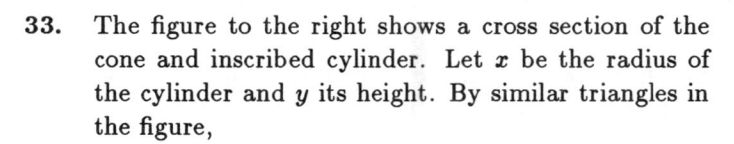

33. The figure to the right shows a cross section of the cone and inscribed cylinder. Let x be the radius of the cylinder and y its height. By similar triangles in the figure,

$$\frac{H}{R} = \frac{y}{R-x}, \text{ so } y = \frac{H}{R}(R-x).$$

We are to maximize the volume $V = \pi x^2 y$ of the cylinder, so we write

$$V = V(x) = \pi x^2 \frac{H}{R}(R-x)$$

$$= \pi \frac{H}{R}(Rx^2 - x^3), \quad 0 \leq x \leq R.$$

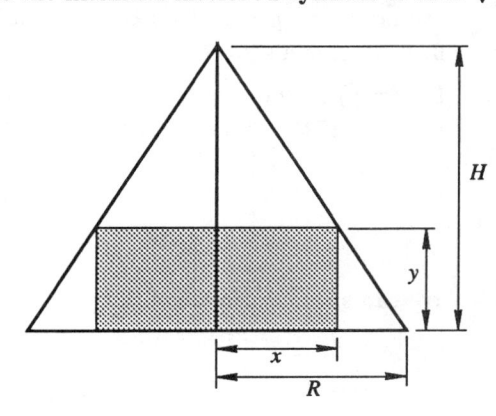

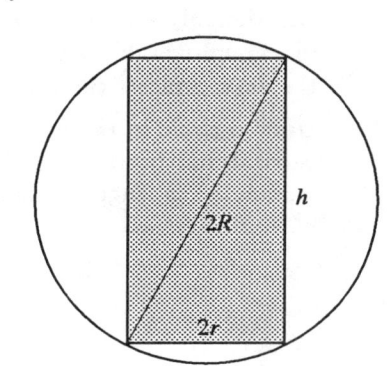

Section 3.6 Applied Maximum-Minimum Problems

Because $V(0) = 0 = V(r)$, V is maximized when $V'(x) = 0$; this leads to the equation $2xR = 3x^2$ and thus to the results $x = \frac{2}{3}R$ and $y = \frac{1}{3}H$.

34. Let the circle have equation $x^2 + y^2 = 1$ and let (x, y) denote the coordinates of the upper right-hand vertex of the trapezoid (Fig. 3.6.25). Then the area A of the trapezoid is the product of its altitude y and the average of the lengths of its two bases, so

$$A = \frac{1}{2}y(2x + 2) \text{ where } y^2 = 1 - x^2.$$

A positive quantity is maximized when its square is maximized, so we maximize instead

$$f(x) = A^2 = (x + 1)^2(1 - x^2)$$
$$= 1 + 2x - 2x^3 - x^4, \qquad 0 \leq x \leq 1.$$

Because $f(0) = 0 = f(1)$, f is maximized when $f'(x) = 0$:

$$0 = 2 - 6x^2 - 4x^3 = 2(1 + x)^2(1 - 2x).$$

But the only solution of $f'(x) = 0$ in the domain of f is $x = 1/2$. Finally, $f(1/2) = 27/16$, so the maximum possible area of the trapezoid is $\frac{3}{4}\sqrt{3}$. This is just over 41% of the area of the circle, so the answer meets the test of plausibility.

35. Draw a circle in the plane with center at the origin and with radius R. Inscribe a rectangle with vertical and horizontal sides, and let (x, y) be its vertex in the first quadrant. The base of the rectangle has length $2x$ and its height is $2y$, so the perimeter of the rectangle is $P = 2x + 2y$. Also $x^2 + y^2 = R^2$, so

$$P = P(x) = 4x + 4\sqrt{R^2 - x^2}, \qquad 0 \leq x \leq R.$$
$$P'(x) = 4 - \frac{4x}{\sqrt{R^2 - x^2}};$$
$$P'(x) = 0 \text{ when } 4\sqrt{R^2 - x^2} = 4x;$$
$$R^2 - x^2 = x^2;$$
$$x^2 = \frac{1}{2}R^2.$$

Because $x > 0$, $x = \frac{1}{2}R\sqrt{2}$. The corresponding value of $P(x)$ is $4R\sqrt{2}$, and $P(0) = 4R = P(R)$. So the former value of x maximizes the perimeter P. Because $y^2 = R^2 - x^2$ and because $R^2 - x^2 = x^2$ at maximum, $y = x$ at maximum. Therefore the rectangle of largest perimeter that can be inscribed in a circle is a square.

36. Let (x, y) be the coordinates of the vertex of the rectangle in the first quadrant. Then, by symmetry, the area of the rectangle is $A = (2x)(2y) = 4xy$. But from the equation of the ellipse we find that

$$y = \frac{3}{5}\sqrt{25 - x^2}, \text{ so}$$
$$A = A(x) = \frac{12}{5}x\sqrt{25 - x^2}, \qquad 0 \leq x \leq 5.$$

We can simplify the algebra by maximizing instead

$$f(x) = \frac{25}{144}A^2 = 25x^2 - x^4;$$

$$f'(x) = 50x - 4x^3;$$
$$f'(x) = 0 \text{ when } x = 0, \ x = \frac{5}{2}\sqrt{2}.$$

Now $A(0) = 0 = A(5)$, whereas $A\left(\frac{5}{2}\sqrt{2}\right) = 30$. So the rectangle of maximum area has base $2x = 5\sqrt{2}$ and height $2y = 3\sqrt{2}$.

37. We are to maximize volume $V = \frac{1}{3}\pi r^2 h$ given $r^2 + h^2 = 100$. The latter relation enables us to write

$$V = V(h) = \frac{1}{3}\pi(100 - h^2)h = \frac{1}{3}\pi(100h - h^3), \qquad 0 \leq h \leq 10.$$

Now $V'(h) = \frac{1}{3}\pi(100 - 3h^2)$, so $V'(h) = 0$ when $3h^2 = 100$, thus when $h = \frac{10}{3}\sqrt{3}$. But $V(h) = 0$ at the endpoints of its domain, so the latter value of h maximizes V, and its maximum value is $\frac{2000}{27}\pi\sqrt{3}$.

38. Put the bases of the poles on the x-axis, one at the origin and the other at $x = 10$. Let the rope touch the ground at the point x. Then the rope reaches straight from $(0, 10)$ to $(x, 0)$ and straight from $(x, 0)$ to $(10, 10)$. In terms of x, its length is

$$\begin{aligned} L(x) &= \sqrt{100 + x^2} + \sqrt{100 + (10 - x)^2} \\ &= \sqrt{100 + x^2} + \sqrt{200 - 20x + x^2}, \qquad 0 \leq x \leq 10. \end{aligned}$$

So

$$L'(x) = \frac{x}{\sqrt{100 + x^2}} + \frac{x - 10}{\sqrt{200 - 20x + x^2}};$$

$L'(x) = 0$ when

$$\begin{aligned} x\sqrt{200 - 20x + x^2} &= (10 - x)\sqrt{x^2 + 100}; \\ x^2(x^2 - 20x + 200) &= \left(100 - 20x + x^2\right)\left(x^2 + 100\right); \\ x^4 - 20x^3 + 200x^2 &= x^4 - 20x^3 + 200x^2 - 2000x + 10000; \\ 2000x &= 10000; \end{aligned}$$

and thus when $x = 5$. Now $L(0) = L(10) = 10\left(1 + \sqrt{2}\right)$, which exceeds $L(5) = 10\sqrt{5}$. So the latter is the length of the shortest possible rope.

39. Let x and y be the two numbers. Then $x \geq 0$, $y \geq 0$, and $x + y = 16$. We are to find both the maximum and minimum values of $x^{1/3} + y^{1/3}$. Because $y = 16 - x$, we seek the extrema of

$$f(x) = x^{1/3} + (16 - x)^{1/3}, \qquad 0 \leq x \leq 16.$$

Now

$$\begin{aligned} f'(x) &= \frac{1}{3}x^{-2/3} - \frac{1}{3}(16 - x)^{-2/3} \\ &= \frac{1}{3x^{2/3}} - \frac{1}{3(16 - x)^{2/3}}; \end{aligned}$$

$f'(x) = 0$ when $(16 - x)^{2/3} = x^{2/3}$, so when $16 - x = x$, and thus when $x = 8$. Now $f(0) = f(16) = 16^{1/3} \approx 2.52$, so $f(8) = 4$ maximizes f whereas $f(0)$ and $f(16)$ yield its minimum.

40. If the base of the L has length x, then the vertical part has length $60 - x$. Place the L with its corner at the origin in the xy-plane, its base on the nonnegative x-axis, and the vertical part on the nonnegative y-axis. The two ends of the L have coordinates $(0, 60 - x)$ and $(x, 0)$, so they are at distance

$$d = d(x) = \sqrt{x^2 + (60 - x)^2}, \qquad 0 \leq x \leq 60.$$

A positive quantity is minimized when its square is minimal, so we minimize

$$f(x) = d^2 = x^2 + (60 - x)^2, \qquad 0 \leq x \leq 60.$$

Section 3.6 Applied Maximum-Minimum Problems

Then $f'(x) = 2x - 2(60 - x) = 4x - 120$; $f'(x) = 0$ when $x = 30$. Now $f(0) = f(60) = 3600$, whereas $f(30) = 1800$. So $x = 30$ minimizes $f(x)$ and thus $d(x)$. The minimum possible distance between the two ends of the wire is therefore $d(30) = 30\sqrt{2}$.

41. If (x, x^2) is a point of the parabola, then its distance from $(0, 1)$ is

$$d(x) = \sqrt{x^2 + (x^2 - 1)^2}.$$

So we minimize

$$f(x) = d^2 = x^4 - x^2 + 1,$$

where the domain of f is the set of all real numbers. But because $f(x)$ is large positive when $|x|$ is large, we will not exclude a minimum if we restrict the domain of f to be an interval of the form $[-a, a]$ where a is a large positive number. On the interval $[-a, a]$ f is continuous and thus has a global minimum, which does not occur at $\pm a$ because $f(\pm a)$ is large positive. Because f' exists, the minimum of f occurs at a point where $f'(x) = 0$:

$$4x^3 - 2x = 0; \qquad 2x(2x^2 - 1) = 0.$$

Hence $x = 0$ or $x = \pm\frac{1}{2}\sqrt{2}$. Now $f(0) = 1$ and at the other two points the value of $f(x)$ is $3/4$. So $x = 0$ actually yields a local maximum value for $f(x)$, and the minimum possible distance is $\sqrt{\frac{3}{4}} = \frac{1}{2}\sqrt{3}$.

42. It suffices to minimize $x^2 + y^2$ given $y = (3x - 4)^{1/3}$. Let $f(x) = x^2 + (3x - 4)^{2/3}$. Then

$$f'(x) = 2x + 2(3x - 4)^{-1/3}.$$

So $f'(x) = 0$ when

$$2x + \frac{2}{(3x - 4)^{1/3}} = 0;$$
$$2x(3x - 4)^{1/3} = -2;$$
$$x^3(3x - 4) = -1.$$

Now $x = 1$ is the only real solution of the last equation, $f'(x)$ does not exist when $x = \frac{4}{3}$, and $f(1) = 2 > \frac{16}{9} = f\left(\frac{4}{3}\right)$. So the point closest to the origin is $\left(\frac{4}{3}, 0\right)$.

43. Examine the plank on the right on Fig. 3.6.10. Let its height be $2y$ and its width (in the x-direction) be z. The total area of the four small rectangles in the figure is then $A = 4 \cdot z \cdot 2y = 8yz$. The circle has radius 1, and by Problem 35 the large inscribed square has dimensions $\sqrt{2}$ by $\sqrt{2}$. Thus

$$\left(\frac{1}{2}\sqrt{2} + z\right)^2 + y^2 = 1;$$

This implies that

$$y = \sqrt{\frac{1}{2} - z\sqrt{2} - z^2}.$$

Therefore

$$A(z) = 8z\sqrt{\frac{1}{2} - z\sqrt{2} - z^2}, \qquad 0 \le z \le 1 - \frac{1}{2}\sqrt{2}.$$

Now $A = 0$ at each endpoint of its domain, and

$$A'(z) = \frac{4\sqrt{2}\left(1 - 3z\sqrt{2} - 4z^2\right)}{\sqrt{1 - 2z\sqrt{2} - 2z^2}}.$$

So $A'(z) = 0$ when $z = \dfrac{-3\sqrt{2} \pm \sqrt{34}}{8}$; we discard the negative solution, and find that when $A(z)$ is maximized,

$$z = \dfrac{-3\sqrt{2} + \sqrt{34}}{8} \approx 0.198539,$$

$$2y = \dfrac{\sqrt{7 - \sqrt{17}}}{2} \approx 0.848071, \text{ and}$$

$$A(z) = \dfrac{\sqrt{142 + 34\sqrt{17}}}{2} \approx 0.673500.$$

The four small planks use just under 59% of the wood that remains after the large plank is cut, a very efficient use of what might be scrap lumber.

44. Place the base of the triangle on the x-axis and its upper vertex on the y-axis. Then its lower right vertex is at the point $\left(\frac{1}{2}, 0\right)$ and its upper vertex is at $\left(0, \frac{1}{2}\sqrt{3}\right)$. It follows that the slope of the side of the triangle joining these two vertices is $-\sqrt{3}$. So this side lies on the straight line with equation

$$y = \sqrt{3}\left(\dfrac{1}{2} - x\right).$$

Let (x, y) be the coordinates of the upper right-hand vertex of the rectangle. Then the rectangle has area $A = 2xy$, so

$$A(x) = \sqrt{3}\left(x - 2x^2\right), \qquad 0 \leq x \leq 1/2.$$

Now $A'(x) = 0$ when $x = 1/4$, and because $A(x) = 0$ at the endpoints of its domain, it follows that the maximum area of such a rectangle is $A(1/4) = \frac{1}{8}\sqrt{3}$.

45. Set up a coordinate system in which the island is located at $(0, 2)$ and the village at $(6, 0)$, and let $(x, 0)$ be the point at which the boat lands. It is clear that $0 \leq x \leq 6$. The trip involves the land distance $6 - x$ traveled at 20 km/h and the water distance $(4 + x^2)^{1/2}$ traveled at 10 km/h. The total time of the trip is then given by

$$T(x) = \dfrac{1}{10}\sqrt{4 + x^2} + \dfrac{1}{20}(6 - x), \qquad 0 \leq x \leq 6.$$

Now

$$T'(x) = \dfrac{x}{10\sqrt{4 + x^2}} - \dfrac{1}{20}.$$

Thus $T'(x) = 0$ when $3x^2 = 4$; because $x \geq 0$, we find that $x = \frac{2}{3}\sqrt{3}$. The value of T there is

$$\dfrac{1}{10}\left(3 + \sqrt{3}\right) \approx 0.473,$$

whereas $T(0) = 0.5$ and $T(6) \approx 0.632$. Therefore the boater should make landfall at $\frac{2}{3}\sqrt{3} \approx 1.155$ km from the point on the shore closest to the island.

46. Set up a coordinate system in which the factory is located at the origin and the power station at (L, W) in the xy-plane—$L = 4500$, $W = 2000$. Part of the path of the power cable will be straight along the river bank and part will be a diagonal running under water. It makes no difference whether the straight part is adjacent to the factory or to the power station, so we assume the former. Thus we suppose that the power cable runs straight from $(0, 0)$ to $(x, 0)$, then straight from $(x, 0)$ to (L, W), where $0 \leq x \leq L$. Let y be the length of the diagonal stretch of the cable. Then by the Pythagorean theorem,

$$W^2 + (L - x)^2 = y^2, \text{ so } y = \sqrt{W^2 + (L - x)^2}.$$

The cost C of the cable is $C = kx + 3ky$ where k is the cost per unit distance of over-the-ground cable. Therefore the total cost of the cable is

$$C(x) = kx + 3k\sqrt{W^2 + (L - x)^2}, \qquad 0 \leq x \leq L.$$

It will not change the solution if we assume that $k = 1$, and in this case we have

$$C'(x) = 1 - \frac{3(L-x)}{\sqrt{W^2 + (L-x)^2}}.$$

Next, $C'(x) = 0$ when $x^2 + (L-x)^2 = 9(L-x)^2$, and this leads to the solution

$$x = L - \frac{1}{4}W\sqrt{2} \text{ and } y = \frac{3}{4}W\sqrt{2}.$$

It is not difficult to verify that the latter value of x yields a value of C smaller than either $C(0)$ or $C(L)$. Answer: Lay the cable $x = 4500 - 500\sqrt{2} \approx 3793$ meters along the bank and $y = 1500\sqrt{2} \approx 2121$ meters diagonally across the river.

47. The distances involved are $|AP| = |BP| = \sqrt{x^2 + 1}$ and $|CP| = 3 - x$. Therefore we are to minimize

$$f(x) = 2\sqrt{x^2 + 1} + 3 - x, \qquad 0 \leq x \leq 3.$$

$$f'(x) = \frac{2x}{\sqrt{x^2+1}} - 1; \ f'(x) = 0 \text{ when } \frac{2x}{\sqrt{x^2+1}} = 1.$$

This leads to the equation $3x^2 = 1$, so $x = \frac{1}{3}\sqrt{3}$. Now $f(0) = 5$, $f(3) \approx 6.32$, and at the critical point, $f(x) = 3 + \sqrt{3} \approx 4.732$. Answer: The distribution center should be located at the point $P(\frac{1}{3}\sqrt{3}, 0)$.

48. (a) $T = \dfrac{1}{c}\sqrt{a^2 + x^2} + \dfrac{1}{v}\sqrt{(s-x)^2 + b^2}$.

(b) $T'(x) = \dfrac{x}{c\sqrt{a^2 + x^2}} - \dfrac{s - x}{v\sqrt{(s-x)^2 + b^2}}$.

$$T'(x) = 0 \text{ when } \frac{x}{c\sqrt{a^2+x^2}} = \frac{s-x}{v\sqrt{(s-x)^2+b^2}};$$

$$\frac{x}{\sqrt{a^2+x^2}} \cdot \frac{\sqrt{(x-s)^2+b^2}}{s-x} = \frac{c}{v};$$

$$\sin \alpha \csc \beta = \frac{c}{v}$$

$$\frac{\sin \alpha}{\sin \beta} = \frac{c}{v} = n.$$

49. We are to minimize total cost

$$C = c_1\sqrt{a^2 + x^2} + c_2\sqrt{(L-x)^2 + b^2}.$$

$$C'(x) = \frac{c_1 x}{\sqrt{a^2+x^2}} - \frac{c_2(L-x)}{\sqrt{(L-x)^2+b^2}};$$

$$C'(x) = 0 \text{ when } \frac{c_1 x}{\sqrt{a^2+x^2}} = \frac{c_2(L-x)}{\sqrt{(L-x)^2+b^2}}.$$

The result in Part (a) is equivalent to the last equation. For Part (b), assume that $a = b = c_1 = 1$, $c_2 = 2$, and $L = 4$. Then we obtain

$$\frac{x}{\sqrt{1+x^2}} = \frac{2(4-x)}{\sqrt{(4-x)^2+1}};$$

$$\frac{x^2}{1+x^2} = \frac{4(16 - 8x + x^2)}{16 - 8x + x^2 + 1};$$

$$x^2(17 - 8x + x^2) = (4 + 4x^2)(16 - 8x + x^2);$$

$$17x^2 - 8x^3 + x^4 = 64 - 32x + 68x^2 - 32x^3 + 4x^4.$$

Therefore we wish to solve $f(x) = 0$ where

$$f(x) = 3x^4 - 24x^4 + 51x^2 - 32x + 64.$$

Now $f(0) = 64$, $f(1) = 62$, $f(2) = 60$, $f(3) = 22$, and $f(4) = -16$. Because $f(3) > 0 > f(4)$, we interpolate to estimate the zero of $f(x)$ between 3 and 4; it turns out that interpolation gives $x \approx 3.58$. Subsequent interpolation yields the more accurate estimate $x \approx 3.45$. (The equation $f(x) = 0$ has exactly two solutions, $x \approx 3.452462314$ and $x \approx 4.559682567$.)

50. Because $x^3 + y^3 = 2000$, $y = (2000 - x^3)^{1/3}$. We want to maximize and minimize total surface area $A = 6x^2 + 6y^2$;

$$A = A(x) = 6x^2 + 6(2000 - x^3)^{2/3}, \qquad 0 \le x \le 10\sqrt[3]{2}.$$

$$A'(x) = \frac{-12[x^2 - x(2000 - x^3)^{1/3}]}{(2000 - x^3)^{1/3}}.$$

Now $A'(x) = 0$ at $x = 0$ and at $x = 10$; $A'(x)$ does not exist at $x = 10\sqrt[3]{2}$, the right-hand endpoint of the domain of A (at that point, the graph of A has a vertical tangent). Now $A(0) = 600 \cdot 2^{2/3} \approx 952.441$ and $A(10\sqrt[3]{2})$ is the same; $A(10) = 1200$. So the maximum surface area is attained when each cube has edge length 10 and the minimum is attained when there is only one cube, of edge length $10\sqrt[3]{2} \approx 12.5992$.

51. Let r be the radius of the sphere and x the edge length of the cube. We are to maximize and minimize total volume

$$V = \frac{4}{3}\pi r^3 + x^3 \text{ given } 4\pi r^2 + 6x^2 = 1000.$$

The latter relation yields $x = \sqrt{\dfrac{1000 - 4\pi r^2}{6}}$, so

$$V = V(r) = \frac{4}{3}\pi r^3 + \left(\frac{500 - 2\pi r^2}{3}\right)^{3/2} \qquad 0 \le r \le r_1 = 5\sqrt{\frac{10}{\pi}}.$$

Next, $V'(r) = 4\pi r^2 - 2\pi r\sqrt{\dfrac{500 - 2\pi r^2}{3}}$, and $V'(r) = 0$ when $4\pi r^2 = 2\pi r\sqrt{\dfrac{500 - 2\pi r^2}{3}}$. So $r = 0$ or $2r = \sqrt{\dfrac{500 - 2\pi r^2}{3}}$. The latter equation leads to

$$r = r_2 = 5\sqrt{\frac{10}{\pi + 6}}.$$

Now $V(0) \approx 2151.66$, $V(r_1) \approx 2973.54$, and $V(r_2) \approx 1743.16$. Therefore, to minimize the sum of the volumes, choose $r = r_2 \approx 5.229$ in. and $x = 2r_2 \approx 10.459$ in. To maximize the sum of their volumes, take $r = r_1 \approx 8.921$ in. and $x = 0$ in.

52. Let the horizontal piece of wood have length $2x$ and the vertical piece have length $y + z$ where y is the length of the part above the horizontal piece and z the length of the part below it. Then

$$y = \sqrt{4 - x^2} \text{ and } z = \sqrt{16 - x^2}.$$

Also the kite area is $A = x(y + z)$; $\dfrac{dA}{dx} = 0$ implies that

$$y + z = \frac{x^2}{y} + \frac{x^2}{z}.$$

Multiply each side of the last equation by yz to obtain

$$y^2z + yz^2 = x^2z + x^2y,$$

so that
$$yz(y+z) = x^2(y+z);$$
$$x^2 = yz;$$
$$x^4 = y^2z^2 = (4-x^2)(16-x^2);$$
$$x^4 = 64 - 20x^2 + x^4;$$
$$20x^2 = 64;$$
$$x = \frac{4}{5}\sqrt{5},\ y = \frac{2}{5}\sqrt{5},\ z = \frac{8}{5}\sqrt{5}.$$

Therefore $L_1 = \frac{8}{5}\sqrt{5} \approx 3.5777$ and $L_2 = 2\sqrt{5} \approx 4.47214$ for maximum area.

53. The graph of $V(x)$ is shown on the right. The maximum volume seems to occur near the point $(4, V(4)) \approx (4, 95.406)$, so the maximum volume is approximately 95.406 cubic feet.

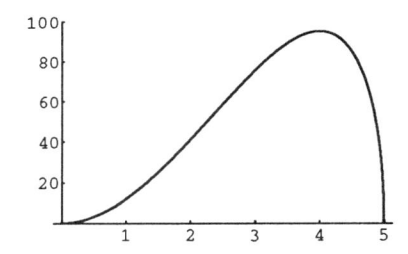

54. The graph of $V(x)$ is shown on the right. The maximum volume seems to occur near the point $(8, V(8)) \approx (8, 269.848)$, so the maximum volume is approximately 269.848 cubic feet.

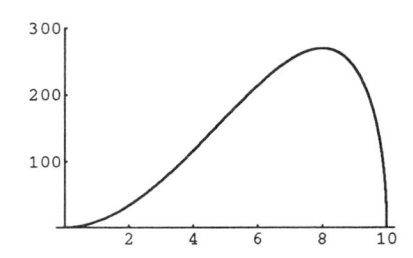

55. Let V_1 and V_2 be the volume functions of problems 53 and 54, respectively. $V_1'(x) = \dfrac{20\sqrt{5}\,(4x - x^2)}{3\sqrt{5-x}}$, which is zero at $x = 0$ and at $x = 4$, and $V_2'(x) = \dfrac{10\sqrt{5}\,(8x - x^2)}{3\sqrt{10-x}}$, which is zero at $x = 0$ and at $x = 8$ as expected. $\dfrac{V_2(8)}{V_1(4)} = 2\sqrt{2}.$

Section 3.7

1. $f'(x) = 6\sin x \cos x$
2. $f'(x) = -8\cos^3 x \sin x$
3. $f'(x) = \cos x - x \sin x$
4. $f'(x) = \dfrac{1}{2\sqrt{x}}\sin x + \sqrt{x}\cos x$
5. $f'(x) = \dfrac{x\cos x - \sin x}{x^2}$
6. $f'(x) = -\dfrac{x^{1/2}\sin x + \frac{1}{2}x^{-1/2}\cos x}{x}$
7. $f'(x) = \cos^3 x - 2\sin^2 x \cos x$
8. $f'(x) = -3\cos^2 x \sin^3 x + 2\cos^4 x \sin x$
9. $g'(t) = 4(1 + \sin t)^3 \cos t$

10. $g'(t) = 6(2 - \cos^2 t)^2 \sin t \cos t$

11. $g'(t) = \dfrac{\sin t - \cos t}{(\sin t + \cos t)^2}$

12. $g'(t) = \dfrac{(1 + \cos t) \cos t + \sin^2 t}{(1 + \cos t)^2} = \dfrac{1}{1 + \cos t}$

13. $f'(x) = 2 \sin x + 2x \cos x - 6x \cos x + 3x^2 \sin x$

14. $f'(x) = \tfrac{1}{2} x^{-1/2} \cos x - x^{1/2} \sin x + \tfrac{1}{2} x^{-3/2} \sin x - x^{-1/2} \cos x$

15. $f'(x) = 3 \cos 2x \cos 3x - 2 \sin 2x \sin 3x$

16. $f'(x) = 7 \cos 5x \cos 7x - 5 \sin 5x \sin 7x$

17. $g'(t) = 3t^2 \sin^2 2t + 4t^3 \sin 2t \cos 2t$

18. $g'(t) = \tfrac{1}{2} t^{-1/2} \cos^3 t - 9 t^{1/2} \cos^2 3t \sin 3t$

19. $g'(t) = -\tfrac{5}{2}(\cos 3t + \cos 5t)^{3/2}(3 \sin 3t + 5 \sin 5t)$

20. $g'(t) = -\dfrac{\sin t \cos t + 3 \sin 3t \cos 3t}{(\sin^2 t + \sin^2 3t)^{3/2}}$

21. $\dfrac{dy}{dx} = \dfrac{1}{\sqrt{x}} \sin \sqrt{x} \cos \sqrt{x}$

22. $\dfrac{dy}{dx} = \dfrac{-2x \sin 2x - \cos 2x}{x^2}$

23. $\dfrac{dy}{dx} = 2x \cos(3x^2 - 1) - 6x^3 \sin(3x^2 - 1)$

24. $\dfrac{dy}{dx} = 12 x^3 \sin^2 x^4 \cos x^4$

25. $\dfrac{dy}{dx} = 2 \cos 2x \cos 3x - 3 \sin 2x \sin 3x$

26. $\dfrac{dy}{dx} = \dfrac{\sin 3x - 3x \cos 3x}{\sin^2 3x}$

27. $\dfrac{dy}{dx} = -\dfrac{3 \sin 5x \sin 3x + 5 \cos 5x \cos 3x}{\sin^2 5x}$

28. $\dfrac{dy}{dx} = -\dfrac{\sin \sqrt{x}}{4\sqrt{x}\sqrt{\cos \sqrt{x}}}$

29. $\dfrac{dy}{dx} = 4x \sin x^2 \cos x^2$

30. $\dfrac{dy}{dx} = -9 x^2 \cos^2 x^3 \sin x^3$

31. $\dfrac{dy}{dx} = \dfrac{\cos 2\sqrt{x}}{\sqrt{x}}$

32. $\dfrac{dy}{dx} = -x^{-2/3} \sin 3 x^{1/3}$

33. $\dfrac{dy}{dx} = \sin x^2 + 2 x^2 \cos x^2$

34. $\dfrac{dy}{dx} = 2x \cos \dfrac{1}{x} + \sin \dfrac{1}{x}$

35. $\dfrac{dy}{dx} = \tfrac{1}{2} x^{-1/2} \sin x^{1/2} + \tfrac{1}{2} \cos x^{1/2}$

36. $\dfrac{dy}{dx} = 2(\sin x - \cos x)(\cos x + \sin x)$

37. $\dfrac{dy}{dx} = \tfrac{1}{2} x^{-1/2}(x - \cos x)^3 + 3 x^{1/2}(x - \cos x)^2(1 + \sin x)$

Section 3.7 Derivatives of Trigonometric Functions

38. $\dfrac{dy}{dx} = \dfrac{\sin\sqrt{x+\sqrt{x}}}{2\sqrt{x}} + \dfrac{\sqrt{x}\left(1+\dfrac{1}{2\sqrt{x}}\right)\cos\sqrt{x+\sqrt{x}}}{2\sqrt{x+\sqrt{x}}}$

39. $\dfrac{dy}{dx} = -2x[\sin(\sin x^2)]\cos x^2$

40. $\dfrac{dy}{dx} = \dfrac{(\cos x)\cos\left(1+\sqrt{\sin x}\right)}{2\sqrt{\sin x}}$

41. $\dfrac{dx}{dt} = 7t^6 \sec^2 t^7$

42. $\dfrac{dx}{dt} = 7t^6 \sec t^7 \tan t^7$

43. $\dfrac{dx}{dt} = 7\sec^2 t \tan^6 t$

44. $\dfrac{dx}{dt} = 14\sec^7 2t \tan 2t$

45. $\dfrac{dx}{dt} = 5t^7 \sec^2 5t + 7t^6 \tan 5t$

46. $\dfrac{dx}{dt} = \dfrac{5t^5 \sec t^5 \tan t^5 - \sec t^5}{t^2}$

47. $\dfrac{dx}{dt} = \dfrac{\sec\sqrt{t} + \sqrt{t}\sec\sqrt{t}\tan\sqrt{t}}{2\sqrt{t}}$

48. $\dfrac{dx}{dt} = \dfrac{\sec^3\sqrt{t} + \sec\sqrt{t}\tan^2\sqrt{t}}{2\sqrt{t}}$

49. $\dfrac{dx}{dt} = \dfrac{2\cot\dfrac{1}{t^2}\csc\dfrac{1}{t^2}}{t^3}$

50. $\dfrac{dx}{dt} = \dfrac{\csc^2\left(\dfrac{1}{\sqrt{t}}\right)}{2t^{3/2}}$

51. $\dfrac{dx}{dt} = \dfrac{5\tan 3t \sec 5t \tan 5t - 3\sec 5t \sec^2 3t}{\tan^2 3t} = 5\cot 3t \sec 5t \tan 5t - 3\csc^2 3t \sec 5t$

52. $\dfrac{dx}{dt} \equiv 0$

53. $\dfrac{dx}{dt} = \sec t \csc t + t\sec t \tan t \csc t - t\sec t \csc t \cot t = t\sec^2 t + \sec t \csc t - t\csc^2 t$

54. $\dfrac{dx}{dt} = 3t^2 \tan^3 t^3 + 9t^5 \sec^2 t^3 \tan^2 t^3$

55. $\dfrac{dx}{dt} = [\sec(\sin t)\tan(\sin t)]\cos t$

56. $\dfrac{dx}{dt} = -7[\csc(\sec 7t)]^2 \sec 7t \tan 7t$

57. $\dfrac{dx}{dt} = \dfrac{\sec t \cos t - \sin t \sec t \tan t}{\sec^2 t} = \cos^2 t - \sin^2 t$

58. $\dfrac{dx}{dt} = \dfrac{(1+\tan t)\sec t \tan t - \sec^3 t}{(1+\tan t)^2} = \dfrac{\sec t \tan t - \sec t}{(1+\tan t)^2}$

59. $\dfrac{dx}{dt} = -\dfrac{5\csc^2 5t}{2\sqrt{1+\cot 5t}}$

60. $\dfrac{dx}{dt} = -\dfrac{\left(\csc\sqrt{t}\right)^{3/2}\cos\sqrt{t}}{4\sqrt{t}}$

61. $\dfrac{dy}{dx} = -x\sin x + \cos x$, so the slope of the tangent at $x = \pi$ is $-\pi\sin\pi + \cos\pi = -1$. Since $y(\pi) = -\pi$, the equation of the tangent line is $y + \pi = -(x - \pi)$, or $y = -x$.

62. $\dfrac{dy}{dx} = -2\cos x \sin x$, so the slope of the tangent at $x = \pi/4$ is $-2\cos(\pi/4)\sin(\pi/4) = -1$. Since $y(\pi/4) = \tfrac{1}{2}$, the equation of the tangent line is $y - \tfrac{1}{2} = -(x - \pi/4)$, or $4y = -4x + 2 + \pi$.

63. $\dfrac{dy}{dx} = \sec^2\left(\dfrac{\pi x}{4}\right)$, so the slope of the tangent at $x = 1$ is $\sec^2\left(\dfrac{\pi}{4}\right) = 2$. Since $y(1) = \dfrac{4}{\pi}$, the equation of the tangent line is $y - \dfrac{4}{\pi} = 2(x - 1)$, or $y = 2x - 2 + \dfrac{4}{\pi}$.

64. $\dfrac{dy}{dx} = 2\sin\left(\dfrac{\pi x}{3}\right)\cos\left(\dfrac{\pi x}{3}\right)$, so the slope of the tangent at $x = 5$ is $2\sin\dfrac{5\pi}{3}\cos\dfrac{5\pi}{3} = -\tfrac{1}{2}\sqrt{3}$. Since $y(5) = \dfrac{9}{4\pi}$, the equation of the tangent line is $y - \dfrac{9}{4\pi} = -\tfrac{1}{2}\sqrt{3}\,(x - 5)$, or $y = -\dfrac{x\sqrt{3}}{2} + \dfrac{9 + 10\pi\sqrt{3}}{4\pi}$.

65. $\dfrac{dy}{dx} = -2\sin 2x$. This derivative is zero at all values of x for which $\sin 2x = 0$; i.e., values of x for which $2x = 0, \pm\pi, \pm 2\pi, \pm 3\pi, \ldots$. Therefore the tangent line is horizontal at points with x-coordinate an integral multiple of $\tfrac{1}{2}\pi$. These are points of the form $(n\pi, 1)$ for any integer n and $(\tfrac{1}{2}m\pi, -1)$ for any odd integer m.

66. $\dfrac{dy}{dx} = 1 - 2\cos x$, which is zero for $x = \left(\tfrac{1}{3}\pi\right) + 2k\pi$ and for $x = -\left(\tfrac{1}{3}\pi\right) + 2k\pi$ for any integer k. The tangent line is horizontal at all points of the form $\left(\pm\tfrac{1}{3}\pi + 2k\pi, y\left(\pm\tfrac{1}{3}\pi + 2k\pi\right)\right)$ where k is an integer.

67. $\dfrac{dy}{dx} = \cos^2 x - \sin^2 x$. This derivative is zero for $x = \tfrac{1}{4}\pi + n\pi$ and at $x = \tfrac{3}{4}\pi + n\pi$ for any integer n. The tangent line is horizontal at all points of the form $\left(n\pi + \tfrac{1}{4}\pi, \tfrac{1}{2}\right)$ and at all points of the form $\left(n\pi + \tfrac{3}{4}\pi, -\tfrac{1}{2}\right)$ where n is an integer.

68. $\dfrac{dy}{dx} = -\dfrac{\sin(2x)}{\left(2 + \sin^2 x\right)^2}$. This derivative is zero at all values of x for which $\sin 2x = 0$; i.e., values of x for which $2x = 0, \pm\pi, \pm 2\pi, \pm 3\pi, \ldots$. Therefore the tangent line is horizontal at points with x-coordinate an integral multiple of $\tfrac{1}{2}\pi$. These are points of the form $\left(n\pi, \tfrac{1}{2}\right)$ for any integer n and $\left(\tfrac{1}{2}m\pi, \tfrac{1}{3}\right)$ for any odd integer m.

69. $\dfrac{dy}{dx} = 1 + 2\cos x = 1$ at every integral multiple of π. Checking the points $(n\pi, n\pi - 2\cos n\pi)$ for $n = -2, -1, 0, 1, \ldots$, we find that the two lines are $y = x \pm 2$.

70. $\dfrac{dy}{dx} = \dfrac{-13\cos x}{(3 + \sin x)^2}$. The two lines are $y \equiv \tfrac{17}{4}$ and $y \equiv \tfrac{15}{2}$.

71. For example, if $f(x) = \sec x = \dfrac{1}{\cos x}$, then
$$f'(x) = -\dfrac{-\sin x}{\cos^2 x} = \dfrac{1}{\cos x} \cdot \dfrac{\sin x}{\cos x} = \sec x \tan x.$$

72. If $g(x) = \cos x$, then
$$\begin{aligned}g'(x) &= \lim_{h\to 0} \dfrac{g(x+h) - g(x)}{h} \\ &= \lim_{h\to 0} \dfrac{\cos x \cos h - \sin x \sin h - \cos x}{h} \\ &= \lim_{h\to 0} \dfrac{1 - \cos h}{h}(-\cos x) - \lim_{h\to 0}\dfrac{\sin h}{h}(\sin x) \\ &= 0 \cdot (-\cos x) - 1 \cdot \sin x = -\sin x.\end{aligned}$$

73. Write $R = R(\alpha) = \frac{1}{32}v^2 \sin 2\alpha$. Then
$$R'(\alpha) = \frac{1}{16}v^2 \cos 2\alpha,$$
which is zero when $\alpha = \pi/4$ (we assume $0 \leq \alpha \leq \pi/2$). Because R is zero at the endpoints of its domain, we conclude that $\alpha = \pi/4$ maximizes the range R.

74. Let h be the altitude of the balloon (in feet) at time t (in seconds) and let θ be its angle of elevation with respect to the observer. From the obvious figure, $h = 300 \tan \theta$, so
$$\frac{dh}{dt} = (300 \sec^2 \theta) \frac{d\theta}{dt}.$$
When $\theta = \pi/4$ and $\frac{d\theta}{dt} = \pi/180$, we have
$$\frac{dh}{dt} = 300 \cdot 2 \cdot \frac{\pi}{180} = \frac{10\pi}{3} \approx 10.47 \text{ ft/s}$$
as the rate of the balloon's ascent then.

75. Let h be the altitude of the rocket (in miles) at time t (in seconds) and let α be its angle of elevation then. From the obvious figure, $h = 2 \tan \alpha$, so
$$\frac{dh}{dt} = (2 \sec^2 \alpha) \frac{d\alpha}{dt}.$$
When $\alpha = 5\pi/18$ and $d\alpha/dt = 5\pi/180$, we have $dh/dt \approx 0.4224$ (mi/s; about 1521 mi/h).

76. Draw a figure in which the airplane is located at $(0, 25000)$ and the fixed point on the ground is located at $(x, 0)$. A line connecting the two produces a triangle with angle θ at $(x, 0)$. This angle is also the angle of depression of the pilot's line of sight, and when $\theta = 65°$, $d\theta/dt = 1.5°/\text{s}$. Now
$$\tan \theta = \frac{25000}{x}, \text{ so } x = 25000 \frac{\cos \theta}{\sin \theta},$$
thus
$$\frac{dx}{d\theta} = -\frac{25000}{\sin^2 \theta}.$$
The speed of the airplane is
$$-\frac{dx}{dt} = \frac{25000}{\sin^2 \theta} \cdot \frac{d\theta}{dt}.$$
When $\theta = \frac{13}{36}\pi$, $\frac{d\theta}{dt} = \frac{\pi}{120}$. So the ground speed of the airplane is
$$\frac{25000}{\sin^2 \left(\frac{13\pi}{36}\right)} \cdot \frac{\pi}{120} \approx 796.81 \text{ (ft/s)}.$$
Answer: About 543.28 mi/h.

77. As in the figure to the right, let θ be the angle of elevation of the observer's line of sight. Then
$$\tan \theta = \frac{20000}{x},$$
so that $x = 20000 \cot \theta$. Thus
$$\frac{dx}{dt} = (-20000 \csc^2 \theta) \frac{d\theta}{dt}.$$

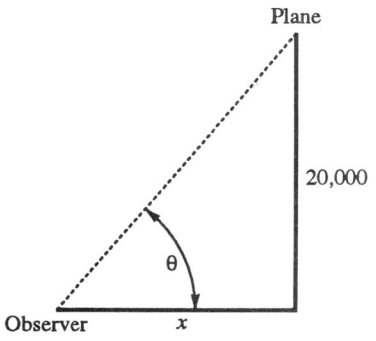

68 Section 3.7 Derivatives of Trigonometric Functions

When $\theta = 60°$, we are given $\dfrac{d\theta}{dt} = 0.5°/\text{s}$; that is, $\dfrac{d\theta}{dt} = \pi/360$ radians per second when $\theta = \pi/3$. We evaluate dx/dt at this time with these values to obtain

$$\frac{dx}{dt} = (-20000)\frac{1}{\sin^2\left(\dfrac{\pi}{3}\right)} \cdot \frac{\pi}{360} = -\frac{2000\pi}{27},$$

approximately -232.71 ft/s. Answer: About 158.67 mi/h.

78. The area of the rectangle is $A = 4xy$, but $x = \cos\theta$ and $y = \sin\theta$, so

$$A = A(\theta) = 4\sin\theta\cos\theta, \qquad 0 \le \theta \le \pi/2.$$

Now $A'(\theta) = 4(\cos^2\theta - \sin^2\theta) = 4\cos 2\theta$, so $A'(\theta) = 0$ when $\cos 2\theta = 0$. Because $0 \le 2\theta \le \pi$, it follows that $2\theta = \pi/2$, so $\theta = \pi/4$. But $A(0) = 0 = A(\pi/2)$ and $A(\pi/4) = 2$, so the latter is the largest possible area of a rectangle inscribed in the unit circle.

79. The cross section of the trough is a trapezoid with short base 2, long base $2 + 4\cos\theta$, and height $2\sin\theta$. Thus its cross-sectional area is

$$A(\theta) = \frac{2 + (2 + 4\cos\theta)}{2} \cdot 2\sin\theta$$
$$= 4(\sin\theta + \sin\theta\cos\theta), \qquad 0 \le \theta \le \pi/2$$

(the real upper bound on θ is $2\pi/3$, but the maximum value of A clearly occurs in the interval $[0, \pi/2]$).

$$A'(\theta) = 4(\cos\theta + \cos^2\theta - \sin^2\theta)$$
$$= 4(2\cos^2\theta + \cos\theta - 1)$$
$$= 4(2\cos\theta - 1)(\cos\theta + 1).$$

The only solution of $A'(\theta) = 0$ in the given domain occurs when $\cos\theta = 1/2$, so that $\theta = \pi/3$. It is easy to verify that this value of θ maximizes the function A.

80. In the situation described in the problem, we have $D = 20\sec\theta$. The illumination of the walkway is then

$$I = I(\theta) = \frac{k}{400}\sin\theta\cos^2\theta, \qquad 0 \le \theta \le \pi/2.$$

$$\frac{dI}{d\theta} = \frac{k\cos\theta}{400}(\cos^2\theta - 2\sin^2\theta);$$

$dI/d\theta = 0$ when $\theta = \pi/2$ and when $\cos^2\theta = 2\sin^2\theta$. The solution θ in the domain of I of the latter equation has the property that $\sin\theta = \sqrt{3}/3$ and $\cos\theta = \sqrt{6}/3$. But $I(0) = 0$ and $I(\theta) \to 0$ as $\theta \to (\pi/2)^-$, so the optimal height of the lamp post occurs when $\sin\theta = \sqrt{3}/3$. This implies that the optimal height is $10\sqrt{2} \approx 14.14$ m.

81. The figure on the right shows a cross section of the sphere-with-cone through the axis of the cone and a diameter of the sphere. Note that $h = r\tan\theta$ and that

$$\cos\theta = \frac{R}{h - R}.$$

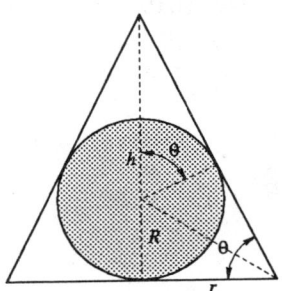

Therefore

$$h = R + R\sec\theta,$$

Section 3.7 Derivatives of Trigonometric Functions

and thus $r = \dfrac{R + R\sec\theta}{\tan\theta}$.

Now $V = \frac{1}{3}\pi r^2 h$, so for θ in the interval $(0, \pi/2)$, we have

$$V = V(\theta) = \frac{1}{3}\pi R^3 \cdot \frac{(1 + \sec\theta)^3}{\tan^2\theta}.$$

Therefore

$$V'(\theta) = \frac{\pi R^3}{3\tan^4\theta}\left[3(\tan^2\theta)(1+\sec\theta)^2 \sec\theta\tan\theta - (1+\sec\theta)^3(2\tan\theta \sec^2\theta)\right].$$

If $V'(\theta) = 0$ then either $\sec\theta = -1$ (so $\theta = \pi$, which we reject), or $\sec\theta = 0$ (which has no solutions), or $\tan\theta = 0$ (so either $\theta = 0$ or $\theta = \pi$, which we also reject), or (after replacement of $\tan^2\theta$ with $\sec^2\theta - 1$)

$$3(\sec^2\theta - 1) - 2\sec\theta - 2\sec^2\theta = 0;$$
$$\sec^2\theta - 2\sec\theta - 3 = 0.$$

It follows that $\sec\theta = 3$ or $\sec\theta = -1$. We reject the latter as before, and find that $\sec\theta = 3$, so $\theta \approx 1.23095$ (radians). The resulting minimum volume of the cone is $\frac{8}{3}\pi R^3$, twice the volume of the sphere!

82. Let L be the length of the crease. Then the right triangle of which L is the hypotenuse has sides $L\cos\theta$ and $L\sin\theta$. Now $20 = L\sin\theta + L\sin\theta\cos 2\theta$, so

$$L = L(\theta) = \frac{20}{(\sin\theta)(1 + \cos 2\theta)}, \qquad 0 < \theta \le \frac{\pi}{4}.$$

Next, $dL/d\theta = 0$ when

$$(\cos\theta)(1 + \cos 2\theta) = (\sin\theta)(2\sin 2\theta);$$
$$(\cos\theta)(2\cos^2\theta) = 4\sin^2\theta\cos\theta;$$

so $\cos\theta = 0$ (which is impossible given the domain of L) or

$$\cos^2\theta = 2\sin^2\theta = 2 - 2\cos^2\theta; \quad \cos^2\theta = \frac{2}{3}.$$

This implies that $\cos\theta = \sqrt{6}/3$ and $\sin\theta = \sqrt{3}/3$. Because $L \to +\infty$ as $\theta \to 0^+$, we have a minimum either at the horizontal tangent just found or at the endpoint $\theta = \pi/4$. The value of L at $\pi/4$ is $20\sqrt{2} \approx 28.28$ and at the horizontal tangent we have $L = 15\sqrt{3} \approx 25.98$. So the shortest crease is obtained when $\cos\theta = \sqrt{6}/3$; that is, for θ approximately $35°\,15'\,52''$. The bottom of the crease should be one-quarter of the way across the page from the lower left-hand corner.

83. Set up coordinates so the diameter is on the x-axis and the equation of the circle is $x^2 + y^2 = 1$; let (x, y) denote the northwest corner of the trapezoid. The chord from $(1, 0)$ to (x, y) forms a right triangle with hypotenuse 2, side z opposite angle θ, and side w; moreover, $z = 2\sin\theta$ and $w = 2\cos\theta$. It follows that

$$y = w\sin\theta = 2\sin\theta\cos\theta \text{ and}$$
$$-x = 1 - w\cos\theta = -\cos 2\theta.$$

Now

$$A = y(1 - x) = (2\sin\theta\cos\theta)(1 - \cos 2\theta)$$
$$= 4\sin\theta\cos\theta\sin^2\theta,$$

and therefore
$$A = A(\theta) = 4\sin^3\theta \cos\theta, \qquad \frac{\pi}{4} \leq \theta \leq \frac{\pi}{2}.$$

$$A'(\theta) = 12\sin^2\theta \cos^2\theta - 4\sin^4\theta$$
$$= (4\sin^2\theta)(3\cos^2\theta - \sin^2\theta).$$

To solve $A'(\theta) = 0$, we note that $\sin\theta \neq 0$, so we must have $3\cos^2\theta = \sin^2\theta$; that is $\tan^2\theta = 3$. It follows that $\theta = \pi/3$. The value of A here exceeds its value at the endpoints, so we have found the maximum value of the area—it is $3\sqrt{3}/4$.

84. Let $\theta = \alpha/2$ (see Fig. 3.7.18 of the text) and denote the radius of the circular log by r. Using the technique of the solution of Problem 82, we find that the area of the hexagon is
$$A = A(\theta) = 8r^2\sin^3\theta \cos\theta, \qquad 0 \leq \theta \leq \pi/2.$$
After some simplifications we also find that
$$\frac{dA}{d\theta} = 8r^2(\sin^2\theta)(4\cos^2\theta - 1).$$
Now $dA/d\theta = 0$ when $\sin\theta = 0$ and when $\cos\theta = 1/2$. When $\sin\theta = 0$, $A = 0$; also, $A(0) = 0 = A(\pi/2)$. Therefore A is maximal when $\cos\theta = 1/2$: $\theta = \pi/3$. When this happens, we find that $\alpha = 2\pi/3$ and that $\beta = \pi - \theta = 2\pi/3$. Therefore the figure of maximal area is a regular hexagon.

85. The area in question is the area of the sector minus the area of the triangle in Fig. 3.7.19 and turns out to be
$$A = \frac{1}{2}r^2\theta - r^2\cos\frac{\theta}{2}\sin\frac{\theta}{2}$$
$$= \frac{1}{2}r^2(\theta - \sin\theta) = \frac{s^2(\theta - \sin\theta)}{2\theta^2}$$
because $s = r\theta$. Now $\dfrac{dA}{d\theta} = \dfrac{s^2(2\sin\theta - \theta\cos\theta - \theta)}{2\theta^3}$, so $\dfrac{dA}{d\theta} = 0$ when $\theta(1 + \cos\theta) = 2\sin\theta$. Let $\theta = 2x$; note that $0 < x \leq \pi$ because $0 < \theta \leq 2\pi$. So the condition that $\dfrac{dA}{d\theta} = 0$ becomes
$$x = \frac{\sin\theta}{1 + \cos\theta} = \tan x.$$
But this equation has no solution in the interval $(0, \pi]$. So the only possible maximum of A must occur at an endpoint of its domain, or where x is undefined because the denominator $1 + \cos\theta$ is zero—and this occurs when $\theta = \pi$. Finally, $A(2\pi) = \dfrac{s^2}{4\pi}$ and $A(\pi) = \dfrac{s^2}{2\pi}$, so the maximum area is attained when the arc is a semicircle.

86. The length of the forest path is $2\csc\theta$. So the length of the part of the trip along the road is $3 - 2\csc\theta \cos\theta$. Thus the total time for the trip is given by
$$T = T(\theta) = \frac{2}{3\sin\theta} + \frac{3 - \dfrac{2\cos\theta}{\sin\theta}}{8}.$$
Note that the range of values of θ is determined by the condition
$$\frac{3\sqrt{13}}{13} \geq \cos\theta \geq 0.$$
After simplifications, we find that
$$T'(\theta) = \frac{3 - 8\cos\theta}{12\sin^2\theta}.$$

Now $T'(\theta) = 0$ when $\cos\theta = 3/8$; that is, when θ is approximately $67°\,58'\,32''$. For this value of θ, we find that $\sin\theta = \frac{1}{8}\sqrt{55}$. There's no problem in verifying that we have found the minimum. Answer: The distance to walk down the road is

$$\left(3 - 2\frac{\cos\theta}{\sin\theta}\right)\bigg|_{\sin\theta = \frac{\sqrt{55}}{8}} = 3 - \frac{6\sqrt{55}}{55} \approx 2.19096 \text{ (km)}.$$

88. $f'(0) = \lim\limits_{h \to 0} \dfrac{f(0+h) - f(0)}{h} = \lim\limits_{h \to 0} \dfrac{h^2 \sin\dfrac{1}{h}}{h} = \cdots .$

Section 3.8

1. $2x - 2y\dfrac{dy}{dx} = 0$, so $\dfrac{dy}{dx} = \dfrac{x}{y}$. Also, $y = \pm\sqrt{x^2 - 1}$, so $\dfrac{dy}{dx} = \pm\dfrac{x}{\sqrt{x^2 - 1}} = \dfrac{x}{y}$.

2. $x\dfrac{dy}{dx} + y = 0$, so $\dfrac{dy}{dx} = -\dfrac{y}{x}$. By substituting $y = x^{-1}$ into the derivative, we get $\dfrac{dy}{dx} = -\dfrac{x^{-1}}{x} = -x^{-2}$, which is the result obtained by explicit differentiation.

3. $32x + 50y\dfrac{dy}{dx} = 0$; $\dfrac{dy}{dx} = -\dfrac{16x}{25y}$. Substituting $y = \pm\frac{1}{5}\sqrt{400 - 16x^2}$ into the derivative, we get $\dfrac{dy}{dx} = \mp\dfrac{16x}{5\sqrt{400 - 16x^2}}$, which is the result obtained by explicit differentiation.

4. $3x^2 + 3y^2\dfrac{dy}{dx} = 0$, so $\dfrac{dy}{dx} = -\dfrac{x^2}{y^2}$. $y = \sqrt[3]{1 - x^3}$, so substitution results in $\dfrac{dy}{dx} = -\dfrac{x^2}{(1 - x^3)^{2/3}}$. Explicit differentiation yields the same answer.

5. $\frac{1}{2}x^{-1/2} + \frac{1}{2}y^{-1/2}\dfrac{dy}{dx} = 0$: $\dfrac{dy}{dx} = -\sqrt{\dfrac{y}{x}}$.

6. $4x^3 + 2x^2 y\dfrac{dy}{dx} + 2xy^2 + 4y^3\dfrac{dy}{dx} = 0$: $(2x^2 y + 4y^3)\dfrac{dy}{dx} = -(4x^3 + 2xy^2)$; $\dfrac{dy}{dx} = -\dfrac{4x^3 + 2xy^2}{2x^2 y + 4y^3}$.

7. $\frac{2}{3}x^{-1/3} + \frac{2}{3}y^{-1/3}\dfrac{dy}{dx} = 0$: $\dfrac{dy}{dx} = -\left(\dfrac{y}{x}\right)^{1/3}$.

8. $y^2 + 2(x - 1)y\dfrac{dy}{dx} = 1$, so $\dfrac{dy}{dx} = \dfrac{1 - y^2}{2y(x - 1)}$.

9. Given: $x^3 - x^2 y = xy^2 + y^3$:
$$3x^2 - x^2\dfrac{dy}{dx} - 2xy = y^2 + 2xy\dfrac{dy}{dx} + 3y^2\dfrac{dy}{dx};$$
$$3x^2 - 2xy - y^2 = (2xy + 3y^2 + x^2)\dfrac{dy}{dx};$$
$$\dfrac{dy}{dx} = \dfrac{3x^2 - 2xy - y^2}{3y^2 + 2xy + x^2}.$$

10. Given: $x^5 + y^5 = 5x^2 y^2$:
$$5x^4 + 5y^4\dfrac{dy}{dx} = 10x^2 y\dfrac{dy}{dx} + 10xy^2$$
$$\dfrac{dy}{dx} = \dfrac{10xy^2 - 5x^4}{5y^4 - 10x^2 y}$$

11. Given: $x\sin y + y\sin x = 1$:
$$x\cos y\dfrac{dy}{dx} + \sin y + y\cos x + \sin x\dfrac{dy}{dx} = 0;$$
$$\dfrac{dy}{dx} = -\dfrac{\sin y + y\cos x}{x\cos y + \sin x}.$$

12. Given: $\cos(x+y) = \sin x \sin y$:
$$-\sin(x+y)\left(1+\frac{dy}{dx}\right) = \sin x \cos y \frac{dy}{dx} + \sin y \cos x;$$
$$\frac{dy}{dx} = -\frac{\sin y \cos x + \sin(x+y)}{\sin(x+y) + \sin x \cos y}$$

13. Given: $\cos^3 x + \cos^3 y = \sin(x+y)$:
$$3\left(\cos^2 x\right)(-\sin x) + 3\left(\cos^2 y\right)(-\sin y)\frac{dy}{dx} = \cos(x+y)\left(1+\frac{dy}{dx}\right);$$
$$\frac{dy}{dx} = -\frac{\cos(x+y) + 3\cos^2 x \sin x}{\cos(x+y) + 3\cos^2 y \sin y}.$$

14. Given: $xy = \tan xy$:
$$x\frac{dy}{dx} + y = (\sec^2 xy)\left(x\frac{dy}{dx} + y\right);$$
$$\frac{dy}{dx} = \frac{y \sec^2 xy - y}{x - x \sec^2 xy} = -\frac{y}{x}.$$

Note: The original equation is of the form $\tan u = u$, which is true only for some isolated constant values of u; under the assumption that $xy = k$ for some constant k, we also obtain $\frac{dy}{dx} = -\frac{y}{x}$.

15. $2x + 2y\frac{dy}{dx} = 0$: $\frac{dy}{dx} = -\frac{x}{y}$. At $(3,-4)$ the tangent has slope $\frac{3}{4}$ and thus equation $y+4 = \frac{3}{4}(x-3)$.

16. $x\frac{dy}{dx} + y = 0$: $\frac{dy}{dx} = -\frac{y}{x}$. At $(4,-2)$ the tangent has slope $\frac{1}{2}$ and thus equation $y+2 = \frac{1}{2}(x-4)$.

17. $x^2\frac{dy}{dx} + 2xy = 1$, so $\frac{dy}{dx} = \frac{1-2xy}{x^2}$. At $(2,1)$ the tangent has slope $-\frac{3}{4}$ and thus equation $3x+4y = 10$.

18. $\frac{1}{4}x^{-3/4} + \frac{1}{4}y^{-3/4}\frac{dy}{dx} = 0$: $\frac{dy}{dx} = (-y/x)^{3/4}$. At $(16,16)$ the tangent has slope -1 and thus equation $x+y = 32$.

19. $y^2 + 2xy\frac{dy}{dx} + 2xy + x^2\frac{dy}{dx} = 0$: $\frac{dy}{dx} = -\frac{2xy + y^2}{2xy + x^2}$. At $(1,-2)$ the slope is zero.

20. $-\frac{1}{(x+1)^2} - \frac{1}{(y+1)^2} \cdot \frac{dy}{dx} = 0$, so $\frac{dy}{dx} = -\frac{(y+1)^2}{(x+1)^2}$. At $(1,1)$ the tangent line has slope -1 and thus equation $y - 1 = -(x-1)$.

21. $24x + 24y\frac{dy}{dx} = 25y + 25x\frac{dy}{dx}$: $\frac{dy}{dx} = \frac{25y - 24x}{24y - 25x}$. At $(3,4)$ the tangent line has slope $4/3$ and thus equation $4x = 3y$.

22. $2x + y + x\frac{dy}{dx} + 2y\frac{dy}{dx} = 0$: $\frac{dy}{dx} = -\frac{2x+y}{x+2y}$. At $(3,-2)$ the tangent line has slope 4 and thus equation $y+2 = 4(x-3)$.

23. $-3x^{-4} - 3y^{-4}\frac{dy}{dx} = 0$: $\frac{dy}{dx} = -\frac{y^4}{x^4}$. At $(1,1)$ the tangent has slope -1, and thus equation $y-1 = -(x-1)$.

24. $3(x^2+y^2)^2\left(2x + 2y\frac{dy}{dx}\right) = 16xy^2 + 16x^2y\frac{dy}{dx}$:
$$\frac{dy}{dx} = \frac{16xy^2 - 6x(x^2+y^2)^2}{6y(x^2+y^2)^2 - 16x^2y}.$$

At $(1,-1)$ the tangent line has slope 1 and thus equation $y+1 = x-1$.

25. $(2/3)x^{-1/3} + (2/3)y^{-1/3}\frac{dy}{dx} = 0$: $\frac{dy}{dx} = -\frac{y^{1/3}}{x^{1/3}}$. At $(8,1)$ the tangent line has slope $-\frac{1}{2}$, and thus equation $y-1 = -\frac{1}{2}(x-8)$, or $2y = 10 - x$.

Section 3.8 Implicit Differentiation and Related Rates

26. $2x - x\dfrac{dy}{dx} - y + 2y\dfrac{dy}{dx} = 0$: $\dfrac{dy}{dx} = \dfrac{y - 2x}{2y - x}$. At $(3, -2)$ the tangent line has slope $\frac{8}{7}$, and thus equation $y + 2 = \frac{8}{7}(x - 3)$, or $7y = 8x - 38$.

27. $2(x^2 + y^2)\left(2x + 2y\dfrac{dy}{dx}\right) = 50x\dfrac{dy}{dx} + 50y$:

$$\dfrac{dy}{dx} = -\dfrac{2x^3 - 25y + 2xy^2}{-25x + 2x^2y + 2y^3}.$$

At $(2, 4)$ the tangent line has slope $\frac{2}{11}$, and thus equation $y - 4 = \frac{2}{11}(x - 2)$, or $11y = 2x + 40$.

28. $2y\dfrac{dy}{dx} = 3x^2 + 14x$: $\dfrac{dy}{dx} = \dfrac{3x^2 + 14x}{2y}$. At $(-3, 6)$ the tangent line has slope $-\frac{5}{4}$ and thus equation $y - 6 = -\frac{5}{4}(x + 3)$ or $4y = 9 - 5x$.

29. $3x^2 + 3y^2\dfrac{dy}{dx} = 9x\dfrac{dy}{dx} + 9y$: $\dfrac{dy}{dx} = \dfrac{3y - x^2}{y^2 - 3x}$.

   (a) At $(2, 4)$ the tangent line has slope $\frac{4}{5}$ and thus equation $y - 4 = \frac{4}{5}(x - 2)$, or $5y = 4x + 12$.

   (b) At a point on the curve at which $\dfrac{dy}{dx} = -1$, $3y - x^2 = -y^2 - 3x$ and $x^3 + y^3 = 9xy$. This pair of simultaneous equations has solutions $x = 0$, $y = 0$ and $x = \frac{9}{2}$ and $y = \frac{9}{2}$, but the derivative does not exist at the point $(0, 0)$. Therefore the tangent line with slope -1 has equation $y - \frac{9}{2} = -(x - \frac{9}{2})$.

30. $2x^2 - 5xy + 2y^2 = (y - 2x)(2y - x)$.

   (a) So if $2x^2 - 5xy + 2y^2 = 0$, then $y - 2x = 0$ or $2y - x = 0$. This is a pair of lines with slope 2 and $\frac{1}{2}$, respectively.

   (b) Differentiating implicitly, we obtain $4x - 5x\dfrac{dy}{dx} - 5y + 4y\dfrac{dy}{dx} = 0$, which gives $\dfrac{dy}{dx} = \dfrac{5y - 4x}{4y - 5x}$, which is 2 if $y = 2x$ and $-\frac{1}{2}$ if $y = -\frac{1}{2}x$.

31. Here $\dfrac{dy}{dx} = \dfrac{2 - x}{y - 2}$, so horizontal tangents can occur only if $x = 2$ and $y \ne 2$. When $x = 2$, the given equation yields $y^2 - 4y - 4 = 0$, so that $y = 2 \pm \sqrt{8}$. Thus there are two points at which the tangent line is horizontal.

32. First, $\dfrac{dy}{dx} = \dfrac{y - x^2}{y^2 - x}$ and $\dfrac{dx}{dy} = \dfrac{y^2 - x}{y - x^2}$. Horizontal tangents require $y = x^2$, and the equation $x^3 + y^3 = 3xy$ of the folium yields $x^3(x^3 - 2) = 0$, so either $x = 0$ or $x = \sqrt[3]{2}$. But dy/dx is not defined at $(0, 0)$, so only at $(\sqrt[3]{2}, \sqrt[3]{4})$ is there a horizontal tangent. By symmetry or by a similar argument, there is a vertical tangent at $(\sqrt[3]{4}, \sqrt[3]{2})$ and nowhere else.

33. Given: $x^2 - xy + y^2 = 9$. The x-intercepts are $(3, 0)$ and $(-3, 0)$. Next, $\dfrac{dy}{dx} = \dfrac{y - 2x}{2y - x}$. The slope of the ellipse at both x-intercepts is 2, and this shows that the tangent lines are parallel. Their equations may be written in the form $y = 2(x - 3)$ and $y = 2(x + 3)$.

34. Here, $\dfrac{dy}{dx} = \dfrac{y - 2x}{2y - x}$ and $\dfrac{dx}{dy} = \dfrac{2y - x}{y - 2x}$. For horizontal tangents, $y = 2x$, and from the original equation $x^2 - xy + y^2 = 9$; it follows upon substitution of $2x$ for y that $x^2 = 3$. So the tangent line is horizontal at $(\sqrt{3}, 2\sqrt{3})$ and at $(-\sqrt{3}, -2\sqrt{3})$. Where there are vertical tangents we must have $x = 2y$, and (as above) it turns out that $y^2 = 3$; there are vertical tangents at $(2\sqrt{3}, \sqrt{3})$ and at $(-2\sqrt{3}, -\sqrt{3})$.

35. From $2(x^2 + y^2)\left(2x + 2y\dfrac{dy}{dx}\right) = 2x - 2y\dfrac{dy}{dx}$ it follows that

$$\dfrac{dy}{dx} = \dfrac{x[1 - 2(x^2 + y^2)]}{y[1 + 2(x^2 + y^2)]}.$$

So $dy/dx = 0$ when $x^2 + y^2 = \frac{1}{2}$, but is undefined when $x = 0$, for then $y = 0$ as well. If $x^2 + y^2 = \frac{1}{2}$, then $x^2 - y^2 = \frac{1}{4}$, so that $x^2 = \frac{3}{8}$, and it follows that $y^2 = \frac{1}{8}$. Consequently there are horizontal tangents at all four points where $|x| = \frac{1}{4}\sqrt{6}$ and $|y| = \frac{1}{4}\sqrt{2}$.

Also $dx/dy = 0$ only when $y = 0$, and if so, then $x^4 = x^2$, so that $x = \pm 1$ (dx/dy is undefined when $x = 0$). So there are vertical tangents at the two points $(-1, 0)$ and $(1, 0)$.

36. Base edge of block: x. Height: y. Volume: $V = x^2 y$. We are given $dx/dt = -2$ and $dy/dt = -3$.

$$\frac{dV}{dt} = x^2 \frac{dx}{dt} + 2xy \frac{dy}{dt}.$$

When $x = 20$ and $y = 15$, $dV/dt = (400)(-3) + (600)(-2) = -2400$. So the rate of flow at the time given is 2400 in.^{3}/h.

37. Suppose that the pile has height $h = h(t)$ at time t (seconds) and radius $r = r(t)$ then. We are given $h = 2r$ and we know that the volume of the pile at time t is

$$V = V(t) = \frac{\pi}{3} r^2 h = \frac{2}{3}\pi r^3. \text{ Now } \frac{dV}{dt} = \frac{dV}{dr} \cdot \frac{dr}{dt}, \text{ so } 10 = 2\pi r^2 \frac{dr}{dt}.$$

When $h = 5$, $r = 2.5$; at that time $\dfrac{dr}{dt} = \dfrac{10}{2\pi (2.5)^2} = \dfrac{4}{5\pi} \approx 0.25645$ (ft/s).

38. Draw a vertical cross section through the center of the tank. Let r denote the radius of the (circular) water surface when the depth of water in the tank is y. From the drawing and the Pythagorean theorem derive the relationship $r^2 + (10 - y)^2 = 100$. Therefore

$$2r\frac{dr}{dt} - 2(10 - y)\frac{dy}{dt} = 0, \text{ and so } r\frac{dr}{dt} = (10 - y)\frac{dy}{dt}.$$

We are to find dr/dt when $y = 5$, given $dy/dt = -3$. At that time, $r^2 = 100 - 25$, so $r = 5\sqrt{3}$. Thus

$$\left. \frac{dr}{dt} \right|_{y=5} = \frac{10 - y}{r} \cdot \left. \frac{dy}{dt} \right|_{y=5} = \frac{5}{5\sqrt{3}}(-3) = -\sqrt{3}.$$

Answer: The radius of the top surface is decreasing at $\sqrt{3}$ ft/s then.

39. With the usual meaning of each variable, we have $V = \pi r^2 h$, and we are given $V = 1$ (constant) and $dh/dt = -0.001$. Therefore $0 = \pi r^2 \dfrac{dh}{dt} + 2\pi r h \dfrac{dr}{dt}$. Consequently $2h \dfrac{dr}{dt} = \dfrac{r}{1000}$, and so $\dfrac{dr}{dt} = \dfrac{r}{2000h}$.

When $r = 8$, $h = \dfrac{1}{\pi r^2} = \dfrac{1}{64\pi}$. At that time, $\dfrac{dr}{dt} = \dfrac{8 \cdot 64\pi}{2000} = \dfrac{32\pi}{125} \approx 0.80425$ (m/h).

40. Let x be the distance from the ostrich to the street light and u the distance from the base of the light pole to the tip of the ostrich's shadow. Draw a figure and so label it; by similar triangles you find that $\dfrac{u}{10} = \dfrac{u - x}{5}$, and it follows that $u = 2x$. We are to find du/dt and $D_t(u - x) = du/dt - dx/dt$. But $u = 2x$, so

$$\frac{du}{dt} = 2\frac{dx}{dt} = (2)(-4) = -8; \qquad \frac{du}{dt} - \frac{dx}{dt} = -8 - (-4) = -4.$$

Answers: (a) $+8$ ft/s; (b) $+4$ ft/s.

41. Let x denote the width of the rectangle; then its length is $2x$ and its area is $A = 2x^2$. Thus $\dfrac{dA}{dt} = 4x \dfrac{dx}{dt}$. When $x = 10$ and $dx/dt = 0.5$, we have

$$\left. \frac{dA}{dt} \right|_{x=10} = (40)(10)(0.5) = 20 \text{ (cm}^2\text{/s)}.$$

42. Let x denote the length of each edge of the triangle. Then the triangle's area is $A(x) = \frac{\sqrt{3}}{4}x^2$, and therefore $\frac{dA}{dt} = \frac{\sqrt{3}}{2}x\frac{dx}{dt}$. Given $x = 10$ and $dx/dt = 0.5$, we find that

$$\left.\frac{dA}{dt}\right|_{x=10} = \frac{\sqrt{3}}{2} \cdot 10 \cdot (0.5) = \frac{5\sqrt{3}}{2} \text{ (cm}^2/\text{s)}.$$

43. Let r denote the radius of the balloon and V its volume at time t (in seconds). Then

$$V = \frac{4}{3}\pi r^3, \text{ so } \frac{dV}{dt} = 4\pi r^2 \frac{dr}{dt}.$$

We are to find dr/dt when $r = 10$, and we are given the information that $dV/dt = 100\pi$. Therefore

$$100\pi = 4\pi(10)^2 \left.\frac{dr}{dt}\right|_{r=10},$$

and so at the time in question the radius is increasing at the rate of $dr/dt = \frac{1}{4} = 0.25$ (cm/s).

44. Because $pV = 1000$, $V = 10$ when $p = 100$. Moreover, $p\frac{dV}{dt} + V\frac{dp}{dt} = 0$. With $p = 100$, $V = 10$, and $dp/dt = 2$, we find that

$$\left.\frac{dV}{dt}\right|_{p=100} = -\frac{V}{p} \cdot \left.\frac{dp}{dt}\right|_{p=100} = -\frac{10}{100} \cdot 2 = -\frac{1}{5}.$$

Therefore the volume is decreasing at 0.2 in.^{3}/s.

45. Place the person at the origin and the kite in the first quadrant at $(x, 400)$ at time t, where $x = x(t)$ and we are given $dx/dt = 10$. Then the length $L = L(t)$ of the string satisfies the equation $L^2 = x^2 + 160{,}000$, and therefore $2L\frac{dL}{dt} = 2x\frac{dx}{dt}$. Moreover, when $L = 500$, $x = 300$. So

$$1000\left.\frac{dL}{dt}\right|_{L=500} = 600 \cdot 10,$$

which implies that the string is being let out at 6 ft/s.

46. Locate the observer at the origin and the balloon in the first quadrant at $(300, y)$, where $y = y(t)$ is the balloon's altitude at time t. Let θ be the angle of elevation of the balloon (in radians) from the observer's point of view. Then $\tan\theta = y/300$. We are given $d\theta/dt = \pi/180$ rad/s. Hence we are to find dy/dt when $\theta = \pi/4$. But $y = 300\tan\theta$, so

$$\frac{dy}{dt} = (300\sec^2\theta)\frac{d\theta}{dt}.$$

Substitution of the given values of θ and $d\theta/dt$ yields the answer

$$\left.\frac{dy}{dt}\right|_{\theta=45°} = 300 \cdot 2 \cdot \frac{\pi}{180} = \frac{10\pi}{3} \approx 10.472 \text{ (ft/s)}.$$

47. Locate the observer at the origin and the airplane at $(x, 3)$, with $x > 0$. We are given dx/dt where the units are in miles, hours, and miles per hour. The distance z between the observer and the airplane satisfies the identity $z^2 = x^2 + 9$, and because the airplane is traveling at 8 mi/min, we find that $x = 4$, and therefore that $z = 5$, at the time 30 seconds after the airplane has passed over the observer. Also $2z\frac{dz}{dt} = 2x\frac{dx}{dt}$, so at the time in question, $10\frac{dz}{dt} = 8 \cdot 480$. Therefore the distance between the airplane and the observer is increasing at 384 mi/h at the time in question.

48. In this problem we have $V = \frac{1}{3}\pi y^2(15-y)$ and $(-100)(0.1337) = \frac{dV}{dt} = \pi(10y-y^2)\frac{dy}{dt}$. Therefore $\frac{dy}{dt} = -\frac{13\cdot 37}{\pi y(10-y)}$. Answers: (a) Approximately 0.2027 ft/min: (b) The same.

49. We use $a = 10$ in the formula given in Problem 42. Then
$$V = \frac{1}{3}\pi y^2(30-y).$$
Hence $(-100)(0.1337) = \frac{dV}{dt} = \pi(20y-y^2)\frac{dy}{dt}$. Thus $\frac{dy}{dt} = -\frac{13\cdot 37}{\pi y(20-y)}$. Substitution of $y = 7$ and $y = 3$ now yields the two answers.

50. When the height of the water at the deep end of the pool is 10 ft, the length of the water surface is 50 ft. So by similar triangles, if the height of the water at the deep end is y feet ($y \geq 10$), then the length of the water surface is $x = 5y$ feet. A cross section of the water perpendicular to the width of the pool thus forms a right triangle of area $5y^2/2$. Hence the volume of the pool is $V(y) = 50y^2$. Now $133.7 = \frac{dV}{dt} = 100y\frac{dy}{dt}$, so when $y = 6$ we have
$$\left.\frac{dy}{dt}\right|_{y=6} = \frac{133.7}{600} \approx 0.2228 \text{ (ft/min)}.$$

51. Let the positive y-axis represent the wall and the positive x-axis the ground, with the top of the ladder at $(0, y)$ and its lower end at $(x, 0)$ at time t. Given: $dx/dt = 4$, with units in feet, seconds, and feet per second. Also $x^2 + y^2 = 41^2$, and it follows that $y\frac{dy}{dt} = -x\frac{dx}{dt}$. Finally, when $y = 9$, we have $x = 40$, so at that time $9\frac{dy}{dt} = -40\cdot 4$. Therefore the top of the ladder is moving downward at $\frac{160}{9}$ ft/s.

52. Let x be the length of the base of the rectangle and y its height. We are given $dx/dt = +4$ and $dy/dt = -3$, with units in centimeters and seconds. The area of the rectangle is $A = xy$, so
$$\frac{dA}{dt} = x\frac{dy}{dt} + y\frac{dx}{dt} = -3x + 4y.$$
Therefore when $x = 20$ and $y = 12$, we have $dA/dt = -12$, so the area of the rectangle is decreasing at the rate of 12 cm^2/s then.

53. Let r be the radius of the cone, h its height. We are given $dh/dt = -3$ and $dr/dt = +2$, with units in centimeters and seconds. The volume of the cone at time t is $V = \frac{1}{3}\pi r^2 h$, so
$$\frac{dV}{dt} = \frac{2}{3}\pi rh\frac{dr}{dt} + \frac{1}{3}\pi r^2\frac{dh}{dt}.$$
When $r = 4$ and $h = 6$, $\frac{dV}{dt} = \frac{2}{3}\cdot 24\pi\cdot 2 + \frac{1}{3}\cdot 16\pi\cdot(-3) = 16\pi$, so the volume of the cone is increasing at the rate of 16π cm^3/s then.

54. Let x be the edge length of the square and $A = x^2$ its area. Given: $\frac{dA}{dt} = 120$ when $x = 10$. But $dA/dt = 2x(dx/dt)$, so $dx/dt = 6$ when $x = 10$. Answer: At 6 in./s.

55. Locate the radar station at the origin and the rocket at $(4, y)$ in the first quadrant at time t, with y in miles and t in hours. The distance z between the station and the rocket satisfies the equation $y^2 + 16 = z^2$, so $2y\frac{dy}{dt} = 2z\frac{dz}{dt}$. When $z = 5$, we have $y = 3$, and because $dz/dt = 3600$ it follows that $dy/dt = 6000$ mi/h.

56. Locate the car at $(x, 0)$, the truck at $(0, y)$ $(x, y > 0)$. Then at 1 P.M. we have $x = 90$ and $y = 80$. We are given that data $dx/dt = 30$ and $dy/dt = 40$, with units in miles, hours, and miles per hour. The distance z between the vehicles satisfies the equation $z^2 = x^2 + y^2$, so

$$z\frac{dz}{dt} = x\frac{dx}{dt} + y\frac{dy}{dt}.$$

Finally, at 1 P.M. $z^2 = 8100 + 6400 = 14500$, so $z = 10\sqrt{145}$ then. So at 1 P.M.

$$\frac{dz}{dt} = \frac{2700 + 3200}{10\sqrt{145}} = \frac{590}{\sqrt{145}}$$

mi/h—approximately 49 mi/h.

58. Let x be the distance between the *Pinta* and the island at time t and y the distance between the *Niña* and the island then. We know that $x^2 + y^2 = z^2$ where $z = z(t)$ is the distance between the two ships; so

$$2z\frac{dz}{dt} = 2x\frac{dx}{dt} + 2y\frac{dy}{dt}.$$

When $x = 30$ and $y = 40$, $z = 50$. It follows from the last equation that $dz/dt = -25$ then. Answer: They are drawing closer at 25 mi/h then.

59. Locate the military jet at $(x, 0)$ with $x < 0$ and the other aircraft at $(0, y)$ with $y \geq 0$. With units in miles, minutes, and miles per minute, we are given $dx/dt = +12$, $dy/dt = +8$, and when $t = 0$, $x = -208$ and $y = 0$. The distance z between the aircraft satisfies the equation $x^2 + y^2 = z^2$, so

$$\frac{dz}{dt} = \frac{1}{\sqrt{x^2 + y^2}}\left(x\frac{dx}{dt} + y\frac{dy}{dt}\right) = \frac{12x + 8y}{\sqrt{x^2 + y^2}}.$$

The closest approach will occur when $dz/dt = 0$: $y = 3x/2$. Now $x(t) = 12t - 280$ and $y(t) = 8t$. So at closest approach we have

$$8t = y(t) = -\frac{3}{2}x(t) = -\frac{3}{2}(12t - 208).$$

Hence at closest approach, $16t = 624 - 36t$, and thus $t = 12$. At this time, $x = -64$, $y = 96$, and $z = 32\sqrt{13} \approx 115.38$ (mi).

60. Let x be the distance from the anchor to the point on the seabed directly beneath the hawsehole; let L be the amount of anchor chain out. We must find dx/dt when $L = 13$ (fathoms), given $dL/dt = -10$. Now $x^2 + 144 = L^2$, so $2L\frac{dL}{dt} = 2x\frac{dx}{dt}$. Consequently, $\frac{dx}{dt} = \frac{L}{x} \cdot \frac{dL}{dt}$. At the time in question in the problem, $x^2 = 13^2 - 12^2$, so $x = 5$. It follows that $dx/dt = -26$ then. Thus the ship is moving at 26 fathoms per minute—about 1.77 mi/h.

61. Let x be the radius of the water surface at time t and y the height of the water remaining at time t. If Q is the amount of water remaining in the tank at time t, then (because the water forms a cone) $Q = Q(t) = \frac{1}{3}\pi x^2 y$. But by similar triangles, $\frac{x}{y} = \frac{3}{5}$, so $x = \frac{3y}{5}$. So

$$Q(t) = \frac{1}{3}\pi \frac{9}{25}y^3 = \frac{3}{25}\pi y^3.$$

We are given $dQ/dt = -2$ when $y = 3$. This implies that when $y = 3$, $-2 = \frac{dQ}{dt} = \frac{9}{25}\pi y^2 \frac{dy}{dt}$. So at the time in question,

$$\left.\frac{dy}{dt}\right|_{y=3} = -\frac{50}{81\pi} \approx -0.1965 \text{ (ft/s)}.$$

Section 3.8 Implicit Differentiation and Related Rates

62. Given $V = \frac{1}{3}\pi(60y^2 - y^3)$, find dy/dt given V, y, and dy/dt. First,

$$\frac{dV}{dt} = \frac{1}{3}\pi(60y - 3y^2)\frac{dy}{dt} = \pi(20y - y^2)\frac{dy}{dt}.$$

So $\dfrac{dy}{dt} = \dfrac{1}{\pi(20y - y^2)} \cdot \dfrac{dV}{dt}$. Therefore, when $y = 5$, we have

$$\left.\frac{dy}{dt}\right|_{y=5} = \frac{(200)(0.1337)}{\pi(100 - 25)} \approx 0.113488 \text{ (ft/min)}.$$

63. Let r be the radius of the water surface at time t, h the depth of water in the bucket then. By similar triangles we find that

$$\frac{r - 6}{h} = \frac{1}{4}, \text{ so } r = 6 + \frac{h}{4}.$$

The volume of water in the bucket then is

$$V = \frac{1}{3}\pi h(36 + 6r + r^2)$$
$$= \frac{1}{3}\pi\left(36 + 36 + \frac{3}{2}h + 36 + 3h + \frac{1}{16}h^2\right).$$
$$= \frac{1}{3}\pi h\left(108 + \frac{9}{2}h + \frac{1}{16}h^2\right).$$

Now $\dfrac{dV}{dt} = -10$; we are to find dh/dt when $h = 12$.

$$\frac{dV}{dt} = \frac{1}{3}\pi\left(108 + 9h + \frac{3}{16}h^2\right)\frac{dh}{dt}.$$

Therefore $\left.\dfrac{dh}{dt}\right|_{h=12} = \dfrac{3}{\pi} \cdot \dfrac{-10}{108 + 9 \cdot 12 + \frac{3 \cdot 12^2}{16}} = -\dfrac{10}{81\pi} \approx -0.0393$ (in./min).

64. Let x denote the distance between the ship and A, y the distance between the ship and B, h the perpendicular distance from the position of the ship to the line AB, u the distance from A to the foot of this perpendicular, and v the distance from B to the foot of the perpendicular. At the time in question, we know that $x = 10.4$, $dx/dt = 19.2$, $y = 5$, and $dy/dt = -0.6$. From the right triangles involved, we see that $u^2 + h^2 = x^2$ and $(12.6 - u)^2 + h^2 = y^2$. Therefore

$$x^2 - u^2 = y^2 - (12.6 - u)^2. \qquad (*)$$

We take $x = 10.4$ and $y = 5$ in Eq. (*); it follows that $u = 9.6$ and that $v = 12.6 - u = 3$. From Eq. (*), we know that

$$x\frac{dx}{dt} - u\frac{du}{dt} = y\frac{dy}{dt} + (12.6 - u)\frac{du}{dt},$$

so

$$\frac{du}{dt} = \frac{1}{12.6}\left(x\frac{dx}{dt} - y\frac{dy}{dt}\right).$$

From the data given, $du/dt \approx 16.0857$. Also, because $h = \sqrt{x^2 - u^2}$, $h = 4$ when $x = 10.4$ and $y = 9.6$. Moreover, $h\dfrac{dh}{dt} = x\dfrac{dx}{dt} - u\dfrac{du}{dt}$, and therefore

$$\left.4\frac{dh}{dt}\right|_{h=4} \approx (10.4)(19.2) - (9.6)(16.0857) \approx 11.3143.$$

Finally, $\dfrac{dh/dt}{du/dt} \approx 0.7034$, so the ship is sailing a course about $35°7'$ north *or* south of east at a speed of $\sqrt{(du/dt)^2 + (dh/dt)^2} \approx 19.67$ mi/h. It is located 9.6 miles east and 4 miles north *or* south of A, or 10.4 miles from A at a bearing of either $67°22'48''$ or $112°37'12''$.

65. Set up a coordinate system in which the radar station is at the origin, the plane passes over it at the point $(0,1)$ (so units on the axes are in miles), and the plane is moving along the graph of the equation $y = x + 1$. Let s be the distance from $(0,1)$ to the plane and let u be the distance from the radar station to the plane. We are given $du/dt = +7$ mi/min. We may deduce from the law of cosines that $u^2 = s^2 + 1 + s\sqrt{2}$. Let v denote the speed of the plane, so that $v = ds/dt$. Then

$$2u\frac{du}{dt} = 2sv + v\sqrt{2} = v\left(2s + \sqrt{2}\right), \text{ and so } v = \frac{2u}{2s + \sqrt{2}} \cdot \frac{du}{dt}.$$

When $u = 5$, $s^2 + s\sqrt{2} - 24 = 0$. The quadratic formula yields the solution $s = 3\sqrt{2}$, and it follows that $v = 5\sqrt{2}$ mi/min; alternatively, $v \approx 424.26$ mi/h.

66. $V(y) = \frac{1}{3}\pi(30y^2 - y^3)$ where the depth is y. Now $\dfrac{dV}{dt} = -k\sqrt{y} = \dfrac{dV}{dy} \cdot \dfrac{dy}{dt}$, and therefore

$$\frac{dy}{dt} = -\frac{k\sqrt{y}}{\dfrac{dV}{dy}} = -\frac{k\sqrt{y}}{\pi(20y - y^2)}.$$

To minimize dy/dt, write $F(y) = dy/dt$. It turns out (after simplification) that

$$F'(y) = \frac{k}{2\pi} \cdot \frac{20y - 3y^2}{(20y - y^2)^2 \sqrt{y}}.$$

So $F'(y) = 0$ when $y = 0$ and when $y = 20/3$. When y is near 20, $F(y)$ is very large; the same is true for y near zero. So $y = 20/3$ minimizes dy/dt, and therefore the answer to part (b) is 6 ft 8 in.

67. Place the pole at the origin in the plane, and let the horizontal strip $0 \leq y \leq 30$ represent the road. Suppose that the person is located at $(x, 30)$ with $x > 0$ and is walking to the right, so $dx/dt = +5$. Then the distance from the pole to the person will be $\sqrt{x^2 + 900}$. Let z be the length of the person's shadow. By similar triangles it follows that $2z = \sqrt{x^2 + 900}$, so $4z^2 = x^2 + 900$, and thus $8z\dfrac{dz}{dt} = 2x\dfrac{dx}{dt}$. When $x = 40$, we find that $z = 25$, and therefore that

$$100\frac{dz}{dt}\bigg|_{z=25} = 40 \cdot 5 = 200.$$

Therefore the person's shadow is lengthening at 2 ft/s at the time in question.

68. Set up a coordinate system in which the officer is at the origin and the van is moving in the positive direction along the line $y = 200$ (so units on the coordinate axes are in feet). When the van is at position $(x, 200)$, the distance from the officer to the van is z, where $x^2 + 200^2 = z^2$, so that $x\dfrac{dx}{dt} = z\dfrac{dz}{dt}$. When the van reaches the call box, $x = 200$, $z = 200\sqrt{2}$, and $dz/dt = 66$. It follows that

$$\frac{dx}{dt}\bigg|_{x=200} = 66\sqrt{2},$$

which translates to about 63.6 mi/h.

Section 3.9

Note: In this section your results may differ from the answers in the last one or two decimal places because of differences in calculators or in methods of solving the equations.

Note: In Problems 1 through 20, we obtained our initial estimate x_0 of the solution by linear interpolation: Write the equation of the straight line that joins $(a, f(a))$ with $(b, f(b))$ and let x_0 be the x-coordinate of the point where this line crosses the x-axis.

1. $x_0 = 2.2$; we use $f(x) = x^2 - 5$.
   Then $x_1 = 2.236363636$, $x_2 = 2.236067997$, and $x_3 = x_4 = 2.236067978$.

2. $x_0 = 1.142857154$; we use $f(x) = x^3 - 2$.
   Then $x_1 = 1.272321429$, $x_2 = 1.260041515$, $x_3 = 1.259921061$, and $x_4 = x_5 = 1.259921050$.

3. $x_0 = 2.322274882$; we use $f(x) = x^5 - 100$.
   Then $x_1 = 2.545482650$, $x_2 = 2.512761734$, $x_3 = 2.511887041$, and $x_4 = x_5 = 2.511886432$.

4. Let $f(x) = x^{3/2} - 10$. Then $x_0 = 4.628863603$. From the iterative formula
   $$x \longleftarrow x - \frac{x^{3/2} - 10}{\frac{3}{2}x^{1/2}}$$
   we obtain $x_1 = 4.641597575$, $x_2 = 4.641588834 = x_3$.

5. 0.25, 0.3035714286, 0.3027758133, 0.3027756377

6. 0.2, 0.2466019417, 0.2462661921, 0.2462661722

7. $x_0 = -0.5$;
   $x_1 = -0.8108695652$, $x_2 = -0.7449619516$, $x_3 = -0.7402438226$, $x_4 = -0.7402217821 = x_5$

8. Let $f(x) = x^3 + 2x^2 + 2x - 10$. Then $x_0 = 1.222222222$, $x_1 = 1.312580677$, $x_2 = 1.308913539$, $x_3 = 1.308907320$, and $x_4 = x_3$.

9. With $f(x) = x - \cos x$, $f'(x) = 1 + \sin x$, and calculator set in *radian* mode, we obtain:
   $x_0 = 0.5854549279$, $x_1 = 0.7451929664$, $x_2 = 0.7390933178$, $x_3 = 0.7390851332$, and $x_4 = x_3$.

10. Let $f(x) = x^2 - \sin x$. Then $f'(x) = 2x - \cos x$. The interpolation formula at the beginning of this solution section yields $x_0 = 0.7956861008$, and the iterative formula
    $$x \longleftarrow x - \frac{x^2 - \sin x}{2x - \cos x}$$
    (with calculator in *radian* mode) yields these results:
    $x_1 = 0.8867915207$, $x_2 = 0.8768492470$, $x_3 = 0.8767262342$, and $x_4 = 0.8767262154 = x_5$.

11. $x_0 = 1.2139964$, $x_1 = 1.232527939$, $x_2 = 1.235594896$, $x_3 = 1.236049696$,
    $x_4 = 1.236117649$, $x_5 = 1.236128116$, $x_6 = 1.236129704$, $x_7 = 1.236129945$,
    $x_8 = 1.236129982$, $x_9 = 1.236129988$, $x_{10} = 1.236129989 = x_{11}$

12. $x_0 = 0.8809986055$, $x_1 = 0.8712142932$, $x_3 = 0.8712215145$, and $x_4 = x_3$.

13. With $x_0 = 2.188405797$ and the iterative formula
    $$x \longleftarrow x - \frac{x^4(x+1) - 100}{x^3(5x + 4)},$$
    we obtain $x_1 = 2.360000254$, $x_2 = 2.339638357$, $x_3 = 2.339301099$, and $x_4 = 2.339301008 = x_5$.

14. $x_0 = 0.7142857143$, $x_1 = 0.8890827860$, $x_2 = 0.8607185590$, $x_3 = 0.8596255544$, and $x_4 = 0.8596240119 = x_5$.

15. The nearest discontinuities of $f(x) = x - \tan x$ are at $\pi/2$ and at $3\pi/2$, approximately 1.571 and 4.712. Therefore the function $f(x) = x - \tan x$ has the intermediate value property on the interval $[2, 3]$. Results: $x_0 = 2.060818494$, $x_1 = 2.027969226$, $x_2 = 2.028752991$, and $x_3 = 2.028757838 = x_4$.

16. Because $7\pi/2 \approx 10.9956$ and $4\pi \approx 12.5663$ are the nearest discontinuities of $f(x) = x - \tan x$, this function has the intermediate value property on the interval $[11, 12]$. Because $f(11) \approx -214.95$ and $f(12) \approx 11.364$, the equation $f(x) = 0$ has a solution in $[11, 12]$. We obtain $x_0 = 11.94978618$ by interpolation, and the iteration
$$x \longleftarrow x - \frac{x + \tan x}{1 + \sec^2 x}$$
of Newton's method yields the successive approximations
$$x_1 = 7.457596948, \quad x_2 = 6.180210620, \quad x_3 = 3.157913273, \quad x_4 = 1.571006986;$$
after many more iterations we arrive at the answer 2.028757838 of Problem 15. The difficulty is caused by the fact that $f(x)$ is generally a very large number, so the iteration of Newton's method tends to alter the value of x excessively. A little experimentation yields the fact that $f(11.08) \approx -0.736577$ and $f(11.09) \approx 0.531158$. We begin anew on the better interval $[11.08, 11.09]$ and obtain $x_0 = 11.08581018$, $x_1 = 11.08553759$, $x_2 = 11.08553841$, and $x_3 = x_2$.

17. $x_0 = 2.105263158$, $x_1 = 2.155592105$, $x_2 = 2.154435311$, $x_3 = 2.154434690 = x_4$.

18. $x_0 = 2.058823529$, $x_1 = 2.095291459$, $x_2 = 2.094551790$, $x_3 = 2.094551482 = x_4$.

19. $x_0 = 1.538461538$, $\quad x_1 = 1.932798309$, $\quad x_2 = 1.819962709$,
    $x_3 = 1.802569044$, $\quad x_4 = 1.802191039$, $\quad x_5 = 1.802190864$,
    $x_6 = 1.802190864 = x_5$.
    The convergence is slow because $|f'(x)|$ is large when x is near 1.8.

20. $x_0 = 0.0512$, $x_1 = 931322.6156$, $x_2 = 745058.0925$, ... —better improve the initial guess! Maybe the (naïve) choice of the midpoint of the interval would be better? Then we obtain $x_0 = 2.5$, $x_1 = 2.16384$, $x_2 = 2.023002449$, $x_3 = 2.000517182$, $x_4 = 2.000000267$, $x_5 = 2.000000000 = x_6$.

22. (b) With $x_0 = 1.5$ we obtain the successive approximations 1.610123, 1.586600, 1.584901, 1.584893, and 1.584893.

23. $x_0 = 0.5$, $x_1 = 0.4387912809$, $x_2 = 0.4526329217$, $x_3 = 0.4496493762$, ..., $x_{14} = 0.4501836113 = x_{15}$.

24. $x_0 = 1.5$, $x_1 = 1.257433430$, $x_2 = 1.225755182$, $x_3 = 1.221432153$, ..., $x_{10} = 1.220745085 = x_{11}$. These are the results obtained by using the first formula. When we use the second formula, we obtain $x_1 = 4.0625$, $x_2 = 271.3789215$, $x_3 = 5423829645$, and x_4 has 39 digits to the left of the decimal point. It may require some ingenuity to find a suitable way to put the equation $f(x) = 0$ into the form $x = G(x)$.

25. Using the first formula, we obtain $x_0 = 0.5$, $x_1 = -1$, $x_2 = 2$, $x_3 = 2.75$, $x_4 = 2.867768595$, ..., $x_{12} = 2.879385242 = x_{13}$. Wrong root! At least the method converged. With the second formula, we find $x_0 = 0.5$, error message on x_1. That's because our pocket computer won't compute the cube root of a negative number. With the alternative formula $x = \sqrt[3]{3x^2 - 1}$, we obtain $x_0 = 0.5$, $x_1 = 0.629960525$, $x_2 = 0.5754446861$, $x_3 = 0.1874852347$, $x_4 = 0.9635358111$, $x_5 = 1.213098128$, ..., $x_{62} = 2.879385240 = x_{63}$. Wrong root again. Actually, we're lucky to get a correct root in any case, because using absolute values in the formula changes it so much that we might be solving the wrong equation!

26. If $f(x) = \dfrac{1}{x} - a$, then Newton's method uses the iteration
$$x \longleftarrow x - \frac{\left(\dfrac{1}{x} - a\right)}{\left(-\dfrac{1}{x^2}\right)} = x + x^2\left(\dfrac{1}{x} - a\right) = 2x - ax^2.$$

27. Let $f(x) = x^5 + x - 1$. Then $f(x)$ is a polynomial, thus is continuous everywhere, and thus has the intermediate value property on every interval. Also $f(0) = -1$ and $f(1) = 1$, so $f(x)$ must assume

the intermediate value 0 somewhere in the interval $[0, 1]$. Thus the equation $f(x) = 0$ has *at least* one solution. Next, $f'(x) = 5x^4 + 1$ is positive for all x, so f is an increasing function. Because f is continuous, its graph can therefore cross the x-axis at most once, and so the equation $f(x) = 0$ has *at most* one solution. Thus it has exactly one solution. Incidentally, Newton's method yields the approximate solution 0.754877666624669276. To four places, 0.7549.

28. 0.8241323123 and -0.8241323123
30. 1.977383029, 3.837467106, and -1.306440008
32. Let $f(x) = x^3 - 5$. Use the iteration

$$x \longleftarrow x - \frac{x^3 - 5}{3x^2}.$$

With $x_0 = 2$, we obtain the sequence of approximations
1.75, 1.710884354, 1.709976429, 1.709975947, 1.709975947.

33. There is only one solution for the following reasons: $x^3 < -1$ if $x < -1$, $x^3 < 0 < \cos x$ if $-1 < x < 0$, x^3 is increasing on $[0, 1]$ whereas $\cos x$ is decreasing there (and their graphs cross in this interval as a consequence of the intermediate value property of continuous functions), and $x^3 > 1 \geq \cos x$ for $x > 1$.

34. The graphs of $y = x$ and $y = \tan x$ show that the smallest positive solution of $f(x) = x - \tan x = 0$ is between π and $3\pi/2$. With initial guess $x = 4.5$ we obtain 4.493613903, 4.493409655, 4.493409458, and 4.493409458.

35. With $x_0 = 3.5$, we obtain the sequence 3.451450588, 3.452461938, 3.452462314, 3.452462314.

36. To find a zero of $f(\theta) = \theta - \frac{1}{2}\sin\theta - \frac{17}{50}\pi$, we use the iteration

$$\theta \longleftarrow \theta - \frac{\theta - \frac{1}{2}\sin\theta - \frac{17}{50}\pi}{1 - \frac{1}{2}\cos\theta}.$$

Here are the results, beginning with $\theta_0 = 1.5$ (86° 56' 37''):
1.569342 (89° 55' 00''), 1.568140 (89° 50' 52''), 1.568140.

37. With $x_0 = 0.25$, Newton's method yields the sequence 0.2259259259, 0.2260737086, 0.2260737138, 0.2260717138. To four places, $x = 0.2261$.

38. This table shows that the equation $f(x) = 0$ has solutions in each of the intervals $(-3, -2)$, $(0, 1)$, and $(1, 2)$.

x	-3	-2	-1	0	1	2	3
$f(x)$	-14	1	4	1	-2	1	16

The next table shows the results of the iteration of Newton's method:

n	x_n	x_n	x_n
0	1.5	0.5	-2.5
1	2.090909091	0.2307692308	-2.186440678
2	1.895903734	0.2540002371	-2.118117688
3	1.861832371	0.2541016863	-2.114914461
4	1.860806773	0.2541016884	-2.114907542
5	1.860805853	0.2541016884	-2.114907541
6	1.860805853		-2.114907541

39. We iterate using the formula
$$x \longleftarrow x - \frac{x + \tan x}{1 + \sec^2 x}.$$

Here is a sequence of simple *Mathematica* commands to find approximations to the four least positive solutions of the given equation, together with the results. (The command **list=g[list]** was executed repeatedly, but deleted from the output to save space.)

> **list={2.0, 5.0, 8.0, 11.0}**
> **f[x_]:=x+Tan[x]**
> **g[x_]:=N[x−f[x]/f'[x],10]**
> **list=g[list]**
> 2.027314579, 4.879393859, 7.975116372, 11.00421012
> 2.028754298, 4.907699753, 7.978566616, 11.01202429
> 2.028757838, 4.913038110, 7.978665635, 11.02548807
> 2.028757838, 4.913180344, 7.978665712, 11.04550306
> 2.028757838, 4.913180439, 7.978665712, 11.06778114
> 2.028757838, 4.913180439, 7.978665712, 11.08205766
> 2.028757838, 4.913180439, 7.978665712, 11.08540507
> 2.028757838, 4.913180439, 7.978665712, 11.08553821
> 2.028757838, 4.913180439, 7.978665712, 11.08553841

40. Plot the graph from -1 to 12 to see that this equation has exactly one solution, and that this solution lies between $x = 10$ and $x = 12$. The solution is approximately 10.9901597, which is 10.9902 rounded to four decimal places.

41. Answer: $w \approx 13.01643877211592461$; to four places $w = 13.0164$.

Chapter 3 Miscellaneous

1. $\dfrac{dy}{dx} = 2x - \dfrac{6}{x^3}$

2. $2y\dfrac{dy}{dx} = 2x$: $\dfrac{dy}{dx} = \dfrac{x}{y}$

3. $\dfrac{dy}{dx} = \dfrac{1}{2\sqrt{x}} - \dfrac{1}{3x^{4/3}}$

4. $\dfrac{dy}{dx} = \frac{5}{2}(x^2 + 4x)^{3/2}(2x+4) = 5(x+2)(x^2+4x)^{3/2}$

5. $\dfrac{dy}{dx} = 7(x-1)^6(3x+2)^9 + 27(x-1)^7(3x+2)^8$

6. $\dfrac{dy}{dx} = \dfrac{(x^2+x+1)(4x^3+2x) - (x^4+x^2)(2x+1)}{(x^2+x+1)^2} = \dfrac{2x^5 + 3x^4 + 4x^3 + x^2 + 2x}{(x^2+x+1)^2}$

7. $\dfrac{dy}{dx} = 4(3x - \tfrac{1}{2}x^{-2})^3(3 + x^{-3})$

8. $\dfrac{dy}{dx} = 10x^9 \sin 10x + 10x^{10} \cos 10x$

9. $x\dfrac{dy}{dx} + y = 0$: $\dfrac{dy}{dx} = -\dfrac{y}{x} = -\dfrac{9}{x^2}$

10. $y = (5x^6)^{-1/2}$: $\dfrac{dy}{dx} = -\tfrac{1}{2}(5x^6)^{-3/2}(30x^5) = -\dfrac{3}{x\sqrt{5x^6}} = -\dfrac{3\sqrt{5}}{5x^4}$

11. $\dfrac{dy}{dx} = -\tfrac{3}{2}(x^3 - x)^{-5/2}(3x^2 - 1)$

12. $\dfrac{dy}{dx} = \tfrac{2}{3}(2x + 1)^{-2/3}(3x - 2)^{1/5} + \tfrac{3}{5}(3x - 2)^{-4/5}(2x + 1)^{1/3} = \dfrac{10(3x - 2) + 9(2x + 1)}{15(2x + 1)^{2/3}(3x - 2)^{4/5}}$
$= \dfrac{48x - 11}{15(2x + 1)^{2/3}(3x - 2)^{4/5}}$

13. $\dfrac{dy}{dx} = \dfrac{dy}{du} \cdot \dfrac{du}{dx} = \dfrac{-2u}{(1 + u^2)^2} \cdot \dfrac{-2x}{(1 + x^2)^2}$. Now $1 + u^2 = 1 + \dfrac{1}{(1 + x^2)^2} = \dfrac{x^4 + 2x^2 + 2}{(1 + x^2)^2}$.
So $\dfrac{dy}{du} = \dfrac{-2u}{(1 + u^2)^2} = \dfrac{-2}{1 + x^2} \cdot \dfrac{(1 + x^2)^4}{(x^4 + 2x^2 + 2)^2} = \dfrac{-2(1 + x^2)^3}{(x^4 + 2x^2 + 2)^2}$.
Therefore $\dfrac{dy}{dx} = \dfrac{-2(1 + x^2)^3}{(x^4 + 2x^2 + 2)^2} \cdot \dfrac{-2x}{(1 + x^2)^2} = \dfrac{4x(1 + x^2)}{(x^4 + 2x^2 + 2)^2}$.

14. $3x^2 = 2\dfrac{dy}{dx}\sin y \cos y$, so $\dfrac{dy}{dx} = \dfrac{3x^2}{2\sin y \cos y}$.

16. $\dfrac{dy}{dx} = \dfrac{15x^4 - 8x}{2(3x^5 - 4x^2)^{1/2}}$

17. $\dfrac{dy}{dx} = \dfrac{dy}{du} \cdot \dfrac{du}{dx} = \dfrac{(u - 1) - (u + 1)}{(u - 1)^2} \cdot \tfrac{1}{2}(x + 1)^{-1/2}$

18. $\dfrac{dy}{dx} = -6(\sin 3x)\cos(2\cos 3x)$

19. $2x^2y\dfrac{dy}{dx} + 2xy^2 = 1 + \dfrac{dy}{dx}$, so $\dfrac{dy}{dx} = \dfrac{1 - 2xy^2}{2x^2y - 1}$.

20. $\dfrac{dy}{dx} = \dfrac{\cos\sqrt{x}}{4\sqrt{x}\sqrt{1 + \sin\sqrt{x}}}$

22. $\dfrac{dy}{dx} = \dfrac{(x^2 + \cos x)(1 + \cos x) - (x + \sin x)(2x - \sin x)}{(x^2 + \cos x)^2} = \dfrac{1 - x^2 - x\sin x + \cos x + x^2\cos x}{(x^2 + \cos x)^2}$

23. $\tfrac{1}{3}x^{-2/3} + \tfrac{1}{3}y^{-2/3}\dfrac{dy}{dx} = 0$, so $\dfrac{dy}{dx} = -\left(\dfrac{y}{x}\right)^{2/3}$.

24. $3x^2 + 3y^2\dfrac{dy}{dx} = x\dfrac{dy}{dx} + y$, so $\dfrac{dy}{dx} = \dfrac{y - 3x^2}{3y^2 - x}$.

26. $\dfrac{dy}{dx} = \left(-2\cos(\sin^2 x)\sin(\sin^2 x)\right)(2\sin x \cos x)$

28. $\dfrac{dy}{dx} = \dfrac{3(1 + \sqrt{x})^2}{2\sqrt{x}}(1 - 2\sqrt[3]{x})^4 + 4(1 - 2\sqrt[3]{x})^3\left(-\tfrac{2}{3}x^{-2/3}\right)(1 + \sqrt{x})^3$

30. $3x^2 - x^2\dfrac{dy}{dx} - 2xy + y^2 + 2xy\dfrac{dy}{dx} - 3y^2\dfrac{dy}{dx} = 0$: $\dfrac{dy}{dx} = \dfrac{3x^2 - 2xy + y^2}{3y^2 - 2xy + x^2}$.

31. $\dfrac{dy}{dx} = (\sin^3 2x)(2)(\cos 3x)(-\sin 3x)(3) + (\cos^2 3x)(3\sin^2 2x)(2\cos 2x)$
$= 6(\cos 3x \sin^2 2x)(\cos 3x \cos 2x - \sin 2x \sin 3x)$
$= 6\cos 3x \cos 5x \sin^2 2x$

32. $\dfrac{dy}{dx} = \tfrac{2}{3}[1 + (2 + 3x)^{-3/2}]^{-1/3}[-\tfrac{9}{2}(2 + 3x)^{-5/2}] = -\dfrac{3}{[1 + (2 + 3x)^{-3/2}]^{1/3}(2 + 3x)^{5/2}}$

33. $\dfrac{dy}{dx} = 5\left[\sin^4\left(x + \dfrac{1}{x}\right)\right]\left[\cos\left(x + \dfrac{1}{x}\right)\right]\left[1 - \dfrac{1}{x^2}\right]$

34. $(x+y)^3 = (x-y)^2$, so $3(x+y)^2\left(1+\dfrac{dy}{dx}\right) = 2(x-y)\left(1-\dfrac{dy}{dx}\right)$;

thus $\dfrac{dy}{dx} = \dfrac{2(x-y) - 3(x+y)^2}{3(x+y)^2 + 2(x-y)} = \dfrac{2(x+y)^{3/2} - 3(x+y)^2}{3(x+y)^2 + 2(x+y)^{3/2}} = \dfrac{2 - 3\sqrt{x+y}}{2 + 3\sqrt{x+y}}.$

36. $\dfrac{dy}{dx} = \dfrac{(x-1)-(x+1)}{(x-1)^2} = -\dfrac{2}{(x-1)^2}$; the slope of the line tangent at $(0,-1)$ is -2; an equation of the tangent line is $y + 1 = -2x$; that is, $2x + y + 1 = 0$.

37. $1 = (2\cos 2y)\dfrac{dy}{dx}$, so $\dfrac{dy}{dx} = \dfrac{1}{2\cos 2y}$. Because $\dfrac{dy}{dx}$ is undefined at $(1, \pi/4)$, there may well be a vertical tangent at that point; sure enough, $\dfrac{dx}{dy} = 0$ at $(1, \pi/4)$. So an equation of the tangent line is $x = 1$.

38. $\dfrac{dy}{dx} = \dfrac{3y - 2x}{4y - 3x}$; at $(2,1)$, the slope is $1/2$. So an equation of the the tangent is $y - 1 = \tfrac{1}{2}(x-2)$; that is, $x = 2y$.

39. $\dfrac{dy}{dx} = \dfrac{2x+1}{3y^2}$; at $(0,0)$, $\dfrac{dx}{dy} = 0$, so the tangent line is vertical. Its equation is $x = 0$.

40. $V(x) = \tfrac{1}{3}\pi(36x^2 - x^3)$: $V'(x) = \pi x(24 - x)$. Now $\dfrac{dV}{dt} = \dfrac{dV}{dx} \cdot \dfrac{dx}{dt}$; when $x = 6$, $36\pi = -108\pi\dfrac{dx}{dt}$, so $dx/dt = -\tfrac{1}{3}$ (in./s) when $x = 6$.

41. Let r be the radius of the sandpile, h its height, each a function of time t. We know that $2r = h$, so the volume of the sandpile at time t is

$$V = \frac{1}{3}\pi r^2 h = \frac{2}{3}\pi r^3.$$

So

$$25\pi = \frac{dV}{dt} = 2\pi r^2 \frac{dr}{dt};$$

substitution of $r = 5$ yields the answer: $dr/dt = \tfrac{1}{2}$ (ft/min) when $r = 5$ (ft).

42. Divide each term in the numerator and denominator by $\sin x$ to obtain

$$\lim_{x\to 0}\frac{x}{\sin x} - \lim_{x\to 0}\frac{1}{\cos x} = 1 - 1 = 0.$$

43. $x\cot 3x = \dfrac{1}{3}\cdot\dfrac{3x}{\sin 3x} \to \dfrac{1}{3}\cdot 1\cdot 1 = \dfrac{1}{3}$ as $x \to 0$.

44. $\dfrac{\sin 2x}{\sin 5x} = \dfrac{2}{5}\cdot\dfrac{\sin 2x}{2x}\cdot\dfrac{5x}{\sin 5x} \to \dfrac{2}{5}$ as $x \to 0$.

45. $x^2\csc 2x \cot 2x = \dfrac{1}{4}\cdot\dfrac{2x}{\sin 2x}\cdot\dfrac{2x}{\sin 2x}\cdot\cos 2x \to \dfrac{1}{4}$ as $x \to 0$.

46. $-1 \leq \sin u \leq 1$ for all u. So

$$-x^2 \leq x^2 \sin\frac{1}{x^2} \leq x^2$$

for all $x \neq 0$. But $x^2 \to 0$ as $x \to 0$, so the limit of the expression caught in the squeeze is also zero.

47. $-1 \leq \sin u \leq 1$ for all u. So

$$-\sqrt{x} \leq \sqrt{x}\sin\frac{1}{x} \leq \sqrt{x}$$

for all $x > 0$. But $\sqrt{x} \to 0$ as $x \to 0^+$, so the limit is zero.

48. $g(x) = x^{1/3}$, $f(x) = x + x^4$; $h'(x) = \tfrac{1}{3}(x + x^4)^{-2/3}(1 + 4x^3)$.

49. $g(x) = x^{-1/2}$, $f(x) = x^2 + 25$.

50. $g(x) = x^{1/2}$, $f(x) = \dfrac{x}{x^2 + 1}$; $h'(x) = \dfrac{1 - x^2}{2x^{1/2}(x^2+1)^{3/2}}$.

51. $g(x) = x^{1/3}$, $f(x) = (x-1)^5$.

52. $g(x) = x^{10}$, $f(x) = \dfrac{x+1}{x-1}$; $h'(x) = -\dfrac{20(x+1)^9}{(x-1)^{11}}$.

53. $g(x) = \cos x$, $f(x) = x^2 + 1$.

54. $T = 2\pi\sqrt{\dfrac{L}{32}}$; $\dfrac{dT}{dL} = \dfrac{\pi}{32}\sqrt{\dfrac{32}{L}}$. So $\dfrac{dT}{dL}\bigg|_{L=4} = \dfrac{\pi\sqrt{2}}{16}$.
Hence when $L = 4$, T is changing at approximately 0.27768 seconds per foot.

55. $\dfrac{dV}{dA} \cdot \dfrac{dA}{dr} = \dfrac{dV}{dr}$. Now $V = \dfrac{4}{3}\pi r^3$ and $A = 4\pi r^2$, so $\dfrac{dV}{dA} \cdot 8\pi r = 4\pi r^2$, and therefore $\dfrac{dV}{dA} = \dfrac{r}{2} = \dfrac{1}{4}\sqrt{\dfrac{A}{\pi}}$.

56. Let (a,b) denote the point of tangency; note that
$$b = a + \frac{1}{a}, \quad a > 0, \text{ and } h'(x) = 1 - \frac{1}{x^2}.$$
The slope of the tangent line can be computed using the two-point formula for slope and by using the derivative. We equate the results to obtain
$$\frac{a + \dfrac{1}{a} - 0}{a - 1} = 1 - \frac{1}{a^2} = \frac{a^2 - 1}{a^2}.$$
It follows that $a^3 + a = (a-1)(a^2 - 1) = a^3 - a^2 - a + 1$. Thus $a^2 + 2a - 1 = 0$, and so $a = -1 + \sqrt{2}$ (the positive root because $a > 0$). Consequently the tangent line has slope $-2(1+\sqrt{2})$ and thus equation
$$y = -2(1 + \sqrt{2})(x - 1).$$

57. Let $y = y(t)$ denote the altitude of the rocket at time t; let $u = u(t)$ denote the angle of elevation of the observer's line of sight at time t. Then $\tan u = y/3$, so that $y = 3\tan u$ and, therefore,
$$\frac{dy}{dt} = (3\sec^2 u)\frac{du}{dt}.$$
When $u = 60°$, we take $du/dt = \dfrac{\pi}{3}$ and find that the speed of the rocket is
$$\frac{dy}{dt}\bigg|_{u=60°} = \frac{3}{\cos^2(\pi/3)} \cdot \frac{\pi}{30} = \frac{2}{5}\pi \approx 1.2566 \text{ (mi/s)},$$
about 4524 mi/h, or about 6635 ft/s.

58. Current production per well: 200 (bbl/day). Number of new wells: x ($x \geq 0$). Production per well: $200 - 5x$. Total production:
$$T = T(x) = (20 + x)(200 - 5x), \quad 0 \leq x \leq 40.$$
Now $T(x) = 4000 + 100x - 5x^2$, so $T'(x) = 100 - 10x$. $T'(x) = 0$ when $x = 10$. $T(0) = 4000$, $T(40) = 0$, and $T(10) = 4500$. So $x = 10$ maximizes $T(x)$. Answer: Ten new wells should be drilled, thereby increasing total production from 4000 bbl/day to 4500 bbl/day.

59. Let the circle be the one with equation $x^2 + y^2 = R^2$ and let the base of the triangle lie on the x-axis; denote the opposite vertex of the triangle by (x, y). The area of the triangle $A = Ry$ is clearly maximal when y is maximal; that is, when $y = R$. To solve this problem using calculus, let θ be the angle of the triangle at $(-R, 0)$. Because the triangle has a right angle at (x, y), its two short sides are $2R\cos\theta$ and $2R\sin\theta$, so its area is
$$A(\theta) = 2R^2 \sin\theta \cos\theta = R^2 \sin 2\theta, \quad 0 \leq \theta \leq \pi/2.$$

60. Let x be the length of the edges of each of the 20 small squares. The first five boxes measure $210-2x$ by $336-2x$ by x. The total volume is then

$$V(x) = 5x(210-2x)(336-2x) + 8x^3, \quad 0 \le x \le 105.$$

Thus $V(x) = 28x^3 - 5460x^2 + 352800x$, and so

$$V'(x) = 84x^2 - 10290x + 352800 = 84(x^2 - 130x + 4200).$$

So $V'(x) = 0$ when $x = 60$ and when $x = 70$. But $V(0) = 0$, $V(60) = 7{,}560{,}000$, $V(70) = 7{,}546{,}000$, and $V(105) = 9{,}261{,}000$. Answer: For maximal volume, make x as large as possible: 105 cm. This yields the maximum volume, $9{,}261{,}000$ cm^3.

61. Let one sphere have radius r; the other, s. We seek the extrema of $A = 4\pi(r^2 + x^2)$ given $\frac{4}{3}\pi(r^3 + s^3) = V$, a constant. We illustrate here the **method of auxiliary variables:**

$$\frac{dA}{dr} = 4\pi\left(2r + 2s\frac{ds}{dr}\right);$$

the condition $dA/dr = 0$ yields $ds/dr = -r/s$. But we also know that $\frac{4}{3}\pi(r^3 + x^3) = V$; differentiation of both sides of this *identity* with respect to r yields

$$\frac{4}{3}\pi\left(3r^2 + 3s^2\frac{ds}{dr}\right) = 0, \text{ and so}$$

$$3r^2 + 3s^2\left(-\frac{r}{s}\right) = 0;$$

$$r^2 - rs = 0.$$

Therefore $r = 0$ or $r = s$. Also, ds/dr is undefined when $s = 0$. So we test these three critical points. If $r = 0$ or if $s = 0$, there is only one sphere, with radius $(3V/4\pi)^{1/3}$ and surface area $(36\pi V^2)^{1/3}$. If $r = s$, then there are two spheres of equal size, both with radius $\frac{1}{2}(3V/\pi)^{1/3}$ and surface area $(72\pi V^2)^{1/3}$. Therefore, for maximum surface area, make two equal spheres. For minimum surface area, make only one sphere.

62. Let x be the length of the edge of the rectangle on the side of length 4 and y the length of the adjacent edges. By similar triangles, $3/4 = (3-y)/x$, so $x = 4 - \frac{4}{3}y$. We are to maximize $A = xy$; that is,

$$A = A(y) = 4y - \frac{4}{3}y^2, \quad 0 \le y \le 3.$$

Now $dA/dy = 4 - \frac{8}{3}y$; $dA/dy = 0$ when $y = \frac{3}{2}$. Because $A(0) = A(3) = 0$, the maximum is $A(2) = 3$ (m^2).

63. Let r be the radius of the cone; let its height be $h = R + y$ where $0 \le y \le R$. (Actually, $-R \le y \le R$, but the cone will have maximal volume if $y \ge 0$.) A central vertical cross section of the figure shows a right triangle from which we read the relation $y^2 = R^2 - r^2$. We are to maximize $V = \frac{1}{3}\pi r^2 h$, so we write

$$V = V(r) = \frac{1}{3}\pi\left[r^2\left(R + \sqrt{R^2 - r^2}\right)\right], \quad 0 \le r \le R.$$

The condition $V'(r) = 0$ leads to the equation $r\left(2R^2 - 3r^2 + 2R\sqrt{R^2 - r^2}\right) = 0$, which has the two solutions $r = 0$ and $r = \frac{2}{3}R\sqrt{2}$. Now $V(0) = 0$, $V(R) = \frac{1}{3}\pi R^3$ (which is one-fourth the volume of the sphere), and $V\left(\frac{2}{3}R\sqrt{2}\right) = \frac{32}{81}\pi R^3$ (which is 8/27 of the volume of the sphere). Answer: The maximum volume is $\frac{32}{81}\pi R^3$.

64. Let x denote the length of the two sides of the corral that are perpendicular to the wall. There are two cases to consider.

Case 1: Part of the wall is used. Let y be the length of the side of the corral parallel to the wall. Then $y = 400 - 2x$, and we are to maximize the area

$$A = xy = x(400 - 2x), \qquad 150 \leq x \leq 200.$$

Then $A'(x) = 400 - 4x$; $A'(x) = 0$ when $x = 100$, but that value of x is not in the domain of A. Note that $A(150) = 15000$ and that $A(200) = 0$.

Case 2: All of the wall is used. Let y be the length of fence added to one end of the wall, so that the side parallel to the wall has length $100 + y$. Then $100 + 2y + 2x = 400$, so $y = 150 - x$. We are to maximize the area

$$A = x(100 + y) = x(250 - x), \qquad 0 \leq x \leq 150.$$

In this case $A'(x) = 0$ when $x = 125$. And in this case $A(150) = 15000$, $A(0) = 0$, and $A(125) = 15625$.

Answer: The maximum area is 15,625 ft^2; to attain it, use all the existing wall and build a square corral.

65. First, $R'(x) = kM - 2kx$; because $k \neq 0$, $R'(x) = 0$ when $x = M/2$. Because $R(0) = 0 = R(M)$ and $R(M/2) > 0$, the latter is the maximum value of $R(x)$. Therefore the incidence of the disease is the highest when half the susceptible individuals are infected.

66. The trapezoid is shown on the right. It has altitude $L \cos \theta$ and the length of its longer base is $L + 2L \sin \theta$, so its area is

$$A(\theta) = L^2(1 + \sin \theta) \cos \theta, \qquad -\pi/6 \leq \theta \leq \pi/2.$$

Now $dA/d\theta = 0$ when

$$1 - \sin \theta - 2 \sin^2 \theta = 0;$$
$$(2 \sin \theta - 1)(\sin \theta + 1) = 0;$$

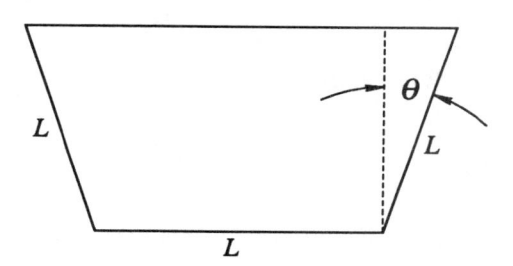

the only solution is $\theta = \pi/6$ because $\sin \theta$ cannot equal -1 in the range of A. But $A(\pi/2)$ is zero, $A\left(-\dfrac{\pi}{6}\right) = \dfrac{\sqrt{3}}{4} L^2$, and $A\left(\dfrac{\pi}{6}\right) = \dfrac{3\sqrt{3}}{4} L^2$. The latter maximizes $A(\theta)$, and the fourth side of the trapezoid then has length $2L$.

67. Let x be the width of the base of the box, so that the base has length $2x$; let y be the height of the box. Then the volume of the box is $V = 2x^2 y$, and for its total surface area to be 54 ft^2, we require $2x^2 + 6xy = 54$. Therefore the volume of the box is given by

$$V = V(x) = 2x^2 \left(\dfrac{27 - x^2}{3x}\right) = \dfrac{2}{3}(27x - x^3), \qquad 0 < x \leq 3\sqrt{3}.$$

Now $V'(x) = 0$ when $x^2 = 9$, so that $x = 3$. Also $V(0) = 0$, so even though $x = 0$ is not in the domain of V, the continuity of V implies that $V(x)$ is near zero for x near zero. Finally, $V(3\sqrt{3}) = 0$, so $V(3) = 36$ (ft^3) is the maximum possible volume of the box.

68. Suppose that the small cone has radius x and height y. Similar triangles that appear in a vertical cross section of the cones show that $\dfrac{x}{H - y} = \dfrac{R}{H}$. Hence $y = H - \dfrac{H}{R} x$, and we seek to maximize the volume $V = \frac{1}{3} \pi x^2 y$. Now

$$V = V(x) = \dfrac{\pi H}{3R}(Rx^2 - x^3), \qquad 0 \leq x \leq R.$$

Chapter 3 Miscellaneous

So $V'(x) = \dfrac{\pi H}{3R}x(2R - 3x)$. $V'(x) = 0$ when $x = 0$ and when $x = \frac{2}{3}R$ (in this case, $y = H/3$). But $V(0) = 0$ and $V(R) = 0$, so $x = \frac{2}{3}R$ maximizes V. Finally, it is easy to find that $V_{max} = \dfrac{4}{27} \cdot \dfrac{\pi}{3} R^2 H$, so the largest fraction of the large cone that the small cone can occupy is $4/27$.

69. Let (x, y) be the coordinates of the vertex of the trapezoid lying properly in the first quadrant, and let θ be the angle that the radius of the circle to (x, y) makes with the x-axis. The bases of the trapezoid have lengths 4 and $4\cos\theta$, and its altitude is $2\sin\theta$, so its area is $A(\theta) = \frac{1}{2}(4 + 4\cos\theta)(2\sin\theta) = 4(1 + \cos\theta)\sin\theta$, with domain $[0, \pi/2]$. Now

$$A'(\theta) = 4(\cos\theta + \cos^2\theta - \sin^2\theta)$$
$$= 4(2\cos^2\theta + \cos\theta - 1)$$
$$= 4(2\cos\theta - 1)(\cos\theta + 1).$$

The only zero of A' in its domain occurs at $\theta = \pi/3$. At the endpoints, we have $A(0) = 0$ and $A(\pi/2) = 4$. But $A(\pi/3) = 3\sqrt{3} \approx 5.196$, so the latter is the maximum possible area of such a trapezoid.

70. The square of the length of PQ is a function of x, $G(x) = (x - x_0)^2 + (y - y_0)^2$, which we are to maximize given the constraint $C(x) = y - f(x) = 0$. Now

$$\dfrac{dG}{dx} = 2(x - x_0) + 2(y - y_0)\dfrac{dy}{dx} \text{ and } \dfrac{dC}{dx} = \dfrac{dy}{dx} - f'(x).$$

When both vanish, $f'(x) = \dfrac{dy}{dx} = -\dfrac{x - x_0}{y - y_0}$. The line containing P and Q has slope

$$\dfrac{y - y_0}{x - x_0} = -\dfrac{1}{f'(x)},$$

and therefore this line is normal to the graph at Q.

72. Let r be the radius of each semicircle and x the length of the straightaway. We wish to maximize $A = 2rx$ given $C = 2\pi r + 2x - 5 = 0$.

$$\dfrac{dA}{dr} = 2r + 2x\dfrac{dr}{dx} \text{ and } \dfrac{dC}{dx} = 2\pi\dfrac{dr}{dx} + 2.$$

When both derivatives are zero, $-r/x = dr/dx = -1/\pi$, and so $x = \pi r$. Also $2\pi r + 2x = 5$, and it follows that $r = \dfrac{5}{4\pi}$ and that $x = \dfrac{5}{4}$. Answer: Design the straightaway 1.25 km long with semicircles at each end.

73. As the diagram to the right suggests, we are to minimize the sum of the lengths of the two diagonals. Fermat's principle of least time may be used here, so we know that the angles at which the roads meet the shore are equal, and thus so are the tangents of those angles: $\dfrac{x}{1} = \dfrac{6 - x}{2}$. It follows that the pier should be built two miles from the point on the shore nearest the first town. A short computation is sufficient to show that this actually yields the global minimum.

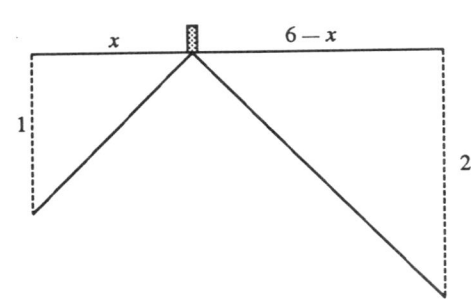

74. The length of each angled path is $\dfrac{2}{\sin\theta}$. The length of the roadway path is $10 - \dfrac{4\cos\theta}{\sin\theta}$. So the total time of the trip will be

$$T = T(\theta) = \dfrac{5}{4} + \dfrac{32 - 12\cos\theta}{24\sin\theta}.$$

90 Chapter 3 Miscellaneous

Note that $\cos\theta$ varies in the range $0 \leq \cos\theta \leq \dfrac{5\sqrt{29}}{29}$, so $21.80° \leq \theta° \leq 90°$. After simplifications,

$$T'(\theta) = \dfrac{12 - 32\cos\theta}{24\sin^2\theta};$$

$T'(\theta) = 0$ when $\cos\theta = 3/8$, so $\theta° \approx 67.98°$. With this value of θ, we find that the time of the trip is

$$T = \dfrac{2\sqrt{55} + 15}{12} \approx 2.486 \text{ (hours)}.$$

Because $T \approx 3.590$ with $\theta° \approx 21.80°$ and $T \approx 2.583$ when $\theta° \approx 90°$, the value $\theta° \approx 69.98°$ minimizes T, and the time saved is about 50.8 minutes.

75. Denote the initial velocity of the arrow by v. First, we have

$$\dfrac{dy}{dx} = m - \dfrac{32x}{v^2}(m^2 + 1);$$

$dy/dx = 0$ when $mv^2 = 32x(m^2+1)$, so that $x = \dfrac{mv^2}{32(m^2+1)}$. Substitution of this value of x in the formula given for y in the problem yields the maximum height

$$y_{\max} = \dfrac{m^2 v^2}{64(m^2+1)}.$$

For part (b), we set $y = 0$ and solve for x to obtain the range

$$R = \dfrac{mv^2}{16(m^2+1)}.$$

For maximum range, we solve $dR/dm = 0$ and find that $m = 1$, so the maximum range occurs when $\tan\alpha = 1$; that is, when $\alpha = \pi/4$.

76. Here we have

$$R = R(\theta) = \dfrac{v^2\sqrt{2}}{16}(\cos\theta\sin\theta - \cos^2\theta) \text{ for } \pi/4 \leq \theta \leq \pi/2.$$

Now

$$R'(\theta) = \dfrac{v^2\sqrt{2}}{16}(\cos^2\theta - \sin^2\theta + 2\sin\theta\cos\theta);$$

$R'(\theta) = 0$ when $\cos 2\theta + \sin 2\theta = 0$, so that $\tan 2\theta = -1$. It follows that $\theta = 3\pi/8$ (67.5°). This yields the maximum range because $R(\pi/4) = 0 = R(\pi/2)$.

78. Result: 1.442249570. Answer: 1.4422.

79. Use the iteration $x_{n+1} = x_n - \dfrac{(x_n)^5 - 75}{5(x_n)^4}$.
Results: $x_0 = 2.20379147$, $x_1 = 2.39896311$, $x_2 = 2.37206492$, $x_3 = 2.37144094$, $x_4 = 2.37144061$. Answer: 2.3714.

80. Alternative method: Solve $x^4 = 100$ using the iteration

$$x \longleftarrow x - \dfrac{x^4 - 1000}{4x^3};$$

with initial estimate $x_0 = 5.558867362$, the results are 5.624546176, 5.623413594, 5.623413252. Answer: 5.6234.

81. With $x_0 = -0.5$, we obtain -0.3333333333, -0.3472222222, -0.3472963532, -0.3472963553. Answer: -0.3473.

82. Linear interpolation gives $x_0 = -1/3$. We iterate using the formula

$$x_{n+1} = x_n - \frac{(x_n)^3 - 4x_n - 1}{3(x_n)^2 - 4}$$

to obtain the sequence -0.2525252525, -0.2541011930, -0.2541016884 of improving approximations. Answer: -0.2541.

83. Linear interpolation gives $x_0 = 0.5$. Sequence of approximations: 0.8108695652, 0.7449619517, 0.7402438226, 0.7402217826, 0.7402217821, 0.7402217821. Answer: 0.7402.

84. Linear interpolation gives $x_0 = -1.222222222$. Approximations: -1.312580677, -1.308913539, -1.308907320, -1.308907320. Answer: -1.3089.

85. Linear interpolation gives $x_0 = -0.5854549279$. If you got -0.9996955062 instead, it's because your calculator was set in degree mode. Change to radians and begin anew. Note also that a quick glance at the graphs of $y = -x$ and $y = \cos x$ shows that the equation $x + \cos x = 0$ has exactly one solution in the interval $[-2, 0]$. We use the Newton's method formula: We iterate

$$x \longleftarrow x - \frac{x + \cos x}{1 - \sin x}$$

and obtain -0.7451929664, -0.7390933178, -0.7390851332, -0.7390851332. Answer: -0.7391

86. Linear interpolation yields $x_0 = -0.7956861008$. Approximations: -0.8867915207, -0.8768492470, -0.8767262342, -0.8767262154, and -0.8767262154. Answer: -0.8767.

87. Linear interpolation yields $x_0 = -1.2139964$. Approximations: -1.236193029, -1.236129989, -1.236129989. Answer: -1.2361.

88. Let $f(x) = 5(x + 1) - \cos x$. Then $f'(x) = 5 + \sin x$, and we iterate using the Newton's method formula

$$x \longleftarrow x - \frac{f(x)}{f'(x)}.$$

Linear interpolation yields the initial estimate -0.8809986055, and the succeeding approximations are -0.8712142932, -0.8712215145, and -0.8712215145. Answer: -0.8712.

89. The volume of a spherical segment of height h is

$$V = \frac{1}{3}\pi h^2 (3r - h)$$

if the sphere has radius r. If ρ is the density of water and the ball sinks to the depth h, then the weight of the water that the ball displaces is equal to the total weight of the ball, so

$$\frac{1}{3}\pi \rho h^2 (3r - h) = \frac{4}{3^2}\pi \rho r^3.$$

Because $r = 2$, this leads to the equation $p(h) = 3h^3 - 18h^2 + 32 = 0$. This equation has at most three [real] solutions because $p(h)$ is a polynomial of degree 3, and it turns out to have exactly three solutions because $p(-2) = -64$, $p(-1) = 11$, $p(2) = -16$, and $p(6) = 32$. Newton's method yields the three approximate solutions $h = -1.215825766$, $h = 1.547852572$, and $h = 5.667973193$. Only one is plausible, so the answer is that the ball sinks to a depth of approximately 1.54785 ft, about 39% of the way up a diameter.

90. The iteration is

$$x \longleftarrow x - \frac{x^2 + 1}{2x} = \frac{x^2 - 1}{2x}.$$

With $x_0 = 2$, the sequence obtained by iteration of Newton's method is 0.75, -0.2917, 1.5685, 0.4654, -0.8415, 0.1734, -2.7970, -1.2197, -0.1999, 2.4009, 0.9922, -0.0078, 63.7100, $\ldots$.

91. Let $f(x) = x^5 - 3x^3 + x^2 - 23x + 19$. Then $f(-3) = -65$, $f(0) = 19$, $f(1) = -5$, and $f(3) = 121$. So there are at least three, and at most five, real solutions. Newton's method produces three real solutions, specifically $r_1 = -2.722493355$, $r_2 = 0.8012614801$, and $r_3 = 2.309976541$. If one divides the polynomial $f(x)$ by $(x - r_1)(x - r_2)(x - r_3)$, one obtains the quotient polynomial $x^2 + (0.38874466)x + 3.770552031$, which has no real roots—the quadratic formula yields the two complex roots $-0.194372333 \pm (1.932038153)i$. Consequently we have found all three real solutions.

92. Let $f(x) = \tan x - \dfrac{1}{x}$. We iterate

$$x \longleftarrow x - \frac{\tan x - \dfrac{1}{x}}{\sec^2 x + \dfrac{1}{x^2}}.$$

The results are shown in the following table. The instability in the last one or two digits is caused by machine rounding and is common.

Answers: To three places, $\alpha_1 = 0.860$ and $\alpha_2 = 3.426$.

```
f[x_]:=Tan[x]-1/x
g[x_]:=N[x-f[x]/f'[x],20]
list={1.0,4.0};
g[list]
```
0.8740469203219249386,   3.622221245370322529
0.8604001629909660496,   3.440232462677783381
0.8603335904117901655,   3.425673797668214504
0.8603335890193797612,   3.425618460245614115
0.8603335890193797636,   3.425618459481728148
0.8603335890193797608,   3.425618459481728146
0.8603335890193797634,   3.425618459481728148

93. The number of summands on the right is variable, and we have no formula for finding its derivative. One thing is certain: Its derivative is *not* $2x^2$.

94. We factor: $z^{3/2} - x^{3/2} = (z^{1/2})^3 - (x^{1/2})^3$
$= (z^{1/2} - x^{1/2})(z + z^{1/2}x^{1/2} + x)$

and $z - x = (z^{1/2})^2 - (x^{1/2})^2 = (z^{1/2} - x^{1/2})(z^{1/2} + x^{1/2})$. Therefore

$$\frac{z^{3/2} - x^{3/2}}{z - x} = \frac{z + z^{1/2}x^{1/2} + x}{z^{1/2} + x^{1/2}} \to \frac{3x}{2x^{1/2}} = \frac{3}{2}x^{1/2} \text{ as } z \to x.$$

96. The volume of the block is $V = x^2y$, and V is constant while x and y are functions of time t (in minutes). So

$$0 = \frac{dV}{dt} = 2xy\frac{dx}{dt} + x^2\frac{dy}{dt}.$$

We are given $dy/dt = -2$, $x = 30$, and $y = 20$, so (from the preceding formula) $dx/dt = 3/2$. Answer: At the time in question, the edge of the base is increasing at 1.5 in./min.

97. The balloon has volume $V = \frac{4}{3}\pi r^3$ and surface area $A = 4\pi r^2$ where r is its radius and V, A, and r

are all functions of time t. We are given $dV/dt = +10$, and we are to find dA/dt when $r = 5$.

$$\frac{dV}{dt} = 4\pi r^2 \frac{dr}{dt}, \text{ so } 10 = 4\pi \cdot 25 \cdot \frac{dr}{dt}.$$

$$\text{Thus } \frac{dr}{dt} = \frac{10}{100\pi} = \frac{1}{10\pi}.$$

$$\text{Also } \frac{dA}{dt} = 8\pi r \frac{dr}{dt}, \text{ and therefore}$$

$$\left.\frac{dA}{dt}\right|_{r=5} = 8\pi \cdot 4 \cdot \frac{1}{10\pi} = 4.$$

Answer: At 4 in.²/s.

98. Let the positive x-axis represent the ground and the positive y-axis the wall. Let x be the distance from the base of the wall to the foot of the ladder; let y be the height of the top of the ladder above the ground. From the Pythagorean theorem we obtain $x^2 + y^2 = 100$, so

$$x\frac{dx}{dt} + y\frac{dy}{dt} = 0.$$

Thus $\dfrac{dy}{dt} = -\dfrac{x}{y} \cdot \dfrac{dx}{dt}$. We are given $\dfrac{dx}{dt} = \dfrac{5280}{3600} = \dfrac{22}{15}$ ft/s, and at the time when $y = 1$, we have

$$x = \sqrt{100 - (0.01)^2} = \sqrt{99.9999}.$$

At that time,

$$\left.\frac{dy}{dt}\right|_{y=0.01} = -\frac{\sqrt{99.9999}}{0.01} \cdot \frac{22}{15} \approx -1466.666 \text{ (ft/s)},$$

almost exactly 1000 mi/h.

99. Let Q be the amount of water in the cone at time t, r the radius of its upper surface, and h its height. From similar triangles we find that $h = 2r$, so

$$Q = \frac{1}{3}\pi r^2 h = \frac{2}{3}\pi r^3 = \frac{1}{12}\pi h^3.$$

Now

$$-50 = \frac{dQ}{dt} = \frac{1}{4}\pi h^2 \frac{dh}{dt}, \text{ so } \frac{dh}{dt} = -\frac{200}{36\pi}.$$

Therefore $\dfrac{dh}{dt} = -\dfrac{50}{9\pi} \approx -1.7684$ ft/min.

100. Let x denote the distance from plane A to the airport, y the distance from plane B to the airport, and z the distance between the two aircraft. Then

$$z^2 = x^2 + y^2 + (3-2)^2 = x^2 + y^2 + 1$$

and $dx/dt = -500$. Now

$$2z\frac{dz}{dt} = 2x\frac{dx}{dt} + 2y\frac{dy}{dt},$$

and when $x = 2$, $y = 2$. Therefore $z = 3$ at that time. Therefore,

$$3 \cdot (-600) = 2 \cdot (-500) + 2 \cdot \left.\frac{dy}{dt}\right|_{x=2},$$

and thus $\left.\dfrac{dy}{dt}\right|_{x=2} = -400$. Answer: Its speed is 400 mi/h.

101. $\dfrac{dV}{dt} = 3\sqrt{y}\,\dfrac{dy}{dt} = -3\sqrt{y}$, so $\dfrac{dy}{dt} = -1$. Answer: At 1 in./min—a constant rate.

102. As in the solution of Problem 99, we find that when the height of water in the tank is y, its volume is $V = \frac{1}{12}\pi y^3$. For part (a), we have

$$+50 - 10\sqrt{y} = \frac{dV}{dt} = \frac{1}{4}\pi y^2 \frac{dy}{dt}.$$

So when $y = 5$,

$$50 - 10\sqrt{5} = \frac{25}{4}\pi \frac{dy}{dt}\bigg|_{y=5},$$

and therefore $\dfrac{dy}{dt}\bigg|_{y=5} = \dfrac{1}{5\pi}(40 - 8\sqrt{5}) \approx 1.40766$ (ft/min). In part (b),

$$\frac{dV}{dt} = 25 - 10\sqrt{y} = \frac{1}{4}\pi y^2 \frac{dy}{dt};$$

$dy/dt = 0$ when $25 = 10\sqrt{y}$, so that $y = 6.25$ (ft) would seem to be the maximum height ever attained by the water. What actually happens is that the water level rises more and more slowly as time passes, approaching the limiting height of 6.25 ft as a right-hand limit, but never reaching it. This is not obvious; you must solve the differential equation last displayed (use the substitution $y = u^2$) and analyze the solution to establish this conclusion.

103. The straight line through $P(x_0, y_0)$ and $Q(a, a^2)$ has slope $\dfrac{a^2 - y_0}{a - x_0} = 2a$, a consequence of the two-point formula for slope and the fact that the line is tangent to the parabola at Q. Hence $a^2 - 2ax_0 + y_0 = 0$. Think of this as a quadratic equation in the unknown a. It has two real solutions when the discriminant is positive: $(x_0)^2 - y_0 > 0$, and this establishes the conclusion in part (b). There are no real solutions when $(x_0)^2 - y_0 < 0$, and this establishes the conclusion in part (c). What if $(x_0)^2 - y_0 = 0$?

This seems a good spot to mention Descartes' Rule of Signs. In a sequence of nonzero numbers, such as

$$-3, \quad -5, \quad * \quad 2, \quad 4, \quad * \quad -1, \quad * \quad 6, \quad 6, \quad 6, \quad * \quad -2, \quad -2, \quad * \quad 12,$$

there are five *sign changes*, marked with asterisks. If some terms of such a sequence are zero, they are simply disregarded in counting the number of sign changes; thus the sequence

$$2, \quad 0, \quad 0, \quad * \quad -3, \quad -4, \quad 0, \quad 0, \quad 0, \quad * \quad 2, \quad 3, \quad * \quad -4, \quad 0,$$

has three sign changes.

Suppose that $p(x)$ is a polynomial with real coefficients, so that the polynomial equation $p(x) = 0$ has the form

$$a_0 x^n + a_1 x^{n-1} + \cdots + a_{n-1} x + a_n = 0.$$

Descartes' Rule of Signs is a classical theorem that states that the number of positive real roots of this equation is never greater than the number of sign changes in the sequence

$$a_0, \ a_1, \ a_2, \ \cdots, \ a_{n-1}, \ a_n,$$

and if less, then is less by an even number. For example, the equation

$$f(x) = x^5 + 3x^3 + x^2 - 23x + 19 = 0$$

of Problem 91 has the sequence 1, 0, −3, −23, 19 of coefficients, which has four sign changes. We already know that there are at least two and at most four positive solutions of the equation, and therefore there are either two or four. Now we consider the related equation

$$f(-x) = (-x)^5 - 3(-x)^3 + (-x)^2 - 23(-x) + 19 = 0,$$

which has the same number of positive roots as the original equation has negative roots. The sequence of coefficients in this equation is −1, 0, 3, 1, 23, 19; there is one sign change, so the original equation has exactly one negative root (because we already know of the existence of at least one).

Chapter 4: Additional Applications of the Derivative
Section 4.2

2. $dy = (x^{-1/2} + x^{-4/3})\, dx$.

4. $dy = -\left(\dfrac{1}{(x-x^{1/2})^2}\right)\cdot(1-\tfrac{1}{2}x^{-1/2})\, dx$.

6. $dy = -\dfrac{x^2+4}{(x^2-4)^2}\, dx$.

8. $dy = -\tfrac{8}{3}x(x^2-1)^{-7/3}\, dx$.

10. $dy = (x^2\cos x + 2x\sin x)\, dx$.

12. $dy = -9(\cos^2 3x \sin 3x)\, dx$.

14. $dy = -\dfrac{2x\sin x + \cos x}{2x^{3/2}}\, dx$.

16. $dy = -3(1+\cos 2x)^{1/2}(\sin 2x)\, dx$

17. $f(x) \approx f(0) + f'(0)(x-0) = 1 + x$

18. $f(x) \approx f(0) + f'(0)(x-0) = 1 - \tfrac{1}{2}x$

19. $f(x) \approx f(0) + f'(0)(x-0) = 1 + 2x$

20. $1 - 3x$

21. $1 - 3x$

22. $f'(x) = -2(1+3x)^{-5/3}$, so $f(x) \approx f(0) + f'(0)(x-0) = 1 - 2x$

23. x

24. 1

25. Let $f(x) = x^{1/3}$. Then $f'(x) = \tfrac{1}{3}x^{-2/3}$. Take $a=27$ and $x=25$. Then $f(x) \approx f(a) + f'(a)(x-a)$, so

$$25^{1/3} = f(25)$$
$$\approx f(27) + f'(27)(25-27)$$
$$= 3 + \tfrac{1}{27}(-2) \approx 2.926.$$

26. Let $f(x) = x^{1/2}$. Then $f'(x) = \tfrac{1}{2}x^{-1/2}$. Take $a=100$ and $x=102$ in the linear approximation formula to obtain

$$\sqrt{102} = f(x) \approx f(a) + f'(a)(x-a)$$
$$= (100)^{1/2} + \dfrac{2}{2\sqrt{100}} = 10.1.$$

27. Let $f(x) = x^{1/4}$; then $f'(x) = \tfrac{1}{4}x^{-3/4}$. Let $a=16$ and let $x=15$. Then

$$(15)^{1/4} = f(x) \approx f(a) + f'(a)(x-a)$$
$$= (16)^{1/4} + \dfrac{1}{4(16)^{3/4}}(-1)$$
$$= 2 - \tfrac{1}{32} = \tfrac{63}{32} = 1.96875.$$

The true value is approximately 1.96798967.

28. Let $f(x) = x^{1/2}$; then $f'(x) = \tfrac{1}{2}x^{-1/2}$. Let $a=81$ and let $x=80$. Then

$$\sqrt{80} = f(x) \approx f(a) + f'(a)(x-a)$$
$$= \sqrt{81} + \dfrac{1}{2\sqrt{81}}(-1)$$
$$= \tfrac{161}{18} \approx 8.944.$$

30. Let $f(x) = x^{3/4}$; then $f'(x) = \tfrac{3}{4}x^{-1/4}$. Let $a=81$ and let $x=80$. Then

$$80^{3/4} = f(x) \approx f(a) + f'(a)(x-a)$$
$$= 81^{3/4} + \dfrac{3}{4}(81)^{-1/4}(-1)$$
$$= 27 - \tfrac{1}{4} = 26.75.$$

32. Let $f(x) = \sin x$; then $f'(x) = \cos x$. Let $a = \pi/6$ and let $x = 8\pi/45$ (32°). Then

$$\sin 32° = \sin(x) \approx \sin(a) + \cos(a)(x-a)$$
$$= \sin\left(\frac{\pi}{6}\right) + \frac{\pi}{90}\cos\left(\frac{\pi}{6}\right)$$
$$= \frac{1}{2} + \frac{\pi}{180}\sqrt{3} \approx 0.53023.$$

Note that the first approximation involves the mathematical error in using the tangent line to approximate the value of the function, whereas the second approximation involves calculator roundoff error.

33. Let $f(x) = \sin x$; then $f'(x) = \cos x$. Let $a = \pi/2$ and let $x = 22\pi/45$ (88°). Then

$$\sin 88° = \sin(x) \approx \sin(a) + \cos(a)(x-a)$$
$$= \sin\left(\frac{\pi}{2}\right) - \frac{\pi}{90}\cos\left(\frac{\pi}{2}\right)$$
$$= 1 - 0 = 1.00000.$$

The true value is approximately 0.99939.

34. $\frac{1}{2} - \frac{\pi}{180}\sqrt{3} \approx 0.46977.$

36. $\frac{2}{3}x^{-1/3}\,dx + \frac{2}{3}y^{-1/3}\,dy = 0$;

$$y^{-1/3}\,dy = -x^{-1/3}\,dx;$$
$$dy/dx = -x^{-1/3}y^{1/3} = -(y/x)^{1/3}.$$

38. Given: $x \sin y = 1$.

$$x(\cos y)\,dy + (\sin y)\,dx = 0;$$
$$x(\cos y)\,dy = -(\sin y)\,dx;$$
$$\frac{dy}{dx} = -\frac{\sin y}{x \cos y} = -\frac{\tan y}{x}.$$

40. If C is the circumference of the circle and r its radius, then $C = 2\pi r$. Thus $dC = 2\pi\,dr$, and so $\Delta C \approx 2\pi\Delta r$. With $r = 10$ and $\Delta r = 0.5$, we obtain $\Delta C \approx 2\pi(0.5) = \pi \approx 3.1416$. This happens to be the exact value as well (because C is a linear function of r).

42. The relationship between the surface area A and the radius r of the sphere is $A = 4\pi r^2$, and hence $dA = 8\pi r\,dr$. Thus $\Delta A \approx 8\pi r\Delta r$. With $r = 5$ and $\Delta r = 0.2$ we obtain $\Delta A \approx 8\pi(5)(0.2) = 8\pi \approx 25.1327$ square inches. The true value is approximately 25.6354 square inches.

44. With volume V, height h, and radius r, we have $V = \frac{1}{3}\pi r^2 h$. Because $r = 14$ is constant, we may think of V as a function of r alone, so that

$$dV = \frac{1}{3}\pi r^2\,dh.$$

With $r = 14$, $h = 7$, and $dh = 0.1$, we find that

$$dV = \frac{1}{3}\pi(196)(0.1) \approx 20.5251.$$

The true value is exactly the same because V is a linear function of h.

46. Because v is constant, R is a function of the angle of inclination θ alone, and hence

$$dR = \frac{1}{8}v^2(\cos 2\theta)\,d\theta.$$

With $\theta = \pi/4$, $d\theta = \pi/180$ (1°), and $v = 80$, we obtain

$$\Delta R \approx \frac{1}{8}(6400)(0)\frac{\pi}{180} = 0.$$

The true value of ΔR is approximately -0.2437.

48. With circumference C and radius r, we have $C = 2\pi r$. So, given $\Delta r = +10$, $\Delta C \approx 20\pi$ (feet). Thus the wire should be lengthened approximately 63 feet.

49. Let V be the volume of the ball. Then $V_{\text{calc}} = \frac{4}{3}(1000\pi) \approx 4188.7902$ cubic inches. $\Delta V \approx 4\pi(10)^2 \frac{1}{16} = 25\pi \approx 78.5398$ cubic inches (the true value of ΔV is approximately 79.0317).

50. With volume V and radius r, we have $V = \frac{4}{3}\pi r^3$, and thus $dV = 4\pi r^2\, dr$. For $|\Delta V| \leq 1$, we require that $4\pi r^2 |\Delta r| \leq 1$, so

$$|\Delta r| \leq \frac{1}{4\pi(10)^2} \approx 0.0008$$

inches. Thus the radius must be measured with error not exceeding 0.0008 inches.

51. With surface area S and radius r, we have $S = 2\pi r^2$, so that $dS = 4\pi r\, dr \approx 4\pi(100)(0.01) = 4\pi$. That is, $\Delta S \approx 12.57$ square meters.

52. With the notation of the preceding solution, we now require that

$$\frac{|dS|}{S} \leq 0.0001;$$

thus, at least approximately,

$$\frac{|4\pi r\, dr|}{|2\pi r^2|} \leq 0.0001.$$

Hence

$$2\left|\frac{dr}{r}\right| \leq 0.0001,$$

which implies that $|dr|/r \leq 0.00005$. Answer: With percentage error not exceeding 0.005%.

53. We plotted $f(x) = x^2$ and its linear approximation $L(x) = 1 + 2(x-1)$ on the interval $[0.5, 1.5]$, and it was clear that the interval $I = (0.58, 1.42)$ would be an adequate answer to this problem. We used Newton's nethod to find a "better" interval, which turns out to be $I = (0.56, 1.44)$.

54. We plotted $f(x) = \sqrt{x}$ and its linear approximation $L(x) = 1 + \frac{1}{2}(x-1)$ on the interval $[0.3, 2.15]$, and it was clear that the interval $I = (0.32, 1.98)$ would be adequate. We used Newton's method to "improve" the answer to $I = (0.306, 2.094)$.

55. We plotted $f(x) = 1/x$ and its linear approximation $L(x) = \frac{1}{2} + \frac{1}{4}(2-x)$ on the interval $[1.73, 2.32]$, and it was clear that the interval was a little too large to be a correct answer. We used Newton's method to find more accurate endpoints, and came up with the answer $I = (1.74, 2.30)$. Or course, any subinterval of this interval containing $a = 2$ is also a correct answer.

56. $I = (6.403, 9.797)$.

58. We plotted $f(x) = \cos x$ and its linear approximation $L(x) = \frac{1}{2}\pi - x$ on the interval $[0.85, 2.25]$, and it was clear that this interval was a little too large to be a correct answer. We used Newton's method to improve our estimate of the desired endpoints and came up with the answer $I = (0.897, 2.245)$. Of course, any subinterval of this interval containing $a = \pi/2$ is also a correct answer.

60. $I = (0.679, 0.878)$.

Section 4.3

1. $f'(x) = -2x$; f is increasing on $(-\infty, 0)$ and decreasing on $(0, +\infty)$. Matching graph: (c).
2. $f'(x) = 2x - 2$; f is increasing on $(1, +\infty)$ and decreasing on $(-\infty, 1)$. Matching graph: (b).
3. $f'(x) = 2x + 4$; f is increasing on $(-2, +\infty)$ and decreasing on $(-\infty, -2)$. Matching graph: (f).
4. $f'(x) = \frac{3}{4}x^2 - 3$; $f'(x) = 0$ when $x = \pm 2$; f is increasing on $(-\infty, -2)$ and on $(2, \infty)$, decreasing on $(-2, +2)$. Matching graph: (a).
5. $f'(x) = x^2 - x - 2 = (x+1)(x-2)$; $f'(x) = 0$ when $x = -1$ and when $x = 2$; f is increasing on $(-\infty, -1)$ and on $(2 + \infty)$, decreasing on $(-1, 2)$. Matching graph: (d).
6. $f'(x) = 2 - \frac{1}{3}x - \frac{1}{3}x^2 = -\frac{1}{3}(x^2 + x - 6) = -\frac{1}{3}(x+3)(x-2)$; $f'(x) = 0$ when $x = -3$ and when $x = 2$. f is increasing on $(-3, 2)$ and decreasing on $(-\infty, -3)$ and on $(2, +\infty)$. Matching graph: (e).
7. $f(x) = 2x^2 + C$; $5 = f(0) = C$: $f(x) = 2x^2 + 5$.
8. $f(x) = 2x^{3/2} + C$; $4 = f(0) = C$: $f(x) = 2x^{3/2} + 4$.
9. $f(x) = -\frac{1}{x} + C$; $1 = f(1) = C - 1$: $f(x) = -\frac{1}{x} + 2$.
10. $f(x) = 4\sqrt{x} + C$; $3 = f(0) = C$: $f(x) = 4\sqrt{x} + 3$.
11. $f'(x) > 0$ for all x, so f is increasing for all x.
12. $f'(x) < 0$ for all x, so f is decreasing for all x.
13. $f'(x) = -4x$, so f is increasing on $(-\infty, 0)$ and decreasing on $(0, +\infty)$.
14. $f'(x) = 8x + 8 = 8(x+1)$. Therefore f is increasing for $x > -1$ and decreasing for $x < -1$.
16. $f'(x) = 3x^2 - 12 = 3(x^2 - 4) = 3(x+2)(x-2)$. Hence f is increasing for $x > 2$ and for $x < -2$, decreasing for x in the interval $(-2, 2)$.
17. $f'(x) = 4x^3 - 4x = 4x(x+1)(x-1)$. The intervals on which $f'(x)$ cannot change sign are $x < -1$, $-1 < x < 0$, $0 < x < 1$, and $1 < x$. Because $f'(-2) = -24$, $f'(-0.5) = 1.5$, $f'(0.5) = -1.5$, and $f'(2) = 24$, we may conclude that f is increasing if $-1 < x < 0$ or if $x > 1$, decreasing for $x < -1$ and for $0 < x < 1$.
18. Because $f'(x) = \dfrac{1}{(x+1)^2}$, $f'(x) > 0$ for all x other than $x = -1$. Hence f is increasing for $x > -1$ and for $x < -1$.
19. $f'(x) = 12x^3 + 12x^2 - 24x = 12x(x+2)(x-1)$, so the only points where $f'(x)$ can change sign are -2, 0, and 1.
20. Note that f is continuous for all x, as is $f'(x) = \dfrac{2x^2 + 1}{(x^2 + 1)^{1/2}}$; also, $f'(x) > 0$ for all x. Hence f is increasing for all x.
21. After simplifications, $f'(x) = \dfrac{4(2-x)}{3x^{2/3}}$. Note that the denominator in $f'(x)$ is positive for all $x \neq 0$ and that $f'(0)$ is not defined (even though f is continuous at $x = 0$). The intervals on which $f'(x)$ cannot change sign are therefore $x < 0$, $0 < x < 2$, and $2 < x$. So f is increasing if $x < 0$ and if $0 < x < 2$, decreasing for $x > 2$. It is also correct to say that f is increasing for all $x < 2$, because for x near zero, $f(x)$ is approximately $8x^{1/3}$, and is therefore increasing on any small open interval containing $x = 0$.
22. $f'(x) = 6(x+2)(x-1)$, so f is increasing for $x < -2$ and for $x > 1$, decreasing for $-2 < x < 1$.
23. After simplifications,
$$f'(x) = \frac{2(x-1)(x-3)}{(x^2-3)^2}.$$

The intervals on which $f'(x)$ cannot change sign are $x < -\sqrt{3}$, $-\sqrt{3} < x < 1$, $1 < x < \sqrt{3}$, $\sqrt{3} < x < 3$, and $3 < x$. Now $f'(-2) = 30$, $f'(0) = 2/3$, $f'(1.5) = -8/3$, $f'(2) = -2$, and $f'(4) = 6/169$. Therefore f is increasing for $x < -\sqrt{3}$, for $-\sqrt{3} < x < 1$, and for $x > 3$; decreasing for $1 < x < \sqrt{3}$ and for $\sqrt{3} < x < 3$.

24. After simplifications,
$$f'(x) = \frac{2}{x^3}(x^2 + 4)(x + 2)(x - 2).$$
Now $f'(-3) = -130/27$, $f'(-1) = 30$, $f'(1) = -30$, and $f'(3) = 130/27$. Therefore f is increasing for $-2 < x < 0$ and for $x > 2$, decreasing for $x < -2$ and for $0 < x < 2$.

25. $f(0) = 0$, $f(2) = 0$, f is continuous for $0 \leq x \leq 2$, and $f'(x) = 2x - 2$ exists for $0 < x < 2$. To find the numbers c satisfying the conclusion of Rolle's theorem, we solve $f'(c) = 0$ to find that $c = 1$ is the only such number.

26. $f(-3) = 81 - 81 = 0 = f(3)$, f is continuous everywhere, and $f'(x) = 18x - 4x^3$ exists for all x, including all x in the interval $(-3, 3)$. Thus f satisfies the hypotheses of Rolle's theorem. To find what value or values c might assume, we solve the equation $f'(x) = 0$ to obtain the three values $c = 0$, $c = \frac{3}{2}\sqrt{2}$, and $c = -\frac{3}{2}\sqrt{2}$. All three of these numbers lie in the interval $(-3, 3)$, so these are the three possible values for the number c whose existence is guaranteed by Rolle's theorem.

27. Because
$$f'(x) = -\frac{4x}{(1 + x^2)^2}$$
exists for all x, f is continuous for $-1 \leq x \leq 1$ and is differentiable on $(-1, 1)$; moreover, it is clear that $f(-1) = 0 = f(1)$. So f satisfies the hypotheses of Rolle's theorem. Finally, $f'(x) = 0$ exactly when $x = 0$, so $c = 0$ is the number whose existence is guaranteed by Rolle's theorem.

28. Here,
$$f'(x) = \frac{10}{3}x^{-1/3} - \frac{5}{3}x^{2/3} = \frac{10 - 5x}{3x^{1/3}};$$
$f'(x)$ exists for all x in $(0, 5)$ and f is continuous on the interval $0 \leq x \leq 5$ (the only point that might cause trouble is $x = 0$ but the limit of f and its value there are the same). Because $f(0) = 0 = f(5)$, there is a solution c of $f(x) = 0$ in $(0, 5)$, and clearly $c = 2$.

29. On the interval $(-1, 0)$, $f'(x) = 1$; on the interval $(0, 1)$, we have $f'(x) = -1$. Because f is not differentiable at $x = 0$, it does not satisfy the hypotheses of Rolle's theorem, so there is no guarantee that the equation $f'(x) = 0$ has a solution—and, indeed, it has no solution in $(-1, 1)$.

30. Because
$$f'(x) = \frac{2}{3(2 - x)^{1/3}} \text{ for } x \neq 2,$$
$f'(x)$ can never be zero, so the conclusion of Rolle's theorem does not hold here. The reason is that $f'(x)$ is not differentiable at every point of the interval $1 \leq x \leq 3$.

31. Because $f(1) = 2 \neq 0$, this function does not satisfy the hypotheses of Rolle's theorem. Neither does the conclusion hold, for $f'(x) = 4x^3 + 2x = 2x(2x^2 + 1)$ is never zero on $(0, 1)$.

32. It is clear that f satisfies the hypotheses of the mean value theorem, for every polynomial is continuous and differentiable everywhere. To find c, we solve
$$f'(c) = \frac{f(1) - f(-1)}{1 - (-1)};$$
thus $3c^2 = 2/2 = 1$, with the two solutions $c = 1/\sqrt{3}$ and $c = -1/\sqrt{3}$. Both these numbers lie in the interval $-1 \leq x \leq 1$, so each is an answer to the problem.

33. Here, $f'(x) = 6x + 6$; $f(-1) = -5$ and $f(1) = 4$. So we are to solve the equation

$$6(c+1) = \frac{4 - (-5)}{1 - (-2)} = 3.$$

It turns out that $c = -1/2$.

34. First,

$$f'(x) = \frac{1}{2(x-1)^{1/2}}$$

exists for all $x > 1$, so f satisfies the hypotheses of the mean value theorem for $2 \leq x \leq 5$. To find c, we solve

$$\frac{1}{2(c-1)^{1/2}} = \frac{(4)^{1/2} - (1)^{1/2}}{5 - 2};$$

thus $2(c-1)^{1/2} = 3$, and so $c = 13/4$. Note: $2 < c < 5$.

35. First, $f'(x) = \frac{2}{3}(x-1)^{-1/3}$ is defined on $(1, 2)$; moreover, f is continuous for $1 \leq x \leq 2$ (the only "problem point" is $x = 1$). To find c, we solve

$$f'(c) = \frac{2}{3(c-1)^{1/3}} = \frac{f(2) - f(1)}{2 - 1} = \frac{1 - 0}{1} = 1.$$

This leads to the equation $(c-1)^{1/3} = 2/3$, and thereby $c = 35/27$. Note that $35/27$ does lie in the given interval.

36. There's no problem with the hypotheses. Next,

$$1 - \frac{1}{c^2} = \frac{5 + (1/5) - (1 + 1)}{5 - 1} = \frac{4}{5}$$

yields the information that $c^2 = 5$, and thus that $c = +\sqrt{5}$ (not $-\sqrt{5}$; it's not in the interval $(1, 5)$).

37. First, $f(x) = |x - 2|$ is not differentiable at $x = 2$, so does not satisfy the hypotheses of the mean value theorem on the given interval $1 \leq x \leq 4$. Wherever $f'(x)$ is defined, its value is 1 or -1, but

$$\frac{f(4) - f(1)}{4 - 1} = \frac{2 - 1}{3} = \frac{1}{3}$$

is never a value of $f'(x)$. So f satisfies neither the hypotheses nor the conclusion of the mean value theorem on the interval $1 \leq x \leq 4$.

38. Because f is not differentiable at $x = 1$, the hypotheses of the mean value theorem do not hold. The only values of $f'(x)$ are 1 (for $x > 1$) and -1 (for $x < 1$). Neither of these is equal to the everage slope of f on the interval $0 \leq x \leq 3$:

$$\frac{f(3) - f(0)}{3 - 0} = \frac{3 - 2}{3} = \frac{1}{3},$$

so the conclusion of the theorem also fails to hold.

39. The greatest integer function is continuous at x if and only if x is not an integer. Consequently all the hypotheses of the mean value theorem fail here: f is discontinuous at -1, 0, and 1, and also $f'(0)$ does not exist because (for one reason) f is not continuous at $x = 0$. Finally, the average slope of the graph of f is 1, but $f'(x) = 0$ wherever it is defined.

40. The function $f(x) = 3x^{2/3}$ is continuous everywhere, but its derivative $f'(x) = 2x^{-1/3}$ does not exist at $x = 0$. Because $f'(x)$ does not exist for *all* x in $(-1, 1)$, this essential hypothesis of the mean value theorem is not satisfied. Moreover, $f'(x)$ is never zero (the average slope of the graph of f on the interval $-1 \leq x \leq 1$), so the conclusion of the theorem also fails to hold.

41. Let $f(x) = x^5 + 2x - 3$. Then $f'(x) = 5x^4 + 2$, so $f'(x) > 0$ for all x. This means that f is an increasing function, and therefore f can have at most one zero in any interval. To show that f has at least one zero in the interval $0 \le x \le 1$, it is sufficient to notice that $f(1) = 0$.

42. Let $f(x) = x^{10} - 1000$. Then $f'(x) = 10x^9$, so $f(x)$ is increasing on the interval $1 \le x \le 2$; therefore $f(x) = 0$ has at most one solution in that interval. But $f(1) = -999 < 0$ and $f(2) = 1024 - 1000 > 0$. As f is continuous, it has the intermediate value property, so $f(x)$ has at least one zero in the given interval. Consequently the equation $x^{10} = 1000$ has exactly one solution in the given interval.

43. Let $g(x) = x^4 - 3x - 20$. Then $g(2) = -10 < 0$ and $g(3) = 52 > 0$. By the intermediate value property of continuous functions, $g(x)$ has at least one zero in $(2, 3)$. Its derivative $g'(x) = 4x^3 - 3$ is also continuous, and is zero only when $x = (3/4)^{1/3}$, approximately 0.91. So $g'(x)$ does not change sign on the interval $2 \le x \le 3$. For $x \ge 2$, $g'(x) = 4x^3 - 3 \ge 4 \cdot 2^3 - 3 = 29 > 0$. Consequently g is increasing on that interval, and so $g(x)$ has at most one zero there. The conclusion is that $g(x) = 0$ has exactly one solution for $2 \le x \le 3$.

44. Because $f'(x) = -3 + \cos x$ is always negative, the graph of f is decreasing on every interval of real numbers, and in particular is decreasing on $[-1, 1]$. Hence the equation $f(x) = 0$ can have *at most* one solution in that interval. Moreover, $f(-1) \approx 3.16 > 0$ and $f(1) \approx -1.16 < 0$. Because f is continuous on $[-1, 1]$, the intermediate value property of continuous functions guarantees that the equation $f(x) = 0$ has *at least* one solution in $[-1, 1]$.

45. The car traveled 35 miles in 18 minutes, which is an average speed of $\frac{250}{3} \approx 83.33$ miles per hour. By the mean value theorem, the car must have been traveling over 83 miles per hour at some time between 3:00 P.M. and 3:18 P.M.

46. A change of 15 miles per hour in 10 minutes is an average change of 1.5 miles per hour per minute, which is an average change of 90 miles per hour per hour. By the mean value theorem, the instantaneous rate of change of velocity must have been exactly 90 miles per hour per hour at some time in the given 10-minute interval.

48. Because $f'(0)$ does not exist, the function $f(x) = x^{2/3}$ does not satisfy the hypotheses of the mean value theorem on the given interval. But consider the equation

$$f'(c) = \frac{f(27) - f(-1)}{27 - (-1)}; \qquad (*)$$

that is,

$$\frac{2}{3c^{1/3}} = \frac{9-1}{28} = \frac{2}{7},$$

which leads to $c^{1/3} = 7/3$, and thus to $c = 343/27$, which is approximately 12.7. Because $-1 < c < 27$, there is indeed a number c satisfying Eq. (*).

49. Because

$$f'(x) = \frac{3}{2}(1+x)^{1/2} - \frac{3}{2} = \frac{3}{2}\left(\sqrt{1+x} - 1\right),$$

it is clear that $f'(x) > 0$ for $x > 0$. Also $f(0) = 0$; it follows that $f(x) > 0$ for all $x > 0$. That is,

$$(1+x)^{3/2} > 1 + \frac{3}{2}x \quad \text{for } x > 0.$$

50. Proof: Suppose that $f'(x)$ is the constant K on the interval $a \le x \le b$. Let $g(x) = Kx + f(a) - Ka$. Then the graph of g is a straight line, and $g'(x) = K$ for all x. Consequently f and g differ by a constant on the interval $a \le x \le b$. But $g(a) = Ka + f(a) - Ka = f(a)$, so $g(x) = f(x)$ for all x in the interval. Therefore the graph of f is a straight line.

51. Proof: Suppose that $f'(x)$ is a polynomial of degree $n - 1$ on the interval $I = \{x \mid a \le x \le b\}$. Then $f'(x)$ has the form

$$f'(x) = a_{n-1}x^{n-1} + a_{n-2}x^{n-2} + \ldots + a_2x^2 + a_1x + x_0$$

where $a_{n-1} \neq 0$. Note that $f'(x)$ is the derivative of the function

$$g(x) = \frac{1}{n}a_{n-1}x^n + \ldots + \frac{1}{2}a_1x^2 + a_0x.$$

By Corollary 2, $f(x)$ and $g(x)$ can differ only by a constant, and this is sufficient to establish that $f(x)$ must also be a polynomial, and one of degree n because the coefficient of x^n in $f(x)$ is nonzero.

52. Suppose that $f(x) = 0$ for $x = x_1, x_2, \ldots, x_k$ in the interval $[a, b]$. By Rolle's theorem, $f'(x) = 0$ for some c_1 in (x_1, x_2), some c_2 in (x_2, x_3), ..., and some c_{k-1} in (x_{k-1}, x_k). The numbers $c_1, c_2, \ldots, c_{k-1}$ are distinct because they come from disjoint intervals, and this proves the desired result.

53. First note that $f'(x) = \frac{1}{2}x^{-1/2}$, and that the hypotheses of the mean value theorem are all satisfied for the given function on the given interval. Thus there does exist a number c between 100 and 101 such that

$$\frac{1}{2c^{1/2}} = \frac{f(101) - f(100)}{101 - 100} = \sqrt{101} - \sqrt{100}.$$

Therefore $1/(2\sqrt{c}) = \sqrt{101} - 10$, and thus we have shown that $\sqrt{101} = 10 + \frac{1}{2\sqrt{c}}$ for some number c in $(100, 101)$. Proof for part (b): If $0 \leq \sqrt{c} \leq 10$, then $0 \leq c \leq 100$; because $c > 100$, we see that $0 \leq \sqrt{c} \leq 10$ is impossible. If $10.5 \leq \sqrt{c}$ then $110.25 \leq c$, which is also impossible because $c < 110$. Therefore $10 < \sqrt{c} < 10.5$. Finally,

$$10 < \sqrt{c} < 10.5 \text{ implies that } 20 < 2\sqrt{c} < 21.$$

Consequently

$$\frac{1}{21} < \frac{1}{2c^{1/2}} < \frac{1}{20},$$

so

$$10 + \frac{1}{21} < \sqrt{101} < 10 + \frac{1}{20}.$$

The decimal expansion of $1/21$ begins $0.047619047619\ldots$, and so $10.0476 < \sqrt{101} < 10.05$.

54. Let $f(x) = x^7 + x^5 + x^3 + 1$. Then $f(-1) = -2$, $f(1) = 4$, and $f'(x) = 7x^6 + 5x^4 + 3x^2$. Now $f'(x) > 0$ for all x except that $f'(0) = 0$, so f is increasing on the set of all real numbers. This information together with the fact that f (continuous) has the intermediate value property establishes that the equation $f(x) = 0$ has exactly one solution (approximately -0.79130272).

55. Let $f(x) = (\tan x)^2$ and let $g(x) = (\sec x)^2$. Then

$$f'(x) = 2(\tan x)(\sec^2 x) \text{ and } g'(x) = 2(\sec x)(\sec x \tan x) = f'(x) \text{ on } (-\pi/2, \pi/2).$$

Therefore there exists a constant C such that $f(x) = g(x) + C$ for all x in $(-\pi/2, \pi/2)$. Finally, $f(0) = 0$ and $g(0) = 1$, so $C = f(0) - g(0) = -1$.

56. The mean value theorem does not apply here because $f'(0)$ does not exist.

57. The average slope of the graph of f on the given interval is

$$\frac{f(2) - f(-1)}{2 - (-1)} = \frac{5 - (-1)}{3} = 2$$

and f satisfies the hypotheses of the mean value theorem there. Therefore $f'(c) = 2$ for some number c, $-1 < c < 2$. This implies that the tangent line to the graph of f at the point $(c, f(c))$ has slope 2 and is therefore parallel to the line with equation $y = 2x$ because the latter line also has slope 2.

58. To show that the graph of $f(x) = x^4 - x^3 + 7x^2 + 3x - 11$ has a horizontal tangent line, we must show that its derivative $f'(x) = 4x^3 - 3x^2 + 14x + 3$ has the value zero at some number c. Now

$f'(x)$ is a polynomial, thus is continuous everywhere, and so has the intermediate value property; moreover, $f'(-1) = -18$ and $f'(0) - 3$, so $f'(c) = 0$ for some number c in $(-1, 0)$. (The value of c is approximately -0.203058.)

59. Use the definition of the derivative:

$$g'(0) = \lim_{h \to 0} \frac{g(0+h) - g(0)}{h}$$
$$= \lim_{h \to 0} \left[\frac{1}{2} + \frac{1}{h} h^2 \sin\left(\frac{1}{h}\right) \right]$$
$$= \lim_{h \to 0} \left[\frac{1}{2} + h \sin\left(\frac{1}{h}\right) \right]$$
$$= \frac{1}{2} + 0 \quad \text{(by the squeeze law)}$$
$$= \frac{1}{2} > 0.$$

If $x \neq 0$ then

$$g'(x) = \frac{1}{2} + 2x \sin\left(\frac{1}{x}\right) - \cos\left(\frac{1}{x}\right).$$

Because $\cos(1/x)$ oscillates between $+1$ and -1 near $x = 0$ and $2x \sin(1/x)$ is near zero for x close to zero, it follows that every interval about $x = 0$ contains subintervals on which $g'(x) > 0$ and subintervals on which $g'(x) < 0$.

61. Let $h(x) = 1 - \frac{1}{2}x^2 - \cos x$. Then $h'(x) = -x + \sin x$. By Example 8, $\sin x < x$ for all $x > 0$, so $h'(x) < 0$ for all $x > 0$. If $x > 0$, then $\frac{h(x) - 0}{x - 0} = h'(c)$ for some $c > 0$, so $h(x) < 0$ for all $x > 0$; that is, $\cos x > 1 - \frac{1}{2}x^2$ for all $x > 0$.

62. (a) Let $j(x) = \sin x - x + \frac{1}{6}x^3$. Then

$$j'(x) = \cos x - 1 + \frac{1}{2}x^2.$$

By Problem 61, $j'(x) > 0$ for all $x > 0$. Also, if $x > 0$, then $\frac{j(x) - 0}{x - 0} = j'(c)$ for some $c > 0$. Hence $j(x) > 0$ for all $x > 0$; that is, $\sin x > x - \frac{1}{6}x^3$ for all $x > 0$.

(b) By part (a) and Example 8,

$$x - \frac{1}{6}x^3 < \sin x < x$$

for all $x > 0$. So

$$\pi/36 - \frac{1}{6}(\pi/36)^3 < \sin \pi/36 < \pi/36;$$
$$0.0871557 < \sin 5° < 0.0872665;$$
$$\sin 5° \approx 0.087.$$

63. (a) Let $K(x) = 1 - \frac{1}{2}x^2 + \frac{1}{24}x^4 - \cos x$. Then

$$K'(x) = -x + \frac{1}{6}x^3 + \sin x = \sin x - (x - \frac{1}{6}x^3).$$

By Problem 62, part (a), $K'(x) > 0$ for all $x > 0$. So if $x > 0$, $\frac{K(x) - 0}{x - 0} = K'(c)$ for some $c > 0$. Therefore $K(x) > 0$ for all $x > 0$. That is,

$$\cos x < 1 - \frac{1}{2}x^2 + \frac{1}{24}x^4 \quad \text{for all } x > 0.$$

(b) By Problem 61 and part (a),

$$1 - \frac{1}{2}x^2 < \cos x < 1 - \frac{1}{2}x^2 + \frac{1}{24}x^4$$

for all $x > 0$. In particular,

$$1 - \frac{1}{2}\left(\frac{\pi}{18}\right)^2 < \cos\frac{\pi}{18} < 1 - \frac{1}{2}\left(\frac{\pi}{18}\right)^2 + \frac{1}{24}\left(\frac{\pi}{18}\right)^4;$$

hence $0.984769 < \cos 10° < 0.984808$. So $\cos 10° \approx 0.985$.

Section 4.4

1. $f'(x) = 2x - 4$; $x = 2$ is the only critical point. Because $f'(x) > 0$ for $x > 2$ and $f'(x) < 0$ for $x < 2$, it follows that $f(2) = 1$ is the global minimum value of $f(x)$.

2. $f'(x) = 6 - 2x$, so $x = 3$ is the only critical point. If $x < 3$ then f is increasing, whereas f is decreasing for $x > 3$, so $f(3) = 9$ is the global maximum value of $f(x)$.

3. $f'(x) = 3x^2 - 6x = 3x(x - 2)$, so $x = 0$ and $x = 2$ are the only critical points. If $x < 0$ or if $x > 2$ then $f'(x)$ is positive, but $f'(x) < 0$ for $0 < x < 2$. So $f(0) = 5$ is a local maximum and $f(2) = 1$ is a local minimum.

4. $f'(x) = 3x^2 - 3 = 3(x + 1)(x - 1)$, so $x = 1$ and $x = -1$ are the only critical points. If $x < -1$ or if $x > 1$, then $f'(x) > 0$, whereas $f'(x) < 0$ on $(-1, 1)$. So $f(-1) = 7$ is a local maximum value and $f(1) = 3$ is a local minimum.

5. $f'(x) = 3x^2 - 6x + 3 = 3(x - 1)^2$, so $x = 1$ is the only critical point of f. $f'(x) > 0$ if $x \neq 1$ so the graph of f is increasing for *all* x, and so f has no extrema of any sort.

6. $f'(x) = 6x^2 + 6x - 36 = 6(x + 3)(x - 2)$, so $x = -3$ and $x = 2$ are the only critical points. If $x < -3$ or if $x > 2$ then $f'(x) > 0$, but $f'(x) < 0$ on the interval $(-3, 2)$. So $f(-3) = 98$ is a local maximum value of $f(x)$ and $f(2) = -27$ is a local minimum value.

7. $f'(x) = -6(x - 5)(x + 2)$; $f'(x) < 0$ if $x < -2$ and if $x > 5$, but $f'(x) > 0$ for $-2 < x < 5$. Hence $f(-2) = -58$ is a local minimum value of $f(x)$ and $f(5) = 285$ is a local maximum value.

8. $f'(x) = -3x^2$, so $x = 0$ is the only critical point. But $f'(x) < 0$ if $x \neq 0$, so f is decreasing everywhere. Therefore there are no extrema.

9. $f'(x) = 4x(x - 1)(x + 1)$; $f'(x) < 0$ for $x < -1$ and on the interval $(0, 1)$, whereas $f'(x) > 0$ for $x > 1$ and on the interval $(-1, 0)$. Consequently, $f(-1) = -1 = f(1)$ is the global minimum value of $f(x)$ and $f(0) = 0$ is a local maximum value.

10. $f'(x) = 15x^2(x + 1)(x - 1)$, so $f'(x) > 0$ if $x < -1$ and if $x > 1$, but $f'(x) < 0$ on $(-1, 0)$ and on $(0, 1)$. Therefore $f(0) = 0$ is not an extremum of $f(x)$, but $f(-1) = 2$ is a local maximum value and $f(1) = -2$ is a local minimum value.

11. $f'(x) = 1 - x^{-2}$, so the critical points are where $x = -1$ and $x = 1$ (horizontal tangents); note that f is not defined at $x = 0$. If $x^2 > 1$ then $f'(x) > 0$, so f is increasing if $x > 1$ and if $x < -1$. If $x^2 < 1$ then $f'(x) < 0$, so f is decreasing on $(-1, 0)$ and on $(0, 1)$. Therefore $f(-1) = -2$ is a local maximum value and $f(1) = 2$ is a local minimum value for $f(x)$. The discontinuity at $x = 0$ is what makes it possible for the minimum to exceed the maximum.

12. $f'(x) = 1 - 9x^{-2}$, so the critical points are where $x = -3$ and $x = 3$ (horizontal tangents); note that f is not defined at $x = 0$. If $x^2 > 9$ then $f'(x) > 0$, so f is increasing if $x > 3$ and if $x < -3$. If $x^2 < 9$ then $f'(x) < 0$, so f is decreasing on $(-3, 0)$ and on $(0, 3)$. Therefore $f(-3) = -6$ is a local maximum value and $f(3) = 6$ is a local minimum value for $f(x)$.

13. Here,
$$f'(x) = 2x - \frac{2}{x^2} = \frac{2(x^3-1)}{x^2} = \frac{2(x-1)(x^2+x+1)}{x^2}.$$
Because $x^2 + x + 1 > 0$ for all x, the only critical point is $x = 1$; note that f is not defined at $x = 0$. Also $f'(x)$ has the sign of $x - 1$, so $f'(x) > 0$ for $x > 1$ and $f'(x) < 0$ for $0 < x < 1$ and for $x < 0$. Consequently $f(1) = 3$ is a local minimum value of $f(x)$. It is not a global minimum; check the behavior of $f(x)$ for x negative and near zero.

14. This is exactly like Problem 13, except that the local minimum of $f(x)$ is $f\left(\sqrt[3]{4}\right) = 3\sqrt[3]{16}$.

15. The only critical point is at $x = 0$, where
$$f'(x) = -\frac{2}{3}x^{-1/3}$$
is not defined, though f is continuous there. If $x > 0$ then $f'(x) < 0$; for $x < 0$, $f'(x) > 0$. Consequently $f(0) = 3$ is a local (indeed, the global) maximum value of $f(x)$.

16. Because $f'(x) = \frac{1}{3}x^{-2/3}$, $f'(x) > 0$ for all x except for x except for $x = 0$, where f is continuous but $f'(x)$ is not defined. Consequently f has no extrema. Examination of the behavior of $f(x)$ and $f'(x)$ for x near zero makes it clear that the graph of f has a vertical tangent at $(0, 4)$.

17. $f'(x) = 2\sin x \cos x$; $f'(x) = 0$ when x is any integral multiple of $\pi/2$. In $(0, 3)$, $f'(x) = 0$ when $x = \pi/2$. Because $f'(x) > 0$ if $0 < x < \pi/2$ and $f'(x) < 0$ if $\pi/2 < x < 3$, $f(x)$ has the global maximum value $f(\pi/2) = 1$.

18. $f'(x) = -2\sin x \cos x$; $f'(x) = 0$ when $x = 0$ and when $x = \pi/2$. f is increasing on $(-1, 0)$ and on $(\pi/2, 3)$, decreasing on $(0, \pi/2)$. So f has a [global] maximum at $(0, 1)$ and a [global] minimum at $(\pi/2, 0)$.

19. $f'(x) = 3\sin^2 x \cos x$; $f'(x) = 0$ when $x = -\pi/2$, 0, or $\pi/2$. f is decreasing on $(-3, -\pi/2)$ and on $(\pi/2, 3)$, increasing on $(-\pi/2, \pi/2)$. So f has a [global] minimum at $(-\pi/2, -1)$ and a [global] maximum at $(\pi/2, 1)$.

20. $f'(x) = -4\cos^3 x \sin x$ vanishes at $\pi/2$ and at π. f is decreasing on $(0, \pi/2)$ and on $(\pi, 4)$, increasing on $(\pi/2, \pi)$. Global minimum at $(\pi/2, 0)$, global maximum at $(\pi, 1)$.

21. $f'(x) = 2\tan x \sec^2 x$; $f'(0) = 0$; f is decreasing on $(-1, 0)$, increasing on $(0, 1)$. Global minimum at $(0, 0)$.

22. $f'(x) = 3\tan^2 x \sec^2 x > 0$ on $(-1, 1)$; no extrema.

23. $f'(x) = x\sin x$; $f'(x) = 0$ at $-\pi$, 0, and π. $f'(x) > 0$ on $(-\pi, \pi)$, $f'(x) < 0$ on $(-5, -\pi)$ and on $(\pi, 5)$. So f has a [global] maximum at (π, π) and a [global] minimum at $(-\pi, -\pi)$.

24. $f'(x) = x\cos x$; $f'(x) = 0$ at $-\pi/2$, 0, and $\pi/2$. $f'(x) > 0$ on $(0, \pi/2)$ and on $(-3, -\pi/2)$. $f'(x) < 0$ on $(-\pi/2, 0)$ and on $(\pi/2, 3)$. So f has a maximum at $(-\pi/2, \pi/2)$ and at $(\pi/2, \pi/2)$, a minimum at $(0, 1)$.

25. $f'(x) = 2\sec^2 x - 2\tan x \sec^2 x = (2\sec^2 x)(1 - \tan x)$. $f'(x) = 0$ when $x = \pi/4$; f is increasing on $(0, \pi/4)$ and decreasing on $(\pi/4, 1)$; maximum at $(\pi/4, 1)$.

26. $f'(x) = -4(1 - 2\sin x)\cos x$. $f'(x) = 0$ when $x = \pi/6$ and when $x = \pi/2$. f is decreasing on $(0, \pi/6)$ and on $(\pi/2, 2)$, increasing on $(\pi/6, \pi/2)$. Minimum at $(\pi/6, 0)$, maximum at $(\pi/2, 1)$.

27. Let x be the smaller of the two numbers; then the other is $x+20$, and their product is $f(x) = x^2 + 20x$. Consequently $f'(x) = 2x + 20$, so $x = -10$ is the only critical point of f. The graph of f is decreasing for $x < -10$, increasing for $x > -10$. Therefore $(-10, -100)$ is the global minimum value of $f(x)$. Answer: The two numbers are -10 and 10.

28. We assume that the length turned upward is the same on each side—call it y. If the width of the gutter is x, then we have the constraint $xy = 18$, and we are to minimize the width $x + 2y$ of the

Section 4.4 The First Derivative Test and Applications

strip. Its width is given by the function

$$f(x) = x + \frac{36}{x}, \quad x > 0,$$

for which

$$f'(x) = 1 - \frac{36}{x^2}.$$

The only critical point in the domain of f is $x = 6$, and if $0 < x < 6$ then $f'(x) < 0$, whereas $f'(x) > 0$ for $x > 6$. Thus $x = 6$ yields the minimum value $f(6) = 12$ of the function f. Answer: The minimum possible width of the strip is 12 inches.

29. Let us minimize

$$g(x) = (x-3)^2 + (3 - 2x - 2)^2 = (x-3)^2 + (1 - 2x)^2,$$

the square of the distance from (x, y) on the line $2x + y = 3$ to the point $(3, 2)$. We have

$$g'(x) = 2(x-3) - 4(1-2x) = 10x - 10,$$

so $x = 1$ is the only critical point of $g(x)$. If $x > 1$ then $g'(x) > 0$, but $g'(x) < 0$ for $x < 1$. Thus $x = 1$ minimizes $g(x)$, and so the point on the line $2x + y = 3$ closest to the point $(3, 2)$ is $(1, 1)$. As an independent check, note that the slope of the line segment joining $(3, 2)$ and $(1, 1)$ is $\frac{1}{2}$, whereas the slope of the line $2x + y = 3$ is -2, so the segment and the line are perpendicular, as suggested by plane geometry.

30. Base of box: x wide, $2x$ long. Height: y. Then the box has volume $2x^2 = 576$, so $y = 288x^{-2}$. Its total surface area is $A = 4x^2 + 6xy$, so we minimize

$$A = A(x) = 4x^2 + \frac{1728}{x}, \quad x > 0.$$

Now

$$A'(x) = 8x - \frac{1728}{x^2},$$

so the only critical point of $A(x)$ occurs when $8x^3 = 1728$; that is, when $x = 6$. It is easy to verify that $A'(x) < 0$ for $0 < x < 6$ and $A'(x) > 0$ for $x > 6$. Therefore $A(6)$ is the global minimum value of $A(x)$. Also, when $x = 6$ we have $y = 8$. Answer: The dimensions of the box of minimal surface area are 6 inches wide by 12 inches long by 8 inches high.

31. Base of box: x wide, $2x$ long. Height: y. Then the box has volume $2x^2 y = 972$, so $y = 486x^{-2}$. Its total surface area is $A = 2x^2 + 6xy$, so we minimize

$$A = A(x) = 2x^2 + \frac{2916}{x}, \quad x > 0.$$

Now

$$A'(x) = 4x - \frac{2916}{x^2},$$

so the only critical point of $A(x)$ occurs when $4x^3 = 2916$; that is, when $x = 9$. It is easy to verify that $A'(x) < 0$ for $0 < x < 9$ and that $A'(x) > 0$ for $x > 9$. Therefore $A(9)$ is the global minimum value of $A(x)$. Answer: The dimensions of the box are 9 inches wide, 18 inches long, 6 inches high.

32. If the radius of the base of the pot is r and its height is h (inches), then we are to minimize the total surface area A given the constraint $\pi r^2 h = 125$. Thus $h = 125/(\pi r^2)$, and so

$$A = \pi r^2 + 2\pi r h = A(r) = \pi r^2 + \frac{250}{r}, \quad r > 0.$$

Now

$$A'(r) = 2\pi r - \frac{250}{r^2};$$

$A'(r) = 0$ when $r^3 = 125\pi$, so that $r = 5/\sqrt[3]{\pi}$. The latter point is the only value of r at which $A'(r)$ can change sign (for $r > 0$), and it is easy to see that $A'(r)$ is positive when r is large positive, whereas $A'(r)$ is negative when r is near zero. Therefore we have located the global minimum of $A(r)$, and it occurs when the pot has radius $r = 5/\sqrt[3]{\pi}$ inches and height $h = 5/\sqrt[3]{\pi}$ inches. Thus the pot will have its radius equal to its height, each approximately 3.414 inches.

33. Let r denote the radius of the pot and h its height. We are given the constraint $\pi r^2 h = 250$, so $h = 250/(\pi r^2)$. Now the bottom of the pot has area πr^2, and thus costs $4\pi r^2$ cents. The curved side of the pot has area $2\pi rh$, and thus costs $4\pi rh$ cents. So the total cost of the pot is

$$C = 4\pi r^2 + 4\pi rh = C(r) = 4\pi r^2 + \frac{1000}{r}, \qquad r > 0.$$

Now

$$C'(r) = 8\pi r - \frac{1000}{r^2};$$

$C'(r) = 0$ when $8\pi r^3 = 1000$, so that $r = 5/\sqrt[3]{\pi}$. It is clear that this is the only (positive) value of r at which $C'(r)$ can change sign, and that $C'(r) < 0$ for r positive and near zero, but $C'(r) > 0$ for r large positive. Therefore we have found the value of r that minimizes $C(r)$. The corresponding value of h is $10/\sqrt[3]{\pi}$, so the pot of minimal cost has height equal to its diameter, each approximately 6.828 centimeters.

34. If $(x, y) = (x, 4 - x^2)$ is a point on the parabola $y = 4 - x^2$, then the square of its distance from the point $(3, 4)$ is

$$h(x) = (x-3)^2 + (4 - x^2 - 4)^2 = (x-3)^2 + x^4.$$

We minimize the distance by minimizing its square:

$$h'(x) = 2(x-3) + 4x^3;$$

$h'(x) = 0$ when $2x^3 + x - 3 = 0$. It is clear that $h'(1) = 0$, so $x - 1$ is a factor of $h'(x)$; $h'(x) = 0$ is equivalent to $(x-1)(2x^2 + 2x + 3) = 0$. The quadratic factor in the last equation is always positive, so $x = 1$ is the only critical point of $h(x)$. Also $h'(x) < 0$ if $x < 1$, whereas $h'(x) > 0$ for $x > 1$, so $x = 1$ yields the global minimum value $h(1) = 5$ for $h(x)$. When $x = 1$ we have $y = 3$, so the point on the parabola $y = 4 - x^2$ closest to $(3, 4)$ is $(1, 3)$, at distance $\sqrt{5}$ from it.

35. If the sides of the rectangle are x and y, then $xy = 100$, so that $y = 100/x$. Therefore the perimeter of the rectangle is

$$P = P(x) = 2x + \frac{200}{x}, \qquad 0 < x.$$

Then

$$P'(x) = 2 - \frac{200}{x^2};$$

$P'(x) = 0$ when $x = 10$ (-10 is not in the domain of $P(x)$). Now $P'(x) < 0$ on $(0, 10)$ and $P'(x) > 0$ for $x > 10$, and so $x = 10$ minimizes $P(x)$. A little thought about the behavior of $P(x)$ for x near zero and for x large makes it clear that we have found the global minimum value for P: $P(10) = 40$. When $x = 10$, also $y = 10$, so the rectangle of minimal perimeter is indeed a square.

36. Let x denote the length of each side of the square base of the solid and let y denote its height. Then its total volume is $x^2 y = 1000$. We are to minimize its total surface area $A = 2x^2 + 4xy$. Now $y = 1000/(x^2)$, so

$$A = A(x) = 2x^2 + \frac{4000}{x}, \qquad x > 0.$$

Therefore

$$\frac{dA}{dx} = 4x - \frac{4000}{x^2}.$$

The derivative is zero when $4x^3 = 4000$; that is, when $x = 10$. Also $A(x)$ is decreasing on $(0, 10)$ and increasing for $x > 10$. So $x = 10$ yields the global minimum value of $A(x)$. In this case, $y = 10$ as well, so the solid is indeed a cube.

37. Let the square base of the box have edge length x and let its height be y, so that its total volume is $x^2 y = 62.5$ and the surface area of this box-without-top will be $A = x^2 + 4xy$. So
$$A = A(x) = x^2 + \frac{250}{x}, \qquad x > 0.$$
Now
$$A'(x) = 2x - \frac{250}{x^2},$$
so $A'(x) = 0$ when $x^3 = 125$: $x = 5$. In this case, $y = 2.5$. Also $A'(x) < 0$ if $0 < x < 5$ and $A'(x) > 0$ if $x > 5$, so we have found the global minimum for $A(x)$. Answer: Square base of edge length 5 inches, height 2.5 inches.

38. Let r denote the radius of the can and h its height (in centimeters). We are to minimize its total surface area $A = 2\pi r^2 + 2\pi rh$ given the constraint $\pi r^2 h = V = 16\pi$. First we note that $h = V/(\pi r^2)$, so we minimize
$$A = A(r) = 2\pi r^2 + \frac{2V}{r}, \qquad r > 0.$$
Now
$$A'(r) = 4\pi r - \frac{2V}{r^2};$$
$A'(r) = 0$ when $4\pi r^3 = 2V = 32\pi$—that is, when $r = 2$. Now $A(r)$ is decreasing on $(0, 2)$ and increasing for $r > 2$, so the global minimum of $A(r)$ occurs when $r = 2$, for which $h = 4$.

39. Let x denote the radius and y the height of the cylinder (in inches). Then its cost (in cents) is $C = 8\pi x^2 + 4\pi xy$, and we also have the constraint $\pi x^2 y = 100$. So
$$C = C(x) = 8\pi x^2 + \frac{400}{x}, \qquad x > 0.$$
Now $dC/dx = 16\pi x - 400/(x^2)$; $dC/dx = 0$ when $x = (25/\pi)^{1/3}$ (about 1.9965 inches) and consequently, when $y = (1600/\pi)^{1/3}$ (about 7.9859 inches). Because $C'(x) < 0$ if $x^3 < 25/\pi$ and $C'(x) > 0$ if $x^3 > 25/\pi$, we have indeed found the dimensions that minimize the total cost of the can. For simplicity, note that $y = 4x$ at minimum: The height of the can is twice its diameter.

40. If the print width is x and its height is y (in inches), then the page area is $A = (x+2)(y+4)$. We are to minimize A given $xy = 30$. Because $y = 30/x$,
$$A = A(x) = 4x + 38 + \frac{60}{x}, \qquad x > 0.$$
Now
$$A'(x) = 4 - \frac{60}{x^2};$$
$A'(x) = 0$ when $x = \sqrt{15}$. But $A'(x) > 0$ for $x > \sqrt{15}$ whereas $A'(x) < 0$ for $x < \sqrt{15}$. Therefore $x = \sqrt{15}$ yields the global minimum value of $A(x)$, which is $38 + 8\sqrt{15}$, approximately 68.98 square inches.

41. Let $(x, y) = (x, x^2)$ denote an arbitrary point on the curve. The square of its distance from $(0, 2)$ is then
$$f(x) = x^2 + (x^2 - 2)^2.$$
Now $f'(x) = 2x(2x^2 - 3)$, and therefore $f'(x) = 0$ when $x = 0$, when $x = -\sqrt{3/2}$, and when $x = +\sqrt{3/2}$. Now $f'(x) < 0$ if $x < -\sqrt{3/2}$ and if $0 < x < \sqrt{3/2}$; $f'(x) > 0$ if $-\sqrt{3/2} < x < 0$ and

if $x > \sqrt{3/2}$. Therefore $x = 0$ yields a local maximum for f; the other two zeros of $f'(x)$ yield its global minimum. Answer: There are exactly two points on the curve that are nearest $(0,2)$; they are $(+\sqrt{3/2}, 3/2)$ and $(-\sqrt{3/2}, 3/2)$.

42. Let $(a,0)$ and $(0,b)$ denote the endpoints of the segment and denote its point of tangency by $(c, 1/c)$. The segment then has slope $-1/c^2$, and therefore

$$\frac{b-0}{0-a} = -\frac{1}{c^2} = \frac{(1/c)-0}{c-a}.$$

It follows that $b = a/c^2$ and that $c = a - c$, so $a = 2c$ and $b = 2/c$. The square of the length of the segment is then

$$f(c) = 4c^2 + \frac{4}{c^2}, \quad c > 0.$$

Now

$$f'(c) = 8c - \frac{8}{c^3};$$

$f'(c) = 0$ when $c = -1$ and when $c = 1$. We reject the negative solution. On the interval $(0,1)$, f is decreasing; f is increasing for $c > 1$. Therefore $c = 1$ gives the segment of minimal length, which is $L = \sqrt{f(1)} = 2\sqrt{2}$.

43. If the dimensions of the rectangle are x by y, and the line segment bisects the side of length x, then the square of the length of the segment is

$$f(x) = \left(\frac{x}{2}\right)^2 + y^2 = \frac{x^2}{4} + \frac{4096}{x^2}, \quad x > 0,$$

because $y = 64/x$. Now

$$f'(x) = \frac{x}{2} - \frac{8192}{x^3}.$$

When $f'(x) = 0$, we must have $x = +8\sqrt{2}$, so that $y = 4\sqrt{2}$. We have found the minimum of f because if $0 < x < 8\sqrt{2}$ then $f'(x) < 0$, and $f'(x) > 0$ if $x > 8\sqrt{2}$. The minimum length satisfies $L^2 = f(8\sqrt{2})$, so that $L = 8$ centimeters.

44. Let y be the height of the cylindrical part and x the length of the radii of both the cylinder and the hemisphere. The total surface area is

$$A = \pi x^2 + 2\pi xy + 2\pi x^2 = 3\pi x^2 + 2\pi xy.$$

But the can must have volume $V = \pi x^2 y + \frac{2}{3}\pi x^3$, so

$$y = \frac{1000 - (2\pi x^3)/3}{\pi x^2}.$$

Therefore

$$A = A(x) = \frac{5}{3}\pi x^2 + \frac{2000}{x}, \quad x > 0.$$

Thus

$$\frac{dA}{dx} = \frac{10}{3}\pi x - \frac{2000}{x^2}.$$

Now $dA/dx = 0$ when $x = (600/\pi)^{1/3} \approx 5.7588$. Because $dA/dx < 0$ for smaller values of x and $dA/dx > 0$ for larger values, we have found the point at which $A(x)$ attains its global minimum value. After a little arithmetic, we find that $y = x$, so the radius of the hemisphere and the radius and height of the cylinder should all be equal to $(600/\pi)^{1/3}$ to attain minimal surface area.

This argument contains the implicit assumption that $y > 0$. If $y = 0$, then

$$x = (1500/\pi)^{1/3} \approx 7.8159, \text{ for which}$$
$$A = (150)(18\pi)^{1/3} \approx 575.747 \text{ cubic inches.}$$

But with $x = y = (600/\pi)^{1/3}$, we have

$$A = (100)(45\pi)^{1/3} \approx 520.940 \text{ cubic inches.}$$

So the solution in the first paragraph indeed yields the dimensions of the can requiring the least amount of material.

45. If the end of the rod projects the distance y into the narrower hall, then we have the proportion $y/2 = 4/x$ by similar triangles. So $y = 8/x$. The square of the length of the rod is then

$$f(x) = (x+2)^2 + \left(4 + \frac{8}{x}\right)^2, \quad x > 0.$$

It turns out that

$$f'(x) = 4 + 2x - \frac{64}{x^2} - \frac{128}{x^3},$$

and that $f'(x) = 0$ when $(x+2)(x^3 - 32) = 0$. The only admissible solution is $x = \sqrt[3]{32}$, which indeed minimizes $f(x)$ by the usual argument. The minimum length is

$$L = \left(20 + 12\sqrt[3]{4} + 12\sqrt[3]{16}\right)^{1/2} \approx 8.323876 \text{ (meters)}.$$

46. By similar triangles, $y/1 = 8/x$, and

$$L_1 + L_2 = L = \left[(x+1)^2 + (y+8)^2\right]^{1/2}.$$

We minimize L by minimizing

$$f(x) = L^2 = (x+1)^2 + \left(8 + \frac{8}{x}\right)^2, \quad x > 0.$$

$$f'(x) = 2 + 2x - \frac{128}{x^3} - \frac{128}{x^2};$$

$f'(x) = 0$ when $2x^3 + 2x^4 - 128 - 128x = 0$, which leads to the equation

$$(x+1)(x-4)(x^2 + 4x + 16) = 0.$$

The only relevant solution is $x = 4$. Because $f'(x) < 0$ for x in the interval $(-1, 4)$ and $f'(x) > 0$ if $x > 4$, we have indeed found the global minimum of f. The corresponding value of y is 2, and the length of the shortest ladder is $L = 5\sqrt{5}$ feet, approximately 11 ft 2 in.

47. If the pyramid has base edge length x and altitude y, then its volume is $V = \frac{1}{3}x^2 y$. From Fig. 4.4.29 we see also that

$$\frac{2y}{x} = \tan\theta \quad \text{and} \quad \frac{a}{y-a} = \cos\theta$$

where θ is the angle that each side of the pyramid makes with its base. It follows, successively, that

$$\left(\frac{a}{y-a}\right)^2 = \cos^2\theta;$$

$$\sin^2\theta = 1 - \cos^2\theta = \frac{(y-a)^2 - a^2}{(y-a)^2}$$

$$= \frac{y^2 - 2ay}{(y-a)^2} = \frac{y(y-2a)}{(y-a)^2}.$$

$$\sin\theta = \frac{(y(y-2a))^{1/2}}{y-a}.$$

$$y = \frac{x\sin\theta}{2\cos\theta} = \left(\frac{x}{2}\right)\left(\frac{(y(y-2a))^{1/2}}{y-a}\right)\left(\frac{y-a}{a}\right);$$

$$2y = \frac{x}{a}\sqrt{(y-2a)}.$$

$$x^2 = \frac{4a^2y^2}{y(y-2a)}.$$

Therefore

$$V = \frac{1}{3}x^2y = V(y) = \frac{4a^2y^2}{3(y-2a)}, \qquad y > 2a.$$

Now

$$\frac{dV}{dy} = \frac{24a^2y(y-2a) - 12a^2y^2}{9(y-2a)^2}.$$

The condition $dV/dy = 0$ then implies that $2(y-2a) = y$, and thus that $y = 4a$. Consequently the minimum volume of the pyramid is

$$V(4a) = \frac{(4a^2)(16a^2)}{(3)(2a)} = \frac{32}{3}a^3.$$

The ratio of the volume of the smallest pyramid to that of the sphere is then

$$\frac{32/3}{4\pi/3} = \frac{32}{4\pi} = \frac{8}{\pi}.$$

48. Let x denote the distance from the noisier of the two discos. Let K be the "noise proportionality" constant. The noise level at x is then

$$N(x) = \frac{4K}{x^2} + \frac{K}{(1000-x)^2}.$$

$$N'(x) = -\frac{8K}{x^3} + \frac{2K}{(1000-x)^3}.$$

Now $N'(x) = 0$ when $4(1000-x)^3 = x^3$; it turns out that

$$x = \frac{(1000)4^{1/3}}{1+4^{1/3}} \approx 613.512.$$

Because the noise level is very high when x is near zero and when x is near 1000, the above value of x minimizes the noise level—the quietest point is about 613.5 feet from the noisier of the two discos.

49. Let z be the length of the segment from the top of the tent to the midpoint of one side of its base. Then $x^2 + y^2 = z^2$. The total surface area of the tent is

$$A = 4x^2 + (4)(\tfrac{1}{2})(2x)(z) = 4x^2 + 4xz = 4x^2 + 4x(x^2+y^2)^{1/2}.$$

Because the (fixed) volume V of the tent is given by

$$V = \frac{1}{3}(4x^2)(y) = \frac{4}{3}x^2y,$$

we have $y = 3V/(4x^2)$, so

$$A = A(x) = 4x^2 + \frac{1}{x}(16x^6 + 9V^2)^{1/2}.$$

Section 4.4 The First Derivative Test and Applications

After simplifications, the condition $dV/dx = 0$ takes the form

$$8x\left(16x^6 + 9V^2\right)^{1/2} - \frac{1}{x^2}\left(16x^6 + 9V^2\right) + 48x^4 = 0,$$

which has solution $x = 2^{-7/6}\sqrt[3]{3V}$. Because this is the only positive solution of the equation, and because it is clear that neither large values of x nor values of x near zero will yield small values of the surface area, this is the desired value of x.

50. By similar triangles in Fig. 4.4.28, we have $y/a = b/x$, and thus $y = ab/x$. If L denotes the length of the ladder, then we minimize

$$L^2 = f(x) = (x+a)^2 + (y+b)^2 = (x+a)^2 + b^2\left(1+\frac{a}{x}\right)^2, \qquad 0 < x.$$

Now

$$f'(x) = 2(x+a) + 2b^2\left(1+\frac{a}{x}\right)\left(-\frac{a}{x^2}\right);$$

$f'(x) = 0$ when $x^3 = ab^2$, so that $x = a^{1/3}b^{2/3}$ and $y = a^{2/3}b^{1/3}$. It's clear that f is differentiable on its domain and that $f(x) \to +\infty$ as $x \to 0^+$ and as $x \to +\infty$. Therefore we have minimized L. With these values of x and y, we find that

$$L = (a^2 + y^2)^{1/2} + (x^2 + b^2)^{1/2} = \left(a^2 + a^{4/3}b^{2/3}\right)^{1/2} + \left(a^{2/3}b^{4/3} + b^2\right)^{1/2}$$
$$= a^{2/3}\left(a^{2/3} + b^{2/3}\right)^{1/2} + b^{2/3}\left(a^{2/3} + b^{2/3}\right)^{1/2} = \left(a^{2/3} + b^{2/3}\right)\left(a^{2/3} + b^{2/3}\right)^{1/2}$$
$$= \left(a^{2/3} + b^{2/3}\right)^{3/2}$$

Note that the answer is dimensionally correct.

Section 4.5

1. $f(x) \to +\infty$ as $x \to +\infty$, $f(x) \to -\infty$ as $x \to -\infty$. Matching graph: 4.5.13(c).
2. $f(x) \to +\infty$ as $x \to +\infty$, $f(x) \to +\infty$ as $x \to -\infty$. Matching graph: 4.5.13(a).
3. $f(x) \to -\infty$ as $x \to +\infty$, $f(x) \to +\infty$ as $x \to -\infty$. Matching graph: 4.5.13(d).
4. $f(x) \to -\infty$ as $x \to +\infty$, $f(x) \to -\infty$ as $x \to -\infty$. Matching graph: 4.5.13(b).
6. The only critical point occurs where $x = \frac{3}{2}$. The graph is increasing if $x < \frac{3}{2}$, decreasing if $x > \frac{3}{2}$.
8. The only critical points occur where $x = -\frac{7}{2}$ and where $x = \frac{5}{3}$. The graph is decreasing between them and increasing otherwise.
10. The critical points occur where $x = -\frac{8}{3}$, where $x = 0$, and where $x = \frac{5}{2}$. The graph is increasing on $(-\infty, -\frac{8}{3})$ and on $(0, \frac{5}{2})$. The graph is decreasing on $(-\frac{8}{3}, 0)$ and on $(\frac{5}{2}, +\infty)$.
12. The critical points occur at $x = -5$, $x = -2$, $x = 0$, $x = 2$, and $x = 5$. The graph of f is decreasing on $(-\infty, -5)$, on $(-2, 0)$, and on $(2, 5)$. The graph is increasing on $(-5, -2)$, on $(0, 2)$, and on $(5, +\infty)$.
14. The critical points occur where $x = -3$, $x = -2$, $x = 0$, $x = 2$, and $x = 3$. The graph of f is decreasing on $(-\infty, -3)$, on $(-2, 0)$, and on $(2, 3)$. It is decreasing on $(-3, -2)$, on $(0, 2)$, and on $(3, +\infty)$.
16. $f'(x) = -8 - 4x$ is positive for $x < -2$, negative for $x > -2$. The graph is a parabola opening downward, vertical axis, vertex (and global maximum) at $(-2, 13)$.
18. The function f is increasing on the set of all real numbers. It has no extrema of any kind.

20. $f'(x) = 3x^2 + 12x + 9 = 3(x+1)(x+3)$ is positive for $x > -1$ and for $x < -3$, negative for $-3 < x < -1$. So there is a local maximum at $(-3, 0)$ and a local minimum at $(-1, -4)$. There are intercepts at $(-3, 0)$ and $(0, 0)$.

22. $f'(x) = 3(x+3)(x-3)$: Local maximum at $(-3, 54)$, local minimum at $(3, -54)$.

24. $f'(x) = 2(x-2)(2x+3)(4x-1)$: Local minima at $(-1.5, 0)$ and at $(2, 0)$, local maximum at $(0.25, 37.515625)$.

26. Here, $f'(x) = \dfrac{10 - 5x}{3x^{1/3}}$ can change sign only at $x = 2$ and at $x = 0$. The function is increasing for $0 < x < 2$, decreasing for $x < 0$ and for $x > 2$. Thus there is a local maximum at $(2, f(2))$ and a local minimum at $(0, 0)$. Note that $f'(0)$ does not exist, but that f is continuous at $x = 0$.

28. $f'(x) = 4x^2(x+3)$ is positive for $x > -3$ and negative for $x < -3$; there is a horizontal tangent but no extremum at $x = 0$. There is a global minimum at $(-3, -27)$.

30. $f'(x) = -1/x^2$ is negative for all $x \ne 0$, so the function is decreasing for all $x \ne 0$; there is an infinite discontinuity at $x = 0$. There are no extrema and no intercepts. Note that as x increases without bound, $f(x)$ approaches zero.

31. $f'(x) = 4x - 3$ changes sign at $x = 3/4$. The function is increasing for $x > 3/4$ and decreasing for $x < 3/4$; it has a global minimum at $(3/4, -81/8)$.

32. The graph is a parabola, opening downward, vertical axis, vertex at $(-5/12, 169/24)$.

34. $f'(x) = 3x^2 + 4$ is positive for all x, so the function is increasing for all x; there are no extrema, and $(0, 0)$ is the only intercept.

36. $f'(x) = 3(x-1)^2$ is positive except at $x = 1$, so the graph is increasing for all x; there are no extrema, and the intercepts are at $(0, -1)$ and $(1, 0)$.

38. $f(x) = (x^2 - 1)^2$; $f'(x) = 4x(x+1)(x-1)$. So $f(x)$ is increasing for $-1 < x < 0$ and for $x > 1$, decreasing if $x < -1$ or if $0 < x < 1$. There are local minima at $(-1, 0)$ and at $(1, 0)$ and a local maximum at $(0, 1)$. These points are also all the intercepts.

40. $f'(x) = 15(x+1)(x-1)(x+2)(x-2)$, so f is increasing if $x < -2$, if $-1 < x < 1$, and if $x > 1$, decreasing if $-2 < x < 1$ and if $1 < x < 2$. So there are local maxima at $(-2, -16)$ and $(1, 38)$, local minima at $(-1, -38)$ and $(2, 16)$. The only intercept is $(0, 0)$.

42. $f'(x) = 4x^2(x-3)$, so f is increasing for $x > 3$, decreasing for $x < 3$. So there is a local (and global) minimum at $(3, -27)$; $(0, 0)$ and $(4, 0)$ are the only intercepts. There is a horizontal tangent at $(0, 0)$ but no extremum there.

44. Here we have
$$f'(x) = -\frac{1}{3x^{2/3}},$$
which is negative for all $x \ne 0$. Though $f'(0)$ is not defined, f is continuous at $x = 0$; careful examination of the behavior of f and f' near zero shows that the graph has a vertical tangent at $(0, 1)$; there are no extrema.

46. In this case
$$f'(x) = \frac{8(x+2)(x-2)}{3x^{1/3}},$$
which is positive for $x > 2$ and for $-2 < x < 0$, negative for $x < -2$ and for $0 < x < 2$. Note that f is continuous at $x = 0$ even though $f'(0)$ does not exist. Moreover, for x near zero, we have
$$f(x) \approx -16x^{2/3} \text{ and } f'(x) \approx -\frac{32}{3x^{1/3}}.$$
Consequently $f'(x) \to -\infty$ as $x \to 0^+$, while $f'(x) \to +\infty$ as $x \to 0^-$. This is consistent with the observation that $f(x) < 0$ for all x near (but not equal to) zero. The origin is a local maximum and there are global minima where $|x| = 2$.

48. After simplifications, we find that
$$f'(x) = \frac{2-3x}{3x^{2/3}(2-x)^{1/3}}.$$
so $f'(x) = 0$ when $x = 2/3$ and $f'(x)$ does not exist at $x = 0$ and at $x = 2$. The graph is increasing for $x < 2/3$ and for $x > 2$, decreasing for $2/3 < x < 2$. There is a vertical tangent at $(0,0)$, which is not an extremum. There's a horizontal tangent at $(2/3, 1.058)$ (ordinate approximate), which is a local maximum. There is a cusp at $(2,0)$, which is also a local minimum. Note that $f(x) \approx x$ for $|x|$ large; this aids in constructing the global sketch of the graph.

49. The graph is shown below. 50. The graph is shown below. 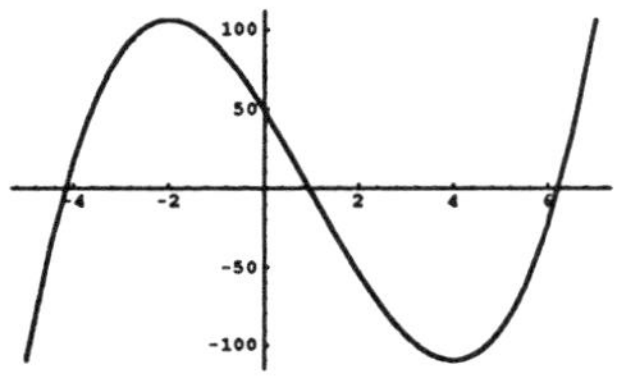 51. The graph is shown below.

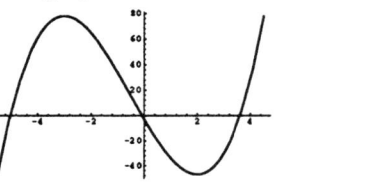

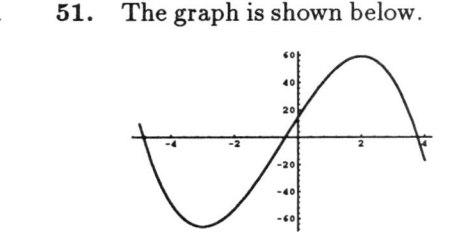

52. The graph is shown below. 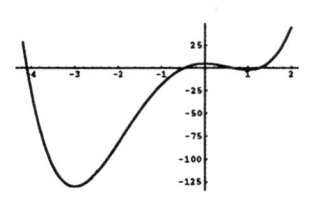 53. The graph is shown below. 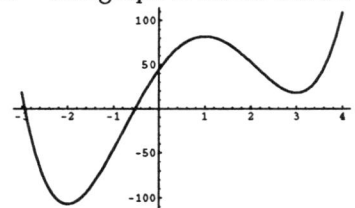 54. The graph is shown below.

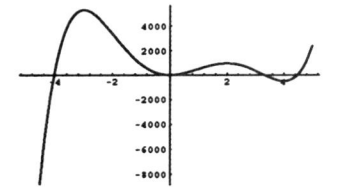

55. $x^3 - 3x + 3 \approx (x + 2.1038)(x^2 - 2.1038x + 1.4260)$.
56. The graph of $y = x^3 - 3x - 2$:

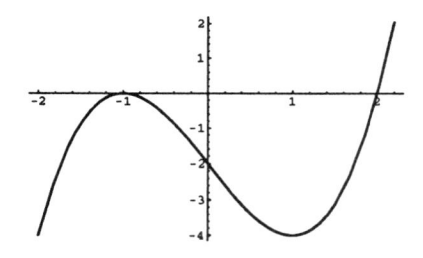

Section 4.6

1. $f'(x) = 8x^3 - 9x^2 + 6$, $f''(x) = 24x^2 - 18x$, $f'''(x) = 48x - 18$
2. $f'(x) = 10x^4 + \frac{3}{2}x^{1/2} + \frac{1}{2}x^{-2}$, $f''(x) = 40x^3 + \frac{3}{4}x^{-1/2} - x^{-3}$, $f'''(x) = 120x^2 - \frac{3}{8}x^{-3/2} + 3x^{-4}$
4. $g'(t) = 2t + \frac{1}{2}(t+1)^{-1/2}$, $g''(t) = 2 - \frac{1}{4}(t+1)^{-3/2}$, $g'''(t) = \frac{3}{8}(t+1)^{-5/2}$
6. $f'(x) = (x+1)^{1/2} + \frac{1}{2}x(x+1)^{-1/2}$, $f''(x) = (x+1)^{-1/2} - \frac{1}{4}x(x+1)^{-3/2}$,
   $f'''(x) = -\frac{3}{4}(x+1)^{-3/2} + \frac{3}{8}x(x+1)^{-5/2}$
8. $f'(x) = \frac{3}{2}x^{-1/2} + 3 + \frac{3}{2}x^{1/2}$, $f''(x) = -\frac{3}{4}x^{-3/2} + \frac{3}{4}x^{-1/2}$, $f'''(x) = \frac{9}{8}x^{-5/2} - \frac{3}{8}x^{-3/2}$
10. $h'(z) = \frac{8z}{(z^2+4)^2}$, $h''(z) = \frac{32 - 24z^2}{(z^2+4)^3}$, $h'''(z) = \frac{96z^3 - 384z}{(z^2+4)^4}$
12. $f'(x) = -4\sin 2x \cos 2x$, $f''(x) = 8\sin^2 2x - 8\cos^2 2x$, $f'''(x) = 64\sin 2x \cos 2x$

116   Section 4.6 Higher Derivatives and Concavity

14. $f'(x) = 2x\cos x - x^2\sin x$, $f''(x) = 2\cos x - 4x\sin x - x^2\cos x$,
$f'''(x) = -2\sin x - 4\sin x - 6x\cos x + x^2\sin x$

16. Given: $x^2 + y^2 = 4$.
$$2x + 2yy'(x) = 0, \text{ so } y'(x) = -\frac{x}{y}.$$
$$y''(x) = -\frac{y - xy'(x)}{y^2} = -\frac{y + (x^2/y)}{y^2} = -\frac{y^2 + x^2}{y^3} = -\frac{4}{y^3}.$$

18. $y'(x) = -(y/x)^{2/3}$; $y''(x) = \frac{2}{3}(y/x^5)^{1/3}$.

20. $y'(x) = -(y/x)^2$; $y''(x) = \frac{2y^2(x+y)}{x^4} = 2(y/x)^3$ (because $x + y = xy$)

22. $\sin^2 x + \cos^2 y = 1$: $2\sin x\cos x - 2y'(x)\sin y\cos y = 0$; $y'(x) = \frac{\sin x\cos x}{\sin y\cos y}$.
$\frac{d^2y}{dx^2}$ can be simplified (with the aid of the original equation) to
$$\frac{\cos^2 x\sin^2 y - \sin^2 x\cos^2 y}{\sin^3 y\cos^3 y} \equiv 0 \text{ if } y \text{ is not an integral multiple of } \pi/2.$$

24. Critical points: $(-3, 389)$ and $(6, -340)$; inflection point: $(1.5, 24.5)$

26. Critical points: $(-6.25, -8701.56)$ and $(3.4, 9271.08)$; inflection point: $(-1.425, 284.76)$

28. Critical point: $(7.5, -1304.69)$; inflection points: $(0, -250)$ and $(5, -875)$

30. Critical points: $(-4\sqrt{2}, 8192\sqrt{2})$ and $(4\sqrt{2}, -8192\sqrt{2})$; inflection points: $(0, 0)$, $(-4, 7168)$, and $(4, -7168)$

32. $f'(x) = -6 - 2x$; $f''(x) = -2$. The only critical point is at $(-3, 14)$, and it is a local maximum point because $f''(-3) = -2 < 0$. There are no inflection points because $f''(x)$ never changes sign.

34. $f'(x) = 3x(x - 2)$; $f''(x) = 6(x - 1)$. There are critical points at $(0, 0)$ and at $(2, -4)$. Now $f''(0) = -6 < 0$, so there is a local maximum at $(0, 0)$; $f''(2) = 6 > 0$, so there is a local minimum at $(2, -4)$. The only possible inflection point is $(1, -2)$, and it is indeed an inflection point because f'' changes sign there.

36. $f'(x) = 4x^3$; $f''(x) = 12x^2$. The only critical point and the only possible inflection point is $(0, 0)$. The second derivative does not identify this point as a local maximum or minimum, and it is not an inflection point because f'' does not change sign there. (It is, of course, the location of the global minimum of f.)

38. $f'(x) = 4x(x + 2)(x - 2)$; $f''(x) = 12x^2 - 16$. The critical points are located at $(-2, -16)$, $(0, 0)$, and $(2, -16)$. Now $f''(-2) > 0$ and $f''(2) > 0$, so $(-2, -16)$ and $(2, -16)$ are local minimum points. But $f''(0) < 0$, so $(0, 0)$ is a local maximum point. The only possible inflection points are where $3x^2 - 4 = 0$; $x = \frac{2}{3}\sqrt{3}$ and $x = -\frac{2}{3}\sqrt{3}$. Because $f''(x) = 4(3x^2 - 4)$, it is clear that $f''(x)$ changes sign at each of these two points, so the corresponding points on the graph are inflection points.

40. $f'(x) = x^2(x + 2)(5x + 6)$ and $f''(x) = 4x(5x^2 + 12x + 6)$. So the critical points occur where $x = 0$, $x = -2$, and $x = -6/5$. Now $f''(0) = 0$, so the second derivative test fails here, but $f'(x) > 0$ for x near zero but $x \ne 0$, so $(0, 0)$ is not an extremum for the graph of f. Next, $f''(-2) = -16 < 0$, so $(-2, 0)$ is a local maximum point; $f''(-6/5) = 5.76 > 0$, so $(-6/5, -3456/3125)$ is a local minimum point. The possible inflection points occur at
$$x = 0, \quad x = \tfrac{1}{5}\left(-6 + \sqrt{6}\right), \text{ and } \tfrac{1}{5}\left(-6 - \sqrt{6}\right).$$
In decimal form these are $x = 0$, $x \approx -0.710$, and $x \approx -1.690$. Because $f''(-2) = -16 < 0$, $f''(-1) = 4 > 0$, $f''(-0.5) = -2.5 < 0$, and $f''(1) = 92 > 0$, each of the three numbers displayed above is the abscissa of an inflection point of the graph of f.

42. Local (indeed, global) maximum point: $(0,1)$; no inflection points

44. Local minimum point: $(0,1)$; no inflection points

46. $f(x) = \sin^3 x$, $-\pi < x < \pi$:

$$f'(x) = 3\sin^2 x \cos x,$$
$$f''(x) = 6\sin x \cos^2 x - 3\sin^3 x = 3(2\cos^2 x - \sin^2 x)\sin x.$$

Minimum at $(-\pi/2, -1)$; maximum at $(\pi/2, 1)$; inflection points at $x = 0$ and at the four solutions of $\tan^2 x = 2$ in $(-\pi, \pi)$.

48. $f(x) = \cos x - \sin x$, $0 < x < \pi$:

$$f'(x) = -\sin x - \cos x, \quad f''(x) = -\cos x + \sin x.$$

$f'(x) = 0$ when $x = 3\pi/4, 7\pi/4$. $f''(x) = 0$ when $x = \pi/4, 5\pi/4$.
$f(\pi/4) = 0$, $f(3\pi/4) = -\sqrt{2}$, $f(5\pi/4) = 0$, $f(7\pi/4) = \sqrt{2}$.
Minimum point: $(3\pi/4, -\sqrt{2})$. Maximum point: $(7\pi/4, \sqrt{2})$.
Inflection points: $(\pi/4, 0)$ and $(5\pi/4, 0)$.

50. $f(x) = 3\sin x - 4\cos x$, $0 < x < 2\pi$:

$$f'(x) = 3\cos x + 4\sin x, \quad f''(x) = -3\sin x + 4\cos x.$$

$f'(x) = 0$ when $\tan x = -\frac{3}{4}$: $x \approx 2.498$, $x \approx 5.640$.
$f''(x) = 0$ when $\tan x = \frac{4}{3}$: $x \approx 0.927$, $x \approx 4.069$.
Maximum: $f(2.498) \approx 5$; minimum: $f(5.640) \approx -5$;
Inflection points $(0.927, f(0.927))$, where $f(0.927) \approx 0$, and $(4.069, f(4.069))$ where $f(4.069) \approx 0$.

52. We assume that the length turned upward is the same on each side—call it y. If the width of the gutter is x, then we have the constraint $xy = 18$, and we are to minimize the width $x + 2y$ of the strip. Its width is given by the function

$$f(x) = x + \frac{36}{x}, \quad x > 0,$$

for which

$$f'(x) = 1 - \frac{36}{x^2} \quad \text{and} \quad f''(x) = \frac{72}{x^3}.$$

The only critical point in the domain of f is $x = 6$, and $f''(x) > 0$ on the entire domain of f. Consequently the graph of f is concave upward for all $x > 0$. Because f is continuous for such x, $f(6) = 12$ is the global minimum of f.

53. Let us minimize

$$g(x) = (x-3)^2 + (3 - 2x - 2)^2 = (x-3)^2 + (1-2x)^2,$$

the square of the distance from the point (x, y) on the line $2x + y = 3$ to the point $(3, 2)$. We have $g'(x) = 2(x-3) - 4(1-2x) = 10x - 10$; $g''(x) = 10$. So $x = 1$ is the only critical point of $g(x)$. Because $g''(x)$ is always positive, the graph of g is concave upward on the set $\mathbb{R}$ of all real numbers, and therefore $(1, g(1)) = (1, 1)$ yields the global minimum for g: The point on the given line closest to $(3, 2)$ is $(1, 1)$.

54. Base of box: x wide, $2x$ long. Height: y. Then the box has volume $2x^2 y = 576$, so $y = 288x^{-2}$. Its total surface area is $A = 4x^2 + 6xy$, so we minimize

$$A = A(x) = 4x^2 + \frac{1728}{x}, \quad x > 0.$$

Now
$$A'(x) = 8x = \frac{1728}{x^2} \quad \text{and} \quad A''(x) = 8 + \frac{3456}{x^3}.$$

The only critical point of $A(x)$ occurs when $8x^3 = 1728$; that is, when $x = 6$. But $A''(x) > 0$ for all $x > 0$, so the graph of $y = A(x)$ is concave upward for all $x > 0$. Therefore $A(6)$ is the global minimum value of $A(x)$. Also, when $x = 6$ we have $y = 8$. Answer: The dimensions of the box of minimal surface area are 6 inches wide by 12 inches long by 8 inches high.

55. Base of box: x wide, $2x$ long. Height: y. Then the box has volume $2x^2y = 972$, so $y = 486x^{-2}$. Its total surface area is $A = 2x^2 + 6xy$, so we minimize
$$A = A(x) = 2x^2 + \frac{2916}{x}, \quad x > 0.$$

Now
$$A'(x) = 4x - \frac{2916}{x^2} \quad \text{and} \quad A''(x) = 4 + \frac{5832}{x^3}.$$

The only critical point of A occurs when $x = 9$, and $A''(x)$ is always positive. So the graph of $y = A(x)$ is concave upward for all $x > 0$; consequently, $(9, A(9))$ is the global minimum point of A. Answer: The dimensions of the box are 9 inches wide, 18 inches long, and 6 inches high.

56. If the radius of the base of the pot is r and its height is h (inches), then we are to minimize the total surface area A given the constraint $\pi r^2 h = 125$. Thus $h = 125/(\pi r^2)$, and so
$$A = \pi r^2 + 2\pi rh = A(r) = \pi r^2 + \frac{250}{r}, \quad r > 0.$$

Hence
$$A'(r) = 2\pi 4 - \frac{250}{r^2} \quad \text{and} \quad A''(r) = 2\pi + \frac{500}{r^3}.$$

Now $A'(r) = 0$ when $r^3 = 125/\pi$, so that $r = 5/\sqrt[3]{\pi}$. This is the only critical point of A, and $A''(r) > 0$ for all r, so the graph of $y = A(r)$ is concave upward for all r in the domain of A. Consequently we have located the global minimum, and it occurs when the pot has radius $r = 5/\sqrt[3]{\pi}$ inches and height $h = 5/\sqrt[3]{\pi}$ inches. Thus the pot will have its radius equal to its height, each approximately 3.414 inches.

57. Let r denote the radius of the pot and h its height. We are given the constraint $\pi r^2 h = 250$, so $h = 250/(\pi r^2)$. Now the bottom of the pot has area πr^2, and thus costs $4\pi r^2$ cents. The curved side of the pot has area $2\pi rh$, and thus costs $4\pi rh$ cents. So the total cost of the pot is
$$C = 4\pi r^2 + 4\pi rh = C(r) = 4\pi r^2 + \frac{1000}{r}, \quad r > 0.$$

Now
$$C'(r) = 8\pi r = \frac{1000}{r^2} \quad \text{and} \quad C''(r) = 8\pi + \frac{2000}{r^3}.$$

$C'(r) = 0$ when $8\pi r^3 = 1000$, so that $r = 5/\sqrt[3]{\pi}$. Because $C''(r) > 0$ for all $r > 0$, the graph of $y = C(r)$ is concave upward on the domain of C. Therefore we have found the value of r that minimizes $C(r)$. The corresponding value of h is $10/\sqrt[3]{\pi}$, so the pot of minimal cost has height equal to its diameter, each approximately 6.828 centimeters.

58. Let x denote the length of each side of the square base of the solid and let y denote its height. Then its total volume is $x^2 y = 1000$. We are to minimize its total surface area $A = 2x^2 + 4xy$. Now $y = 1000/(x^2)$, so
$$A = A(x) = 2x^2 + \frac{4000}{x}, \quad x > 0.$$

Therefore
$$A'(x) = 4x - \frac{4000}{x^2} \quad \text{and} \quad A''(x) = 4 + \frac{8000}{x^3}.$$

The only critical point occurs when $x = 10$, and $A''(x) > 0$ for all x in the domain of A, so $x = 10$ yields the global minimum value of $A(x)$. In this case, $y = 10$ as well, so the solid is indeed a cube.

59. Let the square base of the box have edge length x and let its height be y, so that its total volume is $x^2y = 62.5$ and the surface area of this box-without-top will be $A = x^2 + 4xy$. So

$$A = A(x) = x^2 + \frac{250}{x}, \quad x > 0.$$

Now

$$A'(x) = 2x - \frac{250}{x^2} \quad \text{and} \quad A''(x) = 2 + \frac{500}{x^3}.$$

The only critical point occurs when $x = 5$, and $A''(x) > 0$ for all x in the domain of A, so $x = 5$ yields the global minimum for A. Answer: Square base of edge length $x = 5$ inches, height $y = 2.5$ inches.

60. Let r denote the radius of the can and h its height (in centimeters). We are to minimize its total surface area $A = 2\pi r^2 + 2\pi rh$ given the constraint $\pi r^2 h = V = 16\pi$. First we note that $h = V/(\pi r^2)$, so we minimize

$$A = A(r) = 2\pi r^2 + \frac{2V}{r}, \quad r > 0.$$

Now

$$A'(r) = 4\pi r - \frac{2V}{r^2} \quad \text{and} \quad A''(r) = 4\pi + \frac{4V}{r^3}.$$

The only critical point of A occurs when $4\pi r^3 = 2V = 32\pi$—that is, when $r = 2$. Now $A''(r) > 0$ for all $r > 0$, so the graph of $y = A(r)$ is concave upward for all $r > 0$. Thus the global minimum occurs when $r = 2$ centimeters, for which $h = 4$ centimeters.

61. Let x denote the radius and y the height of the cylinder (in inches). Then its cost (in cents) is $C = 8\pi x^2 + 4\pi xy$, and we also have the constraint $\pi x^2 y = 100$. So

$$C = C(x) = 8\pi x^2 + \frac{400}{x}, \quad x > 0.$$

Now

$$C'(x) = 16\pi x - \frac{400}{x^2} \quad \text{and} \quad C''(x) = 16\pi + \frac{800}{x^3}.$$

The only critical point in the domain of C is $x = \sqrt[3]{25/\pi}$ (about 1.9965 inches) and, consequently, when $y = \sqrt[3]{1600/\pi}$ (about 7.9859 inches). Because $C''(x) > 0$ for all x in the domain of C, we have indeed found the dimensions that minimize the cost of the can. For simplicity, note that $y = 4x$ at the minimum: The height of the can is twice its diameter.

62. Let x denote the width of the print. Then $30/x$ is the height of the print, $x + 2$ is the width of the page, and $(30/x) + 4$ is the height of the page. We minimize the area A of the page, where

$$A = A(x) = (x+2)\left(\frac{30}{x} + 4\right) = 4x + 68 + \frac{60}{x}, \quad 0 < x < \infty.$$

Now

$$A'(x) = 4 - \frac{60}{x^2} \quad \text{and} \quad A''(x) = \frac{120}{x^3}.$$

$A'(x) = 0$ when $x = \sqrt{15}$, and $A''\left(\sqrt{15}\right) = 120/\left(15\sqrt{15}\right) > 0$, so $x = \sqrt{15}$ yields a local minimum of $A(x)$. $A'(x) < 0$ if $0 < x < \sqrt{15}$ and $A'(x) > 0$ if $\sqrt{15} > x$, so $x = \sqrt{15}$ yields the global minimum value of $A(x)$; this minimum value is $4\sqrt{15} + 68 + 60/\sqrt{15} = 8\sqrt{15} + 68 \approx 98.98$ in.^{2}

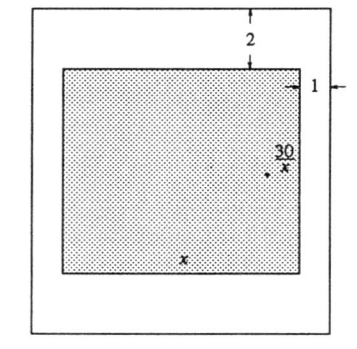

64. Given: $f(x) = 3x^4 - 4x^3 - 5$. Then

$$f'(x) = 12x^3 - 12x^2 = 12x^2(x-1) \quad \text{and} \quad f''(x) = 36x^2 - 24x = 12x(3x-2).$$

So the graph of f is increasing for $x > 1$ and decreasing for $x < 1$ (even though there's a horizontal tangent at $x = 0$), concave upward for $x < 0$ and $x > 2/3$, concave downward on $(0, 2/3)$. There is a global minimum at $(1, -6)$, inflection points at $(0, -5)$ and at $(2/3, -151/27)$. The x-intercepts are approximately -0.906212 and 1.682971.

66. Given: $f(x) = 3x^5 - 5x^3$. Then

$$f'(x) = 15x^4 - 15x^2 = 15x^2(x+1)(x-1) \quad \text{and}$$
$$f''(x) = 60x^3 - 30x = 60x(x+r)(x-r) \quad \text{where} \quad r = \frac{1}{2}\sqrt{2}.$$

The graph is increasing for $x < -1$ and for $x > 1$, decreasing for $-1 < x < 1$ (although there is a horizontal tangent at the origin). It is concave upward on $(-r, 0)$ and on $(r, +\infty)$, concave downward on $(-\infty, -r)$ and on $(0, r)$. Thus there is a local maximum at $(-1, 2)$, a local minimum at $(1, -2)$, and inflection points at $(-r, 7r/4)$, $(0, 0)$, and $(r, -7r/4)$ (the last ordinate is approximately -1.237437). Finally, the x-intercepts are 0, $-\sqrt{5/3}$, and $\sqrt{5/3} \approx 1.29099$.

68. Given: $f(x) = 3x^5 - 25x^3 + 60x$. Then

$$f'(x) = 15x^4 - 75x^2 + 60 = 15(x^2 - 4)(x^2 - 1) \quad \text{and} \quad f''(x) = 60x^3 - 150x = 30x(2x^2 - 5).$$

There are local maxima where $x = -2$ and $x = 1$, local minima where $x = -1$ and $x = 2$. Inflection points occur where $x = 0$, $x = -\sqrt{5/2}$, and $x = \sqrt{5/2}$.

70. Given: $f(x) = (x-1)^2(x+2)^3$. Then

$$f'(x) = (x-1)(x+2)^2(5x+1) \quad \text{and} \quad f''(x) = 2(x+2)(10x^2 + 4x - 5).$$

The zeros of $f''(x)$ are $x = -2$, $x \approx 0.535$, and $x \approx -0.935$. It follows that $(1, 0)$ is a local minimum (from the second derivative test), that $(-0.2, 8.39808)$ is a local maximum, and that $(-2, 0)$ is not an extremum. Also, the second derivative changes sign at each of its zeros, so each of these three zeros is the abscissa of an inflection point on the graph.

72. Given: $f(x) = 2 - (x-3)^{1/3}$. Then

$$f'(x) = -\frac{1}{3(x-3)^{2/3}} \quad \text{and} \quad f''(x) = \frac{2}{9(x-3)^{5/3}}.$$

There is a vertical tangent at $(3, 2)$ but there are no other critical points. The graph is decreasing for all x, concave down for $x < 3$, and concave up for $x > 3$. Because f is continuous for all x, there is an inflection point at $(3, 2)$. The y-intercept is at $(0, 3.44225)$ (ordinate approximate) and the x-intercept is at $(11, 0)$.

74. Given: $f(x) = x^{2/3}(5 - 2x)$. Then

$$f'(x) = \frac{10 - 10x}{3x^{1/3}} \quad \text{and} \quad f''(x) = -\frac{20x + 10}{9x^{4/3}}.$$

If $|x|$ is large, then $f(x) \approx -2x^{5/3}$, which (because the exponent $5/3$ has odd numerator and odd denominator) acts rather like $-2x^3$ for $|x|$ large (at least qualitatively). This aids in determining the behavior of $f(x)$ for $|x|$ large. The graph is decreasing for $x < 0$ and for $x > 1$, increasing on the interval $(0, 1)$. It is concave upward for $x < -0.5$, concave downward for $x > 0$ and on the interval $(-0.5, 0)$. There is a vertical tangent and a local minimum at the origin, a local maximum at $(1, 3)$, an inflection point where $x = -0.5$, a dual intercept at $(0, 0)$, and an x-intercept at $x = 2.5$.

76. Given: $f(x) = x^{1/3}(6-x)^{2/3}$. Then

$$f'(x) = \frac{2-x}{x^{2/3}(6-x)^{1/3}} \quad \text{and} \quad f''(x) = -\frac{8}{x^{5/3}(6-x)^{4/3}}.$$

If $|x|$ is large, then $(6-x)^{2/3} \approx x^{2/3}$, so $f(x) \approx x$ for such x. This aids in sketching the graph, which has a local maximum where $x = 2$, a local minimum at $(6,0)$, vertical tangents at $(6,0)$ and at the origin. It is increasing for $x < 2$ and for $x > 6$, decreasing on the interval $(2,6)$, concave upward for $x < 0$, and concave downward on $(0,6)$ and for $x > 6$. All the intercepts have been mentioned, too.

78. Figure 4.6.33(e)

80. Figure 4.6.33(f)

82. Figure 4.6.33(a)

83. (a) Proof: The result holds when $n = 1$. Suppose that it holds for $n = k$ where $k \geq 1$. Then $f^{(k)}(x) = k!$ if $f(x) = x^k$. Now if $g(x) = x^{k+1}$, then $g(x) = xf(x)$. So by the product rule,

$$g'(x) = xf'(x) + f(x) = x(kx^{k-1}) + x^k = (k+1)x^k.$$

Thus

$$g^{(k+1)}(x) = (k+1)D_x^k(x^k) = (k+1)f^{(k)}(x) = (k+1)(k!) = (k+1)!.$$

That is, whenever the result holds for $n = k$, it follows for $n = k+1$. Therefore, by induction, it holds for all $n \geq 1$.

(b) Since the nth derivative of x^n is constant, any higher order derivative of x^n is zero; the result follows immediately.

84. $f'(x) = \cos x$, $f''(x) = -\sin x$, $f^{(3)} = -\cos x$, and $f^{(4)} = \sin x = f(x)$. It is now clear that

$$f^{(n+4)}(x) = f^{(n)}(x) \quad \text{for all } n \geq 0$$

(we interpret $f^{(0)}(x)$ to mean $f(x)$).

85. $\dfrac{dz}{dx} = \dfrac{dz}{dy} \cdot \dfrac{dy}{dx}$. So $\dfrac{d^2z}{dx^2} = \dfrac{dz}{dy} \cdot \dfrac{d^2y}{dx^2} + \dfrac{dy}{dx} \cdot \dfrac{d^2z}{dy^2} \cdot \dfrac{dy}{dx}$.

86. If $f(x) = Ax^2 + Bx + C$, then $f''(x) = 2A \neq 0$. Because $f''(x)$ never changes sign, $f(x)$ can have no inflection points.

87. If $f(x) = ax^3 + bx^2 + cx + d$ with $a \neq 0$, then $f'(x)$ and $f''(x)$ exist for all x, and $f''(x) = 6ax + 2b$. The latter is zero when and only when $x = -b/3a$, and this is the abscissa of an inflection point because $f''(x)$ changes sign at $x = -b/3a$. Therefore the graph of a cubic polynomial has exactly one inflection point.

88. If $f(x) = Ax^4 + Bx^3 + Cx^2 + Dx + E$, then both $f'(x)$ and $f''(x)$ are continuous for all x, and $f''(x) = 12Ax^2 + 6Bx + 2C$. In order for $f''(x)$ to change sign, we must have $f''(x) = 0$. If so, then (because $f''(x)$ is a quadratic polynomial) either the graph of $f''(x)$ crosses the x-axis in two places or is tangent to it at a single point. In the first case, $f''(x)$ changes sign twice, so there are two points of inflection on the graph of f. In the second case, $f''(x)$ does not change sign, so f has no inflection points. Therefore the graph of a polynomial of degree four has either exactly two inflection points or else none at all.

89. $p = p(V) = \dfrac{RT}{V-b} - \dfrac{a}{V^2}$, so

$$p'(V) = \frac{2a}{V^3} - \frac{RT}{(V-b)^2} \quad \text{and} \quad p''(V) = \frac{2RT}{(V-b)^3} - \frac{6a}{V^4}.$$

From now on, use the constant values $p = 72.8$, $V = 128.1$, and $T = 304$; we already have $n = 1$. Then

$$p = \frac{RT}{V-b} - \frac{a}{V^2},$$

$$\frac{2a}{V^3} = \frac{RT}{(V-b)^2}, \quad \text{and} \quad \frac{3a}{V^4} = \frac{RT}{(V-b)^3}.$$

The last two equations yield

$$\frac{RTV^3}{a(V-b)^2} = 2 = \frac{3(V-b)}{V},$$

and thus $b = \frac{1}{3}V$ and $V - b = \frac{2}{3}V$. Next,

$$a = \frac{V^3 RT}{2(V-b)^2} = \frac{V^3 RT}{2(2V/3)^2} = \frac{9V^3 RT}{8V^2} = \frac{9}{8}VRT.$$

Finally, $\frac{RT}{V-b} = p + \frac{a}{V^2}$, so

$$R = \frac{2V}{3T}\left(p + \frac{a}{V^2}\right) = \frac{2V}{3T}\left(p + \frac{9RT}{8V}\right) = \frac{2Vp}{3T} + \frac{3R}{4}.$$

Therefore $R = \frac{8Vp}{3T}$. We substitute this into the earlier formula for a, in order to determine that $a = \frac{9}{8}VRT = 3V^2 p$. In summary, and using the values given in the problem, we find that

$$b = \frac{1}{3}V = 42.7, \quad a = 3V^2 p \approx 3{,}583{,}859, \quad \text{and} \quad R = \frac{8Vp}{3T} \approx 81.8.$$

Section 4.7

1. $\dfrac{x}{x+1} = \dfrac{1}{1+(1/x)} \to 1$ as $x \to +\infty$.

2. $\dfrac{x^2+1}{x^2-1} = \dfrac{1+(1/x^2)}{1-(1/x^2)} \to 1$ as $x \to -\infty$.

3. $\dfrac{x^2+x-2}{x-1} = \dfrac{(x+2)(x-1)}{x-1} = x+2$ for $x \neq 1$, so $\dfrac{x^2+x-2}{x-1} \to 1+2 = 3$ as $x \to 1$.

4. The numerator approaches -2 as $x \to -1$, whereas the denominator approaches zero. Therefore this limit does not exist.

5. $\dfrac{2x^2-1}{x^2-3x} = \dfrac{2-(1/x^2)}{1-(3/x)} \to 2$ as $x \to +\infty$.

6. $\dfrac{x^2+3x}{x^3-5} = \dfrac{(1/x)+(3/x^2)}{1-(5/x^3)} \to 0$ as $x \to -\infty$.

7. The numerator is equal to the denominator for all $x \neq -1$, so the limit is 1.

8. $\dfrac{5x^3-2x+1}{7x^3+4x^2-2} = \dfrac{5-(2/x^2)+(1/x^3)}{7+(4/x)-(2/x^3)} \to \dfrac{5}{7}$ as $x \to +\infty$.

9. Factor the numerator: $x - 4 = (\sqrt{x}+2)(\sqrt{x}-2)$. Thus the fraction is equal to $\sqrt{x}+2$ if $x \neq 4$. Therefore as $x \to 4$, the fraction approaches $\sqrt{4}+2 = 4$.

10. Divide each term in numerator and denominator by $x^{3/2}$, the highest power of x that appears in any term. The numerator then becomes $2x^{-1/2} + x^{-3/2}$, which approaches 0 as $x \to +\infty$; the denominator becomes $x^{-1/2} - 1$, which approaches -1 as $x \to +\infty$. Therefore the limit is 0.

11. Divide each term in numerator and denominator by x to obtain
$$\frac{\left(\frac{8}{x}\right) - \left(\frac{1}{\sqrt[3]{x^2}}\right)}{\left(\frac{2}{x}\right) + 1} \to 0 \text{ as } x \to -\infty.$$

12. Divide each term in numerator and denominator by x^3 to see that the limit is zero.

13. $\dfrac{4x^2 - x}{x^2 + 9} = \dfrac{4 - (1/x)}{1 + (9/x^2)} \to 4$ as $x \to +\infty$, so the limit is $\sqrt{4} = 2$.

14. Divide each term in numerator and denominator by x, because in effect the "term of largest degree" in the numerator is x. Of course in the numerator we must divide each term under the radical by x^3; the result is that
$$\frac{\sqrt[3]{1 - \frac{8}{x^2} + \frac{1}{x^3}}}{3 - \frac{4}{x}} \to \frac{1}{3} \text{ as } x \to -\infty.$$

15. $\sqrt{x^2 + 2x} - x = \dfrac{x^2 + 2x - x^2}{\sqrt{x^2 + 2x} + x} = \dfrac{2x}{\sqrt{x^2 + 2x} + x} = \dfrac{2}{1 - \sqrt{1 + (2/x)}} \to +\infty$ as $x \to -\infty$.

16. $\lim\limits_{x \to -\infty} \left(2x - \sqrt{4x^2 - 5x}\right) = \lim\limits_{x \to -\infty} \dfrac{4x^2 - (4x^2 - 5x)}{2x + \sqrt{4x^2 - 5x}} = \lim\limits_{x \to -\infty} \dfrac{5x}{2x + \sqrt{4x^2 - 5x}}$
$= \lim\limits_{x \to -\infty} \dfrac{5}{2 + \left(\dfrac{\sqrt{4x^2 - 5x}}{-\sqrt{x^2}}\right)} = \lim\limits_{x \to -\infty} \dfrac{5}{2 - \sqrt{4 - (5/x)}} = -\infty.$

18. Matches 4.7.9 (i)
20. Matches 4.7.9 (d)
22. Matches 4.7.9 (c)
24. Matches 4.7.9 (h)
26. Matches 4.7.9 (b)
28. Matches 4.7.9 (e)

29. There are no critical points and no inflection points. The only intercept is at $(0, -\frac{2}{3})$. The line $x = 3$ is a vertical asymptote and the x-axis is a horizontal asymptote. The graph is decreasing for all x, is concave upward for $x > 3$, and is concave downward for $x < 3$.

30. First,
$$f'(x) = \frac{4}{(5 - x)^2} \text{ and } f''(x) = \frac{8}{(5 - x)^3}.$$
The graph is increasing and concave upward for $x < 5$, increasing and concave downward for $x > 5$. There are no extrema or inflection points, and the y-intercept is $(0, \frac{4}{5})$. The line $x = 5$ is a vertical asymptote and the x-axis is a horizontal asymptote.

31. Here we have
$$f'(x) = -\frac{6}{(x + 2)^3} \text{ and } f''(x) = \frac{18}{(x + 2)^4}.$$
The graph is increasing and concave upward for $x < -2$, decreasing and concave upward for $x > -2$. There are no extrema and no inflection points; the y-intercept is $(0, \frac{3}{4})$. The line $x = -2$ is a vertical asymptote and the x-axis is a horizontal asymptote.

32. First, $f'(x) = -8/(3 - x)^3$ and $f''(x) = -24/(3 - x)^4$. The graph is decreasing and concave downward for $x < 3$, increasing and concave downward for $x > 3$. There are no extrema and no

inflection points. The y-intercept is $(0, -\frac{4}{9})$. The line $x = 3$ is a vertical asymptote and the x-axis is a horizontal asymptote.

33. $f'(x) = -6/(2x-3)^4$ and $f''(x) = 48/(2x-3)^5$. The graph is decreasing and concave downward for $x < \frac{3}{2}$, decreasing and concave upward for $x > \frac{3}{2}$. There are no extrema and no inflection points. The y-intercept is $(0, -\frac{1}{27})$. The line $x = \frac{3}{2}$ is a vertical asymptote and the x-axis is a horizontal asymptote.

34. Here,
$$f'(x) = -\frac{2}{(x-1)^2} \quad \text{and} \quad f''(x) = \frac{4}{(x-1)^3}.$$
The graph is decreasing and concave downward if $x < 1$, decreasing and concave upward if $x > 1$. There are no extrema and no inflection points; the y-intercept is $(0, -1)$ and the only x-intercept is $(-1, 0)$. The line $x = 1$ is a vertical asymptote and the line $y = 1$ is a horizontal asymptote.

35. Here we have
$$f'(x) = \frac{2x}{(x^2+1)^2} \quad \text{and} \quad f''(x) = \frac{2(1-3x^2)}{(x^2+1)^3}.$$
The graph is concave downward if $|x| > 1/\sqrt{3}$, concave upward if $|x| < 1/\sqrt{3}$. It is decreasing for $x < 0$ and increasing if $x > 0$, and the line $y = 1$ is a horizontal asymptote. The origin is a global minimum and the only intercept, and there are points of inflection where $x^2 = \frac{1}{3}$ and $y = \frac{1}{4}$.

36.
$$f'(x) = \frac{2(1-x^2)}{(x^2+1)^2} \quad \text{and} \quad f''(x) = \frac{4x(x^2-3)}{(x^2+1)^3}.$$
The graph is decreasing for $x < -1$ and for $x > 1$, increasing on the interval $(-1, 1)$. It is concave down if $x < -\sqrt{3}$ and if $0 < x < \sqrt{3}$, concave up if $-\sqrt{3} < x < 0$ and if $\sqrt{3} < x$. The origin is the only intercept and is also an inflection point; there are also inflection points at
$$\left(-\sqrt{3}, -\frac{1}{2}\sqrt{3}\right) \quad \text{and at} \quad \left(\sqrt{3}, \frac{1}{2}\sqrt{3}\right).$$
The global maximum is at $(1, 1)$ and the global minimum is at $(-1, -1)$. The x-axis is a horizontal asymptote.

37.
$$f'(x) = -\frac{2x}{(x^2-9)^2} \quad \text{and} \quad f''(x) = \frac{6(x^2+3)}{(x^2-9)^3}.$$
The graph is increasing for $x < -3$ and for $-3 < x < 0$; the graph is decreasing for $0 < x < 3$ and for $3 < x$. It is concave upward if $x < -3$ and if $x > 3$, concave downward on $(-3, 3)$. The only extremum is the local maximum and y-intercept at the point $(0, -\frac{1}{9})$, and there are no points of inflection. The x-axis is a horizontal asymptote and the lines $x = -3$ and $x = 3$ are vertical asymptotes.

38.
$$f'(x) = \frac{x^2+4}{(4-x^2)^2} \quad \text{and} \quad f''(x) = \frac{2x(x^2+12)}{(4-x^2)^3}.$$
The graph is increasing for $x < -2$, for $-2 < x < 2$, and for $2 < x$. It is concave upward for $x < -2$ and for $0 < x < 2$, concave downward for $-2 < x < 0$ and for $x > 2$. The origin is the only intercept and the only inflection point; there are no extrema. The x-axis is a horizontal asymptote, and the lines $x = -2$ and $x = 2$ are vertical asymptotes.

39.
$$f'(x) = -\frac{2x+1}{(x-2)^2(x+3)^2} \quad \text{and} \quad f''(x) = \frac{2(3x^2+3x+7)}{(x-2)^3(x+3)^3}.$$

Note that the numerator of $f''(x)$ is always positive. The graph is increasing for $x < -3$ and for $-3 < x < -\frac{1}{2}$, decreasing for $-\frac{1}{2} < x < 2$ and for $2 < x$. It is concave upward for $x < -3$ and for $x > 2$, concave downward on the interval $(-3, 2)$. There is a local maximum at $(-\frac{1}{2}, -\frac{4}{25})$, but no other extrema and no inflection points. The only intercept is $(0, -\frac{1}{6})$, the x-axis is a horizontal asymptote, and the lines $x = -3$ and $x = 2$ are vertical asymptotes.

40.
$$f'(x) = -\frac{2(2x-1)(x+1)}{x^2(x-2)^2} \quad \text{and} \quad f''(x) = \frac{2(4x^3 + 3x^2 - 6x + 4)}{(x^2 - 2x)^3}.$$

The zeros of $f'(x)$ occur at -1 and 0.5, and the only zero of $f''(x)$ is at $x \approx -1.8517$. The graph is decreasing for $x < -1$, for $0.5 < x < 2$, and for $x > 2$; increasing for $-1 < x < 0$ and for $0 < x < 0.5$. It is concave downward for $x < -1.85^*$ and on $(0, 2)$, concave upward for $x > 2$ and on $(-1.85^*, 0)$. The line $y = 2$ is a horizontal asymptote and the lines $x = 0$ and $x = 2$ are vertical asymptotes. There is a local minimum at $(-1, 1)$, a local maximum at $(0.5, -2)$, and a point of inflection at $(-1.85^*, 1.10^*)$. (*Coordinates approximate.)

41.
$$f'(x) = \frac{x^2 - 1}{x^2} \quad \text{and} \quad f''(x) = \frac{2}{x^3}.$$

The graph is increasing if $x < -1$ and if $x > 1$, decreasing on $(-1, 0)$ and on $(0, 1)$. It is concave downward if $x < 0$ and concave upward if $x > 0$. There is a local maximum at the point $(-1, -2)$ and a local minimum at $(1, 2)$. There are no inflection points The y-axis is a vertical asymptote and the $45°$-line $y = x$ is a slant asymptote.

42.
$$f'(x) = \frac{2(x^3 - 1)}{x^3} \quad \text{and} \quad f''(x) = \frac{6}{x^4}.$$

The graph is concave upward for all $x \neq 0$, is increasing for $x < 0$ and for $x > 1$, and is decreasing on $(0, 1)$. There is a local minimum at $(1, 3)$, but there are no inflection points and no other extrema. The only intercept occurs where $x \approx -0.79$. The y-axis is a vertical asymptote and the line $y = 2x$ is a slant asymptote.

43.
$$f'(x) = \frac{x(x-2)}{(x-1)^2} \quad \text{and} \quad f''(x) = \frac{2}{(x-1)^3}.$$

The graph is increasing for $x < 0$ and for $x > 2$, decreasing on $(0, 1)$ and on $(1, 2)$. It is concave upward if $x > 1$, concave downward if $x < 1$. The origin is a local maximum and the only intercept, the only other extremum is a local minimum at $(2, 4)$, and there are no inflection points. The lines $y = x + 1$ and $x = 1$ are asymptotes.

44.
$$f'(x) = 2 - \frac{2}{(x-1)^3} \quad \text{and} \quad f''(x) = \frac{6}{(x-1)^4}.$$

The graph is increasing for $x < 1$ and for $x > 2$ and decreasing on $(1, 2)$. It is concave upward for $x < 1$ and for $x > 1$. The only extremum is a local minimum at $(2, 4)$, and there are no points of inflection. The origin is the only intercept. The vertical line $x = 1$ and the line $y = 2x - 1$ are asymptotes.

45.
$$f'(x) = -\frac{2}{(x-1)^3} \quad \text{and} \quad f''(x) = \frac{6}{(x-1)^4}.$$

The graph is decreasing for $x > 1$ and increasing for $x < 1$; it is concave upward for all $x \neq 1$. There are no intercepts other than $(0, 1)$, no extrema, and no inflection points. The x-axis is a horizontal asymptote and the line $x = 1$ is a vertical asymptote.

46.
$$f'(x) = -\frac{2x}{(x^2 - 4)^2} \quad \text{and} \quad f''(x) = \frac{6x^2 + 8}{(x^2 - 4)^3}.$$

The graph is increasing for $x < -2$ and on $(-2, 0)$, decreasing on $(0, 2)$ and for $x > 2$. It is concave upward if $|x| > 2$ and concave downward if $|x| < 2$. The only intercept is at the point $(0, -0.25)$, which is also a local maximum; there are no other extrema and no inflection points. The two vertical lines $x = -2$ and $x = 2$ are asymptotes, as is the x-axis.

47.
$$f'(x) = \frac{1}{(x+1)^2} \quad \text{and} \quad f''(x) = -\frac{2}{(x+1)^3}.$$

The graph is increasing for all $x \neq -1$, concave upward if $x < -1$, and concave downward if $x > -1$. There are no extrema and no inflection points. The only intercept is $(0, 0)$. The line $x = -1$ is a vertical asymptote and the line $y = 1$ is a horizontal asymptote.

48.
$$f'(x) = -\frac{3}{(x+1)^4} \quad \text{and} \quad f''(x) = \frac{12}{(x+1)^5}.$$

The graph is decreasing for all $x \neq -1$, concave upward for $x > -1$, and concave downward for $x < -1$. There are no extrema and no inflection points; $(0, 1)$ is the only intercept. The line $x = -1$ is a vertical asymptote and the x-axis is a horizontal asymptote.

49.
$$f(x) = \frac{1}{x^2 - x - 2} = \frac{1}{(x-1)(x-2)} : \quad f'(x) = -\frac{2x-1}{(x+1)^2(x-2)^2} \quad \text{and} \quad f''(x) = \frac{6(x^2 - x + 1)}{(x+1)^3(x-2)^3}.$$

It is useful to notice the discontinuities at $x = -1$ and at $x = 2$, that $f(x) \to 0$ as $x \to +\infty$ and as $x \to -\infty$, and that $f(x) > 0$ for $x > 2$ and for $x < -1$ while $f(x) < 0$ on the interval $(-1, 2)$. The denominator in $f'(x)$ is never negative, so the graph is decreasing for $\frac{1}{2} < x < 2$ and for $2 < x$ and increasing for $x < -1$ and for $-1 < x < \frac{1}{2}$. The graph is concave upward for $x > 2$ and for $x < -1$, concave downward on $(-1, 2)$. There are no inflection points or intercepts, but there is a local maximum at $(\frac{1}{2}, -\frac{4}{9})$. The x-axis is a horizontal asymptote and the lines $x = -1$ and $x = 2$ are vertical asymptotes.

50.
$$f'(x) = -\frac{3x - 1}{(x-1)^2(x+1)^3} \quad \text{and} \quad f''(x) = \frac{4(3x^2 - 2x + 1)}{(x-1)^3(x+1)^4}.$$

The graph is decreasing for $x < -1$, $\frac{1}{3} < x < 1$, and $x > 1$; it is increasing for $-1 < x < \frac{1}{3}$. It is concave downward for $x < 1$ (except at $x = -1$), concave upward for $x > 1$. There is a local maximum at $(\frac{1}{3}, -\frac{27}{32})$ and an intercept at $(0, -1)$, but no other intercepts or extrema and no inflection points. Note that $f(x) \to -\infty$ as $x \to -1$ and as $x \to +1^-$, but $f(x) \to +\infty$ as $x \to +1^+$. Also $f(x) \to 0$ as $|x| \to +\infty$. Thus the lines $x = -1$ and $x = 1$ are vertical asymptotes and the x-axis is a horizontal asymptote.

51.
$$f'(x) = 1 + \frac{4}{x^2} \quad \text{and} \quad f''(x) = -\frac{8}{x^3}.$$

The graph is increasing for all $x \neq 0$, concave upward for $x < 0$, and concave downward for $x > 0$. The only intercepts are $(-2, 0)$ and $(2, 0)$. Because $f(x) \to +\infty$ as $x \to 0^-$ and $f(x) \to -\infty$ as $x \to 0^+$, the y-axis is a vertical asymptote. The line $y = x$ is a slant asymptote, and sketching it helps in drawing the graph of $y = f(x)$. There are no intercepts and no extrema, and the graph resembles that of $y = x$ for $|x|$ large.

52.
$$f'(x) = -\frac{x^2 + 1}{(x^2 - 1)^2} \quad \text{and} \quad f''(x) = \frac{2x(x^2 + 3)}{(x^2 - 1)^3}.$$

The graph is decreasing on $(-\infty, -1)$, on $(-1, 1)$, and on $(1, \infty)$; it is concave upward for $x > 1$ and for $-1 < x < 0$, concave downward for $0 < x < 1$ and for $x < -1$. The only intercept is $(0, 0)$, which is also an inflection point. Note that $f(x) \to 0$ as $|x| \to \infty$, so the x-axis is a horizontal asymptote; $f(x) \to +\infty$ as $x \to -1^+$ and as $x \to +1^+$, while $f(x) \to -\infty$ as $x \to -1^-$ and as $x \to +1^-$, so the lines $x = -1$ and $x = 1$ are vertical asymptotes. There are no extrema.

53.
$$f'(x) = 1 + \frac{8}{x^3} \quad \text{and} \quad f''(x) = -\frac{24}{x^4},$$

By inspection of $f'(x)$ it is clear that the graph is increasing for $x > 0$ and for $x < -2$ and decreasing for $-2 < x < 0$; the graph is also concave downward for all $x \neq 0$. The graph resembles that of $y = x$ for $|x|$ large, and indeed the line $y = x$ is a slant asymptote. There is a local maximum at the point $(-2, 3)$ and an intercept at $(\sqrt[3]{4}, 0)$, but no other intercepts or extrema and no inflection points. As $x \to 0$ we see that $f(x) \to -\infty$, so the y-axis is an asymptote.

54. First note that $f(x) = \dfrac{x^2 - 4 + 5}{x - 2} = x + 2 + \dfrac{5}{x - 2}$. Consequently $f(x) \approx x + 2$ if $|x|$ is large, and consequently the line $y = x + 2$ is a slant asymptote. As $x \to 2^+$, $f(x) \to +\infty$, while $f(x) \to -\infty$ as $x \to 2^-$. Therefore the vertical line $x = 2$ is also an asymptote. Next,

$$f'(x) = 1 - \frac{5}{(x - 2)^2} = \frac{(x - 2)^2 - 5}{(x - 2)^2} \quad \text{and} \quad f''(x) = \frac{10}{(x - 2)^3}.$$

Thus the graph of f is increasing if $(x - 2)^2 > 5$ and decreasing if $(x - 2)^2 < 5$. That is, the graph is increasing for $x < 2 - \sqrt{5}$ and for $x > 2 + \sqrt{5}$, decreasing for $2 - \sqrt{5} < x < 2$ and for $2 < x < 2 + \sqrt{5}$. The graph is concave upward for $x > 2$ and concave downward for $x < 2$. So there is a local maximum where $x = 2 - \sqrt{5}$ and a local minimum where $x = 2 + \sqrt{5}$. The approximate coordinates of these two points are $(-0.236, -0.472)$ and $(4.236, 8.476)$, respectively. There are no other extrema, no inflection points, and $(0, -1/2)$ is the only intercept. The vertical line $x = 2$ is a second asymptote, and $f(x) \to +\infty$ as $x \to 2^+$ while $f(x) \to -\infty$ as $x \to 2^-$.

55. The x-axis is a horizontal asymptote, and there are vertical asymptotes at $x = 0$ and $x = 2$. There are local minima at $(-1.9095, -0.3132)$ and $(1.3907, 3.2649)$ and a local maximum at $(4.5188, 0.1630)$ (all coordinates approximate, of course), and inflection points at $(-2.8119, -0.2768)$ and $(6.0623, 0.1449)$.

56. The line $y = 1$ is a horizontal asymptote and the lines $x = 0$ and $x = 4$ are vertical asymptotes. There is a local minimum at $(-1, 0)$ and inflection points at $(-1.5300, 0.0983)$ and $(2.1540, 0.9826)$. (Numbers with decimal points are approximations.)

57. The x-axis is a horizontal asymptote and there are vertical asymptotes at $x = 0$ and $x = 2$. There are local minima at $(-2.8173, -0.1783)$ and $(1.4695, 5.5444)$ and local maxima at $(-1, 0)$ and $(4.3478, 0.1998)$. There are inflection points at $(-4.3611, -0.1576)$, $(-1.2569, -0.0434)$, and $(5.7008, 0.1769)$. (Numbers with decimal points are approximations.)

58. The horizontal line $y = 1$ is an asymptote, as are the vertical lines $x = 0$ and $x = 2$. There are local maxima at $(-5.6056, 1.1726)$ and $(1.6056, -8.0861)$, $(-1.2994, 0.2289)$, and $(3.6777, 0.1204)$. (Numbers with decimal points are approximations.)

59. The horizontal line $y = 0$ is an asymptote, as are the vertical lines $x = 0$ and $x = 2$. There are local minima at $(-2.6643, -0.2160)$, $(1.2471, 14.1117)$, and $(3, 0)$; there are local maxima at $(-1, 0)$ and $(5.4172, 0.1296)$. There are inflection points at $(-4.0562, -0.1900)$, $(-1.2469, -0.0538)$, $(3.3264, 0.0308)$, and $(7.4969, 0.1147)$. (Numbers with decimal points are approximations.)

60. The horizontal line $y = 0$ is an asymptote, as are the vertical lines $x = 0$ and $x = 2$. There are local minima at $(-1.5125, -1.4172)$ and $(3, 0)$, local maxima at $(1.2904, -25.4845)$ and $(9.2221, 0.0519)$ and inflection points at $(-2.0145, -1.2127)$, $(4.2422, 0.0145)$, and $(14.2106, 0.0460)$. (Numbers with decimal points are approximations.)

61. The x-axis is a horizontal asymptote; there are vertical asymptotes at $x = -0.5321$, $x = 0.6527$, and $x = 2.8794$. There is a local minimum at $(0, 0)$ and a local maximum at $(\sqrt[3]{2}, -0.9008)$. There are no inflection points (Numbers with decimal points are approximations.)

62. The x-axis is a horizontal asymptote; there is a vertical asymptote at $x = -1.1038$. There is a local minimum at $(0, 0)$ and a local maximum at $(2.1544, 4.3168)$. There are inflection points at $(1.8107, 2.9787)$ and $(2.4759, 3.4299)$. (Numbers with decimal points are approximations.)

63. The line $y = x + 3$ is a slant asymptote in both the positive and negative directions; thus there is no horizontal asymptote. There is a vertical asymptote at $x = -1.1038$. There are local maxima at $(-2.3562, -1.8292)$ and $(2.3761, 18.5247)$, local minima at $(0.8212, 0.6146)$ and $(5.0827, 11.0886)$. There are inflection points at $(1.9433, 11.3790)$ and $(2.7040, 16.8013)$. (Numbers with decimal points are approximations.)

64. The line $2y = x$ is a slant asymptote in both the positive and negative directions; thus there is no horizontal asymptote. There is a vertical asymptote at $x = -1.4757$. There is a local maximum at $(-2.9821, -2.1859)$ and a local minimum at $(0.7868, -2.8741)$. There are inflection points at $(-0.2971, 0.7736)$, $(0.5713, 0.5566)$, $(1, -2)$, and $(9.1960, 4.6515)$. (Numbers with decimal points are approximations.)

65. The line $2y = x$ is a slant asymptote in both the positive and negative directions; thus there is no horizontal asymptote. There also are no vertical asymptotes. There is a local maximum at $(0.2201, 0.6001)$, a local minimum at $(0.8222, -2.9691)$, and inflection points at $(-2.2417, -1.2782)$, $(-0.5946, -0.1211)$, $(0.2564, -1.6820)$, and $(0.6701, -2.2501)$. (Numbers with decimal points are approximations.)

66. The line $2y = x$ is a slant asymptote in both the positive and negative directions; thus there is no horizontal asymptote. There also are no vertical asymptotes. There are local maxima at $(-1.1379, 0.4263)$ and $(0.4727, 0.5851)$, local minima at $(0.3948, -0.4939)$ and $(1.2036, -0.7702)$, and inflection points at $(-2.3813, -0.2531)$, $(-0.7752, 0.3733)$, $(0.1896, 0.4866)$, $(0.8903, -0.1458)$, and $(1.5535, -0.4446)$. (Numbers with decimal points are approximations.)

67. The line $2y = x$ is a slant asymptote in both the positive and negative directions; thus there is no horizontal asymptote. There is a vertical asymptote at $x = -1.7277$. There are local maxima at $(-3.1594, -2.3665)$ and $(1.3381, 1.7792)$, local minima at $(-0.5379, -0.3591)$ and $(1.8786, 1.4388)$. There are inflection points at $(0, 0)$, $(0.5324, 0.4805)$, $(1.1607, 1.4294)$, and $(1.4627, 1.6727)$. (Numbers with decimal points are approximations.)

68. The line $6x + 10 = 9y$ is a slant asymptote in both the positive and negative directions; thus there is no horizontal asymptote. There is a vertical asymptote at $x = -0.8529$. There are local maxima at $(-1.3637, -0.0573)$ and $(0.7710, 1.5254)$, local minima at $(0, \frac{3}{2})$ and $(1.1703, 1.4578)$. There are inflection points at $(0.5460, 1.5154)$, $(1.0725, 1.4793)$, $(1.3880, 1.9432)$, and $(1.8247, 2.6353)$. (Numbers with decimal points are approximations.)

69. Sketch the parabola $y = x^2$, but modify it by changing its behavior near $x = 0$: Let $y \to +\infty$ as $x \to 0^+$ and let $y \to -\infty$ as $x \to 0^-$. Using calculus, we compute

$$f'(x) = \frac{2(x^3 - 1)}{x^2} \quad \text{and} \quad f''(x) = \frac{2(x^3 + 2)}{x^3}.$$

It follows that the graph is decreasing for $0 < x < 1$ and for $x < 0$, increasing for $x > 1$. It is concave upward for $x < -\sqrt[3]{2}$ and also for $x > 0$, concave downward for $-\sqrt[3]{2} < x < 0$. The only intercept is at $(-\sqrt[3]{2}, 0)$; this is also the only inflection point. There is a local minimum at $(1, 3)$. The y-axis is a vertical asymptote.

70. Because $f(x) \approx x^3$ when $|x|$ is large, we obtain the graph of f by making "modifications" in the graph of $y = x^3$ at and near the discontinuity of $f(x)$ at $x = 1$. We are aided in sketching the graph of f by finding its x-intercepts—these are approximately -1.654 and 2.172—as well as its y-intercept 12 and its inflection points $(2.22, 1.04)$ and $(-0.75, 6.44)$ (also approximations).

Chapter 4 Miscellaneous

1. $dy = \frac{3}{2}(4x - x^2)^{1/2}(4 - 2x)\,dx$
2. $dy = [24x^2(x^2 + 9)^{1/2} + 4x^3(x^2 + 9)^{-1/2}(2x)]\,dx$
4. $dy = 2x\cos(x^2)\,dx$
6. $dy = \dfrac{\sin 2x - 2x\cos 2x}{\sin^2 2x}\,dx$
7. Let $f(x) = x^{1/2}$; $f'(x) = \frac{1}{2}x^{-1/2}$. Then

$$\sqrt{6401} = f(6400 + 1) \approx f(6400) + 1 \cdot f'(6400)$$
$$= 80 + \frac{1}{160} = \frac{12801}{160} = 80.00625.$$

   (Actually, $\sqrt{6401} \approx 80.00624976$.)

8. Choose $f(x) = \dfrac{1}{x}$; $f'(x) = -\dfrac{1}{x^2}$. Choose $x = 1$ and $\Delta x = 0.000007$. Then

$$\frac{1}{1.000007} = f(x + \Delta x) \approx f(x) + f'(x)\,\Delta x$$
$$= 1 - 0.000007 = 0.999993.$$

9. $(20003)^{10} \approx 2^{10} + 10 \cdot 2^9 \cdot (0.0003) = 1025.536$.
10. $\sqrt[3]{999} = \sqrt[3]{1000} - 1 \cdot \frac{1}{3}(1000)^{-2/3} = 10 - \frac{1}{300} = \frac{2999}{300} \approx 9.996667$.
12. Take $f(x) = x^{1/3}$; then $f'(x) = \frac{1}{3}x^{-2/3}$. Take $x = 64$ and $\Delta x = -2$. Thus

$$(62)^{1/3} = f(x + \Delta x) \approx f(x) + f'(x)\,\Delta x$$
$$= (64)^{1/3} + (-2)\left(\frac{1}{3}\right)(64)^{-2/3} = \frac{95}{24} \approx 3.958.$$

14. Take $f(x) = x^{1/5}$; then $f'(x) = \frac{1}{5}x^{-4/5}$. Take $x = 32$ and $\Delta x = -2$. Then

$$(30)^{1/5} = f(x + \Delta x) \approx f(x) + f'(x)\,\Delta x$$
$$= (32)^{1/5} + (-2)\left(\frac{1}{5}\right)(32)^{-4/5} = 2 - \frac{1}{40} = \frac{79}{40} = 1.975.$$

16. With $f(x) = x^{1/10}$, $f'(x) = \frac{1}{10}x^{-9/10}$, $x = 1024$, and $\Delta x = -24$, we obtain

$$(1000)^{1/10} = f(x + \Delta x) \approx f(x) + f'(x)\,\Delta x$$
$$= (1024)^{1/10} + (-24)\left(\frac{1}{10}\right)(1024)^{-9/10}$$
$$= 2 - \frac{3}{640} = \frac{1277}{640} \approx 1.9953.$$

17. $dV = 3s^2\,ds$, so with $s = 5$ and $\Delta s = 0.1$, we obtain $\Delta V \approx 3(5)^2(0.1) = 7.5$ (cubic inches).

18. With radius r and area $A = \pi r^2$, we have $dA = 2\pi r\, dr$. We take $r = 10$ and $\Delta r = -0.2$ to obtain
$$\Delta A \approx (2\pi)(10)(-0.2) = -4\pi \text{ (cm}^2\text{)}.$$

20. If $V = 1000/p$ then $dV = -1000/p^2$. With $p = 100$ and $\Delta p = -1$, we obtain
$$\Delta V \approx -\frac{1000}{100^2}(-1) = 0.1 \text{ (cubic inches)}.$$

22. Here, $dL = (-13)(10^{30})E^{-14}\, dE$. We take $E = 110$ and $\Delta E = +1$ and obtain
$$dL \approx (-13)(10^{30})\left(110^{-14}\right)(+1) \approx -342 \text{ hours}.$$
The actual decrease is $L(110) - L(111) \approx 2896.6 - 2575.1 \approx 321.5$ (hours).

23. First, $f'(x) = 1 + \dfrac{1}{x^2}$, so $f'(x)$ exists for $1 < x < 3$ and f is continuous for $1 \leq x \leq 3$. So we are to solve
$$\frac{f(3) - f(1)}{3 - 1} = f'(c);$$
that is,
$$\frac{3 - \frac{1}{3} - 1 + 1}{2} = 1 + \frac{1}{c^2}.$$
After simplifications we find that $c^2 = 3$. Therefore, because $1 < c < 3$, $c = +\sqrt{3}$.

24. Every polynomial is continuous and differentiable everywhere, so all hypotheses are met.
$$\frac{f(3) - f(-2)}{3 - (-2)} = \frac{26 - (-14)}{5} = 8 = f'(c) = 3c^2 + 1,$$
so $c^2 = 7/3$. Both roots lie in $(-2, 3)$, so both $+\sqrt{7/3}$ and $-\sqrt{7/3}$ are solutions.

26. Here,
$$\frac{(1)^3 - (-2)^3}{1 - (-2)} = 3 = 3c^2,$$
so $c^2 = 1$. Because $+1$ is not in the interval $(-2, 1)$, only the answer $c = -1$ is correct.

28. $\dfrac{f(4) - f(0)}{4 - 0} = f'(c)$: $\dfrac{2 - 0}{4} = \frac{1}{2}c^{-1/2}$; $c^{-1/2} = 1$; $c = 1$.

29. $f'(x) = 2x - 6$ and $f''(x) = 2$. So the graph is increasoing for $x > 3$, decreasing for $x < 3$, and always concave upward. Thus there is a global minimum at $(3, -5)$, no other extrema, and no inflection points. Because $f(x) \to +\infty$ as $x \to +\infty$ and as $x \to -\infty$, there are two x-intercepts; the y-intercept is at $(0, 4)$.

30. $f'(x) = 6(x - 3)(x + 2)$ and $f''(x) = 6(2x - 1)$. So the graph is increasing for $x < -2$ and for $x > 3$, decreasing for $-2 < x < 3$. It is concave upward for $x > 1/2$ and concave downward for $x < 1/2$. Therefore $(0.5, -18.5)$ is an inflection point. There is a local maximum at $(-2, 44)$, a local minimum at $(3, -81)$, and no other extrema. The intercepts are (about) $(-3.558, 0)$, $(5.058, 0)$, and (exactly) $(0, 0)$.

31. $f'(x) = 15(x^4 - x^2 + 4) > 0$ for all x; $f''(x) = 30x(2x^2 - 1)$, so the graph is concave upward for $-1/\sqrt{2} < x < 0$ and for $x > 1/\sqrt{2}$, concave downward for $x < -1/\sqrt{2}$ and for $0 < x < 1/\sqrt{2}$. There are no extrema, there are inflection points where $f''(x) = 0$, and $(0, 0)$ is the only intercept.

32. Here, $f'(x) = \dfrac{3(1 - x)}{2x^{1/2}}$ and $f''(x) = -\dfrac{3(x + 1)}{4x^{3/2}}$. Begin by noting that $f(x)$ is continuous for $x \geq 0$, though $f'(0)$ is undefined. The graph is increasing for $x < 1$ and decreasing for $x > 1$; it is concave

downward for all $x > 0$. The intercepts are $(0, 0)$ and $(3, 0)$. In sketching the graph it helps to note that $f'(3) \approx -1.732$ and that $f'(x) \to \infty$ as $x \to 0^+$.

33. $f'(x) = \dfrac{1-4x}{3x^{2/3}}$ and $f''(x) = -\dfrac{2(2x+1)}{9x^{5/3}}$.

34. Let $g(x) = x^5 + x - 5$. Then $g(2) = 29 > 0$ while $g(1) = -3 < 0$. Because $g(x)$ is a polynomial, it has the intermediate value property. Therefore the equation $g(x) = 0$ has at least one solution in the interval $1 \leq x \leq 2$. Moreover, $g'(x) = 5x^4 + 1$, so $g'(x) > 0$ for all x. Consequently g is increasing on the set of all real numbers, and so takes on each value—including zero—at most once. We may conclude that the equation $g(x) = 0$ has exactly one solution, and hence that the equation $x^5 + x = 5$ has exactly one solution. (The solution is approximately 1.299152792.)

36. $f'(x) = 100(x+1)^{99}$, $f''(x) = 9900(x+1)^{98}$, and $f'''(x) = 970200(x+1)^{97}$.

38. $h'(y) = \tfrac{3}{2}(3y-1)^{-1/2}$, $h''(y) = -\tfrac{9}{4}(3y-1)^{-3/2}$, and $h'''(y) = \tfrac{81}{8}(3y-1)^{-5/2}$.

40. $g'(x) = -\dfrac{2x}{(x^2+9)^2}$, $g''(x) = \dfrac{6x^2-18}{(x^2+9)^3}$, and $g'''(x) = \dfrac{216x-24x^3}{(x^2+9)^4}$.

42. $f'(z) = \tfrac{1}{3}z^{-2/3} - \tfrac{3}{5}z^{-6/5}$, $f''(z) = -\tfrac{2}{9}z^{-5/3} + \tfrac{18}{25}z^{-11/5}$, and $f'''(z) = \tfrac{10}{27}z^{-8/3} - \tfrac{198}{125}z^{-16/5}$.

44. $g'(t) = 12(3-t)^{-5/2}$, $g''(t) = 30(3-t)^{-7/2}$, and $g'''(t) = 105(3-t)^{-9/2}$.

45. $x^{-2/3} + y^{-2/3}\dfrac{dy}{dx} = 0$, so $\dfrac{dy}{dx} = -(y/x)^{2/3}$.

$$\dfrac{d^2y}{dx^2} = -\dfrac{2}{3}(y/x)^{-1/3} \cdot \dfrac{x(dy/dx)-y}{x^2} = -\dfrac{2}{3} \cdot \dfrac{x(dy/dx)-y}{x^{5/3}y^{1/3}}$$

$$= \dfrac{2}{3} \cdot \dfrac{y+x^{1/3}y^{2/3}}{x^{5/3}y^{1/3}} = \dfrac{2}{3}y^{2/3} \cdot \dfrac{x^{1/3}+y^{1/3}}{x^{5/3}y^{1/3}} = \dfrac{2}{3}(y/x^5)^{1/3}.$$

46. $\dfrac{dy}{dx} = \dfrac{3y-4x}{10y-3x}$; $\dfrac{d^2y}{dx^2} = -\dfrac{1550}{(10y-3x)^3}$.

48. Given: $\sin(xy) = xy$. The only solution of $\sin z = z$ is $z = 0$. Therefore $xy = 0$. Thus $x = 0$ or $y = 0$. This means that the graph of the equation $\sin(xy) = xy$ consists of the coordinate axes. The y-axis is not the graph of a function, so the derivative is defined only for $x \neq 0$, and $dy/dx = 0$ for $x \neq 0$. Therefore also $d^2y/dx^2 = 0$ for $x \neq 0$.

50. $x^5 + xy^4 = 1$: $5x^4 + y^4 + 4xy^3\dfrac{dy}{dx} = 0$, so $\dfrac{dy}{dx} = -\dfrac{5x^4+y^4}{4xy^3}$.

$$\dfrac{d^2y}{dx^2} = -\dfrac{4xy^3(20x^3+4y^3\tfrac{dy}{dx}) - (5x^4+y^4)(4y^3+12xy^2\tfrac{dy}{dx})}{16x^2y^6}$$

$$= \dfrac{20x^4y^3+4y^7+(60x^5y^2+12xy^6)\tfrac{dy}{dx} - 80x^4y^3 - 16xy^6\tfrac{dy}{dx}}{16x^2y^6}$$

$$= \dfrac{4y^7 - 60x^4y^3 + (60x^5y^2 - 4xy^6)\tfrac{dy}{dx}}{16x^2y^6}$$

$$= \dfrac{4y^5 - 60x^4y + (60x^5 - 4xy^4)\tfrac{dy}{dx}}{16x^2y^4}$$

$$= \dfrac{4y^5 - 60x^4y + (4xy^4 - 60x^5) \cdot \left(\dfrac{5x^4+y^4}{4xy^3}\right)}{16x^2y^4}$$

$$= \dfrac{16xy^8 - 240x^5y^4 + 20x^5y^4 + 4xy^8 - 300x^9 - 60x^5y^4}{64x^3y^7}$$

$$= \frac{20xy^8 - 280x^5y^4 - 300x^9}{64x^3y^7} = \frac{5y^8 - 70x^4y^4 - 75x^8}{16x^2y^7}$$
$$= \frac{5(y^8 - 14x^4y^4 - 15x^8)}{16x^2y^7} = \frac{5(y^4 + x^4)(y^4 - 15x^4)}{16x^2y^7}.$$

But $x^4 + y^4 = \dfrac{1}{x}$, so $\dfrac{d^2y}{dx^2} = \dfrac{5(y^4 - 15x^4)}{16x^3y^7}$.

52. $(x^2 - y^2)^2 = 4xy$:

$$2(x^2 - y^2)(2x - 2y\frac{dy}{dx}) = 4x\frac{dy}{dx} + 4y$$
$$(x^2 - y^2) \cdot x - (x^2 - y^2) \cdot y\frac{dy}{dx} = x\frac{dy}{dx} + y$$
$$(x + x^2y - y^3)\frac{dy}{dx} = x^3 - xy^2 - y$$
$$\frac{dy}{dx} = \frac{x(x^2 - y^2) - y}{x + y(x^2 - y^2)} = \frac{x^3 - xy^2 - y}{x + x^2y - y^3}.$$

$$\frac{d^2y}{dx^2} = \frac{(x + x^2y - y^3)\left(3x^2 - x2y\frac{dy}{dx} - y^2 - \frac{dy}{dx}\right) - (x^3 - xy^2 - y)\left(1 + x^2\frac{dy}{dx} + 2xy - 3y^2\frac{dy}{dx}\right)}{(x + x^2y - y^3)^2},$$

which upon simplification and substitution for dy/dx becomes:

$$\frac{d^2y}{dx^2} = \frac{3xy(2 - xy)}{(x + x^2y - y^3)^3}.$$

53. $f'(x) = 4(x - 2)(x^2 + 2x + 4)$ and $f''(x) = 12x^2$.

54. $f(x) = 18x^2 - x^4 = x^2(18 - x^2)$; $f'(x) = 36x - 4x^3 = 4x(3 + x)(3 - x)$; $f''(x) = 12(3 - x^2)$. There are global maxima at $(-3, 81)$ and $(3, 81)$ and a local minimum at $(0, 0)$. The other two x-intercepts are at $(-3\sqrt{2}, 0)$ and $(3\sqrt{2}, 0)$. There are inflection points at $(-\sqrt{3}, 45)$ and $(\sqrt{3}, 45)$.

55. $f'(x) = 2x^3(3x^2 - 4)$ and $f''(x) = 6x^2(5x^2 - 4)$.

56. $f'(x) = \dfrac{3(x - 2)}{2(x - 3)^{1/2}}$ and $f''(x) = \dfrac{3(x - 4)}{4(x - 3)^{3/2}}$. So $(3, 0)$ is a global minimum, an endpoint of the domain, and the graph is vertical there; the graph is increasing for all $x > 3$, has an inflection point at $(4, 4)$, is concave upward if $x > 4$, and is concave downward if $3 < x < 4$.

57. $f'(x) = \dfrac{4(3 - x)}{3(4 - x)^{2/3}}$ and $f''(x) = \dfrac{4(x - 6)}{9(4 - x)^{5/3}}$.

58. $f'(x) = \dfrac{3}{(x + 2)^2}$ and $f''(x) = -\dfrac{6}{(x + 2)^3}$. There are no critical points and no inflection points. The graph is increasing except at the discontinuity at $x = -2$. It is concave upward for $x < -2$ and concave downward for $x > -2$. The vertical line $x = -2$ and the horizontal line $y = 1$ are asymptotes.

59. $f(x) = 1 + \dfrac{5}{x^2 - 4}$, $f'(x) = -\dfrac{10x}{(x^2 - 4)^2}$, and $f''(x) = \dfrac{10(3x^3 + 4)}{(x^2 - 4)^3}$.

60. $f(x) = \dfrac{x}{(x - 2)(x + 1)}$: $f'(x) = -\dfrac{x^2 + 2}{(x^2 - x - 2)^2}$, $f''(x) = \dfrac{2(x^3 + 6x - 2)}{(x + 1)^3(x - 2)^3}$. There are no critical points, but there is an inflection point with the approximate coordinates $(0.3275, -0.1475)$. The graph is decreasing for all x other than -1 and 2, is concave upward on the intervals $(-1, 0.3275)$ and $(2, +\infty)$, and is concave downward on the intervals $(0.3275, 2)$ and $(-\infty, -1)$. The asymptotes are $y = 0$, $x = 2$, and $x = -1$.

61. $f(x) = \dfrac{2x^2}{(x-2)(x+1)}$, $f'(x) = -\dfrac{2x(x+4)}{(x-2)^2(x+1)^2}$, and $f''(x) = \dfrac{4(x^3 + 6x^2 + 4)}{(x^2 - x - 2)^3}$.

62. $f'(x) = \dfrac{x^2(x^2 - 3)}{(x^2 - 1)^2}$ and $f''(x) = \dfrac{2x(x^2 + 3)}{(x^2 - 1)^3}$. Inflection point and lone intercept: $(0,0)$. There is a local minimum where $x = \sqrt{3}$ and a local maximum where $x = -\sqrt{3}$. The graph is concave downward on the intervals $(0, 1)$ and $(-\infty, -1)$, concave upward on the intervals $(-1, 0)$ and $(1, \infty)$. The graph is increasing if $x < -\sqrt{3}$ and if $x > \sqrt{3}$ and is decreasing otherwise. The lines $x = -1$, $x = 1$, and $y = x$ are asymptotes.

63. Here we have $f(x) = x^3(3x - 4)$, $f'(x) = 12x^2(x - 1)$, and $f''(x) = 12x(3x - 2)$. Hence there are intercepts at $(0, 0)$ and $(4/3, 0)$; the graph is increasing for $x > 1$ and decreasing for $x < 1$; it is concave upward for $x > 2/3$ and for $x < 0$, concave downward on the interval $(0, 2/3)$. Consequently there is a global minimum at $(1, -1)$ and inflection points at $(0, 0)$ and $(2/3, -16/27)$. There are no asymptotes, no other extrema, and $f(x) \to +\infty$ as $x \to +\infty$ and as $x \to -\infty$.

64. Here we have $f(x) = x^2(x^2 - 2)$, $f'(x) = 4x(x + 1)(x - 1)$, and $f''(x) = 4(3x^2 - 1)$. So there are intercepts at $(-\sqrt{2}, 0)$, $(0, 0)$, and $(\sqrt{2}, 0)$. The graph is increasing on the intervals $(1, \infty)$ and $(-1, 0)$, decreasing on the intervals $(-\infty, -1)$ and $(0, 1)$. It is concave upward where $x^2 > 1/3$ and concave downward where $x^2 < 1/3$. There are global minima at $(-1, -1)$ and $(1, -1)$ and a local maximum at the origin. There are inflection points at the two points where $x^2 = 1/3$.

65. $f'(x) = -\dfrac{2x}{(x^2 - 1)^2}$ and $f''(x) = \dfrac{6x^2 + 2}{(x^2 - 1)^3}$.

66. First, $f(x) = x(x^2 - 12)$, $f'(x) = 3(x + 2)(x - 2)$, and $f''(x) = 6x$. So there are intercepts at $(2\sqrt{3}, 0)$, $(0, 0)$, and $(-2\sqrt{3}, 0)$. The graph is increasing for $x > 2$ and for $x < -2$; it is decreasing on the interval $(-2, 2)$. It is concave upward for $x > 0$ and concave downward for $x < 0$. There is a local maximum at $(-2, 16)$, a local minimum at $(2, -16)$, and an inflection point at the origin.

67. $f'(x) = 3x(4 - x)$ and $f''(x) = 6(2 - x)$. The abscissas of the x-intercepts are approximately -1.18014, 1.48887, and 5.69127.

68. The only intercept is $(0, 0)$, but $f(x) \to 0$ as $x \to +\infty$ and as $x \to -\infty$, so the x-axis is a horizontal asymptote. The graph is increasing on the interval $(-1, 1)$ and decreasing if $|x| > 1$. It is concave upward on $(-\sqrt{3}, 0)$ and for $x > \sqrt{3}$, concave downward for $x < -\sqrt{3}$ and on the interval $(0, \sqrt{3})$. There is a global maximum at the point $(1, 1/2)$ and a global minimum at $(-1, -1/2)$, inflection points at the origin and at the two points where $x^2 = 3$.

69. Here, $f'(x) = 3(x + 1)(x - 1)$ and $f''(x) = 6x$.

70. We have $f(x) = x^2(x^2 - 12)$, $f'(x) = 4x(x^2 - 6)$, and $f''(x) = 12(x^2 - 2)$. The analysis, results, and graph are qualitatively the same as in the solution of Problem 64.

71. $f(x) = (x - 1)^2(x + 3)$, $f'(x) = (x - 1)(3x + 5)$, and $f''(x) = 6x + 2$.

72. $f(x) = \dfrac{x+1}{x^2}$, $f'(x) = -\dfrac{x+2}{x^3}$, $f''(x) = \dfrac{2(x+3)}{x^4}$. The graph is decreasing for $x > 0$ and for $x < -2$, increasing on the interval $(-2, 0)$. It is concave downward for $x < -3$, concave upward for $x > 0$ and on the interval $(-3, 0)$. The only intercept is $(-1, 0)$ and there is a discontinuity where $x = 0$. There is a global minimum at $(-2, -0.25)$ and an inflection point at $(-3, -2/9)$. As $x \to 0$, $f(x) \to +\infty$, so the y-axis is a vertical asymptote. As $|x| \to +\infty$, $f(x) \to 0$, so the x-axis is a horizontal asymptote.

73. The given function $f(x)$ is expressed as a fraction with constant numerator, so we maximize $f(x)$ by minimizing its denominator $(x + 1)^2 + 1$. It is clear that $x = -1$ does the trick, so the maximum value of $f(x)$ is $f(-1) = 1$.

74. Let k be the proportionality constant for cost; if the pot has radius r and height h, we are to minimize total cost

$$C = k\left[(5)(\pi r^2) + (1)(2\pi rh)\right]$$

subject to the constraint $\pi r^2 h = 1$. Then $h = 1/(\pi r^2)$, so

$$C = C(r) = k\left(5\pi r^2 + \frac{2}{r}\right), \quad r > 0.$$

Now

$$C'(r) = k\left(10\pi r - \frac{2}{r^2}\right);$$

$C'(r) = 0$ when $r = \left(\frac{1}{5\pi}\right)^{1/3}$ and $h = \left(\frac{25}{\pi}\right)^{1/3}$. It's easy to establish in the usual way that these values minimize C, but because $h = 5r$, it seems that the manufacturer will have a marketing problem.

75. Let x represent the width of the base of the box. Then the length of the base is $2x$ and, because the volume of the box is 4500, the height of the box is $4500/(2x^2)$. We minimize the surface area of the box, which is given by

$$f(x) = 2x^2 + 4x \cdot \frac{4500}{2x^2} + 2x \cdot \frac{4500}{2x^2} = 2x^2 + \frac{13500}{x}, \quad 0 < x < \infty.$$

Now $f'(x) = 4x - (13500/x^2)$, so $f'(x) = 0$ when $x = \sqrt[3]{3375} = 15$. Note that $f''(15) > 0$, so surface area is minimized when $x = 15$. The box of minimal surface area is 15 cm wide, 30 cm long, and 10 cm high.

76. Let x represent the edge length of the square base of the box. Because the volume of the box is 324, the box has height $324/x^2$. We minimize the cost C of materials to make the box, where

$$C = C(x) = 3x^2 + 4 \cdot x \cdot \frac{324}{x^2} = 3x^2 + \frac{1296}{x}, \quad 0 < x < \infty.$$

Now $C'(x) = 6x - (1296/x^2)$, so $C(x) = 0$ when $x = \sqrt[3]{1296/6} = 6$. Because $C''(6) > 0$, the cost C is minimized when $x = 6$. The box we seek has a square base 6 in. on a side and height 9 in.

77. Let x represent the width of the base of the box. Then the box has base of length $2x$ and height $200/x^2$. We minimize the cost C of the box, where

$$C = C(x) = 7 \cdot 2x^2 + 5 \cdot \left(6x \cdot \frac{200}{x^2}\right) + 5 \cdot 2x^2 = 24x^2 + \frac{6000}{x}, \quad 0 < x < \infty.$$

Now $C'(x) = 48x - (6000/x^2)$, so $C'(x) = 0$ when $x = \sqrt[3]{125} = 5$. Because $C''(5) > 0$, the cost C is minimized when $x = 5$. The box of minimal cost is 5 in. wide, 10 in. long, and 8 in. high.

78. If the zeros of $f(x)$ are at a, b, and c (with $a < b < c$), apply Rolle's theorem to f' on the two intervals $[a,b]$ and $[b,c]$.

79. If the speed of the truck is v, then the trip time is $T = 1000/v$. So the resulting cost is

$$C(v) = \frac{10000}{v} + (1000)\left(1 + (0.0003)v^{3/2}\right),$$

so that

$$\frac{C(v)}{1000} = \frac{10}{v} + 1 + (0.0003)v^{3/2}.$$

Thus

$$\frac{C'(v)}{1000} = -\frac{10}{v^2} + \frac{3}{2}(0.0003)\sqrt{v}.$$

Then $C'(v) = 0$ when $v = (200,000/9)^{2/5} \approx 54.79$ mi/h. This clearly minimizes the cost, since $C''(v) > 0$ for *all* $v > 0$.

80. The sum in question is

$$S(x) = (x - a_1)^2 + (x - a_2)^2 + \ldots + (x - a_n)^2.$$

Now $S'(x) = 2(x - a_1) + 2(x - a_2) + \ldots + 2(x - a_n)$; $S'(x) = 0$ when $nx = a_1 + a_2 + \ldots + a_n$, so that

$$x = \frac{1}{n}(a_1 + a_2 + \ldots + a_n)$$

—the *average* of the n fixed numbers. It is clear that S is continuous and that $S(x) \to +\infty$ as $|x| \to +\infty$, so $S(x)$ must have a global minimum value. Therefore the value of x shown above minimizes the sum of the squares of the distances.

81. $2y\frac{dy}{dx} = 3x^2 - 6x + 2$, so $\frac{dy}{dx} = \frac{3x^2 - 6x + 2}{2y}$. Now $dy/dx = 0$ when $x = 1 - \frac{1}{3}\sqrt{3}$. After lengthy simplifications, one can show that

$$\frac{d^2y}{dx^2} = \frac{3x^4 - 12x^3 + 12x^2 - 4}{4y^3}.$$

The only zero of $\frac{d^2y}{dx^2}$ in the domain is about 2.4679, and there the graph has the two values $|y| \approx 1.3019$.

82. Let x represent the length of the internal divider. Then the field is x by $2400/x$ ft. We minimize the total length of fencing, given by:

$$f(x) = 3x + \frac{4800}{x}, \quad 0 < x < \infty.$$

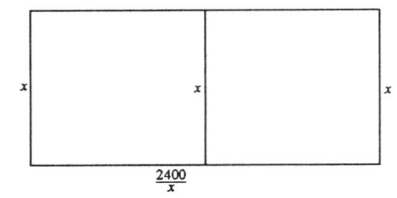

Now $f'(x) = 3 - \frac{4800}{x^2}$, which is zero only when $x = \sqrt{1600} = 40$.
Verification: $f'(x) > 0$ if $x > 40$, and $f'(x) < 0$ if $x < 40$, so f is minimized when $x = 40$. The minimum length of fencing required for this field is 240 feet.

83. Let x represent the length of each of the dividers. Then the field is x by $1800/x$ ft. We minimize the total length of fencing, given by:

$$f(x) = 4x + \frac{3600}{x}, \quad 0 < x < \infty.$$

Now $f'(x) = 4 - \frac{3600}{x^2}$, which is zero only when $x = 30$. Verification: $f'(x) > 0$ if $x > 30$ and $f'(x) < 0$ if $x < 30$, so f is minimized when $x = 30$. The minimum length of fencing required for this field is 240 ft.

84. Let x represent the length of each of the dividers. Then the field is x by $2250/x$ ft. We minimize the total length of fencing, given by:

$$f(x) = 5x + \frac{4500}{x}, \quad 0 < x < \infty.$$

Now $f'(x) = 5 - \frac{4500}{x^2}$, which is zero only when $x = 30$. Verification: $f'(x) > 0$ if $x > 30$ and $f'(x) < 0$ if $x < 30$, so f is minimized when $x = 30$. The minimum length of fencing required for this field is 300 meters.

85. Let x represent the length of each of the dividers. Then the field is x by A/x ft. We minimize the total length of fencing, given by:

$$f(x) = (n+2)x + \frac{2A}{x}, \quad 0 < x < \infty.$$

Now $f'(x) = n+2 - \frac{2A}{x^2}$, which is zero only when $x = \sqrt{\frac{2A}{n+2}}$. Verification: $f'(x) > 0$ if $x > \sqrt{\frac{2A}{n+2}}$ and $f'(x) < 0$ if $x < \sqrt{\frac{2A}{n+2}}$, so f is minimized when $x = \sqrt{\frac{2A}{n+2}}$. The minimum length of fencing required for this field is

$$f\left(\sqrt{\frac{2A}{n+2}}\right) = (n+2)\sqrt{\frac{2A}{n+2}} + \frac{2A\sqrt{n+2}}{\sqrt{2A}}$$
$$= \sqrt{2A(n+2)} + \sqrt{2A(n+2)}$$
$$= 2\sqrt{2A(n+2)} \text{ (ft)}.$$

86. Let L be the line segments with endpoints at $(0,c)$ and $(b,0)$ on the coordinate axes, and suppose that L is tangent to the graph of $y = 1/x^2$ at $(x, 1/x^2)$. We will minimize S, the square of the length of L, where $S = b^2 + c^2$. We compute the slope of L in several ways: as the value of dy/dx at the point of tangency, as the slope of the line segment between $(x, 1/x^2)$ and $(b,0)$, and as the slope of the line segment between $(x, 1/x^2)$ and $(0,c)$:

$$-\frac{2}{x^3} = \frac{\frac{1}{x^2} - 0}{x - b}, \text{ so } x = -2(x-b), \text{ hence } b = \frac{3}{2}x.$$

$$-\frac{2}{x^3} = \frac{\frac{1}{x^2} - c}{x - 0}; \quad -2x = x^3\left(\frac{1}{x^2} - 3\right), \quad cx^2 = 3, \text{ hence } c = \frac{3}{x^2}.$$

Therefore $S(x) = \frac{9}{x^4} + \frac{9x^2}{4}$; $f'(x) = -\frac{36}{x^5} + \frac{9}{2}x$, which is zero only when $x = \sqrt{2}$. Verification: $f'(x) < 0$ if $x < \sqrt{2}$, and $f'(x) > 0$ if $x > \sqrt{2}$. So S, hence the length of L, is minimized when $S = \sqrt{2}$. The length of this shortest line segment is $\frac{3}{2}\sqrt{3}$.

87. From the solution to Problem 86, we see that the area A of this triangle can be written as a function of x as follows:

$$A(x) = \frac{1}{2} \cdot \frac{3}{2}x \cdot \frac{3}{x^2} = \frac{9}{4x}, \text{ with domain } 0 < x < \infty.$$

$A'(x) = -\frac{9}{4x^2}$, which is never zero, so A has no critical points and no endpoints on its domain. Therefore there is neither a maximum nor a minimum area of such a triangle.

88. Let L be the line segment in the first quadrant that is tangent to the graph of $y = 1/x$ at $(x, 1/x)$ and has endpoints $(0, c)$ and $b, 0)$. Compute the slope of L in several ways: as the value of dy/dx at the point of tangency, as the slope of the line segment between $(x, 1/x)$ and $(b, 0)$, and as the slope of the line segment between $(x, 1/x)$ and $(0, c)$:

$$-\frac{1}{x^2} = \frac{\frac{1}{x} - 0}{x - b} \text{ so } b = 2x.$$

$$-\frac{1}{x^2} = \frac{\frac{1}{x} - c}{x} : c - \frac{1}{x} = \frac{1}{x}, \text{ so } c = \frac{2}{x}.$$

Chapter 4 Miscellaneous

Therefore the area A of the triangle is $A = A(x) = \frac{1}{2} \cdot 2x \cdot \frac{1}{x} = 1$. Because A is a constant function, every triangle has both maximal and minimal area.

89. See the solution to Problem 92: Here, $V = 288$ and $n = 3$. The minimal area is 288 in.^{2}

90. See the solution to Problem 92: Here, $V = 800$ and $n = 4$. The minimal area is 600 in.^{2}

91. Let x be the width of the box. Then its length is $5x$, and its height is $225/(5x^2)$. We minimize its surface area A, where

$$A(x) = 10x^2 + \frac{225}{5x^2} \cdot 2(6)x = 10x^2 + \frac{(12)(225)}{5x}, \quad 0 < x < \infty.$$

Now $A'(x) = 20x - \frac{(12)(225)}{5x^2}$, and $A'(x) = 0$ when $x = \sqrt[3]{(6)(225)/50}$. Verification: $A'(x) > 0$ for $x > \sqrt[3]{(6)(225)/50}$, and $A'(x) < 0$ for $x < \sqrt[3]{(6)(225)/50}$, so at this critical point the surface area is minimized. The minimal surface area is 270 cm^2.

92. Let x represent the width of the box. Then the length of the box is nx, and its height is $V/(nx^2)$. We minimize the surface area A of the box, where

$$A = A(x) = 2nx^2 + \frac{V}{nx^2} \cdot 2(n+1)x = 2nx^2 + \frac{2(n+1)V}{nx}, \quad 0 < x < \infty.$$

Now $A'(x) = 4nx - \frac{2(n+1)V}{nx^2}$, and $A'(x) = 0$ when $x = \sqrt[3]{\frac{(n+1)V}{2n^2}}$. Verification: $A'(x) > 0$ for $x > \sqrt[3]{\frac{(n+1)V}{2n^2}}$ and $A'(x) < 0$ for $x < \sqrt[3]{\frac{(n+1)V}{2n^2}}$, so this critical point minimizes A. The value of $A(x)$, simplified, at this minimum point is $3\left(\frac{2(n+1)^2 V^2}{n}\right)^{1/3}$

93.
$$\lim_{x \to \pm\infty} \frac{f(x)}{x} = \lim_{x \to \pm\infty} \frac{(1-x)^{2/3}}{x^{2/3}}$$
$$= \lim_{x \to \pm\infty} \left(\frac{\frac{1}{x} - 1}{1}\right)^{2/3} = +1.$$

$$\lim_{x \to \infty} [f(x) - mx] = \lim_{x \to \infty} \left(x^{1/3}(1-x)^{2/3} - x\right)$$
$$= \lim_{x \to \infty} \frac{\left(x^{1/3}(1-x)^{2/3} - x\right)\left(x^{2/3}(1-x)^{4/3} + x^{4/3}(1-x)^{2/3} + x^2\right)}{x^{2/3}(1-x)^{4/3} + x^{4/3}(1-x)^{2/3} + x^2}$$
$$= \lim_{x \to \infty} \frac{x(1-x)^2 - x^3}{x^{2/3}(1-x)^{4/3} + x^{4/3}(1-x)^{2/3} + x^2}$$
$$= \lim_{x \to \infty} \frac{x - 2x^2}{x^{2/3}(1-x)^{4/3} + x^{4/3}(1-x)^{2/3} + x^2}$$
$$= \lim_{x \to \infty} \frac{\frac{1}{x} - 2}{\left(\frac{1-x}{x}\right)^{4/3} + \left(\frac{1-x}{x}\right)^{2/3} + 1}$$
$$= \frac{0 - 2}{1 + 1 + 1} = -\frac{2}{3}.$$

The limit is the same as $x \to -\infty$. So the graph of $f(x) = x^{1/3}(1-x)^{2/3}$ has the oblique asymptote $y = x - \frac{2}{3}$.

94. Let θ be the angle between your initial path and due north, so that $0 \le \theta \le \pi/2$, and if $\theta = \pi/2$ then you plan to jog around a semicircle and not swim at all. Suppose that you can swim with speed v (in miles per hour). Then you will swim a length of $2\cos\theta$ miles at speed v and jog a length of 2θ miles at speed $2v$, for a total time of

$$T(\theta) = \frac{2\cos\theta}{v} + \frac{2\theta}{2v} = \frac{1}{v}(\theta + 2\cos\theta), \quad 0 \le \theta \le \pi/2.$$

It's easy to verify that this formula is correct even in the extreme case $\theta = \pi/2$. It turns out that although $T'(\theta) = 0$ when $\theta = \pi/6$, this value of θ actually *maximizes* $T(\theta)$; this function has an endpoint minimum not even at $\theta = 0$, but at $\theta = \pi/2$. Answer: Jog all the way.

Chapter 5: The Integral
Section 5.2

2. $\int (3t^4 + 5t - 6)\, dx = \frac{3}{5}t^5 + \frac{5}{2}t^2 - 6t + C$

4. $\int \left(-\frac{1}{t^2}\right) dt = \frac{1}{t} + C$

6. $\int \left(x^{5/2} - \frac{5}{x^4} - \sqrt{x}\right) dx = \frac{2}{7}x^{7/2} + \frac{5}{3}x^{-3} - \frac{2}{3}x^{3/2} + C$

8. $\int \left(\frac{2}{x^{3/4}} - \frac{3}{x^{2/3}}\right) dx = 8x^{1/4} - 9x^{1/3} + C$

10. $\int \left(2x\sqrt{x} - \frac{1}{\sqrt{x}}\right) dx = \frac{4}{5}x^{5/2} - 2x^{1/2} + C$

12. $\int \left(\frac{1}{4}t^5 - \frac{6}{t^2}\right) dt = \frac{1}{24}t^6 + 6t^{-1} + C$

14. $\int \left(4\sqrt[3]{x^2} - \frac{5}{\sqrt[3]{x}}\right) dx = \frac{12}{5}x^{5/3} - \frac{15}{2}x^{2/3} + C$

16. $\int (t+1)^{10}\, dt = \frac{1}{11}(t+1)^{11} + C$

18. $\int \sqrt{z+1}\, dz = \frac{2}{3}(z+1)^{3/2} + C$

20. $\int \sqrt[3]{x}\,(x+1)^3\, dx = \frac{3}{13}x^{13/3} + \frac{9}{10}x^{10/3} + \frac{9}{7}x^{7/3} + \frac{3}{4}x^{4/3} + C$

22. $\int \frac{(3x+4)^2}{\sqrt{x}}\, dx = \int x^{-1/2}(9x^2 + 24x + 16)\, dx$
$\qquad = \int (9x^{3/2} + 24x^{1/2} + 16x^{-1/2})\, dx = \frac{18}{5}x^{5/2} + 16x^{3/2} + 32x^{1/2} + C$

24. $\int \frac{1}{(3z+10)^7}\, dz = -\frac{1}{18}(3z+10)^{-6} + C$

26. $\int \frac{3}{\sqrt{(x-1)^3}}\, dx = -6(x-1)^{-1/2} + C$

28. $\int (2\cos \pi x + 3\sin \pi x)\, dx = \frac{2}{\pi}\sin \pi x - \frac{3}{\pi}\cos \pi x + C$

30. $\int (4\sin 2\pi t - 2\sin 4\pi t)\, dt = -\frac{2}{\pi}\cos 2\pi t + \frac{1}{2\pi}\cos 4\pi t + C$

31. $\frac{1}{2}\sin^2 x + C_1 = -\frac{1}{2}\cos^2 x + C_2$: $\sin^2 x + \cos^2 x + 2C_1 = 2C_2$; $1 + 2C_1 = 2C_2$; $C_2 = C_1 + \frac{1}{2}$.

32. $F_1'(x) = \frac{1}{(1-x)^2}$, $F_2'(x) = \frac{1-x+x}{(1-x)^2} = \frac{1}{(1-x)^2}$.
$F_1(x) - F_2(x) = C_1$ for some constant C_1 on $(-\infty, 1)$; $F_1(x) - F_2(x) = C_2$ for some constant C_2 on $(1, +\infty)$. On either interval, $F_1(x) - F_2(x) = \frac{1-x}{1-x} = 1$.

34. (a) $D_x \tan x = \sec^2 x$; (b) $\int \tan^2 x\, dx = \int (\sec^2 x - 1)\, dx = \tan x - x + C$.

35. $y = \int (2x+1)\, dx = x^2 + x + C$; $y(0) = C = 3$, so $y = x^2 + x + 3$.

36. $y = \frac{1}{4}(x-2)^4 + 1$

38. $y = -\frac{1}{x} + 6$

40. $y = \int \sqrt{x+9}\, dx = \frac{2}{3}(x+9)^{3/2} + C;\quad 0 = y(-4) = \frac{2}{3}(-4+9)^{3/2} + C = \frac{2}{3}\cdot 5\sqrt{5} + C;$
$y(x) = \frac{2}{3}(x+9)^{3/2} - \frac{10}{3}\sqrt{5}.$

42. $y = \int \left(x^4 - 3x + \frac{3}{x^2}\right) dx = \frac{1}{5}x^5 - \frac{3}{2}x^2 - 3x^{-1} + C = \frac{1}{5}x^5 - \frac{3}{2}x^2 - 3x^{-1} + \frac{9}{5}$

44. $y = \int \sqrt{x+5}\, dx = \frac{2}{3}(x+5)^{3/2} + C = \frac{2}{3}(x+5)^{3/2} - 21$

46. $y = \int (2x+3)^{3/2}\, dx = \frac{1}{5}(2x+3)^{5/2} + C = \frac{1}{5}(2x+3)^{5/2} + \frac{257}{5}$

48. $x(t) = 5 - 5t + 5t^2 - 5t^3$

50. $x(t) = 4t^{5/2} + 7t + 5$

52. $x(t) = 4t - 2\cos 2t$

53. The graph is shown below.

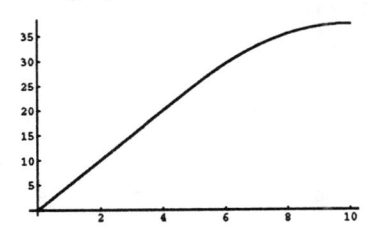

54. The graph is shown below.

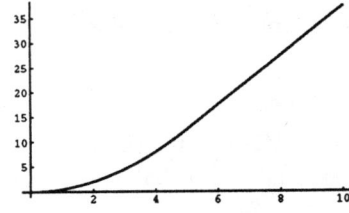

55. The graph is shown below.

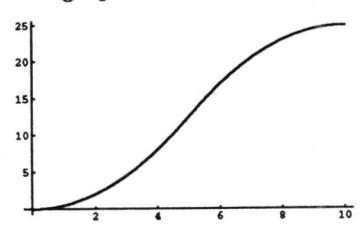

56. The graph is shown below.

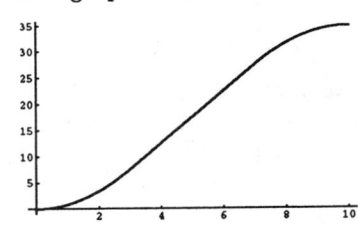

In the solutions for Problems 57–78, unless otherwise indicated, we will take the upward direction to be the positive direction, $s = s(t)$ for position (in feet) at time t (in seconds) with $s = 0$ corresponding to ground level, and $v(t)$ velocity at time t in ft/s, $a = a(t)$ acceleration at time t in ft/s^2. The initial position will be denoted by s_0 and the initial velocity by v_0.

57. Here, $a = -32$, $v(t) = -32t + 96$, $s(t) = -16t^2 + 96t$. The maximum height is reached when $v = 0$, thus when $t = 3$. The maximum height is therefore $s(3) = 144$. The ball remains aloft until $s(t) = 0$ for $t > 0$; $t = 6$. So it remains aloft for six seconds.

58. With initial velocity v_0, here we have

$$a(t) = -32,\ v(t) = -32t + v_0,\ \text{and}\ s(t) = -16t^2 + v_0 t$$

(because $s_0 = 0$). The maximum altitude is attained when $v = 0$, which occurs when $t = v_0/32$. Therefore

$$400 = s(v_0/32) = (-16)(v_0/32)^2 + (v_0)^2/32.$$

It follows that $\frac{1}{64}(v_0)^2 = 400$, and therefore that $v_0 = 160$ (ft/s).

59. Here it is more convenient to take the downward direction as the positive direction. Thus

$$a(t) = +32,\ v(t) = +32t\ (\text{because}\ v_0 = 0),\ \text{and}\ s(t) = 16t^2\ (\text{because}\ s_0 = 0).$$

The stone hits the bottom when $t = 3$, and at that time we have $s = s(3) = 144$. Answer: The well is 144 feet deep.

Section 5.2 Antiderivatives and Initial Value Problems

60. We have $v(t) = -32t + v_0$ and $s(t) = -16t^2 + v_0 t$. Also $0 = s(4)$, so $4v_0 = 256$: $v_0 = 64$. Thus
$$v(t) = -32t + 64 \text{ and } s(t) = -16t^2 + 64t.$$
The height of the tree is the maximum value of $s(t)$, which occurs when $v(t) = 0$; that is, when $t = 2$. Therefore the height of the tree is $s(2) = 64$ (feet).

61. Here, $v(t) = -32t + 48$ and $s(t) = -16t^2 + 48 + 160$. The ball strikes the ground at that value of $t > 0$ for which $s(t) = 0$:
$$0 = s(t) = -16(t - 5)(t + 2), \text{ so } t = 5.$$
Therefore the ball remains aloft for 5 seconds. Its velocity at impact is $v(5) = -112$ (ft/s), so the ball strikes the ground at a speed of 112 ft/s.

62. First ball: $v_0 = 0$, $s_0 = 576$. So $s(t) = -16t^2 + 576$. The first ball strikes the ground at that $t > 0$ for which $s(t) = 0$; $t = 6$. Second ball: The second ball must remain aloft from time $t = 3$ until time $t = 6$, thus for 3 seconds. Reset $t = 0$ as the time it is thrown downward. Then with initial velocity v_0, the second ball has velocity and position
$$v(t) = -32t + v_0 \text{ and } s(t) = -16t^2 + v_0 t + 576$$
at time t. We require that $s(3) = 0$; that is, $0 = s(3) = -144 + 3v_0 + 576$, so that $v_0 = -144$. Answer: The second ball should be thrown straight downward with an initial velocity of 144 ft/s.

63. One solution: Take $s_0 = 960$, $v_0 = 0$. Then
$$v(t) = -32t \text{ and } s(t) = -16t^2 + 960.$$
The ball hits the street for that value of $t > 0$ for which $s(t) = 0$—that is, when $t = 2\sqrt{15}$. It therefore takes the ball approximately 7.746 seconds to reach the street. Its velocity then is $v(2\sqrt{15}) = -64\sqrt{15}$ (ft/s)—approximately 247.87 ft/s (downward), almost exactly 169 miles per hour.

64. Here we have $v(t) = -32t + 320$ and $s(t) = -16t^2 + 320t$. After three seconds have elapsed, the height of the arrow will be $s(3) = 816$ (ft). The height of the arrow will be 1200 feet when $s(t) = 1200$:
$$16t^2 - 320t + 1200 = 0;$$
$$16(t - 5)(t - 15) = 0;$$
$t = 5$ and $t = 15$ are both solutions. So the height of the arrow will be 1200 feet both at $t = 5$ (the arrow is still rising) and at $t = 15$ (the arrow is falling). The arrow strikes the ground at that value of $t > 0$ for which $s(t) = 0$: $t = 20$. So the arrow will strike the ground 20 seconds after it is released.

65. With $v(t) = -32t + v_0$ and $s(t) = -16t^2 + v_0 t$, we have the maximum altitude $s = 225$ occurring when $v(t) = 0$; that is, when $t = v_0/32$. So
$$225 = s(v_0/32) = (-16)(v_0/32)^2 + (v_0)^2/32 = (v_0)^2/64.$$
It follows that $v_0 = +120$. So the initial velocity of the ball was 120 ft/s.

66. It is more convenient to take the downward direction as the positive direction here. Thus
$$v(t) = 9.8t \text{ and } s(t) = 4.9t^2.$$
The rock reaches the water when $s(t) = 98$: $t = +2\sqrt{5}$. So it takes the rock $2\sqrt{5}$ seconds to reach the water. Its velocity as it penetrates the water surface is $v(2\sqrt{5}) \approx 43.8$ (m/s).

67. In this problem, $v(t) = -32t + v_0 = -32t$ and $s(t) = -16t^2 + s_0 = -16t^2 + 400$. The ball reaches the ground when $s = 0$, thus when $16t^2 = 400$: $t = +5$. Ths impact velocity is $v(5) = (-32)(5) = -160$ (ft/s).

68. Here s_0 will be the height of the building, so
$$v(t) = -32t - 25 \text{ and } s(t) = -16t^2 - 25t + s_0.$$
The velocity of impact is -153 ft/s, so we can obtain the time of impact t by solving $v(t) = -153$: $t = 4$. At this time we also have $s = 0$:
$$0 = s(4) = (-16)(16) - (25)(4) + s_0,$$
so that $s_0 = 356$. Answer: The building is 356 feet high.

69. For this problem, we take $s(t) = -16t^2 + 160t$ and $v(t) = -32t + 160$. Because $s = 0$ when $t = 0$ and when $t = 10$, the time aloft is 10 seconds. The velocity is zero at maximum altitude, and that occurs when $32t = 160$: $t = 5$. So the maximum altitude is $s(5) = 400$ (ft).

70. Let $f(t)$ be the altitude of the first ball at time t. Then $f(t) = -16t^2 + h$, so the altitude of the first ball will be $h/2$ when $f(t) = h/2$:
$$t^2 = \frac{h}{32}, \text{ so } t = \frac{1}{8}\sqrt{2h}.$$
Let the second ball have initial velocity v_0 and altitude $s(t)$ at time t. Then $s(t) = -16t^2 + v_0 t$. We require that $s(t) = h/2$ at the above value of t. That is,
$$\frac{h}{2} = (-16)\left(\frac{h}{2}\right) + (v_0)\left(\frac{1}{8}\sqrt{2h}\right).$$
Solution of this equation yields $v_0 = 4\sqrt{2h}$.

71. Because $v_0 = -40$, $v(t) = -32t - 40$. Thus
$$s(t) = -16t^2 - 40t + 555.$$
Now $s(t) = 0$ when $g = \frac{1}{4}\left(-5 + 2\sqrt{145}\right) \approx 4.77$ (s). The speed at impact is $|v(t)|$ for that value of t; that is, $16\sqrt{145} \approx 192.6655$ (ft/s), over 131 miles per hour.

72. In this problem, $v(t) = -gt$ and $s(t) = -\frac{1}{2}gt^2 + h$. The rock strikes the ground when $s(t) = 0$, so that $t = \sqrt{2h/g}$. The speed of the rock then is $\left|-g\sqrt{2h/g}\right| = \sqrt{2gh}$.

73. Bomb equations: $a = -32$, $v = -32t$, $s_B = s = -16t^2 + 800$. Here we have $t = 0$ at the time the bomb is released.
Projectile equations: $a = -32$, $v = -32(t-2) + v_0$, and $s_P = s = -16(t-2)$, $t \geq 2$.
We require $s_B = s_P = 400$ at the same time. The equation $s_B = 400$ leads to $t = 5$, and for $s_P(5) = 400$, we must have $v_0 = 544/3 \approx 181.33$ (ft/s).

74. Let $x(t)$ denote the distance the car has traveled t seconds after the brakes are applied; let $v(t)$ denote its velocity and $a(t)$ its acceleration at time t during the braking. Then we are given $a = -40$, so $v(t) = -40t + 88$ (because 60 mi/h is the same speed as 88 ft/s). The car comes to a stop when $v(t) = 0$; that is, when $t = 2.2$. The car travels the distance $x(2.2) \approx 96.8$. Answer: 96.8 feet.

75. The deceleration $a = k > 0$ is unknown at first. But the velocity of the car is $v(t) = -kt + 88$, and so the distance it travels after the brakes are applied at time $t = 0$ is
$$x(t) = -\frac{1}{2}kt^2 + 88t.$$
But $x = 176$ when $v = 0$, so the stopping time t_1 is $88/k$ because that is the time at which $v = 0$. Therefore
$$176 = -\frac{1}{2}k(88/k)^2 + (88)(88/k) = \frac{3872}{k}.$$

Section 5.2 Antiderivatives and Initial Value Problems

It follows that $k = 22$ (ft/s^2), about $0.69g$.

76. Let $x(t)$ be the altitude (in miles) of the spacecraft at time t (hours), with $t = 0$ corresponding to the time at which the retrorockets are fired; let $v(t) = x'(t)$ be the velocity of the spacecraft at time t. Then $v_0 = -1000$ and x_0 is unknown. But the acceleration constant is $a = +20000$, so

$$v(t) = (20000)t - 1000 \text{ and } x(t) = (10000)t^2 - 1000t + x_0.$$

We want $v = 0$ exactly when $x = 0$—call the time then t_1. Then $0 = (20000)t_1 - 1000$, so $t_1 = 1/20$. Also $x(t_1) = 0$, so

$$0 = (10000)\left(\frac{1}{400}\right) - (1000)\left(\frac{1}{20}\right) + x_0.$$

Therefore $x_0 = 50 - 25 = 25$ miles. (Also $t_1 = 1/20$ of an hour; that is, exactly three minutes.)

77. (a) With the usual coordinate system, the ball has velocity $v(t) = -32t + v_0$ (ft/s) at time t (seconds) and altitude $y(t) = -16t^2 + v_0 t$ (ft). We require $y(T) = 144$ when $v(T) = 0$: $v_0 = 32T$, so

$$144 = -16T^2 + 32T = 16T^2,$$

and thus $T = 3$ and $v_0 = 96$. Answer: 96 ft/s.

(b) Now $v(t) = -\frac{26}{5}t + 96$, $y(t) = -\frac{13}{5}t^2 + 96t$. Maximum height occurs when $v(t) = 0$: $t = \frac{240}{13}$. The maximum height is

$$y\left(\frac{240}{13}\right) = -\frac{13}{5} \cdot \frac{240^2}{13^2} + 96 \cdot \frac{240}{13} = \frac{11520}{13} \approx 886 \text{ ft.}$$

78. Set up a coordinate system in which the Diana moves along the x-axis in the positive direction, with initial position $x_0 = 0$ and initial velocity $v_0 = 0$. Then $\dfrac{dv}{dt} = +0.032$ feet per second per second, so

$$v(t) = (0.032)t + v_0 = (0.032)t.$$

Thus

$$x(t) = (0.016)t^2 + x_0 = (0.016)t^2.$$

The units are in feet, seconds, and feet per second. After one minute we take $t = 60$ to find that $x(60) = 57.6$ (feet). After one hour we take $t = 3600$ to find that $x(3600) = 207360$ (ft)—over 39 miles. After one day we take $t = 86400$; $x(86400) = 119,439,360$ (feet), approximately 22621 miles! At this point the speed of the Diana would be $v(86400) = 2764.8$ feet per second, approximately 1885 miles per hour! After 30 days, the Diana will have traveled well over 20 million miles and will be speeding along in excess of 56000 miles per hour.

Section 5.3

1. $\displaystyle\sum_{i=1}^{5} 3^i = 3^1 + 3^2 + 3^3 + 3^4 + 3^5 = 3 + 9 + 27 + 81 + 243.$

2. $\sqrt{2} + \sqrt{4} + \sqrt{6} + \sqrt{8} + \sqrt{10} + \sqrt{12}$

4. $1 + 3 + 5 + 7 + 9 + 11$

6. $\dfrac{1}{1} - \dfrac{1}{4} + \dfrac{1}{9} - \dfrac{1}{16} + \dfrac{1}{25} - \dfrac{1}{36}$

7. $x + x^2 + x^3 + x^4 + x^5$

8. $x - x^3 + x^5 - x^7 + x^9$

9. $\sum_{n=1}^{5} n^2$
10. $\sum_{n=1}^{6} n \cdot (-1)^{n+1}$
11. $\sum_{k=1}^{5} \frac{1}{k}$
12. $\sum_{i=1}^{5} \frac{1}{i^2}$

13. $\sum_{m=1}^{6} \frac{1}{2^m}$
14. $\sum_{n=1}^{5} \frac{(-1)^{n+1}}{3^n}$
15. $\sum_{n=1}^{5} \left(\frac{2}{3}\right)^n$
16. $\sum_{j=1}^{9} \sqrt{j}$

17. $\sum_{n=1}^{10} \frac{1}{n} x^n$

18. $\sum_{n=1}^{10} \frac{(-1)^{n+1}}{2n-1} x^{2n-1}$

20. -32 22. -231 24. 190

25. $\sum_{i=1}^{6} (i^3 - i^2) = \frac{6^2 \cdot 7^2}{4} - \frac{6 \cdot 7 \cdot 13}{6} = 3^2 \cdot 7^2 - 7 \cdot 13 = 441 - 91 = 350.$

26. 1330

27. $\sum_{i=1}^{100} i^2 = \frac{100 \cdot 101 \cdot 201}{6} = 50 \cdot 101 \cdot 67 = 338,350.$

28. $\frac{10^8}{4} + \frac{10^6}{2} + \frac{10^4}{4} = 25,502,500.$

29. $\lim_{n \to \infty} \frac{1^2 + 2^2 + \cdots + n^2}{n^3} = \lim_{n \to \infty} \sum_{i=1}^{n} \left(\frac{i}{n}\right)^2 \cdot \frac{1}{n} = \int_{0}^{1} x^2 \, dx = \frac{1}{3}.$

30. $\frac{n^4 + 2n^3 + n^2}{4n^4} \to \frac{1}{4}$ as $n \to +\infty$.

31. n^2

32. $\sum_{i=1}^{n} (2i-1)^2 = \sum_{i=1}^{n} 4i^2 - 4i + 1 = 4\left(\frac{1}{3}n^3 + \frac{1}{2}n^2 + \frac{1}{6}n\right) - 4\left(\frac{1}{2}n^2 + \frac{1}{2}n\right) + n = \frac{1}{3}(4n^3 - n).$

33. $\underline{A}_5 = \sum_{i=1}^{5} \frac{i-1}{5} \cdot \frac{1}{5}, \quad \overline{A}_5 = \sum_{i=1}^{5} \frac{i}{5} \cdot \frac{1}{5}.$

34. $\underline{A}_5 = \sum_{i=1}^{5} \frac{2i+3}{5} \cdot \frac{1}{5}, \quad \overline{A}_5 = \sum_{i=1}^{5} \frac{2i+5}{5} \cdot \frac{1}{5}.$

35. $\underline{A}_6 = \sum_{i=1}^{6} \left[2\left(\frac{i-1}{2}\right) + 3\right] \cdot \frac{1}{6}, \quad \overline{A}_6 = \sum_{i=1}^{6} \left[2 \cdot \frac{i}{2} + 3\right] \cdot \frac{1}{6}.$

36. $\underline{A}_6 = \sum_{i=1}^{6} \left[13 - 3 \cdot \frac{i}{2}\right] \cdot \frac{1}{6}, \quad \overline{A}_6 = \sum_{i=1}^{6} \left[13 - 3 \cdot \frac{i-1}{2}\right] \cdot \frac{1}{6}.$

37. $\underline{A}_5 = \sum_{i=1}^{5} \left(\frac{i-1}{5}\right)^2 \cdot \frac{1}{5}, \quad \overline{A}_5 = \sum_{i=1}^{5} \left(\frac{i}{5}\right)^2 \cdot \frac{1}{5}.$

38. $\underline{A}_5 = \sum_{i=1}^{5} \left(\frac{2i+3}{5}\right)^2 \cdot \frac{1}{5}, \quad \overline{A}_5 = \sum_{i=1}^{5} \left(\frac{2i+5}{5}\right)^2 \cdot \frac{1}{5}.$

39. $\underline{A}_5 = \sum_{i=1}^{5} \left[9 - \left(\frac{3i}{5}\right)^2\right] \cdot \frac{1}{5}, \quad \overline{A}_5 = \sum_{i=1}^{5} \left[9 - \left(\frac{3i-3}{5}\right)^2\right] \cdot \frac{1}{5}.$

40. $\underline{A}_8 = \sum_{i=1}^{8} \left[9 - \left(\frac{i}{4} + 1\right)^2\right] \cdot \frac{1}{8}, \quad \overline{A}_8 = \sum_{i=1}^{8} \left[9 - \left(\frac{i-1}{4} + 1\right)^2\right] \cdot \frac{1}{8}.$

41. $\underline{A}_{10} = \sum_{i=1}^{10} \left(\frac{i-1}{10}\right)^3 \cdot \frac{1}{10}, \quad \overline{A}_{10} = \sum_{i=1}^{10} \left(\frac{i}{10}\right)^3 \cdot \frac{1}{10}.$

42. $\underline{A}_{10} = \sum_{i=1}^{10} \sqrt{\frac{i-1}{10}} \cdot \frac{1}{10}, \quad \overline{A}_{10} = \sum_{i=1}^{10} \sqrt{\frac{i}{10}} \cdot \frac{1}{10}.$

45. $\sum_{i=1}^{n} \frac{i}{n^2} = \frac{n(n+1)}{2n^2} \to \frac{1}{2}$ as $n \to \infty$.

46. $\sum_{i=1}^{n} \left(\frac{2i}{n^2}\right)^2 \cdot \frac{2}{n} = \frac{8n(n+1)(2n+1)}{6n^3} \to \frac{8}{3}$ as $n \to \infty$.

47. $\sum_{i=1}^{n} \left(\frac{3i}{n}\right)^3 \cdot \frac{3}{n} = \frac{81n^2(n+1)^2}{4n^4} \to \frac{81}{4}$ as $n \to \infty$.

48. $\sum_{i=1}^{n} \left(\frac{2i}{n} + 2\right) \cdot \left(\frac{2}{n}\right) = \frac{4n(n+1)}{2n^2} + 2n \cdot \frac{2}{n} \to 6$ as $n \to \infty$.

49. $\sum_{i=1}^{n} \left(5 - \frac{3i}{n}\right) \left(\frac{1}{n}\right) = 5n \cdot \frac{1}{n} - \frac{3n(n+1)}{2n^2} \to \frac{7}{2}$ as $n \to \infty$.

50. $\sum_{i=1}^{n} \left(9 - \left(\frac{3i}{n}\right)^2\right) \cdot \frac{3}{n} = 9n \cdot \frac{3}{n} - \frac{27n(n+1)(2n+1)}{6n^3} \to 27 - 9 = 18$ as $n \to \infty$.

51. $\sum_{i=1}^{n} f(x_i)\Delta x = \sum_{i=1}^{n} \frac{h}{b} \cdot \frac{bi}{n} \cdot \frac{b}{n} = \frac{bh}{n^2} \cdot \frac{n(n+1)}{2} \to \frac{1}{2}bh$ as $n \to \infty$.

Section 5.4

1. $\int_1^3 (2x - 1)\, dx$

2. $\int_{-3}^2 (2 - 3x)\, dx$

3. $\int_0^{10} (x^2 + 4)\, dx$

4. $\int_0^3 (x^3 - 3x^2 + 1)\, dx$

5. $\int_4^9 \sqrt{x}\, dx$

6. $\int_0^5 \sqrt{25 - x^2}\, dx$

7. $\int_3^8 \frac{1}{\sqrt{1+x}}\, dx$

8. $\int_0^{\pi/2} \cos 2x\, dx$

9. $\int_0^{1/2} \sin 2\pi x\, dx$

10. $\int_0^{\pi/4} \tan x\, dx$

11. $\sum_{i=1}^{n} f(x_i^*)\Delta x = \sum_{i=1}^{5} (i/5)^2 (1/5) = \frac{1}{125}(5/6)(6)(11) = \frac{11}{25}.$

12. $\sum_{i=1}^{n} f(x_i^*)\Delta x = \sum_{i=1}^{5} (i/5)^3 (1/5) = \frac{1}{625} \cdot \frac{1}{4}(25)(36) = 0.36.$

13. $\sum_{i=1}^{n} f(x_i^*)\Delta x = \sum_{i=1}^{5} \frac{1}{1+i} = 1.45.$

14. $\sum_{i=1}^{n} f(x_i^*)\Delta x = \sum_{i=1}^{5} \sqrt{i} \approx 8.382332.$

16. $\sum_{i=1}^{n} f(x_i^*) \Delta x = \sum_{i=1}^{6} ((1+i/2)^2 + 2(1+i/2))(1/2) = 41.375$

18. $\sum_{i=1}^{n} f(x_i^*) \Delta x = \sum_{i=1}^{5} \left(1 + 2\sqrt{2+(i/5)}\right)(1/5) \approx 4.220102$

19. $\sum_{i=1}^{6} \left(\cos \frac{i\pi}{6}\right) \cdot \frac{\pi}{6} = -\pi/6.$

20. $\sum_{i=1}^{6} \left(\sin \frac{i\pi}{6}\right) \cdot \frac{1}{6} = \frac{1}{3} + \frac{\sqrt{3}}{6}.$

21. $6/25$
22. 0.16
23. $137/60 \approx 2.283333$
24. 6.146264 (rounded)
26. 30.875
28. 4.092967 (rounded)

29. $\sum_{i=1}^{6} \left(\cos \frac{(i-1)\pi}{6}\right) \cdot \frac{\pi}{6} = \frac{\pi}{6}.$

30. $\sum_{i=1}^{6} \left(\sin \pi \cdot \frac{i-1}{6}\right) \cdot \frac{1}{6} = \frac{1}{3} + \frac{\sqrt{3}}{6}.$

31. $33/100$
32. 0.245
33. $6086/3465 \approx 1.756421$
34. 7.505140
36. 35.9375
38. 4.157183 (rounded)

39. $\sum_{i=1}^{6} \left(\cos \frac{(2i-1)\pi}{12}\right) \cdot \frac{\pi}{6} = 0.$

40. $\sum_{i=1}^{6} \left(\sin \pi \cdot \frac{2i-1}{12}\right) \cdot \frac{1}{6} = \frac{\sqrt{2}+\sqrt{6}}{6}.$

41. $\frac{5}{7} + \frac{5}{12} + \frac{5}{17} + \frac{5}{22} + \frac{5}{27} \approx 1.83752795.$

42. 7.81558531 (rounded)

43. $\sum_{i=1}^{n} \left(\frac{2i}{n}\right)^2 \cdot \frac{2}{n} = \frac{8n(n+1)(2n+1)}{6n^3} \to \frac{8}{3}$ as $n \to \infty.$

44. $\sum_{i=1}^{n} \left(\frac{4i}{n}\right)^3 \cdot \frac{4}{n} = \frac{256n^2(n+1)^2}{4n^4} \to 64$ as $n \to \infty.$

45. $\sum_{i=1}^{n} \left(2 \cdot \frac{3i}{n} + 1\right) \cdot \frac{3}{n} = \frac{18n(n+1)}{2n^2} + n \cdot \frac{3}{n} \to 12$ as $n \to \infty.$

46. $\sum_{i=1}^{n} \left[4 - 3\left(1 + \frac{4i}{n}\right)\right] \cdot \frac{4}{n} = \frac{16}{n} \cdot n - \frac{12}{n} \cdot n - \frac{48n(n+1)}{2n^2} \to 4 - 24 = -20$ as $n \to \infty.$

47. $\sum_{i=1}^{n} \left[3 \cdot \left(\frac{3i}{n}\right)^2 + 1\right] \cdot \frac{3}{n} = \frac{81n(n+1)(2n+1)}{6n^3} + n \cdot \frac{3}{n} \to 27 + 3 = 30$ as $n \to \infty.$

48. $\sum_{i=1}^{n} \left[\left(\frac{4i}{n}\right)^3 - \frac{4i}{n}\right] \cdot \frac{4}{n} = \frac{256n^2(n+1)^2}{4n^4} - \frac{16n(n+1)}{2n^2} \to 64 - 8 = 56$ as $n \to \infty.$

49. Take $x_i = \frac{bi}{n}$ and $\Delta x = \frac{b}{n}$. The integral is equal to $\lim_{n \to \infty} \frac{n(n+1)}{2n^2} b^2 = \frac{1}{2}b^2.$

50. Take $x_i = \frac{bi}{n}$ and $\Delta x = \frac{b}{n}$. The integral is equal to $\lim_{n \to \infty} \frac{n^2(n+1)^2}{4n^4} b^4 = \frac{1}{4}b^4.$

Section 5.5

1. $\int_0^1 (3x^2 + 2\sqrt{x} + 3\sqrt[3]{x})\, dx = \left[x^3 + \frac{4}{3}x^{3/2} + \frac{9}{4}x^{4/3}\right]_0^1 = \frac{55}{12}.$

2. $\int_1^3 \frac{6}{x^2}\,dx = \left[-\frac{6}{x}\right]_1^3 = -2 + 6 = 4.$

3. $\int_0^1 x^3(1+x)^2\,dx = \left[\frac{1}{4}x^4 + \frac{2}{5}x^5 + \frac{1}{6}x^6\right]_0^1 = \frac{49}{60}.$

4. $\int_{-2}^{-1} \frac{1}{x^4}\,dx = \left[-\frac{1}{3x^3}\right]_{-2}^{-1} = \frac{7}{24}.$

6. $\int_1^2 (x^4 - x^3)\,dx = \left[\frac{1}{5}x^5 - \frac{1}{4}x^4\right]_1^2 = \frac{49}{20} = 2.45.$

7. $\int_{-1}^0 (x+1)^3\,dx = \left[\frac{1}{4}(x+1)^4\right]_{-1}^0 = \frac{1}{4}.$

8. $\int_1^3 \frac{x^4+1}{x^2}\,dx = \left[\frac{1}{3}x^3 - \frac{1}{x}\right]_1^3 = \frac{28}{3}.$

10. $\int_1^4 \frac{1}{\sqrt{x}}\,dx = \left[2\sqrt{x}\right]_1^4 = 2\sqrt{4} - 2\sqrt{1} = 2.$

12. $\int_0^1 x^{99}\,dx = \left[\frac{1}{100}x^{100}\right]_0^1 = \frac{1}{100}.$

13. $\int_{-1}^1 x^{99}\,dx = \left[\frac{1}{100}x^{100}\right]_{-1}^1 = 0.$

14. $\int_0^4 (7x^{5/2} - 5x^{3/2})\,dx = \left[2x^{7/2} - 2x^{5/2}\right]_0^4 = 192.$

16. $\int_1^2 (x^2+1)^3\,dx = \int_1^2 (x^6 + 3x^4 + 3x^2 + 1)\,dx = \left[\frac{1}{7}x^7 + \frac{3}{5}x^5 + x^3 + x\right]_1^2 = \frac{1566}{35} \approx 44.742857.$

18. $\int_1^3 \frac{10}{(2x+3)^2}\,dx = \left[-\frac{5}{2x+3}\right]_1^3 = \frac{4}{9}.$

19. $\int_1^8 x^{2/3}\,dx = \left[\frac{3}{5}x^{5/3}\right]_1^8 = \frac{93}{5}.$

20. $\int_1^9 (1+\sqrt{x})^2\,dx = \int_1^9 (1 + 2\sqrt{x} + x)\,dx = \left[x + \frac{4}{3}x^{3/2} + \frac{1}{2}x^2\right]_1^9 = \frac{248}{3}.$

22. $\int_0^4 \sqrt{3t}\,dt = \left[\frac{2}{3}t^{3/2}\sqrt{3}\right]_0^4 = \frac{16}{3}\sqrt{3}.$

24. $\int_2^3 \frac{du}{u^2} = \left[-\frac{1}{u}\right]_2^3 = -\frac{1}{3} + \frac{1}{2} = \frac{1}{6}.$

25. $\int_1^4 \frac{x^2-1}{\sqrt{x}}\,dx = \int_1^4 (x^{3/2} - x^{-1/2})\,dx = \left[\frac{2}{5}x^{5/2} - 2x^{1/2}\right]_1^4 = \frac{52}{5}.$

26. $\int_1^4 (t^2 - 2)\sqrt{t}\,dt = \left[\frac{2}{7}t^{7/2} - \frac{4}{3}t^{3/2}\right]_1^4 = \frac{566}{21}.$

27. $\int_4^7 \sqrt{3x+4}\,dx = \left[\frac{2}{9}(3x+4)^{3/2}\right]_4^7 = \frac{122}{9}.$

28. $\int_0^{\pi/2} \cos 2x\,dx = \left[\frac{1}{2}\sin 2x\right]_0^{\pi/2} = 0.$

29. $\int_0^{\pi/4} \sin x \cos x\,dx = \left[\frac{1}{2}(\sin x)^2\right]_0^{\pi/4} = \frac{1}{4}.$

30. $\int_0^{\pi} \sin^2 x \cos x\,dx = \left[\frac{1}{3}\sin^3 x\right]_0^{\pi} = 0.$

148   Section 5.5 Evaluation of Integrals

31. $\int_0^\pi \sin 5x\, dx = \left[-\frac{1}{5}\cos x\right]_0^\pi = \frac{2}{5}.$

32. $\int_0^2 \cos \pi t\, dt = \left[\frac{1}{\pi}\sin \pi t\right]_0^2 = 0.$

33. $\int_0^{\pi/2} \cos 3x\, dx = \left[\frac{1}{3}\sin 3x\right]_0^{\pi/2} = -\frac{1}{3}.$

34. $\int_0^5 \sin \frac{\pi x}{10}\, dx = \left[-\frac{10}{\pi}\cos \frac{\pi x}{10}\right]_0^5 = \frac{10}{\pi}.$

35. $\int_0^2 \cos \frac{\pi x}{4}\, dx = \left[\frac{4}{\pi}\sin \frac{\pi x}{4}\right]_0^2 = \frac{4}{\pi}.$

36. $\int_0^{\pi/8} \sec^2 2t\, dt = \left[\frac{1}{2}\tan 2t\right]_0^{\pi/8} = \frac{1}{2}.$

37. Choose $x_i = i/n$, $\Delta x = 1/n$, $x_0 = 0$, and $x_n = 1$. Then the limit in question is the limit of a Riemann sum for the function $f(x) = 2x - 1$ on the interval $0 \leq x \leq 1$, and its value is therefore

$$\int_0^1 (2x - 1)\, dx = \left[x^2 - x\right]_0^1 = 1 - 1 = 0.$$

38. This limit is the integral of $f(x) = x^2$ on the interval $0 \leq x \leq 1$, and its value is therefore $\frac{1}{3}$.

39. This limit is the integral of $f(x) = x$ on the interval $0 \leq x \leq 1$, and it is therefore equal to $\frac{1}{2}$.

40. This limit is the integral of $f(x) = x^3$ on the interval $0 \leq x \leq 1$, and it is therefore equal to $\frac{1}{4}$.

41. This limit is the integral of $f(x) = \sqrt{x}$ on the interval $0 \leq x \leq 1$, and it is therefore equal to $\frac{2}{3}$.

42. This limit is the integral of $f(x) = \sin \pi x$ on the interval $0 \leq x \leq 1$, and it is therefore equal to $2/\pi$.

43. $\int_{-2}^2 |1 - x|\, dx = 5.$
    The graph is shown below.

44. $\int_{-3}^3 |3x - 2|\, dx = \frac{85}{3}.$
    The graph is shown below.

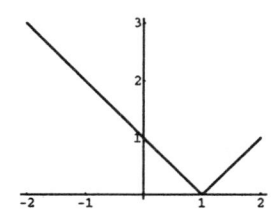

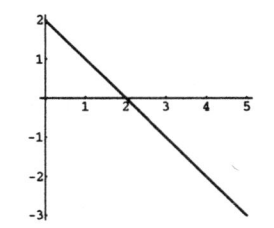

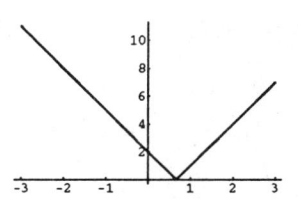

45. $\int_0^5 (2 - |x|)\, dx = -\frac{5}{2}.$
    The graph is shown below.

46. $\int_0^6 |5 - |2x||\, dx = \frac{37}{2} = 18.5.$
    The graph is shown below.

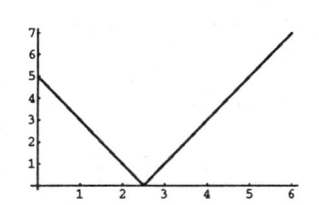

47. $\int_0^5 \sqrt{25-x^2}\, dx = \dfrac{25\pi}{4}.$

The graph is shown below.

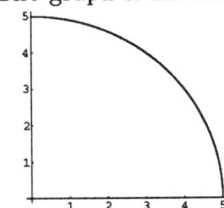

48. $\int_0^6 \sqrt{6x-x^2}\, dx = \dfrac{9\pi}{2}.$

The graph is shown below.

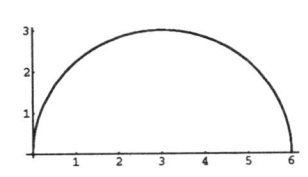

49. $0 \leq x^2 \leq x$ if $0 \leq x \leq 1$. Hence $1 \leq 1 + x^2 \leq 1 + x$ for such x. Therefore
$$1 \leq \sqrt{1+x^2} \leq \sqrt{1+x}$$
if $0 \leq x \leq 1$. Hence, by the comparison property, the inequality in Problem 49 follows.

50. $x \leq x^3 \leq 8$ if $1 \leq x \leq 2$. Hence $1 + x \leq 1 + x^3 \leq 9$ for such x. Therefore
$$\sqrt{1+x} \leq \sqrt{1+x^3} \leq 3$$
if $1 \leq x \leq 2$. The inequality in Problem 50 now follows from the comparison property.

51. $x^2 \leq x$ and $x \leq \sqrt{x}$ if $0 \leq x \leq 1$. So $1 + x^2 \leq 1 + \sqrt{x}$ for such x. Therefore
$$\dfrac{1}{1+\sqrt{x}} \leq \dfrac{1}{1+x^2}$$
if $0 \leq x \leq 1$. The inequality in Problem 51 now follows from the comparison property for definite integrals.

52. $x^2 \leq x^5$ if $x \geq 1$. So $1 + x^2 \leq 1 + x^5$ if $2 \leq x \leq 5$. Therefore
$$\dfrac{1}{1+x^5} \leq \dfrac{1}{1+x^2}$$
if $2 \leq x \leq 5$. The inequality in Problem 52 now follows from the comparison property.

53. $\sin t \leq 1$ for all t. Therefore
$$\int_0^2 \sin\left(\sqrt{x}\right) dx \leq \int_0^2 1\, dx = 2.$$

54. If $0 \leq x \leq \tfrac{1}{4}\pi$, then
$$\dfrac{\sqrt{2}}{2} \leq \cos x \leq 1.$$
Thus $\tfrac{1}{2} \leq \cos^2 x \leq 1$ for such x, and therefore $\tfrac{3}{2} \leq 1 + \cos^2 x \leq 2$ if $0 \leq x \leq \tfrac{1}{4}\pi$. Hence
$$\dfrac{1}{2} \leq \dfrac{1}{1+\cos^2 x} \leq \dfrac{2}{3}$$
if $0 \leq x \leq \tfrac{1}{4}\pi$. So
$$\dfrac{1}{2} \cdot \dfrac{\pi}{4} \leq \int_0^{\pi/4} \dfrac{1}{1+\cos^2 x}\, dx \leq \dfrac{2}{3} \cdot \dfrac{\pi}{4},$$
and the inequality in Problem 54 follows immediately.

55. If $0 \leq x \leq 1$, then
$$1 \leq 1 + x \leq 2;$$
$$\dfrac{1}{2} \leq \dfrac{1}{1+x} \leq 1;$$
$$\dfrac{1}{2} \cdot (1-0) \leq \int_0^1 \dfrac{1}{1+x}\, dx \leq 1 \cdot (1-0).$$

150   Section 5.5   Evaluation of Integrals

So the value of the integral lies between 0.5 and 1.0.

56. If $4 \leq x \leq 9$, then

$$2 \leq \sqrt{x} \leq 3;$$
$$3 \leq 1 + \sqrt{x} \leq 4;$$
$$\frac{1}{4} \leq \frac{1}{1+\sqrt{x}} \leq \frac{1}{3}$$
$$\frac{1}{4} \cdot (9-4) \leq \int_4^9 \frac{1}{1+\sqrt{x}}\,dx \leq \frac{1}{3} \cdot (9-4).$$

Hence the value of the given integral lies between $\frac{5}{4}$ and $\frac{5}{3}$.

57. If $0 \leq x \leq \frac{1}{6}\pi$, then

$$\frac{\sqrt{3}}{2} \leq \cos x \leq 1;$$
$$\frac{3}{4} \leq \cos^2 x \leq 1;$$
$$\frac{3}{4} \cdot \left(\frac{\pi}{6} - 0\right) \leq \int_0^{\pi/6} \cos^2 x\,dx \leq 1 \cdot \left(\frac{\pi}{6} - 0\right).$$

Therefore

$$\frac{\pi}{8} \leq \int_0^{\pi/6} \cos^2 x\,dx \leq \frac{\pi}{6}.$$

58. If $0 \leq x \leq \frac{1}{4}\pi$, then

$$0 \leq \sin x \leq \frac{\sqrt{2}}{2};$$
$$0 \leq \sin^2 x \leq \frac{1}{2};$$
$$0 \leq 2\sin^2 x \leq 1;$$
$$16 \leq 16 + 2\sin^2 x \leq 17;$$
$$4 \leq \sqrt{16 + 2\sin^2 x} \leq \sqrt{17};$$
$$4 \cdot \frac{\pi}{4} \leq \int_0^{\pi/4} \sqrt{16 + 2\sin^2 x}\,dx \leq \frac{\pi\sqrt{17}}{4}.$$

Therefore

$$3.14159 \leq \int_0^{\pi/4} \sqrt{16 + 2\sin^2 x}\,dx \leq 3.2384.$$

63. $1000 + \int_0^{30} V'(t)\,dt = 1000 + \left[(0.4)t^2 - 40t\right]_0^{30} = 160$ (gallons). Alternatively, the tank contains

$$V(t) = (0.4)t^2 - 40t + 1000$$

gallons at time $t \geq 0$, so at time $t = 30$ it contains $V(30) = 160$ gallons.

64. In 1990 the population in thousands was

$$125 + \int_{t=0}^{20} \left(8 + (-0.5)t + (0.03)t^2\right)\,dt = 125 + \left[8t + (0.25)t^2 + (0.01)t^3\right]_0^{20}$$
$$= 125 + 160 + 100 + 80 = 465 \text{ (thousands)}.$$

Section 5.5 Evaluation of Integrals

65. In Fig. 5.5.11 of the text we see that
$$\frac{12-4x}{9} \leq \frac{1}{x} \leq \frac{3-x}{2}.$$
Therefore
$$\frac{2}{3} \leq \int_1^2 \frac{1}{x}\,dx \leq \frac{3}{4}.$$
Another way to put it would be to write
$$\int_1^2 \frac{1}{x}\,dx = 0.708333 \pm 0.041667.$$

For a really sophisticated answer, you could point out that, from the figure, it appears that the low estimate of the integral is about twice as accurate as (has half the error of) the high estimate. So
$$\int_1^2 \frac{1}{x}\,dx \approx \frac{2}{3}\cdot\frac{2}{3} + \frac{1}{3}\cdot\frac{3}{4} \approx 0.6944.$$

66. Because $L(x) \leq f(x) \leq L(x) + 0.07$ if $0 \leq x \leq 1$, it follows that
$$\int_0^1 L(x)\,dx \leq \int_0^1 f(x)\,dx \leq \int_0^1 [L(x)+0.07]\,dx.$$
That is,
$$\frac{3}{4} \leq \int_0^1 \frac{1}{1+x^2}\,dx \leq \frac{41}{50}.$$
Another way to put it would be to write
$$\int_0^1 \frac{1}{1+x^2}\,dx = 0.785 \pm 0.035.$$
Or, for the reasons given in the previous solution,
$$\int_0^1 \frac{1}{1+x^2}\,dx \approx \frac{1}{3}\cdot\frac{41}{50} + \frac{2}{3}\cdot\frac{3}{4} \approx 0.7733.$$

Section 5.6

1. $\frac{1}{2}\int_0^2 x^4\,dx = 16/5.$

2. $\frac{1}{3}\int_1^4 \sqrt{x}\,dx = 14/9$

4. $\frac{1}{4}\int_0^4 8x\,dx = 16.$

6. $\frac{1}{8}\int_{-4}^4 x^2\,dx = 16/3.$

8. $\frac{1}{3}\int_1^4 x^{-1/2}\,dx = 2/3.$

10. $\frac{2}{\pi}\int_0^{\pi/2} \sin 2x\,dx = \frac{2}{\pi}.$

11. $\frac{1}{\pi}\int_0^\pi \sin 2x\,dx = \frac{1}{\pi}\left[-\frac{1}{2}\cos 2x\right]_0^\pi = 0.$

12. $\int_{-1/2}^{1/2} \cos 2\pi t\,dt = \left[\frac{1}{2\pi}\sin 2\pi t\right]_{-1/2}^{1/2} = 0.$

14. $\int_1^2 (y^5 - 1)\,dy = \left[\frac{1}{6}y^6 - y\right]_1^2 = \frac{19}{2}.$

16. $\int_{-1}^1 (x^3+2)^2\,dx = \left[\frac{1}{7}x^7 + x^4 + 4x\right]_{-1}^1 = \frac{58}{7}.$

18. $\int_{-2}^{-1} \frac{x^2 - x + 3}{\sqrt[3]{x}}\,dx = \frac{3}{40}\left(73 - 96\sqrt[3]{4}\right) \approx -5.95429.$

20. $\int_{-1}^{2} |x|\, dx = \int_{-1}^{0} (-x)\, dx + \int_{0}^{2} x\, dx = \frac{5}{2}$.

22. On the interval $-1 \leq x \leq 1$ of integration, the integrand is equal to $x - 2$, so the value of the integral is -4.

24. $\int_{0}^{2} |x - \sqrt{x}|\, dx = \int_{0}^{1} (\sqrt{x} - x)\, dx + \int_{1}^{2} (x - \sqrt{x})\, dx$
$= \left[\frac{2}{3} x^{3/2} - \frac{1}{2} x^2\right]_{0}^{1} + \left[\frac{1}{2} x^2 - \frac{2}{3} x^{3/2}\right]_{1}^{2}$
$= \frac{1}{3}\left(7 - 4\sqrt{2}\right) \approx 0.447715251$.

25. Split the integral into three integrals—one on the interval from -2 to -1, one on the interval from -1 to 1, and one on the interval from 1 to 2.

26. $\int_{0}^{\pi/3} \sin 3x\, dx = \left[-\frac{1}{3} \cos 3x\right]_{0}^{\pi/3} = \frac{2}{3}$.

28. $\int_{5}^{10} \frac{dx}{\sqrt{x-1}} = \left[2\sqrt{x-1}\right]_{5}^{10} = 2$.

29. $\int_{-1}^{0} (1 - x^4)\, dx + \int_{0}^{1} (1 - x^3)\, dx = \left[x - \frac{1}{5} x^5\right]_{-1}^{0} + \left[x - \frac{1}{4} x^4\right]_{0}^{1} = 1 - \frac{1}{5} + 1 - \frac{1}{4} = \frac{31}{20}$.

30. $\int_{0}^{\pi/2} \frac{1}{4}\pi^2 \sin x\, dx + \int_{\pi/2}^{\pi} (\pi x - x^2)\, dx = \left[-\frac{1}{4}\pi^2 \cos x\right]_{0}^{\pi/2} + \left[\frac{1}{2}\pi x^2 - \frac{1}{3} x^3\right]_{\pi/2}^{\pi}$
$= \frac{1}{4}\pi^2 + \frac{1}{2}\pi^3 - \frac{1}{3}\pi^3 - \frac{1}{8}\pi^3 + \frac{1}{24}\pi^3 = \frac{1}{4}\pi^2 + \frac{1}{12}\pi^3$.

31. $\int_{-3}^{0} (x^3 - 9x)\, dx - \int_{0}^{3} (x^3 - 9x)\, dx = \left[\frac{1}{4} x^4 - \frac{9}{2} x^2\right]_{-3}^{0} - \left[\frac{1}{4} x^4 - \frac{9}{2} x^2\right]_{0}^{3} = \frac{81}{4} + \frac{81}{4} = \frac{81}{2}$.

32. $\int_{-3}^{0} (x^3 - 2x^2 - 15x)\, dx - \int_{0}^{5} (x^3 - 2x^2 - 15x)\, dx$
$= \left[\frac{1}{4} x^4 - \frac{2}{3} x^3 - \frac{15}{2} x^2\right]_{-3}^{0} - \left[\frac{1}{4} x^4 - \frac{2}{3} x^3 - \frac{15}{2} x^2\right]_{0}^{5}$
$= \frac{117}{4} + \frac{1375}{12} = \frac{863}{6}$.

33. Height: $s(t) = 400 - 16t^2$. Velocity: $v(t) = -32t$. Time of impact T occurs when $T^2 = 25$, so that $T = 5$.
$$s_{\text{AV}} = \frac{1}{5} \int_{0}^{5} (400 - 16t^2)\, dt = \frac{1}{5}\left[400t - \frac{16}{3} t^3\right]_{0}^{5} = \frac{800}{3} \approx 266.67 \text{ (ft/s)}.$$

34. $P_{\text{AV}} = \frac{1}{10} \int_{0}^{10} (100 + 10t + (0.02)t^2)\, dt = \frac{1}{10}\left[100t + 5t^2 + \frac{0.02}{3} t^3\right]_{0}^{10}$
$= \frac{1}{10}\left(1000 + 500 + \frac{20}{3}\right) = \frac{452}{3} \approx 150.667$.

35. $\frac{1}{10} \int_{0}^{10} 50(10 - t)^2\, dt = \left[-\frac{5}{3}(10 - t)^3\right]_{0}^{10} = \frac{5}{3}(10)^3 \approx 1666.67$ (gallons).

36. $T_{\text{AV}} = \frac{1}{6} \int_{12}^{18} \left(80 + 10 \sin \frac{\pi(t - 10)}{12}\right) dt = \frac{1}{6}\left[80t - \frac{120}{\pi} \cos \frac{\pi(t - 10)}{12}\right]_{12}^{18}$
$= 80 + \frac{10}{\pi}(1 + \sqrt{3}) \approx 88.6984$ (°F, we're sure).

37. $T_{\text{AV}} = \frac{1}{10} \int_{0}^{10} (40x - 4x^2)\, dx = \frac{1}{10}\left[20x^2 - \frac{4}{3} x^3\right]_{0}^{10} = \frac{1}{10}\left(2000 - \frac{4000}{3}\right) = \frac{200}{3}$.

38. If A represents the area of the cross section at distance x from the center of the sphere, then
$$A_{\text{AV}} = \int_{0}^{1} \pi (1 - x^2)\, dx = \pi \left[x - \frac{1}{3} x^3\right]_{0}^{1} = \frac{2}{3}\pi.$$

39. If A represents the area of a cross section of the cone at a distance y from the vertex, then

$$A_{\text{AV}} = \frac{1}{2}\int_0^2 \pi\left(\frac{y^2}{4}\right)dy = \frac{\pi}{8}\left[\frac{1}{3}y^3\right]_0^2 = \frac{\pi}{3}.$$

40. Let $v(t)$ represent velocity of the car. Then $v(t) = at$ and the position of the car at time t is $x(t) = \frac{1}{2}at^2$. So the final velocity, at time $t = T$, is $v(T) = aT$. Average velocity during the T seconds:

$$v_{\text{AV}} = \frac{1}{T}\int_0^T at\, dt = \frac{1}{T}\left[\frac{1}{2}at^2\right]_0^T = \frac{1}{2}aT.$$

The final position, at time $t = T$, is $x(T) = \frac{1}{2}aT^2$. Average position during the T seconds:

$$x_{\text{AV}} = \frac{1}{T}\int_0^T \frac{1}{2}at^2\, dt = \frac{1}{T}\cdot\frac{a}{2}\cdot\left[\frac{1}{3}t^3\right]_0^T = \frac{a}{6T}\cdot T^3 = \frac{1}{6}aT^2.$$

41. Part (a): $A(x) = \frac{1}{2}\cdot 6 \cdot (9 - x^2)$, $-3 \le x \le 3$. Part (b):

$$\frac{1}{6}\int_{-3}^3 A(x)\, dx = 18.$$

Part (c): Such a triangle would have height 6. so there are two such triangles. One has its upper vertex at $(-\sqrt{3}, 6)$ and the other has its upper vertex at $(\sqrt{3}, 6)$.

42. Part (a): $A(x) = x(10 - x)$, $0 \le x \le 10$. Part (b):

$$\frac{1}{10}\int_0^{10} A(x)\, dx = \frac{50}{3}.$$

Part (c): There are two such rectangles. One has base $\frac{1}{3}(15 + 5\sqrt{3})$ and height $\frac{5}{3}(3 - \sqrt{3})$. The other has base $\frac{1}{3}(15 - 5\sqrt{3})$ and height $\frac{5}{3}(3 + \sqrt{3})$.

43. Part (a): $A(x) = 2x\sqrt{16 - x^2}$, $0 \le x \le 4$. Part (b):

$$\frac{1}{4}\int_0^4 A(x)\, dx = \frac{32}{3}.$$

Part (c): $A(x) = \frac{32}{3}$ for two values of x in $[0, 4]$. Thus there are two such rectangles. One has base of length $\frac{4}{3}\sqrt{18 + 6\sqrt{5}} \approx 7.473379$ and the other has base of length $\frac{4}{3}\sqrt{18 - 6\sqrt{5}} \approx 2.854577$.

44. Part (a): $A(x) = 2x\left(16 - x^2\right)$, $0 \le x \le 4$. Part (b):

$$\frac{1}{4}\int_0^4 A(x)\, dx = 32.$$

Part (c): We used *Mathematica* to solve the equation $A(x) = 32$. There are three solutions, approximately -4.42864, 1.07838, and 3.35026, but the first of these solutions is not in the domain of A. Hence there are two such rectangles. One has base of length approximately 2.15676 and the other has base of length approximately 6.70052.

45. $f'(x) = \left(x^2 + 1\right)^{17}$

46. $g'(t) = \left(t^2 + 25\right)^{1/2}$

47. $h'(z) = (z - 1)^{1/3}$

48. $A'(x) = \dfrac{1}{x}$

49. $f'(x) = -x - \dfrac{1}{x}$

50. $G'(x) = \dfrac{x}{x^2 + 1}$

51. $G'(x) = \sqrt{x + 4}$

52. $G'(x) = \sin^3 x$

53. $G'(x) = (x^3 + 1)^{1/2}$

54. First, $f(x) = g(u)$, where $g(u) = \int_0^u (1+t^3)^{1/2} \, dt$ and $u = x^2$. Now $g'(u) = (1+u^3)^{1/2}$, and therefore $f'(x) = g'(u) \dfrac{du}{dx} = 2x \left(1 + x^6\right)^{1/2}$.

56. $f'(x) = \left(1 - \sin^2 x\right)^{1/2} \cos x = |\cos x| \cos x$.

58. $f'(x) = \left(1 + \sin^2 x\right)^3 \cos x$

60. $f'(x) = 5x^4 \left(1 + x^{10}\right)^{1/2}$

61. $dy = \dfrac{1}{x} \, dx$: $y(x) = \displaystyle\int_1^x \dfrac{1}{t} \, dt$.

62. $dy = \dfrac{1}{1+x^2} \, dx$: $y(x) = \dfrac{\pi}{4} + \displaystyle\int_1^x \dfrac{1}{1+t^2} \, dt$.

63. $dy = \sqrt{1+x^2} \, dx$: $y(x) = 10 + \displaystyle\int_5^x \sqrt{1+t^2} \, dt$.

64. $y(x) = 2 + \displaystyle\int_1^x \tan t \, dt$.

66. The average value of the derivative of f is
$$\dfrac{1}{b-a} \int_a^b f'(x) \, dx = \dfrac{1}{b-a} \Big[f(x)\Big]_a^b = \dfrac{f(b) - f(a)}{b - a}.$$

67. Part (a): $g(0) = 0$, $g(2) = 4$, $g(4) = 8$, $g(6) = 4$, $g(8) = -4$, and $g(10) = -8$. Part (b): The function g is increasing on $(0, 4)$ and decreasing on $(4, 10)$. Part (c): Its maximum value is 8 and its minimum value is -8. Part (d): The graph of $g(x)$ is shown on the right.

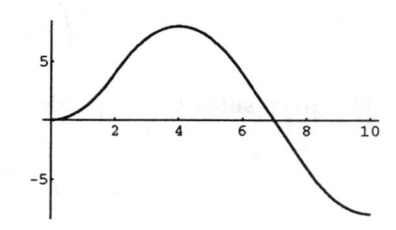

68. Part (a): $g(0) = 0$, $g(2) = 4$, $g(6) = 10$, $g(8) = 3$, and $g(10) = -2$. Part (b): The function g is increasing on $(0, 5)$ and decreasing on $(5, 10)$. Part (c): The global maximum of g is $g(5) = \dfrac{23}{2}$ and the global minimum of g is $g(10) = -2$. Part (d): The graph of $g(x)$ is shown on the right.

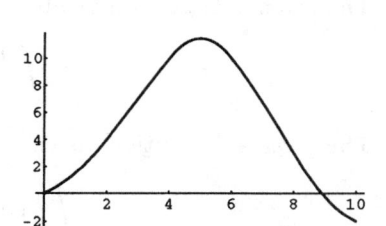

69. Part (a): The function g has local extrema when $x = 0$, π, 2π, 3π, and 4π. Part (b): The global maximum value of g is $g(3\pi) = 3\pi$ and the global minimum is $g(4\pi) = -4\pi$. Part (c): The extrema of f correspond to inflection points of g. The approximate x-coordinates of these points are 2.028758, 4.913180, 7.978666, and 11.085538. Part (d): The graph of $g(x)$ is shown on the right.

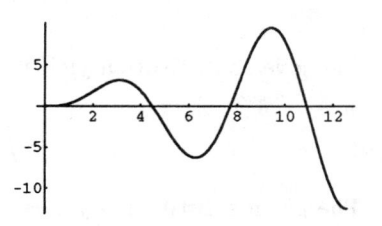

70. Part (a): The function g has local extrema when $x = 0$, π, 2π, 3π, and 4π. Part (b): The global minimum of g is $g(0) = 0$ and the global maximum occurs where $x = \pi$. Part (c): The extrema of f correspond to inflection points of g. The approximate x-coordinates of these points are 4.49493409, 7.725252, and 10.904122. Part (d): The graph of $g(x)$ is shown on the right.

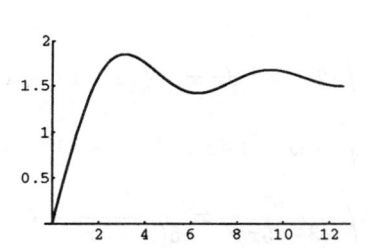

Section 5.7

1. Let $u = 3x - 5$. Then $du = 3\,dx$, so $dx = \tfrac{1}{3}\,du$. Thus

$$\int (3x-5)^{17}\,dx = \int \tfrac{1}{3}u^{17}\,du = \tfrac{1}{54}u^{18} + C = \tfrac{1}{54}(3x-5)^{18} + C.$$

2. Let $u = 4x + 7$. Then $dx = \tfrac{1}{4}\,du$. Thus

$$\int \frac{1}{(4x+7)^6}\,dx = \tfrac{1}{4}\int u^{-6}\,du = -\tfrac{1}{20}u^{-5} + C = -\frac{1}{20(4x+7)^5} + C.$$

3. The given substitution yields

$$\int \tfrac{1}{2}u^{1/2}\,du = \tfrac{1}{3}u^{3/2} + C = \tfrac{1}{3}(x^2+9)^{3/2} + C.$$

4. The given substitution yields

$$\int \tfrac{1}{6}u^{-1/3}\,du = \tfrac{1}{4}u^{2/3} + C = \tfrac{1}{4}(2x^3-1)^{2/3} + C.$$

5. The given substitution yields

$$\int \tfrac{1}{5}\sin u\,du = -\tfrac{1}{5}\cos u + C = -\tfrac{1}{5}\cos 5x + C.$$

6. The given substitution yields

$$\int \tfrac{1}{k}\cos u\,du = \tfrac{1}{k}\sin u + C = \tfrac{1}{k}\sin kx + C.$$

7. The given substitution yields

$$\int \tfrac{1}{4}\sin u\,du = -\tfrac{1}{4}\cos u + C = -\tfrac{1}{4}\cos(2x^2) + C.$$

8. The given substitution yields

$$\int \tfrac{2}{3}\cos u\,du = \tfrac{2}{3}\sin u + C = \tfrac{2}{3}\sin\left(x^{3/2}\right) + C.$$

9. The given substitution yields

$$\int u^5\,du = \tfrac{1}{6}u^6 + C = \tfrac{1}{6}(1-\cos x)^6 + C.$$

10. The given substitution yields

$$\int \tfrac{1}{6}u^{-1/2}\,du = \tfrac{1}{3}u^{1/2} + C = \tfrac{1}{3}\sqrt{5+2\sin 3x} + C.$$

12. $\displaystyle\int (2-x)^5\,dx = -\tfrac{1}{6}(2-x)^6 + C$

14. $\displaystyle\int \sqrt{2x+1}\,dx = \tfrac{1}{3}(2x+1)^{3/2} + C$

16. $\displaystyle\int \frac{dx}{(3-5x)^2} = \frac{1}{5(3-5x)} + C$

18. $\int \cos \frac{\pi t}{3} \, dt = \frac{3}{\pi} \sin \frac{\pi t}{3} + C$

19. $\int \sec 2\theta \tan 2\theta \, d\theta = \frac{1}{2} \sec 2\theta + C$

20. $\int \csc^2 5x \, dx = -\frac{1}{5} \cot 5x + C$

22. $\int 3t \left(1 - 2t^2\right)^{10} dt = -\frac{3}{44} \left(1 - 2t^2\right)^{11} + C$

24. $\int \frac{t}{\sqrt{2t^2 + 1}} \, dt = \frac{1}{2}(2t^2 + 1)^{1/2} + C$

26. $\int \frac{x^2}{\sqrt[3]{x^3 + 1}} \, dx = \frac{1}{2} \left(x^3 + 1\right)^{2/3} + C$

28. $\int t \sec^2 t^2 \, dt = \frac{1}{2} \tan t^2 + C$

30. $\int y^2 \sqrt[3]{2 - 4y^3} \, dy = -\frac{1}{16} \left(2 - 4y^3\right)^{4/3} + C$

32. $\int \sin^5 3z \cos 3z \, dz = \frac{1}{18} \sin^6 3z + C$

34. $\int \sec^3 \theta \tan \theta \, d\theta = \frac{1}{3} \sec^3 \theta + C$

36. $\int \frac{dx}{\sqrt{x}\left(1 + \sqrt{x}\right)^2} = \frac{-2}{1 + \sqrt{x}} + C$

38. $\int \frac{(x+2)\,dx}{(x^2 + 4x + 3)^2} = -\frac{1}{4}(x^2 + 4x + 3)^{-2} + C$

40. $\int \frac{2 - x^2}{(x^3 - 6x + 1)^5} \, dx = \frac{1}{12} \left(x^3 - 6x + 1\right)^{-4} + C$

42. $\int_0^4 \frac{dx}{\sqrt{2x+1}} = \left[\sqrt{2x+1}\right]_0^4 = 2$

44. $\int_1^4 \frac{(1+\sqrt{x})^4}{\sqrt{x}} \, dx = \left[\frac{2}{5}(1+\sqrt{x})^5\right]_1^4 = \frac{422}{5}$

46. $\int_0^{\pi/2} \sin x \cos x \, dx = \left[\frac{1}{2} \sin^2 x\right]_0^{\pi/2} = \frac{1}{2}$

48. $\int_0^{\sqrt{\pi}} t \sin \frac{t^2}{2} \, dt = \left[-\cos \frac{t^2}{2}\right]_0^{\sqrt{\pi}} = 1$

50. $\int_0^{\pi/2} \sec^2 \frac{x}{2} \, dx = \left[2 \tan \frac{x}{2}\right]_0^{\pi/2} = 2$

52. $\int_0^{\pi/2} (\cos x)\sqrt{\sin x} \, dx = \left[\frac{2}{3}(\sin x)^{3/2}\right]_0^{\pi/2} = \frac{2}{3}$

54. $\int_{\pi^2/4}^{\pi^2} \frac{\sin \sqrt{x} \cos \sqrt{x}}{\sqrt{x}} \, dx = \left[(\sin \sqrt{x})^2\right]_{\pi^2/4}^{\pi^2} = -1$

56. $\int \cos^2 x \, dx = \int \frac{1}{2}(1 + \cos 2x)\, dx = \frac{1}{2}(x + \frac{1}{2} \sin 2x) + C$

58. $\int_0^1 \cos^2 \pi t \, dt = \left[\frac{1}{2}t + \frac{\sin 2\pi t}{4\pi}\right]_0^1 = \frac{1}{2}$

60. $\int_0^{\pi/12} \tan^2 3t \, dt = \int_0^{\pi/12} (\sec^2 3t - 1) \, dt = \left[\frac{1}{3}\tan 3t - t\right]_0^{\pi/12} = \frac{4-\pi}{12}$

62. $\int_0^{\pi/2} \cos^3 x \, dx = \int_0^{\pi/2} \cos x(1-\sin^2 x) \, dx = \int_0^{\pi/2} (\cos x - \sin^2 x \cos x) \, dx$
$= \left[\sin x - \frac{1}{3}\sin^3 x\right]_0^{\pi/2} = 1 - \frac{1}{3} = \frac{2}{3}$

64. $\frac{1}{2}\sec^2 \theta + C_2 = \frac{1}{2}(1+\tan^2 \theta) + C_2 = \frac{1}{2}\tan^2 \theta + \frac{1}{2} + C_2$, so $C_1 = \frac{1}{2} + C_2$

66. $\frac{x^2}{2(1-x^2)} - \frac{x^2-1}{2(1-x^2)} = -\frac{1}{2}$, a constant

67. $\int_{-a}^{a} f(x) \, dx = \int_{-a}^{0} f(x) \, dx + \int_0^a f(x) \, dx = -\int_a^0 f(-u) \, du + \int_0^a f(x) \, dx$
$= \int_0^a f(-u) \, du + \int_0^a f(x) \, dx = -\int_0^a f(u) \, du + \int_0^a f(x) \, dx = 0$

68. $\int_{-a}^{a} f(x) \, dx = \int_{-a}^{0} f(x) \, dx + \int_0^a f(x) \, dx = -\int_a^0 f(-u) \, du + \int_0^a f(x) \, dx$
$= \int_0^a f(u) \, du + \int_0^a f(x) \, dx = 2\int_0^a f(x) \, dx$

Section 5.8

1. $\int_{-4}^{4} (16 - x^2) \, dx = \frac{256}{3}$.

2. $\int_{-5}^{5} (25 - x^2) \, dx = \frac{500}{3}$.

3. $\int_0^3 (3x - x^2) \, dx = \frac{9}{2}$.

4. $\int_0^3 (9x - x^3) \, dx = \frac{81}{4}$.

5. $\int_{-2}^{2} (12 - 3x^2) \, dx = 32$.

6. $\int_0^2 (6x - 3x^2) \, dx = 4$.

7. $\int_{-2}^{2} (16 - 4x^2) \, dx = \frac{128}{3}$.

8. $\int_{-2}^{2} (8 - 2x^2) \, dx = \frac{64}{3}$.

9. The two solutions of $6 - x^2 + 3x = 0$ are $a = \frac{3-\sqrt{33}}{2}$ and $b = \frac{3+\sqrt{33}}{2}$, so the area is
$\int_a^b (6 - x^2 + 3x) \, dx = \frac{11}{2}\sqrt{33} \approx 31.595094556$.

10. $\int_0^4 (4x - x^2) \, dx = \frac{32}{3}$.

12. $A = \int_1^3 \frac{1}{(x+1)^2} \, dx = \left[\frac{-1}{x+1}\right]_1^3 = \frac{1}{4}$.

14. $A = \int_{-1}^{2} (x^2 - (-1)) \, dx = \left[\frac{1}{3}x^3 + x\right]_{-1}^{2} = 6.$

16. $A = \int_{0}^{4} (4x - x^2) \, dx = \left[2x^2 - \frac{1}{3}x^3\right]_{0}^{4} = \frac{32}{3}.$

18. First solve $x^4 - 4 = 3x^2$ for $x = -2, x = 2$. The graph of $y = 3x^2$ is above the graph of $y = x^4 - 4$ on the interval $-2 \leq x \leq 2$, so the area is
$$A = \int_{-2}^{2} (3x^2 - x^4 + 4) \, dx = \left[x^3 - \frac{1}{5}x^5 + 4x\right]_{-2}^{2} = 19.2.$$

20. $A = 2\int_{0}^{1} \left(x^{1/3} - x^3\right) dx = 2\left[\frac{3}{4}x^{4/3} - \frac{1}{4}x^4\right]_{0}^{1} = 1.$

21. $\int_{0}^{2} (2x - x^2) \, dx = \frac{4}{3}.$

22. $\int_{-2}^{2} (8 - 2x^2) \, dx = \frac{64}{3}.$

23. $\int_{-5}^{5} (25 - y^2) \, dy = \frac{500}{3}.$

24. $\int_{-4}^{4} (32 - 2y^2) \, dy = \frac{512}{3}.$

25. $\int_{-1}^{3} (2x + 3 - x^2) \, dx = \frac{32}{3}.$

26. $\int_{-2}^{4} (2x + 8 - x^2) \, dx = 36.$

27. $\int_{-2}^{3} (y + 6 - y^2) \, dy = \frac{125}{6}.$

28. $\int_{-4}^{2} (8 - 2y - y^2) \, dy = 36.$

29. $\int_{0}^{1} (\sqrt{x} - x^2) \, dx = \frac{1}{3}.$

30. $\int_{0}^{1} (x^2 - x^3) \, dx = \frac{1}{12}.$

31. $\int_{1}^{25} \left(\frac{1}{12}(-5-x) + \frac{1}{2}\sqrt{x}\right) dx = \frac{16}{3}.$

32. $\int_{-1/2}^{3} (3 + 5x - 2x^2) \, dx = \frac{343}{24}.$

33. $\int_{1/2}^{5/2} (12y - y^2 - 5 - 3y^2) \, dy = \frac{16}{3}.$

34. $\int_{2/3}^{2} (x^2 - 4(x-1)^2) \, dx = \frac{32}{27}.$

35. $\int_{-1}^{2} (-3y^2 + 3y + 6) \, dy = \frac{27}{2}.$

36. $\int_{-2}^{2} (32 - 2x^4) \, dx = \frac{512}{5}.$

37. $\int_{0}^{4} (32\sqrt{x} - x^3) \, dx = \frac{320}{3}.$

38. $\int_{-2}^{0} \left(x^3 - 2x + x^2\right) dx + \int_{0}^{1} \left(2x - x^2 - x^3\right) dx = \dfrac{37}{12}.$

39. $2\int_{0}^{1} \left(x^{2/3} - x^2\right) dx = \dfrac{8}{15}.$

40. $\int_{-\sqrt{6}}^{\sqrt{6}} \left(\dfrac{1}{2}y^2 + 3 - y^2\right) dy = 4\sqrt{6}.$

41. $\int_{-1}^{1} (g(x) - f(x))\, dx = \dfrac{4}{3}.$

42. $\int_{-1}^{1} (g(x) - f(x))\, dx = \dfrac{8}{5}.$

43. $\int_{-1}^{0} (g(x) - f(x))\, dx + \int_{0}^{2} (f(x) - g(x))\, dx = \dfrac{37}{12}.$

44. $\int_{-2}^{0} (g(x) - f(x))\, dx + \int_{0}^{1} (f(x) - g(x))\, dx = \dfrac{37}{12}.$

45. $\int_{-3}^{3} 4x\sqrt{9 - x^2}\, dx = 0;\quad \int_{-3}^{3} 5\sqrt{9 - x^2}\, dx = \dfrac{45}{2}\pi.$

46. If we let $u = x^2$, then $dy = 2x\,dx$ and the new limits of integration will be 0 and 9. The resulting integral is
$$\int_{0}^{9} \dfrac{1}{2}\sqrt{81 - u^2}\, du,$$
which is one-eighth the area of a circle of radius 9. Hence the value of the integral is $\dfrac{81}{8}\pi$.

48. The area of the parabolic segment is $\int_{-1}^{1} (1 - x^2)\, dx = \left[x - \tfrac{1}{3}x^3\right]_{-1}^{1} = \tfrac{2}{3} + \tfrac{2}{3} = \tfrac{4}{3}$, which is four-thirds the area of triangle ABC.

49. The points of intersection are $A(-1, 1)$ and $B(2, 4)$, and C is the point $C(1/2, 1/4)$. The normal line at C has the equation $4x + 4y = 3$. The line through A and B has equation $y = x + 2$. These lines meet at $(-5/8, 11/8)$. The altitude of the triangle ABC from its vertex at C has length $\tfrac{9}{8}\sqrt{2}$ and the base of the triangle has length $3\sqrt{2}$. So the area of the triangle is $\tfrac{27}{8}$. The area of the segment is $\tfrac{9}{2}$, and this is indeed four-thirds the area of the triangle.

50. Let $A_b = \int_{1}^{b} \dfrac{1}{x^2}\, dx$. Then $A_b = \left[-\dfrac{1}{x}\right]_{1}^{b} = 1 - \dfrac{1}{b}$. Therefore $A = \lim_{b \to \infty} A_b = 1.$

51. The graph of $y = 2x^3 - 2x^2 - 12x$ crosses the x-axis where $x = -2$, 0, and 3. The area of the region between the graph and the x-axis in the second quadrant is $32/3$ and the area between the graph and the x-axis in the fourth quadrant is $63/2$ (the value of the integral is $-63/2$). So the total area is $253/6$.

52. First, it is not difficult to show that the integral of $f(x)$ over the interval $-h \leq x \leq h$ is $\dfrac{2}{3}ph^3 + 2rh$. But with $a = -h$, $m = 0$, and $b = h$, we find that
$$\dfrac{h}{3}[f(a) + 4f(m) + f(b)] = \dfrac{2}{3}ph^2 + 2rh$$
as well. Therefore for $a = -h$, $m = 0$, and $b = h$, we have
$$\int_{a}^{b} f(x)\, dx = \dfrac{h}{3}[f(a) + 4f(m) + f(b)].$$
But the right-hand side above depends only on $f(a)$, $f(m)$, $f(b)$, and h, so it is independent of translation along the x-axis. The result in Problem 52 now follows.

53. The area of the loop is

$$2\int_0^5 (5-x)\sqrt{x}\, dx = 2\int_0^5 \left(5x^{1/2} - x^{3/2}\right) dx = 2\left[\frac{10}{3}x^{3/2} - \frac{2}{5}x^{5/2}\right]_0^5 = \frac{40}{3}\sqrt{5}.$$

54. The area of the loop is $2\int_{-3}^0 -x\sqrt{x+3}\, dx = \frac{24}{5}\sqrt{3}$. The minus sign is needed because $x\sqrt{x+3}$ is negative for $-3 \leq x \leq 0$.

55. The curves cross where $x = a \approx -0.824132312$ and where $x = b \approx 0.8324132312$, and the area between them is

$$\int_a^b \left[(\cos x) - x^2\right] dx \approx 1.09475.$$

56. The curves cross where $x = 0$ and where $x = b \approx 2.316934289$, and the area between them is

$$\int_0^b \left[(\sin x) - x^2 + 2x\right] dx \approx 2.90108.$$

57. The curves cross where $x = a = -\left(2^{1/4}\right)$ and where $x = b = 2^{1/4}$, and the area between them is

$$\int_a^b \left(\frac{1}{1+x^2} + 1 - x^2\right) dx = 2 \cdot \left[2^{1/4} - \frac{1}{3}\cdot 2^{3/4} + \arctan\left(2^{1/4}\right)\right] \approx 3.000441.$$

58. The curves cross where $x = a \approx -1.752171779$ and where $x = 2$, and the area between them is

$$\int_a^2 \left(2x - x^2 - x^4 + 16\right) dx \approx 46.801821.$$

59. The curves $y = x^2$ and $y = k - x^2$ cross where $x = a = -\sqrt{k/2}$ and where $x = b = \sqrt{k/2}$. When we solve the equation

$$\int_a^b \left(k - 2x^2\right) dx = 72$$

for k, we find that $k = 18$.

60. By symmetry, it is sufficient to work in the first quadrant. Then the curves $y = k$ and $y = 100 - x^2$ cross at the point $x = b = \sqrt{100 - k}$. When we solve the equation

$$\int_0^b \left(10 - x^2 - k\right) dx = kb + \int_b^{10} \left(100 - x^2\right) dx$$

for k, we find that $k = 50\left(2 - 2^{1/3}\right)$.

Section 5.9

1. $T_4 = 8$, and the true value of the integral is also 8.
2. $T_5 = 2.34$, and the true value of the integral is $\frac{7}{3}$.
3. $T_5 = 0.65$, and the true value of the integral is $\frac{2}{3}$.
4. $T_4 = 0.71$, and the true value of the integral is $\frac{2}{3}$.
5. $T_3 = 0.98$, and the true value of the integral is 1.
6. $T_4 = 1.90$, and the true value of the integral is 2.

7. $M_4 = 8$.
8. $M_5 = 2.33$.
9. $M_5 = 0.67$.
10. $M_4 = 0.65$.
11. $M_3 = 1.01$.
12. $M_4 = 2.05$.
13. $T_4 = 8.75$, $S_4 \approx 8.6667$, integral: $\frac{26}{3}$.
14. $T_4 \approx 65.8594$, $S_4 \approx 63.7500$, integral: 63.75.
15. $T_4 \approx 0.0973$, $S_4 \approx 0.0940$, integral: 0.09375.
16. $T_4 \approx 1.2182$, $S_4 \approx 1.2189$, integral: $\frac{2}{3}(2\sqrt{2}-1) \approx 1.218951417$.
17. $T_6 \approx 3.2599$, $S_6 \approx 3.2411$, integral: approximately 3.241309263.
18. $T_6 \approx 1.0980$, $S_6 \approx 1.1090$, integral: approximately 1.098439868.
19. $T_8 \approx 8.5499$, $S_8 \approx 8.5509$, integral: approximately 8.550733044.
20. $T_{10} \approx 1.150703$, $S_{10} \approx 1.149170$, integral: approximately 1.14915.
22. (a) 28.3; (b) 28.6.
24. (a) $14.33°C$; (b) $14.23°C$.
26. Simpson's approximation with $n = 10$ gives

$$\int_1^{2.7} \frac{1}{x}\,dx \approx 0.993277383 \quad \text{and} \quad \int_1^{2.8} \frac{1}{x}\,dx \approx 1.029651463.$$

The error is in each case less than $\dfrac{(24)(1.8)^5}{(180)(10^4)} \approx 0.000251942$, so the first integral above is less than 0.993530 and the second is greater than 1.029399. Therefore $2.7 < e < 2.8$.

27. With $f(x) = \dfrac{1}{x}$, we have $f''(x) = \dfrac{2}{x}$. The maximum value of $|f''(x)|$ for $1 \le x \le 2$ is 2. So we take $M = 2$, $a = 1$, $b = 2$, and ask for n sufficiently large that

$$\frac{M(b-a)^3}{12n^2} \le 0.0005;$$

thus $n^2 \ge 333.333$, and so $n \ge 18.25$. Therefore $n = 19$ is sufficiently large.

28. $f^{(4)}(x) = \dfrac{24}{x^5}$, and the maximum of $|f^{(4)}(x)|$ for $1 \le x \le 2$ is 24. We take $M = 24$, $a = 1$, $b = 2$, and ask for n large enough that

$$\frac{M(b-a)^5}{180n^4} < 0.000005;$$

thus $n^4 > \dfrac{2}{(15)(0.000005)}$, and therefore $n \ge 14$.

32. (a) 2.0109; (b) 2.1070.

Chapter 5 Miscellaneous

1. $\displaystyle\int \frac{x^5 - 2x + 5}{x^3}\,dx = \tfrac{1}{3}x^3 + \dfrac{2}{x} - \dfrac{5}{2x^2} + C$

2. $\displaystyle\int \sqrt{x}\left(1 + 3x^{1/2} + 3x + x^{3/2}\right)dx = \tfrac{1}{3}x^3 + \tfrac{6}{5}x^{5/2} + \tfrac{3}{2}x^2 + \tfrac{2}{3}x^{3/2} + C$

4. $\displaystyle\int 7(2x+3)^{-3}\,dx = -\tfrac{7}{4}(2x+3)^{-2} + C$

6. $\displaystyle\int 24(6x+7)^{-1/2}\,dx = 8\sqrt{6x+7} + C$

8. $\displaystyle\int 3x^2\left(4+x^3\right)^{1/2}dx = \tfrac{2}{3}\left(4+x^3\right)^{3/2} + C$

10. $\int 3x\left(1+3x^2\right)^{-1/2} dx = \sqrt{1+3x^2} + C$

12. $\int \left(\sin^3 4x \cos 4x\right) dx = \frac{5}{16}\sin^4 4x + C$

14. $\int \sin^2 x \cos x\, dx = \frac{1}{3}\sin^3 x + C$

15. $\int \left(1+x^{1/2}\right)^{-2} x^{-1/2} dx = \int 2u^{-2} du = 2\left(\frac{-1}{u}\right) + C = -\frac{2}{1+\sqrt{x}} + C$

16. $\int \left(1+x^{1/2}\right)^{-2} x^{-1/2} dx = \int (1+u)^{-2}\, 2\, du = -\frac{2}{1+u} + C = -\frac{2}{1+\sqrt{x}} + C$

18. $\int x\left(x^2+1\right)^{14} dx = \int (u-1)\, u^{14}\, du = \int \left(u^{15}-u^{14}\right) du = \frac{1}{16}(x+1)^{16} - \frac{1}{15}(x+1)^{15} + C$

20. $\int x^3 \cos x^4\, dx = \frac{1}{4}\sin x^4 + C$

21. $\int x(4-x)^{1/2} dx = \int -(4-u)(u)^{1/2} du = \int \left(u^{3/2} - 4u^{1/2}\right) du = \frac{2}{5}(4-x)^{5/2} - \frac{8}{3}(4-x)^{3/2} + C$

22. $\int \frac{x+2x^3}{(x^4+x^2)^3}\, dx = \int \frac{1}{2}u^{-3}\, du = -\frac{1}{4}\left(x^4+x^2\right)^{-2} + C$

24. $\int \frac{2x+1}{\sqrt{x^2+x}}\, dx = \int u^{-1/2}\, du = 2\sqrt{x^2+x} + C$

26. $y(x) = 2x^{3/2} + 4$

28. $y(x) = \int \frac{2}{\sqrt{x+5}}\, dx = 4(x+5)^{1/2} + C;\ y(4) = 3 = 12 + C,\ \text{so}\ C = -9;\ y(x) = 4\sqrt{x+5} - 9.$

30. $y = \int (1-\cos x)\, dx = x - \sin x + C;\ y(0) = 0 = 0 + C,\ \text{so}\ y(x) = x - \sin x.$

32. We have acceleration $a = -22500$, so velocity and position (in the usual coordinate system) are
$$v = (-22500)t + v_0 \text{ and } s = (-11250)t^2 + v_0 t + s_0.$$
Here we have $v_0 = 0$ and $x_0 = 450$, so
$$v(t) = (-22500)t \text{ and } x(t) = (-11500)t^2 + 450.$$
The stone strikes the ground when $x(t) = 0$, and this equation has the positive solution $t = 1/5$. The impact speed of the stone is $|v(1/5)| = 4500$ ft/s.

33. The velocity of the automobile for $t \geq 0$ will be given by $v(t) = -40t + v_0$, and its distance traveled will be $x(t) = -20t^2 + v_0 t$, measured from the point at which the brakes are applied. The car comes to a stop when $v(t) = 0$; that is, when $t = (0.025)v_0$. At this time we have $x(t) = 180$, so
$$180 = (-20)(0.025v_0)^2 + (0.025)(v_0)^2,$$
so $v_0 = 120$ ft/s, just under 82 mi/h.

34. With the usual notation, $a = +8$, $v = 8t$, and $s = 4t^2$. When $v = 88$, $t = 11$, so the distance traveled then will be $(4)(11)^2 = 484$ feet.

35. Let g denote the acceleration of gravity on the surface of the planet in question. Then
$$s = -\frac{1}{2}gt^2 + 20.$$
From the equation $0 = -\frac{1}{2}(4g) + 20$ we find that $g = 10$. So
$$s = -5t^2 + 200 \text{ and } v = -10t$$

Chapter 5 Miscellaneous 163

describe the behavior of the falling ball dropped at time $t = 0$. Now $s = 0$ when $t^2 = 40$, so the ball hits the ground after $2\sqrt{10}$ seconds. Its velocity then is $v(2\sqrt{10}) = -20\sqrt{10}$ feet per second. So the time aloft is approximately 6.3246 seconds and the impact speed is about 63.2456 ft/s.

36. First we find the initial velocity the man can impart to a ball he throws straight upward. We make the simplifying assumptions that there is no air resistance, that the ball is actually released at ground level, and that the man gives the ball the same initial velocity on any planet. Then, on the earth,

$$v(t) = -32t + v_0 \text{ and } s(t) = -16t^2 + v_0 t.$$

Now s_{MAX} occurs when $v = 0$, thus when $t = v_0/32$. Consequently

$$144 = s(v_0/32) = -(16)(v_0/32)^2 + (v_0)(v_0/32),$$

and it follows that $(v_0)^2 = (64)(144)$, so that $v_0 = 96$ ft/s.

On the planet of Problem 35, we are to find s_{MAX} given $g = 10$ and $v_0 = 96$. The equations of motion of the ball are now

$$v(t) = -10t + 96 \text{ and } s(t) = -5t^2 + 96t.$$

Now y_{MAX} occurs when $v(t) = 0$: $t = 9.6$. Therefore the ball would reach a maximum height of $s(9.6) = 460.8$ feet on Zorg.

At the polar regions of Mesklin, the equations of motion of the ball are

$$v(t) = -(22500)t + 96 \text{ and } s(t) = -(11250)t^2 + 96t.$$

Now $v(t) = 0$ when $t = 8/1875 \approx 0.00427$, so the maximum height the ball would attain on Mesklin is $s(8/1875) = 128/625$ feet, less than two and one-half inches.

37. Assume that the brakes are applied at time $t = 0$ (seconds), that $s(t)$ is the distance the car subsequently travels, that $v(t)$ is its velocity at time t, and that its constant deceleration is $-a$ (where $a > 0$). Then

$$s = -\frac{1}{2}at^2 + v_0 t \text{ and } v = -at + v_0.$$

Now $v = 0$ when $t = v_0/a$, and it follows from the first equation above that $a = 22$. So $s = -11t^2 + v_0 t$ and $v = -22t + v_0$. But $v = 0$ when $t = 4$, and at this time we have $s = 176$ feet. The point of this problem is that *doubling* the speed *quadruples* the stopping distance.

39. $\sum_{i=1}^{100} 17 = 1700.$

40. $\sum_{k=1}^{100} \left(\frac{1}{k} - \frac{1}{k+1} \right) = 1 - \frac{1}{2} + \frac{1}{2} - \frac{1}{3} + \frac{1}{3} - \frac{1}{4} + \cdots + \frac{1}{98} - \frac{1}{99} + \frac{1}{99} - \frac{1}{100} + \frac{1}{100} - \frac{1}{101} = 1 - \frac{1}{101} = \frac{100}{101}.$

41. $\sum_{n=1}^{10} (3n - 2)^2 = 9 \frac{(10)(11)(21)}{6} - 12 \frac{(10)(11)}{2} + 40 = 2845.$

42. $\sum_{n=1}^{16} \sin \frac{n\pi}{2} = 1 + 0 - 1 + 0 + 1 + 0 - 1 + 0 + \cdots + 0 - 1 = 0.$

43. $\lim_{n \to \infty} \sum_{i=1}^{n} \frac{\Delta x}{\sqrt{x_i^*}} = \int_1^2 x^{-1/2}\, dx = \left[2\sqrt{x} \right]_1^2 = 2\left(\sqrt{2} - 1\right).$

44. $\lim_{n \to \infty} \sum_{i=1}^{n} \left[(x_i^*)^2 - 3x_i^* \right] \Delta x = \int_0^3 (x^2 - 3x)\, dx = \left[\frac{1}{3}x^3 - \frac{3}{2}x^2 \right]_0^3 = -\frac{9}{2}.$

45. $\lim_{n\to\infty} \sum_{i=1}^{n} 2\pi x_i^* \sqrt{1+(x_i^*)^2}\, \Delta x = \int_0^1 2\pi x\sqrt{1+x^2}\, dx = \left[\frac{2}{3}\pi(1+x^2)^{3/2}\right]_0^1 = \frac{2}{3}\pi\left(2\sqrt{2}-1\right).$

46. $\lim_{n\to\infty} \frac{1^{10}+2^{10}+3^{10}+\cdots+n^{10}}{n^{11}} = \int_0^1 x^{10}\, dx = \left[\frac{1}{11}x^{11}\right]_0^1 = \frac{1}{11}.$

48. Note that the limit of a nonnegative quantity cannot be negative.

50. $\int_0^1 (1-x^2)^3\, dx = \int_0^1 (1-3x^2+3x^4-x^6)\, dx = \left[x - x^3 + \frac{3}{5}x^5 - \frac{1}{7}x^7\right]_0^1 = \frac{16}{35}$

51. $\int \left(\sqrt{2x} - \frac{1}{\sqrt{3x^3}}\right) dx = \int \left((\sqrt{2})x^{1/2} - \frac{1}{\sqrt{3}}x^{-3/2}\right) dx = \frac{2\sqrt{2}}{3}x^{3/2} + \frac{2}{\sqrt{3}}x^{-1/2} + C.$

52. $\int \frac{(1+\sqrt[3]{x})^2}{\sqrt{x}}\, dx = \int (x^{-1/2} + 2x^{-1/6} + x^{1/6})\, dx = 2x^{1/2} + \frac{12}{5}x^{5/6} + \frac{6}{7}x^{7/6} + C.$

53. $\int \frac{4-x^3}{2x^2}\, dx = \int \left(\frac{4}{2x^2} - \frac{x^3}{2x^2}\right) dx = \int \left(2x^{-2} - \frac{1}{2}x\right) dx = -\frac{2}{x} - \frac{1}{4}x^2 + C.$

54. $\int_0^1 \frac{dt}{(3-2t)^2}\, dt = \int_3^1 u^{-2}\left(-\frac{1}{2}\right) du = \frac{1}{3}.$

55. You may use the substitution $u = x^{3/2}$, $du = \frac{3}{2}x^{1/2}$.

56. $\int_0^2 x^2\sqrt{9-x^3}\, dx = \left[-\frac{2}{9}(9-x^3)^{3/2}\right]_0^2 = \frac{52}{9}.$

57. Use the substitution $u = \frac{1}{t}$, $du = -\frac{1}{t^2}\, dt$.

58. $\int_1^2 \frac{2t+1}{\sqrt{t^2+t}}\, dt = \left[2(t^2+t)^{1/2}\right]_1^2 = 2\sqrt{2}\left(\sqrt{3}-1\right)$ (using the substitution $u = t^2 + t$).

59. Use the substitution $x = 1 + u^{4/3}$.

60. $\int_0^{\pi/4} \frac{\sin t}{\sqrt{\cos t}}\, dt = \left[-2\sqrt{\cos t}\right]_0^{\pi/4} = 2 - 2^{3/4}$ (using the substitution $y = \cos t$).

61. One easy substitution is $u = 1 + \sqrt{t}$.

62. $\int \frac{1}{u^2}\sqrt[3]{1-\frac{1}{u}}\, du = \frac{3}{4}\left(1-\frac{1}{u}\right)^{4/3} + C$ (using the substitution $x = 1 - \frac{1}{u}$).

63. The substitution $u = 1/x$ works.

64. $A = \int_{-1}^1 (1-x^3)\, dx = \left[x - \frac{1}{4}x^4\right]_{-1}^1 = 2.$

65. Note that the curves cross at $(0,0)$ and at $(1,1)$, and also that $x^4 > x^5$ if $0 < x < 1$.

66. The curves cross at $(3, -\sqrt{3})$ and at $(3, \sqrt{3})$. We take advantage of symmetry—we double a simple integral to obtain the total area:

$$A = 2\int_0^{\sqrt{3}} [y^2 - (3y^2 - 6)]\, dy = 2\left[6y - \frac{2}{3}y^3\right]_0^{\sqrt{3}} = 8\sqrt{3}.$$

67. The curves cross at $(-1,1)$ and at $(1,1)$; we obtain the total area by doubling the integral of $2-x^2-x^4$ over the interval $0 \leq x \leq 1$.

68. The curves cross at $(-1,1)$ and at $(1,1)$; we obtain the total area by doubling the integral of $x^4 - (2x^2 - 1)$ over the interval $0 \leq x \leq 1$, and the total area is $\frac{16}{15}$.

69. The curves cross at $(-3, 25)$ and at $(2, 0)$. The area is the integral of $10 - 5x - (x-2)^2$ over the interval $-3 \leq x \leq 2$.

Chapter 5 Miscellaneous   165

70. The curves cross at $(-1, 1)$ and at $(1, 1)$. By symmetry,

$$A = 2\int_0^1 \left(2 - x^2 - x^{2/3}\right) dx = 2\left[2x - \frac{1}{3}x^3 - \frac{3}{5}x^{5/3}\right]_0^1 = \frac{32}{15}.$$

71. $y = \sqrt{2x - x^2}$ is the semicircle $(x-1)^2 + y^2 = 1$, $y \geq 0$, with center $(1, 0)$ and radius 1. Therefore its area is $\pi/2$.

72. $y^2 = 6x - 5 - x^2$ can be written in the form $(x-3)^2 + y^2 = 2^2$. This is the equation of a circle with radius 2 and center $(3, 0)$. When $x = 1$, $y = 0$; when $x = 5$, $y = 0$. So the given integral is the area of a semicircle of radius 2; its value is therefore 2π.

73. Differentiation of both sides of the given equation yields

$$2x = \left(1 + [f(x)]^2\right)^{1/2}, \text{ so that } 4x^2 = 1 + [f(x)]^2, \text{ and therefore } f(x) = \left(4x^2 - 1\right)^{1/2}.$$

This answer must be tested by substitution in the original equation because it was obtained under the assumption that such a function actually exists.

74. Let $u = h(x)$. Then

$$G(u) = \int_a^u \phi(t)\, dt.$$

So $G'(u) = \phi(u)$. Therefore

$$G'(x) = \phi(u)\frac{du}{dx} = \phi(h(x))\, h'(x).$$

76. $T_6 \approx 2.812254$ and $S_6 \approx 2.828502$. For the exact value:

$$(1 - \cos x)^{1/2} = \sqrt{2}\left(\frac{1 - \cos x}{2}\right)^{1/2} = \sqrt{2}\left|\sin\frac{x}{2}\right|.$$

Therefore

$$\int_0^\pi (1 - \cos x)^{1/2}\, dx = \int_0^\pi \sqrt{2}\left(\frac{1-\cos x}{2}\right)^{1/2} dx = \sqrt{2}\int_0^\pi \left|\sin\frac{x}{2}\right| dx = \left[-2\sqrt{2}\cos\frac{x}{2}\right]_0^\pi = 2\sqrt{2}.$$

77. The graph is concave upward on the interval $1 \leq x \leq 2$, so the integral is trapped between the midpoint and trapezoidal approximations. The graph is concave upward because

$$f''(x) = \frac{2(3x^2 + 3x + 1)}{(x + x^2)^3}$$

is always positive on this interval.

78. First,

$$(x_{i-1})^2 \leq \frac{1}{3}\left((x_{i-1})^2 + x_{i-1}x_i + (x_i)^2\right) \leq (x_i)^2.$$

Therefore $x_{i-1} \leq x_i^* \leq x_i$. Then

$$(x_i^*)^2 (x_i - x_{i-1}) = \frac{1}{3}\left((x_{i-1})^2 + x_{i-1}x_i + (x_i)^2\right)(x_i - x_{i-1}) = \frac{1}{3}\left((x_i)^3 - (x_{i-1})^3\right),$$

and when such expressions are summed for $i = 1, 2, 3, \ldots, n$, the result is $\frac{1}{3}(b^3 - a^3)$.

Chapter 6: Applications of the Integral

Section 6.1

1. $\lim_{n \to \infty} \sum_{i=1}^{n} 2x_i^* \Delta x = \int_0^1 2x \, dx = 1.$

2. $\lim_{n \to \infty} \sum_{i=1}^{n} \frac{\Delta x}{(x_i^*)^2} = \int_1^2 \frac{dx}{x^2} = \frac{1}{2}.$

3. $\lim_{n \to \infty} \sum_{i=1}^{n} (\sin \pi x_i^*) \Delta x = \int_0^1 \sin \pi x \, dx = \frac{2}{\pi}.$

4. $\lim_{n \to \infty} \sum_{i=1}^{n} (3(x_i^*) - 1) \Delta x = \int_{-1}^{3} (3x^2 - 1) \, dx = 24.$

5. $\lim_{n \to \infty} \sum_{i=1}^{n} x_i^* \sqrt{(x_i^*)^2 + 9} \, \Delta x = \int_0^4 x(x^2+9)^{1/2} \, dx = \frac{98}{3}.$

6. $\lim_{n \to \infty} \sum_{i=1}^{n} (x_i^*)^2 \Delta x = \int_2^4 x^2 \, dx = \frac{56}{3}.$

7. $\lim_{n \to \infty} \sum_{i=1}^{n} (2m_i - 1) \Delta x = \int_{-1}^{3} (2x - 1) \, dx = 4.$

8. $\lim_{n \to \infty} \sum_{i=1}^{n} \sqrt{2m_i + 1} \, \Delta x = \int_0^4 \sqrt{2x+1} \, dx = \frac{26}{3}.$

9. $\lim_{n \to \infty} \sum_{i=1}^{n} \frac{m_i}{\sqrt{(m_i)^2 + 16}} \Delta x = \int_{-3}^{0} x(x^2+16)^{-1/2} \, dx = -1.$

10. $\lim_{n \to \infty} \sum_{i=1}^{n} m_i \cos(m_i)^2 \, \Delta x = \int_0^{\sqrt{\pi}} x \cos(x^2) \, dx = \left[\frac{1}{2}\sin(x^2)\right]_0^{\sqrt{\pi}} = 0.$

11. $\lim_{n \to \infty} \sum_{i=1}^{n} 2\pi x_i^* f(x_i^*) \Delta x = \int_1^4 2\pi x f(x) \, dx$

12. $\lim_{n \to \infty} \sum_{i=1}^{n} [f(x_i^*)]^2 \Delta x = \int_{-1}^{1} [f(x)]^2 \, dx$

13. $\lim_{n \to \infty} \sum_{i=1}^{n} \sqrt{1 + [f(x_i^*)]^2} \, \Delta x = \int_0^{10} \left(1 + [f(x)]^2\right)^{1/2} dx$

14. $\lim_{n \to \infty} \sum_{i=1}^{n} 2\pi m_i \sqrt{1 + [f(m_i)]^2} \, \Delta x = \int_{-2}^{3} 2\pi x \left(1 + [f(x)]^2\right)^{1/2} dx$

15. $M = \int_0^{100} \frac{1}{5} x \, dx = \left[\frac{1}{10} x^2\right]_0^{100} = 1000$

16. $M = \int_0^{25} (60 - 2x) \, dx \, dx = \left[60x - x^2\right]_0^{25} = 875$

17. $M = \int_0^{10} x(10 - x) \, dx = \left[5x^2 - \frac{1}{3}x^3\right]_0^{10} = \frac{500}{3}$

18. $M = \int_0^{10} 10 \sin \frac{\pi x}{10} \, dx = \left[-\frac{100}{\pi} \cos \frac{\pi x}{10}\right]_0^{10} = \frac{200}{\pi}$

19. $\int_0^{10} -32t\, dt = -320$ is the net distance; $\int_0^{10} 32t\, dt = 320$ is the total distance.

20. $\int_1^5 (2t + 10)\, dt = 64$ is the net and the total distance.

21. $\int_0^{6.25} (25 - 4t)\, dt + \int_{6.25}^{10} (4t - 25)\, dt = 106.25$ is the total distance.

22. $\int_0^5 |2t - 5|\, dt = 2\int_0^{5/2} (5 - 2t)\, dt = \dfrac{25}{2}$ is the net and the total distance.

23. $\int_{-2}^3 4t^3\, dt = 65$ is the net distance. $\int_0^{-2} 4t^3\, dt + \int_0^3 4t^3\, dt = 97$ is the total distance.

24. Net distance: $-\dfrac{1701}{200}$. Total distance: $\dfrac{1701}{200}$.

26. Net distance: 0. Total distance: 1.

28. Net distance: 2. Total distance: $2\sqrt{2}$.

29. First, $v(t) < 0$ on $(2, 7)$. So the total distance traveled is

$$\int_0^2 v(t)\, dt - \int_2^7 v(t)\, dt + \int_7^{10} v(t)\, dt = 65.$$

The net distance traveled is $\int_0^{10} v(t)\, dt = \dfrac{70}{3}$.

30. Here, $v(t) < 0$ on the interval $(3, 5)$. so the total distance traveled is

$$\int_0^3 v(t)\, dt - \int_3^5 v(t)\, dt + \int_5^6 v(t)\, dt = \dfrac{86}{3}.$$

The net distance traveled is $\int_0^6 v(t)\, dt = 18$.

31. In this problem, $v(t) < 0$ on $(a, b) \approx (0.602750, 2.292402)$, so the total distance traveled is

$$\int_0^a v(t)\, dt - \int_a^b v(t)\, dt + \int_b^3 v(t)\, dt \approx 4.66407.$$

The net distance traveled is $\int_0^3 v(t)\, dt = \dfrac{3}{4}$.

32. Here, $v(t) < 0$ on $(a, b) \approx (1.755640, 4.507903)$, so the total distance traveled is

$$\int_0^a v(t)\, dt - \int_a^b v(t)\, dt + \int_b^5 v(t)\, dt \approx 28.4615.$$

The net distance traveled is $\int_0^5 v(t)\, dt = -\dfrac{25}{12} \approx -2.083333$.

33. In this case, $v(t) < 0$ on $(0, b) \approx (0, 0.860334)$. So the total distance traveled is

$$-\int_0^b v(t)\, dt + \int_b^\pi v(t)\, dt \approx 4.26379.$$

34. In this problem, $v(t) < 0$ on $(a, b) \approx (2.167455, 5.128225)$. So the total distance traveled is

$$\int_0^a v(t)\, dt - \int_a^b v(t)\, dt + \int_b^{2\pi} v(t)\, dt \approx 7.68273.$$

The total distance traveled is $\int_0^{2\pi} v(t)\,dt \approx -0.430408$.

36. $M = \int_0^{10} 2\pi x^2\,dx = \left[\frac{2}{3}\pi x^3\right]_0^{10} = \frac{2000}{3}\pi$.

37. $M = \int_0^5 2\pi x\,(25 - x^2)\,dx = \left[25\pi x^2 - \frac{1}{2}\pi x^4\right]_0^5 = \frac{625}{2}\pi$.

38. $h_{\text{MAX}} = \int_0^5 (-32t + 160)\,dt = 400$ (ft). Check: $h(t) = -16t^2 + 160t + h_0$, so $h(5) = 400$.

39. $\int_{10}^{20} (100 - 3t)\,dt = 550$ (gallons).

40. $\int_0^{20} (13 + t)\,dt = 460$ (thousands of births).

41. $125 + \int_0^{20} \left(8 + \frac{t}{2}\right)\,dt = 385$ (thousands).

43. $r(0) = 0.1 = a - b$, $r(182.5) = a + b$. So $a = 0.3$ and $b = 0.2$. Therefore the average total annual rainfall will be

$$R = \int_0^{365} \left(0.3 - 0.2\cos\frac{2\pi t}{365}\right)\,dt = (0.3)(365) - \frac{36.5}{\pi}\sin(2\pi) = 109.5 \text{ (inches)}.$$

44. Partition the interval $a \leq t \leq b$ into subintervals of equal length $\Delta t = (b - a)/n$ with endpoints $t_0, t_1, t_2, \ldots, t_n$. Choose t_i^* in the ith subinterval, and note that

$$r(t_{i-1}) \leq r(t_i^*) \leq r(t_i)$$

for all meaningful values of i. This inequality persists through formation of sums of such terms (for $i = 1$ to n), and even through taking limits of such (Riemann) sums. Thereby we find that

$$\int_a^b r(t)\,dt \leq \lim_{n \to \infty} \sum_{i=1}^n r(t_i^*)\,\Delta t \leq \int_a^b r(t)\,dt,$$

and therefore $\int_a^b r(t)\,dt = Q$.

45. Let $f(x) = x^{1/3}$; on the interval $0 \leq x \leq 1$, let $x_i = x_i^* = i/n$ and $\Delta x = 1/n$. Then the limit given is

$$\int_0^1 x^{1/3}\,dx = \frac{3}{4}.$$

47. $f(x) = 4\pi x \cdot 100(1 + x)$; $W = \int_0^1 4\pi x^2 \cdot 100(1 + x)\,dx = \frac{7}{12} \cdot 400\pi = \frac{700}{3}\pi$ (lb).

Section 6.2

1. $V = \int_0^1 \pi x^4\,dx = \frac{\pi}{5}$.

2. $V = \int_0^4 \pi x\,dx = 8\pi$.

3. $V = \int_0^4 \pi y\,dy = 8\pi$.

4. $V = \int_{0.1}^{1} \dfrac{\pi}{x^2}\, dx = 9\pi.$

5. $V = \int_{0}^{\pi} \pi \sin^2 x\, dx = \dfrac{\pi}{2} \int_{0}^{\pi} (1 - \cos 2x)\, dx = \dfrac{1}{2}\pi^2.$

6. $V = 2\int_{0}^{3} \pi(9 - x^2)^2\, dx = \dfrac{1296}{5}\pi.$

7. $V = \int_{0}^{1} (\pi x - \pi x^4)\, dx = \dfrac{3}{10}\pi.$

8. $V = \int_{0}^{16} \pi\left[(\tfrac{1}{4}y - 5)^2 - (\sqrt{y} - 5)^2\right] dy = 64\pi.$

9. $V = 2\int_{0}^{2} \left[\pi(8 - x^2)^2 - \pi x^4\right] dx = \dfrac{512}{3}\pi.$

10. $V = \int_{-2}^{3} \pi\left[(y + 6)^2 - (y^2)^2\right] dy = \dfrac{500}{3}\pi.$

11. $V = \int_{-1}^{1} \pi(1 - x^2)^2\, dx = \dfrac{16}{15}\pi.$

12. $V = \int_{0}^{1} \pi(x - x^3)^2\, dx = \dfrac{8}{105}\pi.$

13. $V = \int_{0}^{1} \pi\left(\sqrt{1 - y}\right)^2 dy = \dfrac{\pi}{2}.$

14. $V = \int_{-2}^{2} \pi\left[(6 - x^2)^2 - (2)^2\right] dx = \dfrac{384}{5}\pi.$

15. $V = \int_{2}^{6} \pi\left(\sqrt{6 - y}\right)^2 dy = 8\pi.$

16. $V = \int_{0}^{1} \pi\left[\left(2 + \sqrt{1 - y}\right)^2 - \left(2 - \sqrt{1 - y}\right)^2\right] dy = \dfrac{16}{3}\pi.$

17. $V = \int_{0}^{1} \pi\left[(x - x^3 + 1)^2 - (1)^2\right] dx = \dfrac{121}{210}\pi.$

18. $V = \int_{0}^{2} \pi\left[(4)^2 - (x^2)^2\right] dx = \dfrac{128}{5}\pi.$

19. $V = \int_{0}^{4} \pi(\sqrt{y})^2\, dy = 8\pi.$

20. $V = \int_{0}^{16} \pi(16 - x)\, dx = 128\pi.$

21. $V = \int_{0}^{1} \pi\left[(x^{1/2} + 2)^2 - (x^2 + 2)^2\right] dx = \dfrac{49}{30}\pi \approx 5.131268.$

22. $V = 2\int_{0}^{2} \pi\left[(9 - x^2)^2 - (x^2 + 1)^2\right] dx = \dfrac{640}{3}\pi \approx 670.206433.$
Note how we used the fact that the plane region is symmetric around the y-axis.

23. $V = \int_{0}^{1} \pi\left[(3 - y^2)^2 - (3 - \sqrt{y})^2\right] dy = \dfrac{17}{10}\pi \approx 5.340708.$

24. $V = 2\int_{0}^{4} \pi\left[(4 + \sqrt{y})^2 - (4 - \sqrt{y})^2\right] dy = \dfrac{512}{3}\pi \approx 536.165146.$
Note how we used the fact that the plane region is symmetric around the horizontal line $y = 4$.

25. The volume is $V = \int_{0}^{\pi} \pi \sin^2 x\, dx = \left[\tfrac{1}{2}\pi x - \tfrac{1}{4}\pi \sin 2x\right]_{0}^{\pi} = \tfrac{1}{2}\pi^2.$

26. The volume is $V = \pi \int_{-1}^{1} \pi \cos^2\left(\frac{1}{2}\pi x\right) dx = \left[\frac{1}{2}\pi x + \frac{1}{2}\sin(\pi x)\right]_{-1}^{1} = \pi$.

27. The volume is $V = \int_{0}^{\pi/4} \pi\left(\cos^2 x - \sin^2 x\right) dx = \left[\frac{1}{2}\pi \sin 2x\right]_{0}^{\pi/4} = \frac{1}{2}\pi$.

28. The volume is
$$V = \int_{-\pi/3}^{\pi/3} \pi\left[(\cos^2 x) - \tfrac{1}{4}\right] dx = \tfrac{1}{4}\pi\left[x - \sin 2x\right]_{-\pi/3}^{\pi/3} = \tfrac{1}{12}\pi\left(2\pi + 3\sqrt{3}\right) \approx 3.005283590.$$

29. The volume is
$$V = \int_{0}^{\pi/4} \pi \tan^2 x\, dx = \pi\left[-x + \tan x\right]_{0}^{\pi/4} = \pi - \tfrac{1}{4}\pi^2 \approx 0.674191553.$$

30. The volume is
$$V = \int_{0}^{\pi/4} \pi(1 - \tan^2 x)\, dx = \pi\left[2x - \tan x\right]_{0}^{\pi/4} = \tfrac{1}{2}\pi^2 - \pi \approx 1.793209547.$$

31. The curves intersect in three points, with x-coordinates $a \approx -0.532$, $b \approx 0.653$, and $c \approx 2.879$. Two bounded regions in the plane are formed by these curves. When the one on the left is rotated around the x-axis, the volume swept out is approximately 2.998317. When the one on the right is rotated around the x-axis, the volume swept out is approximately 267.441647. The total volume swept out by the two regions is approximately 270.439964.

32. The curves intersect in two points, with x-coordinates $a \approx -1.283781666$ and $b \approx 1.533751169$. The volume swept out by the region between them, when rotated around the x-axis, is approximately 136.768218962.

33. The curves intersect in two points, with x-coordinates $b \approx 0.824132312$ and $b = -a$. When the region between them is rotated around the x-axis, the volume swept out is
$$V = \int_{a}^{b} \pi\left[(\cos^2 x) - x^2\right] dx = \pi\left[\tfrac{1}{4}\sin 2x + \tfrac{1}{10}\left(5x - 2x^5\right)\right]_{a}^{b} \approx 3.67743.$$

34. The curves intersect in two points, with x-coordinates $a \approx 0.386236871$ and $b \approx 1.964192887$. When the region between them is rotated around the x-axis, the volume swept out is
$$V = \int_{a}^{b} \pi\left[(\sin^2 x) - (x-1)^4\right] dx$$
$$= \pi\left[\tfrac{1}{10}\left(-2x^5 + 10x^4 - 20x^3 + 20x^2 - 5x\right) - \tfrac{1}{4}\sin 2x\right]_{a}^{b} \approx 3.00464.$$

35. $V = \int_{0}^{6} \pi x\, dx - \int_{3}^{6} 2\pi(x-3)\, dx = 9\pi.$

36. First, $y^2 = b^2 - \dfrac{b^2}{a^2}x^2$. Therefore $V = 2\int_{0}^{a} \pi\left(b^2 - \dfrac{b^2}{a^2}x^2\right) dx = \dfrac{4}{3}\pi ab^2$.

37. Here, $x^2 = \dfrac{a^2}{b^2}(b^2 - y^2)$. So $V = 2\int_{0}^{b} \pi \dfrac{a^2}{b^2}(b^2 - y^2)\, dy = \dfrac{4}{3}\pi a^2 b$.

38. $V_b = \int_{1}^{b} \dfrac{\pi}{x^4}\, dx = \dfrac{\pi}{3}\left(1 - \dfrac{1}{b^3}\right)$. Therefore $V = \lim_{b\to\infty} V_b = \dfrac{\pi}{3}$.

39. We set up a coordinate system in which AB is the segment on the x-axis from $x = -a$ to $x = a$. Then $V = 2\int_{0}^{a} 4\left(a^2 - x^2\right) dx = \dfrac{16}{3}a^3$.

40. Let AB be the segment on the x-axis from $x = -a$ to $x = a$. Visualize a cross section of the solid at x and perpendicular to AB. Its radius is then $y = (a^2 - x^2)^{1/2}$, and so it has area $\frac{1}{2}\pi y^2$. Therefore its volume is $V = 2\int_0^a \frac{\pi}{2}(a^2 - x^2)\,dx = \frac{2}{3}\pi a^3$.

41. $V = 2\int_0^a \sqrt{3}\,(a^2 - x^2)\,dx = \frac{4}{3}a^3\sqrt{3}$.

42. $V = \int_0^1 (\sqrt{x} - x^2)^2\,dx = \frac{9}{70}$.

44. Let e denote the length of each edge of the base of the pyramid. Imagine a cross section at level y—height y above the base. Then (by similar triangles)
$$\frac{h-y}{x} = \frac{h}{e},$$
so that the cross-sectional area is $A_y = \left(\frac{h-y}{h}\right)^2 A$. Thus
$$V = \int_0^h \left(1 - \frac{y}{h}\right)^2 A\,dy = \frac{1}{3}Ah.$$

46. Set up a coordinate system with the center of the sphere at the origin and with the axis of the hole coincident with the y-axis. The volume that remains after the hole is drilled is then
$$V = 2\int_0^4 \pi\left[(25 - y^2) - 9\right]dy = \frac{256\pi}{3}.$$

47. See the figure below, which shows the nearest quarter of each of the two cylinders. This implies that the volume of the intersection illustrated is one-eighth of the total volume of their intersection. Note that we have chosen the x-axis and the z-axis as the centerlines of the cylinders; the y-axis is vertical.

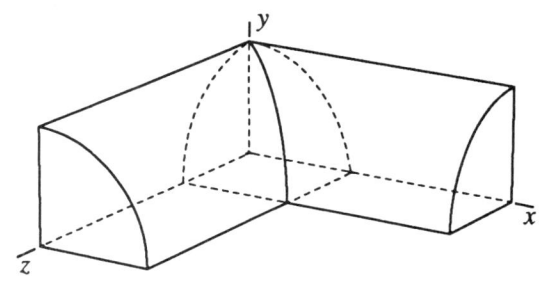

48. $V = \int_{r-h}^{r} \pi(r^2 - y^2)\,dy$.

50. $V \approx \frac{25}{3}\left[\pi(60)^2 + 4\pi(55)^2 + 2\pi(50)^2 + 4\pi(35)^2 + 0\right] = \frac{25}{3}\pi(25{,}600) \approx 670{,}200$ (cubic feet).

52. (a) $x = (y/k)^{1/4}$, so $\pi x^2 = \pi\sqrt{y/k}$.
$$V = \int_0^y \pi\sqrt{y/k}\,dy = \frac{2\pi}{3\sqrt{k}}y^{3/2}.$$

(b) Torricelli's law: $\dfrac{dV}{dt} = -c\sqrt{y}$. Now
$$\frac{dV}{dt} = \frac{dV}{dy}\cdot\frac{dy}{dt}, \quad \text{so} \quad -c\sqrt{y} = \left(\pi\sqrt{y/k}\right)\frac{dy}{dt}.$$

Therefore $\dfrac{dy}{dt} = -\dfrac{c}{\pi}\sqrt{k}$, a constant.

56. The solid can be formed by rotating around the x-axis the plane region above the x-axis and common to the two circles with equations
$$\left(x + \tfrac{1}{2}a\right)^2 + y^2 = a^2 \quad \text{and} \quad \left(x - \tfrac{1}{2}a\right)^2 + y^2 = a^2.$$
Let R denote the half of that region that lies in the first quadrant. The solid of Problem 56 has volume V double that obtained when R is revolved around the x-axis. The curve that forms the upper boundary of R has equation
$$y = f(x) = \tfrac{1}{2}\sqrt{3a^2 - 4ax - 4x^2}, \quad \text{and so}$$
$$V = 2\int_0^{a/2} \pi\left(f(x)\right)^2\,dx = 2\pi\left[\tfrac{3}{4}a^2 x - \tfrac{1}{2}ax^2 - \tfrac{1}{3}x^3\right]_0^{a/2} = \tfrac{5}{12}\pi a^3.$$
Note that the answer is dimensionally correct. Moreover, the solid occupies 31.25% of the volume of either sphere, and thus the answer also passes the test of plausiblility.

Section 6.3

1. $V = \int_0^2 2\pi x\left(x^2\right)dx = 8\pi.$
2. $V = \int_0^4 2\pi x\left(2\sqrt{x}\right)dx = \dfrac{256\pi}{5}.$
3. $V = \int_0^5 2\pi x\left(25 - x^2\right)dx = \dfrac{625\pi}{2}.$
4. $V = \int_0^2 2\pi x\left(8 - 2x^2\right)dx = 16\pi.$
5. $V = \int_0^2 2\pi x\left(8 - 2x^2\right)dx = 16\pi.$
6. $V = \int_0^3 2\pi y\left(9 - y^2\right)dy = \dfrac{81\pi}{2}.$
7. $V = \int_0^1 2\pi y\left(3 - 3y\right)dy = \pi.$
8. $V = \int_0^4 2\pi(5 - y)\left(\sqrt{y} - \tfrac{1}{2}y\right)dy = \dfrac{136\pi}{15}.$
9. $V = \int_0^2 2\pi y\left(\sqrt{\tfrac{y}{2}} - \tfrac{1}{4}y^2\right)dy = \dfrac{6\pi}{5}.$
10. $V = \int_0^3 2\pi x\left(3x - x^2\right)dx = \dfrac{27\pi}{2}.$
11. $V = 2\int_0^2 \left(4x - x^3\right)(2\pi x)\,dx = \dfrac{256\pi}{15}.$
12. $V = \int_0^1 2\pi(y + 2)\left(y^3 - y^4\right)dy = \dfrac{4\pi}{15}.$
13. $V = \int_0^1 2\pi x\left(x - x^3\right)dx = \dfrac{4\pi}{15}.$
14. $V = \int_0^4 2\pi y\left(16 - y^2\right)dy = 128\pi.$
15. $V = \int_0^1 2\pi(2 - x)\left(x - x^3\right)dx = \dfrac{11\pi}{15}.$
16. $V = \int_0^2 2\pi x\left(x^3\right)dx = \dfrac{64\pi}{5}.$
17. $V = \int_0^2 2\pi(3 - x)\left(x^3\right)dx = \dfrac{56\pi}{5}.$
18. $V = \int_0^8 2\pi y\left(2 - y^{1/3}\right)dy = \dfrac{128\pi}{7}.$
19. $V = \int_{-1}^1 2\pi(2 - x)(x^2)\,dx = \dfrac{8\pi}{3}.$ This is one of many examples in which you do *not* obtain the correct answer by doubling the value of the integral from 0 to 1.
20. $V = \int_0^1 2\pi x\left(x - x^2\right)dx = \dfrac{\pi}{6}.$
21. $V = \int_0^1 2\pi y\left(\sqrt{y} - y\right)dy = \dfrac{2\pi}{15}.$
22. $V = \int_0^1 2\pi(2 - y)\left(\sqrt{y} - y\right)dy = \dfrac{8\pi}{15}.$
23. $V = \int_0^1 2\pi(x + 1)\left(x - x^2\right)dx = \dfrac{\pi}{2}.$
24. $V = \int_0^1 2\pi y\left(2 - 2y^2\right)dy = \pi.$
25. $V = \int_{-1}^1 2\pi(1 - y)\left(2 - 2y^2\right)dy = \dfrac{16\pi}{3}.$
26. $V = \int_0^4 2\pi x\left(4x - x^2\right)dx = \dfrac{128\pi}{3}.$
27. $V = \int_0^4 2\pi(x + 1)\left(4x - x^2\right)dx = 64\pi.$
28. $V = \int_0^1 2\pi(y + 1)\left(\sqrt{y} - y^2\right)dy = \dfrac{29\pi}{30}.$

29. The curves cross in the first quadrant at the two points with x-coordinates $a \approx 0.172480093$ and $b \approx 1.891954441$. The volume generated by rotation of R around the y-axis is

$$V = \int_a^b 2\pi x \left(6x - x^2 - x^3 - 1\right) dx \approx 23.299098.$$

30. The curves cross at the two points with x-coordinates $a \approx 0.506585856$ and $b \approx 1.952080163$. The volume generated by rotation of R around the y-axis is

$$V = \int_a^b 2\pi x \left(10x - 5 - x^4\right) dx \approx 39.318469946.$$

31. The curves cross at the two points with x-coordinates $b \approx 0.824132312$ and $a = -b$. The volume generated by rotation of R around the y-axis is

$$V = \int_a^b 2\pi x \left[(\cos x) - x^2\right] dx = \pi \left[2x \sin x + 2\cos x - \tfrac{1}{2}x^4\right]_a^b \approx 1.060269.$$

32. The curves cross at the two points with x-coordinates $a = 0$ and $b \approx 1.405563633$. The volume generated by rotation of R around the y-axis is

$$\int_a^b 2\pi x \left[(\cos x) - (x-1)^2\right] dx = \pi \left[2x \sin x + 2\cos x - \tfrac{1}{2}x^4 + \tfrac{4}{3}x^3 - x^2\right]_a^b \approx 2.75561.$$

33. The curves cross at the two points with x-coordinates $a \approx 0.187072596$ and $b \approx 1.575880679$. The volume generated by rotation of R around the y-axis is

$$V = \int_a^b 2\pi x \left[(\cos x) - 3x^2 + 6x - 2\right] dx = \pi \left[2x \sin x + 2\cos x - \tfrac{3}{2}x^4 + 4x^3 - 2x^2\right]_a^b \approx 8.133345.$$

34. The curves cross at the two points $(-a, 0)$ and $(a, 0)$ where $a \approx 1.7878717268$. The volume generated by rotation of R around the y-axis is

$$V = \int_0^a 2\pi x \cdot (3\cos x + \cos 4x) \, dx = \frac{\pi}{8} \left[48 \cos x + 48x \sin x + \cos 4x + 4x \sin 4x\right]_0^a \approx 12.004897.$$

35. $V = \int_0^r 2\pi x \left(h - \frac{h}{r}x\right) dx.$

36. $V = \int_0^{\sqrt{2ph}} 2\pi y \left(h - \frac{y^2}{2p}\right) dy = \pi p h^2.$

37. $V = 2 \int_0^a 2\pi x \frac{b}{a} \left(a^2 - x^2\right)^{1/2} dx = \frac{4}{3}\pi a^2 b.$

38. $V = \int_0^{\sqrt{2rh-h^2}} 2\pi x \left[\left(r^2 - x^2\right)^{1/2} - (r - h)\right] dx = \frac{\pi h^2}{3}(3r - h).$

39. $V = 2 \int_{b-a}^{b+a} 2\pi x \left(a^2 - (x-b)^2\right)^{1/2} dx.$

40. (a) $V = \int_{-1}^{2} 2\pi(x+2)\left(x+2-x^2\right) dx = \dfrac{45\pi}{2}.$

    (b) $V = \int_{-1}^{2} 2\pi(3-x)\left(x+2-x^2\right) dx = \dfrac{45\pi}{2}.$

41. $V = \int_{-a}^{a} 2\pi(x+a)(2)\left(a^2 - x^2\right)^{1/2} dx = 2\pi^2 a^3.$

42. (b) $V = \int_0^\pi 2\pi x \sin x \, dx = 2\pi^2$.

43. $a^2 + \frac{1}{4}h^2 = b^2$, so $b^2 - a^2 = \frac{1}{4}h^2$. Therefore $V = \frac{4}{3}\pi \left(\frac{1}{4}h^2\right)^{3/2}$. So the answer to part (a) is $V = \frac{1}{6}\pi h^3$.

    (b) The answer involves neither the radius b of the sphere nor the radius a of the hole; it depends only upon the length of the hole.

44. (a) $V = \int_0^{16} \pi[(25-y) - 9] \, dy = 128\pi$.   (b) $V = \int_3^5 2\pi x \left(25 - x^2\right) dx = 128\pi$.

45. Let $f(x) = (5-x)\sqrt{x}$. Part (a): The volume is $V_1 = \int_0^5 \pi (f(x))^2 \, dx = \frac{625}{12}\pi$.

    Part (b): The volume is $V_2 = \int_0^5 4\pi f(x) \, dx = \frac{400}{7}\pi\sqrt{5}$.

    Part (c): $V_3 = \int_0^5 4\pi(5-x)f(x) \, dx = \frac{1600}{21}\pi\sqrt{5}$.

46. Let $f(x) = x\sqrt{x+3}$. Part (a): The volume is $V_1 = \int_{-3}^0 \pi (f(x))^2 \, dx = \frac{27}{4}\pi$.

    Part (b): The volume is $V_2 = \int_{-3}^0 4\pi f(x) \, dx = \frac{576}{35}\pi\sqrt{3}$.

    Part (c): $V_3 = \int_{-3}^0 -4(x+3)\pi f(x) \, dx = \frac{432}{35}\pi\sqrt{3}$.

Section 6.4

1. $\int_0^1 \sqrt{1 + 4x^2} \, dx$
2. $\int_1^3 \sqrt{1 + \frac{25}{4}x^3} \, dx$
3. $\int_0^2 \sqrt{1 + 36x^4 - 72x^3 + 36x^2} \, dx$
4. $\int_{-1}^1 \sqrt{1 + \frac{16}{9}x^{2/3}} \, dx$
5. $\int_0^{100} \sqrt{1 + 4x^2} \, dx$
6. $\int_0^1 \sqrt{4y^2 - 16y + 17} \, dy$
7. $\int_{-1}^2 \sqrt{1 + 16y^6} \, dy$
8. $\int_1^2 \sqrt{1 + 4x^2} \, dx$ or $\int_1^4 \sqrt{1 + \frac{1}{4y}} \, dy$
9. $\int_1^2 \frac{1}{x^2}\sqrt{x^4 + 1} \, dx$
10. $\int_0^2 \frac{2}{\sqrt{4 - x^2}} \, dx$
11. $\int_0^4 2\pi x^2 \sqrt{1 + 4x^2} \, dx$
12. $\int_0^4 2\pi x \sqrt{1 + 4x^2} \, dx$
13. $\int_0^1 2\pi\left(x - x^2\right)\sqrt{4x^2 - 4x + 2} \, dx$
14. $\int_0^1 2\pi\left(4 - x^2\right)\sqrt{1 + 4x^2} \, dx$
15. $\int_0^1 2\pi(2-x)\sqrt{1 + 4x^2} \, dx$
16. $\int_0^1 2\pi\left(x - x^3\right)\sqrt{9x^4 - 6x^2 + 2} \, dx$
17. $\int_1^4 2\pi\sqrt{x}\sqrt{1 + \frac{1}{4x}} \, dx$
18. $\int_1^4 2\pi x\sqrt{1 + \frac{1}{4x}} \, dx$
19. $\int_1^4 2\pi(x+1)\sqrt{1 + \frac{9}{4}x} \, dx$
20. $\int_1^4 2\pi\left(x^{5/2} + 2\right)\sqrt{1 + \frac{25}{4}x^3} \, dx$

21. $\frac{dy}{dx} = 2x\sqrt{x^2 + 1}$. So $L = \int_0^2 \left(1 + 4x^2\left(x^2 + 1\right)\right)^{1/2} dx = \int_0^2 \left(2x^2 + 1\right) dx = \frac{22}{3}$.

22. $\dfrac{dx}{dy} = \sqrt{y-1}$, so $L = \displaystyle\int_1^5 \left(1 + \left(\sqrt{y-1}\right)^2\right)^{1/2} dy = \tfrac{2}{3}\left(5\sqrt{5}-1\right)$.

23. $\dfrac{dy}{dx} = \tfrac{1}{2}x^2 - \tfrac{1}{2}x^{-2}$. Therefore $L = \displaystyle\int_1^3 \tfrac{1}{2}\left(x^2 + x^{-2}\right) dx = \dfrac{14}{3}$.

24. $x = \tfrac{1}{8}y^4 + \tfrac{1}{4}y^{-2}$, $1 \le y \le 2$. Thus $\dfrac{dx}{dy} = \tfrac{1}{2}y^3 - \tfrac{1}{2}y^{-3}$. So

$$L = \int_1^2 \sqrt{1 + \tfrac{1}{4}y^6 - \tfrac{1}{2} + \tfrac{1}{4}y^{-6}}\; dy = \int_1^2 \left(\tfrac{1}{2}y^3 + \tfrac{1}{2}y^{-3}\right) dy = \tfrac{33}{16}.$$

25. $\dfrac{dy}{dx} = \dfrac{6x^4 - 8y}{4x}$. But $8y = \dfrac{2x^6 + 1}{x^2}$, so $\dfrac{dy}{dx} = x^3 - \tfrac{1}{4}x^{-3}$. Therefore $1 + \left(\dfrac{dy}{dx}\right)^2 = \left(x^3 + \tfrac{1}{4}x^{-3}\right)^2$, so

$$L = \int_1^2 \left(x^3 + \tfrac{1}{4}x^{-3}\right) dx = \tfrac{123}{32} = 3.84375.$$

26. $12y\dfrac{dx}{dy} + 12x - 16y^3 = 0$, so $12y^2\dfrac{dx}{dy} + 12xy = 16y^4$. But $12xy = 4y^4 + 3$, so

$$12y^2 \dfrac{dx}{dy} = 16y^4 - 4y^4 - 3 = 12y^4 - 3;$$
$$\dfrac{dx}{dy} = y^2 - \tfrac{1}{4}y^{-2}.$$
$$\text{Thus } 1 + \left(\dfrac{dx}{dy}\right)^2 = \left(y^2 + \tfrac{1}{4}y^{-2}\right)^2.$$
$$L = \int_1^2 \left(y^2 + \tfrac{1}{4}y^{-2}\right) dy = \tfrac{59}{24}.$$

27. $x = \dfrac{y^{3/2}}{\sqrt{8}}$, so $\dfrac{dx}{dy} = \tfrac{3}{2}\sqrt{y/8}$. So $\left(\dfrac{dx}{dy}\right)^2 = \tfrac{9}{32}y$, and consequently

$$\left[1 + \left(\dfrac{dx}{dy}\right)^2\right]^{1/2} = \left(\tfrac{9}{32}y + 1\right)^{1/2}.$$

Therefore
$$L = \int_2^8 \left(\tfrac{9}{32}y + 1\right)^{1/2} dy.$$

28. $2(y-3)\dfrac{dy}{dx} = 12(x+2)^2$, so $\dfrac{dy}{dx} = \dfrac{6(x+2)^2}{y-3}$. Thus

$$1 + \left(\dfrac{dy}{dx}\right)^2 = 1 + \dfrac{36(x+2)^4}{(y-3)^2} = 1 + \dfrac{36(x+2)^4}{4(x+2)^3} = 1 + 9(x+2) = 9x + 19.$$

Therefore
$$L = \int_{-1}^2 (9x+19)^{1/2}\, dx = \dfrac{2}{27}\left(37\sqrt{37} - 10\sqrt{10}\right).$$

29. $A = \displaystyle\int_0^1 2\pi x^{1/2}\left(\dfrac{4x+1}{4x}\right)^{1/2} dx = \dfrac{\pi}{6}\left(5\sqrt{5}-1\right) \approx 5.3304$.

30. $A = \displaystyle\int_1^2 2\pi x^3 \left(1+9x^4\right)^{1/2} dx = \dfrac{\pi}{27}\left(145\sqrt{145} - 10\sqrt{10}\right) \approx 199.48$.

31. $1 + \left(\dfrac{dy}{dx}\right)^2 = (x^4 + \tfrac{1}{4}x^{-4})^2$. Therefore $A = \displaystyle\int_1^2 2\pi x \left(x^4 + \tfrac{1}{4}x^{-4}\right) dx = \tfrac{339}{16}\pi$.

32. $\dfrac{dx}{dy} = \tfrac{1}{2}y^3 - \tfrac{1}{2}y^{-3}$; $1 + \left(\dfrac{dx}{dy}\right)^2 = (\tfrac{1}{2}y^3 + \tfrac{1}{2}y^{-3})^2$. Therefore

$$A = \int_1^2 2\pi y \left(\frac{1}{2}y^3 + \frac{1}{2}y^{-3}\right) dy = \tfrac{67}{10}\pi.$$

33. $A = \displaystyle\int_0^3 \tfrac{2}{3}\pi y^3 (1+y^4)^{1/2}\, dy = \dfrac{\pi}{9}\left(82\sqrt{82} - 1\right) \approx 258.8468$.

34. $A = \displaystyle\int_1^2 2\pi x\sqrt{1+x}\, dx$. Let $u = 1 + x$; then $x = u - 1$ and $dx = du$. As x takes on values from 1 to 2, u takes on values from 2 to 3. So

$$A = \int_2^3 2\pi(u-1)u^{1/2}\, du = \frac{8}{15}\pi\left(6\sqrt{3} - \sqrt{2}\right).$$

35. $\dfrac{dy}{dx} = \dfrac{1-x}{(2x-x^2)^{1/2}}$; $1 + \left(\dfrac{dy}{dx}\right)^2 = \dfrac{1}{2x-x^2}$. So the integrand simplifies to 2π, and

$$A = \int_0^2 2\pi\, dx = 4\pi.$$

36. The length of one arch of the sine curve is

$$L_1 = \int_0^\pi (1 + \cos^2 x)^{1/2}\, dx.$$

To find the arc length of half the ellipse, we take $y = (2 - 2x^2)^{1/2}$, $-1 \le x \le 1$. Then

$$\frac{dy}{dx} = -\frac{2x}{(2x-x^2)^{1/2}}, \text{ so } 1 + \left(\frac{dy}{dx}\right)^2 = \frac{1+x^2}{1-x^2}.$$

Thus

$$L_2 = \int_{-1}^1 \sqrt{\frac{1+x^2}{1-x^2}}\, dx.$$

Let $x = \cos u$. Then $dx = -\sin u\, du$, and

$$L_2 = \int_\pi^0 \sqrt{\frac{1+\cos^2 u}{\sin^2 u}}(-\sin u)\, du = \int_0^\pi (1+\cos^2 u)^{1/2}\, du = L_1 \approx 3.820197789.$$

38. $L = \displaystyle\int_0^1 (1 + 4x^2)^{1/2}\, dx$; $S_{10} \approx 1.47894$. The true value of the integral is

$$L = \frac{1}{4}\left[2\sqrt{5} + \ln\left(2 + \sqrt{5}\right)\right] \approx 1.47894286.$$

39. Change in notation: Temporarily replace r_1 with r and r_2 with s. Then

$$A = \int_r^s 2\pi x\left(1 + \frac{h^2}{(s-r)^2}\right)^{1/2} dx = \left[\pi x^2 \sqrt{1 + \frac{h^2}{(s-r)^2}}\right]_r^s$$

$$= \pi(s-r)(s+r)\frac{\sqrt{(s-r)^2 + h^2}}{s-r} = \pi(s+r)L = (2\pi)\left(\tfrac{1}{2}\right)(r_1+r_2)L = 2\pi\bar{r}L.$$

Section 6.4 Arc Length and Surface Area of Revolution

40. Take $y = f(x) = (r^2 - x^2)^{1/2}$, $-r \leq x \leq r$. Then $\dfrac{dy}{dx} = -\dfrac{x}{\sqrt{r^2 - x^2}}$. So

$$A = \int_{-r}^{r} 2\pi \sqrt{r^2 - x^2} \sqrt{1 + \dfrac{x^2}{r^2 - x^2}}\, dx = 2\pi \int_{-r}^{r} (r^2)^{1/2}\, dx = 4\pi r^2.$$

42. First, $\dfrac{dy}{dx} = -(y/x)^{1/3}$. So $\left(\dfrac{ds}{dx}\right)^2 = 1 + (y/x)^{2/3} = x^{-2/3}$. Therefore

$$A = 2 \int_0^1 (2\pi x)\left(x^{-1/3}\right) dx = \dfrac{12}{5}\pi.$$

44. Let $f(x) = x\sqrt{\dfrac{4 - x^2}{32}}$. Then $1 + (f'(x))^2 = \dfrac{(6 - x^2)^2}{8(4 - x^2)}$. Hence the surface area is

$$A = \int_0^2 2\pi f(x) \dfrac{(6 - x^2)^2}{8(4 - x^2)}\, dx = \pi \left[\dfrac{12x^2 - x^4}{32}\right]_0^2 = \pi.$$

Section 6.5

1. $y^{-1/2} = 2x\, dx$; $2y^{1/2} = x^2 + C$; $y(x) = \tfrac{1}{4}(x^2 + C)^2$.
2. $y(x) = (C - x^2)^{-1}$
4. $y^{-3/2}\, dy = x^{3/2}\, dx$; $-2y^{-1/2} = \tfrac{2}{5}x^{5/2} + K$; $y^{-1/2} = \tfrac{1}{5}(C - x^{5/2})$; $y(x) = 25(C - x^{5/2})^{-2}$.
6. $y(x) = 4 + \dfrac{1}{C - x^4}$
7. $(1 + y^{1/2})\, dy = (1 + x^{1/2})\, dx$; $y + \tfrac{2}{3}y^{3/2} = x + \tfrac{2}{3}x^{3/2} + K$; $3y + 2y^{3/2} = 3x + 2x^{3/2} + C$.
8. $2y^2 + y^4 = 2x^2 + x^4 + C$
10. $2y + \tfrac{3}{2}y^{-2} = x + x^{-1} + C$
12. Two solutions: $y(x) = \tfrac{1}{4}(x + 4)^2$, $y(x) = \tfrac{1}{4}(x - 4)^2$.
13. $4y^3\, dy = 1\, dx$; $y^4 = x + C$. $1 = 0 + C$, so $C = 1$. $y^4 = x + 1$.
14. $xy^2 + 2 = 6x$.
16. $y\, dy = x\, dx$; $\tfrac{1}{2}y^2 = \tfrac{1}{2}x^2 + K$; $y^2 = x^2 + C$. $25 = 9 + C$, so $C = 16$. $y^2 = x^2 + 16$; that is, $y(x) = \sqrt{x^2 + 16}$. (We take the positive sign at the last step because $y(3) > 0$.)
18. $y(x) = x + 1$
19. $y^{-2}\, dy = (3x^2 - 1)\, dx$; $-(y^{-1}) = x^3 - x + K$; $y(x) = \dfrac{1}{C + x - x^3}$. $1 = \dfrac{1}{C}$; $y(x) = \dfrac{1}{1 + x - x^3}$.
20. $(y^2)(5 - 2x^2 - 2x^4) = 1$.
21. We take time t in weeks.

$$P^{1/2}\, dP = -k\, dt;$$
$$2P^{1/2} = C - kt;$$
$$P(t) = (C - kt)^2.$$
$$900 = P(0) = C^2, \text{ so } C = 30 \text{ (not } -30\text{)}.$$
$$P(t) = (30 - kt)^2.$$

Now $441 = P(6) = (30 - 6k)^2$, and it follows that $k = 1.5$. The fish will be gone when $kt = 30$, thus when $t = 20$. Answer: 20 weeks (after time $t = 0$).

22. If $P(t) = \left(\frac{1}{2}ktP_0^{1/2}\right)^2$, then

$$\frac{dP}{dt} = 2\left(\frac{1}{2}kt + P_0^{1/2}\right)\left(\frac{1}{2}k\right) = k\left(\frac{1}{2}kt + P_0^{1/2}\right) = kP^{1/2} \text{ and } P(0) = \left(P_0^{1/2}\right)^2 = P_0.$$

Thus we have verified that the proposed solution satisfies both the differential equation and the associated initial condition.

23. We take time t in years, with $t = 0$ corresponding to the year 1970. The condition $P(10) = 121,000$ yields the fact that $k = 2\sqrt{10}$. It then follows immediately that in the year 2000, the population will be $P(30) = 169,000$. Next we solve the equation $P(t) = 200,000$ to find that this will be the population when $t = 100(\sqrt{2} - 1) \approx 41.4$—that is, in the year 2011.

25. $P(t) = \dfrac{2}{1 - 2kt}$; $4 = P(3) = \dfrac{2}{1 - 6k}$, so $k = \frac{1}{12}$. Now $P(6)$ is undefined, but $P(t) \to +\infty$ as $t \to 6$ from below. So the rabbit population explodes in the second three-month period.

26. First write $v^{-2}\, dv = -k\, dt$, then antidifferentiate to obtain $-\dfrac{1}{v} = C - kt$. Now $v(0) = 40$; it follows that $C = -\frac{1}{40}$, and therefore that $v(t) = \dfrac{40}{40kt + 1}$. If $v(10) = 20$, this implies that $k = \frac{1}{400}$, so that $v(t) = \dfrac{400}{t + 10}$. Thus $v(t) = 5$ when $t + 10 = 80$, so it requires $t = 70$ total seconds for the motorboat to slow to 5 ft/s. Note that $v(t) > 0$ for all t, contrary to experience. Consequently the mathematical model $dv/dt = -kv^2$ must be regarded as unrealistic.

27. Let R denote the radius of the tank. From Eq. (20) of the text we obtain

$$\pi R^2 \frac{dy}{dt} = -a\sqrt{2gy}, \text{ so that } y^{-1/2}\, dy = -2k\, dt \quad (k \text{ constant}, k > 0).$$

It now follows that $2y^{1/2} = -2kt + 2C$, and thus $y(t) = (C - kt)^2$. With time t in hours, we have $9 = y(0) = C^2$, so $|C| = 3$. But $c > 0$ because $k > 0$, so $C = 3$. Thus $y(t) = (3 - kt)^2$. Also $y(1) = 4$, so $4 = (3 - k)^2$; that is, $|3 - k| = 2$, so $k = 1$ or $k = 5$. If $k = 5$ then $y(t) = (3 - 5t)^2$, and this would imply that $y(t) = 0$ when $t = 0.6 < 1$. This is impossible in view of the conditions given in the problem, and therefore $k = 1$. Thus

$$y(t) = (3 - t)^2,$$

and the tank will be empty ($y = 0$) when $t = 3$: 3 hours after the bottom plug is removed.

28. In the notation of Section 6.5 of the text, we have $c = 1$, $g = 32$, $a = \pi/144$, and $A(y) = 9\pi$. So Eq. (20) takes the form

$$9\pi \frac{dy}{dt} = -\frac{\pi}{144}\sqrt{64y}, \text{ and hence } y^{-1/2}\frac{dy}{dt} = -\frac{1}{162}.$$

It follows that $y^{1/2} = C - (t/324)$. Therefore

$$y(t) = \left(C - \frac{t}{324}\right)^2$$

Now $9 = y(0) = C^2$, so $C = 3$ (not -3, else y would never be zero). Thus

$$y(t) = \left(3 - \frac{t}{324}\right)^2$$

where the units are feet and seconds (because those are the units that we used for g and other assorted constants and variables in the problem). The tank will be empty when $y = 0$; that is, when $t = 972$ (s). Hence the tank will require approximately 16 min 12 s to empty.

29. Let R denote the radius of the cone—the radius of the tank at its top. If the height of the water at time t is $y = y(t)$ and the radius of the water surface then is $r = r(t)$, then (by similar triangles)

$$\frac{y}{16} = \frac{r}{R}, \text{ so that } r = \frac{R}{16}y.$$

Thus the area of the water surface at time t is

$$A(y) = \pi r^2 = \frac{\pi r^2}{256}y^2.$$

From Eq. (20) of this section of the text we find that

$$\frac{\pi R^2}{256}y^2 \frac{dy}{dt} = -a\sqrt{2gy},$$

and thus that $y^{3/2}\frac{dy}{dt} = -k$ where k is a positive constant. Hence

$$\frac{2}{5}y^{5/2} = C - kt,$$

and therefore $y = (A - Bt)^{2/5}$ where A and B also are constants. Now $16 = y(0) = A^{2/5}$, so $A = 1024$. (Note that $A \neq -1024$ because $B > 0$ and $y \geq 0$.) Consequently $y(t) = (1024 - Bt)^{2/5}$. Now we take t in hours and use the fact that $y(1) = 9$ to determine that $B = 781$, and thus that

$$y(t) = (1024 - 781t)^{5/2}.$$

The tank will be empty when $t = \frac{1024}{781} \approx 1.31114$ hours after the bottom plug is removed—about 1 h 18 min 40 s.

30. Let R denote the radius of the tank and y the height of the water at time t (seconds). We take $c = 1$, a as the area of the bottom hole, $g = 32$, and $A(y) = \pi R^2$. The volume of water in the tank at time t is $V(t) = \pi R^2 y(t)$ (cubic feet), and from Eq. (20) we find that

$$\pi r^2 \frac{dy}{dt} = -a\sqrt{64y}, \text{ so that } \frac{dy}{dt} = -2ky^{1/2};$$
$$y^{-1/2} dy = -2k \, dt;$$
$$2y^{1/2} = -2kt + 2C;$$
$$y(t) = (C - kt)^2.$$

Now $y(t) = 0$ when $t = C/k = 60T$, so $C = 60kT$:

$$y(t) = (60kT - kt)^2 = k^2(60T - t)^2 = k^2T^2\left(60 - \frac{t}{T}\right)^2.$$

Now conversion of t from seconds to minutes yields

$$y(t) = k^2T^2\left(60 - \frac{60t}{T}\right)^2 = 3600k^2T^2\left(1 - \frac{t}{T}\right)^2.$$

Because $V(t)$ is proportional to $y(t)$, even with V measured in gallons, we find that

$$V(t) = C_1\left(1 - \frac{t}{T}\right)^2;$$

180 Section 6.5 Separable Differential Equations

$V_0 = V(0) = C_1$, so $V(t) = V_0 \left(1 - \dfrac{t}{T}\right)^2$.

31. Let $V(y)$ denote the volume of water in the tank when the water has depth y. Then $\dfrac{dV}{dt} = -C_0\sqrt{y}$ and $V(y) = \displaystyle\int_0^y \pi u^{3/2}\,du$. Therefore

$$\pi y^{3/2} \dfrac{dy}{dt} = -C_0 y^{1/2}$$
$$\pi y\,dy = -C_0\,dt$$
$$\dfrac{1}{2}\pi y^2 = -C_0 t + K_0$$
$$y^2 = -Kt + C.$$

Let $t = 0$ at noon. Then $y(0) = 12$, so $C = 144$. Since $y(1) = 6$, $36 = 144 - K$, so $K = 108$. Therefore $y^2 = 144 - 108t$. When $y = 0$, $t = 4/3$. The tank will be empty at 1:20 P.M.

32. Let a represent the area of the hole and let the volume of water in the tank at depth y be $V(y)$. Then if s represents the time in seconds,

$$V(y) = \int_0^y \pi u\,du = \dfrac{1}{2}\pi y^2 \text{ and } \dfrac{dV}{ds} = -\pi a^2 \sqrt{2gy}.$$
$$\pi y \dfrac{dy}{ds} = -\pi a^2 \sqrt{2gy}.$$
$$\dfrac{dy}{ds} = -a^2\sqrt{2g}\,y^{-1/2}$$
$$y^{1/2}\,dy = -a^2\sqrt{2g}\,ds$$
$$\dfrac{2}{3} y^{3/2} = -a^2 s\sqrt{2g} + C$$

Let $s = 0$ at noon. Then $y(0) = 4$, so

$$\dfrac{2}{3}(8) = C;\quad \dfrac{2}{3} y^{3/2} = -a^2 s\sqrt{2g} + \dfrac{16}{3},\ \text{hence } y(s) = \left(8 - \dfrac{3}{2}a^2 s\sqrt{2g}\right)^{2/3}.$$

Also, $y(3600) = 1$, so

$$1 = y(3600) = \left(8 - 5400 a^2 \sqrt{2g}\right)^{3/2};\ a = \dfrac{\sqrt{14}}{360}.$$

(a) In seconds, $y(t) = \left(8 - \dfrac{7s}{3600}\right)^{2/3}$, so in hours: $y(t) = (8 - 7t)^{2/3}$.

(b) The tank will be empty at $t = 8/7$ hours.

(c) The radius of the hole is $a = \sqrt{14}/360$ ft. In inches: $\sqrt{14}/30 \approx 0.125$ in.

33. Set up a coordinate system in which the center of one end of the tank is located at the point $(0,3)$ in the xy-plane, with the x-axis horizontal and the y-axis vertical, so that the bounding curve of that of the tank has equation $x^2 + (y-3)^2 = 9$; that is, $x^2 + y^2 - 6y = 0$. If the depth of liquid in the tank is y, $0 \le y \le 3$, then we solve this last equation for

$$2x = 2\left(6y - y^2\right)^{1/2}$$

to obtain the width of the upper surface of the liquid then. It follows that we should take

$$A(y) = 10\left(6y - y^2\right)^{1/2}$$

Section 6.5 Separable Differential Equations

in Eq. (20), together with $g = 32$, $c = 1$, and $a = \pi/144$, to obtain

$$10\left(6y - y^2\right)^{1/2} \frac{dy}{dt} = -\frac{\pi}{144}\sqrt{64y}.$$

Note that $y(0) = 3$ with time t in seconds and y in feet. The solution of this differential equation is

$$y(t) = 6 - \left(3\sqrt{3} - \frac{\pi t}{120}\right)^{2/3}$$

Now $y(t) = 0$ when $t = \frac{120}{\pi}\left(6\sqrt{6} - 3\sqrt{3}\right)$, and therefore the tank will be empty after approximately 362.9 seconds—about 6 minutes 2.9 seconds.

34. Set up a coordinate system in which the tank has its lowest point at the origin and its vertical diameter lying on the y-axis, so that the equation of the cross section of the tank in the xy-plane will be $x^2 + (y-4)^2 = 16$. If the liquid in the tank has depth y, then the radius at its surface is $x = \left(8y - y^2\right)^{1/2}$, so in Eq. (20) we take $A(y) = \pi x^2 \left(8y - y^2\right)$, $c = 1$, $g = 32$, and $a = \pi/144$ to obtain

$$A(y) = \pi x^2 = \pi\left(8y - y^2\right).$$

Thus

$$\pi\left(8y - y^2\right)\frac{dy}{dt} = -\frac{\pi}{144}\sqrt{64y};$$

$$\left(8y^{1/2} - y^{3/2}\right) dy = -\frac{1}{18} dt;$$

$$\frac{16}{3}y^{3/2} - \frac{2}{5}y^{5/2} = -\frac{t}{18} + C.$$

When $t = 0$, $y = 8$. It follows that $C = \frac{512}{15}\sqrt{2}$. Thus

$$\frac{16}{3}y^{3/2} - \frac{2}{5}y^{5/2} = -\frac{t}{18} + \frac{512}{15}\sqrt{2}.$$

The tank is empty when $t = 0$. At that time we have $t = \frac{3072}{5}\sqrt{2} \approx 869$ seconds—about 14 minutes 29 seconds.

35. Let $h = f^{-1}$ and let a be the area of the hole. We use $c = 1$, $g = 32$, and $\frac{dy}{dt} = -\frac{1}{10800}$ (feet per second). Then

$$-\frac{1}{10800}A(y) = -a\sqrt{64y}$$

where $A(y) = \pi\left(h(y)\right)^2$. Therefore

$$(h(y))^2 = \frac{86400}{\pi} ay^{1/2},$$

and thus

$$(h(y))^4 = \frac{7464960000}{\pi^2} a^2 y.$$

Finally, because $y = f(x)$ and $x = h(y)$, we have

$$f(x) = \frac{\pi^2}{(86400)^2} x^4.$$

Now $f(1) = 4$, so $86400 a = \pi/2$; it follows that $a = \frac{\pi}{172800} = \pi r^2$ where r is the radius of the hole. Therefore $r = \frac{1}{240\sqrt{3}}$ feet; that is, r is approximately 0.02887 inches.

Section 6.6

1. $W = \int_{-2}^{1} 10\, dx = 30.$

2. $W = \int_{1}^{5} (3x - 1)\, dx = 32.$

3. $W = \int_{1}^{10} \frac{10}{x^2}\, dx = 9.$

4. $W = \int_{0}^{4} -3\sqrt{x}\, dx = -16.$

5. $W = \int_{-1}^{1} \sin \pi x\, dx = 0.$

6. $F = 10x$, so $W = \int_{0}^{-0.4} 10x\, dx = +0.8$ (N·m).

7. $W = \int_{0}^{1} 30x\, dx = 15$ (ft·lb).

8. $W = \int_{0}^{10} 100\, dx = 1000$ (ft·lb).

9. $W = \int_{5000}^{6000} \frac{k}{y^2}\, dy = \frac{k}{30000} \approx 2.816 \times 10^9$ (ft·lb).

10. $W = \int_{0}^{10} (62.4)(y)(25\pi)\, dy = 78000\pi \approx 245{,}044.23$ (ft·lb).

11. A thin circular disk of water at height y above the base of the cone has radius r given (with the aid of similar triangles) by
$$r = \frac{1}{2}(10 - y).$$
Therefore
$$W = \int_{0}^{10} \frac{1}{4}(10 - y)^2 (y)(62.4)\, dy = 13000\pi \approx 40841 \text{ (ft·lb)}.$$

12. By similar triangles, the radius of a circular disk of water at height y above the vertex of the cone is $r = \frac{1}{2}y$. Therefore
$$W = \int_{0}^{10} (62.4)(y)\left(\frac{\pi}{4}y^2\right) dy = 39000\pi \approx 122{,}522.11 \text{ (ft·lb)}.$$

13. Take $y = -10$ as ground level, so that the radius x of a thin horizontal slab of water at height y above ground level satisfies the equation $x^2 = 5y$. Therefore
$$W = \int_{0}^{5} (y + 10)(50)(5\pi y)\, dy = \frac{125{,}000}{3}\pi \approx 130{,}900 \text{ (ft·lb)}.$$

15. $W = (10)(\pi)(25)(10)(62.4) = 156{,}000\pi \approx 490{,}088.454$ (ft·lb).

16. Set up the following coordinate system: The x-axis and y-axis cross at the center of one end of the tank, so that the equation of the circular (vertical) cross section of the tank is $x^2 + y^2 = 9$. Then the gasoline must be lifted to the level $y = 10$. A horizontal cross section of the tank at the level y is a rectangle of length 10 and width $2x$ where x and y satisfy the equation $x^2 + y^2 = 9$ of the end of the tank. Thus we find that $x = (9 - y^2)^{1/2}$. So

(a) The amount of work required to pump all of the gasoline into the cars is:

$$W = \int_{-3}^{3} \left(2\sqrt{9-y^2}\right)(10)(10-y)(45)\,dy$$

$$= 900 \int_{-3}^{3} \left(10\sqrt{9-y^2} - y\sqrt{9-y^2}\right)dy$$

$$= 9000 \cdot \frac{1}{2} \cdot \pi \cdot 9 + 900 \left[\frac{1}{3}(9-y^2)^{3/2}\right]_{-3}^{3}$$

$$= 40500\pi \approx 127{,}234.5 \text{ (ft·lb).}$$

(b) Assume that the tank has a 1.341 hp motor. If it were to operate at 100% efficiency, it would pump all of the gasoline in $40500\pi/((3300)(1.341)) \approx 2.875161$ min, using 1 kW for 2.875161 minutes. This would amount to 0.047919356 kWh, costing 0.345¢. Assuming that the pump in the tank is only 30% efficient, the actual cost would be about 1.15¢.

17. The area of a cross-sectional slice at y is $\pi(100-y^2)$. So the volume of the slice is approximately $\Delta V = \pi(100-y^2)\Delta y$, its weight (the force required to lift the slice) is approximately $(62.4)(100-y^2)\Delta y$, and the work required to lift the slice from its initial position $y = -50$ to its final position y is then approximately $\pi(62.4)(100-y^2)(50-(-y))\Delta y$. Therefore the total work required to fill the tank is

$$W = \int_{-10}^{10} \pi(62.4)(100-y^2)(y+50)\,dy.$$

18. If the origin is put at the center of the hemisphere (that is, where the center would be if the other half of the sphere were present), then the total work required is

$$W = \int_{0}^{10} \pi(100-y^2)(60+y)(50)\,dy$$

$$= 50\pi \int_{0}^{10} (6000 + 100y - 60y^2 - y^3)\,dy$$

$$= (50\pi)(42{,}500) = 2{,}120{,}000\pi \approx 6{,}675{,}884.4 \text{ (ft·lb).}$$

19. Take $y = 0$ at ground level. At time t, $0 \le t \le 50$, the bucket is at height $y = 2t$ and its weight is $F = 100 - \frac{1}{2}t$. So $t = \frac{1}{2}y$, and therefore the work is given by

$$W = \int_{0}^{100} \left(100 - \frac{1}{4}y\right)dy = 8750 \text{ (ft·lb).}$$

20. If y feet of the rope are hanging, then the weight of that part of the rope is $\frac{1}{4}y$. So

$$W = \int_{0}^{100} \frac{1}{4}y\,dy = 1250 \text{ (ft·lb).}$$

21. $\int_{0}^{100} \left(100 + \left(25 - \frac{1}{4}y\right)\right)dy = 11{,}250$ (ft·lb).

22. $W = \int_{x_1}^{x_2} Ap(Ax)\,dx$. Let $V = Ax$; then $dV = A\,dx$. Therefore

$$W = \int_{V_1}^{V_2} pV\,dV.$$

23. $pV^{1.4} = c$. $p_1 = 200$, $V_1 = 50$. $(200)(50^{1.4}) = c = (200)(50^{7/5})$, so

$$p = \frac{c}{V^{1.4}} = (200)\left(\frac{50}{V}\right)^{7/5}$$

Thus

$$W = \int_{50}^{500} (200)\left(\frac{50}{V}\right)^{7/5} dV \quad \text{(in.·lb)};$$

divide by 12 to convert the answer into ft·lb.

24. Set up a coordinate system in which the center of the hemisphere is at the origin, with a diameter lying on the x-axis and the y-axis perpendicular to the base, so that the highest point of the hemisphere has coordinates $(0, 60)$. Now imagine a horizontal thin circular slice of its contents at position y and having radius x, so that $x^2 + y^2 = 3600$. If the thickness of this slice is dy, then its volume is $dV = \pi(3600 - y^2)\,dy$, so its weight is $40\pi(3600 - y^2)\,dy$. This is the force acting on the slice, which is to be lifted a distance $60 - y$, so the work used in lifting this slice is $40\pi(3600 - y^2)(60 - y)\,dy$. Therefore the total work to pump all the liquid to the level of the top of the tank is

$$W = \int_0^{60} 40\pi(3600 - y^2)(60 - y)\,dy = 216{,}000{,}000\pi \quad \text{(ft·lb)}.$$

25. $W = \displaystyle\int_0^1 60\pi(1-y)\sqrt{y}\,dy = 16\pi$ (ft·lb).

26. Set up a coordinate system in which the center of the tank is at the origin and the ground surface coincides with the horizontal line $y = -3$. Imagine a horizontal cross section of the tank at position y, $-3 \le y \le 3$. The equation of the circle $x^2 + y^2 = 9$ gives us the width $2x$ of this rectangular cross section: $2x = 2(9 - y^2)^{1/2}$. The length of the cross section is 20, so if we denote its thickness by dy then its volume is $40(9 - y^2)^{1/2}\,dy$. To fill this slab with gasoline weighing 40 pounds per cubic foot, which is to be lifted the distance $y + 3$ feet, requires $dW = 1600(y+3)(9-y^2)^{1/2}\,dy$ ft·lb of work. So the work required to fill the tank is

$$W = \int_{-3}^{3} 1600(y+3)(9-y^2)^{1/2}\,dy$$

$$= 1600\int_{-3}^{3} y(9-y^2)^{1/2}\,dy + 4800\int_{-3}^{3} (9-y^2)^{1/2}\,dy.$$

The first integral is zero because it involves the evaluation of $(9 - y^2)^{3/2}$ at $y = 3$ and at $y = -3$. The second is the product of 4800 and the area of a semicircle of radius 3, so the answer is that the total work is $21{,}600\pi$ ft·lb.

27. It is convenient to set up a coordinate system in which the center of the tank is at the origin, the x-axis horizontal, and the y-axis vertical. A horizontal cross section at y is circular with radius x satisfying $x^2 + y^2 = 144$, so the answer may be found by evaluating the integral

$$W = \int_{-12}^{12} (50\pi)(y+12)(144 - y^2)\,dy.$$

28. There are a number of ways to work this problem. Here is a way to check your answer by using elementary physics and no calculus. Stage 1: Imagine the chain hanging in the shape of an "L" with 40 feet vertical and 10 feet horizontal, the latter on the floor of the monkey's cage in a neat heap. Stage 2: Cut off this ten-foot length of chain and move it to its final position—hanging from the top of the cage. It weighs 5 pounds and has moved an average distance of 35 feet, so the work to lift this segment of the chain is $S_1 = (5)(35) = 175$ ft·lb. Stage 3: Return to the dangling chain. Cut off its bottom 15 feet and move it to its final position—hanging from the 10-foot segment now hanging from the top of the cage. The top end of this segment is lifted $30 - 15 = 15$ feet and it weighs 7.5 pounds, so the work to lift the second segment is $S_2 = (15)(7.5) = 112.5$ ft·lb. The remaining 25 feet of the chain doesn't move at all. Finally, the monkey lifts her own 20 pounds a distance of 40 feet, so the work involved here is $S_3 = 800$ ft·lb. So the total work in the process is $W = W_1 + W_2 + W_3 = 1087.5$ ft·lb. Of course, to gain the maximum benefit from this problem, you should work it using techniques of calculus.

29. Let the string begin its journey stretched out straight along the x-axis from $x = 0$ to $x = 500\sqrt{2}$. Imagine it reaching its final position by simply pivoting at the origin up to a 45° angle while remaining straight. A small segment of the string initially at location x and of length dx is lifted from $y = 0$ to the final height $y = x/\sqrt{2}$, so the total work done in lifting the string is

$$W = \int_0^{500\sqrt{2}} \frac{x}{16\sqrt{2}} \, dx \quad \text{(ft·oz)}.$$

Divide by 16 to convert the answer into ft·lb. To check the answer without using calculus, note that the string is lifted an average distance of 250 feet. Multiply this by the weight of the string in pounds to obtain the answer in ft·lb.

30. Set up a coordinate system in which the center of the sphere is located at the origin. Then the work to fill the tank is given by

$$W = \int_{-R}^{R} (y+H) \rho \pi \left(R^2 - y^2\right) dy$$

$$= \rho\pi \left[R^2 Hy + \frac{1}{2} R^2 y^2 - \frac{1}{3} H y^3 - \frac{1}{4} y^4 \right]_{-R}^{R}$$

$$= \rho\pi \left(2R^3 H - \frac{2}{3} R^3 H \right) = \frac{4}{3} \pi \rho R^3 H.$$

This is the product of the volume $\frac{4}{3}\pi R^3$ of the tank, the weight density ρ of the liquid, and the distance H from the ground to the center of the tank, and the result in Problem 30 now follows.

31. Set up a coordinate system with the y-axis vertical and the x-axis coinciding with the bottom of one end of the trough. A horizontal section of the trough at y is $2 - y$ feet below the water surface, so the total force on the end of the trough is given by

$$F = \int_0^2 (2)(2-y)(\rho) \, dy = 6\rho = 249.6 \text{ (pounds)}.$$

32. Set up a coordinate system in which the origin is at the lowest point of the triangular end of the trough, the y-axis vertical. A narrow horizontal strip at height y has width $2x = \frac{2}{3}y\sqrt{3}$. Therefore the total force on the end of the trough is given by

$$F = \int_0^{\frac{3}{2}\sqrt{3}} \rho \left(\frac{3}{2}\sqrt{3} - y \right) \left(\frac{2}{3} y \sqrt{3} \right) dy$$

$$= \rho \int_0^{\frac{3}{2}\sqrt{3}} \left(3y - \frac{2}{3} y^2 \sqrt{3} \right) dy$$

$$= \frac{27}{8} \rho = 210.6 \text{ (pounds)}.$$

33. Set up a coordinate system in which one end of the trough lies in the xy-plane with its base on the x-axis and bisected by the y-axis. Thus the trapezoidal end has vertices at the points $(1, 0)$, $(-1, 0)$,

(2,3), and (−2,3). Because the width of a horizontal section at height y is $2x = \frac{2}{3}(y+3)$, the total force on the end of the trough is

$$F = \int_0^3 \rho \frac{2}{3}(y+3)(3-y)\,dy = 12\rho = 748.8 \text{ (pounds)}.$$

34. Describe the end of the tank by the inequality $x^2 + y^2 \leq 16$, so that a horizontal section at level y has width $2x = 2\left(16 - y^2\right)^{1/2}$. Then the total force on the end of the tank is

$$F = \int_{-4}^4 \rho(2)(4-y)\left(16 - y^2\right)^{1/2} dy$$

$$= 2\rho \int_{-4}^4 4\left(16 - y^2\right)^{1/2} dy - 2\rho \int_{-4}^4 y\left(16 - y^2\right)^{1/2} dy$$

$$= (16\rho)(4\pi) = 64\rho\pi = 3200\pi \approx 10053.1 \text{ (pounds)}.$$

35. $F = \displaystyle\int_{-15}^{-10} \rho(-y)(5)\,dy = \frac{625}{2}\rho$ (pounds).

36. Put the origin at the center of the circle. Then

$$F = \int_{-3}^3 2\rho(13-y)\left(9 - y^2\right)^{1/2} dy$$

$$= 26\rho \int_{-3}^3 \left(9 - y^2\right)^{1/2} dy - 2\rho \int_{-3}^3 y\left(9 - y^2\right)^{1/2} dy$$

$$= 117\pi\rho \approx 22{,}936.14 \text{ (pounds)}.$$

37. Place the x-axis along the water surface. Then a horizontal section of the triangle at level y has width $2x = \frac{8}{5}(y+15)$, and hence the total force on the gate is

$$F = \int_{-15}^{-10} -\frac{8}{5}\rho y(y+15)\,dy.$$

38. The equation of the semicircle is $x^2 + y^2 = 16$, $y \leq 0$. So

$$F = \int_{-4}^0 2\rho(10-y)\left(16 - y^2\right)^{1/2} dy$$

$$= 20\rho \int_{-4}^0 \left(16 - y^2\right)^{1/2} dy - 2\rho \int_{-4}^0 y\left(16 - y^2\right)^{1/2} dy$$

$$= \frac{1}{3}\rho(240\pi + 128) \approx 18{,}345.23 \text{ (pounds)}.$$

39. $F = \displaystyle\int_0^{100} (62.4)(200)\left(\frac{y}{100}\right)\left(100^2 + 30^2\right)^{1/2} dy.$

Chapter 6 Miscellaneous

1. Note that $t^2 - t - 2 = (t+1)(t-2)$ is negative on the interval $(-1, 2)$. Therefore the net distance traveled is

$$\int_0^3 (t^2 - t - 2)\,dt = -\tfrac{3}{2},$$

whereas the total distance traveled is
$$-\int_0^2 (t^2 - t - 2)\, dt + \int_2^3 (t^2 - t - 2)\, dt = \tfrac{31}{6}.$$

2. $\int_1^4 |t^2 - 4|\, dt = \int_1^2 (4 - t^2)\, dt + \int_2^4 (t^2 - 4)\, dt = \tfrac{37}{3}.$ This is both net distance and total distance.

3. Net distance: $\int_0^{3/2} \pi \sin\left(\tfrac{\pi}{2}(2t - 1)\right) dt = 1.$

   Total distance: $\int_0^{1/2} -\pi \sin\left(\tfrac{\pi}{2}(2t - 2)\right) dt + \int_{1/2}^{3/2} \pi \sin\left(\tfrac{\pi}{2}(2t - 1)\right) dt = 3.$

4. $V = \int_0^1 x^3\, dx = \tfrac{1}{4}.$

5. $V = \int_1^4 x^{1/2}\, dx = \left[\tfrac{2}{3} x^{3/2}\right]_1^4 = \tfrac{14}{3}.$

6. $V = \int_1^2 x^3\, dx = \tfrac{15}{4}.$

7. $V = \int_0^1 \pi(x^2 - x^4)\, dx = \pi\left(\tfrac{1}{3} - \tfrac{1}{5}\right) = \tfrac{2}{15}\pi.$

8. $V = \int_{-1}^1 x^{100}\, dx = \tfrac{2}{101}.$

9. $V = \int_0^{12} \dfrac{t + 6}{12}\, dt = 12$ (inches).

10. $V = \int_0^1 (2x - x^2 - x^3)^2\, dx = \tfrac{22}{105}.$

11. $V = \int_0^1 \pi\left((2x - x^2)^2 - x^6\right) dx = \tfrac{41}{105}\pi.$

12. The two graphs cross at $(-1, 1)$ and at $(1, 1)$. Because the figure is symmetric about the y-axis, part (b) of the problem is not ambiguous.

    (a) $V = 2\int_0^1 \pi\left((x^2 + 1)^2 - (2x^4)\right)^2 dx = \tfrac{128}{45}\pi.$

    (b) $V = \int_0^1 (2\pi x)(x^2 + 1 - 2x^4)\, dx = \tfrac{5}{6}\pi.$

13. $M = \int_0^{20} \dfrac{\pi}{16}(8.5)\, dx = (10.625)\pi \approx 33.379$ (grams).

14. Write r for r_1 and s for r_2. Sketch a trapezoid in the first quadrant with vertices at $(0, 0)$, $(h, 0)$, (h, s), and $(0, r)$. Then an equation of the top edge of your trapezoid is
$$y = r + \dfrac{s - r}{h} x.$$
The frustum is produced by rotating the trapezoidal region around the x-axis, and its volume is
$$V = \int_0^h \pi\left(r + \dfrac{s - r}{h} x\right)^2 dx = \dfrac{\pi h}{3}(r^2 + rs + s^2) = \dfrac{\pi h}{3}\left((r_1)^2 + r_1 r_2 + (r_2)^2\right).$$

16. Because $(a - h, r)$ lies on the ellipse, $\left(\dfrac{a - h}{a}\right)^2 + \left(\dfrac{r}{b}\right)^2 = 1.$ Therefore $r^2 = \dfrac{2ah - h^2}{a^2} b^2$. And so
$$V = \int_{a-h}^a \pi y^2\, dx = \int_{a-h}^a \pi b^2\left(1 - \dfrac{x^2}{a^2}\right) dx = \pi \dfrac{b^2 h^2}{3a^2}(3a - h).$$

But $r^2 = \dfrac{b^2}{a^2} h(2a-h)$, so $\dfrac{b^2}{a^2} h = \dfrac{r^2}{2a-h}$. Therefore
$$V = \tfrac{1}{3}\pi r^2 h \dfrac{3a-h}{2a-h}.$$

17. The computations are quite similar to those in Problem 16.

18. $V(t) = \displaystyle\int_1^t \pi\left(f(x)\right)^2 dx = \pi\left(1 - \dfrac{1}{t}\right)$, so $V'(t) = \pi\left(f(t)\right)^2 = \dfrac{\pi}{t^2}$. Therefore $f(x) = \dfrac{1}{x}$.

19. $V = \displaystyle\int_1^t \pi\left(f(x)\right)^2 dx = \dfrac{\pi}{6}\left[(1+3t)^2 - 16\right]$. Thus
$$\pi(f(x))^2 = \dfrac{\pi}{6}\left[(2)(1+3x)(3)\right] = \pi(1+3x).$$
Therefore $f(x) = \sqrt{1+3x}$.

20. $V(t) = \displaystyle\int_1^t 2\pi x f(x)\, dx = \tfrac{2}{9}\pi\left((1+3t^2)^{3/2} - 8\right)$, so
$$V'(t) = 2\pi t f(t) = \tfrac{2}{9}\pi \left(\tfrac{3}{2}\sqrt{1+3t^3}\,(6t)\right) = 2\pi t\sqrt{1+3t^2}.$$
Therefore $f(x) = \sqrt{1+3x^2}$.

21. $V = \displaystyle\int_0^1 \pi\left(\left(\sin\dfrac{\pi x}{2}\right) - x\right)(2\pi x)\, dx = \dfrac{24 - 2\pi^2}{3\pi} \approx 0.4521$.

22. If $-1 \leq x \leq 2$, then a thin vertical strip of the region above x is rotated in a circle of radius $x+2$. Therefore the volume generated is
$$V = \int_{-1}^2 2\pi(x+2)(x+2-x^2)\, dx = \tfrac{45}{2}\pi.$$

23. $\dfrac{dy}{dx} = \tfrac{1}{2}x^{1/2} - \tfrac{1}{2}x^{-1/2}$, so
$$1 + \left(\dfrac{dy}{dx}\right)^2 = \left(\tfrac{1}{2}x^{1/2} + \tfrac{1}{2}x^{-1/2}\right)^2. \tag{*}$$
So the length of the curve is
$$L = \int_1^4 \left(\tfrac{1}{2}x^{1/2} + \tfrac{1}{2}x^{-1/2}\right) dx = \tfrac{10}{3}.$$

24. The curve in question lies below the x-axis for $1 \leq x \leq 3$ and above it for $3 \leq x \leq 4$. Thus to find the area in part (a), we compute two integrals and add the results. We also use the formula in Eq. (*) of the solution of Problem 23. The area of the left-hand part of the surface is
$$A_L = \int_1^3 -2\pi\left(\tfrac{1}{3}x^{3/2} - x^{1/2}\right)\left(\tfrac{1}{2}x^{1/2} + \tfrac{1}{2}x^{-1/2}\right) dx = \tfrac{16}{9}\pi.$$
The area of the right-hand part of the surface is
$$A_R = \int_3^4 -\left[-2\pi\left(\tfrac{1}{3}x^{3/2} - x^{1/2}\right)\left(\tfrac{1}{2}x^{1/2} + \tfrac{1}{2}x^{-1/2}\right)\right] dx = \tfrac{7}{9}\pi.$$
The total area, and the answer to part (a), is thus $\tfrac{23}{9}\pi$.

Part (b) is much easier:
$$A = \int_1^4 2\pi x\left(\tfrac{1}{2}x^{1/2} + \tfrac{1}{2}x^{-1/2}\right) dx = \tfrac{256}{15}\pi.$$

Chapter 6 Miscellaneous

25. $\frac{dx}{dy} = \frac{3}{8}\left(\frac{4}{3}y^{1/3} - \frac{4}{3}y^{-1/3}\right)$. So—after some algebra—

$$\left(1 + \left(\frac{dx}{dy}\right)^2\right)^{1/2} = \frac{1}{2}\left(y^{1/3} + y^{-1/3}\right).$$

Therefore
$$L = \frac{1}{2}\int_1^8 \left(y^{1/3} + y^{-1/3}\right) dy = \frac{63}{8}.$$

26. (a) $A = \int_1^8 (2\pi y)\frac{y^{1/3} + y^{-1/3}}{2}\, dy = \frac{2556}{35}\pi.$

(b) As in Problem 24, two integrals are required. The area is

$$A = \int_1^{2\sqrt{2}} -2\pi\frac{3}{8}\left(y^{4/3} - 2y^{2/3}\right)\frac{y^{1/3} + y^{-1/3}}{2}\, dy + \int_{2\sqrt{2}}^8 2\pi\frac{3}{8}\left(y^{4/3} - 2y^{2/3}\right)\frac{y^{1/3} + y^{-1/3}}{2}\, dy$$
$$= \frac{57}{64}\pi + \frac{33}{2}\pi = \frac{1113}{64}\pi \approx 17.39087\pi.$$

27. $L = \int_1^4 2\pi(x-1)\frac{1}{2}\left(x^{1/2} + x^{-1/2}\right) dx = \frac{52}{5}\pi.$

28. $\frac{dy}{dx} = -\frac{x}{\sqrt{r^2 - x^2}}$, so $1 + \left(\frac{dy}{dx}\right)^2 = \frac{r^2}{r^2 - x^2}$. Therefore

$$A = \int_a^b 2\pi\sqrt{r^2 - x^2}\,\frac{r}{\sqrt{(r^2 - x^2)}}\, dx = 2\pi rh.$$

30. We'll provide only half the solution in each part, and no details.

(a) $V = \int_0^1 \pi\left(4x - 4x^6\right) dx = \frac{10}{7}\pi.$

(b) $V = \int_0^1 2\pi x\left(\sqrt{2x} - 2x^3\right) dx = \frac{4}{5}\pi\left(\sqrt{2} - 1\right).$

(c) $V = \int_0^1 \pi\left((2\sqrt{x} + 1)^2 - \left(2x^3 + 1\right)^2\right) dx = \frac{65}{21}\pi.$

(d) $V = \int_0^1 2\pi(2 - x)\left(2\sqrt{x} - 2x^3\right) dx = \frac{38}{15}\pi.$

32. $y = 2x^{3/2} + 2x^{1/2} + C.$ $10 = y(1) = 2 + 2 + C$: $C = 6.$
$y(x) = 2x^{1/2}(x+1) + 6.$

34. $(y+1)^{-1/2}\, dy = 1\, dx;$
$2(y+1)^{1/2} = x + C;$
$y(x) = -1 + \frac{1}{4}(x + C)^2.$

35. $y^{-2}\, dy = 3x^2\, dx;$
$-\frac{1}{y} = x^3 - C;$
$y(x) = \frac{1}{C - x^3}.$ $1 = y(0) = \frac{1}{C}$: $C = 1.$
$y(x) = \frac{1}{1 - x^3}.$

36. $y^{-1/3}\, dy = x^{1/3}\, dx;$

$\frac{3}{2}y^{2/3} = \frac{3}{4}x^{4/3} + C.$ $\frac{3}{2} = \frac{3}{4} + C$: $C = \frac{3}{4}$.

$6y^{2/3} = 3x^{4/3} + 3$;

$2y^{2/3} = x^{4/3} + 1$.

37. $y^2 \, dy = \dfrac{1}{x^2} \, dx$;

$\frac{1}{3}y^3 = -\dfrac{1}{x} + K$;

$y^3 = C - \dfrac{3}{x}$;

$y(x) = \left(C - \dfrac{3}{x}\right)^{1/3}$

38. $y^{1/2} \, dy = x^{-1/2} \, dx$;

$\frac{2}{3}y^{3/2} = 2x^{1/2} + K$;

$y^{3/2} = 3x^{1/2} + C$;

$y(x) = (3\sqrt{x} + C)^{2/3}$.

39. $\dfrac{1}{y^2} \, dy = \cos x \, dx$;

$-\dfrac{1}{y} = K + \sin x$;

$y(x) = \dfrac{1}{C - \sin x}$. $1 = y(0) = \dfrac{1}{C}$: $C = 1$.

$y(x) = \dfrac{1}{1 - \sin x}$.

40. $y^{-1/2} \, dy = \sin x \, dx$;

$2y^{1/2} = C - \cos x$;

$y(x) = \frac{1}{4}(C - \cos x)^2$. $4 = y(0) = \frac{1}{4}(C - 1)^2$: $C = 5$ or $C = -3$.

Two solutions: $y(x) = \frac{1}{4}(5 - \cos x)^2$, $y(x) = \frac{1}{4}(3 + \cos x)^2$.

42. $\frac{2}{7}y^{7/2} + \frac{6}{5}y^{5/2} + 2y^{3/2} + 2y^{1/2} = \frac{2}{7}x^{7/2} + \frac{6}{5}x^{5/2} + 2x^{3/2} + 2x^{1/2} + C$

43. Denote by K the spring constant. Then

$$\int_2^5 K(x - L) \, dx = 5 \int_2^3 K(x - L) \, dx.$$

After applying the fundamental theorem of calculus, we find that

$$(5 - L)^2 - (2 - L)^2 = 5(3 - L)^2 - 5(2 - L)^2.$$

Solve for L: $L = 1$, and therefore the natural length of the spring is 1 foot.

44. Set up a coordinate system in which $x = 50$ corresponds to the position of the windlass and $x = 0$ is the initial position of the beam. Then

$$W = \int_0^{25} [1000 + (5)(50 - x)] \, dx = 29687.5 \text{ (ft·lb)}.$$

45. Here's a quick way to work this problem. The centroid of the oil is initially located at the center of the spherical tank, so to pump the oil to the given height requires lifting its centroid the distance $3R$. The total weight of the oil is

$$F = \tfrac{4}{3}\pi R^3 \rho,$$

so the total work required is $W = (3R)(F) = 4\pi R^4 \rho$ (ft·lb).

46. Set up a coordinate system with the axis of the cone lying on the y-axis and with a diameter of the cone lying on the x-axis. Now a horizontal slice of the cone at height y has radius given by $x = \frac{1}{2}(1-y)$; the units here are in feet. Therefore the work done in building the anthill is

$$W = \int_0^1 \tfrac{1}{4}(150y)\pi(1-y)^2\, dy = \tfrac{25}{8}\pi \approx 9.82 \quad \text{(ft·lb)}.$$

47. $\displaystyle\int_0^R \left(\frac{x}{R}\right)(1)\, dx = \frac{R}{2} = 10{,}454{,}400 \quad \text{(ft·lb)}.$

48. Imagine a thin cylindrical horizontal slab of dirt (or basalt, or whatever) in the hole at distance y from the center of the earth. As it moves from its initial position y to its final position R, its weight varies: If it is at position u, $y \le u \le R$, then its weight will be

$$(350\pi)\left(\frac{u}{R}\right) du$$

where du denotes its thickness. The total work required to lift this slab from its initial position ($u = y$) to the surface ($u = R$) is then

$$\int_y^R 350\pi \frac{u}{R}\, du = \frac{350\pi}{2R}\left(R^2 - y^2\right).$$

Therefore the total work required to lift all the dirt (or basalt, or whatever) from the hole to the surface of the earth is

$$W = \int_0^R \frac{350\pi}{2R}\left(R^2 - y^2\right) dy = \frac{350\pi R^2}{3} \approx 1.60234 \times 10^{17} \quad \text{(ft·lb)}.$$

It is intriguing to note that the answer may be written in the form

$$W = \int_0^R \left(\int_y^R 350\pi \frac{u}{R}\, du\right) dy.$$

49. If the coordinate system is chosen with the origin at the midpoint of the bottom of the dam and with the x-axis horizontal, then the equation of the slanted edge of the dam is $y = 2x - 200$ (with units in feet). Therefore the width of the dam at level y is $2x = y + 200$. Thus the total force on the dam is

$$F = \int_0^{100} \rho(100 - y)(y + 200)\, dy.$$

50. The answer may be obtained from the answer to Problem 49 by multiplying the latter by $\sec 30°$: the force is $2/\sqrt{3}$ times as great, or approximately 8.40622×10^7 pounds The analytical approach here is to introduce the additional factor $\sec(\pi/6)$ into the integral in the solution of Problem 49, but because this factor is a constant, one may as well simply multiply the answer by the same factor.

51. The volume of the solid is

$$V = \int_0^c 2\pi\left(y + \frac{1}{c}\right)\frac{2}{c}\sqrt{y}\, dy = 8\pi\left(\frac{1}{5}c^{3/2} + \frac{1}{3}c^{-1/2}\right).$$

It is clear that there is no maximum volume, because $V \to +\infty$ as $c \to 0^+$. But $V \to +\infty$ as $x \to +\infty$ as well, so there is a minimum volume; $\dfrac{dV}{dc} = 0$ when $c = \tfrac{1}{3}\sqrt{5}$, so this value of c minimizes V.

Chapter 7: Exponential and Logarithmic Functions

Section 7.1

1. (a) $2^3 \cdot 2^4 = 2^{3+4} = 2^7 = 128$. (b) $3^2 \cdot 3^3 = 3^5 = 243$.
   (c) $(2^2)^3 = 64$. (d) $2^{2^3} = 2^8 = 256$.
   (e) $3^5 \cdot 3^{-5} = 3^{5-5} = 3^0 = 1$.

2. (a) $10^{10} \cdot 10^{-10} = 10^{10-10} = 10^0 = 1$. (b) $(2^{12})^{1/3} = 2^{(12/3)} = 2^4 = 16$.
   (c) $3^3 = 27$. (d) $4^5 \cdot 2^{-6} = 2^{10} \cdot 2^{-6} = 2^4 = 16$.
   (e) $6^5 \cdot 3^{-5} = 2^5 \cdot 3^5 \cdot 3^{-5} = 2^5 \cdot 3^0 = 32$.

3. (a) $\log_2 16 = \log_2 2^4 = 4\log_2 2 = 4$. (b) $\log_3 27 = \log_3 3^3 = 3\log_3 3 = 3$.
   (c) $\log_5 125 = \log_5 5^3 = 3\log_5 5 = 3$.

4. (a) $\log_7 7^2 = 2\log_7 7 = 2$. (b) $\log_{10} 1000 = \log_{10} 10^3 = 3\log_{10} 10 = 3$.
   (c) $\log_{12} 12^2 = 2\log_{12} 12 = 2$.

5. (a) $\ln 8 = \ln 2^3 = 3\ln 2$. (b) $\ln 9 = \ln 3^2 = 2\ln 3$.
   (c) $\ln 6 = \ln(2 \cdot 3) = (\ln 2) + (\ln 3)$.

6. (a) $\ln 15 = (\ln 3) + (\ln 5)$. (b) $\ln 72 = \ln(2^3 \cdot 3^2) = 3\ln 2 + 2\ln 3$.
   (c) $\ln 200 = \ln(2^3 \cdot 5^2) = (3\ln 2) + (2\ln 5)$.

7. (a) $\ln \frac{8}{27} = (\ln 2^3) - (\ln 3^3) = 3\ln 2 - 3\ln 3$. (b) $(2\ln 2) + (\ln 3) - (2\ln 5)$.

8. (a) $\ln \frac{27}{40} = \ln(3^3) - \ln(2^3 \cdot 5) = 3\ln 3 - 3\ln 2 - \ln 5$.
   (b) $(\ln 1) - (\ln 90) = 0 - \ln(2 \cdot 3^2 \cdot 5) = -\ln 2 - 2\ln 3 - \ln 5$.

10. If $x = \log_{0.5} 16$, this means that $(0.5)^x = 16$. Take the reciprocal of each side in the last equation to obtain
    $$2^x = \frac{1}{16} = \frac{1}{2^4} = 2^{-4},$$
    then take the base 2 logarithm of the first and last terms above to conclude that $x = -4$. Finally verify this answer by substitution (because the method is predicated on the assumption that x exists—that is, that the logarithm to the base 1/2 of 16 exists).

11. $x = 2$ and $x = 4$. There is also a negative solution.

13. $2^x < e^x < 3^x$ if $x > 0$, whereas $3^x < e^x < 2^x$ if $x < 0$.

14. $2^{-x} < e^{-x} < 3^{-x}$ if $x < 0$, whereas $3^{-x} < e^{-x} < 2^{-x}$ if $x > 0$.

15. Each graph is the reflection of the other across the y-axis.

16. $(0.2)^x < (0.4)^x < (0.6)^x$ if $x < 0$, whereas $(0.6)^x < (0.4)^x < (0.2)^x$ if $x > 0$.

18. $10^{-x} = 10^{-3}$: $x = 3$.

19. $10^{-x} = 10^2$: $x = -2$.

20. $3^{2x} = 3^4$: $2x = 4$, so $x = 2$.

22. $\log_x 16 = 2$ implies that $x^2 = 16$, so that $x = 4$ (only positive numbers other than 1 may be used as bases for logarithms).

24. Apply the natural logarithm to obtain $5x = \ln 7$, so that $x = \frac{1}{5}\ln 7$.

25. Apply the natural logarithm after division of both sides by 3 to obtain $\ln(e^x) = \ln 1$, so that $x = 0$.

26. $2e^{-7x} = 5$: $e^{-7x} = \frac{5}{2}$; $-7x = \ln 5 - \ln 2$; $x = -\frac{1}{7}(\ln 5 - \ln 2)$.

27. $\dfrac{dy}{dx} = xe^x + x^x$.

28. $\dfrac{dy}{dx} = x^3 e^x + 3x^2 e^x$.

29. $\dfrac{dy}{dx} = x^{1/2} e^x + \frac{1}{2} x^{-1/2} e^x$.

30. $\dfrac{dy}{dx} = \dfrac{1}{x} e^x - \dfrac{1}{x^2} e^x$.

31. $\dfrac{dy}{dx} = \dfrac{x-2}{x^3} e^x$.

32. $\dfrac{dy}{dx} = \dfrac{2x-1}{2x^{3/2}} e^x$.

33. $\dfrac{dy}{dx} = 1 + \ln x$.

34. $\dfrac{dy}{dx} = x + 2x \ln x$.

35. $\dfrac{dy}{dx} = \frac{1}{2} x^{1/2} \ln x + x^{-1/2}$.

36. $\dfrac{dy}{dx} = x^{-3/2}\left(1 - \frac{1}{2} \ln x\right)$.

37. $\dfrac{dy}{dx} = \dfrac{1-x}{e^x}$.

38. $\dfrac{dy}{dx} = e^x \left(\dfrac{1}{x} + \ln x\right)$.

40. $y = \frac{1}{3} \ln x$, so $\dfrac{dy}{dx} = \dfrac{1}{3x}$.

41. $\dfrac{dy}{dx} = \dfrac{e^x + e^{-x}}{2\sqrt{e^x - e^{-x}}}$.

42. $\dfrac{dy}{dx} = \dfrac{(4x+5)e^{2x}}{2\sqrt{x+1}}$.

43. $\dfrac{dy}{dx} = e^{3x}(3\cos 4x - 4\sin 4x)$.

44. $\dfrac{dy}{dx} = \dfrac{1}{x} e^{3x}(1 + 3x \ln 4x)$.

45. $y = e^2(3x - 2)$.

46. $y = 2x + 1$.

47. $y = x - 1$.

48. $y = e^{-3}(2e - x)$.

49. $f^{(n)}(x) = 2^n e^{2x}$.

50. $f^{(n)}(x) = (x + n)e^x$.

51. $f'(x) = 0$ when $x = 2$, $f'(x) > 0$ on $(0, 2)$, and $f'(x) < 0$ if $x > 2$. Therefore the global maximum value of f is $f(2) = e^{-2}$.

52. $f'(x) = 0$ when $x = 5$, $f'(x) > 0$ on $(0, 5)$, and $f'(x) < 0$ if $x > 5$. Therefore the global maximum value of f is $f(5) = 2e^{-5/2}$.

53. $f'(x) = 0$ when $x = \frac{1}{2}$ and when $x = 3$. Because $f'(x) < 0$ on $\left(0, \frac{1}{2}\right)$, $f'(x) > 0$ on $\left(\frac{1}{2}, 3\right)$, and $f'(x) < 0$ if $x > 3$, the global minimum value of f is $f\left(\frac{1}{2}\right) = -e^{-1/2}$ and the global maximum value is $f(3) = 9e^{-3}$.

54. $f'(x) = 0$ when $x = \frac{1}{3}$ and when $x = \frac{5}{2}$. Because $f'(x) < 0$ on $\left(0, \frac{1}{3}\right)$, $f'(x) > 0$ on $\left(\frac{1}{3}, \frac{5}{2}\right)$, and $f'(x) < 0$ if $x > \frac{5}{2}$, the global minimum of f is $f\left(\frac{1}{3}\right) = -e^{-1/3}$ and its global maximum is $f\left(\frac{5}{2}\right) = 25 e^{-5/2}$.

55. First, $f'(x) = \dfrac{6\cos x - \sin x}{6 e^{x/6}}$, so the first local maximum point for $x > 0$ occurs when $x = \arctan 6$ and the first local minimum point when $x = \pi + \arctan 6$. The corresponding y-coordinates are, respectively,

$$\dfrac{6}{e^{(\arctan 6)/6} \sqrt{37}} \quad \text{and} \quad -\dfrac{6}{e^{(\pi + \arctan 6)/6} \sqrt{37}}.$$

56. Given $f(x) = e^{-x/6} \sin x$, let $g(x) = e^{-x/6}$ and $h(x) = -e^{-x/6}$. We solve the equation $f(x) = g(x)$ by hand; the x-coordinate of the first point of tangency is $\pi/2$. Similarly, the x-coordinate of the second point of tangency is $3\pi/2$. These are *not* the same as $\arctan 6$ and $\pi + \arctan 6$.

57. Part (a): We solved $2 \cdot 3^t = 8$ to find that $t = (\ln 4)/(\ln 3) \approx 1.26186$. So it takes this population about 1 hour and 16 minutes to quadruple. Part (b): $P'(t) = 2 \cdot 3^t (\ln 3)$, so the rate of change of this population after 4 hours is $P'(4) = 162 \ln 3 \approx 177.975$ million per hour.

58. Part (a): $P(t) = 4 \cdot 2^{t/3} = 12$ when $t = (\ln 27)(\ln 2) \approx 4.75489$. So it requires about 4.75 months for the population to triple. Part (b): At the end of one year the population numbers $P(12) = 64$ rabbits and is then growing at the rate of $P'(12) = \frac{64}{3} \ln 2 \approx 14.7871$ rabbits per month.

59. Part (a): $A(t) = 1000 \cdot (1.08)^t = 2000$ when $t \approx 9.0065$, so the account will double in value in slightly over 9 years. Part (b): At the end of 5 years it will be growing at the rate of $A'(5) \approx 113.08$,

approximately $113.08 per year.

60. $R(t) = 3 \cdot (0.9)^t = 1$ when $t = \dfrac{\ln 3}{\ln(10/9)} \approx 10.4272$, so it will be safe to return to campus after about 10.43 months.

Section 7.2

1. $f'(x) = \dfrac{1}{3x-1} D_x(3x-1) = \dfrac{3}{3x-1}$

2. $f'(x) = -\dfrac{2x}{4-x^2}$

4. $f(x) = 2\ln(1+x)$, so $f'(x) = \dfrac{2}{1+x}$.

6. $f'(x) = \dfrac{2\sin x \cos x}{\sin^2 x} = 2\cot x$

7. $f'(x) = -\dfrac{1}{x}\sin(\ln x)$

8. $f'(x) = 3(\ln x)^2 D_x(\ln x) = \dfrac{3(\ln x)^2}{x}$

10. $f'(x) = \dfrac{1}{\ln x} D_x(\ln x) = \dfrac{1}{x \ln x}$

12. $g'(t) = \tfrac{3}{2} t^{1/2} \ln(t+1) + \dfrac{t^{3/2}}{t+1}$

14. $f'(x) = \dfrac{2\cos x}{2\sin x} = \cot x$

16. $f'(x) = [\cos(\ln 2x)] D_x(\ln 2x) = \dfrac{1}{x}\cos(\ln 2x)$

18. $g'(t) = \tfrac{1}{2} t^{-1/2} [\cos(\ln t)]^2 - 2\sqrt{t}\,[\cos(\ln t)]\dfrac{\sin(\ln t)}{t}$

19. $f(x) = 3\ln(2x+1) + 4\ln(x^2-4)$, so $f'(x) = \dfrac{6}{2x+1} + \dfrac{8x}{x^2-4}$.

20. Given: $f(x) = \ln[(1-x)/(1+x)]^{1/2} = \tfrac{1}{2}\ln\dfrac{1-x}{1+x} = \tfrac{1}{2}[\ln(1-x) - \ln(1+x)]$:

   $f'(x) = \tfrac{1}{2}\left(-\dfrac{1}{1-x} - \dfrac{1}{1+x}\right) = \dfrac{1}{x^2-1}$.

21. Rewrite the given function as $f(x) = \tfrac{1}{2}\left(\ln(4-x^2) - \ln(9+x^2)\right)$.
   Then $f'(x) = \tfrac{1}{2}\left[\dfrac{-2x}{4-x^2} - \dfrac{2x}{9+x^2}\right] = -\dfrac{13x}{(4-x^2)(9+x^2)}$.

22. $f(x) = \tfrac{1}{2}\ln(4x-7) - 3\ln(3x-2)$, so $f'(x) = \dfrac{2}{4x-7} - \dfrac{9}{3x-2} = \dfrac{59-30x}{(4x-7)(3x-2)}$.

24. $f(x) = -x^2 \ln(2x+1)$, so $f'(x) = -\dfrac{2x^2}{2x+1} - 2x\ln(2x+1)$.

25. *Suggestion:* Write $g(t) = 2\ln t - \ln(t^2+1)$.

26. $f(x) = \tfrac{1}{2}\ln(x+1) - 3\ln(x-1)$, so $f'(x) = \dfrac{1}{2(x+1)} - \dfrac{3}{x-1}$.

28. $f(x) = \ln(\sin x) - \ln(\cos x)$, so $f'(x) = \dfrac{\cos x}{\sin x} + \dfrac{\sin x}{\cos x} = \cot x + \tan x$.

30. $\dfrac{dy}{dx} = \dfrac{1}{x}\ln y + \dfrac{\ln x}{y}\cdot\dfrac{dy}{dx}$, so $\dfrac{dy}{dx} = \dfrac{y \ln y}{x(y - \ln x)}$.

32. $x\dfrac{dy}{dx} + y + 2x(\ln y)^2 + \dfrac{2x^2 \ln y}{y} \cdot \dfrac{dy}{dx} = 0$, so $\dfrac{dy}{dx} = -\dfrac{y^2 + 2xy(\ln y)^2}{xy + 2x^2 \ln y}$.

34. $\displaystyle\int \dfrac{dx}{3x+5} = \tfrac{1}{3} \ln |3x+5| + C$.

36. $\displaystyle\int \dfrac{x^2}{4-x^3}\, dx = -\tfrac{1}{3} \int \dfrac{-3x^2}{4-x^3}\, dx = -\tfrac{1}{3} \ln |4 - x^3| + C$.

38. $\displaystyle\int \dfrac{\cos x}{1+\sin x}\, dx = \ln(1 + \sin x) + C$.

40. $\displaystyle\int \dfrac{1}{x \ln x}\, dx = \ln |\ln x| + C$.

42. $\displaystyle\int \dfrac{x}{1-x^2}\, dx = -\tfrac{1}{2} \ln |1 - x^2| + C$.

44. $\displaystyle\int \dfrac{2x+1}{x^2+x+3}\, dx = \tfrac{1}{2} \ln(x^2 + 2x + 3) + C$.

46. $\displaystyle\int \dfrac{\ln(x^3)}{x}\, dx = 3 \int \dfrac{\ln x}{x}\, dx = \tfrac{3}{2} (\ln x)^2 + C$.

48. $\displaystyle\int \dfrac{dx}{x(\ln x)^2} = -(\ln x)^{-1} + C$.

49. The numerator is $\tfrac{1}{3}$ the derivative of the denominator.

50. If $u = 1 + \sqrt{x}$, then $dy = \tfrac{1}{2} x^{-1/2}\, dx$, so $\dfrac{dx}{\sqrt{x}} = 2\, du$. Therefore the integral becomes:
$$\int \dfrac{dx}{\sqrt{x}(1+\sqrt{x})} = \int \dfrac{2}{u}\, du = 2 \ln u + C = 2 \ln(1+\sqrt{x}) + C.$$

51. $\displaystyle\lim_{x \to \infty} \dfrac{\ln \sqrt{x}}{x} = \lim_{x \to \infty} \dfrac{1}{2x} \ln x = 0$.

52. $\displaystyle\lim_{x \to \infty} \dfrac{\ln x^3}{x^2} = \lim_{x \to \infty} \dfrac{3 \ln x}{x^2} = 0$.

54. $\displaystyle\lim_{x \to 0^+} x \ln x = \lim_{u \to \infty} \dfrac{1}{u} \ln\left(\dfrac{1}{u}\right) = \lim_{u \to \infty} -\dfrac{1}{u} \ln u = 0$.

55. *Suggestion:* Make the substitution $x = \dfrac{1}{u^2}$.

56. Simply use the result of Problem 53.

58. $f^{(1)}(x) = x^{-1}$, $f^{(2)}(x) = (-1)x^{-2}$, $f^{(3)}(x) = (-2)(-1)x^{-3}$, $f^{(4)}(x) = (-3)(-2)(-1)x^{-4}$, ..., and, in general, $f^{(n)}(x) = (-1)^{n-1}(n-1)!\, x^{-n}$ for $n \geq 1$. Proof: By induction on n.

59. $\ln R = \ln k + m \ln W$. So

$$\ln(R_1) - \ln(R_2) = m\left(\ln(W_1) - \ln(W_2)\right),$$

and thus

$$\dfrac{1}{m} = \dfrac{\ln(W_1) - \ln(W_2)}{\ln(R_2) - \ln(R_2)}.$$

Using consecutive values of W and R in this formula, we obtain the table shown next. It follows that $m \approx -0.2479$, $k \approx 291.7616$, and we use the formula

$$R = \dfrac{291.7616}{W^{0.2479}}.$$

Section 7.2 The Natural Logarithm

$\ln W$	$\ln R$	$\dfrac{1}{m}$
3.2189	4.8752	
4.2047	4.6347	-4.0996
4.8442	4.4773	-4.0631
5.1648	4.3944	-3.8679
5.4806	4.3175	-4.1041
6.8824	3.9703	-4.0375
	Average:	-4.034

If you compare the data predicted by the formula with the actual data given in the problem, you'll find that the percent error varies between 0.28 and 0.23; very good results.

60. If $P = kV^m$ then $\ln P = \ln k + m \ln V$. From the data given in Fig.7.12, we obtain the results shown below:

$x = \ln V$	$y = \ln P$
0.3784	3.3429
0.9163	2.5878
1.2556	2.1163
1.7457	1.4351
1.9824	1.0986

If $y = mx + b$, then numerical results suggest that $m \approx -1.4$, and it follows that $k \approx 48$. The relation we find is therefore

$$P = 48V^{-1.4},$$

and the table below gives a comparison between the true values of P with those predicted by this formula.

V	P (true)	P (predicted)
1.46	28.3	28.26
2.50	13.3	13.31
3.51	8.3	8.28
5.73	4.2	4.17
7.26	3.0	2.99

62. 1.763

64. Two solutions, 1.615 and 5.329.

66. Three solutions, 1.428, 5.459, and 6.965.

68. Viewing window: $3.439062 \times 10^{15} \leqq x \leqq 3.43064 \times 10^{15}$, $-6.0 \times 10^{-6} \leqq y \leqq 8.0 \times 10^{-6}$. Solution: 3.43×10^{15}.

70. The curves cross near $x = 2.1956108$ and $x = 9.7747251$. The area between them is approximately 86.1489.

72. If $k > 1$, then $0 < \dfrac{1}{k} < 1$, so

$$\lim_{x \to \infty} \frac{\ln x}{x^{1/k}} = 0 \quad \text{and therefore} \quad \lim_{x \to \infty} \frac{(\ln x)^k}{x} = 0.$$

If $0 < k \leq 1$, then

$$0 \leq \lim_{x \to \infty} \frac{(\ln x)^k}{x} \leq \lim_{x \to \infty} \frac{(\ln x)^2}{x} = 0, \quad \text{so} \quad \lim_{x \to \infty} \frac{(\ln x)^k}{x} = 0 \quad \text{for all } k > 0.$$

73. Let $y = 1/x$; $x = 1/y$. Then $\lim_{x \to 0^+} x^k \ln x = \lim_{y \to \infty} \frac{\ln(1/y)}{y^k} = -\lim_{y \to \infty} \frac{\ln y}{y^k} = 0$.

74. Given: $y = f(x) = x \ln x$ for $x > 0$. Then $f'(x) = 1 + \ln x$ and $f''(x) = 1/x$. The critical point occurs where $\ln x = -1$, so $x = 1/e$ and $y = (1/e) \ln(1/e) = -1/e$. There are no possible points of inflection. The graph is decreasing on $(0, 1/e)$ and is increasing if $x > 1/e$. It is concave upward everywhere, and its only intercept is $(1, 0)$. As $x \to 0^+$, $y \to 0$; moreover, $dy/dx \to -\infty$. This helps sketch the graph near the point $(0, 0)$.

75. $\frac{dy}{dx} = x(1 + 2\ln x)$ and $\frac{d^2y}{dx^2} = 3 + 2\ln x$. Both y and $\frac{dy}{dx}$ approach zero as $x \to 0^+$.

76. $\frac{dy}{dx} = \frac{2 + \ln x}{2x^{1/2}}$ and $\frac{d^2y}{dx^2} = -\frac{\ln x}{4x^{3/2}}$. Now $\frac{dy}{dx} = 0$ when $x = 1/(e^2)$ (there, $y = -2/e$). As $x \to 0^+$, $y \to 0$ while $\frac{dy}{dx} \to -\infty$. The graph is increasing for $x > 1/(e^2)$ and decreasing for $0 < x < 1/(e^2)$. It is concave upward on $(0, 1)$, concave downward if $x > 1$. The point $(1, 0)$ is an inflection point and the only intercept. The point where there is a horizontal tangent is in fact a global minimum. Note that the point $(0, 0)$ is not on the graph. It is also helpful to note that $dy/dx = 1$ when $x = 1$.

77. After simplifications, you will find that $\frac{dy}{dx} = \frac{2 - \ln x}{2x^{3/2}}$ and $\frac{d^2y}{dx^2} = \frac{3\ln x - 8}{4x^{5/2}}$.

78. The equation $\ln x = 1$ has a unique solution (because $\ln x$ is an increasing function) and that solution lies in the interval $2.7 \leq x \leq 2.8$ by the result of Problem 26 of Section 5.9 and the intermediate value property of the continuous function $\ln x$. Therefore $2.7 < e < 2.8$.

79. $W = \int_{V_1}^{V_2} p(V)\, dV = \int_{V_1}^{V_2} \frac{nRT}{V}\, dV = nRT(\ln(V_2) - \ln(V_1)) = nRT \ln\left(\frac{V_1}{V_2}\right)$.

80. $\frac{dy}{dx} = -\frac{1}{x^2}$; $\left(1 + \left(\frac{dy}{dx}\right)^2\right)^{1/2} = (1 + x^{-4})^{1/2} = \frac{(x^4 + 1)^{1/2}}{x^2}$. The surface area of the part of the horn over the interval from $x = 1$ to $x = b$ (for $b > 1$) is then

$$A_b = \int_1^b \frac{2\pi}{x^3}(x^4 + 1)^{1/2}\, dx \geq \int_1^b \frac{2\pi}{x^3} x^2\, dx = 2\pi \ln b.$$

Therefore the surface area of Gabriel's horn is infinite because $A_b \to +\infty$ as $b \to +\infty$. Next,

$$V_b = \int_1^b \frac{\pi}{x^2}\, dx = \pi\left(1 - \frac{1}{b}\right) \to \pi \text{ as } b \to +\infty.$$

In summary, the volume is finite although the surface area is infinite.

81. We estimate the integral $\int_{90,000}^{100,000} \frac{1}{\ln x}\, dx$ first with the midpoint rule: $\frac{10,000}{\ln(95,000)} \approx 872.47$; then with the trapezoidal rule: $(5000)\left(\frac{1}{\ln(90,000)} + \frac{1}{\ln(100,000)}\right) \approx 872.60$. The first is an underestimate and the second is an overestimate because the graph of $y = 1/(\ln x)$ is concave upward for $x > 0$. The true value of the integral, incidentally, is approximately 872.5174045.

Section 7.3

1. $f'(x) = e^{2x} D_x(2x) = 2e^{2x}$
2. $f'(x) = 3e^{3x-1}$
4. $f'(x) = -3x^2 e^{4-x^3}$
6. $f'(x) = 2xe^{x^3} + 3x^4 e^{x^3}$
8. $g'(t) = 7(e^{2t} + e^{3t})^6 (2e^{2t} + 3e^{3t})$
10. $g'(t) = \frac{1}{2}(e^t - e^{-t})^{-1/2}(e^t + e^{-t})$
12. $f'(x) = e^{\sin x} + x(\cos x)e^{\sin x}$
14. $f'(x) = -2e^{-x}\sin(e^{-x})\cos(e^{-x})$

16. $f'(x) = e^x \cos 2x - 2e^x \sin 2x$

18. $g'(t) = \dfrac{1}{t} + 2t$

20. $g'(t) = e^t \cos(e^t) \cos(e^{-t}) + e^{-t} \sin(e^t) \sin(e^{-t})$

22. $g'(t) = \dfrac{2e^t}{(1-e^t)^2}$

24. $f'(x) = \dfrac{e^{-1/x}}{x^2}$

26. $f'(x) = \tfrac{1}{2}x^{-1/2}\left(e^{\sqrt{x}} - e^{-\sqrt{x}}\right)$

28. $f'(x) = \left(e^{2x} + e^{-2x}\right)^{-1/2}\left(e^{2x} - e^{-2x}\right)$

30. $f'(x) = -(e^x - e^{-x})\sin(e^x + e^{-x})$

32. $\dfrac{dy}{dx} = \dfrac{1 - ye^{xy}\cos(e^{xy})}{xe^{xy}\cos(e^{xy})}$

34. $\dfrac{dy}{dx} = \dfrac{1}{(1+y)e^y} = \dfrac{y}{x(1+y)}$

36. $\displaystyle\int e^{3x}\,dx = \tfrac{1}{3}e^{3x} + C$

38. $\displaystyle\int xe^{x^2}\,dx = \tfrac{1}{2}e^{x^2} + C$

40. $\displaystyle\int \sqrt{x}\,e^{2x\sqrt{x}} = \tfrac{1}{3}e^{2x\sqrt{x}} + C$

42. $\displaystyle\int (\cos x)e^{\sin x}\,dx = e^{\sin x} + C$

44. $\displaystyle\int (e^x + e^{-x})^2\,dx = \int (e^{2x} + 2 + e^{-2x})\,dx = \tfrac{1}{2}e^{2x} + 2x - \tfrac{1}{2}e^{-2x} + C$

46. $\displaystyle\int e^{2x+3}\,dx = \tfrac{1}{2}e^{2x+3} + C$

48. $\displaystyle\int x^2 e^{1-x^3}\,dx = -\tfrac{1}{3}e^{1-x^3} + C$

49. Suggestion: Let $u = \sqrt{x}$.

50. $\displaystyle\int \dfrac{e^{1/t}}{t^2}\,dt = -e^{1/t} + C$

51. Suggestion: Let $u = 1 + e^x$.

52. Because $e^{a+b} = e^a e^b$, we have $\displaystyle\int e^{x+e^x}\,dx = \int e^x e^{e^x}\,dx = e^{e^x} + C$. Note that e^{e^x} means $e^{(e^x)}$.

54. $\displaystyle\lim_{n\to\infty}\left(1 - \dfrac{1}{n}\right)^n = \dfrac{1}{e}$

56. $\displaystyle\lim_{n\to\infty}\left(1 + \dfrac{2}{3n}\right)^n = e^{2/3}$

58. $\displaystyle\lim_{h\to 0}(1 + 2h)^{1/h} = e^2$

60. $\displaystyle\lim_{x\to\infty}\dfrac{e^x}{\sqrt{x}} = +\infty$

62. $\displaystyle\lim_{x\to\infty} x^2 e^{-x} = 0$

63. $dy/dx = x(2-x)e^{-x}$ and $d^2y/dx^2 = (x^2 - 4x + 2)e^{-x}$. So the graph is increasing on $(0,2)$, decreasing if $x < 0$ or if $x > 2$. It is concave downward if $|x - 2| < \sqrt{2}$ and concave upward if $|x-2| > \sqrt{2}$.

64. First, $dy/dx = 3x^2 e^{-x} - x^3 e^{-x} = x^2(3-x)e^{-x}$ and $d^2y/dx^2 = x(x^2 - 6x + 6)e^{-x}$. Note that $y = 0$ when $x = 0$ and that this is the only intercept. Next, $dy/dx = 0$ when $x = 0$ and when $x = 3$, so there are horizontal tangents at $(0,0)$ and at $\left(3, \dfrac{27}{e^3}\right)$—near the point $(3, 1.344)$. The second derivative vanishes when $x = 0$ and when $x^2 - 6x + 6 = 0$; the latter equation has the two solutions $x = 3 \pm \sqrt{3}$. Consequently there may be inflection points at $(0,0)$, near $(1.268, 0.574)$, and near $(4.732, 0.933)$. The graph is

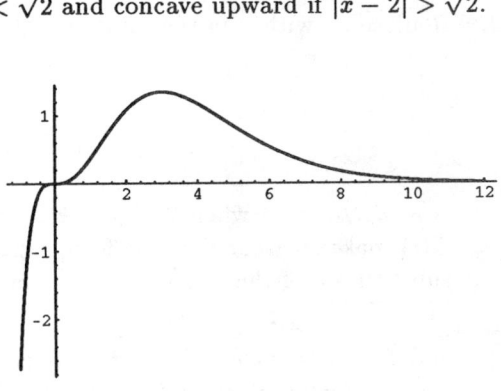

increasing if $x < 3$ and decreasing if $x > 3$. It is concave downward if $x < 0$ and if $|x-3| < \sqrt{3}$, concave upward if both $|x-3| > \sqrt{3}$ and $x > 0$. Because $x^3 e^{-x} \to 0$ as $x \to +\infty$, the x-axis is a horizontal asymptote. The graph is shown above.

65. $dy/dx = -2xe^{-x^2}$ and $d^2y/dx^2 = 2\left(2x^2 - 2\right)e^{-x^2}$.

66. $A = \int_0^1 e^x \, dx = e - 1$.

67. $V = \int_0^1 \pi e^{2x} \, dx = \dfrac{\pi}{2}\left(e^2 - 1\right) \approx 10.0359$.

68. $V = \int_0^1 2\pi x e^{-x^2} \, dx = \dfrac{\pi}{e}(e - 1) \approx 1.986$.

69. $dy/dx = \tfrac{1}{2}(e^x - e^{-x})$. So $\left(1 + (dy/dx)^2\right)^{1/2} = \tfrac{1}{2}(e^x + e^{-x})$. Therefore

$$L = \int_0^1 \tfrac{1}{2}(e^x + e^{-x}) \, dx = \dfrac{e^2 - 1}{2e} \approx 1.1752.$$

70. $A = \displaystyle\int_0^1 (2\pi)\left[\tfrac{1}{2}(e^x + e^{-x})\right]\left[\tfrac{1}{2}(e^x + e^{-x})\right] dx = \dfrac{\pi}{2}\int_0^1 \left(e^{2x} + 2 + e^{-2x}\right) dx$
$= \dfrac{\pi}{4}\left(e^2 + 4 - e^{-2}\right) \approx 8.83865$.

72. $1.309799585804 \approx 1.310$.

74. Three solutions: 0.512, 2.057, and 4.384.

76. Three solutions: 0.291, 0.989, and 1.493.

78. The viewing window is shown in the next figure. The "second solution" of the equation $e^x = x^{10}$ is (approximately) 35.7715. Because of the magnitude of the values of x^{10} and e^x (about 3.43×10^{15}) near that solution, it may be more practical to solve instead the equivalent $x = 10 \ln x$.

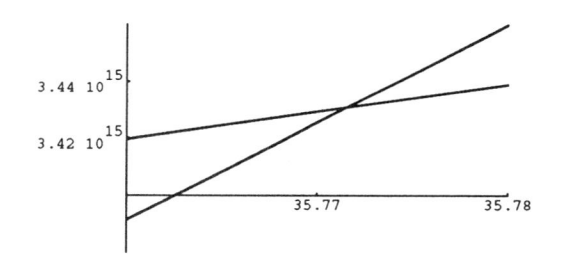

80. Replace x_0 with x in the solution. Then

$$\dfrac{dC}{dt} = \dfrac{A}{(k\pi t)^{1/2}}\left(e^{-\frac{x^2}{4kt}}\right)\left(\dfrac{x^2}{4kt^2} - \dfrac{1}{2t}\right).$$

Now $dC/dt = 0$ when $2tx^2 = 4kt^2$, so $t = 0$ or $t = x^2/(2k)$. The general shape of the graph of $C(t)$ makes it clear that the former yields the minimum and the latter yields the maximum. Then substitution of the latter in the formula for $C(t)$ gives the maximum value of $C(t)$.

81. $f'(x) = (n-x)x^{n-1}e^{-x}$ and $f''(x) = \left((x-n)^2 - n\right)x^{n-2}e^{-x}$. Because $f(x) \geq 0$ for $x \geq 0$, $f(0) = 0$, and $f(x) \to 0$ as $x \to +\infty$, $f(x)$ must have a maximum, and the critical point where $x = n$ is the sole candidate. Evaluate $f(n)$ to obtain the global maximum value of $f(x)$.

Section 7.3 The Exponential Function

82. $e - 1 = \int_0^1 e^x \, dx \approx \frac{1}{6}\left(e^0 + 4\sqrt{e} + e\right);$

$$6e - 6 \approx 1 + 4\sqrt{e} + e;$$
$$5e - 7 \approx 4\sqrt{e};$$
$$25e^2 - 70e + 49 \approx 16e;$$
$$25e^2 - 86e + 49 \approx 0;$$
$$e \approx \tfrac{1}{50}\left(86 + \sqrt{2496}\right);$$

therefore $e \approx 2.7192$.

83. $f(n-1) = (n-1)^n e^{-(n-1)} < n^n e^{-n}$, so $\left(\dfrac{n-1}{n}\right)^n < \dfrac{e^{n-1}}{e^n} = \dfrac{1}{e}$. Therefore

$$e < \left(\frac{n}{n-1}\right)^n = \left(\frac{n-1}{n}\right)^{-n} = \left(1 - \frac{1}{n}\right)^{-n}.$$

Also $f(n+1) = (n+1)^n e^{-(n+1)} < \dfrac{n^n}{e^n}$. Therefore, by similar computations,

$$\left(1 + \frac{1}{n}\right)^n < e.$$

With $n = 1024$, we obtain $2.716957 < e < 2.719611$. Hence we may conclude that $2.716 < e < 2.720$.

84. To avoid subscripts, write p for m_1, q for m_2, A for C_1, and B for C_2. Then with

$$y(x) = Ae^{px} + Be^{qx}, \text{ we obtain}$$
$$y'(x) = Ape^{px} + Bqe^{qx} \text{ and}$$
$$y''(x) = Ap^2 e^{px} + Bq^2 e^{qx}.$$

So

$$ay''(x) + by'(x) + cy(x) = \left(aAp^2 + bAp + cA\right)e^{px} + \left(aBq^2 + bBq + cB\right)e^{qx}$$
$$= A\left(ap^2 + bp + c\right)e^{px} + B\left(aq^2 + bq + c\right)e^{qx}$$
$$= (A)(0)e^{px} + (B)(0)e^{qx} = 0.$$

85. Given $y''(x) + y'(x) - 2y(x) = 0$, we write the associated equation $m^2 + m - 2 = 0$, which has solutions $m_1 = -2$ and $m_2 = 1$. Therefore the function $y(x) = Ae^{-2x} + Be^x$ satisfies the given differential equation for any choice of the constants A and B. The additional information given in the problem is this:

$$5 = y(0) = A + B,$$
$$2 = y'(0) = -2A + B.$$

It follows that $A = 1$ and $B = 4$, and therefore a solution of the given differential equation satisfying the two additional side conditions is $y(x) = e^{-2x} + 4e^x$.

Section 7.4

1. $f'(x) = 10^x \ln 10$

2. $f'(x) = 2^{(1/x^2)}(\ln 2)D_x(1/x^2) = -\dfrac{2}{x^3}2^{(1/x^2)}(\ln 2)$

4. $f(x) = (\log_{10} e)(\ln \cos x) = \dfrac{1}{\ln 10}\ln(\cos x)$, so $f'(x) = \left(\dfrac{1}{\ln 10}\right)\left(\dfrac{-\sin x}{\cos x}\right)$.

6. $f'(x) = (2^x \ln 2)\, 3^{(x^2)} + 2^x 3^{(x^2)}(\ln 3)(2x)$.

8. $f(x) = \log_{100}(10^x) = \log_{100}(100^{1/2})^x = \log_{100}(100^{x/2}) = \tfrac{1}{2}x$, so $f'(x) = \tfrac{1}{2}$.

10. $f'(x) = 7^{(8^x)}(\ln 7)(8^x \ln 8)$

12. $f'(x) = \left(2^{\sqrt{x}}\right)(\ln 2)\left(\tfrac{1}{2}x^{-1/2}\right)$

14. $f'(x) = \left(3^{(1-x^2)^{1/2}}\right)(-x\ln 3)(1-x^2)^{-1/2}$

16. $f(x) = (\log_2 e)(\log_e x) = \dfrac{\ln x}{\ln 2}$, so $f'(x) = \dfrac{1}{x \ln 2}$.

18. $\log_{10}(e^x) = x\log_{10} e$, so $f'(x) = \log_{10} e = \dfrac{1}{\ln 10}$.

20. $f(x) = \log_{10}(\log_{10} x) = (\log_{10} e)(\ln(\log_{10} e)(\ln x))$
$= (\log_{10} e)(\ln(\log_{10} e) + \ln(\ln x)) = \dfrac{1}{\ln 10}(-\ln(\ln 10) + \ln(\ln x))$, so $f'(x) = \dfrac{1}{x(\ln 10)(\ln x)}$.

22. $f'(x) = \pi^x \ln \pi + \pi x^{\pi - 1}$

24. $f'(x) = \pi^{(x^3)}(\ln \pi)(3x^2)$

26. Let $u = -x^2$. Then $du = -2x\, dx$, so $x\, dx = -\tfrac{1}{2}du$. Thus

$$\int x\left(10^{-x^2}\right)dx = -\tfrac{1}{2}\int 10^u\, du = -\dfrac{10^u}{2\ln 10} + C = -\dfrac{10^{-x^2}}{2\ln 10} + C.$$

27. Suggestion: Use the substitution $u = \sqrt{x}$.

28. The substitution $u = 1/x$ yields

$$\int \dfrac{10^{1/x}}{x^2}\, dx = \int -10^u\, du = -\dfrac{10^u}{\ln 10} + C = -\dfrac{10^{1/x}}{\ln 10} + C.$$

29. Suggestion: Use the substitution $u = x^3 + 1$.

30. First write $\log_{10} x$ as $(\log_{10} e)(\ln x)$. The integral becomes

$$(\ln 10)\int \dfrac{1}{x \ln x}\, dx = (\ln 10)(\ln|\ln x|) + C.$$

31. Write $\log_2 x$ as $(\ln x)/(\ln 2)$. Then, if you wish, use the substitution $u = \ln x$.

32. Let $v = 2^x$. Then $dv = (2^x \ln 2)\, dx$, so $2^x\, dx = \dfrac{dv}{\ln 2}$. Then

$$\int (2^x)\, 3^{(2^x)}\, dx = \dfrac{1}{\ln 2}\int 3^v\, dv = \dfrac{3^v}{(\ln 2)(\ln 3)} + C = \dfrac{3^{(2^x)}}{(\ln 2)(\ln 3)} + C.$$

33. $\ln y = \tfrac{1}{2}\ln(x^2 - 4) + \tfrac{1}{4}\ln(2x+1)$, so

$$\dfrac{dy}{dx} = y\left(\dfrac{x}{x^2 - 4} + \dfrac{1}{2(2x+1)}\right) = \left(\dfrac{x}{x^2 - 4} + \dfrac{1}{2(2x+1)}\right)\left((x^2 - 4)\sqrt{2x+1}\right)^{1/2}$$

34. $\ln y = \frac{1}{3}\ln(3-x^2) - \frac{1}{4}\ln(x^4+1)$, so

$$\frac{1}{y}\cdot\frac{dy}{dx} = \frac{-2x}{3(3-x^2)} - \frac{x^3}{x^4+1};$$

$$\frac{dy}{dx} = -\frac{(3-x^2)^{1/2}}{(x^4+1)^{1/4}}\left(\frac{x}{(3-x^2)} + \frac{x^3}{x^4+1}\right).$$

35. $\ln y = x\ln 2$. Therefore $dy/dx = y\ln 2 = 2^x \ln 2$.

36. $\ln y = x\ln x$.

$$\frac{1}{y}\cdot\frac{dy}{dx} = 1 + \ln x.$$

$$\frac{dy}{dx} = x^x(1+\ln x).$$

37. $\ln y = (\ln x)^2$. So $\dfrac{dy}{dx} = (y)\dfrac{2\ln x}{x} = (x^{\ln x})\dfrac{2\ln x}{x}$.

38. $y = (x+1)^{1/x}$. So $\ln y = \dfrac{1}{x}\ln(1+x)$.

$$\frac{1}{y}\cdot\frac{dy}{dx} = -\frac{1}{x^2}\ln(1+x) + \frac{1}{x(1+x)}.$$

$$\frac{dy}{dx} = \frac{x - (1+x)\ln(1+x)}{x^2(1+x)}(1+x)^{1/x}.$$

39. $\ln y = \frac{1}{3}\ln(1+x) + \frac{1}{3}\ln(x+2) - \frac{1}{3}\ln(x^2+1) - \frac{1}{3}\ln(x^2+2)$.

$$\frac{dy}{dx} = \frac{1}{3}(y)\left(\frac{1}{x+1} + \frac{1}{x+2} - \frac{2x}{x^2+1} - \frac{2x}{x^2+2}\right) = -\frac{2x^5+9x^4+8x^3+9x^2+8x-6}{3(x+1)^{2/3}(x+2)^{2/3}(x^2+1)^{4/3}(x^2+2)^{4/3}}.$$

40. $\dfrac{dy}{dx} = (y)\left(\dfrac{1}{2(x+1)} + \dfrac{1}{3(x+2)} + \dfrac{1}{4(x+3)}\right)$

$\qquad = \sqrt{x+1}\sqrt[3]{x+2}\sqrt[4]{x+3}\left(\dfrac{1}{2(x+1)} + \dfrac{1}{3(x+2)} + \dfrac{1}{4(x+3)}\right)$.

41. $\ln y = \sqrt{x}\ln(\ln x)$, so $\dfrac{dy}{dx} = (y)\left(\frac{1}{2}x^{-1/2}\ln(\ln x) + \dfrac{x^{1/2}}{x\ln x}\right) = (\ln x)^{\sqrt{x}}\left(\frac{1}{2}x^{-1/2}\ln(\ln x) + \dfrac{x^{1/2}}{x\ln x}\right)$.

42. $\ln y = x\ln(3+2^x)$:

$$\frac{1}{y}\cdot\frac{dy}{dx} = \ln(3+2^x) + \frac{(x)(2^x \ln 2)}{3+2^x};$$

$$\frac{dy}{dx} = (3+2^x)^x\left(\ln(3+2^x) + \frac{2^x(x\ln 2)}{3+2^x}\right).$$

44. $\ln y = x\ln(x+1)$, so

$$\frac{1}{y}\cdot\frac{dy}{dx} = \frac{x}{x+1} + \ln(x+1).$$

$$\frac{dy}{dx} = (x+1)^x\left(\frac{x}{x+1} + \ln(x+1)\right).$$

46. $\ln y = x \ln\left(1 + \dfrac{1}{x}\right) = x\ln(x+1) - x\ln x$.

$$\frac{dy}{dx} = \left(1 + \frac{1}{x}\right)^x \left(\ln(x+1) + \frac{x}{x+1} - \ln x - 1\right).$$

48. $\ln y = (\sin x)(\ln x)$. Therefore $\dfrac{dy}{dx} = x^{\sin x}\left((\cos x)(\ln x) + \dfrac{1}{x}\sin x\right)$.

50. $\dfrac{dy}{dx} = \dfrac{1 + \ln(\ln x)}{x}(\ln x)^{\ln x}$.

51. $f'(x) = (1 - x\ln 2)\cdot 2^{-x}$, so $f'(x) = 0$ when $x = 1/(\ln 2)$. Because $f'(x) > 0$ to the left of this point and $f'(x) < 0$ to the right, we have found the highest point on the curve; it is $\left(\dfrac{1}{\ln 2}, \dfrac{1}{2^{1/(\ln 2)}\ln 2}\right)$.

52. The curves cross at $x = 0$ and at $x = a \approx 1.578620636$, and the area between them is
$$\int_0^a \left(2^{-x} - (x-1)^2\right)\, dx \approx 0.561770.$$

53. The volume is $\displaystyle\int_0^a \pi\left(2^{-2x} - (x-1)^4\right)\, dx \approx 1.343088216$ where a is the number found in the previous solution.

54. The curves cross where $x \approx 0.623229172$ and where $x \approx 1.721720799$. The area between them is approximately 1.645168.

55. $f'(x) = \dfrac{\cos x - (x\ln x)\sin x}{x}\cdot x^{\cos x}$.

56. Graphical approximation of the coordinates of the local minimum yields the approximate result $(1.44467, 0.692201)$. According to Problem 50, the derivative should be zero when $\ln(\ln x) = -1$, and thus when $x = e^{1/e}$. Sure enough, $e^{1/e} \approx 1.444667861$.

57. By definition of z, x, and y, respectively, we have
$$a^z = c, \quad a^x = b, \quad \text{and} \quad b^y = c.$$
Therefore $a^{xy} = b^y = c = a^z$. Because $a > 0$ and $a \neq 1$, it now follows that $z = xy$.

58. If $y = u^v$ where all are functions of x, then $\ln y = v\ln u$. With $u'(x)$ denoted simply by u', etc., we now have
$$\frac{1}{y}y' = v'\ln u + \frac{vu'}{u}.$$
Thus $y' = u^v v'\ln u + \dfrac{u^v vu'}{u} = vu^{v-1}u' + u^v(\ln u)v'$.

(i) If u is constant, this implies that $\dfrac{dy}{dx} = u^{v(x)}(\ln u)v'(x)$.

(ii) If v is constant, this implies that $\dfrac{dy}{dx} = v(u(x))^{v-1}u'(x)$.

59. If $y = \ln\left(a^{1/x}\right)$ then $y = \dfrac{1}{x}\ln a$.

$$\lim_{x\to\infty} y = \lim_{x\to\infty}\frac{1}{x}(\ln a) = 0.$$
$$\lim_{x\to\infty}\ln\left(a^{1/x}\right) = 0,$$
$$\lim_{x\to\infty} a^{1/x} = e^0 = 1.$$

60. $\ln\left(n^{1/n}\right) = \dfrac{1}{n}\ln n$, and $\dfrac{1}{n}\ln n \to 0$ as $n \to +\infty$. So

$$\lim_{n\to\infty} e^{\left(\frac{1}{n}\ln n\right)} = e^0 = 1$$

because the exponential function is continuous. Therefore

$$\lim_{n\to\infty} n^{1/n} = 1.$$

61. $\ln\left(\dfrac{x^x}{e^x}\right) = x\ln\left(\dfrac{x}{e}\right)$. The latter clearly approaches $+\infty$ as x does, and this is enough to establish the desired result.

62. $\displaystyle\lim_{x\to 0^+} \dfrac{1}{1+2^{1/x}} = \lim_{k\to\infty} \dfrac{1}{1+2^k} = 0.$ $\displaystyle\lim_{x\to 0^-} \dfrac{1}{1+2^{1/x}} = \lim_{k\to -\infty} \dfrac{1}{1+2^k} = 1.$

63. Beginning with the equation $x^y = 2$, we first write $y\ln x = \ln 2$, then differentiate implicitly with respect to x to obtain

$$\frac{y}{x} + \frac{dy}{dx}\ln x = 0.$$

Thus

$$\frac{dy}{dx} = -\frac{y}{x\ln x} = -\frac{\ln 2}{x(\ln x)^2}.$$

Section 7.5

1. The principal at time t is $P(t) = 1000e^{(0.08)t}$. So $P'(t) = 80e^{(0.08)t}$.
    Answers: $P'(5) = \$119.35$ and $P'(20) = \$396.24$.

2. Take $t = 0$ (years) as 1960. Then the population $P(t)$ satisfies the equation

$$P(t) = P_0 e^{kt}$$

where $P_0 = P(0) = 25000$. Now $30000 = P(10) = 25000e^{10k}$, so $10k = \ln(30/25)$. Therefore $k = (0.1)\ln(1.2)$. In the year 2000, the population—under the given assumptions—will be

$$P(40) = (25000)e^{4\ln(1.2)} = (25000)(1.2)^4 = 51840 \text{ individuals.}$$

3. If $P(t)$ is the number of bacteria present at time t (in hours), then

$$P(10) = 6P_0 = P_0 e^{10k}.$$

Therefore $k = (0.1)\ln 6$. If T is the doubling time, then

$$P(T) = 2P_0 = P_0 e^{(0.1)T\ln 6},$$

which we can solve for $T = \dfrac{10\ln 2}{\ln 6} \approx 3.8685$, approximately 3 hours and 52 minutes.

4. Suppose that the skull was formed at time $t = 0$ (in years). Then the amount of ^{14}C it contains at time t will be

$$Q(t) = Q_0 e^{-kt}$$

where Q_0 is the initial amount and $k = \dfrac{\ln 2}{5700} \approx 0.0001216$. We find the value $t = T$ corresponding to "now" by solving

$$Q(T) = \tfrac{1}{6}Q_0: \quad \tfrac{1}{6}Q_0 = Q_0 e^{-kT}, \text{ so } 6 = e^{kT};$$

therefore $T = \dfrac{1}{k}\ln 6 = 5700\,\dfrac{\ln 6}{\ln 2} \approx 14734$, the approximate age of the skull in years.

5. From the equation $Q = Q_0 e^{-kt}$, using t for the age of the relic and $k \approx 0.0001216$ (from Problem 4), we obtain
$$4.6 \times 10^{10} = (5.0 \times 10^{10})\,e^{-kt},$$
and it follows that $t \approx \dfrac{0.0833816}{k} \approx 685.7$ (years). We conclude that the relic is probably not authentic.

6. (a) The principal is multiplied by the factor $1 + \dfrac{rt}{n}$ exactly n times.

   (b) $\displaystyle\lim_{n\to\infty}\left(1 + \dfrac{x}{n}\right)^n = e^x$; this also holds when $x = rt$.

7. $1 + r = \left(1 + \dfrac{0.09}{4}\right)^4$ for quarterly compounding, and in this case we find that (a) $r \approx 9.308\%$. With the aid of similar formulas, we obtain the other four answers.

8. Birth: $t = 0$ (years). Principal at time t:
$$P(t) = 5000 e^{(0.06)t}.$$
At college age, the principal will be $P(18) = \$14{,}723.40$.

9. $(0.30)e^{(100)(1/20)} \approx \$44.52$.

10. If $C(t)$ is the concentration of the drug at time t (hours), then
$$C(t) = C_0 e^{-kt}$$
where $k = \tfrac{1}{5}\ln 2$. We require C_0 so large that $C(1) = (45)(50) = 2250$. Thus $C_0 e^{-k} \geq 2250$; that is, $C_0 \geq 2250 e^k \approx 2584.57$ (mg).

11. Let $S(t)$ represent the sales t weeks after advertising is discontinued, and let $S(0) = S_0$. Then for some constant λ,
$$\dfrac{dS}{dt} = -\lambda S, \text{ so } S(t) = S_0 e^{-\lambda t}.$$
Because $S(1) = 0.95 S_0 = S_0 e^{-\lambda}$, $\lambda = \ln\dfrac{20}{19}$. Therefore at time $t = T$, when sales have declined to 75% of the initial rate,
$$S(T) = \tfrac{3}{4}S_0 = S_0 e^{-\lambda T}:\quad e^{\lambda T} = \tfrac{4}{3};\quad T = \dfrac{\ln(\tfrac{4}{3})}{\lambda} = \dfrac{\ln(\tfrac{4}{3})}{\ln(\tfrac{20}{19})} \approx 5.608.$$
So the company plans to resume advertising about 5.6 weeks (about 39 days) after cessation of advertising.

12. Let L denote the number of words on the basic list at time $t = 0$ (in years)—corresponding to the year A.D. 1400. The number at time $t \geq 0$ is then given by
$$Q(t) = L e^{-kt}.$$
We are given
$$Q(1000) = (0.23)L = L e^{-1000k}, \text{ so}$$
$$k = (0.001)\ln\left(\dfrac{1}{0.23}\right) \approx 0.001469676.$$
In 1998 we would expect that about the fraction $e^{-598k} \approx 0.415$ of the words in the basic list in 1400—about 41.5% of them—would still be in use.

As a matter of independent interest, 87% of the words in the *Prologue* to the *Canterbury Tales* are still in use. You are invited to speculate about the reason for the apparent discrepancy.

13. Let Q denote the amount of radioactive cobalt remaining at time t (in years), with the occurrence of the accident set at time $t = 0$. Then

$$Q = Q_0 e^{-(t \ln 2)/(5.27)}.$$

If T is the number of years until the level of radioactivity has dropped to a hundredth of its initial value, then

$$\frac{1}{100} = e^{-(T \ln 2)/(5.27)},$$

and it follows that $T = (5.27)\dfrac{\ln 100}{\ln 2} \approx 35$ (years).

14. Let $Q(t)$ denote the amount of ^{238}U in the mineral body at time t (in years), with the supposition that the mineral body was formed at time $t = 0$. Then

$$Q(t) = Q_0 e^{-kt} \text{ where } k = \frac{\ln 2}{\tau};$$

τ denotes the half-life of ^{238}U, about 4.51×10^9 years. Let $t = T$ denote "now", so that

$$\frac{Q(T)}{Q_0 - Q(T)} = 0.9.$$

Therefore

$$\frac{e^{-kT}}{1 - e^{-kT}} = 0.9;$$
$$e^{-kT} = 0.9 - (0.9)e^{-kT};$$
$$(1.9)e^{-kT} = 0.9;$$
$$e^{kT} = \frac{19}{9};$$
$$T = \frac{1}{k}\ln\left(\frac{19}{9}\right) \approx 4.86 \times 10^9.$$

Answer: The cataclysm occurred approximately 4.86×10^9 years ago.

15. Let τ denote the half-life of potassium, so that τ is approximately 1.28×10^9. Measure time t also in years, with $t = 0$ corresponding to the time when the rock contained only potassium, and with $t = T$ corresponding to the present. Then at time $t = 0$, the amount of potassium was $Q(0)$ and no argon was present. At present, the amount of potassium is $Q(T)$ and the amount of argon is $A(T)$, where $A(t)$ is the amount of argon in the rock at time t. Now

$$Q(t) = Q_0 e^{(-(t \ln 2)/\tau)}, \text{ so}$$
$$A(t) = \tfrac{1}{9}(Q_0 - Q(t)).$$

We also are given the observation that $A(T) = Q(T)$. Thus

$$Q_0 - Q(t) = 9Q(T), \text{ so } Q(T) = (0.1)Q_0 = Q_0 e^{(-(T \ln 2)/\tau)}.$$

Therefore $\ln 10 = \dfrac{T}{\tau}\ln 2$, and so $T = \dfrac{\ln 10}{\ln 2}(1.28 \times 10^9) \approx 4.2521 \times 10^9$ (years).

16. Let $T = T(t)$ denote the temperature at time t; by Newton's law of cooling, we have

$$\frac{dT}{dt} = k(T - A).$$

Section 7.5 Natural Growth and Decay

Here, $A = 0$, $T(0) = 25$, and $T(20) = 15$. Also $\dfrac{dT}{dt} = kT$, so

$$T(t) = T_0 e^{kt} = 25e^{kt}.$$

Next, $15 = T(20) = 25e^{20k}$, so $k = \tfrac{1}{20}\ln\left(\tfrac{3}{5}\right)$. Now $T(t) = 5$ when $5 = 25e^{kt}$; that is, when $t = -\dfrac{20\ln 5}{\ln\left(\tfrac{3}{5}\right)} \approx 63.01$.

Answer: The buttermilk will be at $5°C$ about one hour and three minutes after putting it on the porch.

17. First, $\dfrac{dA}{dt} = -kA$, so $A(T) = A_0 e^{-kt}$.

$$\tfrac{3}{4}A_0 = A_0 e^{-k}, \text{ so } k = \ln\tfrac{4}{3}.$$

Also

$$\tfrac{1}{2}A_0 = A_0 e^{-kT}$$

where T is the time required for half the sugar to dissolve. So

$$\dfrac{\ln 2}{k} = T = \dfrac{\ln 2}{\ln\left(\tfrac{4}{3}\right)} \approx 2.40942 \text{ (minutes)},$$

so half of the sugar is dissolved in about 2 minutes and 25 seconds.

18. $\dfrac{dI}{dx} = -(1.4)I$, so $I(x) = I_0 e^{-(1.4)x}$.

   (a) $I(x) = \tfrac{1}{2}I_0$: $I_0 e^{-(1.4)x} = \tfrac{1}{2}I_0$; $e^{(1.4)x} = 2$; $x = \dfrac{\ln 2}{1.4} \approx 0.495$ (meters).

   (b) $I(10) = I_0 e^{-(1.4)(10)} \approx (0.000000832)I_0$; that is, about $\dfrac{1}{1,202,600}I_0$.

   (c) $I(x) = (0.01)I_0$: As in Part (a), $x = \dfrac{\ln 100}{1.4} \approx 3.29$ (meters).

19. We begin with the equation $p(x) = (29.92)e^{-x/5}$.

   (a) $p\left(\tfrac{10000}{5280}\right) \approx 20.486$ (inches); $p\left(\tfrac{30000}{5280}\right) \approx 9.604$ (inches).

   (b) If x is the altitude in question, then we must solve

$$15 = (29.92)e^{-x/5};$$
$$x = 5\ln\left(\dfrac{29.92}{15}\right) \approx 3.4524 \text{ (miles)},$$

approximately 18230 feet.

20. $\dfrac{dA}{dt} = -kA$; $A(t) = A_0 e^{-kt}$. With $A_0 = 10S$ and $A(100) = 7S$, $k = \tfrac{1}{100}\ln\left(\tfrac{10}{7}\right)$.

$$A(T) = S; \quad 10Se^{-kT} = S;$$
$$e^{kT} = 10; \quad T = \dfrac{1}{k}\ln 10 = \dfrac{100\ln 10}{\ln\left(\tfrac{10}{7}\right)} \approx 646.$$

   (a) $A(t) = 10Se^{-kt}$ where $k = \tfrac{1}{100}\ln\tfrac{10}{7}$; (b) The site will be safe after 646 days.

21. The decay constant k satisfies the equation $140k = \ln 2$, and so $k = (\ln 2)/140$. Measuring radioactivity as a multiple of the "safe level" 1, it is then $P(t) = 5e^{-kt}$ with t measured in days. When we solve $P(t) = 1$, we find that $t \approx 325.07$, so the room should be safe to enter in a little over 325 days.

22. The projected revenues are $r(t) = (1.85)e^{(0.03)t}$ and the projected budget is $b(t) = 2e^{kt}$ for some constant k (values of both functions are in billions of dollars; remember that in the U.S., a billion is a *thousand* million). In order that $r(7) = b(7)$, we solve to find $k \approx 0.0188626$, so the annual budget increase should be approximately 1.886%.

23. An atom of ^{14}C weighs about $w = 2.338 \times 10^{-23}$ grams. If we take the half-life of ^{14}C to be $\tau = 5700$ years, then at least $70{,}000{,}000/\tau$ half-lives have elapsed since the demise of the dinosaur. Working backwards from "today," 5700 years ago we would expect to find two atoms of ^{14}C, $2 \cdot 5700$ years ago there would be four such atoms, and so on. So the weight of the ^{14}C in the living dinosaur would be at least
$$2^{12000} w \approx 5.3554 \times 10^{3589}$$
grams. By comparison, the earth weighs about 5.988×10^{27} grams. So even if no other elements were present in the dinosaur's body, it would have weighed well over 10^{3560} times as much as the earth. In fact, its weight would have been an extremely large multiple of the total mass of the universe!

Section 7.6

1. Given: $\dfrac{dy}{dx} = y + 1$; $y(0) = 1$.

$$\frac{1}{y+2}\frac{dy}{dx} = 1;$$
$$\ln(y+1) = x + C;$$
$$y + 1 = Ke^x.$$

When $x = 0$, $y = 1$. Therefore $2 = (K)(1) = K$, so the solution is $y(x) = -1 + 2e^x$.

2. $\dfrac{1}{y-2}\dfrac{dy}{dx} = -1$:

$$\ln(y-2) = C_1 - x \quad \text{(see the note below)};$$
$$y - 2 = Ce^{-x};$$
$$y = 2 + Ce^{-x};$$
$$3 = y(0) = 2 + C, \text{ so } C = 1.$$

Answer: $y(x) = 2 + e^{-x}$.

Note: It is correct to write $\ln|y-2| = C_1 - x$. The "other case"—in which $y - 2 < 0$—does not apply in this problem because the initial condition $y(0) = 3$ assures us that $y(x) - 2 > 0$ for at least some values of y for which x is near zero. Thus on any interval containing $x = 0$ on which the solution $y(x)$ is continuous, we will "automatically" obtain the correct solution on that interval. You may wish to experiment with changing the initial condition to $y(0) = -3$, and observe what happens when the absolute value function is "forgotten". In physical applications there are normally no difficulties because the range of values of $y(x)$ is known (or can be estimated) in advance.

3. $\dfrac{1}{2y-3}\dfrac{dy}{dx} = 1$:

$$\tfrac{1}{2}\ln(2y-3) = C + x;$$
$$2y - 3 = Ke^{2x}.$$

Because $y(0) = 2$, it follows that $K = 1$. So $2y - 3 = e^{2x}$, hence $y(x) = \tfrac{1}{2}(e^{2x} + 3)$.

4. $\frac{dy}{dx} = \frac{1}{4} - \frac{y}{16} = -\frac{1}{16}(y-4); \quad y(0) = 20.$

$$\frac{1}{y-4}\frac{dy}{dx} = -\frac{1}{16};$$
$$\ln(y-4) = C_1 - \frac{x}{16};$$
$$y = 4 + Ce^{-x/16}.$$

We are given $20 = y(0) = 4 + C$, so $C = 16$. Answer: $y(x) = 4 + 16e^{-x/16}$.

6. $x(t) = \frac{2}{3} + \frac{10}{3}e^{-3t}$

8. $x(t) = -\frac{3}{4} - \frac{17}{4}e^{-4t}$

10. $v(t) = 10 - 20e^{5t}$

11. Let the population at time t (in years) be $Q(t)$; $t = 0$ corresponds to the year 1980. From the data given in the problem, we know that $\frac{dQ}{dt} = (0.04)Q + 50000; \quad Q(0) = 1{,}500{,}000$.

$$25\frac{dQ}{dt} = Q + 1{,}250{,}000;$$
$$\frac{1}{Q+1{,}250{,}000}\frac{dQ}{dt} = \frac{1}{25};$$
$$\ln(Q+1{,}250{,}000) = (0.04)t + C;$$
$$Q = 1{,}250{,}000 = Ke^{t/25}.$$

Now from the condition $Q(0) = 1{,}500{,}000$ it follows that $1{,}500{,}000 + 1{,}250{,}000 = K$, so

$$Q + 1{,}250{,}000 = 2{,}750{,}000 e^{t/25}.$$

In the year 2000, we have $Q(20) = -1{,}250{,}000 + 2{,}750{,}000 e^{0.8} \approx 4{,}870{,}238$, so the population in the year 2000 will be approximately 4.87 million people.

12. Let $y(t)$ be the temperature of the cake at time t (in minutes); denote by A the temperature of the room. By Newton's law of cooling, we have

$$\frac{dy}{dt} = k(y-A) \quad (k \text{ a constant}).$$

So

$$\frac{1}{y-A}\frac{dy}{dt} = k;$$
$$\ln(y-A) = C_1 + kt;$$
$$y(t) = A + Ce^{kt}.$$

Now $A = 70$ (°F) and $y(0) = 210$ (°F). Thus

$$210 = y(0) = 70 + C : \quad C = 140.$$
$$y(t) = 70 + 140e^{kt}.$$

Also

$$140 = y(30) = 70 + 140e^{30k} :$$
$$70 = 140e^{30k}$$
$$\tfrac{1}{2} = e^{30k};$$
$$k = -\frac{\ln 2}{30}.$$

Now $y(t) = 100$ when $100 = 70 + 140e^{kt}$; $e^{kt} = \frac{3}{14}$; $t = \frac{1}{k}\ln\frac{3}{14} = \frac{30\ln(14/3)}{\ln 2} \approx 66.67$. The cake will be at $100°F$ about one hour and seven minutes after the cake is removed from the oven.

14. In the notation of Problem 13, $\frac{dP}{dt} = rP - c$ and $P(0) = P_0$.

$$\frac{1}{rP-c}\frac{dP}{dt} = 1;$$

$$\frac{1}{r}\ln(rP-c) = C_1 + t;$$

$$\ln(rP-c) = C_2 + rt;$$

$$rP - c = Ce^{rt};$$

$$P(t) = \frac{1}{r}(c + Ce^{rt}).$$

Now $P_0 = P(0) = \frac{1}{r(c+C)}$, so $\frac{C}{r} = P_0 - \frac{c}{r}$. Therefore

$$P(t) = \frac{c}{r} + \left(P_0 - \frac{c}{r}\right)e^{rt}.$$

We are given $P_0 = 3600$; we also require that $P(36) = 0$.

(a) $r = \frac{0.12}{12} = 0.01$: $0 = 100c + (3600 - 100c)e^{0.36}$. Consequently,

$$c = -\frac{3600e^{0.36}}{100(1-e^{0.36})} = (36)\frac{e^{0.36}}{e^{0.36}-1}, \text{ approximately } \$119.08.$$

(b) $r = \frac{0.18}{12} = 0.015$: $0 = \frac{c}{0.015} + \left(3600 - \frac{c}{0.015}\right)e^{0.54}$, so that

$$c = \frac{(0.015)(3600)e^{0.54}}{e^{-0.54}-1}, \text{ approximately } \$129.42.$$

15. Let $P = P(t)$ denote the number of people who have heard the rumor after t days. Then

$$\frac{dP}{dt} = k(100{,}000 - P).$$

It follows that

$$P(t) = 100{,}000 - Ce^{-kt}.$$

But $P(0) = 0$, which implies that $C = 100{,}000$. Therefore

$$P(t) = (100{,}000)\left(1 - e^{-kt}\right).$$

Now $P(7) = 100{,}000\left(1-e^{-7k}\right) = 10000$, and it follows that $k = -\frac{1}{7}\ln(0.9) \approx 0.0150515$. Half the people have heard the rumor when $P(T) = 50{,}000$, so that at that time T, we have

$$\frac{1}{2} = 1 - e^{-kT}; \quad T = \frac{1}{k}\ln 2 \approx 46.$$

Half the population of the city will have heard the rumor forty-six days after the beginning of the rumor.

16. Let $Q(t)$ be the number of pounds of salt in the tank at time t (in seconds). Now $Q(0) = 50$, and

$$\frac{dQ}{dt} = -\frac{5}{1000}Q(t) = -\frac{1}{200}Q(t).$$

Therefore
$$Q(t) = 50e^{-t/200}.$$

Next, $Q(t) = 10$ when $e^{-t/200} = \frac{1}{5}$, so that $t = 200 \ln 5$. So 10 pounds of salt will remain in the tank after approximately 5 minutes and 22 seconds.

18. (a) $\dfrac{1}{v}\dfrac{dv}{dt} = -k$:
$$\ln v = C_1 - kt;$$
$$v(t) = Ce^{-kt}.$$

Now $v_0 = v(0) = C$, and therefore $v(t) = v_0 e^{-kt}$. Because $\dfrac{dx}{dt} = v(t)$, $x(t) = C_2 - \dfrac{1}{k}v_0 e^{-kt}$. Also $x(0) = x_0 = C_2 - \dfrac{1}{k}v_0$, so $C_2 = x_0 + \dfrac{1}{k}v_0$: $x(t) = x_0 + \dfrac{1}{k}v_0\left(1 - e^{-kt}\right)$.

(b) $\lim\limits_{t\to\infty} x(t) = x_0 + \dfrac{1}{k}v_0$, so the total distance traveled is $\dfrac{1}{k}v_0$.

19. In the notation of Problem 18, we have $v = v_0 e^{-kt}$ where we are given $v_0 = 40$. Here, also, $v(10) = 20$, so that $20 = 40e^{-10k}$. It follows that $k = (0.1)\ln 2$, so by Part (b) of Problem 18 the total distance traveled will be $\dfrac{1}{k}v_0 = \dfrac{(40)(10)}{\ln 2}$, approximately 577 feet.

20. First, $\dfrac{dv}{dt} = k(250 - v)$ where k is some positive constant. We use kilometers and seconds in this problem; if $v(0) = 0$, then $v(10) = 100$. We are to find T so that $v(T) = 200$, given $v(0) = 0$.

$$\dfrac{1}{250 - v}\dfrac{dv}{dt} = +k\, dt\,:$$
$$-\ln(250 - v) = C_1 + kt;$$
$$\ln(250 - v) = C_2 - kt;$$
$$250 - v = Ce^{-kt};$$
$$v(t) = 250 - Ce^{-kt}.$$
$$0 = v(0) = 250 = C: \quad C = 250.$$
$$v(t) = 250\left(1 - e^{-kt}\right).$$

Now $100 = v(10) = 250\left(1 - e^{-10k}\right)$, so $1 - e^{-10k} = \dfrac{100}{250} = \dfrac{2}{5}$. So $e^{-10k} = 0.6$, and therefore $k = (0.1)\ln(5/3)$.

$$200 = v(T) = 250\left(1 - e^{-kT}\right);$$
$$\dfrac{4}{5} = 1 - e^{-kT};$$
$$e^{-kT} = \dfrac{1}{5}.$$

Answer: $T = \dfrac{1}{k}\ln 5 = \dfrac{10\ln 5}{\ln(5/3)} \approx 31.51$ (seconds).

22. $\dfrac{dx}{dt} + ax = be^{ct}$, $x(0) = x_0$, $a + c \neq 0$.

$$e^{at}\dfrac{dx}{dt} + axe^{at} = be^{(a+c)t}.$$
$$D_t\left(e^{at}x(t)\right) = be^{(a+c)t}.$$
$$e^{at}x(t) = C + \dfrac{b}{a+c}e^{(a+c)t} \qquad (a+c \neq 0).$$

So $x(t) = Ce^{-at} + \dfrac{b}{a+c}e^{ct}$, and $x_0 = x(0) = C + \dfrac{b}{a+c}$, and hence $C = x_0 - \dfrac{b}{a+c}$.

Therefore $x(t) = \left(x_0 - \dfrac{b}{a+c}\right)e^{-at} + \dfrac{b}{a+c}e^{ct} = x_0 e^{-at} + \dfrac{b}{a+c}(e^{ct} - e^{-at})$.

23. $S(t) = 30e^{(0.05)t}$ (t is in years; $t = 0$ corresponds to age 30).

(a) $\Delta A = A(t + \Delta t) - A(t) \approx (0.06)A(t)\,\Delta t + (0.12)S(t)\,\Delta t$.

$$\frac{dA}{dt} = \lim_{\Delta t \to 0} \frac{\Delta A}{\Delta t} = (0.06)A(t) + (0.12)S(t).$$

$$\frac{dA}{dt} + (-0.06)A(t) = (3.6)e^{(0.05)t}.$$

(b) Now in the result of Problem 22, take $x(t) = A(t)$, $x_0 = 0$; $a = -0.06$, $b = 3.6$, and $c = 0.05$. Then

$$A(t) = -\frac{3.6}{0.01}\left(e^{(0.05)t} - e^{(0.06)t}\right), \text{ so that}$$

$$A(t) = 360\left(e^{(0.06)t} - e^{(0.05)t}\right).$$

Now $A(40) = 360\left(e^{2.4} - e^2\right) \approx 1308.28330$. Because the units in this problem are in thousands of dollars, the answer is that the retirement money available will be $1,308,283.30.

24. Given: $\dfrac{dN}{dt} = k(10000 - N)$:

$$-\frac{dN}{10000 - N} = -k\,dt;$$
$$\ln(10000 - N) = C_1 - kt;$$
$$10000 - N = Ce^{-kt}.$$

On January 1, $t = 0$ and $N = 1000$. On April 1, $t = 3$ and $N = 2000$. On October 1, $t = 9$; we want to determine the value of N then.

$$9000 = Ce^0 = C, \text{ so } N(t) = 10000 - 9000e^{-kt}.$$
$$2000 = 10000 - 9000e^{-3k} \text{ so } 8 = 9e^{-3k}. \text{ Solve for } k: k = \tfrac{1}{3}\ln(\tfrac{9}{8}).$$

So $N(9) = 1000 - 9000e^{-9k} = 1000\left(10 - 9e^{-3\ln(9/8)}\right) \approx 3679$.

25. $\dfrac{dx}{dt} = k(100000 - x(t))$:

$$\frac{-dx}{100000 - x} = -k\,dt;$$
$$\ln(100000 - x) = C_1 - kt;$$
$$100000 - x = Ce^{-kt};$$
$$x(t) = 100000 - Ce^{-kt}.$$

On March 1, $t = 0$ and $x = 20000$. On March 15, $t = 14$ and $x = 60000$.

$$20000 = 100000 - C, \text{ so } C = 80000$$
$$x(t) = 10000\left(10 - 8e^{-kt}\right).$$
$$60000 = x(14) = 10000(10 - 8e^{-14k}). \text{ so } 6 = 10 - 8e^{-14k}. \text{ Solve for } k: k = \tfrac{1}{14}\ln 2.$$

(a) $x(t) = 10000(10 - 8e^{-kt})$ where $k = \frac{1}{14} \ln 2$.

(b) $x(T) = 80000$: Solve $10 - 8e^{-kT} = 2$ for T: $T = \dfrac{1}{k} \ln 4 = 28$. So 80,000 people will be infected on March 29.

(c) $\lim\limits_{t \to \infty} N(t) = 100{,}000$: Eventually everybody gets the flu.

Chapter 7 Miscellaneous

1. $f(x) = \ln 2\sqrt{x} = \ln 2 + \frac{1}{2} \ln x$, so $f'(x) = \dfrac{1}{2x}$.

2. $f'(x) = -\left(x^{-1/2}\right) e^{-2x^{1/2}}$

3. $f'(x) = \dfrac{1 - e^x}{x - e^x}$

4. $f'(x) = \frac{1}{2}\left(x^{-1/2}\right) 10^{\left(x^{1/2}\right)} \ln 10$

5. $f(x) = x \ln 2$, so $f'(x) = \ln 2$.

6. $f(x) = (\log_{10} e)(\ln \sin x)$, so $f'(x) = \dfrac{\cot x}{\ln 10}$.

7. $f'(x) = 3x^2 e^{-1/x^2} + x^3 e^{-1/x^2}\left(2x^{-3}\right) = \left(2 + 3x^2\right) e^{-1/x^2}$.

8. $f'(x) = (\ln x)^2 + 2x(\ln x)\dfrac{1}{x} = (\ln x)(2 + \ln x)$

9. $f'(x) = \dfrac{1}{x} \ln(\ln x) + (\ln x)\left(\dfrac{1}{x \ln x}\right) = \dfrac{1 + \ln(\ln x)}{x}$

10. $f'(x) = (\exp(10^x))(10^x)(\ln 10)$

12. $f(x) = \ln\left(e^x + e^{-x}\right) - \ln\left(e^x - e^{-x}\right)$, so $f'(x) = \dfrac{e^x - e^{-x}}{e^x + e^{-x}} - \dfrac{e^x + e^{-x}}{e^x - e^{-x}} = -\dfrac{4}{e^{2x} - e^{-2x}}$.

13. $f'(x) = \dfrac{(x-1) - (x+1)}{(x-1)^2} \exp\left(\dfrac{x+1}{x-1}\right) = -\dfrac{2}{(x-1)^2} \exp\left(\dfrac{x+1}{x-1}\right)$

14. $f(x) = \frac{1}{2} \ln(1 + x) + \frac{1}{3} \ln\left(2 + x^2\right)$. So $f'(x) = \dfrac{1}{2(1+x)} + \dfrac{2x}{3(2+x^2)}$.

15. First write $f(x) = \frac{3}{2} \ln(x-1) - \frac{3}{2} \ln\left(3 - 4x^2\right)$.

16. $f'(x) = \dfrac{1}{x} \cos(\ln x)$

17. $f'(x) = \left(\exp\left(1 + \sin^2 x\right)^{1/2}\right) \dfrac{1}{2}\left(1 + \sin^2 x\right)^{-1/2}(2 \sin x \cos x)$.

18. $f'(x) = \dfrac{(\ln x)^2 - x(2 \ln x)(1/x)}{(\ln x)^4} = \dfrac{(\ln x) - 2}{(\ln x)^3}$

19. $f'(x) = \dfrac{3^x \cos x + (3^x \ln 3) \sin x}{3^x \sin x} = \dfrac{\cos x + (\ln 3) \sin x}{\sin x} = \cot x + \ln 3$.

20. If $y = (\ln x)^x$ then $\ln y = x \ln(\ln x)$. So $\dfrac{dy}{dx} = y\left(\ln(\ln x) + \dfrac{1}{\ln x}\right)$.

21. Let $y = x^{1/x}$. Then $\ln y = \dfrac{1}{x} \ln x$, so $\dfrac{dy}{dx} = x^{1/x}\left(\dfrac{1 - \ln x}{x^2}\right)$.

22. If $y = x^{\sin x}$ then $\ln y = (\sin x)(\ln x)$.

So $\dfrac{dy}{dx} = (y)\left(\dfrac{1}{x} \sin x + (\cos x)(\ln x)\right) = \left(x^{\sin x}\right)\left(\dfrac{1}{x} \sin x + (\cos x)(\ln x)\right)$.

23. $\ln y = (\ln x)(\ln \ln x)$, so $\dfrac{dy}{dx} = y\left(\dfrac{\ln \ln x}{x} + \dfrac{\ln x}{x \ln x}\right) = \dfrac{1 + \ln(\ln x)}{x}(\ln x)^{\ln x}$.

24. If $y = (\sin x)^{\cos x}$ then $\ln y = (\cos x)\ln(\sin x)$. So
$$\frac{dy}{dx} = (y)\left((-\sin x)\ln(\sin x) + (\cos x)\left(\frac{\cos x}{\sin x}\right)\right) = [(\sin x)^{\cos x}]\left(\frac{\cos^2 x - (\sin^2 x)\ln(\sin x)}{\sin x}\right).$$

26. Let $u = x^{3/2}$. Then $du = \frac{3}{2}x^{1/2}\,dx$, so $x^{1/2}\,dx = \frac{2}{3}\,du$. Therefore
$$\int \frac{x^{1/2}}{1+x^{3/2}}\,dx = \int \frac{2/3}{1+u}\,du = \frac{2}{3}\ln|1+u| + C = \frac{2}{3}\ln\left(1+x^{3/2}\right) + C.$$

27. Note that $D_x\left(1 + 6x - x^2\right) = -2x + 6 = 2(3-x)$.

28. $\displaystyle\int \frac{e^x - e^{-x}}{e^x + e^{-x}}\,dx = \ln\left(e^x + e^{-x}\right) + C.$

30. Let $u = -\dfrac{1}{x^2}$. Then $du = \dfrac{2}{x^3}\,dx$, so $\dfrac{1}{x^3}\,dx = \dfrac{1}{2}\,du$.
$$\int \frac{e^{(-1/x^2)}}{x^3}\,dx = \frac{1}{2}\int e^u\,du = \frac{1}{2}e^u + C = \frac{1}{2}e^{-1/x^2} + C.$$

31. Let $u = \sqrt{x}$.

32. Let $u = \ln x$. Then $du = \dfrac{1}{x}\,dx$, so
$$\int \frac{dx}{x(\ln x)^2} = \int \frac{1}{u^2}\,du = -\frac{1}{u} + C = -\frac{1}{\ln x} + C.$$

33. If necessary, let $u = e^x$.

34. Let $u = \ln x$. Then $du = \dfrac{1}{x}\,dx$, and so
$$\int \frac{1}{x}(1 + \ln x)^{1/2}\,dx = \int (1+u)^{1/2}\,du = \frac{2}{3}(1+u)^{3/2} + C = \frac{2}{3}(1 + \ln x)^{3/2} + C.$$

35. $2^x 3^x = 6^x$, n'est-ce pas?

36. Let $u = x^{2/3}$. Then $du = \frac{2}{3}x^{-1/3}\,dx$, so that $\dfrac{1}{x^{1/3}}\,dx = \frac{3}{2}\,du$. Thus
$$\int \frac{dx}{x^{1/3}\left(1+x^{2/3}\right)} = \int \frac{3/2}{1+u}\,du = \frac{3}{2}\ln|1+u| + C = \frac{3}{2}\ln\left(1+x^{2/3}\right) + C.$$

37. First, $dx = 2t\,dt$, and so $x = t^2 + C$. But $x(0) = 17$, and so $x(t) = t^2 + 17$.

38. $\dfrac{dx}{x} = 2\,dt$; $\ln x = 2t + C_1$; $x = Ce^{2t}$. But $x(0) = 17$, so $C = 17$. Therefore $x(t) = 17e^{2t}$.

39. $dx = e^t\,dt$, so $x = e^t + C$; $x(0) = 2$, so $C = 1$. Hence $x(t) = 1 + e^t$.

40. $e^{-x}\,dx = dt$, so $-e^{-x} = C + t$. Now $-e^{-2} = C + 0$, and so
$$-e^{-x} = -e^{-2} + t;$$
$$e^{-x} = e^{-2} - t;$$
$$-x = \ln\left(e^{-2} - t\right);$$
$$x(t) = -\ln\left(e^{-2} - t\right).$$

41. $\dfrac{dx}{3x-2} = dt$; $\frac{1}{3}\ln|3x-2| = t + C_1$; $\ln|3x-2| = 3t + C_2$; $3x - 2 = Ce^{3t}$;

$x = \frac{1}{3}\left(2 + Ce^{3t}\right)$. Now $3 = \frac{1}{3}(2 + C)$, so $C = 7$. Therefore $x(t) = \frac{1}{3}\left(2 + 7e^{3t}\right)$.

42. $x^{-2}\,dx = t^2\,dt$; $\frac{1}{x} = \frac{1}{3}t^3 + C$. But $1 = \frac{1}{3}(0)^3 + C$, so that $C = 1$. Therefore $x(t) = -\frac{3}{t^3 + 3}$.

43. $\frac{dx}{x} = \cos t\,dt$, so $\ln|x| = C_1 + \sin t$. Consequently $x(t) = Ce^{\sin t}$. Because $x(0) = \sqrt{2}$, $C = \sqrt{2}$. So $x(t) = \sqrt{2}\,e^{\sin t}$.

44. $x^{-1/2}\,dx = dt$: $2x^{1/2} = C + t$. $x(1) = 0$, so $C = -1$, thus $2x^{1/2} = t - 1$. Therefore $x(t) = \left(\frac{t-1}{2}\right)^2$.

45. $\frac{dy}{dx} = \frac{e^{-x}}{2x^{1/2}}(1 - 2x)$; $\frac{d^2y}{dx^2} = \frac{4x^2 - 4x - 1}{4x^{3/2}e^x}$.

Now $\frac{dy}{dx} = 0$ when $x = \frac{1}{2}$, so there is a horizontal tangent at $x = \frac{1}{2}$, $y = 1/\sqrt{2e} \approx 0.43$. Note that $y(0) = 0$ and that $\frac{dy}{dx} \to +\infty$ as $y \to 0^+$. Also $\frac{d^2y}{dx^2} = 0$ when $x = \left(1 + \sqrt{2}\right)/2$, so at the point with approximate coordinates $(1.21, 0.33)$ there is a possible inflection point. As the graph in the answer section shows, the x-axis is a horizontal asymptote.

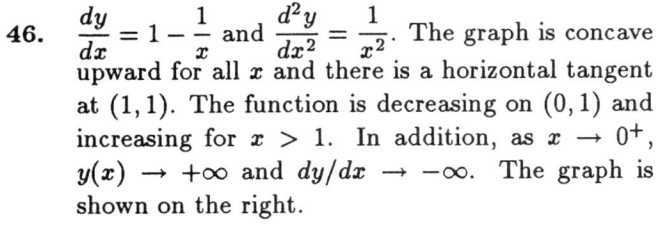

46. $\frac{dy}{dx} = 1 - \frac{1}{x}$ and $\frac{d^2y}{dx^2} = \frac{1}{x^2}$. The graph is concave upward for all x and there is a horizontal tangent at $(1,1)$. The function is decreasing on $(0,1)$ and increasing for $x > 1$. In addition, as $x \to 0^+$, $y(x) \to +\infty$ and $dy/dx \to -\infty$. The graph is shown on the right.

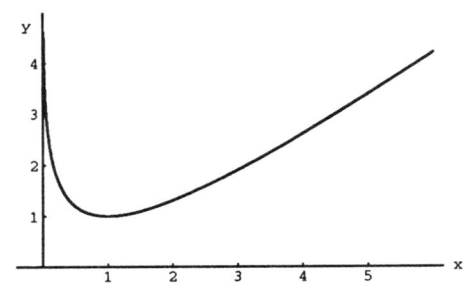

47. $\frac{dy}{dx} = \frac{x^{1/2} - 2}{2x}$; $\frac{d^2y}{dx^2} = \frac{4 - x^{1/2}}{4x^2}$.

There is a horizontal tangent where $x = 4$ and $y = 2 - \ln 4$, approximately $(4, 0.61)$. There is an inflection point where $x = 16$—close to the point $(16, 1.23)$.

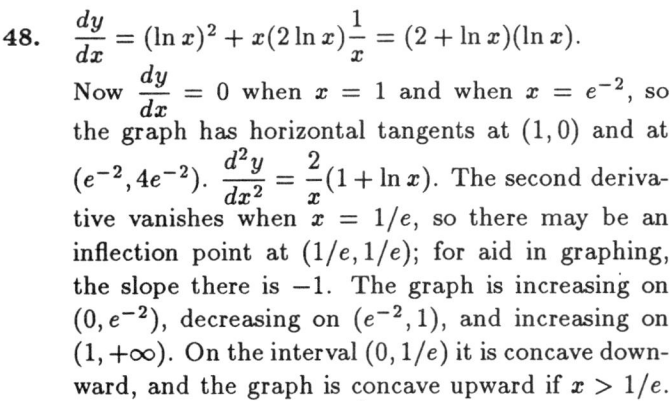

48. $\frac{dy}{dx} = (\ln x)^2 + x(2\ln x)\frac{1}{x} = (2 + \ln x)(\ln x)$.

Now $\frac{dy}{dx} = 0$ when $x = 1$ and when $x = e^{-2}$, so the graph has horizontal tangents at $(1,0)$ and at $(e^{-2}, 4e^{-2})$. $\frac{d^2y}{dx^2} = \frac{2}{x}(1 + \ln x)$. The second derivative vanishes when $x = 1/e$, so there may be an inflection point at $(1/e, 1/e)$; for aid in graphing, the slope there is -1. The graph is increasing on $(0, e^{-2})$, decreasing on $(e^{-2}, 1)$, and increasing on $(1, +\infty)$. On the interval $(0, 1/e)$ it is concave downward, and the graph is concave upward if $x > 1/e$. As $x \to 0^+$, $y \to 0$ and $\frac{dy}{dx} \to +\infty$. The graph is shown on the right.

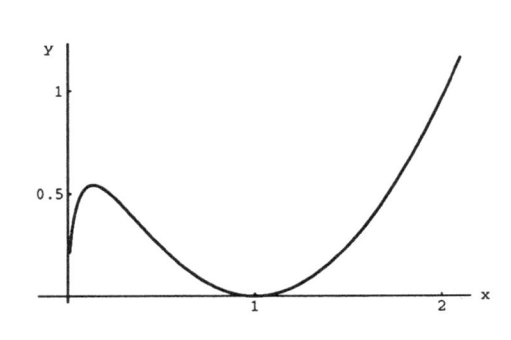

49. $\frac{dy}{dx} = \frac{1}{x^2}e^{-1/x}$ and $\frac{d^2y}{dx^2} = \frac{1 - 2x}{x^4}e^{-1/x}$.

50. Given: $y = \frac{1}{2}x^2 - \frac{1}{4}\ln x$:

$$\frac{dy}{dx} = x - \frac{1}{4x}, \text{ so}$$

$$1 + \left(\frac{dy}{dx}\right)^2 = 1 + x^2 - \frac{1}{2} + \frac{1}{16x^2} = \left(x + \frac{1}{4x}\right)^2.$$

$$L = \int_1^e \left(x + \frac{1}{4x}\right)dx = \frac{2e^2 - 1}{4} \approx 3.44453.$$

51. Revenue from the sale at time t:

$$f(t) = (B)\left(2^{-t/12}\right)\left(2 + \frac{t}{12}\right).$$

$$\frac{1}{B}f'(t) = \frac{1}{12}\left(2^{-t/12}\right) + \left(2 + \frac{t}{12}\right)\left(2^{-t/12}\right)\left(-\frac{\ln 2}{12}\right).$$

Now $f'(t) = 0$ when $2 + \frac{t}{12} = \frac{1}{\ln 2}$: that is, when $t = (12)\left(-2 + \frac{1}{\ln 2}\right)$. But this value of t is negative—so here's the answer: Sell immediately!

52. At time t (in years), the amount to be repaid will be $1000e^{(0.1)t}$. So the profit on selling would be

$$P(t) = 800e^{\left(\frac{1}{2}\sqrt{t}\right)} - 1000e^{(t/10)}.$$
$$P'(t) = 200t^{-1/2}e^{\left(\frac{1}{2}\sqrt{t}\right)} - 100e^{(t/10)}.$$

$P'(t) = 0$ when $2e^{\left(\frac{1}{2}\sqrt{t}\right)} = t^{1/2}e^{(t/10)}$. The iteration

$$t \longleftarrow \left(2e^{\left(\frac{1}{2}\sqrt{t}\right)}e^{(-t/10)}\right)^2$$

yields $t \approx 11.7519$ years as the optimal time to cut and sell. The resulting profit would be $1202.37.

54. We begin with

$$\lim_{x \to 0+} x^k \ln x = 0 \quad \text{if } k > 0.$$
$$\lim_{x \to 0+} x \ln x = 0;$$
$$\lim_{x \to 0+} \ln(x^x) = 0.$$

Because $y = \ln x$ is continuous at $x = 1$, $\lim_{x \to 0+} x^x = 1$.

56. Let $f(x) = a^x$. Then $f'(0) = \lim_{h \to 0} \frac{a^h - a^0}{h} = \lim_{h \to 0} \frac{a^h - 1}{h}$. But $f'(0) = a^0 \ln a = \ln a$. Therefore

$$\lim_{h \to 0} \frac{1}{h}\left(a^h - 1\right) = \ln a.$$

$\ln 2 = \lim_{n \to \infty} n\left(2^{1/n} - 1\right) \approx (1024)\left(2^{1/1024} - 1\right) \approx 0.693382144$ (true value: $\ln 2 \approx 0.693147181$).

57. $\frac{dP}{dt} = 3\sqrt{P}$, so $P^{-1/2}\,dP = -3\,dt$. Therefore

$$2\sqrt{P} = -3t + C,$$
$$P(t) = \left(\frac{C - 3t}{2}\right)^2.$$

Now $900 = P_0 = \frac{1}{4}C^2$, so $C = 60$. Consequently $P = 0$ when $t = 20$. The fish will all be dead in 20 weeks.

58. Let $x(t)$ represent the position of the race car at time t and let $x(0) = 0$. Then the velocity of the car is $v(t) = x'(t)$. We want to find $v(0) = v_0$.

$$\frac{dv}{dt} = -kv,$$
$$v(t) = v_0 e^{-kt}, \text{ as usual.}$$

$$x(t) = C - \frac{v_0}{k}\left(e^{-kt}\right).$$

Since $0 = x(0) = C - \frac{v_0}{k}$, $C = \frac{v_0}{k}$, hence $x(t) = \frac{v_0}{k}\left(1 - e^{-kt}\right)$.

When $t = 0$, $\frac{dv}{dt} = -2$, so $-kv_0 = -2$, hence $k = \frac{2}{v_0}$ and so $x(t) = \frac{(v_0)^2}{2}\left(1 - e^{-2t/v_0}\right)$.

$$\lim_{t\to\infty} v(t) = 0, \text{ so } \lim_{t\to\infty} x(t) = 1800.$$

$$1800 = \lim_{t\to\infty} \frac{(v_0)^2}{2}\left(1 - e^{-2t/v_0}\right) = \frac{(v_0)^2}{2}: \quad (v_0)^2 = 3600; \quad v_0 = 60.$$

The initial velocity of the car was 60 m/s.

59. $\frac{dP}{dt} = rP - c$, $P(0) = P_0$: P_0 is the original amount of the mortgage, $P(t)$ is the balance at time t (in months), c is the amount of the monthly payment, and r is the monthly interest rate.

$$\frac{dP}{rP - c} = dt, \text{ so } \frac{r\, dP}{rP - c} = r\, dt.$$

So $\ln|rP - c| = rt + K_1$. Therefore $rP - c = Ke^{rt}$, and so $P(t) = \frac{1}{r}(c + Ke^{rt})$.

But $P_0 = P(0) = \frac{c + K}{r}$, so $K = rP_0 - c$. Thus $P(t) = \frac{1}{r}\left(c + (rP_0 - c)e^{rt}\right)$.

Now $P_0 = 120{,}000$ (given), and we require $P(300) = 0$. So

$$0 = \frac{1}{r}\left(c + (120{,}000r - c)e^{300r}\right);$$
$$c = (c - 120{,}000r)\, e^{300r};$$
$$c\left(e^{300r} - 1\right) = 120{,}000r e^{300r};$$
$$c = \frac{120{,}000r}{1 - e^{-300r}}.$$

In Part (a), we take $r = (0.08)/12$, and find that the monthly payment will be \$925.21.

In Part (b), we take $r = (0.12)/12$, and find that the monthly payment will be \$1262.87.

60. $\frac{1000\, dv}{5000 - 100v} = dt$, so $\frac{-100\, dv}{5000 - 100v} = -\frac{1}{10}\, dt$:

$$\ln(5000 - 100v) = C_1 - \frac{t}{10}$$
$$5000 - 100v = Ce^{-t/10};$$
$$v(t) = \frac{5000 - Ce^{-t/10}}{100}.$$

Now $0 = v(0) = \frac{5000 - C}{100}$, so $C = 5000$. Therefore $v(t) = 50\left(1 - e^{-t/10}\right)$. Because $\lim_{t\to\infty} v(t) = 50$, the boat can attain any speed up to 50 ft/s (about 34 miles per hour).

61. Let $Q(t)$ denote the temperature at time t, with t in hours and $t = 0$ corresponding to 11:00 P.M., the time of the power failure. Let $A = 20$ be the room temperature. By Newton's law of cooling,

$$\frac{dQ}{dt} = k(A - Q), \text{ so that } \frac{1}{A - Q}\, dQ = k\, dt$$

where k is a positive constant. Next, $\ln(A - Q) = C_1 - kt$, so that $Q(t) = A - Ce^{-kt}$. Now $Q_0 = Q(0) = A - C$, so $C = A - Q_0$. Thus

$$Q(t) = A + (Q_0 - A)e^{-kt}.$$

We are given $Q_0 = -16$, $A = 20$, and $Q(7) = -10$. We must find the value $t = T$ at which $Q(T) = 0$. Now

$$Q(t) = 20 - 36e^{-kt};$$
$$Q(7) = -10 = 20 - 36e^{-7k};$$
$$30 = 36e^{-7k};$$
$$k = \tfrac{1}{7}\ln(1.2).$$

Next, $0 = Q(T) = 20 - 36e^{-kT}$; $20 = 36e^{-kT}$: Therefore $e^{kT} = 1.8$, and thus

$$T = \frac{1}{k}\ln(1.8) = \frac{7\ln(1.8)}{\ln(1.2)} \approx 22.5673.$$

The critical temperature will be reached about 22 hours and 34 minutes after the power goes off; that is, at about 9:34 P.M. on the following day. (The data used in this problem are those obtained during an actual incident of the sort described.)

62. $\dfrac{dA}{dt} = -\dfrac{1}{400}A$; $A(0) = A_0$:

$$\frac{dA}{A} = -\frac{1}{400}dt;$$
$$\ln A = C_1 - \frac{t}{400};$$
$$A(t) = A_0 e^{-t/400}.$$

(a) $\dfrac{A(25)}{A_0} = e^{-25/400} = e^{-1/16} \approx 0.9394$; Answer: About 94%.

(b) $A(T) = \tfrac{1}{2}A_0$ when $e^{-t/400} = \tfrac{1}{2}$: $e^{t/400} = 2$, so $t = 400\ln 2 \approx 277.26$. Answer: About 277 years.

63. Let $x(t)$ denote the distance traveled after t seconds and let $v(t) = dx/dt$ denote the velocity of the car then. We are given $x(0) = 0$, $v(0) = 0$, and $dv/dt = a - \rho v$.

(a) $\dfrac{dv}{a - \rho v} = dt$, so $\dfrac{-\rho\,dv}{a - \rho v} = -\rho\,dt$. Thus

$$\ln(a - \rho v) = C_1 - \rho t, \text{ and so}$$
$$a - \rho v = Ce^{-\rho t}.$$

But $v(0) = 0$, so $C = a$. Moreover, $a - \rho v = ae^{-\rho t}$, so $v(t) = \dfrac{a}{\rho}(1 - e^{-\rho t})$.

(b) Given $a = 17.6$ and $\rho = 0.1$, we are to find $v(10)$ and the limiting velocity $v_{\lim}$.

$$v_{\lim} = \lim_{t \to \infty} \frac{a}{\rho}(1 - e^{-\rho t}) = \frac{a}{\rho} = 176$$

feet per second, exactly 120 miles per hour. And

$$v(10) = \frac{a}{\rho}(1 - e^{-10\rho}) = 176(1 - e^{-1}) \approx 111.2532$$

feet per second, approximately 75.85 miles per hour.

64. Let S be the safe limit and let $R(t)$ be the radiation level at time t (in years).

$$R(t) = 10Se^{-kt}.$$

Chapter 7 Miscellaneous 219

$R(\frac{1}{2}) = 95 = 105e^{-k/2}$; $\frac{9}{10} = e^{-k/2}$; $\frac{k}{2} = \ln \frac{10}{9}$; $k = 2\ln \frac{10}{9}$.

$R(t) = S$ when $10Se^{-kt} = S$: $e^{kt} = 10$; $t = \dfrac{\ln 10}{k} = \dfrac{\ln 10}{2\ln\left(\frac{10}{9}\right)} \approx 10.927$. Radiation will drop to a safe level in just under 11 years.

65. (b) Solve $x^{1/3} = \ln x$, which is equivalent to $x^{1/3} - \ln x = 0$, by iterating:

$$x \longleftarrow x - \dfrac{x^{1/3} - \ln x}{\frac{1}{3}x^{-2/3} - \dfrac{1}{x}}.$$

Beginning with $x_0 = 100$, we get $x_5 \approx 93.354461$.

(c) Suppose that $j(x) = x^{1/p}$ is tangent to the graph of $g(x) = \ln x$ at $(q, \ln q)$:
$q^{1/p} = \ln q$ and $j'(q) = g'(q)$:

$$\frac{1}{p}q^{(1/p)-1} = \frac{1}{q};$$
$$q^{1/p} = p;$$
$$p = \ln q = \ln p^p = p\ln p;$$
$$\ln p = 1, \text{ so } p = e.$$

220   Chapter 7 Miscellaneous

Chapter 8: Further Calculus of Transcendental Functions
Section 8.2

2. (a) $\cos^{-1}\left(\frac{1}{2}\right) = \pi/3$ (b) $\cos^{-1}\left(-\frac{1}{2}\right) = 2\pi/3$
   (c) $\cos^{-1}\left(\frac{1}{2}\sqrt{2}\right) = \pi/4$ (d) $\cos^{-1}\left(-\frac{1}{2}\sqrt{3}\right) = 5\pi/6$

4. (a) $\sec^{-1}(1) = 0$ (b) $\sec^{-1}(-1) = \pi$
   (c) $\sec^{-1}(2) = \pi/3$ (d) $\sec^{-1}(-\sqrt{2}) = 3\pi/4$

6. $f'(x) = \dfrac{e^x}{1 + e^{2x}}$

8. $f'(x) = \dfrac{1}{(1+x^2)\tan^{-1} x}$

10. $f'(x) = \dfrac{x}{1+x^2} + \arctan x$

12. $f'(x) = \dfrac{1}{2\sqrt{x}\,(1+x)}$

14. $f'(x) = \dfrac{2x}{x^4 + 1}$

16. $f'(x) = \dfrac{1}{2x\sqrt{x-1}}$

18. $f'(x) = \dfrac{2\arcsin x}{(1-x^2)^{1/2}}$

20. $f'(x) = \dfrac{x}{|x|(x^2+1)}$

22. $f'(x) = \dfrac{e^{\arcsin x}}{(1-x^2)^{1/2}}$

24. $f(x) = \sec(\sec^{-1} e^x) = e^x$, so $f'(x) = e^x$.

26. $f'(x) = -2\left(\sin^{-1} 2x^2\right)^{-3} \dfrac{4x}{(1-4x^4)^{1/2}}$

28. $\dfrac{dy}{dx} = -\left(1-y^2\right)^{1/2}\left(1-x^2\right)^{-1/2}$; Tangent: $x\sqrt{3} + 3y = 2\sqrt{3}$

30. $\dfrac{dy}{dx} = -\dfrac{(1-y^2)^{1/2}\arcsin x}{(1-x^2)^{1/2}\arcsin y}$; Tangent: $2x\sqrt{3} + 12y = 7\sqrt{3}$

32. $\displaystyle\int_0^{1/2} \dfrac{dx}{\sqrt{1-x^2}} = \arcsin(\tfrac{1}{2}) - \arcsin(0) = \dfrac{\pi}{6}$

34. $\displaystyle\int_{-2}^{-2/\sqrt{3}} \dfrac{dx}{x\sqrt{x^2-1}} = \text{arcsec}\left|\dfrac{-2}{\sqrt{3}}\right| - \text{arcsec}\,|-2| = \dfrac{\pi}{6} - \dfrac{\pi}{3} = -\dfrac{\pi}{6}$

36. Let $x = 4u$. Then $dx = 4\,du$, and so

$$\int_0^{\sqrt{12}} \dfrac{dx}{(16-x^2)^{1/2}} = \int_0^{\sqrt{3}/2} \dfrac{4\,du}{(16-16u^2)^{1/2}} = \int_0^{\sqrt{3}/2} \dfrac{du}{(1-u^2)^{1/2}} = \sin^{-1}\left(\dfrac{\sqrt{3}}{2}\right) - \sin^{-1}(0) = \dfrac{\pi}{3}.$$

37. Suggestion: Let $u = 2x$.

38. Let $u = \tfrac{3}{2}x$. Then $du = \tfrac{3}{2}\,dx$, $3x = 2u$, and

$$\int \dfrac{1}{9x^2+4}\,dx = \int \dfrac{2/3}{4u^2+4}\,du = \tfrac{1}{6}\int \dfrac{du}{u^2+1} = \tfrac{1}{6}\tan^{-1} u + C = \tfrac{1}{6}\tan^{-1}\left(\tfrac{3}{2}x\right) + C.$$

39. Suggestion: Let $x = 5u$.

40. Let $u = \tfrac{2}{3}x$, so that $2x = 3u$ and $dx = \tfrac{3}{2}\,du$. Then

$$\int \dfrac{dx}{x(4x^2-9)^{1/2}} = \int \dfrac{(3/2)\,du}{(3/2)u(9u^2-9)^{1/2}} = \int \dfrac{du}{3u(u^2-1)^{1/2}} = \tfrac{1}{3}\sec^{-1}|u| + C = \tfrac{1}{3}\sec^{-1}\left|\tfrac{2}{3}x\right| + C.$$

41. Suggestion: Let $u = e^x$; note that $e^{2x} = u^2$.

42. Let $u = \frac{1}{5}x^3$; $x^3 = 5u$, $3x^2\,dx = 5\,du$. Then

$$\int \frac{x^2}{x^6+25}\,dx = \frac{5}{3}\int \frac{du}{25u^2+25} = \frac{1}{15}\int \frac{du}{u^2+1} = \frac{1}{15}\tan^{-1}u + C = \frac{1}{15}\tan^{-1}\left(\frac{1}{5}x^3\right)+C.$$

43. Suggestion: Let $u = \frac{1}{5}x^3$.

44. Let $u = x^{3/2}$. Then $du = \frac{3}{2}\sqrt{x}\,dx$, so $\sqrt{x}\,dx = \frac{2}{3}\,du$ and

$$\int \frac{x^{1/2}}{1+x^3}\,dx = \frac{2}{3}\int \frac{du}{1+u^2} = \frac{2}{3}\tan^{-1}u + C = \frac{2}{3}\tan^{-1}\left(x^{3/2}\right)+C.$$

45. Suggestion: Write the denominator in the form $\sqrt{x}\left[1-(\sqrt{x})^2\right]^{1/2}$. Then let $u = \sqrt{x}$.

46. Suggestion: Let $u = \sec x$.

47. Suggestion: Let $u = x^{50}$.

48. Suggestion: Let $u = x^5$.

49. Suggestion: Let $u = \ln x$.

50. $\int \frac{\arctan x}{1+x^2}\,dx = \frac{1}{2}(\arctan x)^2 + C$

51. Suggestion: Let $u = 2x - 1$. Note that $u = -1$ when $x = 0$ and that $u = 1$ when $x = 1$.

52. $\int_0^1 \frac{x^3}{1+x^4}\,dx = \left[\frac{1}{4}\ln\left(1+x^4\right)\right]_0^1 = \frac{1}{4}\ln 2.$

53. Suggestion: Let $u = \ln x$.

54. $\int_1^2 \frac{dx}{x\sqrt{x^2-1}}\,dx = \left[\sec^{-1}|x|\right]_1^2 = \sec^{-1}(2) - \sec^{-1}(1) = \pi/3.$

56. $\cos^{-1}x = C - \sin^{-1}x$ for some constant C on the interval $0 < x < 1$. In particular,

$$C = \cos^{-1}(1/2) + \sin^{-1}(1/2) = \frac{\pi}{3} + \frac{\pi}{6} = \frac{\pi}{2},$$

so $\sin^{-1}x + \cos^{-1}x = \dfrac{\pi}{2}$ for $0 < x < 1$. This formula holds for $x = 0$ and for $x = 1$ as well, and therefore it holds for all x in the closed interval $0 \leq x \leq 1$.

58. If $u = ax$, then $\sqrt{a^2-u^2} = \sqrt{a^2-a^2x^2} = a\sqrt{1-x^2}$ and $du = a\,dx$. Thus

$$\int \frac{1}{\sqrt{a^2-u^2}}\,dx = \int \frac{a}{a\sqrt{1-x^2}}\,dx = \arcsin x + C = \arcsin\left(\frac{u}{a}\right) + C.$$

The hypothesis that $a > 0$ is used in the first step, in which

$$\sqrt{a^2(1-x^2)} = |a|\sqrt{1-x^2} = a\sqrt{1-x^2}.$$

61. If $x > 1$, then

$$\frac{1}{x^2\sqrt{1-\frac{1}{x^2}}} = \frac{1}{x^2\sqrt{\frac{x^2-1}{x^2}}} = \frac{1}{x^2 \cdot \frac{\sqrt{x^2-1}}{|x|}} = \frac{1}{x\sqrt{x^2-1}} = \frac{1}{|x|\sqrt{x^2-1}}.$$

The derivation requires slightly more care in the case $x < -1$ (so that $x < 0$), but generally follows the preceding line of argument.

62. If $x > 1$, then

$$D_x \cos^{-1}\left(\frac{1}{x}\right) = \left(-\frac{1}{\sqrt{1-\frac{1}{x^2}}}\right)\cdot\left(-\frac{1}{x^2}\right) = \frac{1}{x^2\sqrt{1-\frac{1}{x^2}}}.$$

Now proceed as in the solution of Problem 61. And, as in Problem 61, slightly more care is needed in the case $x < -1$. Moreover, in each case you can conclude only that $\sec^{-1} x = \cos^{-1} \frac{1}{x} + C$ for some constant C. The problem is that C may take on one value on the interval $x > 1$ and another in the interval $x < -1$, so you need to verify—perhaps by substitution of $x = 2$ and, later, $x = -2$ in the last equation, that $C = 0$ in each case.

64. (a) We begin with the identity

$$\tan(A + B) = \frac{\tan A + \tan B}{1 - \tan A \tan B}.$$

Let $x = \tan A$ and $y = \tan B$, and suppose that $xy < 1$. We will treat only the case in which x and y are both positive; the other cases are similar. In this case, the formula above shows that $0 < A + B < \pi/2$, so it is valid to apply the inverse tangent function to each side of the above identity to obtain

$$A + B = \arctan \frac{x + y}{1 - xy},$$

and therefore

$$\arctan x + \arctan y = \arctan \frac{x + y}{1 - xy}.$$

(b i) $\arctan \dfrac{(1/2) + (1/3)}{1 - (1/6)} = \arctan(1) = \pi/4.$

(b ii) $\arctan \dfrac{(1/3) + (1/3)}{1 - (1/9)} + \arctan(1/7) = \arctan(3/4) + \arctan(1/7)$

$= \arctan \dfrac{(3/4) + (1/7)}{1 - (3/28)} = \arctan \dfrac{25}{25} = \dfrac{\pi}{4}.$

(b iii) $\arctan \dfrac{(120/119) - (1/239)}{1 + (120/119)(1/239)} = \arctan \dfrac{28561/28441}{28561/28441} = \dfrac{\pi}{4}.$

(b iv) $2 \arctan \dfrac{1}{5} = \arctan \dfrac{2/5}{1 - (1/25)} = \arctan \dfrac{10}{24} = \arctan \dfrac{5}{12};$

$4 \arctan \dfrac{1}{5} = \arctan \dfrac{10/12}{1 - (25/144)} = \arctan \dfrac{120}{119};$

the rest of Part (b iv) follows from Part (b iii)

65. See the figure to the right for the meanings of the variables. We are required to maximize the angle θ, and from the figure and the data given in the problem we may express θ as a function of the distance x of the billboard from the motorist:

$$\theta = \theta(x) = \arctan \frac{16}{x} - \arctan \frac{4}{x}.$$

After simplification,

$$\frac{d\theta}{dx} = -\frac{16}{x^2 + 256} + \frac{4}{x^2 + 16}.$$

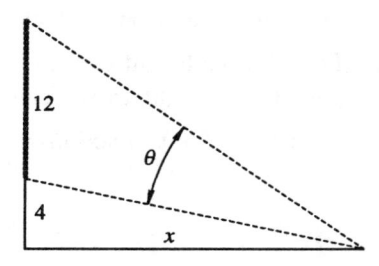

Now $\dfrac{d\theta}{dx} = 0$ certainly yields the maximum value of θ because θ is small for x near zero and for x very large. And $\dfrac{d\theta}{dx}$ vanishes when $4(x^2 + 16) = x^2 + 256$; $\quad 3x^2 = 192$: $\quad x^2 = 64$; $\quad x = +8$.

Answer: The billboard should be placed so that it will be 8 meters from the eyes of passing motorists. As some alert students have pointed out, such a billboard wouldn't be visible long enough to be effective. This illustrates that once you have used mathematics to solve a problem, you must *interpret* the results.

66. See the figure at the right. The problem is to maximize the vertical angle θ subtended at the eye level of the observer by the painting. We will assume that the observer views the painting from some fixed height L above the floor, and from a fixed distance W from the painting. If y is the distance of the bottom of the painting from the floor, then $\theta = \theta_1 + \theta_2$ where

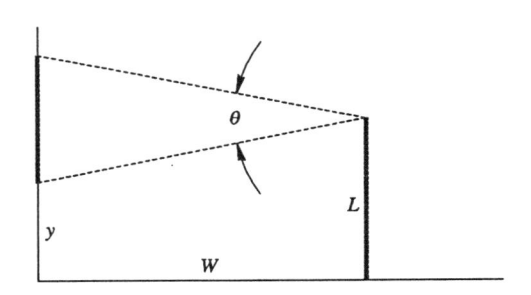

$$\theta_1 = \arctan \frac{y + h - L}{W} \quad \text{and} \quad \theta_2 = \arctan \frac{L - y}{W}.$$

With the aid of the arctangent addition formula of Problem 58, Part (a), we may write (after simplification)

$$\theta = \theta(y) = \arctan \frac{Wh}{W^2 + (y - L)(y - L + h)}.$$

Now θ is maximized when $\tan \theta$ is maximized, and this occurs when the denominator of $\theta(y)$, $f(y) = W^2 + (y - L)(Y - L + h)$, is minimized:

$$f'(y) = y - L + y - L + h = 2y - 2L + h;$$
$$f'(y) = 0 \text{ when } y = L - \frac{h}{2}.$$

This value of y clearly minimizes $f(y)$, and the center of the painting is then at height

$$y + \frac{h}{2} = L - \frac{h}{2} + \frac{h}{2} = L$$

above the floor—exactly at the height of the observer's eyes.

68. By the method of cylindrical shells,

$$V = \int_0^1 (2\pi x) \frac{dx}{1 + x^4} = \pi \left[\arctan (x^2) \right]_0^1 = \frac{\pi^2}{4}.$$

69. The value of the integral is $\tan^{-1}(a)$. As $a \to +\infty$, the value of the integral approaches the total area under the curve, which is therefore $\pi/2$.

70. Let y be the height of the elevator (measured upward from ground level) and let θ be the angle that your line of sight to the elevator makes with the horizontal ($\theta > 0$ if you are looking up, $\theta < 0$ if down). You're to maximize $\frac{d\theta}{dt}$ given $\frac{dy}{dt} = -25$.

$$\tan \theta = \frac{y - 100}{50}, \text{ so } \theta = \tan^{-1} \left(\frac{y - 100}{50} \right).$$

Therefore

$$\frac{d\theta}{dt} = \frac{d\theta}{dy} \cdot \frac{dy}{dt} = -25 \frac{1/50}{1 + ((y - 100)/50)^2} = \frac{(-25)(50)}{2500 + (y - 100)^2}.$$

To find the value of y that maximizes $f(y) = d\theta/dt$, we need only minimize the last denominator above: $y = 100$. Answer: The elevator has maximum apparent speed when it's at eye level.

71. For $x > 1$: $f(x) = \text{arcsec } x + A$:
$$1 = f(2) = \frac{\pi}{3} + 1, \text{ so } A = 1 - \frac{\pi}{3}.$$

For $x < -1$: $f(x) = -\text{arcsec } x + B$;
$$1 = f(-2) = -\frac{2\pi}{3} + B, \text{ so } B = 1 + \frac{2\pi}{3}.$$

Therefore $f(x) = \text{arcsec } x + 1 - \frac{\pi}{3}$ if $x > 1$; $f(x) = -\text{arcsec} x + 1 + \frac{2\pi}{3}$ if $x < -1$.

72. (a) If $|x| < 1$, then
$$D_x \arctan\left(\frac{x}{\sqrt{1-x^2}}\right) = \frac{1}{1 + \frac{x^2}{1-x^2}} \cdot \frac{(1-x^2)^{1/2} + x^2(1-x^2)^{-1/2}}{1-x^2} = \frac{1}{\sqrt{1-x^2}}.$$

Therefore $\arctan\left(\frac{x}{\sqrt{1-x^2}}\right) = C + \arcsin x$ for some constant C if $-1 < x < 1$. Now substitute $x = 0$ to show that $C = 0$.

74. The global maximum of $f(x)$ occurs at approximately $(1.391745, 0.803364)$.

75. The global maximum of $f(x)$ occurs at approximately $(2.689220, 0.928343)$.

76. The global maximum of $f(x)$ occurs at approximately $(8.333265, 1.334530)$.

Section 8.3

1. $\lim\limits_{x \to 1} \dfrac{x-1}{x^2-1} = \lim\limits_{x \to 1} \dfrac{1}{2x} = \tfrac{1}{2}$. Of course, l'Hôpital's rule is not necessary here, but it may be applied.

2. $\lim\limits_{x \to \infty} \dfrac{3x-4}{2x-5} = \lim\limits_{x \to \infty} \tfrac{3}{2} = \tfrac{3}{2}$. Again, there is a simple alternative to l'Hôpital's rule.

3. $\lim\limits_{x \to \infty} \dfrac{2x^2-1}{5x^2+3x} = \lim\limits_{x \to \infty} \dfrac{4x}{10x+3} = \tfrac{2}{5}$.

4. $\lim\limits_{x \to 0} \dfrac{e^{3x}-1}{x} = \lim\limits_{x \to 0} \dfrac{3e^{3x}}{1} = 3$.

5. $\lim\limits_{x \to 0} \dfrac{\sin x^2}{x} = \lim\limits_{x \to 0} 2x \cos x^2 = 0$.

6. $\lim\limits_{x \to 0} \dfrac{1 - \cos \sqrt{x}}{x} = \lim\limits_{x \to 0} \dfrac{\sin x^{1/2}}{2x^{1/2}} = \tfrac{1}{2}$ (because $\dfrac{\sin u}{u} \to 1$ as $u \to 0$).

7. $\lim\limits_{x \to 1} \dfrac{x-1}{\sin x} = \dfrac{0}{\sin 1} = 0$. Note that l'Hôpital's rule does not apply.

8. $\lim\limits_{x \to 0} \dfrac{1-\cos x}{x^3} = \lim\limits_{x \to 0} \dfrac{\sin x}{3x^2}$ if the latter limit exists.

But $\dfrac{\sin x}{3x^2} = \dfrac{1}{3} \cdot \dfrac{\sin x}{x} \cdot \dfrac{1}{x}$, which has no limit as $x \to 0$. Therefore l'Hôpital's rule does not apply.

Try again: $\lim\limits_{x \to 0} \dfrac{1-\cos x}{x^3} = \lim\limits_{x \to 0} \dfrac{\sin^2 x}{x^3(1+\cos x)} = \lim\limits_{x \to 0} \left(\dfrac{\sin x}{x}\right)^2 \cdot \left(\dfrac{1}{x(1+\cos x)}\right)$ which does not exist, because although $\lim\limits_{x \to 0} \left(\dfrac{\sin x}{x}\right)^2 = 1$, $\lim\limits_{x \to 0} \dfrac{1}{x(1+\cos x)}$ does not exist.

9. $\lim\limits_{x \to 0} \dfrac{e^x - x - 1}{x^2} = \lim\limits_{x \to 0} \dfrac{e^x - 1}{2x} = \lim\limits_{x \to 0} \dfrac{e^x}{2} = \tfrac{1}{2}$.

10. $\lim\limits_{z \to \pi/2} \dfrac{1 + \cos 2z}{1 - \sin 2z} = \dfrac{1 + \cos \pi}{1 - \sin \pi} = \dfrac{0}{1} = 0$.

12. $\lim_{x\to 0} \dfrac{x - \arctan x}{x^3} = \lim_{x\to 0} \dfrac{1 - [1/(1+x^2)]}{3x^2} = \lim_{x\to 0} \dfrac{1+x^2-1}{3x^2(1+x^2)} = \lim_{x\to 0} \dfrac{1}{3(1+x^2)} = \tfrac{1}{3}.$

13. $\lim_{x\to\infty} \dfrac{\ln x}{x^{0.1}} = \lim_{x\to\infty} \dfrac{1/x}{(0.1)x^{-0.9}} = \lim_{x\to\infty} \dfrac{10}{x^{0.1}} = 0.$

14. $\lim_{r\to\infty} \dfrac{e^r}{(r+1)^4} = \lim_{r\to\infty} \dfrac{e^r}{4(r+1)^3} = \lim_{r\to\infty} \dfrac{e^r}{12(r+1)^2} = \lim_{r\to\infty} \dfrac{e^r}{24(r+1)} = \lim_{r\to\infty} \dfrac{e^r}{24} = +\infty.$

It is also correct to say that this limit does not exist.

15. $\lim_{x\to 10} \dfrac{\ln(x-9)}{x-10} = \lim_{x\to 10} \dfrac{1}{x-9} = 1.$

16. $\lim_{t\to\infty} \dfrac{t^2+1}{t\ln t} = \lim_{t\to\infty} \dfrac{2t}{1+\ln t} = \lim_{t\to\infty} \dfrac{2}{1/t} = +\infty.$

It is also correct to say that this limit does not exist.

17. $\lim_{x\to 0} \dfrac{e^x + e^{-x} - 2}{x \sin x} = \lim_{x\to 0} \dfrac{e^x - e^{-x}}{x\cos x + \sin x} = \lim_{x\to 0} \dfrac{e^x + e^{-x}}{-x\sin x + 2\cos x} = 1.$

This limit provides an interesting insight into how well pocket calculators can be trusted to give information about limits. Let
$$f(x) = \dfrac{e^x + e^{-x} - 2}{x \sin x}.$$

Here are the results of an experiment:

x	$f(x)$ via TI-30	$f(x)$ via HP-67	$f(x)$ via TRS-80 PC-2
0.1	1.0025036	1.002503604	1.002503614
0.01	1.0000246	1.000026667	1.000024967
0.001	1.0000001	1.000000167	1.000000167
0.0001	0.99	1.000000002	0.9990000017
0.00005	0.96	1.200000000	0.9960000004
0.00004	0.9375	1.250000000	0.9937500003
-0.00001	0.	0.000000000	0.9
0.00001	0.	0.000000000	0.9
0.000001	0.	0.	0.

18. $\lim_{x\to(\pi/2)^-} \dfrac{\tan x}{\ln(\cos x)} = -\infty.$

20. $\lim_{x\to 0} \dfrac{e^x - e^{-x}}{x} = 2.$

22. $\lim_{x\to 2} \dfrac{x^3 - 8}{x^4 - 16} = \tfrac{3}{8}.$

24. $\lim_{x\to\infty} \dfrac{\sqrt{x^2+4}}{x} = 1.$

26. $\lim_{x\to\infty} \dfrac{2^x}{3^x} = 0.$

28. $\lim_{x\to\infty} \dfrac{\sqrt{x^3+x}}{\sqrt{2x^3-4}} = \dfrac{1}{\sqrt{2}}.$

30. $\lim_{x\to\infty} \dfrac{\ln(\ln x)}{x\ln x} = 0.$

32. $\lim_{x\to 0} \dfrac{\sin x - \tan x}{x^3} = -\tfrac{1}{2}.$

34. $\lim_{x\to 0} \dfrac{e^{3x} - e^{-3x}}{2x} = 3.$

36. $\lim_{x\to\pi/2} \dfrac{\sec x}{\tan x} = 1.$

38. $\lim_{x\to 1/2} \dfrac{2x - \sin \pi x}{4x^2 - 1} = \tfrac{1}{2}.$

40. $\lim_{x\to\infty} \dfrac{\arctan 2x}{\arctan 3x} = 1.$

42. $\lim_{x\to 0} \dfrac{\sqrt{1+3x} - 1}{x} = \tfrac{3}{2}.$

44. $\lim_{x\to 0} \dfrac{\sqrt{3+2x} - \sqrt{3+x}}{x} = \dfrac{1}{2\sqrt{3}}.$

46. $\lim_{x\to\pi/4} \dfrac{1 - \tan x}{4x - \pi} = -\tfrac{1}{2}.$

48. $\lim_{x\to 2} \dfrac{x^5 - 5x^2 - 12}{x^{10} - 500x - 24} = \tfrac{1}{77}.$

49. $\lim\limits_{x \to 0} \dfrac{\sin^2 x}{x} = \lim\limits_{x \to 0} (2\sin x \cos x) = 2 \cdot 0 \cdot 1 = 0$, confirmed by the graph shown below.

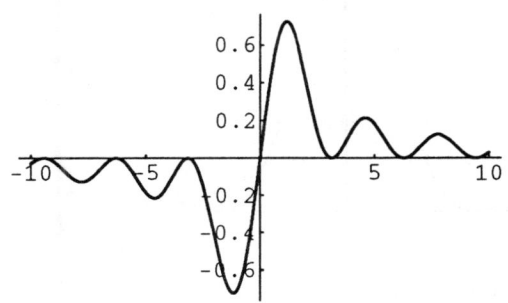

50. By l'Hôpital's rule, $\lim\limits_{x \to 0} \dfrac{\sin^2 x}{x^2} = \lim\limits_{x \to 0} \dfrac{\sin x \cos x}{x} = \lim\limits_{h \to 0} \left(\cos^2 x - \sin^2 x\right) = 1^2 - 0^2 = 1$. The graph, shown next, confirms this computation.

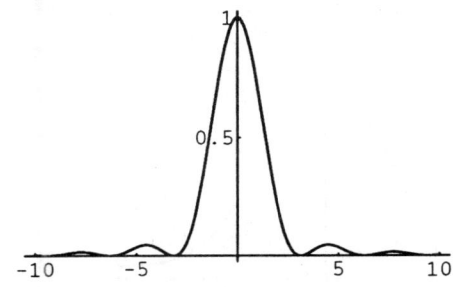

51. By l'Hôpital's rule, $\lim\limits_{x \to \pi} \dfrac{\sin x}{x - \pi} = \lim\limits_{x \to \pi} \dfrac{\cos x}{1} = \cos \pi = -1$. The graph (shown next) confirms this computation.

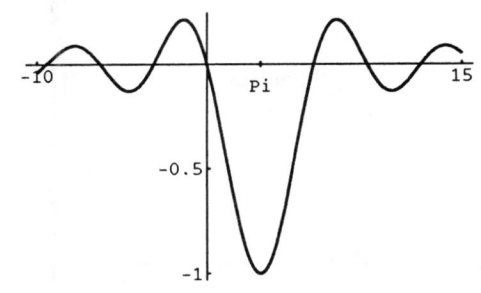

52. By l'Hôpital's rule, $\lim\limits_{x \to \pi/2} \dfrac{\cos x}{2x - \pi} = \lim\limits_{x \to \pi/2} \dfrac{-\sin x}{2} = -\dfrac{1}{2}$. The graph (shown next) confirms this computation.

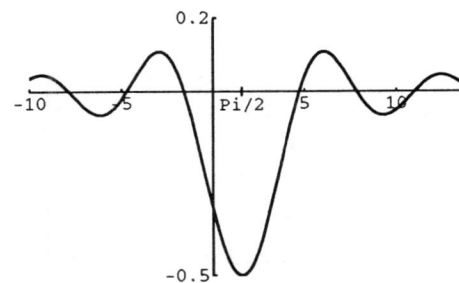

53. We use l'Hôpital's rule twice: $\lim\limits_{x \to 0} \dfrac{1 - \cos x}{x^2} = \lim\limits_{x \to 0} \dfrac{\sin x}{2x} = \lim\limits_{x \to 0} \dfrac{\cos x}{2} = \dfrac{1}{2}$. This result is confirmed by the graph, shown next.

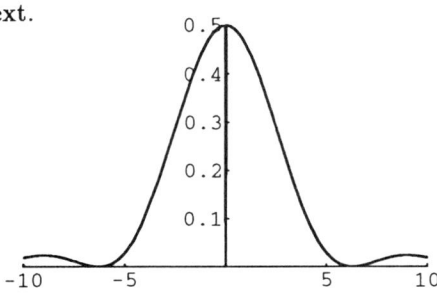

54. Again we use l'Hôpital's rule repeatedly:

$$\lim_{x \to 0} \frac{x - \sin x}{x^3} = \lim_{x \to 0} \frac{1 - \cos x}{3x^2} = \lim_{x \to 0} \frac{\sin x}{6x} = \lim_{x \to 0} \frac{\cos x}{6} = \frac{1}{6}.$$

The graph corroborates this result.

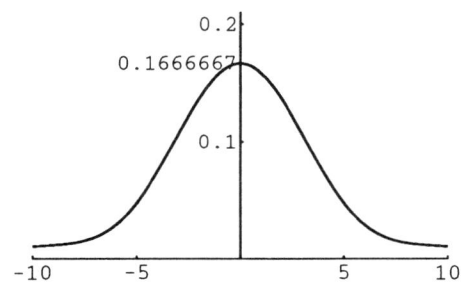

55. Here, l'Hôpital's rule yields $\lim_{x \to \infty} xe^{-x} = \lim_{x \to \infty} \frac{x}{e^x} = \lim_{x \to \infty} \frac{1}{e^x} = 0$. Well, $x = 20$ isn't particularly "close" to $+\infty$, but the graph does suggest that the preceding computation is correct:

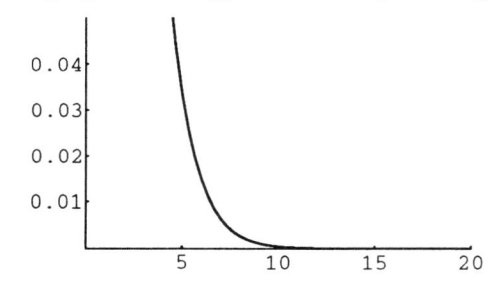

56. l'Hôpital's rule yields $\lim_{x \to \infty} \frac{\sqrt{x}}{e^x} = \lim_{x \to \infty} \frac{1}{2e^x \sqrt{x}} = 0$. The graph of $y = e^{-x}\sqrt{x}$ on $[1, 10]$ supports this result:

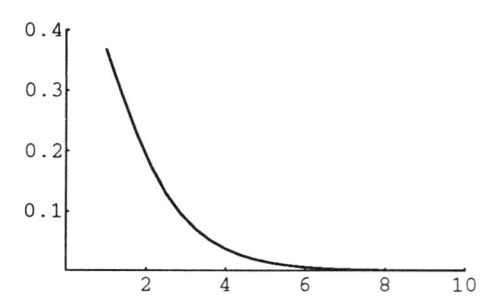

57. By l'Hôpital's rule, $\lim_{x \to \infty} \frac{x}{e^{\sqrt{x}}} = \lim_{x \to \infty} \frac{2\sqrt{x}}{e^{\sqrt{x}}} = \lim_{x \to \infty} \frac{2}{e^{\sqrt{x}}} = 0$, in accord with the graph of $y = xe^{-\sqrt{x}}$,

shown next.

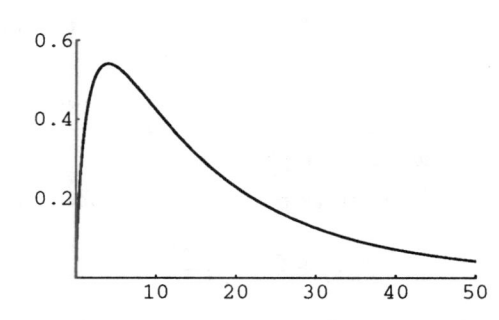

58. Two applications of l'Hôpital's rule yield $\lim\limits_{x\to\infty} \dfrac{x^2}{e^{2x}} = \lim\limits_{x\to\infty} \dfrac{2x}{2e^{2x}} = \lim\limits_{x\to\infty} \dfrac{2}{4e^{2x}} = 0$. The graph (next) confirms this result.

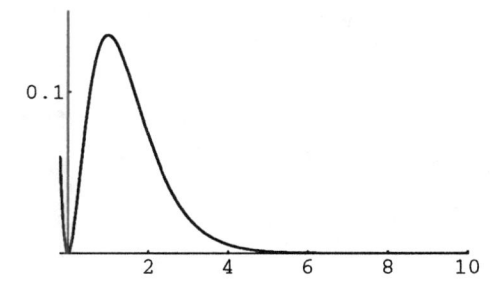

59. Here we find that $\lim\limits_{x\to\infty} \dfrac{\ln x}{x} = \lim\limits_{x\to\infty} \dfrac{1}{x} = 0$. The graph is supportive, but not as conclusive as the algebra.

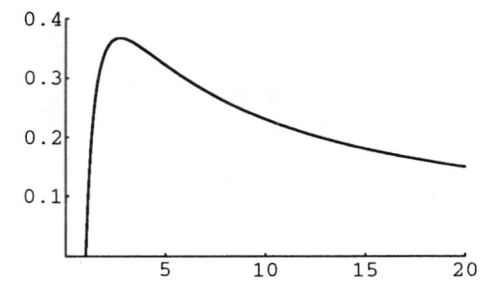

60. By l'Hôpital's rule, $\lim\limits_{x\to\infty} \dfrac{\ln x}{x^{1/2} + x^{1/3}} = \lim\limits_{x\to\infty} \dfrac{1}{\frac{1}{3}x^{1/3} + \frac{1}{2}x^{1/2}} = 0$. The graph supports this computation. For good results, plot it on the interval $1 \leq x \leq 100$.

63. Given: $f(x) = x^n e^{-x}$, where n is a positive integer and $n \geq 2$. So

$$f'(x) = \frac{(n-x)x^{n-1}}{e^x}.$$

It's clear that $f'(x) > 0$ if $0 < x < n$ and that $f'(x) < 0$ if $x > n$. Hence $f(x)$ has a local maximum at $(n, f(n)) = (n, n^n e^{-n})$. Next,

$$f''(x) = \frac{(x^2 - 2nx + n^2 - n)x^{n-2}}{e^x},$$

so $f''(x) = 0$ when $x = n \pm \sqrt{n}$. Because the expression $x^2 - 2nx + n^2 - n$ is quadratic and opens upward, with two distinct positive real zeros, there will be two inflection points on the graph of f. Finally, one application of l'Hôpital's rule yields

$$\lim\limits_{x\to\infty} \frac{x^n}{e^x} = \lim\limits_{x\to\infty} \frac{nx^{n-1}}{e^x}.$$

Section 8.3 Indeterminate Forms and l'Hôpital's Rule

It should be clear that repeated applications of l'Hôpital's rule will eventually yield

$$\lim_{x \to \infty} \frac{n!}{e^x} = 0.$$

Therefore the (positive) x-axis is a horizontal asymptote.

64. Given: $f(x) = x^{-k} \ln x$, where k is an arbitrary positive real number. Now

$$f'(x) = \frac{1 - k \ln x}{x^{k+1}}.$$

The sign of $f'(x)$ is that of $1 - k \ln x$, which is positive if $0 < x < e^{1/k}$ but negative if $x > e^{1/k}$. Hence the graph of f will have a single local maximum where $x = e^{1/k}$. Next,

$$f''(x) = \frac{k^2 \ln x + k \ln x - 2k - 1}{x^{k+2}},$$

and $f''(x) = 0$ when $x = \exp\left(\frac{2k+1}{k^2+k}\right)$, so there is at most one inflection point on the graph of f. Moreover, if x is near zero, then $f''(x) < 0$, whereas $f''(x) > 0$ for large positive values of x. Hence there is exactly one inflection point. Finally, $\lim_{x \to \infty} \frac{\ln x}{x^k} = \lim_{x \to \infty} \frac{1}{kx^k} = 0$, and hence the (positive) x-axis is a horizontal asymptote.

65. $\lim_{x \to 0} \frac{E(x)}{x} = \lim_{x \to 0} \frac{E'(x)}{1} = \lim_{x \to 0} \exp(-x^2) = 1.$

66. $\lim_{x \to 0} \frac{S(x)}{x^3} = \lim_{x \to 0} \frac{S'(x)}{3x^2} = \lim_{x \to 0} \frac{\sin^2 x}{3x^2} = \frac{1}{3}.$

67. By l'Hôpital's rule,

$$\lim_{h \to 0} \frac{f(x+h) - f(x-h)}{2h} = \lim_{h \to 0} \frac{f'(x+h) + f'(x-h)}{2} = \frac{2f'(x)}{2} = f'(x).$$

The continuity of f' is used to establish that $f'(x+h)$ and $f'(x-h)$ both approach $f'(x)$ as $h \to 0$. Note that the primes denote derivatives with respect to h.

68. By l'Hôpital's rule,

$$\lim_{h \to 0} \frac{f(x+h) - 2f(x) + f(x-h)}{h^2} = \lim_{h \to 0} \frac{f'(x+h) - f'(x-h)}{2h}.$$

Now the continuity of f'' and the result of Problem 67 imply that the last expression has limit $f''(x)$ as $h \to 0$. Note that primes denote derivatives with respect to h. Question: What is the purpose of the term $-2f(x)$ in the first numerator?

69. One application of l'Hôpital's rule yields

$$\lim_{x \to 1} \frac{x^{-2/3} + 3(2x^3 - 1)(2x - x^4)^{-1/2}}{4x^{1/3}} = \lim_{x \to 1} \frac{6x^{11/3} - 3x^{2/3} + \sqrt{2x - x^4}}{4x\sqrt{2x - x^4}}.$$

The last fraction is no longer an indeterminate form, and clearly approaches 1 as $x \to 1$.

Section 8.4

1. $\lim_{x \to 0} x \cot x = \lim_{x \to 0} \frac{x \cos x}{\sin x} = (1)(\cos 0) = 1.$

2. $\lim_{x \to 0} \left(\frac{1}{x} - \cot x\right) = 0.$

3. $\lim_{x \to 0} \frac{1}{x} \ln\left(\frac{7x+8}{4x+8}\right) = \frac{3}{8}$.

4. Let $u = \sin x$. Then $\lim_{x \to 0^+} (\sin x)(\ln \sin x) = \lim_{u \to 0^+} u \ln u = \lim_{u \to 0^+} \frac{\ln u}{1/u}$
$$= \lim_{u \to 0^+} \frac{1/u}{-(1/u^2)} = \lim_{u \to 0^+} (-u) = 0.$$

6. $\lim_{x \to \infty} e^{-x} \ln x = 0$.

7. Let $u = 1/x$. Then $\lim_{x \to \infty} x\left(e^{1/x} - 1\right) = \lim_{u \to 0^+} \frac{e^u - 1}{u} = \lim_{u \to 0^+} \frac{e^u}{1} = 1$.

8. $\lim_{x \to 2} \left(\frac{1}{x-2} - \frac{1}{\ln(x-1)}\right) = -\frac{1}{2}$.

9. See the solution to Problem 4.

10. Replace $\cos 3x$ with $\cos^3 x - 3\sin^2 x \cos x$; replace $\tan x$ with $(\sin x)/(\cos x)$.
Then $\lim_{x \to \pi/2} (\tan x)(\cos 3x) = \lim_{x \to \pi/2} (\sin x)\left(\cos^2 x - 3\sin^2 x\right) = -3$.

12. $\lim_{x \to \infty} e^{-x^2}(x - \sin x) = \lim_{x \to \infty} \frac{x - \sin x}{e^{(x^2)}} = \lim_{x \to \infty} \frac{1 - \cos x}{2xe^{(x^2)}} = 0$ because $|\cos x| \le 1$ for all x.

14. $\lim_{x \to 0} \left(\frac{1}{x} - \frac{1}{e^x - 1}\right) = \lim_{x \to 0} \frac{e^x - 1 - x}{x(e^x - 1)} = \lim_{x \to 0} \frac{e^x - 1}{xe^x + e^x - 1} = \lim_{x \to 0} \frac{e^x}{xe^x + e^x + e^x} = \frac{1}{2}$.

15. $\lim_{x \to 1^+} \left(\frac{x}{x^2 + x - 2} - \frac{1}{x-1}\right) = \lim_{x \to 1^+} -\frac{2}{(x-1)(x+1)}$.

16. $\lim_{x \to \infty} (\sqrt{x+1} - \sqrt{x}) = \lim_{x \to \infty} \frac{x+1-x}{\sqrt{x+1}+\sqrt{x}} = \lim_{x \to \infty} \frac{1}{\sqrt{x+1}+\sqrt{x}} = 0$.

18. $\lim_{x \to \infty} \left(\sqrt{x^2+x} - \sqrt{x^2-x}\right) = \lim_{x \to \infty} \frac{(x^2+x)-(x^2-x)}{\sqrt{x^2+x}+\sqrt{x^2-x}} = \lim_{x \to \infty} \frac{2x}{\sqrt{x^2+x}+\sqrt{x^2-x}}$
$$= \lim_{x \to \infty} \frac{2}{\sqrt{1+(1/x)}+\sqrt{1-(1/x)}} = 1.$$

20. Let $y = x^x$. By the result of Problem 4, $\ln y \to 0$ as $x \to 0^+$. Therefore $\lim_{x \to 0^+} x^x = \lim_{x \to 0^+} y = e^0 = 1$.

22. Let $y = \left(x + \frac{1}{x}\right)^x$. Then
$$\ln y = x \ln\left(1 + \frac{1}{x}\right) = x \ln\left(\frac{x+1}{x}\right) = x[\ln(x+1) - \ln x] = \frac{\ln(x+1) - \ln x}{1/x}.$$

Now apply l'Hôpital's rule to find that
$$\lim_{x \to \infty} \ln y = \lim_{x \to \infty} \frac{\ln(x+1) - \ln x}{1/x} = \lim_{x \to \infty} \frac{x - (x+1)}{-(x+1)/x} = \lim_{x \to \infty} \frac{x}{x+1} = 1.$$

Therefore $y \to e$ as $x \to +\infty$.

24. Use the technique of the solution of Problem 22; the limit is 1.

25. The limit of the natural logarithm of the expression in question is $-1/6$. A calculator estimate of this limit is particularly misleading.

26. $\lim_{x \to 0^+} (1 + 2x)^{1/(3x)} = e^{2/3}$.

28. $\lim_{x \to 0^+} (\sin x)^{\sec x} = 0$.

30. $\lim_{x \to \pi/2} (\tan x - \sec x) = 0$.

32. $\lim_{x \to 1^+} (x-1)^{\ln x} = 1$.

34. Let $Q = x^5 - 3x^4 + 17$. Then $Q^{1/5} - x = \dfrac{Q - x^5}{Q^{4/5} + Q^{3/5}x + Q^{2/5}x^2 + Q^{1/5}x^3 + x^4}$. The numerator is just $-3x^4 + 17$. Now *carefully* divide each term in numerator and denominator by x^4; put this divisor within each radical in the denominator. Then let x increase without bound to see that the limit is $-3/5$.

35. (b) $f(x) \to 0$ as $x \to 0^+$ and $f(x) \to 1$ as $x \to +\infty$.

(c) The highest point on the graph of f is $(e, e^{1/e})$.

36. (b) $f(x) \to 0$ as $x \to 0^+$ and $f(x) \to 1$ as $x \to +\infty$.

(c) The highest point on the graph of f is $\left(\sqrt{e}, \exp(1/(2e))\right)$.

37. (b) $f(x) \to 0$ as $x \to 0^+$ and $f(x) \to 1$ as $x \to +\infty$.

(c) The highest point on the graph of f is $(e, e^{2/e})$.

38. (b) Given: $f(x) = x^{-x}$. We begin by finding the limit of x^x as $x \to 0^+$. Note that $\ln x^x = x \ln x$. Hence $\lim_{x \to 0^+} x \ln x = \lim_{x \to 0^+} \dfrac{\ln x}{1/x} = \lim_{x \to 0^+} \dfrac{1/x}{-1/x^2} = \lim_{x \to 0^+} (-x) = 0$, and therefore $x^x \to 1$ as $x \to 0^+$. Clearly $x^x \to +\infty$ as $x \to +\infty$. Therefore $\lim_{x \to 0^+} f(x) = 1$ and $\lim_{x \to \infty} f(x) = 0$.

(c) The highest point on the graph of f is $(e^{-1}, e^{1/e})$. The easiest way to find this is to maximize $g(x) = \ln(f(x)) = -x \ln x$. (The natural logarithm is an increasing function, so the positive function $f(x)$ is maximized by that value of x that maximizes $\ln f(x)$.)

39. (b) Let $g(x) = \ln f(x)$. Then $\lim_{x \to 0^+} g(x) = \lim_{x \to 0^+} \dfrac{\ln(1+x^2)}{x} = \lim_{x \to 0^+} \dfrac{2x}{1+x^2} = 0$. Therefore $f(x) \to 1$ as $x \to 0^+$. Similarly, $g(x) \to 0$ as $x \to +\infty$, so $f(x) \to 1$ as $x \to +\infty$.

(c) We used Newton's method to solve $g'(x) = 0$, and thereby found the highest point on the graph of f to be approximately $(1.980291, 2.236120)$.

40. (b) Let $g(x) = \ln f(x) = \dfrac{\ln(1 + 1/x^2)}{1/x}$. Then $\lim_{x \to 0^+} g(x) = \lim_{x \to 0^+} \dfrac{2x}{1+x^2} = 0$. Similarly, $g(x) \to 0$ as $x \to +\infty$. Therefore $f(x) \to 1$ as $x \to 0^+$ and also as $x \to +\infty$.

(c) We used Newton's method to determine that the highest point on the graph of f is approximately $(0.50498, 2.23612)$.

41. (b) Given: $f(x) = (x + \sin x)^{1/x}$, let $g(x) = \ln f(x) = \dfrac{\ln(x + \sin x)}{x}$. Then, by l'Hôpital's rule, $\lim_{x \to \infty} g(x) = \lim_{x \to \infty} \dfrac{1 + \cos x}{x + \sin x} = 0$, so $f(x) \to 1$ as $x \to +\infty$. But $f(x)$ is not indeterminate as $x \to 0^+$. In fact, it's clear that $f(x) \to 0$ as $x \to 0^+$.

(c) We used Newton's method to discover that the highest point on the graph of f is approximately $(1.20960, 1.87936)$.

42. Let $g(x) = \ln f(x) = (\cos x - 1)x^2$. Then $\lim_{x \to 0^+} g(x) = \lim_{x \to 0^+} \dfrac{-\sin x}{2x} = \lim_{x \to 0^+} \dfrac{-\cos x}{2} = -\tfrac{1}{2}$. Therefore $f(x) \to e^{-1/2}$ as $x \to 0^+$. Moreover, $f(x)$ is not indeterminate as $x \to +\infty$; it is clear that $e^{1/x^2} \to 1$ as $x \to +\infty$; meanwhile, the exponent $\cos x - 1$ takes on various values between 0 and -2, so $f(x) \to 1$ as $x \to +\infty$.

49. Graphically it is clear that $f(x) \to +\infty$ as $x \to 0^+$ and that $f(x) \to 1$ as $x \to +\infty$. The graph also shows a corner point at $(1, 0)$ much like the one on the graph of $y = |x|$, so there's a global minimum at $(1, 0)$. We were not able to accurately determine the inflection points graphically, so we applied Newton's method to $f''(x)$ to find their abscissas to be (approximately) 1.116390596 and 8.928007697. By "zooming" we found a local maximum near $(5.83120, 1.10215)$.

50. $f(x) \to 1$ as $x \to 0^+$, $f(x) \to 0$ as $x \to 1$, and $f(x) \to 1$ as $x \to +\infty$. There is a local maximum near $(0.06599, 1.44467)$. Can you *analytically* (using the derivative) find the exact coordinates of this extremum? (It's possible but it isn't easy.)

51. $f(x) \to +\infty$ as $x \to 0^+$, $f(x) \to 1$ as $x \to 1$ (there is a corner point at $(1,1)$ shaped like the graph of $y = -|x|$, so f is not differentiable there), and $f(x) \to +\infty$ as $x \to +\infty$.

Section 8.5

1. $f'(x) = 3\sinh(3x - 2)$

2. $f'(x) = \frac{1}{2}x^{-1/2}\cosh x^{1/2}$

4. $f'(x) = -2e^{2x}\operatorname{sech} e^{2x}\tanh e^{2x}$

6. $f'(x) = \dfrac{3\cosh 3x}{\sinh 3x} = 3\coth 3x$

8. $f'(x) = \dfrac{1}{x}\sinh(\ln x)$

10. $f'(x) = \dfrac{\operatorname{sech}^2 x}{1 + \tanh^2 x}$

12. $f'(x) = 4\sinh^3 x \cosh x$

14. $f'(x) \equiv 0$ because $\cosh^2 x - \sinh^2 x = 1$ for all x.

16. $\displaystyle\int \cosh^2 3u\, du = \int \tfrac{1}{2}(1 + \cosh 6u)\, du = \tfrac{1}{2}(u + \tfrac{1}{6}\sinh 6u) + C = \tfrac{1}{2}u + \tfrac{1}{6}\sinh 3u \cosh 3u + C$

17. $\displaystyle\int \tanh^2 3x\, dx = \int (1 - \operatorname{sech}^2 dx)\, dx = x - \tfrac{1}{3}\tanh 3x + C$

18. Let $u = \sqrt{x}$. Then $du = \tfrac{1}{2}x^{-1/2}\, dx$, so that $x^{-1/2}\, dx = 2\, du$. Therefore
$$\int \dfrac{\operatorname{sech}\sqrt{x}\tanh\sqrt{x}}{\sqrt{x}}\, dx = \int 2\operatorname{sech} u\tanh u\, du = -2\operatorname{sech} u + C = -2\operatorname{sech}\sqrt{x} + C.$$

19. If necessary, let $u = 2x$.

20. $\displaystyle\int \tanh 3x\, dx = \int \dfrac{\sinh 3x}{\cosh 3x}\, dx = \tfrac{1}{3}\ln(\cosh 3x) + C$

21. If necessary, let $u = \cosh x$.

22. $\displaystyle\int \sinh^4 x\, dx = \int (\sinh^2 x)^2\, dx = \int \tfrac{1}{4}(\cosh 2x - 1)^2\, dx = \tfrac{1}{4}\int (\cosh^2 2x - 2\cosh 2x + 1)\, dx$
$= \tfrac{1}{4}\int \left(\tfrac{1}{2}(\cosh 4x + 1) - 2\cosh 2x + 1\right) dx = \tfrac{1}{32}\sinh 4x - \tfrac{1}{4}\sinh 2x + \tfrac{3}{8}x + C$

24. $\displaystyle\int \operatorname{sech} x\, dx = \int \dfrac{2}{e^x + e^{-x}}\, dx = \int \dfrac{2e^x}{e^{2x} + 1}\, dx = 2\arctan e^x + C$

26. Let $u = \ln x$; $du = \dfrac{1}{x}\, dx$, and so
$$\int \dfrac{\sinh(\ln x)}{x}\, dx = \int \sinh u\, du = \cosh u + C = \cosh(\ln x) + C$$

27. The integrand is merely $\tfrac{1}{4}\operatorname{sech}^2 x$.

28. $\displaystyle\int \dfrac{e^x + e^{-x}}{e^x - e^{-x}}\, dx = \ln|e^x - e^{-x}| + C_1 = -\ln 2 + \ln|e^x - e^{-x}| + C = \ln|\sinh x| + C$

30. $f'(x) = \dfrac{2x}{\left((x^2+1)^2 - 1\right)^{1/2}} = \dfrac{2x}{(x^4 + 2x^2)^{1/2}} = \dfrac{2x}{|x|(x^2+2)^{1/2}}$

32. $f'(x) = \left(\dfrac{1}{1-(x^2+1)}\right) \cdot \left(\dfrac{x}{(x^2+1)^{1/2}}\right) = -\dfrac{1}{x(x^2+1)^{1/2}}$

34. $f'(x) = -\dfrac{e^x}{e^x(1+e^{2x})^{1/2}} = -\dfrac{1}{(1+e^{2x})^{1/2}}$

36. $f'(x) = \dfrac{1}{x(1+(\ln x)^2)^{1/2}}$

38. $f'(x) = -\left(\tanh^{-1} 3x\right)^{-2} D_x \tanh^{-1} 3x = -\left(\dfrac{1}{(\tanh^{-1} 3x)^2}\right) \cdot \left(\dfrac{3}{1-9x^2}\right)$

39. Let $x = 3u$; then $dx = 3\,du$.

40. Let $u = \tfrac{2}{3}y$. Then $y = \tfrac{3}{2}u$, $dy = \tfrac{3}{2}\,du$, and $4y^2 - 9 = 9(u^2 - 1)$. So
$$\int \dfrac{dy}{(4y^2-9)^{1/2}} = \int \dfrac{(3/2)\,du}{2(u^2-1)^{1/2}} = \tfrac{1}{2}\int \dfrac{du}{(u^2-1)^{1/2}} = \tfrac{1}{2}\cosh^{-1} u + C = \tfrac{1}{2}\cosh^{-1}\left(\dfrac{2y}{3}\right) + C.$$

41. Let $x = 2u$; then $dx = 2\,du$, and so
$$\int_{1/2}^{1} \dfrac{dx}{4-x^2} = \int_{1/4}^{1/2} \dfrac{2}{4(1-u^2)}\,du = \left[\tfrac{1}{4}\ln\left(\dfrac{1+u}{1-u}\right)\right]_{1/4}^{1/2} = \tfrac{1}{4}\left(\ln 3 - \ln \tfrac{5}{3}\right) = \tfrac{1}{4}\ln \tfrac{9}{5} \approx 0.14695.$$

42. Let $x = 2u$; then $dx = 2\,du$, $u = \dfrac{x}{2}$, and
$$\int_{5}^{10} \dfrac{dx}{4-x^2} = \int_{5/2}^{5} \dfrac{2\,du}{4(1-u^2)} = \tfrac{1}{2}\left[\coth^{-1} u\right]_{5/2}^{5} = \tfrac{1}{2}\left[\tfrac{1}{2}\ln\left(\dfrac{u+1}{u-1}\right)\right]_{5/2}^{5}$$
$$= \tfrac{1}{4}\left(\ln \tfrac{6}{4} - \ln \tfrac{7}{3}\right) = \tfrac{1}{4}\ln \tfrac{9}{14} \approx -0.110458.$$

43. Let $u = \tfrac{3}{2}x$.

44. Let $x = 5u$; then $dx = 5\,du$, and so
$$\int \dfrac{dx}{x(x^2+25)^{1/2}} = \int \dfrac{5\,du}{5u(25u^2+25)^{1/2}} = \tfrac{1}{5}\int \dfrac{du}{u(u^2+1)^{1/2}}$$
$$= -\tfrac{1}{5}\operatorname{csch}^{-1}|u| + C = -\tfrac{1}{5}\operatorname{csch}^{-1}\left|\dfrac{x}{5}\right| + C.$$

45. Let $u = e^x$.

46. Let $u = x^2$. Then $du = 2x\,dx$, $x\,dx = \tfrac{1}{2}\,du$, and thus
$$\int \dfrac{x\,dx}{(x^4-1)^{1/2}} = \tfrac{1}{2}\int \dfrac{du}{(u^2-1)^{1/2}} = \tfrac{1}{2}\cosh^{-1} u + C = \tfrac{1}{2}\cosh^{-1}(x^2) + C.$$

47. $\displaystyle\int \dfrac{dx}{(1-e^{2x})^{1/2}} = \int \dfrac{e^x\,dx}{e^x(1-e^{2x})^{1/2}} = -\operatorname{sech}^{-1}(e^x) + C$

48. Let $u = \sin x$; then $du = \cos x\,dx$, and so
$$\int \dfrac{\cos x}{(1+\sin^2 x)^{1/2}}\,dx = \int \dfrac{1}{(1+u^2)^{1/2}}\,du = \sinh^{-1} u + C = \sinh^{-1}(\sin x) + C.$$

49. Proof:
$$\sinh x \cosh y + \cosh x \sinh y = \tfrac{1}{4}(e^x - e^{-x})(e^y + e^{-y}) + \tfrac{1}{4}(e^x + e^{-x})(e^y - e^{-y})$$
$$= \tfrac{1}{4}(e^x e^y - e^{-x}e^y + e^x e^{-y} - e^{-x}e^{-y} + e^x e^y + e^{-x}e^y - e^x e^{-y} - e^{-x}e^{-y})$$
$$= \tfrac{1}{4}(2e^x e^y - 2e^{-x}e^{-y})$$
$$= \sinh(x+y).$$

50. Divide each term in the identity $\cosh^2 x - \sinh^2 x = 1$ by $\cosh^2 x$ (which is never zero) to obtain the identity in (5). The derivation of the identity in (6) is obtained similarly.

51. By (8), $\cosh(x+y) = \cosh x \cosh y + \sinh x \sinh y$. Therefore
$$\cosh 2x = \cosh^2 x + \sinh^2 x, \text{ and so}$$
$$\cosh 2x = \cosh^2 x + \cosh^2 x - 1 = 2\cosh^2 x - 1.$$
Consequently $\cosh^2 x = \frac{1}{2}(1 + \cosh 2x)$.

52. If $x(t) = A\cosh kt + B\sinh kt$, then
$$x'(t) = kA\sinh kt + kB\cosh kt \text{ and}$$
$$x''(t) = k^2 A \cosh kt + k^2 B \sinh kt = k^2 x(t).$$

53. If $y = \cosh x$, then $\dfrac{dy}{dx} = \sinh x$, so that
$$1 + \left(\frac{dy}{dx}\right)^2 = 1 + \sinh^2 x = \cosh^2 x.$$

So the arc length in question is
$$L = \int_0^a (\cosh^2 x)^{1/2}\, dx = \sinh a.$$

54. By the "slab" method, we find that
$$V = \int_0^\pi \pi \sinh^2 x\, dx = \frac{\pi}{2}\int_0^\pi (\cosh 2x - 1)\, dx = \frac{\pi}{2}\left[\frac{1}{2}\sinh 2x - x\right]_0^\pi$$
$$= \frac{\pi}{2}\left(\frac{1}{2}\sinh 2\pi - \pi\right) = \frac{\pi}{8}(e^{2\pi} - e^{-2\pi}) - \frac{1}{2}\pi^2 \approx 205.3515.$$

56. (a) $\lim\limits_{x\to 0} \dfrac{\sinh x}{x} = \lim\limits_{x\to 0} \dfrac{\cosh x}{1} = 1.$

    (b) $\lim\limits_{x\to\infty} \tanh x = \lim\limits_{x\to\infty} \dfrac{e^x - e^{-x}}{e^x + e^{-x}} = \lim\limits_{x\to\infty} \dfrac{1 - e^{-2x}}{1 + e^{-2x}} = 1.$

    (c) $\lim\limits_{x\to\infty} \dfrac{\cosh x}{e^x} = \lim\limits_{x\to\infty} \dfrac{e^x + e^{-x}}{2e^x} = \lim\limits_{x\to\infty} \dfrac{1 + e^{-2x}}{2} = \frac{1}{2}.$

57. $z = \sinh^{-1} 1$: $\sinh z = 1$;
$$e^z - e^{-z} = 2;$$
$$e^{2z} - 2e^z - 1 = 0:$$
$$e^z = \frac{2 \pm \sqrt{4+4}}{2} = 1 \pm \sqrt{2}$$
$$z = \ln\left(1 + \sqrt{2}\right) \approx 0.8813736$$

62. $x = \sinh y = \frac{1}{2}(e^y - e^{-y})$;
$$2x = e^y - e^{-y};$$
$$(e^y)^2 - 2xe^y - 1 = 0;$$
$$e^y = \frac{1}{2}\left(2x \pm (4x^2 + 4)^{1/2}\right) = x \pm (x^2 + 1)^{1/2}.$$

Because $e^y > 0$ for all y, the positive sign is the only correct choice. Therefore $y = \sinh^{-1} x = \ln\left|x + (x^2+1)^{1/2}\right|$ for all x.

64. (a) We are to prove that
$$\coth^{-1} x = \tfrac{1}{2} \ln\left(\frac{x+1}{x-1}\right) \text{ if } |x| > 1.$$

Section 8.5 Hyperbolic Functions and Inverse Hyperbolic Functions

By one of the formulas in the text, the left-hand side above has derivative
$$\frac{1}{1-x^2}$$
The derivative of the right-hand side is
$$\left(\tfrac{1}{2}\right)\left(\frac{x-1}{x+1}\right)\left(\frac{x-1-x-1}{(x-1)^2}\right) = -\frac{1}{x^2-1} = \frac{1}{1-x^2}.$$
Therefore
$$\coth^{-1} x = \frac{1}{2}\ln\frac{x+1}{x-1} + C \text{ for } |x| > 1.$$

(b) If $u = \coth^{-1}(2)$, then $\coth u = 2$. So
$$2 = \frac{e^u + e^{-u}}{e^u - e^{-u}};$$
$$2e^u - 2e^{-u} = e^u + e^{-u};$$
$$e^u = 3e^{-u}; \quad e^{2u} = 3; \quad 2u = \ln 3.$$

Therefore $u = \tfrac{1}{2}\ln 3$. Now substitute $x = 2$ in the result of Part (a):
$$\tfrac{1}{2}\ln 3 = \tfrac{1}{2}\ln \tfrac{3}{1} + C.$$
So $C = 0$ here as well. This establishes the desired result.

66. The curves cross near $x = -0.725264$ and $x = 2.085186$. The area between them is approximately 2.78045.

67. Note that $e^{-2x}\tanh x = \dfrac{1 - e^{-2x}}{1 + e^{2x}}$. Therefore $f(x) \to 0$ as $x \to +\infty$. We used Newton's method to find that the highest point on the graph of f is near $(0.440687, 0.171573)$.

68. Use l'Hôpital's rule to show that $f(x) \to 0$ as $x \to +\infty$; this is relatively easy. The high point on the graph of f is near $(0.841843, 0.329655)$.

70. (a) We let $f(k) = 30 + \dfrac{1}{k}(-1 + \cosh(100k)) - 50$ and solve the equation $f(k) = 0$ by Newton's method to discover that $k \approx 0.00394843545331550515$.

(b) We then let $y(x) = 30 + \dfrac{1}{k}(-1 + \cosh(kx))$, so that $\sqrt{1 + [(y'(x))^2} = \cosh(kx)$, and therefore the approximate length of the high-voltage line is
$$2\int_0^{100} \cosh kx\, dx \approx 205.237 \quad \text{(ft)}.$$

Chapter 8 Miscellaneous

2. $f'(x) = \dfrac{7}{1 + 49x^2}$

4. $g'(t) = \dfrac{e^t}{1 + e^{2t}}$

6. $f'(x) = \dfrac{2}{\sqrt{1 + 4x^2}}$

8. $h'(u) = -\dfrac{1}{u^2 - 1}$

10. $f'(x) = -\dfrac{1}{x^2+1}$

12. $f'(x) = \sec^{-1} x^2 + x\left(\dfrac{2x}{x^2(x^4-1)^{1/2}}\right) = \sec^{-1} x^2 + \dfrac{2}{(x^4-1)^{1/2}}$

14. $f'(x) = \left(\dfrac{1}{(1-(1-x^2))^{1/2}}\right)\cdot\left(\dfrac{-x}{(1-x^2)^{1/2}}\right) = -\dfrac{x}{|x|(1-x^2)^{1/2}}$

16. $f'(x) = \dfrac{\sinh x}{\cosh x} = \tanh x$

18. $f'(x) = \left(\dfrac{1}{(x^2-1+1)^{1/2}}\right)\cdot\left(\dfrac{x}{(x^2-1)^{1/2}}\right) = \dfrac{x}{|x|(x^2-1)^{1/2}}$

20. $f'(x) = \dfrac{1}{1-(1-x^2)^2}(-2x) = \dfrac{2}{x^3 - 2x}$

22. $\displaystyle\int \dfrac{dx}{1+4x^2} = \tfrac{1}{2}\arctan 2x + C$

24. $\displaystyle\int \dfrac{dx}{4+x^2} = \tfrac{1}{2}\arctan\left(\dfrac{x}{2}\right) + C$

26. Let $u = x^2$; $\displaystyle\int \dfrac{x}{1+x^4}\,dx = \tfrac{1}{2}\arctan(x^2) + C$.

27. Let $u = \tfrac{2}{3}x$; $x = \tfrac{3}{2}u$, $dx = \tfrac{3}{2}du$, and $9 - 4x^2 = 9 - 9u^2$, so that

$$\int \dfrac{dx}{\sqrt{9-4x^2}} = \tfrac{3}{2}\int \dfrac{du}{3\sqrt{1-u^2}} = \tfrac{1}{2}\arcsin\left(\dfrac{2x}{3}\right) + C.$$

28. Let $u = \tfrac{2}{3}x$; $\displaystyle\int \dfrac{1}{9+4x^2}\,dx = \tfrac{3}{2}\int \dfrac{1}{9+9u^2}\,du = \tfrac{1}{6}\arctan u + C = \tfrac{1}{6}\arctan\left(\dfrac{2x}{3}\right) + C$.

29. Let $u = x^3$.

30. Let $u = \sin x$; $du = \cos x\,dx$. Then

$$\int \dfrac{\cos x}{1+\sin^2 x}\,dx = \int \dfrac{du}{1+u^2} = \arctan(\sin x) + C.$$

31. Let $u = 2x$; $x = \tfrac{1}{2}u$ and $dx = \tfrac{1}{2}du$. Then

$$\int \dfrac{1}{x\sqrt{4x^2-1}}\,dx = \int \dfrac{du}{u\sqrt{u^2-1}} = \sec^{-1}|2x| + C.$$

32. Let $u = x^2$; $x = \sqrt{u}$ and $dx = \dfrac{1}{2\sqrt{u}}du$. Then

$$\int \dfrac{dx}{x\sqrt{x^4-1}} = \int \dfrac{du}{2\sqrt{u}\sqrt{u}\sqrt{u^2-1}} = \tfrac{1}{2}\int \dfrac{du}{u\sqrt{u^2-1}} = \tfrac{1}{2}\sec^{-1}(x^2) + C.$$

Note: The *method* is valid for $x > 1$ (we assumed that $x > 0$ in writing $x = \sqrt{u}$); the *answer* can be verified for all $|x| > 1$ by differentiation.

33. Note that $|e^x| = e^x$. Therefore $\displaystyle\int \dfrac{dx}{(e^{2x}-1)^{1/2}} = \int \dfrac{e^x\,dx}{e^x(e^{2x}-1)^{1/2}} = \sec^{-1}(e^x) + C.$

34. $\displaystyle\int x^2 \cosh x^3\,dx = \tfrac{1}{3}\sinh x^3 + C.$

36. $\displaystyle\int \operatorname{sech}^2(3x-2)\,dx = \tfrac{1}{3}\tanh(3x-2) + C$

38. Let $u = 2x$; $\displaystyle\int \dfrac{dx}{\sqrt{4x^2-1}} = \tfrac{1}{2}\int \dfrac{du}{(u^2-1)^{1/2}} = \tfrac{1}{2}\cosh^{-1}(2x) + C$ if $x \geq \tfrac{1}{2}$.

$$\int \frac{dx}{\sqrt{4x^2-1}} = -\tfrac{1}{2}\cosh^{-1}(-2x)+C \text{ if } x\le -\tfrac{1}{2}.$$

39. Let $x=\tfrac{3}{2}u$; then $dx=\tfrac{3}{2}du$, $u=\tfrac{2}{3}x$, and $\displaystyle\int \frac{dx}{\sqrt{4x^2+9}} = \tfrac{3}{2}\int \frac{du}{3\sqrt{x^2+1}} = \tfrac{1}{2}\sinh^{-1}\left(\frac{2x}{3}\right)+C.$

40. Let $u=x^2$; then $du=2x\,dx$, and the integral becomes $\tfrac{1}{2}\displaystyle\int \frac{du}{\sqrt{u^2+1}} = \tfrac{1}{2}\sinh^{-1}(x^2)+C.$

41. $\displaystyle\lim_{x\to 2}\frac{x-2}{x^2-4} = \lim_{x\to 2}\frac{1}{2x} = \tfrac{1}{4}.$

42. $\displaystyle\lim_{x\to 0}\frac{\sin 2x}{x} = \lim_{x\to 0} 2\cos 2x = 2.$

43. $\displaystyle\lim_{x\to\pi}\frac{1+\cos x}{(x-\pi)^2} = \lim_{x\to\pi}\frac{-\sin x}{2(x-\pi)} = \lim_{x\to\pi}\frac{-\cos x}{2} = \tfrac{1}{2}.$

44. $\displaystyle\lim_{x\to 0}\frac{x-\sin x}{x^3} = \lim_{x\to 0}\frac{1-\cos x}{3x^2} = \lim_{x\to 0}\frac{\sin x}{6x} = \tfrac{1}{6}$

45. $\displaystyle\lim_{t\to 0}\frac{(\arctan t - \sin t)}{t^3} = \lim_{t\to 0}\frac{\left(\frac{1}{1+t^2}-\cos t\right)}{3t^2} = \lim_{t\to 0}\frac{\left(-\frac{2t}{(1+t^2)^2}+\sin t\right)}{6t}$
$= \displaystyle\lim_{t\to 0}\tfrac{1}{6}\left(\frac{\sin t}{t}-\frac{2}{(1+t^2)^2}\right) = \tfrac{1}{6}(1-2) = -\tfrac{1}{6}.$

46. $\displaystyle\lim_{x\to\infty}\frac{\ln(\ln x)}{\ln x} = \lim_{x\to\infty}\frac{\left(\frac{1}{x\ln x}\right)}{\left(\frac{1}{x}\right)} = \lim_{x\to\infty}\frac{1}{\ln x} = 0.$

47. $\displaystyle\lim_{x\to 0}(\cot x)\ln(1+x) = \lim_{x\to 0}\frac{\ln(1+x)}{\tan x} = \lim_{x\to 0}\frac{1}{(1+x)\sec^2 x} = 1.$

48. $\displaystyle\lim_{x\to 0^+}\left(e^{1/x}-1\right)\tan x = \lim_{x\to 0^+}\frac{e^{1/x}-1}{\cot x} = \lim_{x\to 0^+}\frac{\left(\frac{1}{x^2}\right)(e^{1/x})}{\cot x\,\csc x} = \lim_{x\to 0^+}\left(\frac{\sin^2 x}{x^2}\right)\left(\frac{e^{1/x}}{\cos x}\right)$
$= \displaystyle\lim_{x\to 0^+}\frac{e^{1/x}}{\cos x} = +\infty.$

49. $\displaystyle\lim_{x\to 0}\left(\frac{1}{x^2}-\frac{1}{1-\cos x}\right) = \lim_{x\to 0}\frac{1-\cos x - x^2}{x^2(1-\cos x)} = \lim_{x\to 0}\frac{\sin x - 2x}{2x(1-\cos x)+x^2\sin x}$
$= \displaystyle\lim_{x\to 0}\frac{\left(\frac{\sin x}{x}-2\right)}{2(1-\cos x)+x\sin x} = -\infty.$

50. $\displaystyle\lim_{x\to\infty}\left(\frac{x^2}{x+2}-\frac{x^3}{x^2+3}\right) = \lim_{x\to\infty}\frac{x^4+3x^2-x^4-2x^3}{x^3+2x^2+3x+6} = \lim_{x\to\infty}\frac{-2+\frac{3}{x}}{1+\frac{2}{x}+\frac{3}{x^2}+\frac{6}{x^3}} = -2.$

51. $\displaystyle\lim_{x\to\infty}\left(\sqrt{x^2-x+1}-\sqrt{x}\right) = \lim_{x\to\infty}\frac{x^2-x+1-x}{\sqrt{x^2-x+1}+\sqrt{x}} = \lim_{x\to\infty}\frac{x^2-2x+1}{\sqrt{x^2-x+1}+\sqrt{x}}$
$= \displaystyle\lim_{x\to\infty}\frac{x-2+\frac{1}{x}}{\sqrt{1-\frac{1}{x}+\frac{1}{x^2}}+\sqrt{\frac{1}{x}}} = +\infty.$

52. $\displaystyle\lim_{x\to\infty}\ln\left(x^{1/x}\right) = \lim_{x\to\infty}\frac{\ln x}{x} = 0.$ Therefore $\displaystyle\lim_{x\to\infty} x^{1/x} = 1.$

53. $\lim_{x \to \infty} \ln\left(e^{2x} - 2x\right)^{1/x} = \lim_{x \to \infty} \frac{\ln\left(e^{2x} - 2x\right)}{x} = \lim_{x \to \infty} \frac{2e^{2x} - 2}{e^{2x} - 2x} = \lim_{x \to \infty} \frac{2 - 2e^{-2x}}{1 - 2xe^{-2x}} = 2.$

   Therefore $\lim_{x \to \infty} \left(e^{2x} - 2x\right)^{1/x} = e^2$.

54. $\lim_{x \to \infty} \ln\left(1 - e^{(-x^2)}\right)^{1/x^2} = \lim_{x \to \infty} \frac{\ln\left(1 - e^{(-x^2)}\right)}{x^2} = \lim_{x \to \infty} \frac{2xe^{(-x^2)}}{2x\left(1 - e^{(-x^2)}\right)}$

   $= \lim_{x \to \infty} \frac{e^{(-x^2)}}{1 - \left(e^{(-x^2)}\right)} = 0.$

   Therefore $\lim_{x \to \infty} \left(1 - e^{(-x^2)}\right)^{1/x^2} = 1$.

55. One of our most challenging problems. First let $u = 1/x$. It is then sufficient to evaluate

    $$L = \lim_{u \to 0^+} \frac{(1+u)^{1/u} - e}{u}.$$

    Apply l'Hôpital's rule once:

    $$L = \lim_{u \to 0^+} (1+u)^{1/u} \left(\frac{u - (1+u)\ln(1+u)}{u^2(1+u)}\right).$$

    Now apply the product rule for limits!

    $$L = e \lim_{u \to 0^+} \frac{u - (1+u)\ln(1+u)}{u^2(1+u)}.$$

    Finally apply l'Hôpital's rule twice to the limit that remains. The answer in the text follows without any more difficulties.

57. By the method of cylindrical shells,

    $$V = \int_0^{1/\sqrt{2}} 2\pi x \, \frac{dx}{\sqrt{1 - x^4}}.$$

    Let $u = x^2$, so that $du = 2x\,dx$. Then

    $$V = \int_0^{1/2} \frac{\pi \, du}{\sqrt{1 - u^2}} = \pi \left(\arcsin\left(\tfrac{1}{2}\right) - \arcsin(0)\right) = \tfrac{1}{6}\pi^2.$$

58. By the method of cylindrical shells,

    $$V = \int_0^1 2\pi x \, \frac{1}{\sqrt{x^4 + 1}} \, dx.$$

    Let $u = x^2$. Then $du = 2x\,dx$, and we obtain

    $$V = \int_0^1 \frac{\pi}{\sqrt{u^2 + 1}} \, du = \pi \left(\sinh^{-1}(1) - \sinh^{-1}(0)\right) = \pi \sinh^{-1}(1) = \pi \ln\left(1 + \sqrt{2}\right) \approx 2.7689.$$

60. See the solution to Problem 52 of Section 8.5.

    $$x(t) = A \cosh kt + B \sinh kt;$$
    $$x'(t) = kA \sinh kt + kB \cosh kt.$$

    (a) $x(0) = 1$, $x'(0) = 0$. It follows that $A = 1$ and that $kB = 0$. Therefore $A = 1$ and $B = 0$.

(b) $x(0) = 0$, $x'(0) = 1$. Thus $A = 0$ and $kB = 1$. Therefore $A = 0$ and $B = 1/k$.

61. It's clear from the sketch on the right that the least positive solution is larger than $3\pi/2$ and smaller than 2π. So we use the iteration of Newton's method with initial estimate $x_0 = 5$. The formula is
$$x \longleftarrow x - \frac{\cos x \, \cosh x - 1}{\cos x \, \sinh x - \sin x \, \cosh x}.$$

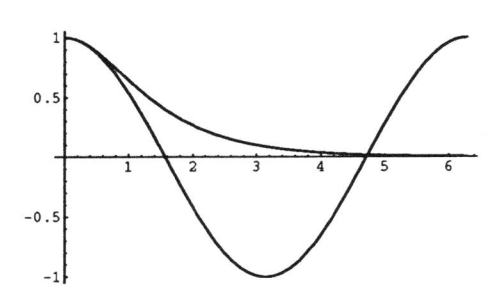

Here are the (rounded) results:
$$x_0 = 5.0$$
$$x_1 = 4.782556376$$
$$x_2 = 4.732575187$$
$$x_3 = 4.730047035$$
$$x_4 = 4.730040745 = x_5.$$

Answer: The least positive solution of $\cos x \, \cosh x = 1$ is approximately 4.730040745.

Chapter 9: Techniques of Integration
Section 9.2

1. Let $u = 2 - 3x$ and apply Formula (1) of Fig. 9.1.

2. Let $u = 1 + 2x$. $\displaystyle\int \frac{dx}{(1+2x)^2} = \frac{1}{2}\int \frac{du}{u^2} = -\frac{1}{2u} + C = -\frac{1}{2(1+2x)} + C.$

4. Let $u = 5 + 2t^2$. $\displaystyle\int \frac{5t}{5+2t^2}\,dt = \frac{5}{4}\int \frac{du}{u} = \frac{5}{4}\ln|u| + C = \frac{5}{4}\ln(5+2t^2) + C.$

6. Let $u = x^2$. $\displaystyle\int x \sec^2 x^2\,dx = \frac{1}{2}\int \sec^2 u\,du = \frac{1}{2}\tan u + C = \frac{1}{2}\tan x^2 + C.$

7. Let $u = \sqrt{y}$.

8. Let $u = \pi(2x+1)$. $\displaystyle\int \sin \pi(2x+1)\,dx = \frac{1}{2\pi}\int \sin u\,du = -\frac{1}{2\pi}\cos u + C = -\frac{1}{2\pi}\cos \pi(2x+1) + C.$

10. Let $u = 4 + \cos 2x$. $\displaystyle\int \frac{\sin 2x}{4 + \cos 2x}\,dx = -\frac{1}{2}\int \frac{du}{u} = -\frac{1}{2}\ln|u| + C = -\frac{1}{2}\ln(4 + \cos 2x) + C.$

12. Let $u = \sqrt{x+4}$. $\displaystyle\int \frac{e^{\sqrt{x+4}}}{\sqrt{x+4}}\,dx = \int 2e^u\,du = 2e^u + C = 2e^{\sqrt{x+4}} + C.$

13. Let $u = \ln t$.

14. Let $u = 1 - 9t^2$. $\displaystyle\int \frac{t}{\sqrt{1-9t^2}}\,dt = -\frac{1}{18}\int u^{-1/2}\,du = -\left(\frac{1}{18}\right)(2)\sqrt{u} + C = -\frac{1}{9}\left(1 - 9t^2\right)^{1/2} + C.$

16. Let $u = 1 + e^{2x}$. $\displaystyle\int \frac{e^{2x}}{1+e^{2x}}\,dx = \frac{1}{2}\int \frac{du}{u} = \frac{1}{2}\ln|u| + C = \frac{1}{2}\ln\left(1 + e^{2x}\right) + C$

17. Let $u = e^{2x}$.

18. Let $u = \tan^{-1} x$. $\displaystyle\int \frac{e^{\arctan x}}{1 + x^2}\,dx = \int e^u\,du = e^u + C = e^{\arctan x} + C.$

19. Let $u = x^2$.

20. Let $u = \sin 2x$. $\displaystyle\int \sin^3 2x \cos 2x\,dx = \frac{1}{2}\int u^3\,du = \left(\frac{1}{2}\right)\left(\frac{1}{4}\right)u^4 + C = \frac{1}{8}\sin^4 2x + C.$

21. Let $u = \tan 3x$.

22. Let $u = 2t$. $\displaystyle\int \frac{1}{1+4t^2}\,dt = \frac{1}{2}\int \frac{du}{1+u^2} = \frac{1}{2}\arctan u + C = \frac{1}{2}\arctan 2t + C.$

23. Let $u = \sin \theta$.

24. Let $u = 1 + \tan \theta$. $\displaystyle\int \frac{\sec^2 \theta}{1 + \tan \theta}\,d\theta = \int \frac{du}{u} = \ln|u| + C = \ln|1 + \tan \theta| + C.$

25. Let $v = 1 + \sqrt{x}$. $\displaystyle\int \frac{(1+\sqrt{x})^4}{\sqrt{x}}\,dx = 2\int v^4\,dv = \frac{2}{5}v^5 + C = \frac{2}{5}\left(1 + \sqrt{x}\right)^5 + C.$

26. Let $u = t^{2/3} - 1$. $\displaystyle\int t^{-1/3}\sqrt{t^{2/3} - 1}\,dt = \frac{3}{2}\int \sqrt{u}\,du = u^{3/2} + C = \left(t^{2/3} - 1\right)^{3/2} + C.$

27. Let $u = \arctan t$.

28. Let $u = 1 + \sec 2x$. $\displaystyle\int \frac{\sec 2x \tan 2x}{(1 + \sec 2x)^{3/2}}\,dx = \int \frac{1}{2}u^{-3/2}\,du = -u^{-1/2} + C = -\frac{1}{\sqrt{1 + \sec 2x}} + C.$

29. Let $w = e^x$; $dw = e^x\,dx$; $dx = \dfrac{1}{w}\,dw$.

$\displaystyle\int \frac{1}{\sqrt{e^{2x} - 1}}\,dx = \int \frac{dw}{w(w^2 - 1)^{1/2}} = \sec^{-1}|w| + C = \sec^{-1}(e^x) + C.$

30. Let $u = e^{x^2}$. Then $u^2 - 1 = e^{2x^2} - 1$, $x^2 = \ln u$, and $2x\,dx = \dfrac{1}{u}\,du.$

$$\int \frac{x}{\sqrt{e^{2x^2}-1}}\,dx = \tfrac{1}{2}\int \frac{du}{u\sqrt{u^2-1}} = \tfrac{1}{2}\sec^{-1}|u| + C = \tfrac{1}{2}\sec^{-1}\left(e^{x^2}\right) + C.$$

31. $\displaystyle\int x^2\sqrt{x-2}\,dx = \int (u+2)^2 u^{1/2}\,du = \int \left(u^{5/2} + 4u^{3/2} + 4u^{1/2}\right)du$

$\qquad = \tfrac{2}{7}u^{7/2} + \tfrac{8}{5}u^{5/2} + \tfrac{8}{3}u^{3/2} + C = \tfrac{2}{7}(x-2)^{7/2} + \tfrac{8}{5}(x-2)^{5/2} + \tfrac{8}{3}(x-2)^{3/2} + C$

$\qquad = (x-2)^{3/2}\left(\tfrac{2}{7}(x-2)^2 + \tfrac{8}{5}(x-2) + \tfrac{8}{3}\right) + C$

$\qquad = \tfrac{1}{105}(x-2)^{3/2}\left(30\left(x^2 - 4x + 4\right) + 168(x-2) + 280\right) + C$

$\qquad = \tfrac{2}{105}(x-2)^{3/2}\left(15x^2 + 24x + 32\right) + C.$

32. $\displaystyle\int \frac{x^2}{\sqrt{x+3}}\,dx = \int \frac{(u-3)^2}{u^{1/2}}\,du = \int \left(u^{3/2} - 6u^{1/2} + 9u^{-1/2}\right)du$

$\qquad = \tfrac{2}{5}u^{5/2} - 4u^{3/2} + 18u^{1/2} + C$

$\qquad = \tfrac{2}{5}(x+3)^{5/2} - 4(x+3)^{3/2} + 18(x+3)^{1/2} + C$

$\qquad = \tfrac{2}{5}\left(x^2 - 4x + 24\right)\sqrt{x+3} + C.$

33. $\displaystyle\int \frac{x}{\sqrt{2x+3}}\,dx = \tfrac{1}{4}\int \left(u^{1/2} - 3u^{-1/2}\right)du = \tfrac{1}{4}\left(\tfrac{2}{3}u^{3/2} - 6u^{1/2}\right) + C$

$\qquad = \tfrac{1}{6}(2x+3)^{3/2} - \tfrac{3}{2}(2x+3)^{1/2} + C = \tfrac{1}{3}(x-3)\sqrt{2x+3} + C.$

34. $\displaystyle\int x\sqrt[3]{x-1}\,dx = \int (u+1)\,u^{1/3}\,du = \int \left(u^{4/3} + u^{1/3}\right)du$

$\qquad = \tfrac{3}{7}u^{7/3} + \tfrac{3}{4}u^{4/3} + C = \left(3u^{4/3}\right)\cdot\left(\dfrac{4u+7}{28}\right) + C$

$\qquad = \left(\dfrac{3(x-1)^{4/3}}{28}\right)\cdot (4x+3) + C = \tfrac{3}{28}(x-1)^{1/3}\left(4x^2 - x - 3\right) + C.$

35. $\displaystyle\int \frac{x}{\sqrt[3]{x+1}}\,dx = \int \left(u^{2/3} - u^{-1/3}\right)du.$

36. With $a = 10$, $u = 3x$, and $dx = \tfrac{1}{3}du$, we get

$\displaystyle\int \frac{1}{100 + 9x^2}\,dx = \tfrac{1}{3}\int \frac{1}{a^2 + u^2}\,du = \frac{1}{3a}\arctan\frac{u}{a} + C = \tfrac{1}{30}\arctan\tfrac{3}{10}x + C.$

37. With $a = 10$, $u = 3x$, and $dx = \tfrac{1}{3}du$, we get

$\displaystyle\int \frac{1}{100 - 9x^2}\,dx = \tfrac{1}{3}\int \frac{1}{a^2 - u^2}\,du = \frac{1}{6a}\ln\left|\frac{u+a}{u-a}\right| + C = \tfrac{1}{60}\ln\left|\frac{3x+10}{3x-10}\right| + C.$

38. With $a = 3$, $u = 2x$, and $dx = \tfrac{1}{2}du$, we obtain

$\displaystyle\int \sqrt{9 - 4x^2}\,dx = \tfrac{1}{2}\int \left(a^2 - u^2\right)^{1/2}du = \frac{u}{4}\left(a^2 - u^2\right)^{1/2} + \tfrac{1}{4}a^2\arcsin\frac{u}{a} + C$

$\qquad = \dfrac{x}{2}\left(9 - 4x^2\right)^{1/2} + \tfrac{9}{4}\arcsin\tfrac{2}{3}x + C.$

39. With $a = 2$, $u = 3x$, and $dx = \tfrac{1}{3}dx$, we get

$\displaystyle\int \sqrt{4 + 9x^2}\,dx = \tfrac{1}{3}\int \left(a^2 + u^2\right)^{1/2}du = \frac{u}{6}\left(a^2 + u^2\right)^{1/2} + \tfrac{1}{6}a^2\ln\left|u + \left(a^2 + u^2\right)^{1/2}\right| + C$

$\qquad = \tfrac{1}{2}x\left(4 + 9x^2\right)^{1/2} + \tfrac{2}{3}\ln\left|3x + \left(4 + 9x^2\right)^{1/2}\right| + C.$

40. With $a = 3$, $u = 4x$, and $dx = \tfrac{1}{4}du$, we obtain

$\displaystyle\int \frac{dx}{\sqrt{16x^2 + 9}} = \tfrac{1}{4}\int \frac{du}{\left(u^2 + a^2\right)^{1/2}} = \tfrac{1}{4}\ln\left|u + \left(u^2 + a^2\right)^{1/2}\right| + C = \tfrac{1}{4}\ln\left|4x + \left(16x^2 + 9\right)^{1/2}\right| + C.$

41. With $a = 3$, $u = 4x$, and $dx = \tfrac{1}{4}du$, we obtain

242   Section 9.2 Integral Tables and Simple Substitutions

$$\int \frac{x^2}{\sqrt{16x^2+9}}\,dx = \tfrac{1}{64}\int \frac{u^2}{(u^2+a^2)^{1/2}}\,du$$
$$= \tfrac{1}{64}\left(\frac{u}{2}(u^2+a^2)^{1/2} - \tfrac{1}{2}a^2 \ln\left|u+(u^2+a^2)^{1/2}\right|\right) + C$$
$$= \frac{x}{32}(16x^2+9)^{1/2} - \tfrac{9}{128}\ln\left|4x+(16x^2+9)^{1/2}\right| + C.$$

42. With $a = 5$, $u = 4x$, and $dx = \tfrac{1}{4}du$, we get
$$\int \frac{x^2}{\sqrt{25+16x^2}}\,dx = \tfrac{1}{64}\int \frac{u^2}{(u^2+a^2)^{1/2}}\,du$$
$$= \tfrac{1}{64}\left(\frac{u}{2}(u^2+a^2)^{1/2} - \tfrac{1}{2}a^2\ln\left|u+(u^2+a^2)^{1/2}\right|\right) + C$$
$$= \frac{x}{32}(25+16x^2)^{1/2} - \tfrac{25}{128}\ln\left|4x+(25+16x^2)^{1/2}\right| + C.$$

43. With $a = 5$, $u = 4x$, and $dx = \tfrac{1}{4}du$, we get
$$\int x^2\sqrt{25-16x^2}\,dx = \tfrac{1}{64}\int u^2(a^2-u^2)^{1/2}\,du$$
$$= \tfrac{1}{64}\left(\frac{u}{8}(2u^2-a^2)(a^2-u^2)^{1/2} + \tfrac{1}{8}a^4 \arcsin\frac{u}{a}\right) + C$$
$$= \frac{x}{128}(32x^2-25)(25-16x^2)^{1/2} + \tfrac{625}{512}\arcsin\frac{4x}{5} + C.$$

44. Let $u = x^2$, $a = 2$. Then $du = 2x\,dx$, and we find that
$$\int x(4-x^4)^{1/2}\,dx = \tfrac{1}{2}\int (a^2-u^2)^{1/2}\,du \quad \text{(which by Formula (54) of the endpapers)}$$
$$= \frac{u}{4}(a^2-u^2)^{1/2} + \tfrac{1}{4}a^2 \sin^{-1}\left(\frac{u}{a}\right) + C$$
$$= \tfrac{1}{4}x^2(4-x^2)^{1/2} + \sin^{-1}\left(\tfrac{1}{2}x^2\right) + C.$$

45. Let $u = \tfrac{1}{3}e^x$. Then
$$\int e^x(9+e^{2x})^{1/2}\,dx = 9\int (1+u^2)^{1/2}\,du \quad \text{(which by Formula (44) of the endpapers)}$$
$$= \frac{9u}{2}(u^2+1)^{1/2} + \tfrac{9}{2}\ln\left|u+(u^2+1)^{1/2}\right| + C$$
$$= \tfrac{3}{2}e^x\left(\tfrac{1}{9}e^{2x}+1\right)^{1/2} + \tfrac{9}{2}\ln\left|\tfrac{1}{3}e^x + \left(\tfrac{1}{9}e^{2x}+1\right)^{1/2}\right| + C.$$

46. Let $u = \sin x$, $du = \cos x\,dx$. Use Formula (50) of the endpapers to obtain
$$\int \frac{\cos x}{(\sin^2 x)\sqrt{1+\sin^2 x}}\,dx = \int \frac{1}{u^2(1+u^2)^{1/2}}\,du = -\frac{1}{u}(u^2+1)^{1/2} + C = -\frac{(1+\sin^2 x)^{1/2}}{\sin x} + C$$

47. With $u = x^2$, we obtain $\int \frac{\sqrt{x^4-1}}{x}\,dx = \tfrac{1}{2}\int \frac{(u^2-1)^{1/2}}{u}\,du$. Now apply Formula (47).

48. Let $u = 4e^x$. Then $du = 4e^x\,dx$, $e^x\,dx = \tfrac{1}{4}du$, $e^{2x} = \tfrac{1}{16}u^2$, and $e^{3x}\,dx = \tfrac{1}{64}u^2\,du$. Take $a = 5$.
$$\int \frac{e^{3x}}{\sqrt{25+16e^{2x}}}\,dx = \tfrac{1}{64}\int \frac{u^2}{(a^2-u^2)^{1/2}}\,du.$$
Now apply Formula (49). The final answer may be written in the form
$$\tfrac{1}{128}\left(4e^x\sqrt{25+16e^{2x}} - 25\ln\left|4e^x + \sqrt{25+16e^{2x}}\right|\right) + C.$$

49. The substitution $u = \ln x$ leads to

$$\int \frac{(\ln x)^2}{x} \sqrt{1+(\ln x)^2} \, dx = \int u^2 \left(1+u^2\right)^{1/2} du \qquad \text{(which by Formula (48))}$$
$$= \tfrac{1}{8} \left[(\ln x)\left(2(\ln x)^2+1\right)\left((\ln x)^2+1\right)^{1/2} - \ln\left|(\ln x)+\left((\ln x)^2+1\right)^{1/2}\right| \right] + C.$$

50. Let $u = 2x^3$. Use Formula (48):
$$\int x^8 \sqrt{4x^6-1} \, dx = \tfrac{1}{24} \int u^2 \left(u^2-1\right)^{1/2} du$$
$$= \tfrac{1}{24} \left(\tfrac{u}{8}\left(2u^2-1\right)\left(u^2-1\right)^{1/2} - \tfrac{1}{8} \ln\left|u+\left(u^2-1\right)^{1/2}\right| \right) + C$$
$$= \tfrac{1}{192}\left(2x^3\left(8x^6-1\right)\left(4x^6-1\right)^{1/2} - \ln\left|2x^3+\left(4x^6-1\right)^{1/2}\right| \right) + C.$$

51. Is x really equal to $\sqrt{u}$ for all x in $[-1, 1]$?

52. $\displaystyle \int \frac{dx}{x^2+4x+5} = \int \frac{dx}{(x+2)^2+1} = \tan^{-1}(x+2) + C.$

53. With $u = x-1$ and $du = dx$, $(2x-x^2)^{1/2} = (1-(x-1)^2)^{1/2} = (1-u^2)^{1/2}$. Therefore
$$\int \frac{1}{\sqrt{2x-x^2}} \, dx = \int \frac{du}{(1-u^2)^{1/2}} = \sin^{-1} u + C = \sin^{-1}(x-1) + C.$$

Section 9.3

1. $\begin{bmatrix} u = x & dv = e^{2x}\, dx \\ du = dx & v = \tfrac{1}{2}e^{2x} \end{bmatrix}$ $\qquad \displaystyle\int xe^{2x}\, dx = \tfrac{1}{2}xe^{2x} - \int \tfrac{1}{2}e^{2x}\, dx = \tfrac{1}{2}xe^{2x} - \tfrac{1}{4}e^{2x} + C.$

2. $\begin{bmatrix} u = x^2 & dv = e^{2x}\, dx \\ du = 2x\, dx & v = \tfrac{1}{2}e^{2x} \end{bmatrix}$ $\qquad \displaystyle\int x^2 e^{2x}\, dx = \tfrac{1}{2}x^2 e^{2x} - \int xe^{2x}\, dx.$

   Now either repeat the steps of Problem 1 or use its result to get the final answer:
$$\int x^2 e^{2x}\, dx = \tfrac{1}{4}\left(2x^2-2x+1\right)e^{2x} + C.$$

3. $\begin{bmatrix} u = t & dv = \sin t\, dt \\ du = dt & v = -\cos t \end{bmatrix}$ $\qquad \displaystyle\int t \sin t\, dt = -t\cos t + \int \cos t\, dt.$

4. $\begin{bmatrix} u = t^2 & dv = \sin t\, dt \\ du = 2t\, dt & v = -\cos t \end{bmatrix}$ $\qquad \displaystyle\int t^2 \sin t\, dt = -t^2 \cos t + 2\int t\cos t\, dt.$

5. $\begin{bmatrix} u = x & dv = \cos 3x\, dx \\ du = dx & v = \tfrac{1}{3}\sin 3x \end{bmatrix}$

6. $\begin{bmatrix} u = \ln x & dv = x\, dx \\ du = \tfrac{1}{x}dx & v = \tfrac{1}{2}x^2 \end{bmatrix}$ $\qquad \displaystyle\int x \ln x\, dx = \tfrac{1}{2}x^2 \ln x - \tfrac{1}{2}\int \frac{x^2}{x}\, dx = \tfrac{1}{2}x^2 \ln x - \tfrac{1}{4}x^2 + C.$

7. $\begin{bmatrix} u = \ln x & dv = x^3\, dx \\ du = \tfrac{1}{x}dx & v = \tfrac{1}{4}x^4 \end{bmatrix}$ $\qquad \displaystyle\int x^3 \ln x\, dx = \tfrac{1}{4}x^4 \ln x - \tfrac{1}{16}x^4 + C.$

8. $\begin{bmatrix} u = \cos 3z & dv = e^{3z}\, dz \\ du = -3\sin 3z\, dz & v = \tfrac{1}{3}e^{3z} \end{bmatrix}$ $\qquad \displaystyle\int e^{3z} \cos 3z\, dz = \tfrac{1}{3}e^{3z}\cos 3z + \int e^{3z}\sin 3z\, dz.$

   Next choose:

   $\begin{bmatrix} u = \sin 3z & dv = e^{3z}\, dz \\ du = 3\cos 3z\, dz & v = \tfrac{1}{3}e^{3z} \end{bmatrix}$ $\displaystyle\int e^{3z} \cos 3z\, dz = \tfrac{1}{3}e^{3z}\cos 3z + \tfrac{1}{3}e^{3z}\sin 3z - \int e^{3z}\cos 3z\, dz.$

Now solve for the original integral and add a constant:
$$\int e^{3z} \cos 3z \, dz = \tfrac{1}{6}(\cos 3z + \sin 3z) \, e^{3z} + C.$$

9. Choose $u = \tan^{-1} x$, $dv = dx$.

10. $\begin{bmatrix} u = \ln x & dv = \dfrac{1}{x^2} dx \\ du = \dfrac{1}{x} dx & v = -\dfrac{1}{x} \end{bmatrix}$ $\displaystyle\int \dfrac{\ln x}{x^2} dx = -\dfrac{1}{x} \ln x + \int \dfrac{1}{x^2} dx = -\dfrac{1}{x} \ln x - \dfrac{1}{x} + C.$

11. Choose $u = \ln y$, $dv = \sqrt{y} \, dy$.

12. $\begin{bmatrix} u = x & dv = \sec^2 x \, dx \\ du = dx & v = \tan x \end{bmatrix}$ $\displaystyle\int x \sec^2 x \, dx \, dx = x \tan x - \int \tan x \, dx = x \tan x + \ln |\cos x| + C.$

13. Choose $u = (\ln t)^2$ and $dv = dt$. The necessity of integrating $\ln t$ then arises; a second integration by parts is necessary, and works well with the choices $u = \ln t$, $dv = dt$.

14. $\begin{bmatrix} u = (\ln t)^2 & dv = t \, dt \\ du = 2(\ln t)(1/t) \, dt & v = \tfrac{1}{2} t^2 \end{bmatrix}$ $\displaystyle\int t(\ln t)^2 \, dt = \tfrac{1}{2}(t \ln t)^2 - \int t \ln t \, dt.$

Then apply the result (or method) of the solution of Problem 6 to obtain the final answer:
$$\int t \, (\ln t)^2 \, dt = \tfrac{1}{4} t^2 \left(2(\ln t)^2 - 2 \ln t + 1 \right) + C.$$

15. Choose $u = x$ and $dv = \sqrt{x+3} \, dx$.

16. $\begin{bmatrix} u = x^2 & dv = x \left(1 - x^2\right)^{1/2} dx \\ du = 2x \, dx & v = -\tfrac{1}{3} \left(1 - x^2\right)^{3/2} \end{bmatrix}$ $\displaystyle\int x^3 \sqrt{1 - x^2} \, dx = -\tfrac{1}{3} x^2 \left(1 - x^2\right)^{3/2} - \tfrac{2}{15} \left(1 - x^2\right)^{5/2} + C.$

17. Choose $u = x^3$, $dv = x^2 \left(x^3 + 1 \right)^{1/2} dx$.

18. $\begin{bmatrix} u = \sin \theta & dv = \sin \theta \, d\theta \\ du = \cos \theta \, d\theta & v = -\cos \theta \end{bmatrix}$ $\displaystyle I = \int \sin^2 \theta \, d\theta = -\sin \theta \cos \theta + \int \cos^2 \theta \, d\theta$
$$= -\sin \theta \cos \theta + \int 1 \, d\theta - \int \sin^2 \theta \, d\theta$$
$$= -\sin \theta \cos \theta + \theta - I.$$

Now solve for I to find that
$$\int \sin^2 \theta \, d\theta = \tfrac{1}{2}(\theta - \sin \theta \cos \theta) + C.$$

19. Choose $u = \csc \theta$, $dv = \csc^2 \theta \, d\theta$. Replace $\cot^2 \theta$ with $\csc^2 \theta - z$ in the resulting integral to obtain
$$I = -\csc \theta \cot \theta + \int \csc \theta \, d\theta - I$$

where I is the original integral. Solve for I and use Formula 15 of the endpapers to obtain the answer.

20. $\begin{bmatrix} u = \sin(\ln t) & dv = dt \\ du = (1/t) \cos(\ln t) \, dt & v = t \end{bmatrix}$ $\displaystyle I = \int \sin(\ln t) \, dt = t \sin(\ln t) - \int \cos(\ln t) \, dt.$

Now let $u = \cos(\ln t)$ and $dv = dt$. We find that
$$I = t \sin(\ln t) - t \cos(\ln t) - I.$$

Section 9.3 Integration by Parts

Solve for I to obtain
$$\int \sin(\ln t)\, dt = \frac{t}{2}\left(\sin(\ln t) - \cos(\ln t)\right) + C.$$

21. Choose $u = \arctan x$, $dv = x^2\, dx$. Note that we simplify the resulting new integrand by division of denominator into numerator:
$$\int x^2 \arctan x\, dx = \tfrac{1}{3}x^3 \arctan x - \tfrac{1}{3}\int \left(x - \frac{x}{x^2+1}\right) dx = \tfrac{1}{3}x^3 \arctan x - \tfrac{1}{6}x^2 + \tfrac{1}{6}\ln(1+x^2) + C.$$

22. Choose $u = \ln(1+x^2)$, $dv = dx$. Then
$$\int \ln(1+x^2)\, dx = x\ln(1+x^2) - 2\int \frac{x^2}{x^2+1}\, dx$$
$$= x\ln(1+x^2) - 2\int \frac{x^2+1}{x^2+1}\, dx + 2\int \frac{dx}{x^2+1}$$
$$= x\ln(1+x^2) - 2x + 2\tan^{-1} x + C.$$

23. Let $u = \sec^{-1}\sqrt{x}$, $dv = dx$.

24. $\left[\begin{array}{ll} u = \tan^{-1}\sqrt{x} & dv = x\, dx \\ du = \dfrac{dx}{2x^{1/2}(1+x)} & v = \dfrac{1}{2}x^2 - \dfrac{1}{2} \end{array}\right]$ Note the clever choice of v!

$$\int x \tan^{-1}\sqrt{x}\, dx = \tfrac{1}{2}(x^2-1)\tan^{-1}\sqrt{x} - \tfrac{1}{4}\int \frac{x^2-1}{x^{1/2}(x+1)}\, dx$$
$$= \tfrac{1}{2}(x^2-1)\tan^{-1}\sqrt{x} - \tfrac{1}{4}\int (x^{1/2} - x^{-1/2})\, dx$$
$$= \tfrac{1}{2}(x^2-1)\tan^{-1}\sqrt{x} - \tfrac{1}{6}x^{3/2} + \tfrac{1}{2}\sqrt{x} + C.$$

25. Choose $u = \tan^{-1}\sqrt{x}$ and $dv = dx$. To simplify the resulting computations, choose $v = x+1$.

26. $\left[\begin{array}{ll} u = x^2 & dv = \cos 4x\, dx \\ du = 2x\, dx & v = \tfrac{1}{4}\sin 4x \end{array}\right]$ $\quad \int x^2 \cos 4x\, dx = \tfrac{1}{4}x^2 \sin 4x - \tfrac{1}{2}\int x\sin 4x\, dx.$

In the integral on the right-hand side, now choose $u = x$ and $dv = \sin 4x\, dx$. You'll then obtain
$$\int x^2 \cos 4x\, dx = \tfrac{1}{4}x^2 \sin 4x + \tfrac{1}{8}x\cos 4x - \tfrac{1}{8}\int \cos 4x\, dx$$
$$= \tfrac{1}{4}x^2 \sin 4x + \tfrac{1}{8}x\cos 4x - \frac{1}{32}\sin 4x + C.$$

27. Choose $u = x$, $dv = \csc^2 x\, dx$. Then
$$\int x\csc^2 x\, dx = -x\cot x + \int \cot x\, dx$$
$$= -x\cot x + \ln|\sin x| + C.$$

28. Choose $u = \tan^{-1} x$, $dv = x\, dx$. Then $du = \dfrac{dx}{1+x^2}$; we choose $v = \tfrac{1}{2}x^2 + \tfrac{1}{2} = \tfrac{1}{2}(x^2+1)$ for the purpose of providing a fortuitous cancellation:
$$\int x\tan^{-1} x\, dx = \tfrac{1}{2}(x^2+1)\tan^{-1} x - \tfrac{1}{2}\int \frac{x^2+1}{1+x^2}\, dx = \tfrac{1}{2}(x^2+1)\tan^{-1} x - \tfrac{1}{2}x + C.$$

This sly trick—a clever choice for v—is rarely useful. Try it with the integral of $\ln(x+1)$.

29. $\begin{bmatrix} u = x^2 & dv = x\cos(x^2)\,dx \\ du = 2x\,dx & v = \frac{1}{2}\sin(x^2) \end{bmatrix}$
$\int x^3 \cos(x^2)\,dx = \frac{1}{2}x^2 \sin(x^2) - \int x \sin(x^2)\,dx$
$= \frac{1}{2}x^2 \sin(x^2) + \frac{1}{2}\cos(x^2) + C.$

30. If a and b are real and $i^2 = -1$, then

$$\int e^{(a+bi)x}\,dx = \frac{e^{(a+bi)x}}{a+bi} + C.$$

But

$$\frac{e^{(a+bi)x}}{a+bi} = \frac{a-bi}{a^2+b^2} e^{ax}(\cos bx + i\sin bx)$$
$$= \frac{e^{ax}}{a^2+b^2}(a\cos bx + b\sin bx) + i\frac{e^{ax}}{a^2+b^2}(-b\cos bx + a\sin bx).$$

Also,

$$\int e^{(a+bi)x}\,dx = \int e^{ax}(\cos bx + i\sin bx)\,dx$$
$$= \int e^{ax}\cos bx\,dx + i\int e^{ax}\sin bx\,dx.$$

We equate real and imaginary parts to obtain

$$\int e^{ax}\cos bx\,dx = \frac{e^{ax}}{a^2+b^2}(a\cos bx + b\sin bx) + C \quad \text{and}$$
$$\int e^{ax}\sin bx\,dx = \frac{e^{ax}}{a^2+b^2}(a\sin bx - b\cos bx) + C$$

In particular, with $a = -3$ and $b = 4$, we obtain

$$\int e^{-3x}\sin 4x\,dx = -\frac{e^{-3x}}{25}(3\sin 4x + 4\cos 4x) + C.$$

31. Choose $u = \ln x$ and $dv = x^{-3/2}\,dx$. Then

$$\int \frac{\ln x}{x^{3/2}}\,dx = -2x^{-1/2}\ln x + 2\int x^{-3/2}\,dx$$
$$= -2x^{-1/2}\ln x - 4x^{-1/2} + C$$
$$= -\frac{2}{\sqrt{x}}(2 + \ln x) + C.$$

32. Let $u = x^4$ and $dv = \dfrac{x^3}{(1+x^4)^{3/2}}\,dx$. Then

$$\int \frac{x^7}{(1+x^4)^{3/2}}\,dx = -\frac{1}{2}x^4(1+x^4)^{-1/2} + 2\int x^3(1+x^4)^{-1/2}\,dx$$
$$= -\frac{1}{2}x^4(1+x^4)^{-1/2} + (1+x^4)^{1/2} + C.$$

33. Let $u = x$ and $dv = \cosh x\,dx$. Then

$$\int x \cosh x\,dx = x\sinh x - \int \sinh x\,dx = x\sinh x - \cosh x + C.$$

34. First method:

$$\int e^x \cosh x \, dx = \tfrac{1}{2} \int (e^{2x} + 1) \, dx = \tfrac{1}{4} e^{2x} + \tfrac{1}{2} x + C_1$$
$$= \tfrac{1}{4}(e^{2x} + 1) - \tfrac{1}{4} + \tfrac{1}{2}x + C_1 = \tfrac{1}{4} e^x \left(e^x + e^{-x} \right) + \tfrac{1}{2}x + C$$
$$= \tfrac{1}{2} e^x \cosh x + \tfrac{1}{2} x + C.$$

Second method: Presented because no integration by parts is used in the first method, although what follows is somewhat artificial.

$$\begin{bmatrix} u = e^x & dv = \cosh x \, dx \\ du = e^x \, dx & v = \sinh x \end{bmatrix} \qquad J = \int e^x \cosh x \, dx = e^x \sinh x - \int e^x \sinh x \, dx.$$

Now $e^x \sinh x = \tfrac{1}{2}(e^{2x} - 1) = \tfrac{1}{2}(e^{2x} + 1) - 1 = e^x \cosh x - 1$. Therefore

$$J = e^x \sinh x - J + \int 1 \, dx; \text{ it follows that } \int e^x \cosh x \, dx = \tfrac{1}{2} e^x \sinh x + \tfrac{1}{2} x + C.$$

35. Let $t = x^2$. Then $dt = 2x \, dx$, so $\tfrac{1}{2} t \, dt = x^3 \, dx$. This substitution transforms the given integral into

$$I = \tfrac{1}{2} \int t \sin t \, dt.$$

Then integrate by parts: Let $u = t$, $dv = \sin t \, dt$. Thus $du = dt$ and $v = -\cos t$, and hence

$$2I = -t \cos t + \int \cos t \, dt = -t \cos t + \sin t + C.$$

Therefore

$$\int x^3 \sin x^2 \, dx = \tfrac{1}{2} \left(-x^2 \cos x^2 + \sin x^2 \right) + C.$$

36. Let $t = x^4$. Then $dt = 4x^3 \, dx$, so $x^7 = \tfrac{1}{4} t \, dt$. Thus the given integral becomes

$$I = \tfrac{1}{4} \int t \cos t \, dt.$$

Now let $u = t$ and $dv = \cos t \, dt$, so that $du = dt$ and $v = \sin t$. Hence

$$4I = t \sin t - \int \sin t \, dt = t \sin t + \cos t + C.$$

Therefore

$$I = \tfrac{1}{4} \left(x^4 \sin x^4 + \cos x^4 \right) + C.$$

37. Let $t = \sqrt{x}$, so that $x = t^2$ and $dx = 2t \, dt$. Thus

$$I = \int \exp\left(-\sqrt{x}\right) dx = \int 2t \exp(-t) \, dt.$$

Now let $u = 2t$ and $dv = \exp(-t) \, dt$. Then $du = 2 \, dt$ and $v = -\exp(-t)$. Hence

$$I = -2t \exp(-t) + \int 2 \exp(-t) \, dt = -2t \exp(-t) - 2 \exp(-t) + C.$$

Therefore

$$I = -2\sqrt{x} \exp\left(-\sqrt{x}\right) - 2 \exp\left(-\sqrt{x}\right) + C.$$

38. Let $t = x^{3/2}$. Then $dt = \frac{3}{2}x^{1/2}\,dx$, so $t\,dt = \frac{3}{2}x^2\,dx$. Therefore
$$I = \int x^2 \sin x^{3/2}\,dx = \frac{2}{3}\int t\sin t\,dt = \frac{2}{3}(-t\cos t + \sin t) + C.$$
(The integration by parts is the same as in the solution of Problem 35.) Therefore
$$I = \frac{2}{3}\left(-x^{3/2}\cos x^{3/2} + \sin x^{3/2}\right) + C.$$

39. $\int_0^{\pi/2} 2\pi x \cos x\,dx = \pi(\pi - 2).$

40. $\int_0^{\pi} 2\pi x \sin x\,dx = 2\pi^2.$

41. $\int_1^{e} 2\pi x \ln x\,dx = \frac{1}{2}\pi\left(e^2 + 1\right).$

42. $\int_0^1 2\pi x e^{-x}\,dx = 2\pi\left(1 - 2e^{-1}\right).$

43. The curves intersect at the point (a, b) in the first quadrant for which $a \approx 0.824132312$. The volume is
$$\int_0^a 2\pi x\left((\cos x) - x^2\right)\,dx \approx 1.06027.$$

44. The curves intersect where $x = 0$ and where $x = a \approx 3.110367680$. The volume is
$$\int_0^a 2\pi x(10x - x^2 - e^x + 1)\,dx \approx 209.907.$$

45. The curves intersect where $x = 0$ and where $x = a \approx 2.501048238$. The volume is
$$\int_0^a 2\pi x\left(2x - x^2 + \ln(x+1)\right)\,dx \approx 22.7894.$$

46. $\int 2x \arctan x\,dx = (x^2 + 1)\tan^{-1} x - x + C.$

One may add any convenient constant to v. Here's why: Let K be any constant. Then
$$\int u\,d(v + K) = u(v + K) - \int (v + K)\,du$$
$$= uv + uK - \int v\,du - \int K\,du$$
$$= uv + uK - \int v\,du - Ku$$
$$= uv - \int v\,du = \int u\,dv.$$

47. First choose $u = xe^x$ and $dv = \cos x\,dx$. This yields
$$I = \int xe^x \cos x\,dx = xe^x \sin x - \int (x + 1)e^x \sin x\,dx.$$
Now choose $u = (x+1)e^x$ and $dv = \sin x\,dx$;
$$I = xe^x \sin x + (x+1)e^x \cos x - \int (x+2)e^x \cos x\,dx$$
$$= xe^x \sin x + (x+1)e^x \cos x - 2\int e^x \cos x\,dx - I.$$

Thus
$$2I = xe^x \sin x + (x+1)e^x \cos x - 2\int e^x \cos x \, dx.$$

Compute the right-hand integral by parts separately, then solve for I:
$$I = \tfrac{1}{2}xe^x \cos x + \tfrac{1}{2}(x-1)e^x \sin x + C.$$

48. Given: Constants A and B, neither zero, $A \neq B$, and $J = \int \sin Ax \cos Bx \, dx.$

    Let $u = \sin Ax$ and $dv = \cos Bx \, dx$. Result:
    $$J = \frac{1}{B}\sin Ax \sin Bx + \frac{A}{B}\int \cos Ax \sin Bx + C.$$

    In the second integral, let $u = \cos Ax$ and $dv = \sin Bx \, dx$ (the other choice doesn't work). You will find that
    $$J = \frac{1}{B}\sin Ax \sin Bx + \frac{A}{B^2}\cos Ax \cos Bx + \frac{A^2}{B^2}J.$$

    Now solve for J to obtain
    $$J = \frac{B}{B^2 - A^2}\sin Ax \sin Bx + \frac{A}{B^2 - A^2}\cos Ax \cos Bx + C.$$

    In particular, we get the integral in Problem 40 by choosing $A = 3$ and $B = 1$, thus obtaining
    $$\int \sin 3x \cos x \, dx = -\tfrac{1}{8}\sin 3x \sin x - \tfrac{3}{8}\cos 3x \cos x + C.$$

    See Problems 49–52 of Section 9.3 for a "better" way, which yields the antiderivative in the alternative form $-\tfrac{1}{8}\cos 4x - \tfrac{1}{4}\cos 2x + C.$

49. Let $u = x^n$ and $dv = e^x \, dx$. Then $du = nx^{n-1}\, dx$ and $v = e^x$. The desired reduction formula is an immediate consequence.

50. $\begin{bmatrix} u = x^{n-1} & dv = xe^{-x^2}\, dx \\ du = (n-1)x^{n-2}\, dx & v = -\tfrac{1}{2}e^{-x^2} \end{bmatrix}$ $\quad \int x^n e^{-x^2}\, dx = -\tfrac{1}{2}x^{n-1}e^{-x^2} + \dfrac{n-1}{2}\int x^{n-2}e^{-x^2}\, dx.$

51. Let $u = (\ln x)^n$, $dv = dx$.

52. $\begin{bmatrix} u = x^n & dv = \cos x \, dx \\ du = nx^{n-1}\, dx & v = \sin x \end{bmatrix}$ $\quad \int x^n \cos x \, dx = x^n \sin x - n \int x^{n-1}\sin x \, dx.$

53. $\begin{bmatrix} u = \sin^{n-1} x & dv = \sin x \, dx \\ du = (n-1)\sin^{n-2} x \cos x \, dx & v = -\cos x \end{bmatrix}$

    $$I_n = \int \sin^n x \, dx$$
    $$= -\sin^{n-1} x \cos x + \int (n-1)\sin^{n-2} x \cos^2 x \, dx$$
    $$= -\sin^{n-1} x \cos x + (n-1)I_{n-2} - (n-1)I_n$$
    (upon replacement of $\cos^2 x$ with $1 - \sin^2 x$).

    Therefore, $nI_n = -\sin^{n-1} x \cos x + (n-1)I_{n-2}$; that is,
    $$\int \sin^n x \, dx = -\frac{1}{n}\sin^{n-1} x \cos x + \frac{n-1}{n}\int \sin^{n-2} x \, dx.$$

54. $\begin{bmatrix} u = \cos^{n-1} x & dv = \cos x\, dx \\ du = -(n-1)\cos^{n-2} x \sin x\, dx & v = \sin x \end{bmatrix}$

$$I_n = \int \cos^n x\, dx$$
$$= \cos^{n-1} x \sin x + \int (n-1)\cos^{n-2} x \sin^2 x\, dx$$
$$= \cos^{n-1} x \sin x + (n-1)I_{n-2} - (n-1)I_n$$

(upon replacement of $\sin^2 x$ with $1 - \cos^2 x$)

Therefore, $nI_n = \cos^{n-1} x \sin x + (n-1)I_{n-2}$; that is,

$$\int \cos^n x\, dx = \frac{1}{n}\cos^{n-1} x \sin x + \frac{n-1}{n}\int \cos^{n-2} x\, dx.$$

55. $\displaystyle\int_0^1 x^3 e^x\, dx = \left[x^3 e^x\right]_0^1 - 3\int_0^1 x^2 e^x\, dx$

$$= e - 3\left[x^2 e^x\right]_0^1 + 6\int_0^1 x e^x\, dx$$
$$= e - 3e + 6\left[x e^x\right]_0^1 - 6\left[e^x\right]_0^1$$
$$= e - 3e + 6e - 6e + 6 = 6 - 2e \approx 0.563436.$$

56. Let J_n denote $\displaystyle\int_0^1 x^n e^{-x^2}\, dx$. Then from the solution of Problem 42 we conclude that

$$J_n = -\frac{1}{2e} + \frac{n-1}{2}J_{n-2}.$$

Therefore

$$J_5 = -\frac{1}{2e} + 2J_3 = -\frac{1}{2e} - \frac{2}{2e} + 2\int_0^1 x e^{-x^2}\, dx$$
$$= -\frac{1}{2e} - \frac{1}{e} + 2\left[-\frac{1}{2}e^{-x^2}\right]_0^1$$
$$= -\frac{3}{2e} + 1 - \frac{1}{e} = \frac{2e-5}{2e} \approx 0.0803014.$$

57. $\displaystyle\int (\ln x)^3\, dx = x(\ln x)^3 - 3\int x(\ln x)^2\, dx - 2\int x \ln x\, dx - \int 1\, dx.$

So $\displaystyle\int_1^e (\ln x)^3\, dx = \left[x(\ln x)^3 - 3x(\ln x)^2 + 6x(\ln x) - 6x\right]_1^e = e - 3e + 6e - 6e + 6 = 6 - 2e \approx 0.563436.$

58. Let $S_{2n} = \displaystyle\int_0^{\pi/2} \sin^{2n} x\, dx$. By the solution of Problem 45, $S_{2n} = \dfrac{2n-1}{2n}S_{2n-2}$.

Repeated application of this formula yields

$$S_{2n} = \left(\frac{2n-1}{2n}\right)\cdot\left(\frac{2n-3}{2n-2}\right) S_{2n-4}$$
$$= \left(\frac{2n-1}{2n}\right)\cdot\left(\frac{2n-3}{2n-2}\right)\cdot\left(\frac{2n-5}{2n-4}\right) S_{2n-6} = \cdots$$
$$= \left(\frac{2n-1}{2n}\right)\cdot\left(\frac{2n-3}{2n-2}\right)\cdot\left(\frac{2n-5}{2n-4}\right)\cdots\frac{3}{4}\cdot\frac{1}{2}\int_0^{\pi/2} 1\, dx$$
$$= \left(\frac{2n-1}{2n}\right)\cdot\left(\frac{2n-3}{2n-2}\right)\cdots\frac{5}{6}\cdot\frac{3}{4}\cdot\frac{1}{2}\cdot\frac{\pi}{2}.$$

The other derivation is similar.

64. **(a)** Area:

$$A = \int_0^\pi \tfrac{1}{2}x^2 \sin x\, dx = \left[\tfrac{1}{2}\left(-x^2 \cos x + 2\int x \cos x\, dx\right)\right]_0^\pi$$

$$= \left[-\tfrac{1}{2}x^2 \cos x + x \sin x - \int \sin x\, dx\right]_0^\pi$$

$$= \left[-\tfrac{1}{2}x^2 \cos x + x \sin x + \cos x\right]_0^\pi$$

$$= \tfrac{1}{2}\pi^2 - 1 - 1 = \frac{\pi^2 - 4}{2}.$$

(b) Volume:

$$V = \int_0^\pi 2\pi x \cdot \tfrac{1}{2}x^2 \sin x\, dx = \pi \int_0^\pi x^3 \sin x\, dx$$

$$= \pi\left[-x^3 \cos x + 3\int x^2 \cos x\, dx\right]_0^\pi$$

$$= \pi\left[-x^3 \cos x + 3\left(x^2 \sin x - 2\int x \sin x\, dx\right)\right]_0^\pi$$

$$= \pi\left[-x^3 \cos x + 3x^2 \sin x - 6(-x \cos x + \sin x)\right]_0^\pi$$

$$= \pi\left[-x^3 \cos x + 3x^2 \sin x + 6x \cos x - 6 \sin x\right]_0^\pi$$

$$= \pi\left(\pi^3 - 6\pi\right) = \pi^4 - 6\pi^2 = \pi^2\left(\pi^2 - 6\right).$$

65. Volume: $V = \int_0^\pi \pi\left(\tfrac{1}{2}x^2 \sin x\right)^2 dx = \frac{\pi}{4}\int_0^\pi x^4 \sin^2 x\, dx = \frac{\pi}{8}\int_0^\pi x^4(1 - \cos 2x)\, dx.$

Let $u = 2x$: $x = \tfrac{1}{2}u$, $dx = \tfrac{1}{2}du$.

$$V = \frac{\pi}{8}\int_0^{2\pi} \frac{u^4}{16}(1 - \cos u) \cdot \tfrac{1}{2}du$$

$$= \frac{\pi}{256}\int_0^{2\pi} \left(u^4 - u^4 \cos u\right) du$$

$$= \frac{\pi}{256}\left(\left[\tfrac{1}{5}u^5\right]_0^{2\pi} - \int_0^{2\pi} u^4 \cos u\, du\right)$$

$$= \frac{\pi}{256}\left(\tfrac{32}{5}\pi^5 - \left[u^4 \sin u - 4\int u^3 \sin u\, du\right]_0^{2\pi}\right)$$

$$= \frac{\pi^6}{40} - \frac{\pi}{256}\left[u^4 \sin u - 4\left(-u^3 \cos u + 3\{u^2 \sin u - 2[-u \cos u + \sin u]\}\right)\right]_0^{2\pi}$$

$$= \frac{\pi^6}{40} - \frac{\pi}{256}\left[4(2\pi)^3 - 24(2\pi)\right]$$

$$= \frac{\pi^6}{40} - \frac{\pi^4}{8} + \frac{3\pi^2}{16} = \frac{\pi^2}{80}\left(2\pi^4 - 10\pi^2 + 15\right).$$

Section 9.4

1. $\int \sin^2 2x\, dx = \int \dfrac{1-\cos 4x}{2}\, dx = \dfrac{x}{2} - \dfrac{1}{8}\sin 4x + C.$

2. $\int \cos^2 5x\, dx = \int \dfrac{1+\cos 10x}{2}\, dx = \dfrac{x}{2} + \dfrac{1}{20}\sin 10x + C.$

3. $\int \sec^2 \dfrac{x}{2}\, dx = 2\tan \dfrac{x}{2} + C.$

4. $\int \tan^2 \dfrac{x}{2}\, dx = \int \left(\sec^2 \dfrac{x}{2} - 1\right) dx = \left(2\tan \dfrac{x}{2}\right) - x + C.$

5. $\int \tan 3x\, dx = \tfrac{1}{3}\ln|\sec 3x| + C.$

6. $\int \cot 4x\, dx = \tfrac{1}{4}\ln|\sin 4x| + C.$

7. $\int \sec 3x\, dx = \tfrac{1}{3}\ln|\sec 3x + \tan 3x| + C.$

8. $\int \csc 2x\, dx = -\tfrac{1}{2}\ln|\csc 2x + \cot 2x| + C.$

9. $\int \dfrac{dx}{\csc^2 x} = \int \sin^2 x\, dx = \int \dfrac{1-\cos 2x}{2}\, dx = \tfrac{1}{2}x - \tfrac{1}{4}\sin 2x + C.$

10. $\int \sin^2 x \cot^2 x\, dx = \int \cos^2 x\, dx = \int \dfrac{1+\cos 2x}{2}\, dx = \tfrac{1}{2}x + \tfrac{1}{4}\sin 2x + C.$

11. $\int \sin^3 x\, dx = \int (\sin x)(1-\cos^2 x)\, dx = \int (\sin x - \cos^2 x \sin x)\, dx = \tfrac{1}{3}\cos^3 x - \cos x + C.$

12. $\int \sin^4 x\, dx = \int (\sin^2 x)^2\, dx = \tfrac{1}{4}\int (1-\cos 2x)^2\, dx$
    $= \tfrac{1}{4}\int \left(1 - 2\cos 2x + \tfrac{1}{2}(1+\cos 4x)\right) dx = \tfrac{3}{8}x - \tfrac{1}{4}\sin 2x + \tfrac{1}{32}\sin 4x + C.$

13. $\int \sin^2 \theta \cos^3 \theta\, d\theta = \int (\sin^2 \theta)(1-\sin^2 \theta)(\cos \theta)\, d\theta$
    $= \int (\sin^2 \theta \cos \theta - \sin^4 \theta \cos \theta)\, d\theta = \tfrac{1}{3}\sin^3 \theta - \tfrac{1}{5}\sin^5 \theta + C.$

14. $\int \sin^3 t \cos^3 t\, dt = \int (\sin^3 t)(1-\sin^2 t)(\cos t)\, dt$
    $= \int (\sin^3 t \cos t - \sin^5 t \cos t)\, dt = \tfrac{1}{4}\sin^4 t - \tfrac{1}{6}\sin^6 t + C.$

15. $\int \cos^5 x\, dx = \int (\cos x)(1-\sin^2 x)^2\, dx$
    $= \int (\sin^4 x \cos x - 2\sin^2 x \cos x + \cos x)\, dx = \tfrac{1}{5}\sin^5 x - \tfrac{2}{3}\sin^3 x + \sin x + C.$

16. $\int \dfrac{\sin t}{\cos^3 t}\, dt = \dfrac{1}{2\cos^2 t} + C.$

17. $\int \dfrac{\sin^3 x}{\sqrt{\cos x}}\, dx = \int (\sin x)(1-\cos^2 x)(\cos x)^{-1/2}\, dx$
    $= \int \left((\cos x)^{-1/2}\sin x - (\cos x)^{3/2}\sin x\right) dx = \tfrac{2}{5}(\cos x)^{5/2} - 2(\cos x)^{1/2} + C.$

18. $\int \sin^3 3\phi \cos^4 3\phi\, d\phi = \int (\sin 3\phi)(1-\cos^2 3\phi)(\cos^4 3\phi)\, d\phi$
    $= \int (\cos^4 3\phi \sin 3\phi - \cos^6 3\phi \sin 3\phi)\, d\phi = \tfrac{1}{21}\cos^7 3\phi - \tfrac{1}{15}\cos^5 3\phi + C.$

19. $\int \sin^5 2z \cos^2 2z \, dz = \int (\sin 2z)(1 - \cos^2 2z)^2 \cos^2 2z \, dz$
$= \int (\cos^6 2z \sin 2z - 2\cos^4 2z \sin 2z + \cos^2 2z \sin 2z) \, dz$
$= -\frac{1}{14} \cos^7 2z + \frac{1}{5} \cos^5 2z - \frac{1}{6} \cos^3 2z + C.$

20. $\int \sin^{3/2} x \cos^3 x \, dx = \int \left(\sin^{3/2} x\right)(1 - \sin^2 x)(\cos x) \, dx$
$= \int \left(\sin^{3/2} x \cos x - \sin^{7/2} x \cos x\right) dx = \frac{2}{5} \sin^{5/2} x - \frac{2}{9} \sin^{9/2} x + C.$

21. $\int \frac{\sin^3 u}{\cos^2 u} \, du = \int \frac{1 - \cos^2 u}{\cos^2 u} \sin u \, du = \int \left((\cos u)^{-2} \sin u - \sin u\right) du.$

22. $\cos^6 u = (\cos^2 u)^3 = \frac{1}{8}(1 + \cos 2u)^3 = \frac{1}{8}(1 + 3\cos 2u + 3\cos^2 2u + \cos^3 2u)$
$= \frac{1}{8}\left(1 + 3\cos 2u + \frac{3}{2}(1 + \cos 4u) + (1 - \sin^2 2u)(\cos 2u)\right).$
Thus the antiderivative—simplified—is $\frac{5}{16}\theta + \frac{1}{16}\sin 8\theta + \frac{3}{256}\sin 16\theta - \frac{1}{192}\sin^3 8\theta + C.$

23. $\int \sec^4 t \, dt = \int (1 + \tan^2 t) \sec^2 t \, dt = \frac{1}{3} \tan^3 t + \tan t + C.$

24. $\int \tan^3 x \, dx = \int (\sec^2 x - 1) \tan x \, dx$
$= \int ((\sec x)(\sec x \tan x) - \tan x) \, dx = \frac{1}{2} \sec^2 x + \ln|\cos x| + C.$

25. $\int \cot^3 2x \, dx = \int (\cot 2x)(\csc^2 2x - 1) \, dx.$

26. $\int \tan\theta \sec^4\theta \, d\theta = \int (\sec^3\theta)(\sec\theta \tan\theta) \, d\theta = \frac{1}{4} \sec^4\theta + C.$

27. $\int \tan^5 u \sec^2 u \, du = \frac{1}{6} \tan^6 u + C.$

28. $\int \cot^3 x \csc^2 x \, dx = -\frac{1}{4} \cot^4 x + C.$

29. $\int \csc^6 v \, dv = \int (\csc v)^2 (1 + \cot^2 v)^2 \, dv = \int (\cot^4 v \csc^2 v + 2\cot^2 v \csc^2 v + \csc^2 v) \, dv.$

30. $\int \frac{\sec^4 t}{\tan^2 t} \, dt = \int \frac{1 + \tan^2 t}{\tan^2 t} \sec^2 t \, dt = \int (\sec^2 t + \tan^{-2} t \sec^2 t) \, dt$
$= \tan t - \frac{1}{\tan t} + C = \tan t - \cot t + C.$

31. $\int \frac{\tan^3 \theta}{\sec^4 \theta} \, d\theta = \int (\sec\theta)^{-4}(\sec^2\theta - 1)(\tan\theta) \, d\theta$
$= \int ((\sec\theta)^{-3} \sec\theta \tan\theta - (\sec\theta)^{-5} \sec\theta \tan\theta) \, d\theta.$

32. $\int \frac{\cot^3 x}{\csc^2 x} \, dx = \int \frac{\cos^3 x}{\sin^3 x} \sin^2 x \, dx = \int \frac{\cos^3 x}{\sin x} \, dx = \int \frac{(1 - \sin^2 x)(\cos x)}{\sin x} \, dx$
$= \int \left(\frac{\cos x}{\sin x} - \sin x \cos x\right) dx = \ln|\sin x| + \frac{1}{2} \cos^2 x + C.$

33. $\int \tan^3 t \sec^{-1/2} t \, dt = \int (\tan t)(\sec^2 t - 1)(\sec t)^{-1/2} \, dt$
$= \int \left((\sec t)^{3/2}(\tan t) - (\sec t)^{-1/2}(\tan t)\right) dt$
$= \int \left((\sec t)^{1/2}(\sec t \tan t) - (\sec t)^{-3/2}(\sec t)(\tan t)\right) dt.$

34. $\int \dfrac{1}{\cos^4 2x}\, dx = \int \sec^4 2x\, dx = \int (\tan^2 2x + 1) \sec^2 2x\, dx = \tfrac{1}{6}\tan^3 2x + \tfrac{1}{2}\tan 2x + C.$

35. $\int \dfrac{\cot\theta}{\csc^3\theta}\, d\theta = \int \dfrac{\cos\theta}{\sin\theta} \sin^3\theta\, d\theta = \tfrac{1}{3}\sin^3\theta + C.$

36. $\int \sin^2 3\alpha \cos^2 3\alpha\, d\alpha = \int \left(\dfrac{1-\cos 6\alpha}{2}\right)\left(\dfrac{1+\cos 6\alpha}{2}\right) d\alpha = \tfrac{1}{4}\int (1-\cos^2 6\alpha)\, d\alpha$
$= \tfrac{1}{4}\int \left(1 - \dfrac{1+\cos 12\alpha}{2}\right) d\alpha = \tfrac{1}{8}\alpha - \tfrac{1}{96}\sin 12\alpha + C.$

37. $\int \cos^3 5t\, dt = \int (1-\sin^2 5t)\cos 5t\, dt = \int (\cos 5t - \sin^2 5t \cos 5t)\, dt.$

38. $\int \tan^4 x\, dx = \int (\sec^2 x - 1)\tan^2 x\, dx = \int (\tan^2 x \sec^2 x - (\sec^2 x - 1))\, dx$
$= \tfrac{1}{3}\tan^3 x - \tan x + x + C.$

39. $\int \cot^4 3t\, dt = \int (\csc^2 3t - 1)\cot^2 3t\, dt = \int (\cot^2 3t \csc^2 3t - (\csc^2 3t - 1))\, dt.$

40. $\int \tan^2 2t \sec^4 2t\, dt = \int (\tan^2 2t)(\tan^2 2t + 1)\sec^2 2t\, dt = \int (\tan^4 2t \sec^2 2t + \tan^2 2t \sec^2 2t)\, dt$
$= \tfrac{1}{10}\tan^5 2t + \tfrac{1}{6}\tan^3 2t + C.$

41. $\int \sin^5 2t \cos^{3/2} 2t\, dt = \int (1-\cos^2 2t)^2 \cos^{3/2} 2t \sin 2t\, dt$
$= \int (\cos^{3/2} 2t \sin 2t - 2\cos^{7/2} 2t \sin 2t + \cos^{11/2} 2t \sin 2t)\, dt.$

42. $\int \cot^3\theta \csc^{3/2}\theta\, d\theta = \int (\csc^2\theta - 1)(\csc^{1/2}\theta)(\csc\theta \cot\theta)\, d\theta$
$= \int ((\csc\theta)^{5/2}(\csc\theta \cot\theta) - (\csc\theta)^{1/2}(\csc\theta \cot\theta))\, d\theta$
$= -\tfrac{2}{7}(\csc\theta)^{7/2} + \tfrac{2}{3}(\csc\theta)^{3/2} + C.$

43. $\dfrac{\tan x}{\sec x} = \sin x$ and $\dfrac{\sin x}{\sec x} = \sin x \cos x.$

44. $\dfrac{\cot x}{\sin x} = \csc x \cot x$ and $\dfrac{\csc x}{\sin x} = \csc^2 x$, so $\int \dfrac{\cot x + \csc x}{\sin x}\, dx = -\csc x - \cot x + C.$

45. The area is $\int_0^\pi \sin^3 x\, dx = \int_0^\pi (1-\cos^2 x)\sin x\, dx = \left[\tfrac{1}{3}\cos^3 x - \cos x\right]_0^\pi = \tfrac{4}{3}.$

46. The area is $\int_{-\pi/4}^{\pi/4} (\cos^2 x - \sin^2 x)\, dx = \int_{-\pi/4}^{\pi/4} \cos 2x\, dx = \left[\tfrac{1}{2}\sin 2x\right]_{-\pi/4}^{\pi/4} = 1.$

47. The area is
$\int_{\pi/4}^{\pi} (\sin^2 x - \sin x \cos x)\, dx = \int_{\pi/4}^{\pi} (\tfrac{1}{2}(1-\cos 2x) - \sin x \cos x)\, dx$
$= \left[\tfrac{1}{2}x - \tfrac{1}{4}\sin 2x - \tfrac{1}{2}\sin^2 x\right]_{\pi/4}^{\pi} = \tfrac{1}{2} + \tfrac{3}{8}\pi.$

48. The area is
$\int_{\pi/4}^{5\pi/4} (\sin^3 x - \cos^3 x)\, dx = \int_{\pi/4}^{5\pi/4} ((1-\cos^2 x)\sin x - (1-\sin^2 x)\cos x)\, dx$
$= \left[\tfrac{1}{3}\cos^3 x - \cos x + \tfrac{1}{3}\sin^3 x - \sin x\right]_{\pi/4}^{5\pi/4} = \tfrac{5}{3}\sqrt{2}.$

49. 0

Section 9.4 Trigonometric Integrals

50. 0

51. The volume is

$$\int_0^\pi \pi \sin^4 x \, dx = \pi \int_0^\pi \left(\frac{1-\cos 2x}{2}\right)^2 dx = \tfrac{1}{4}\pi \int_0^\pi \left(1 - 2\cos 2x + \tfrac{1}{2}(1+\cos 4x)\right) dx$$
$$= \tfrac{1}{4}\pi \left[x - \sin 2x + \tfrac{1}{2}x + \tfrac{1}{8}\sin 4x\right]_0^\pi = \tfrac{3}{8}\pi^2.$$

52. The volume is

$$\int_{-\pi/4}^{\pi/4} \left(\pi \cos^4 x - \pi \sin^4 x\right) dx = \pi \int_{-\pi/4}^{\pi/4} \left(\cos^2 x + \sin^2 x\right)\left(\cos^2 x - \sin^2 x\right) dx$$
$$= \pi \int_{-\pi/4}^{\pi/4} \cos 2x \, dx = \pi \left[\tfrac{1}{2}\sin 2x\right]_{-\pi/4}^{\pi/4} = \pi.$$

53. The volume is

$$\int_{-\pi/3}^{\pi/3} \left(4\pi - \pi \sec^2 x\right) dx = \pi \left[4x - \tan x\right]_{-\pi/3}^{\pi/3}$$
$$= \tfrac{1}{3}\pi \left(8\pi - 6\sqrt{3}\right) \approx 15.4361.$$

54. The volume is

$$\int_{-\pi/3}^{\pi/3} \left(\pi(4\cos x)^2 - \pi \sec^2 x\right) dx = \pi \left[8x + 4\sin 2x - \tan x\right]_{-\pi/3}^{\pi/3}$$
$$= \frac{2\pi \left(8\pi + 3\sqrt{3}\right)}{3} \approx 63.520686325.$$

55. (a) The area of R is $\displaystyle\int_0^{\pi/4} \left(\sec^2 x - \tan^2 x\right) dx = \int_0^{\pi/4} 1 \, dx = \frac{\pi}{4}.$

(b) The volume of revolution is

$$\int_0^{\pi/4} \left(\pi \sec^4 x - \pi \tan^4 x\right) dx = \pi \int_0^{\pi/4} \left(\sec^2 x + \tan^2 x\right)\left(\sec^2 x - \tan^2 x\right) dx$$
$$= \pi \int_0^{\pi/4} \left(2\sec^2 x - 1\right) dx = \pi \left[2\tan x - x\right]_0^{\pi/4}$$
$$= \frac{\pi(8-\pi)}{4} \approx 3.815784207.$$

56. The arc-length element is

$$ds = \sqrt{1 + (-\tan x)^2} \, dx = |\sec x| \, dx = \sec x \, dx$$

because $\sec x$ is nonnegative on $[0, \pi/4]$. So the length of the graph is

$$\int_0^{\pi/4} \sec x \, dx = \left[\ln|\sec x + \tan x|\right]_0^{\pi/4} = \ln\left(1 + \sqrt{2}\right) \approx 0.881373587.$$

57. $\tan x \sec^4 x = (\sec x)^3 D_x(\sec x)$
$= \left(\tan x \sec^2 x\right)\left(\tan^2 x + 1\right)$
$= (\tan x)^3 D_x(\tan x) + (\tan x)^1 D_x(\tan x).$

58. (1) $\int \cot^3 x \, dx = \int (\cot x)(\csc^2 x - 1) \, dx = -\frac{1}{2}\cot^2 x - \ln|\sin x| + C_1$;

(2) $\int \cot^3 x \, dx = \int \frac{\cos^3 x}{\sin^3 x} \, dx = \int \frac{(\cos x)(1 - \sin^2 x)}{\sin^3 x} \, dx = \int \left(\frac{\cos x}{\sin^3 x} - \frac{\cos x}{\sin x}\right) dx$
$= -\frac{1}{2\sin^2 x} - \ln|\sin x| + C_2$.

The difference in the two antiderivatives is $\frac{1}{2} + C_1 - C_2 = C$ (a constant). Therefore the two results are equivalent.

59. $\sin 3x \cos 5x = \frac{1}{2}(\sin 8x - \sin 2x)$.

60. $\int \sin 2x \sin 4x \, dx = \frac{1}{2}\int (\cos 2x - \cos 6x) \, dx = \frac{1}{4}\sin 2x - \frac{1}{12}\sin 6x + C$.

61. $\cos x \cos 4x = \frac{1}{2}(\cos 3x + \cos 5x)$.

62. (a) $\int_0^{2\pi} \sin mx \sin nx \, dx = \frac{1}{2}\int_0^{2\pi} (\cos(n-m)x - \cos(n+m)x) \, dx$
$= \frac{1}{2}\left[\frac{\sin(n-m)x}{n-m} - \frac{\sin(n+m)x}{n+m}\right]_0^{2\pi} = 0$.

The derivations for Parts (b) and (c) are similar.

68. Mathematica 2.2.1 gives $-x + \frac{23}{15}\tan x - \frac{11}{15}\sec^2 x \tan x + \frac{1}{5}\sec^4 x \tan x + C$.
Derive 2.56 gives $\tan x - \frac{1}{3}\tan^3 x + \frac{1}{5}\tan^5 x - x + C$.

Section 9.5

1. $\int \frac{x^2}{x+1} \, dx = \int \left(x - 1 + \frac{1}{x+1}\right) dx = \frac{1}{2}x^2 - x + \ln|x+1| + C$.

2. $\int \frac{x^3}{2x-1} \, dx = \int \left(\frac{1}{2}x^2 + \frac{1}{4}x + \frac{1}{8} + \frac{1}{8}\left(\frac{1}{2x-1}\right)\right) dx = \frac{1}{6}x^3 + \frac{1}{8}x^2 + \frac{1}{8}x + \frac{1}{16}\ln|2x-1| + C$.

3. $\frac{1}{x^2 - 3x} = \frac{1}{x(x-3)} = \frac{1}{3}\left(\frac{1}{x-3} - \frac{1}{x}\right)$.

4. $\int \frac{x}{x^2 + 4x} \, dx = \int \frac{1}{x+4} \, dx = \ln|x+4| + C$.

5. $\frac{1}{x^2 + x - 6} = \frac{1}{(x+3)(x-2)} = \frac{1}{5}\left(\frac{1}{x-2} - \frac{1}{x+3}\right)$.

6. $\int \frac{x^3}{x^2 + x - 6} \, dx = \int \left(x - 1 + \frac{7x-6}{(x+3)(x-2)}\right) dx = \frac{1}{2}x^2 - x + \frac{27}{5}\ln|x+3| + \frac{8}{5}\ln|x-2| + C$.

7. $\frac{1}{x^3 + 4x} = \frac{1}{x(x^2+4)} = \frac{A}{x} + \frac{Bx+C}{x^2+4}$ yields $A = \frac{1}{4}$, $B = -\frac{1}{4}$, and $C = 0$.

So $\int \frac{1}{x^3 + 4x} \, dx = \frac{1}{4}\ln|x| - \frac{1}{8}\ln(x^2+4) + C$.

8. $\frac{1}{(x+1)(x^2+1)} = \frac{A}{x+1} + \frac{Bx+C}{x^2+1}$ yields $A = \frac{1}{2}$, $B = -\frac{1}{2}$, and $C = \frac{1}{2}$.

So $\int \frac{1}{(x+1)(x^2+1)} \, dx = \frac{1}{2}\ln|x+1| - \frac{1}{4}\ln(x^2+1) + \frac{1}{2}\arctan x + C$.

9. $\frac{x^4}{x^2+4} = x^2 - 4 + \frac{16}{x^2+4}$.

10. $\frac{1}{(x^2+1)(x^2+4)} = \frac{Ax+B}{x^2+1} + \frac{Cx+D}{x^2+4}$ yields $A = C = 0$, $B = \frac{1}{3}$, and $D = -\frac{1}{3}$.

Thus $\int \frac{1}{(x^2+1)(x^2+4)} dx = \frac{1}{3} \arctan x - \frac{1}{6} \arctan\left(\frac{x}{2}\right) + C.$

11. $\frac{x-1}{x+1} = \frac{x+1-2}{x+1}.$

12. $\int \frac{2x^3-1}{x^2+1} dx = \int \left(2x - \frac{2x}{x^2+1} - \frac{1}{x^2+1}\right) dx = x^2 - \ln(x^2+1) - \arctan x + C.$

13. Rewrite the integrand as $1 - \frac{1}{(x+1)^2}.$

14. $\int \frac{2x-4}{x^2-x} dx = \int \left(\frac{4}{x} - \frac{2}{x-1}\right) dx = 4\ln|x| - 2\ln|x-1| + C = 2\ln\left|\frac{x^2}{x-1}\right| + C.$

15. $\frac{1}{x^2-4} = \frac{1}{4}\left(\frac{1}{x-2} - \frac{1}{x+2}\right).$

16. After division:
$$\int \frac{x^4}{x^2+4x+4} dx = \int \left(x^2 - 4x + 12 - (16)\frac{2x+3}{(x+2)^2}\right) dx$$
$$= \tfrac{1}{3}x^3 - 2x^2 + 12x - 16\int \frac{2x+4-1}{(x+2)^2} dx$$
$$= \tfrac{1}{3}x^3 - 2x^2 + 12x - 16\int \left(\frac{2}{x+2} - \frac{1}{(x+2)^2}\right) dx$$
$$= \tfrac{1}{3}x^3 - 2x^2 + 12x - \frac{16}{x+2} - 32\ln|x+2| + C.$$

17. $\frac{x+10}{2x^2+5x-3} = \frac{3}{2x-1} - \frac{1}{x+3}.$

18. $\int \frac{x+1}{x^3-x^2} dx = \int \left(-\frac{2}{x} - \frac{1}{x^2} + \frac{2}{x-1}\right) dx = 2\ln\left|\frac{x-1}{x}\right| + \frac{1}{x} + C.$

19. $\frac{x^2+1}{x^3+2x^2+x} = \frac{1}{x} + \frac{0}{x+1} - \frac{2}{(x+1)^2}.$

20. $\int \frac{x^2+x}{x^3-x^2-2x} dx = \int \frac{x(x+1)}{x(x^2-x-2)} dx = \int \frac{x+1}{(x+1)(x-2)} dx = \int \frac{1}{x-2} dx = \ln|x-2| + C.$

21. $\frac{4x^3-7x}{x^4-5x^2+4} = \frac{A}{x-2} + \frac{B}{x+2} + \frac{C}{x-1} + \frac{D}{x+1}$ yields $A = \tfrac{3}{2} = B$, $C = \tfrac{1}{2} = D$.

22. $\int \frac{2x^2+3}{x^4-2x^2+1} dx = \int \left(-\tfrac{1}{4}\left(\frac{1}{x-1}\right) + \tfrac{5}{4}\left(\frac{1}{(x-1)^2}\right) + \tfrac{1}{4}\left(\frac{1}{x+1}\right) + \tfrac{5}{4}\left(\frac{1}{(x+1)^2}\right)\right) dx$
$= \tfrac{1}{4}\ln\left|\frac{x+1}{x-1}\right| - \frac{5x}{2(x^2-1)} + C.$

23. $\frac{x^2}{(x+2)^3} = \frac{1}{x+2} - \frac{4}{(x+2)^2} + \frac{4}{(x+2)^3}.$

24. $\int \frac{x^2+x}{(x^2-4)(x+4)} dx = \int \left[\tfrac{1}{4}\left(\frac{1}{x-2} - \frac{1}{x+2}\right) + \frac{1}{x+4}\right] dx = \tfrac{1}{4}\ln\left|\frac{x-2}{x+2}\right| + \ln|x+4| + C.$

25. $\frac{1}{x^3+x} = \frac{A}{x} + \frac{Bx+C}{x^2+1}$ leads to $A = 1$, $B = -1$, $C = 0$.

26. $\int \frac{6x^3-18x}{(x^2-1)(x^2-4)} dx = \int \left(\frac{1}{x-2} + \frac{2}{x-1} + \frac{2}{x+1} + \frac{1}{x+2}\right) dx$
$= \ln|x-2| + 2\ln|x-1| + 2\ln|x+1| + \ln|x+2| + C = \ln\left|(x^2-4)(x^2-1)^2\right| + C.$

27. $\frac{x+4}{x^3+4x} = \frac{A}{x} + \frac{Bx+C}{x^2+4}$ leads to $A = C = 1$, $B = -1$; thus we must find the antiderivative of $\frac{1}{x^2+4}$. Use Formula 17 of the endpapers, or write the integrand in the form $\frac{1/4}{(x/2)^2+1}.$

258   Section 9.5 Rational Functions and Partial Fractions

28. $\dfrac{4x^4+x+1}{x^5+x^4} = \dfrac{A}{x} + \dfrac{B}{x^2} + \dfrac{C}{x^3} + \dfrac{D}{x^4} + \dfrac{E}{x+1}$ yields $A = B = C = 0$, $D = 1$, and $E = 4$.

So $\displaystyle\int \dfrac{4x^4+x+1}{x^5+x^4}\,dx = \int\left(\dfrac{1}{x^4} + \dfrac{4}{x+1}\right)dx = -\tfrac{1}{3}x^{-3} + 4\ln|x+1| + C.$

29. $\dfrac{x}{(x+1)(x^2+1)} = \dfrac{A}{x+1} + \dfrac{Bx+C}{x^2+1}$ leads to $A = -\tfrac{1}{2}$ and $B = C = \tfrac{1}{2}.$

30. $\displaystyle\int \dfrac{x^2+2}{(x^2+1)^2}\,dx = \int\left(\dfrac{1}{x^2+1} + \dfrac{1}{(x^2+1)^2}\right)dx$

$= \tan^{-1}x + \displaystyle\int \dfrac{\sec^2 u}{\sec^4 u}\,du \quad (x = \tan u)$

$= \tan^{-1}x + \tfrac{1}{2}\displaystyle\int (1+\cos 2u)\,du$

$= \tan^{-1}x + \tfrac{1}{2}(u + \sin u \cos u) + C = \tfrac{3}{2}\tan^{-1}x + \dfrac{x}{2(x^2+1)} + C.$

31. $\dfrac{x^2-10}{2x^4+9x^2+4} = \dfrac{Ax+B}{2x^2+1} + \dfrac{Cx+D}{x^2+4}$ yields $A = C = 0$, $B = -3$, and $D = 2$.

32. $\displaystyle\int \dfrac{x^2}{x^4-1}\,dx = \int \tfrac{1}{4}\left(\dfrac{1}{x-1}\right) - \tfrac{1}{4}\left(\dfrac{1}{x+1}\right) + \tfrac{1}{2}\left(\dfrac{1}{x^2+1}\right)dx = \tfrac{1}{4}\ln\left|\dfrac{x-1}{x+1}\right| + \tfrac{1}{2}\tan^{-1}x + C.$

33. $\dfrac{x^3+x^2+2x+3}{(x^2+2)(x^2+3)} = \dfrac{Ax+B}{x^2+2} + \dfrac{Cx+D}{x^2+3}$ yields the equation (actually, the *identity*)

$$Ax^3 + Bx^2 + 3Ax + 3B + Cx^3 + Dx^2 + 2Cx + 2D = x^3 + x^2 + 2x + 3,$$

and thus the simultaneous equations

$$\begin{aligned} A \quad\quad\; + C \quad\quad\;\; &= 1, \\ B \quad\quad\; + D &= 1, \\ 3A \quad\quad + 2C \quad\quad\;\; &= 2, \\ 3B \quad\quad + 2D &= 3. \end{aligned}$$

These equations have solution $A = D = 0$, $B = C = 1$, and the partial fraction decomposition of the integrand gives:

$$\int \dfrac{x^3+x^2+2x+3}{x^4+5x^2+6}\,dx = \int\left(\dfrac{1}{x^2+2} + \dfrac{x}{x^2+3}\right)dx = \dfrac{1}{\sqrt{2}}\arctan\dfrac{x}{\sqrt{2}} + \tfrac{1}{2}\ln(x^2+3) + C.$$

34. $\displaystyle\int \dfrac{x^2+4}{(x^2+1)^2(x^2+2)}\,dx = \int\left(-\dfrac{2}{x^2+1} + \dfrac{3}{(x^2+1)^2} + \dfrac{2}{x^2+2}\right)dx.$

The first term in the integrand presents no problem, and by Formula 17 of the endpapers the third yields

$$\sqrt{2}\arctan\left(\tfrac{1}{2}x\sqrt{2}\right) + C_3.$$

For the second term, we use the substitution $x = \tan z$. Then

$$\int \dfrac{3}{(x^2+1)^2}\,dx = 3\int \dfrac{\sec^2 z}{\sec^4 z}\,dz = 3\int \tfrac{1}{2}(1+\cos 2z)\,dz$$

$$= \tfrac{3}{2}(z + \sin z \cos z) + C_2 = \tfrac{3}{2}\left(\tan^{-1}x + \dfrac{x}{1+x^2}\right) + C_2.$$

When we assemble this work, we find:

$$\int \dfrac{x^2+4}{(x^2+1)^2(x^2+2)}\,dx = \dfrac{3x}{2(1+x^2)} - \tfrac{1}{2}\tan^{-1}x + \sqrt{2}\tan^{-1}\left(\tfrac{1}{2}x\sqrt{2}\right) + C.$$

35. The partial fraction decomposition of the integrand is $1 + \dfrac{\frac{1}{2}}{x-1} + \dfrac{\frac{5}{2}}{(x-1)^2} + \dfrac{\frac{3}{2}x+2}{x^2+1}$.

36. The partial fraction decomposition of the integrand is $\dfrac{1}{x-1} + \dfrac{1}{x+2} + \dfrac{1}{(x-1)^2} + \dfrac{1}{(x+2)^2}$. The antiderivative is $\ln|x-1| + \ln|x+2| - \dfrac{1}{x-1} - \dfrac{1}{x+2} + C$.

37. Let $x = e^{2t}$. Then $dx = 2e^{2t}\,dt$; $e^{4t}\,dt = \frac{1}{2}x\,dx$.

$$\int \frac{e^{4t}}{(e^{2t}-1)^3}\,dt = \frac{1}{2}\int \frac{x}{(x-1)^3}\,dx = \frac{1}{2}\int\left(\frac{1}{(x-1)^2} + \frac{1}{(x-1)^3}\right)dx$$
$$= -\frac{1}{4}\left(\frac{2}{x-1} + \frac{1}{(x-1)^2}\right) + C = -\frac{2x-1}{4(x-1)^2} + C = \frac{1-2e^{2t}}{4(e^{2t}-1)^2} + C.$$

38. Let $u = \sin\theta$. Then

$$\int \frac{\cos\theta}{\sin^2\theta - \sin\theta - 6}\,d\theta = \int \frac{1}{u^2-u-6}\,du = \int \frac{1}{5}\left(\frac{1}{u-3} - \frac{1}{u+2}\right)du$$
$$= \frac{1}{5}\ln\left|\frac{u-3}{u+2}\right| + C = \frac{1}{5}\ln\left|\frac{-3+\sin\theta}{2+\sin\theta}\right| + C.$$

39. The substitution $x = \ln t$, $t = e^x$ results in:

$$\int \frac{1+\ln t}{t(3+2\ln t)^2}\,dt = \int \frac{1+x}{(3+2x)^2}\,dx = \frac{1}{2}\int \frac{2+2x}{(3+2x)^2}\,dx$$
$$= \frac{1}{2}\int \frac{3+2x}{(3+2x)^2}\,dx - \frac{1}{2}\int \frac{1}{(3+2x)^2}\,dx$$
$$= \frac{1}{4}\ln|3+2x| + \frac{1}{4(3+2x)} + C = \frac{1}{4}\left(\ln|3+2\ln t| + \frac{1}{3+2\ln t}\right) + C.$$

40. Let $u = \tan t$; $du = \sec^2 t\,dt$. Then

$$\int \frac{\sec^2 t}{\tan^3 t + \tan^2 t}\,dt = \int \frac{1}{u^3+u^2}\,du = \int\left(-\frac{1}{u} + \frac{1}{u^2} + \frac{1}{u+1}\right)du$$
$$= \ln\left|\frac{u+1}{u}\right| - \frac{1}{u} + C = \ln\left|\frac{1+\tan t}{\tan t}\right| - \cot t + C$$
$$= \ln|1+\cot t| - \cot t + C.$$

41. The partial fraction decomposition of the integrand is $\dfrac{3}{x} - \dfrac{2}{x-3}$, and therefore

$$\int_1^2 \frac{x-9}{x^2-3x}\,dx = 5\ln 2.$$

42. $\displaystyle\int_0^2 \left(\frac{1}{x+1} - \frac{2}{x-3}\right)dx = 3\ln 3$.

43. $\displaystyle\int_1^2 \left(\frac{5}{\frac{3}{x}} - \frac{\frac{4}{3}}{x-3} - \frac{\frac{7}{3}}{x+3}\right)dx = \frac{1}{3}(23\ln 2 - 7\ln 5) \approx 1.558773255$.

44. $\displaystyle\int_2^5 \left(\frac{1}{x} + \frac{2}{(x+4)^2}\right)dx = \frac{1}{9} - \ln 2 + \ln 5$.

45. $\displaystyle\int_1^2 2\pi x \cdot \frac{x-9}{x^2-3x}\,dx = 2\pi\int_1^2\left(1 - \frac{6}{x-3}\right)dx = 2\pi(1 + 6\ln 2) \approx 32.414218391$.

260   Section 9.5 Rational Functions and Partial Fractions

46. $\int_0^2 2\pi x \cdot \dfrac{x+5}{3+2x-x^2}\,dx = 2\pi \int_0^2 \left(\dfrac{6}{3-x} - 1 - \dfrac{1}{x+1}\right) dx$

$= 2\pi \Big[-6\ln|3-x| - x - \ln|x+1|\Big]_0^2$

$= 2\pi(-2 + 5\ln 3) \approx 21.947552338.$

47. $\int_1^2 2\pi x \cdot \dfrac{3x-15-2x^2}{x^3-9x}\,dx = 2\pi \int_1^2 \left(\dfrac{7}{x+3} - 2 - \dfrac{4}{x-3}\right) dx$

$= 2\pi \Big[7\ln|x+3| - 2x - 4\ln|x-3|\Big]_1^2$

$= 2\pi(7\ln 5 - 2 - 10\ln 2) \approx 14.668684089.$

48. $\int_2^5 2\pi x \cdot \dfrac{x^2+10x+16}{x^3+8x^2+16x}\,dx = 2\pi \int_2^5 \left(\dfrac{2}{x+4} + 1 - \dfrac{8}{(x+4)^2}\right) dx$

$= 2\pi \Big[2\ln|x+4| + x + \dfrac{8}{x+4}\Big]_2^5$

$= 2\pi\left(\dfrac{23}{9} + 2\ln 3 - 2\ln 2\right) \approx 21.152253938.$

49. $\int_1^2 \pi \left(\dfrac{x-9}{x^2-3x}\right)^2 dx = \pi \int_1^2 \left(\dfrac{4}{x} - \dfrac{4}{x-3} + \dfrac{9}{x^2} + \dfrac{4}{(x-3)^2}\right) dx$

$= \pi\Big[4\ln|x| - 4\ln|x-3| - \dfrac{9}{x} - \dfrac{4}{x-3}\Big]_1^2$

$= \pi\left(\dfrac{13}{2} + 8\ln 2\right) \approx 37.841040971.$

50. $\int_0^2 \pi\left(\dfrac{x+5}{3+2x-x^2}\right)^2 dx = \pi \int_0^2 \left(\dfrac{1}{x+1} - \dfrac{1}{x-3} + \dfrac{1}{(x+1)^2} + \dfrac{4}{(x-3)^2}\right) dx$

$= \pi\Big[\ln|x+1| - \ln|x-3| - \dfrac{1}{x+1} - \dfrac{4}{x-3}\Big]_0^2$

$= \pi\left(\dfrac{10}{3} + 2\ln 3\right) \approx 17.374760102.$

51. Let V be the volume of the solid. Then

$V = \int_0^1 \pi y^2\,dx = \pi \int_0^1 x^2 \left(\dfrac{1-x}{1+x}\right) dx$

$= \pi \int_0^1 \left(-x^2 + 2x - 2 + \dfrac{2}{x+1}\right) dx$

$= \pi\Big[-\tfrac{1}{3}x^3 + x^2 - 2x + 2\ln|x+1|\Big]_0^1$

$= \pi\left(-\tfrac{1}{3} + 1 - 2 + 2\ln 2\right) = \tfrac{2}{3}\pi(3\ln 2 - 2) \approx 0.166382.$

52. (a) The volume of revolution around the x-axis is

$\int_0^1 \pi \cdot \dfrac{x^4(1-x)^2}{(1+x)^2}\,dx = \pi \int_0^1 \left(x^4 - 4x^3 + 8x^2 - 12x + 16 - \dfrac{20}{x+1} + \dfrac{4}{(x+1)^2}\right) dx$

$= \pi\Big[\tfrac{1}{5}x^5 - x^4 + \tfrac{8}{3}x^3 - 6x^2 + 16x - 20\ln|x+1| - \dfrac{4}{x+1}\Big]_0^1$

$= \pi\left(\dfrac{208}{15} - 20\ln 2\right) \approx 0.011696324.$

(b) The volume of revolution around the y-axis is

$2\int_0^1 2\pi x \cdot \dfrac{x^2(1-x)}{1+x}\,dx = 2\pi \int_0^1 \left(4 - 4x + 4x^2 - 2x^3 - \dfrac{4}{x+1}\right) dx$

$= 2\pi\Big[4x - 2x^2 + \tfrac{4}{3}x^3 - \tfrac{1}{2}x^4 - 4\ln|x+1|\Big]_0^1$

$= 2\pi\left(\dfrac{17}{6} - 4\ln 2\right) \approx 0.381669648.$

53. $\int \left(\dfrac{93}{x-7} + \dfrac{49}{x-5} - \dfrac{44}{x} + \dfrac{280}{x^2}\right) dx = 93\ln|x-7| + 49\ln|x-5| - 44\ln|x| - \dfrac{280}{x} + C.$

54. $\int \left(\dfrac{323}{x+3} - \dfrac{291}{x+7} - \dfrac{384}{(x+3)^2} - \dfrac{1324}{(x+7)^2}\right) dx = 323\ln|x+3| - 291\ln|x+7| + \dfrac{384}{x+3} + \dfrac{1324}{x+7} + C.$

55. $\int \left(\dfrac{48}{(x-4)^2} - \dfrac{104}{3(x-4)} + \dfrac{567}{16(x-3)} - \dfrac{39}{2(x+5)^2} - \dfrac{37}{48(x+5)}\right) dx$

    $= -\dfrac{48}{x-4} + \dfrac{39}{2(x+5)} + \dfrac{567\ln|x-3|}{16} - \dfrac{104\ln|x-4|}{3} - \dfrac{37\ln|x+5|}{48} + C.$

56. $\int \left(\dfrac{2660}{(x-3)^3} - \dfrac{504}{(x-3)} - \dfrac{375}{(x-2)^2} + \dfrac{1125}{2(x-2)} - \dfrac{15}{(x+2)^2} - \dfrac{117}{2(x+2)}\right) dx$

    $= -\dfrac{2660}{(x-3)} + \dfrac{30(13x+24)}{x^2-4} - 504\ln|x-3| + \dfrac{1125}{2}\ln|x-2| - \dfrac{117}{2}\ln|x+2| + C.$

58. $x(t) = \dfrac{10e^{10t}}{9 + e^{10t}}$

60. $x(t) = \dfrac{3e^{12t} - 3}{2e^{12t} + 2}$

62. $x(t) = \dfrac{65 + 45e^{11t}}{26 - 15e^{11t}}$

64. $N(t) = 10000$ when $t = \dfrac{\ln 4}{0.15} \approx 9.24$ (days).

66. $P(t) = 200$ when $t = 50\ln(1.125) \approx 5.89$ (months).

68. Solve:

$$10000\dfrac{dx}{dt} = x^2 - 100x;$$

$$\dfrac{dx}{x(x-100)} = \dfrac{1}{10000} dt$$

$$\left(-\dfrac{1}{100}\left(\dfrac{1}{x}\right) + \dfrac{1}{100}\left(\dfrac{1}{x-100}\right)\right) dx = \dfrac{1}{10000} dt;$$

$$\left(\dfrac{1}{x-100} - \dfrac{1}{x}\right) dx = \dfrac{1}{100} dt;$$

$$\ln\left(\dfrac{x-100}{x}\right) = C_1 + (t/100);$$

$$\dfrac{x-100}{x} = Ce^{t/100}.$$

(a) $x(0) = 25$: $\dfrac{-75}{25} = C$: $C = -3$.

$$\dfrac{x-100}{x} = -3e^{t/100};$$

$$1 - \dfrac{100}{x} = -3e^{t/100};$$

$$\dfrac{100}{x} = 1 + 3e^{t/100};$$

$$x(t) = \dfrac{100}{1 + 3e^{t/100}}. \qquad \lim_{t\to\infty} x(t) = 0.$$

(b) $x(0) = 150$: $\dfrac{50}{150} = C$: $C = \tfrac{1}{3}$.

$$\dfrac{x-100}{x} = \tfrac{1}{3}e^{t/100};$$

262   Section 9.5 Rational Functions and Partial Fractions

$$1 - \frac{100}{x} = \tfrac{1}{3}e^{t/100};$$
$$\frac{100}{x} = 1 - \tfrac{1}{3}e^{t/100};$$
$$x(t) = \frac{100}{1 - \tfrac{1}{3}e^{t/100}},$$

Notice that as t approaches $100 \ln 3$ from below, the denominator approaches zero, hence $x(t) \to +\infty$. So "doomsday" occurs at $t = 100 \ln 3 \approx 109.86$ (months).

Section 9.6

1. Let $x = 4 \sin u$. Then $16 - x^2 = 16 \cos^2 u$ and $dx = 4 \cos u\, du$.
$$\int \frac{1}{\sqrt{16 - x^2}}\, dx = \int \frac{4 \cos u}{4 \cos u}\, du = u + C = \arcsin \frac{x}{4} + C$$

2. Let $x = \tfrac{2}{3} \sin u$. Then $4 - 9x^2 = 4 \cos^2 u$ and $dx = \tfrac{2}{3} \cos u\, du$.
$$\int \frac{1}{\sqrt{4 - 9x^2}}\, dx = \tfrac{1}{3} \int \frac{\cos u}{\cos u}\, du = \tfrac{1}{3} u + C = \tfrac{1}{3} \arcsin \frac{3x}{2} + C$$

3. Let $x = 2 \sin u$. Then $4 - x^2 = 4 \cos^2 u$ and $dx = 2 \cos u\, du$.
$$\int \frac{1}{x^2 \sqrt{4 - x^2}}\, dx = \int \frac{2 \cos u}{(4 \sin^2 u)(2 \cos u)}\, du = \tfrac{1}{4} \int \csc^2 u\, du = -\tfrac{1}{4} \cot u + C = -\frac{\sqrt{4 - x^2}}{4x} + C$$

4. Let $x = 5 \sec u$. Then $x^2 - 25 = 25(\sec^2 u - 1) = 25 \tan^2 u$ and $dx = 5 \sec u \tan u\, du$.
$$\int \frac{1}{x^2 \sqrt{x^2 - 25}}\, dx = \int \frac{5 \sec u \tan u}{(25 \sec^2 u)(5 \tan u)}\, du = \tfrac{1}{25} \int \cos u\, du = \tfrac{1}{25} \sin u + C = \frac{\sqrt{x^2 - 25}}{25x} + C$$

5. Let $x = 4 \sin u$. Then $16 - x^2 = 16 \cos^2 u$ and $dx = 4 \cos u\, du$.
$$\int \frac{x^2}{\sqrt{16 - x^2}}\, dx = \int \frac{16 \sin^2 u}{4 \cos u}(4 \cos u)\, du = \int 8(1 - \cos 2u)\, du$$
$$= 8u - 8 \sin u \cos u + C = 8 \arcsin \frac{x}{4} - \tfrac{1}{2} x \sqrt{16 - x^2} + C$$

6. Let $x = \tfrac{3}{2} \sin u$. Then $9 - 4x^2 = 9 \cos^2 u$ and $dx = \tfrac{3}{2} \cos u\, du$.
$$\int \frac{x^2}{\sqrt{9 - 4x^2}}\, dx = \tfrac{9}{8} \int \sin^2 u\, du = \tfrac{9}{16} \int (1 - \cos 2u)\, du$$
$$= \tfrac{9}{16}(u - \sin u \cos u) + C = \tfrac{9}{16} \arcsin \frac{2x}{3} - \frac{x}{8} \sqrt{9 - 4x^2} + C$$

7. Let $x = \tfrac{3}{4} \sin u$. Then $9 - 16x^2 = 9 \cos^2 u$ and $dx = \tfrac{3}{4} \cos u\, du$.
$$\int \frac{1}{(9 - 16x^2)^{3/2}}\, dx = \int \frac{1}{27 \cos^3 u}\left(\tfrac{3}{4} \cos u\right) du = \tfrac{1}{36} \int \sec^2 u\, du = \tfrac{1}{36} \tan u + C = \frac{x}{9\sqrt{9 - 16x^2}} + C$$

8. Let $x = \tfrac{5}{4} \tan u$. Then $25 + 16x^2 = 25 + 25 \tan^2 u = 25 \sec^2 u$ and $dx = \tfrac{5}{4} \sec^2 u\, du$.
$$\int \frac{1}{(25 + 16x^2)^{3/2}}\, dx = \int \frac{1}{125 \sec^3 u}\left(\tfrac{5}{4} \sec^2 u\right) du$$
$$= \tfrac{1}{100} \int \cos u\, du = \tfrac{1}{100} \sin u + C = \frac{x}{25\sqrt{25 + 16x^2}} + C$$

9. Let $x = \sec u$. Then $x^2 - 1 = \tan^2 u$ and $dx = \sec u \tan u\, du$.

$$\int \frac{\sqrt{x^2-1}}{x^2}\, dx = \int \frac{\sin^2 u}{\cos u}\, du = \int (\sec u - \cos u)\, du$$
$$= \ln|\sec u + \tan u| - \sin u + C = \ln\left|x + \sqrt{x^2-1}\right| - \frac{1}{x}\sqrt{x^2-1} + C$$

10. Let $x = 2\sin u$. Then $dx = 2\cos u\, du$ and $\sqrt{4-x^2} = 2\cos u$.

$$\int x^3\sqrt{4-x^2}\, dx = \int 32\sin^3 u \cos^2 u\, du = 32\int (\sin u)(\cos^2 u - \cos^4 u)\, du$$
$$= 32\left(\tfrac{1}{5}\cos^5 u - \tfrac{1}{3}\cos^3 u\right) + C = \tfrac{32}{15}\left(3\left(\frac{\sqrt{4-x^2}}{2}\right)^5 - 5\left(\frac{\sqrt{4-x^2}}{2}\right)^3\right) + C$$
$$= \tfrac{4}{15}\left(\tfrac{3}{4}(4-x^2)(4-x^2)^{3/2} - 5(4-x^2)^{3/2}\right) + C$$
$$= -\tfrac{1}{15}(4-x^2)^{3/2}(3x^2 + 8) + C$$

11. Let $x = \tfrac{3}{2}\tan u$. Then $9 + 4x^2 = 9\sec^2 u$ and $dx = \tfrac{3}{2}\sec^2 u\, du$.

$$\int x^3\sqrt{9+4x^2}\, dx = \int \tfrac{243}{16}\tan^3 u\, \sec^3 u\, du = \int \tfrac{243}{16}(\sec^4 u - \sec^2 u)(\sec u \tan u)\, du$$
$$= \tfrac{243}{80}\sec^5 u - \tfrac{81}{16}\sec^3 u + C = \tfrac{1}{80}(9+4x^2)^{5/2} - \tfrac{3}{16}(9+4x^2)^{3/2} + C$$

12. Let $x = 5\tan u$. Then $dx = 5\sec^2 u\, du$ and $\sqrt{x^2+25} = \sqrt{25\tan^2 u + 25} = 5\sec u$.

$$\int \frac{x^3}{\sqrt{x^2+25}}\, dx = \int \frac{125\tan^3 u}{5\sec u}(5\sec^2 u)\, du$$
$$= 125\int \tan^3 u \sec u\, du = 125\int (\tan u)(\sec^2 u - 1)(\sec u)\, du$$
$$= 125\int\Big((\sec^2 u)(\sec u \tan u) - \sec u \tan u\Big)\, du$$
$$= 125\left(\tfrac{1}{3}\sec^3 u - \sec u\right) + C = \tfrac{1}{3}\sqrt{x^2+25}(x^2 - 50) + C$$

13. Let $x = \tfrac{1}{2}\sin\theta$. Then $1 - 4x^2 = \cos^2\theta$, and the integrand becomes $\csc\theta - \sin\theta$.

14. Let $x = \tan v$. Then $\sqrt{1+x^2} = \sec v$ and $dx = \sec^2 v\, dv$.

$$\int \frac{1}{\sqrt{1+x^2}}\, dx = \int \frac{\sec^2 v}{\sec v}\, dv = \ln|\sec v + \tan v| + C = \ln\left|x + \sqrt{1+x^2}\right| + C$$

15. Let $x = \tfrac{3}{2}\tan\theta$. The integrand becomes $\tfrac{1}{2}\sec\theta$.

16. Let $x = \tfrac{1}{2}\tan z$. Then $2x = \tan z$, $1 + 4x^2 = \sec^2 z$, and $dx = \tfrac{1}{2}\sec^2 z\, dz$.

$$\int \sqrt{1+4x^2}\, dx = \int \tfrac{1}{2}(\sec z)(\sec^2 z)\, dz = \tfrac{1}{2}\int \sec^3 z\, dz$$

Now do a moderately difficult integration by parts, or apply Formula 28 of the endpapers, to obtain

$$\int \sqrt{1+4x^2}\, dx = \tfrac{1}{4}(\sec z \tan z + \ln|\sec z + \tan z|) + C$$
$$= \tfrac{1}{4}\left(2x\sqrt{1+4x^2} + \ln\left|2x + \sqrt{1+4x^2}\right|\right) + C$$

17. Let $x = 5\sin\theta$. Then $25 - x^2 = 25\cos^2\theta$ and $dx = 5\cos\theta\,d\theta$.

$$\int \frac{x^2}{\sqrt{25 - x^2}}\,dx = \int 25\sin^2\theta\,d\theta = 25\int \tfrac{1}{2}(1 - \cos 2\theta)\,d\theta$$
$$= \tfrac{25}{2}\left(\theta - \tfrac{1}{2}\sin 2\theta\right) + C = \tfrac{25}{2}(\theta - \sin\theta\,\cos\theta) + C$$
$$= \tfrac{25}{2}\left(\arcsin\left(\tfrac{x}{5}\right) - \tfrac{x}{25}\sqrt{25 - x^2}\right) + C$$

18. Let $x = 5\sin u$. Then $\sqrt{25 - x^2} = 5\cos u$ and $dx = 5\cos u\,du$.

$$\int \frac{x^3}{\sqrt{25 - x^2}}\,dx = \int \frac{125\sin^3 u}{5\cos u}(5\cos u)\,du$$
$$= 125\int \sin^3 u\,du = 125\int (1 - \cos^2 u)(\sin u)\,du$$
$$= 125\left(\tfrac{1}{3}\cos^3 u - \cos u\right) + C = \tfrac{125}{3}(\cos u)(\cos^2 u - 3) + C$$
$$= \tfrac{25}{3}\sqrt{25 - x^2}\left(\tfrac{25 - x^2}{25} - 3\right) + C = -\tfrac{1}{3}(x^2 + 50)\sqrt{25 - x^2} + C$$

19. Use the substitution $x = \tan u$ to transform the integrand into $\tan^2 u\,\sec u = \sec^3 u - \sec u$, then apply Formulas 14 and 28 of the endpapers.

20. Let $x = \tan u$. Then $1 + x^2 = \sec^2 u$ and $dx = \sec^2 u\,du$.

$$\int \frac{x^3}{\sqrt{1 + x^2}}\,dx = \int \sec u\,\tan^3 u\,du = \int (\sec u)(\sec^2 u - 1)(\tan u)\,du$$
$$= \int \left((\sec^2 u)(\sec u\,\tan u) - \sec u\,\tan u\right)du$$
$$= \tfrac{1}{3}(\sec u)(\sec^2 u - 3) + C = \tfrac{1}{3}(x^2 - 2)\sqrt{1 + x^2} + C$$

21. Use the substitution $x = \tfrac{2}{3}\tan z$, then proceed as in the solution to Problem 19.

22. Let $x = \sin z$. Then $\sqrt{1 - x^2} = \cos z$ and $dx = \cos z\,dz$.

$$\int (1 - x^2)^{3/2}\,dx = \int \cos^4 z\,dz$$
$$= \tfrac{1}{4}\int (1 + \cos 2z)^2\,dz = \tfrac{1}{4}\int \left(1 + 2\cos 2z + \tfrac{1}{2}(1 + \cos 4z)\right)dz$$
$$= \tfrac{1}{4}\left(\tfrac{3}{2}z + \sin 2z + \tfrac{1}{8}\sin 4z\right) + C = \tfrac{3}{8}z + \tfrac{1}{2}\sin z\,\cos z + \tfrac{1}{16}\sin 2z\,\cos 2z + C$$
$$= \tfrac{3}{8}z + \tfrac{1}{2}\sin z\,\cos z + \tfrac{1}{8}(\sin z\,\cos z)(\cos^2 z - \sin^2 z) + C$$
$$= \tfrac{3}{8}z + \tfrac{1}{2}\sin z\,\cos z + \tfrac{1}{8}\sin z\,\cos^3 z - \tfrac{1}{8}\sin^3 z\,\cos z + C$$
$$= \tfrac{3}{8}\arcsin x + \tfrac{1}{2}x\sqrt{1 - x^2} + \tfrac{1}{8}x(1 - x^2)^{3/2} - \tfrac{1}{8}x^3\sqrt{1 - x^2} + C$$
$$= \tfrac{1}{8}\left(3\arcsin x + x(5 - 2x^2)\sqrt{1 - x^2}\right) + C$$

23. The substitution $x = \tan\theta$ transforms the integrand into $\cos\theta$.

24. Let $x = 2\sin u$. Then $4 - x^2 = 4 - 4\sin^2 u = 4\cos^2 u$ and $dx = 2\cos u\,du$.

$$\int \frac{1}{(4 - x^2)^2}\,dx = \int \frac{2\cos u}{16\cos^4 u}\,du = \tfrac{1}{8}\int \sec^3 u\,du$$
$$= \tfrac{1}{16}(\sec u\,\tan u + \ln|\sec u + \tan u|) + C$$
$$= \tfrac{1}{16}\left(\frac{\sin u}{\cos^2 u} + \ln\left|\frac{1 + \sin u}{\cos u}\right|\right) + C$$
$$= \tfrac{1}{16}\left(\frac{2x}{4 - x^2} + \ln\left|\frac{2 + x}{\sqrt{4 - x^2}}\right|\right) + C$$
$$= \tfrac{1}{32}\left(\frac{4x}{4 - x^2} + \ln\left|\frac{2 + x}{2 - x}\right|\right) + C$$

25. The substitution $x = 2\sin u$ transforms the integral into $\frac{1}{32}\int \sec^5 u\, du$. Application of Formula 37 of the endpapers transforms this integral into

$$\frac{1}{32}\int \frac{1}{4}\sec^3 u \tan u\, du + \frac{3}{4}\int \sec^3 u\, du.$$

Then Formula 28 from the endpapers yields the antiderivative

$$\frac{1}{128}\sec^3 u \tan u + \frac{3}{256}\sec u \tan u + \frac{3}{256}\ln|\sec u + \tan u| + C.$$

Finally make the replacements $\sec u = \dfrac{2}{\sqrt{4-x^2}}$ and $\tan u = \dfrac{x}{\sqrt{4-x^2}}$ to obtain the final answer.

26. Let $x = \frac{3}{2}\tan z$. Then $2x = 3\tan z$, $4x^2 + 9 = 9\sec^2 z$ and $dx = \frac{3}{2}\sec^2 z\, dz$.

$$\int \frac{dx}{(4x^2+9)^3} = \frac{3}{2}\int \frac{\sec^2 z}{729\sec^6 z}\, dz = \frac{1}{486}\int \cos^4 z\, dz.$$

Now proceed exactly as in the solution to Problem 22 to obtain

$$\frac{1}{3888}\left(3z + 4\sin z \cos z + \sin z \cos^3 z - \sin^3 z \cos z\right) + C.$$

Next replace z with $\arctan(\frac{2}{3}x)$, $\sin z$ with $\dfrac{2x}{\sqrt{4x^2+9}}$, and $\cos z$ with $\dfrac{3}{\sqrt{4x^2+9}}$, to obtain

$$\int \frac{1}{(4x^2+9)^3}\, dx = \frac{1}{1296}\left(\tan^{-1}\left(\frac{2x}{3}\right) + \frac{6x(4x^2+15)}{(4x^2+9)^2}\right) + C.$$

27. Let $x = \frac{3}{4}\tan u$. Then $9 + 16x^2 = 9 + 9\tan^2 u = 9\sec^2 u$ and $dx = \frac{3}{4}\sec^2 u\, du$. The integrand becomes $\frac{9}{4}\sec^3 u$. The rest is routine.

28. Use the substitution $x = \frac{3}{4}\tan u$ to obtain $\frac{81}{4}\int \sec^5 u\, du$. With the aid of Formula 37 of the endpapers, we next obtain

$$\int (9+16x^2)^{3/2}\, dx = \frac{81}{4}\left(\frac{1}{4}\sec^3 u \tan u + \frac{3}{8}\sec u \tan u + \frac{3}{8}\ln|\sec u + \tan u|\right) + C$$

$$= \frac{1}{4}x\left(9+16x^2\right)^{3/2} + \frac{27}{8}x\left(9+16x^2\right)^{1/2} + \frac{243}{32}\ln\left|4x + \sqrt{9+16x^2}\right| + C.$$

(We have allowed the constant $-\frac{243}{32}\ln 3$ to be "absorbed" by the constant C.)

29. Let $x = 5\sec u$. Then $x^2 - 25 = 25\tan^2 u$ and $dx = 5\sec u \tan u\, du$.

$$\int \frac{\sqrt{x^2-25}}{x}\, dx = \int \frac{1}{5}(\cos u)\sqrt{25\sec^2 u - 25}\,(5\sec u \tan u)\, du$$

$$= \int 5\tan^2 u\, du = \int (5\sec^2 u - 5)\, du$$

$$= 5\tan u - 5u + C = \sqrt{x^2-25} - 5\sec^{-1}\left|\frac{x}{5}\right| + C$$

30. Let $x = \frac{4}{3}\sec u$. Then $9x^2 - 16 = 16\sec^2 u - 16 = 16\tan^2 u$ and $dx = \frac{4}{3}\sec u \tan u\, du$.

$$\int \frac{\sqrt{9x^2-16}}{x}\, dx = \int 4\tan^2 u\, du = \int (4\sec^2 u - 4)\, du$$

$$= 4\tan u - 4u + C = \sqrt{9x^2-16} - 4\sec^{-1}\left|\frac{3x}{4}\right| + C$$

31. Let $x = \sec u$. Then $x^2 - 1 = \tan^2 x$ and $dx = \sec u \tan u \, du$.

$$\int x^2 \sqrt{x^2-1} \, dx = \int \sec^3 u \tan^2 u \, du = \int (\sec^5 u - \sec^3 u) \, du$$
$$= \tfrac{1}{4} \sec^3 u \tan u - \tfrac{1}{8} \sec u \tan u - \tfrac{1}{8} \ln|\sec u + \tan u| + C$$

—with the aid of Formula 37 of the endpapers. Then replace $\tan u$ with $\sqrt{x^2-1}$ and $\sec u$ with x to obtain the final version of the answer.

32. Let $x = \tfrac{3}{2} \sec u$. Then $4x^2 - 9 = 9\tan^2 u$ and $dx = \tfrac{3}{2} \sec u \tan u \, du$;

$$\int \frac{x^2}{\sqrt{4x^2-9}} \, dx = \int \tfrac{9}{8} \sec^3 u \, du$$

and the rest is routine; the answer is

$$\tfrac{1}{8} x \sqrt{4x^2-9} + \tfrac{9}{16} \ln\left|2x + \sqrt{4x^2-9}\right| + C.$$

33. Let $x = \tfrac{1}{2} \sec u$. Then $(4x^2-1)^{-3/2} = (\sec^2 u - 1)^{-3/2} = \cot^3 u$ and $dx = \tfrac{1}{2} \sec u \tan u \, du$.

$$\int \frac{1}{(4x^2-1)^{3/2}} \, dx = \tfrac{1}{2} \int (\sin u)^{-2}(\cos u) \, du = -\tfrac{1}{2} \csc u + C = -\frac{x}{\sqrt{4x^2-1}} + C$$

34. Let $x = \tfrac{3}{2} \sec u$. Then $\sqrt{4x^2-9} = \sqrt{9\sec^2 u - 9} = 3 \tan u$ and $dx = \tfrac{3}{2} \sec u \tan u \, du$.

$$\int \frac{1}{x^2 \sqrt{4x^2-9}} \, dx = \tfrac{2}{9} \int \cos u \, du = \tfrac{2}{9} \sin u + C = \frac{\sqrt{4x^2-9}}{9x} + C$$

35. Let $x = \sqrt{5} \sec u$. Then $\sqrt{x^2-5} = \sqrt{5} \tan u$ and $dx = \sqrt{5} \sec u \tan u \, du$.

$$\int \frac{\sqrt{x^2-5}}{x^2} \, dx = \int \frac{\tan^2 u}{\sec u} \, du = \int (\sec u - \cos u) \, du$$
$$= -\sin u + \ln|\sec u + \tan u| + C = -\frac{1}{x}\sqrt{x^2-5} + \ln\left|x + \sqrt{x^2-5}\right| + C$$

36. Given $(a^2 x^2 - b^2)^{3/2}$ with a and b positive, let $x = \dfrac{b}{a} \sec u$. Then $\sqrt{a^2 x^2 - b^2} = b \tan u$, and therefore

$$\int (a^2 x^2 - b^2)^{3/2} \, dx = \frac{b^4}{a} \int \sec u \tan^4 u \, du = \frac{b^4}{a} \int (\sec^5 u - 2\sec^3 u + \sec u) \, du.$$

We now use Formula 37 of the endpapers; after simplification, the resulting antiderivative is

$$\frac{b^4}{8a} \left(2 \sec^3 u \tan u - 5 \sec u \tan u + 3 \ln|\sec u + \tan u|\right) + C.$$

Now $\sec u = \dfrac{ax}{b}$ and $\tan u = \dfrac{1}{b}\sqrt{a^2 x^2 - b^2}$. Substitution in the antiderivative and simplification lead to the answer

$$\tfrac{1}{8}\left(2a^2 x^3 - 5b^2 x\right)\sqrt{a^2 x^2 - b^2} + \frac{3b^4}{8a} \ln\left|ax + \sqrt{a^2 x^2 - b^2}\right| + C.$$

With $a = 2$ and $b = \sqrt{5}$, we obtain

$$\int (4x^2 - 5)^{3/2} \, dx = \tfrac{1}{8}\left(8x^3 - 25x\right)\sqrt{4x^2-5} + \tfrac{75}{16} \ln\left|2x + \sqrt{4x^2-5}\right| + C.$$

37. The substitution $x = 5\sinh u$ yields

$$\int \frac{dx}{\sqrt{25+x^2}}\,dx = \int \frac{5\cosh u}{5\cosh u}\,du = \int 1\,du = u + C = \sinh^{-1}\left(\frac{x}{5}\right) + C.$$

38. Let $x = \sinh u$. Then $1 + x^2 = \cosh^2 u$ and $dx = \cosh u\,du$.

$$\int \sqrt{1+x^2}\,dx = \int \cosh^2 u\,du$$
$$= \tfrac{1}{4}\sinh 2u + \frac{u}{2} + C \quad \text{(by Formula 85, endpapers)}$$
$$= \tfrac{1}{2}(\sinh u \cosh u + u) + C$$
$$= \tfrac{1}{2}\left(x\sqrt{1+x^2} + \sinh^{-1} x\right) + C$$

39. Let $x = 2\cosh u$. Then $\sqrt{x^2 - 4} = 2\sinh u$ and $dx = 2\sinh u\,du$. The integrand is transformed into $\tanh^2 u$, and (by Formula 86 of the endpapers) the antiderivative is

$$u - \tanh u + C = \cosh^{-1}\left(\frac{x}{2}\right) - \frac{1}{x}\sqrt{x^2 - 4} + C.$$

40. Let $x = \tfrac{1}{3}\sinh u$. Then $9x^2 = \sinh^2 u$, $\sqrt{1 + 9x^2} = \cosh u$, and $dx = \tfrac{1}{3}\cosh u\,du$.

$$\int \frac{dx}{\sqrt{1+9x^2}}\,dx = \tfrac{1}{3}\int \frac{\cosh u}{\cosh u}\,du = \tfrac{1}{3}u + C = \tfrac{1}{3}\sinh^{-1}(3x) + C$$

41. Let $x = \sinh u$. Then $\sqrt{1+x^2} = \cosh u$ and $dx = \cosh u\,du$. Thus

$$\int x^2 \sqrt{1+x^2}\,dx = \int \sinh^2 u \cosh^2 u\,du.$$

We proceed with the aid of several of the formulas from Section 9.5 of the text, and obtain

$$\int \tfrac{1}{2}(\cosh 2u - 1)\tfrac{1}{2}(\cosh 2u + 1)\,du = \tfrac{1}{4}\int (\cosh^2 2u - 1)\,du$$
$$= \tfrac{1}{4}\int \left(\tfrac{1}{2}(\cosh 4u + 1) - 1\right)du$$
$$= \tfrac{1}{4}\int \left(\tfrac{1}{2}\cosh 4u - \tfrac{1}{2}\right)du$$
$$= \tfrac{1}{32}\sinh 4u - \tfrac{1}{8}u + C$$
$$= \tfrac{1}{32}(2\sinh 2u \cosh 2u) - \tfrac{1}{8}\sinh^{-1} x + C$$
$$= \tfrac{1}{16}(2\sinh u \cosh u)(\cosh^2 u + \sinh^2 u) - \tfrac{1}{8}\sinh^{-1} x + C$$
$$= \tfrac{1}{8}x\sqrt{1+x^2}(1 + x^2 + x^2) - \tfrac{1}{8}\sinh^{-1} x + C$$
$$= \tfrac{1}{8}\left(x\sqrt{1+x^2}(1 + 2x^2) - \sinh^{-1} x\right) + C$$

44. Given: $y = x^2$ on the interval $0 \le x \le 1$;

$$\frac{dy}{dx} = 2x, \quad \text{so}\quad 1 + \left(\frac{dy}{dx}\right)^2 = 1 + 4x^2.$$

The arc length is therefore

$$L = \int_0^1 \sqrt{1 + 4x^2}\,dx.$$

Now let $x = \frac{1}{2}\tan u$. The integrand becomes $\frac{1}{2}\sec^3 u$, the antiderivative is

$$\frac{1}{4}\left(2x\sqrt{1+4x^2} + \ln\left|2x + \sqrt{1+4x^2}\right|\right) + C,$$

and it follows that

$$L = \tfrac{1}{4}\left(2\sqrt{5} + \ln\left(2+\sqrt{5}\right)\right) \approx 1.47894286.$$

45. $A = \displaystyle\int_0^1 2\pi x^2\sqrt{1+4x^2}\,dx$. Let $x = \frac{1}{2}\tan u$. This yields the transformation

$$I = \int x^2\sqrt{1+4x^2}\,dx = \tfrac{1}{8}\int \sec^3 u\,\tan^2 u\,du = \tfrac{1}{8}\int\left(\sec^5 u - \sec^3 u\right)du.$$

Apply Formula 37 of the endpapers with $n = 5$, then Formula 28:

$$I = \tfrac{1}{32}\left(\sec^3 u\,\tan u - \tfrac{1}{2}\sec u\,\tan u - \tfrac{1}{2}\ln|\sec u + \tan u|\right) + C$$
$$= \tfrac{1}{64}\left(4x\left(1+4x^2\right)^{3/2} - 2x\left(1+4x^2\right)^{1/2} - \ln\left|2x + \sqrt{1+4x^2}\right|\right) + C.$$

Now to obtain A, substitute $x = 1$, subtract the value when $x = 0$, and finally multiply by 2π; the result is that

$$A = \frac{\pi}{32}\left(18\sqrt{5} - \ln\left(2+\sqrt{5}\right)\right) \approx 3.80973.$$

46. The length of one arch of the sine curve is

$$S = \int_0^\pi \sqrt{1+\cos^2 x}\,dx.$$

To obtain the length of the upper half of the ellipse, take

$$y = \sqrt{2-2x^2}, \qquad -1 \le x \le 1.$$

Then $\dfrac{dy}{dx} = -\dfrac{2x}{\sqrt{2-2x^2}}$, so—after algebraic simplification—the arc length is

$$E = \int_{-1}^1 \frac{\sqrt{1+x^2}}{\sqrt{1-x^2}}\,dx.$$

Let $x = \cos u$. Then

$$E = \int_\pi^0 \frac{\sqrt{1+\cos^2 u}}{\sqrt{1-\cos^2 u}}(-\sin u)\,du = \int_0^\pi \sqrt{1+\cos^2 u}\,du = S.$$

47. Given $y = \ln x$, it follows that the arc length element is $ds = \dfrac{1}{x}\sqrt{x^2+1}\,dx$, so the arc length in question is

$$L = \int_1^2 \frac{1}{x}\sqrt{x^2+1}\,dx.$$

The substitution $x = \sinh u$ can be made to work, but we prefer to use $x = \tan u$. This results in the definite integral

$$L = \int_{x=1}^{x=2} (\csc u + \sec u\,\tan u)\,du,$$

and the value of this integral may be simplified to

$$\sqrt{5} - \sqrt{2} + \ln\left(2+2\sqrt{2}\right) - \ln\left(1+\sqrt{5}\right) \approx 1.222016177.$$

48. $A = \int_1^2 2\pi x \frac{\sqrt{x^2+1}}{x} dx = 2\pi \int_1^2 \sqrt{x^2+1}\, dx$. The substitution $x = \tan u$ transforms the antidifferentiation problem into

$$2\pi \int \sec^3 z\, dz = \pi(\sec z \tan z + \ln|\sec z + \tan z|) + C = \pi\left(x\sqrt{x^2+1} + \ln\left|x + \sqrt{x^2+1}\right|\right) + C.$$

Substitution of the limits $x = 1$ and $x = 2$ yields the answer:

$$A = \pi\left(2\sqrt{5} - \sqrt{2} + \ln\left(2 + \sqrt{5}\right) - \ln\left(1 + \sqrt{2}\right)\right) \approx 11.37314434.$$

49. After algebraic simplification, the surface area integral takes the form

$$A = 4\pi \int_{a-b}^{a+b} \frac{bx}{\sqrt{b^2 - (x-a)^2}}\, dx.$$

The substitution $x = a + b\sin\theta$ leads to the desired result.

50. Let $x = 3\tan u$. Then $\sqrt{9+x^2} = 3\sec u$ and $dx = 3\sec^2 u\, du$. The area is given by

$$A = \int_0^4 \sqrt{9+x^2}\, dx = \int_{x=0}^{x=4} 9\sec^3 u\, du$$

$$= \tfrac{9}{2}\left[\sec u \tan u + \ln|\sec u + \tan u|\right]_{x=0}^{x=4}$$

$$= \tfrac{9}{2}\left[\tfrac{1}{9}x\sqrt{9+x^2} + \ln\left(x + \sqrt{9+x^2}\right)\right]_0^4 = 10 + \tfrac{9}{2}\ln 3 \approx 14.943755.$$

51. $A = 4\pi \int_0^{\pi/2} (\sin x)\sqrt{1 + \cos^2 x}\, dx$. With $u = \cos x$ and $du = -\sin x\, dx$, we obtain

$$A = 4\pi \int_0^1 \sqrt{1+u^2}\, du.$$

To find the antiderivative, we let $u = \sinh z$, $du = \cosh z\, dz$. Then we obtain

$$A = 4\pi \int_{u=0}^{u=1} \cosh^2 z\, dz = \left[2\pi(z + \sinh z \cosh z)\right]_{u=0}^{u=1}$$

$$= 2\pi\left[\sinh^{-1} u + u\sqrt{1+u^2}\right]_0^1 = 2\pi\left(\sinh^{-1}(1) + \sqrt{2}\right)$$

$$= 2\pi\left(\sqrt{2} + \ln\left(1 + \sqrt{2}\right)\right) \approx 14.4236.$$

52. After it is simplified, the surface area integral should become

$$A = \frac{4\pi b}{a^2} \int_0^a \sqrt{a^4 - x^2(a^2 - b^2)}\, dx.$$

To find the antiderivative, let $x = \dfrac{a^2 \sin u}{\sqrt{a^2 - b^2}}$. Note that $\arcsin w \approx w$ if $w \approx 0$.

53. Modify the solution to Problem 50 for the case $b > a$ as follows: Let $x = \dfrac{a^2 \tan u}{\sqrt{b^2 - a^2}}$. Note that $\ln(1+h) \approx h$ if $h \approx 0$.

54. You should find that the arc length element is $ds = \dfrac{\sqrt{x}}{\sqrt{x-1}}\, dx$. After using the suggested substitution, it turns out that the antiderivative is

$$\left(\sqrt{x}\sqrt{x-1} + \ln\left(\sqrt{x} + \sqrt{x-1}\right)\right) + C,$$

and that the value of the definite integral is approximately equal to 3.620184.

55. One integral that yields the cost (in millions of dollars) is

$$C = \int_2^5 \frac{x}{\sqrt{x-1}}\, dx.$$

The substitution $x = \sec^2\theta$ yields the antiderivative

$$\tfrac{2}{3}\sec^2\theta \tan\theta + \tfrac{4}{3}\tan\theta + C = \tfrac{2}{3}x\sqrt{x-1} + \tfrac{4}{3}\sqrt{x-1} + C.$$

It follows that the total cost of the road will be $\tfrac{20}{3}$ million dollars.

56. Let ρ denote the weight of the string in pounds per foot. The arc length element of the string is $ds = \tfrac{1}{10}\sqrt{100+x^2}\, dx$, so the total work to lift the string is given by

$$W = \int_0^{100} \tfrac{1}{20}x^2 \left(\tfrac{\rho}{10}\right) \sqrt{100+x^2}\, dx = \frac{\rho}{200}\int_0^{100} x^2\sqrt{100+x^2}\, dx.$$

The substitution $x = 10\tan\theta$ yields

$$W = 50\rho \int_{x=0}^{x=100} \left(\sec^5\theta - \sec^3\theta\right)\, d\theta$$

$$= 50\rho \left[\tfrac{1}{4}\sec^3\theta \tan\theta - \tfrac{1}{8}\sec\theta \tan\theta - \tfrac{1}{8}\ln|\sec\theta + \tan\theta|\right]_{x=0}^{x=100}.$$

After substitution of $\tfrac{1}{10}x$ for $\tan\theta$ and $\tfrac{1}{10}\sqrt{100+x^2}$ for $\sec\theta$, and noting that $\rho = \tfrac{1}{256}$, we find that the total work is approximately 493.097 ft·lb.

Section 9.7

1. $\displaystyle\int \frac{1}{x^2+4x+5}\, dx = \int \frac{1}{(x+2)^2+1}\, dx = \arctan(x+2) + C.$

2. $\displaystyle\int \frac{2x+5}{x^2+4x+5}\, dx = \int \frac{2x+4}{x^2+4x+5}\, dx + \int \frac{1}{x^2+4x+5}\, dx = \ln(x^2+4x+5) + \arctan(x+2) + C.$

3. $\displaystyle\int \frac{5-3x}{x^2+4x+5}\, dx = \int \left(\frac{-6-3x}{x^2+4x+5} + \frac{11}{x^2+4x+5}\right) dx$
$= -\tfrac{3}{2}\ln(x^2+4x+5) + 11\arctan(x+2) + C.$

4. Let $u = x+2$: $x = u-2$ and $dx = du$. Thus

$$\int \frac{x+1}{(x^2+4x+5)^2}\, dx = \int \frac{u-1}{(u^2+1)^2}\, du.$$

Next let $u = \tan\theta$. Then $du = \sec^2\theta\, d\theta$, and

$$\int \frac{x+1}{(x^2+4x+5)^2}\, dx = \int \frac{\tan\theta - 1}{\sec^2\theta}\, d\theta = \int (\sin\theta \cos\theta - \cos^2\theta)\, d\theta$$

$$= \tfrac{1}{2}\sin^2\theta - \tfrac{1}{2}\theta - \tfrac{1}{2}\sin\theta\cos\theta + C$$

$$= \frac{u^2}{2(1+u^2)} - \tfrac{1}{2}\arctan u - \frac{u}{2(1+u^2)} + C$$

$$= \frac{x^2+3x+2}{2(x^2+4x+5)} - \tfrac{1}{2}\arctan(x+2) + C.$$

5. First, $3 - 2x - x^2 = 4 - (x+1)^2$, so we let $x = -1 + 2\sin u$, so that $x + 1 = 2\sin u$. Then $4 - (x+1)^2 = 4 - 4\sin^2 u = 4\cos^2 u$, so

$$\int \frac{1}{\sqrt{3 - 2x - x^2}}\, dx = \int \frac{2\cos u}{2\cos u}\, du$$

$$= u + C = \arcsin\left(\frac{x+1}{2}\right) + C.$$

6. The substitution of the solution of Problem 5 yields

$$\int \frac{x+3}{\sqrt{3 - 2x - x^2}}\, dx = \int \frac{2 + 2\sin u}{2\cos u}(2\cos u)\, du$$

$$= 2u - 2\cos u + C = 2\arcsin\left(\frac{x+1}{2}\right) - \sqrt{3 - 2x - x^2} + C.$$

7. First, $3 - 2x - x^2 = 4 - (x+1)^2$, so we let $x = -1 + 2\sin u$: $x + 1 = 2\sin u$, $dx = 2\cos u\, du$. Then $4 - (x+1)^2 = 4 - 4\sin^2 u = 4\cos^2 u$, so

$$\int x\sqrt{3 - 2x - x^2}\, dx = \int (-1 + 2\sin u)(2\cos u)(2\cos u)\, du$$

$$= \int (-4\cos^2 u + 8\cos^2 u \sin u)\, du$$

$$= \int (-2 - 2\cos 2u + 8\cos^2 u \sin u)\, du$$

$$= -2u - 2\sin u \cos u - \tfrac{8}{3}\cos^3 u + C$$

$$= -2\arcsin\left(\frac{x+1}{2}\right) - \tfrac{1}{2}(x+1)\sqrt{3 - 2x - x^2} - \tfrac{1}{3}(3 - 2x - x^2)^{3/2} + C.$$

8. We begin with the observation that $4x^2 + 4x - 3 = (2x+1)^2 - 4$, so we let $x = -\tfrac{1}{2} + \sec u$: $dx = \sec u \tan u\, du$ and $(2x+1)^2 - 4 = 4\tan^2 u$.

$$\int \frac{1}{4x^2 + 4x - 3}\, dx = \int \frac{\sec u \tan u}{4\tan^2 u}\, du = \tfrac{1}{4}\int \frac{\sec u}{\tan u}\, du = \tfrac{1}{4}\int \csc u\, du$$

$$= -\tfrac{1}{4}\ln|\csc u + \cot u| + C = -\tfrac{1}{4}\ln\left|\frac{2x+3}{\sqrt{4x^2 + 4x - 3}}\right| + C$$

$$= \tfrac{1}{8}\ln\left|\frac{4x^2 + 4x - 3}{4x^2 + 12x + 9}\right| + C.$$

9. With the substitution of the solution of Problem 8, we obtain

$$\int \frac{3x+2}{4x^2 + 4x - 3}\, dx = \tfrac{1}{2}\int \frac{6\sec u + 1}{4\tan^2 u}(\sec u \tan u)\, du$$

$$= \tfrac{1}{8}\int \left(\frac{6\sec^2 u}{\tan u} + \frac{\sec u}{\tan u}\right) du$$

$$= \tfrac{3}{4}\ln|\tan u| + \tfrac{1}{16}\ln\left|\frac{4x^2 + 4x - 3}{4x^2 + 12x + 9}\right| + C$$

$$= \tfrac{3}{8}\ln\left|4x^2 + 4x - 3\right| + \tfrac{1}{16}\ln\left|\frac{4x^2 + 4x - 3}{4x^2 + 12x + 9}\right| + C$$

(the constant $-\tfrac{3}{2}\ln 2$ has been "absorbed" by C).

10. Because $4x^2 + 4x - 3 = (2x+1)^2 - 4$, we let $x = -\frac{1}{2} + \sec u$: $dx = \sec u \tan u\, du$, $2x+1 = 2\sec u$, and $(2x+1)^2 - 4 = 4\tan^2 u$.

$$\int \sqrt{4x^2 + 4x - 3}\, dx = \int 2\sec u \tan^2 u\, du = 2\int (\sec^3 u - \sec u)\, du$$
$$= \sec u \tan u - \ln|\sec u + \tan u| + C$$
$$= \tfrac{1}{4}(2x+1)(4x^2 + 4x - 3)^{1/2} - \ln\left|2x+1+\sqrt{4x^2+4x-3}\right| + C$$

(the constant $\ln 2$ has been "absorbed" by C).

11. We note that $x^2 + 4x + 13 = (x+2)^2 + 9$. Therefore

$$\int \frac{1}{x^2 + 4x + 13}\, dx = \int \frac{1}{(x+2)^2 + 9}\, dx = \tfrac{1}{9}\int \frac{1}{((x+2)/3)^2 + 1}\, dx$$
$$= \tfrac{1}{3}\arctan\left(\frac{x+2}{3}\right) + C.$$

12. $\displaystyle \int \frac{1}{\sqrt{2x - x^2}}\, dx = \int \frac{1}{\sqrt{1 - (x-1)^2}}\, dx = \sin^{-1}(x-1) + C.$

13. $3 + 2x - x^2 = 4 - (x-1)^2 = 4 - 4\sin^2 u$ if we let $x = 1 + 2\sin u$. Then $dx = 2\cos u\, du$, and therefore

$$\int \frac{1}{3 + 2x - x^2}\, dx = \int \frac{2\cos u}{4\cos^2 u}\, du = \tfrac{1}{2}\int \sec u\, du$$
$$= \tfrac{1}{2}\ln|\sec u + \tan u| + C = \tfrac{1}{2}\ln\left|\frac{x+1}{\sqrt{3+2x-x^2}}\right| + C.$$

14. Because $8 + 2x - x^2 = 9 - (x-1)^2$, we use the substitution $x = 1 + 3\sin u$, $dx = 3\cos u\, du$ to obtain $8 + 2x - x^2 = 9 - 9\sin^2 u$.

$$\int x\sqrt{8 + 2x - x^2}\, dx = \int (1 + 3\sin u)\sqrt{9\cos^2 u}\,(3\cos u)\, du = 9\int (\cos^2 u + 3\cos^2 u \sin u)\, du$$
$$= 9\int \tfrac{1}{2}(1 + \cos 2u)\, du - 9\cos^3 u + C$$
$$= \tfrac{9}{2}u + \tfrac{9}{2}\sin u \cos u - 9\cos^3 u + C$$
$$= \tfrac{9}{2}\sin^{-1}\left(\frac{x-1}{3}\right) + \tfrac{1}{2}(x-1)\sqrt{8+2x-x^2} - \tfrac{1}{3}(8+2x-x^2)^{3/2} + C.$$

15. Let $x = -1 + \tan u$: $dx = \sec^2 u\, du$, $x^2 + 2x + 2 = (x+1)^2 + 1 = \sec^2 u$, and $2x - 5 = 2\tan u - 7$.

$$\int \frac{2x - 5}{x^2 + 2x + 2}\, dx = \int \frac{2\tan u - 7}{\sec^2 u}(\sec^2 u)\, du$$
$$= 2\ln|\sec u| - 7u + C = \ln(x^2 + 2x + 2) - 7\arctan(x+1) + C.$$

16. Since $4x^2 + 4x - 15 = (2x+1)^2 - 16$, we let $2x + 1 = 4\sec z$. Then $x = \tfrac{1}{2}(-1 + 4\sec z)$ and $dx = 2\sec z \tan z\, dz$.

$$\int \frac{2x - 1}{4x^2 + 4x - 15}\, dx = \int \frac{4\sec z - 2}{16\tan^2 z}(2\sec z \tan z)\, dz$$
$$= \tfrac{1}{4}\int \frac{(2\sec z - 1)\sec z}{\tan z}\, dz$$
$$= \tfrac{1}{2}\int \frac{\sec^2 z}{\tan z}\, dz - \tfrac{1}{4}\int \csc z\, dz$$
$$= \tfrac{1}{2}\ln|\tan z| - \tfrac{1}{4}\ln|\csc z - \cot z| + C_1.$$

With the aid of the reference triangle to the right, we can "translate" the expression above into a function of the original variable x. Thus we find the antiderivative to be

$$\tfrac{1}{2}\ln\frac{\sqrt{4x^2+4x-15}}{4} - \tfrac{1}{4}\ln\frac{2x+1-4}{\sqrt{4x^2+4x-15}} + C_1,$$

which can be simplified to

$$\tfrac{1}{8}\ln|2x-3| - \tfrac{3}{8}\ln|2x+5| + C.$$

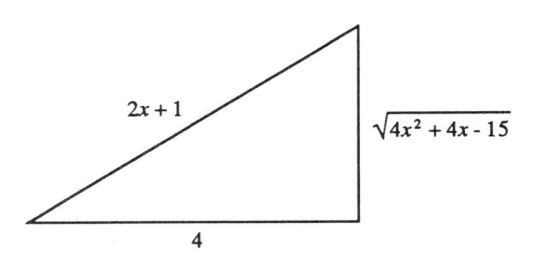

17. As $5+12x-9x^2 = 9-(3x-2)^2$, we let $x = \tfrac{2}{3}+\sin u$. This transforms the integral into

$$\int \frac{(2+3\sin u)\cos u}{9\cos u}\,du = \tfrac{2}{9}u - \tfrac{1}{9}(3\cos u) + C.$$

Then use the facts that $u = \sin^{-1}\left(x-\tfrac{2}{3}\right)$ and $\cos u = \tfrac{1}{3}\sqrt{5+12x-9x^2}$.

18. Because $9x^2+12x+8 = (3x+2)^2+4$, we let $x = \tfrac{2}{3}(\tan u - 1)$ to transform the integral into

$$\tfrac{4}{3}\int (\tan u - 2)\sqrt{4\sec^2 u}\sec^2 u\,du = \tfrac{8}{3}\int (\sec^2 u)(\sec u \tan u)\,du - \tfrac{16}{3}\int \sec^3 u\,du$$

$$= \tfrac{8}{9}\sec^3 u - \tfrac{8}{3}(\sec u \tan u + \ln|\sec u + \tan u|) + C_1.$$

Now $2\sec u = \sqrt{9x^2+12x+8}$, so the antiderivative can be written in terms of x as

$$\tfrac{1}{9}(9x^2+12x+8)^{3/2} - \tfrac{2}{3}(3x+2)\sqrt{9x^2+12x+8} - \tfrac{8}{3}\ln\frac{|3x+2+\sqrt{9x^2+12x+8}|}{2} + C_1$$

$$= \tfrac{1}{9}(9x^2+12x+8)^{3/2} - \tfrac{2}{3}(3x+2)\sqrt{9x^2+12x+8} - \tfrac{8}{3}\ln\left|3x+2+\sqrt{9x^2+12x+8}\right| + C.$$

19. First, $9+16x-4x^2 = 25-(2x-4)^2$. Then use the trigonometric substitution $x = 2 + \tfrac{5}{2}\sin u$.

$$\int (7-2x)\sqrt{9+16x-4x^2}\,dx = \int\left(\tfrac{75}{2}\cos^2 u - \tfrac{125}{2}\cos^2 u \sin u\right) du$$

$$= \tfrac{25}{12}(9u + 9\sin u \cos u + 10\cos^3 u) + C.$$

20. Here, $x^2+2x+5 = (x+1)^2+4$, so let $x = -1+2\tan u$. Then

$$\int \frac{2x+3}{\sqrt{x^2+2x+5}}\,dx = \int \frac{2x+2}{\sqrt{x^2+2x+5}}\,dx + \int \frac{1}{\sqrt{x^2+2x+5}}\,dx$$

$$= 2\sqrt{x^2+2x+5} + \int \frac{1}{\sqrt{x^2+2x+5}}\,dx$$

$$= 2\sqrt{x^2+2x+5} + \int \frac{2\sec^2 u}{2\sec u}\,du$$

$$= 2\sqrt{x^2+2x+5} + \ln|\sec u + \tan u| + C_1$$

$$= 2\sqrt{x^2+2x+5} + \ln\left|\frac{x+1+\sqrt{x^2+2x+5}}{2}\right| + C_1$$

$$= 2\sqrt{x^2+2x+5} + \ln\left|x+1+\sqrt{x^2+2x+5}\right| + C.$$

21. Let $x = 3+3\sin z$. Then $(6x-x^2)^{3/2} = \left(9-(x-3)^2\right)^{3/2} = 27\cos^3 z$.

$$\int \frac{x+4}{(6x-x^2)^{3/2}}\,dx = \int \left(\tfrac{7}{9}\sec^2 z + \frac{\sin z}{3\cos^2 z}\right) dz.$$

22. Let $x = \tan u$. Then

$$\int \frac{x-1}{(x^2+1)^2}\, dx = \int \frac{\tan u - 1}{\sec^4 u} \sec^2 u\, du = \int \left(\frac{\tan u}{\sec^2 u} - \frac{1}{\sec^2 u}\right) du = \int (\cos u \sin u - \cos^2 u)\, du$$

$$= \tfrac{1}{2}\sin^2 u - \tfrac{1}{2}u - \tfrac{1}{2}\sin u \cos u + C$$

$$= \frac{x^2}{2(x^2+1)} - \tfrac{1}{2}\tan^{-1} x - \frac{x}{2(x^2+1)} + C$$

$$= \frac{x(x-1)}{2(x^2+1)} - \tfrac{1}{2}\tan^{-1} x + C.$$

23. The substitution $u = 2x + 3$ transforms the integral into $\tfrac{1}{4}\int \frac{2u}{(u^2+4)^2}\, du$, which presents no difficulties.

24. Let $x = \sin v$. Then

$$\int \frac{x^3}{(1-x^2)^4}\, dx = \int \frac{\sin^3 v}{\cos^8 v} \cos v\, dv$$

$$= \int (\cos^{-7} v \sin v - \cos^{-5} v \sin v)\, dv$$

$$= \tfrac{1}{6}\cos^{-6} v - \tfrac{1}{4}\cos^{-4} v + C$$

$$= \frac{1}{6(1-x^2)^3} - \frac{1}{4(1-x^2)^2} + C.$$

25. We note that $x^2 + x + 1 = \tfrac{3}{4}\left(\tfrac{4}{3}\left(x+\tfrac{1}{2}\right)^2 + 1\right)$. This suggests that we attempt to obtain

$$\tfrac{4}{3}\left(x + \tfrac{1}{2}\right)^2 = \tan^2 u,$$

which we accomplish by using the substitution

$$x = \tfrac{1}{2}\left(-1 + \sqrt{3}\tan u\right).$$

This leads to

$$\int \frac{3x-1}{x^2+x+1}\, dx = \int \left(3 \tan u - \tfrac{5}{3}\sqrt{3}\right) du,$$

and only the final answer is complicated.

26. The substitution of the solution of Problem 25 yields

$$\int \frac{3x-1}{(x^2+x+1)^2}\, dx = \tfrac{4}{9}\sqrt{3} \int \left(3\sqrt{3}\, \frac{\sec u \tan u}{\sec^3 u} - 5\cos^2 u\right) du$$

$$= -2\cos^2 u - \tfrac{10}{9}\sqrt{3}\, (u + \sin u \cos u) + C,$$

and resubstitution and simplification lead to the answer

$$\int \frac{3x-1}{(x^2+x+1)^2}\, dx = -\frac{5x+7}{3(x^2+x+1)} - \tfrac{10}{9}\sqrt{3} \arctan\left(\tfrac{1}{3}\sqrt{3}\,(2x+1)\right) + C.$$

27. Let $x = 2\sec u$ to transform the integral into

$$\tfrac{1}{8}\int (\csc^3 u - \csc u)\, du.$$

Then use Formulas 15 and 29 of the endpapers.

28. Because $x - x^2 = \frac{1}{4}\left(1 - (2x-1)^2\right)$, we want $2x - 1 = \sin u$: Let $x = \frac{1}{2}(1 + \sin u)$. This yields

$$\int (x - x^2)^{2/3}\, dx = \frac{1}{16}\int \cos^4 u\, du.$$

Then we apply Formula 34 of the endpapers to obtain

$$\int (x - x^2)^{3/2}\, dx = \frac{1}{128}\left(3u + 4\sin u\cos u + \sin u\cos^3 u - \sin^3 u\cos u\right) + C$$

$$= \frac{3}{128}\sin^{-1}(2x-1) - \frac{1}{64}(16x^3 - 24x^2 + 2x + 3)\sqrt{x - x^2} + C.$$

29. $\dfrac{x^2 + 1}{x^3 + x^2 + x} = \dfrac{A}{x} + \dfrac{Bx + C}{x^2 + x + 1}$ leads to $A = 1$, $B = 0$, and $C = -1$, and thus

$$\int \frac{x^2 + 1}{x^3 + x^2 + x}\, dx = \ln|x| - \tfrac{2}{3}\sqrt{3}\,\tan^{-1}\left(\tfrac{1}{3}\sqrt{3}(2x+1)\right) + C.$$

30. $\dfrac{x^2 + 2}{(x^2 + 1)^2} = \dfrac{Ax + B}{x^2 + 1} + \dfrac{Cx + D}{(x^2 + 1)^2}$ leads to $A = C = 0$, $B = D = 1$, and so to the problem of computing

$$\int \left(\frac{1}{x^2 + 1} + \frac{1}{(x^2 + 1)^2}\right) dx.$$

Let $x = \tan u$. We thereby find that

$$\int \frac{x^2 + 2}{(x^2 + 1)^2}\, dx = \tan^{-1} x + \int \frac{\sec^2 u}{\sec^4 u}\, du$$

$$= \tan^{-1} x + \tfrac{1}{2}\int (1 + \cos 2u)\, du$$

$$= \tan^{-1} x + \tfrac{1}{2}(u + \sin u\cos u) + C = \tfrac{3}{2}\tan^{-1} x + \frac{x}{2(x^2 + 1)} + C.$$

31. $\dfrac{2x^2 + 3}{x^4 - 2x^2 + 1} = \dfrac{A}{x - 1} + \dfrac{B}{(x-1)^2} + \dfrac{C}{x + 1} + \dfrac{D}{(x+1)^2}$ leads to $A = -\tfrac{1}{4}$, $B = \tfrac{5}{4}$, $C = \tfrac{1}{4}$, and $D = \tfrac{5}{4}$, and thus:

$$\int \frac{2x^2 + 3}{x^4 - 2x^2 + 1} = \tfrac{1}{4}\ln\left|\frac{x+1}{x-1}\right| - \frac{5x}{2(x^2 - 1)} + C.$$

32. $\dfrac{x^2 + 4}{(x^2 + 1)^2(x^2 + 2)} = \dfrac{Ax + B}{x^2 + 1} + \dfrac{Cx + D}{(x^2 + 1)^2} + \dfrac{Ex + F}{x^2 + 2}$ leads to $A = C = E = 0$, $B = -2$, $D = 3$, and $F = 2$. So we must perform the integration indicated below:

$$\int \left(-\frac{2}{x^2 + 1} + \frac{3}{(x^2 + 1)^2} + \frac{2}{x^2 + 2}\right) dx.$$

The first expression in the integrand presents no problem, and by Formula 17 of the endpapers the third yields

$$\sqrt{2}\,\arctan\left(\tfrac{1}{2}x\sqrt{2}\right) + C_3.$$

For the second expression, we use the substitution $x = \tan z$. Then

$$\int \frac{3}{(x^2 + 1)^2}\, dx = 3\int \frac{\sec^2 z}{\sec^4 z}\, dz$$

$$= 3\int \tfrac{1}{2}(1 + \cos 2x)\, dz = \tfrac{3}{2}(z + \sin z\cos z) + C_2$$

$$= \tfrac{3}{2}\left(\tan^{-1} x + \frac{x}{1 + x^2}\right) + C_2.$$

276   Section 9.7 Integrals Containing Quadratic Polynomials

When we assemble all this information, we find that

$$\int \frac{x^2+4}{(x^2+1)^2(x^2+2)} = \frac{3x}{2(1+x^2)} - \tfrac{1}{2}\tan^{-1} x + \sqrt{2}\tan^{-1}\left(\tfrac{1}{2}x\sqrt{2}\right) + C.$$

33. First write the integrand in the form

$$\tfrac{3}{2}\left(\frac{2x+2}{(x^2+2x+5)^2}\right) - \frac{2}{(x^2+2x+5)^2}.$$

The first of these is easy to integrate, so we'll examine only the second. Forget the presence of the factor -2 temporarily and make the substitution $x = -1 + 2\tan u$:

$$\int \frac{1}{\left((x+1)^2+4\right)^2}\,dx = \int \frac{2\sec^2 u}{(4\sec^2 u)^2}\,du$$

$$= \tfrac{1}{8}\int \cos^2 u\,du = \tfrac{1}{16}\int (1+\cos 2u)\,du$$

$$= \tfrac{1}{16}(u + \sin u \cos u) + C$$

$$= \tfrac{1}{16}\left(\tan^{-1}\left(\frac{x+1}{2}\right) + \frac{2x+2}{x^2+2x+5}\right) + C.$$

34. $\displaystyle\int \frac{x^3-2x}{x^2+2x+2}\,dx = \int x - 2 + \frac{4}{1+(x+1)^2}\,dx = \tfrac{1}{2}x^2 - 2x + 4\arctan(x+1) + C.$

Originally, Problem 34 was supposed to read

$$\int \frac{x^3-2x}{(x^2+2x+2)^2}\,dx,$$

which is somewhat more challenging. The antiderivative in this case is

$$\tfrac{1}{2}\ln(x^2+2x+2) - \arctan(x+1) + \frac{2(x+1)}{x^2+2x+2} + C.$$

35. Let $u = a\tan\theta$, so that $du = a\sec^2\theta\,d\theta$. Then

$$\int \frac{1}{(a^2+u^2)^n}\,du = \int \frac{a\sec^2\theta}{a^{2n}\sec^{2n}\theta}\,d\theta$$

$$= \frac{1}{a^{2n-1}}\int \frac{1}{\sec^{2n-2}\theta}\,d\theta = \frac{1}{a^{2n-1}}\int \cos^{2n-2}\theta\,d\theta.$$

36. This derivation is similar to the one above.

37. The area of R is $\displaystyle\int_0^5 \frac{1}{x^2-2x+5}\,dx = \left[\tfrac{1}{2}\arctan\left(\tfrac{1}{2}[x-1]\right)\right]_0^5 = \tfrac{1}{4}\pi.$

38. The volume generated by rotation of R around the y-axis is

$$\int_0^5 2\pi x \cdot \frac{1}{x^2-2x+5}\,dx = \pi\left[\arctan\left(\tfrac{1}{2}[x-1]\right) + \ln\left(x^2-2x+5\right)\right]_0^5$$

$$= \pi\left(\tfrac{1}{2}\pi + 2\ln 2\right) \approx 9.289974381.$$

39. The volume generated by rotation of R around the x-axis is

$$\int_0^5 \pi\cdot\left(\frac{1}{x^2-2x+5}\right)^2 dx = \left[\tfrac{1}{16}\pi\left(\frac{2(x-1)}{x^2-2x+5} + \arctan\left(\tfrac{1}{2}[x-1]\right)\right)\right]_0^5$$

$$= \tfrac{1}{160}\pi(8+5\pi) \approx 0.465504770.$$

40. The area of R is

$$\int_1^4 \frac{1}{4x^2 - 20x + 29}\, dx = \left[\tfrac{1}{4}\arctan\left(\tfrac{1}{2}[2x-5]\right)\right]_1^4$$
$$= \tfrac{1}{2}\arctan\left(\tfrac{3}{2}\right) \approx 0.491396862.$$

41. The volume generated by rotation of R around the y-axis is

$$\int_1^4 2\pi x \cdot \frac{1}{4x^2 - 20x + 29}\, dx = \tfrac{1}{4}\pi\left[5\arctan\left(\tfrac{1}{2}[2x-5]\right) + \ln(4x^2 - 20x + 20)\right]_1^4$$
$$= \tfrac{5}{2}\pi\arctan\left(\tfrac{3}{2}\right) \approx 7.718843852.$$

42. The volume generated by rotation of R around the x-axis is

$$\int_1^4 \pi\left(\frac{1}{4x^2 - 20x + 29}\right)^2 dx = \tfrac{1}{32}\pi\left[\arctan\left(\tfrac{1}{2}[2x-5]\right) + \frac{2(2x-5)}{4x^2 - 20x + 29}\right]_1^4$$
$$= \tfrac{1}{208}\pi\left[6 + 13\arctan\left(\tfrac{3}{2}\right)\right] \approx 0.283593961.$$

43. First, $y = \tfrac{19}{4} + \sqrt{R^2 - (x+1)^2}$ where $R = \sqrt{377/16}$. It follows that $\dfrac{dy}{dx} = -\dfrac{x+1}{\sqrt{R^2 - (1+x)^2}}$ and hence the length of the road is given by

$$S = \int_0^3 R\left(R^2 - (1+x)^2\right)^{-1/2} dx$$
$$= R\left[\sin^{-1}\left(\frac{1+x}{R}\right)\right]_0^3 = -\tfrac{1}{4}\sqrt{377}\arctan\tfrac{20}{21} \approx 3.6940487.$$

Thus the length of the road is just over 3.69 miles.

44. (a) $\displaystyle\int_0^3 \frac{10R\,dx}{(1+x)\sqrt{R^2 - (1+x)^2}} = 10\left[\ln\frac{1+x}{R + \sqrt{R^2 - (1+x)^2}}\right]_0^3$
$= 10\ln\left(21 + \sqrt{377}\right) - 30\ln 2 \approx 16.198.$

(b) $\displaystyle\int_0^3 \tfrac{10}{3}\sqrt{13}\,\frac{1}{1+x}\, dx = \tfrac{10}{3}\sqrt{13}\left[\ln(1+x)\right]_0^3 = \tfrac{20}{3}\sqrt{13}\ln 2 \approx 16.661.$

45. $\dfrac{3x+2}{x^3 + x^2 - 2} = \dfrac{1}{x-1} - \dfrac{x}{x^2 + 2x + 2} = \dfrac{1}{x-1} - \dfrac{x+1}{x^2 + 2x + 2} + \dfrac{1}{1 + (x+1)^2}.$

46. $\dfrac{1}{x^3 + 8} = \dfrac{A}{x+2} + \dfrac{Bx + C}{x^2 - 2x + 4}$ leads to $A = \tfrac{1}{12}$, $B = -\tfrac{1}{12}$, and $C = \tfrac{1}{3}$. Thus

$$\int \frac{1}{x^3 + 8}\, dx = \tfrac{1}{12}\int\left(\frac{1}{x+2} + \frac{4-x}{x^2 - 2x + 4}\right) dx$$
$$= \tfrac{1}{12}\int\left(\frac{1}{x+2} - \tfrac{1}{2}\left(\frac{2x-2}{x^2 - 2x + 4}\right) + \frac{3}{x^2 - 2x + 4}\right) dx.$$

Note that $x^2 - 2x + 4 = (x-1)^2 + 3$, and with the aid of Formula 17 of the endpapers we obtain the final answer; after simplification, it is

$$\int \frac{1}{x^3 + 8}\, dx = \tfrac{1}{24}\ln\left|\frac{x^2 + 4x + 4}{x^2 - 2x + 4}\right| + \tfrac{1}{12}\sqrt{3}\arctan\left(\tfrac{1}{3}\sqrt{3}\,(x-1)\right) + C.$$

47. The integrand is $x + \dfrac{2x^2 + x}{x^3 - 1}$. The partial fraction decomposition $\dfrac{2x^2 + x}{x^3 - 1} = \dfrac{A}{x - 1} + \dfrac{Bx + C}{x^2 + x + 1}$ yields the values $A = B = C = 1$. Therefore

$$I = \int \dfrac{x^4 + 2x^2}{x^3 - 1}\, dx = \int \left(x + \dfrac{1}{x - 1} + \dfrac{x + 1}{x^2 + x + 1} \right) dx.$$

The third expression poses a minor problem; here's one way to find the antiderivative in question:

$$J = \int \dfrac{x + 1}{x^2 + x + 1}\, dx = \tfrac{1}{2} \int \dfrac{2x + 2}{x^2 + x + 1}\, dx = \tfrac{1}{2} \int \left(\dfrac{2x + 1}{x^2 + x + 1} + \dfrac{1}{x^2 + x + 1} \right) dx.$$

The first of these two is easy; for the second, note that $x^2 + x + 1 = \left(x + \tfrac{1}{2}\right)^2 + \left(\tfrac{1}{2}\sqrt{3}\right)^2$ and apply Formula 17 of the endpapers. The final answer is:

$$\int \dfrac{x^4 + 2x^2}{x^3 - 1}\, dx = \tfrac{1}{2}x^2 + \ln|x - 1| + \tfrac{1}{2}\ln\left(x^2 + x + 1\right) + \tfrac{1}{3}\sqrt{3}\tan^{-1}\left(\tfrac{1}{3}\sqrt{3}\,(2x + 1)\right) + C.$$

48. (a) $a = \sqrt{2},\ b = -\sqrt{2}$ (or vice versa).

(b) The partial fraction decomposition $\dfrac{x^2 + 1}{x^4 + 1} = \dfrac{Ax + B}{x^2 + x\sqrt{2} + 1} + \dfrac{Cx + D}{x^2 - x\sqrt{2} + 1}$ leads to $A = C = 0$, $B = D = \tfrac{1}{2}$. Write

$$x^2 + x\sqrt{x} + 1 = \tfrac{1}{2}\left(\left(x\sqrt{2} + 1\right)^2 + 1\right) \text{ and } x^2 - x\sqrt{x} + 1 = \tfrac{1}{2}\left(\left(x\sqrt{2} - 1\right)^2 + 1\right).$$

Then

$$\int_0^1 \dfrac{x^2 + 1}{x^4 + 1}\, dx = \tfrac{1}{2}\int_0^1 \left(\dfrac{2}{\left(x\sqrt{2} + 1\right)^2 + 1} + \dfrac{2}{\left(x\sqrt{2} - 1\right)^2 + 1} \right) dx$$

$$= \tfrac{1}{2}\sqrt{2}\left[\arctan\left(x\sqrt{2} + 1\right) + \arctan\left(x\sqrt{2} - 1\right) \right]_0^1$$

$$= \tfrac{1}{2}\sqrt{2}\left[\arctan \dfrac{2^{3/2}x}{1 - (2x^2 - 1)} \right]_0^1 = \tfrac{1}{2}\sqrt{2}\left(\lim_{x \to 1^-} \arctan \dfrac{2^{1/2}x}{1 - x^2} \right) = \dfrac{\pi}{4}\sqrt{2}.$$

49. $x^4 + x^2 + 1 = \left(x^2 + x + 1\right)\left(x^2 - x + 1\right)$. (It follows that $10^{12} + 10^6 + 1 = 1{,}000{,}001{,}000{,}001$ is composite.) And

$$\dfrac{2x^3 + 3x}{x^4 + x^2 + 1} = \dfrac{Ax + B}{x^2 + x + 1} + \dfrac{Cx + D}{x^2 - x + 1}$$

yields the values $A = 1$, $B = -\tfrac{1}{2}$, $C = 1$, and $D = \tfrac{1}{2}$. So

$$\int \dfrac{2x^3 + 3x}{x^4 + x^2 + 1}\, dx = \tfrac{1}{2}\int \left(\dfrac{2x - 1}{x^2 + x + 1} + \dfrac{2x + 1}{x^2 - x + 1} \right) dx$$

$$= \tfrac{1}{2}\int \left(\dfrac{2x + 1}{x^2 + x + 1} - \dfrac{2}{x^2 + x + 1} + \dfrac{2x - 1}{x^2 - x + 1} + \dfrac{2}{x^2 - x + 1} \right) dx$$

$$= \tfrac{1}{2}\left(\ln\left(x^2 + x + 1\right) + \ln\left(x^2 - x + 1\right) \right) + \int \left(\dfrac{1}{\left(x - \tfrac{1}{2}\right)^2 + \tfrac{3}{4}} - \dfrac{1}{\left(x + \tfrac{1}{2}\right)^2 + \tfrac{3}{4}} \right) dx$$

$$= \tfrac{1}{2}\ln\left(x^4 + x^2 + 1\right) + \tfrac{2}{3}\sqrt{3}\int \left(\dfrac{\tfrac{2}{3}\sqrt{3}}{\left(\dfrac{2x - 1}{\sqrt{3}}\right)^2 + 1} - \dfrac{\tfrac{2}{3}\sqrt{3}}{\left(\dfrac{2x + 1}{\sqrt{3}}\right)^2 + 1} \right) dx$$

$$= \tfrac{1}{2}\ln\left(x^4 + x^2 + 1\right) + \tfrac{2}{3}\sqrt{3}\left(\arctan\left(\dfrac{2x - 1}{\sqrt{3}}\right) - \arctan\left(\dfrac{2x + 1}{\sqrt{3}}\right) \right) + C$$

$$= \tfrac{1}{2}\ln\left(x^4 + x^2 + 1\right) + \dfrac{2\sqrt{3}}{3}\arctan\left(\dfrac{\sqrt{3}}{3}\left(2x^2 + 1\right)\right) + C.$$

Section 9.7 Integrals Containing Quadratic Polynomials

50. The partial fraction decomposition of the integrand yields, after we combine the two terms with denominators $x + \sqrt{2}$ and $x - \sqrt{2}$, $\dfrac{4x}{x^2 - 2} - \dfrac{4(x - 2)}{x^2 - 2x + 2}$.
The antiderivative is $2\ln|x^2 - 2| - 4\arctan(1 - x) - 2\ln(x^2 - 2x + 2) + C$.

51. The partial fraction decomposition of the integrand is $\dfrac{7}{x - 1} - \dfrac{6x - 5}{(x^2 + 2x + 2)^2}$.
The antiderivative is $7\ln|x - 1| + \tfrac{11}{2}\arctan(x + 1) + \dfrac{11x + 17}{2(x^2 + 2x + 2)} + C$.

52. The partial fraction decomposition of the integrand is $\dfrac{7x + 3}{(x^2 + 1)^2} - \dfrac{4x - 5}{x^2 + 6x + 10}$.
The antiderivative is $\dfrac{3x - 7}{2(x^2 + 1)} + \tfrac{3}{2}\arctan x + 17\arctan(x + 3) - 2\ln(x^2 + 6x + 10) + C$.

53. The partial fraction decomposition of the integrand is $\dfrac{7}{8(x - 5)} + \dfrac{9}{8(x + 3)} + \dfrac{3x - 4}{(4x^2 + 4x + 5)^2}$.
The antiderivative is $\tfrac{7}{8}\ln|x - 5| + \tfrac{9}{8}\ln|x + 3| - \tfrac{11}{64}\arctan\left(\tfrac{1}{2}[2x + 1]\right) - \dfrac{22x + 23}{32(4x^2 + 4x + 5)} + C$.

54. The partial fraction decomposition of the integrand is $\dfrac{4(x + 3)}{(x^2 + 6x + 10)^2} - \dfrac{x + 6}{(4x^2 + 4x + 5)^2}$.
The antiderivative is $-\dfrac{2}{x^2 + 6x + 10} - \dfrac{22x + 7}{32(4x^2 + 4x + 5)} - \tfrac{11}{64}\arctan\left(\tfrac{1}{2}[2x + 1]\right) + C$.

Section 9.8

1. $\displaystyle\int_4^\infty x^{-3/2}\,dx = \lim_{t\to\infty}\left[\dfrac{2}{x^{1/2}}\right]_t^4 = 1$.

2. $\displaystyle\int_1^\infty x^{-2/3}\,dx = \lim_{t\to\infty}\left[3x^{1/3}\right]_1^t$ diverges.

4. $\displaystyle\int_0^8 x^{-2/3}\,dx = \lim_{t\to 0}\left[3x^{1/3}\right]_t^8 = 6$.

6. $\displaystyle\int_3^\infty (x + 1)^{-1/2}\,dx = \lim_{t\to\infty}\left[2\sqrt{x + 1}\right]_3^t$ diverges.

7. $\displaystyle\int_5^\infty (x - 1)^{-3/2}\,dx = \lim_{t\to\infty}\left[-\dfrac{2}{\sqrt{x - 1}}\right]_5^t = 1$.

8. $\displaystyle\int_0^4 (4 - x)^{-1/2}\,dx = \lim_{t\to 4}\left[-2\sqrt{4 - x}\right]_0^t = 4$.

10. $\displaystyle\int_0^3 \dfrac{1}{(x - 3)^2}\,dx = \lim_{t\to 3^-}\left[-\dfrac{1}{x - 3}\right]_0^t$ diverges.

12. $\displaystyle\int_{-\infty}^0 \dfrac{1}{\sqrt{4 - x}}\,dx = \lim_{t\to -\infty}\left[-2\sqrt{4 - x}\right]_t^0$ diverges.

13. Integrate from -1 to 0, from 0 to 8. If both integrals converge add the results.

14. $\displaystyle\int_{-4}^4 \dfrac{1}{(x + 4)^{2/3}}\,dx = \lim_{t\to -4}\left[3(x + 4)^{1/3}\right]_{-4}^4 = 6$.

16. $\int_{-\infty}^{\infty} \frac{x}{(x^2+4)^{3/2}} dx = \int_{-\infty}^{0} \frac{x}{(x^2+4)^{3/2}} dx + \int_{0}^{\infty} \frac{x}{(x^2+4)^{3/2}} dx$
$= \lim_{s \to -\infty} \left[-\frac{1}{\sqrt{x^2+4}}\right]_{s}^{0} + \lim_{t \to \infty} \left[-\frac{1}{\sqrt{x^2+4}}\right]_{0}^{t} = 0.$

18. $\int_{0}^{\infty} e^{-(x+1)} dx = \lim_{t \to \infty} \left[-e^{-(x+1)}\right]_{0}^{t} = \frac{1}{e}.$

20. $\int_{0}^{2} \frac{x}{x^2-1} dx = \int_{0}^{1} \frac{x}{x^2-1} dx + \int_{1}^{2} \frac{x}{x^2-1} dx$ diverges since $\int_{0}^{1} \frac{x}{x^2-1} dx = \lim_{t \to 1^-} \left[\frac{1}{2}\ln(1-x^2)\right]_{0}^{t}$ diverges.

21. $\left[-\frac{1}{9}(3x+1)e^{-3x}\right]_{0}^{\infty} = \frac{1}{9}.$

22. $\left[\frac{1}{2}e^{2x}\right]_{-\infty}^{2} = \frac{1}{2}e^4.$

23. $\left[-\frac{1}{2}\exp(-x^2)\right]_{0}^{\infty} = \frac{1}{2}.$

24. $2\left[-\frac{1}{2}\exp(-x^2)\right]_{0}^{\infty} = 1.$

25. $\left[\arctan x\right]_{0}^{\infty} = \frac{\pi}{2}.$

26. $\left[\frac{1}{2}\ln(x^2+1)\right]_{0}^{\infty} = +\infty.$

27. This integral does not converge.

28. This integral diverges to $+\infty$.

29. This integral diverges to $+\infty$.

30. This integral diverges to $+\infty$.

31. $\left[-\frac{1}{\ln x}\right]_{2}^{\infty} = \frac{1}{\ln 2}.$

32. $\left[-\frac{1+\ln x}{x}\right]_{1}^{\infty} = 1.$

33. $\left[2\sqrt{\sin x}\right]_{0}^{\pi/2} = 2.$

34. This integral diverges to $+\infty$.

35. $\left[(x \ln x) - x\right]_{0}^{1} = -1.$

36. This integral diverges to $-\infty$.

37. This integral diverges to $-\infty$.

38. $\left[\frac{1}{2}e^{-x}(\sin x - \cos x)\right]_{0}^{\infty} = \frac{1}{2}.$

39. $\int_{0}^{1} \frac{1}{x^2+x} dx = +\infty; \int_{1}^{\infty} \left(\frac{1}{x} - \frac{1}{x+1}\right) dx = \left[\ln x - \ln(x+1)\right]_{1}^{\infty} = \ln 2.$

40. $\int_{0}^{1} \frac{1}{x^2+x^4} dx = +\infty; \int_{1}^{\infty} \left(\frac{1}{x^2} - \frac{1}{x^2+1}\right) dx = \left[-\frac{1}{x} - \arctan x\right]_{1}^{\infty} = \frac{4-\pi}{4}.$

41. $\int_{0}^{1} \frac{1}{(1+x)\sqrt{x}} dx = \left[2\arctan(\sqrt{x})\right]_{0}^{1} = \frac{\pi}{2};$
$\int_{1}^{\infty} \frac{1}{(1+x)\sqrt{x}} dx = \left[2\arctan(\sqrt{x})\right]_{1}^{\infty} = \frac{\pi}{2}.$

42. $\int_{0}^{1} \frac{1}{x^{2/3}(1+x^{2/3})} dx = \left[3\arctan(x^{1/3})\right]_{0}^{1} = \frac{3\pi}{4};$

Section 9.8 Improper Integrals

$$\int_1^\infty \frac{1}{x^{2/3}(1+x^{2/3})}\,dx = \left[3\arctan\left(x^{1/3}\right)\right]_1^\infty = \frac{3\pi}{4}.$$

43. This integral converges exactly when $k < 1$. For such k, its value is $\left[\dfrac{x^{1-k}}{1-k}\right]_0^1 = \dfrac{1}{1-k}$.

44. This integral converges exactly when $k > 1$. For such k, its value is $\left[\dfrac{x^{1-k}}{1-k}\right]_1^\infty = \dfrac{1}{k-1}$.

45. This integral converges exactly when $k > -1$. For such k, its value is

$$\left[\frac{x\ln x}{k+1} - \frac{x^{k+1}}{(k+1)^2}\right]_0^1 = -\frac{1}{(k+1)^2}.$$

46. Note that $\displaystyle\int \frac{1}{x(\ln x)^k}\,dx = \frac{(\ln x)^{1-k}}{1-k} + C$. If $1-k > 0$, then the improper integral will diverge because $(\ln x)^{1-k} \to +\infty$ as $x \to +\infty$. If $1-k < 0$, then the improper integral will diverge because $(\ln x)^{1-k} = \dfrac{1}{(\ln x)^{k-1}} \to +\infty$ as $x \to 1^+$. The integral clearly diverges if $k=1$. Therefore this integral converges for *no* values of k.

47. Let $u = x^{t-1}$ and $dv = e^{-x}\,dx$. Then $du = (t-1)x^{t-2}\,dx$ and $v = -e^{-x}$. So

$$\int_0^\infty x^{t-1}e^{-x}\,dx = \left[-x^{t-1}e^{-x}\right]_0^\infty + (t-1)\int_0^\infty x^{t-2}e^{-x}\,dx.$$

The evaluation bracket is zero at both limits of integration, so we have shown that

$$\Gamma(t) = (t-1)\Gamma(t-1)$$

if $t > 1$. Replace t with $x+1$ to conclude that $\Gamma(x+1) = x\Gamma(x)$ if $x > 0$.

50. Volume: $V = \displaystyle\int_1^\infty \frac{\pi}{x^2}\,dx = \pi$.

52. $\displaystyle\int_0^\infty \frac{1+x}{1+x^2}\,dx$ dominates $\displaystyle\int_0^\infty \frac{x}{1+x^2}\,dx$, which diverges.

54. Integrate by parts with $u = 10+t$, $dv = e^{-t/10}\,dt$ to obtain the answer \$200,000.

56. The force exerted on m by dy is $\dfrac{Gm\delta}{a^2+y^2}\,dy$. The horizontal component of that force is

$$dF = \frac{Gm\delta}{r^2}(\cos\theta)\,dy.$$

So the total horizontal force is

$$F = \int_{-\infty}^\infty \frac{Gm\delta}{r^2}(\cos\theta)\,dy.$$

Now $r^2 = a^2 + y^2$ and $\cos\theta = \dfrac{a}{r}$. So $\cos\theta = \dfrac{a}{\sqrt{a^2+y^2}}$: $F = 2\displaystyle\int_0^\infty \frac{Gm\delta a}{(a^2+y^2)^{3/2}}\,dy$.

With the aid of Formula 52 of the endpapers of the text, we find that

$$F = 2Gm\delta a\left[\frac{y}{a^2\sqrt{a^2+y^2}}\right]_0^\infty = \frac{2Gm\delta}{a}\left(\lim_{y\to\infty}\frac{y}{\sqrt{a^2+y^2}}\right) = \frac{2Gm\delta}{a}.$$

58. We need to evaluate $V = \displaystyle\int_0^\infty \pi[\exp(-x^2)]^2\,dx = \int_0^\infty \pi\exp(-2x^2)\,dx$.

Let $x = u/\sqrt{2}$. Then $V = \displaystyle\int_{u=0}^\infty \frac{1}{\sqrt{2}}\pi e^{-u^2}\,du = \frac{\pi}{\sqrt{2}}\int_0^\infty e^{-u^2}\,du = \frac{\pi}{\sqrt{2}}\cdot\frac{\sqrt{\pi}}{2} = \left(\frac{\pi}{2}\right)^{3/2}$.

59. The volume is $V = \int_0^\infty 2\pi x \exp(-x^2)\, dx = \left[-\pi \exp(-x^2) \right]_0^\infty = \pi$.

60. If n is a positive integer, then
$$\Gamma\left(n + \tfrac{1}{2}\right) = \Gamma\left(n - \tfrac{1}{2} + 1\right) = \left(n - \tfrac{1}{2}\right)\Gamma\left(n - \tfrac{1}{2}\right) = \frac{2n-1}{2}\Gamma\left(n - 1 + \tfrac{1}{2}\right).$$

So
$$\Gamma\left(1 + \tfrac{1}{2}\right) = \tfrac{1}{2}\Gamma\left(\tfrac{1}{2}\right) = \tfrac{1}{2}\sqrt{\pi}$$
$$\Gamma\left(2 + \tfrac{1}{2}\right) = \tfrac{3}{2}\Gamma\left(\tfrac{1}{2}\right) = \tfrac{3}{2}\cdot\tfrac{1}{2}\cdot\sqrt{\pi},$$
$$\Gamma\left(3 + \tfrac{1}{2}\right) = \tfrac{5}{2}\Gamma\left(\tfrac{3}{2}\right) = \tfrac{5}{2}\cdot\tfrac{3}{2}\cdot\tfrac{1}{2}\cdot\sqrt{\pi} \text{ and, by induction,}$$
$$\Gamma\left(n + \tfrac{1}{2}\right) = \frac{(2n-1)(2n-3)\cdots 5\cdot 3\cdot 1}{2^n}\sqrt{\pi}.$$

Here is the inductive step. Suppose that $\Gamma\left(k + \tfrac{1}{2}\right) = \dfrac{(2k-1)(2k-3)\cdots 5\cdot 3\cdot 1}{2^k}\sqrt{\pi}$ for some integer $k \geq 1$. Then
$$\Gamma\left(k + 1 + \tfrac{1}{2}\right) = \frac{2(k+1) - 1}{2}\cdot \Gamma\left(k + \tfrac{1}{2}\right)$$
$$= \frac{2k+1}{2}\cdot \frac{(2k-1)(2k-3)\cdots 5\cdot 3\cdot 1}{2^k}\sqrt{\pi}$$
$$= \frac{(2k+1)(2n-1)\cdots 5\cdot 3\cdot 1}{2^{k+1}}\sqrt{\pi}.$$

61. (a) $\begin{bmatrix} u = x^{k-1} & dv = xe^{-x^2}\, dx \\ du = (k-1)x^{k-2}\, dx & v = -\tfrac{1}{2}e^{-x^2} \end{bmatrix}$
$$\int_0^\infty x^k e^{-x^2}\, dx = \left[-\frac{x^{k-1}}{2}e^{-x^2}\right]_0^\infty + \frac{k-1}{2}\int_0^\infty x^{k-2}e^{-x^2}\, dx = \frac{k-1}{2}\int_0^\infty x^{k-2}e^{-x^2}\, dx.$$

(b) If $n = 1$, then
$$\int_0^\infty x^{n-1}e^{-x^2}\, dx = \int_0^\infty e^{-x^2}\, dx = \tfrac{1}{2}\sqrt{\pi} \text{ (by Problem 35)}$$
$$= \tfrac{1}{2}\Gamma\left(\tfrac{1}{2}\right) \text{ (also by Problem 35).}$$

If $n = 2$, then
$$\int_0^\infty x^{n-1}e^{-x^2}\, dx = \int_0^\infty xe^{-x^2}\, dx = \left[-\tfrac{1}{2}e^{-x^2}\right]_0^\infty = \tfrac{1}{2} = \tfrac{1}{2}\Gamma(1) \text{ because } \Gamma(1) = 0! = 1.$$

If $n = 3$, then
$$\int_0^\infty x^{n-1}e^{-x^2}\, dx = \frac{n-2}{2}\int_0^\infty x^{n-3}e^{-x^2}\, dx \text{ (by Part (a))}$$
$$= \tfrac{1}{2}\int_0^\infty e^{-x^2}\, dx = \tfrac{1}{2}\cdot \tfrac{1}{2}\sqrt{\pi}$$
$$= \tfrac{1}{2}\Gamma\left(\tfrac{3}{2}\right) \text{ because } \Gamma\left(\tfrac{3}{2}\right) = \tfrac{1}{2}\Gamma\left(\tfrac{1}{2}\right) = \tfrac{1}{2}\sqrt{\pi}.$$

Assume that for some integer $k \geq 3$,
$$\int_0^\infty x^{n-1}e^{-x^2}\, dx = \tfrac{1}{2}\Gamma\left(\frac{n}{2}\right) \text{ for all } n,\ 1 \leq n \leq k.$$

Section 9.8 Improper Integrals

Then
$$\int_0^\infty x^k e^{-x^2}\, dx = \frac{k-1}{2} \int_0^\infty x^{k-2} e^{-x^2}\, dx = \frac{k-1}{2} \cdot \tfrac{1}{2}\Gamma\left(\frac{k-1}{2}\right) = \tfrac{1}{2}\Gamma\left(\frac{k+2}{2}\right)$$

(because $\Gamma(x+1) = x\,\Gamma(x)$). Therefore, by induction, $\int_0^\infty x^{n-1} e^{-x^2}\, dx = \tfrac{1}{2}\Gamma\left(\frac{n}{2}\right)$ for all $n \geq 1$.

62. $\int_0^\infty 10000 e^{-(0.06)t}\, dt = \left[-\frac{10000}{0.06} e^{-(0.06)t}\right]_0^\infty = \frac{10000}{0.06} \approx \$166{,}666.67.$

Chapter 9 Miscellaneous

2. $\int \dfrac{\sec^2 t}{1 + \tan t}\, dt = \ln|1 + \tan t| + C$

4. $\int \dfrac{\csc x \cot x}{1 + \csc^2 x}\, dx = -\tan^{-1}(\csc x) + C$

6. $\int \csc^4 x\, dx = \int (1 + \cot^2 x)(\csc^2 x)\, dx = \int (\csc^2 x + \cot^2 x \csc^2 x)\, dx = -\cot x - \tfrac{1}{3}\cot^3 x + C$

7. Integration by parts: Let $u = x$, $dv = \tan^2 x\, dx = (\sec^2 x - 1)\, dx$.

8. First write $\cos^2 x = \tfrac{1}{2}(1 + \cos 2x)$. Integrate what you can, and then integrate $x^2 \cos 2x$ by parts: Let $u = x^2$ and $dv = \cos x\, dx$. This leads to the integration of $x \sin 2x$, which also works well by parts. You should get
$$\int x^2 \cos^2 x\, dx = \tfrac{1}{6} x^3 + \tfrac{1}{4} x^2 \sin 2x + \tfrac{1}{4} x \cos 2x - \tfrac{1}{8} \sin 2x + C.$$

9. Substitution: Let $u = 2 - x^3$.

10. Let $x = 2 \tan u$:
$$\int \frac{1}{\sqrt{x^2 + 4}}\, dx = \int \sec u\, du = \ln|\sec u + \tan u| + C$$
$$= \ln\left|\tfrac{1}{2}\sqrt{x^2 + 4} + \tfrac{1}{2}x\right| + C_1 = \ln\left|x + \sqrt{x^2+4}\right| + C.$$

11. Let $x = 5 \tan \theta$: $\int \dfrac{x^2}{\sqrt{25 + x^2}}\, dx = \int 25\left(\sec^3 \theta - \sec \theta\right) d\theta.$

12. Let $u = \sin x$: $\int (\cos x)\sqrt{4 - \sin^2 x}\, dx = \int \sqrt{4 - u^2}\, du.$ Now let $u = 2 \sin \theta$.
$$\int (\cos x)\sqrt{4 - \sin^2 x}\, dx = \int 4 \cos^2 \theta\, d\theta = 2 \sin^{-1}\left(\tfrac{1}{2}\sin x\right) + \tfrac{1}{2}(\sin x)\sqrt{4 - \sin^2 x} + C$$

13. Write $x^2 - x + 1 = \left(x - \tfrac{1}{2}\right)^2 + \tfrac{3}{4}$, then apply Formula 17 from the endpapers.

14. First write $x^2 + x + 1 = \left(x + \tfrac{1}{2}\right)^2 + \tfrac{3}{4} = \tfrac{3}{4}\left(\tfrac{4}{3}\left(x + \tfrac{1}{2}\right)^2 + 1\right) = \tfrac{3}{4}(u^2 + 1)$ where $u = \dfrac{2x+1}{\sqrt{3}}$. Then let $u = \tan \theta$, and the integrand becomes $\tfrac{3}{4} \sec^3 \theta$. Apply Formula 28 from the endpapers.
$$\int \sqrt{x^2 + x + 1}\, dx = \tfrac{1}{4}(2x + 1)\sqrt{x^2 + x + 1} + \tfrac{3}{8}\ln\left|2x + 1 + 2\sqrt{x^2 + x + 1}\right| + C.$$

15. $3x^2 - 4x + 11 = \tfrac{1}{3}\left((3x - 2)^2 + 29\right).$

16. $\int \frac{x^4+1}{x^2+2} dx = \int \left(x^2 - 2 + \frac{5}{x^2+2}\right) dx = \frac{1}{3}x^3 - 2x + \frac{5}{2}\sqrt{2}\tan^{-1}\left(\frac{1}{2}x\sqrt{2}\right) + C.$

17. $\int \sqrt{x^4 + x^7}\, dx = \int x^2\sqrt{1+x^3}\, dx$

18. Let $x = u^2$: $\int \frac{\sqrt{x}}{1+x} dx = \int \left(2 - \frac{2}{1+u^2}\right) du = 2\sqrt{x} - 2\tan^{-1}\sqrt{x} + C.$

19. Use the substitution $u = \sin x$.

20. $\int \frac{\cos 2x}{\cos x} dx = \int \frac{2\cos^2 x - 1}{\cos x} dx = 2\sin x - \ln|\sec x + \tan x| + C.$

21. Let $u = \ln(\cos x)$, then compute du.

22. Let $x^2 = \sin u$:
$$\int \frac{x^7}{\sqrt{1-x^4}} dx = \int \tfrac{1}{2}\sin^3 u\, du = \tfrac{1}{6}(\cos u)(\cos^2 u - 3) + C = -\tfrac{1}{6}(x^4 + 2)\sqrt{1-x^4} + C.$$

23. $\begin{bmatrix} u = \ln(1+x) & dv = dx \\ du = \dfrac{1}{1+x} dx & v = x+1 \end{bmatrix}$
$\int \ln(1+x)\, dx = (x+1)\ln(1+x) - \int 1\, dx$
$= (x+1)\ln(1+x) - x + C.$

24. $\begin{bmatrix} u = \sec^{-1} x & dv = x\, dx \\ du = \dfrac{1}{|x|\sqrt{x^2-1}} dx & v = \tfrac{1}{2}x^2 \end{bmatrix}$
$\int x\sec^{-1} x\, dx = \tfrac{1}{2}x^2 \sec^{-1} x - \tfrac{1}{2}\int \dfrac{x^2}{|x|\sqrt{x^2-1}} dx$

For $x > 1$, $\int \dfrac{x^2}{|x|\sqrt{x^2-1}} dx = \int x(x^2-1)^{-1/2} dx = \sqrt{x^2-1} + C.$

For $x < -1$, $\int \dfrac{x^2}{|x|\sqrt{x^2-1}} dx = \int -x(x^2-1)^{-1/2} dx = -\sqrt{x^2-1} + C.$ So
$$\int x\sec^{-1} x\, dx = \tfrac{1}{2}\left(x^2 \sec^{-1} x - \frac{|x|}{x}\sqrt{x^2-1}\right) + C.$$

25. Let $x = 3\tan u$.

26. The substitution $x = 2\sin u$ yields
$$\int \frac{x^2}{\sqrt{4-x^2}} dx = \int 4\sin^2 u\, du = 2\int (1 - \cos 2u)\, du$$
$$= 2u - 2\sin u \cos u + C = 2\arcsin \frac{x}{2} - \frac{x}{2}\sqrt{4-x^2} + C.$$

27. $2x - x^2 = 1 - (1-x)^2$. Now let $x = 1 - \cos u$.

28. $\int \frac{4x-2}{x^3-x} dx = \int \left(\frac{2}{x} - \frac{3}{x+1} + \frac{1}{x-1}\right) dx$
$= 2\ln|x| - 3\ln|x+1| + \ln|x-1| + C = \ln\left|\frac{x^2(x-1)}{(x+1)^3}\right| + C.$

29. Write the integrand in the form $x^2 + 2 - \dfrac{4}{2-x^2}$. Then use Formula 18 from the endpapers, the method of partial fractions, or a trigonometric or hyperbolic substitution.

30. $\int \dfrac{\sec x \tan x}{\sec x + \sec^2 x} dx = \int \dfrac{\tan x}{1 + \sec x} dx = \int \dfrac{\sin x}{1 + \cos x} dx = -\ln(1 + \cos x) + C.$

31. Let $x = -1 + \tan u$: $\int \dfrac{x}{(x^2+2x+2)^2} dx = \int \dfrac{-1+\tan u}{\sec^2 u} du = \int (-\cos^2 u + \sin u \cos u)\, du$, and the rest is routine.

Chapter 9 Miscellaneous

32. The least common multiple of 2, 3, and 4 is 12, so let $u = x^{1/12}$.

$$\int \frac{x^{1/3}}{x^{1/2} + x^{1/4}}\, dx = \int \frac{12 u^{12}}{u^3 + 1}\, du = \int 12\left(u^9 - u^6 + u^3 - 1 + \frac{1}{u^3 + 1}\right) du$$

$$= \int \left(12\left(u^9 - u^6 + u^3 - 1\right) + \frac{4}{u+1} - \frac{4u - 8}{u^2 - u + 1}\right) du \quad \text{(partial fractions)}.$$

Now proceed much as in the last part of the solution to Problem 8, Section 9.8.

$$\int \frac{x^{1/3}}{x^{1/2} + x^{1/4}}\, dx = \tfrac{6}{5} u^{10} - \tfrac{12}{7} u^7 + 3u^4 - 12u + 4\ln|u+1|$$
$$- 2\ln\left|u^2 - u + 1\right| + 4\sqrt{3}\arctan\left(\tfrac{1}{3}\sqrt{3}(2u-1)\right) + C$$
$$= \tfrac{6}{5} x^{5/6} - \tfrac{12}{7} x^{7/12} + 3x^{1/3} - 12 x^{1/2} + 4\ln\left(1 + x^{1/12}\right)$$
$$- 2\ln\left(1 - x^{1/12} + x^{1/6}\right) + 4\sqrt{3}\arctan\left(\tfrac{1}{3}\sqrt{3}\left(2x^{1/12} - 1\right)\right) + C.$$

33. $\dfrac{1}{1 + \cos 2\theta} = \tfrac{1}{2}\sec^2 \theta$.

34. $\displaystyle\int \frac{\sec x}{\tan x}\, dx = \int \csc x\, dx = \ln|\csc x - \cot x| + C.$

35. $\sec^3 x \tan^3 x = \sec^5 x \tan x - \sec^3 x \tan x$.

36. $\begin{bmatrix} u = \tan^{-1} x & dv = x^2\, dx \\ du = \dfrac{1}{1+x^2} dx & v = \tfrac{1}{3} x^3 \end{bmatrix}$ $\displaystyle\int x^2 \tan^{-1} x\, dx = \tfrac{1}{3} x^3 \tan^{-1} x - \tfrac{1}{3}\int \left(x - \frac{x}{1+x^2}\right) dx$
$$= \tfrac{1}{3} x^3 \tan^{-1} x - \tfrac{1}{6} x^2 + \tfrac{1}{6}\ln\left(1 + x^2\right) + C.$$

37. *Suggestion*: Develop a reduction formula for $\displaystyle\int x (\ln x)^n\, dx$ by parts; take $u = (\ln x)^n$ and $dv = x\, dx$. Then apply your formula iteratively to evaluate the given antiderivative. You should find that

$$\int x (\ln x)^n\, dx = \tfrac{1}{2} x^2 (\ln x)^n - \frac{n}{2} \int x (\ln x)^{n-1}\, dx.$$

38. Let $x = \tan\theta$: $\displaystyle\int \csc\theta\, d\theta = \ln|\csc\theta - \cot\theta| + C = \ln\dfrac{\sqrt{x^2 + 1} - 1}{x} + C.$

39. Let $u = e^x$, then $u = \tan z$ to obtain $\displaystyle\int e^x \sqrt{1 + e^{2x}}\, dx = \int \sec^3 z\, dz.$

40. Note that $4x - x^2 = 4 - (x-2)^2$; let $x - 2 = 2\sin u$. Then

$$\int \frac{x}{\sqrt{4x - x^2}}\, dx = \int 2(1 + \sin u)\, du = 2(u - \cos u) + C = 2\arcsin\frac{x-2}{2} - \sqrt{4x - x^2} + C.$$

41. Let $x = 3\sec\theta$.

42. Let $u = 7x + 1$: $\displaystyle\int \frac{x}{(7x+1)^{17}}\, dx = -\frac{112x + 1}{11760 (7x+1)^{16}} + C.$

43. Use the method of partial fraction decomposition.

44. Divide denominator into numerator, then use the method of partial fraction decomposition.

$$\int \frac{4x^3 - x + 1}{x^3 + 1}\, dx = 4x - \tfrac{2}{3}\ln|x+1| + \tfrac{1}{3}\ln|x^2 - x + 1| - \tfrac{4}{3}\sqrt{3}\tan^{-1}\left(\tfrac{1}{3}\sqrt{3}(2x - 1)\right) + C.$$

45. Write the integrand as $\sec^3 x - \sec x$, then apply the formulas of the endpapers.

46. Here is a quick way to obtain the partial fraction decomposition: $\dfrac{x^2+2x+2}{(x+1)^3} = \dfrac{(x+1)^2+1}{(x+1)^3}$.

$$\int \dfrac{x^2+2x+2}{(x+1)^3}\,dx = \int\left(\dfrac{1}{x+1} + \dfrac{1}{(x+1)^3}\right)dx = \ln|x+1| - \dfrac{1}{2(x+1)^2} + C.$$

47. The partial fraction decomposition of the integrand is $\dfrac{1}{x+1} + \dfrac{2}{x^4}$.

48. $\displaystyle\int \dfrac{8x^2-4x+7}{(x^2+1)(4x+1)}\,dx = \int\left(-\dfrac{1}{x^2+1} + \dfrac{8}{4x+1}\right)dx = 2\ln|4x+1| - \tan^{-1}x + C.$

49. The partial fraction decomposition of the integrand has the form

$$\dfrac{A}{x-1} + \dfrac{Bx+C}{x^2+x+1} + \dfrac{D}{(x-1)^2} + \dfrac{Ex+F}{(x^2+x+1)^2}.$$

The simultaneous equations are

$$\begin{aligned}
A + B &&&&&&&&&&&= 3 \\
A - B + C + D &&&&&&&&&&&= -1 \\
A &&- C + 2D + E &&&&&&&&&= 2 \\
-A - B &&+ 3D - 2E + F &&&&&&&&&= -12 \\
-A + B - C + 2D + E - 2F &&&&&&&&&&&= -2 \\
-A &&+ C + D &&+ F &&&&&&&&&= 1
\end{aligned}$$

Their solution: $A = 1$, $B = 2$, $C = 1$, $D = -1$, $E = 4$, and $F = 2$. None of the antiderivatives is difficult.

$$\int \dfrac{3x^5 - x^4 + 2x^3 - 12x^2 - 2x + 1}{(x^3-1)^2}\,dx = \ln|x-1| + \ln(x^2+x+1) + \dfrac{1}{x-1} - \dfrac{2}{x^2+x+1} + C.$$

50. $\displaystyle\int \dfrac{x}{x^4+4x^2+8}\,dx = \int \dfrac{x}{(x^2+2)^2+4}\,dx = \tfrac{1}{4}\int \dfrac{x}{((x^2+2)/2)^2+1}\,dx = \tfrac{1}{4}\arctan\left(\dfrac{x^2+2}{2}\right) + C.$

51. Consider instead $\displaystyle\int (\ln x)^n\,dx$, where n is a positive integer.

$$\begin{bmatrix} u = (\ln x)^n & dv = dx \\ du = \dfrac{n}{x}(\ln x)^{n-1}\,dx & v = x \end{bmatrix} \qquad \int (\ln x)^n\,dx = x(\ln x)^n - n\int(\ln x)^{n-1}\,dx.$$

Hence

$$\int (\ln x)^6\,dx = x(\ln x)^6 - 6\int (\ln x)^5\,dx$$

$$= x(\ln x)^6 - 6\left(x(\ln x)^5 - 5\int(\ln x)^4\,dx\right)$$

$$= \cdots$$

$$= x(\ln x)^6 - 6x(\ln x)^5 + 6\cdot 5x(\ln x)^4 - 6\cdot 5\cdot 4x(\ln x)^3$$
$$\quad + 6\cdot 5\cdot 4\cdot 3x(\ln x)^2 - 6\cdot 5\cdot 4\cdot 3\cdot 2x(\ln x) + 6\cdot 5\cdot 4\cdot 3\cdot 2\int (\ln x)^0\,dx$$

$$= x(\ln x)^6 - 6x(\ln x)^5 + 30x(\ln x)^4 - 120x(\ln x)^3 + 360x(\ln x)^2 - 720x(\ln x) + 720x + C.$$

52. Let $x = u^3$: $\displaystyle\int \dfrac{(1+x^{2/3})^{3/2}}{x^{1/3}}\,dx = 3\int u(1+u^2)^{3/2}\,du = \tfrac{3}{5}(1+u^2)^{5/2} + C = \tfrac{3}{5}(1+x^{2/3})^{5/2} + C.$

54. Let $x = u^6$: $\int \dfrac{1}{x^{3/2}(1+x^{1/3})}\,dx = 6\int \dfrac{1}{u^4(1+u^2)}\,du.$

Next let $u = \tan z$:

$$\int \dfrac{1}{x^{3/2}(1+x^{1/3})}\,dx = 6\int \dfrac{\sec^2 z}{\tan^4 z\,\sec^2 z}\,dz = 6\int \cot^4 z\,dz$$

$$= 6\int (\csc^2 z - 1)\cot^2 z\,dz = 6\int \left(\cot^2 z\,\csc^2 z - (\csc^2 z - 1)\right)\,dz$$

$$= 6\left(-\tfrac{1}{3}\cot^3 z + \cot z + z\right) + C = 6\left(\dfrac{1}{u} + \arctan u - \dfrac{1}{3u^3}\right) + C$$

$$= 6x^{-1/6} + 6\tan^{-1}\left(x^{1/6}\right) - 2x^{-1/2} + C.$$

55. $\tan^3 z = (\tan z)(\sec^2 z - 1) = (\tan z)(\sec^2 z) - \tan z.$

56. Use Formula 39 of the endpapers; alternatively, repeated use of the half-angle formulas and other trigonometric identities may be used to transform the integral as follows:

$$\int \sin^2\omega\,\cos^4\omega\,d\omega = \tfrac{1}{8}\int \left(1 + \cos 2\omega - \tfrac{1}{2}(1+\cos 4\omega) - (\cos 2\omega)(1 - \sin^2 2\omega)\right)\,d\omega$$

$$= \tfrac{1}{8}\left(\tfrac{1}{2}\omega - \tfrac{1}{4}\sin 2\omega\,\cos 2\omega + \tfrac{1}{6}\sin^3 2\omega\right) + C.$$

57. Because $e^{2x^2} = \left(e^{x^2}\right)^2$, let $u = e^{x^2}$. Then the pattern will become clear.

58. Note that $\dfrac{\cos^3 x}{\sqrt{\sin x}} = \dfrac{(1-\sin^2 x)(\cos x)}{\sqrt{\sin x}} = (\sin x)^{-1/2}\cos x - (\sin x)^{3/2}\cos x.$ So

$$\int \dfrac{\cos^3 x}{\sqrt{\sin x}}\,dx = \tfrac{2}{5}(\sin x)^{1/2}\left(5 - \sin^2 x\right) + C.$$

59. Use integration by parts; choose as dv the "most difficult part of the integrand that one can actually integrate": $u = x^2$, $dv = xe^{-x^2}\,dx.$

60. Let $u = \sqrt{x}$: $\int \sin\sqrt{x}\,dx = \int 2u\sin u\,du.$ Now use integration by parts:

$\begin{bmatrix} p = 2u & dq = \sin u\,du \\ dp = 2\,du & q = -\cos u \end{bmatrix}$ $\int \sin\sqrt{x}\,dx = -2u\cos u + 2\sin u + C = 2\left(\sin\sqrt{x} - \sqrt{x}\cos\sqrt{x}\right) + C.$

61. Use integration by parts with $u = \arcsin x$ and $dv = \dfrac{1}{x^2}\,dx.$ Then apply Formula 60 of the endpapers, or use the trigonometric substitution $x = \sin u$.

62. Let $x = 3\sec u$: $\int \sqrt{x^2 - 9}\,dx = 9\int \sec u\,\tan^2 u\,du = 9\int (\sec^3 u - \sec u)\,du.$ Apply Formulas 14 and 28 of the endpapers to obtain

$$\int \sqrt{x^2 - 9}\,dx = \tfrac{9}{2}\left(\sec u\,\tan u - \ln|\sec u + \tan u|\right) + C_1$$

$$= \tfrac{9}{2}\left(\tfrac{1}{9}x\sqrt{x^2-9} - \ln\left|\tfrac{1}{3}x + \tfrac{1}{3}\sqrt{x^2-9}\right|\right) + C_1$$

$$= \tfrac{1}{2}x\sqrt{x^2-9} - \tfrac{9}{2}\ln\left|x + \sqrt{x^2-9}\right| + C.$$

63. Let $x = \sin u$: $\int x^2\sqrt{1-x^2}\,dx = \int \tfrac{1}{4}(2\sin u\,\cos u)^2\,du = \int \tfrac{1}{4}\sin^2(2u)\,du = \int \tfrac{1}{8}(2 - \cos 4u)\,du.$

288   Chapter 9   Miscellaneous

64. Because $2x - x^2 = 1 - (x-1)^2$, let $x = 1 + \sin u$:

$$\int x\sqrt{2x - x^2}\, dx = \int (1 + \sin u)(\cos^2 u)\, du = \int \left(\frac{1 + \cos 2u}{2} + \cos^2 u \sin u\right) du$$

$$= \tfrac{1}{2}u + \tfrac{1}{2}\sin u \cos u - \tfrac{1}{3}\cos^3 u + C$$

$$= \tfrac{1}{2}\sin^{-1}(x-1) + \tfrac{1}{2}(x-1)\sqrt{2x - x^2} - \tfrac{1}{3}(2x - x^2)^{3/2} + C$$

$$= \tfrac{1}{2}\sin^{-1}(x-1) + \tfrac{1}{6}\sqrt{2x - x^2}(2x^2 - x - 3) + C.$$

65. Write $\dfrac{x - 2}{(2x + 1)^2} = \dfrac{2x + 1}{2(2x + 1)^2} - \dfrac{5}{2(2x + 1)^2}$.

66. $\displaystyle\int \dfrac{2x^2 - 5x - 1}{x^3 - 2x^2 - x + 2}\, dx = \int \left(\dfrac{1}{x + 1} + \dfrac{2}{x - 1} - \dfrac{1}{x - 2}\right) dx = \ln\left|\dfrac{(x+1)(x-1)^2}{x - 2}\right| + C.$

68. Let $u = \sin x$: $\displaystyle\int \dfrac{\cos x}{\sin^2 x - 3\sin x + 2}\, dx = \int \dfrac{1}{u^2 - 3u + 2}\, du = \int \left(-\dfrac{1}{u - 1} + \dfrac{1}{u - 2}\right) du$

$$= \ln\left|\dfrac{u - 2}{u - 1}\right| + C = \ln\left(\dfrac{2 - \sin x}{1 - \sin x}\right) + C.$$

69. Partial fraction decomposition: $\dfrac{2x^3 + 3x^2 + 4}{(x + 1)^4} = \dfrac{2}{x + 1} - \dfrac{3}{(x + 1)^2} + \dfrac{5}{(x + 1)^4}.$

70. Let $u = \tan x$: $\displaystyle\int \dfrac{\sec^2 x}{\tan^2 x + 2\tan x + 2}\, dx = \int \dfrac{1}{u^2 + 2u + 2}\, du = \int \dfrac{1}{1 + (u + 1)^2}\, du$

$$= \tan^{-1}(u + 1) + C = \tan^{-1}(1 + \tan x) + C.$$

71. Partial fraction decomposition: $\dfrac{x^3 + x^2 + 2x + 1}{x^4 + 2x^2 + 1} = \dfrac{x + 1}{x^2 + 1} + \dfrac{x}{(x^2 + 1)^2}.$

72. $\begin{bmatrix} u = \cos 3x & dv = \sin x\, dx \\ du = -3\sin 3x\, dx & v = -\cos x \end{bmatrix}$ $I = \displaystyle\int \sin x \cos 3x\, dx = -\cos x \cos 3x - 3\int \sin 3x \cos x\, dx.$

Now use integration by parts again:

$\begin{bmatrix} u = \sin 3x & dv = \cos x\, dx \\ du = 3\cos 3x\, dx & v = \sin x \end{bmatrix}$

$$I = -\cos x \cos 3x - 3\left(\sin x \sin 3x - 3\int \sin x \cos 3x\, dx\right) = -\cos x \cos 3x - 3\sin x \sin 3x + 9I;$$

$$8I = \cos x \cos 3x + 3\sin x \sin 3x;\quad I = \tfrac{1}{8}(\cos x \cos 3x + 3\sin x \sin 3x) + C.$$

Alternative solution: $\sin(A + B) = \sin A \cos B + \cos A \sin B$;
$\sin(A - B) = \sin A \cos B - \cos A \sin B$.

So $\sin A \cos B = \tfrac{1}{2}(\sin(A + B) + \sin(A - B))$. In particular,

$$\sin x \cos 3x = \tfrac{1}{2}(\sin 4x + \sin(-2x)) = \tfrac{1}{2}\sin 4x - \tfrac{1}{2}\sin 2x.$$

So $\displaystyle\int \sin x \cos 3x\, dx = -\tfrac{1}{8}\cos 4x + \tfrac{1}{4}\cos 2x + C.$

73. Let $u = x^3 - 1$; the rest is routine.

74. $\begin{bmatrix} u = \ln(x^2 + 2x) & dv = dx \\ du = \dfrac{2x + 2}{x^2 + 2x}\, dx & v = x + 2 \end{bmatrix}$

$$\int \ln(x^2 + 2x)\, dx = (x + 2)\ln(x^2 + 2x) - \int \dfrac{(2x + 2)(x + 2)}{x(x + 2)}\, dx$$

$$= (x + 2)\ln(x^2 + 2x) - \int \dfrac{2x + 2}{x}\, dx = (x + 2)\ln(x^2 + 2x) - 2x - 2\ln x + C.$$

76. Let $x = \tan^3 z$. $\int \dfrac{1}{x^{2/3}(1+x^{2/3})}\,dx = \int \dfrac{3\tan^2 z \sec^2 z}{\sec^2 z \tan^2 z}\,dz = 3z + C = 3\tan^{-1}(x^{1/3}) + C$.

77. Use the identity $\sin 2x = 2\sin x \cos x$.

78. Because $\tfrac{1}{2}(1+\cos t)^{1/2} = \cos^2(\tfrac{1}{2}t)$,

$$\int \sqrt{1+\cos t}\,dt = \sqrt{2}\int \sqrt{\dfrac{1+\cos t}{2}}\,dt = \sqrt{2}\int \cos(\tfrac{1}{2}t)\,dt = 2\sqrt{2}\sin(\tfrac{1}{2}t) + C,$$

which may also be written in the form $2\sqrt{1-\cos t} + C$.

Note: We took the positive square root in the computations above. If this problem had been a definite integral, we'd need to see whether the values of t made $\cos(t/2)$ positive or negative to know which sign to take.

79. Multiply numerator and denominator of the integrand by $\sqrt{1-\sin t}$.

80. Let $u = \tan t$:

$$\int \dfrac{\sec^2 t}{1-\tan^2 t}\,dt = \int \dfrac{du}{1-u^2} = \tfrac{1}{2}\int\left(\dfrac{1}{1-u} + \dfrac{1}{1+u}\right)du = \tfrac{1}{2}\ln\left|\dfrac{1+u}{1-u}\right| + C = \tfrac{1}{2}\ln\left|\dfrac{1+\tan t}{1-\tan t}\right| + C.$$

81. Use integration by parts with $u = \ln(x^2 + x + 1)$ and—if you wish—$v = x + \tfrac{1}{2}$ (this will save some trouble later).

82. Let $u = e^x$: $\int e^x \sin^{-1}(e^x)\,dx = \int \sin^{-1} u\,du$. Now do an integration by parts with $p = \sin^{-1} u$, $dq = du$:

$$\int e^x \sin^{-1}(e^x)\,dx = u\sin^{-1} u - \int u(1-u^2)^{-1/2}\,du$$
$$= u\sin^{-1} u + \sqrt{1-u^2} + C = e^x \sin^{-1}(e^x) + \sqrt{1-e^{2x}} + C.$$

83. Use integration by parts, with $u = \arctan x$, $dv = x^{-2}\,dx$. The new integrand has the partial fraction decomposition $\dfrac{1}{x} - \dfrac{x}{x^2+1}$.

84. Let $x = 5\sec u$. $\int \dfrac{x^2}{\sqrt{x^2-25}}\,dx = 25\int \sec^3 u\,du$.

Application of Formula 28 from the endpapers and subsequent resubstitution yields

$$\int \dfrac{x^2}{\sqrt{x^2-25}}\,dx = \tfrac{1}{2}\left(x\sqrt{x^2-25} + 25\ln\left|x + \sqrt{x^2-25}\right|\right) + C$$

(an extra constant in the logarithmic term has been absorbed by the constant C of integration).

85. The partial fraction decomposition of the integrand is $\dfrac{x}{x^2+1} - \dfrac{x}{(x^2+1)^2}$, and integration of these terms presents no difficulties.

86. Because $6x - x^2 = 9 - (x-3)^2$, we use the substitution $x = 3 + 3\sin u$:

$$\int \dfrac{1}{x\sqrt{6x-x^2}}\,dx = \tfrac{1}{3}\int \dfrac{1}{1+\sin u}\,du$$
$$= \tfrac{1}{3}\int \dfrac{1-\sin u}{\cos^2 u}\,du = \tfrac{1}{3}\int\left(\sec^2 u - \dfrac{\sin u}{\cos^2 u}\right)du$$
$$= \tfrac{1}{3}\left(\tan u - \dfrac{1}{\cos u}\right) + C = \dfrac{-1+\sin u}{3\cos u} + C = \dfrac{x-6}{3\sqrt{6x-x^2}} + C.$$

87. Let $x = 2\tan\theta$; $\int \dfrac{3x+2}{(x^2+4)^{3/2}}\,dx = \int\left(\tfrac{1}{2}\cos u + \tfrac{3}{2}\sin u\right)du$, and the rest is routine.

88. $\begin{bmatrix} u = \ln x & dv = x^{3/2}\,dx \\ du = \dfrac{1}{x}\,dx & v = \tfrac{2}{5}x^{5/2} \end{bmatrix}$ $\qquad \int x^{3/2}\ln x\,dx = \tfrac{2}{25}x^{5/2}(-2 + 5\ln x) + C.$

89. Let $u = 1 + \sin^2 x$. $\int \dfrac{\sqrt{1 + \sin^2 x}}{\sec x \csc x}\,dx = \tfrac{1}{2}\int \sqrt{u}\,du.$

90. Let $u = \sqrt{\sin x}$. $\int \dfrac{e^{\sin x}}{(\sec x)\sqrt{\sin x}}\,dx = \int 2e^u\,du = 2e^u + C = 2e^{\sqrt{\sin x}} + C.$

91. Use integration by parts. A good choice is $u = x$, $dv = e^x \sin x\,dx$. One must then antidifferentiate both $e^x \sin x$ and $e^x \cos x$, but here Formulas 67 and 68 of the endpapers may be used, or integration by parts will suffice for each.

92. $\begin{bmatrix} u = x^{3/2} & dv = x^{1/2}e^{x^{3/2}}\,dx \\ du = \tfrac{3}{2}x^{1/2}\,dx & v = \tfrac{2}{3}e^{x^{3/2}} \end{bmatrix}$ $\qquad \int x^2 e^{x^{3/2}}\,dx = \tfrac{2}{3}\left(x^{3/2} - 1\right)e^{x^{3/2}} + C.$

93. $\begin{bmatrix} u = \arctan x & dv = (x+1)^{-3}\,dx \\ du = \dfrac{1}{1+x^2}\,dx & v = -\tfrac{1}{2}(x-1)^{-2} \end{bmatrix}$

$\int \dfrac{\arctan x}{(x-1)^3}\,dx = -\tfrac{1}{2}(\arctan x)(x-1)^{-2} + \tfrac{1}{2}\int \dfrac{1}{(1+x^2)(x-1)^2}\,dx$

$\qquad = -\tfrac{1}{2}(\arctan x)(x-1)^{-2} + \int \tfrac{1}{2}\left(\dfrac{x}{1+x^2} - \dfrac{1}{x-1} + \dfrac{1}{(x-1)^2}\right)dx.$

94. $\begin{bmatrix} u = \ln(1+\sqrt{x}) & dv = dx \\ du = \dfrac{1}{2\sqrt{x}(1+\sqrt{x})}\,dx & v = x - 1 \end{bmatrix}$ $\int \ln(1+\sqrt{x})\,dx = (x-1)\ln(1+\sqrt{x}) - \tfrac{1}{2}x + \sqrt{x} + C.$

95. $3 + 6x - 9x^2 = 4 - (3x-1)^2$, so let $x = \tfrac{1}{3}(1 + 2\sin u)$. $\int \dfrac{2x+3}{\sqrt{3+6x-9x^2}}\,dx = \tfrac{1}{9}\int (11 + 4\sin u)\,du.$

96. $\int \dfrac{1}{\sqrt{e^{2x}-1}}\,dx = \int \dfrac{e^x}{e^x\sqrt{(e^x)^2-1}}\,dx = \operatorname{arcsec}|e^x| + C = \operatorname{arcsec}(e^x) + C.$

97. Let $u = x - 1$: $\int \dfrac{x^4}{(x-1)^2}\,dx = \int \dfrac{(u+1)^4}{u^2}\,du = \int \left(u^2 + 4u + 6 + \dfrac{4}{u} + \dfrac{1}{u^2}\right)du.$

98. $\begin{bmatrix} u = \tan^{-1}\sqrt{x} & dv = x^{3/2}\,dx \\ du = \dfrac{1}{2\sqrt{x}(1+x)}\,dx & v = \tfrac{2}{5}x^{5/2} \end{bmatrix}$

$\int x^{3/2}\tan^{-1}\sqrt{x}\,dx = \tfrac{2}{5}x^{5/2}\tan^{-1}\sqrt{x} - \tfrac{1}{5}\int \dfrac{x^2 - 1 + 1}{x+1}\,dx$

$\qquad = \tfrac{2}{5}x^{5/2}\tan^{-1}\sqrt{x} - \tfrac{1}{10}x^2 + \tfrac{1}{5}x - \tfrac{1}{5}\ln|x+1| + C.$

99. Use integration by parts with $u = \sec^{-1}\sqrt{x}$, $dv = dx$.

100. Let $u = x^2$: $\int x\sqrt{\dfrac{1-x^2}{1+x^2}}\,dx = \tfrac{1}{2}\int \sqrt{\dfrac{1-u}{1+u}}\,du.$

Now let $v^2 = \dfrac{1-u}{1+u}$; $u = \dfrac{1-v^2}{1+v^2}$ and $du = -\dfrac{4v}{(1+v^2)^2}\,dv.$

$\int x\sqrt{\dfrac{1-x^2}{1+x^2}}\,dx = -\tfrac{1}{2}\int \dfrac{4v^2}{(1+v^2)^2}\,dv.$

Chapter 9 Miscellaneous 291

Finally let $v = \tan z$.

$$\int x\sqrt{\frac{1-x^2}{1+x^2}}\, dx = -2\int \sin^2 z\, dz = \sin z \cos z - z + C = \tfrac{1}{2}\sqrt{1-x^4} - \tan^{-1}\frac{1-x^2}{\sqrt{1+x^2}} + C.$$

101. The area is $A = \int_0^1 2\pi \cosh^2 x\, dx = 2\pi\left(\tfrac{1}{4}\sinh 2 + \tfrac{1}{2} - \tfrac{1}{4}\sinh 0 - 0\right) = \dfrac{\pi}{4}\left(e^2 - \dfrac{1}{e^2} + 4\right) \approx 8.83865.$

102. The length of the curve is $L = \int_0^1 \sqrt{1+e^{-2x}}\, dx$. Let $e^{-x} = \tan u$.

$$L = \int_{x=0}^{x=1} -\frac{\sec^3 u}{\tan u}\, du = -\int_{x=0}^{x=1} (\csc u + \sec u \tan u)\, du$$

$$= \left[-\ln|\csc u - \cot u| - \sec u\right]_{x=0}^{x=1}$$

$$= \left[-\ln\left|\frac{\sqrt{1+e^{-2x}}-1}{e^{-x}}\right| - \sqrt{1+e^{-2x}}\right]_0^1$$

$$= \sqrt{2} + \ln\left(\sqrt{2}-1\right) - \ln\left(\sqrt{e^2+1}-e\right) - \frac{1}{e}\sqrt{e^2+1} \approx 1.1927014.$$

103. $A_t = \int_0^t 2\pi e^{-x}\sqrt{1+e^{-2x}}\, dx$. Let $u = e^{-x}$. Then

$$A_t = \int_1^{e^{-t}} 2\pi u\sqrt{1+u^2}\left(-\frac{1}{u}\right)\, du = \int_p^1 2\pi\sqrt{1+u^2}\, du \quad \text{(where } p = e^{-t}\text{)}.$$

Let $u = \tan z$. Then

$$A_t = \int_{u=p}^{u=1} 2\pi\sqrt{1+\tan^2 z}\, \sec^2 z\, dz$$

$$= \pi\Big[\sec z \tan z + \ln|\sec z + \tan z|\Big]_{u=p}^{u=1}$$

$$= \pi\left(\sqrt{2} + \ln\left(1+\sqrt{2}\right) - e^{-t}\sqrt{1+e^{-2t}} - \ln\left|e^{-t}+\sqrt{1+e^{-2t}}\right|\right).$$

$\lim_{t\to\infty} A_t = \pi\left(\sqrt{2} + \ln\left(1+\sqrt{2}\right)\right) \approx 7.2118.$

104. $A_t = \int_1^t \dfrac{2\pi}{x^3}\sqrt{x^4+1}\, dx$. Let $x^2 = \tan u$. Then

$$A_t = \pi\int_{x=1}^t \frac{\sec u}{\tan^2 u}\sec^2 u\, du = \pi\int_{x=1}^t \left(\frac{\cos u}{\sin^2 u} + \sec u\right)\, du$$

$$= \pi\Big[-\csc u + \ln|\sec u + \tan u|\Big]_{x=1}^{x=t} = \pi\left[-\frac{\sqrt{x^4+1}}{x^2} + \ln\left(x^2 + \sqrt{x^4+1}\right)\right]_{x=1}^{x=t}$$

$$= \pi\left(\ln\left(\frac{t^2+\sqrt{t^4+1}}{1+\sqrt{2}}\right) + \sqrt{2} - \frac{\sqrt{t^4+1}}{t^2}\right).$$

$\lim_{t\to+\infty} A_t = +\infty$ because for large t, $\dfrac{\sqrt{t^4+1}}{t^2} \approx 1$ and $\ln\left(t^2+\sqrt{t^4+1}\right) \approx \ln\left(2t^2\right)$.

105. Surface area: $A = \int_1^2 2\pi\sqrt{x^2-1}\sqrt{\dfrac{2x^2-1}{x^2-1}}\, dx = 2\pi\int_1^2 \sqrt{2x^2-1}\, dx$. Let $\sqrt{2}\, x = \sec u$:

$$\int 2\pi\sqrt{x^2-1}\sqrt{\frac{2x^2-1}{x^2-1}}\, dx = \frac{\pi}{\sqrt{2}}\left(\sec u \tan u - \ln|\sec u + \tan u|\right) + C.$$

106. (a) Use integration by parts with $u = (\ln x)^n$ and $dv = x^m\, dx$.

(b) Application of the formula and simplification of the result yields $\dfrac{17e^4 + 3}{128} \approx 7.2747543$.

108. Answer: $\dfrac{8}{693} \approx 0.011544$.

109. The area is $A = 2\displaystyle\int_0^2 x^{5/2}(2-x)^{1/2}\,dx$. Use the suggested substitution $x = 2\sin^2\theta$. This results in $A = 64\displaystyle\int_0^{\pi/2} \sin^6\theta \cos^2\theta\, d\theta$. Then the formula of Problem 108 gives the answer $\tfrac{5}{4}\pi$.

110. Clearly $\dfrac{t^4(1-t)^4}{1+t^2} > 0$ for $0 < t < 1$. Hence $\displaystyle\int_0^1 \dfrac{t^4(1-t)^4}{1+t^2}\,dt > 0$. After division, the integral becomes $\displaystyle\int_0^1 \left(t^6 - 4t^5 + 5t^4 + 4 - \dfrac{4}{t^2+1}\right)dt$, and its value is $\tfrac{22}{7} \approx \pi$. Consequently $\pi < \tfrac{22}{7}$ (Why?).

112. $\sqrt{1 + (dy/dx)^2} = \sqrt{1+\sqrt{x}}$; the curve's length is $L = \displaystyle\int_0^1 \sqrt{1+\sqrt{x}}\,dx$. Let $x = \tan^4 u$.

$$L = \int_0^{\pi/4} 4\sqrt{1+\tan^2 u}\,\tan^3 u\,\sec^2 u\, du = 4\int_0^{\pi/4} \sec^3 u\,\tan^3 u\, du$$

$$= 4\int_0^{\pi/4} (\sec^3 u)(\sec^2 u - 1)\tan u\, du = 4\int_0^{\pi/4}(\sec^4 u - \sec^2 u)(\sec u \tan u)\,du$$

$$= \left[\tfrac{4}{5}\sec^5 u - \tfrac{4}{3}\sec^3 u\right]_0^{\pi/4} = \tfrac{4}{5}(4\sqrt{2}-1) - \tfrac{4}{3}(2\sqrt{2}-1) = \tfrac{8}{15}(1+\sqrt{2}) \approx 1.28758.$$

113. Its length is $L = \displaystyle\int_1^4 \sqrt{1 + x^{-1/2}}\,dx = \int_1^4 \dfrac{\sqrt{1+\sqrt{x}}}{x^{1/4}}\,dx$. Now let $x = u^4$.

$$L = \int_1^{\sqrt{2}} \dfrac{\sqrt{1+u^2}}{u}\,4u^3\,du = 4\int_1^{\sqrt{2}} u^2\sqrt{1+u^2}\,du.$$

Next, let $u = \tan z$:

$$L = 4\int_{\pi/4}^{\arctan\sqrt{2}} (\sec^5 z - \sec^3 z)\,dz$$

$$= \left[\sec^3 z \tan z - (\tfrac{1}{2}\sec z \tan z + \tfrac{1}{2}\ln|\sec z + \tan z|)\right]_{\pi/4}^{\arctan\sqrt{2}}$$

$$= \tfrac{5}{2}\sqrt{6} - \tfrac{3}{2}\sqrt{2} + \tfrac{1}{2}\ln\left(\dfrac{1+\sqrt{2}}{\sqrt{3}+\sqrt{2}}\right) \approx 3.869983.$$

114. Let $Q(t)$ denote the amount of water (in cubic feet) in the tank at time $t \geq 0$, and $y(t)$ the depth of water then. Because the radius then is $\tfrac{1}{2}y(t)$, it follows that

$$Q(t) = \dfrac{\pi (y(t))^3}{12}.$$

We also know that $Q(0) = 0$, and by Torricelli's law that

$$\dfrac{dQ}{dt} = 50 - 10\sqrt{y(t)}.$$

But

$$\dfrac{dQ}{dt} = \dfrac{dQ}{dy}\cdot\dfrac{dy}{dt} = \dfrac{3\pi}{12}(y(t))^2 \dfrac{dy}{dt},$$

and therefore
$$\frac{dy}{dt} = \frac{50 - 10\sqrt{y}}{(\pi/4)\, y^2}.$$

Let T denote the time required to fill the tank. Then
$$T = \int_0^T 1\, dt = \int_{t=0}^{t=T} \frac{(\pi/4)\, y^2}{50 - 10\sqrt{y}}\, dy = \int_0^9 \frac{(\pi/4)\, y^2}{10\,(5 - \sqrt{y})}\, dy = \frac{\pi}{40} \int_0^9 \frac{y^2}{5 - \sqrt{y}}\, dy.$$

The substitution $y = x^2$ yields
$$T = \frac{\pi}{40} \int_0^3 \frac{2x^5}{5 - x}\, dx$$
$$= -\frac{\pi}{20} \int_0^3 \left(x^4 + 5x^3 + 25x^2 + 125x + 625 + \frac{3125}{x - 5} \right) dx$$
$$= \frac{\pi}{400} \left(62500 \ln (5/2) - 56247 \right) \approx 8.020256 \text{ (seconds)}.$$

115. Let $u = e^x$. $\displaystyle\int \frac{1}{1 + e^x + e^{-x}}\, dx = \int \frac{1}{u^2 + u + 1}\, du.$

116. (a) The iteration
$$x \longleftarrow x - \frac{x^3 + x + 1}{3x^2 + 1} = \frac{2x^3 - 1}{3x^2 + 1}$$

with initial value $x_0 = -0.5$ yields the approximate root -0.682327804.

(b) If we let r denote the root obtained in Part (a), division yields the quotient $x^2 + rx + (r^2 + 1)$; that is, the irreducible quadratic factor is
$$x^2 - (0.6823278)\, x + 1.4655712$$

(coefficients approximate, of course).

(c) Let $q = r^2 + 1$. The partial fraction decomposition of the integrand is $\displaystyle\frac{A}{x - r} + \frac{Bx + C}{x^2 + rx + q}$ where $A = \dfrac{1}{3r^2 + 1}$, $B = -\dfrac{1}{3r^2 + 1}$, and $C = -\dfrac{2r}{3r^2 + 1}$. This yields the antiderivative
$$\frac{1}{3r^2 + 1} \left[\ln\left| \frac{r - 1}{r} \right| + \tfrac{1}{2} \ln \left| \frac{q}{1 + r + q} \right| + \frac{3r}{2w} \left(\tan^{-1}\left(\frac{r}{2w} \right) - \tan^{-1}\left(\frac{r + 2}{2w} \right) \right) \right] + C$$

where $w = \tfrac{1}{2}\sqrt{3r^2 + 4}$. With $r = -0.6823279038$, we find that $q \approx 1.465571232$, $w \approx 1.16154140$, and thereby that
$$\int_0^1 \frac{1}{x^3 + x + 1}\, dx \approx 0.6303193226.$$

117. Answer *and* hint intentionally omitted.

118. With the recommended substitution, the numerator is $\tfrac{1}{2}\, du$, so
$$\int \frac{1 + 2x^2}{x^5 (1 + x^2)^3}\, dx = \tfrac{1}{2} \int u^{-3}\, du = -\tfrac{1}{4} u^{-2} + C = -\frac{1}{4\, (x^4 + x^2)^2} + C.$$

Note: A partial fraction decomposition results in
$$\int \frac{1 + 2x^2}{x^5 (1 + x^2)^3}\, dx = \frac{1}{2x^2} - \frac{1}{4x^4} - \frac{1}{2\, (x^2 + 1)} - \frac{1}{4\, (x^2 + 1)^2} + C.$$

119. $\displaystyle\int \sqrt{\tan\theta}\, d\theta = \int \frac{\sqrt{u}}{1+u^2}\, du = \int \frac{2x^2}{1+x^4}\, dx.$

121. Let $3x - 2 = u^2$: $\displaystyle\int x^3\sqrt{3x-2}\, dx = \int \left(\frac{u^2+2}{3}\right)^3 \cdot u \cdot \tfrac{2}{3}u\, du$

122. Let $u^3 = x^2 + 1$:

$$\int x^3\sqrt[3]{x^2+1}\, dx = \int \tfrac{3}{2}\left(u^6 - u^3\right) du = \tfrac{3}{2}\left(\tfrac{1}{7}u^7 - \tfrac{1}{4}u^4\right) + C$$
$$= \tfrac{3}{14}(x^2+1)^{7/3} - \tfrac{3}{8}(x^2+1)^{4/3} + C = \tfrac{3}{56}(x^2+1)^{4/3}(4x^2 - 3) + C$$

124. Let $x - 1 = u^2$:

$$\int x^2(x-1)^{3/2}\, dx = \int (2u^8 + 4u^6 + 2u^4)\, du = \tfrac{2}{9}(x-1)^{9/2} + \tfrac{4}{7}(x-1)^{7/2} + \tfrac{2}{5}(x-1)^{5/2} + C$$

126. Let $u^3 = x^4 + 1$.

$$\int x^7\sqrt[3]{x^4-1}\, dx = \tfrac{3}{4}\int (u^6 - u^3)\, du = \tfrac{3}{4}\left(\tfrac{1}{7}u^7 - \tfrac{1}{4}u^4\right) + C = \tfrac{3}{112}(x^4-1)^{4/3}(4x^4 + 3) + C$$

128. Let $u^2 = x + 1$: $\displaystyle\int \frac{x}{\sqrt{x+1}}\, dx = \int \frac{(u^2-1)\,2u\, du}{u} = \tfrac{2}{3}u^3 - 2u + C = \tfrac{2}{3}(x+1)^{3/2} - 2\sqrt{x+1} + C.$

130. $\displaystyle\int \sqrt{1+\sqrt{x}}\, dx = \tfrac{4}{15}(3\sqrt{x} - 2)(1+\sqrt{x})^{3/2} + C.$

131. Let $u^2 = 1 + e^{2x}$:

$$\int \sqrt{1+e^{2x}}\, dx = \int \frac{u^2}{u^2 - 1}\, du = u + \tfrac{1}{2}\ln\frac{u-1}{u+1} + C = \sqrt{1+e^{2x}} + \tfrac{1}{2}\ln\frac{\sqrt{1+e^{2x}} - 1}{\sqrt{1+e^{2x}} + 1} + C.$$

132. $dy/dx = x^{1/2}$, so $\sqrt{1+(dy/dx)^2} = \sqrt{1+x}$: $\displaystyle A = \int_3^8 2\pi \cdot \tfrac{2}{3}x^{3/2}\sqrt{1+x}\, dx.$ Let $x = u^2$:

$$A = \int_{\sqrt{3}}^{2\sqrt{2}} \tfrac{4}{3}\pi u^3\sqrt{1+u^2} \cdot 2u\, du = \tfrac{8}{3}\pi \int_{\sqrt{3}}^{2\sqrt{2}} u^4\sqrt{1+u^2}\, du$$
$$= \tfrac{8}{3}\pi \left(\tfrac{1}{48}\left[3\ln\left(u+\sqrt{u^2+1}\right) + (8u^5 + 2u^3 - 3u)\sqrt{u^2+1}\right]_{\sqrt{3}}^{2\sqrt{2}}\right)$$
$$= \tfrac{\pi}{6}\left(\ln\left(4\sqrt{2} - 3\sqrt{3} - 2\sqrt{6} + 6\right) + 1050\sqrt{2} - 50\sqrt{3}\right) \approx 732.39$$

133. Area: $A = 2\displaystyle\int_0^1 x\sqrt{1-x}\, dx.$ For variety, let $x = \sin^2\theta$.

$$A = 2\int_0^{\pi/2} (\sin^2\theta)(\cos\theta)(2\sin\theta\cos\theta)\, d\theta$$
$$= 4\int_0^{\pi/2} (\cos^2\theta - \cos^4\theta)\sin\theta\, d\theta$$
$$= 4\left[\tfrac{1}{5}\cos^5\theta - \tfrac{1}{3}\cos^3\theta\right]_0^{\pi/2} = \tfrac{8}{15}.$$

134. Area: $A = 2\displaystyle\int_0^1 x\sqrt{\frac{1-x}{1+x}}\, dx = \left[2\arctan\sqrt{\frac{1-x}{1+x}} + (x^2 - x + 2)\sqrt{\frac{1-x}{1+x}}\right]_0^1 = \frac{4-\pi}{2} \approx 0.429204.$

135. $\int \dfrac{1}{1+\cos\theta}\, d\theta = \int 1\, du = u + C = \tan\dfrac{\theta}{2} + C = \dfrac{1-\cos\theta}{\sin\theta} + C = \csc\theta - \cot\theta + C.$

136. $\int \dfrac{1}{5+4\cos\theta}\, d\theta = \int \dfrac{2}{u^2+9}\, du = \tfrac{2}{3}\arctan\left(\dfrac{u}{3}\right) + C = \tfrac{2}{3}\arctan\left(\tfrac{1}{3}\tan\dfrac{\theta}{2}\right) + C.$

137. $\int \dfrac{1}{1+\sin\theta}\, d\theta = \int \dfrac{2}{(u+1)^2}\, du = -\dfrac{2}{1+u} + C = -\dfrac{2}{1+\tan\dfrac{\theta}{2}} + C = -\dfrac{2+2\cos\theta}{1+\sin\theta+\cos\theta} + C.$

138. $\int \dfrac{1}{(1-\cos\theta)^2}\, d\theta = \int \dfrac{u^2+1}{2u^4}\, du = -\dfrac{1}{2u} - \dfrac{1}{6u^3} + C = -\tfrac{1}{6}\left(\dfrac{3(1+\cos\theta)}{\sin\theta} + \dfrac{(1+\cos\theta)^3}{\sin^3\theta}\right) + C$

139. $\int \dfrac{1}{\sin\theta+\cos\theta}\, d\theta = \int \dfrac{2}{1+2u-u^2}\, du = \dfrac{\sqrt{2}}{2}\ln\left|\dfrac{u+\sqrt{2}-1}{u-\sqrt{2}-1}\right| + C.$

140. $\int \dfrac{1}{2+\sin\phi+\cos\phi}\, d\phi = \int \dfrac{2}{u^2+2u+3}\, du = \sqrt{2}\arctan\left(\dfrac{\sqrt{2}}{2}(u+1)\right) + C.$

141. $\int \dfrac{\sin\theta}{2+\cos\theta}\, d\theta = \int \dfrac{4u}{(u^2+3)(u^2+1)}\, du = \int \left(\dfrac{2u}{u^2+1} - \dfrac{2u}{u^2+3}\right) du.$ I prefer the "easy" way!

142. $\int \dfrac{\sin\theta - \cos\theta}{\sin\theta + \cos\theta}\, d\theta = -2\int \dfrac{u^2+2u-1}{(u^2+1)(u^2-2u-1)}\, du$

$= \ln\left|\dfrac{u^2+1}{u+\sqrt{2}-1}\right| - \ln|u-\sqrt{2}-1| + C = -\ln|\sin\theta+\cos\theta| + C.$

Chapter 10: Polar Coordinates and Plane Curves
Section 10.1

1. The given line has slope $-\frac{1}{2}$.

2. The given line has slope $\frac{3}{4}$, so the answer is $y - 2 = -\frac{4}{3}(x+3)$; that is, $4x + 3y + 6 = 0$.

3. The radius has slope $-\frac{4}{3}$ and is normal to the tangent, so the tangent has slope $\frac{3}{4}$.

4. By implicit differentiation, $\frac{dy}{dx} = \frac{1}{2y}$; in particular, the slope of the tangent at $(6, -3)$ is $-\frac{1}{6}$. So the tangent line has equation $y + 3 = -\frac{1}{6}(x - 6)$; that is, $x + 6y + 12 = 0$.

5. By implicit differentiation, $\frac{dy}{dx} = -\frac{x}{2y}$. The slope of the tangent at $(2, -1)$ is 1, so the normal there has slope -1.

6. The slope of the segment is $-\frac{3}{4}$ and its midpoint is $(1, -1)$, so the perpendicular bisector has equation $y + 1 = \frac{4}{3}(x - 1)$; that is, $4x - 3y = 7$.

7. Write the equation in the form $x^2 + 2x + 1 + y^2 = 5$.

8. The equation can be written as $(x - 0)^2 + (y - 2)^2 = 3^2$, so the circle has center $(0, 2)$ and radius 3.

9. Write the equation in the form $x^2 - 4x + 4 + y^2 + 6y + 9 = 16$.

10. Write the equation in the form $x^2 + 8x + 16 + y^2 - 6y + 9 = 25$ to conclude that the center is at $(-4, 3)$ and the radius is 5.

11. The given equation may be written in the form $\left(x - \frac{1}{2}\right)^2 + (y - 0)^2 = 1^2$.

12. Write the equation in the form $(x - 0)^2 + \left(y - \frac{3}{2}\right)^2 = 2^2$.

13. Complete the squares as follows: $2x^2 + 2y^2 - 2x + 6y = 13$;
$$x^2 + y^2 - x + 3y = \tfrac{13}{2};$$
$$x^2 - x + \tfrac{1}{4} + y^2 + 3y + \tfrac{9}{4} = \tfrac{36}{4};$$
$$\left(x - \tfrac{1}{2}\right)^2 + \left(y + \tfrac{3}{2}\right)^2 = 3^2.$$
Thus the center is at $\left(\frac{1}{2}, -\frac{3}{2}\right)$ and the radius is 3.

14. Center: $\left(\frac{2}{3}, 0\right)$; radius: 1.

16. Center: $\left(\frac{2}{3}, \frac{3}{2}\right)$; radius: 12.

18. The graph consists of the single point $\left(-\frac{3}{2}, -\frac{1}{2}\right)$ because the equation can be written in the form $\left(x + \frac{3}{2}\right)^2 + \left(y + \frac{1}{2}\right)^2 = 0$.

19. Complete the squares as follows: $x^2 + y^2 - 6x - 10y + 84 = 0$;
$$x^2 - 6x + 9 + y^2 - 10y + 25 + 50 = 0;$$
$$(x - 3)^2 + (y - 5)^2 = -50.$$
It follows that there are no points on the graph.

20. Write the equation in the form $\left(x - \frac{1}{3}\right)^2 + \left(y + \frac{1}{3}\right)^2 = -1$ to see that there are no points on the graph.

21. Note that $\sqrt{(x+1)^2 + (y+2)^2}$ must be equal to the distance between the two points $(-1, -2)$ and $(2, 3)$.

22. The line has slope 1, so the radius to the point of tangency has slope -1. The radius is a segment of the line with equation $y + 2 = -(x - 2)$; that is, $x + y = 0$. The point of tangency is the simultaneous solution of the equations of the two lines: $x = -2$, $y = 2$—therefore they meet at $(-2, 2)$. The length of the radius is the distance from $(2, -2)$ to $(-2, 2)$, which is $4\sqrt{2}$. Therefore the equation of the circle is $(x - 2)^2 + (y + 2)^2 = 32$.

23. Let (a,b) denote the point of tangency. The line containing the radius as a segment has slope $-\frac{1}{2}$, and also must have slope $(b-6)/(a-6)$. Because we know also that $b = 2a - 4$, we may now solve for the coordinates $(a,b) = (\frac{26}{5}, \frac{32}{5})$. Then the rest is routine.

24. Use the fact that the perpendicular bisector of a chord passes through the center of the circle. (Some hardware stores sell a simple tool for finding the center of a dowel rod by means of this principle.) We plan to find equations of two lines containing such bisectors, then to solve them simultaneously (the tool does this geometrically) to find the coordinates of the center of the circle.

    Chord 1: $(4,6)$ to $(-2,-2)$. Slope: $4/3$. Midpoint: $(1,2)$. Equation of perpendicular bisector: $3x + 4y = 11$.

    Chord 2: $(-2,-2)$ to $(5,-1)$. Slope: $1/7$. Midpoint: $(3/2, -3/2)$. Equation of perpendicular bisector: $7x + y = 9$.

    Center of circle: The bisectors meet at $(1,2)$; it follows that the radius of the circle is 5 and therefore that its equation is $(x-2)^2 + (y-2)^2 = 25$.

25. The squares of the distances are equal, so $P(x,y)$ satisfies $(x-3)^2 + (y-x)^2 = (x-7)^2 + (y-4)^2$. Expand and simplify to obtain the answer.

26. The point $P(x,y)$ satisfies the equation $\sqrt{(x+2)^2 + (y-1)^2} = \frac{1}{2}\sqrt{(x-4)^2 + (y+2)^2}$. Now square both sides of this equation and simplify; you'll obtain $x^2 + 8x + y^2 - 4y = 0$. Complete the square as usual:
$$(x+4)^2 + (y-2)^2 = 20.$$
The locus is therefore a circle with center $(-4,2)$ and radius $2\sqrt{5}$.

27. The point $P(x,y)$ must satisfy the equation $(x+3)^2 + (y-2)^2 = 9\left((x-5)^2 + (y-10)^2\right)$. Expand and simplify to obtain
$$x^2 + y^2 - 12x - 22y + 139 = 0.$$
This may be recast in the standard form
$$(x-6)^2 + (y-11)^2 = 18,$$
so the locus is a circle with center at $(6,11)$ and radius $3\sqrt{2}$.

28. The point $P(x,y)$ satisfies the equation $x + 3 = \sqrt{(x-3)^2 + y^2}$. Expand and simplify to obtain $y^2 = 12x$: The locus is a parabola, opening to the right, with its vertex at the origin, and symmetric about the x-axis.

29. The point $P(x,y)$ satisfies the equation
$$\sqrt{(x-4)^2 + y^2} + \sqrt{(x+4)^2 + y^2} = 10.$$
First write this equation in the form
$$\sqrt{(x-4)^2 + y^2} = 10 - \sqrt{(x+4)^2 + y^2}.$$
Then square both sides to obtain
$$(x-4)^2 + y^2 = 100 - 20\sqrt{(x+4)^2 + y^2} + (x+4)^2 + y^2.$$
Simplify, then isolate the radical on one side of the resulting equation (this is the standard technique for solving an equation involving the sum or difference of two square roots); the result is
$$-16x - 100 = -20\sqrt{(x+4)^2 + y^2}.$$

Next divide each term by 4 and then square both sides again:
$$16x^2 + 200x + 625 = 25\left(x^2 + 8x + 16 + y^2\right).$$

Expand and simplify to obtain $9x^2 + 25y^2 = 225$. Finally write the equation in the form
$$(x/5)^2 + (y/3)^2 = 1.$$

It now becomes obvious that the figure is bounded, symmetric about the coordinate axes, and has intercepts $(-5, 0)$, $(5, 0)$, $(0, 3)$, and $(0, -3)$. If x increases in magnitude then y must decrease in magnitude, and vice versa; it's easy to believe that the graph resembles a flattened circle. It's actually an ellipse, the topic of Section 10.7.

30. The solution of this problem is almost exactly the same as that of Problem 29. Begin with the equation
$$\sqrt{x^2 + (y-3)^2} + \sqrt{x^2 + (y+3)^2} = 10.$$
A bit of algebra yields $(x/4)^2 + (y/5)^2 = 1$.

31. If $P(a, b)$ is the point of tangency, then $b = a^2$, and the slope of the tangent line can be measured in two different ways. They are equal, and we thereby obtain
$$\frac{1 - a^2}{2 - a} = 2a.$$
We find two solutions: $a = 2 - \sqrt{3}$ and $a = 2 + \sqrt{3}$. But $b = a^2$, so $b = 7 - 4\sqrt{3}$ or $b = 7 - 4\sqrt{3}$. Thus we obtain the two answers given in the text.

32. Let $P(a, a^2)$ be the point where the line meets the parabola. The slope of the tangent line there is $2a$, so the slope of the normal line can be measured in two different ways, yielding
$$-\frac{1}{2a} = \frac{a^2 - 2}{a + 1}.$$
It follows that $2a^3 - 3a + 1 = 0$, which has the three solutions $a = 1$, $a = \frac{1}{2}\left(-1 + \sqrt{3}\right)$, and $a = \frac{1}{2}\left(-1 - \sqrt{3}\right)$. The slope of the normal is $-\dfrac{1}{2a}$, and the corresponding three values are therefore $-\frac{1}{2}$, $-\frac{1}{2}\left(1 + \sqrt{3}\right)$, and $\frac{1}{2}\left(\sqrt{3} - 1\right)$. The three lines have the corresponding equations
$$y - 2 = -\tfrac{1}{2}(x + 1),$$
$$y - 2 = -\tfrac{1}{2}\left(1 + \sqrt{3}\right)(x + 1), \text{ and}$$
$$y - 2 = \tfrac{1}{2}\left(\sqrt{3} - 1\right)(x + 1).$$

33. By the second condition, all such lines have slope 4. The slope of $xy = 4$ at the point (x, y) is $\dfrac{dy}{dx} = -\dfrac{4}{x^2}$, so a line normal to $xy = 4$ at $(a, b) = (a, 4/a)$ must have slope $\tfrac{1}{4}a^2$. Because this must also equal 4, we find the two solutions $a = 4$ and $a = -4$, and thereby the equations of the two lines.

34. The second condition means that all such lines have slope 3. If such a line is tangent to the graph of $y = x^3$ at the point (a, a^3), its slope must also be $3a^2 = 3$. Thus $a = 1$ or $a = -1$. Thus there are two such lines:
$$y - 1 = 3(x - 1) \quad \text{(through } (1, 1) \text{ with slope 3)} \quad \text{and}$$
$$y + 1 = 3(x + 1) \quad \text{(through } (-1, -1) \text{ with slope 3)}.$$

35. Begin with the equation $x^2\left(1 - e^2\right) - 2p\left(1 + e^2\right)x + y^2 = -p^2\left(1 - e^2\right)$, and proceed as in Case 2 of Section 10.1 of the text. Be careful with minus signs, and at some strategic point "let" h, a, and b have the values shown in the answer section of the text.

Section 10.1 Analytic Geometry and the Conic Sections

Section 10.2

2. (a) $(r, \theta) = (\sqrt{2}, 5\pi/4)$ or $(-\sqrt{2}, \pi/4)$.
   (b) $(r, \theta) = (2, -\pi/6)$ or $(-2, 5\pi/6)$.
   (c) $(r, \theta) = (2\sqrt{2}, \pi/4)$ or $(-2\sqrt{2}, 5\pi/4)$.
   (d) $(r, \theta) = (2, 2\pi/3)$ or $(-2, -\pi/3)$.
   (e) $(r, \theta) = (2, -\pi/4)$ or $(-2, 3\pi/4)$.
   (f) $(r, \theta) = (2\sqrt{3}, 5\pi/6,)$ or $(-2\sqrt{3}, -\pi/6)$.

4. Answer: $r \sin \theta = 6$; a better form is $r = 6 \csc \theta, 0 < \theta < \pi$.

6. Answer: $r = 5, 0 \leq \theta \leq 2\pi$.

8. Answer: $r^2 \left(\cos^2 \theta - \sin^2 \theta \right) = 1$; that is, $r^2 = \sec 2\theta$ or $r = \sqrt{|\sec 2\theta|}$.

   The two branches of the hyperbola may be described as follows:

   $$r = \sqrt{\sec 2\theta}, \quad -\pi/4 < \theta < \pi/4;$$
   $$r = -\sqrt{\sec 2\theta}, \quad -\pi/4 < \theta < \pi/4.$$

   In essence, one may write $r = \pm \sqrt{\sec 2\theta}, \quad -\pi/4 < \theta < \pi/4$.

10. Answer: $r = \dfrac{4}{\sin \theta + \cos \theta}$. It would be best to restrict the values of θ to the range $-\pi/4 < \theta < 3\pi/4$.

12. Given: $\theta = 3\pi/4$. Then $\sin \theta = \frac{1}{2}\sqrt{2}$, so that $\sin^2 \theta = \frac{1}{2}$;
    $$2r^2 \sin^2 \theta = r^2;$$
    $$2y^2 = x^2 + y^2;$$
    $$x^2 = y^2.$$

    But $\theta \neq \pi/4$; this rules out the equation $y = x$. So the answer is $y = -x$.

13. Begin by multiplying each side of the equation by r.

14. First, $r^3 = 2r^2 \sin \theta \cos \theta$: $\left| \left(x^2 + y^2 \right)^{3/2} \right| = |2xy|$;
    $$\left(x^2 + y^2 \right)^3 = 4x^2 y^2.$$

    Verify that squaring both sides didn't introduce extraneous roots, so that we don't end up with more graph than we began with.

15. Divide each side of the equation by 2, then apply a familiar identity to make the work easier.

16. First, $r^2 = 2r + r \sin \theta$, so $x^2 + y^2 = 2\sqrt{x^2 + y^2} + y$. Hence

    $$\left(x^2 + y^2 - y \right)^2 = \left(2\sqrt{x^2 + y^2} \right)^2 = 4x^2 + 4y^2;$$
    $$x^4 + 2x^2 y^2 + y^4 - 2x^2 y - 2y^3 + y^2 = 4x^2 + 4y^2;$$
    $$x^4 + 2x^2 y^2 + y^4 - 2x^2 y - 2y^3 - 4x^2 - 3y^2 = 0.$$

17. First multiply each side by $\cos \theta$.

18. Given: $r^2 = \cos 2\theta$. It follows that $r^4 = r^2 \left(\cos^2 \theta - \sin^2 \theta \right)$, and so $\left(x^2 + y^2 \right)^2 = x^2 - y^2$. The graph of this equation resembles the one shown in the solution of Problem 46 below.

20. $y = 3$; $r \sin \theta = 3$, $\quad \pi/2 < \theta < 3\pi/2$

22. $y = x - 2$; $r \left(\cos \theta - \sin \theta \right) = 2$, $\quad -5\pi/4 < \theta < \pi/4$

24. $(x - 3)^2 + y^2 = 9$; $r = 6 \cos \theta$

26. $(x - 3)^2 + (y - 4)^2 = 25$; $r = 6 \cos \theta + 8 \sin \theta$

28. $(x-5)^2 + (y+2)^2 = 25$; $r^2 - 10r\cos\theta + 4r\sin\theta + 4 = 0$
29. Matches Fig. 10.2.17.
30. Matches Fig. 10.2.15.
31. Matches Fig. 10.2.18.
32. Matches Fig. 10.2.16.
33. Matches Fig. 10.2.20.
34. Matches Fig. 10.2.22.
35. Matches Fig. 10.2.19.
36. Matches Fig. 10.2.21.
37. Given $r = a\cos\theta + b\sin\theta$, multiply both sides by r and convert to rectangular coordinates to obtain, successively,

$$x^2 + y^2 = ax + by;$$
$$x^2 - ax + \tfrac{1}{4}a^2 + y^2 - by + \tfrac{1}{4}b^2 = \tfrac{1}{2}(a^2 + b^2);$$
$$\left(x - \frac{a}{2}\right)^2 + \left(y - \frac{b}{2}\right)^2 = \frac{a^2 + b^2}{4}.$$

Thus the graph is a circle with center $(a/2, b/2)$ and radius $\tfrac{1}{2}\sqrt{a^2+b^2}$—unless $a = b = 0$, in which case the graph consists of the single point $(0,0)$.

38. The (rectangular-coordinates) graph of $y = a + b\cos x$ crosses the x-axis when $\cos x = -a/b$. Because $0 < a < b$, one solution of this equation lies in the second quadrant and the other lies in the third quadrant. Between these two angles, y is negative. Hence the equation $r = a + b\cos\theta$ produces negative values of r if $\arccos(-a/b) < \theta < 2\pi - \arccos(-a/b)$, and it is these values of r that produce an "inner loop."

40. Multiply each side by r, then complete the square to obtain the equation
$$(x-1)^2 + (y-1)^2 = 2.$$

The graph is a circle with center at $(1,1)$ and radius $\sqrt{2}$. It has no symmetries of the sort mentioned; its graph is shown on the right.

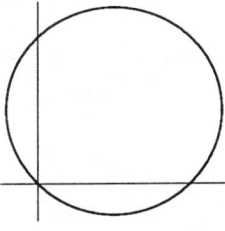

42. Given:
$$r = 1 - \sin\theta.$$

The graph is symmetric about the y-axis. It appears at the right.

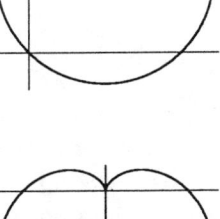

44. Given:
$$r = 4 + 2\cos\theta.$$

This graph is symmetric about the x-axis. It is shown on the right.

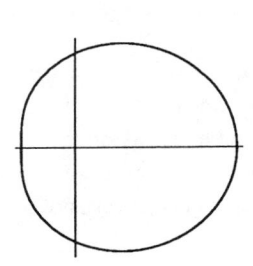

46. Given:
$$r^2 = 4\cos 2\theta.$$

Note that there is no graph when $\cos 2\theta < 0$; that is, for $\pi/4 < \theta < 3\pi/4$ and for $5\pi/4 < \theta < 7\pi/4$. The graph is symmetric about both coordinate axes and about the origin, and is shown on the right.

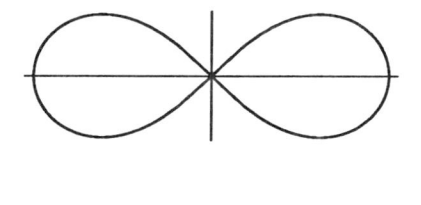

48. Note that r is zero when the angle θ is a multiple of $\pi/3$, and that $|r|$ is maximal between those values. The graph is symmetric about the y-axis and it appears on the right.

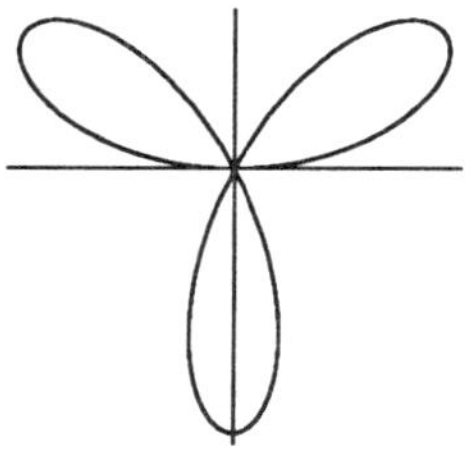

50. Given:
$$r = 3\theta.$$

There are no symmetries. The graph is an equally spaced spiral, shown on the right.

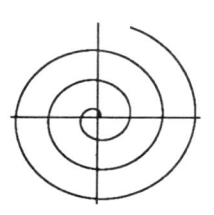

52. Given:
$$r^2 = 4\sin\theta.$$

The graph is symmetric about the x-axis, the y-axis, and the origin. It is shown at the right.

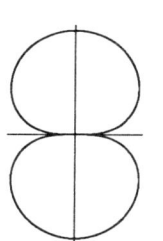

54. The graph of the circle with equation $r = \sin\theta$ is shown as a dashed curve in the figure at the right, whereas the graph of the equation $r^2 = 3\cos^2\theta$ is shown as a solid curve. The three points of intersection are

$$r = \tfrac{1}{2}\sqrt{3}, \quad \theta = \pi/3,$$
$$r = \tfrac{1}{2}\sqrt{3}, \quad \theta = 2\pi/3, \text{ and}$$
$$r = 0.$$

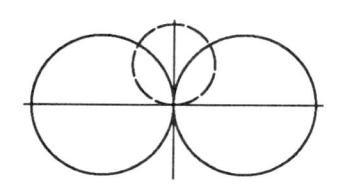

55. The graph of $r = \sin\theta$ is shown as a dashed curve in the figure to the right. The other graph—that of the equation $r = \cos 2\theta$—is shown as a solid curve. The Answer section of the text gives the polar coordinates of the four points of intersection.

56. The graph of $r = 1 + \cos\theta$ is shown as a dashed curve in the figure to the right and the graph of $r = 1 - \sin\theta$ is shown as a solid curve. The graphs meet at three points:
$$\left(\tfrac{1}{2}\left(2-\sqrt{2}\right), 3\pi/4\right),$$
$$\left(\tfrac{1}{2}\left(2+\sqrt{2}\right), -\pi/4\right),$$
and $(0,0)$.

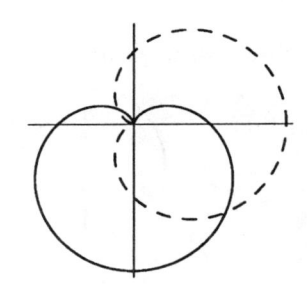

57. The graph of $r = 1 - \cos\theta$ is shown as a dashed curve in the figure at the right and the graph of $r^2 = 4\cos\theta$ is shown as a solid curve. The four intersection points are given in the Answer section.

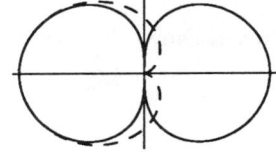

58. The graph of $r^2 = 4\sin\theta$ is shown as a dashed curve in the figure to the right and the graph of $r^2 = 4\cos\theta$ is a solid curve. The five intersection points are the origin and the four points for which $r = 8^{1/4}$ and θ is an odd multiple of $\pi/4$.

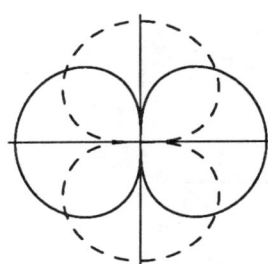

60. $x^4 + 2x^2y^2 + y^4 + 2x^3 + 2xy^2 = y^2$.

61. The given equation has polar form $a^2r^2 = (r^2 - br\sin\theta)^2$. Expand the right-hand side and cancel r^2 to obtain
$$a^2 = r^2 - 2br\sin\theta + b^2\sin^2\theta = (r - b\sin\theta)^2.$$
It follows that $r = \pm a + b\sin\theta$, and hence the graph is a limaçon.

62. The graphs of $r = 1 + \cos\theta$ and $r = -1 + \cos\theta$ are sketched side-by-side below.

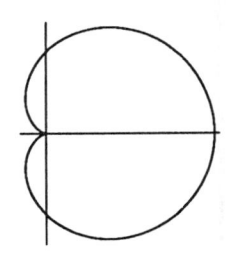

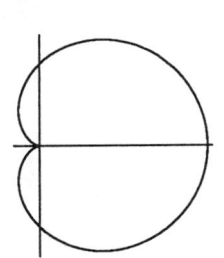

Section 10.3

1. The area is shown below:

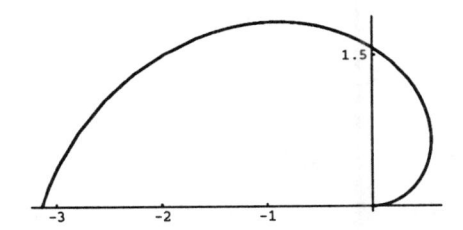

2. The area is shown below:

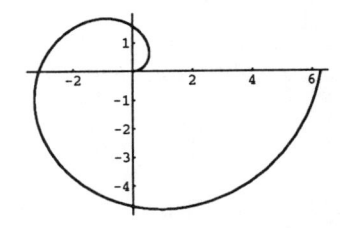

3. The area is shown below:

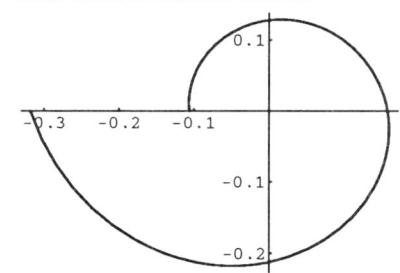

4. The area is shown below:

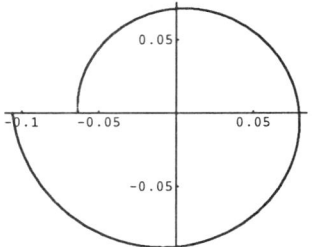

5. The area is shown below:

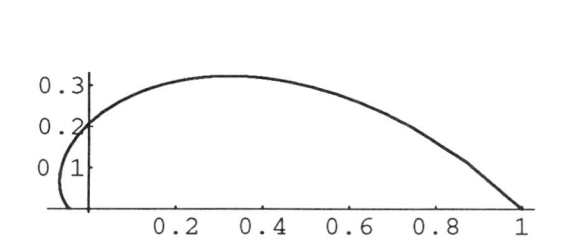

6. The area is shown below:

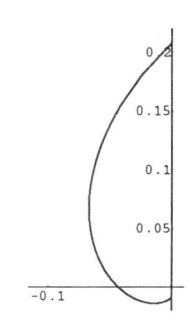

7. $A = 2\int_0^{\pi/2} \frac{1}{2}\left(4\cos^2\theta\right)\,d\theta.$

8. $A = \frac{1}{2}\int_0^\pi 16\sin^2\theta\,d\theta = 4\int_0^\pi (1-\cos 2\theta)\,d\theta = 4\left[\theta - \frac{1}{2}\sin 2\theta\right]_0^\pi = 4\pi.$

9. $A = 2\int_0^\pi \frac{1}{2}(1+\cos\theta)^2\,d\theta.$

10. $A = \int_0^{2\pi} \frac{1}{2}(4)(1-\sin\theta)^2\,d\theta = 2\int_0^{2\pi}\left(1 - 2\sin\theta + \frac{1}{2}(1-\cos 2\theta)\right)d\theta$
$= \left[2\theta + 4\cos\theta + \theta - \frac{1}{2}\sin 2\theta\right]_0^{2\pi} = 6\pi.$

11. $A = 2\int_0^\pi \frac{1}{2}(2-\cos\theta)^2\,d\theta.$

12. $A = \frac{1}{2}\int_0^{2\pi}\left(9 + 12\sin\theta + 4\sin^2\theta\right)d\theta = \left[\frac{9}{2}\theta - 6\cos\theta + \theta - \frac{1}{2}\sin 2\theta\right]_0^{2\pi} = 11\pi.$

13. $A = \frac{1}{2}\int_0^\pi 16\cos^2\theta\,d\theta = 4\int_0^\pi (1+\cos 2\theta)\,d\theta = 4\left[\theta + \frac{1}{2}\sin 2\theta\right]_0^\pi = 4\pi.$

14. $A = \frac{1}{2}\int_0^{2\pi} 25\left(1 + 2\sin\theta + \sin^2\theta\right)d\theta = \frac{25}{4}\int_0^{2\pi}(2 + 4\sin\theta + 1 - \cos 2\theta)\,d\theta$
$= \frac{25}{4}\left[3\theta - 4\cos\theta - \frac{1}{2}\sin 2\theta\right]_0^{2\pi} = \frac{75}{2}\pi.$

15. $A = \frac{1}{2}\int_0^{2\pi}\left(9 - 6\cos\theta + \cos^2\theta\right)d\theta = \frac{1}{4}\int_0^{2\pi}(18 - 12\cos\theta + 1 + \cos 2\theta)\,d\theta$
$= \frac{1}{4}\left[19\theta - 12\sin\theta + \frac{1}{2}\sin 2\theta\right]_0^{2\pi} = \frac{19}{2}\pi.$

16. $A = \frac{1}{2}\int_0^{2\pi}(10 + 6\sin\theta + 6\cos\theta + 2\sin\theta\cos\theta)\,d\theta = \frac{1}{2}\left[10\theta - 6\cos\theta + 6\sin\theta + \sin^2\theta\right]_0^{2\pi} = 10\pi.$

Section 10.3 Area Computations in Polar Coordinates

17. The graph of the given curve is shown on the right. The area within one loop is

$$A = 2 \int_0^{\pi/4} \tfrac{1}{2} (2 \cos \theta)^2 \, d\theta.$$

18. The graph of the given curve is shown on the right. The area within one loop is

$$A = \int_0^{\pi/3} 9 \sin^2 3\theta \, d\theta$$
$$= \tfrac{9}{2} \int_0^{\pi/3} \tfrac{1}{2}(1 - \cos 6\theta) \, d\theta$$
$$= \left[\tfrac{9}{4}\theta - \tfrac{3}{8} \sin 6\theta \right]_0^{\pi/3} = \tfrac{3}{4}\pi.$$

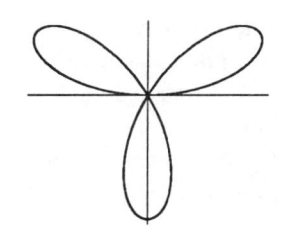

19. The graph of the given curve is shown on the right. The area within each of the eight loops is

$$A = 2 \int_0^{\pi/8} \tfrac{1}{2} (4 \cos^2 4\theta) \, d\theta.$$

20. The graph of the given curve is shown on the right. The area within each of the five loops is

$$A = \tfrac{1}{2} \int_0^{\pi/5} \sin^2 5\theta \, d\theta$$
$$= \tfrac{1}{4} \int_0^{\pi/5} (1 - \cos 10\theta) \, d\theta$$
$$= \tfrac{1}{4} \left[\theta - \tfrac{1}{10} \sin 10\theta \right]_0^{\pi/5} = \tfrac{1}{20}\pi.$$

21. The graph of $r^2 = 4 \sin 2\theta$ appears on the right. The area within each loop is

$$A = \tfrac{1}{2} \int_0^{\pi/2} 4 \sin 2\theta \, d\theta.$$

22. The graph of $r^2 = 4 \cos 2\theta$ is shown on the right. The area within each of the loops is

$$A = \tfrac{1}{2} \int_{-\pi/4}^{\pi/4} 4 \cos 2\theta \, d\theta$$
$$= \left[\sin 2\theta \right]_{-\pi/4}^{\pi/4} = 2.$$

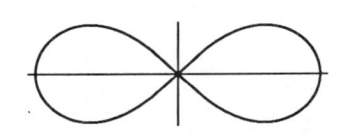

23. $A = \int_0^{\pi} 2 \sin \theta \, d\theta = 4.$

24. $A = \int_{-\pi/12}^{\pi/12} 9(1 + \cos 12\theta)\, d\theta = \frac{3}{2}\pi.$

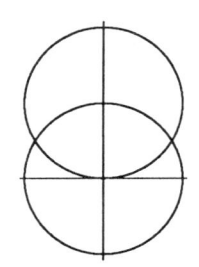

25. The two curves are shown on the right. The region in question has area

$$A = \frac{1}{2} \int_{\pi/6}^{5\pi/6} \left(4 \sin^2 \theta - 1\right) d\theta.$$

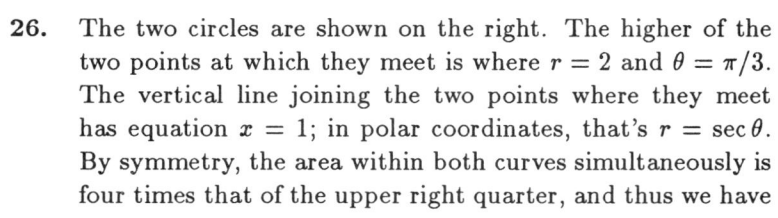

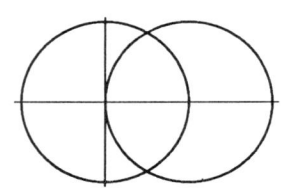

26. The two circles are shown on the right. The higher of the two points at which they meet is where $r = 2$ and $\theta = \pi/3$. The vertical line joining the two points where they meet has equation $x = 1$; in polar coordinates, that's $r = \sec \theta$. By symmetry, the area within both curves simultaneously is four times that of the upper right quarter, and thus we have

$$A = (4)\left(\tfrac{1}{2}\right)\int_0^{\pi/3} \left(4 - \sec^2 \theta\right) d\theta$$
$$= \tfrac{2}{3}\left(4\pi - 3\sqrt{3}\right).$$

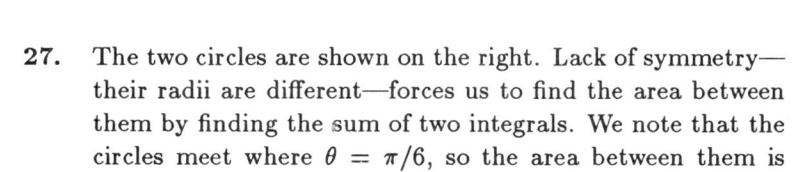

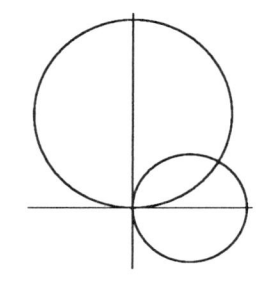

27. The two circles are shown on the right. Lack of symmetry—their radii are different—forces us to find the area between them by finding the sum of two integrals. We note that the circles meet where $\theta = \pi/6$, so the area between them is given by

$$A = \tfrac{1}{2}\left(\int_0^{\pi/6} 3\sin^2\theta\, d\theta + \int_{\pi/6}^{\pi/2} \cos^2 \theta\, d\theta\right).$$

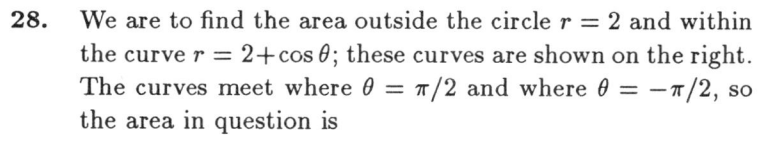

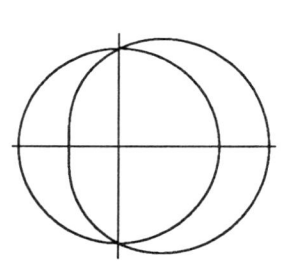

28. We are to find the area outside the circle $r = 2$ and within the curve $r = 2 + \cos \theta$; these curves are shown on the right. The curves meet where $\theta = \pi/2$ and where $\theta = -\pi/2$, so the area in question is

$$A = \tfrac{1}{2} \int_{-\pi/2}^{\pi/2} \left((2+\cos\theta)^2 - 2^2\right) d\theta$$
$$= \int_0^{\pi/2} \left(4\cos\theta + \tfrac{1}{2}(1+\cos 2\theta)\right) d\theta$$
$$= \left[4\sin\theta + \tfrac{1}{2}\theta + \tfrac{1}{4}\sin 2\theta\right]_0^{\pi/2} = \tfrac{1}{4}(\pi + 16).$$

29. The two curves meet where $\theta = \pi/6$ and $\theta = 5\pi/6$. So the area between them is

$$A = \tfrac{1}{2}\int_{\pi/6}^{5\pi/6} \left((3+2\sin\theta)^2 - 16\right) d\theta.$$

30. The two curves meet where $\theta = \pi/6$ and $\theta = -\pi/6$. By symmetry, the area outside the circle and within the lemniscate is

$$A = 2\int_0^{\pi/6} (2\cos 2\theta - 1)\, d\theta = 2\left[\sin 2\theta - \theta\right]_0^{\pi/6} = \tfrac{1}{3}\left(3\sqrt{3} - \pi\right).$$

31. The curves, shown on the right, intersect where $\theta = \pi/8$. By symmetry, the area between them is
$$A = 4\int_0^{\pi/8} \tfrac{1}{2}\sin 2\theta \, d\theta.$$

32. The graph of $r = 1 - 2\sin\theta$ is shown on the right. The total area it encloses is
$$A_T = \int_{-\pi/2}^{\pi/6} (1 - 2\sin\theta)^2 \, d\theta$$
$$= \tfrac{1}{2}\left(4\pi + 3\sqrt{3}\right) \approx 8.881261518.$$
The small enclosed area is
$$A_S = \int_{\pi/6}^{\pi/2} (1 - 2\sin\theta)^2 \, d\theta$$
$$= \tfrac{1}{2}\left(2\pi - 3\sqrt{3}\right) \approx 0.543516442.$$
Therefore the area between them is
$$A_T - A_S = \pi + 3\sqrt{3} \approx 8.337745076.$$

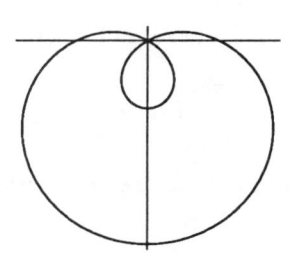

33. The two curves meet where $\theta = 2\pi/3$ and where $\theta = 4\pi/3$. The area within the cardioid but outside the circle is
$$A = \int_0^{2\pi/3} \left((2 + 2\cos\theta)^2 - 1\right) d\theta = \int_0^{2\pi/3} (3 + 8\cos\theta + 2(1 + \cos 2\theta))\, d\theta$$
$$= \left[5\theta + 8\sin\theta + \sin 2\theta\right]_0^{2\pi/3} = \tfrac{10}{3}\pi + \tfrac{7}{2}\sqrt{3} \approx 16.53415334.$$

34. The two curves meet at the origin, at the point with Cartesian coordinates $(-2, 0)$, and at the two points where $\cos\theta = 3 - 2\sqrt{2}$. Let the least positive value of θ that satisfies the latter equation be denoted by ω. Then the area within the figure-8 curve but outside the cardioid is given by
$$A = \int_0^{\omega} \left(4\cos\theta - (1 - \cos\theta)^2\right) d\theta = \int_0^{\omega} \left(6\cos\theta - 1 - \tfrac{1}{2}(1 + \cos 2\theta)\right) d\theta$$
$$= \left[6\sin\theta - \tfrac{3}{2}\theta - \tfrac{1}{4}\sin 2\theta\right]_0^{\omega}$$
$$= 12\sqrt{3\sqrt{2} - 4} - \tfrac{3}{2}\omega - \left(3 - 2\sqrt{2}\right)\sqrt{3\sqrt{2} - 4} \approx 3.7289587.$$

35. The region in question is symmetric about the line $y = x$, so we integrate over half the region and double:
$$A = 2\int_0^{\pi/4} 2\cos^2\theta \, d\theta = 2\int_0^{\pi/4} (1 + \cos 2\theta) \, d\theta = \tfrac{1}{2}(\pi + 2).$$

36. The region is symmetric about the y-axis, so we integrate over the part in the first quadrant and double. The two curves cross when $\theta = \pi/6$ and $\theta = 5\pi/6$, so the area is
$$A = \int_{\pi/6}^{\pi/2} \left((2 + 2\sin\theta)^2 - 9\right) d\theta$$
$$= \int_{\pi/6}^{\pi/2} (8\sin\theta + 2(1 - \cos\theta) - 5) \, d\theta = \cdots = \tfrac{9}{2}\sqrt{3} - \pi \approx 4.65263598.$$

37. The Cartesian equation of the curve is $\left(x - \tfrac{1}{2}\right)^2 + \left(y - \tfrac{1}{2}\right)^2 = \left(\tfrac{1}{2}\sqrt{2}\right)^2$. So the graph is a circle of radius $\tfrac{1}{2}\sqrt{2}$.

38. By symmetry, the area common to all three circles is
$$A = \int_0^{\pi/6} 4\sin^2\theta\, d\theta + \int_{\pi/6}^{\pi/4} 1\, d\theta = \tfrac{1}{12}\left(5\pi - 6\sqrt{3}\right) \approx 0.44297.$$

40. One way to solve this problem is to let one circle have polar equation $r = 2a\cos\theta$ and the other have polar equation $r = a$. The first circle then has center at $x = a$ on the x-axis and passes through the origin; the second has center at the origin and passes through the center of the first. They meet where $\theta = \pi/4$ and where $\theta = -\pi/4$, and the area within either that is outside the other is
$$A_1 = \int_0^{\pi/4}\left(4a^2\cos^2\theta - a^2\right)d\theta = a^2\int_0^{\pi/4}\left(2(1+\cos 2\theta) - 1\right)d\theta = a^2\Big[\theta + \sin 2\theta\Big]_0^{\pi/4} = \tfrac{1}{4}a^2(\pi + 4).$$

Let A denote the area within both circles. Each circle has area πa^2, so
$$2\pi a^2 = (A_1 + A) + (A_1 + A). \text{ Therefore}$$
$$A = \pi a^2 - A_1 = \tfrac{1}{4}a^2(3\pi - 4).$$

41. (a) $\tfrac{5}{2}\left(1 - e^{-2\pi/5}\right)^2 \approx 1.279458764;$ (b) $\tfrac{5}{2}e^{-2n\pi/5}\left(e^{2\pi/5} - 1\right)^2$

42. Let $r(t) = 2e^{-\theta/10}$. R_1 has area
$$a_1 = 4\pi - \int_0^{2\pi} \tfrac{1}{2}[r(t)]^2\, dt = 4\pi - 10(1 - e^{-2\pi/5})$$

and R_2 has area
$$a_2 = \int_0^{2\pi} \tfrac{1}{2}[r(t)]^2\, dt - \pi = 10(1 - e^{-2\pi/5}) - \pi.$$

and, indeed, $a_1 + a_2 = 3\pi$.

43. The point of intersection in the second quadrant is located where $\theta = \alpha \approx 2.326839$. Using symmetry, the total area of the shaded region R is approximately
$$2\int_0^\alpha \tfrac{1}{2}(e^{-t/5})^2\, dt + 2\int_\alpha^\pi \tfrac{1}{2}[2(1+\cos t)]^2\, dt \approx 1.58069.$$

44. The point of intersection in the first quadrant is located where $\theta = \alpha \approx 0.217075400$ and the point of intersection in the second quadrant is located where $\theta = \beta \approx 2.924517254$. So the total area of the shaded region R is approximately
$$\int_\alpha^\beta \tfrac{1}{2}(3 + \cos 4t)^2\, dt + \int_\beta^{2\pi+\alpha} \tfrac{1}{2}(3 + 3\sin t)^2\, dt \approx 17.2661.$$

Section 10.4

1. Solve the first equation for $t = x - 1$; substitute into the second: $y = 2(x-1) - 1 = 2x - 3$.
   Answer: $y = 2x - 3$.

2. Because $t^2 = x - 1$, $y = 2(x-1) - 1$; thus $y = 2x - 3$ with domain $x \geq 1$.

4. First, $x^2 = t$, so $y = 3x^2 - 2$, $x \geq 0$.

6. We solve for $t = y + 2$, so $x = (y+2)^2 + 3(y+2)$. Thus $x = y^2 + 7y + 10$. We complete the square to obtain $\left(y + \frac{7}{2}\right)^2 = x + \frac{9}{4}$. The graph is therefore a parabola, opening to the right, with axis the line $y = -\frac{7}{2}$ and with vertex at $\left(-\frac{9}{4}, -\frac{7}{2}\right)$.

7. From $x = e^t$ we may conclude that $y = 4e^{2t} = 4x^2$. So the answer is $y = 4x^2$, $x > 0$.

8. First, $x/2 = e^t = 2/y$, so $xy = 4$; $x > 0$, $y > 0$.

10. $1 + \sinh^2 t = \cosh^2 t$, hence because $\cosh t > 0$ for all t, we get $y = +\sqrt{1 + x^2}$.

11. Given: $x = 2\cosh t$, $y = 3\sinh t$. Then $(x/2)^2 = 1 + (y/3)^2$, which we may write in the standard form $\left(\frac{x}{2}\right)^2 - \left(\frac{y}{3}\right)^2 = 1$. But $x \geq 2$, so the graph is the right branch only of the hyperbola with center at $(0,0)$ and with vertices at $(-2, 0)$ and $(2, 0)$.

12. $1 + \tan^2 t = \sec^2 t$, hence we get $x^2 = 1 + y^2$.

14. $(x-3)^2 + (y-5)^2 = 4$, a circle with center $(3,5)$ and radius 2.

15. $y = 1 - x$, $0 \leq x \leq 1$.

16. $y = 1 - x^2$, $-1 \leq x \leq 1$.

17. First, $\dfrac{dy}{dx} = \dfrac{dy/dt}{dx/dt} = \dfrac{9t^2}{4t} = \dfrac{9t}{4}$. So when $t = 1$, the slope is $9/4$ at the point $P(3, 5)$ of tangency. Thus an equation of the tangent line is $9x - 4y = 7$. The second derivative is $\dfrac{9}{16t}$, so the curve is concave upward at the point where $t = 1$.

18. $dy/dx = -\tan t$; the point of tangency is $\left(\frac{1}{4}\sqrt{2}, \frac{1}{4}\sqrt{2}\right)$, and the slope there is -1. The equation of the tangent line may be written in the form $x + y = \frac{1}{2}\sqrt{2}$. The second derivative is $\frac{1}{3}\sec^4 t \csc t$, so the curve is concave upward at the point of tangency.

20. $dy/dx = -e^{-2t}$; the point of tangency is $(1, 1)$ and the slope there is -1. An equation of the tangent line is $x + y = 2$. The second derivative is $2e^{-3t}$, so the graph is concave upward everywhere.

21. Here, $dr/d\theta = \sqrt{3}e^{\theta\sqrt{3}}$. Therefore $\cot\psi = \dfrac{1}{r} \cdot \dfrac{dr}{d\theta} = \left(e^{-\theta\sqrt{3}}\right)\left(\sqrt{3}\right)\left(e^{\theta\sqrt{3}}\right) = \sqrt{3}$. Therefore $\tan\psi = 1/\sqrt{3}$, and therefore $\psi = \pi/6$, a constant, independent of the value of θ.

22. We use the equation $\cot\psi = \dfrac{1}{r} \cdot \dfrac{dr}{d\theta}$ from the text. Here, $\dfrac{dr}{d\theta} = -\dfrac{1}{\theta^2}$. And because $r = 1/\theta$, $\cot\psi = (\theta)\left(\dfrac{-1}{\theta^2}\right) = -\dfrac{1}{\theta}$. When $\theta = 1$, $\cot\psi = -1$. Therefore $\psi = 3\pi/4$.

24. $dr/d\theta = \sin\theta$. So $\cot\psi = (\sin\theta)/(1 - \cos\theta)$. Now when $\theta = \pi/3$, $\cot\psi = \sqrt{3}$. Consequently $\psi = \pi/6$.

25. There are horizontal tangents at $(1, 2)$ and $(1, -2)$. There is a vertical tangent line at $(0, 0)$. There is no tangent line at the other x-intercept $(3, 0)$ because the curve crosses itself with two different slopes there, namely the slopes $\pm\sqrt{3}$.

26. There are horizontal tangents at $(\pm 1/\sqrt{2}, \pm 1)$ (all four combinations). The tangent line is vertical at $(-1, 0)$ and at $(1, 0)$. There is no tangent line at $(0, 0)$ because the curve crosses itself with slopes ± 2 there.

27. There are horizontal tangents at the points corresponding to $\theta = \pm\pi/3$. The corresponding value of r is $\frac{3}{2}$, and the rectangular coordinates of these two points are $\left(\frac{3}{4}, \pm\frac{3}{4}\sqrt{3}\right)$. There is a vertical tangent at $(2, 0)$. If a line tangent to the curve C at the point P is simply a line through P that approximates the curve's shape very *very* well at and near P, then there is a horizontal tangent line at $(0, 0)$.

28. There are horizontal tangents at the four points $\left(\pm\frac{1}{2}\sqrt{6}, \pm\frac{1}{2}\sqrt{2}\right)$. There are vertical tangents at $(\pm 2, 0)$ but no tangent at the third x-intercept $(0, 0)$; at that point, the curve crosses itself with slopes $+1$ and -1.

29. You should find that

$$\frac{dy}{dx} = -2e^{3t}$$

and that $\frac{d^2y}{dx^2} = 6e^{4t}.$

The graph is shown at the right.

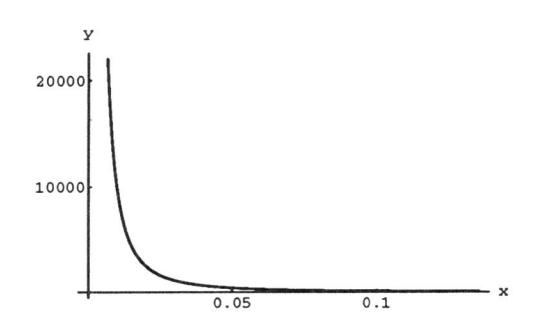

30. Answer: $x = \dfrac{3t}{1+t^3}$, $y = \dfrac{3t^2}{1+t^3}$, $0 \leq t < +\infty$.

31. If the slope at $P(x,y)$ is m, then $2y\dfrac{dy}{dx} = 4p$, so $y = \dfrac{2p}{dy/dx} = \dfrac{2p}{m}$. Therefore $4px = y^2 = \dfrac{4p^2}{m^2}$, and so $x = \dfrac{p}{m^2}$, $y = \dfrac{2p}{m}$.

34. $|OC| = a - b$. So C has coordinates $x = (a-b)\cos t$, $y = (a-b)\sin t$. The arc length from the point of tangency to $A(a,0)$ is the same as that to P; denote it by s. Note that $s = ta$. Let α be the angle OCP and θ the angle supplementary to α, so that $\theta = \pi - \alpha$. Then $s = b\theta$. So $ta = b\theta$. The radius b is at the angle $-(\theta - t) = t - \theta$ from the horizontal, so P has coordinates

$$x = (a-b)\cos t + b\cos(t-\theta), \quad y = (a-b)\sin t + b\sin(t-\theta).$$

Now $\theta = \dfrac{a}{b}t$, so $t - \theta = t - \dfrac{a}{b}t = \dfrac{b-a}{b}t$. Hence P has the coordinates given in the statement of the problem.

36. (a) If $x = \cos^3 t$ and $y = \sin^3 t$, then

$$x^{2/3} + y^{2/3} = \cos^2 t + \sin^2 t = 1.$$

So the hypocycloid lies on the graph $x^{2/3} + y^{2/3} = 1$. But $\cos^3 t$ and $\sin^3 t$ take on all values from -1 to 1, so the hypocycloid is the entire graph $x^{2/3} + y^{2/3} = 1$.

(b) $dx/dt = -3\cos^2 t \sin t$ and $dy/dt = 3\sin^2 t \cos t$. So $dy/dx = -\tan t$ and $dx/dt = -\cot t$. Note that $dy/dx = 0$ at each multiple of π and that $dx/dy = 0$ at each odd multiple of $\pi/2$. Horizontal tangents: $t = 0$ gives $(1,0)$, whereas $t = \pi$ gives $(-1,0)$. Vertical tangents: $t = \pi/2$ gives $(0,1)$ and $t = 3\pi/2$ gives $(0,-1)$. Let y' denote dy/dx. Then $\dfrac{d^2y}{dx^2} = \dfrac{dy'/dt}{dx/dt}$. Here,

$$\frac{dy'}{dt} = -\sec^2 t, \quad \text{so} \quad \frac{d^2y}{dx^2} = \frac{1}{3\cos^4 t \sin t}.$$

Therefore $\dfrac{d^2y}{dx^2}$ has the same sign as $\sin t$; thus the graph of the hypocycloid is concave upward for $0 < t < \pi/2$ and for $\pi/2 < t < \pi$; it is concave downward for $\pi < t < 3\pi/2$ and for $3\pi/2 < t < 2\pi$. The graph is shown above.

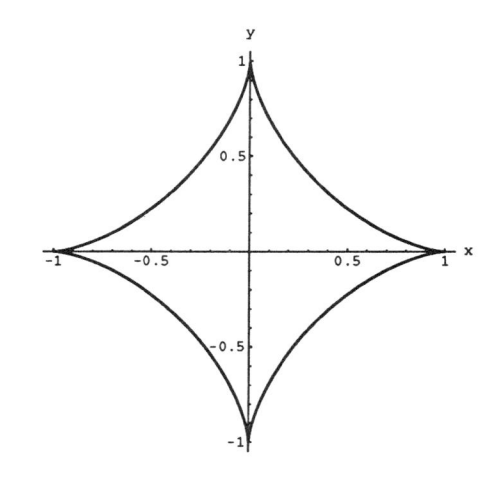

41. Given: $x^5 + y^5 = 5x^2y^2$. Substitute $y = tx$ to obtain $x^5 + t^5x^5 = 5x^4t^2$, then solve for

$$x = \frac{5t^2}{1+t^5}, \quad y = \frac{5t^3}{1+t^5}, \quad 0 \leq t < +\infty.$$

42. Draw a figure in which the segment lies in the third quadrant and makes the angle θ with the [negative] x-axis. Drop perpendiculars from the midpoint of the segment to the coordinate axes. If (x, y) is that midpoint, then we see by various right triangles that

$$x = -a\sin\theta \quad \text{and} \quad y = a\sin\theta.$$

It is now easy to identify the locus as a circle with center $(0,0)$ and radius a.

Section 10.5

1. Note first that $y = 2t^2 + 1$ is always positive, so the curve lies entirely above the x-axis. Moreover, as t goes from -1 to 1, $dx = 3t^2\,dt$ is positive, so the area is $A = \int_{-1}^{1} (2t^2 + 1)(3t^2)\,dt = \frac{22}{5}$.

2. $A = \int_0^{\ln 2} 3e^{2t}\,dt = \frac{9}{2}$.

3. $A = \int_0^{\pi} \sin^3 t\,dt = \frac{4}{3}$.

4. $A = \int_1^0 -3e^{2t}\,dt = \frac{3}{2}(e^2 - 1)$.

5. $A = +\int_0^{\pi} e^t \sin t\,dt = \frac{1}{2}(e^{\pi} + 1)$.

6. $A = \int_1^0 -(2t+1)e^t\,dt = e + 1$.

7. $V = \int_{-1}^{1} \pi(2t^2 + 1)^2 (3t^2)\,dt$.

8. $V = \int_0^{\ln 2} \pi(e^{-2t})(3e^{3t})\,dt = 3\pi$.

9. $V = \int_0^{\pi} \pi \sin^5 t\,dt$.

10. $V = \int_{\pi}^{0} -\pi e^{2t} \sin t\,dt = \frac{\pi}{5}(e^{2\pi} + 1)$.

11. $L = \int_5^{12} \sqrt{4+t}\,dt$.

12. $L = \int_0^1 \sqrt{t^2 + t^4}\,dt = \frac{1}{3}(2\sqrt{2} - 1)$.

13. $\left(\frac{dx}{dt}\right)^2 + \left(\frac{dy}{dt}\right)^2 = 2$, so $L = \int_{\pi/4}^{\pi/2} \sqrt{2}\,dt$.

14. $L = \int_0^{\pi} \sqrt{2}e^t\,dt = (e^{\pi} - 1)\sqrt{2}$.

15. $L = \int_0^{4\pi} \frac{1}{2}\sqrt{5}e^{\theta/2}\,d\theta$.

16. $L = \int_{2\pi}^{4\pi} \sqrt{1+\theta^2}\, d\theta$
    $= 2\pi\sqrt{1+16\pi^2} + \tfrac{1}{2}\ln\left(4\pi + \sqrt{1+16\pi^2}\right) - \pi\sqrt{1+4\pi^2} - \tfrac{1}{2}\ln\left(2\pi + \sqrt{1+4\pi^2}\right)$,
    which is approximately equal to 59.563022.

17. $A = \int_1^4 (2\pi)\left(2\sqrt{t}\right)\sqrt{\dfrac{t+1}{t}}\, dt = 4\pi \int_1^4 \sqrt{t+1}\, dt$.

18. $A = \int_1^2 16\pi\sqrt{t}\,(4t + t^{-2})\, dt = \tfrac{16}{5}\pi\left(2 + 27\sqrt{2}\right)$.

19. $A = 2\int_0^1 2\pi t^3 \sqrt{9t^4 + 4}\, dt$.

20. $A = \int_0^3 (2\pi)(2t+1)\sqrt{4t^2 + 4t + 5}\, dt$. The substitution $u = 2t + 1$ converts this integral into
    $A = 2\pi \int_1^7 \tfrac{1}{2}u\sqrt{u^2 + 4}\, du = \dfrac{\pi}{3}\left(53\sqrt{53} - 5\sqrt{5}\right)$.

21. $A = \int_0^\pi (2\pi)\left(4\sin^2\theta\right)(4)\, d\theta$.

22. $A = \int_0^{\pi/2} 2\pi\left(e^\theta \cos\theta\right)\left(\sqrt{2}\,e^\theta\right) dt = \tfrac{2}{5}\pi\sqrt{2}\,(e^\pi - 2)$.

23. $V = \int_{t=0}^{2\pi} \pi y^2\, dx = \pi a^3 \int_0^{2\pi} (1 - \cos t)^3\, dt$.

24. $ds = a\sqrt{2(1 - \cos t)}\, dt = 2a\sqrt{\dfrac{1 - \cos t}{2}}\, dt = 2a \sin\left(\dfrac{t}{2}\right) dt$.
    Therefore $A = \int_0^{2\pi} 4\pi a^2 (1 - \cos t)\sin\left(\dfrac{t}{2}\right) dt = 8\pi a^2 \int_0^{2\pi} \sin^3\left(\dfrac{t}{2}\right) dt = \tfrac{64}{3}\pi a^2$.

25. (a) $A = 2\int_0^\pi (b\sin t)(a\sin t)\, dt$. (b) $V = 2\int_0^\pi (b^2 \sin^2 t)(a\sin t)\, dt$.

26. $A = 2\int_{-\sqrt{3}}^0 (t^3 - 3t)(2t)\, dt = \tfrac{24}{5}\sqrt{3}$.

27. First, ds can be simplified to $\sqrt{1 + t^2}\, dt$. Therefore $L = \int_0^{2\pi} \sqrt{1 + t^2}\, dt$. Now use the substitution $t = \tan u$.

28. $A = \int_0^{2\pi} 2\pi a\,(b + a\cos t)\, dt = 4\pi^2 ab$.

29. $A = 4\int_0^{\pi/2} (a\sin^3 t)(3a\cos^2 t)(\sin t)\, dt$.

30. Because $ds = 3a\,|\sin t \cos t|\, dt$, we have $L = 4\int_0^{\pi/2} 3a\sin t \cos t\, dt = 6a$.

31. Here, $ds = 3a\,|\sin t \cos t|\, dt$, so $A = (4\pi)(3a)\int_0^{\pi/2} (\sin t \cos t)(a\sin^3 t)\, dt$.

32. First, $r^2 + \left(\dfrac{dr}{d\theta}\right)^2$ can be simplified to $\dfrac{2a^2}{\cos 2\theta}$. So
    $A = 4\pi \int_0^{\pi/4} (r\cos\theta)\sqrt{\dfrac{2a^2}{\cos 2\theta}}\, d\theta = 4\pi \int_0^{\pi/4} 2a^2 \cos\theta\, d\theta = 4\pi a^2 \sqrt{2}$.

33. The area is $A = 2\int_0^3 (3t - \tfrac{1}{3}t^3)\, 2t\sqrt{3}\, dt$.

34. $ds = (t^2 + 3)\, dt$, so the arc length is $L = \int_{-3}^{3} (t^2 + 3)\, dt = 36$.

35. The volume is $V = \int_0^3 \pi\left(3t - \tfrac{1}{3}t^3\right)^2 2t\sqrt{3}\, dt$.

36. The surface area is $A = \int_0^3 2\pi\left(3t - \tfrac{1}{3}t^3\right)(t^2 + 3)\, dt = 81\pi$.

38. $ds = 2a\left|\sin\dfrac{t}{2}\right| dt$, so the surface area is

$$A = \int_{t=0}^{2\pi} 2\pi x\, ds = \int_0^{2\pi} 2\pi a\,(t - \sin t)\, 2a \sin\frac{t}{2}\, dt$$

$$= 4\pi a^2 \int_0^{2\pi}\left(2\cdot\frac{t}{2} - 2\sin\frac{t}{2}\cos\frac{t}{2}\right)\sin\frac{t}{2}\, dt$$

$$= 8\pi a^2\left[-t\cos\frac{t}{2} + 2\sin\frac{t}{2} - \tfrac{2}{3}\sin^3\frac{t}{2}\right]_0^{2\pi} = 16\pi^2 a^2.$$

39. The volume is

$$V = 2\pi\int_{t=0}^{2\pi} a^2(t - \sin t)(1 - \cos t)\cdot a(1 - \cos t)\, dt$$

$$= 2\pi a^3\left[\tfrac{3}{4}t^2 - 2t\sin t + \tfrac{1}{4}t\sin 2t - 2\cos t + \tfrac{1}{8}\cos 2t - \tfrac{1}{3}(1 - \cos t)^3\right]_{t=0}^{2\pi}$$

$$= 2\pi a^3 (3\pi^2) = 6\pi^3 a^3.$$

40. (b) First, the arc-length element is $ds = \sqrt{[x'(t)]^2 + [y'(t)]^2}\, dt = \sqrt{a^2 t^2}\, dt = |at|\, dt = at\, dt$. So the length of the involute from $t = 0$ to $t = \pi$ is

$$\int_{t=0}^{\pi} 1\, ds = \int_0^{\pi} at\, dt = \tfrac{1}{2}\pi^2 a.$$

41. We will compute the area of the part of the region above the x-axis, then double the result. On the left we see a quarter-circle of radius πa, with area

$$A_1 = \tfrac{1}{4}\pi(\pi a)^2 = \tfrac{1}{4}\pi^3 a^2.$$

On the right, the area between the involute and the x-axis can be found with an integral:

$$A_2 = \int_0^{\pi}(-y(t)\cdot x'(t))\, dt$$

$$= \left[\tfrac{1}{12}(3t^2\sin 2t - 3\sin 2t + 6t\cos 2t + 2t^3)\,a^2\right]_0^{\pi} = \tfrac{1}{6}\pi(\pi^2 + 3)\,a^2.$$

But we must subtract the area of the part of the water tank above the x-axis, the area of a semicircle of radius a: $A_3 = \tfrac{1}{2}\pi a^2$. So the total area of the region the cow can graze is

$$A = 2(A_1 + A_2 - A_3) = \tfrac{5}{6}\pi^3 a^2.$$

42. If you look carefully at the figure, you see that there is a problem at the extreme left. Each involute moves away from the y-axis very briefly, then moves back toward it.

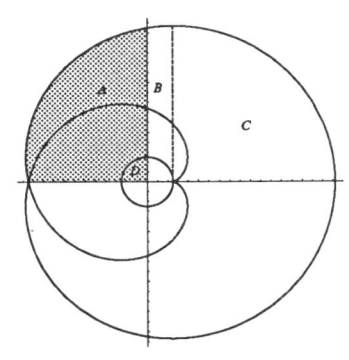

We can avoid this problem by finding the area that the cow can graze in the third quadrant by integrating not $y\,dx$, but instead $x\,dy$. To find the limits of integration on the parameter t, we need to know the value t_1 of t at which the involute crosses the negative x-axis (where the two involutes cross) and the value t_2 of t at which the outer involute crosses the positive y-axis. Newton's method yields

$$t_1 \approx 4.4934094579 \quad \text{and} \quad t_2 \approx 6.121250466898.$$

So the area of the shaded region is

$$\int_{t=t_1}^{t_2} x(t) \cdot y'(t)\,dt \approx (23.106)a^2.$$

The area of the region bounded below by the x-axis, on the left by the y-axis, on the right by the line $x = a$ (the dotted line in the figure) and above by the outer involute, is

$$B = \int_{t=t_1}^{2\pi} (-y(t) \cdot x'(t))\,dt \approx (6.256)a^2.$$

The area of the quarter-circle bounded below by the x-axis, on the left by the line $x = a$, and on the right and above by the circular arc of radius $2\pi a$ is

$$C = \tfrac{1}{4}\pi(2\pi a)^2 = \pi^3 a^2 \approx (31.006)a^2.$$

We can obtain the total area that the cow can graze by doubling the sum of the areas A, B, and C, but then we need to subtract the area occupied by the water tank, the area $D = \pi a^2 \approx (3.142)a^2$ of a circle of radius a. So the area the cow can graze is

$$2(A + B + C) - D \approx (117.596)a^2.$$

43. Given $r(t) = 3\sin 3\theta$, remember that roses with *odd* coefficients are swept out *twice* in the interval $0 \leqq \theta \leqq 2\pi$, so we should integrate $ds = \sqrt{[r(\theta)]^2 + [r'(\theta)]^2}\,d\theta = \sqrt{45 + 36\cos 6\theta}\,d\theta$ from 0 to π to obtain the total length of the rose:

$$\int_{\theta=0}^{\pi} 1\,ds = \int_{0}^{\pi} \sqrt{45 + 36\cos 6\theta}\,d\theta \approx 20.0473.$$

44. Two integrals are required. The surface area is

$$\int_{\theta=0}^{\pi/3} 2\pi x\,ds - \int_{\theta=\pi/3}^{\pi/2} 2\pi x\,ds.$$

The minus sign is needed because $x(\theta) = r(\theta)\cos\theta$ is negative if $\pi/3 \leqq \theta \leqq \pi/2$. The total surface area is approximately 64.912.

314   Section 10.5 Integral Computations with Parametric Curves

45. Given $r(\theta) = 2\cos 2\theta$, remember than a rose with an even coefficient n of θ has $2n$ "petals," and is swept out as θ ranges from 0 to 2π. The arc length element in this case is $ds = \sqrt{10 - 6\cos 4\theta}\, d\theta$, and the length of the graph is

$$\int_0^{2\pi} \sqrt{10 - 6\cos 4\theta}\, d\theta \approx 19.37689.$$

46. When the rose of Problem 45 is rotated around the x-axis, the entire surface is generated twice. To obtain each part of the surface once, we will rotate the part of the rose from $\theta = 0$ to $\theta = \pi/4$ and, separately, the part from $\theta = \pi/4$ to $\pi/2$. We will set up an integral for each surface area, add the results, and double the sum. With $x(\theta) = r(\theta)\sin\theta$ and the arc length element ds of Problem 45, we get the integrals

$$\int_{\theta=0}^{\pi/4} 2\pi y\, ds \approx 5.46827 \quad \text{and} \quad \int_{\theta=\pi/4}^{\pi/2} (-2\pi y)\, ds \approx 16.1232,$$

for a total area of approximately 43.1829.

47. Given: $r(\theta) = 5 + 9\cos\theta$, the arc length element is $ds = \sqrt{106 + 90\cos\theta}\, d\theta$, and so the total length of the limaçon is

$$\int_0^{2\pi} \sqrt{106 + 90\cos\theta}\, d\theta \approx 61.0036.$$

48. The limaçon of Problem 47 is to be rotated around the x-axis. To find the surface area generated, we need to know where $r(\theta) = 0$. The solution is $\theta_1 = \cos^{-1}\left(-\frac{5}{9}\right) \approx 2.159827297$. So the surface area is

$$\int_{\theta=0}^{\theta_1} 2\pi y\, ds - \int_{\theta=\theta_1}^{\pi} 2\pi y\, ds.$$

The minus sign is needed because $y < 0$ on the part of the limaçon from $\theta = \theta_1$ to π. And we stop at $\theta = \pi$ because the same surface is swept out a second time for $\pi \leq \theta \leq 2\pi$. The resulting surface area is approximately $830.393 + 29.868 = 860.261$.

49. Given: $r(\theta) = \cos(7\theta/3)$. To sweep out all seven "petals" of this quasi-rose, you need to let θ vary from 0 to 3π. The length of the graph is

$$\int_0^{3\pi} \sqrt{\tfrac{1}{9}(29 - 20\cos(14\theta/3))}\, d\theta \approx 16.3428.$$

50. The length of the graph of this curve is $\displaystyle\int_0^{2\pi} \sqrt{\cos^2 t + 4\cos^2 2t}\, dt \approx 9.42943$.

51. (a) When the curve of Problem 50 is rotated around the x-axis, the surface generated is swept out twice. We will rotate the part of the curve in the first quadrant around the x-axis and double the result to get the total surface area $\displaystyle 2\int_{t=0}^{\pi/2} 2\pi y\, ds \approx 16.0570$.

(b) To find the volume of revolution around the x-axis, we evaluate

$$2\int_0^{\pi/2} \pi[y(t)]^2 \cdot x'(t)\, dt = \int_0^{\pi/2} 4\pi(\sin^2 t \cos t - \sin^4 t \cos t)\, dt$$

$$= \left[4\pi\left(\tfrac{1}{3}\sin^3 t - \tfrac{1}{5}\sin^5 t\right)\right]_0^{\pi/2} = \tfrac{16}{15}\pi.$$

52. Now the curve of Problems 50 and 51 is to be rotated around the y-axis. We will use the same part of the curve (the part in the first quadrant) and double the answer.

(a) The surface area generated is

$$2\int_0^{\pi/2} 2\pi x(t)\sqrt{\cos^2 t + 4\cos^2 2t}\, dt \approx 17.7205.$$

Section 10.5 Integral Computations with Parametric Curves

(b) Using the method of cylindrical shells, the volume enclosed by that surface is

$$2\int_0^{\pi/2} 2\pi x(t)y(t)x'(t)\,dt = 4\pi \int_0^{\pi/2} 2\sin^2 t \cos^2 t\,dt$$
$$= 4\pi \int_0^{\pi/2} \tfrac{1}{2}(1-\cos^2 2t)\,dt = 2\pi \int_0^{\pi/2} \left(1 - \frac{1+\cos 4t}{2}\right) dt$$
$$= 2\pi \int_0^{\pi/2} \left(\tfrac{1}{2} - \tfrac{1}{2}\cos 4t\right) dt = 2\pi \left[\tfrac{1}{2}t - \tfrac{1}{8}\sin 4t\right]_0^{\pi/2} = \tfrac{1}{2}\pi^2.$$

53. The arc-length element is $ds = \sqrt{25\cos^2 5t + 9\sin^2 3t}\,dt$, and the entire Lissajous curve is obtain by letting t range from 0 to 2π. Hence the length of the graph is

$$\int_0^{2\pi} \sqrt{25\cos^2 5t + 9\sin^2 3t}\,dt \approx 24.603.$$

54. The length of the graph is $\int_0^{2\pi} \sqrt{464 - 320\cos 3t}\,dt \approx 130.743.$

Section 10.6

1. The value of p is 3, so the parabola has equation $y^2 = 12x$.

2. Here, $p = 2$, so the parabola has equation $x^2 = -8y$. It opens downward and its vertex is at the origin.

3. Here, $p = 2$, so the equation is $(x-2)^2 = -8(y-3)$.

4. The value of p is 2, so this parabola has equation $(y+1)^2 = -8(x+1)$. Its vertex is at the point $(-1,-1)$ and it opens to the left.

6. Here, $p = 1$, so the parabola has equation

$$(y-2)^2 = 4x.$$

Its graph is shown at the right.

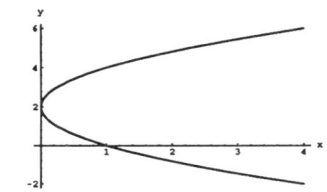

7. Here, we have $p = \tfrac{3}{2}$, so this parabola has equation $x^2 = -6\left(y + \tfrac{3}{2}\right)$.

8. In this problem we find that $p = 1$, so the equation of the parabola is
$$(y+1)^2 = -4(x-2).$$
Its graph is shown at the right.

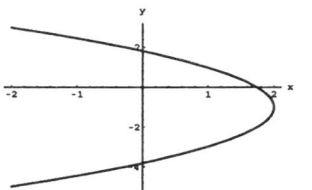

10. Here we have $p = 1$, so this parabola has equation
$$(y-1)^2 = 4(x+3)$$
and its graph is shown at the right.

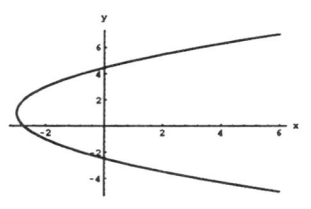

11. Given: $y^2 = (4)(3)(x)$. We see that $p = 3$, the vertex is at $V(0,0)$, the directrix is the line $x = -3$, the focus is $F(3,0)$, and the axis is the line $y = 0$.

12. Because $x^2 = -(4)(2)(y)$, we have $p = 2$. The parabola opens downward, its vertex is $V(0,0)$, its directrix is the line $y = 2$, its focus is $F(0,-2)$, and its axis is the y-axis.

14. Because $x^2 = (4)(\frac{7}{4})(y)$, $p = \frac{7}{4}$. This parabola opens upward, its vertex is at $(0,0)$, its directrix has equation $y = -\frac{7}{4}$, its focus is $(0, \frac{7}{4})$, and its axis is the y-axis.

16. The given equation may be written in the form
$$y^2 + 6y + 9 = 2x - 6;$$
$$(y+3)^2 = (4)(\tfrac{1}{2})(x-3).$$
So $p = \frac{1}{2}$; vertex $(3,-3)$; directrix $x = \frac{5}{2}$; focus at $(\frac{7}{2}, -3)$; axis the horizontal line $y = -3$. The graph is on the right.

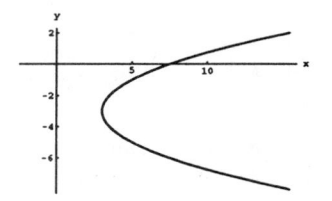

18. The given equation can be put in the form
$$\left(y - \tfrac{3}{2}\right)^2 = (-4)\left(\tfrac{9}{16}\right)(x-1).$$
Thus the vertex is $(1, \frac{3}{2})$, the directrix is $x = \frac{25}{16}$, the focus is $(\frac{7}{16}, \frac{3}{2})$, and the axis is $y = \frac{3}{2}$. The graph is shown at the right.

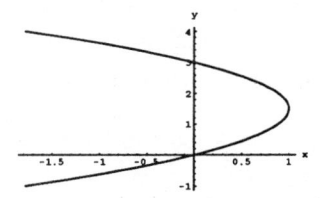

19. Note that this is a maximum-minimum problem, and recall that a distance is minimized when its square is minimized.

20. One method: Let (a, b) denote the vertex. From the data given in the problem, the parabola has equation
$$(x-a)^2 = -4p(y-b).$$
Moreover, its axis is the line $x = 3$, so that $a = 3$:
$$(x-3)^2 = -4p(y-b).$$
From the fact that both $(4,3)$ and $(6,-5)$ satisfy this last equation, we find that
$$1 = -4p(3-b) \quad \text{and} \quad 9 = -4p(-5-b).$$
These equations have the simultaneous solution $b = 4$, $p = \frac{1}{4}$. Therefore the equation of the parabola may be written in the form
$$(x-3)^2 = -(y-4);$$
if you prefer it in expanded form, $y + x^2 - 6x + 5 = 0$.

22. Set up coordinates so that the parabola has vertex $V(-p, 0)$. Then the equation of the comet's orbit is
$$y^2 = 4p(x+p).$$
The line $y = x$ meets the orbit of the comet at the point (a, b) (say), which is $100\sqrt{2}$ million miles from the origin (which is also where both the sun and the focus of the parabola are located). Therefore
$$a^2 = 4p(a+p) \quad \text{and} \quad \sqrt{a^2 + a^2} = \left(100\sqrt{2}\right)(10^6) = 10^8\sqrt{2}.$$
It follows that $a = 10^8$. Next, $a^2 = 4p(a+p)$. We apply the quadratic formula to find that $p = \frac{1}{2}(\sqrt{2} - 1)(10^8)$. The vertex is at distance p from the focus; therefore, by the result of Problem 19, the closest approach is approximately 20.71 million miles.

23. We continue the notation of the preceding solution. Solve the equation of the orbit for x:

$$x = \frac{1}{4p}y^2 - p.$$

The area A_3 swept out by the orbit in three days is then

$$A_3 = \tfrac{1}{2}(100)(100) - \int_{2p}^{100} \left(\frac{1}{4p}y^2 - p\right) dy.$$

It follows that

$$A_3 = 5000 - \frac{1}{12p}\left(10^6 - 8p^3\right) + 100p - 2p^2 \approx 2475.469.$$

The area of the "quarter-parabola" is $A_Q = \int_0^{2p} \left(p - \frac{1}{4p}y^2\right) dy$, and this is $\tfrac{4}{3}p^2 \approx 571.9096$. It now follows that the comet will reach its point of closest approach in roughly 0.693 more days; that is, in about 16 hrs 38 min.

26. $v_0 = 50$, $g = 9.8$, $\alpha = \pi/4$; Range: $\dfrac{(v_0)^2}{g}\sin 2\alpha = \dfrac{50^2}{9.8} \approx 255.1$ (meters).

    Maximum height: $\dfrac{(v_0 \sin\alpha)^2}{2g} = \dfrac{2500(0.5)}{2(9.8)} \approx 63.776$ (meters)

27. $\dfrac{(v_0)^2}{g}\sin 2\alpha = 125$: $\sin 2\alpha = \dfrac{125(9.8)}{50^2} = 0.49$; $\alpha \approx 14°40'13''$, $75°19'47''$.

28. (a) $\alpha = \pi/6$: Range: $\dfrac{2500}{9.8} \cdot \dfrac{\sqrt{3}}{2} \approx 220.9$ meters

    Time aloft: $T = \dfrac{2v_0 \sin\alpha}{3} = \dfrac{100(0.5)}{9.8} \approx 5.102$ seconds.

    (b) $\alpha = \pi/3$: Range: $\dfrac{2500}{9.8} \cdot \dfrac{\sqrt{3}}{2} \approx 220.9$ meters

    Time aloft: $T = \dfrac{100}{9.8} \cdot \dfrac{\sqrt{3}}{2} \approx 8.837$ seconds.

30. Consider the following figure:

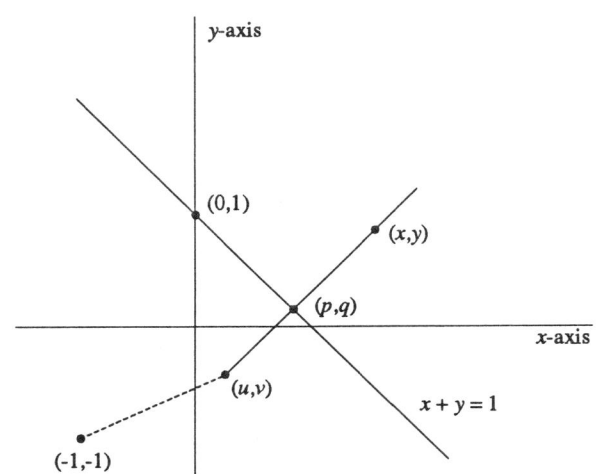

Let L be the line $x + y = 1$, let (u, v) be a point equidistant from the point $(-1, -1)$ and line L, and let M be the line through (u, v) that is perpendicular to line L. The distance from (u, v) to line L is the distance from (u, v) to the point of intersection of the lines L and M; call this point of intersection (p, q). The slope of L is -1, so the slope of M is $+1$.

First write p and q in terms of u and v: Because the slope of M is 1, $q - v = p - u$, and because the point (p, q) lies on line L, $p + q = 1$. So

$$1 - p - v = p - u;$$
$$p = \tfrac{1}{2}(1 + u - v) \text{ and } q = \tfrac{1}{2}(1 - u + v).$$

Now equate the distance between (u, v) and $(-1, -1)$ with the distance between (u, v) and (p, q):

$$(u + 1)^2 + (v + 1)^2 = (u - p)^2 + (v - q)^2$$
$$= \left(u + \frac{v - u - 1}{2}\right)^2 + \left(v + \frac{u - v - 1}{2}\right)^2.$$

Now, in order to write the equation of the curve in terms of x and y, replace (u, v) by (x, y), and expand:

$$4(x + 1)^2 + 4(y + 1)^2 = (2x + y - x - 1)^2 + (2y + x - y - 1)^2;$$
$$4x^2 + 8x + 4 + 4y^2 + 8y + 4 = 2(x^2 + 2xy + y^2 - 2x - 2y + 1);$$
$$2x^2 + 12x + 2y^2 + 12y - 4xy + 6 = 0;$$
$$x^2 - 2xy + y^2 + 6x + 6y + 3 = 0.$$

The coefficient of x is 6, so $D = 6$.

Section 10.7

1. The location of the vertices makes it clear that the center of the ellipse is at $(0, 0)$. Therefore its equation may be written in the standard form

$$\left(\frac{x}{4}\right)^2 + \left(\frac{y}{5}\right)^2 = 1.$$

2. Because $c = 5$ and $a = 13$, we find that $b = 12$; thus the equation is

$$\left(\frac{x}{13}\right)^2 + \left(\frac{y}{12}\right)^2 = 1.$$

4. We immediately have $a = 6$ and $b = 4$, so the equation is

$$\left(\frac{x}{4}\right)^2 + \left(\frac{y}{6}\right)^2 = 1.$$

5. Because $e = 0.75$ and $b^2 = a^2(1 - e^2) = a^2 - c^2$, it follows that $c = 3$. But $a = c/e$, so $a = 4$ and finally $b = \sqrt{7}$. So the equation is

$$\frac{x^2}{16} + \frac{y^2}{7} = 1.$$

6. We have $c = 4$ and $e = \tfrac{2}{3}$. So $a = c/e = 6$ and $b = \sqrt{a^2 - c^2} = 2\sqrt{5}$. Thus the equation of the ellipse is

$$\frac{x^2}{20} + \frac{y^2}{36} = 1.$$

7. First, $a = 10$ and $e = \frac{1}{2}$. So $c = ae = 5$ and thus $b^2 = 100 - 25 = 75$. So the equation is
$$\frac{x^2}{100} + \frac{y^2}{75} = 1.$$

8. We have $b = 5$ and $e = \frac{1}{2}$. Thus $a = 2c$; moreover, $a^2 = b^2 + c^2$. So $4c^2 = 25 + c^2$, and it follows that $c = \frac{5}{3}\sqrt{3}$ and $a = \frac{10}{3}\sqrt{3}$. Therefore the ellipse has equation
$$\frac{x^2}{25} + \frac{3y^2}{100} = 1.$$

9. From the information given in the problem, we see that $8 = a/e$ and $a = 2/e$. It follows that $e = \frac{1}{2}$, and so $a = 4$ and $c = 2$. Consequently $b^2 = 12$, and therefore the equation is
$$\frac{x^2}{16} + \frac{y^2}{12} = 1.$$

10. First, $c = 4$ and $9 = c/e^2$; therefore $e = \frac{2}{3}$. So $a = c/e = 6$; $b^2 = a^2 - c^2 = 20$. Equation:
$$\frac{x^2}{20} + \frac{y^2}{36} = 1.$$

11. Were the center at the origin, the equation would be $\frac{x^2}{16} + \frac{y^2}{4} = 1$. Because the center is at $C(2,3)$, the translation principle implies that the equation is in fact
$$\left(\frac{x-2}{4}\right)^2 + \left(\frac{y-3}{2}\right)^2 = 1.$$

12. First, $a = 4$ and $e = \frac{3}{4}$. So $c = ae = 3$ and $b^2 = a^2 - c^2 = 16 - 9 = 7$; therefore the ellipse has equation
$$\frac{(x-1)^2}{16} + \frac{(y+2)^2}{7} = 1.$$

13. "Move" the center first to the origin to obtain the equation $\frac{x^2}{25} + \frac{y^2}{16} = 1$. Then apply the translation principle to obtain the answer.

14. First we note that the center is $C(-3, 2)$. It follows that $b = 3$ and $c = 2$, so that $a^2 = 13$. Therefore the equation is
$$\frac{(x+3)^2}{9} + \frac{(y-2)^2}{13} = 1.$$

15. "Move" the center to the origin: This moves the foci to $(-3, 0)$ and $(3, 0)$. It's then easy to find that $a = c/e = 9$ and that $b^2 = a^2 - c^2 = 72$. So the equation of the ellipse is
$$\frac{(x-1)^2}{81} + \frac{(y-2)^2}{72} = 1.$$

16. In standard form, the equation of this ellipse is
$$\frac{x^2}{4} + \frac{y^2}{16} = 1.$$
So the major axis is vertical, $b = 2$, $a = 4$, the minor axis is of length 4, and the major axis is of length 8. The center is at the origin. Foci: $(0, -2\sqrt{3})$ and $(0, 2\sqrt{3})$. Its graph is shown at the right.

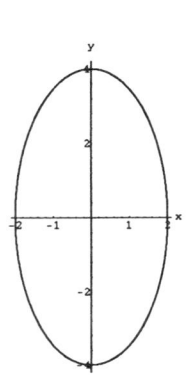

18. The equation can be written in the form
$$\frac{(x-3)^2}{9} + \frac{y^2}{4} = 1.$$
So this ellipse has a horizontal axis, its center is at the point $C(3,0)$, $a = 3$, $b = 2$, the major axis is of length 6 and the minor axis is of length 4; finally, $c^2 = 9 - 4 = 5$, so the foci are at $(3 - \sqrt{5}, 0)$ and $(3 + \sqrt{5}, 0)$. The graph is shown at the right.

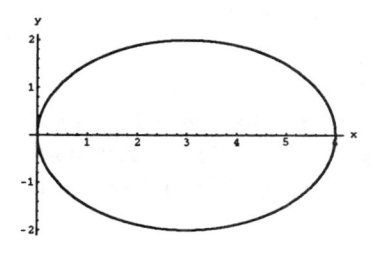

19. The equation can be put in the standard form $\left(\frac{x}{2}\right)^2 + \left(\frac{y-4}{3}\right)^2 = 1$. The rest is routine.

20. The standard form of the equation is
$$\frac{(x+3)^2}{3} + \frac{(y-4)^2}{2} = 1.$$
Therefore the axis is horizontal and the center is at $C(-3, 4)$. The parameters are $a = \sqrt{3}$, $b = \sqrt{2}$; so the major axis has length $2\sqrt{3}$ and the minor axis has length $2\sqrt{2}$. The foci are at $(-4, 4)$ and $(-2, 4)$. The graph is shown at the right.

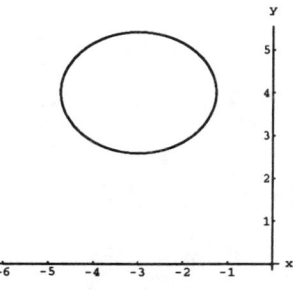

21. (a) In the usual notation, we have $e = 0.999925$ and $a - c = 0.13$ (A.U.). Now
$$b^2 = a^2 - c^2 = (a+c)(a-c), \text{ and } a = c/e.$$
It follows that
$$\frac{c}{e} - c = 0.13, \text{ and thereby that } c = (0.13)\frac{999925}{75} \approx 1733.203333.$$
Thus $a = c/e \approx 1733.246664$, and so $b \approx 12.25577415$. The maximum distance between Kahoutek and the sun is therefore $2a - 0.13 \approx 3466.363328$ (A.U.)—about 3466.36 A.U., about 322,000,000,000 miles, about 20 light-days.

22. In the usual notation, we have $2a = 0.467 + 0.307 = 0.774$. So $a = 0.387$, $e = 0.206$. Therefore $c = ae = 0.079722$, and
$$b = \sqrt{a^2 - c^2} \approx 0.378699621;$$
we'll use $b = 0.3787$. Therefore the ellipse has major axis 0.774, minor axis 0.7574; in terms of percentages, a is about 2.2% greater than b. Is this a nearly circular orbit? Decide for yourself: Compare the circle (on the left) below, with diameter 0.7657, with the ellipse (on the right) below with the shape of the orbit of the planet.

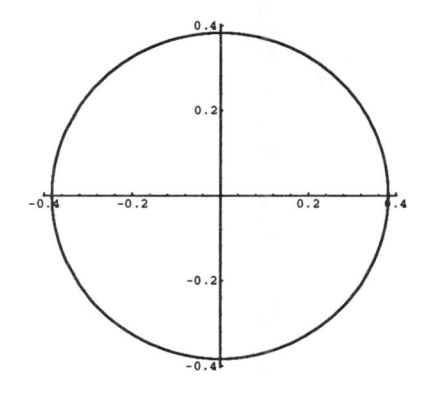

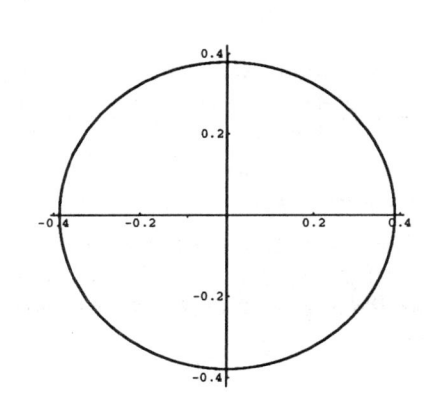

Section 10.7 The Ellipse

26. The equation $|PF_1| + |PF_2| = 2a$ becomes $\sqrt{(x+c)^2 + y^2} + \sqrt{(x-c)^2 + y^2} = 2a$. The rest is more-or-less routine, though tedious.

27. The location of the given points and the information about "horizontal and vertical axes" tells us that this ellipse must be centered at $(1,0)$. So first "move" the data: Assume that the ellipse passes through $(-2,0)$ and $(2,0)$ and also that it contains the points $(-1,2)$ and $(-1,-2)$. Let $(-c,0)$ and $(c,0)$ denote its foci. This ellipse has equation

$$\frac{x^2}{4} + \frac{y^2}{b^2} = 1,$$

and the distance formula yields $b^2 = \frac{16}{3}$. Now translate to the true center $(1,0)$ to obtain the answer.

28. Begin with the equation

$$\sqrt{(x-3)^2 + (y+3)^2} + \sqrt{(x+3)^2 + (y-3)^2} = 10.$$

This leads to the equation $16x^2 + 18xy + 16y^2 = 175$.

Section 10.8

1. It follows that $c = 4$, $a = 1$, and $b^2 = 15$. So the standard equation is

$$x^2 - \frac{1}{15}y^2 = 1.$$

2. The foci are $(0,-3)$ and $(0,3)$, the vertices are $(0,-2)$ and $(0,2)$. So $c = 3$, $a = 2$; $b^2 = c^2 - a^2 = 5$, so the equation is

$$\tfrac{1}{4}y^2 - \tfrac{1}{5}x^2 = 1.$$

3. From the information given, $c = 5$ and $b/a = 3/4$, so (because $a^2 + b^2 = c^2$) $a = 4$ and $b = 3$. Now the answer is clear.

4. First, $a = 3$, and $b/a = 3/4 = b/3$, so $b = 9/4$. So the equation of the hyperbola is

$$\tfrac{1}{9}x^2 - \tfrac{16}{81}y^2 = 1.$$

5. It may make the work simpler to begin by interchanging the information about x and y, then interchanging x and y as the final step. This method gives us vertices at $(-5,0)$ and $(5,0)$, and asymptotes $y = x$ and $y = -x$. So $a = 5$ and $b = a = 5$; $c = \sqrt{25 + 25} = 5\sqrt{2}$. This hyperbola would have equation $x^2/25 - y^2/25 = 1$; we interchange x and y to obtain the answer.

6. We see immediately that $a = 3$, that $x = ea = 5$; so $b = 4$ because $b^2 = c^2 - a^2 = 16$. Therefore the equation is

$$\tfrac{1}{9}x^2 - \tfrac{1}{16}y^2 = 1.$$

7. Let us interchange x and y in the data given in the problem, then restore their meanings with a second interchange at the last step. That is, we assume the foci to be at $(-6,0)$ and $(6,0)$, and that the eccentricity is $e = 2$. It follows that $c = 6$, and thus that $a = c/e = 3$. Thus $b^2 = c^2 - a^2 = 27$, and this hyperbola would have equation $x^2/9 - y^2/27 = 1$. Now we interchange x and y to obtain the correct answer.

8. Because $a = 4$, the equation must be of the form $\frac{1}{16}x^2 - \frac{1}{b^2}y^2 = 1$. Because $(8,3)$ lies on the hyperbola, $\frac{64}{16} - \frac{9}{b^2} = 1$, and it follows that $b^2 = 3$. Therefore the equation of this hyperbola is

$$\frac{x^2}{16} - \frac{y^2}{3} = 1.$$

9. First, $c = 4$; next, $4/e^2 = 1$, so $e = 2$. But $a/e = 1$, so $a = 2$. Finally, $b^2 = 12$. The answer is now easy to write.

10. We have $c = 9$; also, $4 = c/e^2$, so $e = 3/2$. Next, $a = c/e = 6$, so $b^2 = c^2 - a^2 = 45$. Hence the equation is
$$\frac{y^2}{36} - \frac{x^2}{45} = 1.$$

11. First "move" the data so that the center is at the origin. In order, we see that $a = 3$, $e = 2$, $c = 6$, and $b^2 = 27$. This hyperbola would have equation $x^2/9 - y^2/27 = 1$. But we translate to obtain the answer by replacing x with $x - 2$ and y with $y - 2$.

12. Move the center to the origin; this yields the new data to the effect that the vertices are at $(-3, 0)$ and $(3, 0)$, and that the foci are at $(-5, 0)$ and $(5, 0)$. It follows that $a = 3$, $c = 5$, and $b = 4$. Replace x with $x + 1$ and y with $y - 3$ to obtain the equation
$$\frac{(x+1)^2}{9} - \frac{(y-3)^2}{16} = 1.$$

13. We "move" the data so that the center is at $(0, 0)$: Replace x with $x - 1$ and y with $y + 2$. The translated hyperbola has vertices at $(0, 3)$ and $(0, -3)$ and asymptotes $3x = 2y$ and $3x = -2y$. Now let's interchange x and y. One asymptote then has equation $y = 2x/3$, so $b/a = 2/3$. But $a = 3$, so $b = 2$. The equation of this hyperbola is $x^2/9 - y^2/4 = 1$. But we must interchange x and y again and then replace y with $y + 2$ and x with $x - 1$; this gives the answer.

14. The center of the given hyperbola lies at the intersection of the asymptotes; their equation has the simulatneous solution $(3, -1)$. We translate the center to the origin; this moves the given focus to $(5, 0)$. The transverse axis is horizontal; also, $c = 5$. The equation of one of the translated asymptotes is $y = 3x/4$. Now $b/a = 3/4$, so $b = 3a/4$. But $c^2 = b^2 + a^2 = \frac{25}{16}a^2$, so $a = 4$; it follows that $b = 3$. We remember to correct for the earlier translation, thereby finding the equation of this hyperbola to be
$$\frac{(x-3)^2}{16} - \frac{(y+1)^2}{9} = 1.$$

15. The equation given can be written in the form $(x - 1)^2 - (y - 2)^2 = 1$.

16. Write $(x + 2)^2 - 2y^2 = 4$, thus $\dfrac{(x+2)^2}{4} - \dfrac{y^2}{2} = 1$. So $a = 2$, $b = \sqrt{2}$, and $c^2 = a^2 + b^2 = 6$. Therefore the center is at the point $(-2, 0)$, the foci are at $(-2 + \sqrt{6}, 0)$ and $(-2 - \sqrt{6}, 0)$, and the asymptotes have the equations
$$y = \left| \tfrac{1}{2}\sqrt{2}\,(x + 2) \right|.$$

The graph is shown at the right.

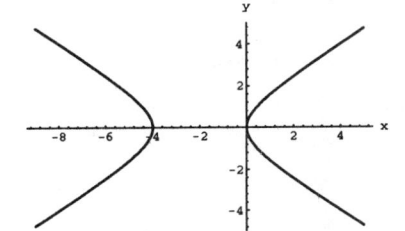

18. The given equation takes the alternative form
$$(x - 1)^2 - (y - 3)^2 = 1.$$

So $a = 1 = b$ and $x = \sqrt{2}$. The center is at $(1, 3)$ and the foci are at $(1 - \sqrt{2}, 3)$ and $(1 + \sqrt{2}, 3)$. The asymptotes have equations $y = 2 + x$ and $y = 4 - x$. The graph is shown at the right.

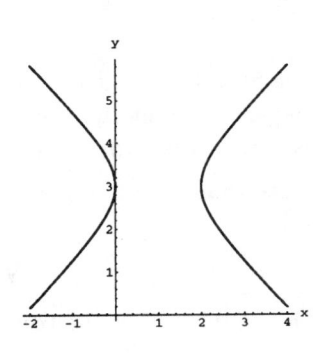

20. The given equation can be put into the form

$$4(y-1)^2 - 9(x+1)^2 = 36; \text{ that is,}$$

$$\left(\frac{y-1}{3}\right)^2 - \left(\frac{x+1}{2}\right)^2 = 1.$$

Hence $a = 3$ and $b = 2$; the transverse axis is vertical, and $c = \sqrt{13}$. The center is at $(-1,1)$, the foci are at $(-1, 1+\sqrt{13})$ and $(-1, 1-\sqrt{13})$. Finally, the asymptotes have equations

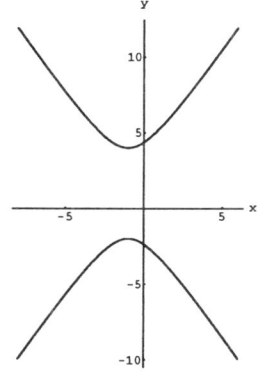

$$2y = 3x + 5, \qquad 2y = -3x - 1.$$

The graph is shown at the right.

22. First show that the equation of the tangent at $P_0(x_0, y_0)$ is

$$y - y_0 = \left(\frac{b^2 x_0}{a^2 y_0}\right)(x - x_0).$$

If $y_0 = 0$, use dx/dy rather than dy/dx to get the desired result.

24. We begin with $0 < a < c$ and $b = \sqrt{c^2 - a^2}$. Let $F_1 = F_1(-c, 0)$ and $F_2 = F_2(c, 0)$. Suppose that $P = P(x, y)$ satisfies the condition stated in the problem. Then the equation

$$|PF_1| - |PF_2| = 2a \text{ leads to}$$

$$\sqrt{(x+c)^2 + y^2} = 2a + \sqrt{(x-c)^2 + y^2}.$$

Square both sides of this equation:

$$4cx - 4a^2 = 4a\sqrt{(x-c)^2 + y^2}$$

is what you will obtain after simplification. Divide each side by 4 and square again; after further simplification, you'll have

$$c^2 x^2 - 2a^2 cx + a^4 = a^2 x^2 - 2a^2 cx + a^2 c^2 + a^2 y^2.$$

In succession, then, you can write

$$(c^2 - a^2) x^2 = a^2 (c^2 - a^2) + a^2 y^2;$$
$$b^2 x^2 = a^2 b^2 + a^2 y^2 \quad (\text{where } b^2 = a^2 - c^2);$$
$$b^2 x^2 - a^2 y^2 = a^2 b^2;$$
$$\frac{x^2}{a^2} - \frac{y^2}{b^2} = 1. \qquad (*)$$

We have the implicit assumption that $x > 0$, so $x \geq c$. So we have obtained the *right* branch of the hyperbola. But the equation $|PF_2| - |PF_1| = 2a$ yields the *left* branch, and so the locus of $P(x,y)$ is indeed the *entire* hyperbola with equation $(*)$.

25. Note that $a^2 = \frac{9}{2} + \frac{9}{2}$, so that $a = 3$; therefore $2a = 6$. Then

$$\sqrt{(x-5)^2 + (y-5)^2} + 6 = \sqrt{(x+5)^2 + (y+5)^2}.$$

Now apply either the technique or the formula of the solution of Problem 24.

26. Suppose that the plane is at $P(x,y)$, that A is at $(-50,0)$, and that B is at $(50,0)$. Let T_A and T_B denote the times for the signals from A and B (respectively) to reach the plane. Then $T_A - T_B = 400$. But
$$|PA| = 980T_A \quad \text{and} \quad |PB| = 980T_B,$$
so $|PA|/980 = 400 + |PB|/980$, and hence $|PA| - |PB| = (980)(400) = 392{,}000$ (ft). Now $b^2 = c^2 - a^2$, so (still in feet)
$$a = 196{,}000,$$
$$c = 264{,}000, \quad \text{and}$$
$$b = (4000)\sqrt{1955} \approx 176{,}861.53.$$
In miles, $a \approx 37.1212$, $b \approx 33.4965$, and $c = 50$. The hyperbola on which the plane must lie has approximate equation
$$\frac{x^2}{1377.984} - \frac{y^2}{1122.016} = 1.$$
Now the plane also lies on the line $y = 50$, so when this value is substituted into the equation of the hyperbola we find that
$$x^2 \approx 4448.317, \quad \text{so that} \quad x \approx 66.6957.$$
In our coordinate system, the plane is located approximately at the point $(66.6957, 50)$ (now we stay exclusively in miles). Thus the plane is 16.6957 miles *east* of B and 50 miles north of B; alternatively, it is about 52.7138 miles from B in the direction $18°27'54''$ east of north.

27. With the same coordinate system as in the previous solution, let $B = |AP|$ and $E = |BP|$, in feet. Then
$$\frac{D}{980} + \frac{E}{980} = 600 \quad \text{and} \quad \frac{D}{980} = \frac{E}{980} + 400.$$
Find D and E, observe in the process that $D = 5E$, and note that $P(x, y)$ satisfies both the equations $D = |AP|$ and $E = |BP|$. You should find that (in feet) $x \approx 218{,}272.73$.

Chapter 10 Miscellaneous

2. Circle, center $\left(\frac{1}{2}, \frac{1}{2}\right)$, radius $\frac{1}{2}\sqrt{2}$.

4. Given: $y^2 = 4(x + y)$. Thus $y^2 - 4y + 4 = 4x + 4 = 4(x + 1)$; it follows that
$$(y - 2)^2 = 4(x + 1).$$
So the graph is a parabola; it has directrix $x = -2$, axis $y = 2$, vertex at $(-1, 2)$, focus at $(0, 2)$, and it opens to the right.

6. The equation can be written in the form
$$(x - 1)^2 + 2(y + 2)^2 = 1,$$
and therefore the graph is an ellipse with center $(1, -2)$, major axis horizontal and of length 2, minor axis of length $\sqrt{2}$.

8. The equation can be written in the form
$$(y - 1)^2 - (x - 1)^2 = 1.$$
Therefore the graph is a hyperbola with center $(1, 1)$, foci at the points $\left(1, 1 - \sqrt{2}\right)$ and $\left(1, 1 + \sqrt{2}\right)$, vertices at $(1, 2)$ and $(1, 0)$, vertical transverse axis of length 2, horizontal conjugate axis of length 2, eccentricity $e = \sqrt{2}$, directrices $y = 1 + \frac{1}{2}\sqrt{2}$ and $y = 1 - \frac{1}{2}\sqrt{2}$, and asymptotes $y = x$ and $x + y = 2$.

10. The given equation can be written in the form
$$\frac{(y-1)^2}{4} - \frac{(x+1)^2}{9} = 1.$$
So the graph is a hyperbola with center $(-1,1)$. Because $c = \sqrt{13}$, the foci are at the points
$$\left(-1, 1+\sqrt{13}\right) \quad \text{and} \quad \left(-1, 1-\sqrt{13}\right).$$
The vertices are at $(-1, 3)$ and $(-1, -1)$. The transverse axis is vertical, of length 4, and the conjugate axis is horizontal, of length 6. The eccentricity is $\frac{1}{2}\sqrt{13}$, the directrices are
$$y = 1 + \tfrac{4}{13}\sqrt{13} \text{ and } y = 1 - \tfrac{4}{13}\sqrt{13},$$ 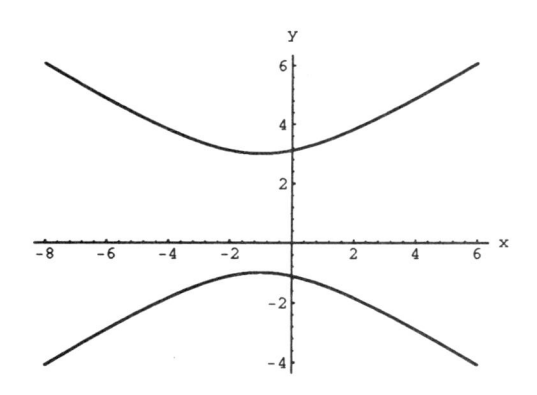
and the asymptotes have the equations $3y = 2x + 5$ and $3y = -2x + 1$. The graph is shown above.

12. After you complete the square to obtain $(y-3)^2 = -4(x+1)$, it is now clear that the graph is a parabola, opening to the left, with its vertex at $(1, 3)$.

13. The equation can be written in the form
$$\frac{(x-1)^2}{4} - \frac{y^2}{9} = 1,$$
so this is the equation of a hyperbola with center at $(1, 0)$ and horizontal transverse axis.

14. The graph consists of the two horizontal lines $y = \pm 1$ together with the two vertical lines $x = \pm 2$.

15. The equation can be written in the form $(x-4)^2 + (y-1)^2 = 1$; this is a circle with center $(4, 1)$ and radius 1.

16. This equation can be written in the form
$$\left(\frac{x-1}{2}\right)^2 + (y-2)^2 = 1,$$
so this is an equation of the ellipse with center $(1, 2)$, horizontal major axis of length 4, and vertical minor axis of length 2.

17. The given equation can be written in the form
$$\left((x-2)^2 + (y-2)^2\right) \cdot (x+y)^2 = 0.$$
Thus either $(x-2)^2 + (y-2)^2 = 0$ or $(x+y)^2 = 0$. In the former case, the only way for the sum of two squares to be zero is if each is zero, so $(x, y) = (2, 2)$ is the only point contributed to the graph by that factor. In the latter case, $y = -x$, so this straight line is also on the graph.

18. The graph of $x - 1 = (y+2)^2$ is a parabola opening to the right with vertex at $(1, -2)$.

20. Multiply each side by r to obtain the equation $y = -x$.

22. Multiply each side by r to obtain $y^2 = x$. This is the equation of a parabola with axis the x-axis, opening to the right, with vertex $(0, 0)$, directrix $x = -\frac{1}{4}$, and focus $(\frac{1}{4}, 0)$.

24. Given: $r = 2(\cos\theta - 1)$. Then
$$-\tfrac{1}{4}r = \tfrac{1}{2}(1 - \cos\theta) = \sin^2\left(\frac{\theta}{2}\right), \text{ so } r = -4\sin^2\left(\frac{\theta}{2}\right).$$
The graph is shown on the right.

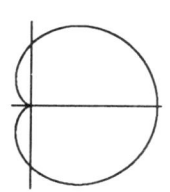

326   Chapter 10 Miscellaneous

26. Given: $r\theta = 1$; that is, $r = 1/\theta$. This is a spiral, and the part of the graph for $\theta > 0$ is shown on the right. The part of the graph for $\theta < 0$ is the reflection of that graph around the y-axis.

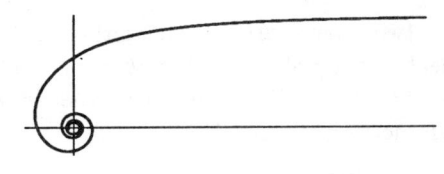

28. Given: $r = \dfrac{1}{1+\cos\theta}$. In Cartesian coordinates we obtain $y^2 = -2x + 1$, so it is a parabola with focus at $(0,0)$, directrix $x = 1$, and the vertex is at $(0, \frac{1}{2})$. It opens to the left and its axis is the x-axis.

30. Given: $r = \dfrac{4}{1-2\cos\theta}$. In Cartesian coordinates we obtain $y^2 = 3x^2 + 16x + 16$: a hyperbola with one focus at $(0,0)$ and one directrix the vertical line $x = -2$. Its center is $(-\frac{8}{3}, 0)$, the other focus is at $(-\frac{16}{3}, 0)$, the other directrix has equation $x = -\frac{10}{3}$, and the vertices are $(-\frac{4}{3}, 0)$ and $(-4, 0)$. The hyperbola has a horizontal transverse axis of length $\frac{8}{3}$.

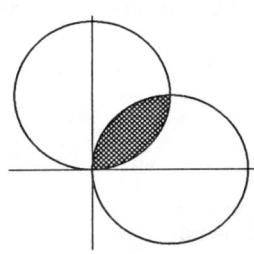

31. The region whose area is sought is shown at the right.

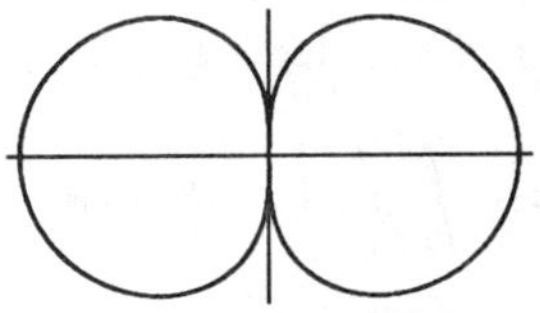

32. The graph of $r^2 = 4\cos\theta$ is shown on the right. By symmetry, its area is
$$A = \int_{-\pi/2}^{\pi/2} 4\cos\theta\, d\theta = 8.$$

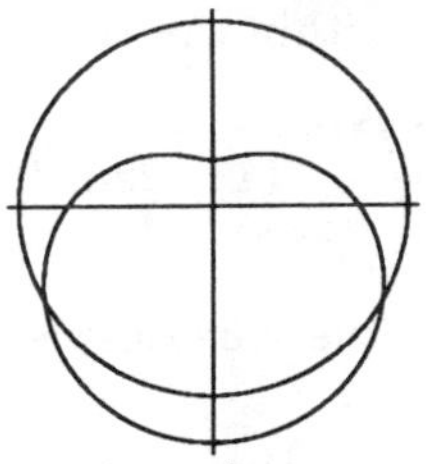

33. The two regions are shown on the right.

34. The two regions are shown at the right. The curves cross at the points where $\sin\theta = 0$ and where $\cos\theta = \sin\theta$. We obtain the two solutions $r = 0$ and $r = \sqrt{2}$, $\theta = \pi/4$. The area of the small region is
$$A_S = \tfrac{1}{2}\int_0^{\pi/4}\left((2\sin 2\theta) - (2\sin\theta)^2\right)d\theta,$$
which turns out to be $\frac{1}{4}(4 - \pi) \approx 0.214602$. The area of the large region is
$$A_L = \int_0^{\pi/2}\sin 2\theta\, d\theta = 1.$$
Therefore the total area outside the circle but within the lemniscate is $\frac{1}{4}(8-\pi) \approx 1.214602$.

35. The two curves are shown at the right. They meet where θ is an odd integral multiple of $\pi/8$.

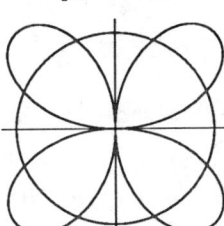

Chapter 10 Miscellaneous 327

36. The two curves are shown at the right. They meet at the pole and where $\theta = \pi/3$. The area outside the cardioid but within the circle is, by symmetry,

$$A = \int_0^{\pi/3} \left(9\cos^2\theta - (1+\cos\theta)^2\right) d\theta = \pi.$$

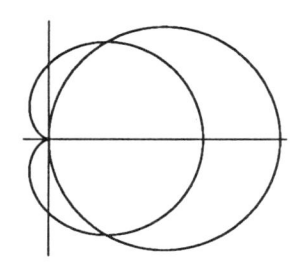

37. The circle and the cardioid are shown at the right. They intersect only at the pole.

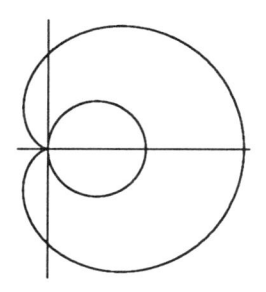

38. The graph of $r = 1 - 2\sin\theta$ is shown on the right. The curve passes through the pole when $\theta = \frac{1}{6}\pi$ and again when $\theta = \frac{5}{6}\pi$. The area within the smaller loop is

$$A_S = \tfrac{1}{2}\int_{\pi/6}^{5\pi/6} (1 - 2\sin\theta)^2 \, d\theta = \pi - \tfrac{3}{2}\sqrt{3}.$$

The area within the large loop is

$$A_L = \int_{-\pi/2}^{\pi/6} (1 - 2\sin\theta)^2 \, d\theta = 2\pi + \tfrac{3}{2}\sqrt{3}.$$

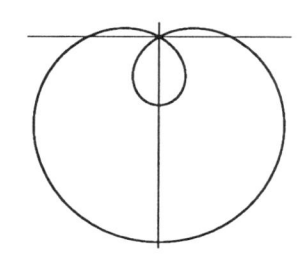

Therefore the area between the loops is exactly $\pi + 3\sqrt{3}$, which is approximately 8.337745.

40. $x^2 - y^2 = 1$: Hyperbola;

        center at $(0,0)$,
    vertices at $(-1,0)$ and $(1,0)$.

The graph is shown at the right.

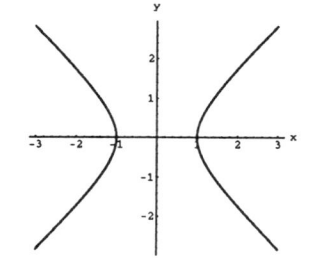

42. Note that neither x nor y is ever negative. So first we write

$$\sqrt{x} + \sqrt{y} = 1, \quad \text{then}$$
$$y = \left(1 - \sqrt{x}\right)^2, \quad 0 \leq x \leq 1.$$

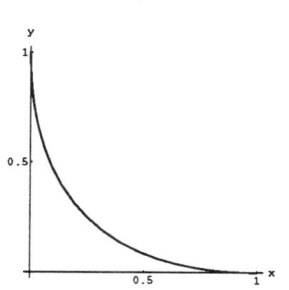

The graph is shown at the right.

44. $dy/dx = (dy/dt)/(dx/dt) = 3t^2/2t = 3t/2$. When $t = 1$, we have $x = 1$, $y = 1$, and $dy/dx = 3/2$. So an equation of the tangent line is $2y + 1 = 3x$.

46. $dy/dx = -e^{-t}/e^t = -e^{-2t}$. When $t = 0$, we have $x = 1$, $y = 1$, and $dy/dx = -1$. One equation of the tangent line is therefore $x + y = 2$.

48. $dr/d\theta = \cos\theta$. By the formula in Equation (9) of Section 12.1,
$$\frac{dy}{dx} = \frac{\cos\theta + 2\sin\theta\,\cos\theta}{\cos^2\theta - \sin^2\theta - \sin\theta}.$$

At $\theta = \pi/3$, $dy/dx = -1$. Also
$$x = r\cos\theta = \tfrac{1}{4}\left(2+\sqrt{3}\right) \quad \text{and} \quad r\sin\theta = \tfrac{1}{4}\left(3+2\sqrt{3}\right).$$

So an equation of the tangent line is $x + y = \tfrac{1}{4}\left(5 + 3\sqrt{3}\right)$.

50. $A = \displaystyle\int_{t=0}^{10} y\,dx = \int_0^{10} e^{-t}e^t\,dt = 10.$

52. $A = \displaystyle\int_0^1 \sinh^2 t\,dt = \frac{e^4 - 4e^2 - 1}{8e^2} \approx 0.4067151.$

54. $dx/dt = -\tan t$, $dy/dt = 1$. So $ds = \sqrt{1+\tan^2 t}\,dt = +\sec t\,dt$. Therefore
$$L = \int_0^{\pi/4} \sec t\,dt = \ln\left(1+\sqrt{2}\right).$$

56. $dr/d\theta = \cos\theta$; $ds = \sqrt{r^2 + (dr/d\theta)^2}\,d\theta = d\theta$. So $L = \displaystyle\int_0^\pi d\theta = \pi$.

58. $dx/dt = 2t$, $dy/dt = 3$. So $ds = \sqrt{9+4t^2}\,dt$.
$$A = \int_{t=0}^2 2\pi y\,ds = \int_0^2 (2\pi)(3t)\sqrt{9+4t^2}\,dt = \left[\left(\frac{3\pi}{4}\right)\left(\frac{2}{3}\right)(9+4t^2)^{3/2}\right]_0^2 = 49\pi.$$

60. $dr/d\theta = 4\sin\theta$; $y = r\sin\theta$. $ds = \sqrt{r^2 + (dr/d\theta)^2}\,d\theta = 4\,d\theta$. Therefore the surface area is
$$A = \int_0^{\pi/2}(2\pi)(4\sin\theta\,\cos\theta)(4)\,d\theta = 16\pi.$$

62. $dx/dt = e^t(\cos t - \sin t)$; $dy/dt = e^t(\sin t + \cos t)$. After simplification, $ds = \sqrt{2}\,e^t\,dt$. Therefore
$$A = \int_0^{\pi/2}(2\pi)(e^t\sin t)\left(\sqrt{2}e^t\right)dt = \tfrac{2}{5}\pi\sqrt{2}\left(1+2e^\pi\right) \approx 84.026264.$$

(Use Formula 67 of the endpapers to avoid a lengthy integration by parts.)

66. From $r^2 = 2a^2\cos 2\theta$ we find that $2r\dfrac{dr}{d\theta} = -4a^2\sin 2\theta$, and thus that $\dfrac{dr}{d\theta} = -\dfrac{1}{r}(2a^2\sin 2\theta)$. So
$$r^2 + \left(\frac{dr}{d\theta}\right)^2 = r^2 + \frac{4a^4\sin^2 2\theta}{r^2}$$
$$= \frac{r^4 + 4a^4\sin^2 2\theta}{r^2}$$
$$= \frac{4a^4\cos^2 2\theta + 4a^4\sin^2 2\theta}{r^2} = \frac{4a^4}{r^2}.$$

Therefore $ds = \dfrac{2a^2}{|r|}\,d\theta$.
$$A = 2\int_{\theta=0}^{\pi/4} 2\pi y\,ds = 4\pi\int_0^{\pi/4}\frac{2a^2}{r}\,y\,d\theta = 4\pi\int_0^{\pi/4}\frac{2a^2}{r}\,r\sin\theta\,d\theta = 4\pi a^2\left(2-\sqrt{2}\right).$$

68. First show that
$$\left(\frac{dx}{dt}\right)^2 + \left(\frac{dy}{dt}\right)^2 = 4(a-b)^2 \sin^2\left(\frac{at}{2b}\right).$$

Then show that
$$x^2 + y^2 = (a-b)^2 + b^2 + 2b(a-b)\cos\left(\frac{at}{b}\right).$$

Next show that $x^2 + y^2 = a^2$ when $\cos(at/b) = 1$; that is, when $t = 0$ and when $t = 2\pi b/a$ (these are "consecutive" in order to obtain correct limits of integration for one arch). Finally evaluate
$$L = \int_0^{2\pi b/a} 2(a-b)|\sin(at/2b)|\, dt$$
to obtain the result given in the text for the arc length.

69. If the point C were on the x-axis, then a Cartesian equation for the circle would be
$$(x-p)^2 + y^2 = p^2; \text{ that is, } x^2 - 2px + y^2 = 0.$$

In polar form, its equation could be written as
$$r^2 = 2px = 2pr\cos\theta; \text{ i.e., } r = 2p\cos\theta.$$

Because the radius to C makes the angle α with the x-axis, the actual equation we seek is therefore
$$r = 2p\cos(\theta - \alpha).$$

70. From the figure at the right, we see that matters would be greatly simplified if we were to rotate 45° counterclockwise to obtain the situation shown in the following figure. Then the parabola in the second figure has equation
$$r = \frac{2^{3/2}}{1 - \cos\theta}.$$

Therefore the parabola in the first figure has equation
$$r = \frac{2^{3/2}}{1 - \cos(\theta + (\pi/4))}.$$

After a considerable amount of algebra we find that we can write the Cartesian equation of the first parabola in the form
$$x^2 + 2xy + y^2 - 8x + 8y - 16 = 0.$$

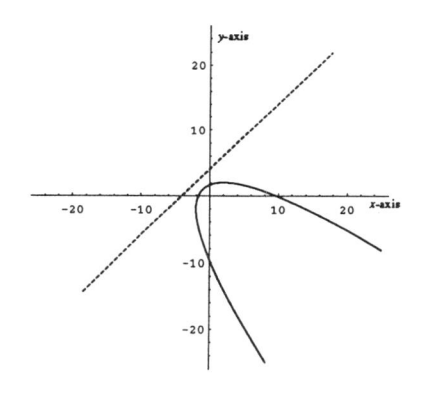

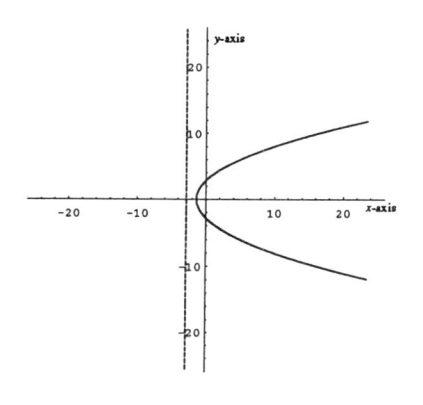

72. Use implicit differentiation.

74. As indicated by the figure at the right, we consider only the case in which $a > b$. Recall that

$$c^2 = a^2 - b^2.$$

(a) We are to maximize and minimize the expression $x^2 + y^2$ given the side condition $\dfrac{x^2}{a^2} + \dfrac{y^2}{b^2} = 1$. Now $y^2 = b^2\left(1 - \dfrac{x^2}{a^2}\right)$, so we consider

$$f(x) = x^2 + b^2 - \frac{b^2 x^2}{a^2}, \qquad -a \leq x \leq a.$$

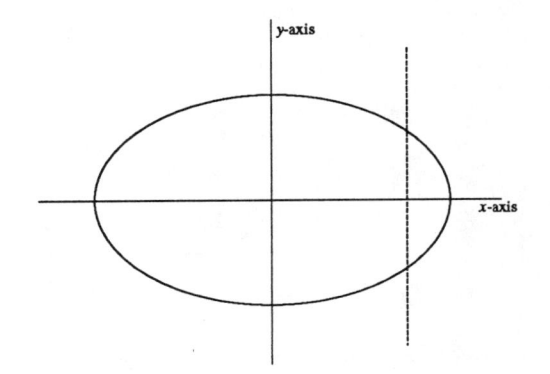

Then $f'(x) = 2x\left(1 - \dfrac{b^2}{a^2}\right)$. It is clear that $f'(x) = 0$ when $x = 0$; the other critical points occur when $x = -a$ and $x = a$. It follows immediately that the farthest points are $(a, 0)$ and $(-a, 0)$ and that the nearest are $(0, b)$ and $(0, -b)$.

(b) Introduce a vertical v-axis through $x = c$. Write the polar equation of the ellipse in the xv-coordinate system:

$$r = \frac{pe}{1 + e\cos\theta}, \qquad 0 < e < 1.$$

It's clear that r is minimized when $1 + e\cos\theta$ is maximized; that is, when $\theta = 0$. Also $\theta = \pi$ maximizes r. Therefore the point nearest $(c, 0)$ is $(a, 0)$ and the point farthest from $(c, 0)$ is $(-a, 0)$.

75. *Suggestion:* Use the figure below, and let θ be the angle that the segment QR makes with the x-axis. Write Q and R in terms of a, b, and θ, then write x and y in terms of those variables where $P(x, y)$ is a typical point on the locus.

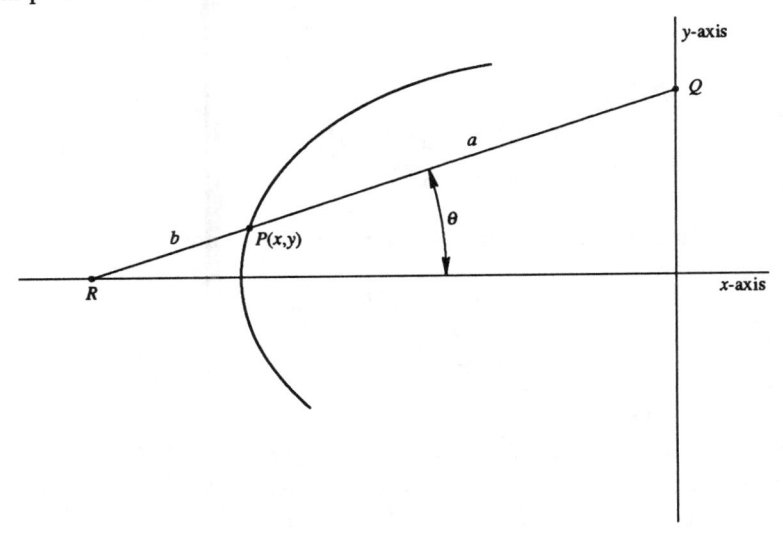

Chapter 10 Miscellaneous 331

76. We use the figure below. Note that we introduce a uv-coordinate system; in the rest of this discussion, all coordinates will be uv-coordinates.

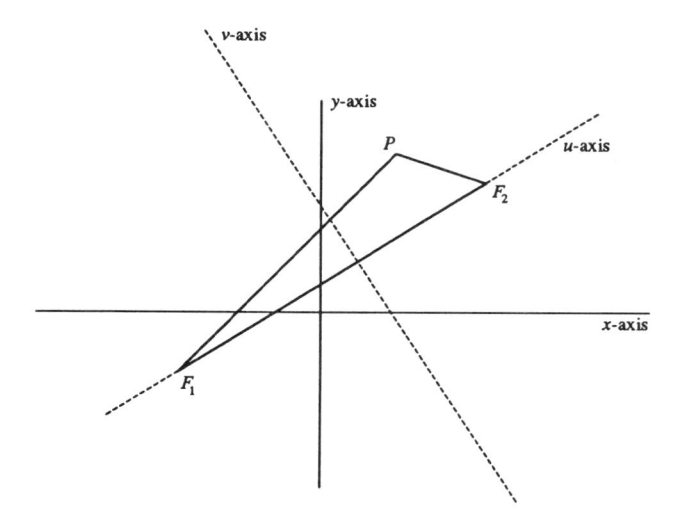

Choose the new axes so that $F_1 = F_1(c, 0)$ and $F_2 = F_2(-c, 0)$, $c > 0$. Suppose that $P = P(u, v)$. Then

$$|PF_2| = 2a + |PF_1|,$$

and therefore

$$\sqrt{(u+c)^2 + v^2} = 2a + \sqrt{(u-c)^2 + v^2}.$$

Consequently

$$(u+c)^2 + v^2 = 4a^2 + 4a\sqrt{(u-c)^2 + v^2} + (u-c)^2 + v^2.$$

Successive simplifications produce

$$4uc - 4a^2 = 4a\sqrt{(u-c)^2 + v^2};$$
$$uc - a^2 = a\sqrt{(u-c)^2 + v^2};$$
$$u^2c^2 - 2a^2uc + a^4 = a^2u^2 - 2a^2uc + a^2c^2 + a^2v^2;$$
$$u^2c^2 - a^2u^2 - a^2v^2 = a^2c^2 - a^4;$$
$$u^2(c^2 - a^2) - a^2v^2 = a^2(c^2 - a^2).$$

Now $|F_1 F_2| > 2a$, so $c > a$. Thus $c^2 - a^2 = b^2$ for some $b > 0$. Hence

$$b^2 u^2 - a^2 v^2 = a^2 b^2; \text{ that is,}$$
$$\frac{u^2}{a^2} - \frac{v^2}{b^2} = 1.$$

Therefore the locus of $P(u, v)$ is a hyperbola with vertices $(a, 0)$ and $(-a, 0)$ and foci $(c, 0)$ and $(-c, 0)$ (because $c^2 = a^2 + b^2$), and therefore the hyperbola has foci F_1 and F_2. Finally, if a circle with radius r_2 is centered at F_2 and another with radius r_1 is centered at F_1, with r_2 and r_1 satisfying the equation $r_2 = 2a + r_1$, then the two circles will intersect at a point on the hyperbola. You may thereby construct by straightedge-and-compass methods as many points lying on the hyperbola as you please.

78. Let $P = P(x,y)$; we have $F_1(-a, 0)$, $F_2(a, 0)$, and $|PF_1|\,|PF_2| = a^2$. Then

$$\sqrt{(x+a)^2 + y^2}\sqrt{(x-a)^2 + y^2} = a^2.$$

It follows after considerable algebraic simplification that

$$(x^2 + y^2)^2 = 2a^2(x^2 - y^2).$$

In polar coordinates,

$$r^4 = 2a^2 r^2 (\cos^2\theta - \sin^2\theta), \text{ and so}$$
$$r^2 = 2a^2 \cos 2\theta.$$

This is the equation of a lemniscate; its graph is exactly the same—for the choice of scale for which $a = \sqrt{2}$—as the one shown in the figure accompanying the solution to Problem 46 of Section 10.2.

79. The equation may be written in the form

$$(x+2)^2 - \tfrac{1}{3}y^2 = 1,$$

so the graph is a hyperbola with a vertical directrix. In the notation at the beginning of Section 10.8, we have $a = 1$ and $b = \sqrt{3}$, so $c^2 = a^2 + b^2 = 4$, and therefore $c = 2$. The eccentricity is then $e = c/a = 2$.

80. When $r = 0$, $\sec\theta = 2\cos\theta$, so $|\theta| = \pi/4$. The loop of the strophoid is obtained when θ ranges between these two values, so the area of the loop is (by symmetry)

$$A = \int_0^{\pi/4} (\sec^2\theta - 4\cos\theta\sec\theta + 4\cos^2\theta)\,d\theta = \Big[\tan\theta - 2\theta + \sin 2\theta\Big]_0^{\pi/4} = \frac{4-\pi}{2}.$$

81. The polar equation takes the form

$$r = \frac{3\sin\theta\,\cos\theta}{\sin^3\theta + \cos^3\theta}.$$

To obtain the area A described in the problem, we evaluate

$$A = \tfrac{1}{2}\int_0^{\pi/2} r^2\,d\theta = 9\int_0^{\pi/4} \frac{\sec^2\theta\,\tan^2\theta}{(1+\tan^3\theta)^2}\,d\theta.$$

The substitution $u = \tan\theta$ transforms this integral into

$$A = 3\int_0^1 \frac{3u^2}{(1+u^3)^2}\,du = \tfrac{3}{2}.$$

82. Here, the loop has polar equation

$$r = \frac{5\cos^2\theta\,\sin^2\theta}{\cos^5\theta + \sin^5\theta} \quad\text{for}\quad 0 \le \theta \le \pi/2.$$

Therefore the area it bounds is

$$A = 25\int_0^{\pi/4} \frac{\cos^4\theta\,\sin^4\theta}{(\cos^5\theta + \sin^5\theta)^2}\,d\theta.$$

The substitution $u = \tan\theta$ transforms this integral into
$$A = 25\int_0^1 \frac{u^4}{(1+u^5)^2}\,du = \tfrac{5}{2}.$$

83. The equation of the conic can be written
$$x^2 + Bxy + Cy^2 + Dx + Ey + F = 0.$$

So $25 + 5D + F = 0$,
$25 - 5D + F = 0$. So $D = 0$ and $F = -25$.

Also $16C + 4E + F = 0$,
$16C - 4E + F = 0$. So $E = 0$ and $F = -16C$.

So $16C = 25$: $C = \tfrac{25}{16}$. The equation of the conic is thus
$$x^2 + Bxy + \tfrac{25}{16}y^2 - 25 = 0;$$
$$16x^2 + 16By + 25y^2 = 400.$$

The discriminant is $256B^2 - 1600 = 64(4B^2 - 25)$.

If $B < \tfrac{5}{2}$, the conic is an ellipse.

If $B = \tfrac{5}{2}$, the conic has equation $16x^2 + 40y + 25y^2 = 400$;
$(4x + 5y)^2 = 400$;
$4x + 5y = \pm 20$;
$y = -\tfrac{4}{5}x \pm 20$: two parallel lines.

If $B < \tfrac{5}{2}$, the conic is a hyperbola.

Chapter 11: Infinite Series
Section 11.2

2. $a_n = 5n - 3$

4. $a_n = \dfrac{(-1)^{n+1}}{2^n}$

6. $a_n = \dfrac{1}{n^2 + 1}$

8. $a_n = 5 \cdot \left(1 + \dfrac{1 - (-1)^n}{2}\right)$

9. $a_n = \dfrac{2n}{5n - 3} = \dfrac{2}{5 - \dfrac{3}{n}} \to \dfrac{2}{5}$ as $n \to +\infty$.

10. $\lim\limits_{n \to \infty} \dfrac{(1/n^2) - 1}{(2/n^2) + 3} = -\dfrac{1}{3}$.

11. Divide each term in numerator and denominator by n^3.

12. $\lim\limits_{n \to \infty} \dfrac{n}{10 + (1/n^2)}$ does not exist.

13. Show that if $|x| < 1$, then $x^n \to 0$ as $n \to +\infty$.

14. $\lim\limits_{n \to \infty} \left(2 - \left(-\tfrac{1}{2}\right)^n\right) = 2 - \lim\limits_{n \to \infty} \left(-\tfrac{1}{2}\right)^n = 2 - 0 = 2$.

16. $0 \leq 1 + (-1)^n \leq 2$ for all n, so $0 \leq \dfrac{1 + (-1)^n}{\sqrt{n}} \leq \dfrac{2}{\sqrt{n}}$ for all n. So by the squeeze law, the limit is 0.

18. $-1 \leq \sin n \leq 1$ for all n, so by the squeeze law, $\lim\limits_{n \to \infty} \dfrac{\sin n}{3^n} = 0$.

20. $1 \leq 2 + \cos n \leq 3$ for all n, so $\sqrt{1/n} \leq a_n \leq \sqrt{3/n}$ for all n. So by the squeeze law,
$$\lim_{n \to \infty} \sqrt{\dfrac{2 + \cos n}{n}} = 0.$$

22. $a_n = n \cos \pi n = n$ if n is even, $-n$ if n is odd. Because $\{a_n\}$ has no upper bound (and no lower bound), it therefore diverges.

24. $\tfrac{1}{2}, 2, \tfrac{1}{2}, 2, \ldots$ diverges.

26. $a_n = \dfrac{(\ln 2/\ln n) + 1}{(\ln 3/\ln n) + 1} \to 1$ as $n \to \infty$.

28. Let $x = 1/n$. Then $\lim\limits_{n \to \infty} a_n = \lim\limits_{x \to 0^+} \dfrac{\sin x}{x} = 1$.

30. Apply l'Hôpital's rule thrice to $\lim\limits_{x \to \infty} \dfrac{x^3}{e^{x/10}}$ to get the limit 0.

32. $a_n = \dfrac{1 - e^{-2n}}{1 + e^{-2n}} \to 1$ as $n \to \infty$.

34. $\ln a_n = \dfrac{1}{n} \ln(2n + 5)$ and $\lim\limits_{x \to \infty} \dfrac{1}{x} \ln(2x + 5) = 0$. Therefore $\lim\limits_{n \to \infty} a_n = e^0 = 1$.

35. Use the method of solution of Problem 26.

36. $\ln a_n = -\dfrac{1}{n} \ln(0.001) = \dfrac{1}{n} \ln(1000) \to 0$ as $n \to \infty$.

37. Use the method of solution of Problem 26.

38. $\ln a_n = n \ln \left(1 - \dfrac{2}{n^2}\right)$. Replace n with x, then apply l'Hôpital's rule to obtain the limit zero. Therefore $\{a_n\}$ has limit 1.

39. $\ln a_n = \dfrac{3}{n}\ln\left(\dfrac{2}{n}\right) = \dfrac{3(\ln 2 - \ln n)}{n} \to 0.$

40. $\lim\limits_{x\to\infty} \ln\left((x^2+1)^{1/x}\right) = \lim\limits_{x\to\infty} \dfrac{\ln(x^2+1)}{x} = \lim\limits_{x\to\infty} \dfrac{2x}{x^2+1} = 0.$ Therefore $\lim\limits_{n\to\infty} (n^2+1)^{1/n} = 1$, and therefore $\lim\limits_{n\to\infty} (-1)^n (n^2+1)^{1/n}$ does not exist.

41. Write $a_n = (-1)^n \left(\dfrac{n^2-2}{n^2+3}\right)^n$; use the technique of solution of Problem 32.

42. $\lim\limits_{n\to\infty} a_n = \lim\limits_{x\to\infty} \dfrac{(2/3)^x}{1 - x^{1/x}} = \lim\limits_{x\to\infty} \dfrac{x^2 (2/3)^x \ln(2/3)}{((\ln x) - 1) x^{1/x}}$ by l'Hôpital's rule. And

$$\lim\limits_{x\to\infty} x^2 (2/3)^x = \lim\limits_{x\to\infty} \dfrac{x^2}{(3/2)^x} = \lim\limits_{x\to\infty} \dfrac{2x}{(3/2)^x \ln(3/2)} = \lim\limits_{x\to\infty} \dfrac{2}{(3/2)^x (\ln(3/2))^2} = 0.$$

Thus
$$\lim\limits_{x\to\infty} \dfrac{x^2 (2/3)^x \ln(2/3)}{((\ln x) - 1) x^{1/x}} = 0,$$

and therefore $\lim\limits_{n\to\infty} \dfrac{(2/3)^n}{1 - n^{1/n}} = 0$.

43. $\lim\limits_{n\to\infty} \dfrac{n-2}{n+13} = \lim\limits_{n\to\infty} \dfrac{1 - \dfrac{2}{n}}{1 + \dfrac{13}{n}} = \dfrac{\left(\lim\limits_{n\to\infty} 1\right) - 2\cdot\left(\lim\limits_{n\to\infty} \dfrac{1}{n}\right)}{\left(\lim\limits_{n\to\infty} 1\right) + 13\cdot\left(\lim\limits_{n\to\infty} \dfrac{1}{n}\right)} = \dfrac{1 - 2\cdot 0}{1 + 13\cdot 0} = 1.$

44. $\lim\limits_{n\to\infty} \dfrac{2n+3}{5n-17} = \tfrac{2}{5}.$

46. The limit is

$$\lim\limits_{n\to\infty}\left(\dfrac{n^3-5}{8n^3+7n}\right)^{1/3} = \left(\lim\limits_{n\to\infty}\dfrac{n^3-5}{8n^3+7n}\right)^{1/3}$$

$$= \left(\lim\limits_{n\to\infty}\dfrac{1 - \dfrac{5}{n^3}}{8 + \dfrac{7}{n^2}}\right)^{1/3} = \left(\dfrac{\left(\lim\limits_{n\to\infty} 1\right) - 5\cdot\left(\lim\limits_{n\to\infty}\dfrac{1}{n^3}\right)}{\left(\lim\limits_{n\to\infty} 8\right) + 7\cdot\left(\lim\limits_{n\to\infty}\dfrac{1}{n^2}\right)}\right)^{1/3}$$

$$= \left(\dfrac{1 - 5\cdot 0}{8 + 7\cdot 0}\right)^{1/3} = \left(\tfrac{1}{8}\right)^{1/3} = \tfrac{1}{2}.$$

47. Because $\lim\limits_{n\to\infty} -\dfrac{1}{\sqrt{n}} = 0$ and because $f(x) = e^x$ is continuous at $x=0$, the value of the limit is $f(0) = 1$.

48. Let $x = 1/n$. Then $x \to 0^+$ as $n \to +\infty$. So

$$\lim\limits_{n\to\infty} n\sin\dfrac{2}{n} = \lim\limits_{x\to 0^+} \dfrac{\sin 2x}{x} = \lim\limits_{x\to 0^+} \dfrac{2\cos 2x}{1}$$

by l'Hôpital's rule. Hence the limit is 2.

49. Because $\lim\limits_{n\to\infty} \dfrac{n-1}{n+1} = 1$, and because $f(x) = 4\arctan x$ is continuous at $x = 1$, the limit is $4\arctan 1 = \pi$.

50. Because $\lim\limits_{n\to\infty} \dfrac{3n-1}{4n+1} = \tfrac{3}{4}$, and because $f(x) = 3\sin^{-1}\sqrt{x}$ is continuous at $x = \tfrac{3}{4}$, the limit is $f\left(\tfrac{3}{4}\right) = \pi$.

51. Without loss of generality, suppose that $A > 0$. Let $\epsilon = A/2$. Then there exists a positive integer N such that, if $n \geq N$, then $|a_n - A| < \epsilon$. That is, if $n \geq N$ then
$$\frac{A}{2} < a_n < \frac{3A}{2}.$$
Thus for every odd integer $n \geq N$,
$$-\frac{3A}{2} < (-1)^n a_n < -\frac{A}{2}$$
and for every even integer $n \geq N$,
$$\frac{A}{2} < (-1)^n a_n < \frac{3A}{2}.$$
Any number L that aspires to be the limit of the sequence $\{(-1)^n a_n\}$ must, therefore, lie in both the intervals $(-3A/2, -A/2)$ and $(A/2, 3A/2)$—but these two intervals have no points in common, so no such number L can exist. Therefore $\{(-1)^n a_n\}$ diverges.

52. To say that
$$\lim_{n \to \infty} a_n = +\infty$$
means that, for every interval of the form $(c, +\infty)$, there exists a positive integer N such that, if $n \geq N$, then a_n is in the interval $(c, +\infty)$. If $\{a_n\}$ is an unbounded increasing sequence, then, no matter how large the number c, $a_k > c$ for some integer k. But then $a_n > c$ for all $n \geq k$, so that a_n is in the interval $(c, +\infty)$ for all $n \geq k$. This is what $\lim_{n \to \infty} a_n = +\infty$ means.

53. If L exists, then $L = \frac{1}{2} \cdot \left(L + \frac{A}{L}\right)$. Now express L in terms of A.

54. See the hint in the previous problem.

55. (b) $G_1 = G_2 = G_3 = 1$ and $G_{n+1} = G_n + G_{n-2}$ for $n \geq 3$. The first few terms of the sequence are
$$1, 1, 1, 2, 3, 4, 6, 9, 13, 19, 28, 41, 60, 88, 129, 189, 277, 406, 595, \text{ and } 872.$$

57. (a) Clearly $a_1 < 4$. Suppose that $a_k < 4$ for some integer $k \geq 1$. Then
$$a_{k+1} = \tfrac{1}{2}(a_k + 4) < \tfrac{1}{2}(4 + 4) < 4.$$
Therefore, by induction, $a_n < 4$ for all integers $n \geq 1$. Next, $a_2 = 3$, so $a_1 < a_2$. Suppose that $a_k < a_{k+1}$ for some integer $k \geq 1$. Then
$$a_k + 4 < a_{k+1} + 4;$$
$$\tfrac{1}{2}(a_k + 4) < \tfrac{1}{2}(a_{k+1} + 4);$$
$$a_{k+1} < a_{k+2}.$$
Therefore, by induction, $a_n < a_{n+1}$ for all integers $n \geq 1$.

(b) The limit is 4.

58. Much as in Example 13, you can show that $\{a_n\}$ is a bounded (by 2) increasing sequence, and therefore converges to [say] L. Then, again as in Example 13,
$$L = \lim_{n \to \infty} a_{n+1} = \lim_{n \to \infty} \sqrt{2 + a_n} = \sqrt{2 + L}.$$
Hence $L^2 = L + 2$, and it follows that $L = -1$ or $L = 2$. It is clear that $L > 0$, and therefore $a_n \to 2$ as $n \to \infty$.

Section 11.3

1. Geometric, ratio $\frac{1}{3}$, first term 1; sum $\frac{1}{1-\frac{1}{3}} = \frac{3}{2}$.

2. Geometric, ratio $\frac{1}{e}$, sum $\frac{e}{e-1}$.

4. $\lim_{n \to \infty} (0.5)^{1/n} = 1 \neq 0$: This series diverges by the nth-term test.

6. Geometric, ratio $-\frac{1}{4}$, sum $\frac{4}{5}$.

7. Geometric, ratio $\frac{1}{3}$.

8. Geometric, ratio $\frac{2}{3}$, sum 1.

10. $\lim_{x \to \infty} x^{1/x} = 1 \neq 0$. This series diverges by the nth-term test.

12. Geometric, ratio $\frac{e}{10}$, sum $\frac{e}{10-e}$.

13. Geometric, ratio $r = -\frac{3}{e}$. The series diverges because $|r| > 1$.

14. $\sum_{n=0}^{\infty} \left(\frac{3}{4}\right)^n = 4$, $\sum_{n=0}^{\infty} \left(\frac{2}{4}\right)^n = 2$. Therefore $\sum_{n=0}^{\infty} \frac{3^n - 2^n}{4^n} = 4 - 2 = 2$.

16. $\sum_{n=0}^{\infty} \frac{1}{2^n} = 1$. So $\sum_{n=1}^{k} \left(\frac{2}{n} - \frac{1}{2^n}\right) > \left(\sum_{n=1}^{k} \frac{2}{n}\right) - 1$ for all positive integers k.

    Because the harmonic series diverges to $+\infty$, so does $\sum_{n=1}^{\infty} \frac{2}{n}$, and therefore so does the given series.

18. $\lim_{x \to \infty} \frac{x^{1/2}}{\ln(x+1)} = +\infty$ by l'Hôpital's rule. Therefore the given series diverges by the nth-term test.

19. $\frac{\frac{1}{5}}{1-\frac{1}{5}} - \frac{\frac{1}{7}}{1-\frac{1}{7}} = \frac{1}{4} - \frac{1}{6} = \frac{1}{12}$.

20. $\left(\frac{9}{10}\right)^n \to 0$ as $n \to +\infty$, so the given series diverges by the nth-term test.

22. The series is geometric with ratio $r = \frac{\pi}{e}$, and it diverges because $|r| > 1$.

24. Geometric, ratio $\frac{99}{100}$, first term 1: sum 100.

26. Diverges.

28. Diverges by the nth-term test ($2^{1/n} \to 1$ as $n \to +\infty$).

30. The series diverges by the nth-term test for divergence, because $\lim_{n \to \infty} \frac{2n}{\sqrt{4n^2+3}} = 1 \neq 0$.

31. The series diverges by the nth-term test for divergence, because $\lim_{n \to \infty} \frac{n^2-1}{3n^2+1} = \frac{1}{3} \neq 0$.

32. This is a geometric series with first term sin 1 and ratio sin 1; the latter is approximately 0.841470985, so the series converges to $\frac{\sin 1}{1 - \sin 1} \approx 5.3079935164$.

33. This is a geometric series with nonzero first term and ratio tan 1; the latter is approximately $1.5574077 > 1$, so this series diverges.

34. This is a geometric series with nonzero first term and ratio arcsin 1; the latter is approximately $1.5707963 > 1$, so this series diverges.

35. This is a geometric series with first term arctan 1 and ratio arctan $1 = \frac{\pi}{4} < 1$, so this series converges to $\frac{\pi}{4-\pi} \approx 3.6597923663$.

36. This series diverges by the nth-term test for divergence, because $\lim_{n \to \infty} \arctan n = \frac{\pi}{2} \neq 0$.

40. $0.252525\ldots = \frac{1}{4}\left(1 + 10^{-2} + 10^{-4} + 10^{-6} + \ldots\right) = \frac{1}{4}\left(\frac{1}{1 - \frac{1}{100}}\right) = \frac{25}{99}$.

42. $\frac{307}{909}$

44. This series is geometric with ratio $2x$, so it converges if $|2x| < 1$; that is, if $-\frac{1}{2} < x < \frac{1}{2}$. For such values of x, its sum is $2x/(1 - 2x)$.

45. This series is geometric with ratio $x/3$, so it converges if $|x/3| < 1$; that is, if $-3 < x < 3$. For such x, its sum is $x/(3 - x)$.

46. This series is geometric with ratio $x - 1$, so it converges if $|x - 1| < 1$; that is, if $0 < x < 2$. For such x, its sum is $(x - 1)/(2 - x)$.

47. This series is geometric with ratio $(x - 2)/3$, so it converges if $|x - 2| < 3$; that is, if $-1 < x < 5$. For such x, its sum is $(x - 2)/(5 - x)$.

48. This series is geometric with ratio $x^2/(x^2 + 1)$. Because $0 \leq \frac{x^2}{x^2 + 1} < 1$ for all [real numbers] x, this series converges for all x. Its sum is x^2.

49. This series is geometric with ratio $5x^2/(x^2 + 16)$, so it converges if $5x^2/(x^2 + 16) < 1$; that is, if $-2 < x < 2$. For such x, its sum is $5x^2/(16 - 4x^2)$.

50. The nth partial sum is $S_n = \frac{1}{2} - \frac{1}{4n + 2}$, which approaches $\frac{1}{2}$ as $n \to +\infty$.

52. The nth partial sum is $\ln(n + 1)$, which approaches $+\infty$ as $n \to +\infty$. So this series diverges to $+\infty$.

54. The nth partial sum is $S_n = \frac{3}{4} - \frac{1}{2n + 2} - \frac{1}{2n + 4}$, which approaches $\frac{3}{4}$ as $n \to +\infty$.

56. The nth partial sum is $S_n = 1 - \frac{1}{(n+1)^2}$, which approaches 1 as $n \to +\infty$.

58. The nth partial sum is $\frac{1}{2} - \frac{1}{n+1} + \frac{1}{n+2}$, which approaches $\frac{1}{2}$ as $n \to +\infty$.

60. The nth partial sum is $\frac{3}{4} - \frac{1}{n-1} + \frac{1}{n+2}$, which approaches $\frac{3}{4}$ as $n \to +\infty$.

62. If $\sum (a_n + b_n)$ were a convergent series, then—because $\sum a_n$ is convergent—the series

$$\sum (a_n + b_n - a_n) = \sum b_n$$

would also converge, contrary to hypothesis.

64. Total distance traveled:

$$D = a + 2ra + 2r^2 a + 2r^3 a + 2r^4 a + \ldots$$
$$= -a + 2a\left(1 + r + r^2 + r^3 + r^4 + \ldots\right)$$
$$= -a + \frac{2a}{1 - r} = \frac{-a + ar + 2a}{1 - r} = a\frac{1 + r}{1 - r}.$$

65. $T = \sqrt{\frac{2h}{g}} + 2\left(\sqrt{\frac{2rh}{g}} + \sqrt{\frac{2r^2 h}{g}} + \sqrt{\frac{2r^3 h}{g}} + \ldots\right)$

$= \sqrt{\frac{2h}{g}} + 2\sqrt{\frac{2h}{g}}\left(r^{1/2} + r + r^{3/2} + r^2 + \ldots\right)$

$= \sqrt{\frac{2h}{g}}\left(1 + 2\frac{r^{1/2}}{1 - r^{1/2}}\right)$

$= \sqrt{\frac{2h}{g}} \frac{1 + r^{1/2}}{1 - r^{1/2}}.$

Now take $h = a = 4$, $g = 32$, and $r = 0.64$ to get $T = 4.5$ seconds.

66. $1 + 0.9 + (0.9)^2 + (0.9)^3 + \ldots = 10$ (billion dollars).

67. $M_1 = (0.95) M_0$, $M_2 = (0.95) M_1 = (0.95)^2 M_0$, and so on. Therefore $M_n = (0.95)^n M_0$.

68. Suppose that Mary tosses first. Here are her winning patterns and their respective probabilities:

    | H | $\frac{1}{2}$ |
    | T T H | $\frac{1}{2^3}$ |
    | T T T T H | $\frac{1}{2^5}$ |
    | T T T T T T H | $\frac{1}{2^7}$ |
    | $\vdots$ | $\vdots$ |

    Evidently Mary's probability of winning the game is the sum of the probabilities in the right-hand column. This sum is a geometric series with first term 0.5 and ratio 0.25, therefore its sum is $\frac{2}{3}$.

69. Peter's probability of winning is the sum of:

    The probability he wins in the first round;

    The probability that everyone tosses tails on the first round and Peter wins in the second round;

    The probability that everyone tosses tails on the first two rounds and Peter wins in the third round;

    ....

    Thus his probability of winning is $\frac{1}{2} + \frac{1}{2^4} + \frac{1}{2^7} + \frac{1}{2^{10}} + \cdots = \frac{4}{7}$.

    Similarly, the probability that Paul wins is $\frac{2}{7}$ and the probability that Mary wins is $\frac{1}{7}$.

70. Let X denote 1, 2, 3, 4, or 5. Peter (who goes first) has these winning patterns and their probabilities:

    | 6 | $\frac{1}{6}$ |
    | X X X 6 | $\frac{5^3}{6^4}$ |
    | X X X X X 6 | $\frac{5^6}{6^7}$ |
    | X X X X X X X X 6 | $\frac{5^9}{6^{10}}$ |
    | $\vdots$ | $\vdots$ |

    So his probability of winning the game is the sum of the geometric series with first term $\frac{1}{6}$ and ratio $\frac{125}{216}$, and so his probability of winning the game is $\frac{36}{91} \approx 0.3956$. Paul (who is second) wins with probability $\frac{30}{91} \approx 0.3297$ and Mary wins with probability $\frac{25}{91} \approx 0.2747$.

71. The amount of light transmitted is

    $$\frac{I}{2^4} + \frac{I}{2^6} + \frac{I}{2^8} + \frac{I}{2^{10}} + \cdots,$$

    and is therefore $\frac{I}{12}$, or $\frac{1}{12}$ of the incident light.

Section 11.4

2. $\sin x = \dfrac{x}{1!} - \dfrac{x^3}{3!} + \dfrac{x^5}{5!}\cos z$ for some z between 0 and x.

4. $\dfrac{1}{1-x} = 1 + x + x^2 + x^3 + x^4 + \dfrac{x^5}{(1-z)^6}$ for some z between 0 and x.

6. $\ln(1+x) = x - \dfrac{1}{2}x^2 + \dfrac{1}{3}x^3 - \dfrac{1}{4}x^4 + \dfrac{x^5}{5(1+z)^5}$ for some z between 0 and x.

8. $\arctan x = x + \dfrac{6z^2 - 2}{3!\,(1+z^2)^3}x^3$ for some z between 0 and x.

10. $f(x) = -7 + 5x - 3x^2 + x^3$.

12. $\cos x = \dfrac{1}{2}\sqrt{2} - \dfrac{\sqrt{2}}{1!\,2}\left(x - \dfrac{\pi}{4}\right) - \dfrac{\sqrt{2}}{2!\,2}\left(x - \dfrac{\pi}{4}\right)^2 + \dfrac{\sqrt{2}}{3!\,2}\left(x - \dfrac{\pi}{4}\right)^3 + \dfrac{1}{4!}\left(x - \dfrac{\pi}{4}\right)^4 \cos z$

for some z between $\pi/4$ and x.

14. $\sqrt{x} = 10 + \dfrac{x - 100}{1!\,20} - \dfrac{(x-100)^2}{2!\,4000} + \dfrac{3(x-100)^3}{3!\,800{,}000} - \dfrac{15}{4!\,16 z^{7/2}}(x - 100)^4$

for some z between 0 and x.

16. $\tan x = 1 + \dfrac{2}{1!}\left(x - \dfrac{\pi}{4}\right) + \dfrac{4}{2!}\left(x - \dfrac{\pi}{4}\right)^2 + \dfrac{16}{3!}\left(x - \dfrac{\pi}{4}\right)^3 + \dfrac{80}{4!}\left(x - \dfrac{\pi}{4}\right)^4 + \dfrac{Q(z)}{5!}\left(x - \dfrac{\pi}{4}\right)^5$

for some z between $\pi/4$ and x, where $Q(z) = 16\sec^6 z + 88\sec^4 z \tan^2 z + 16\sec^2 z \tan^4 z$.

18. $\sin x = 1 - \dfrac{1}{2}\left(x - \dfrac{\pi}{2}\right)^2 + \dfrac{1}{24}\left(x - \dfrac{\pi}{2}\right)^4 + \dfrac{\cos z}{5!}\left(x - \dfrac{\pi}{2}\right)^5$ for some z between $\pi/2$ and x.

20. $\dfrac{1}{\sqrt{1-x}} = 1 + \dfrac{1}{2}x + \dfrac{3}{8}x^2 + \dfrac{5}{16}x^3 + \dfrac{35}{128}x^4 - \dfrac{945}{2^5\,5!\,(1-z)^{11/2}}x^5$ for some z between 0 and x.

21. $1 - x + \dfrac{1}{2!}x^2 - \dfrac{1}{3!}x^3 + \dfrac{1}{4!}x^4 - \cdots$

22. $1 + 2x + \dfrac{1}{2!}4x^2 + \dfrac{1}{3!}8x^3 + \dfrac{1}{3!}16x^4 + \cdots$

23. $1 - 3x + \dfrac{1}{2!}9x^2 - \dfrac{1}{3!}27x^3 + \dfrac{1}{4!}81x^4 - \cdots$

24. $1 + x^3 + \dfrac{1}{2!}x^6 + \dfrac{1}{3!}x^9 + \dfrac{1}{4!}x^{12} + \cdots$

25. $\sin 2x = 2x - \dfrac{(2x)^3}{3!} + \dfrac{(2x)^5}{5!} - \dfrac{(2x)^7}{7!} + \dfrac{(2x)^9}{9!} - \cdots$

$= \displaystyle\sum_{n=0}^{\infty} \dfrac{(-1)^n 2^{2n+1} x^{2n+1}}{(2n+1)!} = 2x - \dfrac{4x^3}{3} + \dfrac{4x^5}{15} - \dfrac{8x^7}{315} + \dfrac{4x^9}{2835} - \cdots$.

26. $\dfrac{1}{2}x - \dfrac{1}{3!\,2^3}x^3 + \dfrac{1}{5!\,2^5}x^5 - \dfrac{1}{7!\,2^7}x^7 + \cdots$

27. $x^2 - \dfrac{1}{3!}x^6 + \dfrac{1}{5!}x^{10} - \dfrac{1}{7!}x^{14} + \dfrac{1}{9!}x^{18} - \cdots$

28. $\sin^2 x = \tfrac{1}{2}(1 - \cos 2x)$

$= \tfrac{1}{2}\left(1 - \left[1 - \dfrac{x^2}{2!} + \dfrac{x^4}{4!} - \dfrac{x^6}{6!} + \cdots\right]\right)$

$= \dfrac{x^2}{2!\,2} - \dfrac{x^4}{4!\,2} + \dfrac{x^6}{6!\,2} - \dfrac{x^8}{8!\,2} + \cdots = \displaystyle\sum_{n=0}^{\infty} \dfrac{(-1)^n x^{2n+2}}{(2n+2)!\,2}$.

29.

n	$f^{(n)}(x)$	$f^{(n)}(0)$
0	$\ln(1+x)$	0
1	$(1+x)^{-1}$	1
2	$-(1+x)^{-2}$	-1
3	$2(1+x)^{-3}$	2
4	$-6(1+x)^{-4}$	-6
5	$24(1+x)^{-5}$	$4!$
6	$-120(1+x)^{-6}$	$-(5!)$
7	$720(1+x)^{-7}$	$6!$
$\vdots$	$\vdots$	$\vdots$

Answer: $x - \frac{1}{2}x^2 + \frac{1}{3}x^3 - \frac{1}{4}x^4 + \frac{1}{5}x^5 - \ldots$

30. $1 + x + x^2 + x^3 + x^4 + x^5 + \ldots$

32. $1 - \frac{1}{2!}\left(x - \frac{\pi}{2}\right)^2 + \frac{1}{4!}\left(x - \frac{\pi}{2}\right)^4 - \frac{1}{6!}\left(x - \frac{\pi}{2}\right)^6 + \ldots$

34. $1 + \frac{2x}{1!} + \frac{4x^2}{2!} + \frac{8x^3}{3!} + \frac{16x^4}{4!} + \ldots$

36. $1 + 2x + 3x^2 + 4x^3 + 5x^4 + 6x^5 + \ldots$

38. $-\left(x - \frac{\pi}{2}\right) + \frac{1}{3!}\left(x - \frac{\pi}{2}\right)^3 - \frac{1}{5!}\left(x - \frac{\pi}{2}\right)^5 + \ldots$

40.

n	$f^{(n)}(x)$	$f^{(n)}(0)$
0	$(1+x)^{1/2}$	1
1	$\frac{1}{2}(1+x)^{-1/2}$	$\frac{1}{2}$
2	$-\frac{1}{4}(1+x)^{-3/2}$	$-\frac{1}{4}$
3	$\frac{3}{8}(1+x)^{-5/2}$	$\frac{3}{8}$
4	$-\frac{(5)(3)}{2^4}(1+x)^{-7/2}$	$\frac{15}{16}$
$\vdots$	$\vdots$	$\vdots$

For large n, then, $f^{(n)}(0) = \dfrac{(2n-3)(2n-5)\cdots(5)(3)(1)}{2^n}(-1)^{n+1}$ and the answer is

$$1 + \frac{1}{1!\,2^1}x - \frac{1}{2!\,2^2}x^2 + \frac{3}{3!\,2^3}x^3 - \frac{5\cdot 3}{4!\,2^4}x^4 + \ldots \;.$$

45. Here is a plot of e^{-x} and its Taylor polynomials, center zero, of degrees 3, 5, and 7.

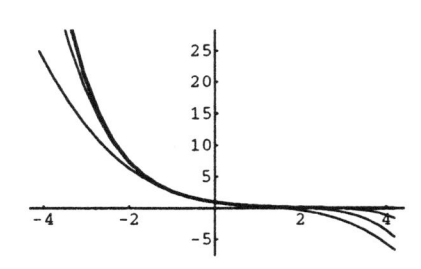

46. Here is a plot of $\sin x$ and its Taylor polynomials, center zero, of degrees 3, 5, and 7.

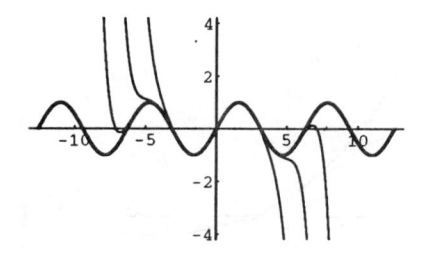

47. Here is a plot of $\cos x$ and its Taylor polynomials, center zero, of degrees 3, 4, and 5.

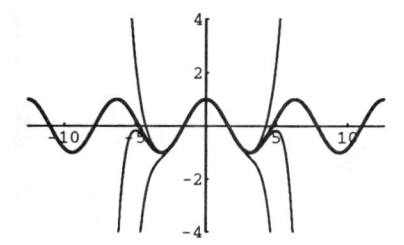

48. Here is a plot of $\ln(1+x)$ and its Taylor polynomials, center zero, of degrees 3, 4, and 5.

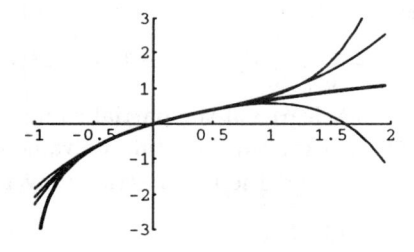

49. Here is a plot of $1/(1+x)$ and its Taylor polynomials, center zero, of degrees 2, 3, and 4.

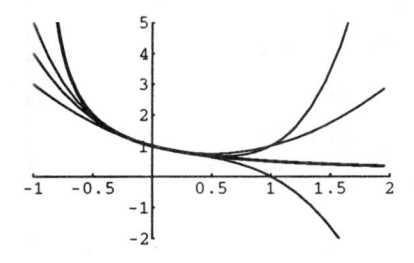

50. Here is a plot of $1/(1-x^2)$ and its Taylor polynomials, center zero, of degrees 2, 3, and 4.

Section 11.4 Taylor Series and Taylor Polynomials

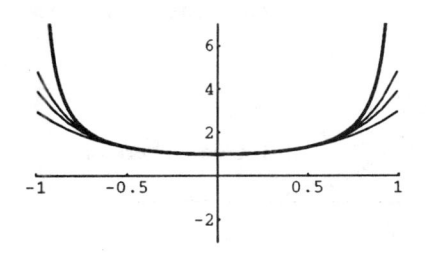

51. Here is a plot of $g(x)$ and the partial sums of the series for $f(x)$ of degrees 1, 2, and 3.

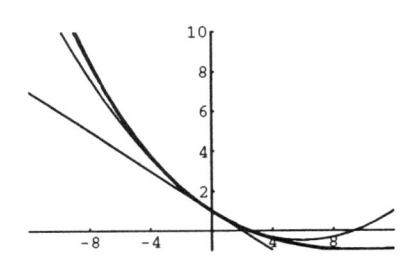

52. Given: $\alpha = \tan^{-1}(1/5)$.

   (a) $\tan 2\alpha = \dfrac{\frac{1}{5}+\frac{1}{5}}{1-\frac{1}{25}} = \frac{5}{12}$.

   (b) $\tan 4\alpha = \dfrac{\frac{5}{12}+\frac{5}{12}}{1-\frac{25}{144}} = \frac{120}{119}$.

   (c) $\tan\left(\dfrac{\pi}{4} - 4\alpha\right) = \dfrac{1-\frac{120}{119}}{1+\frac{120}{119}} = -\frac{1}{239}$.

   (d) $\tan\left(\dfrac{\pi}{4} - 4\alpha\right) = -\frac{1}{239}$:

   $\dfrac{\pi}{4} - 4\alpha = -\arctan\frac{1}{239}$;

   $4\arctan\frac{1}{5} - \arctan\frac{1}{239} = \dfrac{\pi}{4}$.

57. $\cos(-x) = 1 - \dfrac{1}{2!}(-x)^2 + \dfrac{1}{4!}(-x)^4 - \dfrac{1}{6!}(-x)^6 + \ldots = 1 - \dfrac{1}{2!}x^2 + \dfrac{1}{4!}x^4 - \dfrac{1}{6!}x^6 + \ldots = \cos x$.

59. The first column of the table gives the degree of the partial sum, the second column its value using the Maclaurin series of Problem 56, and the third column its value using the Maclaurin series of the second series of Problem 58. It is clear that the latter series converges much more rapidly to $\ln 2$.

5	0.783333333	0.693146047
10	0.645634921	0.693147181
15	0.725371850	0.693147181
20	0.668771403	0.693147181
25	0.712747500	0.693147181
30	0.676758138	0.693147181

Section 11.5

1. $\displaystyle\int_0^\infty \dfrac{x}{x^2+1}\,dx = \left[\tfrac{1}{2}\ln(x^2+1)\right]_0^\infty = +\infty$. Therefore the given series diverges.

2. $\displaystyle\int_0^\infty xe^{-x^2}\,dx = \left[-\tfrac{1}{2}e^{-x^2}\right]_0^\infty = \tfrac{1}{2} < \infty$. Therefore the given series converges.

3. $\displaystyle\int_0^\infty (x+1)^{-1/2}\,dx = \left[2\sqrt{x+1}\right]_0^\infty = +\infty$.

4. $\displaystyle\int_0^\infty (x+1)^{-4/3}\,dx = \left[-3(x+1)^{-1/3}\right]_0^\infty = 3 < \infty$. Therefore the given series converges.

5. $\displaystyle\int_0^\infty \dfrac{1}{x^2+1}\,dx = \left[\arctan x\right]_0^\infty = \dfrac{\pi}{2}$.

6. $\int_1^\infty \frac{1}{x(x+1)} dx = \ln 2 < \infty$, so the series converges.

7. $\int_2^\infty \frac{1}{x \ln x} dx = \Big[\ln(\ln x)\Big]_2^\infty = +\infty$.

8. $\int_1^\infty \frac{\ln x}{x} dx = +\infty$, and so the given series diverges.

9. $\int_0^\infty 2^{-x} dx = \left[\frac{1}{2^x \ln 2}\right]_0^\infty = \frac{1}{\ln 2}$.

10. $\int_0^\infty xe^{-x} dx = 1 < \infty$, so the given series converges.

12. $\int_1^\infty \frac{1}{17x - 13} dx = +\infty$, so the given series diverges.

13. $\int_1^\infty \frac{\ln x}{x^2} dx = \left[-\frac{1}{x}(1 + \ln x)\right]_1^\infty = 1$. (Integrate by parts; use l'Hôpital's rule to get the limit.)

14. $\int_1^\infty \frac{x+1}{x^2} dx = +\infty$, so the given series diverges.

16. $\int_1^\infty \frac{dx}{x^3 + x} = \int_1^\infty \left(\frac{1}{x} - \frac{x}{x^2+1}\right) dx = \Big[(\ln x) - \tfrac{1}{2}\ln(x^2+1)\Big]_1^\infty = \tfrac{1}{2}\left[\ln \frac{x^2}{x^2+1}\right]_1^\infty = \tfrac{1}{2}\ln 2 < \infty$,
and therefore the given series converges.

18. $\int_1^\infty \ln\left(\frac{x+1}{x}\right) dx = \Big[(x+1)\ln(x+1) - x \ln x\Big]_1^\infty = \left[\ln \frac{(x+1)^{x+1}}{x^x}\right]_1^\infty$.

    Now $\frac{(x+1)^{x+1}}{x^x} = (x+1)\left(\frac{x+1}{x}\right)^x = (x+1)\left(1 + \frac{1}{x}\right)^x$. Because $\left(1 + \frac{1}{x}\right)^x \to e$ as $x \to +\infty$,
    $\lim_{x \to \infty} \frac{(x+1)^{x+1}}{x^x} = +\infty$. Therefore the given series diverges.

19. Let $J = \int_1^\infty \ln\left(1 + \frac{1}{x^2}\right) dx$. Integrate by parts: With $u = \ln(1 + x^{-2})$ and $dv = dx$, we find that

    $$J = \Big[x \ln(1 + x^{-2})\Big]_1^\infty + 2\int_1^\infty \frac{dx}{1+x^2}$$
    $$= \lim_{x \to \infty} \frac{\ln(1 + x^{-2})}{1/x} - \ln 2 + \Big[2\tan^{-1} x\Big]_1^\infty$$
    $$= \left(\lim_{u \to 0^+} \frac{\ln(1+u^2)}{u}\right) + \pi - \frac{\pi}{2} - \ln 2 = \frac{\pi}{2} - \ln 2 < \infty,$$

    so the series converges.

20. $\int_1^\infty \frac{2^{1/x}}{x^2} dx = \frac{1}{\ln 2} < \infty$, so the series converges.

22. $\int_1^\infty \frac{x}{(4x^2+5)^{3/2}} dx = \left[-\frac{1}{4\sqrt{4x^2+5}}\right]_1^\infty < \infty$. Therefore the given series converges.

24. $\int_2^\infty \frac{1}{x}(\ln x)^{-2} dx = \left[-\frac{1}{\ln x}\right]_2^\infty = \frac{1}{\ln 2}$. Therefore the given series converges.

26. $\int_1^\infty \frac{x+1}{x+100} dx = \int_1^\infty \left(1 - \frac{99}{x+100}\right) dx = \Big[x - 99\ln(x+100)\Big]_1^\infty = +\infty$ because, by l'Hôpital's
    rule, $\lim_{x \to \infty} \frac{x}{99\ln(x+100)} = \lim_{x \to \infty} \frac{x+100}{99}$. So the given series diverges.

28. $\int_1^\infty (x+1)^{-3} dx = \left[-\tfrac{1}{2}(x+1)^{-2}\right]_1^\infty = \tfrac{1}{8} < \infty$. Therefore the given series converges.

Section 11.5 The Integral Test   345

29. The series converges because $\int_1^\infty \dfrac{\arctan x}{x^2+1}\,dx = \left[\tfrac{1}{2}(\arctan x)^2\right]_1^\infty = \tfrac{3}{32}\pi^2 < \infty$.

30. The series diverges because $\int_3^\infty \dfrac{1}{x(\ln x)(\ln(\ln x))}\,dx = \left[\ln(\ln(\ln x))\right]_3^\infty = +\infty$.

32. This is not a positive term series; $\sin n$ is negative for infinitely many positive integral values of n. (Exercise: Prove this assertion.). After you study absolute convergence, you will see how to apply the integral test to prove that this series does indeed converge.

34. The terms of the series are not monotonically decreasing. For example, the third term is about 4.9×10^{-6} but the fourth term is about 1.3×10^{-3}.

36. Because
$$\int \frac{x}{(x^2+1)^p}\,dx = -\frac{1}{2(p-1)(x^2+1)^{p-1}} + C$$
if $p \neq 1$ and
$$\int \frac{x}{x^2+1}\,dx = \tfrac{1}{2}\ln(x^2+1) + C,$$
the given series converges exactly when $p > 1$.

38. Because
$$\int \frac{1}{x(\ln x)(\ln(\ln x))^p}\,dx = -\frac{1}{(p-1)(\ln(\ln x))^{p-1}} + C$$
and
$$\int \frac{1}{x(\ln x)(\ln(\ln x))}\,dx = \ln(\ln(\ln x)) + C,$$
this series converges exactly when $p > 1$.

39. We require $R_n < 0.0001$. This will hold provided that
$$\int_n^\infty \frac{1}{x^2}\,dx < 0.0001$$
because R_n cannot exceed the integral. So we require
$$\left[-\frac{1}{x}\right]_n^\infty < 0.0001;$$
that is, that $n > 10000$.

40. $n = 100$.

42. We require $R_n < (2)(10^{-11})$. This will hold provided that
$$\int_n^\infty \frac{1}{x^6}\,dx < (2)(10^{-11})$$
because R_n cannot exceed the integral by Theorem 2. So we require
$$\left[-\frac{1}{5x^5}\right]_n^\infty < (2)(10^{-11}),$$
and it follows that $n^5 > 10^{10}$, and thus that $n > 100$. We therefore choose $n = 101$. The exact value of the sum is $\dfrac{\pi^6}{945} \approx 1.017343061984$.

44. $n = 32$; 1.202

46. $n = 13$; 1.0083493

48. The series converges exactly when $p > e$.

50. Show that $c_n - c_{n+1} = \int_n^{n+1} \frac{1}{x}\,dx - \frac{1}{n+1} > 0$. A better approximation is $\gamma \approx 0.577215664902$.

Section 11.6

1. Because $n^2 + n + 1 > n^2$ if $n > 0$, this series converges by comparison with the p-series for which $p = 2$.

2. Diverges by limit-comparison with the harmonic series.

4. Converges by limit-comparison with the p-series for which $p = \frac{3}{2}$.

6. Converges by limit-comparison with the p-series for which $p = 2$.

7. Diverges by limit-comparison with the harmonic series.

8. Converges by limit-comparison with the p-series for which $p = 2$.

10. Diverges by limit-comparison with the harmonic series.

12. Converges by comparison with the geometric series with ratio $\frac{1}{5}$.

13. Diverges by *careful* limit-comparison with the harmonic series.

14. Diverges by limit-comparison with the harmonic series.

16. Converges by comparison with the geometric series with ratio $\frac{1}{3}$.

18. Converges by comparison with the geometric series wtih ratio $\frac{1}{3}$.

19. Because $n^2 \ln n > n^2$ if $n \geq 3$, this series converges by comparison with the p-series for which $p = 2$.

20. Converges by comparison with the p-series for which $p = 2$.

22. Diverges by limit-comparison with the harmonic series.

24. Diverges by limit-comparison with the harmonic series.

25. Converges by comparison with the p-series for which $p = 2$. To show this, show that $\ln n < n$ if $n > 2$ and that $e^n > n^3$ if $n > 4$. To do the latter, sketch the graph of $f(x) = e^x - x^3$. Obtain an estimate of its largest x-intercept (it's approximately 4.5364) and show that the graph of $f(x)$ is increasing for all larger values of x.

26. Diverges by limit-comparison with the harmonic series.

28. Converges by comparison with the geometric series with ratio $\frac{1}{2}$.

30. Converges by comparison or by limit-comparison with the convergent geometric series $\sum_{n=1}^{\infty} \frac{1}{e^n}$.

32. Converges by limit-comparison with the p-series with $p = \frac{4}{3}$.

34. Show that $\ln n < n$ if $n \geq 1$. Then the given series converges by comparison with the p-series for which $p = 2$.

36. The series converges because it is dominated by the convergent p-series $\sum 1/n^4$.

38. The sum of the first ten terms is approximately 0.404054799773. The error is approximately 0.00001542.

40. The sum of the first ten terms (subscripts 2 through 11) is approximately 1.2248932892. The error is approximately 0.3947.

42. $n = 9$; 0.62

44. $n = 198$; 1.47

45. Because $\sum a_n$ converges, $a_n \to 0$ as $n \to +\infty$. So, using also the hypothesis that $a_n > 0$ for all n, there exists an integer K such that $0 < a_n < \pi$ for all $n \geq K$. But $\sin x < x$ for all $x > 0$, so

$$0 < \sin(a_n) < a_n$$

for all $n \geq K$. So the convergent series $\sum_{n=K}^{\infty} a_n$ dominates $\sum_{n=K}^{\infty} \sin(a_n)$. Adjoining a finite number of terms to the beginning of an infinite series cannot affect its convergence or divergence, only its sum. Therefore $\sum_{n=1}^{\infty} \sin(a_n)$ converges.

46. Let $f(x) = x - (\ln x)^8$. Then $f'(x) = 1 - \dfrac{8}{x}(\ln x)^7$. Now $f'(x) < 0$ when $8(\ln x)^7 < x$. By Newton's method we find that $8(\ln x)^7 = x$ when x is approximately 2.3104 and when x is approximately 4.18853×10^{10}. (In order to obtain the latter solution, apply Newton's method to the equation $\ln x = (x/8)^{1/7}$.) It is easy to show that $f'(x) > 0$ if $x > 4.2 \times 10^{10}$. Next, also by Newton's method, show that $f(x) = 0$ when x is about equal to 3.1752 and when x is approximately 2.1491×10^{11}. When all this information is assembled, you can see that

$$f(x) > 0 \text{ if } x > 2.1492 \times 10^{11}.$$

Therefore $(\ln n)^8 < n$ for all $n > 2.1492 \times 10^{11}$, and so

$$\frac{1}{(\ln n)^8} > \frac{1}{n} \text{ if } n > 2.1492 \times 10^{11}.$$

48. $\sum a_n$ eventually dominates $\sum c_n a_n$ because $c_n \leq 1$ for all sufficiently large values of n.

50. First, $1 + 2 + 3 + 4 + \ldots + n = \dfrac{n(n+1)}{2}$, and so $\dfrac{1}{1+2+3+\ldots+n} = \dfrac{2}{n(n+1)} = \dfrac{2}{n} - \dfrac{2}{n+1}$.
So the sum of the first k terms of the given series is

$$S_k = 2\left(1 - \frac{1}{k+1}\right).$$

Therefore the sum of the series is 2.

51. The summand is approximately $1/(\ln n)$. Make this statement precise with the approximate inequalities (in order to apply the comparison test), or see if the limit-comparison test can be applied successfully.

Section 11.7

1. This series meets both criteria of the alternating series test, and therefore it converges.

2. This series meets both criteria of the alternating series test, and therefore it converges.

4. This series meets both criteria of the alternating series test, and therefore it converges.

6. The first term of this series is smaller in magnitude than its second. But one can show by induction that if the first term is omitted, then the remaining terms steadily decrease in magnitude, with limit zero. Changing the first term of a series cannot affect its convergence or divergence, only its sum, and therefore this series converges.

7. Because $n/(\ln n) \to +\infty$ as $n \to \infty$, this series diverges by the nth-term test for divergence.

8. If a_n denotes the nth term of this series, then

$$|a_1| < |a_2| < |a_3| > |a_4| > |a_5| > |a_6| > \cdots,$$

and one can show that after the first two exceptions, the terms of this series steadily decreasing in magnitude and have limit zero. Changing the first two terms of a series cannot affect its convergence or divergence, so this series converges by the alternating series test.

10. If a_n denotes the nth term of this series, then

$$|a_1| < |a_2| = |a_3| > |a_4| > |a_5| > |a_6| > |a_7| > \cdots,$$

and one can show that after the first two exceptions, the terms of this series steadily decreasing in magnitude and have limit zero. Changing the first two terms of a series cannot affect its convergence or divergence, so this series converges by the alternating series test.

12. This series diverges by the nth-term test for divergence, because $(n\pi/10)^{n+1} \to +\infty$ as $n \to \infty$.

13. This series has the same sequence of partial sums as the series

$$\sum_{n=1}^{\infty} \frac{(-1)^{n+1}}{(2n-1)^{2/3}} = 1 - \frac{1}{3^{2/3}} + \frac{1}{5^{2/3}} - \frac{1}{7^{2/3}} + \frac{1}{9^{2/3}} - \cdots,$$

and the latter series converges by the alternating series test. So the series given in Problem 13 also converges.

14. This series converges by the alternating series test, as the numerators of the terms are $-1, 1, -1, 1, -1, \ldots$ and the denominators are steadily increasing as $n \to \infty$.

16. Because $n \sin(\pi/n) \to \pi \neq 0$ as $n \to \infty$, this series diverges by the n-th term test for divergence.

18. This series diverges because, if $a > 1$, then $\lim_{n \to \infty} \frac{a^n}{n^4} = +\infty$. Hence the terms of the given series do not approach zero.

20. Converges by the ratio test.

22. Diverges by limit-comparison with the harmonic series.

23. Converges conditionally—Theorem 1 for convergence, a careful limit-comparison with the harmonic series to show that the given series is not absolutely convergent.

24. Converges by comparison with the p-series for which $p = 2$; the given series also converges absolutely.

26. Converges absolutely by the ratio test.

28. Converges absolutely by the ratio test (the limit in the ratio test is $\frac{1}{e}$, and $-1 < \frac{1}{e} < 1$).

29. Diverges by the nth-term test.

30. Converges absolutely by the ratio test.

32. Diverges by the nth-term test.

34. Converges absolutely by the ratio test (the limit in the ratio test is $\frac{3}{4}$).

35. Diverges by the nth-term test: $\ln(1/n) = -\ln n$.

36. Converges absolutely by the ratio test (the limit there is $\frac{1}{4}$).

38. Claim: $f(x) = \frac{1}{x} \arctan x$ is decreasing for $x \geq 2$. The reason is that

$$f'(x) = \frac{x - (1+x^2)\arctan x}{x^2(1+x^2)},$$

so $f'(x) < \frac{x - (1+x^2)}{x^2(1+x^2)}$ if $x \geq 2$;

thus for $x \geq 2$, $f'(x) < \frac{2x - (1+x^2)}{x^2(1+x^2)} = -\frac{(x-1)^2}{x^2(x^2+1)} < 0.$

Therefore $f(x) = \frac{1}{x} \arctan x$ is decreasing for $x \geq 2$, so the given series converges by Theorem 1. But the convergence is conditional because

$$\sum_{n=1}^{\infty} \frac{1}{n} \arctan n$$

diverges by limit-comparison with the harmonic series.

40. The ratio test yields the limit $\frac{2}{3}$, so the given series converges absolutely.

42. The given series converges absolutely by the root test (the limit obtained is zero).

43. The sum of the first five terms of the series is approximately 0.904412037 and the sixth term is approximately -0.004629630. Hence the sum of the series lies between 0.899782406 and 0.904412038. We have only two-place accuracy; all we can say is that the sum of the series rounds to 0.90.

44. The sum of the first eight terms of the series is approximately 0.2499618961 and its ninth term is approximately 0.000050805, so the sum of the series lies between 0.249961895 and 0.250012702. Hence we have four-place accuracy; the sum of the series rounds to 0.2500. Incidentally, this is a geometric series with first term $\frac{1}{3}$ and ratio $-\frac{1}{3}$, so its sum is exactly $\frac{1}{4}$.

45. The sum of the first six terms is approximately 0.631944444 and the seventh term is approximately 0.000198413, so the sum of this series lies between 0.631944443 and 0.632142859. Thus we have three-place accuracy; the sum of this series rounds to 0.632. The exact value of the sum is $1 - e^{-1}$.

46. The sum of the first seven terms is approxiately 0.783430568 and the eighth term is approximately $-5.9604645 \times 10^{-8}$, so the sum of this series lies between 0.783430507 and 0.783430569, so we have six-place accuracy; the sum of the given series rounds to 0.783431.

47. The sum of the first 12 terms of this series is approximately 0.653210678 and the thirteenth term is approximately 0.076923076, so the sum of this series lies between 0.653210677 and 0.730133756. We have only one-place accuracy; the sum of this series rounds to 0.7. The exact value of its sum is $\ln 2 \approx 0.693147181$.

48. The sum of the first 15 terms of this series is approximately 0.820635507 and its sixteenth term is exactly -0.00390625, so its sum lies between 0.820635506 and 0.824541758. Hence its sum rounds to 0.82. The exact value of its sum is $\frac{1}{12}\pi^2 \approx 0.822467033$.

49. The seventh term of the given series is approximately 0.000416493, so we should obtain three-place accuracy. The alternating series remainder estimate reveals that the sum of this series lies between 0.946767823 and 0.947184318, so to three places its sum is 0.947. The exact value of its sum is $\frac{7}{720}\pi^4$.

50. The seventh term of the given series is approximately 0.000059499, so we should obtain four-place accuracy. The alternating series remainder estimate reveals that the sum of this series lies between 0.972080062 and 0.972139563, so its sum rounds to 0.9721.

51. The seventh term of the given series (corresponding to $n = 6$) is approximately 0.000021701, so the sum of the first six terms (corresponding to $0 \leq n \leq 5$) rounds correctly to 0.6065.

52. The sum of the first five terms (corresponding to $0 \leq n \leq 4$) of the series is approximately 0.540302579 and the sixth term (corresponding to $n = 5$) is approximately $-2.755731922 \times 10^{-7}$, so we have five-place accuracy; the sum of the series rounds to 0.54030.

54. The sixth term of the series is approximately $-1.666666667 \times 10^{-7}$, so the sum of the first five terms yields seven-place accuracy; the fifth partial sum rounds correctly to 0.0953102.

57. Let $a_n = b_n = \dfrac{(-1)^{n+1}}{\sqrt{n}}$.

58. This is merely the contrapositive of Theorem 3, so its proof is the same.

59. The ratio test yields $\rho = 0$ for every value of a. Therefore the series $\displaystyle\sum_{n=0}^{\infty} \dfrac{a^n}{n!}$ converges for every a.

By the nth-term test for divergence, it follows that $\displaystyle\lim_{n \to \infty} \dfrac{a^n}{n!} = 0$ for all real number values of a.

60. (a) The ratio test gives limit r, and $|r| < 1$.

(b) Show that $(1-r)S = \dfrac{r}{1-r}$.

Section 11.8

1. The radius of convergence is
$$R = \lim_{n \to \infty} \left|\frac{n}{n+1}\right| = 1.$$
and the series clearly diverges when $x = \pm 1$. Hence the interval of convergence is $(-1, 1)$.

2. The radius of convergence is
$$R = \lim_{n \to \infty} \frac{\sqrt{n+1}}{\sqrt{n}} = 1.$$
The series diverges if $x = 1$ (it dominates the harmonic series) and converges when $x = -1$ (by the alternating series test), so the interval of convergence is $[-1, 1)$.

3. The radius of convergence is
$$R = \lim_{n \to \infty} \frac{2n}{n+1} = 2.$$
When $x = \pm 2$, the series diverges by the nth-term test. Hence the interval of convergence is $(-2, 2)$.

4. The radius of convergence is
$$R = \lim_{n \to \infty} \frac{5\sqrt{n+1}}{\sqrt{n}} = 5.$$
When $x = 5$, then the series converges by the alternating series test. When $x = -5$, it diverges because it dominates the harmonic series. Hence the interval of convergence is $(-5, 5]$.

6. The radius of convergence is
$$R = \lim_{n \to \infty} \frac{(n+1)^{n+1}}{n^n} = \lim_{n \to \infty} (n+1)\left(\frac{n+1}{n}\right)^n = +\infty$$
because
$$\lim_{n \to \infty} \left(\frac{n+1}{n}\right)^n = \lim_{n \to \infty} \left(1 + \frac{1}{n}\right)^n = e > 0.$$
Therefore the interval of convergence is $(-\infty, +\infty)$.

7. The radius of convergence is
$$R = \lim_{n \to \infty} \frac{(n+1)^3}{3n^3} = \frac{1}{3}.$$
When $x = \frac{1}{3}$, the series converges because it is a p-series with $p = 3 > 1$. When $x = -\frac{1}{3}$, the series converges by the alternating series test. Hence the interval of convergence is $\left[-\frac{1}{3}, \frac{1}{3}\right]$.

8. The radius of convergence is
$$R = \lim_{n \to \infty} \frac{\sqrt{2n+3}}{4\sqrt{2n+1}} = \frac{1}{4}.$$
When $x = \frac{1}{4}$, the series converges by the alternating series test. When $x = -\frac{1}{4}$, it diverges by limit comparison with the divergent p-series $\sum n^{-1/2}$. Hence its interval of convergence is $\left(-\frac{1}{4}, \frac{1}{4}\right]$.

9. The radius of convergence is
$$R = \lim_{n \to \infty} \frac{\sqrt{n}}{2\sqrt{n+1}} = \frac{1}{2}.$$
When $x = \pm\frac{1}{2}$, the series diverges by the nth-term test for divergence, so its interval of convergence is $\left(-\frac{1}{2}, \frac{1}{2}\right)$.

10. The radius of convergence is $R = \lim_{n \to \infty} \frac{(3n+2)n^2}{(3n-1)(n+1)^2} = 1$. When $x = \pm 1$, the series diverges by the nth-term test for divergence, so its interval of convergence is $(-1, 1)$.

11. The radius of convergence is
$$R = \lim_{n \to \infty} \frac{2n(n+2)^3}{(n+1)^4} = 2.$$
When $x = \pm 2$ the series converges absolutely by limit-comparison with the convergent p-series $\sum n^{-2}$, so its interval of convergence is $[-2, 2]$.

12. The radius of convergence is
$$R = \lim_{n \to \infty} \frac{10 n^{10}}{(n+1)^{10}} = 10.$$
When $x = \pm 10$, the series diverges by the nth-term test for divergence, so its interval of convergence is $(-10, 10)$.

13. The radius of convergence is
$$R = \lim_{n \to \infty} \frac{3 \ln n}{\ln(n+1)} = 3.$$
When $x = \pm 3$, the series diverges by the nth-term test for divergence, so its interval of convergence is $(-3, 3)$.

14. The radius of convergence is
$$R = \lim_{n \to \infty} \frac{(n+1)\ln(n+1)}{4n \ln n} = \tfrac{1}{4}.$$
When $x = -\tfrac{1}{4}$, the series diverges by the integral test. When $x = \tfrac{1}{4}$, it converges by the alternating series test. Hence the interval of convergence is $\left(-\tfrac{1}{4}, \tfrac{1}{4}\right]$.

16. $0 \leq x \leq 1$

18. The ratio test leads to the limit $|x| \left(\lim_{n \to \infty} \left(\frac{n}{n+1} \right)^n \right) = \frac{|x|}{e}$. So the series converges on the interval $(-e, e)$ and diverges if $|x| > e$. Only if we borrow the result of Miscellaneous Problem 61 of this chapter is it easy to test convergence at the endpoints $-e$ and e: For large values of n,
$$\frac{n!}{n^n} e^n \approx \frac{\sqrt{2\pi n}\, (n/e)^n}{n^n} e^n = \sqrt{2\pi n} \to +\infty,$$
so this series diverges at the endpoints; the interval of convergence really is $(-e, e)$.

20. The ratio test yields the limit $2|x|$, so the series converges on $\left(-\tfrac{1}{2}, \tfrac{1}{2}\right)$ and diverges if $|x| > \tfrac{1}{2}$. Again, use of the result of Miscellaneous Problem 61 gives us information about the behavior of the series at the endpoints; for large n,
$$\left(\frac{1 \cdot 3 \cdot 5 \cdots (2n+1)}{n!\, 2^n} \right) \left(\frac{n!\, 2^n}{n!\, 2^n} \right) = \frac{(2n+1)!}{(n!)^2\, n^{2n}}$$
$$\approx \frac{(2\pi(n+1))^{1/2} ((2n+1)/e)^{2n+1}}{2\pi n\, (n/e)^{2n}\, 2^{2n}} \approx \frac{(2n+1)^{2n+1}}{\sqrt{2\pi n}\, e\, (2n)^{2n}}$$
$$= \frac{(1 + (1/2n))^{2n}\,(2n+1)}{e\sqrt{2\pi n}} \approx \frac{2n+1}{\sqrt{2\pi n}} \to +\infty,$$
so this series diverges at the endpoints; the interval of convergence really is $\left(-\tfrac{1}{2}, \tfrac{1}{2}\right)$.

22. $1 \leq x \leq 3$

24. $(-\infty, +\infty)$

26. $-8 < x \leq 12$

28. $(-2, 2)$

29. The radius of convergence is
$$R = \lim_{n \to \infty} \frac{n!(2n+2)!}{(2)(n+1)!(2n)!} = \lim_{n \to \infty} \frac{(2n+2)(2n+1)}{2n} = \infty.$$

Therefore the interval of convergence is $(-\infty, +\infty)$.

30. The radius of convergence is
$$R = \lim_{n \to \infty} \frac{3n+2}{2n+1} = \tfrac{3}{2}.$$

Hence the series converges if $|x| < \tfrac{3}{2}$ and diverges if $|x| > \tfrac{3}{2}$. If $x = \tfrac{3}{2}$, then the nth term of the series is
$$a_n = \frac{1}{2} \cdot \frac{3}{5} \cdot \frac{5}{8} \cdots \frac{2n-1}{3n-1} \cdot \frac{3}{2} < \left(\frac{2}{3}\right)^n \cdot \frac{3}{2} = \left(\frac{2}{3}\right)^{n-1},$$

so the given series $\sum a_n$ converges by comparison with a convergent geometric series. If $x = -\tfrac{3}{2}$, then the resulting series converges absolutely by the same argument. Hence the interval of convergence is $\left[-\tfrac{3}{2}, \tfrac{3}{2}\right]$.

31. Here we have
$$f(x) = \frac{x}{1-x} = x + x^2 + x^3 + x^4 + \cdots$$
with interval of convergence $(-1, 1)$.

32. Here we can force $f(x)$ to be the sum of a geometric series:
$$f(x) = \frac{1}{10+x} = \frac{\tfrac{1}{10}}{1+\tfrac{1}{10}x}$$
$$= \frac{1}{10} - \frac{x}{10^2} + \frac{x^2}{10^3} - \frac{x^3}{10^4} + \cdots = \sum_{n=0}^{\infty} \frac{(-1)^n x^n}{10^{n+1}},$$
and the interval of convergence is $(-10, 10)$.

33. The series is
$$x^2 - \frac{3x^3}{1!} + \frac{3^2 x^4}{2!} - \frac{3^3 x^5}{3!} + \cdots = \sum_{n=0}^{\infty} \frac{(-1)^n 3^n x^{n+2}}{n!},$$
with interval of convergence $(-\infty, +\infty)$.

34. One solution: By the method of partial fractions,
$$\frac{x}{9-x^2} = \frac{1}{2}\left(\frac{1}{3-x} - \frac{1}{3+x}\right),$$
which is the sum of two geometric series, each of which converges on $(-3, 3)$. Hence their sum series
$$\sum_{n=1}^{\infty} \frac{x^{2n-1}}{3^{2n}} = \frac{x}{3^2} + \frac{x^3}{3^4} + \frac{x^5}{3^6} + \frac{x^7}{3^8} + \cdots$$
represents $f(x)$ on the interval $(-3, 3)$.

35. Replace x with x^2 in the Maclaurin series for $\sin x$ to obtain
$$\sum_{n=0}^{\infty} \frac{(-1)^n x^{4n+2}}{(2n+1)!} = x^2 - \frac{x^6}{3!} + \frac{x^{10}}{5!} - \frac{x^{14}}{7!} + \cdots$$
with interval of convergence $(-\infty, +\infty)$.

36. The Maclaurin series for $\cos x$, with x replaced with $4x$, yields
$$f(x) = 1 - \frac{4^2 x^2}{2!2} + \frac{4^4 x^4}{4!2} - \frac{4^6 x^6}{6!2} + \cdots.$$

38. $(1+x^2)^{3/2} = 1 + \frac{3}{2}x^2 + \frac{3}{8}x^4 - \frac{1}{16}x^6 + (3)\frac{(1)(3)}{4!\,2^4}x^8 - (3)\frac{(1)(3)(5)}{5!\,2^5}x^{10} + (3)\frac{(1)(3)(5)(7)}{6!\,2^6}x^{12}$
$- (3)\frac{(1)(3)(5)(7)(9)}{7!\,2^7}x^{14} + \cdots;$

the limit in the ratio test is x^2, so the radius of convergence is 1.

40. $(9+x^3)^{-1/2} = \sum_{n=0}^{\infty} \frac{(-1)^n (2n)!\, x^{3n}}{(n!)^2\, 2^{2n}\, 3^{2n+1}}$; the ratio test gives limit $\frac{1}{9}|x|^3$; the radius of convergence is therefore $9^{1/3}$.

42. $f(x) = \frac{1}{3} - \frac{1}{5}x^2 + \frac{1}{7}x^4 - \frac{1}{9}x^6 + \cdots$; the ratio test yields the limit x^2, and therefore the radius of convergence is 1.

43. Integrate $t^3 - \frac{1}{3!}t^9 + \frac{1}{5!}t^{15} - \frac{1}{7!}t^{21} + \cdots$.

44. $f(x) = \int_0^x \frac{\sin t}{t}\, dt = \int_0^x \left(1 - \frac{1}{3!}t^2 + \frac{1}{5!}t^4 - \frac{1}{7!}t^6 + \cdots\right) dt$
$= \left[t - \frac{t^3}{3!\,3} + \frac{t^5}{5!\,5} - \frac{t^7}{7!\,7} + \cdots\right]_0^x = x - \frac{x^3}{3!\,3} + \frac{x^5}{5!\,5} - \frac{x^7}{7!\,7} + \cdots.$

Note: The interval of convergence is $(-\infty, +\infty)$.

46. $f(x) = x - \frac{x^3}{3^2} + \frac{x^5}{5^2} - \frac{x^7}{7^2} + \frac{x^9}{9^2} - \cdots$; the interval of convergence is $-1 \leq x \leq 1$.

48. $\tanh^{-1} x = x + \frac{1}{3}x^3 + \frac{1}{5}x^5 + \frac{1}{7}x^7 + \frac{1}{9}x^9 + \cdots$; the interval of convergence is $(-1, 1)$.

49. Let $f(x) = \sum_{n=0}^{\infty} x^n$, $-1 < x < 1$. Then $xf'(x) = \frac{x}{(1-x)^2} = \sum_{n=1}^{\infty} nx^n$.

50. Differentiate $f(x)$ of Problem 49 twice, then multiply by x^2 to obtain

$$x^2 f''(x) = \sum_{n=1}^{\infty} n(n-1)x^n = \frac{2x^2}{(1-x)^3}.$$

51. Differentiate $f(x)$ of Problem 49 once, then multiply by x to obtain the series of Problem 49. Differentiate again and again multiply by x to obtain

$$\frac{x(1+x)}{(1-x)^3} = \sum_{n=1}^{\infty} n^2 x^n.$$

52. $2;\ \frac{3}{2}$

58. Multiply the series for $J_0(x)$ by x to obtain

$$xJ_0(x) = \sum_{n=0}^{\infty} \frac{(-1)^n x^{2n+1}}{2^{2n}(n!)^2}.$$

Termwise integration is "legal," and in this case, legal on the set of all real numbers. Hence

$$\int xJ_0(x)\, dx = \sum_{n=0}^{\infty} \frac{(-1)^n x^{2n+2}}{2 \cdot 2^{2n}(n+1)(n!)^2} = \sum_{n=0}^{\infty} \frac{(-1)^n x^{2n+2}}{2^{2n+1} n!(n+1)!} + C = J_1(x) + C.$$

64. We begin by replacing $\sin xt$ with its Maclaurin series:

$$\int_0^{\infty} e^{-t} \sin xt\, dt = \int_0^{\infty} e^{-t} \left(xt - \frac{x^3 t^3}{3!} + \frac{x^5 t^5}{5!} - \frac{x^7 t^7}{7!} + \cdots\right) dt$$
$$= x\int_0^{\infty} te^{-t}\, dt - \frac{x^3}{3!}\int_0^{\infty} t^3 e^{-t}\, dt + \frac{x^5}{5!}\int_0^{\infty} t^5 e^{-t}\, dt - \frac{x^7}{7!}\int_0^{\infty} t^7 e^{-t}\, dt + \cdots$$
$$= x - x^3 + x^5 - x^7 + \cdots = \frac{x}{1+x^2}$$

provided that $|x| < 1$.

66. $f(x) = \sum_{n=0}^{\infty} a_n x^n$: $f(0) = a_0 = \dfrac{f^{(0)}(0)}{0!}$.

$f'(x) = \sum_{n=1}^{\infty} n a_n x^{n-1}$: $f'(0) = a_1 = \dfrac{f^{(1)}(0)}{1!}$, and so on.

Section 11.9

1. Use the binomial series for $4(x+1)^{1/3}$; take $x = \tfrac{1}{64}$.

2. First,
$$(630)^{1/4} = (5)\left(\tfrac{630}{625}\right)^{1/4} = (5)\left(\tfrac{126}{125}\right)^{1/4} = (5)\left(1 + \tfrac{1}{125}\right)^{1/4}.$$
$$(1+x)^{1/4} = 1 + \tfrac{1}{4}x - \tfrac{(1)(3)}{2!\,4^2}x^2 + \tfrac{(1)(3)(7)}{3!\,4^3}x^3 - \tfrac{(1)(3)(7)(11)}{4!\,4^4}x^4 + \cdots.$$

To satisfy the condition $|R_n| < 0.0005$, it is sufficient to take the first two terms of the binomial series. Therefore
$$(630)^{1/4} \approx (5)\left(1 + \tfrac{1}{(4)(125)}\right) = 5.01;$$

in fact, $5.00886 \leq (630)^{1/4} \leq 5.01000$. Answer: 5.010. (The true value is approximately 5.00997014.)

4. We use the series
$$e^{-x} = 1 - \tfrac{1}{1!}x + \tfrac{1}{2!}x^2 - \tfrac{1}{3!}x^3 + \cdots.$$

To insure that $|R_n| < 0.0005$, we impose the condition that
$$\dfrac{(0.2)^{n+1}}{(n+1)!} < \dfrac{1}{2000},$$

and it suffices to take $n = 3$. We find that
$$e^{-0.2} \approx 1 - \tfrac{0.2}{1!} + \tfrac{(0.2)^2}{2!} - \tfrac{(0.2)^3}{3!} \approx 0.818666667.$$

Answer: 0.819. (The true value is approximately 0.818730753.)

6. First,
$$\ln(1+x) = x - \tfrac{1}{2}x^2 + \tfrac{1}{3}x^3 - \tfrac{1}{4}x^4 + \cdots$$

if $-1 < x \leq 1$; the error term in using the Taylor polynomial $P_n(x)$ to approximate $\ln(1+x)$ cannot exceed
$$\dfrac{t^{n+1}}{n+1} \text{ for } 0 < t \leq 1.$$

With $t = 0.1$, we require that the error not exceed 0.0005; this will hold for $n \geq 2$, so we choose $n = 2$. Thus
$$\ln(1.1) \approx 0.1 - \tfrac{1}{2}(0.1)^2 = 0.95.$$

Answer: 0.095 (the true value is approximately 0.09531018).

8. First,
$$\cos x = 1 - \tfrac{1}{2!}x^2 + \tfrac{1}{4!}x^4 - \cdots;$$

the error term in using the Taylor polynomial $P_n(x)$ to approximate $\cos x$ cannot exceed

$$\frac{|x|^{n+1}}{(n+1)!},$$

and here we have $x = \dfrac{\pi}{20} < 0.1571$. For error less than 0.0005, we need $n \geq 3$; we take $n = 4$, and the error will not exceed 0.000000798. Result: $\cos(\pi/20) \approx 0.9876883615$. (The true value is approximately 0.9876883406.)

10. First,

$$\cos x = 1 - \frac{1}{2!}x^2 + \frac{1}{4!}x^4 - \cdots ;$$

the error term in using the Taylor polynomial $P_n(x)$ to approximate $\cos x$ cannot exceed

$$\frac{|x|^{n+1}}{(n+1)!},$$

and here we have $x = \dfrac{\pi}{36} < 0.0873$. For error less than 0.0005, we need $n \geq 2$; we take $n = 2$, and the error will not exceed 0.000111. Result: $\cos(\pi/36) \approx 0.9961922823$. (The true value is approximately 0.9961946981.)

12. From the Maclaurin series for the sine function, we find that

$$\frac{\sin x}{\sqrt{x}} = x^{-1/2}\left(x - \frac{x^3}{3!} + \frac{x^5}{5!} - \cdots\right)$$

$$= x^{1/2} - \frac{x^{5/2}}{3!} + \frac{x^{9/2}}{5!} - \frac{x^{13/2}}{7!} + \cdots ;$$

it follows that

$$\int_0^1 \frac{\sin x}{\sqrt{x}}\, dx = \frac{2}{3} - \frac{2}{3!\cdot 7} + \frac{2}{5!\cdot 11} - \frac{2}{7!\cdot 15} + \cdots .$$

A calculator shows that

$$\frac{2}{n!\cdot(2n+1)} < 0.00005$$

if $n \geq 7$ (but not if $n = 5$). Hence

$$\int_0^1 \frac{\sin x}{\sqrt{x}}\, dx \approx \frac{2}{3} - \frac{2}{3!\cdot 7} + \frac{2}{5!\cdot 11} \approx 0.6206.$$

(The exact answer actually rounds to 0.6205.)

13. The Maclaurin series for the arctangent function yields

$$\frac{\arctan x}{x} = 1 - \tfrac{1}{3}x^2 + \tfrac{1}{5}x^4 - \tfrac{1}{7}x^6 + \cdots .$$

It follows that

$$\int_0^{1/2} \frac{\arctan x}{x}\, dx = \frac{1}{2} - \frac{1}{2^3\cdot 3^2} + \frac{1}{2^5\cdot 5^2} - \frac{1}{2^7\cdot 7^2} + \cdots .$$

The least odd positive integer n for which

$$\frac{1}{2^n\cdot n^2} < 0.00005$$

is $n = 9$, so four terms of the last series yield

$$\int_0^{1/2} \frac{\arctan x}{x}\, dx \approx 0.4872,$$

which agrees, to four places, with the exact answer.

14. Here we have

$$\int_0^1 \sin x^2\, dx = \int_0^1 \left(x^2 - \frac{x^6}{3!} + \frac{x^{10}}{5!} - \cdots\right) dx$$

$$= \left[\frac{x^3}{3} - \frac{x^7}{3!\cdot 7} + \frac{x^{11}}{5!\cdot 11} - \frac{x^{15}}{7!\cdot 15} + \cdots\right]_0^1$$

$$= \frac{1}{3} - \frac{1}{3!\cdot 7} + \frac{1}{5!\cdot 11} - \frac{1}{7!\cdot 15} + \cdots.$$

Now the least odd positive integer n for which

$$\frac{1}{n!\cdot(2n+1)} < 0.00005$$

is $n = 7$. Hence three terms of the last series yield the four-place approximation

$$\int_0^1 \sin x^2\, dx \approx 0.3103.$$

16. The binomial series yields

$$(1+x^4)^{-1/2} = 1 - \frac{\frac{1}{2}}{1!}x^4 + \frac{\frac{1}{2}\cdot\frac{3}{2}}{2!}x^8 - \frac{\frac{1}{2}\cdot\frac{3}{2}\cdot\frac{5}{2}}{3!}x^{12}$$

$$+ \frac{3\cdot 5\cdot 7}{4!\cdot 2^4}x^{16} - \frac{3\cdot 5\cdot 7\cdot 9}{5!\cdot 2^5}x^{20} + \cdots.$$

Then term-by-term integration yields

$$\int_0^{1/2} \frac{1}{\sqrt{1+x^4}}\, dx = \frac{1}{2} - \frac{1}{2^6\cdot 5} + \frac{3}{2!\cdot 2^{11}\cdot 9} - \frac{3\cdot 5}{3!\cdot 2^{16}\cdot 13} + \frac{3\cdot 5\cdot 7}{4!\cdot 2^{21}\cdot 17} - \cdots.$$

Now

$$\frac{3}{2!\cdot 2^{11}\cdot 9} \approx 0.0008 \quad \text{but} \quad \frac{3\cdot 5}{3!\cdot 2^{16}\cdot 13} \approx 0.000003,$$

so three terms of the last series yield the approximation

$$\int_0^{1/2} \frac{1}{\sqrt{1+x^4}}\, dx \approx 0.4970.$$

18. The binomial series yields

$$(1+x^3)^{1/2} = 1 + \frac{1}{2}x^3 - \frac{1}{2!\cdot 2^2}x^6 + \frac{3}{3!\cdot 2^3}x^9 - \frac{3\cdot 5}{4!\cdot 2^4}x^{12} + \cdots.$$

Then term-by-term integration yields

$$\int_0^{1/2} \sqrt{1+x^3}\, dx = \frac{1}{2} + \frac{1}{1!\cdot 4\cdot 2^5} - \frac{1}{2!\cdot 7\cdot 2^9} + \frac{3}{3!\cdot 10\cdot 2^{13}} - \frac{3\cdot 5}{4!\cdot 13\cdot 2^{17}} + \cdots.$$

With the aid of a calculator, we find that

$$\frac{1}{2!\cdot 7\cdot 2^9} \approx 0.00014, \quad \text{whereas} \quad \frac{3}{3!\cdot 10\cdot 2^{13}} \approx 0.0000061.$$

Therefore three terms of the last series yield the approximation

$$\int_0^{1/2} \sqrt{1+x^3}\, dx \approx 0.5077.$$

19. The Maclaurin series for e^x yields

$$\exp(-x^2) = \frac{1}{0!} - \frac{x^2}{1!} + \frac{x^4}{2!} - \frac{x^6}{3!} + \cdots,$$

and then term-by-term integration gives

$$\int_0^1 \exp(-x^2)\,dx = 1 - \frac{1}{1!\cdot 3} + \frac{1}{2!\cdot 5} - \frac{1}{3!\cdot 7} + \cdots.$$

Next,

$$\frac{1}{6!\cdot 13} \approx 0.0001, \quad \text{and} \quad \frac{1}{7!\cdot 15} \approx 0.000013,$$

so six terms of the last series yield

$$\int_0^1 \exp(-x^2)\,dx \approx 0.7468.$$

20. The Maclaurin series for $\cos x$ yields

$$\frac{1-\cos x}{x^2} = \frac{1}{2!} - \frac{x^2}{4!} + \frac{x^4}{6!} - \frac{x^6}{8!} + \cdots.$$

Then term-by-term integration gives the series

$$\int_0^1 \frac{1-\cos x}{x^2}\,dx = \frac{1}{2!} - \frac{1}{4!\cdot 3} + \frac{1}{6!\cdot 5} - \frac{1}{8!\cdot 7} + \frac{1}{10!\cdot 9} - \cdots.$$

Next,

$$\frac{1}{6!\cdot 5} \approx 0.00028, \quad \text{whereas} \quad \frac{1}{8!\cdot 7} \approx 0.0000035.$$

Therefore three terms of the last series are enough to give four-place accuracy:

$$\int_0^1 \frac{1-\cos x}{x^2}\,dx \approx 0.4864.$$

22. First, the binomial series yields

$$(1+x^3)^{-1/2} = 1 - \frac{1}{2}x^3 + \frac{3}{2!\cdot 2^2}x^6 - \frac{3\cdot 5}{3!\cdot 2^3}x^9 + \frac{3\cdot 5\cdot 7}{4!\cdot 2^4}x^{12} - \cdots.$$

Then term-by-term integration gives

$$\int_0^{1/2} \frac{x}{\sqrt{1+x^3}}\,dx = \frac{1}{8} - \frac{1}{320} + \frac{3}{16384} - \frac{5}{360448} + \frac{5}{4194304} - \cdots.$$

Now

$$\frac{5}{360448} \approx 0.000014, \quad \text{but} \quad \frac{5}{4194304} \approx 0.0000012,$$

So only four terms of the last series are need to give four-place accuracy:

$$\int_0^{1/2} \frac{x}{\sqrt{1+x^3}}\,dx \approx 0.1220.$$

24. $\dfrac{x-\sin x}{x^3\cos x} = \dfrac{x^3/3! - x^5/5! + x^7/7! - \cdots}{x^3 - x^5/2! + x^7/4! - \cdots} = \dfrac{1/3! - x^2/5! + \cdots}{1 - x^2/2! + \cdots} \to \dfrac{1}{6}$ as $x \to 0$.

26. The limit can be simplified to $\displaystyle\lim_{x\to 0} \dfrac{2/3! - 2x^2/5! + \cdots}{1/3 - x^2/5 + \cdots} = \left(\dfrac{2}{3!}\right)\left(\dfrac{3}{1}\right) = 1.$

28. The limit can be simplified to $\lim_{x \to 1} 2\left(1 - \frac{1}{2}(x-1) + \frac{1}{3}(x-1)^2 - \cdots\right) = 2$.

29. The Taylor series with center $\pi/2$ for $f(x) = \sin x$ is

$$\sin x = \frac{1}{0!} - \frac{1}{2!}\left(x - \frac{\pi}{2}\right)^2 + \frac{1}{4!}\left(x - \frac{\pi}{2}\right)^4 - \cdots.$$

We convert $80°$ into $x = 4\pi/9$, and substitution yields the series

$$\sin 80° = 1 - \frac{1}{2!}\left(\frac{\pi}{18}\right)^2 + \frac{1}{4!}\left(\frac{\pi}{18}\right)^4 - \cdots.$$

For four-place accuracy, we need

$$\frac{1}{n!}\left(\frac{\pi}{18}\right)^n < 0.00005,$$

and the smallest even positive integer for which this inequality holds is $n = 4$. Thus only two terms of the series are needed to show that, to four places, $\sin 80° \approx 0.9848$.

30. The Taylor series for $f(x) = \cos x$ with center $\pi/4$ is

$$\cos x = \frac{\sqrt{2}}{2}\left[\frac{1}{0!} - \frac{1}{1!}\left(x - \frac{\pi}{4}\right) - \frac{1}{2!}\left(x - \frac{\pi}{4}\right)^2 + \frac{1}{3!}\left(x - \frac{\pi}{4}\right)^3 + \frac{1}{4!}\left(x - \frac{\pi}{4}\right)^4 - \frac{1}{5!}\left(x - \frac{\pi}{5}\right)^5 - \cdots\right].$$

After we convert $35°$ to radians and substitute, we find that some care with signs is needed because

$$x - \frac{\pi}{4} = \frac{7\pi}{36} - \frac{\pi}{4} = -\frac{\pi}{18}$$

is negative, and some of the exponents in the Taylor series are odd. We obtain

$$\cos 35° = \frac{\sqrt{2}}{2}\left[1 + \frac{\pi}{18} - \frac{1}{2!}\left(\frac{\pi}{18}\right)^2 - \frac{1}{3!}\left(\frac{\pi}{18}\right)^3 + \frac{1}{4!}\left(\frac{\pi}{18}\right)^4 + \frac{1}{5!}\left(\frac{\pi}{18}\right)^5 - \frac{1}{6!}\left(\frac{\pi}{18}\right)^6 - \frac{1}{7!}\left(\frac{\pi}{18}\right)^7 + \cdots\right].$$

Normally one cannot combine terms in an infinite series without affecting its convergence or its sum. For example, the series

$$1 - \tfrac{1}{2} - \tfrac{1}{2} + \tfrac{1}{3} + \tfrac{1}{3} + \tfrac{1}{3} - \tfrac{1}{4} - \tfrac{1}{4} - \tfrac{1}{4} - \tfrac{1}{4} + \tfrac{1}{5} + \tfrac{1}{5} + \tfrac{1}{5} + \tfrac{1}{5} + \tfrac{1}{5} - \tfrac{1}{6} - \cdots$$

clearly diverges because its sequence of partial sums oscillates between the two values 1 and 0, but insertion of parentheses yields the series

$$\left(1 - \tfrac{1}{2} - \tfrac{1}{2}\right) + \left(\tfrac{1}{3} + \tfrac{1}{3} + \tfrac{1}{3} - \tfrac{1}{4} - \tfrac{1}{4} - \tfrac{1}{4} - \tfrac{1}{4}\right) + \left(\tfrac{1}{5} + \tfrac{1}{5} + \tfrac{1}{5} + \tfrac{1}{5} + \tfrac{1}{5} - \tfrac{1}{6} - \cdots - \tfrac{1}{6}\right) + \left(\tfrac{1}{7} + \cdots\right),$$

which converges to zero. One can show that if the terms of a series are decreasing in magnitude with limit zero (as in our present solution) then pairs (or triples, or quadruples) of consecutive terms may be grouped without affecting the convergence or the sum of the series. What is not permitted is the grouping of arbitrarily large numbers of terms, as in the numerical example given here. We will take the series for $\cos 35°$ here and group pairs of terms—the first two positive terms, then the next two negative terms, and so on—to obtain an alternating series. Then, for four-place accuracy, we observe that

$$\frac{1}{4!}\left(\frac{\pi}{18}\right)^4 + \frac{1}{5!}\left(\frac{\pi}{18}\right)^5 \approx 0.00004,$$

which is enough for four-place accuracy. Thus we find that

$$\cos 35° \approx \frac{\sqrt{2}}{2}\left[1 + \frac{\pi}{18} - \frac{1}{2}\left(\frac{\pi}{18}\right)^2 - \frac{1}{6}\left(\frac{\pi}{18}\right)^3\right] \approx 0.8191.$$

We pushed the envelope a little too hard here; the true value of the answer rounds to 0.8192.

31. First we find that
$$\cos x = \frac{\sqrt{2}}{2}\left[\frac{1}{0!} - \frac{1}{1!}\left(x - \frac{\pi}{4}\right) - \frac{1}{2!}\left(x - \frac{\pi}{4}\right)^2 + \frac{1}{3!}\left(x - \frac{\pi}{4}\right)^3 + \frac{1}{4!}\left(x - \frac{\pi}{4}\right)^4 - \frac{1}{5!}\left(x - \frac{\pi}{5}\right)^5 - \cdots\right].$$

We convert 47° to radians and substitute to find that $\cos 47°$ is the sum of the series
$$\frac{\sqrt{2}}{2}\left[1 - \frac{\pi}{90} - \frac{1}{2!}\left(\frac{\pi}{90}\right)^2 + \frac{1}{3!}\left(\frac{\pi}{90}\right)^3 + \frac{1}{4!}\left(\frac{\pi}{90}\right)^4 - \frac{1}{5!}\left(\frac{\pi}{90}\right)^5 - \cdots\right].$$

We make this into an alternating series by grouping terms 2 and 3, terms 4 and 5, and so on. Let $x = \pi/90$. For six-place accuracy, we find that
$$\frac{x^3}{3!} + \frac{x^4}{4!} \approx 0.000007 \quad \text{and} \quad \frac{x^5}{5!} + \frac{x^6}{6!} \approx 0.00000000043,$$

so the first five terms of the (ungrouped) series—through exponent 4—yield the required six-place accuracy: $\cos 47° \approx 0.681998$.

32. The Taylor series for the sine function with center $\pi/3$ is
$$\frac{\sqrt{3}}{2} + \frac{1}{2}\left(x - \frac{\pi}{3}\right) - \frac{\sqrt{3}}{2!\cdot 2}\left(x - \frac{\pi}{3}\right)^2 - \frac{1}{3!\cdot 2}\left(x - \frac{\pi}{3}\right)^3$$
$$+ \frac{\sqrt{3}}{4!\cdot 2}\left(x - \frac{\pi}{3}\right)^4 + \frac{1}{5!\cdot 2}\left(x - \frac{\pi}{3}\right)^5 - \frac{\sqrt{3}}{6!\cdot 2}\left(x - \frac{\pi}{3}\right)^6 - \cdots,$$

and 58° translates into $x = 29\pi/90$ radians, so that
$$y = x - \frac{\pi}{3} = -\frac{\pi}{90}.$$

Hence
$$\sin 58° = \frac{\sqrt{3}}{2} - \frac{1}{2}y - \frac{\sqrt{3}}{2\cdot 2}y^2 + \frac{1}{3!\cdot 2}y^3 + \frac{\sqrt{3}}{4!\cdot 2}y^4 - \frac{1}{5!\cdot 2}y^5 - \frac{\sqrt{3}}{6!\cdot 2}y^6 + \cdots.$$

We proceed to group terms in pairs, much as in the solution of Problem 30. For six-place accuracy, we find that
$$\frac{1}{3!\cdot 2}y^3 + \frac{\sqrt{3}}{4!\cdot 2}y^4 \approx 0.0000036,$$

which is not sufficient for the needed accuracy, but
$$\frac{1}{5!\cdot 2}y^5 + \frac{\sqrt{3}}{6!\cdot 2}y^6 \approx 0.0000000002,$$

quite enough. We sum the series through the terms up to degree 4 to find that $\sin 58° \approx 0.848048$.

33. Note that $e^{0.1} < 1.2 = \frac{6}{5}$, and if $|x| \leq 0.1$, then the Taylor series remainder estimate yields
$$\frac{e^z}{120}x^5 \leq \frac{6}{600}\left(\frac{1}{10}\right)^5 = 10^{-7} < 0.5 \times 10^{-5},$$

so five-place accuracy is assured.

34. The Taylor series remainder estimate yields
$$\frac{\cos z}{720}x^6 \leq \frac{10^{-6}}{720} \approx 1.4 \times 10^{-9} < 0.5 \times 10^{-8},$$

so eight-place accuracy is guaranteed (too conservative, as usual; you actually get 10-place accuracy).

35. The Taylor series remainder estimate is difficult to work with; we will use the cruder alternating series remainder estimate:
$$\frac{(0.1)^5}{5} = 0.5 \times 10^{-5},$$

36. so five-place accuracy is assured.

    The alternating series remainder estimate gives

    $$\frac{3}{16} \cdot (0.1)^3 = 1.875 \times 10^{-4} < 0.5 \times 10^{-3},$$

    so three-place accuracy is obtained.

37. Clearly $|e^z| < \frac{5}{3}$ if $|z| < 0.5$. Hence the Taylor series remainder estimate yields

    $$\left|\frac{e^z}{120}x^5\right| \leq \frac{5}{3 \cdot 120}\left(\frac{1}{2}\right)^5 \approx 0.434 \times 10^{-3},$$

    so three-place accuracy can be obtained if $|x| \leq 0.5$. And

    $$e^{1/3} \approx 1 + \frac{1}{3} + \frac{1}{18} + \frac{1}{486} + \frac{1}{1944} \approx 1.39.$$

48. You should obtain the equations

    $$(a_0)^2 = 1, \quad 2a_0a_1 = 1, \quad (a_1)^2 + 2a_0a_2 = 0,$$
    $$2a_0a_3 + 2a_1a_2 = 0, \quad \text{and} \quad 2a_0a_4 + 2a_1a_3 + (a_2)^2 = 0.$$

    Put $x = 0$; this shows that $a_0 = 1$ (not -1). Then there is no difficulty in solving for $a_1 = \frac{1}{2}$, $a_2 = -\frac{1}{8}$, $a_3 = \frac{1}{16}$, and $a_4 = -\frac{5}{128}$.

54. Here we have

    $$\int_0^{1/2} \frac{x+2}{x^2+x+1}\,dx = \int_0^{1/2}(2 - x - x^2 + 2x^3 - x^4 - x^5 + \cdots)\,dx$$
    $$= \left[2x - \tfrac{1}{2}x^2 - \tfrac{1}{3}x^3 + \tfrac{2}{4}x^4 - \tfrac{1}{5}x^5 - \tfrac{1}{6}x^6 + \tfrac{2}{7}x^7 - \cdots\right]_0^{1/2}$$
    $$= 1 - \frac{1}{2 \cdot 2^2} - \frac{1}{3 \cdot 2^3} + \frac{2}{4 \cdot 2^4} - \frac{1}{5 \cdot 2^5} - \frac{1}{6 \cdot 2^6} + \frac{2}{7 \cdot 2^7} - \cdots.$$

    As in the solution of Problem 30, we may group terms in order to regard this as an alternating series. For maximum error 0.005,

    $$\frac{1}{5 \cdot 2^5} + \frac{1}{6 \cdot 2^6} \approx 0.009, \quad \text{but} \quad \frac{1}{7 \cdot 2^7} + \frac{1}{8 \cdot 2^8} \approx 0.001,$$

    so summing the first six terms of the preceding series yields the approximation

    $$\int_0^{1/2} \frac{x+2}{x^2+x+1}\,dx \approx 0.86.$$

    Mathematica 2.2.2, given the input

    ```
    Integrate[ (x + 1)/(x^2 + x + 1), x ],
    ```

    responds with the antiderivative

    $$(\sqrt{3})\arctan\left(\frac{2x+1}{\sqrt{3}}\right) + \frac{1}{2}\ln(x^2 + x + 1),$$

    which leads to the exact value of the integral:

    $$(\sqrt{3})\arctan\left(\frac{2}{\sqrt{3}}\right) + \frac{1}{2}\ln\left(\frac{7}{4}\right) - \frac{\pi}{2\sqrt{3}}.$$

That is, approximately 0.8574003712690524814.

55. A series approximation to the integrand is

$$1 - x^2 + x^6 - x^8 + x^{12} - x^{14} + \cdots + x^{60} - x^{62},$$

clearly far more terms than we need for two-place accuracy. Term-by-term integration of this series yields

$$\int_0^{1/2} \frac{1}{1+x^2+x^4}\,dx \approx 0.459239825,$$

and numerical integration with *Mathematica* 2.2.2 yields

```
NIntegrate[ 1/(1 + x^2 + x^4), {x, 0, 0.5} ]
0.459240
```

56. A series approximation to the integrand is

$$1 - x^4 + x^{12} - x^{16} + x^{24} - x^{28} + \cdots + x^{240} - x^{244},$$

again far more terms than we need for two-place accuracy. Term-by-term integration of this series yields

$$\int_0^{1/2} \frac{1}{1+x^4+x^8}\,dx \approx 0.493759,$$

and numerical integration with *Mathematica* 2.2.2 yields

```
NIntegrate[ 1/(1 + x^4 + x^8), {x, 0, 0.5} ]
0.493759
```

Chapter 11 Miscellaneous

1. $a_n = \dfrac{1 + (1/n^2)}{1 + (4/n^2)}.$

2. $\frac{8}{7}$

4. $a_n = 0$ for all n, so the limit is zero.

6. $\left\{ \left(-\frac{1}{2}\right)^n \right\} \to 0$, hence so does $\{a_n\}$.

7. $-1 \leq \sin x \leq 1$ for all x, so $\{a_n\} \to 0$ by the squeeze theorem.

8. $(\ln n)/n$ approaches zero, and therefore the answer is 1.

10. Apply l'Hôpital's rule thrice to obtain the limit zero.

12. Multiply numerator and denominator by e^{-n} and use the fact that n/e^n approaches zero; thus the answer is -1.

13. Because e^n/n increases without bound and e^{-n}/n approaches zero, the limit does not exist (it is also correct to say that the given expression approaches $+\infty$).

14. Take the logarithm, let $n = 1/u$, and take the limit as u approaches zero from above. With the aid of l'Hôpital's rule, the answer is 4, and so the original expression has limit e^4.

16. The ratio test involves finding the limit of

$$\left(\frac{n}{n+1}\right)^n (n+1)$$

as n increases without bound. The first factor approaches $1/e$, so the limit is $+\infty$. Therefore the series diverges.

18. The given series converges by comparison with the geometric series having ratio $\frac{3}{4}$.

20. The given series converges by comparison with the p-series for which $p = \frac{3}{2}$ and use of the fact that $0 < \sin\dfrac{1}{n} < 1$ for all $n \geq 1$.

22. The given series diverges by the nth term test: $\lim\limits_{n \to \infty} -\dfrac{2}{n^2} = 0$, and therefore $\lim\limits_{n \to \infty} 2^{-(2/n^2)} = 1 \neq 0$.

24. $10^{1/n} \to 1$ as $n \to +\infty$, so the given series diverges by the nth-term test.

26. The minimum value of $f(n) = \left(\dfrac{n+1}{n}\right)^n$ is 2 if n is restricted to be a positive integer. (A proof of this is outlined below.) Moreover, for each $n \geq 1$, $n < 2^{n+2}$. Therefore

$$1 < \left(\frac{1}{n}\right)(2)\left(2^{n+1}\right) \quad \text{for all} \ n \geq 1.$$

So

$$n+1 < \frac{n+1}{n}\left(\frac{n+1}{n}\right)^n \left(\left(\frac{n+1}{n}\right)^n\right)^{n+1} \quad \text{if} \ n \geq 1.$$

It follows that

$$n+1 < \left(\frac{n+1}{n}\right)^{n^2+2n+1};$$

$$(n+1)\, n^{(n+1)^2} < (n+1)^{(n+1)^2};$$

$$n^{n^2+2n+1} < (n+1)^{n(n+2)};$$

$$n^{(n+1)/n} < (n+1)^{(n+2)/(n+1)};$$

$$n^{1+(1/n)} < (n+1)^{1+(1/(n+1))}.$$

So the sequence with n^{th} term $\dfrac{1}{n^{1+(1/n)}}$ is strictly monotone decreasing, positive, and dominated by the sequence with n^{th} term $1/n$. Hence it also has limit zero. Therefore, by the alternating series test, the given series converges.

To prove the first assertion of this solution, one method is to show that if

$$f(x) = \left(\frac{x+1}{x}\right)^x, \quad x \geq 1,$$

then $f'(x) > 0$ for all $x \geq 1$. Another method is to show (by induction on n, possibly) that

$$\left(\frac{n+1}{n}\right)^n < \left(\frac{n+2}{n+1}\right)^{n+1} \quad \text{for all} \ n \geq 1.$$

28. $\lim\limits_{x \to \infty} x \sin\dfrac{1}{x} = \lim\limits_{u \to 0^+} \dfrac{\sin u}{u} = 1$, so the given series diverges by the nth-term test.

30. $\displaystyle\int_3^\infty \dfrac{1}{x(\ln x)(\ln \ln x)^2}\, dx = \left[-\dfrac{1}{\ln \ln x}\right]_3^\infty = \dfrac{1}{\ln \ln 3} < +\infty$, so the given series converges by the integral test.

31. Is this not the Maclaurin series for $f(x) = e^{2x}$?

32. Limit: $\frac{3}{2}|x|$. Interval of convergence: $\left(-\frac{2}{3}, \frac{2}{3}\right)$.

34. Limit: $\frac{1}{4}|2x - 3|$. Interval of convergence: $\left(-\frac{1}{2}, \frac{7}{2}\right)$.

36. Limit: $|2x-1|$. Interval of convergence: $0 \leq x \leq 1$.
38. Limit: $|x|$. Interval of convergence: $-1 \leq x < 1$.
40. Limit: $|x-1|$. Interval of convergence: $(0, 2)$.
42. Limit by the ratio test: $|\ln x|$. This limit is less than 1 if $1/e < x < e$. This series diverges for $x = 1/e$ and for $x = e$, and therefore the interval of convergence is $(1/e, e)$.
43. Use the ratio test.
44. $271801/99990$
46. If $\sum a_n$ converges, then $\{a_n\} \to 0$. So $a_n \leq 1$ for all $n \geq N$ (where N is some sufficiently large integer). So the series $\sum a_n$ (eventually) dominates $\sum (a_n)^2$; therefore the latter series also converges.
48. (a) $F_1 = 1 < 2^1$ and $F_2 = 1 < 2^2$. If $n \geq 2$, then $F_{n+1} = F_n + F_{n-1}$, so $F_n > 0$ for all $n \geq 1$. Moreover, if $F_n \leq 2^n$ and $F_{n-1} \leq 2^{n-1}$, then

$$F_{n+1} \leq 2^n + 2^{n-1} < 2^n + 2^n = 2^{n+1}.$$

Therefore, by induction, $F_n \leq 2^n$ for all $n \geq 1$. Hence

$$\sum_{n=1}^{\infty} 2^n x^n \text{ dominates } \sum_{n=1}^{\infty} F_n x^n.$$

Because the former converges absolutely for $|x| < \frac{1}{2}$, so does the latter.

(b)
$$\begin{aligned}
(1 - x - x^2)&\left(F_1 x + F_2 x^2 + F_3 x^3 + F_4 x^4 + \cdots\right) \\
&= F_1 x + F_2 x^2 + F_3 x^3 + F_4 x^4 + F_5 x^5 + \cdots \\
&\quad - F_1 x^2 - F_2 x^3 - F_3 x^4 - F_4 x^5 - \cdots \\
&\quad - F_1 x^3 - F_2 x^4 - F_3 x^5 - \cdots \\
&\quad \cdots \\
&= F_1 x + (F_2 - F_1) x^2 + (F_3 - F_2 - F_1) x^3 \\
&\quad + (F_4 - F_3 - F_2) x^4 \\
&\quad + (F_5 - F_4 - F_3) x^5 + \cdots \\
&= x + (1-1) x^2 + (0) x^3 + (0) x^4 + (0) x^5 + \cdots \\
&= x.
\end{aligned}$$

Therefore $F(x) = \dfrac{x}{1 - x - x^2}$.

Note: Application of the ratio test to the given power series yields the limit $\frac{1}{2}\left(1 + \sqrt{5}\right)|x|$, so the radius of convergence of the series for $F(x)$ is actually $\dfrac{1}{\tau} = \frac{1}{2}\left(\sqrt{5} - 1\right) \approx 0.618034$.

50. We test $\displaystyle\sum_{n=1}^{\infty} \ln\left(1 + \frac{1}{n^2}\right)$, using the integral test, with integration by parts:

$$\begin{bmatrix} u = \ln\left(1 + \dfrac{1}{x^2}\right) & dv = dx \\ du = -\dfrac{2}{x(x^2+1)} dx & v = x \end{bmatrix} \quad \int \ln\left(1 + \frac{1}{x^2}\right) dx = x \ln\left(1 + \frac{1}{x^2}\right) + 2\tan^{-1} x + C.$$

It follows that $\displaystyle\int_1^{\infty} \ln\left(1 + \frac{1}{x^2}\right) dx = \frac{\pi}{2} - \ln 2 < +\infty$. Therefore the series in question converges by the integral test. And so, by definition, the given infinite product also converges. The integral test remainder estimate for the series yields

$$\pi - (n+1)\ln\left(1 + \frac{1}{(n+1)^2}\right) - 2\tan^{-1}(n+1) \leq R_n \leq \pi - n\ln\left(1 + \frac{1}{n^2}\right) - 2\tan^{-1} n.$$

With $n = 100$, the upper and lower estimates differ by about 0.000099005, and we have

$$0.0099008285 \leq R_n \leq 0.0099998336.$$

Now $S_{100} \approx 1.291896397$, so the sum of the series is trapped between 1.301797226 and 1.301896231. We apply the exponential function and thereby may conclude that

$$3.675897152 < \prod_{n=1}^{\infty}\left(1 + \frac{1}{n^2}\right) < 3.676261103.$$

So, to three places, the value of the infinite product is 3.676.

52. $\ln(1+x) = x - \frac{1}{2}x^2 + \frac{1}{3}x^3 - \frac{1}{4}x^4 + \cdots$. For three-place accuracy, we need the first five terms of this series, and we find that

$$0.182266666 < \ln(1.2) < 0.182330667.$$

So $\ln(1.2) = 0.182$ to three places.

53. $\displaystyle\int_0^{0.5}\left(1 - x^2 + \frac{x^4}{2!} - \frac{x^6}{3!} + \cdots\right) dx = \left[x - \frac{1}{3}x^3 + \frac{1}{2!\,5}x^5 - \frac{1}{3!\,7}x^7 + \cdots\right]_0^{0.5}$

$$= \frac{1}{2} - \frac{1}{3 \cdot 2^3} + \frac{1}{2!\,5 \cdot 2^5} - \frac{1}{3!\,7 \cdot 2^7} + \cdots$$

$$= \sum_{n=1}^{\infty}\frac{(-1)^{n+1}}{n!\,(2n+1)\cdot 2^{2n+1}} \approx 0.461281006413.$$

54. $\displaystyle\int_0^{0.5}\left(1 + \frac{1}{3}x^4 - \frac{1}{9}x^8 + \frac{5}{81}x^{12} - \frac{10}{243}x^{16} + \frac{22}{729}x^{20} - \cdots\right) dx$

$$= \left[x + \frac{1}{15}x^5 - \frac{1}{81}x^9 + \frac{5}{1053}x^{13} - \frac{10}{4131}x^{17} + \frac{22}{15309}x^{21} - \cdots\right]_0^{0.5}$$

$$= \frac{1}{2} + \frac{1}{15 \cdot 2^5} - \frac{1}{81 \cdot 2^9} + \frac{5}{1053 \cdot 2^{13}} - \frac{10}{4131 \cdot 2^{17}} + \cdots \approx 0.502059782500.$$

55. $\displaystyle\int_0^1\left(1 - \frac{1}{2}x + \frac{1}{6}x^2 - \frac{1}{24}x^3 + \frac{1}{120}x^4 - \frac{1}{720}x^5 + \cdots\right) dx$

$$= \left[x - \frac{1}{4}x^2 + \frac{1}{18}x^3 - \frac{1}{96}x^4 + \frac{1}{600}x^5 - \frac{1}{4320}x^6 + \cdots\right]_0^1$$

$$1 - \frac{1}{2!\,2} + \frac{1}{3!\,3} - \frac{1}{4!\,4} + \frac{1}{5!\,5} - \frac{1}{6!\,6} + \cdots \approx 0.796599599297.$$

57. $\displaystyle\cos 2xt = \sum_{k=0}^{\infty}\frac{(-1)^k 2^{2k} x^{2k}}{(2k)!} t^{2k}.$

$$\int_0^{\infty} t^{2n} e^{-t^2}\, dt = \left[-\frac{1}{2}t^{2n-1} e^{-t^2}\right]_0^{\infty} + \frac{1}{2}(2n-1)\int_0^{\infty} t^{2n-2} e^{-t^2}\, dt$$

(this comes from an integration by parts with $u = t^{2n-1}$). It now follows that

$$\int_0^{\infty} t^{2n} e^{-t^2}\, dt = \frac{(2n)!}{n!\,2^{2n+1}}\sqrt{\pi} \quad \text{for all } n \geq 0.$$

Therefore

$$\int_0^\infty e^{-t^2} \cos 2xt\, dt = \int_0^\infty \left(\sum_{k=0}^\infty \frac{(-1)^k\, 2^{2k} x^{2k}}{(2k)!} t^{2k} e^{-t^2} \right) dt$$

$$= \sum_{k=0}^\infty \left((-1)^k \frac{2^{2k}}{(2k)!} x^{2k} \int_0^\infty t^{2k} e^{-t^2}\, dt \right)$$

$$= \sum_{k=0}^\infty \left(\frac{(-1)^k\, 2^{2k} x^{2k}}{(2k)!} \right) \left(\frac{(2k)!}{k!\, 2^{2k+1}} \right) \sqrt{\pi}$$

$$= \sum_{k=0}^\infty (-1)^k \frac{x^{2k}}{k!\, 2} \sqrt{\pi}$$

$$= \tfrac{1}{2}\sqrt{\pi} \sum_{k=0}^\infty (-1)^k \frac{(x^2)^k}{k!} = \tfrac{1}{2}\sqrt{\pi}\, e^{-x^2}.$$

58. $\displaystyle \int_0^x \frac{dt}{1-t^2} = \int_0^x \left(1 + t^2 + t^4 + t^6 + \cdots \right) dt$

$$= \left[t + \frac{1}{3} t^3 + \frac{1}{5} t^5 + \frac{1}{7} t^7 + \cdots \right]_0^x$$

$$= x + \frac{1}{3} x^3 + \frac{1}{5} x^5 + \frac{1}{7} x^7 + \cdots = \sum_{n=0}^\infty \frac{x^{2n+1}}{2n+1}.$$

60. $a_0 = 0$, $a_1 = 1$, $a_2 = 0$, and $a_3 = \tfrac{1}{3}$.

64. $\displaystyle P_k = \prod_{n=2}^k \frac{n^2}{n^2 - 1} = \left(\frac{2 \cdot 2}{1 \cdot 3} \right) \left(\frac{3 \cdot 3}{2 \cdot 4} \right) \left(\frac{4 \cdot 4}{3 \cdot 5} \right) \cdots \left(\frac{k \cdot k}{(k-1) \cdot (k+1)} \right) = \frac{2k}{k+1} \to 2$ as $k \to \infty$.

So $\displaystyle \prod_{n=2}^\infty \frac{n^2}{n^2 - 1} = 2$.

Extra: Here's a nice problem contributed by one of our students.

Test for convergence: $\displaystyle \sum_{n=1}^\infty \frac{1}{(2^1)(2^{1/2})(2^{1/3}) \cdots (2^{1/n})}$.

65. We compute as follows: Let $x = \sqrt{5}$. Then

$$x^2 = 5;$$
$$x^2 - 4 = 1;$$
$$x - 2 = \frac{1}{2 + x};$$
$$x = 2 + \frac{1}{2 + x};$$

the continued fraction in the answer section now follows.

66. The sum of the series is

$$S = 1 + \tfrac{1}{2} - \tfrac{2}{3} + \tfrac{1}{4} + \tfrac{1}{5} - \tfrac{2}{6} + \tfrac{1}{7} - \cdots = f(1)$$

where

$$f(x) = x + \tfrac{1}{2} x^2 - \tfrac{2}{3} x^3 + \tfrac{1}{4} x^4 + \tfrac{1}{5} x^5 - \tfrac{2}{6} x^6 + \tfrac{1}{7} x^7 + \cdots;$$
$$f'(x) = 1 + x - 2x^2 + x^3 + x^4 - 2x^5 + x^6 + \cdots, \quad -1 < x < 1.$$

Absolute convergence on $-1 < x < 1$ lets us rearrange and sum:

$$f'(x) = \frac{1 + x - 2x^2}{1 - x^3} = \frac{2x + 1}{x^2 + x + 1}.$$

It follows that $f(x) = C + \ln(x^2 + x + 1); 0 = f(0) = C$, so

$$f(x) = \ln(x^2 + x + 1), \quad 1 < x < 1.$$

But the original series converges if $-1 \leq x \leq 1$, so by a theorem of Abel, its sum is $\ln(x^2 + x + 1)$ for $-1 \leq x \leq 1$. Therefore the sum of the series is $S = f(1) = \ln 3$.

Chapter 12: Vectors, Curves, and Surfaces in Space
Section 12.1

1. $\mathbf{v} = \langle 3-1, 5-2 \rangle = \langle 2, 3 \rangle$
2. $\mathbf{v} = \langle 1-(-2), 4-(-3) \rangle = \langle 3, 7 \rangle$
3. $\mathbf{v} = \langle -5-5, -10-10 \rangle = \langle -10, -20 \rangle$
4. $\mathbf{v} = \langle 15-(-10), -25-20 \rangle = \langle 35, -45 \rangle$
5. $\langle 1, -2 \rangle + \langle 3, 4 \rangle = \langle 4, 2 \rangle$
6. $\langle 4-2, 2+5 \rangle = \langle 2, 7 \rangle$
7. $(3\mathbf{i} + 5\mathbf{j}) + (2\mathbf{i} - 7\mathbf{j}) = 5\mathbf{i} + (-2)\mathbf{j} = 5\mathbf{i} - 2\mathbf{j}$
8. $(7\mathbf{i} + 5\mathbf{j}) + (-10\mathbf{i}) = -3\mathbf{i} + 5\mathbf{j}$
10. $|\mathbf{a}| = 5$, $|-2\mathbf{b}| = 10$, $|\mathbf{a} - \mathbf{b}| = 5\sqrt{2}$, $\mathbf{a} + \mathbf{b} = \langle -1, 7 \rangle$, and $3\mathbf{a} - 2\mathbf{b} = \langle 17, 6 \rangle$.
12. $2\sqrt{65}$, $12\sqrt{5}$, $20\sqrt{2}$, and $\langle 4, -8 \rangle$.
14. $\sqrt{29}$, $2\sqrt{37}$, $\sqrt{2}$, $3\mathbf{i} - 11\mathbf{j}$, and $4\mathbf{i} - 3\mathbf{j}$.
16. $\sqrt{2}$, $4\sqrt{2}$, $3\sqrt{2}$, $\mathbf{i} + \mathbf{j}$, and $-7\mathbf{i} - 7\mathbf{j}$.
18. $|\mathbf{a}| = 13$; choose $\mathbf{u} = \frac{5}{13}\mathbf{i} - \frac{12}{13}\mathbf{j}$; $\mathbf{v} = -\frac{5}{13}\mathbf{i} + \frac{12}{13}\mathbf{j}$.
20. $\mathbf{u} = \frac{7}{25}\mathbf{i} - \frac{24}{25}\mathbf{j}$, $\mathbf{v} = -\frac{7}{25}\mathbf{i} + \frac{24}{25}\mathbf{j}$.
21. $\langle 3, -2 \rangle - \langle 3, 2 \rangle = \langle 0, -4 \rangle = -4\mathbf{j}$.
22. $\mathbf{j}$
24. $-5\mathbf{i}$
26. $\mathbf{a} \cdot \mathbf{b} = (3)(0) + (3)(-1) = -3 \neq 0$; $\mathbf{a}$ and $\mathbf{b}$ are not perpendicular to each other.
27. $\mathbf{a} \cdot \mathbf{b} = (2)(8) + (-1)(4) = 12 \neq 0$; not perpendicular.
28. $\mathbf{a} \cdot \mathbf{b} = 120 - 120 = 0$; $\mathbf{a}$ and $\mathbf{b}$ are perpendicular.
29. $r\langle 2, 3 \rangle + s\langle 3, 4 \rangle = \langle 1, 0 \rangle$: $\quad 2r + 3s = 1$ and $3r + 4s = 0$; $\quad r = -4$, $s = 3$.
    Hence $\mathbf{i} = -4\mathbf{a} + 3\mathbf{b}$. Similarly, $\mathbf{j} = 3\mathbf{a} - 2\mathbf{b}$.
30. $\mathbf{i} = 9\mathbf{b} - 7\mathbf{a}$ and $\mathbf{j} = 5\mathbf{b} - 4\mathbf{a}$.
31. $\langle 2, -3 \rangle = r\langle 1, 1 \rangle + s\langle 1, -1 \rangle$: $\quad r = -\frac{1}{2}$ and $s = \frac{5}{2}$.
32. $\mathbf{c} = 37\mathbf{a} - 13\mathbf{b}$.
34. (a) $12\mathbf{i} - 20\mathbf{j}$; (b) $\frac{3}{4}\mathbf{i} - \frac{5}{4}\mathbf{j}$
36. $\langle c, 2 \rangle \cdot \langle c, -8 \rangle = c^2 - 16$; $c^2 - 16 = 0$ when $c = 4$ and when $c = -4$.
37. $(2c\mathbf{i} - 4\mathbf{j}) \cdot (3\mathbf{i} + c\mathbf{j}) = 0$ when $6c - 4c = 0$, thus when $c = 0$.
40. $(r + s)\langle a_1, a_2 \rangle = \langle (r+s)a_1, (r+s)a_2 \rangle$
    $= \langle ra_1 + sa_1, ra_2 + sa_2 \rangle$
    $= \langle ra_1, ra_2 \rangle + \langle sa_1, sa_2 \rangle$
    $= r\langle a_1, a_2 \rangle + s\langle a_1, a_2 \rangle = r\mathbf{a} + s\mathbf{a}$.
43. With $\mathbf{T}_1 = \langle T_1 \cos 30°, T_1 \sin 30° \rangle$, $\mathbf{T}_2 = \langle -T_2 \cos 30°, T_2 \sin 30° \rangle$, and $\mathbf{F} = \langle 0, -100 \rangle$, the "equation of balance" $\mathbf{T}_1 + \mathbf{T}_2 + \mathbf{F} = \mathbf{0}$ yields $T_1 = T_2 = 100$.
44. With $\mathbf{T}_1 = \langle T_1 \cos 30°, T_1 \sin 30° \rangle$, $\mathbf{T}_2 = \langle -T_2 \cos 45°, T_2 \sin 45° \rangle$, and $\mathbf{F} = \langle 0, -50 \rangle$, the equation $\mathbf{T}_1 + \mathbf{T}_2 + \mathbf{F} = \mathbf{0}$ yields
$$T_1 = \frac{100}{1 + \sqrt{3}} \quad \text{and} \quad T_2 = \frac{50\sqrt{6}}{1 + \sqrt{3}}.$$

Thus $T_1 \approx 36.602540378$ and $T_2 \approx 44.828773608$.

45. With $\mathbf{T}_1 = \langle T_1 \cos 40°, T_1 \sin 40° \rangle$, $\mathbf{T}_2 = \langle -T_2 \cos 55°, T_2 \sin 55° \rangle$, and $\mathbf{F} = \langle 0, -125 \rangle$, the equation $\mathbf{T}_1 + \mathbf{T}_2 + \mathbf{F} = 0$ yields

$$T_1 = \frac{125 \cos 55°}{\cos 55° \sin 40° + \cos 40° \sin 55°} \approx 71.970925645$$

and

$$T_2 = \frac{125 \cos 40°}{\cos 55° \sin 40° + \cos 40° \sin 55°} \approx 96.121326055.$$

46. With $\mathbf{T}_1 = \langle \frac{3}{5}T_1, \frac{4}{5}T_1 \rangle$, $\mathbf{T}_2 = \langle -\frac{4}{5}T_2, \frac{3}{5}T_2 \rangle$, and $\mathbf{F} = \langle 0, -150 \rangle$, the balance equation $\mathbf{T}_1 + \mathbf{T}_2 + \mathbf{F} = 0$ yields $T_1 = 120$ and $T_2 = 90$.

47. Begin with the equation $500\mathbf{i} = \mathbf{v}_a - 25\sqrt{2}\,\mathbf{i} - 25\sqrt{2}\,\mathbf{j}$.

48. Use $\mathbf{v}_a = \mathbf{v}_g - \mathbf{w} = \langle -500, 0 \rangle - 25\sqrt{2}\langle -1, -1 \rangle$.

50. Denote the vertices of the triangle by $A(a_1, a_2)$, $B(b_1, b_2)$, and $C(c_1, c_2)$. Compute the vectors $\overrightarrow{AB}$, $\overrightarrow{BC}$, $\overrightarrow{CA}$, and their sum in terms of the coordinates $a_1, a_2, \ldots, c_2$.

52. $\overrightarrow{AM_1} + \overrightarrow{M_1B} = \overrightarrow{AB}$, $\overrightarrow{CM_2} + \overrightarrow{M_2A} = \overrightarrow{CA}$, and $\overrightarrow{AB} + \overrightarrow{BC} + \overrightarrow{CA} = 0$.
But $\overrightarrow{AM_1} = \overrightarrow{M_1B}$ and $\overrightarrow{AM_2} = \overrightarrow{M_2C}$. So $2\overrightarrow{AM_1} + 2\overrightarrow{M_2A} + \overrightarrow{BC} = 0$.
Also $\overrightarrow{AM_1} + \overrightarrow{M_2A} + \overrightarrow{M_1M_2} = 0$. Therefore $-2\overrightarrow{M_1M_2} + \overrightarrow{BC} = 0$; that is, $\overrightarrow{M_1M_2} = \frac{1}{2}\overrightarrow{BC}$.

53. Alternative suggestion: Let Q be the points where the diagonals cross. Then $\overrightarrow{QC} = r\overrightarrow{AQ}$ and $\overrightarrow{QD} = s\overrightarrow{BQ}$ for some scalars r and s. Apply the result of Problem 50 to such triangles as ABC and ABD to show that $r = s = \frac{1}{2}$. Note that if the vectors $\mathbf{u}$ and $\mathbf{v}$ are not parallel but $\mathbf{u} = r\mathbf{v}$, then $r = 0$.

54. We use the notation indicated in the figure to the right. First,

$$\overrightarrow{AB} + \overrightarrow{BC} + \overrightarrow{CD} + \overrightarrow{DA} = 0.$$

So

$$2\overrightarrow{AP} + 2\overrightarrow{BQ} + 2\overrightarrow{CR} + 2\overrightarrow{DS} = 0.$$

Consequently,

$$\overrightarrow{AP} + \overrightarrow{BQ} = -\left(\overrightarrow{CR} + \overrightarrow{DS}\right);$$
$$\overrightarrow{PB} + \overrightarrow{BQ} = -\left(\overrightarrow{RD} + \overrightarrow{DS}\right);$$
Therefore $\overrightarrow{PQ} = -\overrightarrow{RS}$.

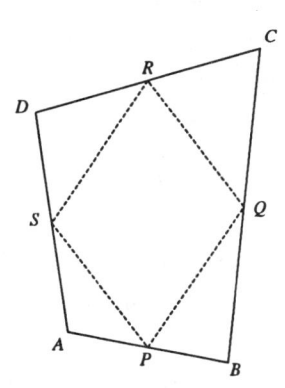

So the two sides PQ and RS are parallel. (one is a scalar multiple of the other) and of equal length (the scalar is -1). We may now conclude that $PQRS$ is a parallelogram.

Section 12.2

2. $\langle 1, 4, -1 \rangle$; $\langle -15, -16, 26 \rangle$; -13; 9; $\frac{1}{5}\langle -\sqrt{5}, 0, \sqrt{20} \rangle$
4. $9\mathbf{i} - 3\mathbf{j} + 3\mathbf{k}$; $-14\mathbf{i} - 21\mathbf{j} + 43\mathbf{k}$; -34; $3\sqrt{21}$; $(2\mathbf{i} - 3\mathbf{j} + 5\mathbf{k})/\sqrt{38}$
6. (a) $3\mathbf{i} - \mathbf{j} + 4\mathbf{k}$; (b) $-\mathbf{i} - 18\mathbf{j} + 17\mathbf{k}$; (c) -11; (d) $5\sqrt{2}$; (e) $\frac{1}{14}\sqrt{14}\,(\mathbf{i} - 2\mathbf{j} + 3\mathbf{k})$

7. $80°$
8. $145°$
9. $90°$ (exactly)
10. $127°$
11. $98°$
12. $142°$
14. $\text{comp}_\mathbf{b}\mathbf{a} = -\frac{13}{10}\sqrt{2}$; $\text{comp}_\mathbf{a}\mathbf{b} = -\frac{13}{5}\sqrt{5}$.
16. $\text{comp}_\mathbf{b}\mathbf{a} = -\frac{34}{\sqrt{83}}$; $\text{comp}_\mathbf{a}\mathbf{b} = -\frac{34}{\sqrt{38}}$.
18. Both are $-\frac{11}{14}\sqrt{14}$
19. $x^2 + y^2 + z^2 - 6x - 2y - 4z = 11$
20. $x^2 + y^2 + z^2 + 4x - 2y + 10z + 23 = 0$
21. $x^2 + y^2 + z^2 - 10x - 8y + 2z + 7 = 0$
22. $x^2 + y^2 + z^2 - 8x - 10y + 4z + 7 = 0$
23. $x^2 + y^2 + z^2 = 4z$
24. $x^2 + y^2 + z^2 - 6x + 8y - 6z + 18 = 0$
26. $(x-4)^2 + \left(y - \frac{9}{2}\right)^2 + (z+5)^2 = \frac{85}{4}$. Center: $\left(4, \frac{9}{2}, -5\right)$. Radius: $\frac{1}{2}\sqrt{85}$.
28. $x^2 + y^2 + z^2 - \frac{7}{2}x - \frac{9}{2}y - \frac{11}{2}z = 0$: $\left(x - \frac{7}{4}\right)^2 + \left(y - \frac{9}{4}\right)^2 + \left(z - \frac{11}{4}\right)^2 = \frac{49}{16} + \frac{81}{16} + \frac{121}{16} = \frac{251}{16}$; center $\left(\frac{7}{4}, \frac{9}{4}, \frac{11}{4}\right)$, radius $\frac{1}{4}\sqrt{251}$.
29. The xy-plane
30. $x = 0$: The yz-plane.
32. $xy = 0$: The union of the yz-plane and the xz-plane.
34. $x^2 + y^2 + z^2 + 7 = 0$: No points satisfy this equation.
35. The single point $(0,0,0)$
36. $(x-1)^2 + y^2 + z^2 = 0$: The single point $(1,0,0)$.
37. $(x-3)^2 + (y+4)^2 + (z-0)^2 = 0$: The single point $(3,-4,0)$.
38. The z-axis
39. $\mathbf{b} = \frac{3}{2}\mathbf{a}$, so $\mathbf{a}$ and $\mathbf{b}$ are parallel; $\mathbf{a} \cdot \mathbf{b} = 84$, so $\mathbf{a}$ and $\mathbf{b}$ are not perpendicular.
40. Each of $\mathbf{b} = r\mathbf{a}$ and $\mathbf{a} = s\mathbf{b}$ leads to a contradiction, so $\mathbf{a}$ and $\mathbf{b}$ are not parallel; $\mathbf{a} \cdot \mathbf{b} = 24$, so $\mathbf{a}$ and $\mathbf{b}$ are not perpendicular.
41. $\mathbf{a} = -\frac{4}{3}\mathbf{b}$, so $\mathbf{a}$ and $\mathbf{b}$ are parallel; $\mathbf{a} \cdot \mathbf{b} = -600$, so $\mathbf{a}$ and $\mathbf{b}$ are not perpendicular.
42. Each of $\mathbf{b} = r\mathbf{a}$ and $\mathbf{a} = r\mathbf{b}$ leads to a contradiction, so $\mathbf{a}$ and $\mathbf{b}$ are not parallel; $\mathbf{a} \cdot \mathbf{b} = 0$, so $\mathbf{a}$ and $\mathbf{b}$ are perpendicular.
43. $\overrightarrow{QR} = 3\overrightarrow{PQ}$, so P, Q, and R are collinear.
44. $\overrightarrow{QR} = -3\overrightarrow{PQ}$, so P, Q, and R are collinear.
45. All three angles are exactly $60°$.
46. $\angle A \approx 56°$, $\angle B = 90°$, $\angle C \approx 34°$
47. $\angle A \approx 79°$, $\angle B \approx 64°$, $\angle C \approx 37°$
48. $\angle A = 90°$, $\angle B \approx 68°$, $\angle C \approx 22°$

50. $\cos\alpha = -\dfrac{1}{\sqrt{46}}$; $\cos\beta = \dfrac{3}{\sqrt{46}}$; $\cos\gamma = -\dfrac{6}{\sqrt{46}}$.
So the direction angles are approximately 1.71878, 1.11261, and 2.65654.

52. $\alpha \approx 74.2188°$, $\beta \approx 49.2535°$, $\gamma = 45°$

53. $\overrightarrow{PQ} = \langle 3, 1, 0\rangle$, $\overrightarrow{F} = \langle 1, 0, -1\rangle$: $W = \overrightarrow{F} \cdot \overrightarrow{PQ} = 3$.

54. $\langle 2, -3, 5\rangle \cdot \langle -6, -5, 9\rangle = 48$

55. $40(\cos 40°) \cdot 1000 \cdot (0.239) \approx 7323.385$ (cal) (less than 8 Cal)

56. $200(\sec 5°) \cdot 10 \cdot (22/15)/550 \approx 5.353706$ (hp)

58. If θ is the angle between $\mathbf{a}$ and $\mathbf{b}$, then $\cos\theta = \dfrac{\mathbf{a}\cdot\mathbf{b}}{|\mathbf{a}|\,|\mathbf{b}|}$. Therefore, because $-1 \leq \cos\theta \leq 1$, $\dfrac{\mathbf{a}\cdot\mathbf{b}}{|\mathbf{a}|\,|\mathbf{b}|} \leq 1$. Consequently $\mathbf{a}\cdot\mathbf{b} \leq |\mathbf{a}|\,|\mathbf{b}|$.

59. Begin with the observation that $|\mathbf{a}+\mathbf{b}|^2 = (\mathbf{a}+\mathbf{b})\cdot(\mathbf{a}+\mathbf{b})$.

61. The simultaneous equations $\mathbf{u}\cdot\mathbf{w} = 0 = \mathbf{v}\cdot\mathbf{w}$ yield the scalar equations
$$w_1 + 2w_2 - 3w_3 = 0,$$
$$2w_1 + w_3 = 0,$$
which in turn yield $w_2 = -\tfrac{7}{2}w_1$ and $w_3 = -2w_1$ where w_1 is an arbitrary nonzero scalar. For example, $\mathbf{w} = \langle 2, -7, -4\rangle$.

62. The angle between $\overrightarrow{OP}$ and $\mathbf{i}$ is $\arccos\left(\tfrac{1}{3}\sqrt{3}\right) \approx 0.955316618$, about $54°\ 44'\ 8.2''$.

64. We think of $\mathbf{a}$, $\mathbf{b}$, and $\mathbf{c}$ as having the same initial point. Now
$$\mathbf{c} = \frac{b\mathbf{a} + a\mathbf{b}}{a + b}$$
is a linear combination of $\mathbf{a}$ and $\mathbf{b}$, so $\mathbf{c}$ lies in the plane determined by $\mathbf{a}$ and $\mathbf{b}$. Let ϕ denote the angle between the vectors $\mathbf{a}$ and $\mathbf{c}$. Note that $\cos\phi = \dfrac{\mathbf{a}\cdot\mathbf{c}}{|\mathbf{a}|\,|\mathbf{c}|}$. Now
$$\mathbf{a}\cdot\mathbf{c} = \frac{\mathbf{a}\cdot(b\mathbf{a} + a\mathbf{b})}{a+b} = \frac{a^2 b + a^2 b \cos\theta}{a+b}$$
where θ is the angle between $\mathbf{a}$ and $\mathbf{b}$. So
$$\mathbf{a}\cdot\mathbf{c} = \frac{a^2 b}{a+b}(1 + \cos\theta) = \frac{2a^2 b}{a+b}\cos^2\left(\frac{\theta}{2}\right).$$
But $|\mathbf{a}| = a$; moreover,
$$|\mathbf{c}| = \frac{\sqrt{(b\mathbf{a}+a\mathbf{b})\cdot(b\mathbf{a}+a\mathbf{b})}}{a+b}$$
$$= \frac{\sqrt{b^2 a^2 + 2ab(\mathbf{a}\cdot\mathbf{b}) + a^2 b^2}}{a+b}$$
$$= \frac{\sqrt{2a^2 b^2 + 2a^2 b^2 \cos\theta}}{a+b}$$
$$= \frac{ab}{a+b}\sqrt{4\left(\frac{1+\cos\theta}{2}\right)} = \frac{2ab}{a+b}\cos(\theta/2).$$
Therefore $\cos\phi = 2\dfrac{a^2 b}{a+b}\cos^2(\theta/2)\dfrac{a+b}{2a^2 b\cos(\theta/2)} = \cos(\theta/2)$. It now follows that $\phi = \theta/2$. Similarly, the angle between the vectors $\mathbf{b}$ and $\mathbf{c}$ is also equal to $\theta/2$. Consequently $\mathbf{c}$ bisects the angle between $\mathbf{a}$ and $\mathbf{b}$.

Alternative proof (using some geometry): Both $b\mathbf{a}$ and $a\mathbf{b}$ have length $|\mathbf{a}||\mathbf{b}|$. So they form two sides of a rhombus. Their sum is a diagonal of the rhombus, and a theorem of geometry tells us that each diagonal of a rhombus bisects the angles at its ends.

66. See the figure below.

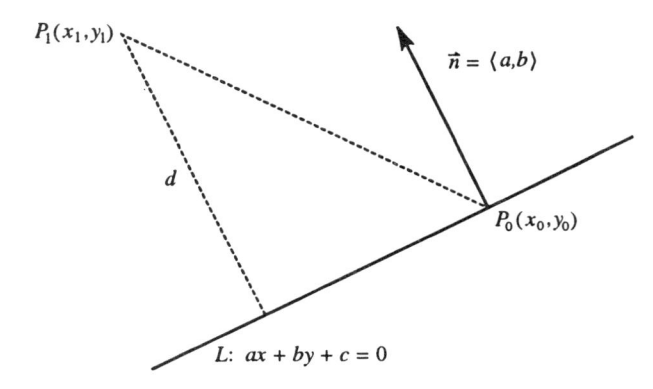

Given: d is the perpendicular distance from P_1 to L. Then

$$d = \left|\text{comp}_{\vec{n}}\left(\overrightarrow{P_0P_1}\right)\right| = \frac{\left(\vec{n} \cdot \overrightarrow{P_0P_1}\right)}{|\vec{n}|}$$

$$= \frac{|ax_1 - ax_0 + by_1 - by_0|}{\sqrt{a^2+b^2}}.$$

Because P_0 is on L, $ax_0 + by_0 + c = 0$. Then the result of Problem 48 follows.

68. $\overrightarrow{AP} = \langle x-1, y-3, z-5\rangle$. But $\vec{n}$ is perpendicular to $\overrightarrow{AP}$, so $\vec{n} \cdot \overrightarrow{AP} = 0$; this leads to the equation $x - y + 2z = 8$. In the language of geometry, we'd say that the locus of $P(x,y,z)$ is the plane through the point A perpendicular to the vector $\vec{n}$.

70. If $A = (0,0,0)$, $B = (1,1,0)$, and $C = \left(\frac{1}{2}, \frac{1}{2}, \frac{1}{2}\right)$, then the angle between $\overrightarrow{CA}$ and $\overrightarrow{CB}$ is approximately 1.910633236; that is, about $109°\ 28'\ 16.4''$.

Section 12.3

1. $\mathbf{a} \times \mathbf{b} = \begin{vmatrix} \mathbf{i} & \mathbf{j} & \mathbf{k} \\ 5 & -1 & -2 \\ -3 & 2 & 4 \end{vmatrix} = (-4+4)\mathbf{i} - (20-6)\mathbf{j} + (10-3)\mathbf{k}$.

2. $4\mathbf{i} + 6\mathbf{j} + 9\mathbf{k}$

4. $-24\mathbf{j} - 24\mathbf{k}$

5. $\langle 2, -3, 0\rangle \times \langle 4, 5, 0\rangle = \langle 0, 0, 22\rangle$

6. $\langle -5, 2, 0\rangle \times \langle 7, -11, 0\rangle = \langle 0, 0, 41\rangle$

7. $\mathbf{c} = \mathbf{a} \times \mathbf{b} = \langle 36, -9, 12\rangle$, so $\mathbf{v} = -\mathbf{u} = \dfrac{\mathbf{c}}{|\mathbf{c}|} = \frac{1}{13}\langle 12, -3, 4\rangle$.

8. $\mathbf{c} = \mathbf{a} \times \mathbf{b} = \langle 1, 1, -1\rangle$, so $\mathbf{v} = -\mathbf{u} = \dfrac{\mathbf{c}}{|\mathbf{c}|} = \frac{1}{3}\langle \sqrt{3}, \sqrt{3}, -\sqrt{3}\rangle$.

11. You should find that $(\mathbf{a} \times \mathbf{b}) \times \mathbf{c} = -\mathbf{i} + \mathbf{j}$ while $\mathbf{a} \times (\mathbf{b} \times \mathbf{c}) = -\mathbf{k}$.

12. Let $\mathbf{a} = \mathbf{i}$, $\mathbf{b} = \mathbf{j}$, and $\mathbf{c} = \mathbf{i} + \mathbf{j}$.

14. $\overrightarrow{PQ} = \langle 0, -1, 1\rangle$ and $\overrightarrow{PR} = \langle -1, 0, 1\rangle$. So the area A of the triangle PQR is given by

$$A = \tfrac{1}{2}|\overrightarrow{PQ} \times \overrightarrow{PR}| = \tfrac{1}{2} \text{ ABS} \begin{vmatrix} \mathbf{i} & \mathbf{j} & \mathbf{k} \\ 0 & -1 & 1 \\ -1 & 0 & 1 \end{vmatrix} = \tfrac{1}{2}|\langle -1, -1, -1\rangle| = \tfrac{1}{2}\sqrt{3}.$$

(Because of the standard notation for determinants, we're using the programming language function ABS(x) = $|x|$ for clarity here.)

16. $\overrightarrow{OP} = \langle 1, 1, 0 \rangle$, $\overrightarrow{OQ} = \langle 1, 0, 1 \rangle$, and $\overrightarrow{OR} = \langle 0, 1, 1 \rangle$. Hence the volume V of the parallelepiped is given by

$$V = |\overrightarrow{OP} \times \overrightarrow{OQ} \cdot \overrightarrow{OR}| = \text{ABS} \begin{vmatrix} 1 & 1 & 0 \\ 1 & 0 & 1 \\ 0 & 1 & 1 \end{vmatrix} = 2.$$

17. $V = \left| \overrightarrow{OP} \cdot \overrightarrow{OQ} \times \overrightarrow{OR} \right|$ where $\overrightarrow{OP} = \langle 1, 3, -2 \rangle$, $\overrightarrow{OQ} = \langle 2, 4, 5 \rangle$, and $\overrightarrow{OR} = \langle -3, -2, 2 \rangle$.

18. $\overrightarrow{PQ} = \langle 1, 1, 7 \rangle$ and $\overrightarrow{PR} = \langle -4, -5, 4 \rangle$. $\overrightarrow{PQ} \times \overrightarrow{PR} = \langle 39, -32, -1 \rangle$. $\vec{n} = \langle 39, -32, -1 \rangle / \sqrt{2546}$. $\overrightarrow{OP} = \langle 1, 3, -2 \rangle$; $\left| \vec{n} \cdot \overrightarrow{OP} \right| = 55/\sqrt{2546}$, which is approximately 1.09002.

19. $(\overrightarrow{AB} \times \overrightarrow{AC}) \cdot \overrightarrow{AD} = 0$, so the four given points are coplanar.

20. $(\overrightarrow{AB} \times \overrightarrow{AC}) \cdot \overrightarrow{AD} = 0$, so the four given points are coplanar.

21. $(\overrightarrow{AB} \times \overrightarrow{AC}) \cdot \overrightarrow{AD} = -6 \neq 0$, so the four given points are not coplanar. The volume of the pyramid is 1.

22. $(\overrightarrow{AB} \times \overrightarrow{AC}) \cdot \overrightarrow{AD} = 54 \neq 0$, so the four given points are not coplanar. The volume of the pyramid is 9.

24. The side of length 255 is represented by the vector $\vec{r} = \langle 227.20666, 115.76758, 0 \rangle$ and the side of length 225 by the vector $\vec{s} = \langle 4.97678, 80.56982, 0 \rangle$. Now $\vec{r} \times \vec{s} = \langle 0, 0, 17729.85027 \rangle$, so the area of the triangle is

$$A = \tfrac{1}{2} |\vec{r} \times \vec{s}| = \tfrac{1}{2}(17729.85027) = 8864.925$$

square feet (all these numbers are, of course, approximate).

26. Name the vertices consecutively counterclockwise around the pentagon thus:

$O(0, 0)$, $S(175, 0)$, P, Q, and R.

Then $P = (3.3, 557522, 153.208889)$,
$Q = (188.650855, 249.627030)$, and
$R = (-42.752518, 117.461578)$.

To find the area we compute $\overrightarrow{OS} \times \overrightarrow{OP} = \langle 0, 0, 26811.55558 \rangle$,
$\overrightarrow{OP} \times \overrightarrow{OQ} = \langle 0, 0, 46873.17475 \rangle$, and
$\overrightarrow{OQ} \times \overrightarrow{OR} = \langle 0, 0, 32831.41121 \rangle$.

The area of the pentagon is half the sum of the magnitudes of these three vectors, and is thus 53258.071 (all data approximate, of course).

30. $V = \dfrac{1}{6} \left| \overrightarrow{AP} \cdot \overrightarrow{AQ} \times \overrightarrow{AR} \right|$ and $V = \dfrac{d}{3} \cdot \dfrac{1}{2} \left| \overrightarrow{PQ} \times \overrightarrow{PR} \right|$. Therefore $d = \dfrac{\left| \overrightarrow{AP} \cdot \overrightarrow{AP} \times \overrightarrow{AR} \right|}{\left| \overrightarrow{PQ} \times \overrightarrow{PR} \right|}$.

Here, $\overrightarrow{AP} = \langle 1, 3, 0 \rangle$, $\overrightarrow{AQ} = \langle 2, -1, 3 \rangle$, and $\overrightarrow{AR} = \langle -1, 0, 1 \rangle$. The value of the scalar triple product is -16, $\overrightarrow{PQ} \times \overrightarrow{PR}$ turns out to equal $\langle 5, -7, -11 \rangle$, and therefore $d = \tfrac{16}{195}\sqrt{195} \approx 1.14578$.

34. First, $(\mathbf{a} \times \mathbf{b}) \times (\mathbf{c} \times \mathbf{d})$ is perpendicular to $\mathbf{a} \times \mathbf{b}$ and $\mathbf{a} \times \mathbf{b}$ is perpendicular to $\mathbf{a}$ and to $\mathbf{b}$. So $(\mathbf{a} \times \mathbf{b}) \times (\mathbf{c} \times \mathbf{d})$ lies in the plane determined by $\mathbf{a}$ and $\mathbf{b}$; that is,

$$(\mathbf{a} \times \mathbf{b}) \times (\mathbf{c} \times \mathbf{d}) = r_1 \mathbf{a} + r_2 \mathbf{b}.$$

(If $\mathbf{a}$ is parallel to $\mathbf{b}$, then $\mathbf{a} \times \mathbf{b} = \mathbf{0}$; in this case, take $r_1 = 0 = r_2$.) The other case follows by symmetry (or by interchanging $\mathbf{a}$ with $\mathbf{c}$ and $\mathbf{b}$ with $\mathbf{d}$ in the above proof).

Section 12.4

2. $x - 3 = -2t$, $y + 4 = 7t$, $z - 5 = 3t$

4. $x = 17 - 17t$, $y = 13t - 13$, $z = 31t - 13$

5. A vector parallel to the line is $\overrightarrow{P_1P_2} = \langle -6, 3, 5 \rangle$. If $\langle x, y, z \rangle$ is on the line through P_1 and P_2 then

$$\langle x, y, z \rangle = \overrightarrow{OP_1} + t\,\overrightarrow{P_1P_2}$$

where $O = (0, 0, 0)$ is the origin. That is,

$$\langle x, y, z \rangle - \langle 0, 0, 0 \rangle = t\,\langle -6, 3, 5 \rangle;$$

it follows that parametric equations of the line in question are

$$x = -6t, \quad y = 3t, \quad z = 5t.$$

6. $\langle x, y, z \rangle = \langle 0, 0, 0 \rangle + t\,\langle 3, -13, 3 \rangle$ yields $x = 3t + 3$, $y = 5 - 13t$, $z = 3t + 7$.

7. $\langle x, y, z \rangle = \langle 3, 5, 7 \rangle + t\,\langle 3, 0, -3 \rangle$ yields $x = 3t + 3$, $y \equiv 5$, $z = 7 - 3t$.

8. $\langle x, y, z \rangle = \langle 29, -47, 13 \rangle + t\langle 44, 100, -80 \rangle$ yields $x = 44t + 29$, $y = 100t - 47$, $z = 13 - 80t$.

10. $x = 2 + 2t$, $y = 5 - 2t$, $z = -7 + 15t$; $\quad \dfrac{x - 2}{2} = \dfrac{y - 5}{-2} = \dfrac{z + 7}{15}$.

11. A line perpendicular to the xy-plane is parallel to the unit vector $\mathbf{k}$. The x- and y-coordinates of all points on such a line are the same (in this case, $x = y = 1$) and the z-coordinates of such points are arbitrary. Parametric equations: $x = 1$, $y = 1$, $z = t$. Symmetric equations: $x - 1 = 0 = y - 1$.

12. A normal to the plane: $\mathbf{n} = \langle 1, 1, 1 \rangle$. A vector equation of the line: $\mathbf{0} + t\,\mathbf{n} = \langle t, t, t \rangle$. Answers: $x = t$, $y = t$, $z = t$; $\quad x = y = z$.

14. The line contains $Q(3, 3, 1)$ (set $t = 1$) and $R(0, 2, 2)$ (set $t = 0$). Now $\overrightarrow{RQ} = \langle 3, 1, -1 \rangle$ and $\overrightarrow{OP} = \langle 2, -1, 5 \rangle$; therefore $\overrightarrow{OP} + t\,\overrightarrow{RQ} = \langle 2, -1, 5 \rangle + t\,\langle 3, 1, -1 \rangle$.
Answers: $x = 2 + 3t$, $y = -1 + t$, $z = 5 - t$; $\quad \dfrac{x - 2}{3} = \dfrac{y + 1}{1} = \dfrac{z - 5}{-1}$.

15. A vector parallel to L_1 is $\mathbf{v}_1 = \langle 1, 2, 3 \rangle$ and a vector parallel to L_2 is $\mathbf{v}_2 = \langle 1, -2, 1 \rangle$. It is then clear that L_1 and L_2 are not parallel. Simultaneous solution of the equations

$$x - 2 = \frac{y + 1}{2} = \frac{z - 3}{3},$$
$$\frac{x - 5}{3} = \frac{y - 1}{2} = z - 4$$

yields $(x, y, z) = (2, -1, 3)$, so L_1 and L_2 meet at that single point.

16. A vector parallel to L_1 is $\mathbf{v}_1 = \langle 4, 1, -2 \rangle$ and a vector parallel to L_2 is $\mathbf{v}_2 = \langle 6, -3, 8 \rangle$. These vectors are not parallel because $\mathbf{v}_1 \times \mathbf{v}_2 = \langle 2, -44, -18 \rangle \neq \mathbf{0}$. Hence L_1 and L_2 are not parallel. When we solve their equations simultaneously, we find the single solution $(x, y, z) = (7, 5, -3)$, so the two lines meet in a single point.

17. A vector parallel to L_1 is $\mathbf{v}_1 = \langle 2, 2, 3 \rangle$ and a vector parallel to L_2 is $\mathbf{v}_2 = \langle 3, 3, 5 \rangle$. These vectors are not parallel because $\mathbf{v}_1 \times \mathbf{v}_2 = \langle 1, -1, 0 \rangle$. Hence L_1 and L_2 are not parallel. Their equations have no simultaneous solution, so L_1 and L_2 are skew lines.

18. A vector parallel to L_1 is $\mathbf{v}_1 = \langle 3, 2, 5 \rangle$ and a vector parallel to L_2 is $\mathbf{v}_2 = \langle 3, 5, 17 \rangle$. The two lines are not parallel because $\mathbf{v}_1 \times \mathbf{v}_2 = \langle 9, -36, 9 \rangle \neq \mathbf{0}$. The equations of L_1 and L_2 have no simultaneous solution, so L_1 and L_2 are skew lines.

19. A vector parallel to L_1 is $\mathbf{v}_1 = \langle 6, 4, -8 \rangle$ and a vector parallel to L_2 is $\mathbf{v}_2 = \langle 9, 6, -12 \rangle = \tfrac{3}{2}\mathbf{v}_1$, so L_1 and L_2 are parallel. They do not intersect because $(7, -5, 9)$ lies on L_1 but not on L_2.

20. A vector parallel to L_1 is $\mathbf{v}_1 = \langle 12, 20, -28 \rangle$ and a vector parallel to L_2 is $\mathbf{v}_2 = \langle 9, 15, -21 \rangle = \frac{3}{4}\mathbf{v}_1$, so L_1 and L_2 are parallel. In fact, they coincide because the point $(13, -7, 11)$ satisfies the equations of both lines.

21. The equation of the plane has the form $x + 2y + 3z = D$ for some constant D. Because $(0, 0, 0)$ is in the plane, $D = 0$.

22. $2x - 7y - 3z = 19$

24. $y = 12$

26. $2x + 2y - z = 3$

28. $x - 3y + 2z = 14$

30. $x + y - 2z = -2$

32. $15x - 9y - z = 16$

33. Two points on L are $(7, 3, 5)$ and $(4, 7, 7)$, so two vectors parallel to the plane are $\mathbf{a} = \langle 5, -1, -1 \rangle$ and $\mathbf{b} = \langle 2, 3, 1 \rangle$. Hence a normal to that plane is $\mathbf{n} = \mathbf{a} \times \mathbf{b} = \langle 2, -7, -17 \rangle$. It follows that an equation of the plane is $2x - 7y + 17z = 78$.

34. Two points on L are $(17, 23, 35)$ and $(8, 37, -6)$, so two vectors parallel to the plane are $\mathbf{a} = \langle 4, 30, 6 \rangle$ and $\mathbf{b} = \langle -5, 44, -35 \rangle$. Hence a normal to that plane is $\mathbf{n} = \mathbf{a} \times \mathbf{b} = \langle -1314, 110, 326 \rangle$. It follows that an equation of the plane is $657x - 55y - 163z = 4199$.

35. The four given equations have no simultaneous solution, so the line and the plane are parallel.

36. The four given equations have no simultaneous solution, so the line and the plane are parallel.

37. The four given equations have the unique simultaneous solutions $x = \frac{9}{2}$, $y = \frac{9}{4}$, $z = \frac{17}{4}$, $t = \frac{3}{4}$, so the line and the plane are not parallel and meet at the point $\left(\frac{9}{2}, \frac{9}{4}, \frac{17}{4}\right)$.

38. The four given equations have the unique simultaneous solutions $x = \frac{237}{20}$, $y = \frac{3}{4}$, $z = \frac{63}{10}$, $t = \frac{21}{20}$. Hence the line and the plane are not parallel and meet at the point $\left(\frac{237}{20}, \frac{3}{4}, \frac{63}{10}\right)$.

39. A normal to the first plane is $\mathbf{i}$ and a normal to the second is $\mathbf{i} + \mathbf{j} + \mathbf{k}$. If θ is the angle between these two normals (by definition, this is the angle between the planes) then
$$\cos \theta = \frac{\langle 1, 0, 0 \rangle \cdot \langle 1, 1, 1 \rangle}{\sqrt{3}},$$
therefore $\theta = \arccos\left(1/\sqrt{3}\right)$ (about $54°44'8''$).

40. Normals: $\langle 2, -1, 1 \rangle$ and $\langle 1, 1, -1 \rangle$. If θ is the angle between the two planes then it follows immediately that $\cos \theta = 0$, and therefore the angle between the two planes is $\pi/2$.

42. Normals to the two given planes are $\mathbf{m} = \langle 2, 1, 1 \rangle$ and $\mathbf{n} = \langle 3, -1, -1 \rangle$. Hence the angle between them, and thus the angle between the planes, is
$$\theta = \arccos\left(\tfrac{2}{33}\sqrt{66}\right) \approx 60.50379°.$$

43. The cross product of the obvious two normals to the two planes is $\mathbf{v} = \langle 0, -1, 1 \rangle$. So the line of intersection has vector equation
$$\langle x, y, z \rangle = \langle 10, 0, 0 \rangle + t\,\mathbf{v},$$
and thus parametric equations $x = 10$, $y = -t$, $z = t$. Technically, this line doesn't have symmetric equations, but elimination of t yields its Cartesian equations
$$x = 10, \qquad y + z = 0.$$

44. If the equation $z = 0$ is adjoined to the equations of the two planes, the resulting system has simultaneous solution $(x, y, z) = (2, -1, 0)$, so this is one point on the line of intersection. Similarly,

using $z = 1$ in place of $z = 0$ yields a second point of intersection, $(2, 0, 1)$. Hence the line is parallel to $\mathbf{v} = \langle 0, 1, 1 \rangle$. It has vector equation $\langle x, y, z \rangle = \langle 2, -1, 0 \rangle + t\mathbf{v}$, which yield the parametric equations
$$x \equiv 2, \quad y = t - 1, \quad z = t.$$
Elimination of the parameter yields the Cartesian equations $x = 2, \ y = z - 1$.

45. The planes of Problem 41 are parallel and distinct, so there is no line of intersection.

46. If the equation $z = 0$ is adjoined to the equations of the two planes, the resulting system has simultaneous solution $(x, y, z) = \left(\frac{7}{5}, \frac{6}{5}, 0\right)$, so this is one point on the line of intersection. Similarly, using $z = 1$ in place of $z = 0$ yields a second point of intersection, $\left(\frac{7}{5}, \frac{1}{5}, 1\right)$. Hence the line is parallel to $\mathbf{v} = \langle 0, -1, 1 \rangle$. It has vector equation $\langle x, y, z \rangle = \frac{1}{5}\langle 7, 6, 0 \rangle + t\mathbf{v}$ and thus parametric equations
$$x \equiv \tfrac{7}{5}, \quad y = \tfrac{6}{5} - t, \quad z = t.$$
Elimination of the parameter yields the Cartesian equations
$$x = \tfrac{7}{5}, \quad y = \tfrac{6}{5} - z.$$

47. Use the fact that $\langle 2, 1, -5 \rangle$ is parallel to the line.

48. $x - 5y - 2z = -14$

49. The xy-plane has equation $z = 0$, so the plane with equation $3x + 2y - z = 6$ meets it in the line with equation $3x + 2y = 6$. Two points on this line are $P(2, 0, 0)$ and $Q(0, 3, 0)$. In order to contain the third point $R(1, 1, 1)$, the plane in question must have normal vector $\overrightarrow{PQ} \times \overrightarrow{PR} = \langle 3, 2, 1 \rangle$. Hence it has an equation of the form $3x + 2y + z = D$ for some constant D. Because the point $(1, 1, 1)$ is in the plane, $D = 6$.

50. Take $z = 1$ to see that $Q(1, 1, 1)$ lies in the line of intersection; take $z = 3$ to see that $R(1, 3, 3)$ does as well. Then a normal vector to the plane is $\overrightarrow{PQ} \times \overrightarrow{PR} = \langle -10, 0, 0, \rangle$. The plane is therefore perpendicular to the x-axis; because it contains the point $P(1, 3, -2)$, it meets the x-axis at $x = 1$. So its equation is simply $x = 1$ (y and z are arbitrary).

52. Suppose that the lines meet at (x, y, z). Then the simultaneous equations that result have solution $P(1, -1, 2)$ The first line also contains $Q(2, 1, 3)$ and the second also contains $R(3, 5, 6)$. A normal to the plane is $\overrightarrow{PQ} \times \overrightarrow{PR} = \langle 2, -2, 2 \rangle$; use $\langle 1, -1, 1 \rangle$ instead. Answer: $x - y + z = 4$.

54. Here is an alternative to the *Suggestion*: $\mathbf{n} = \langle a, b, c \rangle$ is normal to the plane. Assume $a \neq 0$; then $P_1(d/a, 0, 0)$ is in the plane and $\overrightarrow{P_0 P_1} = \langle (d/a) - x_0, -y_0, -z_0 \rangle$. The component of $\overrightarrow{P_0 P_1}$ in the direction of $\mathbf{n}$ is
$$\text{comp}_\mathbf{n} \overrightarrow{P_0 P_1} = \frac{d - ax_0 - by_0 - cz_0}{\sqrt{a^2 + b^2 + c^2}}.$$
The result of Problem 36 now follows immediately. If $a = 0$ then repeat this argument using b or c, whichever is nonzero.

56. $D = \frac{7}{5}\sqrt{2}$.

57. Can you find vectors $\mathbf{V}_1$ and $\mathbf{V}_2$ parallel to L_1 and L_2, respectively? Is there a vector $\mathbf{n}$ normal both to $\mathbf{V}_1$ and to $\mathbf{V}_2$? Does $\mathbf{n}$ determine a plane containing L_1?

58. You may assume without loss of generality that $a \neq 0$. Then the point $(-d_1/a, 0, 0)$ lies on the first plane. The desired result now follows.

60. It is easy to find two points on L_1; one pair is $P_1 = (7, 11, 13)$ and $Q_1 = (9, 6, 19)$. So a vector parallel to L_1 is $\mathbf{v}_1 = \langle 2, -5, 6 \rangle$. Next, to find two points on L_2, we adjoin equations such as $x = 4$ and $x = -4$ to the equations of the two planes and solve for the two points $P_2 = (4, -3, -2)$ and $Q_2 = (-4, 23, 17)$ on L_2. Hence a vector parallel to L_2 is $\mathbf{v}_2 = \langle 8, -26, -19 \rangle$. So a common normal to L_1 and L_2 is
$$\mathbf{n} = \mathbf{v}_1 \times \mathbf{v}_2 = \langle 251, 86, -12 \rangle.$$

A vector that "connects" L_1 with L_2 is $\mathbf{c} = \overrightarrow{P_1P_2} = \langle 3, 14, 15 \rangle$. The distance between L_1 and L_2 is the length of the projection of $\mathbf{c}$ in the direction of $\mathbf{n}$, which is

$$\frac{|\mathbf{c} \cdot \mathbf{n}|}{|\mathbf{v}|} = \frac{1777}{\sqrt{70541}} \approx 6.6906239652.$$

61. A vector parallel to L is $\mathbf{v} = \langle 3, -9, 1 \rangle$. Three points in the plane $\mathcal{P}$ are $P = (0,0,0)$, $Q = (5,7,3)$, and $R = (4,-1,2)$. A normal to $\mathcal{P}$ is $\mathbf{n} = \overrightarrow{PQ} \times \overrightarrow{PR} = \langle 17, 2, -33 \rangle$. The angle between $\mathbf{n}$ and $\mathbf{v}$ is

$$\theta = \arccos\left(\frac{\mathbf{n} \cdot \mathbf{v}}{|\mathbf{n}||\mathbf{v}|}\right) = \frac{\pi}{2},$$

so L and $\mathcal{P}$ are parallel.

62. A vector parallel to L is $\mathbf{v} = \langle 13, -23, 4 \rangle$. The three points $P = (0,0,0)$, $Q = (9,7,11)$, and $R = (3,1,-4)$ lie in the plane $\mathcal{P}$. A normal to $\mathcal{P}$ is $\mathbf{n} = \overrightarrow{PQ} \times \overrightarrow{PR} = \langle -39, 69, -12 \rangle$. The angle between $\mathbf{n}$ and $\mathbf{v}$ is

$$\theta = \arccos\left(\frac{\mathbf{n} \cdot \mathbf{v}}{|\mathbf{n}||\mathbf{v}|}\right) = \pi,$$

so that L and $\mathbf{n}$ are parallel; thus L and $\mathcal{P}$ are perpendicular. To find where they meet, we solve the simultaneous equations

$$x = 16 + 13r = 9s + 3t,$$
$$y = -18 - 23r = 7s + t,$$
$$z = 23 + 4r = 11s - 4t$$

for $(x, y, z) = (3, 5, 19)$.

63. A vector parallel to L is $\mathbf{v} = \langle 5, 10, 20 \rangle$. Three points in $\mathcal{P}$ are $P = (0,0,0)$, $Q = (2,-1,4)$, and $R = (5,2,-3)$. A normal to $\mathcal{P}$ is $\mathbf{n} = \overrightarrow{PQ} \times \overrightarrow{PR} = \langle -5, 26, 9 \rangle$. The angle between $\mathbf{v}$ and $\mathbf{n}$ is

$$\theta = \arccos\left(\frac{\mathbf{n} \cdot \mathbf{v}}{|\mathbf{n}||\mathbf{v}|}\right) = \arccos\left(\frac{83}{\sqrt{16422}}\right) \approx 0.8662518464.$$

We convert to degrees and subtract from $90°$ to obtain the angle between L and $\mathcal{P}$; it is approximately $40.3674°$. We solve the equations of L and $\mathcal{P}$ simultaneously to find their point of intersection; it is $(7, 1, 1)$.

64. A vector parallel to L is $\mathbf{v} = \langle -6, 3, 3 \rangle$. Three points in $\mathcal{P}$ are $P = (0,0,0)$, $Q = (7,4,-5)$, and $R = (3,-2,6)$. So a normal to $\mathcal{P}$ is $\mathbf{n} = \overrightarrow{PR} \times \overrightarrow{PQ} = \langle -14, 57, 26 \rangle$. The angle between $\mathbf{v}$ and $\mathbf{n}$ is

$$\theta = \arccos\left(\frac{\mathbf{n} \cdot \mathbf{v}}{|\mathbf{n}||\mathbf{v}|}\right) = \arccos\left(\frac{111}{\sqrt{24726}}\right) \approx 0.7870967836.$$

We convert to degrees and subtract from $90°$ to obtain the angle between L and $\mathcal{P}$; it is approximately $44.9027°$. Finally, we solve the equations of L and $\mathcal{P}$ simultaneously to find that they meet at the point $(13, 0, 7)$.

65. Three points on $\mathcal{P}_1$ are $P_1 = (0,0,0)$, $Q_1 = (5,3,2)$, and $R_1 = (7,8,5)$. So a normal to $\mathcal{P}_1$ is

$$\mathbf{n}_1 = \overrightarrow{P_1Q_1} \times \overrightarrow{P_1R_1} = \langle -1, -11, 19 \rangle.$$

Three points on $\mathcal{P}_2$ are $P_2 = (-1,7,4)$, $Q_2 = (11,18,11)$, and $R_2 = (0,19,11)$. So a normal to $\mathcal{P}_2$ is

$$\mathbf{n}_2 = \overrightarrow{P_2Q_2} \times \overrightarrow{P_2R_2} = \langle -7, -77, 133 \rangle = 7\mathbf{n}_1.$$

Because their normals are parallel, the planes are parallel as well. Do they coincide? Yes, if and only if P_1 lies on $\mathcal{P}_2$. But it is easy to show that P_1 satisfies the equations of $\mathcal{P}_2$ with $s = \frac{1}{7}$ and $t = -\frac{5}{7}$. Hence the two planes are not only parallel, they coincide. The angle between them is zero.

66. Three points on $\mathcal{P}_1$ are $P_1 = (7,3,9)$, $Q_1 = (6,10,11)$, and $R_1 = (8,15,14)$. So a normal to $\mathcal{P}_1$ is

$$\mathbf{n}_1 = \overrightarrow{P_1Q_1} \times \overrightarrow{P_1R_1} = \langle 11,\, 7,\, -19 \rangle.$$

Three points on $\mathcal{P}_2$ are $P_2 = (5,3,4)$, $Q_2 = (5,22,11)$, and $R_2 = (12,11,11)$. So a normal to $\mathcal{P}_2$ is

$$\mathbf{n}_2 = \overrightarrow{P_2Q_2} \times \overrightarrow{P_2R_2} = \langle 77,\, 49,\, -133 \rangle = 7\mathbf{n}_1.$$

Because their normals are parallel, the planes are parallel as well. Do they coincide? Yes, if and only if P_1 lies on $\mathcal{P}_2$. But it is easy to show that P_1 does *not* satisfy the equations of $\mathcal{P}_2$. Hence the two planes are parallel and distinct; the angle between them is zero.

67. Three points on $\mathcal{P}_1$ are $P_1 = (0,0,0)$, $Q_1 = (7,8,7)$, and $R_1 = (1,12,5)$. So a normal to $\mathcal{P}_1$ is

$$\mathbf{n}_1 = \overrightarrow{P_1R_1} \times \overrightarrow{P_1Q_1} = \langle 44,\, -28,\, -76 \rangle.$$

Three points on $\mathcal{P}_2$ are $P_2 = (0,0,0)$, $Q_2 = (-3,7,-2)$, and $R_2 = (4,4,11)$. So a normal to $\mathcal{P}_2$ is

$$\mathbf{n}_2 = \overrightarrow{P_2Q_2} \times \overrightarrow{P_2R_2} = \langle 85,\, 25,\, -40 \rangle = 7\mathbf{n}_1.$$

The angle between the planes is the angle between their normals,

$$\theta = \arccos\left(\frac{\mathbf{n}_1 \cdot \mathbf{n}_2}{|\mathbf{n}_1||\mathbf{n}_2|}\right) = \arccos\left(\frac{374}{\sqrt{200718}}\right) \approx 0.5830408732.$$

In degrees, the angle is approximately $33.4057813183°$.

The line of intersection of $\mathcal{P}_1$ and $\mathcal{P}_2$ is parallel to

$$\mathbf{v} = \tfrac{1}{20}(\mathbf{n}_1 \times \mathbf{n}_2) = \langle -39,\, 235,\, 64 \rangle.$$

One way to proceed is to find a point at which $\mathcal{P}_1$ intersects $\mathcal{P}_2$. We solved the system

$$x = 7s + t = -3u + 4v,$$
$$y = 8s + 12t = 7u + 4v,$$
$$z = 7s + 5t = -2u + 11v$$

to find

$$x = -\tfrac{65}{18}v, \qquad y = \tfrac{1175}{54}v, \qquad z = \tfrac{160}{27}v.$$

Then the choice $v = 54$ gives a point of intersection with integral coordinates, $P = (-195, 1175, 320)$. A vector equation of the line of intersection is then

$$\langle x,\, y,\, z \rangle = \langle -195,\, 1175,\, 320 \rangle + t\,\mathbf{v},$$

and so parametric equations of this line are

$$x = -39t - 195, \quad y = 235t + 1175, \quad z = 64t + 320.$$

Remember that parametric equations of lines are not unique. A simple substitution allows you to present the parametric equations of this line in the simpler form

$$x = -39t, \quad y = 235t, \quad z = 64t.$$

68. Three points on $\mathcal{P}_1$ are $P_1 = (7,3,5)$, $Q_1 = (9,2,9)$, and $R_1 = (14,7,10)$. So a normal to $\mathcal{P}_1$ is

$$\mathbf{n}_1 = \overrightarrow{P_1Q_1} \times \overrightarrow{P_1R_1} = \langle -21,\, 18,\, 15 \rangle.$$

Three points on $\mathcal{P}_2$ are $P_2 = (11, 7, 10)$, $Q_2 = (16, 6, 8)$, and $R_2 = (15, 11, 15)$, so a normal to $\mathcal{P}_2$ is
$$\mathbf{n}_2 = \overrightarrow{P_2 R_2} \times \overrightarrow{P_2 Q_2} = \langle 3, -33, 24 \rangle.$$

The angle between these normals is
$$\theta = \arccos\left(\frac{\mathbf{n}_1 \cdot \mathbf{n}_2}{|\mathbf{n}_1||\mathbf{n}_2|}\right) = \arccos\left(\frac{\sqrt{33}}{2\sqrt{155}}\right) \approx 1.3379919122,$$

approximately $76.661289593°$. The planes meet at the point $(7, 3, 5)$ because this point clearly satisfies the equations of $\mathcal{P}_1$ and, less clearly, satisfies those of $\mathcal{P}_2$ with the choices of $s = 0$ and $t = -1$. The line of intersection of the two planes has direction
$$\mathbf{v} = \langle -21, 18, 15 \rangle \times \langle 3, -33, 24 \rangle = \langle 927, 549, 639 \rangle = 9\langle 103, 61, 71 \rangle.$$

A vector equation of the line of intersection is
$$\langle x, y, z \rangle = \langle 7, 3, 5 \rangle + t\langle 103, 61, 71 \rangle,$$

which leads to the parametric equations
$$x = 103t + 7, \quad y = 61t + 3, \quad z = 71t + 5.$$

Section 12.5

1. Note that $y^2 + z^2 \equiv 1$. The steady change in x implies that this curve is the helix of Fig. 12.5.17.

2. Note that $x^2 + y^2 = 1$. The periodic behavior of z indicates that this curve has the graph shown in Fig. 12.5.18, which resembles the cord used to tighten certain drums.

3. Because $x^2 + y^2 = z^2$ and z increases steadily, this curve winds around the cone not quite visible in Fig. 12.5.16.

4. It's easy to show that $x^2 + y^2 + z^2 \equiv 1$. Hence this must be the curve shown in Fig. 12.5.15.

5. Note that $\mathbf{r}$ is a constant vector.

6. $\mathbf{r}'(t) = \langle 2t, -3t^2 \rangle$, $\mathbf{r}''(t) = \langle 2, -6t \rangle$. So $\mathbf{r}'(2) = \langle 4, -12 \rangle$ and $\mathbf{r}''(2) = \langle 2, -12 \rangle$.

8. $\mathbf{r}'(t) = \langle -\sin t, \cos t \rangle$ and $\mathbf{r}''(t) = \langle -\cos t, -\sin t \rangle$.
   So $\mathbf{r}'\left(\frac{\pi}{4}\right) = \left\langle -\frac{\sqrt{2}}{2}, \frac{\sqrt{2}}{2} \right\rangle$ and $\mathbf{r}''\left(\frac{\pi}{4}\right) = \left\langle -\frac{\sqrt{2}}{2}, -\frac{\sqrt{2}}{2} \right\rangle$.

10. $\mathbf{r}'(t) = \langle -5\sin t, 4\cos t \rangle$, $\mathbf{r}''(t) = \langle -5\cos t, -4\sin t \rangle$. So $\mathbf{r}'(\pi) = \langle 0, -4 \rangle$ and $\mathbf{r}''(\pi) = \langle 5, 0 \rangle$.

12. $\mathbf{v}(t) = 2t\langle 3, 4, -12 \rangle$; $\mathbf{a}(t) = 2\langle 3, 4, -12 \rangle$; $v(t) = |26t|$.

14. $\mathbf{v}(t) = \langle e^t, 2e^{2t}, 2e^{3t} \rangle$; $\mathbf{a}(t) = \langle e^t, 4e^{2t}, 9e^{3t} \rangle$; $v(t) = \sqrt{e^{2t} + 4e^{4t} + 9e^{3t}}$.

16. $\mathbf{v}(t) = \langle 12, 10\cos 2t, 10\sin 2t \rangle$; $\mathbf{a}(t) = \langle 0, -20\sin 2t, 20\cos 2t \rangle$; $v(t) = \sqrt{244}$.

18. $\int_1^e \langle \tfrac{1}{t}, -1 \rangle \, dt = \Big[\langle \ln t, -t \rangle \Big]_1^e = \langle 1, 1 - e \rangle$.

20. $\int_0^1 \langle e^t, -te^{-t^2} \rangle \, dt = \Big[\langle e^t, \tfrac{1}{2} e^{-t^2} \rangle \Big]_0^1 = \left\langle e - 1, \dfrac{1 - e}{2e} \right\rangle$.

21. $(3\mathbf{i}) \cdot (2\mathbf{i} - 5t\mathbf{j}) + (3t\mathbf{i} - \mathbf{j}) \cdot (-5\mathbf{j}) = 11$.

22. $\langle 1, 2t \rangle \cdot \langle t^2, -t \rangle + \langle t, t^2 \rangle \cdot \langle 2t, -1 \rangle = t^2 - 2t^2 + 2t^2 - t^2 = 0$.

24. Using Theorem 2, we obtain
$$\mathbf{u}(t) \cdot \mathbf{v}'(t) + \mathbf{u}'(t) \cdot \mathbf{v}(t) = \langle t, t^2, t^3 \rangle \cdot \langle -2\sin 2t, 2\cos 2t, -3e^{-3t} \rangle + \langle 1, 2t, 3t^2 \rangle \cdot \langle \cos 2t, \sin 2t, e^{-3t} \rangle$$
$$= 3(t^2 - t^3)e^{-3t} + (1 + 2t^2)\cos 2t.$$

25. $\mathbf{v}(t) = \langle 0, 0, 1 \rangle$ and $\mathbf{r}(t) = \langle 1, 0, t \rangle$.

26. $\mathbf{v}(t) = \langle 2t, 0, 4 \rangle$ and $\mathbf{r}(t) = \langle t^2, 3, 4t \rangle$.

28. $\mathbf{v}(t) = \langle t, 7-t, 3t \rangle$ and $\mathbf{r}(t) = \langle 5 + \frac{1}{2}t^2, 7t - \frac{1}{2}t^2, \frac{3}{2}t^2 \rangle$.

30. $\mathbf{v}(t) = \langle 3t^2, 4 - 5t, 4t^3 - 5 \rangle$ and $\mathbf{r}(t) = \langle t^3 + 3, 4 + 4t - \frac{5}{2}t^2, t^4 - 5t \rangle$.

32. $\mathbf{v}(t) = \langle \frac{1}{2}t^2, 1 - e^{-t}, 5 \rangle$ and $\mathbf{r}(t) = \langle 3 + \frac{1}{6}t^3, 3 + t + e^{-t}, 5t \rangle$.

34. $\mathbf{v}(t) = \langle -1 + 3\cos 3t, -3\sin 3t, 4t - 7 \rangle$ and $\mathbf{r}(t) = \langle 3 - t - \sin 3t, 3 + \cos 3t, 2t^2 - 7t \rangle$.

36. $D_t(\mathbf{u}(t) \cdot \mathbf{v}(t)) = \mathbf{u}(t) \cdot \mathbf{v}'(t) + \mathbf{u}'(t) \cdot \mathbf{v}(t)$
$$= \langle t, t^2, t^3 \rangle \cdot \langle e^t, -\sin t, \cos t \rangle + \langle 1, 2t, 3t^2 \rangle \cdot \langle e^t, \cos t, \sin t \rangle$$
$$= (t+1)e^t + (t^3 + 2t)\cos t + 2t^2 \sin t.$$

The components of the vector $D_t(\mathbf{u}(t) \times \mathbf{v}(t))$ are

$$(t^3 + 2t)\sin t - 2t^2 \cos t, \quad (t^3 + 3t^2)e^t - \sin t - t\cos t, \quad \text{and} \quad \cos t - t\sin t - t^2 e^t - 2te^t.$$

37. Given $\mathbf{u}(t) = \langle 0, 3, 4t \rangle$ and $\mathbf{v}(t) = \langle 5t, 0, -4 \rangle$, we have

$$\mathbf{u}(t) \times \mathbf{v}(t) = \langle -12, 20t^2, -15t \rangle,$$

with derivative

$$\langle 0, 40t, -15 \rangle = \langle 0, 20t, -15 \rangle + \langle 0, 20t, 0 \rangle$$
$$= \langle 0, 3, 4t \rangle \times \langle 5, 0, 0 \rangle + \langle 0, 0, 4 \rangle \times \langle 5t, 0, -4 \rangle$$
$$= \mathbf{u}(t) \times \mathbf{v}'(t) + \mathbf{u}'(t) \times \mathbf{v}(t).$$

38. Write $\mathbf{u} = \langle u_1, u_2, u_3 \rangle$ and $\mathbf{v} = \langle v_1, v_2, v_3 \rangle$ and, for simplicity, suppress the independent variable t. Thus we obtain

$$D_t[\mathbf{u} \times \mathbf{v}] = D_t[\langle u_2v_3 - u_3v_2, u_3v_1 - u_1v_3, u_1v_2 - u_2v_1 \rangle]$$
$$= \langle u_2v_3' + u_2'v_3 - u_3v_2' - u_3'v_2, u_3v_1' + u_3'v_1 - u_1v_3' - u_1'v_3, u_1v_2' + u_1'v_2 - u_2v_1' - u_2'v_1 \rangle$$
$$= \langle u_2v_3' - u_3v_2', u_3v_1' - u_1v_3', u_1v_2' - u_2v_1' \rangle + \langle u_2'v_3 - u_3'v_2, u_3'v_1 - u_1'v_3, u_1'v_2 - u_2'v_1 \rangle$$
$$= \langle u_1, u_2, u_3 \rangle \times \langle v_1', v_2', v_3' \rangle + \langle u_1', u_2', u_3' \rangle \times \langle v_1, v_2, v_3 \rangle$$
$$= \mathbf{u} \times \mathbf{v}' + \mathbf{u}' \times \mathbf{v}.$$

39. Note that the position vector $\mathbf{r}(t)$ of the point has constant magnitude, and therefore $\mathbf{r}(t) \cdot \mathbf{r}(t) = C$, a constant. Now differentiate each side of this last identity with respect to t.

40. Let $\mathbf{v}(t)$ denote the velocity vector of the moving particle. If the speed $|\mathbf{v}(t)|$ of the particle is constant, then $\mathbf{v}(t) \cdot \mathbf{v}(t) = C$ where C is a constant. Now differentiate each side of this identity with respect to time.

43. Suppose that a projectile is launched from the point (x_0, y_0), with y_0 denoting its initial height above the surface of the earth. Let α be the angle of inclination from the horizontal of its initial velocity vector $\mathbf{v}_0$, with $\alpha > 0$ if the initial velocity vector points generally upward. Suppose also that the motion of the projectile takes place sufficiently close to the surface of the earth that we may assume the acceleration g of gravity to be constant. If we also ignore air resistance, then we may derive the equations of motion of the projectile:

$$x = (v_0 \cos \alpha)t + x_0, \tag{1}$$
$$y = -\tfrac{1}{2}gt^2 + (v_0 \sin \alpha)t + y_0. \tag{2}$$

We will use these in several of the next few solutions. To solve Problem 43, first derive the formula $(v_0)^2 = \dfrac{Rg}{\sin 2\alpha}.$

44. Now $dy/dt = 0$ when $gt = v_0 \sin \alpha$, so y_{max} occurs when $t = \dfrac{1}{g} v_0 \sin \alpha$; therefore

$$y_{max} = \frac{1}{2g}(v_0 \sin \alpha)^2.$$

Also $y = 0$ when $t = 0$ and when $t = \dfrac{1}{g}(2v_0 \sin \alpha)$. So the range is given by

$$R = \frac{1}{g}(v_0)^2 \sin 2\alpha.$$

Given the data of the problem—$\alpha = \pi/3$ and $R = 5280$—we find that

$$v_0 = (32)\left(110\sqrt{3}\right)^{1/2} \approx 441.7 \ (\text{ft/s}) \text{ and}$$
$$y_{max} = 1320\sqrt{3} \approx 2286.31 \ (\text{ft});$$

that is, about 0.433 miles.

46. As a consequence of either Problem 22 or Problem 23,

$$R = \frac{1}{g}(v_0)^2 \sin 2\alpha, \quad \text{so}$$
$$\frac{dR}{d\alpha} = \frac{2}{g}(v_0)^2 \cos 2\alpha.$$

Now $dR/d\alpha = 0$ when $\cos 2\alpha = 0$, so that $\alpha = \pi/4$ is the angle that maximizes the range R.

47. The maximum altitude y_{max} occurs when $dy/dx = 0$. To keep the notation simple, we write v for v_0. Then $dy/dx = 0$ when $\dfrac{-gt + v \sin \alpha}{v \cos \alpha} = 0$, so that $t = (v \sin \alpha)/g$. We use this value of t in Equation (2) to find that

$$y_{max} = \frac{1}{2g}(v_0 \sin \alpha)^2.$$

Finally, as before, $R = \dfrac{(v_0 \sin 2\alpha)^2}{2g}$. Results:

(a) $y_{max} = 100$, $R = 400\sqrt{3} \approx 692.82$ (ft);
(b) $y_{max} = 200$, $R = 800$;
(c) $y_{max} = 300$, $R = 400\sqrt{3}$.

48. Here we take $v = v_0 = 160$, $g = 32$, and $R = 600$. We also require that $y_{max} \geq 300$. Now

$$\frac{v^2 \sin 2\alpha}{g} = R = 600, \quad \text{so}$$
$$\sin 2\alpha = \frac{Rg}{v^2} = \frac{(600)(32)}{(160)(160)} = \frac{3}{4}.$$

It follows that $\alpha \approx 0.424031$ or $\alpha \approx 1.146765$; therefore

$$\alpha \approx 24°17'43'' \quad \text{or} \quad \alpha \approx 65°42'17''.$$

Now (from Problem 22) $y_{max} = (v \sin \alpha)^2/(2g)$. If α has the smaller of the two values shown above, then $y_{max} \approx 67.71$ feet—too low. If $\alpha \approx 65°42'17''$, then $y_{max} \approx 332.29$ feet, and so $y_{max} > 300$, as desired. Answer: Exactly $\frac{1}{2}(\pi - \sin^{-1}(0.75))$; about $65°42'17''$.

49. See the diagram at the right.

$$\mathbf{a} = -(9.8)\mathbf{j},$$
$$\mathbf{v}(t) = v_0\mathbf{i} - (9.8)t\,\mathbf{j}, \text{ and}$$
$$\mathbf{r}(t) = v_0 t\,\mathbf{i} + \left(100 - (4.9)t^2\right)\mathbf{j}.$$

At the time T of impact,

$$v_0 T = 1000 \text{ and } 100 - (4.9)T^2 = 0.$$

We solve for T: $T = \frac{10}{7}\sqrt{10}$; so

$$v_0 = \frac{7000}{10\sqrt{10}} \approx 221.36 \text{ m/s}.$$

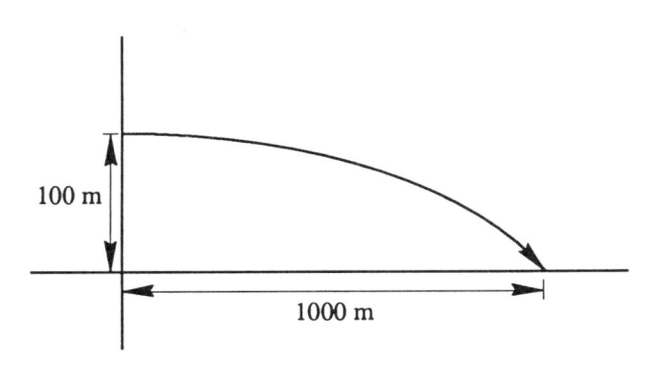

50. See the diagram at the right. Given:

$$\mathbf{a} = -9.8\,\mathbf{j}$$
$$\mathbf{v}(t) = (v_0 \cos\alpha)\,\mathbf{i} + (v_0 \sin\alpha - 9.8t)\,\mathbf{j}$$
$$\mathbf{r}(t) = (v_0 \cos\alpha)\,t\,\mathbf{i} + \left(v_0 t \sin\alpha - 4.9t^2\right)\mathbf{j}$$

We require that at at the time T of interception,

$$800 - 4.9T^2 = 400$$
$$(v_0 \cos\alpha)\,T = 800 \text{ and}$$
$$v_0 T \sin\alpha - 4.9T^2 = 400$$

Solve: $T = \frac{20}{7}\sqrt{10} \approx 9.035$, $\alpha = \pi/4$, and $v_0 = 28\sqrt{10}\sqrt{2} \approx 125.22$ m/s.

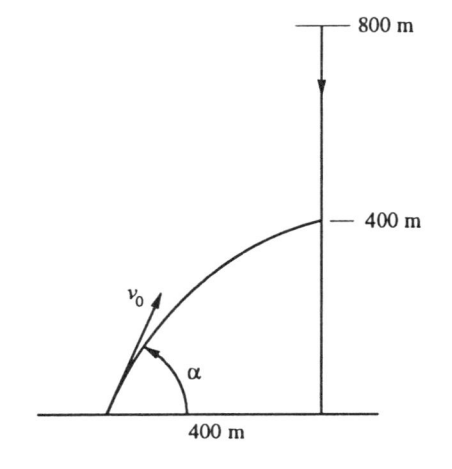

51. The height of the bomb is $y(t) = 800 - 4.9(t+1)^2$. At time of interception, $800 - 4.9(t+1)^2 = 400$, $(v_0 \cos\alpha)\,t = 800$, and $v_0 t \sin\alpha - 4.9t^2 = 400$.

52. The equations of motion of the projectile are

$$x(t) = (100\cos\alpha)\,t \text{ and } y(t) = -16t^2 + (1000\sin\alpha)\,t + 500$$

if we take the gun at position $(0, 500)$ in the usual coordinate system. We want $x(T) = 20,000$ when $y(T) = 0$. The first of these conditions implies that $T = 20\sec\alpha$, and the second yields

$$-16T^2 + (1000\sin\alpha)\,T + 500 = 0.$$

Substitution for T in the last equation gives

$$64u^2 - 200u + 59 = 0 \text{ where } u = \tan T.$$

This quadratic equation has two solutions, yielding

$$u \approx 2.795193, \quad \alpha \approx 70.314970°, \quad T \approx 59.3737 \text{ (sec)} \text{ and}$$
$$u \approx 0.329807, \quad \alpha \approx 18.252934°, \quad T \approx 21.0597 \text{ (sec)}.$$

Either initial angle will "work", but the second is likely to be much more accurate.

56. The point has position vector $\mathbf{r}(t) = R\langle\cos(f(t)), \sin(f(t))\rangle$ for some function f, where R is the radius of the circle. Now

$$\mathbf{v}(t) = Rf'(t)\langle -\sin(f(t)), \cos(f(t))\rangle, \text{ so}$$
$$(\mathbf{r}\cdot\mathbf{v})(t) = R^2 f'(t)(-\sin(f(t))\cos(f(t)) + \sin(f(t))\cos(f(t))) = 0.$$

Therefore $\mathbf{r}(t)$ and $\mathbf{v}(t)$ are perpendicular.

58. $\mathbf{r}(t) = \langle a\cos\omega t, b\sin\omega t\rangle$;
$\mathbf{v}(t) = \langle -a\omega\sin\omega t, b\omega\cos\omega t\rangle$,
$\mathbf{a}(t) = \langle -a\omega^2\cos\omega t, -b\omega^2\sin\omega t\rangle = -\omega^2\langle a\cos\omega t, b\sin\omega t\rangle$.

Therefore $\mathbf{a}(t) = c\mathbf{r}(t)$ where $c = -\omega^2 < 0$. So $\mathbf{F}(t)$ is a force directed toward the origin and has magnitude proportional to distance from the origin.

60. If $\mathbf{a}(t) = \langle 0,0\rangle$ then $\mathbf{v}(t) = \mathbf{C} = \langle c_1, c_2\rangle$. So

$$\mathbf{r}(t) = \langle c_1 t + c_3, c_2 t + c_4\rangle.$$

The path of the particle is then parametrized by

$$x = c_1 t + c_3, \quad y = c_2 t + c_4.$$

and is therefore a straight line. Moreover, the speed of the particle is $|\mathbf{v}(t)| = \sqrt{(c_1)^2 + (c_2)^2}$, a constant. This concludes the proof.

62. Because $\mathbf{F} = k\mathbf{r}$, $\mathbf{r}$ and $\mathbf{a}$ are parallel. So

$$D_t(\mathbf{r}\times\mathbf{v}) = (\mathbf{r}\times\mathbf{a}) + (\mathbf{v}\times\mathbf{v}) = 0 + 0 = 0.$$

Therefore $\mathbf{r}\times\mathbf{v} = \mathbf{C}$, a constant vector. Consequently the vector $\mathbf{r}$ is always perpendicular to the constant vector $\mathbf{C}$. This holds for every point on the trajectory of the particle, and thus every point on the trajectory lies in the plane through the origin with normal vector $\mathbf{C}$.

63. With north the direction of the positive x-axis, west the direction of the positive y-axis, and upward the direction of the positive z-axis, the baseball has acceleration $\mathbf{a}(t) = \langle 0.1, 0, -32\rangle$, initial velocity $\mathbf{v}_0 = \langle 0, 0, 160,\rangle$, and initial position $\mathbf{r}_0 = \langle 0, 0, 0,\rangle$. It follows that its position vector is

$$\mathbf{r}(t) = \langle (0.05)t^2, 0, 160t - 16t^2\rangle.$$

The ball returns to the ground at that positive value of t for which the third component of $\mathbf{r}(t)$ is zero: $t = 5$. At that time the first component of $\mathbf{r}(t)$ is 1.25, so the ball lands 1.25 feet north of the point from which it was thrown.

64. We assume that the baseball is hit directly down the left-field foul line and that this is the direction of due north. We assume also that the acceleration due to spin is directed due east. Then the acceleration vector of the baseball is

$$\mathbf{a}(t) = \langle 2, 0, -32\rangle.$$

The initial velocity of the baseball is $\mathbf{v}_0 = \langle 0, 96\cos 15°, 96\sin 15°\rangle$, so its velocity vector is

$$\mathbf{v}(t) = \left\langle 2t, 24\left(1+\sqrt{3}\right)\sqrt{2}, 24\left(-1+\sqrt{3}\right)\sqrt{2} - 32t\right\rangle.$$

The initial position of the baseball is $\mathbf{r}_0 = \langle 0, 0, 0\rangle$ in our coordinate system, so the baseball has position vector

$$\mathbf{r}(t) = \left\langle t^2, 24t\left(1+\sqrt{3}\right)\sqrt{2}, 24t\left(-1+\sqrt{3}\right)\sqrt{2} - 16t^2\right\rangle.$$

The ball strikes the ground when the third component of $\mathbf{r}(t)$ is zero; that is, when

$$t = \tfrac{3}{2}\left(\sqrt{6} - \sqrt{2}\right).$$

At this time the x-component of $\mathbf{r}(t)$ is $18 - 9\sqrt{3} \approx 2.411543$, so the ball hits the ground just under 2 ft 5 in. from the foul line.

65. The acceleration of the projectile is $\mathbf{a}(t) = \langle 2, 0, -32 \rangle$; in the "obvious" coordinate system, its initial velocity is $\mathbf{v}_0 = \langle 0, 200, 160 \rangle$ and its initial position is $\mathbf{r}_0 = \langle 0, 0, 384 \rangle$. Hence its velocity vector is

$$\mathbf{v}(t) = \langle 2t, 200, 160 - 32t \rangle$$

and its position vector is

$$\mathbf{r}(t) = \langle t^2, 200t, 384 + 160t - 16t^2 \rangle.$$

The projectile strikes the ground when the z-component of $\mathbf{r}$ is zero; that is, when $t = -2$ (which we reject) and when $t = 12$. At that time, its position is $\mathbf{r}(12) = \langle 144, 2400, 0 \rangle$, so it lands 2400 ft north and 144 ft east of the firing position. The projectile reaches its maximum altitude when the z-component of $\mathbf{v}(t)$ is zero; that is, when $t = 5$. Its position then is $\mathbf{r}(5) = \langle 25, 1000, 784 \rangle$, so its maximum altitude is 784 ft.

66. Situate the gun at the origin, north the positive y-direction, east the positive x-direction, upward the positive z-direction. Assume that the gun is fired at time $t = 0$ (seconds) with angle α of elevation and lateral deviation θ measured counterclockwise from the positive y-axis. Note that θ will be rather close to zero. If T is the time of impact of a shell at the point $(0, 5000, 0)$, it is then easy to derive the equations

$$T = 6000 \cos\alpha \sin\theta,$$
$$T \cos\alpha \cos\theta = 10, \quad \text{and}$$
$$4T = 125 \sin\alpha.$$

To obtain a first approximation to a solution, assume that $\theta = 0$. The displayed equations then imply that

$$\sin 2\alpha = \tfrac{16}{25} \quad \text{and} \quad T = 10 \sec\alpha.$$

The first of these equations has two first-quadrant solutions:

$$\alpha \approx 19.89590975° \quad \text{and} \quad \alpha \approx 70.10409025°.$$

The corresponding values of T are

$$T \approx 10.63476324 \quad \text{and} \quad T \approx 29.38476324 \quad \text{(seconds)}.$$

One may now continue in a very pragmatic way: Fire the gun due north with the smaller value of α. It's easy to show that the shell won't clear the hill. So the larger value of α must be used in any case. If the gun is fired due north with the larger value of α, the shell will strike the ground at

$$(x, y, z) \approx (71.95535922, 5000, 0).$$

So swivel the gun counterclockwise through an angle of

$$\theta = \arctan\left(\frac{71.95535922}{5000}\right) \approx 0.8244907643°$$

and *really* fire it this time. The results:

$$T = 29.38476324 \quad \text{and point of impact} \quad (x, y, z) \approx (0.0074499339, 4999.482323, 0.000001).$$

Section 12.5 Curves and Motion in Space

This is certainly close enough! You can also verify that the shell easily clears the hill unless the hill has an abnormal shape (the shell reaches a maximum altitude of more than 3450 feet).

A more sophisticated solution might proceed as follows. Obtain the approximate values of α and T using $\theta = 0$. Beginning with those values, iterate the following versions of the first equations (this is a method of repeated substitution):

$$T = \frac{125}{4} \sin \alpha,$$
$$\theta = \arcsin\left(\frac{T}{6000 \cos \alpha}\right),$$
$$\alpha = \arccos\left(\frac{10}{T \cos \theta}\right).$$

A few iterations of these equations, in the order given, results in convergence to the values

$$T \approx 29.38430462,$$
$$\alpha \approx 70.10161954°, \text{ and}$$
$$\theta \approx 0.8244650319°.$$

The point of impact is $(-0.0000000078, 5000, 0.0000011)$ if these values are used. The errors in x and z are undoubtedly roundoff errors.

Section 12.6

1. $\int_0^\pi \sqrt{(6\cos 2t)^2 + (6\sin 2t)^2 + 64}\, dt = 10\pi.$

2. $(dx/dt)^2 + (dy/dt)^2 + (dz/dt)^2 = (1+t^2)^2$; integrate ds from $t=0$ to $t=1$ to obtain $\frac{4}{3}$.

4. $(ds/dt)^2 = t^2 + (1/t)^2 + 2 = (t+t^{-1})^2$; integrate ds from $t=1$ to $t=2$ to get $s = \frac{3}{2} + \ln 2$.

6. $(ds/dt)^2 = 2e^{2t} + e^{-2t} + 4 = (2e^t + e^{-t})^2$; integrate ds from $t=0$ to $t=1$ to get $s = 2e - e^{-1} - 1$.

8. The curvature at x is $\dfrac{|6x|}{(1+9x^4)^{3/2}}$; at $(-1,-1)$, its value is $\dfrac{3}{50}\sqrt{10}$.

10. The curvature is $\dfrac{|(1)(2) - (0)(7)|}{(1^2 + 7^2)^{3/2}} = \dfrac{1}{250}\sqrt{2}.$

12. $\frac{5}{9}$

14. The curvature at x is $f(x) = \dfrac{x}{(x^2+1)^{3/2}}$. So $f'(x) = \dfrac{1-2x^2}{(x^2+1)^{5/2}}$;

    $f'(x) = 0$ when $x = 1/\sqrt{2}$. Now $f(x) \to 0$ as x approaches zero from above and also as x increases without bound, so the value $x = 1/\sqrt{2}$ maximizes the curvature. Finally, its maximum value is $\frac{2}{9}\sqrt{3}$; this occurs at the point $\left(\frac{1}{2}\sqrt{2}, -\frac{1}{2}\ln 2\right)$.

16. The curvature at x is $f(x) = \dfrac{2|x|^3}{(x^4+1)^{3/2}}$. It suffices to consider the case in which $x > 0$; if so, then

    $$f'(x) = \dfrac{6x^2(1-x^4)}{(x^4+1)^{5/2}}.$$

    It follows that $x = 1$ maximizes $f(x)$, its maximum value is $1/\sqrt{2}$, and the points on the graph of the equation $xy = 1$ where the curvature is maximal are $(1,1)$ and $(-1,-1)$.

17. $\mathbf{r}(t) = \langle t, t^3 \rangle$; $\mathbf{v}(t) = \langle 1, 3t^2 \rangle$. $\mathbf{T} = \dfrac{\mathbf{i} + 3t^2\mathbf{j}}{\sqrt{9t^4+1}}$; $\mathbf{N} = \dfrac{3t^2\mathbf{i} - \mathbf{j}}{\sqrt{9t^4+1}}$. At $(-1,-1)$, we therefore have
$$\mathbf{T} = \frac{\mathbf{i}}{10}\sqrt{10} + \frac{3\mathbf{j}}{10}\sqrt{10} \quad \text{and} \quad \mathbf{N} = \frac{3\mathbf{i}}{10}\sqrt{10} - \frac{\mathbf{j}}{10}\sqrt{10}.$$

18. $\mathbf{T} = \dfrac{\langle 3,-2 \rangle}{\sqrt{13}}$; $\mathbf{N} = \dfrac{\langle -2,-3 \rangle}{\sqrt{13}}$.

20. $\mathbf{T} = \dfrac{\langle 1,1 \rangle}{\sqrt{2}}$; $\mathbf{N} = \dfrac{\langle 1,-1 \rangle}{\sqrt{2}}$.

22. $\mathbf{a}(t) = \langle -3\pi^2 \sin \pi t, -3\pi^2 \cos \pi t \rangle$. So $a_T = 0$, $a_N = 3\pi^2$.

24. $a_T = dv/dt = \dfrac{(18 \sinh 3t \cosh 3t)}{\sqrt{\sinh^2 3t + \cosh^2 3t}}$; $a_N = v^2 = \dfrac{9}{\sqrt{\sinh^2 3t + \cosh^2 3t}}$.

26. $a_T = dv/dt = e^t \sqrt{2}$. From the equation $a_N \mathbf{N} = \mathbf{a} - a_T \mathbf{T}$ we find that $a_N = e^t \sqrt{2}$ as well.

30. The curvature at $(0,1)$ is $\dfrac{1}{2\sqrt{2}}$, so $\rho = 2\sqrt{2}$.

32. $\mathbf{v}(t) = \langle 1,2,3 \rangle$, $\mathbf{a}(t) = 0$; the curvature is $\dfrac{|\mathbf{v} \times \mathbf{a}|}{v^3} = 0$.

33. $\mathbf{v} = \mathbf{i} + \mathbf{j}\cos t - \mathbf{k}\sin t$; $\mathbf{a} = -\mathbf{j}\sin t - \mathbf{k}\cos t$. So $\mathbf{v} \times \mathbf{a} = -\mathbf{i} + \mathbf{j}\cos t - \mathbf{k}\sin t$. Therefore
$$|\mathbf{v} \times \mathbf{a}| = \sqrt{2} \quad \text{and} \quad |\mathbf{v}| = \sqrt{2},$$
and so the curvature is $\tfrac{1}{2}$.

34. $\mathbf{v} = \langle 1, 2t, 3t^2 \rangle$; $\mathbf{a} = \langle 0, 2, 6t \rangle$. So $\mathbf{v} \times \mathbf{a} = \langle 6t^2, -6t, 2 \rangle$. $v = \sqrt{1 + 4t^2 + 9t^4}$; $|\mathbf{v} \times \mathbf{a}| = \sqrt{36t^4 + 36t^2 + 4}$. Thus the curvature is $\dfrac{2\sqrt{9t^4 + 9t^2 + 1}}{(9t^4 + 4t^2 + 1)^{3/2}}$.

36. The curvature is $\dfrac{\sqrt{t^4 + 5t^2 + 8}}{(t^2 + 2)^{3/2}}$.

38. $v = \sqrt{2}$ so $a_T = 0$. $|\mathbf{v} \times \mathbf{a}| = \sqrt{2}$ and the curvature is the constant $\tfrac{1}{2}$. Therefore $a_N = 1$.

39. $\mathbf{v} = \langle 1, 2t, 3t^2 \rangle$ and $\mathbf{a} = \langle 0, 2, 6t \rangle$. $v = \sqrt{1 + 4t^2 + 9t^4}$; $\dfrac{dv}{dt} = \dfrac{4t + 18t^3}{\sqrt{1 + 4t^2 + 9t^4}}$.
$\mathbf{v} \times \mathbf{a} = \langle 6t^2, -6t, 2 \rangle$; $|\mathbf{v}| = \sqrt{9t^4 + 4t^2 + 1}$.
So $a_T = \dfrac{4t + 18t^3}{\sqrt{1 + 4t^2 + 9t^4}}$ and $a_N = \kappa v^2 = \dfrac{2\sqrt{9t^4 + 9t^2 + 1}}{\sqrt{9t^4 + 4t^2 + 1}}$.

40. $|\mathbf{v} \times \mathbf{a}| = \sqrt{6}e^{2t}$, $v = |\mathbf{v}| = \sqrt{3}e^t$, and the curvature is $\tfrac{1}{3}\sqrt{2}e^{-t}$.
Therefore $\dfrac{dv}{dt} = a_T = \sqrt{3}e^t$ and $a_N = \sqrt{2}e^t$.

42. $\mathbf{T}(1,1,1) = \dfrac{\langle 1,2,3 \rangle}{\sqrt{14}}$ and $\mathbf{N}(1,1,1) = \dfrac{\langle -11,-8,9 \rangle}{\sqrt{266}}$.

44. $\mathbf{T} = \tfrac{1}{19}\langle 6,6,7 \rangle$ and $\mathbf{N} = \tfrac{1}{12}\sqrt{2}\langle -6,6,0 \rangle$.

45. $v(t) = \sqrt{3}e^t$, $\mathbf{T} = \tfrac{1}{3}\sqrt{3}\langle 1,1,1 \rangle$, and the curvature is $\tfrac{1}{3}\sqrt{2}e^{-t}$.

46. The curvature is $\dfrac{a\omega^2}{a^2\omega^2 + b^2}$. Also $\dfrac{dv}{dt} = 0$, so $a_T = 0$. Next, $a_N = \kappa v^2 = a\omega^2$. It follows that
$$\mathbf{T}(t) = \dfrac{\langle -a\omega \sin \omega t, a\omega \cos \omega t, b \rangle}{\sqrt{a^2\omega^2 + b^2}}; \quad \mathbf{N}(t) = -\langle \cos \omega t, \sin \omega t, 0 \rangle; \quad a_T = 0; \quad a_N = a\omega^2.$$

48. Because $s = 2t$, $t = s/2$. Answer: $x = 2\cos(s/2)$, $y = 2\sin(s/2)$, $z = 0$.

49. $s = s(t) = \int_0^t ds = \int_0^t \sqrt{9\sin^2 t + 9\cos^2 t + 16}\, dt = 5t$. Therefore $t = s/5$ and the rest is easy.

50. $\mathbf{v}(t) = \langle 1, f'(t), 0\rangle$; $\mathbf{a}(t) = \langle 0, f''(t), 0\rangle$. $\mathbf{v} \times \mathbf{a} = \langle 0, 0, f''(t)\rangle$; $|\mathbf{v}| = \sqrt{1 + (f'(t))^2}$, $|\mathbf{v} \times \mathbf{a}| = |f''(t)|$.
Therefore $\kappa(t) = \dfrac{|\mathbf{v} \times \mathbf{a}|}{v^3} = \dfrac{|f''(t)|}{\left(1 + (f'(t))^2\right)^{3/2}}$. Now simply replace t with x.

54. At $\left(\tfrac{3}{2}, \tfrac{3}{2}\right)$,
$$\mathbf{N} = \tfrac{1}{2}\sqrt{2}\,\langle -1, 1\rangle, \qquad \mathbf{T} = -\tfrac{1}{2}\sqrt{2}\,\langle 1, 1\rangle, \qquad \text{and} \qquad \kappa = \tfrac{8}{3}\sqrt{2}.$$
The osculating circle at $\left(\tfrac{3}{2}\ \tfrac{3}{2}\right)$ has equation $8x^2 - 21x + 8y^2 - 21y + 27 = 0$.

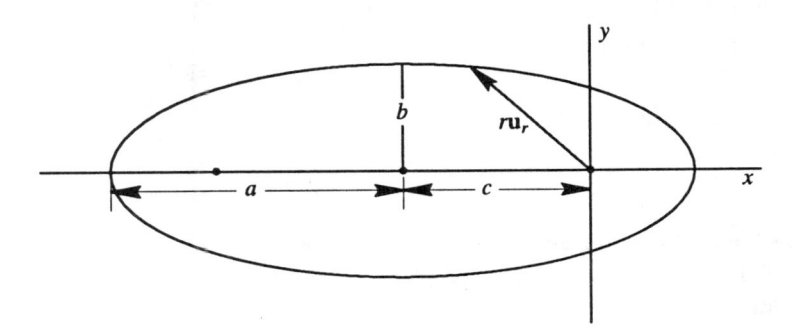

56. See the figure above.

(a) $\mathbf{v} = \dfrac{dr}{dt}\mathbf{u}_r + r\dfrac{d\theta}{dt}\mathbf{u}_\theta$. $v = |\mathbf{v}| = \sqrt{\left(\dfrac{dr}{dt}\right)^2 + r^2\left(\dfrac{d\theta}{dt}\right)^2}$.

At perigee and at apogee, $\dfrac{dr}{dt} = 0$. So $v = \left|r\dfrac{d\theta}{dt}\right| = r\dfrac{d\theta}{dt}$.

(b) $\tfrac{1}{2}r^2\dfrac{d\theta}{dt}$ is constant. And $\int_0^T \tfrac{1}{2}r^2\dfrac{d\theta}{dt}\,dt = \pi ab$. Hence $\dfrac{T}{2}r^2\dfrac{d\theta}{dt} = \pi ab$. Therefore $r\dfrac{d\theta}{dt} = \dfrac{2\pi ab}{rT}$.

At perigee and at apogee, then, $v = \dfrac{2\pi ab}{rT}$ by part (a).

58. With the usual meanings of the symbols, we have $b^2 = a^2(1 - e^2)$. With the aid of a calculator and the result of Problem 3, we obtain these results: Its velocity at apogee is approximately 18.2007 miles per second; at perigee, it is approximately 18.8189 miles per second.

60. 5.38 miles per second; 1.79 miles per second.

61. Equation (11), when applied to the moon, yields $(26.32)^2 = k(238{,}850)^3$.

For a satellite with period $T = \tfrac{1}{24}$ (of a day—one hour), it yields $1^2 = kr^3$ where r is the radius of the orbit of the satellite. Divide the second of these equations by the first and solve for $r \approx 3165$ miles, about 795 miles below the earth's surface. So it can't be done.

62. Equation (11) applied to the Earth-Sun system (in years and miles) yields
$$(1)^2 = k(92{,}956{,}000)^3.$$
Applied to the Jupiter-Sun system it yields
$$(11.86)^2 = kr^3$$
where r is the major semiaxis of Jupiter's orbit. Division of the second of these equations by the first yields
$$r^3 = (92{,}956{,}000)^3 (11.86)^2,$$

so that $r \approx 483{,}430{,}000$ (miles).

Section 12.7

1. A plane with intercepts $x = \frac{20}{3}$, $y = 10$, $z = 2$.

2. A plane perpendicular to the xy-plane (if you prefer, parallel to the z-axis). It meets the x-axis at $x = 10$ and the y-axis at $y = 15$.

4. A cylinder whose rulings are lines parallel to the z-axis. It meets the xy-plane in the hyperbola $x^2 - y^2 = 9$. The graph is shown at the right.

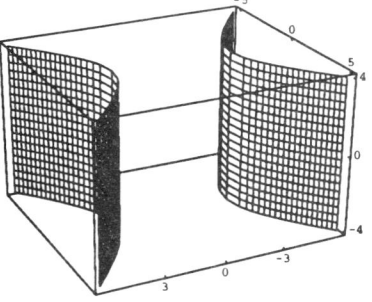

6. In polar form this equation would be $z = 4r^2$, which shows that its graph is a surface of revolution about the z-axis. The surface meets the xz-plane in the parabola $z = 4x^2$, so the surface is a (circular) paraboloid.

7. An elliptic paraboloid. The graph is shown below.

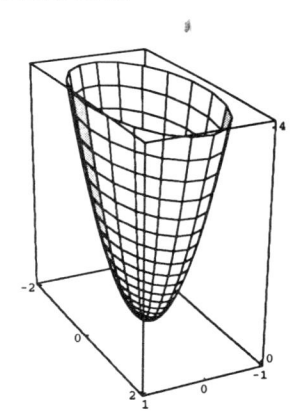

8. An elliptic cylinder. Its rulings are lines parallel to the z-axis and each cross section parallel to the xy-plane is an ellipse. The graph is shown below.

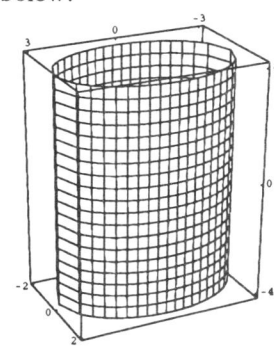

10. A circular cylinder with axis the x-axis.

11. In polar coordinates the equation takes the form $2z = r^2$, so the graph is a paraboloid, vertex at the origin, opening upward.

12. Circular paraboloid, vertex at $(1, 0, 0)$, opening in the positive x-direction.

14. Parabolic cylinder parallel to the y-axis; its trace in the xz-plane is the parabola $y^2 = 4x$ with vertex $(0, 0)$ and opening in the positive x-direction. The graph is shown at the right.

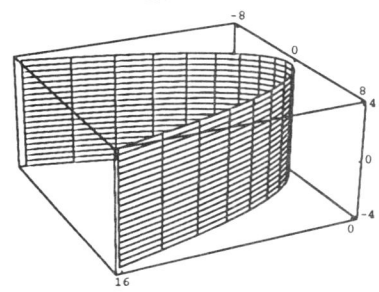

16. Parabolic cylinder, parallel to the z-axis; its trace in the xz-plane is the parabola with vertex $x = 9$ and $z = 0$ and opening in the negative x-direction. The graph is shown at the right.

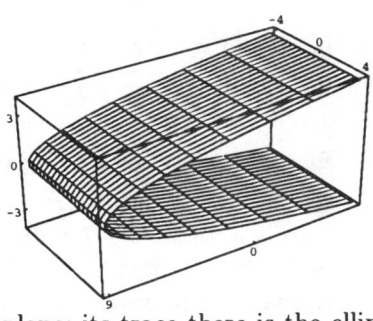

17. $x^2 + (y/2)^2 = 1$: An elliptical cylinder, perpendicular to the xy-plane; its trace there is the ellipse with center $(0, 0)$ and with intercepts $(-1, 0)$, $(0, 2)$, $(1, 0)$, and $(0, -2)$.

18. Circular cylinder, radius 2, axis the y-axis.

20. Hyperbolic paraboloid. The graph is shown below.

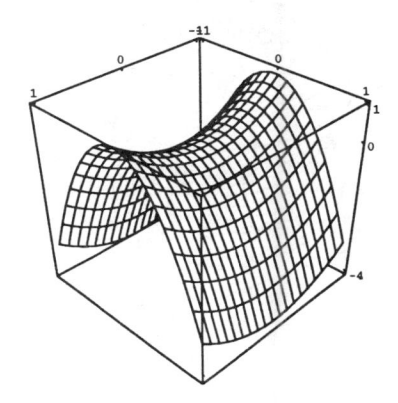

22. A cylinder having the graph $x = \sin y$ as its trace in the xy-plane. The graph is shown below.

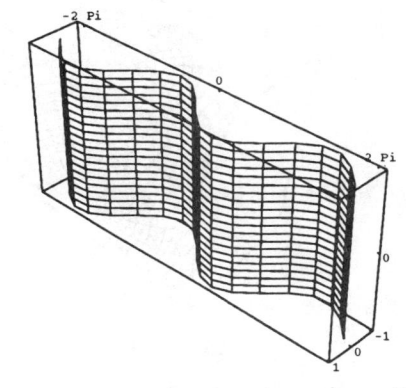

24. An ellipsoid centered at the origin. Its intercepts are located where $|x| = 2$, $|y| = 1$, and $|z| = \sqrt{2}$.

26. Hyperboloid of two sheets. The graph is shown at the right.

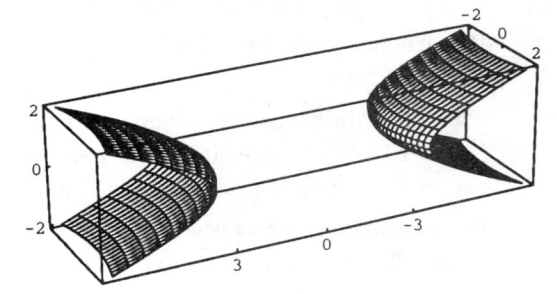

28. A hyperboloid of one sheet. Its graph is shown on the right.

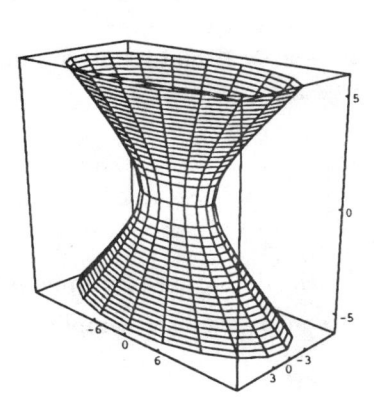

30. An ellipsoid centered at the origin.

Section 12.7 Cylinders and Quadric Surfaces

32. Replace x by $\sqrt{x^2+y^2}$. Answer: The ellipsoid with equation $4x^2 + 9y^2 + 4z^2 = 36$.

34. Replace x by $\sqrt{x^2+y^2}$. Answer: A paraboloid opening along the negative z-axis and with equation $z = 4 - x^2 - y^2$.

36. Replace x by $\sqrt{x^2+y^2}$. Equation: $z^2\left(x^2+y^2\right) = 1$.

38. Given: $y^2 - 2yz + 2z^2 = 1$. This is an ellipse in the yz-plane; in the appropriately rotated (through about 0.447 radians, or about 25.6°) uv-coordinate system, its equation takes the form $(0.38)u^2 + (2.62)v^2 = 1$ (the coefficients are approximate). Solution: Replace y by $\pm\sqrt{x^2+y^2}$. Answer: The resulting equation is

$$x^2 + y^2 \pm 2z\sqrt{x^2+y^2} + 2z^2 = 1.$$

The portion of the graph for $y \geq 0$, (cut so that the inside is visible) is shown below on the left; the entire surface appears below on the right.

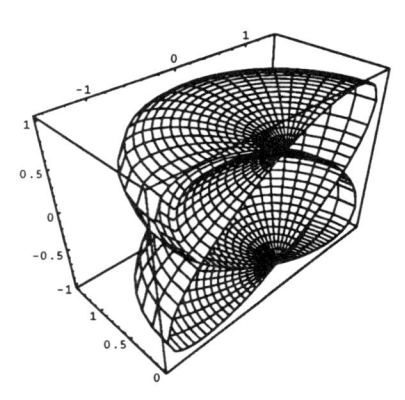

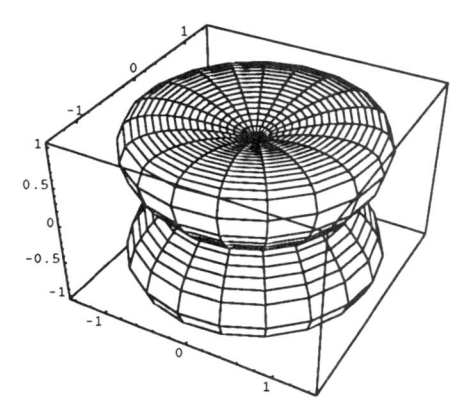

40. $4x^2 = y^2 + z^2$

42. Ellipses centered on the z-axis provided the planes are not too far from the origin.

44. Ellipses centered at the origin in planes above the xy-plane (there is no graph below the xy-plane).

46. Hyperbolas (both branches), except that the trace in the xy-plane itself consists of the coordinate axes.

48. The traces in horizontal planes are hyperbolas (the degenerate case, two intersecting straight lines, if $z = \pm 1$). The traces in planes parallel to the xz-plane are circles. The traces in planes parallel to the yz-plane are hyperbolas (the degenerate case, two intersecting straight lines, if $x = \pm 1$).

50. Intersection: $1-y^2 = y^2+z^2$. To get the projection into the yz-plane, set $x = 0$. Result: $2y^2+z^2 = 1$ — an ellipse.

52. Projection of the intersection: $2x^2 + 3z^2 = 5 - 3x^2 - 2z^2$. That is, $x^2 + z^2 = 1$: a circle.

54. Introduce uv-coordinates in the plane $z = ky$ by $u = x$ and v-axis the line $z = ky$, $x = 0$. Then $u = x$ and $v = \sqrt{y^2+z^2}$. Given the point (x,y,z) on the curve of intersection of $z = ky$ and $x^2 + y^2 = 1$, find its uv-coordinates: The first coordinate is u, the second is v;

$$\begin{aligned}au^2 + bv^2 &= ax^2 + b\left(y^2+z^2\right) \\ &= \left(ax^2+ay^2\right) + (b-a)y^2 + bz^2 \\ &= a + (b-a)y^2 + bk^2y^2 \\ &= a + \left(b-a+bk^2\right)y^2,\end{aligned}$$

which will be constant provided that $b - a + bk^2 = 0$. This leads to $a = 1$, $b = \dfrac{1}{1+k^2}$. That is, after strenuous algebraic simplifications,

$$u^2 + \frac{v^2}{1+k^2} = 1.$$

Because this is the equation of an ellipse in the uv-plane, it is indeed an ellipse in xyz-space.

56. $\lambda_1 = 4$, $\lambda_2 = 6$: ellipse
58. $\lambda_1 = -5$, $\lambda_2 = 10$: hyperbola
60. $\lambda_1 = 13$, $\lambda_2 = 52$: ellipse
62. $\lambda_1 = -2$, $\lambda_2 = 4$: hyperbolic paraboloid
64. $\lambda_1 = 5$, $\lambda_2 = 10$: elliptic paraboloid
66. $\lambda_1 = 0$, $\lambda_2 = 25$: parabolic cylinder ($z = (3x + 4y)^2$)
68. $\lambda_1 = 1$, $\lambda_2 = 3$, $\lambda_3 = 5$: ellipsoid
70. $\lambda_1 \approx 0.492097$, $\lambda_2 \approx 3.24436$, $\lambda_3 \approx 6.26354$: ellipsoid
72. $\lambda_1 = -3$, $\lambda_2 = 3$, $\lambda_3 = 6$: hyperboloid

Section 12.8

2. $(0, -3, -1)$
4. $\left(-\frac{3}{2}\sqrt{3}, -\frac{3}{2}, -1\right)$
6. $\left(2, -2\sqrt{3}, 6\right)$
8. $(0, 0, -3)$
10. $\left(-1, \sqrt{3}, 2\sqrt{3}\right)$
12. $\left(-\frac{3}{2}\sqrt{2}, -\frac{3}{2}\sqrt{6}, -3\sqrt{2}\right)$
13. Cylindrical: $(0, \pi/2, 5)$; spherical: $(5, 0, \pi/2)$
14. Cylindrical: $(0, \pi/2, -3)$; spherical: $(3, \pi, 0)$
16. Cylindrical: $(2\sqrt{2}, -\pi/4, 0)$; spherical: $(2\sqrt{2}, \pi/2, -\pi/4)$
18. Cylindrical: $(\sqrt{2}, 3\pi/4, -1)$; spherical: $\left(\sqrt{3}, \cos^{-1}\left(-1/\sqrt{2}\right), -\pi/4\right)$
20. Cylindrical: $\left(\sqrt{5}, \tan^{-1}(1/2), -2\right)$; spherical: $\left(3, \cos^{-1}(-2/3), \tan^{-1}(1/2)\right)$
22. Cylindrical: $\left(2\sqrt{5}, \tan^{-1}(-2), -12\right)$; spherical: $\left(2\sqrt{41}, \cos^{-1}\left(-\sqrt{41}/6\right), \tan^{-1}(-2)\right)$
24. The plane $y = -x$.
26. The sphere of radius 5 centered at the origin.
28. The lower nappe of the cone $z^2 = 3r^2$, vertex at the origin, axis the z-axis, opening downward.
30. The negative z-axis.
32. $-2x^2 - 2y^2 + z^2 = 4$: This is a hyperboloid of two sheets.
34. $x^2 + y^2 + (z - 2)^2 = 4$: This is the spherical surface with center $(0, 0, 2)$ and radius 2.
36. The graph consists of two spherical surfaces centered at $(0, 0, 0)$, one of radius 1, the other of radius 3.
38. Because the only (real) solution of the equation $\rho^3 + 4\rho = 0$ is $\rho = 0$, the graph consists of the single point $(0, 0, 0)$.
40. Cylindrical equation: $r = 2\cos\theta$. Spherical equation: $\rho\sin\phi = 2\cos\theta$.
42. $r(\cos\theta + \sin\theta) = 4$; $\rho\sin\phi\cos\theta + \rho\sin\phi\sin\theta = 4$.
44. $z = r^2\cos 2\theta$; $\cos\phi = \rho\sin^2\phi\cos 2\theta$.
46. The graph is a hemispherical surface: the upper half of the spherical surface with center $(0, 0, 0)$ and radius 2. To see a graph, execute the *Mathematica* command

```
ParametricPlot3D[ {2*Sin[phi]*Cos[theta], 2*Sin[phi]*Sin[theta],
    2*Cos[phi]}, {phi, 0, Pi/2}, {theta, 0, 2*Pi} ];
```

48. The *solid* cylinder with vertical side $r = 3$, base in the plane $z = -2$, top in the plane $z = 2$. To see a figure, execute the *Mathematica* commands

```
p1 = ParametricPlot3D[ {3*Cos[theta], 3*Sin[theta], z},
    {theta, 0, 2*Pi}, {z, -2, 2} ];
p2 = ParametricPlot3D[ {r*Cos[theta], r*Sin[theta], 2},
    {theta, 0, 2*Pi}, {r, 0, 3} ];
Show[ p1, p2 ]
```

50. This looks just like the figure in Problem 46, except that it is solid—filled-in rather than hollow.

52. This solid region is bounded above by the sphere of radius 10 centered at the origin and bounded below by the 30°-cone, opening upward, with vertex at the origin. To see a figure, execute the *Mathematica* commands

```
p1 = ParametricPlot3D[ {10*Sin[phi]*Cos[theta], 10*Sin[phi]*Sin[theta],
    10*Cos[phi]}, {phi, 0, Pi/6}, {theta, 0, 2*Pi} ];
p2 = ParametricPlot3D[ {r*Cos[theta], r*Sin[theta], r*Sqrt[3]},
    {r, 0, 5}, {theta, 0, 2*Pi} ];
Show[ p1, p2 ]
```

54. Replace y by r: $r^2 - z^2 = 1$.

56. Take $\rho = 3960$ (miles).   Atlanta: $\phi = 56.25°$, $\theta = -84.40°$.

San Francisco: $\phi = 52.22°$, $\theta = -122.42°$.

Therefore Atlanta is at $P_1(x_1, y_1, z_1)$ where $x_1 \approx 321.3$, $y_1 \approx -3276.9$, and $z_1 \approx 2200.1$; San Francisco is at $P_2(x_2, y_2, z_2)$ where $x_2 \approx -1677.8$, $y_2 \approx -2642.0$, and $z_2 \approx 2426.0$.

The cosine of the central angle between the two cities is then $\dfrac{\left(\overrightarrow{OP_1} \times \overrightarrow{OP_2}\right)}{\left|\overrightarrow{OP_1}\right|\left|\overrightarrow{OP_2}\right|} \approx 0.858073636$.

This means that the angle itself is about $30.89903595°$; that is, about 0.5392897386 radians. The arc length between the two cities is the product of the radius of the earth and this angle (in radians), and that's approximately 2135.587365. Answer: The great circle distance between San Francisco and Atlanta is about 2136 miles.

57. With $R = 3960$ as the radius of the earth, the rectangular coordinates of Fairbanks are about $(-1427.54, -897.23, 3583.12)$ and those of St. Petersburg about $(1711.90, 1005.57, 3426.35)$. As a consequence, the central angle between the two cities is roughly 0.569519185 (about $32.6310°$), and multiplication of the angle by R gives the great circle distance—about 2255 miles.

58. The 62nd parallel is at (approximately) $z = 3496.47$; for such points we have the cylindrical equation

$$r = \sqrt{R^2 - z^2} \approx 1859.1$$

(the units are all miles). The angular difference in longitude is $178.28°$, so the distance along the parallel is given by $s = r\theta$ where θ is the radian measure of $178.28°$. Answer: About 5785 miles.

59. We found the rectangular coordinates of the point of the journey nearest the North Pole to be approximately $(x, y, z) = (15.99750973, 26.41463504, 3959.879587)$. The central angle between this point and the North Pole has cosine z/R where $R = 3960$; that angle turns out to be about 0.00779839 radians. Multiply by R to get the closest approach to the North Pole in great circle terms, hardly different from the straight-line distance.

60. Either (1): $\quad 0 \leq z \leq H, \quad 0 \leq r \leq \frac{R}{H}z, \quad 0 \leq \theta \leq 2\pi$

or (2): $\quad 0 \leq r \leq R, \quad \frac{H}{R}r \leq z \leq H, \quad 0 \leq \theta \leq 2\pi.$

62. Maximize z given $ax + by + cz = 0$ and $x^2 + y^2 + z^2 = r^2$: $r = 3960$ is the radius of the earth and $ax + by + cz = 0$ is the equation of the plane through New York, London, and the center of the earth. We found $a = -8.93709 \times 10^6$, $b = 3.80960 \times 10^6$, and $c = 7.10888 \times 10^6$. The Lagrange multiplier method yields:

$$x = -\frac{acr}{\sqrt{a^2+b^2}\sqrt{a^2+b^2+c^2}}, \quad y = -\frac{bcr}{\sqrt{a^2+b^2}\sqrt{a^2+b^2+c^2}}, \quad \text{and} \quad z = \frac{r\sqrt{a^2+b^2}}{\sqrt{a^2+b^2+c^2}}.$$

The latitude of this point is $53.806°$, somewhat farther north than London ($51.5°$).

Chapter 12 Miscellaneous

6. $x = 2t+1,\ y = -t-1,\ z = 3t; \quad \frac{x-1}{2} = \frac{y+1}{-1} = \frac{z}{3}.$

8. $x + y + 2 = 0$

10. For $i = 1$ and $i = 2$, the line L_i passes through the point $P_i\,(x_i, y_i, z_i)$ and is parallel to the vector $\mathbf{v}_i = \langle a_i, b_i, c_i \rangle$. Let L be the line through P_1 parallel to $\mathbf{v}_2$. Now, by definition, the lines L_1 and L_2 are skew if and only they are not coplanar. But L_1 and L_2 are coplanar if and only if the plane determined by L_1 and L is the same as the plane determined by L_2 and L; that is, if and only if the plane determined by L_1 and L is the same as the plane that contains the segment P_1P_2 and the line L. Thus L_1 and L_2 are coplanar if and only if $\overrightarrow{P_1P_2}$, $\mathbf{v}_1$, and $\mathbf{v}_2$ are coplanar, and this condition is equivalent (by a theorem from early in Chapter 13) to the condition

$$|\overrightarrow{P_1P_2} \cdot \mathbf{v}_1 \times \mathbf{v}_2| = 0.$$

That is, L_1 and L_2 are coplanar if and only if $\begin{vmatrix} x_1 - x_2 & y_1 - y_2 & z_1 - z_2 \\ a_1 & b_1 & c_1 \\ a_2 & b_2 & c_2 \end{vmatrix} = 0.$ This establishes the conclusion given in Problem 10.

12. $P = (3, 2, 1)$, $Q = (2, 3, -1)$, and $|\overrightarrow{PQ}| = \sqrt{6}$.

14. Let Q_1 be the foot of the perpendicular from the point $P_1\,(x_1, y_1, z_1)$ to the plane with equation $ax + by + cz + d = 0$; also let the point Q be determined by the vector equation

$$\overrightarrow{OQ} = \overrightarrow{OQ_1} - \overrightarrow{OP_1}.$$

Then Q is the foot of the perpendicular from the origin O to the plane with equation

$$a(x + x_1) + b(y + y_1) + c(z + z_1) + d = 0$$

(a translate of the original plane by $-OP_1$, using our translation principle)—that is,

$$ax + by + cz + d_1 = 0 \quad \text{where} \quad d_1 = ax_1 + by_1 + cz_1 + d.$$

Hence, with the aid of the result of Problem 13,

$$D = |\overrightarrow{P_1Q_1}| = |\overrightarrow{OQ}| = \frac{|d_1|}{\sqrt{a^2+b^2+c^2}} = \frac{|ax_1 + by_1 + cz_1 + d|}{\sqrt{a^2+b^2+c^2}}.$$

16. $x + 2y + 3z = 6$

18. In the figure to the right, the parallelogram has adjacent sides **a** and **b**. Its diagonals are $\mathbf{p} = \mathbf{a} + \mathbf{b}$ and $\mathbf{q} = \mathbf{b} - \mathbf{a}$. So

$$\mathbf{p} \cdot \mathbf{q} = (\mathbf{a} + \mathbf{b}) \cdot (\mathbf{b} - \mathbf{a})$$
$$= \mathbf{a} \cdot \mathbf{b} - \mathbf{a} \cdot \mathbf{a} + \mathbf{b} \cdot \mathbf{b} - \mathbf{a} \cdot \mathbf{b}$$
$$= -|\mathbf{a}|^2 + |\mathbf{b}|^2 = 0.$$

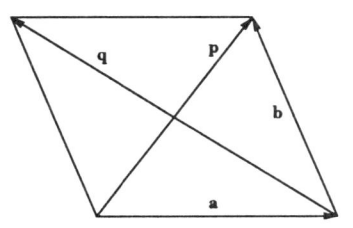

(Here we use the fact that the parallelogram is a rhombus, so that $|\mathbf{a}| = |\mathbf{b}|$.) Therefore **p** and **q** are perpendicular to each other.

20. First show that $a = -\omega^2 r$; conclude that

$$-\omega^2 x = x'' \quad \text{and} \quad -\omega^2 y = y'',$$

so that $x(t) = A\cos\omega t + B\sin\omega t$ and $y(t) = C\cos\omega t + D\sin\omega t$. Then use the given initial data to find A, B, C, and D.

22. Trajectory: $x = (v_0 \cos\alpha)t$, $y = -\frac{1}{2}gt^2 + (v_0 \sin\alpha)t$. Determine when $y = \frac{1}{3}x\sqrt{3}$; you should get impact time

$$t_1 = \frac{2v_0}{g}\left(\sin\alpha - \frac{\sqrt{3}}{3}\cos\alpha\right).$$

Now find the point of impact, and thus the range R as a function of the angle α: You should obtain

$$R = R(\alpha) = \tfrac{2}{3}\sqrt{3}\,(v_0 \cos\alpha)\,t_1.$$

Finally show that $dR/d\alpha = 0$ when $\tan 2\alpha = -\sqrt{3}$.

24. At $t = 1$, we have $\mathbf{r} = \langle 1, 1, \frac{4}{3}\rangle$, $\mathbf{v} = \langle 1, 2, 2\rangle$, $\mathbf{a} = \langle 0, 2, 1\rangle$, $\mathbf{T} = \langle \frac{1}{3}, \frac{2}{3}, \frac{2}{3}\rangle$, curvature $\frac{1}{9}$, $v = 3$, $dv/dt = 2$, $a_T = 2$, $a_N = 1$, and $\mathbf{N} = \langle -\frac{2}{3}, \frac{2}{3}, -\frac{1}{3}\rangle$.

For a normal to the osculating plane, let $\mathbf{n} = 3\,(\mathbf{N} \times \mathbf{T}) = \langle 2, 1, -2\rangle$. It follows that an equation of the plane is $6x + 3y - 6z = 1$.

26. By the definition in Problem 18, the osculating plane at the point $P_0 = \mathbf{r}(t_0)$ is the plane through P_0 that is perpendicular to the vectors **T** and **N**. These latter vectors are scalar multiples of $\mathbf{r}'(t_0)$ and $\mathbf{r}''(t_0)$, respectively. We therefore let $\mathbf{v}_1 = \mathbf{r}'(t_0)$ and $\mathbf{v}_2 = \mathbf{r}''(t_0)$. Then—recalling the determinant for the scalar triple product—the desired equation for the osculating plane is a consequence of the conclusion of Problem 19.

28. $\dfrac{dx}{dt} = \dfrac{dr}{dt}\cos\theta - (r\sin\theta)\dfrac{d\theta}{dt}$ and $\dfrac{dy}{dt} = \dfrac{dr}{dt}\sin\theta + (r\cos\theta)\dfrac{d\theta}{dt}$. Now show that

$$\left(\frac{dx}{dt}\right)^2 + \left(\frac{dy}{dt}\right)^2 + \left(\frac{dz}{dt}\right)^2 = \left(\frac{dr}{dt}\right)^2 + \left(r\left(\frac{d\theta}{dt}\right)\right)^2 + \left(\frac{dz}{dt}\right)^2.$$

32. If **r** moves in a fixed plane with unit normal **n**, it follows that either $\mathbf{B} = \mathbf{n}$ or $\mathbf{B} = -\mathbf{n}$, so that $d\mathbf{B}/ds = \mathbf{0}$. Therefore τ is identically zero for such a curve because $|\mathbf{N}| = 1 \neq 0$.

34. Replace y by r to obtain $(r - 1)^2 + z^2 = 1$. Simplify this to $r^2 - 2r + z^2 = 0$, then convert to the rectangular equation $x^2 + y^2 + z^2 = 2\sqrt{x^2 + y^2}$.

35. Replace y^2 by $x^2 + y^2$.

36. $A = |\mathbf{a} \times \mathbf{b}|$, so $\mathbf{a} \times \mathbf{b} = \mathbf{i}(A\cos\alpha) + \mathbf{j}(A\cos\beta) + \mathbf{k}(A\cos\gamma)$ where α, β, and γ are the direction cosines of $\mathbf{a} \times \mathbf{b}$. By assumption, the (signed) projections of A into the three coordinate planes are $A_x = A\cos\alpha$, $A_y = A\cos\beta$, and $A_z = A\cos\gamma$. Hence $\mathbf{a} \times \mathbf{b} = A_x\mathbf{i} + A_y\mathbf{j} + A_z\mathbf{k}$, and so

$$A^2 = |\mathbf{a} \times \mathbf{b}|^2 = (A_x)^2 + (A_y)^2 + (A_z)^2.$$

38. It suffices to show that the intersection K of the elliptical cylinder $\left(\dfrac{x}{a}\right)^2 + \left(\dfrac{y}{b}\right)^2 = 1$ (z arbitrary) with the plane $Ax + By + Cz = 0$ (with A and B not both zero) is itself an ellipse. This is done in the solution of Problem 33..

39. Without loss of generality, we may assume that the ellipse in the xy-plane is centered at the origin, and by rotation (if necessary) that the plane containing the curve K has equation has equation $z = by + c$ (that is, the normal to the plane has **i**-component zero). Then the ellipse has an equation of the form
$$Ax^2 + Bxy + Cy^2 + D = 0$$
where $B^2 - 4AC < 0$. Parametrize the plane with a uv-coordinate system that projects vertically onto the xy-coordinate system in the plane:
$$u = x, \quad v = \sqrt{1 + b^2}\, y.$$
This parametrization preserves distance; that is,
$$\sqrt{x^2 + y^2 + (z-c)^2}$$
on the plane is
$$\sqrt{u^2 + v^2} = \sqrt{x^2 + (1+b^2)y^2} = \sqrt{x^2 + b^2 y^2 + y^2} = \sqrt{x^2 + (z-c)^2 + y^2}.$$
Now take a point (x, y, z) on the intersection of the plane and the cylinder. The equation
$$Ax^2 + Bxy + Cy^2 + D = 0$$
takes the form
$$Au^2 + Bu\,\dfrac{v}{\sqrt{1+b^2}} + C\,\dfrac{v^2}{1+b^2} + D = 0;$$
that is,
$$Au^2 + \dfrac{B}{\sqrt{1+b^2}}\, uv + \dfrac{C}{1+b^2}\, v^2 + D = 0.$$
Is this the equation of an ellipse? We check the discriminant:
$$\left(\dfrac{B}{\sqrt{1+b^2}}\right)^2 - \dfrac{4AC}{1+b^2} = \dfrac{B^2 - 4AC}{1+b^2} < 0.$$
Because the discriminant is negative, the curve K is an ellipse.

40. Because $z = ax^2 + by^2$ is a paraboloid (not a hyperboloid), we know that $ab > 0$. The projection into the xy-plane of the intersection K has the equation $ax^2 - Ax + by^2 - By = 0$. We may also assume that $a > 0$ and $b > 0$ (multiply through by -1 if necessary). It follows by completing squares that this projection is either empty, a single point, or an ellipse. In the latter case, it follows from Problem 32 that K is an ellipse.

41. The intersection of $z = Ax + By$ with the ellipsoid
$$\left(\dfrac{x}{a}\right)^2 + \left(\dfrac{y}{b}\right)^2 + \left(\dfrac{z}{c}\right)^2 = 1$$
has the simultaneous equations
$$\left(\dfrac{x}{a}\right)^2 + \left(\dfrac{y}{b}\right)^2 + \dfrac{A^2 x^2 + 2ABxy + B^2 y^2}{c^2} = 1, \qquad z = Ax + By.$$

The first of these two equations is the equation of the projection of the intersection into the xy-plane; write it in the form
$$Px^2 + Qxy + Ry^2 = 1$$
and show that its discriminant is negative—this shows that the projection is an ellipse. It follows from the result of Problem 32 that the intersection itself must be an ellipse. (Of course, if the plane is tangent to the ellipse or misses it altogether, then the intersection is not an ellipse—it is either empty or else consists of a single point).

44. The curvature is
$$\kappa(t) = \frac{|x'(t)y''(t) - x''(t)y'(t)|}{\left[(x'(t))^2 + (y(t))^2\right]^{3/2}} = \frac{|\sinh^2 t - \cosh^2 t|}{(\sinh^2 t + \cosh^2 t)^{3/2}}$$
$$= \frac{1}{(\sinh^2 t + \cosh^2 t)^{3/2}} = \frac{1}{(\cosh 2t)^{3/2}}.$$

For maximal curvature, minimize the denominator; when $\cosh 2t$ is minimal, $t = 0$; $(x, y) = (1, 0)$. At no point is the curvature minimal because at no point is $\cosh 2t$ maximal.

46. The curvature is
$$\kappa(t) = \frac{|x'(t)y''(t) - x''(t)y'(t)|}{\left[(x'(t))^2 + (y(t))^2\right]^{3/2}} = \frac{ab\sin^2 t + ab\cos^2 t}{(a^2\sin^2 t + b^2\cos^2 t)^{3/2}} = \frac{ab}{(a^2\sin^2 t + b^2\cos^2 t)^{3/2}}.$$

$$\kappa'(t) = \tfrac{3}{2}ab\left(a^2\sin^2 t + b^2\cos^2 t\right)^{-5/2}\left(2a^2\sin t\cos t - 2b^2\sin t\cos t\right) = \frac{3ab(\sin t\cos t)(a^2 - b^2)}{(a^2\sin^2 t + b^2\cos^2 t)^{5/2}}.$$

$\kappa'(t) = 0$ when $t = 0,\ \pi/2,\ \pi,\ 3\pi/2$: $\kappa(0) = \dfrac{ab}{b^3} = \dfrac{a}{b^2} = \kappa(\pi)$, and $\kappa(\pi/2) = \dfrac{ab}{a^3} = \dfrac{b}{a^2} = \kappa(3\pi/2)$. Because $a > b$, κ is maximal when $t = 0$ and when $t = \pi$—at $(\pm a, 0)$— and minimal when $t = \pi/2$ and when $t = 3\pi/2$—at $(0, \pm b)$.

48. The curvature is $f(\theta) = \dfrac{\theta^2 + 2}{(\theta^2 + 1)^{3/2}}$. If θ is large, then $f(\theta) \approx \dfrac{1}{\theta}$, hence $f(\theta) \to 0$ as $\theta \to \infty$.

49. Because $y(x) = Ax + Bx^3 + Cx^5$ is an odd function, the condition $y(1) = 1$ will imply that $y(-1) = -1$. Because $y'(x) = A + 3Bx^2 + 5Cx^4$ is an even function, the condition $y'(1) = 0$ will imply that $y'(-1) = 0$ as well. Because the graph of y is symmetric about the origin, the condition that the curvature is zero at $(1, 1)$ will imply that it is also zero at $(-1, -1)$. The curvature at (x, y) is
$$\frac{|6Bx + 20Cx^3|}{\left(1 + (A + 3Bx^2 + 5Cx^4)^2\right)^{3/2}}$$
by Problem 50 in Section 13.5, so the curvature at $(1, 1)$ will be zero when $|6B + 20C| = 0$. Thus we obtain the simultaneous equations
$$\begin{array}{rcrcrcl} A & + & B & + & C & = & 1, \\ A & + & 3B & + & 5C & = & 0, \\ & & 3B & + & 10C & = & 0. \end{array}$$

These are easy to solve for $A = \tfrac{15}{8}$, $B = -\tfrac{5}{4}$, and $C = \tfrac{3}{8}$. Thus the equation of the connecting curve is $y = \tfrac{15}{8}x - \tfrac{5}{4}x^3 + \tfrac{3}{8}x^5$.

50. See the solution of Problem 40 of Section 13.7.

51. This is a variation of Problem 36.

Chapter 13: Partial Differentiation

Section 13.2

1. The xy-plane
2. The xy-plane
3. All points of the xy-plane other than $(0,0)$
4. All points of the xy-plane other than the line $y = x$
5. All points of the xy-plane
6. All points (x, y) for which $x \geq 0$ (the "right half-plane")
7. All points (x, y) such that $x^2 + y^2 \leq 1$; that is, all points on and within the unit circle centered at the origin
8. All points of the xy-plane other than the y-axis (where $x = 0$)
9. The domain is the coordinate plane.
10. The points in the plane for which $x^2 - y^2 > 1$. This set consists of the points strictly to the right of the right branch of the hyperbola $x^2 - y^2 = 1$ together with the points strictly to the left of the left branch of that hyperbola.
11. All points of the xy-plane for which $y > x$; that is, all points above the line with equation $y = x$
12. The points in the plane on or within the circle with equation $x^2 + y^2 = 4$; that is, the points of the disk of radius 2 and centered at the origin.
14. All points in the plane other than the origin $(0,0)$.
15. All points in the plane except for those on either of the the two lines $y = x$ and $y = -x$.
16. All points in space that lie strictly above (one might say "within") the paraboloid with equation $z = x^2 + y^2 = r^2$; this is a circular paraboloid with "vertex" at the origin, symmetric about the z-axis, and opening upward.
18. All points in space for which $xyz > 0$. This consists of the interior of the first octant (the points where x, y, and z are all positive) together with three other octants (one where x is positive and y and z are both negative, etc.).
19. All points (x, y, z) of space for which $x^2 + y^2 < z$; that is, all points below the paraboloid with equation $x = x^2 + y^2$
20. All points (x, y, z) of space for which $2 \leq x^2 + y^2 + z^2 \leq 4$; that is, all points on and between the spheres of radius $\sqrt{2}$ and 2 centered at the origin $(0,0,0)$
22. The plane $z = x$, which passes through the y-axis at a $45°$ angle to the xy-plane.
23. The plane that meets the xz-plane in the line $z = x$ and the yz-plane in the line $z = y$.
24. The upper nappe of the $45°$ cone $z = r$, symmetric about the nonnegative z-axis and opening upward.
26. The paraboloid $z = 4 - r^2$ with highest point $(0,0,4)$, symmetric about the z-axis and opening downward.
28. The cylinder $z = 16 - y^2$ with rulings parallel to the x-axis and having the parabola $z = 16 - y^2$ as its trace in the yz-plane.
29. The lower nappe of a $45°$ cone with vertex at $(0,0,10)$, symmetric about the z-axis, and with cylindrical equation $z = 10 - r$.
30. Write $4x^2 + 9y^2 + z^2 = 36$ to see that the graph is the *lower* half of an ellipsoidal surface centered at the origin and with intercepts $(3,0,0)$, $(-3,0,0)$, $(0,2,0)$, $(0,-2,0)$, $(0,0,6)$, and $(0,0,-6)$.

32. Some typical level curves of
$$f(x,y) = x^2 - y^2$$
are shown at the right.

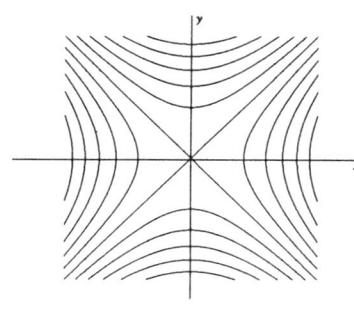

34. Some typical level curves of
$$f(x,y) = y - x^2$$
are shown at the right.

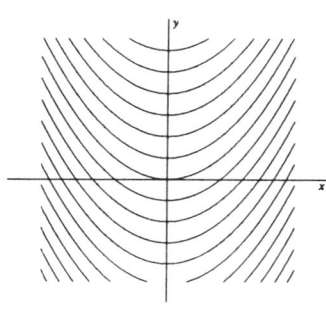

35. The level curves are vertical translates of the graph of $y = x^3$.
36. The level curves are vertical translates of the graph of $y = \cos x$.
38. The level curves are circles centered at $(3, -2)$.
40. The level curves are circles centered at the origin.
41. The level surfaces are circular paraboloids $z = C + r^2$ symmetric about the z-axis and opening upward. They are vertical translates of the "standard" parabolic surface with equation $z = r^2$.
42. The level surfaces are the lower nappes of 45° cones with cylindrical equations $z = C - r$, symmetric about the z-axis and opening downward.
44. The level surfaces are circular hyperboloids of two sheets symmetric about the z-axis, both nappes of the 45° cone $z = r$ with vertex at $(0,0,0)$ and symmetric about the z-axis, and circular hyperboloids of one sheet symmetric about the z-axis.
46. The level surfaces are concentric circular cylinders with axis the y-axis and with rulings straight lines parallel to the y-axis.
47. Matches Fig. 13.2.32
48. Matches Fig. 13.2.31
49. Matches Fig. 13.2.30
50. Matches Fig. 13.2.27
51. Matches Fig. 13.2.28
52. Matches Fig. 13.2.29
53. Matches Fig. 13.2.41
54. Matches Fig. 13.2.39
55. Matches Fig. 13.2.42
56. Matches Fig. 13.2.40
57. Matches Fig. 13.2.44
58. Matches Fig. 13.2.43

Section 13.3

2. 31
4. 0
6. $\frac{5}{7}$
8. 0
10. 0
12. 0
14. $\frac{2}{7}$
16. $\arcsin\left(-\frac{1}{2}\sqrt{2}\right) = \frac{1}{4}\pi$
18. $2x, 2y$
20. $2xy^3, 3x^2y^2$
21. 0
22. The limit does not exist because the denominator is approaching zero and the numerator is not.
23. $\frac{1}{3}$
24. The limit does not exist because the denominator is approaching zero and the numerator is not.
25. The limit is $\ln(1+0+0) = 0$.
26. This limit does not exist.
27. This limit is 1 because $(\sin z)/z \to 1$ as $z \to 0$.
28. Because $\ln x$ is continuous at $x = 1$ and $\sin x$ is continuous at $x = 0$, this limit has the value $\sin(\ln(1+0+0)) = 0$.
29. This limit is zero.
30. $-\pi/2$
31. All points above (not "on") the graph of $y = -x$.
32. All points on and within the circle with equation $x^2 + y^2 = 1$.
33. All points *outside* the circle with equation $x^2 + y^2 = 1$.
34. All points below (not "on") the graph of $y = 2x$.
35. All points in the xy-plane other than the origin $(0,0)$.
36. All points in the xy-plane other than those on the line $y = -x$.
40. This limit is 1 because $(\sin z)/z \to 1$ as $z \to 0$.
41. $\dfrac{\rho^3 \sin^2\phi \cos\phi \sin\theta \cos\theta}{\rho^2}$ has no limit as $\rho \to 0$ because this fraction is zero on the positive x-axis (where $\phi = \pi/2$ and $\theta = 0$) but is $\frac{1}{8}\sqrt{2} \neq 0$ on the half-line $z = y = x > 0$ (where $\phi = \theta = \frac{1}{4}\pi$).
42. $\lim\limits_{\rho \to 0} \arctan\left(\dfrac{1}{\rho^2}\right) = \lim\limits_{u \to +\infty} \arctan u = \dfrac{\pi}{2}$.
43. $\dfrac{x^2 - m^2 x^2}{x^2 + m^2 x^2}$ has limit $\dfrac{1-m^2}{1+m^2}$ as $x \to 0$, and hence the given limit does not exist.
44. $\dfrac{x^3 + y^3}{x^2 + y^2}$ has limit $\dfrac{1+m^3}{1+m^2}$ as $x \to 0$, and hence the given limit does not exist.
45. If $y = z = 0$, then $\dfrac{x+y+z}{x^2+y^2+z^2} = \dfrac{1}{x}$ has no limit as $x \to 0$. Hence the given limit does not exist.
46. If $y = z = 0$, then $\dfrac{x^2+y^2-z^2}{x^2+y^2+z^2} = 1$, but if $x = y = 0$, then $\dfrac{x^2+y^2-z^2}{x^2+y^2+z^2} = -1$. Hence the given limit does not exist.
49. $\dfrac{xy}{2x^2+3y^2} = \dfrac{m}{2+3m^2}$ on the line $y = mx$.
51. On the line $x = 1$, $f(x,y)$ has limit 1. On the line $y = 1$, $f(x,y)$ has limit $\frac{1}{3}$. Therefore f has no limit at $(1,1)$ and consequently f cannot be defined at $(1,1)$ to be continuous there.

53. We let $\theta \to +\infty$, so that $(x, y) \to (0, 0)$ along the hyperbolic spiral. Then

$$\frac{xy}{x^2 + y^2} = \sin\theta \cos\theta$$

takes on all values from $-\frac{1}{2}$ to $+\frac{1}{2}$ repeatedly and infintely often as $\theta \to +\infty$. Hence the given limit does not exist as $(x, y) \to (0, 0)$ along the hyperbolic spiral $r\theta = 1$.

Section 13.4

2. $f_x(x, y) = \sin y, \ f_y(x, y) = x\cos y$
4. $f_x(x, y) = (2x + x^2 y)e^{xy}, \ f_y(x, y) = x^3 e^{xy}$
6. $f_x(x, y) = \dfrac{y^3 - x^2 y}{(x^2 + y^2)^2}, \ f_y(x, y) = \dfrac{x^3 - xy^2}{(x^2 + y^2)^2}$
8. $f_x(x, y) = 14(x - y)^{13}, \ f_y(x, y) = -14(x - y)^{13}$
10. $f_x(x, y) = \dfrac{y}{1 + x^2 y^2}, \ f_y(x, y) = \dfrac{x}{1 + x^2 y^2}$
12. $f_x(x, y, z) = 2x, \ f_y(x, y, z) = 3y^2, \ f_z(x, y, z) = 4z^3$
14. $f_x(x, y, z) = 4x^3, \ f_y(x, y, z) = -16z, \ f_z(x, y, z) = -16y$
16. $\dfrac{\partial f}{\partial u} = (4u - 4u^3 - 6uv^2)e^{-u^2 - v^2}, \ \dfrac{\partial f}{\partial v} = (6v - 4u^2 v - 6v^3)e^{-u^2 - v^2}$
18. $\dfrac{\partial f}{\partial u} = 2ve^{uv}\cos uv, \ \dfrac{\partial f}{\partial v} = 2ue^{uv}\cos uv$
20. $\dfrac{\partial f}{\partial r} = \left(-2r - st(1 - r^2 - s^2 - t^2)\right)e^{-rst}$, etc.
22. $z_{xy} = z_{yx} = 10x + 4y^3$
24. $z_{xy} = z_{yx} = (1 - 3xy + x^2 y^2)e^{-xy}$
26. $z_{xy} = z_{yx} = 810x^2 y^2 (x^3 + y^3)^8$
28. $z_{xy} = z_{yx} = (x^2 y + xy^2)\sec xy + 2(x + y)\sec xy \tan xy + 2(x^2 y + xy^2)\sec xy \tan^2 xy$
30. $z_{xy} = z_{yx} = \cos xy - xy\sin xy + \dfrac{1 - x^2 y^2}{(1 + x^2 y^2)^2}$
31. A normal to the plane at (x, y, z) is $\langle 2x, 2y, -1 \rangle$. So a normal to the plane at $(3, 4, 25)$ is $\langle 6, 8, -1 \rangle$. Therefore an equation of the tangent plane is $6x + 8y - z = 25$.
32. $z_x(x, y) = -x/z$ and $z_y(x, y) = -y/z$. So a normal to the surface at $(4, -3, 5)$ is $\langle -\frac{4}{5}, \frac{3}{5}, -1 \rangle$. Therefore an equation of the tangent plane there is $4x - 3y + 5z = 50$.
34. $2x + 2y - \pi z = 4 - \pi$
36. $z = 3x + 4y$
38. $z = 1$
40. $3x - 4y - 5z = 0$
41. $f(x, y) = x^2 y^3 + C$
42. No such function f because $f_{xy} \neq f_{yx}$
43. No such function f because $f_{xy} \neq f_{yx}$
44. $f(x, y) = \sin x \sin y$
45. Matches Fig. 13.4.14
46. Matches Fig. 13.4.17

47. Matches Fig. 13.4.13
48. Matches Fig. 13.4.12
49. Matches Fig. 13.4.15
50. Matches Fig. 13.4.16
52. Because $z_x = e^{x+y} = z_y$, all subsequent partial derivatives must also be equal to e^{x+y}.
54. You should find that $g_{xy}(x,y) = \cos xy - xy \sin xy$ and that $g_{xxy}(x,y) = -2y \sin xy - xy^2 \cos xy$.
55. You should find that $u_{xx} = -n^2 e^{-n^2 kt} \sin nx$.
56. You should find that $u_{xx} = -m^2 e^{-(m^2+n^2)kt} \sin mx \cos ny$.
58. (a) You should obtain $u_{xx} = \dfrac{y^2 - x^2}{(x^2+y^2)^2}$.

   (b) $u_{xx} + u_{yy} = \dfrac{1}{u} \neq 0$, so this function does not satisfy Laplace's equation.

   (c) You should obtain $u_{xx} = \dfrac{2xy}{(x^2+y^2)^2}$.

   (d) You should obtain $u_{xx} = e^{-x} \sin y$.

Solutions to Problems 59 through 62 intentionally omitted.

63. $P_V = -\dfrac{nRT}{V^2}$, $V_T = \dfrac{nR}{P}$, and $T_P = \dfrac{V}{nR}$.

64. Let $P(a,b,c)$ be a point on the upper nappe of the cone, for which $z = z(x,y) = \sqrt{x^2+y^2}$. Thus $c = \sqrt{a^2+b^2}$. We assume that a and b are not both zero. It turns out that $z_x(P) = \dfrac{a}{c}$ and $z_y(P) = \dfrac{b}{c}$. So an equation of the tangent plane is

$$\frac{a(x-a)}{\sqrt{a^2+b^2}} + \frac{b(y-b)}{\sqrt{a^2+b^2}} - \left(z - \sqrt{a^2+b^2}\right) = 0;$$

this can be simplified to $z = \dfrac{ax+by}{\sqrt{a^2+b^2}}$. When $x = 0$ and $y = 0$, we have $z = 0$. Therefore the tangent plane at $P(a,b,c)$ passes through the origin. The same result for the lower nappe of the cone follows by symmetry.

66. Let $P(a,b,c)$ be a point on the paraboloid $z = x^2 + y^2$. Note that $c = a^2 + b^2$, $z_x(P) = 2a$, and $z_y(P) = 2b$. Thus the tangent plane at P has equation

$$2a(x-a) + 2b(y-b) - (z-c) = 0;$$

substitution of $a^2 + b^2$ for c yields the equation

$$2(ax + by) = z + a^2 + b^2.$$

In the xy-plane, we have $z = 0$, so the tangent plane meets the xy-plane in the line with equation

$$2ax + 2by = a^2 + b^2.$$

Now $(x,y) = (a/2, b/2)$ satisfies this equation, so the point $Q(a/2, b/2)$ is on the line. The line has slope $-a/b$, so the normal to the line has slope b/a. The segment OQ has this slope, so OQ is a perpendicular from the origin O to this line. Its length is $\frac{1}{2}\sqrt{a^2+b^2}$, so the line is tangent to the circle with center O and that same radius. The equation of that circle is therefore $x^2 + y^2 = \frac{1}{2}(a^2+b^2)$, and the result in the problem now follows.

69. (a) $\dfrac{\partial f_1}{\partial x} = \cos x \, \sinh(\pi - y)$, $\dfrac{\partial^2 f_1}{\partial x^2} = -\sin x \, \sinh(\pi - y)$.

   $\dfrac{\partial f_1}{\partial y} = -\sin x \, \cosh(\pi - y)$, $\dfrac{\partial^2 f_1}{\partial y^2} = \sin x \, \sinh(\pi - y)$.

   Clearly $\dfrac{\partial^2 f_1}{\partial x^2} + \dfrac{\partial^2 f_1}{\partial y^2} = 0$.

   (b) $\dfrac{\partial^2 f_2}{\partial x^2} = 4\sinh 2x \, \sin 2y$.

   (c) $\dfrac{\partial^2 f_3}{\partial x^2} = -9 \sin 3x \, \sinh 3y$.

   (d) $\dfrac{\partial^2 f_4}{\partial x^2} = -16 \sinh 4(\pi - x) \, \sin 4y$.

Solution to Problem 70 intentionally omitted.

Section 13.5

2. $(0, 0, 4)$

4. $(-1, 0, -1)$

6. $(4, -3, 35)$

8. $(0, 1, -2)$ and $(0, -1, 2)$

10. $(1, -1, -1)$.

12. $(0, 0, 0)$, $(1, 2, 4/e)$, $(1, -2, -4/e)$, $(-1, 2, -4/e)$, $(-1, -2, 2/e)$

13. The only possible extremum is $f(1, 1) = 1$. Put $x = 1 + h$, $y = 1 + k$. Then $f(x, y) = h^2 + k^2 + 1$, so that $(1, 1)$ yields 1 as the global minimum value of f.

14. The only possible extremum is $f(3, -4) = 25$. Put $x = 3 + h$, $y = -4 + k$. Then $f(x, y) = 25 - h^2 - k^2$, so that $(3, -4)$ yields 25 as the global maximum of f.

16. The surface clearly opens downward. There are two equally high global extrema, at $(1, 1, 2)$ and $(-1, -1, 2)$; there is a saddle point at $(0, 0, 0)$.

17. This surface clearly opens upward. The lowest point is at $(2, 3, -50)$. There is a local minimum at $(-1, 3, -23)$ and a saddle point at $(0, 3, -18)$.

18. Here, $f(x, y) \approx 3x^4 + 6y^4$ when either $|x|$ or $|y|$ is large, and therefore f has a global minimum but no global maximum. The critical points yield the values $f(0, 0) = 7$, $f(0, 1) = 9$, $f(-1, 0) = 6$, and $f(-1, 1) = 8$. Therefore $f(-1, 0) = 7$ is the global minimum value of $z = f(x, y)$.

20. We maximize $f(x, y)$ by minimizing $g(x, y) = 10 - 2x - 4y + x^2 + y^4$ and vice versa. The only critical point of g occurs at $(1, 1)$. Because $f(x, y) \approx 0$ when either $|x|$ or $|y|$ is large, $g(1, 1) = 6$ is the minimum value of $g(x, y)$. Therefore the absolute maximum value of $z = f(x, y)$ is $f(1, 1) = \frac{1}{6}$.

21. The only critical point of $f(x, y)$ occurs at $(1, -2)$. Because $f(x, y) \approx e^{-x^2 - y^2}$ when either $|x|$ or $|y|$ is large and because $f(x, y) > 0$ for all x and y, f has no global minimum value, so in this case it has the global maximum value e^5.

22. The only critical point occurs at $(0, 0)$. By an argument like the one in the preceding solution, $f(x, y)$ has the global maximum value 1 there.

24. Global maximum: $f(0, 1) = 1 = f(1, 1)$. Global minimum: $f\left(\frac{1}{2}, 0\right) = -\frac{1}{4}$.

26. Maximum: $f(0, 2) = 2 = f(2, 0)$. Minimum: $f\left(\frac{1}{2}, \frac{1}{2}\right) = -\frac{1}{2}$.

28. Global maximum: 2, which occurs at the two points $(1, \sqrt{2})$ and $(1, -\sqrt{2})$. Global minimum: -2, which occurs at $(-1, \sqrt{2})$ and at $(-1, -\sqrt{2})$.

29. The square of the distance is
$$f(x,y) = x^2 + y^2 + [(169 - 12x - 4y)/3]^2;$$
$f(x,y)$ has only one critical point, at $(12,4)$, and the point on the plane closest to $Q(0,0,0)$ is $(12,4,3)$.

30. The square of the distance is
$$f(x,y) = (x-9)^2 + (y-9)^2 + (18 - 2x - 2y)^2;$$
$f(x,y)$ has only one critical point, at $(5,5)$, and the point on the plane closest to $Q(9,9,9)$ is $(5,5,7)$.

31. The square of the distance is
$$f(x,y) = (x-7)^2 + (y+7)^2 + (49 - 2x - 3y)^2;$$
$f(x,y)$ has only one critical point, at $(15,5)$, and the point on the plane closest to $Q(7,-7,0)$ is $(15,5,4)$.

32. The square of the distance is
$$f(x,y) = x^2 + y^2 + \frac{64}{x^2 y^2};$$
the only critical point of $f(x,y)$ in the first quadrant is $(2,2)$, and the point in the first octant and on the surface that is closest to $Q(0,0,0)$ is $(2,2,2)$.

33. The square of the distance is
$$f(x,y) = x^2 + y^2 + \frac{16}{x^4 y^4};$$
the only critical point of $f(x,y)$ in the first quadrant is $(\sqrt{2}, \sqrt{2})$, and the point in the first octant and on the surface that is closest to $Q(0,0,0)$ is $(\sqrt{2}, \sqrt{2}, 1)$.

34. The square of the distance is
$$f(x,y) = x^2 + y^2 + \frac{8}{x^4 y^8};$$
the only critical point of $f(x,y)$ in the first quadrant is $(1, \sqrt{2})$, and the point in the first octant and on the surface that is closest to $Q(0,0,0)$ is $(1, \sqrt{1}, 1/\sqrt{2})$.

35. Maximize $f(x,y) = xy(120 - x - y)$ where $x > 0$ and $y > 0$. The only critical point of $f(x,y)$ there is at $(40, 40)$, and by an argument like the one in Example 7, this yields the maximum of $f(x,y)$. The three numbers are 40, 40, and 40, and the maximum possible product of three positive numbers with sum 120 is 64000.

36. If the dimensions of the box are x by y by z, then we are to maximize box volume $V = xyz$ given $4x + 4y + 4z = 6$. Thus we maximize
$$V(x,y) = xy\left(\tfrac{3}{2} - x - y\right)$$
on the plane triangle for which $x \geq 0$, $y \geq 0$, and $x + y \leq \tfrac{3}{2}$. Because $V(x,y) = 0$ on the boundary of this triangle, the global maximum of $V(x,y)$ occurs at its only interior critical point, at $(\tfrac{1}{2}, \tfrac{1}{2})$. With these dimensions, $z = \tfrac{1}{2}$ as well, and the maximum possible volume of such a box is therefore $\tfrac{1}{8}$.

37. If the dimensions of the box are x by y by z, then we are to minimize total surface area
$$A(x,y) = 2xy + 2(x+y)\frac{1000}{xy}$$

Section 13.5 Maxima and Minima of Functions of Several Variables where $x > 0$ and $y > 0$. The only critical point of $A(x, y)$ is at $(10, 10)$, and by an argument like the one in Example 7, this yields the global minimum value of $A(x, y)$. When $x = 10 = y$, we find that $z = 10$, so the box of minimal total surface area is a cube measuring 10 in. along each edge.

38. If the dimensions of the box are x by y by z, then we are to minimize total surface area

$$A(x, y) = xy + 2(x + y)\frac{4000}{xy}$$

where $x > 0$ and $y > 0$. The only critical point of $A(x, y)$ is at $(20, 20)$, and by an argument like the one in Example 7, this yields the global minimum value of $A(x, y)$. When $x = 20 = y$, we find that $z = 10$, so the box of minimal total surface area has base 20 by 20 cm and height 10 cm.

39. Suppose that the base of the box measures x by y inches and that its height is z inches. The cost of its bottom is $6xy$ cents, its front and back cost $5xz$ cents each, and its sides cost $5yz$ cents each. Hence we are to minimize

$$f(x, y) = 6xy + 2 \cdot 5 \cdot (x + y)\frac{600}{xy}$$

where $x > 0$ and $y > 0$. Ths only critical point of $f(x, y)$ is at $(10, 10)$, and when $x = 10 = y$, we find that $z = 6$. Hence the least expensive such box has base 10 by 10 in. and height 6 in.

40. Suppose that the base of the box measures x by y feet and that its height is z feet. Its top and bottom cost \$$3xy$ each, its front and back cost \$$4xz$ each, and its other two sides cost \$$yz$ each. Hence we are to minimize

$$f(x, y) = 6xy + 2 \cdot 4 \cdot (x + y)\frac{48}{xy}$$

where $x > 0$ and $y > 0$. The only critical point of $f(x, y)$ is at $(4, 4)$, and when $x = 4 = y$, we find that $z = 3$. Hence the least expensive such box has base 4 by 4 ft and its height is 3 ft.

41. Suppose that the base of the box measures x by y inches and that its height is z inches. Its top and bottom thus cost $3xy$ cents each, its front and back cost $6xz$ cents each, and its two ends cost $9yz$ cents each. Because $z = 750/(xy)$, we are to minimize

$$f(x, y) = 6xy + 12x\frac{750}{xy} + 18y\frac{750}{xy}$$

where $x > 0$ and $y > 0$. The only critical point of $f(x, y)$ is at $(15, 10)$, and at this point we find that $z = 5$. Hence the least expensive such box is 15 in. wide, 10 in. deep, and 5 in. high.

42. Assuming that the top and four sides of the box have unit cost per square meter, then the cost of the box is $2xy + xy + 2xz + 2yz$. But $z = 12/(xy)$, so we are to minimize

$$f(x, y) = 3xy + 2(x + y)\frac{12}{xy}$$

where $x > 0$ and $y > 0$. The only critical point of $f(x, y)$ is at $(2, 2)$, and this point yields minimum cost by an argument like the one in Example 7. When $x = y = 2$, we find that $z = 3$, so the least expensive such box will have base 2 by 2 m and height 3 m.

43. Frontage: x. Depth: y. Height: z. We are to minimize cost $C = 2(2xz + xy) + 8yz$ given $xyz = 8000$. Begin by expressing C as a function of x and y alone.

44. See the diagram at the right. We minimize the cost C:
$C = 28xy + 10yz + 10xz + 2xy$ given $xyz = 24,000$:

$$C(x, y) = 30xy + 10(x + y)\left(\frac{24000}{xy}\right)$$
$$= 30xy + \frac{24000}{x} + \frac{24000}{y}.$$

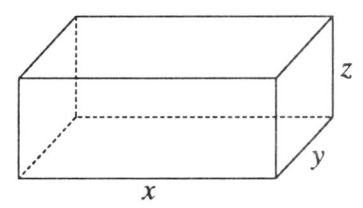

Both partial derivatives vanish at $x = y = 20$, $z = 60$. The least expensive aquarium has a square base 20 in. by 20 in.; its height is 60 in.

45. We maximize the volume $V = xyz$ given $x + 3y + 7z = 11$.
$$V(y, z) = (11 - 3y - 7z) yz = 11yz - 3y^2 z - 7yz^2.$$
The critical points of V are $(0,0)$, $(0, \frac{11}{7})$, $(\frac{11}{3}, 0)$, and $(\frac{11}{9}, \frac{11}{21})$. The volume is maximized when $x = \frac{11}{3}$, $y = \frac{11}{9}$, and $z = \frac{11}{21}$; the maximal volume is $\frac{1331}{567} \approx 2.347443$.

46. We maximize volume $V(x,y) = cxy \left(1 - \frac{x}{a} - \frac{y}{b}\right)$; the critical points are $(0,0)$, $(0,b)$, $(a,0)$, and $\left(\frac{a}{3}, \frac{b}{3}\right)$. The maximum volume is $\frac{abc}{27}$, for $x = \frac{a}{3}$, $y = \frac{b}{3}$, and $z = \frac{c}{3}$.

47. If the box has length x and its other two dimensions are y and z, then its girth is $2y + 2z$. The post office condition then amounts to $x + 2y + 2z \leq 108$; of course, to get the largest possible box, we take $x + 2y + 2z = 108$. The volume V of the box takes the form
$$V = V(y, z) = (108 - 2y - 2z) yz,$$
and the condition that $V_y(y,z) = 0 = V_z(y,z)$ leads to the equation $(z - 54)^2 = (y - 54)^2$. The possibility that $z - 54 = -(y - 54)$ leads to an absurdity, so $y = z$, and the answer in the text follows.

48. If the cylinder has radius x and height ("length") y, the post office will interpret its girth as its circumference $2\pi x$. So we are to maximize $V = \pi x^2 y$ given $2\pi x + y = 108$. Write $V = V(x) = \pi x^2 (108 - 2\pi x)$ and apply methods of single-variable calculus to find that V is maximized when $x = \frac{36}{\pi} \approx 11.459$ and $y = 36$. It then follows that the maximum value of V is $\frac{36^3}{\pi} \approx 14{,}851$ (in.^{3}).

Question: If you could persuade a post office employee to measure the girth the "other" way to obtain $4x + 2y$, would he or she then accept a box of larger volume than that given above?

49. Maximize $V = V(x,y) = 4xy(1 - x^2 - y^2)$ with domain the circular disk $x^2 + y^2 \leq 1$.

50. Use the hemisphere $x^2 + y^2 + z^2 = R^2$, $z \geq 0$. We are to maximize $V = (2x)(2y)(z)$ given $x^2 + y^2 + z^2 = R^2$, with each of x, y, and z in the closed interval $[0, R]$.
$$V = V(x,y) = 4xy\sqrt{R^2 - x^2 - y^2};$$
$$V_x(x,y) = \frac{4R^2 y - 8x^2 y - 4y^3}{\sqrt{R^2 - x^2 - y^2}} \quad \text{and} \quad V_y(x,y) = \frac{4R^2 x - 8xy^2 - 4x^3}{\sqrt{R^2 - x^2 - y^2}}.$$
Both partials are zero when $4y(R^2 - 2x^2 - y^2) = 0$ and $4x(R^2 - 2y^2 - x^2) = 0$. Because neither $x = 0$ nor $y = 0$ can yield a maximum, we find that $2x^2 + y^2 = R^2 = x^2 + 2y^2$. It follows that $x = y$, and subsequently that $x = y = z = \frac{1}{3}R\sqrt{3}$. Answer: $V_{\max} = 4xyz = \frac{4}{9}R^3\sqrt{3}$.

51. See the diagram at the right. We minimize the surface area $A = 2 \cdot 2\pi \frac{r}{2} \sqrt{r^2 + z^2} + 2\pi r h$ given fixed volume $V = \frac{2}{3}\pi r^2 z + \pi r^2 h$:
$$A(r, z) = 2\pi r \left(\frac{V}{\pi r^2} - \frac{2z}{3} + \sqrt{r^2 + z^2}\right).$$
When $\frac{\partial A}{\partial z} = 0$, $2r = z\sqrt{5}$ and $\sqrt{r^2 + z^2} = \frac{3}{2}z$. After considerable algebraic manipulation, we discover that when $\frac{\partial A}{\partial r} = 0$, $r^2 = \frac{5}{4}z^2$;
since $z \neq 0$, $z = \left(\frac{12V}{25\pi}\right)^{1/3}$, $r = \frac{\sqrt{5}}{2}\left(\frac{12V}{25\pi}\right)^{1/3}$, and
$h = \left(\frac{20V}{9\pi}\right)^{1/3} - \left(\frac{24V}{225\pi}\right)^{1/3} \approx (0.56719) V^{1/3}.$

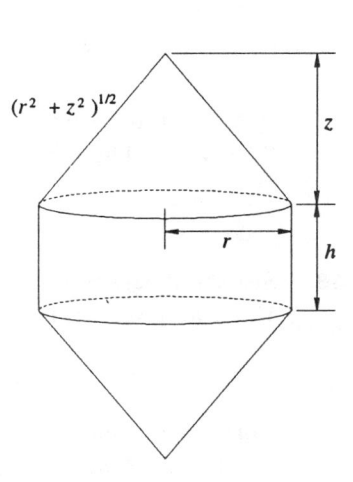

At this point $z = \left(\dfrac{12V}{25\pi}\right)^{1/3} \approx (0.534602)\,V^{1/3}$ and $r = \dfrac{\sqrt{5}}{2}z \approx (0.597703)\,V^{1/3}$. The minimum value of the surface area there is (after more algebraic simplification) $A = \left(18\pi\sqrt{5}V^2\right)^{1/3}$.

52. See the diagram at the right. We maximize the area

$$A(x,y) = xy + \dfrac{x}{4}\sqrt{(24 - x - 2y)^2 - x^2}.$$

Both partial derivatives are zero at points

$$(0,-12),\ (0,4),\ \left(24\left(2\pm\sqrt{3}\right),4\left(3\pm\sqrt{3}\right)\right).$$

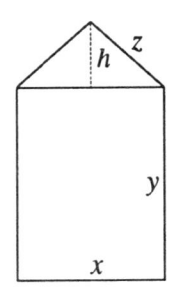

The only possible point at which A is maximized is $\left(24(2-\sqrt{3}),4(3-\sqrt{3})\right)$; at that point the area is approximately 38.58 square feet.

53. See the solution of Problem 56, to follow. The answer follows immediately.

54. We minimize $f(x,y) = (x-a_1)^2 + (y-b_1)^2 + (x-a_2)^2 + (y-b_2)^2 + (x-a_3)^2 + (y-b_3)^2$:
$\dfrac{\partial f}{\partial x} = 2(x-a_1) + 2(x-a_2) + 2(x-a_3)$ and $\dfrac{\partial f}{\partial y} = 2(y-b_1) + 2(y-b_2) + 2(y-b_3)$.
Both partial derivatives vanish when $x = \frac{1}{3}(a_1+a_2+a_3)$ and $y = \frac{1}{3}(b_1+b_2+b_3)$.

55. See the diagram at the right. We minimize the area

$$A = xh + 2wy$$

given fixed volume

$$V = \tfrac{1}{2}xhy.$$

Using the Pythagorean theorem, we see that

$$h = \tfrac{1}{2}\sqrt{4w^2 - x^2}.$$

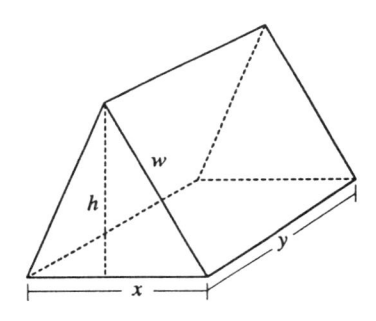

So we minimize

$$A(x,w) = \tfrac{1}{2}x\sqrt{4w^2-x^2} + \dfrac{8Vw}{x\sqrt{4w^2-x^2}} = \dfrac{x^2(4w^2-x^2) + 16Vw}{2x\sqrt{4w^2-x^2}}.$$

Both partial derivatives are zero when $x = 2^{5/6}V^{1/3}$, $w = 2^{1/3}V^{1/3}$, $y = 2^{1/3}V^{1/3}$, and $h = 2^{-1/6}V^{1/3}$. The minimum area is $2^{2/3}\cdot 3V^{2/3}$.

56. See the diagram at the right. We maximize the volume $V = xyz$ given $x^2 + y^2 + z^2 = L^2$:

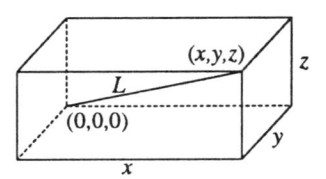

$$V = V(x,y) = xy\sqrt{L^2 - x^2 - y^2}.$$

Both partial derivatives vanish when $x = y$ (since both x and y are positive), so by symmetry, $x = y = z$. Hence $x = L\sqrt{3}$, and the maximum volume is $3L^3\sqrt{3}$.

58. Suppose that the cubes have edges x, y, and z, respectively. We are to maximize and minimize $A = 6x^2 + 6y^2 + 6z^2$ given $x^3 + y^3 + z^3 = V$ (a constant). Note that x, y, and z are also nonnegative. Write
$$A = A(x, y) = 6x^2 + 6y^2 + 6(V - x^3 - y^3)^{2/3}.$$

Then $A_x(x, y) = 0 = A_y(x, y)$ at the following points:

$$\begin{aligned}
x = 0, \ y = 0, \ z = V^{1/3}: \quad & A = 6V^{2/3}. \\
x = 0, \ y = (V/2)^{1/3} = z: \quad & A = 12(V/2)^{2/3}. \\
y = 0, \ x = (V/2)^{1/3} = z: \quad & A = 12(V/2)^{2/3}. \\
x = y = z = (V/3)^{1/3}: \quad & A = 18(V/3)^{2/3}.
\end{aligned}$$

The coefficients of $V^{2/3}$ in the above expressions for A are, in the same order, 6, 7.56, 7.56, and 8.65 (the last three are approximations). So, to obtain the maximum surface area, make three equal cubes, each of edge length $(V/3)^{1/3}$. A single cube of edge length $V^{1/3}$ has minimal surface area.

59. See the diagram below.

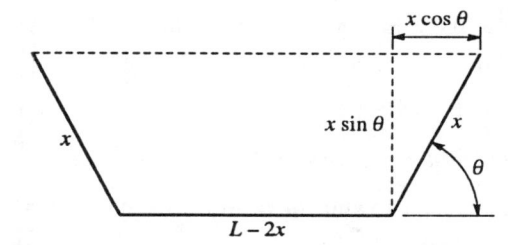

We maximize the cross-sectional area
$$\begin{aligned}
A(x, \theta) &= (L - 2x + x \cos \theta)(x \sin \theta) \\
&= Lx \sin \theta - 2x^2 \sin \theta + x^2 \sin \theta \cos \theta, \quad 0 \leq \theta \leq \pi, \ 0 \leq x \leq \tfrac{1}{2}L.
\end{aligned}$$
$$\frac{\partial A}{\partial x} = L \sin \theta - 4x \sin \theta - 2x \sin \theta \cos \theta = (L - 4x - 2x \cos \theta) \sin \theta \quad \text{and}$$
$$\frac{\partial A}{\partial \theta} = Lx \cos \theta - 2x^2 \cos \theta + x^2 \cos^2 \theta - x^2 \sin^2 \theta = \left(L \cos \theta - 2x \cos \theta + x \cos^2 \theta - x \sin^2 \theta\right) \cdot x.$$

Now $\sin \theta \neq 0$ and $x \neq 0$, so solve $L - 4x - 2x \cos \theta = 0$ and $L \cos \theta - 2x \cos \theta + x \cos^2 \theta - x \sin^2 \theta = 0$:
$$x = \frac{7L \pm L\sqrt{5}}{22} \approx \begin{cases} (0.21654)L \\ (0.41982)L \end{cases}; \quad \cos \theta = \frac{-3 \mp 2\sqrt{5}}{7 \pm \sqrt{5}} \approx \begin{cases} -0.809017 \\ 0.309017 \end{cases}; \quad \theta = \begin{cases} \tfrac{4}{5}\pi \ (144°) \\ \tfrac{2}{5}\pi \ (72°) \end{cases}.$$

When $x = \dfrac{7 + \sqrt{5}}{22}L$, $\theta = \tfrac{4}{5}\pi$, and $A \approx (-0.04424)L^2$. And when $x = \dfrac{7 - \sqrt{5}}{22}L$, $\theta = \tfrac{2}{5}\pi$, and $A \approx (0.130534)L^2$. So the maximum value of A is approximately $(0.130534)L^2$, obtained with $x = \dfrac{7 - \sqrt{5}}{22}L$ and $\theta = \tfrac{2}{5}\pi$.

Section 13.6

2. $dw = w_x \, dx + w_y \, dy = -2xe^{-x^2-y^2} \, dx - 2ye^{-x^2-y^2} \, dy.$
4. $dw = (ye^{x+y} + xye^{x+y}) \, dx + (xe^{x+y} + xye^{x+y}) \, dy.$
6. $dw = (z^2 - 2xy) \, dx + (2yz - x^2) \, dy + (2xz + y^2) \, dz.$
8. $dw = (yz \cos xyz) \, dx + (xz \cos xyz) \, dy + (xy \cos xyz) \, dz.$

10. $dw = ye^{uv}\,dx + xe^{uv}\,dy + xyve^{uv} + xyue^{uv}\,dv$.

12. $dw = \dfrac{s\,dr + r\,ds}{1 + rs}$.

14. $dw = \dfrac{-2t\,ds + 2s\,dt}{(s-t)^2}$.

16. $dw = \left(1 - 2p^2\right) qre^{-(p^2+q^2+r^2)}\,dp + \left(1 - 2q^2\right) pre^{-(p^2+q^2+r^2)}\,dq + \left(1 - 2r^2\right) pqe^{-(p^2+q^2+r^2)}\,dr$.

18. Let $w = f(x,y) = \sqrt{x^2 - y^2}$. $dw = w_x\,dx + w_y\,dy = \dfrac{x}{w}\,dx - \dfrac{y}{w}\,dy$.

    Take $x = 13$, $y = 5$, $dx = 0.2$, and $dy = -0.1$: $dw = \tfrac{13}{12}(0.2) - \tfrac{5}{12}(-0.1) = \tfrac{31}{120}$.

    So $\Delta f = f(Q) - f(P) \approx \tfrac{31}{120} \approx 0.2583$ (the true value is approximately 0.2568).

19. $df = -\dfrac{dx + dy}{(1 + x + y)^2}$, so $\Delta f \approx -\dfrac{0.02 + 0.05}{(1 + 3 + 6)^2} = -0.0007$ (the true value is approximately -0.000695).

20. Answer: -0.15 (true value: about -0.1555).

22. $df = \dfrac{(x+y+z)yz - xyz}{(x+y+z)^2}\,dx + \dfrac{(x+y+z)xz - xyz}{(x+y+z)^2}\,dy + \dfrac{(x+y+z)xy - xyz}{(x+y+z)^2}\,dz$. Take $x = 2$, $y = 3$, $z = 5$, $dx = -0.02$, $dy = 0.03$, and $dz = -0.03$. Then $\Delta f \approx \tfrac{1}{10}(-0.24 + 0.21 - 0.09) = -0.012$. (The true value is approximately -0.012323.)

24. Given $f(x,y) = (x-y)\cos 2\pi xy$, we have

    $$df = [\cos 2\pi xy - 2\pi y(x-y)\sin 2\pi xy]\,dx + [\cos 2\pi xy + 2\pi x(x-y)\sin 2\pi xy]\,dy,$$

    and when $x = 1$, $y = 0.5$, $dx = 0.1$, and $dy = -0.1$, we have $df = -0.2$. Also $f(1, 0.4) = -0.5$, so $f(1.1, 0.4) \approx -0.7$. (The true value of $f(1.1, 0.4)$ is closer to -0.6508.)

26. Let $w = f(x,y,z) = x^{1/2} y^{1/3} x^{1/4}$. Take $x = 25$, $y = 27$, $z = 16$, $\Delta x = 1$, $\Delta y = 1$, and $\Delta z = 1$. Then

    $$\begin{aligned}(26)^{1/2}(28)^{1/3}(17)^{1/4} &= f(x + \Delta x, y + \Delta y, z + \Delta z) \\ &\approx f(x,y,z) + w_x \Delta x + w_y \Delta y + w_z \Delta z \\ &= f(x,y,z) + \tfrac{1}{2}x^{-1/2}y^{1/3}z^{1/4}\,\Delta x + \tfrac{1}{3}y^{-2/3}x^{1/2}z^{1/4}\,\Delta y + \tfrac{1}{4}z^{-3/4}x^{1/2}y^{1/3}\,\Delta z \\ &= (5)(3)(2) + \tfrac{6}{10} + \tfrac{10}{27} + \tfrac{15}{32} = \tfrac{135817}{4320} \approx 31.4391\end{aligned}$$

    (true value: about 31.4402).

28. Let $w = f(x,y) = \dfrac{x^{1/3}}{y^{1/5}}$; $x = 27$, $y = 32$, $\Delta x = -2 = \Delta y$. Answer: $\tfrac{6401}{4320} \approx 1.4817$.

29. Let $f(x,y,z) = (x^2 + y^2 + z^2)^{1/2}$. Then

    $$df(x,y,z,dx,dy,dz) = \dfrac{x\,dx + y\,dy + z\,dz}{\sqrt{x^2 + y^2 + z^2}},$$

    so $df(3, 4, 12, 0.1, 0.2, -0.3) \approx -0.1923$. Hence

    $$f(3.1, 4.2, 11.7) \approx f(3, 4, 12) - 0.1923 = 12.8077.$$

    (The true value of $f(3.1, 4.2, 11.7)$ is approximately 12.8117.)

30. Let $f(x,y,z) = (x^2 + 2y^2 + 2z^2)^{1/3}$. Then

    $$df(x,y,z,dx,dy,dz) = \dfrac{2x\,dx + 4y\,dy + 4z\,dz}{3(x^2 + 2y^2 + 2z^2)^{2/3}},$$

    so $df(5, 5, 5, 0.1, 0.2, 0.3) \approx 0.1467$. Hence

    $$f(5.1, 5.2, 5.3) \approx f(5, 5, 5) + 0.1467 = 5.1467.$$

(The true value of $f(5.1, 5.2, 5.3)$ is approximately 5.1460.)

31. Think of y as implicitly defined as a function of x by means of the equation $2x^3 + 2y^3 = 9xy$. It follows that
$$\frac{dy}{dx} = \frac{3y - 2x^2}{2y^2 - 3x}$$
and therefore that the slope of the line tangent to the graph of $2x^3 + 2y^3 = 9xy$ at the point $(1, 2)$ is $\frac{4}{5}$. The straight line through $(1, 2)$ with that slope has equation
$$y = 2 + \tfrac{4}{5}(x - 1);$$
when $x = 1.1$, we have $y_{\text{curve}} - y_{\text{line}} = 2 + \tfrac{4}{5}(0.1) = 2.08$. The true value of y is approximately 2.0757625.

32. Write $f(x, y) = 4x^4 + 4y^4 - 17x^2 y^2 = 0$. Then
$$df = (16x^3 - 34xy^2)\, dx + (16y^3 - 34x^2 y)\, dy = 0.$$
We substitute $x = 2$, $y = 4$, and $dy = -0.1$, then solve for $dx = -0.05$. Hence the desired x-coordinate is $x + dx = 2 = 0.05 = 1.95$. This is also the exact value of the x-coordinate.

33. The area of the rectangle is $A = xy$ where x is the length of the base of the rectangle and y is its height. Here we have $dA = y\, dx + x\, dy$, so that with the data given in Problem 30,
$$dA = (15)(\pm 0.1) + (10)(\pm 0.1),$$
and therefore $|dA| \leq 1.5 + 1 = 2.5$ (cm^2).

34. (a) The volume of the cylinder is $V(r, h) = \pi r^2 h$, so
$$dV(r, h, dr, dh) = 2\pi rh\, dr + \pi r^2\, dh.$$
With $r = 3$, $h = 9$, $dr = \pm 0.1$, and $dh = \pm 0.1$, we find that
$$dV = (117\pi) \cdot (\pm 0.1) = \pm(11.7)\pi \approx \pm 36.7566.$$

(b) The total surface area of the cylinder is $A(r, h) = 2\pi rh + 2\pi r^2$, so
$$dA(r, h, dr, dh) = (2\pi h + 4\pi r)\, dr + 2\pi r\, dh.$$
With $r = 3$, $h = 9$, $dr = \pm 0.1$, and $dh = \pm 0.1$, we find that
$$dA = \pm(3.6)\pi \approx \pm 11.3097.$$

So the maximum possible error in measuring the volume of the cylinder is approximately 36.7566 cm^3 and the maximum possible error in measuring its total surface area is approximately 11.3097 cm^2.

36. $|dA| \leq 18$ (cm^2).

38. -229.768 (cm^3)

39. $dT = 2\pi \left(\tfrac{1}{2}\right) \sqrt{\dfrac{g}{L}} \left(\dfrac{1}{g}\right) dL + 2\pi \left(\tfrac{1}{2}\right) \sqrt{\dfrac{g}{L}} \left(-\dfrac{L}{g^2}\right) dg = \pi \sqrt{\dfrac{g}{L}} \left(\dfrac{1}{g} dL - \dfrac{L}{g^2} dg\right).$
With $L = 2$, $\Delta L = \tfrac{1}{12}$, $g = 32$, and $\Delta g = 0.2$, we find that $dT \approx 17\pi/1920$—an *increase* in the period of about 0.0278 seconds.

42. In the second part of the problem, take $w = 2$, $h = 4$, $dw = 0.1$, and $dh = 0.1$. Then dS turns out to be exactly $-\tfrac{1}{8}$. Thus we estimate the sag to be $S = 1 + (-0.125) = 0.875$ inches. Because $k = 128$, the true value is about 0.884 inches.

43. In part (b), you should find that $f_x(0,0) = f_y(0,0) = 0$.

47. The function $f(x,y) = \left(\sqrt[3]{x} + \sqrt[3]{y}\right)^3$ is continuous everywhere because it is the composition of the sum of continuous functions. At the origin we can compute its partial derivative with respect to x as follows:
$$f_x(0,0) = \lim_{h \to 0} \frac{f(0+h, 0) - f(0,0)}{h} = 1;$$
similarly, $f_y(0,0) = 1$. So only the plane $z = x+y$ can approximate the graph of $f(x,y)$ at and near $(0,0)$. But the line L_1 in the vertical plane $y = x$, through $(0,0,0)$, and tangent to the graph of f has slope
$$\lim_{x \to 0} \frac{f(x,x) - f(0,0)}{x\sqrt{2}} = 4\sqrt{2},$$
whereas the line L_2 in the vertical plane $y = x$, through $(0,0,0)$, and tangent to the graph of $z = x+y$ has slope $\sqrt{2}$. Because no plane through $(0,0,0)$ approximates the graph of f accurately near $(0,0)$, the function f is not differentiable at $(0,0)$.

Section 13.7

1. $\dfrac{dw}{dt} = \dfrac{dw}{dx} \cdot \dfrac{dx}{dt} + \dfrac{dw}{dy} \cdot \dfrac{dy}{dt} = -2xe^{-x^2-y^2} - yt^{-1/2}e^{-x^2-y^2} = -(2t+1)e^{-t^2-t}$.

2. $\dfrac{dw}{dt} = 0$.

4. $\dfrac{dw}{dt} = \dfrac{2t}{1+t^2}$.

6. $w_s = (4s-t)\sin st + (2s^2 t - st^2 - t^3)\cos st$; $w_t = -(s+2t)\sin st + (2s^3 - s^2 t - st^2)\cos st$.

8. $w_s = 4s^3 + 8s^3 t^2$; $w_t = 4s^4 t - 4t^3$.

10. $r_x = y^2 + z^2 + 2(xy + yz + xz) - 4x - 2y - 2z$;
$r_y = x^2 + z^2 + 2(xy + yz + xz) - 2x - 4y - 2z$;
$r_z = x^2 + y^2 + 2(xy + yz + xz) - 2x - 2y - 4z$.

11. $\dfrac{\partial r}{\partial x} = \dfrac{(2y + 3z)\sqrt{xy^2 z^3}}{2x(x+2y+3z)^{3/2}} \cos \dfrac{\sqrt{xy^2 z^3}}{\sqrt{x+2y+3z}}$,

$\dfrac{\partial r}{\partial y} = \dfrac{(x + y + 3z)\sqrt{xy^2 z^3}}{y(x+2y+3z)^{3/2}} \cos \dfrac{\sqrt{xy^2 z^3}}{\sqrt{x+2y+3z}}$,

$\dfrac{\partial r}{\partial z} = \dfrac{(3x + 6y + 6z)\sqrt{xy^2 z^3}}{2z(x+2y+3z)^{3/2}} \cos \dfrac{\sqrt{xy^2 z^3}}{\sqrt{x+2y+3z}}$.

12. $\dfrac{\partial r}{\partial x} = ye^{xy-yz} - ze^{yz-xz} + (z-y)e^{xz-xy}$,

$\dfrac{\partial r}{\partial y} = ze^{yz-xz} - xe^{xz-xy} + (x-z)e^{xy-xz}$,

$\dfrac{\partial r}{\partial z} = xe^{xz-xy} - ye^{xy-yz} + (y-x)e^{yz-xz}$.

13. $\dfrac{\partial p}{\partial u} = \dfrac{\partial p}{\partial x}\dfrac{\partial x}{\partial u} + \dfrac{\partial p}{\partial y}\dfrac{\partial y}{\partial u}$,

$\dfrac{\partial p}{\partial v} = \dfrac{\partial p}{\partial x}\dfrac{\partial x}{\partial v} + \dfrac{\partial p}{\partial y}\dfrac{\partial y}{\partial v}$,

$\dfrac{\partial p}{\partial w} = \dfrac{\partial p}{\partial x}\dfrac{\partial x}{\partial w} + \dfrac{\partial p}{\partial y}\dfrac{\partial y}{\partial w}$.

14. $\dfrac{\partial p}{\partial u} = \dfrac{\partial p}{\partial x}\dfrac{\partial x}{\partial u} + \dfrac{\partial p}{\partial y}\dfrac{\partial y}{\partial u} + \dfrac{\partial p}{\partial z}\dfrac{\partial z}{\partial u}$,

$$\frac{\partial p}{\partial v} = \frac{\partial p}{\partial x}\frac{\partial x}{\partial v} + \frac{\partial p}{\partial y}\frac{\partial y}{\partial v} + \frac{\partial p}{\partial z}\frac{\partial z}{\partial v}.$$

15. $\dfrac{\partial p}{\partial x} = \dfrac{\partial p}{\partial u}\dfrac{\partial u}{\partial x} + \dfrac{\partial p}{\partial v}\dfrac{\partial v}{\partial x} + \dfrac{\partial p}{\partial w}\dfrac{\partial w}{\partial x}$,

$\dfrac{\partial p}{\partial y} = \dfrac{\partial p}{\partial u}\dfrac{\partial u}{\partial y} + \dfrac{\partial p}{\partial v}\dfrac{\partial v}{\partial y} + \dfrac{\partial p}{\partial w}\dfrac{\partial w}{\partial y}$,

$\dfrac{\partial p}{\partial z} = \dfrac{\partial p}{\partial u}\dfrac{\partial u}{\partial z} + \dfrac{\partial p}{\partial v}\dfrac{\partial v}{\partial z} + \dfrac{\partial p}{\partial w}\dfrac{\partial w}{\partial z}$.

16. $\dfrac{\partial p}{\partial x} = \dfrac{\partial p}{\partial v}\dfrac{\partial v}{\partial x} + \dfrac{\partial p}{\partial w}\dfrac{\partial w}{\partial x}$,

$\dfrac{\partial p}{\partial y} = \dfrac{\partial p}{\partial v}\dfrac{\partial v}{\partial y} + \dfrac{\partial p}{\partial w}\dfrac{\partial w}{\partial y}$,

$\dfrac{\partial p}{\partial z} = \dfrac{\partial p}{\partial v}\dfrac{\partial v}{\partial z} + \dfrac{\partial p}{\partial w}\dfrac{\partial w}{\partial z}$,

$\dfrac{\partial p}{\partial t} = \dfrac{\partial p}{\partial v}\dfrac{\partial v}{\partial t} + \dfrac{\partial p}{\partial w}\dfrac{\partial w}{\partial t}$.

17. $\dfrac{\partial p}{\partial x} = \dfrac{dp}{dw}\dfrac{\partial w}{\partial x},\ \dfrac{\partial p}{\partial y} = \dfrac{dp}{dw}\dfrac{\partial w}{\partial y},\ \dfrac{\partial p}{\partial z} = \dfrac{dp}{dw}\dfrac{\partial w}{\partial z},\ \dfrac{\partial p}{\partial u} = \dfrac{dp}{dw}\dfrac{\partial w}{\partial u},\ \dfrac{\partial p}{\partial v} = \dfrac{dp}{dw}\dfrac{\partial w}{\partial v}$.

18. $\dfrac{\partial p}{\partial s} = \dfrac{\partial p}{\partial x}\dfrac{\partial x}{\partial s} + \dfrac{\partial p}{\partial y}\dfrac{\partial y}{\partial s} + \dfrac{\partial p}{\partial u}\dfrac{\partial u}{\partial s} + \dfrac{\partial p}{\partial v}\dfrac{\partial v}{\partial s}$,

$\dfrac{\partial p}{\partial t} = \dfrac{\partial p}{\partial x}\dfrac{\partial x}{\partial t} + \dfrac{\partial p}{\partial y}\dfrac{\partial y}{\partial t} + \dfrac{\partial p}{\partial u}\dfrac{\partial u}{\partial t} + \dfrac{\partial p}{\partial v}\dfrac{\partial v}{\partial t}$.

20. Let $F(x,y,z) = x^3 + y^3 + z^3 - xyz$. Then $z_x = -\dfrac{F_x}{F_z} = -\dfrac{3x^2 - yz}{3z^2 - xy}$ and $z_y = -\dfrac{F_y}{F_z} = -\dfrac{(3y^2 - xz)}{3z^2 - xy}$.

22. $z_x = -\dfrac{y^2}{5z^4 + y}$ and $z_y = -\dfrac{2xy + z}{5z^4 + y}$.

24. $\dfrac{\partial z}{\partial x} = -\dfrac{yz - \cos(x+y+z)}{xy - \cos(x+y+z)}$,

$\dfrac{\partial z}{\partial y} = -\dfrac{xz - \cos(x+y+z)}{xy - \cos(x+y+z)}$.

25. $w_x = 6x$ and $w_y = 6y$.

27. $w_x = y\ln\left(\sqrt{x^3 + y^3} + (x^2 + y^2)^{1/3}\right) + \dfrac{2x^2 y}{3\left(\sqrt{x^3 + y^3} + (x^2 + y^2)^{1/3}\right)(x^2 + y^2)^{2/3}}$

$+ \dfrac{3x^3 y}{2\left(\sqrt{x^3 + y^3} + (x^2 + y^2)^{1/3}\right)\sqrt{x^3 + y^3}}$,

$w_y = x\ln\left(\sqrt{x^3 + y^3} + (x^2 + y^2)^{1/3}\right) + \dfrac{2xy^2}{3\left(\sqrt{x^3 + y^3} + (x^2 + y^2)^{1/3}\right)(x^2 + y^2)^{2/3}}$

$+ \dfrac{3xy^3}{2\left(\sqrt{x^3 + y^3} + (x^2 + y^2)^{1/3}\right)\sqrt{x^3 + y^3}}$.

29. $x + 2y + 2z = 9$

31. $x - y - z = 0$

33. Let $x = x(t)$ denote the length of each edge of the square base of the block of ice; let $y = y(t)$ denote its height. Then its volume is $V = x^2 y$, and

$$\frac{dV}{dt} = 2xy\frac{dx}{dt} + x^2\frac{dy}{dt}.$$

Section 13.7 The Chain Rule

Then substitution of the data $x = 24$ (in.), $y = 12$, $dx/dt = -3$, and $dy/dt = -2$ yields $dV/dt = -2880$ (in.^{3}/h).

34. Let $x = x(t)$ denote the length of each edge of the square base of the box and let $y = y(t)$ denote its height. Then its volume is $V = x^2 y$ and its surface area is $A = 2x^2 + 4xy$. Hence

$$\frac{dV}{dt} = 2xy\frac{dx}{dt} + x^2\frac{dy}{dt} \quad \text{and} \quad \frac{dA}{dt} = 4(x+y)\frac{dx}{dt} + 4x\frac{dy}{dt}.$$

Substitution of the given data $x = 100$ (cm), $y = 100$, $dx/dt = 2$, and $dy/dt = -3$ yields these results: At the time in question, $dV/dt = -10000$ (cm^3/min) and $dA/dt = 400$ (cm^2/min).

35. Let $r = r(t)$ denote the radius of the conical sandpile and $h = h(t)$ its height. Then its volume is $V = \frac{1}{3}\pi r^2 h$, so

$$\frac{dV}{dt} = \frac{\pi}{3}\left(r^2\frac{dh}{dt} + 2rh\frac{dr}{dt}\right).$$

Then substitution of the given data $h = 5$ (ft), $r = 3$, $dr/dt = 0.7$, and $dh/dt = 0.4$ yields the result that the volume of the sandpile is increasing at $\frac{26}{5}\pi$ (ft^3/min) at the time in question.

36. The volume of the block is $V = xyz$ and its total surface area is $A = 2(xy + xz + yz)$. So

$$\frac{dV}{dt} = yz\frac{dx}{dt} + xz\frac{dy}{dt} + xy\frac{dz}{dt} \quad \text{and} \quad \frac{dA}{dt} = 2(y+z)\frac{dx}{dt} + 2(x+z)\frac{dy}{dt} + 2(x+y)\frac{dz}{dt}.$$

Now substitution of the given data $x = 300$ (cm), $y = 200$, $z = 100$, $dx/dt = 1$, $dy/dt = 2$, and $dz/dt = -2$ yields $dV/dt = -40000$ (cm^3/min) and $dA/dt = -400$ (cm^2/min) at the time in question.

37. For this gas sample, we have $V = 10$ when $p = 2$ and $T = 300$. Substitution in the equation $pV = nRT$ yields $nR = \frac{1}{15}$. Moreover, with t in minutes, we have

$$V = \frac{nRT}{p}, \quad \text{so} \quad \frac{dV}{dt} = nR\left(\frac{1}{p}\frac{dT}{dt} - \frac{T}{p^2}\frac{dp}{dt}\right).$$

Now substitution of $nR = \frac{1}{15}$, $V = 10$, $p = 2$, $t = 200$, $dT/dt = 10$, and $dp/dt = 1$ yields the conclusion that the volume of the gas sample is decreasing at $\frac{14}{3}$ L/min at the time in question.

38. From the equation

$$\frac{1}{R} = \frac{1}{R_1} + \frac{1}{R_2} + \frac{1}{R_3}$$

and the given data $R_1 = R_2 = 100$, $R_3 = 200$, we find that $R = 40$ Ω. Also from this equation we find (with t in seconds) that

$$\frac{1}{R^2}\frac{dR}{dt} = \frac{1}{R_1^2}\frac{dR_1}{dt} + \frac{1}{R_2^2}\frac{dR_2}{dt} + \frac{1}{R_3^2}\frac{dR_3}{dt}.$$

Then substitution of the previous data and the additional data $dR_1/dt = dR_2/dt = 1$ and $dR_3/dt = -2$ yields the result that R is increasing at 0.24 Ω/s at the time in question.

44. $w_u = 2w_x + w_y$ and $w_v = w_x - w_y$. So

$$w_{uu} = 2\frac{\partial w_x}{\partial u} + \frac{\partial w_y}{\partial u} = 2(w_{xx}x_u + w_{xy}y_u) + (w_{yx}x_u + w_{yy}y_u) = 4w_{xx} + 2w_{xy} + 2w_{xy} + w_{yy}.$$

$w_{vv} = w_{xx}x_v + w_{xy}y_v - w_{yx}x_v - w_{yy}y_v = w_{xx} - w_{xy} - w_{xy} + w_{yy}$.

Therefore $w_{uu} + w_{vv} = 5w_{xx} + 2w_{xy} + 2w_{yy}$.

50. $w_u = w_x e^u \cos v + w_y e^u \sin v$ and $w_v = -w_x e^u \sin v + w_y e^u \cos v$. So

$$e^{-2u}\left((w^u)^2 + (w_v)^2\right) = e^{-2u}\Big[e^{2u}\Big((w_x)^2 \cos^2 v + 2w_x w_y \sin v \cos v$$
$$+ (w_y)^2 \sin^2 v + (w_x)^2 \sin^2 v - 2w_x w_y \sin v \cos v + (w_y)^2 \cos^2 v\Big)\Big]$$
$$= (w_x)^2 + (w_y)^2.$$

52. Show that $w_x = \dfrac{4xy^2}{(x^2+y^2)^2} f'(u)$ and that $w_y = -\dfrac{4x^2 y}{(x^2+y^2)^2} f'(u)$.

56. From $F(p,V,T) = 0$ and Theorem 3, we find that
$$\frac{\partial V}{\partial p} = -\frac{F_p}{F_V}, \quad \frac{\partial V}{\partial T} = -\frac{F_T}{F_V}, \quad \frac{\partial p}{\partial V} = -\frac{F_V}{F_p}, \quad \text{and} \quad \frac{\partial p}{\partial T} = -\frac{F_T}{F_p}.$$
It now follows that
$$\frac{\alpha}{\beta} = -\frac{V_T}{V_p} = -\frac{F_T/F_V}{F_p/F_V} = -\frac{F_T}{F_p} = \frac{\partial p}{\partial T},$$
which is what we were supposed to show.

57. First,
$$\frac{\partial p}{\partial T} = \frac{\alpha}{\beta} = \frac{1.8 \times 10^6}{3.9 \times 10^4} = \frac{600}{13}.$$
Hence a 5°C-increase in temperature multiplies the initial pressure (1 atm) by $\frac{3000}{13} \approx 230.77$, so the bulb will burst.

58. The result
$$T'(u,v,w) = \begin{bmatrix} a_1 & b_1 & c_1 \\ a_2 & b_2 & c_2 \\ a_3 & b_3 & c_3 \end{bmatrix}$$
follows immediately.

59. Here we have
$$T'(\rho, \phi, \theta) = \begin{bmatrix} \sin\phi\cos\theta & \rho\cos\phi\cos\theta & -\rho\sin\phi\sin\theta \\ \sin\phi\sin\theta & \rho\cos\phi\sin\theta & \rho\sin\phi\cos\theta \\ \cos\phi & -\rho\sin\phi & 0 \end{bmatrix};$$
$$|T'(\rho,\phi,\theta)| = \rho^2 \sin^3\phi \sin^2\theta + \rho^2 \sin\phi\cos^2\phi\cos^2\theta$$
$$+ \rho^2 \cos^2\phi \sin\phi \sin^2\theta + \rho^2 \sin^3\phi \cos^2\theta$$
$$= \rho^2 \left(\sin^2\phi + \sin\phi \cos^2\phi \right) = \rho^2 \sin\phi.$$

61. Here we compute
$$\begin{bmatrix} F_x & F_y & F_z \end{bmatrix} \begin{bmatrix} \sin\phi\cos\theta & \rho\cos\phi\cos\theta & -\rho\sin\phi\sin\theta \\ \sin\phi\sin\theta & \rho\cos\phi\sin\theta & \rho\sin\phi\cos\theta \\ \cos\phi & -\rho\sin\phi & 0 \end{bmatrix} = \begin{bmatrix} \dfrac{\partial q}{\partial \rho} & \dfrac{\partial q}{\partial \phi} & \dfrac{\partial q}{\partial \theta} \end{bmatrix},$$
which has first component
$$\frac{\partial q}{\partial \rho} = F_x \sin\phi\cos\theta + F_y \sin\phi\sin\theta + F_z \cos\phi,$$
second component
$$\frac{\partial q}{\partial \phi} = F_x \rho\cos\phi\cos\theta + F_y \rho\cos\phi\sin\theta - F_z \rho\sin\phi,$$
and third component
$$\frac{\partial q}{\partial \theta} = -F_x \rho\sin\phi\sin\theta + F_y \rho\sin\phi\cos\theta.$$

Section 13.8

1. $\langle 3, -7 \rangle$
2. $\langle 12, 30 \rangle$
4. $\langle \frac{1}{8}\pi\sqrt{2}, -\frac{3}{8}\pi\sqrt{2} \rangle$
6. $\langle \frac{12}{13}, \frac{3}{13}, \frac{4}{13} \rangle$
8. $\langle 4, 0, -3 \rangle$
10. $\langle 160, -240, 400 \rangle$
11. $\mathbf{u} = \dfrac{\mathbf{i}+\mathbf{j}}{\sqrt{2}}$; $f(x,y) = \langle 2x+2y, 6y+2x \rangle$. $\nabla f(2,1) = \langle 6, 10 \rangle$; $D_{\mathbf{u}}f(P) = 8\sqrt{2}$.
12. 0
14. $-\frac{7}{30}$
16. $\frac{4}{3}\sqrt{3}$
18. $D_{\mathbf{u}}f(P) = \dfrac{1}{\sqrt{17}}$.
20. $\nabla f(1,1,-2) = \langle -\frac{1}{2}, -\frac{1}{2}, 1 \rangle$; $\mathbf{u} = \frac{1}{13}\langle 3, 4, -12 \rangle$. So $D_{\mathbf{u}}f(P) = -\frac{31}{26}$.
22. The maximum value is $\dfrac{1}{\sqrt{5}}$; it occurs in the direction $\langle 2, 1 \rangle$.
23. $\{\nabla f\}(3,4) = \langle \frac{6}{25}, \frac{8}{25} \rangle$, a vector of magnitude $\frac{2}{5}$. The latter is the maximal directional derivative of f and the former is the direction in which it occurs.
24. $\{\nabla f\}(\pi/3, \pi/4) = \langle 3, -4 \rangle$, a vector of magnitude 5. The latter is the maximal directional derivative of f and the former is the direction in which it occurs.
26. Maximum: $\sqrt{3}$. Direction: $\langle 1, -1, -1 \rangle$.
28. $\{\nabla f\}(7,5,5) = 19^{-1/2}\langle 2, 1, 2 \rangle$, a vector of magnitude $3/\sqrt{19}$. The latter is the maximal direction derivative of f, and the direction in which it occurs is $\langle 2, 1, 2 \rangle$. Because most people expect "direction" to be given by a *unit* vector, it is probably better to say that the direction is $\langle \frac{2}{3}, \frac{1}{3}, \frac{2}{3} \rangle$.
29. Let $f(x,y) = \exp(25 - x^2 - y^2) - 1$. Then $\{\nabla f\}(3,4) = \langle -6, -8 \rangle$, so $\langle 3, 4 \rangle$ is normal to the given curve at $(3, 4)$. So an equation of the line normal to the curve at that point is $3x + 4y = 25$.
30. Let $F(x,y) = 2x^2 + 3y^2 - 35$; we are given $P(2,3)$. $\nabla F = \langle 4x, 6y \rangle$; $\nabla F(2,3) = \langle 8, 18 \rangle$. Answer: $8(x-2) + 18(y-3) = 0$; that is, $4x + 9y = 35$.
32. $6x + 18y + 15z = 73$
34. $4x + 23y + 17z = 25$
35. $\nabla(au + bv) = \left\langle \dfrac{\partial}{\partial x}(au+bv), \dfrac{\partial}{\partial y}(au+bv) \right\rangle$
$= \langle au_x + bv_x, au_y + bv_y \rangle = a\langle u_x, u_y \rangle + b\langle v_x, v_y \rangle$
$= a\,\nabla u + b\,\nabla v.$
36. $\nabla(uv) = \left\langle \dfrac{\partial}{\partial x}(uv), \dfrac{\partial}{\partial y}(uv) \right\rangle$
$= \langle u_x v + uv_x, u_y v + uv_y \rangle = \langle u_x v, u_y v \rangle + \langle uv_x, uv_y \rangle$
$= v\,\nabla u + u\,\nabla v.$
37. $\nabla\left(\dfrac{u}{v}\right) = \left\langle \dfrac{\partial}{\partial x}\left(\dfrac{u}{v}\right), \dfrac{\partial}{\partial y}\left(\dfrac{u}{v}\right) \right\rangle$
$= \left\langle \dfrac{u_x v - uv_x}{v^2}, \dfrac{u_y v - uv_y}{v^2} \right\rangle = \dfrac{1}{v^2}\left(\langle u_x v, u_y v \rangle - \langle uv_x, uv_y \rangle\right)$

$$= \frac{v\,\nabla u - u\,\nabla v}{v^2}.$$

38. $\nabla u^n = \left\langle \dfrac{\partial}{\partial x} u^n, \dfrac{\partial}{\partial y} u^n \right\rangle = \langle nu^{n-1} u_x, nu^{n-1} u_y \rangle$

    $= nu^{n-1} \langle u_x, u_y \rangle = nu^{n-1}\,\nabla u.$

39. We mimic the development of Eqs. (16) through (18) in Section 13.8. Then, if ϕ is the angle between ∇f at the point P and the unit vector $\mathbf{u}$, then the formula in Eq. (7) gives

    $$D_{\mathbf{u}} f(P) = \nabla f(P) \cdot \mathbf{u} = |\nabla f(P)| \cos\phi$$

    because $|\mathbf{u}| = 1$. The minimum value of $\cos\phi$ is -1, and thus occurs when $\phi = \pi$. This will be the case when $\mathbf{u}$ is the particular unit vector $-\nabla f(P)/|\nabla f(P)|$ that points in the direction opposite that of the gradient vector itself.

44. $\nabla W = -2\langle x,y,z\rangle$; $\nabla W(3,-4,5) = \langle -6, 8, -10\rangle$. The required unit vector is $\mathbf{u} = \dfrac{\langle 3,-4,12\rangle}{13}$.
    Answers: (a) $-\tfrac{170}{13}$; (b) $\langle -3,4,-5\rangle$; $10\sqrt{2}$.

46. Let $F(x,y,z) = 2x^2 + 3y^2 - z$. The equation $F(x,y,z) = 0$ has the paraboloid as its graph. The vector $\mathbf{n} = \langle 4,-3,-1\rangle$ is normal to the plane. $\nabla F = \langle 4x, 6y, -1\rangle$, and we merely require that ∇F be parallel to $\mathbf{n}$. This leads to $x = 1$, $y = -\tfrac{1}{2}$, and (through $F(x,y,z) = 0$) to $z = \tfrac{11}{4}$. So an equation of the required plane is $4(x-1) - 3\left(y + \tfrac{1}{2}\right) - \left(z - \tfrac{11}{4}\right) = 0$; that is, $16x - 12y - 4z = 11$.

47. Let $F(x,y,z) = z^2 - x^2 - y^2$ and $G(x,y,z) = 2x + 3y + 4z + 2$. Then the cone is the graph of $F(x,y,z) = 0$ and the plane is the graph of $G(x,y,z) = 0$. At the given point $P(3,4,-5)$, we have

    $$\nabla F(3,4,-5) = \langle -6,-8,-10\rangle \quad\text{and}\quad \nabla G(3,4,-5) = \langle 2,3,4\rangle.$$

    Hence a normal to the plane is $\mathbf{n} = \langle -6,-8,-10\rangle \times \langle 2,3,4\rangle$, which turns out to equal $\langle -2, 4, -2\rangle$. We'll use $\langle 1,-2,1\rangle$ instead; the plane has Cartesian equation $x - 2y + z + 10 = 0$.

48. Let $F(x,y,z) = z^2 - x^2 - y^2$ and $G(x,y,z) = 2x + 3y + 4z + 2$. First,

    $$\nabla F \times \nabla G = \langle -8y - 6z,\; 4z + 8x,\; -6x + 4y\rangle.$$

    For the tangent line to be horizontal, we require $-6x + 4y = 0$—that is, $3x = 2y$. So we have the three equations

    $$3x = 2y,$$
    $$z^2 = x^2 + y^2, \quad\text{and}$$
    $$2x + 3y + 4z = -2.$$

    Their simultaneous solution yields the answers:

    Low point: $x = \dfrac{52 + 16\sqrt{13}}{39} \approx 2.812534,$

    $y = \dfrac{26 + 8\sqrt{13}}{13} \approx 4.218801,$

    $z = \dfrac{-8 - 2\sqrt{13}}{3} \approx -5.070368.$

    High point: $x = \dfrac{52 - 16\sqrt{13}}{39} \approx -0.145867,$

    $y = \dfrac{26 - 8\sqrt{13}}{13} \approx -0.218801,$

    $z = \dfrac{-8 + 2\sqrt{13}}{3} \approx -0.262966.$

50. (a) $z = 500 - (0.003)x^2 - (0.004)y^2$: $\nabla z = \langle(-0.006)x, -(0.008)y\rangle$. The value of the gradient at your position on the hill is $\mathbf{v} = \nabla z(-100,-100) = \langle 0.6, 0.8 \rangle$. The direction vector representing the northwest direction is $\mathbf{n} = \langle -\frac{1}{2}\sqrt{2}, \frac{1}{2}\sqrt{2}\rangle$. So your initial rate of climb at $(-100,-100,430)$ in the direction of $\mathbf{n}$ is $D_{\mathbf{n}}z(-100,-100) = \mathbf{v} \cdot \mathbf{n} = -\frac{3}{10}\sqrt{2} + \frac{4}{10}\sqrt{2} = \frac{1}{10}\sqrt{2} \approx 0.1414$ feet per foot. The initial angle of climb is $\arctan\left(\frac{1}{10}\sqrt{2}\right) \approx 0.1405$ radians, or about $8°2'58''$.

(b) Repeat part (a), except now you head northeast. The direction vector representing the northeast direction is $\mathbf{n} = \frac{1}{2}\sqrt{2}\langle 1, 1\rangle$. So your initial rate of climb at $(-100,-100,430)$ in the direction of $\mathbf{n}$ is $D_{\mathbf{n}}z(-100,-100) = \mathbf{v} \cdot \mathbf{n} = \frac{3}{10}\sqrt{2} + \frac{4}{10}\sqrt{2} = \frac{7}{10}\sqrt{2} \approx 0.9898$ feet per foot. The initial angle of climb is $\arctan\left(\frac{7}{10}\sqrt{2}\right) \approx 0.780$ radians, or about $44°42'38''$.

51. The hill is steepest in the direction of $\nabla z(-100,-100) = \langle 0.6, 0.8 \rangle$. The slope of the hill in that direction is $|\langle 0.6, 0.8\rangle| = 1$, making your initial angle of climb $45°$. The compass heading of this direction is $\pi/2 - \arctan\frac{4}{3}$ radians, or about $36°52'12''$.

52. (a) $\nabla z = \dfrac{\langle -0.06x, -0.14y\rangle}{\left(1 + (0.00003)x^2 + (0.00007)y^2\right)^2}$. The slope of this hill at the point $(100, 100, 500)$ in the northwest direction is $\nabla z(100,100) \cdot \dfrac{\sqrt{2}}{2}\langle -1, 1\rangle = -\sqrt{2}$. Your initial rate of *descent* is $\sqrt{2}$ feet per foot, and the angle of descent is about $54°44'8''$.

(b) In the northeast direction, the initial rate of descent is $-\dfrac{5\sqrt{2}}{2}$, and the descent angle is about $74°12'25''$.

53. $\nabla z\big|_{(100,100)} = \langle -\frac{3}{2}, -\frac{7}{2}\rangle$ is the initial direction. The compass heading is $270° - \left(\arctan\left(\frac{7}{3}\right)\right)° \approx 203°11'55''$. $|\nabla z(100,100)| = \frac{1}{2}\sqrt{58}$. The initial angle of climb is about $75°17'8''$.

55. Let
$$f(x,y) = \tfrac{1}{1000}\left(3x^2 - 5xy + y^2\right).$$
Then
$$\nabla f(x,y) = \tfrac{1}{1000}\langle 6x - 5y, 2y - 5x\rangle,$$
and so $\nabla f(100,100) = \langle \frac{1}{10}, -\frac{3}{10}\rangle$.

Part (a): A unit vector in the northeast direction is $\mathbf{u} = \langle 1, 1\rangle/\sqrt{2}$, so the directional derivative of f at $(100,100)$ in the northeast direction is
$$\langle \tfrac{1}{10}, -\tfrac{3}{10}\rangle \cdot \langle 1, 1\rangle/\sqrt{2} = -\tfrac{1}{10}\sqrt{2}.$$
Hence you will initially be descending the hill, at an angle of $-\arctan\left(\frac{1}{10}\sqrt{2}\right)$, approximately $8.049467°$.

Part (b): A unit vector in the direction $30°$ north of east is $\mathbf{u} = \frac{1}{2}\langle \sqrt{3}, 1\rangle$, so the directional derivative of f at $(100,100)$ in the direction of $\mathbf{u}$ is
$$\langle \tfrac{1}{10}, -\tfrac{3}{10}\rangle \cdot \langle \sqrt{3}, 1\rangle/2 = -\tfrac{1}{20}\left(3 - \sqrt{3}\right).$$
Hence you will initially be descending the hill, at an angle of approximately $3.627552°$.

58. $\mathbf{v}(t) = \left\langle \dfrac{dr}{dt}\cos\theta - \dfrac{d\theta}{dt}r\sin\theta,\ \dfrac{dr}{dt}\sin\theta + \dfrac{d\theta}{dt}r\cos\theta \right\rangle$.

59. $\dfrac{dx}{dt} = \dfrac{d\phi}{dt}\rho\cos\phi\cos\theta + \dfrac{d\rho}{dt}\sin\phi\cos\theta - \dfrac{d\theta}{dt}\rho\sin\phi\sin\theta,$

$\dfrac{dy}{dt} = \dfrac{d\phi}{dt}\rho\cos\phi\sin\theta + \dfrac{d\rho}{dt}\sin\phi\sin\theta + \dfrac{d\theta}{dt}\rho\sin\phi\cos\theta,$

$\dfrac{dz}{dt} = \dfrac{d\rho}{dt}\cos\phi - \dfrac{d\phi}{dt}\rho\sin\phi.$

Section 13.9

1. The equations to be solved are

$$2 = 2\lambda x,$$
$$1 = 2\lambda y,$$
$$x^2 + y^2 = 1.$$

   Maximum: $\sqrt{5}$, at $\left(\frac{2}{5}\sqrt{5}, \frac{1}{5}\sqrt{5}\right)$; minimum: $-\sqrt{5}$, at $\left(-\frac{2}{5}\sqrt{5}, -\frac{1}{5}\sqrt{5}\right)$

2. The equations to be solved are

$$1 = 2\lambda x,$$
$$1 = 8\lambda y,$$
$$x^2 + 4y^2 = 1.$$

   Maximum: $\frac{1}{2}\sqrt{5}$, at $\left(\frac{2}{5}\sqrt{5}, \frac{1}{10}\sqrt{5}\right)$; minimum: $-\frac{1}{2}\sqrt{5}$, at $\left(-\frac{2}{5}\sqrt{5}, -\frac{1}{10}\sqrt{5}\right)$

3. The method leads to the simultaneous equations $2x = 2\lambda x$ and $2y + 2\lambda y = 0$. Their solutions: $x = 0$ or $\lambda = 1$.

4. $\langle 2x, 2y \rangle = \lambda \langle 2, 3 \rangle$ leads to $x = \frac{12}{13}$, $y = \frac{18}{13}$. The minimum is $\frac{36}{13}$, and there is no maximum.

6. The method yields $\langle 8x, 18y \rangle = \lambda \langle 2x, 2y \rangle$. It follows that one of x and y is zero. So the minimum occurs at $(-1, 0)$ and at $(1, 0)$, where the value of f is 4. The maximum value is 9, and occurs at $(0, 1)$ and at $(0, -1)$.

8. We obtain $\langle 3, 2, 1 \rangle = \lambda \langle 2x, 2y, 2z \rangle$. Solutions: $x^2 = \frac{9}{14}$, $y = \frac{2}{3}x$, $z = \frac{1}{3}x$. Maximum: $\sqrt{14}$. Minimum: $-\sqrt{14}$.

9. You should find that $2\lambda x = 8\lambda y = 18\lambda z = 1$. This leads to $z^2 = \frac{16}{49}$ while $x = 9z$ and $y = \frac{9}{4}z$.

10. We obtain $\langle yz, xz, xy \rangle = \lambda \langle 2x, 2y, 2z \rangle$. There are fourteen solutions! If $xyz \neq 0$, take all possible combinations of sign in $\langle x, y, z \rangle$ where $x^2 = y^2 = z^2 = \frac{1}{3}$. If one of the variables is zero, the six solutions that result are $(1, 0, 0)$, $(-1, 0, 0)$, $(0, 1, 0)$, $(0, -1, 0)$, $(0, 0, 1)$, and $(0, 0, -1)$. Only the first eight lead to extrema. For the maximum of f, take either three plus signs or one to obtain $\frac{1}{9}\sqrt{3}$. To obtain the minimum, take two plus signs or none to obtain $-\frac{1}{9}\sqrt{3}$.

11. The equations to be solved are

$$y = 2\lambda x,$$
$$x = 2\lambda y,$$
$$2 = 2\lambda z,$$
$$x^2 + y^2 + z^2 = 36.$$

   The solutions are $(0, 0, -6)$, $(0, 0, 6)$, $(-4, 4, -2)$, $(4, -4, -2)$, $(-4, -4, 2)$, and $(4, 4, 2)$. Maximum: 20, at $(4, 4, 2)$ and at $(-4, -4, 2)$; minimum: -20, at $(-4, 4, -2)$ and at $(4, -4, -2)$

12. The equations to be solved are

$$1 = \lambda(2x - 6y),$$
$$-1 = \lambda(2y - 6x),$$
$$1 = -\lambda,$$
$$z = x^2 - 6xy + y^2.$$

There is only one solution. There is no maximum because $x - y + z$ can be made arbitrarily large by choosing $x = M$, a large positive real number, $y = -M$, and $z = x^2 - 6xy + y^2 = 8M^2$, so that $f(x,y,z) = 2M + M^2$. Minimum: $-\frac{1}{8}$, at $\left(-\frac{1}{8}, \frac{1}{8}, \frac{1}{8}\right)$

13. The equations to be solved are
$$2xy^2z^2 = 2\lambda x,$$
$$2x^2yz^2 = 8\lambda y,$$
$$2x^2y^2z = 18\lambda z,$$
$$x^2 + 4y^2 + 9z^2 = 27.$$

Solutions: $(0, y, z)$, $(x, 0, z)$, $(x, y, 0)$, and all eight of $\left(\pm 3, \pm\frac{3}{2}, \pm 1\right)$. Maximum: $81/4$, at all eight of the last critical points. Minimum 0, at all of the other critical points.

14. The equations to be solved are
$$4x^3 = 2\lambda x,$$
$$4y^3 = 2\lambda y,$$
$$4z^3 = 2\lambda z,$$
$$x^2 + y^2 + z^2 = 6.$$

The solutions are $(\pm\sqrt{2}, \pm\sqrt{2}, \pm\sqrt{2})$ (all eight combinations), $(0, \pm\sqrt{3}, \pm\sqrt{3})$ (all four combinations), $(\pm\sqrt{3}, 0, \pm\sqrt{3})$ (all four combinations), $(\pm\sqrt{3}, \pm\sqrt{3}, 0)$ (all four combinations), $(0, 0, \pm\sqrt{6})$, $(0, \pm\sqrt{6}, 0)$, and $(\pm\sqrt{6}, 0, 0)$. Maximum: 36, at the last six critical points; minimum: 12, at the first eight critical points.

16. We let $g(x, y, z) = x^2 + y^2 - 1$ and $h(x, y, z) = 2x + 2y + z - 5$. The equation $\nabla f = \lambda \nabla g + \mu \nabla h$ then takes the form
$$\langle 0, 0, 1 \rangle = \lambda \langle 2x, 2y, 0 \rangle + \mu \langle 2, 2, 1 \rangle.$$
It follows that $\lambda x = -1 = \lambda y$; because $\lambda \neq 0$, $x = y$. So $x = y = \frac{1}{2}\sqrt{2}$ or $x = y = -\frac{1}{2}\sqrt{2}$. In the first case we see that $z = 5 - 2\sqrt{2}$; in the second, $z = 5 + 2\sqrt{2}$. It follows that the maximum is $5 + 2\sqrt{2}$ and that the minimum is $5 - 2\sqrt{2}$.

17. The equations to be solved are
$$0 = \lambda + 2\mu x,$$
$$0 = \lambda + 2\mu y,$$
$$1 = \lambda,$$
$$x + y + z = 1,$$
$$x^2 + y^2 = 1.$$

There are only two solutions. The maximum is $1 + \sqrt{2}$, at $(-1/\sqrt{2}, -1/\sqrt{2}, 1 + \sqrt{2})$; the minimum is $1 - \sqrt{2}$, at $(1/\sqrt{2}, 1/\sqrt{2}, 1 - \sqrt{2})$.

18. The equations to be solved are
$$1 = \lambda,$$
$$0 = \lambda + 8\mu y,$$
$$0 = \lambda + 18\mu z,$$
$$x + y + z = 12,$$
$$4y^2 + 9z^2 = 36,$$

with only two solutions. The maximum is $12+\sqrt{13}$, at $\left(12+\sqrt{13},\, -9/\sqrt{13},\, -4/\sqrt{13}\right)$; the minimum is $12-\sqrt{13}$, at $\left(12-\sqrt{13},\, 9/\sqrt{13},\, 4/\sqrt{13}\right)$.

19. The equations to be solved are

$$2x = 3\lambda,$$

$$2y = 4\lambda,$$

$$3x + 4y = 100.$$

The only solution is $(12, 16)$. Clearly there can be no maximum, so $(12, 16)$ is the point on $3x+4y = 100$ that is closest to the origin.

20. If the base of the box measures x by y and its height is z, then we are to minimize $7xy+10yz+10xz$ given the constraint $xyz = 700$. The equations to be solved are

$$7y + 10z = \lambda yz,$$

$$7x + 10z = \lambda xz,$$

$$10x + 10y = \lambda xy,$$

$$xyz = 700.$$

The only (real) solution is $(10, 10, 7)$, so the least expensive such box has base 10 in. by 10 in. and height 7 in.

21. We are to minimize $x^2 + y^2 + z^2$ given $12x + 4y + 3z = 169$. The Lagrange multiplier equations are

$$2x = 12\lambda,$$

$$2y = 4\lambda,$$

$$2z = 3\lambda,$$

$$12x + 4y + 3z = 169.$$

The only solution is $(12, 4, 3)$, and this is the point on the given plane closest to the origin.

22. We are to minimize $(x-9)^2 + (y-9)^2 + (z-9)^2$ given $2x + 2y + z = 27$. The Lagrange multiplier equations are

$$2(x-9) = 2\lambda,$$

$$2(y-9) = 2\lambda,$$

$$2(z-9) = \lambda,$$

$$2x + 2y + z = 27.$$

The only solution is $(5, 5, 7)$, so this is the point on the given plane closest to $(9, 9, 9)$.

23. We are to minimize $(x-7)^2 + (y+7)^2 + z^2$ given $2x+3y+z = 49$. The Lagrange multiplier equations are

$$2(x-7) = 2\lambda,$$

$$2(y+7) = 3\lambda,$$

$$2z = \lambda,$$

$$2x + 3y + z = 49.$$

The only solution is $(15, 5, 4)$, so this is the point on the given plane closest to $(7, -7, 0)$.

24. We are to minimize $x^2 + y^2 + z^2$ given $xyz = 8$. The Lagrange multiplier equations are

$$2x = \lambda yz,$$
$$2y = \lambda xz,$$
$$2z = \lambda xy,$$
$$xyz = 8.$$

The only (real) solutions are $(-2, -2, 2)$, $(2, -2, -2)$, $(-2, 2, -2)$, and $(2, 2, 2)$. Only the last of these is in the first octant, but all four yield the same global minimum value 12 of the square of the distance from the surface to $(0, 0, 0)$.

25. We are to minimize $x^2 + y^2 + z^2$ given $x^2 y^2 z = 4$. The Lagrange multiplier equations are

$$2x = 2\lambda xy^2 z,$$
$$2y = 2\lambda x^2 yz,$$
$$2z = \lambda x^2 y^2,$$
$$x^2 y^2 z = 4.$$

There are only four real solutions: $(\pm\sqrt{2}, \pm\sqrt{2}, 1)$. Although only one of these points lies in the first octant, all four yield the same global minimum value $\sqrt{5}$ for the distance from the given surface to $(0, 0, 0)$.

26. We are to minimize $x^2 + y^2 + z^2$ given $x^4 y^8 z^2 = 8$. The Lagrange multiplier equations are

$$2x = 4\lambda x^3 y^8 z^2,$$
$$2y = 8\lambda x^4 y^7 z^2,$$
$$2z = 2\lambda x^4 y^8 z,$$
$$x^4 y^8 z^2 = 8.$$

There are 56 solutions, but only eight are real; they are $(\pm 1, \pm\sqrt{2}, \pm 1/\sqrt{2})$. Only one of these lies in the first octant, but all eight yield the same global minimum value $\frac{7}{2}$ of the square of the distance from the given surface to $(0, 0, 0)$.

27. We are to maximize xyz given x, y, and z are positive and $x + y + z = 120$. The Lagrange multiplier equations are

$$yz = \lambda,$$
$$xz = \lambda,$$
$$xy = \lambda,$$
$$x + y + z = 120.$$

If we ignore the restriction that x, y, and z must all be positive, we obtain the four solutions $(120, 0, 0)$, $(0, 120, 0)$, $(0, 0, 120)$, and $(40, 40, 40)$. The last of these produces the maximum possible value 64000 of the product xyz.

28. If the dimensions of the box are x by y by z, then we are to maximize xyz given the constraint $4x + 4y + 4z = 6$. The Lagrange multiplier equations are

$$yz = \lambda,$$
$$xz = \lambda,$$
$$xy = \lambda,$$
$$4x + 4y + 4z = 6.$$

There are four solutions: $(\frac{3}{2}, 0, 0,)$, $(0, \frac{3}{2}, 0)$, $(0, 0, \frac{3}{2})$, and $(\frac{1}{2}, \frac{1}{2}, \frac{1}{2})$. The last of these yields the maximum volume, $\frac{1}{8}$.

29. If the dimensions of the box are x by y by z, then we are to minimize $2xy + 2yz + 2xz$ given the constraint $xyz = 1000$. The Lagrange multiplier equations are

$$2(y + z) = \lambda yz,$$
$$2(x + z) = \lambda xz,$$
$$2(x + y) = \lambda xy,$$
$$xyz = 1000.$$

The only real solution is $(10, 10, 10)$, so the box in question measures 10 in. along each edge.

30. If the base of the box measures x by y and its height is z, then we are to minimize $xy + 2xz + 2yz$ given $xyz = 4000$. The Lagrange multiplier equations are

$$y + 2z = \lambda yz,$$
$$x + 2z = \lambda xz,$$
$$2x + 2y = \lambda xy,$$
$$xyz = 4000.$$

The only real solution is $(20, 20, 10)$, so the box in question has base 20 cm by 20 cm and height 10 cm.

31. If the base of the box measures x by y and its height is z, then we are to minimize $6xy + 10xz + 10yz$ given $xyz = 600$. The Lagrange multiplier equations are

$$6y + 10z = \lambda yz,$$
$$6x + 10z = \lambda xz,$$
$$10x + 10y = \lambda xy,$$
$$xyz = 600.$$

The only real solution is $(10, 10, 6)$, so the least expensive such box has base 10 in. by 10 in. and height 6 in.

32. If the base of the box measures x by y and its height is z, then we are to minimize $6xy + 8xz + 8yz$ given $xyz = 48$. The Lagrange multiplier equations are

$$6y + 8z = \lambda yz,$$
$$6x + 8z = \lambda xz,$$
$$8x + 8y = \lambda xy,$$
$$xyz = 48.$$

The only real solution is $(4,4,3)$, so the least expensive such box has base 4 ft by 4 ft and height 3 ft.

33. If the base of the box measures x by y and its height is z, then we are to minimize $6xy + 12xz + 18yz$ given $xyz = 750$. The Lagrange multiplier equations are

$$6y + 12z = \lambda yz,$$

$$6x + 18z = \lambda xz,$$

$$12x + 18y = \lambda xy,$$

$$xyz = 750.$$

The only real solution is $(15, 10, 5)$, so the least expensive such box has base 15 in. by 10 in. and height 5 in.

34. If the base of the box measures x by y and its height is z, then we are to minimize $3xy + 2xz + 2yz$ given the constraint $xyz = 12$. The Lagrange multiplier equations are

$$3y + 2z = \lambda yz,$$

$$3x + 2z = \lambda xz,$$

$$2x \pm 2y = \lambda xy,$$

$$xyz = 12.$$

The only real solution is $(2, 2, 3)$, so the least expensive such box has base 2 m by 2 m and height 3 m.

36. Maximize A by maximizing

$$f(x,y,z) = A^2 = s(s-x)(s-y)(s-z)$$

given the constraint $g(x,y,z) = 2s - x - y - z = 0$ (where s is constant). The method yields

$$\langle s(s-y)(s-z), s(s-x)(s-z), s(s-x)(s-y) \rangle = \lambda \langle 1, 1, 1 \rangle.$$

Therefore

$$s(s-x)(s-y) = s(s-x)(s-z) = s(s-y)(s-z).$$

Now $s \neq 0$, so

$$s^2 - sx - sy + xy = s^2 - sy - sz + yz = s^2 - sx - sz + xz;$$

it follows that

$$x(s-z) = y(s-z) \quad \text{and} \quad y(s-x) = z(s-x).$$

If $s = x$ (say), the triangle degenerates to a line segment:

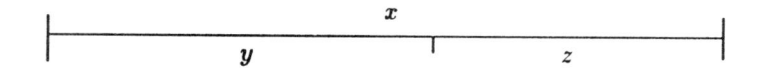

This yields minimum area zero. So at maximum, all three of $s-x$, $s-y$, and $s-z$ are positive. It follows that $x = y = z$, and therefore that the triangle with fixed perimeter and maximum area is an equilateral triangle.

38. Maximize and minimize $f(x,y) = x^2 + y^2$ given the constraint $g(x,y) = x^2 + xy + y^2 - 3 = 0$. The method yields
$$\langle 2x, 2y \rangle = \lambda \langle 2x + y, 2y + x \rangle.$$

Following the suggestion given in the problem, we obtain the simultaneous equations
$$2(\lambda - 1)x + \lambda y = 0,$$
$$\lambda x + 2(\lambda - 1)y = 0.$$

Now $x = y = z = 0$ is ruled out, so nontrivial solutions exist only in case the determinant of the system above is zero:
$$4(\lambda - 1)^2 - \lambda^2 = 0,$$
so that $2(\lambda - 1) = \pm \lambda$.

(a) $2\lambda - 2 = -\lambda$ implies that $\lambda = \frac{2}{3}$;
(b) $2\lambda - 2 = \lambda$ implies that $\lambda = 1$.

In ths first case, $x = y$; in the second, $y = -x$. So in the first case, $(1, 1)$ and $(-1, -1)$ may yield extrema; in the second case, we must examine $(\sqrt{3}, -\sqrt{3})$ and $(-\sqrt{3}, \sqrt{3})$. But the value of f at both points obtained in the first case is 2 and its value at both points of the second case is 6. Therefore the points on the ellipse $x^2 + xy + y^2 = 3$ nearest the origin are $(1, 1)$ and $(-1, -1)$; the two points farthest from the origin are $(\sqrt{3}, -\sqrt{3})$ and $(-\sqrt{3}, \sqrt{3})$.

40. Maximize and minimize $f(x,y) = (x-1)^2 + (y-1)^2$ given $g(x,y) = 4x^2 + 9y^2 - 36 = 0$. The method yields
$$\langle 2(x-1), 2(y-1) \rangle = \lambda \langle 8x, 18y \rangle.$$

The (eventual) answer is that the nearest point—with all the following data approximate—is
$$(1.249987537, 1.818122492), \quad \text{at distance} \quad 0.8554637225;$$

the farthest point is
$$(-2.907018204, -0.494073841), \quad \text{at distance} \quad 4.182947273.$$

Comment: To obtain these answers, we had to eliminate the four points $(-3, 0)$, $(3, 0)$, $(0, 2)$, and $(0, -2)$. Then we solved the resulting equation $25x^4 - 90x^3 - 108x^2 + 810x - 729 = 0$ by numerical methods, and verified that it has only two real solutions.

42. Answers: The highest point is at $x = \dfrac{-15 - 9\sqrt{5}}{20} \approx -1.75623059$,

$y = \dfrac{-15 - 9\sqrt{5}}{10} \approx -3.51248118$,

$z = \dfrac{9 + 3\sqrt{5}}{4} \approx 3.92705098$.

The lowest point is at $x = \dfrac{-15 + 9\sqrt{5}}{20} \approx 0.256230590$,

$y = \dfrac{-15 + 9\sqrt{5}}{10} \approx 0.512461179$,

$z = \dfrac{9 - 3\sqrt{5}}{4} \approx 0.572949017$.

Section 13.9 Lagrange Multipliers; Constrained Maximum-Minimum Problems

44. Minimize $f(x, y, z) = xy + 3xz + 7yz$ given $g(x, y, z) = xyz - 12 = 0$ and $h(x, y, z) = x - 3y = 0$ (because $y/2 = x/6$).

Results: To minimize f, take $x = 2\sqrt[3]{36} \approx 6.603854498$,
$$y = \tfrac{2}{3}\sqrt[3]{36} \approx 2.201284833, \text{ and}$$
$$z = \tfrac{1}{4}\sqrt[3]{36} \approx 0.825481812.$$

The minimum value of f is $4(36)^{2/3} \approx 43.61089$; therefore the minimum cost is about 44 cents.

46. Lagrange multiplier method: We maximize $(x-u)^2 + (y-v)^2 + (z-w)^2$ subject to the constraints
$x^2 + y^2 - z = 0$,
$u^2 + v^2 - w = 0$,
$x + y + z - 12 = 0$, and
$u + v + x - 12 = 0$.

Solve the simultaneous equations $2(x-u) = 2\lambda x + \mu$,
$$2(y-v) = 2\lambda y + \mu,$$
$$2(z-w) = -\lambda + \mu,$$
$$-2(x-u) = 2\eta u + \zeta,$$
$$-2(y-v) = 2\eta v + \zeta, \text{ and}$$
$$-2(z-w) = -\eta u + \zeta \text{ to obtain the four cases below.}$$

Case (1): If $\lambda = 1$: $u = v$ and $x = y$.

Case (2): If $\eta = 1$: $u = v$ and $x = y$.

Case (3): If $u = v$: $\lambda = 1$ or $x = y$, so $x = y$.

Case (4): If $x = y$: $u = v$.

Therefore $x = y$ and $u = v$. So since $x^2 + y^2 + x + y = 12$,
$$x^2 + x - 6 = 0;$$
$$x = -3 \text{ or } x = 2.$$

Similarly, $u = -3$ or $u = 2$. Thus we obtain the two points $(2, 2, 8)$ and $(-3, -3, 18)$. So the center of the ellipse is $\left(-\tfrac{1}{2}, -\tfrac{1}{2}, 13\right)$. The other axis is perpendicular to this one and lies in the horizontal line through the center of the ellipse. A vector $\mathbf{V}$ parallel to that line satisfies $\langle -5, -5, 10 \rangle \cdot \mathbf{V} = 0$ and $\mathbf{V} = \langle a, b, 0 \rangle$. So $b = -a$. Choose $\mathbf{V} = \langle 1, -1, 0 \rangle$. This second line has symmetric equations
$$x - \tfrac{1}{2} = \tfrac{1}{2} - y, \ z = 13.$$

So $x + y = 1$, $z = 13$. This line meets the paraboloid when $x^2 + (1-x)^2 = 13$: at the points $(3, -2, 13)$ and $(-2, 3, 13)$. The first axis has length $\sqrt{150} = 5\sqrt{6} \approx 12.247$. The second has length $\sqrt{50} = 5\sqrt{2}$, so it is the minor axis. Answers: $\tfrac{5}{2}\sqrt{6}$ and $\tfrac{5}{2}\sqrt{2}$.

Note: A simpler solution, which does not use the method of Lagrange multipliers, is the following: If θ is the angle between the xy-plane and the plane $x + y + z = 12$, then
$$\cos\theta = \frac{\langle 1,1,1 \rangle \cdot \langle 1,0,0 \rangle}{|\langle 1,1,1 \rangle|\,|\langle 1,0,0 \rangle|} = \frac{1}{\sqrt{3}},$$

so $\sec\theta = \sqrt{3}$.

The projection of the ellipse into the xy-plane has equation
$$x^2 + y^2 + x + y = 12;$$
$$(2x+1)^2 + (2y+1)^2 = 50;$$
$$\left(x + \tfrac{1}{2}\right)^2 + \left(y + \tfrac{1}{2}\right)^2 = \tfrac{25}{2}.$$

This is a circle with center $\left(-\frac{1}{2}, -\frac{1}{2}\right)$ and radius $\frac{5}{2}\sqrt{2}$. So the major semiaxis of the ellipse will have length $\left(\frac{5}{2}\sqrt{2}\right)\sec\theta = \frac{5}{2}\sqrt{6}$ and minor semiaxis of lenth $\frac{5}{2}\sqrt{2}$.

50. See the diagram below.

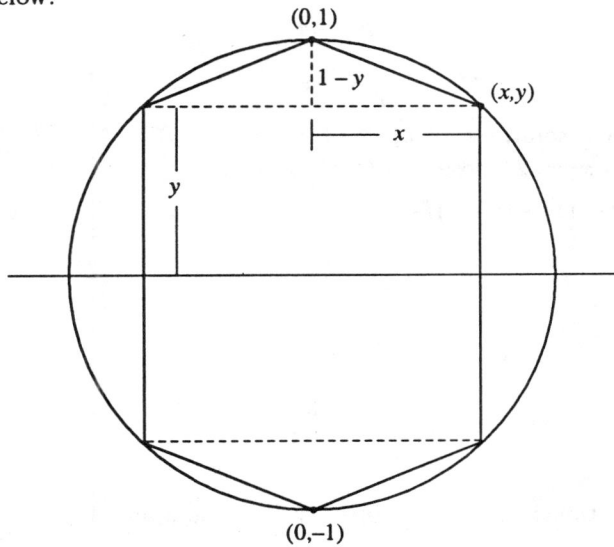

We maximize $V = 2\pi x^2 y + \frac{2}{3}\pi x^2 (1-y)$ given $x^2 + y^2 = 1$, $(x, y > 0)$. Maximize instead

$$E = 3x^2 y + x^2 - x^2 y = 2x^2 y + x^2. \text{ Then}$$
$$4xy + 2x = 2\lambda x \text{ and } 2x^2 = 2\lambda y, \quad \lambda \neq 0.$$

We obtain $y = \dfrac{-1 + \sqrt{13}}{6} \approx 0.434$ and $x = \dfrac{\sqrt{22 + 2\sqrt{13}}}{6} \approx 0.901$.

Answer: radius $\dfrac{\sqrt{22 + 2\sqrt{13}}}{6}$ and height $\dfrac{-1 + \sqrt{13}}{6}$.

51. We minimize the square $x^2 + y^2$ of the distance from (x, y) to $(0, 0)$ given the constraint $y = (x-1)^2$. The Lagrange multiplier equations are

$$2x = 2\lambda(x - 1),$$
$$2y = -\lambda,$$
$$(x - 1)^2 = y.$$

There is only one real solution (which can be found by Newton's method): $(0.4102455, 0.3478104)$, and this is the point of the parabola that is closest to the origin.

52. We are to find the global extrema of $(x-3)^2 + (y-2)^2$ given $4x^2 + 9y^2 = 36$. The Lagrange multiplier equations are

$$2(x - 3) = 8\lambda x,$$
$$2(y - 2) = 18\lambda y,$$
$$4x^2 + 9y^2 = 36.$$

There are only two real solutions, so the point of the ellipse closest to $(3, 2)$ is approximately $(2.35587, 1.23825)$, at approximate distance 2.66147, and the point farthest from $(3, 2)$ is approximately $(-2.88144, -0.55670)$, at approximate distance 2.93472.

Section 13.9 Lagrange Multipliers; Constrained Maximum-Minimum Problems

53. We minimize $(x-1)^2 + (y-4)^2$ given $xy = 24$ (and $x > 0$). The Lagrange multiplier equations

$$2(x-1) = \lambda y,$$
$$2(y-4) = \lambda x,$$
$$xy = 24,$$

which have the two real solutions $(x, y) = (4, 6)$ and $(x, y) \approx (-5.53383, -4.33696)$. Hence the first-quadrant point on $xy = 24$ closest to $(1, 4)$ is $(4, 6)$.

54. We are to minimize $(x-1)^2 + (y-2)^2 + (z-3)^2$ given $xyz = 1$. The Lagrange multiplier equations are

$$2(x-1) = \lambda yz,$$
$$2(y-2) = \lambda xz,$$
$$2(z-3) = \lambda xy,$$
$$xyz = 1.$$

There are four real solutions; their approximate values and approximate distances from $(1, 2, 3)$ are

$(0.17608, 1.92462, 2.95084)$, distance: 3.52741;

$(-0.66477, -0.45145, 3.33213)$, distance: 3.42765;

$(-0.84758, 2.61087, -0.45345)$, distance: 2.77376;

$(2.06775, -0.79105, -0.61136)$, distance: 2.29676.

So the point on $xyz = 1$ closest to $(1, 2, 3)$ is approximately $(2.06775, -0.79105, -0.61136)$.

55. We are to find the extrema of $x^2 + y^2 + z^2$ given

$$(x-1)^2 + (y-2)^2 + (z-3)^2 = 36.$$

The Lagrange multiplier equations are

$$2x = 2\lambda(x-1),$$
$$2y = 2\lambda(y-2),$$
$$2z = 2\lambda(x-3),$$
$$(x-1)^2 + (y-2)^2(z-3)^2 = 36.$$

There are only two solutions. The point of the sphere that is closest to $(0, 0, 0)$ is approximately $(-0.60357, -1.20713, -1.81070)$, at approximate distance 2.25834; the point farthest from $(0, 0, 0)$ is approximately $(2.60357, 5.20713, 7.81070)$, at approximate distance 9.74166.

56. We are to find the extrema of $x^2 + y^2 + z^2$ given $4x^2 + 9y^2 + z^2 = 36$. The Lagrange multiplier equations are

$$2x = 8\lambda x,$$
$$2y = 18\lambda y,$$
$$2z = 2\lambda z,$$
$$4x^2 + 9y^2 + z^2 = 36.$$

There are six solutions. The two solutions $(0, \pm 2, 0)$ are the closest, at distance 2 from the origin. The two solutions $(0, 0, \pm 6)$ are the farthest, at distance 6 from the origin. The other two solutions $(\pm 3, 0, 0)$ are not extrema.

57. Let (x, y) be a point of the ellipse $4x^2 + 9y^2 = 36$ and let (u, v) be a point of the line $x + y = 10$. We are to find the extrema of $(x - u)^2 + (y - v)^2$ given $4x^2 + 9y^2 = 36$ and $u + v = 10$. The Lagrange multiplier equations are

$$2(x - u) = 8\lambda x,$$

$$-2(x - u) = \mu,$$

$$2(y - v) = 18\lambda y,$$

$$-2(y - v) = \mu,$$

$$4x^2 + 9y^2 = 36,$$

$$u + v = 10.$$

There are only two real solutions. The first is the point $(x, y) \approx (2.49615, 1.10940)$, which is closest, at approximate distance 3.48501 from the point $(u, v) \approx 5.69338, 4.30662)$ of the line. The point $(x, y) \approx (-2.49615, -1.10940)$ is farthest, at approximate distance 6.94268 from the point $(u, v) \approx (4.30662, 5.69338)$ of the line.

58. To simplify this problem, let's think of the way the Lagrange multiplier method works. We conclude that we need to find the points of the ellipsoid at which the normal vector is also normal to the given plane. The plane has normal $\langle 2, 3, 1 \rangle$, so such points (x, y, z) of the ellipsoid satisfy the equations

$$8x = 2\lambda,$$

$$18y = 3\lambda,$$

$$2z = \lambda,$$

$$4x^2 + 9y^2 + z^2 = 36.$$

The only solutions of these equations are

$$\left(-\sqrt{3}, -\tfrac{2}{3}\sqrt{3}, -2\sqrt{3}\right) \quad \text{and} \quad \left(\sqrt{3}, \tfrac{2}{3}\sqrt{3}, 2\sqrt{3}\right).$$

The first of these is farthest from the plane and the second is closest (as the nearest point is clearly in the first octant).

If we let (x, y, z) be a point on the ellipsoid and (u, v, w) be a point on the plane, and try to find the extrema of $(x - u)^2 + (y - v)^2 + (z - w)^2$ (as in the solution of Problem 57), the Lagrange multiplier equations are

$$2(x - u) = 8\lambda x,$$

$$-2(x - u) = 2\mu,$$

$$2(y - v) = 18\lambda y,$$

$$-2(y - v) = 3\mu,$$

$$2(z - w) = 2\lambda z,$$

$$-2(z - w) = \mu,$$

$$4x^2 + 9y^2 + z^2 = 36,$$

$$2u + 3v + w = 10.$$

Neither *Mathematica* 2.2 nor *Mathematica* 3.0 was able to solve this system, either exactly or approximately.

59. If all four upper vertices lie on the given paraboloid, then the sides of the box will be parallel to the coordinate planes. If (x,y,z) is the vertex of the box on the paraboloid in the first octant, then we are to maximize box volume $4xyz$ given $x^2 + 2y^2 + z = 9$. The Lagrange multiplier equations are

$$4yz = 2\lambda x,$$

$$4xz = 4\lambda y,$$

$$4xy = \lambda,$$

$$x^2 + 2y^2 + z = 9.$$

This system has nine solutions, five of which have at least one coordinate equl to zero (thus yielding the box of minimal volume). The other four solutions are $(\pm\frac{3}{2}, \pm\frac{3}{2}\sqrt{2}, \frac{9}{2})$, only one of which lies in the first octant. This point yields the maximum possible volume of the box, $\frac{81}{4}\sqrt{2} \approx 28.637825$.

60. We are to maximize and minimze z given the two constraints $4x + 9y + z = 0$ and $2x^2 + 3y^2 - z = 0$. The Lagrange multiplier equations are

$$0 = 4\lambda + 4\mu x,$$

$$0 = 9\lambda + 6\mu y,$$

$$1 = \lambda - \mu,$$

$$4x + 9y + z = 0,$$

$$2x^2 + 3y^2 - z = 0.$$

These equations can be solved by hand; the only solutions are $(0,0,0)$ and $(-2,-3,35)$. The former is the lowest point of the ellipse and the latter is its highest point.

Section 13.10

1. $f(x,y) = 2(x+1)^2 + (y-2)^2 - 1$.
2. $12 - 6x = 0 = -12 - 4y$ at $(2,-3)$. $AC - B^2 = 24 > 0$; $z = -6 < 0$. So f has a local maximum at $(2,-3)$.
4. $y + 3 = 0 = x - 2$ at $(2,-3)$. $AC - B^2 = -1 < 0$, so f has no extrema.
6. $x + 2y + 2 = 0 = x + y - 2$ at $(6,-4)$. $AC - B^2 = -8 < 0$, so f has no extrema.
7. $x^2 + y = 0 = x + y^2$ at $(0,0)$ and at $(-1,-1)$. At the first critical point, $AC - B^2 = -9 < 0$; no extremum there. At $(-1,-1)$, $AC - B^2 = 27$ and $A = -6$. Therefore f has the local maximum value 4 at $(-1,-1)$.
8. At $(1,1)$, $AC - B^2 = 8 > 0$, but $A = 2$, so f has a local minimum at $(1,1)$. At the point $(-\frac{1}{3}, -\frac{1}{3})$, $AC - B^2 < 0$, so there is no extremum at that point.
10. No extremum at $(0,0)$; local maximum at $(1,1)$.
12. Both partials vanish when $y = -x$ and $3x^2 - 6x = 0$, thus the only critical points are $(0,0)$ and $(2,-2)$. $\Delta = 36x - 36$, so $(0,0)$ is not an extremum and $(2,-2)$ is a local minimum.
14. $3x^2 + 6y + 6 = 0 = 6x + 6y$ is equivalent to $y = -x$ and (simultaneously) $x^2 - 2x + 2 = 0$. The latter equation has no real solutions, so f has no extrema of any sort.

16. The equations $6x + 12y - 6 = 0 = 12x + 6y^2 + 6$ lead to $x = 1 - 2y$ and $y^2 - 4y + 3 = 0$, and thus $(-1, 1)$ and $(-5, 3)$ are the only two critical points. But $\Delta = 72y - 144$, so the first is not an extremum and the second yields a local minimum for f.

18. When both partials vanish, we have $x = 2y$ and $2x = y^3$. The critical points are therefore $(0, 0)$, $(4, 2)$, and $(-4, -2)$. Now $\Delta = 48y^2 - 64$, so $(0, 0)$ is not an extremum. The other two critical points yield local maxima for f.

20. Both partials are zero when $6(x - 2)(x + 1) = 0 = 3(y^2 - 1)$; $\Delta = 36y(2x - 1)$. Results: $(-1, 1)$ and $(2, -1)$ are not extrema, $(-1, -1)$ yields a local maximum, and $(2, 1)$ yields a local minimum.

22. Local (indeed, global) minimum at $(0, 0)$; no extremum at either of the other two critical points $(0, 1)$ and $(0, -1)$.

26. $-10t + 12s - 2 = 0 = 12t - 10s$ when $s = \frac{6}{11}$ and $t = \frac{5}{11}$. The theorem (Section 14.10) guarantees that f has a local minimum at that point. The two closest points are $\left(\frac{5}{11}, \frac{16}{11}, \frac{10}{11}\right)$ on the line parametrized by t and $\left(\frac{12}{11}, -\frac{5}{11}, \frac{17}{11}\right)$ on the line parametrized by s.

28. Classification of the critical points:

(x, y)	A	B	C	Δ	Classification	z
$(0, 0)$	$2e$	0	$4e$	$8e^2$	Local minimum	0
$(0, 1)$	-2	0	-8	16	Local maximum	2
$(0, -1)$	-2	0	-8	16	Local maximum	2
$(1, 0)$	-4	0	2	-8	Saddle point	1
$(-1, 0)$	-4	0	2	-8	Saddle point	1

The following diagram gives a geometric summary of the critical points of the function.

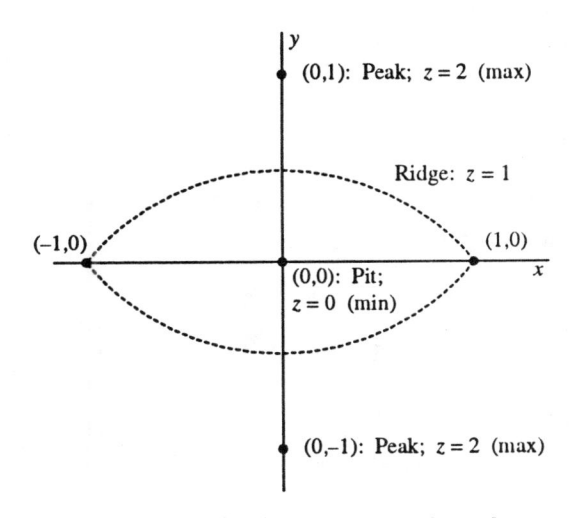

34. At the point with polar coordinates (r, θ), f takes on the value
$$\left(r^2 \sin \theta \cos \theta\right)\left(\cos^2 \theta - \sin^2 \theta\right) = \tfrac{1}{2} r^2 \sin 2\theta \cos 2\theta = \tfrac{1}{4} r^2 \sin 4\theta.$$

As you walk around the z-axis on this surface, the sine function gives you four high spots and four low spots, so the graph near the origin is another dog saddle.

36. Both partials are zero when $4x^3 + 8x - 16 = 0 = -2y$. We solve the first of these equations by Newton's method, obtaining the solution $x \approx 1.1795$. (There is no other solution because

Section 13.10 Second Derivative Test for Functions of Two Variables

$h(x) = 4x^3 + 8x - 16$ has a positive first derivative.) Thus the only critical point is close to $(1, 1895, 0)$. But $\Delta < 0$ for all (x, y) because $\Delta = -24x^2 - 16$. Hence the critical point we found does not yield an extremum; f has no extrema.

38. The only critical point is near $(1.1795, 1.1795)$. Because $\Delta = -96x^2 - 64$ is always negative, there are no extrema.

Chapter 13 Miscellaneous

1. Transform the problem into polar form. Then the limit is $\lim_{r \to 0} r^2 \sin\theta \cos\theta = 0$.

2. The spherical form of the expression is $\rho \left(\sin^3 \phi \cos^3 \theta + \sin^3 \phi \sin^3 \theta - \cos^3 \phi \right)$.

3. On the line $y = x$, g takes on the value $\frac{1}{2}$ (except at $x = 0$, where its value is zero). So as (x, y) approaches $(0, 0)$ along this line, $g(x, y)$ does not approach $g(0, 0)$. Therefore, by definition, g is not continuous at $(0, 0)$.

4. $g_x(0,0) = \lim_{h \to 0} \dfrac{g(h, 0) - g(0, 0)}{h} = \lim_{h \to 0} \dfrac{1}{h} \left(\dfrac{(h)(0)}{h^2 + 0^2} - 0 \right) = 0.$

6. If so, then $12xy = f_{xy}(x, y)$ would equal $f_{yx}(x, y) = 16xy$.

7. The paraboloid is a level surface of $f(x, y, z) = x^2 + y^2 - z$ with gradient $\langle 2a, 2b, -1 \rangle$ at the point $(a, b, a^2 + b^2)$. The normal line through that point thus has parametric equations

$$x = 2at + a, \quad y = 2bt + b, \quad z = a^2 + b^2 - t.$$

Set $x = 0 = y$ and $z = 1$, solve the last equation for t, and substitute in the other two to find

$$2a(a^2 + b^2) - a = 0 = 2b(a^2 + b^2) - b.$$

It then follows that $a^2 + b^2 = \frac{1}{2}$ or $a = 0 = b$.

8. $z = 0$.

10. You should obtain $u_{xx} = \dfrac{4\pi^2}{(4\pi kt)^{5/2}} \left(x^2 - 2kt \right) e^{-x^2/4kt}$.

12. $f_x(0, 0) = 0$, $f_y(0, 0) = 0$; $f_{xx}(0, 0) = 0$ and $f_{yy}(0, 0) = 0$. But $f_{xy}(0, 0) = -1 \neq 1 = f_{yx}(x, y)$.

14. Let the base of the box have dimensions x by y; let z denote the height of the box. We are to maximize its volume $V = xyz$ given that its total surface area satisfies the equation $A = xy + 2yz + 2xz = 300$. The Lagrange multiplier method leads to

$$\langle yz, xz, xy \rangle = \lambda \langle y + 2z, x + 2z, 2x + 2y \rangle.$$

It turns out that $x = 2z = y$, so that $x = 10$, $y = 10$, and (height) $z = 5$ are the dimensions of the box of maximal volume.

16. First find the equation of the tangent plane. Let (a, b, c) be the point of tangency; note that $abc = 1$. Let $F(x, y, z) = xyz - 1$; then $\nabla F = \langle yz, xz, xy \rangle$, so that a normal to the plane is

$$\nabla F(a, b, c) = \langle bc, ac, ab \rangle,$$

and the plane therefore has equation $bc(x - a) + ac(y - b) + ab(z - c) = 0$; that is, $bcx + acy + abz = 3$. Its intercepts are $x_0 = \dfrac{3}{bc}$, $y_0 = \dfrac{3}{ac}$, and $z_0 = \dfrac{3}{ab}$. By the formula $V = \frac{1}{3}hB$, its volume is $\frac{9}{2}$.

18. You should find that

$$V_p = \dfrac{V^3(V - b)}{aV - 2ab - pV^3} \quad \text{and that} \quad V_T = \dfrac{(82.06) V^3}{pV^3 - aV + 2ab}.$$

Now $\Delta V \approx dV = V_T \Delta T + V_p \Delta p$. We take $\Delta p = 0.1$, $p = 1$, $T = 313$, $\Delta T = -10$, $a = 3,590,000$, $b = 42.7$, and $V = 25,600$. We find that $\Delta V \approx -3394.86$ cm^3. (The true value is approximately -3098.264 cm^3.)

20. First sphere: S_1 is the level surface $f(x, y, z) = x^2 + y^2 + z^2 - a^2 = 0$.

    Second sphere: S_2 is the level surface $g(x, y, z) = (x - c)^2 + y^2 + z^2 - b^2 = 0$.

    Set $z = 0$ to obtain the intersection of the two spheres with the xy-plane. The resulting two circles meet at two points, one of which (P, say) has coordinates

    $$x = \frac{a^2 - b^2 + c^2}{2c}, \quad y = \sqrt{a^2 - x^2}, \quad z = 0.$$

    Now $\nabla f = \langle 2x, 2y, 2z \rangle$ is normal to S_1 at P and $\nabla g = \langle 2(x - c), 2y, 2z \rangle$ is normal to S_2 at P. Because the angle θ between the two planes is the same as the angle between ∇f and ∇g, we find that

    $$\cos \theta = \frac{(\nabla f) \cdot (\nabla g)}{|\nabla f| |\nabla g|} = \frac{a^2 - cx}{ab} = \frac{a^2 + b^2 - c^2}{2ab}.$$

22. Write $w = w(u, v) = \int_u^v f(t)\, dt$ where $u = g(x)$, $v = h(x)$. Then $F(x) = w(u(x), v(x))$. Consequently $F'(x) = w_u u_x + w_v v_x = -f(u) g'(x) + f(v) h'(x) = f(h(x)) h'(x) - f(g(x)) g'(x)$.

25. $z = 500 - (0.003) x^2 - (0.004) y^2$. $\nabla z = \langle -(0.006) x, -(0.008) y \rangle$. $\nabla z |_{(-100, -100)} = \langle \frac{3}{5}, \frac{4}{5} \rangle$. So in order to maintain a constant altitude, you should move in the direction of either $\langle -4, 3 \rangle$ or $\langle 4, -3 \rangle$.

26. First, $\nabla f = -2kf(x, y) \langle x, 2y \rangle$. The shark's path: $\mathbf{r} = \mathbf{r}(t) = \langle x(t), y(t) \rangle$. The shark's direction: $\mathbf{v} = d\mathbf{r}/dt = \langle dx/dt, dy/dt \rangle$. That $\mathbf{v}$ is parallel to ∇f implies that $\langle dx/dt, dy/dt \rangle$ is also parallel to $\langle x, 2y \rangle$. Therefore

    $$\langle dx/dt, dy/dt \rangle = s \langle x, 2y \rangle$$

    for some scalar s. Consequently

    $$s = \frac{1}{x} \cdot \frac{dx}{dt} = \frac{1}{2y} \cdot \frac{dy}{dt}.$$

    Now forget s and solve the differential equation:

    $$C + \ln x = \tfrac{1}{2} \ln y;$$
    $$\ln y = 2 \ln x + 2C$$
    $$y = cx^2 : \text{ a parabola.}$$

28. $(0, b)$, $(0, -b)$, $(a, 0)$, $(-a, 0)$.

29. Note that $f_x(0, y) = -y$ and that $f_y(x, 0) = x$; moreover, $f(x, 2x) = -\frac{6}{5} x^2$ while $f(2x, x) = \frac{6}{5} x^2$. Therefore the origin is not an extreme point.

30. We minimize $f(x, y, z) = x^2 + y^2 + z^2$ given $xy + 1 - z = 0$. The Lagrange multiplier method leads to $\langle 2x, 2y, 2z \rangle = \lambda \langle y, x, -1 \rangle$. Then it turns out that the closest point is $(0, 0, 1)$.

32. Maximize $f(x, y, z) = (x - 1)^2 + y^2 + z^2$ given the condition $g(x, y, z) = x^2 + y^2 + z^2 - 1 = 0$. The Lagrange multiplier technique yields

    $$\langle 2(x - 1), 2y, 2z \rangle = \lambda \langle 2x, 2y, 2z \rangle.$$

    We find that $y = 0 = z$ and that either $x = 1$ or $x = -1$. Therefore the longest chord with one endpoint at $(1, 0, 0)$ has its other endpoint at $(-1, 0, 0)$ and so its length is 2.

34. See the diagram below.

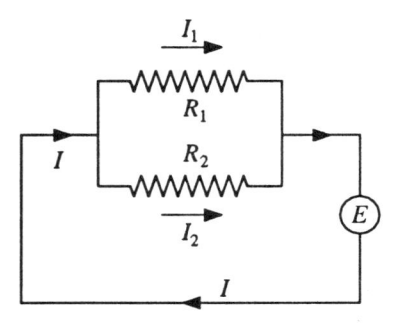

Let $x = I_1$ and $y = I_2$. Minimize $f(x,y) = R_1 x^2 + R_2 y^2$ given the constraint $g(x,y) = x+y-I = 0$ (I, R_1, and R_2 are all constants). The Lagrange multiplier method gives the vector equation $\langle 2R_1 x, 2R_2 y \rangle = \lambda \langle 1, 1 \rangle$. It follows without any difficulty that

$$I_1 = x = \frac{R_2 I}{R_1 + R_2} \quad \text{and} \quad I_2 = y = \frac{R_1 I}{R_1 + R_2}.$$

The resistance R of the parallel circuit satisfies the equation $E = IR$, but $E = R_1 I_1 = R_2 I_2$, so

$$IR = \frac{R_1 R_2 I}{R_1 + R_2};$$
$$R = \frac{R_1 R_2}{R_2 + R_2};$$
$$\frac{1}{R} = \frac{R_1 + R_2}{R_1 R_2} = \frac{1}{R_1} + \frac{1}{R_2}.$$

36. (a) Maximize $f(x,y,z) = x+y+z$ given the constraint $g(x,y,z) = x^2 + y^2 + z^2 - a^2 = 0$. The Lagrange multiplier method yields $\langle 1,1,1 \rangle = \lambda \langle 2x, 2y, 2z \rangle$. Now $\lambda \neq 0$, so $x = y = z$; it follows that f is maximized at the point $x = y = z = \frac{1}{3} a \sqrt{3}$ and that its maximum value is $a\sqrt{3}$.

(b) It follows that $|x+y+z| \leq a\sqrt{3}$ for every point (x,y,z) on the sphere. Therefore it follows that $(x+y+z)^2 \leq 3a^2 = 3(x^2 + y^2 + z^2)$ for all (x,y,z) on the sphere. Because a is arbitrary, and because every point (x,y,z) lies on some sphere, we may conclude that

$$(x+y+z)^2 \leq 3(x^2 + y^2 + z^2)$$

for any three real numbers x, y, and z.

38. First, $\left(\frac{1}{2}, \frac{5}{6}\right)$ is a local maximum of f if f is restricted to the hypotenuse of the triangle. But examination of the behavior of f on the vertical line $x = \frac{1}{2}$ establishes that $\left(\frac{1}{2}, \frac{5}{6}\right)$ is not an extremum of f proper. Results: There is a global maximum value 0 at $(0,0)$, a global minimum value -3 at $(3,0)$, and no other extrema. You could describe $\left(\frac{1}{2}, \frac{5}{6}\right)$ as a "half-saddle."

40. We seek the extrema of $f(x,y) = x^2 y^2$ given the constraint $g(x,y) = x^2 + 4y^2 - 24 = 0$. The Lagrange multiplier method gives the following results: The maximum value 36 of f occurs at the four points $(2\sqrt{3}, \sqrt{3})$, $(-2\sqrt{3}, \sqrt{3})$, $(2\sqrt{3}, -\sqrt{3})$, and $(-2\sqrt{3}, -\sqrt{3})$. The minimum value 0 of f occurs at the four points $(2\sqrt{6}, 0)$, $(-2\sqrt{6}, 0)$, $(0, \sqrt{6})$, and $(0, -\sqrt{6})$.

42. Global minimum at $(4, -2)$; no other extrema and no saddle points.

44. No extrema; some sort of saddle point at $(1, -1)$ and at $(-1, 1)$.

46. Global minimum -2 at $(1, -2)$ and at $(-1, -2)$; saddle point at $(0, -2)$.

48. Local minimum at $(0,0)$, local maximum at $\left(-\frac{2}{3}, \frac{2}{3}\right)$, saddle points at $\left(-\frac{2}{3}, 0\right)$ and $\left(0, \frac{2}{3}\right)$. No global extrema.

50. Global minimum value 0 at $(0,0)$, global maximum value $2/e$ at $(1,0)$ and at $(-1,0)$. Saddle points at $(0,1)$ and at $(0,-1)$.

Chapter 14: Multiple Integrals
Section 14.1

1. (a) $f(1,-2) \cdot 1 + f(2,-2) \cdot 1 + f(1,-1) \cdot 1 + f(2,-1) \cdot 1 + f(1,0) \cdot 1 + f(2,0) \cdot 1 = 198$
   (b) $f(2,-1) \cdot 1 + f(3,-1) \cdot 1 + f(2,0) \cdot 1 + f(3,0) \cdot 1 + f(2,1) \cdot 1 + f(3,1) \cdot 1 = 480$
2. (a) $f(1,-1) \cdot 1 + f(2,-1) \cdot 1 + f(1,0) \cdot 1 + f(2,0) \cdot 1 + f(1,1) \cdot 1 + f(2,1) \cdot 1 = 144$
   (b) $f(2,-2) \cdot 1 + f(3,-2) \cdot 1 + f(2,-1) \cdot 1 + f(3,-1) \cdot 1 + f(2,0) \cdot 1 + f(3,0) \cdot 1 = 570$
3. $f\left(\frac{1}{2},\frac{1}{2}\right) + f\left(\frac{3}{2},\frac{1}{2}\right) + f\left(\frac{3}{2},\frac{1}{2}\right) + f\left(\frac{3}{2},\frac{3}{2}\right) = 8$
4. $f\left(\frac{1}{2},\frac{1}{2}\right) + f\left(\frac{3}{2},\frac{1}{2}\right) + f\left(\frac{3}{2},\frac{1}{2}\right) + f\left(\frac{3}{2},\frac{3}{2}\right) = 4$
5. $f(2,-1) \cdot 2 + f(4,-1) \cdot 2 + f(2,0) \cdot 2 + f(4,0) \cdot 2 = 88$
6. $f(1,1) + f(2,1) + f(1,2) + f(2,2) + f(1,3) + f(2,3) = 43$
7. $\frac{1}{4}\pi^2 \left[f\left(\frac{1}{4}\pi,\frac{1}{4}\pi\right) + f\left(\frac{3}{4}\pi,\frac{1}{4}\pi\right) + f\left(\frac{1}{4}\pi,\frac{3}{4}\pi\right) + f\left(\frac{3}{4}\pi,\frac{3}{4}\pi\right) \right] = \frac{1}{2}\pi^2$
8. $\frac{1}{6}\pi \left[f\left(\frac{1}{4},\frac{1}{6}\pi\right) + f\left(\frac{3}{4},\frac{1}{6}\pi\right) + f\left(\frac{1}{4},\frac{1}{2}\pi\right) + f\left(\frac{3}{4},\frac{1}{2}\pi\right) + f\left(\frac{1}{4},\frac{5}{6}\pi\right) + f\left(\frac{3}{4},\frac{5}{6}\pi\right) \right] = \frac{1}{2}\pi$
9. f is increasing in the positive x-direction and the positive y-direction, and therefore $L \leq M \leq U$.
10. f is decreasing in the positive x-direction and the positive y-direction, and therefore $u \leq M \leq L$.
11. $\int_0^2 \int_0^4 (3x + 4y)\, dx\, dy = \int_0^2 (24 + 16y)\, dy = 80.$
12. $\int_0^3 \int_0^2 x^2 y\, dx\, dy = \int_0^3 \frac{8}{3} y\, dy = 12.$
14. $\int_{-2}^1 \int_2^4 x^2 y^3\, dy\, dx = \int_{-2}^1 (64x^2 - 4x^2)\, dx = 180.$
16. $\int_0^2 \left(\frac{56}{3} y^2 - 34\right) dy = -\frac{164}{9}.$
18. $\int_1^3 \left(20x - 4x^3\right) dx = 0.$
20. $\int_0^{\pi/2} \cos x\, dx = 1.$
22. $\int_0^1 \frac{16}{3} e^y\, dy = \frac{16}{3}(e - 1).$
24. $\int_0^1 (e-1)\, e^y\, dy = (e-1)^2.$
26. $\int_0^{\pi/2} (y-1)\, dy = \frac{1}{8}\pi(\pi - 4).$
28. $\int_1^e \frac{1}{x}\, dx = 1.$
30. $\int_1^2 \left(x \ln 3 + \frac{4}{x}\right) dx = \frac{3}{2} \ln 3 + 4 \ln 2.$
31. $\int_{-1}^1 \int_{-2}^2 (2xy - 3y^2)\, dy\, dx = \int_{-1}^1 -16\, dx = -32.$ Other integral: $\int_{-2}^2 \int_{-1}^1 (2xy - 3y^2)\, dx\, dy.$
32. $\int_0^\pi \int_{-\pi/2}^{\pi/2} (\sin x \cos y)\, dy\, dx = \int_0^\pi 2 \sin x\, dx = 4.$
34. $\int_0^{\ln 2} \int_0^{\ln 3} e^x e^y\, dy\, dx = \int_0^{\ln 2} 2e^x\, dx = 2.$

35. $\int_0^1 \int_0^1 x^n y^n \, dx \, dy = \int_0^1 \frac{1}{n+1} y^n \, dy = \frac{1}{(n+1)^2} \to 0$ as $n \to +\infty$.

36. Note that whatever the choice of (x_i^*, y_i^*), $f(x_i^*, y_i^*) = c$, and hence $f(x_i^*, y_i^*) \Delta A_i$ is equal to the area of R_i for each i.

37. If $0 \leq x \leq \pi$ and $0 \leq y \leq \pi$, then $0 \leq f(x,y) \leq \sin \pi = 1$. Hence every Riemann sum lies between $0 \cdot \text{area}(R)$ and $1 \cdot \text{area}(R)$.

Section 14.2

1. $\int_0^1 \left[y + xy\right]_0^x dx = \int_0^1 (x + x^2) \, dx = \frac{5}{6}$.

2. $\int_0^2 (2x + 2x^2) \, dx = \frac{28}{3}$.

3. $\int_0^1 \left(\frac{1}{2} + y - \frac{3}{2}y^2\right) dy = \frac{1}{2}$.

4. $\int_0^2 \left[\frac{1}{2}x^2 + xy\right]_{y/2}^1 dy = \int_0^2 \left(\frac{1}{2} + y - \frac{5}{8}y^2\right) dy = \frac{4}{3}$.

6. $\frac{3}{20}$

7. $\int_0^1 \int_x^{\sqrt{x}} (2x - y) \, dy \, dx = \int_0^1 \left[2xy - \frac{1}{2}y^2\right]_x^{\sqrt{x}} dx = \int_0^1 \left(2x^{3/2} - \frac{1}{2}x - 2x^2 + \frac{1}{2}x^2\right) dx$
$= \left[\frac{4}{5}x^{5/2} - \frac{1}{4}x^2 - \frac{1}{2}x^3\right]_0^1 = \frac{1}{20}$.

8. $\frac{64}{5}$

10. 36

12. $\pi/4$

14. $2(e-1)$

15. $\int_{-2}^2 \int_{x^2}^4 xy \, dy \, dx = 0$.

16. $\int_{-\sqrt{6}}^{\sqrt{6}} \int_{-4}^{2-x^2} x^2 \, dy \, dx = \int_{-\sqrt{6}}^{\sqrt{6}} 6x^2 - x^4 \, dx = \frac{48}{5}\sqrt{6}$.

17. $\int_{-2}^2 \int_{x^2}^{8-x^2} x \, dy \, dx = \int_{-2}^2 (8x - 2x^3) \, dx = 0$.

18. $\int_{-1}^1 \int_{y^2-1}^{1-y^2} y \, dx \, dy = \int_{-1}^1 (2y - 2y^3) \, dy = 0$.

19. $\int_0^\pi \int_0^{\sin x} x \, dy \, dx = \int_0^\pi x \sin x \, dx = \left[\sin x - x \cos x\right]_0^\pi = \pi$.

20. $\int_{-\pi/2}^{\pi/2} \int_0^{\cos x} \sin x \, dy \, dx = \int_{-\pi/2}^{\pi/2} \sin x \cos x \, dx = \left[\frac{1}{2}\sin^2 x\right]_{-\pi/2}^{\pi/2} = 0$.

21. $\int_1^e \int_1^x \frac{1}{y} \, dy \, dx = \int_1^e \ln x \, dx = \left[x \ln x - x\right]_1^e = 1$.

22. $\int_0^1 \int_0^{\sqrt{1-x^2}} xy \, dy \, dx = \int_0^1 \frac{1}{2}x(1 - x^2) \, dx = \frac{1}{8}$.

23. $\int_0^1 \int_{-2y}^y (1 - x) \, dx \, dy = \int_0^1 \frac{1}{2}(3y^2 + y^3) \, dy = 2$.

24. $\int_0^3 \int_{2x}^{9-x} (9-y)\, dy\, dx = \int_0^3 \tfrac{1}{2}(81 - 36x + 3x^2)\, dx = 54.$

26. $\int_0^1 \int_y^{y^{1/4}} (x-1)\, dx\, dy = -\tfrac{2}{15}.$
The region is shown at the right.

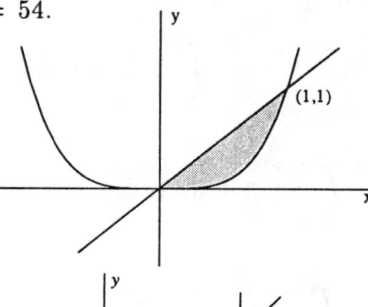

28. 0

30. $\dfrac{e-1}{2e}$

32. $\int_0^{\sqrt{\pi}} \int_0^x (\sin x^2)\, dy\, dx = 1.$
The region is shown at the right.

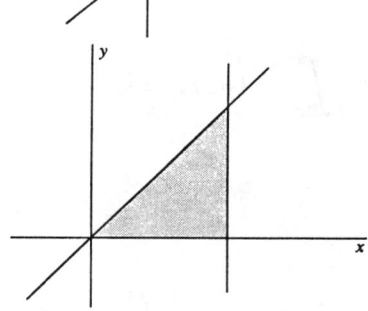

34. $\sqrt{2} - 1.$

35. The curves bound two bounded plane regions. The integral of the one on the left is approximately
$$\int_{-0.53209}^{0.65270} \int_{3x^2}^{x^3+1} x\, dy\, dx = 0.02767.$$
The integral of the region on the right is approximately
$$\int_{0.652704}^{2.87939} \int_{3x^2}^{x^3+1} x\, dy\, dx = 7.92408.$$

36. $\int_{-1.28378}^{1.53375} \int_{x^4}^{x+4} x\, dy\, dx \approx 1.89303.$

37. $\int_{-1.18921}^{1.18921} \int_{x^2-1}^{1/(1+x^2)} x\, dy\, dx = 0.$

38. $\int_{-1.75217}^{2} \int_{x^4-16}^{2x-x^2} x\, dy\, dx \approx 8.87135.$

39. $\int_{-0.824132}^{0.824132} \int_{x^2}^{\cos x} x\, dy\, dx = 0.$

40. $\int_0^{2.316934} \int_{x^2-2x}^{\sin x} x\, dy\, dx \approx 3.39454.$

41. Because $f(x,y) = x$ is symmetric around the y-axis, the value of the integral is zero.

42. It would be slightly simpler to evaluate
$$4 \int_0^1 \int_0^1 x^2\, dy\, dx = \tfrac{4}{3}.$$

43. Because $f(x,y) = xy$ is symmetric around the y-axis, the value of the integral is zero.

44. Because $f(x,y) = x^2 + y^2$ is symmetric around the coordinate axes, it would be somewhat simpler to evaluate
$$4 \int_0^1 \int_0^1 (x^2 + y^2)\, dx\, dy = \tfrac{8}{3}.$$

Section 14.3

1. The area is $A = \int_0^1 \int_{y^2}^{y} 1 \, dx \, dy = \frac{1}{6}$.

2. $\frac{3}{10}$

4. $A = \int_1^3 \int_{2x+3}^{6x-x^2} 1 \, dy \, dx = \frac{4}{3}$.

6. $\frac{2}{3}$

7. $A = \int_{-2}^2 \int_{2x^2-3}^{x^2+1} 1 \, dy \, dx = \frac{32}{3}$.

8. $\frac{64}{3}$

10. $\pi - \frac{2}{3}$

11. 2

12. 36

13. The volume is $V = \int_0^1 \int_0^2 (y + e^x) \, dy \, dx = \int_0^1 \left[\frac{1}{2}y^2 + ye^x\right]_0^2 dx$
$= \int_0^1 (2 + 2e^x) \, dx = \left[2x + 2e^x\right]_0^1 = 2 + 2e - 2 = 2e$.

14. $V = \int_0^\pi \int_0^\pi (3 + \cos x + \cos y) \, dy \, dx = \int_0^\pi \left[3y + y\cos x + \sin y\right]_0^\pi dx$
$= \int_0^\pi (3\pi + \pi \cos x) \, dx = \left[3\pi x + \pi \sin x\right]_0^\pi = 3\pi^2$.

16. $V = \int_0^2 \int_0^{4-2y} (3x + 2y) \, dx \, dy = \int_0^2 \left[\frac{3}{2}x^2 + 2xy\right]_0^{4-2y} dy = \int_0^2 (24 - 16y + 2y^2) \, dy = \frac{64}{3}$.

18. $V = \int_0^1 \int_0^{\sqrt{y}} (1 + x + y) \, dx \, dy = \frac{79}{60}$.

20. $V = \int_{-2}^2 \int_{y^2}^4 y^2 \, dx \, dy = \frac{128}{15}$.

22. $\frac{837}{70}$

23. 19

24. $\frac{1427}{420}$

26. $\frac{13}{70}$

27. $\int_0^2 \int_0^{6-3x} (6 - 3x - 2y) \, dy \, dx = \int_0^2 \left(9 - 9x + \frac{9}{4}x^2\right) dx = 6$.

28. $\int_0^2 \int_{y/2}^{(4-y)/2} (8 - 4x - 2y) \, dx \, dy = \int_0^2 (9 - 8y + 2y^2) \, dy = \frac{16}{3}$.

29. $\int_2^4 \int_1^{9-2y} xy \, dx \, dy = \int_2^4 (4 - y - 18y^2 + 2y^3) \, dy = 24$.

30. $\int_{-3}^5 \int_{(x-5)/2}^{(5-x)/2} (25 - x^2 - y^2) \, dy \, dx = \int_{-3}^5 \left(\frac{1375}{12} - \frac{75}{4}x - \frac{25}{4}x^2 + \frac{13}{12}x^3\right) dx = \frac{1792}{3}$.

31. $\int_{-1}^1 \int_{-\sqrt{1-x^2}}^{\sqrt{1-x^2}} (x + 1) \, dy \, dx = \int_{-1}^1 2(x+1)\sqrt{1-x^2} \, dx = \pi$.

32. $\int_{-3}^3 \int_{-\sqrt{9-x^2}}^{\sqrt{9-x^2}} (9 - x^2 - y^2) \, dy \, dx = \int_{-3}^3 \frac{4}{3}(9-x^2)^{3/2} \, dx = \frac{81}{2}\pi$.

33. $\int_{-1}^{1}\int_{-\sqrt{1-x^2}}^{\sqrt{1-x^2}} 2\sqrt{4-x^2-y^2}\,dy\,dx = \left(\frac{32}{3} - 4\sqrt{3}\right)\pi.$

34. $\int_{-1}^{1}\int_{-\sqrt{1-x^2}}^{\sqrt{1-x^2}} \left[\sqrt{2-x^2-y^2} - (x^2+y^2)\right] dy\,dx \approx 2.258652488356396218.$

37. The volume is $V = \int_{0}^{1}\int_{0}^{\sqrt{1-y^2}} \sqrt{1-y^2}\,dx\,dy.$

38. $\int_{0}^{\pi}\int_{-\sin x}^{\sin x} 2\sin x\,dy\,dx = 2\pi.$

40. $V = \frac{4}{3}\pi abc$

42. Region of integration: $x^2 + y^2 \le 4$. Volume: 24π.

44. Region of integration: $(x/2)^2 + y^2 \le 1$. Volume: 4π.

47. $\int_{-\pi/2}^{\pi/2}\int_{-\cos x}^{\cos x} (4-x^2-y^2)\,dy\,dx = \frac{208}{9} - \pi^2 \approx 13.241506710022.$

48. $\int_{-\pi/2}^{\pi/2}\int_{-\cos x}^{\cos x} \cos y\,dy\,dx = \int_{-\pi/2}^{\pi/2} 2\sin(\cos x)\,dx \approx 3.572974963900.$

Mathematica 3.0 reports that the exact answer is
$$4\ \mathtt{HypergeometricPFQ}\left[\{1\}, \left\{\frac{3}{2}, \frac{3}{2}\right\}, -\frac{1}{4}\right].$$

Section 14.4

1. $A = \int_{0}^{2\pi}\int_{0}^{1} r\,dr\,d\theta.$

2. $\frac{9}{4}\pi$

4. $A = \int_{-\pi/4}^{\pi/4}\int_{0}^{2\cos 2\theta} r\,dr\,d\theta = \pi/2.$

6. $4 + \dfrac{\pi}{4}$

7. $A = 2\int_{\pi/6}^{\pi/2}\int_{0}^{1-2\sin\theta} r\,dr\,d\theta.$

8. $\frac{81}{2}\pi$

10. $\frac{3}{2}\pi$

12. $\frac{1}{2}\pi a^4$

13. $\int_{0}^{\pi/2}\int_{0}^{1} \dfrac{r}{1+r^2}\,dr\,d\theta$

14. $\frac{1}{2}\pi(2-\sqrt{3}) \approx 0.4208936$

16. $\int_{\pi/4}^{\pi/2}\int_{0}^{\csc\theta} r^3\cos^2\theta\,dr\,d\theta = \frac{1}{12}.$

18. $2\sqrt{2} + 2\ln(\sqrt{2}-1) \approx 1.06568$

19. The volume is $V = \int_{0}^{2\pi}\int_{0}^{1} (2 + r\cos\theta + r\sin\theta)\,r\,dr\,d\theta = \int_{0}^{2\pi}\left[r^2 + \frac{1}{3}r^3\cos\theta + \frac{1}{3}r^3\sin\theta\right]_{0}^{1}d\theta$
$= \int_{0}^{2\pi} \left(1 + \frac{1}{3}\cos\theta + \frac{1}{3}\sin\theta\right)d\theta = \left[\theta + \frac{1}{3}\sin\theta - \frac{1}{3}\cos\theta\right]_{0}^{2\pi} = 2\pi.$

20. $V = \int_0^{2\pi} \int_0^2 (2 + r\cos\theta) \, r \, dr \, d\theta = 8\pi$.

21. Note that the correct limits of integration on θ are 0 and π (*not* 0 and 2π).

22. $V = \int_0^{2\pi} \int_0^{1+\cos\theta} (1 + r\cos\theta) \, r \, dr \, d\theta = \frac{1}{6} \int_0^{2\pi} (3 + 9\cos^2\theta + 2\cos^4\theta) \, d\theta = \frac{11}{4}\pi$.

24. $V = 3 \int_0^{2\pi} \int_0^2 r(4 - r^2) \, dr \, d\theta = 24\pi$.

26. $V = 2 \int_0^{\pi/2} \int_0^2 r^2 \cos\theta \, dr \, d\theta = \frac{16}{3}$.

28. Domain of integration: the disk $x^2 + y^2 \leq 1$. $V = \int_0^{2\pi} \int_0^1 r(1 - r^2) \, dr \, d\theta = \frac{1}{2}\pi$.

29. $V = \int_0^{2\pi} \int_0^{a/\sqrt{2}} \left(\sqrt{a^2 - r^2} - r\right) r \, dr \, d\theta$.

30. $V = \int_0^{\pi} \int_0^{2a \sin\theta} r^3 \, dr \, d\theta = \frac{3}{2}\pi a^4$.

31. $V = \int_0^{\pi/2} \int_0^{\sqrt{2 \sin 2\theta}} r^3 \, dr \, d\theta$.

32. $V = \int_0^{2\pi} \int_0^2 2r\sqrt{18 - 2r^2} \, dr \, d\theta = \frac{2}{3}\pi \left(54\sqrt{2} - 10\sqrt{10}\right) \approx 93.7131973$.

34. The polar form of the integral is $\int_0^{\pi/2} \int_0^{\infty} \frac{r}{(1+r^2)^2} \, dr \, d\theta$.

36. $\int_0^{2\pi} \int_0^3 (18 - 2r^2) \, r \, dr \, d\theta = 81\pi$.

37. $\int_0^{2\pi} \int_0^2 (4 - r^2) \, r \, dr \, d\theta = 8\pi$.

38. $\int_0^{2\pi} \int_0^2 (r\cos\theta + r\sin\theta + 3) \, r \, dr \, d\theta = 12\pi$.

39. $\int_0^{2\pi} \int_0^2 (12 - 3r^2) \, r \, dr \, d\theta = 24\pi$.

40. $\int_0^{2\pi} \int_0^2 \left(2\sqrt{20 - r^2} - 2r^2\right) r \, dr \, d\theta = \int_0^{2\pi} \left[-\frac{1}{4}r^2 - \frac{2}{3}(20 - r^2)^{3/2}\right]_0^2 d\theta$

$= \int_0^{2\pi} \frac{80\sqrt{5} - 152}{3} \, d\theta = \frac{2}{3}\pi \left(80\sqrt{5} - 152\right) \approx 56.308730092$.

Section 14.5

2. $(2, 3)$

4. $M_y = \int_0^3 x(3 - x) \, dx = \frac{9}{2}$.

   The area of the region is the same, so $\bar{x} = 1$. By symmetry, $\bar{y} = 1$ as well. Answer: $(1, 1)$.

6. $M = 1$, $M_x = \frac{1}{2} \int_0^1 x^2 \, dx + \frac{1}{2} \int_1^2 (2 - x)^2 \, dx = \frac{1}{2} \left[\frac{1}{3}x^3\right]_0^1 + \frac{1}{2} \left[-\frac{1}{3}(2 - x)^3\right]_1^2 = \frac{1}{3}$.

   Hence $\bar{y} = \frac{1}{3}$. By symmetry, $\bar{x} = 1$.

8. By symmetry, $\bar{x} = 0$. $M_x = \frac{1}{2}\int_{-3}^{3}\left(9^2 - (x^2)^2\right)dx = \frac{972}{5}$. The area of the region is 36, so $\bar{y} = \frac{27}{5}$.

10. By symmetry, $\bar{x} = 0$. $M_x = \frac{1}{2}\int_{-2}^{2}(x^2+1)^2 dx = \frac{206}{15}$. The area of the region is $\frac{28}{3}$, so $\bar{y} = \frac{103}{70}$.

11. $M = \int_0^1\int_0^{1-x} xy\,dy\,dx = \frac{1}{24}$, $M_y = \int_0^1\int_0^{1-x} x^2 y\,dy\,dx = \frac{1}{60}$.
    Therefore $\bar{x} = \frac{2}{5}$; $\bar{y} = \frac{2}{5}$ by symmetry.

12. $M = \frac{1}{12}$, $M_y = \frac{1}{20}$, $M_x = \frac{1}{60}$.

14. $M = \int_{-3}^{3}\int_0^{9-y^2} x^2\,dx\,dy = \frac{23328}{35}$, $M_y = \int_{-3}^{3}\int_0^{9-y^2} x^3\,dx\,dy = \frac{139968}{35}$.
    So $\bar{x} = 6$; $\bar{y} = 0$ by symmetry.

16. $M = \int_0^1\int_{x^2}^{\sqrt{x}}(x^2+y^2)\,dy\,dx = \frac{6}{35}$, $M_y = \int_0^1\int_{x^2}^{\sqrt{x}}(x^3+xy^2)\,dy\,dx = \frac{55}{504}$.
    Hence $\bar{x} = \frac{275}{432}$. By symmetry, $\bar{y} = \bar{x}$.

18. $M = \int_1^e\int_0^{\ln x} x\,dy\,dx = \frac{e^2+1}{4}$.
    $M_y = \int_1^e\int_0^{\ln x} x^2\,dy\,dx = \frac{2e^3+1}{9}$, $M_x = \int_1^e\int_0^{\ln x} xy\,dy\,dx = \frac{e^2-1}{8}$.

20. $M = 2\int_0^1\int_0^{e^{-x^2}} xy\,dy\,dx = \frac{e^2-1}{4e^2}$. $M_x = 2\int_0^1\int_0^{e^{-x^2}} xy^2\,dy\,dx = \frac{e^3-1}{9e^3}$.
    Hence $\bar{y} = \frac{4(e^2+e+1)}{9e(e+1)}$. By symmetry, $\bar{x} = 0$.

21. $M = a^3$, $M_y = M_x = \frac{7}{12}a^4$.

22. We assume that $a > 0$. Then
    $$M = \int_0^a\int_0^{a-x}(x^2+y^2)\,dy\,dx = \frac{1}{6}a^4, \quad M_x = \int_0^a\int_0^{a-x}(x^2 y + y^3)\,dy\,dx = \frac{1}{15}a^5.$$
    Because of the symmetry of x, y, and density in the region, it follows that $M_y = M_x$. Therefore $\bar{x} = \frac{2}{5}a = \bar{y}$.

24. $M = \int_{-1}^{3}\int_{x^2}^{2x+3} x^2\,dy\,dx = \frac{96}{5}$, $M_x = \frac{3616}{35}$, $M_y = \frac{544}{15}$, $\bar{x} = \frac{17}{9}$, $\bar{y} = \frac{113}{21}$.

26. $M = \frac{2}{3}a^3$, $M_x = \frac{1}{8}\pi a^4$, $M_y = 0$; $\bar{x} = 0$, $\bar{y} = \frac{3}{16}\pi a$.

28. $M = \frac{5}{3}\pi$, $M_x = 0$, $M_y = \frac{7}{4}\pi$, $\bar{x} = \frac{21}{20}$, $\bar{y} = 0$.

30. $M = 2\int_0^{\pi/3}\int_2^{1+2\cos\theta} r^2\,dr\,d\theta = \frac{1}{9}\left(45\sqrt{3} - 2\pi\right)$.
    $M_x = 0$ because of symmetry around the x-axis. $M_y = \frac{1}{60}(160\pi + 327\sqrt{3}) \approx 17.81725732$.
    So $M \approx 7.962122$, $\bar{y} = 0$, and $\bar{x} = \frac{981\sqrt{3} + 480\pi}{900\sqrt{3} - 120\pi} \approx 2.713622$.

32. $I_0 = \frac{2}{5}a^5$.

33. $I_0 = \int_{-\pi/2}^{\pi/2}\int_0^{2\cos\theta} kr^3\,dr\,d\theta = \frac{3}{2}k\pi$.

34. $\sqrt{3} + \frac{4}{3}\pi \approx 5.90841$.

36. $I_x = \int_0^a\int_0^a (y^2)(x+y)\,dy\,dx = \frac{5}{12}a^5$.

Section 14.5 Applications of Double Integrals

$M = a^3$ as in Problem 11. Therefore $\hat{y} = \sqrt{\dfrac{I_x}{M}} = \dfrac{a}{6}\sqrt{15}$, about $(0.6455)a$.

By symmetry of the lamina and its density in x and y, $\hat{x} = \hat{y}$.

38. We found $M = \dfrac{96}{5}$ in Problem 14. $I_x = \dfrac{84256}{135} \approx 624.12$ and $I_y = \dfrac{8032}{105} \approx 76.495$. Therefore $\hat{x} = \sqrt{251/63} \approx 1.996$ and $\hat{y} = \sqrt{2633/81} \approx 5.701$.

40. $M = k\pi$ by inspection. With the aid of Formula 113 from the endpapers of the text, $I_y = \dfrac{5}{4}k\pi$ and $I_x = \dfrac{1}{4}k\pi$. Therefore $\hat{x} = \dfrac{1}{2}\sqrt{5}$ and $\hat{y} = \dfrac{1}{2}$.

41. $M_y = \displaystyle\int_0^r x\sqrt{r^2-x^2}\,dx = \dfrac{1}{3}r^3$. $A = \dfrac{1}{4}\pi r^2$, and so $\bar{x} = \dfrac{4r}{3\pi}$. By symmetry $\bar{y} = \bar{x}$, so the centroid is located at the point $\left(\dfrac{4r}{3\pi}, \dfrac{4r}{3\pi}\right)$.

42. By Pappus' first theorem, $\left(\dfrac{1}{4}\pi r^2\right)(2\pi x) = \dfrac{2}{3}\pi r^3$. Therefore $\bar{x} = \dfrac{r^3/3}{\pi r^2/4} = \dfrac{4r}{3\pi}$.

By repeating the argument with x replaced by y, or by symmetry, $\bar{y} = \bar{x}$.

43. Because $y = \sqrt{r^2-x^2}$, $1 + \left(\dfrac{dy}{dx}\right)^2 = \dfrac{r^2}{r^2-x^2}$. So $M_y = \displaystyle\int_0^r x\dfrac{r}{\sqrt{r^2-x^2}}\,dx = r^2$. The length of the quarter-circle is $\dfrac{1}{2}\pi r$, so $\bar{x} = 2r/\pi$. By symmetry, $\bar{y} = \bar{x}$.

44. By Pappus's second theorem, $\left(\dfrac{1}{2}\pi r\right)(2\pi x) = 2\pi r^2$, so—with the aid of symmetry—$\bar{x} = \dfrac{2r}{\pi} = \bar{y}$.

45. $M_y = \displaystyle\int_0^r x\left(h - \dfrac{hx}{r}\right)dx = \dfrac{1}{6}hr^2$. $A = \dfrac{1}{2}rh$, and therefore $\bar{x} = \dfrac{1}{3}r$. By interchanging the roles of x and y, we find that $\bar{y} = \bar{x}$.

Next, the midpoint of the hypotenuse is $(r/2, h/2)$, and its slope is $-h/r$. The line from $(0,0)$ to that midpoint has equation $y = \dfrac{h}{r}x$.

If $x = r/3$, then $y = h/3$, so $(r/3, h/3)$ is on this line. The distance from $(0,0)$ to $(r/3, h/3)$ is $D_1 = \dfrac{1}{3}\sqrt{r^2+h^2}$; the distance from $(0,0)$ to $(r/2, h/2)$ is $D_2 = \dfrac{1}{2}\sqrt{r^2+h^2}$. Therefore $D_1/D_2 = 2/3$, as was to be proved.

46. $V = \left(2\pi\dfrac{r}{3}\right)\left(\dfrac{1}{2}rh\right) = \dfrac{1}{3}\pi r^2 h$.

47. $A = \left(2\dfrac{\pi r}{2}\right)\sqrt{r^2+h^2} = \pi r\sqrt{r^2+h^2} = \pi r L$.

48. (a) Notational change: Write r for r_1 and s for r_2. Then the slanted side of the triangle has equations $y = \dfrac{h}{s-r}(x-r)$ and $x = r + \dfrac{s-r}{h}y$. Hence $M_y = \displaystyle\int_0^s hx\,dx + \int_s^r \dfrac{h}{s-r}x(x-r)\,dx$, and the value of the integral—after tricky simplifications—is $M_y = \dfrac{1}{6}h\left(r^2+rs+s^2\right)$.

Next, $M_x = \displaystyle\int_0^h y\left(r + \dfrac{s-r}{h}y\right)dy = \dfrac{1}{6}h^2(r+2s)$.

The area of the trapezoid is $A = sh + \dfrac{1}{2}h(r-s) = \dfrac{1}{2}h(r+s)$, so we finally find that

$$\bar{x} = \dfrac{r^2+rs+s^2}{3(r+s)}, \qquad \bar{y} = \dfrac{h(r+2s)}{3(r+s)}.$$

(b) By Pappus's first theorem, $V = 2\pi\bar{x}A = 2\pi M_y = \dfrac{1}{3}\pi h\left(r^2+rs+s^2\right)$.

49. With the same notational change as in the solution to Problem 48, the radius of revolution is $\dfrac{1}{2}(r+s)$, so the lateral area is $A = 2\pi\left(\dfrac{r+s}{2}\right)\sqrt{(s-r)^2+h^2} = \pi(r+s)L$.

50. The lateral surface is generated by revolving around the axis of the cylinder a vertical line of length h. Its midpoint is at $(r, h/2)$ and the radius of the circle through which the midpoint moves is r, so the lateral surface area is $A = (2\pi r)h$.

440   Section 14.5 Applications of Double Integrals

Alternatively, from Problem 49, $A = \pi(r_1 + r_2)L = \pi(2r)h$.

51. The semicircular region has centroid (x,y) where $x = 0$ by symmetry and (by work we've done earlier) $y = b + \dfrac{4a}{3\pi}$, so, for the semicircular region, $M_x = \left(b + \dfrac{4a}{3\pi}\right)\left(\tfrac{1}{2}\pi a^2\right)$.

For the rectangle, we have $M_x = \tfrac{1}{2}b(2ab) = ab^2$.

The sum of these two moments is the moment of the entire region: $M_x = \tfrac{2}{3}a^3 + \tfrac{1}{2}\pi a^2 b + ab^2$.

When we divide this moment by the area $2ab + \tfrac{1}{2}\pi a^2$ of the entire region, we find that

$$\bar{y} = \frac{4a^2 + 3\pi ab + 6b^2}{12b + 3\pi a}.$$

Of course $\bar{x} = 0$ by symmetry.

For Part (b), we use the fact that the radius of revolution is $\bar{y}$, so the volume generated by rotation about the x-axis is

$$V = 2\pi\bar{y}A = 2\pi\bar{y}\left(2ab + \tfrac{1}{2}\pi a^2\right) = \pi\bar{y}\left(4ab + \pi a^2\right) = a\bar{y}(4b + \pi a) = \tfrac{1}{3}a\bar{y}(12b + 3\pi a);$$

that is, $V = \tfrac{1}{3}\pi a\left(4a^2 + 3\pi ab + 6b^2\right)$.

52. (a) $A = \displaystyle\int_0^h \sqrt{2py}\, dy = \tfrac{2}{3}h^{3/2}\sqrt{2p}$. Now $r^2 = 2ph$, so $A = \tfrac{2}{3}h\sqrt{2ph} = \tfrac{2}{3}rh$.

$M_y = \displaystyle\int_0^h \tfrac{1}{2}(2py)\, dy = \tfrac{1}{2}ph^2$, so $\bar{x} = \dfrac{ph^2/2}{2rh/3} = \dfrac{3ph}{4r}$. But $ph = \tfrac{1}{2}r^2$, so $\bar{x} = \tfrac{3}{8}r$.

(b) $V = 2\pi\bar{x}A = 2\pi M_y = \pi ph^2$. But $ph = \tfrac{1}{2}r^2$, so $V = \tfrac{1}{2}\pi r^2 h$.

53. $A = \displaystyle\int_0^\infty e^{-x}\, dx = 1$, $M_y = \displaystyle\int_0^\infty xe^{-x}\, dx = 1$, $M_x = \tfrac{1}{2}\displaystyle\int_0^\infty e^{-2x}\, dx = \tfrac{1}{4}$.

56. Let k denote the (constant) density of the racquet. It is easy to show that the area of the racquet is $A = \tfrac{1}{2}$, so that its mass is $M = \tfrac{1}{2}k$. In the computation of

$$I_y = 2\int_0^{\pi/4}\int_0^{\sqrt{\cos 2\theta}} kr(1 + r\cos\theta)^2\, dr\, d\theta,$$

we integrate, substitute, and are then confronted with three integrals:

$$J_1 = \int_0^{\pi/4} \tfrac{1}{4}\cos 2\theta\, d\theta = \tfrac{1}{4};$$

no difficulty here. The second of the three (which arises from the third term the way most people work the problem) is somewhat more challenging:

$$J_2 = \int_0^{\pi/4} \tfrac{1}{4}(\cos 2\theta)^2(\cos\theta)^2\, d\theta = \frac{3\pi + 8}{192}.$$

The real challenge is

$$J_3 = \int_0^{\pi/4} \tfrac{2}{3}(\cos 2\theta)^{2/3}(\cos\theta)\, d\theta.$$

Replace $\cos 2\theta$ by $1 - 2\sin^2\theta$. Then let $u = \sin^{-1}\left(\sqrt{2}\sin^2\theta\right)$. This unlikely substitution transforms the integral in question into

$$J_3 = \int_0^{\pi/2} \tfrac{1}{12}\sqrt{2}(1 + \cos 2u)^2\, du = \frac{\pi}{16}\sqrt{2}.$$

After the tedious arithmetic involved in assembling all this information, we find that
$$I_y = \frac{k}{96}\left(56 + 3\pi\left(1 + 4\sqrt{2}\right)\right).$$

Therefore $x = \frac{1}{4}\left(\pi\left(1 + 4\sqrt{2}\right) + (56/3)\right)^{1/2}$. That is, x is approximately 1.572811795.

57. Mass:
$$M = \int_0^\pi \int_0^{2\sin\theta} r^2 \sin\theta \, dr \, d\theta = \int_0^\pi \tfrac{8}{3}\sin^4\theta \, d\theta = \pi;$$
$$M_y = \int_0^\pi \int_0^{2\sin\theta} r^3 \sin\theta \cos\theta \, dr \, d\theta = \int_0^\pi 4\sin^5\theta \cos\theta \, d\theta = 0;$$
$$M_x = \int_0^\pi \int_0^{2\sin\theta} r^3 \sin^2\theta \, dr \, d\theta = \int_0^\pi 4\sin^6\theta \, d\theta = \frac{5\pi}{4};$$
$\overline{x} = 0$, $\overline{y} = \dfrac{5}{4}$.

58. Mass:
$$M = \int_0^\pi \int_0^{2\sin\theta} r^3 \sin\theta \, dr \, d\theta = \int_0^\pi 4\sin^5\theta \, d\theta = \frac{64}{15};$$
$$M_y = \int_0^\pi \int_0^{2\sin t} r^4 \sin\theta \cos\theta \, dr \, d\theta = \int_0^\pi \tfrac{32}{5}\sin^6\theta \cos\theta \, d\theta = 0;$$
$$M_x = \int_0^\pi \int_0^{2\sin t} r^4 \sin^2\theta \, dr \, d\theta = \int_0^\pi \tfrac{32}{5}\sin^7\theta \, d\theta = \frac{1024}{175};$$
$\overline{x} = 0$, $\overline{y} = \dfrac{48}{35}$.

59. Mass:
$$M = \int_0^{\pi/2} \int_0^{2\cos\theta} r^2 \cos\theta \, dr \, d\theta = \int_0^{\pi/2} \tfrac{8}{3}\cos^4\theta \, d\theta = \frac{\pi}{2};$$
$$M_y = \int_0^{\pi/2} \int_0^{2\cos\theta} r^2 \cos^2\theta \, dr \, d\theta = \int_0^{\pi/2} 4\cos^6\theta \, d\theta = \frac{5\pi}{8};$$
$$M_x = \int_0^{\pi/2} \int_0^{2\cos\theta} r^3 \cos\theta \sin\theta \, dr \, d\theta = \int_0^{\pi/2} 4\sin\theta \cos^5\theta \, d\theta = \frac{2}{3};$$
$\overline{x} = \dfrac{5}{4}$, $\overline{y} = \dfrac{4}{3\pi}$.

60. Mass:
$$M = \int_0^{\pi/2} \int_0^{2\cos\theta} r^5 \cos^2\theta \sin^2\theta \, dr \, d\theta = \int_0^{\pi/2} \tfrac{32}{3}\cos^8\theta \sin^2\theta \, dr \, d\theta = \frac{7\pi}{48};$$
$$M_y = \int_0^{\pi/2} \int_0^{2\cos\theta} r^6 \cos^3\theta \sin^2\theta \, dr \, d\theta = \int_0^{\pi/2} \tfrac{128}{7}\cos^{10}\theta \sin^2\theta \, dr \, d\theta = \frac{3\pi}{16};$$
$$M_x = \int_0^{\pi/2} \int_0^{2\cos\theta} r^6 \cos^2\theta \sin^3\theta \, dr \, d\theta = \int_0^{\pi/2} \tfrac{128}{7}\cos^9\theta \sin^3\theta \, dr \, d\theta = \frac{32}{105};$$
$\overline{x} = \dfrac{9}{7}$, $\overline{y} = \dfrac{512}{245\pi}$.

Section 14.6

1. $\iiint_T f(x,y,z)\, dV = \int_0^1 \int_0^3 \int_0^2 (x+y+z)\, dx\, dy\, dz = \int_0^1 \int_0^3 \left[\tfrac{1}{2}x^2 + xy + xz\right]_0^2 dy\, dz$

    $= \int_0^1 \int_0^3 (2 + 2x + 2y)\, dy\, dz = \int_0^1 \left[2y + y^2 + xyz\right]_0^3 dz$

    $= \int_0^1 (15 + 6z)\, dz = \left[15z + 3z^2\right]_0^1 = 18.$

2. $\int_0^\pi \int_0^\pi \tfrac{1}{2}\pi^2 y \sin z\, dy\, dz = \int_0^\pi \tfrac{1}{4}\pi^4 \sin z\, dz = \tfrac{1}{2}\pi^4.$

4. $\int_{-2}^6 \int_0^2 (4 + 4y + 4z)\, dy\, dz = \int_{-2}^6 (8 + 8z)\, dz = \left[8z + 4z^2\right]_{-2}^6 = 192.$

6. $\int_0^3 \int_0^{2-(2x/3)} \int_0^{6-2x-3y} (2x + 3y)\, dz\, dy\, dx = \int_0^3 \int_0^{2-(2x/3)} (12x + 18y - 4x^2 - 12xy - 9y^2)\, dy\, dx$

    $= \int_0^3 \left[12xy + 9y^2 - 4x^2 y - 6xy^2 - 3y^3\right]_0^{2-(2x/3)} dx = 18.$

8. $\int_{-1}^1 \int_{-2}^2 \int_0^{4-y^2} (2x + z)\, dz\, dy\, dx = \int_{-1}^1 \int_{-2}^2 \left[2yz + \tfrac{1}{2}z^2\right]_0^{4-y^2} dy\, dx$

    $= \int_{-1}^1 \int_{-2}^2 (8y - 2y^3 + 8 - 4y^2 + \tfrac{1}{2}y^4)\, dy\, dx$

    $= \int_{-1}^1 \left[8y + 4y^2 - \tfrac{4}{3}y^3 - \tfrac{1}{2}y^4 + \tfrac{1}{10}y^5\right]_{-2}^2 dx$

    $= \int_{-1}^1 \left(32 - \tfrac{64}{3} + \tfrac{32}{5}\right) dx = \tfrac{512}{15}.$

10. $\int_{-1}^1 \int_{-2}^2 \int_{y^2}^{8-y^2} z\, dz\, dy\, dx = \int_{-1}^1 \int_{-2}^2 (32 - 8y^2)\, dy\, dx = \int_{-1}^1 \left(128 - \tfrac{128}{3}\right) dx = \tfrac{512}{3}.$

12. $\tfrac{128}{5}$

14. $V = \int_0^1 \int_0^{1-x} \int_0^{x^2+y^2} 1\, dz\, dy\, dx = \tfrac{1}{6}.$

16. $\tfrac{128}{3}$

18. $\tfrac{8}{3}$

20. $\tfrac{16}{3}$

22. $M_{yz} = 0 = M_{xz};\ M_{xy} = \tfrac{1}{4}\pi R^4.$

24. $M = \tfrac{8}{3},\ M_{yz} = 0 = M_{xz},\ M_{xy} = \tfrac{16}{15}.$

26. $I_z = 2 \int_0^2 \int_{x^2}^4 \int_0^y (x^2 + y^2)\, dz\, dy\, dx = \tfrac{15872}{63}.$

28. $\tfrac{1}{2}\pi R^4 H$

30. $I_z = \tfrac{149}{12}$

34. $M = ka^5,\ M_{yz} = \tfrac{7}{12}ka^6,\ \bar{x} = \bar{y} = \bar{z} = \tfrac{7}{12}a.$

35. The integrand is $k(x^2 + y^2 + z^2)(x^2 + y^2).$

36. $M = \tfrac{1}{2}k,\ M_{yz} = \tfrac{1}{4}k = M_{xz}$ (by symmetry), $M_{xy} = \tfrac{1}{3}k.$

38. $I_z = \tfrac{2}{5}Ma^5;\ M$ is the mass of the constant-density sphere.

39. $V = 2\int_0^1 \int_0^x \int_0^{\sqrt{1-x^2}} 1\, dz\, dy\, dx = \tfrac{2}{3}.\ M_{xy} = \tfrac{1}{4},\ M_{yz} = M_{xz} = \tfrac{3}{32}\pi.$

40. $\frac{16}{45}$
41. 24π
42. 4π
44. $V = \pi$
46. Mass:
$$M = \int_{-1}^{2} \int_{y^2}^{y+2} \int_{-\sqrt{z-y^2}}^{\sqrt{z-y^2}} 1 \, dx \, dz \, dy$$
$$= \int_{-1}^{2} \int_{y^2}^{y+2} 2\sqrt{z-y^2} \, dz \, dy$$
$$= \int_{-1}^{2} \tfrac{4}{3}(2+y-y^2)^{3/2} \, dy = \frac{81\pi}{32}.$$

By symmetry, $\overline{x} = 0$. Next,
$$M_{xz} = \int_{-1}^{2} \int_{y^2}^{y+2} \int_{-\sqrt{z-y^2}}^{\sqrt{z-y^2}} y \, dx \, dz \, dy$$
$$= \int_{-1}^{2} \int_{y^2}^{y+2} 2y\sqrt{z-y^2} \, dz \, dy$$
$$= \int_{-1}^{2} \tfrac{4}{3}y(2+y-y^2)^{3/2} \, dy = \frac{81\pi}{64},$$

and hence $\overline{y} = \frac{1}{2}$. Finally,
$$M_{xy} = \int_{-1}^{2} \int_{y^2}^{y+2} \int_{-\sqrt{z-y^2}}^{\sqrt{z-y^2}} z \, dx \, dz \, dy$$
$$= \int_{-1}^{2} \int_{y^2}^{y+2} 2z\sqrt{z-y^2} \, dz \, dy$$
$$= \int_{-1}^{2} \tfrac{4}{15}(12 + 12y + y^2 - y^3 - 2y^4)\sqrt{2+y-y^2} \, dy = \frac{567\pi}{128},$$

and therefore $\overline{z} = \frac{7}{4}$. Therefore the centroid of the parabolic segment of Example 5 is located at the point $\left(0, \frac{1}{2}, \frac{7}{4}\right)$.

47. The volume of the pyramid T of Example 2 is
$$V = \int_0^2 \int_0^{(6-3x)/2} \int_0^{6-3x-2y} 1 \, dz \, dy \, dx$$
$$= \int_0^2 \int_0^{(6-3x)/2} (6 - 3x - 2y) \, dy \, dx$$
$$= \int_0^2 \left[\tfrac{3}{2}(6-3x)(2-x) - \tfrac{1}{4}(6-3x)^2\right] \, dx = 6.$$

The average value of $\delta(x, y, z) = z$ on T is therefore
$$\overline{\delta} = \frac{1}{V} \int_0^2 \int_0^{(6-3x)/2} \int_0^{6-3x-2y} z \, dz \, dy \, dx$$
$$= \frac{1}{6} \int_0^2 \int_0^{(6-3x)/2} \tfrac{1}{2}(6-3x-2y)^2 \, dy \, dx$$
$$= \frac{1}{6} \int_0^2 \tfrac{9}{4}(2-x)^3 \, dx = \frac{3}{2}.$$

48. The average value of $x^2 + y^2 + z^2$ on T is

$$\bar{d} = \frac{1}{1} \int_0^1 \int_0^1 \int_0^1 (x^2 + y^2 + z^2) \, dz \, dy \, dx$$

$$= \int_0^1 \int_0^1 (x^2 + y^2 + \tfrac{1}{3}) \, dy \, dz$$

$$= \int_0^1 \tfrac{1}{3}(3x^2 + 2) \, dx = 1.$$

49. Because the centroid of T is at the point $C\left(\tfrac{1}{2}, \tfrac{1}{2}, \tfrac{1}{2}\right)$, the average of the squared distance of points of the cube T from C is

$$\bar{d} = \frac{1}{1} \int_0^1 \int_0^1 \int_0^1 \left[(x - \tfrac{1}{2})^2 + (y - \tfrac{1}{2})^2 + (z - \tfrac{1}{2})\right] dz \, dy \, dx$$

$$= \int_0^1 \int_0^1 (x^2 + y^2 - x - y + \tfrac{7}{12}) \, dy \, dx$$

$$= \int_0^1 (x^2 - x + \tfrac{5}{12}) \, dx = \frac{1}{4}.$$

50. The average value of $\delta(x, y, z) = x + y + z$ on the cube T of Problem 48 is

$$\bar{\delta} = \frac{1}{1} \int_0^1 \int_0^1 \int_0^1 (x + y + z) \, dz \, dy \, dx$$

$$= \int_0^1 \int_0^1 (x + y + \tfrac{1}{2}) \, dy \, dx$$

$$= \int_0^1 (x + 1) \, dx = \frac{3}{2}.$$

51. Recall that the pyramid of Example 2 has volume $V = 6$ (see the solution of Problem 47). Hence the average value of $x^2 + y^2 + z^2$ on the pyramid is

$$\bar{d} = \frac{1}{V} \int_0^2 \int_0^{(6-3x)/2} \int_0^{6-3x-2y} (x^2 + y^2 + z^2) \, dz \, dy \, dx$$

$$= \frac{1}{6} \int_0^2 \int_0^{(6-3x)/2} \left[\tfrac{1}{3}(6 - 3x - 2y)^3 + (6 - 3x - 2y)(x^2 + y^2)\right] dy \, dx$$

$$= \frac{1}{6} \int_0^2 \tfrac{9}{32}(x - 2)^2(23x^2 - 60x + 60) \, dx = \frac{49}{10}.$$

52. Using the result in the text that the centroid of the pyramid T is located at $\left(\tfrac{2}{5}, \tfrac{3}{5}, \tfrac{12}{5}\right)$ and the result of Problem 47 that T has volume $V = 6$, we find that the average of the square distance of points of T from its centroid is

$$\bar{d} = \frac{1}{V} \int_0^2 \int_0^{(6-3x)/2} \int_0^{6-3x-2y} \left[(x - \tfrac{2}{5})^2 + (y - \tfrac{3}{5})^2 + (z - \tfrac{12}{5})^2\right] dz \, dy \, dx$$

$$= \frac{1}{6} \int_0^2 \int_0^{(6-3x)/2} \left(\tfrac{582}{25} - \tfrac{1131}{25}x + \tfrac{204}{5}x^2 - 12x^3 - \tfrac{854}{25}y \right.$$

$$\left. + \tfrac{242}{5}xy - 20x^2y + \tfrac{114}{5}y^2 - 15xy^2 - \tfrac{14}{3}y^3\right) dy \, dx$$

$$= \frac{1}{6} \int_0^2 \left(\tfrac{1341}{50} - \tfrac{1323}{25}x + \tfrac{1467}{25}x^2 - \tfrac{162}{5}x^3 + \tfrac{207}{32}x^4\right) dx = \frac{67}{25}.$$

53. The integral is

$$\int_0^1 \int_0^1 \int_0^1 \sqrt{x^2 + y^2 + z^2} \, dz \, dy \, dx.$$

Derive 2.56 had some difficulties with the exact evaluation of this integral, but approximated it quite accurately. *Mathematica* 3.0 returned the exact answer in less than half a minute (using a Macintosh PowerPC 7600), but complained that it was unable to verify convergence.

Section 14.7

1. $V = \int_0^{2\pi} \int_0^2 \int_{r^2}^4 r \, dz \, dr \, d\theta = 2\pi \int_0^2 (4r - r^3) \, dr = 2\pi \left[2r^2 - \frac{1}{4}r^4\right]_0^2 = 8\pi.$

2. By symmetry, $\bar{x} = \bar{y} = 0$. With unit density we have
$$M_{xy} = \int_0^{2\pi} \int_0^2 \int_{r^2}^4 rz \, dz \, dr \, d\theta = \pi \int_0^2 (16r - r^5) \, dr = \pi \left[8r^2 - \frac{1}{6}r^6\right]_0^2 = \frac{64}{3}\pi.$$
So $\bar{z} = \frac{8}{3}$.

4. Use the sphere $r^2 + z^2 \leq a^2$, $0 \leq \theta \leq 2\pi$. We find its moment of inertia about the x-axis:
$$I_z = \int_0^{2\pi} \int_0^a \int_{-\sqrt{a^2-r^2}}^{\sqrt{a^2-r^2}} r^3 \, dz \, dr \, d\theta = 2\pi \int_0^a 2r^3 \sqrt{a^2 - r^2} \, dr.$$
Let $r = a \sin u$. This substitution yields
$$I_z = 4\pi a^5 \int_0^{\pi/2} (\cos^2 u - \cos^4 u)(\sin u) \, du = 4\pi a^5 \left[\frac{1}{5}\cos^5 u - \frac{1}{3}\cos^3 u\right]_0^{\pi/2} = \frac{8}{15}\pi a^5.$$
The answer may also be written in the form $I_z = \frac{2}{5}Ma^5$ where M is the mass of the sphere.

6. By symmetry, $\bar{x} = \bar{y} = 0$.
$$M_{xy} = \int_0^{2\pi} \int_0^1 \int_0^{\sqrt{4-r^2}} rz \, dz \, dr \, d\theta = \pi \int_0^1 r(4 - r^2) \, dr = \pi \left[2r^2 - \frac{1}{4}r^4\right]_0^1 = \frac{7}{4}\pi.$$
$$M = \int_0^{2\pi} \int_0^1 \int_0^{\sqrt{4-r^2}} r \, dz \, dr \, d\theta = 2\pi \left[-\frac{1}{3}(4-r^2)^{3/2}\right]_0^1 = \frac{2}{3}\pi \left(8 - 3\sqrt{3}\right).$$
Now $\bar{z}$ can be simplified to $\frac{21}{296}\left(8 + 3\sqrt{3}\right)$.

7. Mass: $M = \int_0^{2\pi} \int_0^a \int_0^h rz \, dz \, dr \, d\theta = \pi \int_0^a rh^2 \, dr = \left[\frac{1}{2}\pi r^2 h^2\right]_0^a = \frac{1}{2}\pi a^2 h^2.$

8. By symmetry, $\bar{x} = \bar{y} = 0$. $M_{xy} = \int_0^{2\pi} \int_0^a \int_0^h rz^2 \, dz \, dr \, d\theta = 2\pi \int_0^a \frac{1}{3} rh^3 \, dr = \frac{1}{3}\pi a^2 h^3.$
Therefore $\bar{z} = \frac{2}{3}h$.

9. $I_z = \int_0^{2\pi} \int_0^a \int_0^h r^3 z \, dz \, dr \, d\theta = \pi \int_0^a r^3 h^2 \, dr = \frac{1}{4}\pi a^4 h^2$; alternatively, $I_z = \frac{1}{2}Ma^2.$

10. The diagram at the right shows the intersection of the xy-plane with the sphere and the cylinder. The plane and sphere intersect in the curve $r = 2$ and the cylindrical equation of the sphere is $r^2 + z^2 = 4$. The plane intersects the cylinder in the curve $r = 2\cos\theta$. Thus the volume V of their intersection is given by

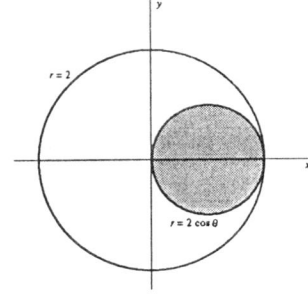

$$V = 4\int_0^{\pi/2}\int_0^{2\cos\theta}\int_0^{\sqrt{4-r^2}} r\, dz\, dr\, d\theta$$

$$= 4\int_0^{\pi/2}\int_0^{2\cos\theta} r\sqrt{4-r^2}\, dr\, d\theta$$

$$= 4\int_0^{\pi/2}\left[-\tfrac{1}{3}(4-r^2)^{3/2}\right]_0^{2\cos\theta} d\theta$$

$$= \tfrac{32}{3}\int_0^{\pi/2}(1-\sin^3\theta)\, d\theta = \tfrac{16}{9}(3\pi-4).$$

11. $V = \tfrac{81}{2}\pi$, $M_{xy} = \tfrac{243}{2}\pi$, and $M_{xz} = 0 = M_{yz}$ by symmetry.

12. $V = 24\pi$, $M_{xy} = 128\pi$, and the centroid is at $(0, 0, \tfrac{16}{3})$.

14. $V = \int_{-\pi/2}^{\pi/2}\int_0^{2\cos\theta}\int_{r^2}^{2r\cos\theta} r\, dz\, dr\, d\theta = \pi/2.$

16. Let k denote the density of the cylinder and h its height. Then $m = \pi a^2 h k$. We choose coordinates so that the z-axis is the axis of symmetry of the cylinder and its base rests on the xy-plane. Then

$$I_z = \int_0^{2\pi}\int_0^a\int_0^h kr^3\, dz\, dr\, d\theta = \tfrac{1}{2}\pi a^4 h k = (\pi a^2 h k)(\tfrac{1}{2}a^2) = \tfrac{1}{2}ma^2.$$

17. Position the cylinder with its base in the xy-plane and symmetric about the z-axis. Then it's described by the inequalities $0 \le \theta \le 2\pi$, $0 \le r \le a$, $0 \le z \le h$. Moreover, note that the square of the distance of a point (x, y, z) from the x-axis is

$$y^2 + z^2 = r^2\sin^2\theta + z^2.$$

Therefore

$$I_x = \int_0^{2\pi}\int_0^a\int_0^h \delta\left(r^3\sin^2\theta + rz^2\right) dz\, dr\, d\theta = \cdots = \frac{\pi\delta a^2 h\,(3a^2+4h^2)}{12}.$$

18. $M_{xy} = \tfrac{3}{8}Ma$; the centroid is at $(0, 0, \tfrac{3}{8}a)$.

20. If the cone is located with its base in the xy-plane and symmetric about the z-axis, then $M_{xy} = \tfrac{1}{4}Mh$ where M is its mass and H is its altitude. It follows that its centroid is at $(0, 0, H/4)$.

22. Locate the hemisphere with its base in the xy-plane and symmetric about the z-axis. It follows that $M = \tfrac{1}{4}k\pi a^4$ and $M_{xy} = \tfrac{2}{15}\pi k a^5$; its centroid is at $(0, 0, \tfrac{8}{15}a)$.

23. $V = \int_0^{2\pi}\int_0^{\pi/4}\int_0^{\sec\phi} \rho^2\sin\phi\, d\rho\, d\phi\, d\theta = 2\pi\int_0^{\pi/4}\tfrac{1}{3}\sec^3\phi\sin\phi\, d\phi = \dfrac{\pi}{3}.$

24. If the hemisphere is located with its base in the xy-plane and symmetric about the z-axis, integrate $\rho^3\sin\phi\cos\phi$ with the following limits of integration to obtain M_{xy}:

$$0 \le \rho \le H\sec\phi,\quad 0 \le \phi \le \tan^{-1}(R/H),\quad 0 \le \theta \le 2\pi.$$

25. $M_{xy} = \tfrac{1}{8}\pi a^4$

26. $I_z = \tfrac{1}{30}\pi a^5(8 - 5\sqrt{2})$

27. Suggestion: Use the sphere with (spherical coordinates) boundary surface $\rho = 2a\cos\phi$ and compute I_x. The square of the distance of the point (x, y, z) from the x-axis is

$$y^2 + z^2 = \rho^2 - x^2 = \rho^2\left(1 - \sin^2\phi\cos^2\theta\right).$$

28. $I_z = \frac{1016}{21}\pi a^7$

30. Description: Begin with cardioid in the xz-plane with its cusp at the origin, its axis of symmetry the z-axis, and containing the point $(0,0,2)$. Rotate the cardioid about the z-axis to obtain the surface. It resembles an inverted apple. Its volume is $\frac{8}{3}\pi$.

32. Use the same limits of integration as in Example 4, but integrate instead $(\rho \sin \phi)^2 \rho^2 \sin \phi \, d\rho \, d\phi \, d\theta$.
    Result:
    $$I_z = \frac{67}{480}\pi a^5 \approx V(0.498a)^2,$$
    where V denotes the volume of the ice cream cone.

34. The moment of inertia of the ice-cream cone around the z-axis is
    $$\Phi_z = \int_0^{2\pi} \int_0^{\pi/6} \int_0^{2a\cos\phi} (\rho\cos\phi)(\rho\sin\phi)^2 \rho^2 \sin\phi \, d\rho \, d\phi \, d\theta$$
    $$= \int_0^{2\pi} \int_0^{\pi/6} \tfrac{32}{3} a^6 \cos^7\phi \sin^3\phi \, d\phi \, d\theta$$
    $$= \int_0^{2\pi} \tfrac{47}{480} a^6 \, d\theta = \frac{47\pi a^6}{240}.$$

35. The mass of the star is
    $$m_1 = \int_0^{2\pi} \int_0^{\pi} \int_0^{a} k\left[1 - (\rho/a)^2\right] \rho^2 \sin\phi \, d\rho \, d\phi \, d\theta$$
    $$= \int_0^{2\pi} \int_0^{\pi} \tfrac{2}{15} k a^3 \sin\phi \, d\phi \, d\theta$$
    $$= \int_0^{2\pi} \tfrac{4}{15} k a^2 \, d\theta = \frac{8k\pi a^3}{15}.$$
    The mass of the "similar star" is
    $$m_2 = \frac{4k\pi a^3}{3},$$
    and the ratio of m_1 to m_2 is therefore $\frac{2}{5}$.

36. The moment of inertia around the z-axis of the gaseous star of Problem 35 is
    $$\Phi_z = \int_0^{2\pi} \int_0^{\pi} \int_0^{a} k(\rho\sin\phi)^2 \left[1 - (\rho/a)^2\right] \rho^2 \sin\phi \, d\rho \, d\phi \, d\theta$$
    $$= \int_0^{2\pi} \int_0^{\pi} \tfrac{2}{35} k a^5 \sin^3\phi \, d\phi \, d\theta$$
    $$= \int_0^{2\pi} \tfrac{8}{105} k a^5 \, d\theta = \frac{16k\pi a^5}{105}.$$

37. The value of the integral in part (a) is
    $$\int_0^{2\pi} \int_0^{\pi} \int_0^{a} \exp(-\rho^3) \rho^2 \sin\phi \, d\rho \, d\phi \, d\theta = \int_0^{2\pi} \int_0^{\pi} \tfrac{1}{3}[1 - \exp(-a^3)] \sin\phi \, d\phi \, d\theta$$
    $$= \int_0^{2\pi} \tfrac{2}{3}[1 - \exp(-a^3)] \, d\theta = \tfrac{4}{3}\pi \left(1 - e^{-a^3}\right).$$

Part (b): It is now clear that the limit of the last expression as $a \to \infty$ is $\frac{4}{3}\pi$.

38. First we integrate the given integrand over the spherical ball of radius a centered at the origin. The result is

$$f(a) = \int_0^{2\pi} \int_0^{\pi} \int_0^a \rho \exp(-\rho^2) \rho^2 \sin\phi \, d\rho \, d\phi \, d\theta$$

$$= \int_0^{2\pi} \int_0^{\pi} \tfrac{1}{2}\left[1 - (1+a^2)\exp(-a^2)\right] \sin\phi \, d\phi \, d\theta$$

$$= \int_0^{2\pi} \left[1 - (1+a^2)\exp(-a^2)\right] d\theta = 2\pi\left[1 - (1+a^2)\exp(-a^2)\right].$$

And the limit of this expression, as $a \to \infty$, is clearly 2π.

39. We use the ball of radius a and volume $V = \frac{4}{3}\pi a^3$ centered at the origin. The average distance of points of this ball from its center is then

$$\bar{d} = \frac{1}{V}\int_0^{2\pi}\int_0^{\pi}\int_0^a \rho^3 \sin\phi \, d\rho \, d\phi \, d\theta$$

$$= \frac{1}{V}\int_0^{2\pi}\int_{0^\pi} \tfrac{1}{4}a^4 \sin\phi \, d\phi \, d\theta$$

$$= \frac{1}{V}\int_0^{2\pi} \tfrac{1}{2}a^4 \, d\theta = \frac{\pi a^4}{V} = \frac{3a}{4}.$$

40. We use the ball of radius a and volume $V = \frac{4}{3}\pi a^3$ centered at the point with Cartesian coordinates $(0,0,a)$ on the positive z-axis. The boundary of this ball is the spherical surface described by

$$\rho = 2a\cos\phi, \qquad 0 \leq phi \leq \tfrac{1}{2}\pi, \qquad 0 \leq \theta \leq 2\pi.$$

The average distance of points of this ball from the origin (its "south pole") is then

$$\bar{d} = \frac{1}{V}\int_0^{2\pi}\int_0^{\pi/2}\int_0^{2a\cos\phi} \rho^3 \sin\phi \, d\rho \, d\phi \, d\theta$$

$$= \frac{1}{V}\int_0^{2\pi}\int_0^{\pi/2} 4a^4 \cos^4\phi \sin\phi \, d\phi \, d\theta$$

$$= \frac{1}{V}\int_0^{2\pi} \tfrac{4}{5}a^4 \, d\theta = \frac{8\pi a^4}{5V} = \frac{6a}{5}.$$

Section 14.8

1. $\sqrt{1 + (z_x)^2 + (z_y)^2} = \sqrt{11}$. The area of the ellipse is 6π, so the answer is $6\pi\sqrt{11}$.

2. $\sqrt{1 + (z_x)^2 + (z_y)^2} = 3$. The area of the plane region is therefore given by the integral

$$\int_0^1 (\sqrt{x} - x^2) \, dx = \left[\tfrac{2}{3}x^{3/2} - \tfrac{1}{3}x^3\right]_0^1 = \tfrac{1}{3},$$

so the answer is 1.

4. $\sqrt{1+(z_x)^2+(z_y)^2} = \sqrt{1+x^2}$. So the answer is

$$\int_0^1 \int_0^x \sqrt{1+x^2}\, dy\, dx = \int_0^1 x\sqrt{1+x^2}\, dx = \left[\tfrac{1}{3}(1+x^2)^{3/2}\right]_0^1 = \tfrac{1}{3}\left(2\sqrt{2}-1\right) \approx 0.609476.$$

5. $A = \iint_R \sqrt{1+1+4y^2}\, dy\, dx = \int_0^2 \sqrt{2+4y^2}\, dy = \tfrac{1}{2}\left(6\sqrt{2} + \ln\left(3+2\sqrt{2}\right)\right) \approx 5.124.$

6. $\tfrac{1}{6}\sqrt{2}\,(3\sqrt{3}-1) \approx 0.989.$

8. $2\pi\sqrt{14}$

10. $A = \tfrac{1}{6}\pi\left(17\sqrt{17}-1\right) \approx 36.1769.$

11. $A = 2\pi \int_0^4 \sqrt{r^2+4r^4}\, dr.$

16. $A = 2a^2(\pi-2)$, about 18% of the total surface area.

18. You should find that $\mathbf{N} = \langle a^2 \sin^2\phi\cos\theta,\, a^2\sin^2\phi\sin\theta,\, a^2\sin\phi\cos\phi\rangle.$

20. You should find that the normal vector $\mathbf{N}$ has components

$$(-4a^2\sin^2\phi\cos\theta)\cos 2\phi,\quad (-4a^2\sin^2\phi\sin\theta)\cos 2\phi,\quad \text{and}\quad 8a^2\sin^3\phi\cos\phi.$$

22. The area in question is given by

$$A = \int_0^{2\pi}\int_0^{\pi/6} a^2\sin\phi\, d\phi\, d\theta = \left[2\pi - a^2\cos\phi\right]_0^{\pi/6} = 2\pi a^2\left(1-\tfrac{1}{3}\sqrt{3}\right),$$

about 21.13% of the total surface area.

25. a) The surface area is

$$\int_{-1}^1 \int_{-1}^1 \sqrt{1+4x^2+4y^2}\, dy\, dx \approx 7.44626.$$

b) Taking advantage of symmetry, the surface area is

$$4\int_0^1 \int_0^{1-x} \sqrt{1+4x^2+4y^2}\, dy\, dx \approx 3.00463.$$

26. a) The surface area is

$$\int_{-1}^1 \int_{-1}^1 \sqrt{2}\, dy\, dx = 4\sqrt{2} \approx 5.65685.$$

b) Taking advantage of symmetry, the surface area is

$$4\int_0^1 \int_0^{1-x} \sqrt{2}\, dy\, dx = 2\sqrt{2} \approx 2.82843.$$

27. a) The surface area is

$$\int_{-1}^1 \int_{-1}^1 \sqrt{1+x^2+y^2}\, dy\, dx \approx 5.12316.$$

b) Taking advantage of symmetry, the surface area is

$$4\int_0^1 \int_0^{1-x} \sqrt{1+x^2+y^2}\, dy\, dx \approx 2.30231,$$

28. a) The surface area is

$$\int_{-1}^1 \int_{-1}^1 \frac{2}{\sqrt{4-x^2-y^2}}\, dy\, dx \approx 17.6411.$$

b) Taking advantage of symmetry, the surface area is

$$4\int_0^1 \int_0^{1-x} \frac{2}{\sqrt{4-x^2-y^2}}\, dy\, dx \approx 2.09159.$$

29. The surface area of the ellipsoid is

$$\int_0^{2\pi} \int_0^{\pi} (4\sin\phi)\sqrt{36\cos^2\phi\cos^4\theta + 9\cos^2\theta\sin^2\phi + 4\sin^2\phi}\, d\phi\, d\theta \approx 111.5458.$$

30. b) The area is

$$\int_0^{2\pi} \int_0^{2\pi} \sqrt{\frac{(5-3\cos 2\psi)(3+2\cos\psi)^2}{2}}\, d\psi\, d\theta \approx 182.62295.$$

c) If $f(x) = \sqrt{1 - \frac{1}{4}(x-3)^2}$ (its graph is the upper half of the ellipse), then the length of the ellipse is

$$2\int_1^5 \sqrt{1 + [f'(x)]^2}\, dx \approx 9.68845.$$

Section 14.9

2. $x = \frac{1}{7}(u + 2v)$, $y = \frac{1}{7}(v - 3u)$; $J_T = \dfrac{\partial(x,y)}{\partial(u,v)} = \frac{1}{7}$.

4. $x = \frac{1}{2}\sqrt{u+v}$, $y = \frac{1}{2}\sqrt{u-v}$, and $J_T = \dfrac{\partial(x,y)}{\partial(u,v)} = -\dfrac{1}{8\sqrt{u^2-v^2}}$.

6. Compute and simplify $(u/2)^2 + (v/2)^2$. Then it becomes easy to see that

$$x = \frac{2u}{u^2+v^2} \quad \text{and} \quad v = -\frac{2v}{u^2+v^2}.$$

Finally, $J_T = \dfrac{\partial(x,y)}{\partial(u,v)} = \dfrac{4}{(u^2+v^2)^2}$.

7. $J_T = \dfrac{\partial(x,y)}{\partial(u,v)} = -\frac{1}{5}$.

8. $x = \sqrt{\dfrac{u}{v}}$, $y = \sqrt{uv}$, $J_T = \dfrac{\partial(x,y)}{\partial(u,v)} = \dfrac{1}{2v}$, and $A = \dfrac{\ln 2}{2}$.

10. First, $x = (u^2v)^{-1/3}$, $y = (uv^2)^{-1/3}$, and $J_T = \dfrac{\partial(x,y)}{\partial(u,v)} = \dfrac{1}{3u^2v^2}$. It follows that the area of the region is $\frac{1}{8}$.

12. By methods like those used in the solution of Problem 6, we find that $x = \dfrac{2u}{u^2+v^2}$, and that $y = \dfrac{2v}{u^2+v^2}$. The Jacobian is $\dfrac{-4}{(u^2+v^2)^2}$ and the area is $\frac{1}{8}$.

13. The Jacobian is $6r$.

14. The Jacobian is abc, and the resulting triple integral is the product of abc with the rectangular coordinates triple integral for the volume of a sphere of radius 1. Thereby we find that $V = \frac{4}{3}\pi abc$.

15. $x = \sqrt{\dfrac{vw}{u}}$, $y = \sqrt{\dfrac{uw}{v}}$, and $z = \sqrt{\dfrac{uv}{2}}$. The Jacobian of the transformation is $\dfrac{1}{2\sqrt{uvw}}$.

16. $r = \sqrt{z}$, $t = \sqrt{\dfrac{z}{x^2+y^2}}$, and $\theta = \arctan\left(\dfrac{y}{x}\right)$. The Jacobian of the transformation is $2(r/t)^3$. The volume of R turns out to be $45\pi/8$.

17. The Jacobian of the first transformation is -2 and that of the second is $r\sqrt{3}$.

19. The spherical integral is $\displaystyle\lim_{a\to\infty}\int_0^{2\pi}\int_0^{\pi}\int_0^{a} \rho^3 e^{-k\rho^2}\sin\phi\,d\rho\,d\phi\,d\theta$.

20. The Jacobian is $abc\rho^2 \sin\phi$.

22. The transformation $u = xy$, $v = y/x$ yields $x = \sqrt{u/v}$, $y = \sqrt{uv}$, and

$$\frac{\partial(u,v)}{\partial(x,y)} = \begin{vmatrix} y & x \\ -\dfrac{y}{x^2} & \dfrac{1}{x} \end{vmatrix} = \frac{2y}{x} = 2v.$$

It follows that the area of the region is

$$\int_1^2 \int_1^2 2v\,dv\,du = 3,$$

$$M_x = \int_1^2\int_1^2 2u^{1/2}v^{3/2}\,d\,du = \tfrac{8}{15}\left(17 - 6\sqrt{2}\right),$$

$$M_y = \int_1^2\int_1^2 2u^{1/2}v^{1/2}\,dv\,du = \tfrac{8}{9}\left(9 - 4\sqrt{2}\right),$$

and hence $\bar{x} = \tfrac{8}{27}\left(9 - 4\sqrt{2}\right) \approx 0.990562$ and $\bar{y} = \tfrac{8}{45}\left(17 - 6\sqrt{2}\right) \approx 1.513728$.

23. The transformation $u = xy$, $v = xy^3$ yields $= \sqrt{u^3/v}$, $y = \sqrt{v/u}$, and

$$\frac{\partial(u,v)}{\partial(x,y)} = \begin{vmatrix} y & x \\ y^3 & 3xy^2 \end{vmatrix} = 2xy^3 = 2v.$$

Hence the area of the region is

$$\int_2^4\int_3^6 \frac{1}{2v}\,dv\,du = \ln 2,$$

$$M_x = \int_2^4\int_3^6 \frac{1}{2\sqrt{uv}}\,dv\,du = 6\sqrt{6} - 8\sqrt{3},$$

$$M_y = \int_2^4\int_3^6 \frac{u^{3/2}}{2v^{3/2}}\,dv\,du = \frac{1}{15}\left(72\sqrt{3} - 40\sqrt{6}\right).$$

Therefore $\bar{x} \approx 2.570697$ and $\bar{y} =\approx 1.212631$.

24. The transformation $y = ux^2$, $x = vy^2$ yields $x = u^{-2/3}v^{-1/3}$, $y = u^{-1/3}v^{-2/3}$, and

$$\frac{\partial(u,v)}{\partial(x,y)} = \begin{vmatrix} -\dfrac{2y}{x^3} & \dfrac{1}{x^2} \\ \dfrac{1}{y^2} & -\dfrac{2x}{y^3} \end{vmatrix} = \frac{3}{x^2y^2} = \frac{3}{u^2v^2}.$$

Hence the area of the region is

$$\int_1^2\int_1^2 \frac{3}{u^2v^2}\,dv\,du = \tfrac{3}{4},$$

$$M_x = \int_1^2\int_1^2 \frac{3}{u^{7/2}v^{8/3}}\,dv\,du = \tfrac{27}{160}\left(9 - 2^{4/3} - 2^{5/3}\right),$$

$$M_y = \int_1^2 \int_1^2 \frac{3}{u^{8/2}v^{7/3}}\, dv\, du = \frac{27}{160}\left(9 - 2^{4/3} - 2^{5/3}\right).$$

Therefore $\bar{x} = \bar{y} = \frac{9}{40}\left(9 - 2^{4/3} - 2^{5/3}\right) \approx 0.743705$.

25. The transformation $x = a\rho \sin\phi \cos\theta$, $y = b\rho \sin\phi \sin\theta$, $z = c\rho \cos\phi$ yields

$$\frac{\partial(x,y,z)}{\partial(\rho,\phi,\theta)} = \begin{vmatrix} a\sin\phi\cos\theta & a\rho\cos\phi\cos\theta & -a\rho\sin\phi\sin\theta \\ b\sin\phi\sin\theta & b\rho\cos\phi\sin\theta & b\rho\sin\phi\cos\theta \\ c\cos\phi & -c\rho\sin\phi & 0 \end{vmatrix} = abc\rho^2 \sin\phi.$$

Now $x^2 + y^2 = (\rho^2 \sin^2\phi)(a^2 \cos^2\theta + b^2 \sin^2\theta)$, and hence

$$I_z = \int_0^{2\pi} \int_0^\pi \int_0^1 (\delta abc\rho^4 \sin^3\phi)(a^2 \cos^2\theta + b^2 \sin^2\theta)\, d\rho\, d\phi\, d\theta = \tfrac{4}{15}\pi \delta abc(a^2 + b^2)$$
$$= \tfrac{1}{5}M(a^2 + b^2)$$

where M is the mass of the ellipsoid. By symmetry,

$$I_x = \tfrac{1}{5}M(b^2 + c^2) \quad \text{and} \quad I_y = \tfrac{1}{5}M(a^2 + c^2).$$

26. First,

$$\frac{\partial(x,y,z)}{\partial(r,\theta,t)} = \frac{2r^3}{t^3}$$

so the volume of the solid is

$$V = \int_0^{2\pi} \int_1^2 \int_1^2 \frac{2r^3}{t^3}\, dr\, dt\, d\theta = \tfrac{45}{8}\pi.$$

Clearly $\bar{x} = \bar{y} = 0$, so we need only calculate

$$M_{xy} = \int_0^{2\pi} \int_1^2 \int_1^2 \frac{2r^5}{t^3}\, dr\, dt\, d\theta = \tfrac{63}{4}\pi,$$

and it follows that the centroid of the solid is located at the point $(0, 0, \tfrac{14}{5})$. Its moment of inertia around the z-axis is

$$I_z = \int_0^{2\pi} \int_1^2 \int_1^2 \frac{2r^5}{t^5}\, dr\, dt\, d\theta = \tfrac{315}{32}\pi,$$

its moment of inertia around the y-axis is

$$I_y = \int_0^{2\pi} \int_1^2 \int_1^2 \frac{2r^3}{t^3}\left(r^4 + \frac{r^2 \cos^2\theta}{t^2}\right) dr\, dt\, d\theta = \tfrac{3375}{64}\pi,$$

and by symmetry, $I_x = I_y$.

27. The average distance $\bar{d}$ of points of the ellipsoid from its center (at $(0,0,0)$) is

$$\frac{1}{V}\int_0^{2\pi} \int_0^\pi \int_0^1 (abc\rho^2 \sin\phi)\rho\sqrt{(a\sin\phi\cos\theta)^2 + (b\sin\phi\sin\theta)^2 + (c\cos\phi)^2}\, d\rho\, d\phi\, d\theta$$

where $V = \tfrac{4}{3}\pi abc$ is the volume of the ellipsoid. For example, if $a = 4$, $b = 3$, and $c = 2$, we find that $\bar{d} \approx 2.30027$.

Chapter 14 Miscellaneous

1. $\int_0^1 \int_0^{x^3} (1+x^2)^{-1/2} \, dy \, dx$

2. $1 - \cos(1) \approx 0.4597$

4. $\int_0^4 \int_0^{y^{3/2}} x \cos y^4 \, dx \, dy$

6. 1

7. $V = \int_0^1 \int_u^{2-y} (x^2 + y^2) \, dx \, dy.$

8. 384π

10. The domain of the integral will be the elliptical region bounded by the ellipse whose equation is $(x/2)^2 + y^2 = 1$. Let us use the transformation $x = 2r\cos\theta$, $y = r\sin\theta$. The Jacobian of this transformation is $2r$. The difference in the z-values of the two paraboloids turns out to be $8(1 - r^2)$, and the volume of the region between them is 8π.

12. $V = 8$

13. Use the same transformation as in the solution of Problem 10.

15. The polar form of the integral is $\int_0^{\pi/4} \int_0^{\tan\theta} \dfrac{r}{(1+r^2)^2} \, dr \, d\theta.$

16. $M = \frac{6}{35}$; $M_y = \frac{55}{504} = M_x$; the centroid is at the point $\left(\frac{275}{432}, \frac{275}{432}\right) \approx (0.636574, 0.636574)$.

18. $M = \frac{1}{2}(\ln 2)^2$; $M_y = -1 + 2\ln 2$; $M_x = \frac{1}{6}(\ln 2)^3$. Centroid: $\bar{x} = \dfrac{-2 + 4\ln 2}{(\ln 2)^2}$, $\bar{y} = \frac{1}{3}\ln 3$.

20. $M = \frac{32}{9}$, $M_y = \frac{64}{15}$, and $M_x = 0$. Centroid: $(6/5, 0)$.

22. Note that $\bar{x} = \bar{y}$. The area of the quarter-ring is $A = \frac{1}{4}(\pi b^2 - \pi a^2) = \frac{1}{4}\pi(b^2 - a^2)$, and the volume generated by its rotation about the x-axis is $V = \frac{2}{3}\pi b^3 - \frac{2}{3}\pi a^3$. Therefore
$$V = \tfrac{2}{3}\pi(b^3 - a^3) = (2\pi\bar{y})\frac{\pi}{4}(b^2 - a^2).$$

   a) Consequently $\bar{y} = \dfrac{(2/3)\pi(b^3 - a^3)}{(1/2)\pi^2(b^2 - a^2)} = \dfrac{4(b^2 + ab + a^2)}{3\pi(b+a)} = \bar{x}.$

   b) $\lim\limits_{b \to a} \bar{x} = \dfrac{12a^2}{(3\pi)(2a)} = \dfrac{2a}{\pi} = \lim\limits_{b \to a} \bar{y}.$

24. $V = \frac{1}{12}$

25. $V = \int_0^{2\pi} \int_0^1 \left(r\sqrt{5-r^2} - 2r^2\right) dr \, d\theta.$

26. Assume unit density. Then $M = V = \int_0^{2\pi} \int_0^{\pi/3} \int_0^a \rho^2 \sin\phi \, d\rho \, d\phi \, d\theta = \frac{1}{3}\pi a^3$. $M_{xy} = \frac{3}{16}\pi a^4$; the centroid is at $(0, 0, 9a/16)$.

27. Suggestion: Place the cone with its vertex at the origin and with the z-axis its natural axis of symmetry. Then use cylindrical coordinates.

28. $M = \frac{1}{48}a^6$

30. $V = \frac{1}{12}\pi a^3$

32. $V = 2\int_0^{\pi/2} \int_0^{2a\cos\theta} 2\pi r^2 \cos\theta \, dr \, d\theta = 2\pi^2 a^3.$

33. $V = \int_0^\pi \int_0^{1+\cos\theta} 2\pi r^2 \sin\theta \, dr \, d\theta.$

34. $2\pi^2 a^2 b$

35. Let's instead use the disk of radius a and center $(b,0)$ in the xz-plane, with $b > a > 0$, and rotate this disk around the z-axis to generate the torus. It should be easier to parametrize that way. Indeed, it's very little trouble to find that points (x,y,z) of the solid torus are described by

$$x = b\cos u + w\cos v \cos u, \quad y = b\sin u + w\cos v \sin u, \quad z = w\sin v$$

where $0 \leq u \leq 2\pi$, $0 \leq v \leq 2\pi$, and $0 \leq w \leq a$. To find the moment of inertia of the torus— let's assume that it has density δ—around its natural axis of symmetry, the z-axis, all we need to calculate are the Jacobian of the coordinate transformation and the value of $x^2 + y^2$, both expressed in terms of the angles u and v and the length w. It turns out that the former is $w(b + w\cos v)$ and the latter is $(b + w\cos v)^2$. So the moment of inertia in question is

$$\int_0^{2\pi} \int_0^{2\pi} \int_0^a \delta w(b + w\cos v)^3 \, dw \, dv \, du = \tfrac{1}{2}\delta \pi^2 a^2 b(3a^2 + 4b^2) = \tfrac{1}{4}M(3a^2 + 4b^2),$$

where M is the mass of the torus.

36. $\tfrac{2}{3}a$

38. $\dfrac{224}{27\pi} \approx 2.6408$

42. The average distance of points of the cone from its vertex is $\dfrac{(H^2 + R^2)^{3/2} - H^3}{2R^2} = \dfrac{L^3 - H^3}{2R^2}$ where L is the slant height of the cone.

44. $\tfrac{1}{6}\pi \left(17\sqrt{17} - 1\right) \approx 36.1769$

46. $8(\pi - 2)$

48. The surface area can be written in the form

$$A = 4\int_0^1 \int_0^{\sqrt{1-x^2}} \sqrt{1 + x^2} \, dy \, dx = 4\int_0^1 \sqrt{1 - x^4} \, dx;$$

this is the integral we choose to approximate. We use Simpson's approximation and obtain the estimate 3.49608, though very many subintervals are needed.

50. $A = 4a^2$

51. Use the transformation $u = xy$, $v = x^2 - y^2$; its Jacobian is $-2\sqrt{4u^2 + v^2}$.

52. The Jacobian of the transformation is 2; the integral becomes $\displaystyle\int_0^1 \int_{-v}^v 2e^{u/v} \, du \, dv = e - \dfrac{1}{e} \approx 2.3504$.

53. The Jacobian of the transformation is $abc\rho^2 \sin\phi$.

55. b) Integration by parts:

$$\begin{bmatrix} u = 8\sqrt{3}\arcsin\dfrac{1}{\sqrt{3-x^2}} & dv = dx \\ du = 8\sqrt{3}\dfrac{x}{(3-x^2)\sqrt{2-x^2}} \, dx & v = x \end{bmatrix}$$

$$A = \left[8x\sqrt{3}\arcsin\dfrac{1}{\sqrt{3-x^2}}\right]_0^1 - 8\sqrt{3}\int_0^1 \dfrac{x^2}{(3-x^2)\sqrt{2-x^2}} \, dx$$

$$= 8\sqrt{3}\arcsin\dfrac{1}{\sqrt{2}} - 8\sqrt{3}\int_0^1 \dfrac{x^2}{(3-x^2)\sqrt{2-x^2}} \, dx$$

$$= 2\pi\sqrt{3} - 8\sqrt{3}\int_0^1 \dfrac{x^2}{(3-x^2)\sqrt{2-x^2}} \, dx.$$

Now let $x = \sqrt{2}\sin\theta$:

$$A = 2\pi\sqrt{3} - 8\sqrt{3}\int_0^{\pi/4} \frac{2\sin^2\theta}{(3-2\sin^2\theta)}\,d\theta$$

$$= 2\pi\sqrt{3} - 8\sqrt{3}\int_0^{\pi/4} \frac{1-\cos 2\theta}{3-2\sin^2\theta}\,d\theta = \frac{1}{2}\int \frac{1-\cos\phi}{2+\cos\phi}\,d\phi. \quad (\phi = 2\theta)$$

Finally substitute $u = \tan\left(\dfrac{\theta}{2}\right)$ to (eventually) obtain $A = 4\pi\left(\sqrt{3}-1\right)$.

58. The average squared distance $\overline{d}$ of points of the ellipsoid from its center (at $(0,0,0)$) is

$$\frac{1}{V}\int_0^{2\pi}\int_0^{\pi}\int_0^1 (abc\rho^2\sin\phi)\rho^2\left[(a\sin\phi\cos\theta)^2 + (b\sin\phi\sin\theta)^2 + (c\cos\phi)^2\right]\,d\rho\,d\phi\,d\theta$$

where $V = \frac{4}{3}\pi abc$ is the volume of the ellipsoid. With the aid of a computer algebra system, we find that $\overline{d} = \frac{1}{5}(a^2 + b^2 + c^2)$. Compare this with the result of Problem 27 of Section 14.9; also examine the answer in the case that the ellipsoid is a sphere: $a = b = c$.

59. Locate the cube C as shown in the following figure, with one vertex at the origin and the opposite vertex at the point $(1,1,1)$ in space. Let L be the line through these two points; we will rotated C around the line L to generate the solid S. We also install a coordinate system on L; it becomes the w-axis, with $w = 0$ at the origin and $w = \sqrt{3}$ at the point with Cartesian coordinates $(1,1,1)$; thus distance is measured on the w-axis in exactly the same way it is measured on the three Cartesian coordinate axes.

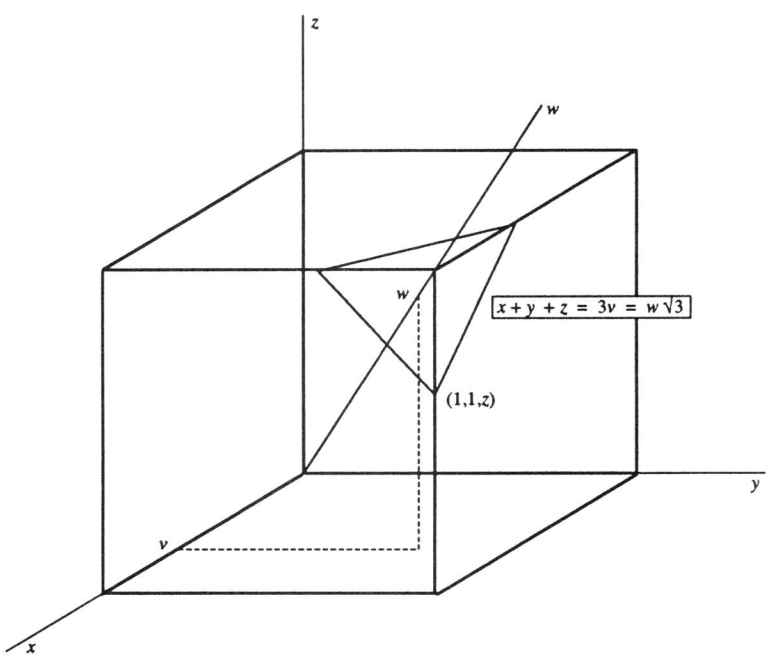

Choose a point v on the x-axis with $\frac{1}{2} \leqq v \leqq 1$. We first deal with the case $\frac{2}{3} \leqq v \leqq 1$. Then the point with Cartesian coordinates (v,v,v) determines a point $w = v\sqrt{3}$ on the w-axis, and the plane normal to the w-axis at this point intersects C in a triangle, also shown in the preceding figure. It is clear that the plane has equation $x + y + z = 3v = w\sqrt{3}$ and that it meets one edge of the cube at the point $(1,1,z)$ for some z between 0 and 1. In fact, because $(1,1,z)$ satisfies the equation of the plane, it follows that $z = -2 + w\sqrt{3}$.

456   Chapter 14 Miscellaneous

When the cube is rotated, the resulting solid S meets the plane $x + y + z = 3v$ in a circular disk centered at (v, v, v), and the radius of this disk is the distance from (v, v, v) to $(1, 1, z)$, which is

$$\sqrt{(v-1)^2 + (v-1)^2 + (w\sqrt{3} - 2 - v)^2} = \sqrt{2(v-1)^2 + (3v - 2 - v)^2}$$
$$= \sqrt{6(v-1)^2} = (1-v)\sqrt{6} = \left(1 - \tfrac{1}{3}w\sqrt{3}\right)\sqrt{6}.$$

Now we turn to the case $\tfrac{1}{2} \leq v \leq \tfrac{2}{3}$. In this case the plane through (v, v, v) normal to the w-axis meets the surface of the cube in a semi-regular hexagon, one in which each interior angle is $2\pi/3$ and whose sides are of only two different lengths a and b, alternating as one moves around the hexagon. Such a hexagon is shown in the next figure.

One of the vertices of this hexagon is located at the point $(1, y, 0)$ on one edge of the cube. The distance from (v, v, v) to this point is the radius of the circular disk in which the plane normal to the w-axis at (v, v, v) meets the solid S. It is easy to show that $y = 3v - 1$, and it follows that the distance in question is

$$\sqrt{(v-1)^2 + (2v-1)^2 + v^2} = \sqrt{6v^2 - 6v + 2} = \sqrt{2w^2 - 2w\sqrt{3} + 2}.$$

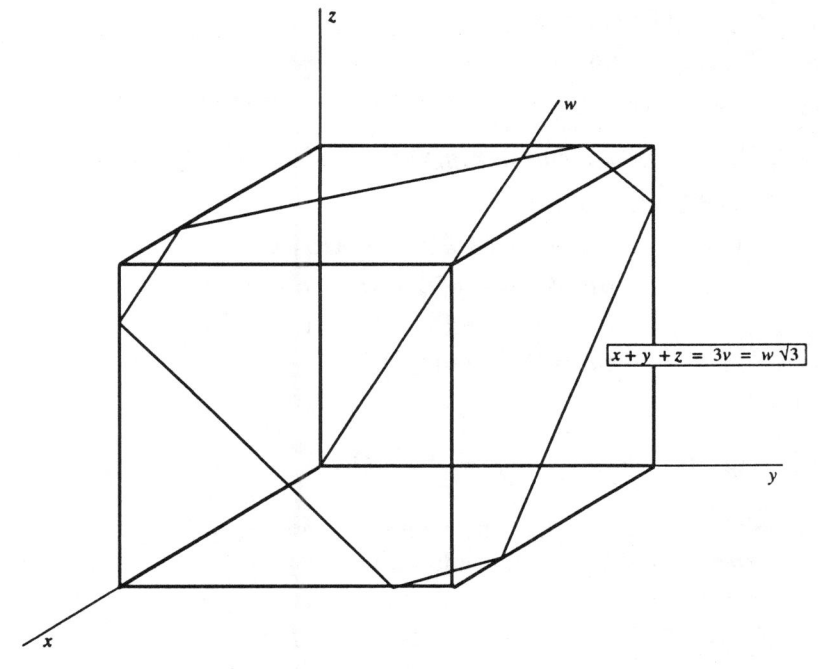

By considering only values of v for which $\tfrac{1}{2} \leq v \leq 1$, we obtain only half of the solid S, so we now can find the volume V of S as follows. We shift to coordinates on the w-axis, and remember that $dw = \sqrt{3}\, dv$; the result is that

$$V = 2\int_{v=1/2}^{2/3} \pi\left(2w^2 - 2w\sqrt{3} + 2\right)\sqrt{3}\, dw + 2\int_{v=2/3}^{1} 6\pi\left(1 - \tfrac{1}{3}w\sqrt{3}\right)^2 \sqrt{3}\, dw.$$

The adjusted limits of integration are $w = \tfrac{1}{2}\sqrt{3}$ to $\tfrac{2}{3}\sqrt{3}$ in the first integral and $w = \tfrac{2}{3}\sqrt{3}$ to $\sqrt{3}$ in the second, and a computer algebra program promptly reports that the value of V is $\pi/\sqrt{3}$.

Chapter 14 Miscellaneous

Chapter 15: Vector Calculus
Section 15.1

11. Matches Fig. 15.1.8
12. Matches Fig. 15.1.9
13. Matches Fig. 15.1.10
14. Matches Fig. 15.1.7

16. $\operatorname{div} \mathbf{F}(x,y,z) = 3 - 2 - 4 = -3$; $\operatorname{curl} \mathbf{F}(x,y,z) = \begin{vmatrix} \mathbf{i} & \mathbf{j} & \mathbf{k} \\ \frac{\partial}{\partial x} & \frac{\partial}{\partial y} & \frac{\partial}{\partial z} \\ 3x & -2y & -4z \end{vmatrix} = 0.$

17. $\operatorname{div} \mathbf{F}(x,y,z) = 0$; $\operatorname{curl} \mathbf{F}(x,y,z) = \begin{vmatrix} \mathbf{i} & \mathbf{j} & \mathbf{k} \\ \frac{\partial}{\partial x} & \frac{\partial}{\partial y} & \frac{\partial}{\partial z} \\ yz & xz & xy \end{vmatrix} = \langle x-x, y-y, z-z \rangle = 0.$

18. $\operatorname{div} \mathbf{F}(x,y,z) = 2x + 2y + 2z$; $\operatorname{curl} \mathbf{F}(x,y,z) = 0$.

20. $\operatorname{div} \mathbf{F}(x,y,z) = 12$; $\operatorname{curl} \mathbf{F}(x,y,z) = \langle 2, 3, 1 \rangle$.

22. $\operatorname{div} \mathbf{F}(x,y,z) = e^{xz}\cos y - e^{xy}\sin z$; $\operatorname{curl} \mathbf{F}(x,y,z) = \langle xe^{xy}\cos z - xe^{xz}\sin y, -ye^{xy}\cos z, ze^{xz}\sin y \rangle$.

24. $\operatorname{div} \mathbf{F}(x,y,z) = 2xe^{-z} + 3y^2 \ln x + \cosh y$; $\operatorname{curl} \mathbf{F}(x,y,z) = \langle z\sinh y, -x^2 e^{-z}, \frac{1}{x}y^3 \rangle$.

26. Write $\mathbf{F} = \langle P, Q, R \rangle$ and $\mathbf{G} = \langle S, T, U \rangle$. Then
$$\begin{aligned}\operatorname{div}(a\mathbf{F}+b\mathbf{G}) &= \operatorname{div}\langle aP+bS, aQ+bT, aR+bU\rangle \\ &= aP_x + bS_x + aQ_y + bT_y + aR_z + bU_z \\ &= a(P_x + Q_y + R_z) + b(S_x + T_y + U_z) \\ &= (a\operatorname{div}\mathbf{F}) + (b\operatorname{div}\mathbf{G}).\end{aligned}$$

32. Write $\mathbf{F} = \langle P, Q, R \rangle$. Then
$$\operatorname{div}(\operatorname{curl}\mathbf{F}) = \operatorname{div}\langle R_y - Q_z, P_z - R_x, Q_x - P_y \rangle = R_{yx} - Q_{zx} + P_{zy} - R_{xy} + Q_{xz} - P_{yz} = 0$$

provided $R_{yx} = R_{xy}$, $Q_{zx} = Q_{xz}$, and $P_{zy} = P_{yz}$; these equations hold in any region where (say) all second-order partial derivatives are continuous, a condition that normally holds in applications.

34. $\nabla f \times \nabla g = \begin{vmatrix} \mathbf{i} & \mathbf{j} & \mathbf{k} \\ f_x & f_y & f_z \\ g_x & g_y & g_z \end{vmatrix} = \langle f_y g_z - f_z g_y, f_z g_x - f_x g_z, f_x g_y - f_y g_x \rangle.$

Therefore
$$\begin{aligned}\operatorname{div}(\nabla f \times \nabla g) &= f_{yx}g_z + f_y g_{zx} - f_{zx}g_y - f_z g_{yx} \\ &\quad + f_{zy}g_x + f_z g_{xy} - f_{xy}g_z - f_x g_{zy} \\ &\quad + f_{xz}g_y + f_x g_{yz} - f_{yz}g_x - f_y g_{xz} = 0\end{aligned}$$

wherever the mixed second-order partial derivatives of both f and g are equal: $f_{xy} = f_{yx}$, and so on.

36. $\mathbf{a} \times \mathbf{r} = \begin{vmatrix} \mathbf{i} & \mathbf{j} & \mathbf{k} \\ a_1 & a_2 & a_3 \\ x & y & z \end{vmatrix} = \langle a_2 z - a_3 y, a_3 x - a_1 z, a_1 y - a_2 x \rangle$ where $\mathbf{a} = \langle a_1, a_2, a_3 \rangle$.

Therefore $\operatorname{div}(\mathbf{a} \times \mathbf{r}) = 0 + 0 + 0 = 0$ and

$$\text{curl}\,(\mathbf{a}\times\mathbf{r}) = \begin{vmatrix} \mathbf{i} & \mathbf{j} & \mathbf{k} \\ \frac{\partial}{\partial x} & \frac{\partial}{\partial y} & \frac{\partial}{\partial z} \\ a_2 z - a_3 y & a_3 x - a_1 z & a_1 y - a_2 x \end{vmatrix} = \langle 2a_1, 2a_2, 2a_3\rangle = 2\mathbf{a}.$$

38. $\nabla \times \dfrac{1}{r^3}\mathbf{r} = \dfrac{1}{r^3}\begin{vmatrix} \mathbf{i} & \mathbf{j} & \mathbf{k} \\ \frac{\partial}{\partial x} & \frac{\partial}{\partial y} & \frac{\partial}{\partial z} \\ x & y & z \end{vmatrix} = \dfrac{1}{r^3}\langle 0,0,0\rangle = \mathbf{0}.$

40. $\dfrac{1}{r} = (x^2 + y^2 + z^2)^{-1/2}$, so $\nabla\left(\dfrac{1}{r}\right) = -\dfrac{1}{2}(x^2+y^2+z^2)^{-3/2}\langle 2x, 2y, 2z\rangle = -\dfrac{1}{r^3}\langle x,y,z\rangle = -\dfrac{1}{r^3}\mathbf{r}.$

41. $\text{div}\,(r\mathbf{r}) = \text{div}\left(\sqrt{x^2+y^2+z^2}\,\langle x,y,z\rangle\right)$
$= \dfrac{\partial}{\partial x}\left(x\sqrt{x^2+y^2+z^2}\right) + \dfrac{\partial}{\partial y}\left(y\sqrt{x^2+y^2+z^2}\right) + \dfrac{\partial}{\partial z}\left(z\sqrt{x^2+y^2+z^2}\right)$
$= 3\sqrt{x^2+y^2+z^2} + \dfrac{x^2}{\sqrt{x^2+y^2+z^2}} + \dfrac{y^2}{\sqrt{x^2+y^2+z^2}} + \dfrac{z^2}{\sqrt{x^2+y^2+z^2}} = 3r + r = 4r.$

42. $\text{div}\,(\text{grad}\,r) = \text{div}\left((x^2+y^2+z^2)^{-1/2}\langle x,y,z\rangle\right)$
$= \dfrac{\partial}{\partial x}\left(x(x^2+y^2+z^2)^{-1/2}\right) + \dfrac{\partial}{\partial y}\left(y(x^2+y^2+z^2)^{-1/2}\right) + \dfrac{\partial}{\partial z}\left(z(x^2+y^2+z^2)^{-1/2}\right)$
$= (x^2+y^2+z^2)^{-1/2} - \dfrac{x^2}{(x^2+y^2+z^2)^{3/2}} - \dfrac{y^2}{(x^2+y^2+z^2)^{3/2}} - \dfrac{z^2}{(x^2+y^2+z^2)^{3/2}} \neq 0.$

44. $\text{grad}\,(r^{10}) = \text{grad}\left((x^2+y^2+z^2)^5\right)$
$= \langle 5(x^2+y^2+z^2)^4(2x), 5(x^2+y^2+z^2)^4(2y), 5(x^2+y^2+z^2)^4(2z)\rangle$
$= 10(x^2+y^2+z^2)^4\langle x,y,z\rangle = 10r^8\mathbf{r}.$

Section 15.2

1. $dx = 4\,dt$, $dy = 3\,dt$, and $ds = 5\,dt$. Also $f(t) = (4t-1)^2 + (3t+1)^2 = 25t^2 - 2t + 2.$

   Therefore $\displaystyle\int_C f(x,y)\,ds = \int_{-1}^{1}(25t^2 - 2t + 2)(5)\,dt = \dfrac{310}{3};$

   $\displaystyle\int_C f(x,y)\,dx = \dfrac{248}{3}$ and $\displaystyle\int_C f(x,y)\,dy = 62.$

2. $(5\sqrt{5}-1)/12$, $1/2$, and $2/3$.

4. Note that $ds = dt$. So $\displaystyle\int_C (2x-y)\,ds = \int_0^{\pi/2}(2\sin t - \cos t)\,dt = 1;$

   $\displaystyle\int_C (2x-y)\,dx = \int_0^{\pi/2}\left(2\sin t\cos t - \dfrac{1+\cos 2t}{2}\right)dt = \dfrac{4-\pi}{4};$

   $\displaystyle\int_C (2x-y)\,dy = \int_0^{\pi/2}(-2\sin^2 t + \sin t\cos t)\,dt = \dfrac{1-\pi}{2}.$

6. Parametrize C: $x = t$, $y = t^2$, $-1 \leq t \leq 2$. Then $\displaystyle\int_C xy\,dx + (x+y)\,dy = \int_{-1}^{2}(3t^3 + 2t^2)\,dt = \dfrac{69}{4}.$

7. Use y as the parameter.

8. Parametrize C: $x = t^2$, $y = t^3$, $1 \leq t \leq 2$. Then $\displaystyle\int_C y\sqrt{x}\,dx + x\sqrt{x}\,dy = \int_1^2 5t^5\,dt = \dfrac{105}{2}.$

10. If $f(x,y) = \frac{1}{2}x^2 + 2xy - \frac{1}{2}y^2$, then $\nabla f = \langle x+2y, 2x-y \rangle$. Therefore the given integral is independent of the path. Hence $\int_C (x+2y)\,dx + (2x-y)\,dy = f(-2,-1) - f(3,2) = -9$.

12. If $u(x,y,z) = xyz$, then $\nabla u = \mathbf{F}$. Therefore the value of the integral is $u(4,2,-1) - u(2,-1,3) = -2$.

13. $\int_C \mathbf{F} \cdot \mathbf{T}\,ds = \int_{t=0}^{\pi} (y\,dx - x\,dy + z\,dz) = \int_0^{\pi} (\cos^2 t + \sin^2 t + 4t)\,dt = \pi + 2\pi^2$.

14. $\mathbf{F} = \nabla u$ where $u(x,y,z) = x^2 + 3xy + y^2 + z^3$; the value of the integral is 71.

16. C is parallel to $\langle 2,3,3 \rangle$, so C may be parametrized by
$$\mathbf{r}(t) = \langle 1,-1,2 \rangle + \langle 2t, 3t, 3t \rangle = \langle 2t+1, 3t-1, 3t+2 \rangle;$$
that is, we let $x = 2t+1$, $y = 3t-1$, and $z = 3t+2$ for $0 \le x \le 1$. Then $ds = \sqrt{22}\,dt$, so
$$\int_C xyz\,ds = \int_0^1 (2t+1)(3t-1)(3t+2)\sqrt{22}\,dt = 7\sqrt{22}.$$

18. $12\sqrt{65}(2\sqrt{2} - 1)$

19. If the wire has constant density k, then the total mass of the wire is $M = \pi a k$ and the mass of a segment of length ds is $dm = k\,ds$. Parametrize the wire as follows:
$$x = a\cos\theta,\quad y = a\sin\theta,\quad 0 \le \theta \le \pi.$$
Then compute $M_x = \int_C y\,dm$.

20. Use the parametrizations and other notation given in the preceding solution.
$$I_x = \int_C y^2\,dm = \tfrac{1}{2}\pi a^3 k = \tfrac{1}{2}Ma^2 \text{ and } I_y = \int_C x^2\,dm = \tfrac{1}{2}\pi a^3 k = \tfrac{1}{2}Ma^2.$$

22. With the parametrization of the helical wire given in Problem 21, we find that $ds = 5\,dt$ and thus that $dm = 5k\,dt$. The mass of the wire is
$$m = \int_0^{2\pi} 5k\,dt = 10k\pi$$
and its moment of intertia around the z-axis is
$$I_z = \int_0^{2\pi} 5k[(x(t))^2 + (y(t))^2]\,dt = 90k\pi = 9m.$$

24. With the parametrization given in Problem 24, we find that
$$ds = \sqrt{2 - 2\cos t}\,dt = 2\left|\sin\frac{t}{2}\right|dt.$$
So the mass of the wire is
$$m = \int_0^{2\pi} 2k\sin\frac{t}{2}\,dt = \left[-4k\cos\frac{t}{2}\right]_0^{2\pi} = 8k.$$
Its moment around the y-axis is
$$M_y = \int_0^{2\pi} kx(t)\,ds = \left[\tfrac{2}{3}k\left(\sin\frac{3t}{2} + 9\sin\frac{t}{2} - 6t\cos\frac{t}{2}\right)\right]_0^{2\pi} = 8\pi k$$

and its moment around the x-axis is

$$M_x = \int_0^{2\pi} ky(t)\,ds = \left[\frac{2}{3}k\left(\cos\frac{3t}{2} - 9\cos\frac{t}{2}\right)\right]_0^{2\pi} = \frac{32k}{3}.$$

Hence

$$\bar{x} = \frac{M_y}{m} = \pi \quad \text{and} \quad \bar{y} = \frac{M_x}{m} = \frac{4}{3}.$$

Its moment of inertia around the x-axis is

$$I_x = \int_0^{2\pi} (y[t])^2\,k\,ds = \left[\tfrac{1}{15}k\left(25\cos\frac{3t}{2} - 3\cos\frac{5t}{2} - 150\cos\frac{t}{2}\right)\right]_0^{2\pi} = \frac{256k}{15} = \frac{32m}{15}.$$

25. From the given parametrization we find that $ds = \frac{3}{2}|\sin 2t|\,dt$, and hence

$$I_0 = 4\int_0^{\pi/2} k(\cos^6 t + \sin^6 t)\,ds = \left[\frac{3}{64}k(-\cos 6t - 7\cos 2t)\right]_0^{\pi/2} = 3k.$$

Because the mass of the wire is

$$m = 4\int_0^{\pi/2} k\,ds = \left[-3k\cos 2t\right]_0^{\pi/2} = 6k,$$

we can also write $I_0 = m/2$.

26. We use the parametrization $x = a\cos t$, $y = a\sin t$, $0 \le t \le 2\pi$. Then $ds = a\,dt$ and the length of C is $2\pi a$, so the average distance of points of this circle from its center is

$$\bar{d} = \frac{1}{2\pi a}\int_0^{2\pi} a^2\,dt = a.$$

27. We use the parametrization given in the solution of Problem 26. The law of cosines gives the distance from $(a,0)$ to the points (x,y) of the circle as $2a\sin(t/2)$, so the average distance of points of the circle from $(a,0)$ is

$$\bar{d} = \frac{1}{2\pi a}\int_0^{2\pi} 2a^2 \sin\frac{t}{2}\,dt = \frac{4a}{\pi}.$$

28. We use the parametrization of the cycloid given in Problem 24. Then $ds = 2\sin(t/2)$, and so the cycloidal arch has length

$$\int_0^{2\pi} 2\sin\frac{t}{2}\,dt = 8.$$

Hence the average distance of points of the cycloidal arch from $(0,0)$ is

$$\bar{d} = \frac{1}{8}\int_0^{2\pi} (t^2 + 2 - 2\cos t - 2t\sin t)^{1/2}\,2\sin\frac{t}{2}\,dt \approx 3.55252.$$

29. We use the parametrization of the astroid given in Problem 25, for which $ds = \frac{3}{2}\sin 2t\,dt$ so long as $0 \le t \le \pi/2$. The part of the astroid in the first quadrant has length $\frac{3}{2}$, so the average distance of points of the astroid from $(0,0)$ is

$$\bar{d} = \frac{2}{3}\int_0^{\pi/2}(\cos^6 t + \sin^6 t)\frac{3}{2}\sin 2t\,dt = -\frac{1}{32}\left[\cos 6t + 7\cos 2t\right]_0^{\pi/2} = \frac{1}{2}.$$

30. We use the parametrization of the helix given in Problem 21. Then $ds = 5\,dt$, so the length of the helix is 10π. Because
$$[x(t)]^2 + [y(t)]^2 + [z(t)]^2 = 9 + 16t^2,$$
the average distance of points of the helix from $(0,0,0)$ is
$$\bar{d} = \frac{1}{10\pi}\int_0^{10\pi} 5\sqrt{9+16t^2}\,dt$$
$$= \frac{1}{10\pi}\left[\frac{5t}{2}\sqrt{9+16t^2} + \frac{45}{8}\operatorname{arcsinh}\frac{4t}{3}\right]_0^{10\pi}$$
$$= \frac{1}{2}\sqrt{9+64\pi^2} + \frac{9}{16\pi}\operatorname{arcsinh}\frac{8\pi}{3} \approx 13.160900458.$$

31. With the given parametrization, we find that $ds = \sqrt{2}\,e^{-t}\,dt$ and that
$$\sqrt{[x(t)]^2+[y(t)]^2} = e^{-t}.$$
The length of the spiral is
$$\int_0^\infty \sqrt{2}\,e^{-t}\,dt = \left[-\sqrt{2}\,e^{-t}\right]_0^\infty = \sqrt{2},$$
so the average distance of points of the spiral from $(0,0)$ is
$$\bar{d} = \frac{1}{\sqrt{2}}\int_0^\infty \sqrt{2}\,e^{-2t}\,dt = \frac{1}{2}.$$

32. The work done in moving along a path on the sphere is zero because $\mathbf{F}$ is normal to the sphere. Therefore $\mathbf{F}\cdot\mathbf{T}$ is identically zero on any path on the sphere. Let C denote the straight line segment from $(1,0,0)$ to $(5,0,0)$. Then
$$W = \int_C \mathbf{F}\cdot d\mathbf{r} = \int_C \mathbf{F}\cdot\mathbf{i}\,ds = \tfrac{4}{5}k.$$

25. (a) $W = \displaystyle\int_0^1 \frac{ky}{1+y^2}\,dy;$ (b) $W = \displaystyle\int_1^0 \frac{kx}{1+x^2}\,dx.$

34. Let C denote the unit circle $x^2+y^2=1$; parametrize C: $\mathbf{r}(t) = \langle \cos t, \sin t\rangle$, $0 \leq t \leq \pi$.

Write $\mathbf{F} = \langle a,b\rangle$. Then the work done in moving a particle uniformly once counterclockwise around C is
$$W = \int_0^{2\pi} \langle a,b\rangle\cdot\langle-\sin t, \cos t\rangle\,dt = \Big[a\cos t + b\sin t\Big]_0^{2\pi} = 0.$$

36. We assume that the particle moves uniformly, so that its path may be parametrized as follows: $\mathbf{r}(t) = \langle \cos t, \sin t\rangle$, $0 \leq t \leq 2\pi$. Then
$$W = \int_0^{2\pi}\langle -\sin t, \cos t\rangle\cdot\langle -\sin t, \cos t\rangle\,dt = \int_0^{2\pi}(\sin^2 t + \cos^2 t)\,dt = 2\pi.$$

38. Parametrization: $x = t$, $y = t$, $100 \geq t \geq 0$.
$$W = \int_{100}^0 \langle 0, -150\rangle\cdot\langle 1,1\rangle\,dt = \Big[-150t\Big]_{100}^0 = 15{,}000 \text{ (ft-lb)}.$$

39. Parametrization: $x = 100\sin t$, $y = 100\cos t$, $\pi/2 \geq t \geq 0$.

$$W = \int_{\pi/2}^{0} \langle 0, -150\rangle \cdot \langle 100\cos t, -100\sin t\rangle \, dt = \left[-15,000 \cos t\right]_0^{\pi/2} = 15,000 \quad \text{(ft-lb)}.$$

40. Parametrization: $x = 10t$, $y = t^2$, $10 \geq t \geq 0$.

$$W = \int_{10}^{0} \langle 0, -150\rangle \cdot \langle 10, 2t\rangle \, dt = \left[-150t^2\right]_{10}^{0} = 15,000 \quad \text{(ft-lb)}.$$

41. We parametrize the helical ramp R with position vector $\mathbf{r}(t)$ having components

$$x(t) = 25\cos t, \quad y(t) = 25\sin t, \quad z(t) = \frac{10t}{\pi}, \quad 0 \leq t \leq 10\pi.$$

Then $ds = (5/\pi)\sqrt{4 + 25\pi^2}\, dt$, so the work done by $\mathbf{F}$ on the person sliding down this ramp is

$$W = \int_R \mathbf{F} \cdot d\mathbf{r} = \int_0^{10\pi} \frac{2000}{\pi}\, dt = 20000 \quad \text{(ft} \cdot \text{lb)}.$$

Section 15.3

1. If $\nabla f = \mathbf{F} = \langle 2x + 3y, 3x + 2y\rangle$ then $f_x(x,y) = 2x + 3y$, so $f(x,y) = x^2 + 3xy + g(y)$. Then $3x + g'(y) = f_y(x,y) = 3x + 2y$, so we may choose $g(y) = y^2$. Answer: One potential function for $\mathbf{F}$ is $f(x,y) = x^2 + 3xy + y^2$.
2. $f(x,y) = 2x^2 - xy + 3y^2$
4. $f(x,y) = x^2y^2 + x^3 + y^4$
5. Not conservative: $P_y = 2 \neq 3 = Q_x$.
6. Not conservative: $P_y = 4x^2 - 20y^3 \neq 3x^2 - 20y^3 = Q_x$.
8. $f(x,y) = x + y^2 + e^{xy}$
10. $f(x,y) = \frac{1}{2}x^2 + x\arctan y + \frac{1}{2}\ln(1 + y^2)$
11. Not conservative: $P_y = -x\sin y + \cos y \neq -y\sin x + \cos x = Q_x$.
12. Not conservative: $P_y = e^{x-y}(1+x)(1-y) \neq e^{x-y}(1+x)(1+y) = Q_x$.
14. $f(x,y) = e^x \sin y + x\tan y$
16. $f(x,y) = xy^{-2/3} + x^{-3/2}y = \dfrac{x^{5/2} + y^{5/3}}{y^{2/3}x^{3/2}}$
22. $\dfrac{\partial}{\partial y}(y^2 + 2xy) = 2y + 2x = \dfrac{\partial}{\partial x}(x^2 + 2xy)$, so the integral is path-independent in the entire plane. If $\mathbf{F}(x,y) = \langle y^2 + 2xy, x^2 + 2xy\rangle$, then $\mathbf{F}$ is the gradient of $f(x,y) = xy^2 + x^2y$, so the value of the integral is $f(1,2) - f(0,0) = 4 + 2 = 6$.
24. $\left[x\cos y\right]_{(0,0)}^{(2,\pi)} = 2\cos\pi = -2$
26. $\left[xe^y + ye^x\right]_{(0,0)}^{(1,-1)} = \dfrac{1}{e} - e$
28. $f(x,y,z) = x^2 - xy - xz + y^2 + z^2$
30. Parametrize the upper semicircle C_1 as follows: $x = \cos t$, $y = \sin t$, $0 \leq t \leq \pi$.
    Parametrize the lower semicircle C_2 as follows: $x = \cos t$, $y = -\sin t$, $0 \leq t \leq \pi$.

On C_1, $\mathbf{T} = \langle -y, x \rangle$; on C_2, $\mathbf{T} = \langle y, -x \rangle$. In either case we have $ds = dt$. Finally, $\mathbf{F} \cdot \mathbf{T} = 1$ on C_1; but on C_2, $\mathbf{F} \cdot \mathbf{T} = -1$. Therefore

$$\int_{C_1} \mathbf{F} \cdot \mathbf{T} \, ds = \int_0^\pi 1 \, dt = \pi; \quad \int_{C_2} \mathbf{F} \cdot \mathbf{T} \, ds = -\pi.$$

There is no such function $f(x, y)$, for if there were then $\int_C \mathbf{F} \cdot \mathbf{T} \, ds$ would be independent of the path.

32. Choose g such that $\mathbf{F} = \nabla g$. Then $P = g_x$, $Q = g_y$, and so on. Assume as usual that the second-order partial derivatives of g are continuous to obtain the desired conclusion.

34. You should find that $f(x, y, z) = xyz + \frac{1}{2} y^2 + z$.

35. (b) $\int_C \mathbf{F} \cdot \mathbf{T} \, ds = f(B) - f(A) = \theta_2 - \theta_1$.

   (c) $\mathbf{F}$ is not conservative on any rectangle that contains both C_1 and C_2 because $\mathbf{F}$ is not defined at $(0, 0)$.

36. $\mathbf{F} = \nabla f$ where

$$f(x, y, z) = -\frac{k}{\sqrt{x^2 + y^2 + z^2}}.$$

Because f depends only on the distance $\sqrt{x^2 + y^2 + z^2}$ of the point (x, y, z) from the origin, it now follows that

$$W = \int_C \mathbf{F} \cdot \mathbf{T} \, ds = f(r_2) - f(r_1) = k \left(\frac{1}{r_1} - \frac{1}{r_2} \right).$$

37. Substitution of the given data in the formula of Problem 36 (and remembering to convert kilometers into meters) yields $W \approx 8.04 \times 10^{10}$ N·m.

38. Substitution of the given data in the formula of Problem 36 (and remembering to convert kilometers into meters) yields $W \approx 3.05 \times 10^{12}$ N·m.

Section 15.4

1. $\int_{-1}^1 \int_{-1}^1 (2x - 2y) \, dy \, dx = \int_{-1}^1 4x \, dx = 0.$

2. $\iint_R (-2y - 2y) \, dA = \int_0^1 \int_0^{1-y} (-4y) \, dx \, dy = -\frac{2}{3}.$

4. $\int_0^1 \int_{x^2}^x (y + 2y) \, dy \, dx = \frac{1}{5}.$

6. $\int_0^{2\pi} \int_0^3 (2 - 2r \sin \theta) \, r \, dr \, d\theta = 18\pi.$

7. $\int_0^\pi \int_0^{\sin x} 1 \, dy \, dx$

8. $\iint_R (e^x \cos y - e^x \cos y) \, dA = 0.$

10. $Q_x - P_y = 0$, so the value of the integral is zero.

12. $Q_x - P_y = 0$.

13. Let C denote the circle with the parametrization given in the problem. The area of the circular disk it bounds is given by

$$A = \oint_C x \, dy = \oint_C (a \cos t)(a \cos t) \, dt = a^2 \int_0^{2\pi} \tfrac{1}{2}(1 + \cos 2t) \, dt = \pi a^2.$$

14. The region under the first arch in the first quadrant is bounded by the curve C, which we write as the union of C_1 and C_2 where C_1 has the parametrization

$$x = a(t - \sin t), \quad y = a(1 - \cos t), \quad 0 \le t \le 2\pi$$

and C_2 has the parametrization

$$x = t, \quad y = 0, \quad 0 \le t \le 2\pi a.$$

Because C is to have the positive orientation, we must reverse direction of the parametrization of C_1 or else change the sign of the integral. In any case, the area of the region is

$$A = \oint_C x \, dy = -\int_0^{2\pi} a^2 (t - \sin t)(\sin t) \, dt + \int_0^{2\pi a} 0 \, dt = 3\pi a^2.$$

16. The area is $\frac{5}{12}$.

17. $Q_x - P_y = 3 + 2 = 5$ and the domain of the double integral is a region bounded by an ellipse with semiaxes $a = 3$ and $b = 2$, so $W = 5\pi ab = 30\pi$.

18. $Q_x - P_y = 2y - 2y = 0$, so $W = 0$.

19. $Q_x - P_y = 21x^2y^2 - 15x^2y^2 = 6x^2y^2$, so the work is

$$W = \int_0^3 \int_0^{6-2x} 6x^2y^2 \, dy \, dx = \int_0^3 \left[2x^2y^3\right]_0^{6-2x} dx$$

$$= \int_0^3 2x^2(6-2x)^3 \, dx = \left[144x^3 - 108x^4 + \tfrac{144}{5}x^5 - \tfrac{8}{3}x^6\right]_0^3 = \tfrac{972}{5}.$$

20. $Q_x - P_y = 6xy - 2xy = 4xy$, so $W = 0$ by symmetry. Check:

$$W = \int_{-2}^2 \int_0^{\sqrt{4-x^2}} 4xy \, dy \, dx = \int_{-2}^2 (8x - 2x^3) \, dx = 0.$$

21. $\nabla \cdot \mathbf{F} = 2 + 3 = 5$ and the domain of the double integral is bounded by an ellipse with semiaxes $a = 3$ and $b = 2$, so $\phi = 6\pi ab = 30\pi$.

22. $\nabla \cdot \mathbf{F} = 3x^2 + 3y^2$, so

$$\phi = 4 \int_0^2 \int_0^{\sqrt{4-x^2}} (3x^2 + 3y^2) \, dy \, dx$$

$$= 4 \int_0^2 \left[3x^2 y + y^3\right]_0^{\sqrt{4-x^2}} dx$$

$$= 4 \int_0^2 2(2 + x^2)\sqrt{4-x^2} \, dx$$

$$= \left[2(2x + x^3)\sqrt{4-x^2} + 48 \arcsin \frac{x}{2}\right]_0^2 = 24\pi.$$

23. $\nabla \cdot \mathbf{F} = 3 + 2 = 5$ and the domain of the double integral is a triangle with base 3 and height 6, so $\phi = 5 \cdot \frac{1}{2} \cdot 3 \cdot 6 = 45$.

24. $\nabla \cdot \mathbf{F} = 3y^2 + 4 + 3x^2 - 4 = 3x^2 + 3y^2$, so

$$\phi = \int_{-2}^{2} \int_{0}^{\sqrt{4-x^2}} (3x^2 + 3y^2) \, dy \, dx = 12\pi$$

(the details of the integration are almost exactly those shown in the solution of Problem 22).

30. (a) $\left(0, \dfrac{4a}{3\pi}\right)$; (b) $\left(\dfrac{4a}{3\pi}, \dfrac{4a}{3\pi}\right)$.

32. Parametrize the boundary curve C as follows: $x = a\cos t$, $y = a\sin t$, $0 \le t \le 2\pi$. Then

$$I_0 = \frac{\rho}{3}\int_0^{2\pi}(a^4\sin^4 t + a^4\cos^4 t)\,dt = \tfrac{4}{3}\rho a^4 \int_0^{\pi/2}(\sin^4 t + \cos^4 t)\,dt$$
$$= \tfrac{4}{3}\rho a^4 (2)\left(\tfrac{1}{2}\right)\left(\tfrac{3}{4}\right)\left(\tfrac{1}{2}\right)\pi \quad \text{(by Integral Formula 113)}$$
$$= \left(\tfrac{1}{2}a^2\right)(\rho\pi a^2) = \tfrac{1}{2}Ma^2.$$

34. $A = \displaystyle\oint_C x\,dy = \int_0^{\pi} 2\sin t \cos^2 t \, dt = \tfrac{4}{3}.$

39. (a) The area of the triangle is

$$A = 3 \cdot \frac{1}{2} \cdot \left(1 \cdot \sin\frac{2\pi}{3} - 0 \cdot \cos\frac{2\pi}{3}\right) = \frac{3\sqrt{3}}{4}.$$

(b) The area of the pentagon is

$$A = 5 \cdot \frac{1}{2} \cdot \left(1 \cdot \sin\frac{2\pi}{5} - 0 \cdot \cos\frac{2\pi}{5}\right) = \frac{5\sqrt{10 + 2\sqrt{5}}}{8} \approx 2.377641291.$$

Section 15.5

1. $dS = \sqrt{3}\,dy\,dx$, so

$$\iint_S f(x,y,z)\,dS = \int_0^1 \int_0^{1-x} (x+y)\sqrt{3}\,dy\,dx = \tfrac{1}{3}\sqrt{3}.$$

2. $dS = \sqrt{14}\,dy\,dx$, so

$$\iint_S f(x,y,z)\,dS = \int_0^3 \int_0^{(6-2x)/3} xyz\sqrt{14}\,dy\,dx = \tfrac{9}{5}\sqrt{14}.$$

3. $dS = r\sqrt{14}\,dr\,d\theta$, so

$$\iint_S f(x,y,z)\,dS = \int_0^{2\pi}\int_0^3 (2r\cos\theta + 3r\sin\theta)\left(r\sqrt{14}\right)dr\,d\theta = 27\pi\sqrt{14}.$$

4. $dS = r\sqrt{2}\,dr\,d\theta$, so

$$\iint_S f(x,y,z)\,dS = \int_0^{2\pi}\int_0^2 r^3\sqrt{2}\,dr\,d\theta = 8\pi\sqrt{2}.$$

5. $dS = r\sqrt{1+4r^2}\,dr\,d\theta$, so

$$\iint_S f(x,y,z)\,dS = \int_0^{2\pi}\!\!\int_0^2 (1+r^2\sin\theta\cos\theta)r\sqrt{1+4r^2}\,dr\,d\theta = \tfrac{1}{6}\pi\left(17\sqrt{17}-1\right).$$

6. $dS = \sin\phi\,d\phi\,d\theta$, so
$$\iint_S f(x,y,z)\,dS = \int_0^{2\pi}\!\!\int_0^{\pi/2} \sin^3\phi\cos\phi\,d\phi\,d\theta = \tfrac{1}{2}\pi.$$

7. $dS = r\sqrt{3}\,dr\,d\theta$, so
$$I_z = \iint_S \delta(x^2+y^2)\,dS = \int_0^{2\pi}\!\!\int_0^3 r^3\sqrt{3}\,dr\,d\theta = \tfrac{81}{2}\pi\sqrt{3}.$$

8. $dS = r\,dr\,d\theta$, so
$$I_z = \iint_S \delta(x^2+y^2)\,dS = \int_0^{2\pi}\!\!\int_0^5 r^3\,dr\,d\theta = \tfrac{625}{2}\pi.$$

9. $dS = 1\,dy\,d\theta$, so
$$I_z = \iint_S \delta(x^2+y^2)\,dS = \int_0^{2\pi}\!\!\int_{-1}^1 (\cos^2\theta + y^2)\,dy\,d\theta = \tfrac{10}{3}\pi.$$

10. $dS = r\sqrt{2}\,dr\,d\theta$, so
$$I_z = \iint_S \delta(x^2+y^2)\,dS = \int_0^{2\pi}\!\!\int_2^5 r^3\sqrt{2}\,dr\,d\theta = \tfrac{609}{2}\pi\sqrt{2}.$$

11. $dS = 25\sin\phi\,d\phi\,d\theta$, so
$$I_z = \iint_S \delta(x^2+y^2)\,dS = \int_0^{2\pi}\!\!\int_0^{\arctan(4/3)} 625\sin^3\phi\,d\phi\,d\theta$$
$$= \tfrac{1}{6}\pi\left[1625 + 625\cos\left(3\arctan\tfrac{4}{3}\right)\right] = \frac{520}{3}\pi.$$

12. $dS = 25\sin\phi\,d\phi\,d\theta$, so
$$I_z = \iint_S \delta(x^2+y^2)\,dS = 2\int_0^{2\pi}\!\!\int_{\arctan(3/4)}^{\pi/2} 625\sin^3\phi\,d\phi\,d\theta$$
$$= \tfrac{1}{3}\pi\left[4500 - 625\cos\left(3\arctan\tfrac{3}{4}\right)\right] = \frac{4720}{3}\pi.$$

13. Parametrize S as follows: $z = 3\cos\phi$, $0 \leq \phi \leq \tfrac{1}{2}\pi$, $0 \leq \theta \leq 2\pi$. An upper unit normal for S is $\mathbf{n} = \tfrac{1}{3}\langle x, y, z\rangle$, $dS = 9\sin\phi\,d\phi\,d\theta$, and $\mathbf{F}\cdot\mathbf{n} = 3\sin^2\phi$. Hence
$$\iint_S \mathbf{F}\cdot\mathbf{n}\,dS = \int_0^{2\pi}\!\!\int_0^{\pi/2} 27\sin^3\phi\,d\phi\,d\theta = 36\pi.$$

14. $\iint_S \mathbf{F}\cdot\mathbf{n}\,dS = \iint_S x\,dy\,dz + y\,dz\,dx + z\,dx\,dy$. Let D be the region in the uv-plane bounded by the u-axis, the v-axis, and the line $2u + 2v = 3$. A suitable parametrization for S is then
$$\mathbf{r}(u,v) = \langle u, v, 3 - 2u - 2v\rangle.$$

Section 15.5 Surface Integrals

Now $\frac{\partial(x,y)}{\partial(u,v)} = 1$, $\frac{\partial(z,x)}{\partial(u,v)} = 2$, and $\frac{\partial(y,z)}{\partial(u,v)} = 1$. Therefore the integral takes the form

$$\iint_D (2x+2y+z)\,du\,dv = \iint_D (2u+2v+3-2u-2v)\,du\,dv = \iint_D 3\,du\,dv = 3(\text{area}(D)) = \tfrac{27}{8}.$$

15. Parametrize S by $\mathbf{r}(u,v) = \langle u, v, 3u+2 \rangle$ on the disk D: $u^2 + v^2 \leq 4$. Then

$$\frac{\partial(y,z)}{\partial(u,v)} = -3, \quad \frac{\partial(z,x)}{\partial(u,v)} = 0, \quad \text{and} \quad \frac{\partial(x,y)}{\partial(u,v)} = 1.$$

Therefore

$$\iint_S \mathbf{F} \cdot \mathbf{n}\, dS = \iint_D (-6y + 3z)\, du\, dv = \iint_D (-6v + 9u + 6)\, du\, dv$$
$$= \int_0^{2\pi} \int_0^2 (6 - 6r\sin\theta + 9r\cos\theta)\, r\, dr\, d\theta = \int_0^{2\pi} (12 - 16\sin\theta + 24\cos\theta)\, d\theta = 24\pi.$$

16. $\frac{16}{3}\pi$

18. 44π

19. On the bottom face of the cube (where $z = 0$, $0 \leq x \leq 1$, $0 \leq y \leq 1$), we take unit normal $\mathbf{n} = -\mathbf{k}$. But then $\mathbf{F} \cdot \mathbf{n} = -3z \equiv 0$ on the bottom face, so the flux across that surface is zero. It is also zero on the other two faces that lie in the coordinate planes. On the upper surface (where $z = 1$, $0 \leq x \leq 1$, $0 \leq y \leq 1$, we take unit normal $\mathbf{n} = \mathbf{k}$, and so $\mathbf{F} \cdot \mathbf{n} = 3z \equiv 3$. So the flux across that surface is $3 \cdot 1^2 = 3$. Similarly, the flux across the face $y = 1$, $0 \leq x \leq 1$, $0 \leq z \leq 1$ is 2 and the flux across the face $x = 1$, $0 \leq y \leq 1$, $0 \leq z \leq 1$ is 1. Therefore $\phi = 6$.

20. On the top of the hemisphere, we take unit normal $\mathbf{n} = \tfrac{1}{2}\langle x, y, z \rangle$. The parametrization

$$x = 2\sin\phi\cos\theta, \quad y = 2\sin\phi\sin\theta, \quad z = 2\cos\phi$$

($0 \leq \phi \leq \pi/2$, $0 \leq \theta \leq 2\pi$) yields $dS = 4\sin\phi\, d\phi\, d\theta$. Then we find that

$$\mathbf{F} \cdot \mathbf{n} = (4\sin\phi)\left[2\cos^2\phi + (-1 + 5\cos 2\theta)\sin^2\phi\right],$$

and it turns out that the flux across the top surface is zero. On the base of the hemisphere, we take unit normal $\mathbf{n} = -\mathbf{k}$, and $\mathbf{F} \cdot \mathbf{n} = -z \equiv 0$, so the flux across the base is also zero.

21. On each of the three faces of the pyramid that lie in the coordinate planes, $\mathbf{F} \cdot \mathbf{n} \equiv 0$, so the flux across each of those faces is zero. On the fourth face, we take unit normal $\mathbf{n} = \langle 3, 4, 1 \rangle/\sqrt{26}$ and find that

$$\mathbf{F} \cdot \mathbf{n} = \frac{3x - 4y}{\sqrt{26}} \quad \text{and} \quad dS = \sqrt{26}\, dx\, dy.$$

Hence the total flux across S is

$$\phi = \iint_S \mathbf{F} \cdot \mathbf{n}\, dS = \int_0^4 \int_0^{(12-3x)/4} (3x - 4y)\, dy\, dx$$
$$= \int_0^4 \left[-\tfrac{1}{8}(12-3x)^2 + \tfrac{3}{4}x(12-3x)\right] dx = \left[9x^2 - \tfrac{9}{8}x^3 - 18x\right]_0^4 = 0.$$

22. 32π

23. Checkpoints: The flux across the lower surface is -243π and the flux across the upper surface is 1701π.

24. On the top surface T, where $z = 3$, $0 \le r \le 3$, $0 \le \theta \le 3$, we take unit normal $\mathbf{n} = \mathbf{k}$, so that $\mathbf{F} \cdot \mathbf{n} = 3z^2 \equiv 27$. Hence the flux across T is

$$\iint_T \mathbf{F} \cdot \mathbf{n}\, dS = 27 \cdot \pi \cdot 3^2 = 243\pi$$

because T is a circular disk of radius 3. On the lower surface C (the cone), where $z = r$, $0 \le r \le 3$, $0 \le \theta \le 2\pi$, we find the (Cartesian) outer unit normal

$$\mathbf{n} = \frac{\langle x, y, -z \rangle}{\sqrt{x^2 + y^2 + z^2}},$$

and with the aid of the equation $z = \sqrt{x^2 + y^2} = r$, we find that

$$\mathbf{F} \cdot \mathbf{n} = \frac{\sqrt{2}}{2}\left(\cos^3\theta + \sin^3\theta\right) r^2 - \frac{3\sqrt{2}}{2} r^2 \quad \text{and} \quad dS = r\sqrt{2}\, dr\, d\theta.$$

Hence the flux across C is

$$\iint_C \mathbf{F} \cdot \mathbf{n}\, dS = \int_0^{2\pi} \int_0^3 \left(\cos^3\theta + \sin^3\theta - 3\right) r^3\, dr\, d\theta = -\frac{243}{2}\pi.$$

Therefore the total flux across S is $\frac{243}{2}\pi$.

26. $M = \pi k a^2 \sqrt{2}$, $M_{xy} = \frac{2}{3}\pi k a^3 \sqrt{2}$, the centroid is at $\left(0, 0, \frac{2}{3}a\right)$, and $I_z = \frac{1}{2}\sqrt{2}\pi k a^4 = \frac{1}{2} M a^2$.

27. Checkpoints: $M = \frac{1}{6}\pi\delta\left((4a^2+1)^{3/2} - 1\right)$; $M_{xy} = \frac{1}{60}\pi\delta\left(1 + (24a^4 + 2a^2 - 1)\sqrt{4a^2+1}\right)$.

28. Assume unit density; $V = (2 - \sqrt{2})\pi a^2$; $M_{xy} = \frac{1}{2}\pi a^3$. Centroid: $\left(0, 0, \frac{1}{4}(2+\sqrt{2})a\right)$.

29. Checkpoints: $A = 4\pi - 8$, $M_{yz} = \frac{16}{3}$, $M_{xy} = 2\pi$.

30. $I_z = a\delta \int_0^{2\pi} \int_0^{2\pi} (b + a\cos\psi)^3\, d\psi\, d\theta$.

31. $dS = \sqrt{1 + 4y^2}$, so

$$I_z = \iint_S \delta(x^2 + y^2)\, dS = \int_{-1}^1 \int_{-2}^2 (x^2 + y^2)\sqrt{1 + 4y^2}\, dy\, dx = \frac{115}{12}\sqrt{17} + \frac{13}{48}\sinh^{-1} 4.$$

32. $dS = \sqrt{1 + 4x^2 + 4y^2}$, so

$$I_z = \iint_S \delta(x^2 + y^2)\, dS = \int_{-1}^1 \int_{-1}^1 (x^2 + y^2)\sqrt{1 + 4x^2 + 4y^2}\, dy\, dx$$

$$= \frac{1}{480}\left[2184 + 338\sinh^{-1}\left(\tfrac{2}{5}\sqrt{5}\right) + 16\tan^{-1}\left(\tfrac{4}{3}\right) + 169\ln 5\right].$$

34. The formula is

$$\iint_S P\, dy\, dz + Q\, dz\, dx + R\, dx\, dy = \iint_D \left(P - Q\frac{\partial x}{\partial y} - R\frac{\partial x}{\partial z}\right) dy\, dz.$$

35. The temperature within the ball is $u(x, y, z) = 4(x^2 + y^2 + z^2)$. With position vector $\mathbf{r} = \langle x, y, z\rangle$ for points of B, we find that

$$\mathbf{q} = -K\,\nabla u = -2 \cdot 4\langle 2x, 2y, 2z\rangle = -16\langle x, y, z\rangle = -16\mathbf{r}.$$

A normal to the concentric spherical surface S of radius 3 is $\mathbf{n} = \frac{1}{3}\mathbf{r}$, so

$$\mathbf{q} \cdot \mathbf{n} = -\tfrac{16}{3}(x^2 + y^2 + z^2) = -\tfrac{16}{3} \cdot 9 = -48.$$

Because S is a spherical surface of radius 3, we then find that the rate of heat flow across S is

$$\iint_S \mathbf{q} \cdot \mathbf{n} \, dS = -\iint_S 48 \, dS = -48 \cdot 4\pi \cdot 3^2 = -1728\pi.$$

36. The temperature within the cylinder is $u(x, y, z) = 4(x^2 + y^2)$, so

$$\mathbf{q} = -K \nabla u = -2 \cdot 4 \langle 2x, 2y, 0 \rangle = -16 \langle x, y, 0 \rangle.$$

A unit normal for the inner cylindrical surface is $\mathbf{n} = \frac{1}{3}\langle x, y, 0 \rangle$, so that $\mathbf{q} \cdot \mathbf{n} = -48$. Hence the rate of flow of heat across the inner surface is

$$\iint_S \mathbf{q} \cdot \mathbf{n} \, dS = -48 \cdot 2\pi \cdot 3 \cdot 10 = -2880\pi.$$

37. The given parametrization yields $\mathbf{N} = \langle -2bu^2 \cos v, -2au^2 \sin v, abu \rangle$, so the area of the paraboloid is

$$A = \int_0^{2\pi} \int_0^c u\sqrt{(2au\sin v)^2 + (2bu\cos v)^2 + (ab)^2} \, du \, dv$$

$$= \int_0^{2\pi} \frac{[(ab)^2 + 2(ac)^2 + 2(bc)^2 - 2(a^2 - b^2)c^2 \cos 2v]^{3/2} - (ab)^3}{6[a^2 + b^2 - (a^2 - b^2)\cos 2v]} \, dv.$$

We believe the last integral to be nonelementary (*Mathematica* 3.0 uses elliptic functions to compute its antiderivative), but with $a = 4$, $b = 3$, and $c = 2$ we find that its value is

$$\int_0^{2\pi} \frac{-1728 + (344 - 56\cos 2v)^{3/2}}{6(25 - 7\cos 2v)} \, dv \approx 194.703.$$

To find I_z, we insert the factor $\delta[(au\cos v)^2 + (bu\sin v)^2]$ into the previous integrand (with $\delta \equiv 1$); with $a = 4$, $b = 3$, and $c = 2$ a numerical integration produces the result $I_z \approx 5157.17$.

38. Using the given parametrization, we find that

$$\mathbf{N} = \langle bc\sin^2 u \cos v, \, ac\sin^2 u \sin v, \, ab\sin u \cos u \rangle$$

and thus that

$$|\mathbf{N}| = (\sin u)\sqrt{(bc\sin u \cos v)^2 + (ac\sin u \sin v)^2 + (ab\cos u)^2}.$$

Hence (using $a = 4$, $b = 3$, $c = 2$, and density $\delta \equiv 1$) the area of the ellipsoid is

$$A = \int_0^{2\pi} \int_0^\pi |\mathbf{N}| \, du \, dv \approx 111.546$$

and its moment of inertia around the z-axis is

$$I_z = \int_0^{2\pi} \int_0^\pi [(a\sin u \cos v)^2 + (b\sin u \sin v)^2] \cdot |\mathbf{N}| \, du \, dv \approx 847.811.$$

39. The given parametrization yields

$$|\mathbf{N}| = (\cosh u)\sqrt{(b\cosh u \cos v)^2 + (a\cosh u \sin v)^2 + (ab\sinh u)^2},$$

and hence (using $a = 4$, $b = 3$, $c = 2$, and density $\delta \equiv 1$) we find that the hyperboloid has surface area

$$A = \int_0^{2\pi} \int_{-c}^{c} |\mathbf{N}| \, du \, dv \approx 1057.35$$

and moment of inertia around the z-axis

$$I_z = \int_0^{2\pi} \int_{-c}^{c} (\cosh^2 u)[(a\cos v)^2 + (b\sin v)^2] \cdot |\mathbf{N}|\, du\, dv \approx 98546.9.$$

40. The given parametrization of the Möbius strip yields

$$|\mathbf{N}| = \sqrt{16 + \tfrac{3}{4}t^2 + 8t\cos\left(\tfrac{1}{2}\theta\right) + \tfrac{1}{2}t^2 \cos\theta},$$

and thus it has area

$$A = \int_0^{2\pi} \int_{-1}^{1} |\mathbf{N}|\, dt\, d\theta \approx 50.3986$$

and moment of inertia around the z-axis

$$I_z = \int_0^{2\pi} \int_{-1}^{1} (x^2 + y^2) \cdot |\mathbf{N}|\, dt\, d\theta \approx 831.47.$$

Section 15.6

1. First, div $\mathbf{F} = 3$. So $\iiint_B \text{div } \mathbf{F}\, dV = \iiint_B 3\, dV = (3)\left(\tfrac{4}{3}\right)(\pi)(1)^3 = 4\pi$.

   A unit normal is $\mathbf{n} = \langle x, y, z \rangle$, and $\mathbf{F} \cdot \mathbf{n} = 1$. So $\iint_S \mathbf{F} \cdot \mathbf{n}\, dS = (1)(4\pi)(1)^2 = 4\pi$.

   Both values are 4π; this verifies the divergence theorem in this special case.

2. Here, div $\mathbf{F} = 4\sqrt{x^2 + y^2 + z^2}$ and $\mathbf{F} \cdot \mathbf{n} = 9$. Each integral in the divergence theroem has the value 324π.

3. Each integral is equal to 24.

4. Here, div $\mathbf{F} = y + z + x$; on the face where $z = 0$, $0 \leq x \leq 2$, and $0 \leq y \leq 2$, we have $\mathbf{F} \cdot \mathbf{n} = 0$. On the opposite face we find that $\mathbf{F} \cdot \mathbf{n} = 2x$. The surface integral of $\mathbf{F} \cdot \mathbf{n}$ on that face is equal to 8. Similar results hold on the other four faces, and both integrals in the divergence theorem are equal to 24.

5. Both values are $\tfrac{1}{2}$.

6. Let B denote the cube $0 \leq x \leq 2$, $0 \leq y \leq 2$, $0 \leq z \leq 2$.

   $$\iint_S \mathbf{F} \cdot \mathbf{n}\, dS = \iiint_B \text{div } \mathbf{F}\, dV = \iiint_B (2x + 2y + 2z)\, dV = 48$$

   (because it is double the integral in Problem 4).

7. Let C denote the solid cylinder. Then

   $$\iint_S \mathbf{F} \cdot \mathbf{n}\, dS = \iiint_C (3x^2 + 3y^2 + 3z^2)\, dV = 3\int_0^{2\pi} \int_0^3 \int_{-1}^{4} (r^2 + z^2)\, r\, dz\, dr\, d\theta.$$

8. Let B denote the region bounded by the paraboloid and the plane. In cylindrical coordinates, div $F = 4r^2$. And

   $$\iint_S \mathbf{F} \cdot \mathbf{n}\, dS = \iiint_B \text{div } \mathbf{F}\, dV = \int_0^{2\pi} \int_0^{25} \int_0^{\sqrt{25-z}} 4r^3\, dr\, dz\, d\theta = 2\pi \int_0^{25} (25 - z)^2\, dz = \tfrac{31250}{3}\pi.$$

9. Let T denote the solid tetrahedron. Then

   $$\iint_S \mathbf{F} \cdot \mathbf{n}\, dS = \iiint_T (2x + 1)\, dV = \int_0^1 \int_0^{1-x} \int_0^{1-x-y} (2x + 1)\, dz\, dy\, dx = \tfrac{1}{4}.$$

10. Let B denote the solid bounded by S; note that div $\mathbf{F} = x^2 + y^2$. So

$$\iint_S \mathbf{F} \cdot \mathbf{n}\, dS = \iiint_B \text{div } \mathbf{F}\, dV = \int_0^{2\pi} \int_0^3 \int_{r^2}^9 r^3\, dz\, dr\, d\theta = \tfrac{243}{2}\pi.$$

18. $\dfrac{\partial g}{\partial \mathbf{n}} = (\boldsymbol{\nabla} g) \cdot \mathbf{n}$, so $f\dfrac{\partial g}{\partial \mathbf{n}} = (f\boldsymbol{\nabla} g) \cdot \mathbf{n}$. Thus

$$\iint_S f\frac{\partial g}{\partial \mathbf{n}}\, dS = \iint_S (f\boldsymbol{\nabla} g)\cdot \mathbf{n}\, dS = \iiint_T \text{div } (f\boldsymbol{\nabla} g)\, dV$$
$$= \iiint_T \left(\frac{\partial}{\partial x}\left(f\frac{\partial g}{\partial x}\right) + \frac{\partial}{\partial y}\left(f\frac{\partial g}{\partial y}\right) + \frac{\partial}{\partial z}\left(f\frac{\partial g}{\partial z}\right)\right)\, dV$$
$$= \iiint_T (fg_{xx} + f_x g_x + fg_{yy} + f_y g_y + fg_{zz} + f_z g_z)\, dV$$
$$= \iiint_T \left((f)(\boldsymbol{\nabla}^2 g) + (\boldsymbol{\nabla} f) \cdot (\boldsymbol{\nabla} g)\right)\, dV.$$

21. $\mathbf{B} = -\iint_S p\mathbf{n}\, dS = -\iiint_T \boldsymbol{\nabla} p\, dV = -\iiint_T \boldsymbol{\nabla}(\rho g z)\, dV$
$= -\rho g \iiint_T \boldsymbol{\nabla} z\, dV = -\rho g \iiint_T \mathbf{k}\, dV = -\rho g V \mathbf{k} = -mg\mathbf{k} = -\omega \mathbf{k}.$

23. Let B denote the region bounded by the paraboloid and the plane. In cylindrical coordinates, div $\mathbf{F} = 4\sqrt{r^2 + z^2}$. And

$$\iint_S \mathbf{F}\cdot \mathbf{n}\, dS = \iiint_B \text{div } \mathbf{F}\, dV$$
$$= \int_0^{2\pi} \int_0^{25} \int_0^{\sqrt{25-z}} 4r\sqrt{r^2 + z^2}\, dr\, dz\, d\theta$$
$$= \tfrac{8}{3}\pi \int_0^{25} \left((25 - z + z^2)^{3/2} - z^3\right)\, dz.$$

Let $J = \displaystyle\int_0^c \left((z-a)^2 + b^2\right)^{3/2} dz.$

Later we will use the following values: $b = \tfrac{3}{2}\sqrt{11}$, $a = \tfrac{1}{2}$, and $c = 25 = a^2 + b^2$.

The substitution $z = a + b\tan u$ yields

$$J = b^4 \int_{z=0}^c \sec^5 u\, du.$$

We evaluate J with the aid of Integral Formulas 37 and 28 of the endpapers; after much algebra and arithmetic we find that
$$J = \frac{12982620 + 29403\ln 11}{128}.$$

It follows that the value of the original integral—the answer to this problem—is

$$\frac{\pi(482620 + 29403\ln 11)}{48} \approx 36201.9672.$$

Section 15.7

1. Because **n** is to be the upper unit normal, we have
$$\mathbf{n} = \mathbf{n}(x, y, z) = \tfrac{1}{2}\langle x, y, z\rangle.$$

The boundary curve C of the hemispherical surface S has the parametrization
$$x = 2\cos\theta, \quad y = 2\sin\theta, \quad 0 \le \theta \le 2\pi.$$

Therefore
$$\iint_S (\text{curl }\mathbf{F}) \cdot \mathbf{n}\, dS = \int_C 3y\, dx - 2x\, dy + xyz\, dz = \int_0^{2\pi} (-12\sin^2\theta - 8\cos^2\theta)\, d\theta = -20\pi.$$

2. Parametrize the boundary curve C as follows:
$$x = 2\cos t, \quad y = 2\sin t, \quad z = 4, \quad 0 \le t \le 2\pi.$$

Then
$$\iint_S (\text{curl }\mathbf{F}) \cdot \mathbf{n}\, dS = \int_C \mathbf{F}\cdot\mathbf{T}\, ds = \int_C 2y\, dx + 3x\, dy + e^z\, dz = \int_0^{2\pi} (-8\sin^2 t + 12\cos^2 t)\, dt = 4\pi.$$

4. Parametrize the boundary curves as follows:
$$C_1: \quad x = \cos t, \quad y = \sin t, \quad z = 1, \quad 0 \le t \le 2\pi;$$
$$C_2: \quad x = \cos t, y = -\sin t, \quad z = 3, \quad 0 \le t \le 2\pi.$$

Then
$$\iint_S (\text{curl }\mathbf{F}) \cdot \mathbf{n}\, dS = \int_{C_1} \mathbf{F}\cdot\mathbf{T}\, ds + \int_{C_2} \mathbf{F}\cdot\mathbf{T}\, ds = \int_0^{2\pi} (2\sin^2 t - 2\cos^2 t)\, dt = 0.$$

6. Use for the surface the disk S: $x^2 + y^2 \le 4$, $z = 4$; use $\mathbf{n} = \mathbf{k}$ for the normal. Then we have curl $\mathbf{F} = \langle 2, -4, -3\rangle$, and hence $(\text{curl }\mathbf{F})\cdot\mathbf{n} = -3$. Therefore
$$\int_C \mathbf{F}\cdot\mathbf{T}\, ds = \iint_S (\text{curl }\mathbf{F}) \cdot \mathbf{n}\, dS = \iint_S (-3)\, dS = (-3)\,(\text{area}\,(S)) = -27\pi.$$

7. Parametrize S (the elliptical region bounded by C) as follows:
$$x = z = r\cos t, \quad y = r\sin t, \quad 0 \le r \le 2, \quad 0 \le t \le 2\pi.$$

Then $\mathbf{r}_r \times \mathbf{r}_t = \langle -r, 0, r\rangle$, $dS = r\sqrt{2}\, dr\, dt$; the upper unit normal for S is
$$\mathbf{n} = \tfrac{1}{2}\sqrt{2}\langle -1, 0, 1\rangle,$$

and curl $\mathbf{F} = \langle 3, 2, 1\rangle$. So $(\text{curl }\mathbf{F})\cdot\mathbf{n} = -\sqrt{2}$. Hence
$$\int_C \mathbf{F}\cdot\mathbf{T}\, ds = \iint_S (\text{curl }\mathbf{F}) \cdot \mathbf{n}\, dS = \int_0^{2\pi}\int_0^2 (-2r)\, dr\, dt = -8\pi.$$

8. The upper unit normal to the triangle bounded by C is
$$\mathbf{n} = \tfrac{1}{2}\sqrt{2}\langle 0, -1, 1\rangle,$$

and consequently $(\text{curl }\mathbf{F})\cdot\mathbf{n} = 0$. Therefore the value of the line integral is zero.

10. Let E be the ellipse bounded by C. Now E lies in the plane with equation $-y + z = 0$, so has upper unit normal
$$\mathbf{n} = \tfrac{1}{2}\sqrt{2}\,\langle 0, -1, 1\rangle.$$
Next, curl $\mathbf{F} = \langle -2z, -2x, -2y\rangle$, so $(\text{curl}\,\mathbf{F})\cdot\mathbf{n} = \sqrt{2}\,(x - y)$. The projection of E into the xy-plane may be described this way:
$$x^2 + (y - 1)^2 = 1, \quad z = 0;$$
alternatively, by $r = 2\sin t$ $(0 \le t \le \pi)$, $z = 0$. Thus
$$\int_C \mathbf{F}\cdot\mathbf{T}\,ds = \iint_E (\text{curl}\,\mathbf{F})\cdot\mathbf{n}\,dS = \iint_E \sqrt{2}\,(x - y)\,dS.$$
A parametrization of E is
$$\mathbf{w}\,(r, t) = \langle r\cos t, r\sin t, r\sin t\rangle, \quad 0 \le t \le \pi,\ \ 0 \le r \le 2\sin t.$$
Next we find that $\mathbf{n} = \mathbf{w}_r \times \mathbf{w}_t = \langle 0, -r, r\rangle$. Therefore $dS = r\sqrt{2}\,dr\,dt$. Consequently,
$$\iint_E \sqrt{2}\,(x - y)\,dS = \int_0^\pi \int_0^{2\sin t} \sqrt{2}\,r\,(\cos t - \sin t)\,r\sqrt{2}\,dr\,dt.$$
Answer: -2π.

12. $f(x, y, z) = 3xy^3 - 5x^2 z^2$

14. $f(x, y, z) = \tfrac{1}{5}\left(x^2 + y^2 + z^2\right)^{5/2}$

18. As suggested, let $\mathbf{F} = \phi\mathbf{a}$, where $\mathbf{a}$ is an arbitrary constant vector. Then
$$\int_C (\phi\mathbf{a})\cdot\mathbf{T}\,ds = \iint_S (\text{curl}\,(\phi\mathbf{a}))\cdot\mathbf{n}\,dS = \iint_S ((\phi)(\text{curl}\,\mathbf{a}) + ((\nabla\phi)\times\mathbf{a}))\cdot\mathbf{n}\,dS = \iint_S (\nabla\phi\times\mathbf{a})\cdot\mathbf{n}\,dS.$$
Write $\mathbf{T} = \langle T_1, T_2, T_3\rangle$ and $\mathbf{n} = \langle n_1, n_2, n_3\rangle$. If $\mathbf{a} = \mathbf{i}$ then
$$\int_C \phi T_1\,ds = \iint_S (-\phi_z\mathbf{j} - \phi_y\mathbf{k})\cdot\mathbf{n}\,dS = \iint_S (-\phi_z n_2 - \phi_y n_3)\,dS.$$
But $(\mathbf{n}\times\nabla\phi)_1 = -n_2\phi_z - n_3\phi_y$. Therefore
$$\int_C \phi T_1\,ds = \iint_S (\mathbf{n}\times\nabla\phi)_1\,dS.$$
The same argument holds for the second and third components of all the vectors involved. Add the results to obtain the conclusion in Problem 18.

21. Beginning with the *suggestion* given in the problem, we find that
$$\phi_x = \lim_{h\to 0}\frac{\phi(x + h) - \phi(x)}{h} = \lim_{h\to 0}\frac{1}{h}\int_x^{x+h} P\,dx = \lim_{h\to 0}\frac{h\cdot P(x^*)}{h} = P(x)$$
by the average value theorem (x^* is between x and $x + h$). The same argument holds for ϕ_y and ϕ_z; adding the results establishes that $\nabla\phi = \mathbf{F} = \langle P, Q, R\rangle$.

22. Another of the glories of Western civilization.
$$\mathbf{L} = \iint_S (\mathbf{r} - \mathbf{r}_0)\times(-\rho g z\mathbf{n})\,dS = \rho g\iiint_V \text{curl}\,(z(\mathbf{r} - \mathbf{r}_0))\,dV \quad \text{(by Problem 20)}.$$
But $\text{curl}\,(z(\mathbf{r} - \mathbf{r}_0)) = (\nabla z)\times(\mathbf{r} - \mathbf{r}_0) + z(\text{curl}\,(\mathbf{r} - \mathbf{r}_0))$. It follows immediately that $\nabla z = \mathbf{k}$ and that $\text{curl}\,(\mathbf{r} - \mathbf{r}_0) = \mathbf{0}$. Thus
$$\mathbf{L} = \rho g\iiint_V \mathbf{k}\times(\mathbf{r} - \mathbf{r}_0)\,dV = \rho g\mathbf{k}\times\left(\iiint_V \mathbf{r}\,dV - \mathbf{r}_0 V\right).$$
consequently $\mathbf{L} = \mathbf{0}$ as desired, because $\mathbf{r}_0 = \dfrac{1}{V}\iiint_V \mathbf{r}\,dV$.

Chapter 15 Miscellaneous

1. C is part of the graph of $y = \frac{4}{3}x$ and $ds = \frac{5}{3}dx$. So $\int_C (x^2 + y^2) \, ds = \int_0^3 \left(x^2 + \left(\frac{4}{3}x\right)^2\right) \frac{5}{3} \, dx = \frac{125}{3}$.

2. $\frac{52}{35}$

4. 115

6. Let $g(x, y, z) = xy^2 + \frac{1}{2}z^2$. Then $\nabla g \cdot d\mathbf{r}$ is the integrand.

7. If $\nabla \phi = \langle x^2y, xy^2 \rangle$ then $\phi_x = x^2y$, so that $\phi(x,y) = \frac{1}{3}x^3y + g(y)$. Thus $\phi_y = \frac{1}{3}x^3 + g'(y) = xy^2$. This is impossible unless x is constant, but x is not constant on C.

8. If k is the density of the wire, then its mass is $M = 2\pi a k$.

   (a) $I_z = I_0 = \int_{\theta=0}^{2\pi} r^2 \, dm = 2\pi a^3 k = Ma^2$.

   (b) $I_x = \int_{\theta=0}^{2\pi} y^2 \, dm = \pi a^3 k = \frac{1}{2}Ma^2$.

10. Parametrize C: $x = t$, $y = t^2$, $z = t^3$, $1 \le z \le 2$.

    $$W = \int_C P\,dx + Q\,dy + R\,dz = \int_C z\,dx - x\,dy + y\,dz = \int_1^2 (t^3 - 2t^2 + 3t^4)\,dt = \frac{1061}{60}.$$

12. Choose $P(x,y) = 0$ and $Q(x,y) = x^2$. Then
    $$\int_C x^2\,dy = \iint_D 2x\,dA$$
    where D is the region enclosed by C. We will integrate from $-\pi$ to π to avoid the cusp:
    $$\int_C x^2\,dy = \int_{-\pi}^{\pi} \int_0^{1+\cos\theta} (2r\cos\theta)(r)\,dr\,d\theta = \frac{5}{2}\pi.$$

16. Note that if $P_y < Q_x$ at some point of D, then $Q_x - P_y > 0$ on a small region R surrounding that point, so that
    $$\iint_R (Q_x - P_y)\,dA > 0.$$

18. On S, $\mathbf{F}(x,y,z) = a^2 \langle x, y, z \rangle$. Also, $\mathbf{n} = \frac{1}{a}\langle x, y, z \rangle$ is the outer unit normal to S at (x,y,z). Therefore
    $$\iint_S \mathbf{F} \cdot \mathbf{n}\,dS = \iint_S \frac{1}{a}a^2(x^2 + y^2 + z^2)\,dS = \iint_S a^3\,dS = a^3(\text{area}(S)) = 4\pi a^5.$$

19. Checkpoints: The flux across the upper surface is 60π and the flux across the lower surface is 12π.

20. The average distance is
    $$\bar{d} = \frac{1}{\text{area}(S)} \iint_S f(x,y,z)\,dS$$
    where $f(x, y, z)$ is the distance between the fixed point P and the point (x, y, z) of the surface S. Now let P be the "North Pole" $(0, 0, a)$ of the sphere with radius a centered at the origin. If another point on the sphere is at distance w from P and its spherical coordinates are (ρ, ϕ, θ) then the law of cosines implies that
    $$w^2 = a^2 + \rho^2 - 2a\rho\cos\phi.$$
    But ρ is constant on this sphere: $\rho = a$. Therefore the average distance we seek is
    $$\frac{1}{4\pi a^2} \int_0^{2\pi} \int_0^{\pi} \sqrt{2a^2 - 2a^2\cos\phi}\, a^2 \sin\theta \sin\phi\,d\phi\,d\theta = \frac{2\pi a^2}{4\pi a^2} \int_0^{\pi} a\sqrt{2(1-\cos\phi)}\sin\phi\,d\phi = \frac{4}{3}a.$$

24. Centroid: $\left(0, 0, \frac{3}{8}a\right)$

Appendices
Appendix A

1. $|3 - 17| = |-14| = 14$
2. $|-3| - |17| = 3 - 17 = -14$
3. $\left|-0.25 - \frac{1}{4}\right| = |-0.5| = 0.5$
4. $|5| - |-7| = 5 - 7 = -2$
5. $|(-5)(4 - 9)| = |(-5)(-5)| = |25| = 25$
6. $\dfrac{|-6|}{|4| + |-2|} = \dfrac{6}{4 + 2} = 1$
7. $|(-3)^3| = |-27| = 27$
8. $|3 - \sqrt{3}| = 3 - \sqrt{3}$ because $3 - \sqrt{3} > 0$.
9. $\left|\pi - \frac{22}{7}\right| = \frac{22}{7} - \pi$ because $\pi - \frac{22}{7} \approx -0.001264 < 0$.
10. $-|7 - 4| = -|3| = -3$
11. $|x - 3| = 3 - x$ because $x - 3 < 0$.
12. $6 < x < 8$, so $|x - 5| + |x - 10| = x - 5 + 10 - x = 5$.
13. $2x < 4$, so $x < 2$. Answer: $(-\infty, 2)$.
14. $4x < -1$, so $x < -\frac{1}{4}$. Answer: $\left(-\infty, -\frac{1}{4}\right)$.
15. $3x \geq 21$, so $x \geq 7$. Answer: $[7, +\infty)$.
16. $2x \leq 4$, so $x \leq 2$. Answer: $(-\infty, 2]$.
17. $3x > -5$, so $x > -\frac{5}{3}$. Answer: $\left(-\frac{5}{3}, +\infty\right)$.
18. $5x < 15$, so $x < 3$. Answer: $(-\infty, 3)$.
19. $-8 < 2x < 2$, so $-4 < x < 1$. Answer: $(-4, 1)$.
20. $9 \leq 3x \leq 15$, so $3 \leq x \leq 5$. Answer: $[3, 5]$.
21. $-11 \leq -2x < -3$; $3 < 2x \leq -11$; $\frac{3}{2} < x \leq \frac{11}{2}$. Answer: $\left(\frac{3}{2}, \frac{11}{2}\right]$.
22. $2 < -5x < 6$; $-6 < 5x < -2$; $-\frac{6}{5} < x < -\frac{2}{5}$. Answer: $\left(-\frac{6}{5}, -\frac{2}{5}\right)$.
23. $-5 < 3 - 2x < 5$; $-8 < -2x < 2$; $-2 < 2x < 8$; $-1 < x < 4$. Answer: $(-1, 4)$.
24. $-4 \leq 5x + 3 \leq 4$; $-7 \leq 5x \leq 1$; $-\frac{7}{5} \leq x \leq \frac{1}{5}$. Answer: $\left[-\frac{7}{5}, \frac{1}{5}\right]$.
25. We solve instead $|1 - 3x| \leq 2$: $-2 \leq 3x - 1 \leq 2$; $-1 \leq 3x \leq 3$; $-\frac{1}{3} \leq x \leq 1$. So the solution set of the original inequality is $\left(-\infty, -\frac{1}{3}\right) \cup (1, +\infty)$.
26. Case (1): $7x - 1 \geq 0$; that is, $x \geq \frac{1}{7}$. Thus $1 < 7x - 1 < 3$; $2 < 7x < 4$; $\frac{2}{7} \leq x \leq \frac{4}{7}$.
    Case (2): $7x - 1 < 0$; that is, $x < \frac{1}{7}$. Then $1 < 1 - 7x < 3$; $0 < -7x < 2$; $-2 < 7x < 0$; $-\frac{2}{7} < x < 0$.
    Answer: $\left(-\frac{2}{7}, 0\right) \cup \left(\frac{2}{7}, \frac{4}{7}\right)$.
27. Case (1): $4 - 5x \geq 0$; that is, $x \leq \frac{4}{5}$. Then $2 \leq 4 - 5x \leq 4$; $-2 \leq -5x \leq 0$; $0 \leq 5x \leq 2$; $0 \leq x \leq \frac{2}{5}$.
    Case (2): $4 - 5x < 0$; that is, $x > \frac{4}{5}$. Then $2 \leq 5x - 4 \leq 4$; $6 \leq 5x \leq 8$; $\frac{6}{5} \leq x \leq \frac{8}{5}$.
    Answer: $\left[0, \frac{2}{5}\right] \cup \left[\frac{6}{5}, \frac{8}{5}\right]$.
28. $1/(2x + 1) > 3$ implies that $2x + 1 > 0$, so $1 > 3 \cdot (2x + 1) = 6x + 3$; $-2 > 6x$; $x < -\frac{1}{3}$. But $2x + 1 > 0$, so $x > -\frac{1}{2}$. Answer: $\left(-\frac{1}{2}, -\frac{1}{3}\right)$.
29. $2/(7 - 3x) \leq -5$ implies that $7 - 3x < 0$, so $2 \geq -5 \cdot (7 - 3x) = -35 + 15x$; $15x \leq 37$; $x \leq \frac{37}{15} \approx 2.4667$. But $7 - 3x < 0$, so $x < \frac{7}{3} \approx 12.3333$. Answer: $\left(\frac{7}{3}, \frac{37}{15}\right]$.
30. First, $|3x - 4| > 2$. We solve instead $|3x - 4| \leq 2$: $-2 \leq 3x - 4 \leq 2$; $2 \leq 3x \leq 6$; $\frac{2}{3} \leq x \leq 2$. So the original inequality has solution set $\left(-\infty, \frac{2}{3}\right) \cup (2, +\infty)$.

31. If $x \neq \frac{1}{5}$, then $|1 - 5x| > 0$, so
$$\frac{1}{|1 - 5x|} > 0 > -\frac{1}{3}.$$
Answer: $\left(-\infty, \frac{1}{5}\right) \cup \left(\frac{1}{5}, +\infty\right)$.

33. $(x + 2)(x - 4) < 0$, so either
$$x > -2 \quad \text{and} \quad x > 4 \quad \text{or} \quad x < 4 \quad \text{and} \quad x < 4.$$
Hence $x > 4$ or $x < -2$. Answer: $(-\infty, -2) \cup (4, +\infty)$.

35. $(2x - 1)(2x - 3) \geq 0$, so either
$$x \geq \tfrac{1}{2} \quad \text{and} \quad x \geq \tfrac{3}{2} \quad \text{or} \quad x \leq \tfrac{1}{2} \quad \text{and} \quad x \leq \tfrac{3}{2}.$$
Therefore $x \leq \tfrac{1}{2}$ or $x \geq \tfrac{3}{2}$. Answer: $\left(-\infty, \tfrac{1}{2}\right] \cup \left[\tfrac{3}{2}, +\infty\right)$.

41. If $0 < a$ and $0 < b$, then $0 + 0 < a + b$, so $a + b$ is positive.

42. If $0 < a$ and b is positive, then $0 \cdot b < a \cdot b$, so $0 < ab$. Therefore ab is positive.

43. If a and b are both negative, then $a < 0$, so $a \cdot b > 0 \cdot b$, and thus ab is positive. If a is positive and b is negative, then $b < 0$, so $a \cdot b < a \cdot 0 = 0$. Hence ab is negative.

44. If $a < b$ and a and b are both negative, then $a < b < 0$. By Problem 43, ab is positive, so $1/(ab)$ is positive (else $ab \cdot 1/(ab) < 0$). Therefore
$$\frac{1}{ab} \cdot a < \frac{1}{ab} \cdot b;$$
that is, $1/b < 1/a$. The proof is similar if a and b are both positive.

47. Suppose first that $|a| < b$. Then there are two cases.

    Case (1): $a \geq 0$. Then $a < b$ and $b > 0$, so $-b < 0 < a < b$, so $-b < a < b$.

    Case (2): $a < 0$. Then $-a < b$, so $b > 0$. Thus $-b < a < 0 < b$, so $-b < a < b$.

    Therefore, if $|a| < b$, then $-b < a < b$.

    Next we suppose that $-b < a < b$. Again there are two cases.

    Case (1): $a \geq 0$. Then $a = |a|$, so $|a| < b$.

    Case (2): $a < 0$. Then $|a| = -a$. But from the hypotheses $-b < a < b$, it follows that $(-1)(-b) > (-1) \cdot a > (-1) \cdot b$, so $-b < -a < b$. Therefore $-b < |a| < b$, and therefore $|a| < b$.

    Therefore, if $-b < a < b$, then $|a| < b$. ◀

Appendix B

1. Both the segments AB and BC have the same slope 1.
2. Both the segments AB and BC have the same slope $-\tfrac{1}{2}$.
3. AB has slope -2 but BC has slope $-\tfrac{4}{3}$.
4. AB has slope 1 but BC has slope $\tfrac{8}{7}$.
5. Both AB and CD have slope $-\tfrac{1}{2}$; both BC and DA have slope 2. This parallelogram is a rectangle!
6. Both AB and CD have slope $-\tfrac{1}{3}$; both BC and DA have slope $\tfrac{2}{3}$.
7. AB has slope 2 and AC has slope $-\tfrac{1}{2}$.
8. AB has slope -1 and BC has slope 1.

9. $m = \frac{2}{3}$, $b = 0$ 10. $m = -1$, $b = 1$ 11. $m = 2$, $b = 3$
12. $m = -\frac{3}{4}$, $b = \frac{3}{2}$ 13. $m = -\frac{2}{5}$, $b = \frac{3}{5}$ 14. $x = 7$ 15. $y = -5$
16. The points $(2,0)$ and $(0,-3)$ lie on L, so the slope of L is $\frac{3}{2}$. An equation of L is $2y = 3x - 6$.
17. The slope of L is 2, so an equation of L is $y - 3 = 2(x - 5)$.
18. $2y + 7 = x$
19. The slope of L is -1; an equation is $y - 2 = 4 - x$.
20. $y = 6x + 7$.
21. The slope of L is -2; equation: $y - 5 = -2(x - 1)$.
22. The *other* line has slope $-\frac{1}{2}$, so L has slope 2 and therefore equation $y - 4 = 2(x + 2)$.
23. The segment has slope 2 and midpoint $(1,6)$; the line L has slope $-\frac{1}{2}$, and one equation of L is $x + 2y = 13$.
24. The given line L_1 has slope 1; every perpendicular has slope -1, including the line L_2 through $(2,1)$ perpendicular to L_1. An equation of L_2 is therefore $y - 2 = 1 - x$, and L_2 meets L_1 where $y = 3 - x$ and $y = x + 1$ are simultaneously true: at $(1,2)$. The distance from $(2,1)$ to $(1,2)$ is the answer, $\sqrt{2}$.
25. The parallel lines have slope 5, so the line $y = -\frac{1}{5}x + 1$ is perpendicular to them both. It meets the line $y = 5x + 1$ at $(0,1)$ and the line $y = 5x + 9$ at $(\frac{-20}{13}, \frac{17}{13})$, and the distance between these two points is
$$\sqrt{\left(\tfrac{20}{13}\right)^2 + \left(\tfrac{4}{13}\right)^2} = \tfrac{4}{13}\sqrt{26} \approx 1.568929.$$
26. A rough sketch shows that the fourth vertex D must lie in the first quadrant, and that D is the intersection of the lines L_1 and L_2, where L_1 passes through C and is parallel to AB whereas L_2 passes through A and is parallel to BC. The point-slope equations of L_1 and L_2 are
$$y - 1 = -6(x - 3) \quad \text{and} \quad y - 6 = \frac{1}{3}(x + 1),$$
respectively. Their simultaneous solution yields $D = (2,7)$. (If the word "consecutive" is omitted from Problem 26, then there are three possible locations for the point D.)
27. Strategy: Find the equations of the diagonals, solve these equations simultaneously to find where the diagonals cross, and show that this point is the midpoint of each diagonal.
28. Show that AB is parallel to CD, that BC is parallel to AD, that AB and CD have the same length, that AD and BC have the same length, and that AC is perpendicular to BD by showing that the product of their slopes is -1.
29. The midpoint of AB is $P(\frac{5}{2},3)$ and the midpoint of BC is $Q(5,4)$. The slope of PQ is $\frac{2}{5}$, the same as the slope of AC, and hence PQ is parallel to AC.
30. The midpoint of BC is $Q(5,4)$, so the line containing $A(2,1)$ and Q has equation $y = x - 1$. The other two medians lie on the lines $y = 3$ and $y = -2x + 11$. The point $(4,3)$, obtained by simultaneous solution of these two equations, also lies on the first line.
31. The slope of $P_1 M$ is
$$\frac{y_1 - \bar{y}}{x_1 - \bar{x}} = \frac{y_1 - \frac{1}{2}(y_1 + y_2)}{x_1 - \frac{1}{2}(x_1 + x_2)} = \frac{2y_1 - y_1 - y_2}{2x_1 - x_1 - x_2} = \frac{y_1 - y_2}{x_1 - x_2},$$
and the slope of MP_2 is the same.
32. The slope of the tangent line is $-\left(\dfrac{x_0}{y_0}\right)$, so it has equation
$$y - y_0 = -\frac{x_0}{y_0}(x - x_0); \qquad y_0 y - (y_0)^2 = -x_0 x + (x_0)^2;$$
$$x_0 x + y_0 y = (x_0)^2 + (y_0)^2 = r^2.$$

33. Because F and K satisfy a linear equation, $K = mF + b$ for some constants m and b. Use the data given in Problem 33 to find m and b.

34. Begin with the fact that $L = mC + b$ for some constants m and b. The data given in Problem 34 yield
$$124.942 = 20m + b \text{ and } 125.134 = 110m + b.$$
It follows that $m = \frac{192}{90000}$ and $b = \frac{187349}{1500}$. Thus, approximately, $L = (0.00213)C + 124.899$.

35. If s denotes weekly sales in gallons and p the selling price per gallon, then $s = mp + b$ for some constants m and b. From the data given in Problem 35 we have
$$980 = (1.69)m + b \text{ and } 1220 = (1.49)m + b.$$
Simultaneous solution of these equations yields $m = -1200$, $b = 3008$, and therefore $s = s(p) = -1200p + 3008$. At \$1.56 per gallon one expects to sell $s(1.56) = 1136$ gallons per week.

36. They are not parallel; they meet at $(137, 227.2)$.

37. $x = -2.75$, $\quad y = 3.5$
38. $x = \frac{41}{34}$, $\quad y = -\frac{19}{34}$
39. $x = \frac{37}{6}$, $\quad y = -\frac{1}{2}$
40. $x = \frac{25}{4}$, $\quad y = \frac{3}{2}$
41. $x = \frac{22}{5}$, $\quad y = -\frac{1}{5}$
42. $x = -\frac{12}{5}$, $\quad y = \frac{41}{5}$
43. $x = -\frac{7}{4}$, $\quad y = \frac{33}{8}$
44. $x = \frac{1}{6}$, $\quad y = \frac{11}{6}$
45. $x = \frac{119}{12}$, $\quad y = -\frac{19}{4}$
46. $x = \frac{59}{11}$, $\quad y = -\frac{12}{11}$

48. If $C = 0$ then the graph is the entire xy-plane. If $C \neq 0$ then the graph is the *empty set*—it contains no points.

Appendix C

1. $40 \cdot \frac{\pi}{180} = \frac{2\pi}{9}$ (rad)
2. $-\frac{3\pi}{4}$
4. $210 \cdot \frac{\pi}{180} = \frac{7\pi}{6}$
6. $\frac{\pi}{10} \cdot \frac{180}{\pi} = 18°$
7. $\frac{2\pi}{5} \cdot \frac{180}{\pi} = 72°$
8. $540°$
10. $\frac{23\pi}{60} \cdot \frac{180}{\pi} = 69°$

	x	$\sin x$	$\cos x$	$\tan x$	$\cot x$	$\sec x$	$\csc x$
11.	$-\frac{1}{3}\pi$	$-\frac{1}{2}\sqrt{3}$	$\frac{1}{2}$	$-\sqrt{3}$	$-\frac{1}{3}\sqrt{3}$	2	$-\frac{2}{3}\sqrt{3}$
12.	$\frac{3}{4}\pi$	$\frac{1}{2}\sqrt{2}$	$-\frac{1}{2}\sqrt{2}$	-1	-1	$-\sqrt{2}$	$\sqrt{2}$
13.	$\frac{7}{6}\pi$	$-\frac{1}{2}$	$-\frac{1}{2}\sqrt{3}$	$\frac{1}{3}\sqrt{3}$	$\sqrt{3}$	$-\frac{2}{3}\sqrt{3}$	-2
14.	$\frac{5}{3}\pi$	$-\frac{1}{2}\sqrt{3}$	$\frac{1}{2}$	$-\sqrt{3}$	$-\frac{1}{3}\sqrt{3}$	2	$-\frac{2}{3}\sqrt{3}$

15. $\sin x = 0$ when x is an integral multiple of π.
16. $\sin x = 1$ for $x = \frac{1}{2}(4n + 1)\pi$ where n is an integer.
17. $\sin x = -1$ for $x = \frac{1}{2}(4n + 3)\pi$ where n is an integer.
18. $\cos x = 0$ when x is an odd integral multiple of $\pi/2$.
19. $\cos x = 1$ when x is an integral multiple of 2π.
20. $\cos x = -1$ when x is an odd integral multiple of π.
21. $\tan x = 0$ when x is an integral multiple of π.
22. $\tan x = 1$ for $x = \frac{1}{4}(4k + 1)\pi$ where k is an integer.

23. $\tan x = -1$ for $x = \frac{1}{4}(4k+3)\pi$ where k is an integer.

24. See the figure at the right.
$\sin x = -\frac{3}{5}$, $\cos x = -\frac{4}{5}$, $\tan x = \frac{3}{4}$,
$\csc x = -\frac{5}{3}$, $\sec x = -\frac{5}{4}$, $\cot x = \frac{4}{3}$.

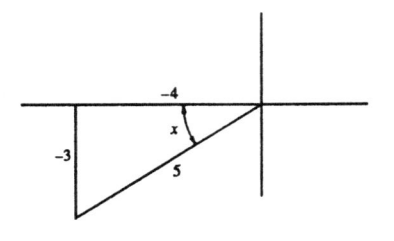

25. See the figure at the right.
$\sin x = -\frac{3}{5}$, $\cos x = \frac{4}{5}$, $\tan x = -\frac{3}{4}$,
$\csc x = -\frac{5}{3}$, $\sec x = \frac{5}{4}$, $\cot x = -\frac{4}{3}$.

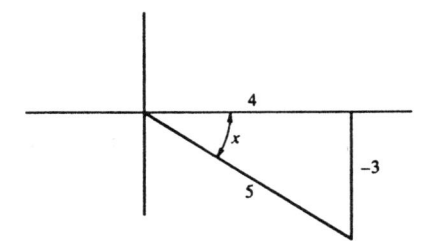

29. $\sin(5\pi/6) = \sin(\pi/6) = 1/2$
30. $\cos(7\pi/6) = -\cos(\pi/6) = -\frac{1}{2}\sqrt{3}$
31. $\sin(11\pi/6) = \sin(-\pi/6) = -\sin(\pi/6) = -1/2$
32. $\cos(19\pi/6) = \cos(7\pi/6) = -\cos(\pi/6) = -\frac{1}{2}\sqrt{3}$
33. $\sin(2\pi/3) = \sin(\pi/3) = \frac{1}{2}\sqrt{3}$
34. $\cos(4\pi/3) = -\cos(\pi/3) = -1/2$
35. $\sin(5\pi/3) = \sin(-\pi/3) = -\sin(\pi/3) = -\frac{1}{2}\sqrt{3}$
36. $\cos(10\pi/3) = \cos(4\pi/3) = -\cos(\pi/3) = -1/2$
37. (a) $\cos\left(\frac{\pi}{2} - \theta\right) = \cos\left(\frac{\pi}{2}\right)\cos\theta + \sin\left(\frac{\pi}{2}\right)\sin\theta = 0 \cdot \cos\theta + 1 \cdot \sin\theta = \sin\theta$.
40. $\tan(\pi \pm \theta) = \tan(\pm\theta)$ (because the tangent function is periodic with period π) and $\tan(\pm\theta) = \pm\tan(\theta)$ because the tangent function is odd (the quotient of an odd function and an even function).

43. $3\sin^2 x - 1 + \sin^2 x = 2$:
$4\sin^2 x = 3$;
$\sin x = \pm\frac{1}{2}\sqrt{3}$
$x = \frac{1}{3}\pi$, $x = \frac{2}{3}\pi$.

44. $\sin^2 x = \cos^2 x$:
$\tan^2 x = 1$;
$\tan x = \pm 1$;
$x = \frac{1}{4}\pi$, $x = \frac{3}{4}\pi$.

45. $2\cos^2 x + 3 - 3\cos^2 x = 3$:
$\cos^2 x = 0$;
$x = \frac{1}{2}\pi$.

46. $2\sin^2 x + \cos x = 2$:
$2 - 2\cos^2 x + \cos x = 2$;
$(\cos x)(2\cos x - 1) = 0$;
$\cos x = 0$ or $\cos x = \frac{1}{2}$;
$x = \frac{1}{2}\pi$, $x = \frac{1}{3}\pi$.

47. $8\sin^2 x \cos^2 x = 1$:
$(2\sin x \cos x)^2 = \frac{1}{2}$;
$\sin 2x = \pm\frac{1}{2}\sqrt{2}$;
$2x = \frac{1}{4}\pi, \frac{3}{4}\pi, \frac{5}{4}\pi, \frac{7}{4}\pi$;
$x = \frac{1}{8}\pi, \frac{3}{8}\pi, \frac{5}{8}\pi, \frac{7}{8}\pi$.

48. $\cos 2\theta - 3\cos\theta = -2$:
$2\cos^2\theta - 1 - 3\cos\theta = -2$;
$(2\cos\theta - 1)(\cos\theta - 1) = 0$;
$\cos\theta = \frac{1}{2}$ or $\cos\theta = 1$;
$\theta = \frac{1}{3}\pi$, $\theta = 0$.

Appendix D

1. Given $\epsilon > 0$, choose $\delta = \epsilon$. If $0 < |x - a| < \delta$ then $|x - a| < \epsilon$. Therefore $\lim\limits_{x \to a} x = a$.

2. Given $\epsilon > 0$, choose $\delta = \epsilon/3$. If $0 < |x - 2| < \delta$ then $|3x - 6| < 3\delta = \epsilon$. Therefore $\lim_{x \to 2} 3x = 6$.

3. Let $\delta = \epsilon$.

4. Given $\epsilon > 0$, choose $\delta = \epsilon/2$. If $0 < |x - (-3)| < \delta$ then $|2x + 6| < 2\delta$, so $|(2x + 1) - (-5)| < \epsilon$. Therefore, by definition, $\lim_{x \to -3} (2x + 1) = -5$.

5. Given $\epsilon > 0$, let δ be the minimum of 1 and $\epsilon/3$. If $|x - 1| < \delta$ then $|x - 1| < 1$. So

$$-1 < x - 1 < 1;$$
$$1 < x + 1 < 3;$$
$$|x + 1| < 3.$$

Moreover, if $|x - 1| < \delta$, then $|x - 1| < \epsilon/3$. Hence

$$|x^2 - 1| = |x + 1|\,|x - 1| < 3 \cdot \frac{\epsilon}{3} = \epsilon.$$

Therefore, by definition, $\lim_{x \to 1} x^2 = 1$.

6. Case (1): $a > 0$. Given $\epsilon > 0$, let δ be the minimum of $3a$ and $\epsilon/(5a)$. If $|x - a| < \delta$, then

$$|x - a| < 3a;$$
$$-3a < x - a < 3a;$$
$$-a < x + a < 5a;$$
$$|x + a| < 5a.$$

Moreover, if $|x - a| < \delta$, then $|x - a| < \epsilon/(5a)$. Hence $|x^2 - a^2| = |x + a|\,|x - a| < 5a \cdot \dfrac{\epsilon}{5a} = \epsilon$. Therefore, by definition, $\lim_{x \to a} x^2 = a^2$ if $a > 0$.

Case (2): $a < 0$; the argument is similar.

Case (3): $a = 0$. Given $\epsilon > 0$, choose δ to be the minimum of 1 and ϵ. If $|x - 0| < \delta$, then

$$|x^2 - 0^2| = x^2 < |x| \quad \text{(because } |x| < 1\text{).} \quad \text{Hence}$$
$$|x^2 - 0^2| < |x - 0| < \delta \leq \epsilon.$$

Therefore, by definition, $\lim_{x \to a} x^2 = a^2$ if $a = 0$.

7. Given $\epsilon > 0$, let $\delta = \epsilon/k$ where you will choose a suitably large positive integer later in the proof so that the inequalities will work. Then go back through the proof and replace k by this integer. Write it neatly and turn it in for a perfect grade. This is a standard technique in ϵ-δ proofs.

8. Suppose first that $a > 0$. Given $\epsilon > 0$, choose δ to be the minimum of $a/2$ and $a^3\epsilon/10$. Why? We need

$$\left|\frac{1}{x^2} - \frac{1}{a^2}\right| < \epsilon,$$

which would hold provided that

$$\left|\frac{a^2 - x^2}{a^2 x^2}\right| < \epsilon.$$

This would follow from

$$\frac{|a + x|\,|a - x|}{a^2 x^2} < \epsilon,$$

which in turn would follow from

$$|x - a| < \frac{a^2 x^2 \epsilon}{|x + a|}.$$

Appendix D   481

This means that we must control the values of both $|x+a|$ and a^2x^2. For the former, we ensure that $|x+a|$ is not large by making x close to a: We require that $a/2 < x < 3a/2$ by ensuring that $\delta < a/2$. If so, it is easy to show that

$$\tfrac{1}{4}a^2 < x^2 < \tfrac{9}{4}a^2 \text{ and also that } \frac{2}{5a} < \frac{1}{x+a} < \frac{2}{3a}.$$

It then follows that

$$|x - a| < \tfrac{1}{10}a^3\epsilon.$$

So it suffices to ensure also that $\delta \leq \tfrac{1}{10}a^3\epsilon$. Thus we choose δ to be the minimum of $\tfrac{1}{2}a$ and $\tfrac{1}{10}a^3\epsilon$. The desired inequalities then follow.

9. The solution resembles that of Problem 8.

10. The desired inequality $\left|\dfrac{1}{\sqrt{x}} - \dfrac{1}{\sqrt{a}}\right| < \epsilon$ follows from $|\sqrt{a} - \sqrt{x}| < \epsilon\sqrt{ax}$, and we keep x from becoming negative or zero (or too close to zero) by requiring that $a/2 < x < 3a/2$. We ensure this by requiring that $\delta < a/2$. We obtain the inequality $|\sqrt{a} - \sqrt{x}| < \epsilon\sqrt{ax}$ from

$$|\sqrt{a} + \sqrt{x}|\,|\sqrt{a} - \sqrt{x}| < \epsilon\sqrt{ax}\,(\sqrt{a} + \sqrt{x});$$

that is,

$$|x - a| < \epsilon\sqrt{ax}\,(\sqrt{a} + \sqrt{x}).$$

It suffices that

$$\delta < \epsilon\sqrt{ax}\,(\sqrt{a} + \sqrt{x}),$$

and this can be assured by choosing $\delta < 3a^{3/2}\epsilon/4$, as this implies the last displayed inequality. So choose δ to be the minimum of $a/2$ and $3a^{3/2}\epsilon/4$.

11. Given $\epsilon > 0$, note that $\epsilon/2$ is also positive. Choose δ_1 so that

$$|f(x) - L| < \epsilon/2 \text{ if } 0 < |x - a| < \delta_1;$$

choose δ_2 so that

$$|f(x) - M| < \epsilon/2 \text{ if } 0 < |x - a| < \delta_2.$$

Then for such x we have

$$|L - f(x)| + |f(x) - M| < \frac{\epsilon}{2} + \frac{\epsilon}{2} = \epsilon,$$

so by the triangle inequality

$$|L - M| = |L - f(x) + f(x) - M| < \epsilon.$$

Thus L and M differ by an amount smaller than any positive number. Therefore $L = M$.

12. If $C = 0$ then the result follows immediately. If $C \neq 0$, then, given $\epsilon > 0$, there exists $\delta > 0$ so that $|f(x) - L| < \epsilon/|C|$ if $0 < |x - a| < \delta$. It follows that

$$|Cf(x) - CL| = |C|\,|f(x) - L| < \epsilon.$$

13. First deal with the case $L > 0$. The desired inequality follows from $|f(x) - L| < \epsilon L f(x)$. But $f(x)$ can be forced to lie between $L/2$ and $3L/2$ by choosing δ sufficiently small, and now the choice of δ is clear: Merely ensure that $\delta < L^2\epsilon/2$.

14. This is solved much as is Problem 6. Note that there are exactly n terms in the larger factor in the identity given in Problem 14.

16. Let $\epsilon = \tfrac{1}{2}f(a)$. Note that $f(x) \to f(a)$ as $x \to a$ by hypothesis. Now choose δ such that

$$|f(x) - f(a)| < \epsilon \text{ if } 0 < |x - a| < \delta.$$

For such x, we have $-\epsilon < f(x) - 2\epsilon < \epsilon$, so $\epsilon < f(x) < 3\epsilon$. Therefore $f(x) > 0$ if x is in the interval $(a - \delta, a + \delta)$.

Appendix H

1. $\int_0^1 x^2\,dx = \tfrac{1}{3}.$

2. $\int_{-1}^3 8x\,dx = \left[4x^2\right]_{-1}^3 = 32.$

3. $\int_0^2 x\sqrt{4-x^2}\,dx = \left[-\tfrac{1}{3}\left(4-x^2\right)^{3/2}\right]_0^2 = \tfrac{8}{3}.$

4. $\int_0^3 \dfrac{x}{\sqrt{16+x^2}}\,dx = \left[\sqrt{16+x^2}\right]_0^3 = 1.$

5. $\int_0^{\pi/2} \sin x \cos x\,dx = \left[\tfrac{1}{2}\sin^2 x\right]_0^{\pi/2} = \tfrac{1}{2}.$

6. $\int_0^{\pi} \sqrt{\sin^2 x + \cos^2 x}\,dx = \pi.$

7. $\int_0^2 \sqrt{x^4+x^7}\,dx = \left[\tfrac{2}{9}\left(1+x^3\right)^{3/2}\right]_0^2 = \tfrac{52}{9}.$

Typeset by $\mathcal{A}\mathcal{M}\mathcal{S}$-TeX

TEST ITEM FILE

FIFTH EDITION
CALCULUS
WITH ANALYTIC GEOMETRY

CONTENTS

Chapter 1   Functions and Graphs
- Section 1.1: Functions and Graphs   1
- Section 1.2: The Coordinate Plane and Straight Lines   3
- Section 1.3: Graphs of Equations and Functions   4
- Section 1.4: A Brief Catalog of Functions   5

Chapter 2   Prelude to Calculus
- Section 2.1: Tangent Lines and the Derivative—A First Look   6
- Section 2.2: The Limit Concept   10
- Section 2.3: More About Limits   11
- Section 2.4: The Concept of Continuity   12

Chapter 3   The Derivative
- Section 3.1: The Derivative and Rates of Change   15
- Section 3.2: Basic Differentiation Rules   16
- Section 3.3: The Chain Rule   18
- Section 3.4: Derivatives of Algebraic Functions   20
- Section 3.5: Maxima and Minima of Functions on Closed Intervals   23
- Section 3.6: Applied Maximum-Minimum Problems   24
- Section 3.7: Derivatives of Trigonometric Functions   27
- Section 3.8: Implicit Differentiation and Related Rates   30
- Section 3.9: Successive Approximations and Newton's Law   34

Chapter 4   Additional Applications of the Derivative
- Section 4.2: Increments, Differentials, and Linear Approximation   36
- Section 4.3: Increasing and Decreasing Functions and the Mean Value Theorem   37
- Section 4.4: The First Derivative Test   41

Section 4.5:	Graphs of Polynomials	47
Section 4.6:	Higher Derivatives and Concavity	47
Section 4.7:	Curve Sketching and Asymptotes	48

Chapter 5   The Integral

Section 5.2:	Antiderivatives and Initial Value Problems	51
Section 5.3:	Elementary Area Computations	57
Section 5.4:	Reimann Sums and the Integral	59
Section 5.5:	Evaluation of Integrals	60
Section 5.6:	Average Values and the Fundamental Theorem of Calculus	61
Section 5.7:	Integration by Substitution	63
Section 5.8:	Areas of Plane Regions	65
Section 5.9:	Numerical Integration	66

Chapter 6   Applications of the Integral

Section 6.2:	Volumes by the Method of Cross Sections	67
Section 6.3:	Volume by the Method of Cylindrical Shells	69
Section 6.4:	Arc Length and Surface Area of Revolution	71
Section 6.5:	Separable Differential Equations	72
Section 6.6:	Force and Work	73

Chapter 7   Exponential and Logarithmic Functions

Section 7.1:	Exponentials, Logarithms, and Inverse Functions	75
Section 7.2:	The Natural Logarithm	76
Section 7.3:	The Exponential Function	78
Section 7.4:	General Exponential and Logarithmic Functions	80
Section 7.5:	Natural Growth and Decay	81

Chapter 8   Further Calculus of Transcendental Functions

Section 8.2:	Inverse Trigonometric Functions	82
Section 8.3:	Indeterminate Forms and l'Hôpital's Rule;	
Section 8.4:	Additional Indeterminate Forms	84
Section 8.5:	Hyperbolic Functions	85

Chapter 9   Techniques of Integration
    Section 9.2 through 9.7: Techniques of Integration   86
    Section 9.8:   Improper Integrals   93

Chapter 10   Polar Coordinates and Conic Sections
    Section 10.3:   Area in Polar Coordinates   95
    Section 10.4:   Parametric Curves;
    Section 10.5:   Integral Computations with
                     Parametric Curves   98

Chapter 11   Infinite Series
    Part 1:   Numerical Sequences and Series   97
    Part 2:   Power Series and Taylor Series   99

Chapter 12   Parametric Curves and Vectors in the Plane
    Section 12.1:   Parametric Curves   107
    Section 12.2:   Integral Computations with
                     Parametric Curves;
    Section 12.3:   Vectors in the Plane   108
    Section 12.4:   Motion and Vector-Valued
                     Functions   110
    Section 12.5:   Curves and Motion Space;
    Section 12.6:   Curvature and Acceleration   113

Chapter 13   Partial Differentiation
    Section 13.4:   Partial Derivatives;
    Section 13.5:   Maxima and Minima of Functions
                     of Several Variables   117
    Section 13.6:   Increments and Differentials;
    Section 13.7:   The Chain Rule   120
    Section 13.8:   Directional Derivatives and the
                     Gradient Vector   121
    Section 13.9:   Lagrange Multipliers and
                     Constrained Maximum-Minimum
                     Problems   123
    Section 13.10:   The Second Derivative Test for
                     Functions of Two Variables   127

Chapter 14   Multiple Integrals
    Section 14.1:   Double Integrals;
    Section 14.2:   Double Integrals Over More General
                     Regions;

Section 14.3:	Area and Volume by Double Integration	128
Section 14.4	Double Integrals in Polar Coordinates	131
Section 14.6:	Triple Integrals;	
Section 14.7:	Integration in Cylindrical and Spherical Coordinates	135
Applications of Multiple Integrals		136
Section 14.8:	Surface Area	140

Chapter 15   Vector Analysis
Section 15.1:	Vector Fields;	
Section 15.2:	Line Integrals;	
Section 15.3:	Independence of Path	142
Section 15.4:	Green's Theorem;	
Section 15.5:	Surface Integrals;	
Section 15.6:	The Divergence Theorem;	
Section 15.7:	Stokes' Theorem	143

Answers to Test Questions   151

Chapter 1 Test Questions

Section 1: Functions and Graphs

1. (E) Given $f(x) = (x - 1)^3$, find:
   (a) $f(3)$; (b) $f(a + 1)$; (c) $f(x^2)$; (d) $f(2a)$

2. Given $g(x) = x^3 - 1$, find:
   (E) (a) $g(-1)$; (E) (b) $g(3a)$;
   (M) (c) $g(x + h) - g(x)$

3. (E) Write without absolute value symbols:
   (a) $|-3 - 8|$; (b) $-|-\pi|$; (c) $|-x^2|$

4. Solve these inequalities:
   (E) (a) $|x^2 - 1| > 0$; (E) (b) $|4x - 3| < 1$;
   (E) (c) $2x - 3 \leq 9$; (M) (d) $\frac{1}{x} < \frac{1}{2}$

5. (E) Solve the inequality $x^2 + 3x - 4 > 0$.

6. (E) True or false: $\sqrt{2} = 1.414$. Justify your answer.

7. (E) True or false: $\pi = \frac{22}{7}$. Justify your answer.

8. (M) Solve the inequality $\frac{x}{x + 1} < 3$.

9. (M) Solve the inequality $|x - 1| < |x - 2|$.

10. (M) A farmer uses 1000 meters of fencing to build a rectangular corral. One side of the corral has length x. Express the area A of the corral as a function of x.

11. (M) Solve for x: $x^3 - x < 0$.

12. (E) Find the largest domain (of real numbers) on which the given formula determines a function:

(a) $f(x) = x^3 - 3x$; (b) $g(x) = \dfrac{1}{\sqrt{x^2 + 1}}$;

(c) $h(t) = \sqrt{t} + t^{-2}$; (d) $p(z) = z^{1/3}$

13. (M) A triangle has sides of lengths 3, 4, and 5. A rectangle is inscribed in the triangle with the base of the rectangle on the long side of the triangle and a corner on each of the other two sides. Express the area A of the rectangle as a function of its height x.

14. (D/N) A regular hexagon is inscribed in a circle of radius r. Express the area A of the hexagon as a function of r.

15. (M) Express the area A of an equilateral triangle as a function of the length s of each of its sides.

16. (D/N) An arrow is shot vertically into the air. At time t (in seconds), its height is $h(t) = 320t - 16t^2$ (in feet); the arrow is released from the bow at time $t = 0$. (a) How high is the arrow exactly three seconds after it is released from the bow? (b) At what time is the arrow exactly 1200 ft above the ground? (c) How many seconds after its release does the arrow strike the ground?

17. (M) Express the distance between the point $(3, 0)$ and the point $P(x, y)$ of the parabola $y = x^2$ as a function of x.

18. (M) The sum of the radii of two circles is 10. Express the total area A of the two circles as a function of the radius r of one of the circles.

19. (D/T) Write a small positive real number. Write a smaller one. Is there a smallest positive real number? Justify your answer.

Section 1.2: The Coordinate Plane and Straight Lines

1. (E) Write the point-slope equation of the straight line passing through $(2, 3)$ and $(4, 7)$.

2. (E) Write an equation of the vertical line through $(3, -5)$.

3. (E) Write the point-slope equation of the straight line with slope -2 and y-intercept $(0, 5)$.

4. (M) Shade in the points (x, y) in the coordinate plane for which $x < y$.

5. (E) Find both intercepts of the straight line with equation $3x + 4y = 36$.

6. (M) Write the slope-intercept equation of the straight line through the origin $(0, 0)$ and perpendicular to the line with equation $x + 3y = 5$.

7. (M) Shade in the points (x, y) of the coordinate plane for which $xy = 0$.

8. (E) Determine if the lines $2x + 3y = 7$ and $3x - 2y = 8$ are perpendicular or not.

9. (E) Find the coordinates of the midpoint of the line segment joining $(3, 7)$ and $(10, -1)$.

10. (D/A) Is there a triangle in the coordinate plane with no side parallel to a coordinate axis, all sides of integral length, and every vertex at a point whose coordinates are both integers?

Section 1.3: Graphs of Equations and Functions

1. (E) Write an equation of the circle with center (2, −3) and radius 6.

2. (E) Find the distance between the points (1, 1) and (−2, 5).

3. (M) Find the center and radius of the circle with equation
$$x^2 - 6x + y^2 + 4y = 3.$$

4. (M) Shade the points (x, y) in the coordinate plane for which the inequality $x^2 + y^2 \geq 4$ holds true.

5. (M) Find the coordinates of the highest point on the parabola with equation $y = 64x - 4x^2$.

6. (M) Find the center and radius of the circle with equation
$$x^2 + 4x + y^2 - 6y + 12 = 0.$$

7. (M) What is the maximum value of $x - x^2$?

8. (M) A farmer has a long straight wall and 400 meters of fencing. What is the maximum rectangular area she can enclose using part of the wall to form one side of the rectangle?

9. (M) Sketch the graph of $f(x) = x^2 - 2x + 2$.

10. (D/N) The function $f(x) = \dfrac{1}{x^2 + 2x + 2}$ has a maximum value, and only one. Find it.

11. (D/N) A rectangle in the first quadrant has one side on the x-axis, one on the y-axis, and the corner opposite the origin on

the graph of the straight line with equation $y = 10 - x$. What is the maximum possible area of such a rectangle?

12. (M) Sketch an accurate graph of $y = \dfrac{|x|}{x}$.

13. (D/N) Sketch the graph of $f(x) = 2x + |x|$, with special attention to its shape at and near $(0, 0)$.

Section 1.4: A Brief Catalog of Functions

1. (E) Given $f(x) = \sqrt{x}$ and $g(x) = x - 1$, find the formula and the domain of

    (a) $f + g$;   (b) $f - g$;   (c) $f \cdot g$;   (d) $\dfrac{f}{g}$

2. (E) Given $f(x) = \sin x$ and $g(x) = \cos x$, find the formula and the domain of

    (a) $f + g$;   (b) $f - g$;   (c) $f \cdot g$;   (d) $\dfrac{f}{g}$

3. (M) Give a convincing reason why $f(x) = \sin x$ is not a polynomial.

4. (M) Prove that the quotient of two rational functions is a rational function.

5. (E) Prove that the sum of two polynomials is a polynomial.

6. (D/N) Give a convincing reason why $g(x) = 2^x$ cannot possibly be a polynomial.

7. (D/T) Give an example of two trigonometric functions whose sum is a polynomial.

8. (D/N) Prove or disprove: If $p(x)$ is a polynomial of degree $n \geq 2$, then $q(x) = p(x) - p(x-1)$ is a polynomial and the degree of $q(x)$ is $n - 1$.

Chapter 2 Test Questions

Section 2.1: Tangent Lines and the Derivative—A First Look

1. (E) Use the definition of the derivative to find $f'(x)$ given $f(x) = x^2 - 1$.

2. (E) Write an equation of the line tangent to the graph of the function $p(x) = 3x^2 - 6x$ at the point $(2, 0)$.

3. (E) Write an equation of the line tangent to the graph of $y = x^2$ at the point $(3, 9)$.

4. (E) Find $g'(z)$ given $g(z) =$
   (a) $z^2 - 5z + 7;$ (b) $z - \left(\dfrac{z}{4}\right)^2$

5. (M) Use the definition of the derivative to find $g'(x)$ given $g(x) = (x - 1)^2$.

6. (M) Write the slope-intercept equation of the straight line that is tangent to the graph of $g(x) = x^2 - 2x + 5$ at the point $(1, 4)$.

7. (M) Write an equation of the straight line that is tangent to the graph of $y = x^3$ at the point $(2, 8)$.

8. (M) Use the definition of the derivative to find $f'(x)$ given $f(x) = x^2 + x + 1$.

9. (M) Use the definition of the derivative to find $g'(x)$ given $g(x) = x^3 - 1$.

10. (D/N) Write an equation of the straight line normal to the graph of $f(x) = x^2 + 2x - 1$ at the point $(2, 7)$.

11. (M) Find the slope of the straight line tangent to the graph of $y = 2x(1 - x)$ at the point $(1, 0)$.

12. (M) State the definition of the derivative of the function f. Then use this definition to find $f'(x)$ given $f(x) = x^2 + 3x$.

13. (M) State the definition of the derivative of the function f. Then use this definition to find $f'(x)$ given $f(x) = x^2 - x$.

14. (M) Find all points on the graph of $y = x^2 - 3x$ at which the slope of the tangent line is 1.

15. (M) Write an equation of the straight line through $(2, 0)$ tangent to the graph of $y = \frac{1}{x}$.

16. (D/T) Find an equation of every straight line tangent to the graph of $y = x^3$ at two different points, or show by your work that there are no such lines.

17. (M) Use the definition of the derivative to find $f'(x)$ given
$$f(x) = \frac{x}{x + 1}.$$

18. (D/N) Write an equation of the straight line that is tangent to the graph of $y = x^2$ and also passes through the point $(5, 9)$.

19. (M) Find all points on the graph of $y = x^3 - x$ at which the tangent line is horizontal.

7

20. (D/N) Prove that no straight line can be tangent to the graph of $y = x^4$ at two different points.

21. (M) State the definition of the derivative $f'(x)$ of the function $f(x)$. Then use the definition of the derivative to find $g'(x)$ given
$$g(x) = \frac{1}{x-1}.$$

22. (E) Write the slope-intercept equation of the straight line normal to the graph of $y = x^2$ at the point $(-1/2, 1/4)$.

23. (M) Find all points on the graph of $y = x^3$ at which the slope of the tangent line is 12.

24. (M) If $y = x^3$ then $dy/dx = 3x^2$. Write an equation of the line normal to the graph of $y = x^3$ at the point $(-2, -8)$.

25. (M) Use the definition of the derivative to compute $g'(x)$ given $g(x) = x^4$.

26. (E) Find all points on the graph of $y = x^3$ at which the tangent line has slope 27.

27. (E) Find all points on the graph of $y = x^3 - 3x$ at which the tangent line is horizontal.

28. (E) Find all points on the graph of $y = x^3$ at which the slope of the tangent line is 48.

29. (D/N) Find the slope of each line through the point $P(3, 8)$ that is also tangent to the graph of $y = x^2$.

30. (D/T) Find *any* one function $h(x)$ such that $h'(x) = 12x - 8$.

31. (M) Write an equation of the straight line passing through the point (3, 5) and tangent to the graph of $y = x^2$. (If there is more than one such line, write an equation of each of them.)

32. (M) Write an equation of the straight line tangent to the graph of $f(x) = 1/x$ at the point (1, 1).

33. (M) Find all points on the graph of $y = x^3 - 12x$ at which the tangent line is horizontal.

34. (D/N) Find the coordinates of the point at which the line tangent to the graph of $y = x^2$ at (a, b) meets the x-axis.

35. (M) The derivative of $f(x) = 1/x$ is

$$f'(x) = -\frac{1}{x^2}.$$

Write an equation for the straight line passing through the point (1, 0) and tangent to the graph of $y = 1/x$.

36. (D/T) Two straight lines through the origin (0, 0) are tangent to the graph of $y = x^2 + 2x + 1$. One of these lines is the x-axis. Write an equation of the *other* line.

37. (D/N) Find the coordinates of the point at which the line tangent to the graph of $y = x^3$ at (a, b) meets the x-axis.

38. (D/A) Find the coordinates of the point at which the line tangent to the graph of $y = x^5$ at (a, b) meets the x-axis.

39. (D/T) Use the definition of the derivative to find $f'(x)$ given $f(x) = \sqrt{x}$.

40. (D/N) How many straight lines that pass through the point (0, 1) are normal to the graph of $y = x^2$?

41. (D/N) Prove that no straight line can be tangent to the graph of $y = x^2$ at two different points.

42. (D/N) Write an equation of each straight line through $(3, -1)$ that is also tangent to the graph of $y = 1/x$ at some point.

43. (D/T) How many straight lines pass through the point $(0, 2)$ and are also tangent to the graph of $y = x^2$?

44. (D/A) The function $f(x) = \dfrac{x}{x^2 + 1}$ has a maximum value, and only one. Find it.

45. (D/A) Given: The *arbitrary* point (a, b) in the coordinate plane. Show that there is at least one straight line through (a, b) also tangent at some point to the graph of $y = x^3$.

Section 2.2: The Limit Concept

1. (E) Evaluate $\lim\limits_{x \to 5} \dfrac{x^2 - 25}{x - 5}$.

2. (M) Evaluate $\lim\limits_{x \to 4} \dfrac{x - 4}{\sqrt{x} - 2}$.

3. (M) Evaluate $\lim\limits_{x \to 2} \dfrac{\frac{1}{x} - \frac{1}{2}}{x - 2}$.

4. (M) Evaluate $\lim\limits_{h \to 0} \dfrac{(3 + h)^4 - 81}{h}$.

5. (E) Evaluate $\lim\limits_{x \to 9} \dfrac{\sqrt{x} - 3}{x - 9}$.

6. (E) Evaluate $\lim\limits_{x \to 3} \dfrac{2x - 6}{x^2 - 4x + 3}$.

7. (D/N) Evaluate $\lim\limits_{h \to 0} \dfrac{\sqrt{x + h + 5} - \sqrt{x + 5}}{h}$.

8. (M) Evaluate $\lim\limits_{h \to 0} \dfrac{\dfrac{1}{8 + 3h} - \dfrac{1}{8}}{h}$.

9. (E) Evaluate $\lim\limits_{x \to 3} \dfrac{x^2 - x - 6}{x - 3}$.

10. (E) Evaluate $\lim\limits_{x \to 16} \dfrac{\sqrt{x} - 4}{x - 16}$.

11. (M) Evaluate $\lim\limits_{h \to 0} \dfrac{[2(x + h) + 3]^3 - [2x + 3]^3}{h}$.

12. (M) Evaluate $\lim\limits_{x \to 1} \dfrac{x^4 - 1}{x^3 - 1}$.

Section 2.3: More About Limits

1. (E) Evaluate $\lim\limits_{x \to 3^+} \sqrt{x^2 - 9}$.

2. (E) Evaluate $\lim\limits_{x \to \infty} \left(\dfrac{3x^2 + 2x}{x + 5} - 3x \right)$.

3. (E) Evaluate $\lim\limits_{x \to 2} \dfrac{x^3 - 8}{x^2 - 4}$.

4. (M) Evaluate $\lim\limits_{x \to \infty} \left(\sqrt{x^2 + 10x} - x \right)$.

5. (E) Evaluate $\lim\limits_{x \to 3} \dfrac{x - 3}{\dfrac{1}{x} - \dfrac{1}{3}}$.

6. (E) Give an example of a function (by stating its rule in the form of a formula (or formulas) that has the following property: This function has a left-hand and a right-hand limit as $x \to 3$, but the limit of this function as $x \to 3$ does not exist.

7. (E) Evaluate $\lim\limits_{x \to 5^-} \dfrac{x - 5}{|x - 5|}$.

8. (M) Evaluate $\lim\limits_{h \to 0} \dfrac{\sqrt{5 + h} - \sqrt{5}}{h}$.

9. (E) Evaluate $\lim\limits_{x \to \infty} \dfrac{x^4 + 6x - 7}{5x^4 + 7x^2 - 16}$.

Section 2.4: The Concept of Continuity

1. (E) Prove that the equation $x^5 + 2x = 7$ has a solution.

2. (E) Select a value for the function g at $x = 3$ so that g will be continuous there, given

$$g(x) = \frac{6x^2 - 54}{x - 3} \quad \text{if} \quad x \neq 3.$$

3. (E) Prove that the equation $x^5 + x = 1$ has at least one solution.

4. (D/T) Prove that the equation $2x^5 - 10x + 5 = 0$ has exactly three (real) solutions.

5. (E) Show that the equation $x^5 - 2x^2 + x + 1 = 0$ has a solution.

6. (M) Sketch the graph of $f(x) = \dfrac{x^2 - 3x + 2}{x - 1}$; discuss any discontinuities of f in detail.

7. (M) The sum of the squares of two nonnegative real numbers is 18. Write the sum of the two numbers as a function of one of them. What is the domain of this function? Explain why it must have a global minimum value.

8. (M) Given: The equation $x^5 + x = 1$. Find exactly how many (real) solutions this equation has.

9. (D/T) Find the number of (real) solutions of the equation $x^7 + 5x^3 = 13$. Give a convincing justification of your answer, written in complete sentences, and show your knowledge of calculus.

10. (M) Let $h(x) = x^4 - x^3 + 7x^2 + 3x + 1$. Prove that the graph of h has at least one horizontal tangent line.

11. (D/T) Give an example (a carefully labelled picture will suffice) of a function whose domain is the closed interval [0, 1] but which has neither a maximum nor a minimum value there.

12. (M) Can the function $f(x) = \dfrac{x^2 - 16}{x - 4}$ be modified very slightly to become continuous on the set of all real numbers? Explain in detail—show your knowledge of calculus. Specifically, where *can* it be made continuous (and how), and where can it not be made continuous (and why)?

13. (D/T) (a) Give an example of a function f continuous on the closed interval [−1, 2] such that $f'(1)$ does not exist.
(b) List the global extreme values of your example of part (a).
(c) Explain why the function given in *every* correct answer to part (a) will have a global maximum value on [−1, 2].

14. (M) Prove that the equation $x^5 + x^3 = 1$ has a solution.

15. (M) Prove that the equation $x^5 - 3x^2 + 1 = 0$ has a solution.

16. (E) Given: $f(x) = x^3$. Is f continuous at $x = 4$? Justify your answer. Is f continuous at $x = 0$? Justify your answer.

17. (E) Given: $g(x) = x + 1$ if $x \geq 3$; $g(x) = 7 - x$ if $x < 3$. Is g continuous at $x = 3$? Justify your answer.

18. (E) Given: $h(x) = x^2 + 1$ if $x > 2$; $h(x) = 3x$ if $x \leq 2$. Is h continuous at $x = 2$? Justify your answer.

19. (E) Given: $j(x) = x^2$. Is j continuous on the interval [0, 1]? Justify your answer.

20. (M) Give an example of a function (by stating its rule in the form of a formula or formulas) that has the following property: This function has both a value at $x = 3$ and a limit as $x \to 3$, but this function is not continuous at $x = 3$.

21. (D/N) Consider the function f defined as follows:
$$f(x) = \frac{x - 2}{x^2 - 2x} \quad \text{if } x \neq 0, 2;$$
$f(0) = C$ and $f(2) = D$. Discuss the continuity of f. In particular, explain as specifically as possible the effects that various choices of C and D will have on the continuity of f.

22. (D/N) Suppose that f is continuous, $f(0) \geq 0$, and $f(1) \leq 1$. Prove that there is some value of x such that $f(x) = x$.

Chapter 3 Test Questions

Section 3.1: The Derivative and Rates of Change

1. (E) A ball thrown vertically upward at time $t = 0$ (seconds) has height $y(t) = 96t - 16t^2$ (ft) at time t. Find its height when its velocity is zero.

2. (E) A particle moves along the x-axis; at time t its location is $x(t) = 3t^2 - 6t + 1$. Find its position when its velocity is zero.

3. (E) At time $t = 0$ (seconds), a race-car begins to speed down a track; it travels $10t^2$ feet in the first t seconds. What is its velocity when $t = 10$?

4. (E) Find the rate of change of the volume V of a cube with respect to the length x of one edge.

5. (M) Find the rate of change of the surface area A of a cube with respect to the length x of one edge.

6. (D/T) Water leaks from a tank in such a way that the volume of water in the tank at time t (minutes) is $(80 - t)^2$ (liters). (a) Find the average rate at which water leaks from the tank. (b) Find the instantaneous rate of change of water in the tank at time $t = 40$.

7. (D/T) You drop a ball from a cliff above the sea. Its height above the ocean, in feet, t seconds after you throw it is $s(t) = -16t^2 + 16t + 320$. (a) Find the average velocity of the ball from time $t = 2$ to time $t = 2 + h$. (b) Find the instantaneous velocity of the ball at time $t = 2$. (c) Find the maximum height that the ball attains.

8. (D/T) Given: $f(x) = x^2 + 3x$. (a) Find the average rate of change in values of f with respect to x as x changes from 2 to 3. (b) Find the average rate of change in values of f with respect to x as x changes from 2 to $2 + h$. (c) Find the instantaneous rate of change of f with respect to x at $x = 2$.

Section 3.2: Basic Differentiation Rules

1. (E) Find $f'(x)$ given $f(x) =$
   (a) $12x^5 - 7x^3 + 7x^2 - 14x + 24$
   (b) $\dfrac{x + 2}{x + 3}$
   (c) $(x^5 + x)^2$
   (d) x^{-1}

2. (E) Given: $D_x \sin x = \cos x$. Find $g'(x)$ given $g(x) =$
   (a) $x^3 \sin x$
   (b) $(\sin x)^2$
   (c) $\dfrac{1}{\sin x}$
   (d) $(\sin x)(x \sin x)$

3. Find one function $h(x)$ such that $h'(x) =$
    (E) (a) $3x^2 + 4x^3$ (E) (b) $\dfrac{1}{x^2}$

    (E) (c) $16x^7$ (M) (d) $2x(x^2 + 3) + (x^2 + 4) \cdot 2x$

4. (M) Given: $D_x \ln x = \dfrac{1}{x}$. Find $j'(x)$ given $j(x) =$
    (a) $x \ln x - x$ (b) $x^5 \ln x$
    (c) $(\ln x)^2$ (d) $\dfrac{1 - x}{\ln x}$

5. (E) Write an equation of the straight line tangent to the graph of $y = x^5$ at the point $(2, 32)$.

6. (M) Write an equation of the straight line tangent to the graph of $y = \dfrac{6}{1 - x^2}$ at the point $P(2, -2)$.

7. (M) Find any one function $h(x)$ such that $h'(x) = \dfrac{x^3 - x}{x}$.

8. (M) Find three different functions all of which have derivative $f(x) = 7x^6 + 1$.

9. (D/N) Write an equation of the straight line that is simultaneously tangent to the graph of $f(x) = x^2$ and to the graph of $g(x) = x^{-1}$.

10. (M) Write an equation of the straight line through $(6, 0)$ that is tangent to the graph of $f(x) = x^{-1}$.

11. (D/N) Use the definition of the derivative to find $f'(x)$ given $f(x) = (x - 1)^{-1}$.

12. (D/N) There is at least one line through the point (1, 4) tangent to the graph of $f(x) = x^2 + 3x + 1$. Write the point-slope equation of each such line.

13. (M) Two lines through the origin are tangent to the graph of $y = x^2 + 3$. Write the slope-intercept equation of each line.

14. (D/N) Find $g'(x)$ given $g(x) = \dfrac{\frac{1}{x} + \frac{1}{x^2}}{x - 1}$.

15. (M) Write an equation of the straight line that is tangent to the graph of $y = x^3$ at the point (2, 8).

Section 3.3: The Chain Rule

1. (E) Find $f'(x)$ given $f(x) =$
   (a) $(x^2 + 1)^5$
   (b) $\dfrac{x}{(x^2 + 1)^5}$
   (c) $(x^5 + x)^{19}$
   (d) $(x^4 + 1)^5 (x^5 + 1)^4$

2. (M) Given: $D_x \sin x = \cos x$. Find $g'(x)$ given $g(x) =$
   (a) $\sin(x^4)$
   (b) $(\sin x)^4$
   (c) $x^3 \sin x^3$
   (d) $(\sin x)(\sin x^2)$

3. (E) Given: $D_x \sin x = \cos x$. Find $g'(x)$ given $g(x) =$
   (a) $\sin 2\pi x$
   (b) $(\sin x)^{100}$
   (c) $\sin(x^{100})$
   (d) $(x \sin x)^{4/3}$

4. (E) Given $h(x)$ as indicated below, follow this procedure:
   A. Express $h(x)$ in the form $f(g(x))$ where $f(x)$ and $g(x)$ are simpler than $h(x)$.
   B. Compute $f'(x)$ and $g'(x)$.

C. Write the correct expression for $f'(g(x))$.
D. Finally write $h'(x) = f'(g(x)) \cdot g'(x)$.

You may use the fact that $D_x \sin x = \cos x$.

(a) $h(x) = \sin(x^2)$ (b) $h(x) = (\sin x)^7$
(c) $h(x) = (x^2 + 1)^{10}$ (d) $h(x) = (x^3 + x^2)^7$
(e) $h(x) = \sin 3x$ (f) $h(x) = \sin(x^2 + 1)$
(g) $h(x) = \sin(\sin x)$ (h) $h(x) = (x + 1)^{100}$

5. (M) Note: $D_x \sin x = \cos x$. Find $f'(x)$ if $f(x) =$
(a) $(x^3 + 3)^4$ (b) $(x \sin x^2)^7$
(c) $\sin x^7$ (that is, $\sin(x^7)$)
(d) $\sin^7 x$ (that is, $(\sin x)^7$)
(e) $(\sin 5x)^3$ (f) $x^2 \sin^3 4x$
(g) $\sin 7x$ (h) $\sin 7x \sin 8x$

6. (M) Find the derivatives. Note: $D_x \sin x = \cos x$.
(a) $F(x) = (1 - 2 \sin x)^4$
(b) $G(t) = (\sin t^7)^{19}$
(c) $H(z) = (\sin z \sin 3z)^9$

7. (M) Find any one function $f(x)$ such that $f'(x) =$
(a) $3x^2(x^3 + 1)^7$ (b) $x^2 \cos x^3$
(c) $\dfrac{x}{(x^2 + 1)^3}$ (d) $\cos 10x$

8. (M) For each function given below, its derivative can be computed in two ways—one way using the chain rule, another way not using the chain rule. Compute the derivative of each function in both these ways and verify that the results are the same.

(a) $f(x) = (x^2 + 1)^2 = x^4 + 2x^2 + 1$
(b) $g(x) = (x^3)^4 = x^{12}$
(c) $h(x) = (x^4 + 1)^{-1} = \dfrac{1}{x^4 + 1}$

(d) $j(x) = (x + 2)^3 = x^6 + 6x^2 + 12x + 8$
(e) $p(x) = (2x)^{10} = 1024x^{10}$

9. (M) Given: $D_x \tan x = \sec^2 x$ (which means $(\sec x)^2$) and $D_x \sec x = \sec x \tan x$. Find $g'(x)$ given $g(x) =$
   (a) $\sec x^2$ (which means $\sec(x^2)$)
   (b) $\tan^3 x$ (which means $(\tan x)^3$)
   (c) $\sec \dfrac{1}{x}$
   (d) $\sec x \tan x$

10. (D/T) Suppose that $f(x) = 3x + 2$. Find two different functions g such that $g(f(x)) = f(g(x))$ for all x.

11. (D/N) Suppose that $f(x) = x^2$. Find two different functions g of the form $g(x) = Ax + B$ such that $g(f(x)) = f(g(x))$ for all x.

12. (M) Two lines of slope 24 are tangent to the graph of the function $f(x) = (2x - 1)^3$. Write the slope-intercept equation of both of these lines.

Section 3.4: Derivatives of Algebraic Functions

1. (E) Find $f'(x)$ given $f(x) =$
   (a) $x^{5/3}$
   (b) $4x^{-1/2}$
   (c) $(x^2 + 1)^{1/2}$
   (d) $(x^{3/2} + 1)^{2/3}$

2. (M) Given: $D_x \sin x = \cos x$. Find $g'(x)$ given $g(x) =$
   (a) $\sqrt{\sin x}$
   (b) $\sin \sqrt{x}$
   (c) $x^4(1 + \sin x)^{3/2}$
   (d) $\sin(x + x^{1/2} + 1)$

3. (M) Given: $D_x \sec x = \sec x \tan x$ and $D_x \tan x = \sec^2 x$ (which means $(\sec x)^2$). Find $h'(x)$ given $h(x) =$

(a) $\sec \sqrt{x}$ (b) $\sqrt{\sec x}$

(c) $\sec^7 x$ (which means $(\sec x)^7$)

(d) $\sec x^7$ (which means $\sec(x^7)$)

(e) $\tan^8 x$ (f) $\tan x^8$

4. (D/N) Find any one function $h(x)$ such that
$$h'(x) = \frac{x}{\sqrt{1-x^2}}.$$

5. (E) Find $f'(x)$ given $f(x) = x^7 + x^\pi + 7^\pi$.

6. (M) Given: $D_x \sin x = \cos x$. Find $g'(x)$ given $g(x) =$

(a) $\sqrt{x^2+1}$ (b) $\dfrac{x}{\sqrt{1-x^2}}$

(c) $\sqrt{\sin x}$ (d) $\sin \sqrt{x}$

7. (M) Find the derivative of $f(x) = (x^4)^{1/2} = x^2$ with the chain rule and without it, then verify that the two answers are the same.

8. (M) For each of the seven functions that follow, the derivative f' can be found in two ways: With the product or quotient rule, or by first simplifying the function algebraically to avoid use of either of these rules. Verify that the resulting derivatives are the same in each case.

(a) $f(x) = (x^3)(x^4)$

(b) $f(x) = (3x^2)(x^{1/2})$

(c) $f(x) = \dfrac{x+1}{x}$

(d) $f(x) = \dfrac{x^2+1}{x}$

(e) $f(x) = \dfrac{x}{x+1}$

(f) $f(x) = (x^2 + 1)(x - 1)$

(g) $f(x) = (x^{-1/2})(x^{-1/2})$

9. (D/T) Use the definition of the derivative to show directly that if $f(x) = \dfrac{x}{g(x)}$ and g is a positive-valued differentiable function, then $f'(x) = \dfrac{g(x) - xg'(x)}{[g(x)]^2}$.

10. (M) Each function given here can be differentiated in two different ways; for example, the function of part (a) can be differentiated using either the power rule or the product rule. Differentiate each function in two different ways, then verify that the results are the same.

(a) $f(x) = x^3 \cdot x^4 = x^7$
(b) $g(x) = \dfrac{1}{x^5} = x^{-5}$

(c) $h(x) = 3x = x + x + x$
(d) $p(x) = x^{1/2} \cdot x^{1/2} = x$

(e) $q(x) = \dfrac{1}{x^2} = x^{-1} \cdot x^{-1}$
(f) $r(x) = -(x^7) = (-x)^7$

11. (E) The derivative of the given function can be found in two ways: With the aid of the chain rule and without its aid. Find the derivative both ways and verify that the results are the same.

(a) $f(x) = (x^3)^4 = x^{12}$

(b) $g(x) = (x^2 + 1)^{-1} = \dfrac{1}{x^2 + 1}$

12. (D/T) The graph of a certain 4th-degree polynomial passes through the points $(0, 0)$ and $(2, 4)$. Moreover, there is a certain straight line that is tangent to the graph of this polynomial at both these points. Find a formula for this polynomial. [Note: The answer is not unique; in fact, there are infinitely many such polynomials.]

13. (D/N) A motorcyclist riding along the road $y = x^2$ is at point (a, b) when she sees a deer standing at point $(1, -4)$ illuminated by her headlight. Find (a, b).

Section 3.5: Maxima and Minima of Functions on Closed Intervals

1. (E) Find the absolute maximum and absolute minimum value of $f(x) = x^3 + x - 1$ on the interval $[0, 1]$.

2. (E) Find the global maximum and global minimum value of $f(x) = x^3 - 3x$ on the interval $[0, 2]$.

3. (M) Locate and identify the extrema of $h(x) = \dfrac{x - 1}{x + 1}$ on the interval $[0, 2]$.

4. (M) Find and identify the global extrema of $h(x) = \dfrac{x}{x^2 + 1}$ on the interval $[0, 2]$.

5. (E) Find and identify the extrema of $h(x) = 2x^3 - 3x^2 - 12x + 4$ on the closed interval $[0, 3]$.

6. (E) Find the maximum and minimum values of $g(x) = x^{1/3}$ on the closed interval $[-1, 8]$.

7. (E) Find the maximum and minimum values of $g(x) = x^{2/3}$ on the closed interval $[-1, 8]$.

8. (E) Find the global maximum and minimum values of the function $g(x) = x^3 - 3x$ on the interval $[-2, 4]$.

Section 3.6: Applied Maximum-Minimum Problems

1. (E) Use the derivative to find the maximum possible area of a rectangle with perimeter 180 meters.

2. (M) A rectangular corral has an internal divider parallel to two opposite sides, and 1200 meters of fencing will be used to make the corral (including the divider). What is the maximum possible area that such a corral can have?

3. (M) The sum of the squares of two nonnegative real numbers x and y is 18. What is the minimum possible value of $x + y$?

4. (E) What is the greatest amount by which a number in the interval $[0, 1]$ can exceed its cube?

5. (M) A farmer has 600 yards of fencing with which to build a rectangular corral. He will use a long straight wall to form one side of the corral (to save fencing). What is the maximum possible area that can be enclosed in this way?

6. (E) Two nonnegative numbers have sum 1. What is the maximum possible value of the sum of their squares?

7. (D/N) The stiffness of a rectangular beam is proportional to the product of its width and the cube of the height of its cross section. What shape beam should be cut from a circular log of radius R to maximize the stiffness of the beam?

8. (D/T) Find the shape of the right circular cylinder of maximal surface area (including the top and the bottom) inscribed in a sphere of radius R.

9. (D/N) Two cubes have total volume 250 cm^3. What is the maximum possible surface area they can have? The minimum? Verify the nature of the extrema that you find.

10. (M) A rectangle has each diagonal of length 5. What is the maximum possible perimeter of such a rectangle?

11. (E) The product of two positive integers is 1600. What is the minimum possible value of their sum?

12. (M) A rectangle has its base on the x-axis and its upper two vertices on the graph of $y = 12 - x^2$. What is the maximum possible area of such a rectangle? Verify that you have found the maximum.

13. (D/N) The sum of the two nonnegative numbers x and y is 8. Find the maximum possible value of the expression $x^2 + y^3$. *Verify* that you have indeed found the maximum.

14. (D/N) A mass of clay of volume 432 in.³ is formed into two cubes. What is the minimum possible total surface area of the two cubes? What is the maximum?

15. (M) A rancher has 1700 meters of fencing with which to build two widely separated corrals; one is to be square, and the other is to be twice as long as it is wide. What is the maximum possible total area that the rancher can thereby enclose?

16. (D/T) Find the maximum possible volume of a right circular cylinder inscribed in a sphere of radius R.

17. (M) A farmer has 480 meters of fencing. He wishes to enclose a rectangular plot of land and to divide the plot into three equal rectangles with two parallel lengths of fence down the middle. What dimensions will maximize the enclosed area? Be sure to verify that you have found the *maximum* enclosed area.

18. (M) The sum of two nonnegative numbers is 10. Find the minimum possible value of the sum of their cubes.

19. (E) The sum of two nonnegative numbers is 48. What is the smallest possible value of the sum of their squares?

20. (M) A rectangle has a line of fixed length L reaching from one vertex to the midpoint of one of the far sides. What is the maximum possible area of such a rectangle?

21. (D/N) Write an equation of the straight line through the point $(7, 1)$ that cuts off the least area from the first quadrant. Be sure to verify that your area is *minimal*.

22. (D/T) A circle is dropped into the graph of the parabola $y = x^2$. How small can the radius of the circle be and yet allow the circle to touch the parabola at two different points?

23. (E) Find the point on the graph of $y = \sqrt{x}$ that is closest to the point $(3, 0)$. Be sure to verify that it is indeed closest.

24. (M) A rectangular box is to have a base three times as long as it is wide. The total surface area of the box is to be 20 ft^3. Find the maximum possible volume of such a box.

25. (M) A circular sector is bounded by two radii of the circle (each of length r) and by a circular arc of length s. The area of such a figure is known to be $\frac{1}{2}rs$. Find the value of r that will produce such a sector of maximum possible area, given that its perimeter must be 100.

26. (D/N) Find two nonnegative numbers whose sum is 4 such that the sum of the square of one and the cube of the other is (a) maximal; (b) minimal.

27. (M) A right circular cone has a slant height of 10 ft. Find the maximum possible volume of such a cone. Verify that your answer is maximal.

28. (M) A rectangular poster is to contain 8250 cm² of print in the shape of a smaller rectangle; the margins at top and bottom must each be 22 cm, and those at the sides must each be 15 cm. What are the dimensions of such a poster having the least possible total area?

29. (D/N) A wastebasket is to have as its base an equilateral triangle, its sides are to be vertical, and its volume is to be 8 ft³. What is the minimum possible surface area of such a wastebasket?

30. (M) Write the number 33 as the sum of two nonnegative real numbers such that the product of one number with the square of the other is maximal.

31. (E) Find the coordinates of the point or points on the curve $2y^2 = 5x + 5$ which is (are) closest to the origin $(0, 0)$.

32. (M) A railroad will operate a special excursion train if at least 200 people subscribe. The fare will be $8 per person if 200 people subscribe, but will decrease 1 cent for each additional person who subscribes. What number of passengers will bring the railroad the maximum revenue?

Section 3.7: Derivatives of Trigonometric Functions

1. (E) Find $f'(x)$ given $f(x) =$
   (a) $\sin 7x$
   (b) $\cos 5x^2$
   (c) $(\sin 7x)^3$
   (d) $\sqrt{3 \cos 3x}$

2. (E) Find $f'(x)$ given $f(x) =$
   (a) $\sin^2 x \cos^2 x$ (b) $\dfrac{\sin 2x}{\cos 3x}$
   (c) $\sin x \cos 3x$ (d) $\cos(\cos x)$

3. (E) Find $g'(x)$ given $g(x) =$
   (a) $x^2 \sin x^3$ (b) $\sin^7 x \cos x$
   (c) $\cos^4 x^4$ (d) $\sin(x^3 + x^2 + x + 1)$

4. (E) Find $h'(x)$ given $h(x) =$
   (a) $\sec(x^2 + 5x)$ (b) $\sec^5(x^2 + 5x)$
   (c) $\sec 3x \tan 5x$ (d) $\tan^3 x^3$

5. (M) Find $j'(x)$ given $j(x) =$
   (a) $\sin x \cos x \sec x$ (b) $\sec^2 x - \tan^2 x$
   (c) $\dfrac{\sin x + \cos x}{\sec x + \tan x}$ (d) $\sec^4 \sqrt{x}$

6. (E) Because $\sin 2x = 2 \sin x \cos x$ is an *identity*, differentiation of each side of this identity with respect to x will yield another true identity. Do so to discover the new identity.

7. (M) Verify that $f(x) = \sin^2 x$ and $g(x) = -\cos^2 x$ have the same derivative on the set **R** of all real numbers. We will see that this implies that $f(x)$ and $g(x)$ differ by a constant. Find that constant.

8. (E) Find $f'(x)$ given $f(x) =$
   (a) $\csc^3 x$ (b) $\cot 7x^2$
   (c) $\csc 3x \cot 5x$ (d) $\cot^3 x^4$

9. (M) Find $g'(x)$ given $g(x) =$
   (a) $x^6 \cot 7x$
   (b) $\sqrt{\csc x \cot x}$
   (c) $\dfrac{1 + \cot x}{1 + \csc x}$
   (d) $\csc^8 x \cot^4 x$

10. (E) Given: $D_x \ln x = \dfrac{1}{x}$. Find $g'(x)$ given $g(x) =$
    (a) $\ln(\cos x)$
    (b) $\ln(\sin x + \cos x)$
    (c) $\sin(\ln x)$
    (d) $\ln(\sec x + \tan x)$

11. (E) Given: There is a constant $e \approx 2.71828$ such that $D_x e^x = e^x$. Find $h'(x)$ given $h(x) =$
    (a) $e^{\sin x}$
    (b) $\sin(e^x)$
    (c) $e^{\tan x}$
    (d) $(\sec e^x)^{11}$

12. (E) Find any one function $F(x)$ such that $F'(x) =$
    (a) $\cos 2x$
    (b) $\sin^3 x \cos x$
    (c) $x^2 \cos x^3$
    (d) $\sec 2x \tan 2x$

13. (M) Find any one function $G(x)$ such that $G'(x) =$
    (a) $\sec^4 x \tan x$
    (b) $\sin x \sec^2 x$
    (c) $x \sec x^2 \tan x^2$
    (d) $(\cos x)\sqrt{\sin x}$

14. (D/N) A triangle has two sides of length 1 and the angle between these two sides is θ. Express the area of the triangle as a function of θ, then find the maximum possible area of such a triangle using calculus.

15. (M) Evaluate $\lim\limits_{x \to 0} \dfrac{\tan 3x}{7x}$.

16. (M) Evaluate $\lim\limits_{x \to 0} \dfrac{1 - \cos x}{x^2}$.

17. (D/T) An isosceles triangle is inscribed in a circle of radius 5. Determine the maximum possible area of the triangle. Include a verification that you have actually *maximized* the area of the triangle.

18. (E) Find any *one* function f such that
$$f'(x) = 2x \sin x^2 + 3x^2 \cos x^3.$$

19. (D/T) Two circles lie in the same plane and their centers are 13 ft apart. One circle has radius 1 ft; the other has radius 6 ft. A string is wrapped tightly around the two circles, touching part but not all of each, and not crossing itself. Find to three-place accuracy the length of the string.

Section 3.8: Implicit Differentiation and Related Rates

1. (E) The function $y = y(x)$ is defined implicitly by the equation $xy^3 - 3x^3y = 2$. Find dy/dx. Then find the slope of the straight line tangent to the graph of $y = y(x)$ at the point $(1, 2)$.

2. (E) The function $y = y(x)$ is defined implicitly by means of the equation $x^5 + y^5 = 5x^2y^2 - 3$. Find and simplify dy/dx.

3. (E) Find dy/dx given $x^{2/3} + y^{2/3} = 1$.

4. (M) Find dy/dx and d^2y/dx^2 given $x^{1/3} + y^{1/3} = 1$. Simplify the second derivative as much as you can.

5. (E) Find dy/dx given $xy + y^2 + x^3 = 7$.

6. (E) Write an equation of the straight line tangent to the graph of $x^3 + 2xy + y^3 = 13$ at the point $(1, 2)$.

7. (M) Find all points on the curve with equation $x^2 + xy + y^2 = 3$ at which the tangent line is horizontal.

8. (M) Find all points on the curve with equation $x^2 - xy + y^2 = 3$ at which the tangent line is horizontal.

9. (M) Write an equation of the straight line normal to the graph of the equation $x^2 + xy + y^2 = 1$ at the point $(1, -1)$.

10. (M) Given: $x^4 + y^4 + 2 = 4xy^3$. Find all points on the graph of this equation at which the tangent line is horizontal.

11. (M) Find all points on the graph of $x^2y + 2 = xy^2$ at which the tangent line is horizontal.

12. (E) Find and simplify dy/dx given $x^2y^2 = x^2 + y^4$.

13. (E) Find and simplify dy/dx given $y = \sin(x^2 + y)$.

14. (M) Find and simplify d^2y/dx^2 given $x^4 + y^4 = 1$.

15. (M) Find all points on the graph of $x^3 + y^3 = 3xy$ at which the tangent line is vertical.

16. (M) A square is expanding; its area is increasing at 120 in.²/s. How fast is each edge increasing when each edge has length 10?

17. (M) Each edge of a square is increasing at the rate of 10 in./s. How fast is its area increasing when each edge has length 50 in.?

18. (D/N) The base of a rectangle is growing larger at the rate of 5 cm/min while its altitude is growing smaller at the rate of 3 cm/min. At what rate is the area of the rectangle changing when its base is 40 cm long and its altitude is 90 cm?

19. (D/N) If a hemispherical bowl of radius 12 cm is filled with water to a depth of x centimeters, the volume of liquid in the bowl turns out to be $V = \frac{1}{3}\pi(36x^2 - x^3)$ cubic centimeters. Suppose that water is poured into the bowl at the rate of 72π cm³/s. How fast is the water level in the bowl rising when $x = 2$ cm?

20. (E) A right triangle has short sides of lengths x and y; x is increasing at the rate of 1 m/s while y is decreasing at the rate of 2 m/s. At what rate is the area of the triangle changing when $x = 12$ m and $y = 5$ m?

21. (M) Two straight roads intersect at right angles. At 10 A.M. a car passes through the intersection heading due east at 30 mi/h. At 11 A.M. a truck passes through the intersection heading due north at 40 mi/h. How fast are the two vehicles separating from one another at 1 P.M.?

22. (M) Sand is pouring from a pipe at the rate of 12 m³/s. If the falling sand forms a conical pile on the ground whose altitude is always 1/3 the radius of the base, how fast is the altitude increasing when the pile is 20 m high?

23. (M) A ladder 13 ft long is sliding down a vertical wall while its base slides horizontally along the ground. The top of the ladder is moving at 12 ft/s when it is 5 ft above the ground. How fast is the base of the ladder moving then?

24. (M) Sand falling from a hopper at 10π ft³/s forms a conical sandpile whose radius is always equal to its height. How fast is the radius increasing when the radius is 5 ft?

25. (D/N) A telephone pole is 15 ft away from a street light; the latter is 20 ft above the ground. A squirrel runs up the telephone pole at 8 ft/s. How fast is the squirrel's shadow

traveling along the (level) ground when the squirrel is 18 ft above the ground?

26. (M) The sides of an equilateral triangle are lengthening at the rate of 3 cm/min. How fast is the area of the triangle increasing when its sides are each 8 cm long?

27. (E) Each edge of a cube is increasing in length at 2 cm/s. How fast is the volume of the cube increasing when the volume is 1000 cm^3?

28. (D/N) A circular oil slick spreads on the surface of the ocean, the result of a spill of 10 ft^3 of oil. When its radius is 50 ft, its radius is increasing at the rate of 2 ft/s. How fast is the thickness of the slick changing then?

29. (D/T) Two aircraft approach Foley Field at the same constant altitude. The first aircraft is moving south at 250 km/h while the second is moving west at 600 km/h. At what rate is the distance between them changing when the first aircraft is 60 km from the field and the second is 25 km from the field?

30. (M) Show that the graph of $x^5y + xy^5 = 1$ has no horizontal tangents.

31. (M) The graph of the equation $x^2 - xy + y^2 = 9$ intersects the y-axis at two points. Find the equations of the tangent lines to this graph at these two points, then show that these two lines are parallel.

32. (D/T) Water is draining from a spherical tank of radius 10 ft in such a way that the water level is falling at the constant rate of 2 ft/min. How fast is the area of the (top) water surface changing when its radius is 7 ft?

33. (M) A baseball diamond is a square 90 ft on a side. A runner is running from second base to third base. When he is halfway between these bases, he is running at a speed of 18 ft/s. How fast is the distance between the runner and home plate changing then?

34. (D/N) A rocket is launched vertically and is tracked by a radar station located on the ground 4 km from the launch site. What is the speed of the rocket at the instant when its distance from the radar station is 5 km if this distance is increasing at the rate of 3600 km/h then?

35. (D/T) Find d^2y/dx^2 given $\sqrt{x} + \sqrt{y} = 1$. Simplify your answer as much as you can.

Section 3.9: Successive Approximations and Newton's Method

1. (M) Use Newton's method to approximate $\sqrt[3]{2}$ with three digits correct to the right of the decimal point.

2. (D/N) The equation $x^3 + 3x - 5 = 0$ has only one (real) solution. Use Newton's method to find it with five digits to the right of the decimal correct.

3. (D/T) Given: The equation $x^5 - 5x^3 + 10x = 0$. Find exactly how many (real) solutions this equation has. Then use Newton's method to find each with three digits to the right of the decimal correct.

4. (M) Use Newton's method to approximate $\sqrt[10]{1000}$ with three digits to the right of the decimal correct.

5. (D/T) The equation $x^3 + 7x = 1$ has exactly one real

solution. Find the interval of length 1 with integer endpoints that contains that solution. Take the midpoint of that interval as an initial estimate of the solution of the equation and then use Newton's method once to improve that estimate.

6. (D/N) Use Newton's method to find all solutions of the equation

$$x^4 = \frac{1}{x+1}$$

with three digits correct to the right of the decimal. [*Suggestion:* Sketch the graphs of $y = x^4$ and $y = 1/(x+1)$, and deduce how many points of intersection the graphs have.]

7. (D/T) Use Newton's method to find all real solutions of the equation $x^5 + 2x = 1$ with six digits to the right of the decimal correct.

8. (D/T) Prove that the equation $x^7 - 3x^3 + 1 = 0$ has a (real) solution. Then closely approximate one solution by Newton's method.

9. (M) Use Newton's method to find the value of x for which $\cos x = x$ with three places to the right of the decimal correct. [*Remember:* Set your calculator in *radian* mode.]

10. (D/T) Use Newton's method to find (approximately) *all* (real) solutions of the equation $2x^3 + 5x = 4$. Give a valid argument to show that you have indeed found all solutions.

11. (M) Use Newton's method once to improve the initial guess $x_0 = 4$ for the solution of the equation $3 + x \sin x = 0$. [*Remember:* Set your calculator in *radian* mode.]

12. (D/N) Use Newton's method to approximate $\sqrt[3]{122}$ with three digits correct to the right of the decimal point.

Chapter 4 Test Questions

Section 4.2: Increments, Differentials, and Linear Approximation

1. (E) Use the linear approximation theorem ("approximation by differentials") to estimate $\sqrt{16.01}$.

2. (E) Use the linear approximation formula to estimate $\sqrt{99.99}$.

3. (E) Use the tangent line (linear approximation) method to estimate $\sqrt[5]{31}$.

4. (E) Use the linear approximation formula to estimate $\sqrt{102}$.

5. (E) Use the tangent line approximation ("method of differentials") to estimate $\sqrt{8.9}$.

6. (E) Use methods of calculus to find a decimal approximation to the cube root of 28.

7. (M) Use differentials to approximate $\dfrac{1}{1.000\,000\,000\,004}$.

8. (E) Use either differentials or Newton's method to estimate the cube root of 26.

9. (M) A simple pendulum of length L feet has a period of oscillation T (in seconds) given by $T = 2\pi\sqrt{\dfrac{L}{32}}$. Suppose that you increase the length of a pendulum from 1 ft to 1.01 ft. Use the linear approximation theorem ("method of differentials")

to estimate the resulting increase in the period of the pendulum.

10. (M) Use differentials to estimate $\sqrt[3]{999}$. *Note:* Do *not* use a calculator until you have completed all your work. You may then use a calculator to check your answer.

11. (M) Use methods of calculus to approximate $\sqrt{24.97}$.

12. (M) Use methods of calculus to estimate $\sqrt[4]{81}$.

13. (E) Use the linear approximation theorem to estimate $(2.001)^{10}$.

14. (M) Use the linear approximation theorem to approximate $\sin(0.01)$.

15. (M) Use differentials to approximate $\cos(0.01)$.

16. (M) Use differentials to approximate $\sin\left(\frac{\pi}{6} + 0.02\right)$.

Section 4.3: Increasing and Decreasing Functions
and the Mean Value Theorem

1. (E) Find the intervals on which $f(x) = 4x^5 - 5x^4$ is increasing and those on which it is decreasing.

2. (E) Find the intervals on which $f(x) = x^4 + 4x^3$ is increasing and those on which it is decreasing.

3. (E) Find the intervals on which $f(x) = x^3 - 27x$ is increasing and those on which it is decreasing.

4. (M) Find the intervals on which $f(x) = 3x^5 - 5x^3$ is increasing and those on which it is decreasing.

5. (M) Find the intervals on which $f(x) = x^{2/3}$ is increasing and those on which it is decreasing.

6. (M) Find the intervals on which $f(x) = \dfrac{x^2}{x-1}$ is increasing and those on which it is decreasing.

7. (D/N) Find the intervals on which $f(x) = \dfrac{x^2 - 1}{x^2 + 1}$ is increasing and those on which it is decreasing.

8. (D/N) Find the intervals on which $f(x) = \sin x$ is increasing and those on which it is decreasing using methods of calculus.

9. (D/N) Find the intervals on which $f(x) = \sin^2 x$ is increasing and those on which it is decreasing.

10. (M) Find the intervals on which $f(x) = x^{1/3}$ is increasing and those on which it is decreasing.

11. (E) (a) State the mean value theorem. (b) Find the number whose existence is guaranteed by the mean value theorem when that theorem is applied to the function $f(x) = x^3$ on $[0, 2]$.

12. (E) Find the number whose existence is guaranteed by the mean value theorem when that theorem is applied to $f(x) = \sqrt{x}$ on the interval $[0, 4]$.

13. (E) Find the number whose existence is guaranteed by the mean value theorem when that theorem is applied to $f(x) = x^4$ on the interval $[0, 2]$.

14. (M) State the mean value theorem. Then find the number whose existence is guaranteed by the mean value theorem when that theorem is applied to $f(x) = x^{1/3}$ on the interval $[0, 27]$.

15. (M) (a) State the mean value theorem. (b) Find the number whose existence is guaranteed by the mean value theorem when that theorem is applied to $f(x) = x + \dfrac{1}{x}$ on the interval $[2, 3]$.

16. (E) The mean value theorem asserts that if f is continuous on $[a, b]$ and differentiable on (a, b), then there exists a number c in (a, b) that satisfies a certain equation. (a) Write that equation. (b) Find that value of c if $f(x) = x^3$, $a = 0$, and $b = 3$.

17. (M) Find the number whose existence is guaranteed by the mean value theorem when that theorem is applied to $f(x) = x^3 + x + 1$ on the interval $[-1, 2]$.

18. (M) (a) State the mean value theorem. (b) Find the number whose existence is guaranteed by the mean value theorem when that theorem is applied to $f(x) = x - \dfrac{1}{x}$ on the interval $[1, 3]$.

19. (D/N) State the mean value theorem. Then find the number whose existence is guaranteed by that theorem when it is applied to the function $f(x) = \cos x$ on the interval $[0, \pi]$.

20. (M) Find all functions $F(x)$ such that $F'(x) =$
    (a) $(\sin x)^4 \cos x$ (b) $x^4 \cos x^5$

21. (M) State the mean value theorem. Then find the number whose existence is guaranteed by that theorem when it is applied to the function $f(x) = (x - 1)^{2/3}$ on the interval $[1, 2]$.

22. (M) State the mean value theorem. Then find the number whose existence is guaranteed by that theorem when it is applied to the function $f(x) = x^3 + x - 4$ on the interval $[-2, 3]$.

23. (D/N) Find the number whose existence is guaranteed by the mean value theorem when it is applied to the function $f(x) = \frac{11}{5} x^5$ on the interval $[-1, 2]$.

24. (D/N) Find the number whose existence is guaranteed by the mean value theorem when that theorem is applied to $f(x) = \sin x$ on the interval $[0, \pi]$.

25. (D/T) Suppose that the function f is differentiable on the interval $[-1, 2]$, that $f(-1) = -1$, and that $f(2) = 5$. Prove that there is a point on the graph of f at which the tangent line is parallel to the straight line with equation $y = 2x$.

26. (D/T) Use the mean value theorem to prove that $\sin x < x$ if $x > 0$. [*Suggestion*: Consider the function $f(x) = x - \sin x$.]

27. (D/N) A function f satisfies the hypotheses of the mean value theorem on the interval $[3, 7]$, $f'(x) \geq 5$ for all x in $[3, 7]$, and $f(7) = 10$. What does the mean value theorem enable you to conclude about $f(3)$? Be as explicit as possible.

28. (D/N) A function f satisfies the hypotheses of the mean value theorem on the interval $[5, 9]$, $f(9) = 23$, and $f'(x) < 2$ for all x in the interval $[5, 9]$. State as explicitly as possible what the mean value theorem enables you to conclude about $f(5)$.

Section 4.4:   The First Derivative Test

1.   (M) How should one choose two positive numbers with product 2 in order to minimize the sum of their squares? Use the first derivative test to verify that you have found the minimum.

2.   (E) What point on the parabola $y = x^2$ is closest to the point $(3, 0)$? Use the first derivative test to verify that you have found the minimum.

3.   (M) The cost of operating a certain truck (gas, oil, insurance, and depreciation) is $15 + \frac{1}{9}s$ cents/mi when the truck travels at a speed of s miles per hour. In addition, the driver is paid \$9 per hour. What is the most economical speed at which to operate the truck for a 600-mile trip? Use the first derivative test to verify that you have found the minimum.

4.   (M) A rectangular box with square base and no top is to have a volume of exactly 1000 cm³. What is the minimum possible surface area of such a box? Use the first derivative test to verify that you have found the minimum.

5.   (M) The potential energy of a diatomic molecule is given by
$$U(x) = k\left[\left(\frac{R}{x}\right)^{12} - 2\left(\frac{R}{x}\right)^{6}\right]$$
where k and R are positive constants and x is the distance between the atoms. For what value of x is $U(x)$ a minimum? Use the first derivative test to verify that you have found the minimum.

6.   (E) Find the minimum possible value of the sum of a real number and its square. Use the first derivative test to verify that you have found the minimum.

7. (M) What is the maximum possible volume of a right circular cylinder with total surface area 600π cm^2? Verify that you have indeed found the global maximum.

8. (E) Find the maximum value of $f(x) = 4x^3 - 3x^4$. Use the first derivative test to verify that you have found the maximum.

9. (M) An aquarium has a base made of slate costing 8 cents/in.^{2} and four glass sides costing 3 cents/in.^{2} The volume of the aquarium is to be 36,000 in.^{3} Find the dimensions of the least expensive such aquarium. Use the first derivative test to verify that you have found the minimum.

10. (M) The sum of two positive numbers is 160. What is the maximum possible value of their product? Use the first derivative test to verify that you have found the maximum.

11. (M) Find the maximum value that the slope of a line tangent to the graph of $f(x) = \dfrac{x}{x^2 + 1}$ can have. Use the first derivative test to verify that you have found the maximum.

12. (D/T) The numbers $a_1, a_2, a_3, \ldots, a_n$ are fixed. Find a simple formula for that number x such that the sum of the squares of the distances from x to the n fixed numbers is as small as possible. Use the first derivative test to verify that you have found the minimum.

13. (D/T) A poster is to contain 96 in.^{2} of print, and each copy must have 3-in. margins at top and bottom and 2-in. margins on each side. What are the dimensions of such a poster having the least possible area? Use the first derivative test to verify that you have found the minimum.

14. (D/T) A handbill is to contain 384 cm² of print, and each copy must have 6-cm margins at top and bottom and 4-cm margins on each side. What are the dimensions of such a handbill having the least possible area? Use the first derivative test to verify that you have found the minimum.

15. (D/T) The pages of a book are each to contain 30 in.² of print, and each page must have 2-in. margins at top and bottom and 1-in. margins on each side. What are the dimensions of such a page having the least possible total area? Use the first derivative test to verify that you have found the minimum.

16. (D/T) A storage building is to be shaped like a box with a square base (its floor). The floor costs \$3/m², the walls cost \$7/m², and the flat roof costs \$5/m². The volume of the building is to be 12,544 m³. What is the shape of the least expensive such building? Use the first derivative test to verify that you have found the minimum.

17. (M) What is the maximum possible area of a rectangle inscribed in the ellipse $x^2 + 4y^2 = 4$ with the sides of the rectangle parallel to the coordinate axes? Use the first derivative test[22] to verify that you have found the maximum.

18. (D/N) A right triangle has sides 3, 4, and 5 m long. A rectangle is inscribed in the triangle in the "obvious" way—with two adjacent sides of the rectangle lying on the two short sides of the triangle. What is the area of the largest possible such rectangle? Use the first derivative test to verify that you have found the maximum.

19. (D/T) A wall 8 m high stands 4 m away from a wall building. What is the length of the shortest ladder that will lean over the wall and touch the building? Use as independent variable the

angle that the ladder makes with the ground. Use the first derivative test to verify that you have found the minimum.

20. (D/N) Show that the rectangular solid with square base, fixed total volume $V > 0$, and of minimum total surface area, is a cube. Use the first derivative test to verify that you have found the minimum.

21. (D/N) Three sides of a trapezoid have length L, a constant. What should be the length of the fourth side if the trapezoid is to have maximum area? Use the first derivative test to verify that you have found the maximum.

22. (M) A rectangular sheet of thin metal is 5 m wide and 8 m long. Four small equal squares are cut from its corners and the projections of the resulting cross-shaped piece of metal are bent upward and welded to make an open-topped box with a rectangular base. What is the maximum possible volume of such a box? Use the first derivative test to verify that you have found the maximum.

23. (D/T) Consider the parabolas $y = \frac{1}{2}x^2 + 2$ and $y = x^2$.

Let R denote the plane region that they bound. At each point P on the first parabola, and in R, the tangent line at P determines a segment called a *tangential segment*. Find the longest tangential segment. Use the first derivative test to verify that you have found the maximum.

24. (D/N) Two straight highways meet at right angles. A historical monument stands 1 km from one highway and 2 km from the other. The state plans to build a straight road from one highway to the other passing directly beside the monument. What is the shortest length such a road can have? Use the first derivative test to verify that you have found the minimum.

25. (M) A box with no top has a square base and total surface area 24 ft². What is the maximum possible volume of such a box? Use the first derivative test to verify that you have found the maximum.

26. (D/T) A mass of clay of volume V is to be formed into two solid spheres. For what distribution of clay is the total surface area of the spheres a maximum? A minimum? Use the first derivative test to verify that you have found the global extrema.

27. (M) The base of a rectangle lies on the x-axis and its two upper vertices lie on the graph of the circle $x^2 + y^2 = 16$. Find the maximum possible area of such a rectangle. Use the first derivative test to verify that you have found the maximum.

28. (D/T) If a and b are two positive numbers, then their *arithmetic mean* is the familiar $\frac{1}{2}(a + b)$; their *geometric mean* is $\sqrt{ab}$. Use calculus to prove that the arithmetic mean is never less than the geometric mean for positive numbers a and b. [*Suggestion:* Minimize

$$f(x) = \sqrt{ax} - \frac{1}{2}(a + x), \quad x > 0.$$

Then interpret the results.]

29. (D/N) Microcomputers that can be sold for $4000 each can be manufactured by a plant for a total cost of $C(x) = \frac{5}{2}x^2 - \frac{1}{3}x^3$ millions of dollars for x thousand machines. The capacity of the plant is 6000 machines per year. Find the number of machines that should be built each year to maximize the annual profit of the plant. Use the first derivative test to verify that you have found the maximum.

30. (D/N) A box with no top must have a base twice as long as it is wide, and the total surface area of the box is to be 54 m^2. What is the maximum possible volume of such a box? Use the first derivative test to verify that you have found the maximum.

31. (D/N) You plan to build a playing field in the shape of a rectangle with a semicircular region at each end, so that races can be held around the perimeter of the field. If you want the perimeter of the field to be 1000 m, what dimensions should your field have to maximize the area of the rectangular portion of the field? Use the first derivative test to verify that you have found the maximum.

32. (D/T) You are in the forest at point A, which is 3 mi from the closest point on a long straight road. You want to get as quickly as possible to point B, which is on the road and 5 mi from you "as the crow flies." If you can walk 4 mi/h on the road but only 1 mi/h in the forest, where should you meet the road to minimize the time of your journey? Use the first derivative test to verify that you have found the minimum.

33. (D/N) Find the maximum possible volume of a pyramid with square base inscribed in a sphere of radius R.

34. (D/T) A rectangular stage is to be constructed with the greatest possible area, subject to the condition that lighting will be placed along three sides of the stage and only 240 m of lighting is available. What should be the dimensions of the stage?

35. (D/T) Find the maximum possible curved surface area of a right circular cylinder inscribed in a sphere of radius R.

36. (D/T) The sum of two nonnegative real numbers is 28. What is the maximum possible value of the sum of the square of one of the numbers and the cube of the other?

37. (D/N) Given $f(x) = x^4 - 8x^3 + 18x^2 + 1$, find the intervals on which f is increasing and those on which it is decreasing.

Section 4.5: Graphs of Polynomials

General instructions: Sketch the graph of the given function. Show and label all extrema and indicate clearly where the function is increasing and where it is decreasing. Find all intercepts unless the arithmetic is really impossible.

1. (E) $f(x) = 4x^5 - 5x^4$
2. (E) $f(x) = x^4 + 4x^3$
3. (E) $f(x) = x^3 - 27x$
4. (E) $g(x) = 3x^5 - 5x^3$
5. (E) $g(x) = x^3 - 3x^2 - 9x$
6. (E) $h(x) = x^3 - 3x$
7. (M) $g(x) = x^4 - 3x^2 + 7$
8. (E) $h(x) = 3x^4 - 4x^3$
9. (E) $f(x) = x^4 - 12x^2$
10. (E) $h(x) = x^4 - 2x^2$
11. (E) $f(x) = x^4 - 4x^3$
12. (M) $f(x) = -x^3 + 6x^2 - 10$
13. (E) $g(x) = 2x^3 - 3x^2$
14. (M) $h(x) = x^4 - 2x^2 + 1$

Section 4.6: Higher Derivatives and Concavity

General Instructions: Sketch the graph of the given function. Show clearly where each graph is increasing, where decreasing, where concave upward, and where concave downward. Locate, identify, and label all extrema and inflection points. Find all intercepts unless the arithmetic is really too difficult.

1. (E) $f(x) = 4x^5 - 5x^4$

2. (E) $f(x) = x^4 + 4x^3$

3. (E) $f(x) = x^3 - 27x$

4. (E) $f(x) = 3x^5 - 5x^3$

5. (M) $g(x) = \dfrac{x^2}{x - 1}$

6. (M) $g(x) = \dfrac{x^2}{x^2 - 1}$

7. (M) $f(x) = x^{1/3}$

8. (M) $g(x) = x^{2/3}$

9. (E) $h(x) = x^3 - 3x^2 - 9x$

10. (E) $h(x) = x^3 - 3x$

11. (M) $f(x) = x^4 - 8x^2 + 7$

12. (E) $f(x) = 3x^4 - 4x^3$

13. (D/N) $f(x) = \dfrac{x^2 - 1}{x^2 + 1}$. Note: $f'(x) = \dfrac{4x}{(x^2 + 1)^2}$ and $f''(x) = \dfrac{4 - 4x^2}{(x^2 + 1)^3}$.

14. (D/N) $g(x) = \dfrac{x}{1 + x^2}$

15. (M) $h(x) = x + \dfrac{1}{x}$

16. (D/N) $f(x) = \dfrac{x}{x^2 - 1}$

17. (M) $f(x) = x^4 - 12x^2$

18. (M) $g(x) = x^4 - 2x^2$

19. (M) $g(x) = 2x^3 - 3x^2$

Section 4.7: Curve Sketching and Asymptotes

General Instructions for Problems 1 through 13: Sketch the graph of the given function. Show clearly where each graph is increasing, where decreasing, where concave upward, and where concave downward. Locate, *identify, and label all extrema and inflection points. Find and label all asymptotes. Pay special attention to the behavior of the function when $|x|$ is large and when x is close to any discontinuity of the function. Find all intercepts unless the arithmetic is really too difficult.*

1. (E) $g(x) = \dfrac{x^2}{x - 1}$

2. (E) $g(x) = \dfrac{x^2}{x^2 - 1}$

3. (E) $f(x) = x^{1/3}$

4. (E) $g(x) = x^{2/3}$

5. (M) $f(x) = \dfrac{x^2 - 1}{x^2 + 1}$. Note: $f'(x) = \dfrac{4x}{(x^2 + 1)^2}$ and

$$f''(x) = \dfrac{4 - 4x^2}{(x^2 + 1)^3}.$$

6. (E) $g(x) = \dfrac{x}{1 + x^2}$

7. (E) $h(x) = x + \dfrac{1}{x}$

8. (E) $f(x) = \dfrac{x}{x^2 - 1}$

9. (E) $g(x) = x^2 + \dfrac{1}{x}$

10. (E) $f(x) = \dfrac{x + 3}{x - 3}$

11. (E) $g(x) = \dfrac{x}{4 - x^2}$

12. (M) $h(x) = \dfrac{x^3 - 8}{x}$

13. (E) $k(x) = \dfrac{4(x - 1)}{x^2 + 1}$

14. (M) Find all asymptotes of the graph of
$g(x) = \dfrac{2x^3 - 2x + 1}{x^2 - 1}$.

15. (M) Use asymptotes, but no calculus, to sketch the graph of $f(x) = \dfrac{1}{x^3 - x^2}$.

16. (D/T) Sketch the graph of a function that satisfies all of these conditions simultaneously:
    (a) $\lim\limits_{x \to \infty} f(x) = 2$;
    (b) $\lim\limits_{x \to -\infty} f(x) = 0$;
    (c) $\lim\limits_{x \to -1} f(x) = -\infty$;
    (d) $f'(x) > 0$ if $x < -2$;
    (e) $f'(x) < 0$ if $-2 < x < -1$;
    (f) $f'(x) > 0$ if $x > -1$;
    (g) $f'(-2) = 0$;
    (h) $f''(x) > 0$ if $x < -3$;
    (i) $f''(-3) = 0$;
    (j) $f''(x) < 0$ if $-3 < x < -1$ and if $-1 < x$.

17. (D/N) Suppose that $f(x)$ is a cubic polynomial that has three distinct real roots. Prove that the solutions of $f'(x) = 0$ are real and distinct.

18. (D/T) The function f is defined for $x > 0$ and has an infinite discontinuity at $x = 1$. Moreover,
$$f'(x) = \frac{\ln x - 1}{(\ln x)^2} \quad \text{and} \quad f''(x) = \frac{2 - \ln x}{x(\ln x)^3}.$$
Finally, $f(e) = e$. Sketch the graph of f as accurately as you can.

19. (D/T) The function f is defined on the set of all real numbers other than $x = 1$; it has an infinite discontinuity there. Given $f(0) = 0$ and
$$f'(x) = \frac{x^2 - 2x}{(x - 1)^2},$$
sketch the graph of f as accurately as you can.

Chapter 5 Test Questions

Section 5.2: Antiderivatives and Initial Value Problems

General Instructions, problems 1 through 32: Evaluate the indicated antiderivative.

1. (E) $\displaystyle\int x^5 \sin x^6 \, dx$

2. (E) $\displaystyle\int \sin^4 x \cos x \, dx$

3. (E) $\displaystyle\int 2x \cos x^2 \, dx$

4. (E) $\displaystyle\int x^2 (x^3 + 1)^{10} \, dx$

5. (M) $\displaystyle\int \frac{x+1}{x^5} \, dx$

6. (M) $\displaystyle\int \sqrt{x} \cos x\sqrt{x} \, dx$

7. (E) $\displaystyle\int \sin x \cos^7 x \, dx$

8. (M) $\displaystyle\int \left(x - \frac{1}{x}\right)^2 dx$

9. (E) $\displaystyle\int \cos 2x - \sin 2x \, dx$

10. (E) $\displaystyle\int x^5 (x^6 - 1)^7 \, dx$

11. (E) $\displaystyle\int t \cos t^2 \, dt$

12. (E) $\displaystyle\int (7u^3 + 7) \, du$

51

13. (E) $\int (x+1)^5 \, dx$

14. (E) $\int \cos 7x \, dx$

15. (M) $\int \sin t \cos t \, dt$

16. (E) $\int 3x^2 \cos x^3 \, dx$

17. (M) $\int \dfrac{\cos x}{\sin^3 x} \, dx$

18. (M) $\int \dfrac{x+1}{\sqrt{x}} \, dx$

19. (M) $\int \dfrac{2x}{\sqrt{x^2+1}} \, dx$

20. (M) $\int \dfrac{7}{(x+1)^2} \, dx$

21. (M) $\int \dfrac{x^3+4}{x^2} \, dx$

22. (M) $\int \dfrac{2x^2}{\sqrt{x^3+5}} \, dx$

23. (E) $\int x^2(x^7 - x^5) \, dx$

24. (E) $\int (\sin x)^{99} \cos x \, dx$

25. (M) $\int \sqrt{x+1} \, dx$

26. (M) $\int z^2(z^3+1)^{1/3} \, dz$

27. (M) $\int x^4(x^5+7)^{99} \, dx$

28. (D/N) $\int \sin 2x \sin x \, dx$

29. (M) $\displaystyle\int x\sqrt{1-x^2}\,dx$ 　　30. (E) $\displaystyle\int 2t\sin t^2\,dt$

31. (M) $\displaystyle\int \frac{1}{x^2}\cos\frac{1}{x}\,dx$ 　　32. (M) $\displaystyle\int \frac{1}{\sqrt{x}}\cos\sqrt{x}\,dx$

General Instructions, problems 33 through 40: Solve the given initial-value problem.

33. (E) $\dfrac{dy}{dx} = 2x + 1;\quad y(0) = 3$

34. (E) $\dfrac{dy}{dx} = (x - 2)^3;\quad y(2) = 1$

35. (E) $\dfrac{dy}{dx} = \sqrt{x};\quad y(4) = 0$

36. (E) $\dfrac{dy}{dx} = \dfrac{1}{x^2};\quad y(1) = 5$

37. (M) $\dfrac{dy}{dx} = \dfrac{1}{\sqrt{x+2}};\quad y(2) = -1$

38. (M) $\dfrac{dy}{dx} = x\sqrt{9+x^2};\quad y(-4) = 0$

39. (E) $\dfrac{dy}{dx} = \cos 2x;\quad y(0) = 1$

40. (M) $\dfrac{dy}{dx} = \sec x \tan x;\quad y(0) = 2$

41. (D/N) An ostrich egg is dropped from an altitude of 14,400 ft above the earth's surface. Ignore air resistance, take $g = 32$ ft/s^2, and find both how long the egg stays aloft and what its impact velocity is.

42. (D/N) A rock is dropped from a balloon hovering at 4800 ft above the ground. Neglect air resistance, take $g = 32$ ft/s^2, and find both how long it takes for the rock to reach the ground and its impact velocity.

43. (D/T) A punter kicked the football straight upward and the sportscaster reported that the ball had a "hang time" of 4.0 seconds. How high did the ball go and what was its initial velocity?

44. (D/T) An arrow shot vertically upward reached a maximum height of 1920 ft. What was its initial velocity?

45. (D/N) A ball is thrown upward with an initial velocity of 64 ft/s. How high does it go?

46. (D/N) A stone dropped from a height of 1 ft near the north pole of the planet Mesklin strikes the ground 0.001 s later. Find the value of the acceleration g of gravity there and also find the impact velocity of the stone.

47. (D/N) A ball is thrown upward with initial velocity 144 ft/s. How high will it go?

48. (M) A stone is dropped from the top of a building 960 ft high. How long will it remain aloft? What will its impact velocity be?

49. (D/T) A crossbow bolt shot upward remained aloft for 48 s. What was its initial velocity, and how high did it go?

50. (D/N) A stone dropped into a well hits the bottom 6 s later. How deep is the well?

51. (D/N) A croquet ball is thrown upward from the top of a building 960 ft high with an initial velocity of 48 ft/s. How high will it go? How long will it remain aloft?

52. (D/N) A watermelon is thrown vertically upward from the ground. Neglect air resistance and take the acceleration of gravity to be 32 ft/s^2. With what initial velocity must the watermelon be thrown so that its maximum altitude is 4096 ft? In such a case, how long will the watermelon remain aloft?

53. (D/N) A very dense planet has g = 15,000 ft/s^2 for the acceleration of gravity at its surface. If a stone is dropped there from an altitude of 3 ft, how long will it remain aloft? With what speed will the stone strike the ground?

54. (D/N) When its brakes are applied, a certain automobile decelerates at 11 ft/s^2. Suppose that its initial velocity is 60 mi/h (88 ft/s). How long will the automobile travel before coming to a stop? How far will it travel?

55. (D/N) An arrow is shot upward from the surface of the moon, where the acceleration of gravity is 5.2 ft/s^2. The initial velocity of the arrow is 1040 ft/s. How high will the arrow go, and how long will it remain aloft?

56. (D/N) A zucchini is dropped from the top of a tall building. Its speed at impact is 256 ft/s. Ignore air resistance, take g = 32 ft/s^2, and find the height of the building.

57. (D/T) When the space shuttle first leaves the ground, its acceleration is a (constant) 60 ft/s². How long does it take the shuttle to reach a height of 3 mi (under the assumption that it climbs vertically)? How fast is it traveling then?

58. (D/T) In a panic stop, a certain car leaves skid marks 420 ft long. This car is known to have constant deceleration under such circumstances, and in an experiment under similar conditions the car left skid marks 105 ft long when the brakes were applied at 30 ft/s. How fast was the car moving when the brakes were applied in the panic stop?

59. (D/N) A stone is thrown vertically upward from the surface of a very small planet where the value of g, the acceleration of gravity, is 5 ft/s². The initial velocity of the stone is 100 ft/s. How high does the stone go and how long does it remain aloft?

60. (D/N) A ball thrown vertically upward from the earth's surface reaches a maximum altitude of 225 ft. Take $g = 32$ ft/s², ignore air resistance, and compute the initial velocity of the ball.

61. (D/T) The maximum deceleration of a certain freight train is 1 ft/s². If it is traveling at 60 mi/h, what is the minimum time in which it can come to a stop? How far will it travel during that time?

62. (D/N) On March 6, 1992, Schroeder told Charlie Brown that a baseball dropped from the height of Charlie's waist would strike the ground at a speed of 9.45 mi/h. How high, to the nearest inch, is Charlie Brown's waist?

63. (D/N) A particle is traveling with acceleration $a(t) =$

$\sqrt{4 + 3t}$ ft/s². At time $t = 0$ its velocity is zero and its location is also zero. Determine its position at time $t = 4$ seconds.

Section 5.3: Elementary Area Computations

1. (E) The plane region R is bounded by the graph of $y = 3x^2$, the x-axis, and the lines $x = 0$ and $x = 1$. Approximate the area A of R by dividing the interval $[0, 1]$ into four equal-length subintervals, inscribing rectangles in R with bases these subintervals, and adding the areas of the rectangles.

2. (M) The plane region R is bounded by the graph of $y = 3x^2$, the x-axis, and the lines $x = 0$ and $x = 1$. Find the exact area A of R as follows: (a) Divide the interval $[0, 1]$ into n equal-length subintervals. (b) Inscribe n rectangles in R having these subintervals as their bases. (c) Sum to find the total area A_n of the inscribed rectangles in terms of n. (d) Find the limit A of A_n as $n \to +\infty$.

3. (M) The plane region R is bounded above by the graph of $y = 1/x$, below by the x-axis, and on the sides by the lines $x = 1$ and $x = 2$. Obtain an accurate overestimate and an accurate underestimate of the area A of R as follows: (a) Divide the interval $[1, 2]$ into four equal-length subintervals. (b) Inscribe four rectangles in R whose bases are these subintervals, and sum their areas to obtain an underestimate of A. (c) Circumscribe four similar rectangles around R, and sum their areas to obtain an overestimate of A.

4. (M) Consider the triangle in the plane bounded below by the x-axis, on the right by the vertical line $x = u > 0$, and above by the line $y = mx$ $(m > 0)$. (a) Write the area A of the triangle as a function of u. (b) Find $A'(u)$. (c) Compare

the functions $A'(x)$ and $y(x) = mx$. State exactly the difference between them.

5. (E) Write in summation notation:
   (a) $1 + 3 + 5 + 7 + \cdots + 101$
   (b) $1 + 4 + 7 + 10 + \cdots + 100$
   (c) $2^2 + 4^2 + 6^2 + 8^2 + \cdots + 50^2$
   (d) $\dfrac{1}{1} + \dfrac{1}{4} + \dfrac{1}{9} + \cdots + \dfrac{1}{400}$

6. (E) Evaluate:
   (a) $\sum_{n=1}^{200} n$ (b) $\sum_{n=1}^{50} (2n-1)$
   (c) $\sum_{n=1}^{100} (n^2 - 3n)$ (d) $\sum_{n=1}^{100} n^2$

7. (M) The region R is bounded above by the graph of $y = x^3$ and below by the x-axis over the interval $[0, 2]$. Obtain an overestimate and an underestimate of its area A by dividing the interval $[0, 2]$ into $n = 4$ equal-length subintervals and adding areas of rectangles, with bases these subintervals, inscribed in R and circumscribed about R.

8. (M) The region R is bounded above by the graph of $y = x^4$ and below by the x-axis over the interval $[0, 1]$. Obtain an overestimate and an underestimate of its area A by dividing the interval $[0, 1]$ into $n = 5$ equal-length subintervals and adding areas of rectangles, with bases these subintervals, inscribed in R and circumscribed about R.

9. (M) The region R is bounded above by the graph of $y = x^{1/2}$ and below by the x-axis over the interval $[0, 1]$. Obtain an overestimate and an underestimate of its area A by dividing the

interval [0, 1] into n = 5 equal-length subintervals and adding areas of rectangles, with bases these subintervals, inscribed in R and circumscribed about R.

10. (D/A) The region R is bounded above by the graph of $y = x^{3/2}$ and below by the x-axis over the interval [0, 1]. Obtain an overestimate and an underestimate of its area A by dividing the interval [0, 1] into n = 10 equal-length subintervals and adding areas of rectangles, with bases these subintervals, inscribed in R and circumscribed about R.

Section 5.4: Riemann Sums and the Integral

1. (E) Write and evaluate one Riemann sum for $f(x) = x^2$ over the interval [1, 2] using a partition of that interval into n = 5 equal-length subintervals.

2. (E) Evaluate $\lim_{n \to \infty} \dfrac{\sqrt{1} + \sqrt{2} + \sqrt{3} + \cdots + \sqrt{n}}{n\sqrt{n}}$ by interpreting it as the limit of Riemann sums for some continuous function f defined on [0, 1].

3. (E) Evaluate $\lim_{n \to \infty} \dfrac{\sin \frac{\pi}{n} + \sin \frac{2\pi}{n} + \sin \frac{3\pi}{n} + \cdots + \sin \frac{n\pi}{n}}{n}$ by interpreting it as the limit of Riemann sums for some continuous function f defined on [0, 1].

4. (E) Use the definition of the definite integral to evaluate $\int_1^3 2x\, dx$. Note: $\sum_{i=1}^{n} i = \dfrac{n(n+1)}{2}$.

Section 5.5: Evaluation of Integrals

General Instructions: In Problems 1 through 12, evaluate the given definite integral with the aid of the evaluation theorem.

1. (M) $\displaystyle\int_{3}^{5} x\sqrt{x^2 - 9}\, dx$

2. (M) $\displaystyle\int_{0}^{\pi} (\sin 4x)^6 \cos 4x\, dx$

3. (M) $\displaystyle\int_{-1}^{1} (x^2 + 1)^4\, dx$

4. (E) $\displaystyle\int_{1}^{3} \frac{6}{x^2}\, dx$

5. (E) $\displaystyle\int_{0}^{\pi/2} \cos x\, dx$

6. (E) $\displaystyle\int_{-1}^{1} \sqrt{x + 1}\, dx$

7. (E) $\displaystyle\int_{-2}^{-1} \frac{1}{x^2}\, dx$

8. (E) $\displaystyle\int_{0}^{1} (x^3 - x^2)\, dx$

9. (E) $\displaystyle\int_{1}^{4} \frac{1}{\sqrt{x}}\, dx$

10. (E) $\displaystyle\int_{0}^{\pi} \sin \frac{x}{4}\, dx$

11. (D/N) $\displaystyle\int_{0}^{1} \sqrt{x^4 + x^7}\, dx$

12. (E) $\displaystyle\int_{0}^{\pi} \cos x\, dx$

Section 5.6: Average Values and the
              Fundamental Theorem of Calculus

1. (E) Find the average value of $f(x) = x^3$ on $[0, 4]$.

2. (E) Find the average value of $g(x) = \sin x$ on $[0, \pi]$.

3. (E) Find the average value of $h(x) = \sec^2 x$ on $[0, \pi/4]$.

4. (M) Find the average value of $f(x) = \dfrac{1}{x^2}$ on $[1, 2]$.

5. (M) Find the average value of $f(x) = \dfrac{1}{x^2}$ on $[1, 100]$.

6. (E) Find the average value of $g(x) = \sqrt{x}$ on $[0, 4]$.

7. (E) Find the average value of $h(x) = \cos x$ on $[0, 2\pi]$.

8. (M) Find the average value of $f(x) = x(x^2 + 1)^3$ on $[-1, 1]$.

9. (M) Suppose that f is continuous for all $x \geq 0$, that $f(0) = 0$ and $f(x) > 0$ if $x > 0$, and that if $u \geq 0$ then
$$u^3 = \int_0^u f(x)\, dx.$$

Find $f(x)$.

10. (E) Find $F'(x)$ given $F(x) = \displaystyle\int_3^x \dfrac{1}{1 + u^3}\, du$.

11. (D/N) Find $G'(x)$ given $G(x) = \int_{2}^{x^3} \sqrt{u^4 + 1}\ du$.

12. (D/N) Evaluate $\int_{0}^{4} \sqrt{16 - x^2}\ dx$ without use of the fundamental theorem of calculus.

13. (E) Find $H'(x)$ given $H(x) = \int_{0}^{2} tx^3\ dt$.

14. (M) Find $G'(x)$ given $G(x) = $

  (a) $\int_{0}^{x} \sqrt{1 + t}\ dt$ (b) $\int_{0}^{x^2} \sqrt{1 + t}\ dt$

15. (D/N) Evaluate $\lim_{x \to \infty} e^{-x^2} \int_{0}^{x} e^{t^2}\ dt$.

16. (M) Given: $\lim_{n \to \infty} \sum_{i=1}^{n} \frac{1}{n} \cdot \sin\left(\frac{\pi i}{n}\right) = \int_{0}^{1} f(x)\ dx$. Find the formula of the function f, then use the fundamental theorem of calculus to evaluate the integral.

Section 5.7: Integration by Substitution

General Instructions: Use the indicated substitution to help evaluate the given definite or indefinite integral.

1. (E) $\displaystyle\int x^3(1 + x^4)^{3/2}\, dx;\quad u = x^4$

2. (E) $\displaystyle\int x^3(1 + x^4)^{3/2}\, dx;\quad u = 1 + x^4$

3. (E) $\displaystyle\int \frac{\sin x}{(1 + \cos x)^7}\, dx;\quad u = \cos x$

4. (E) $\displaystyle\int \frac{\sin x}{(1 + \cos x)^7}\, dx;\quad u = 1 + \cos x$

5. (E) $\displaystyle\int (\sec 6x)^2\, dx;\quad u = 6x$

6. (E) $\displaystyle\int \sec^7 x \tan x\, dx;\quad u = \sec^6 x$

7. (M) $\int x\sqrt{x+1}\, dx;\quad u = x+1$

8. (E) $\int \cos 8x\, dx;\quad u = 8x$

9. (E) $\int_0^1 \dfrac{x^3}{\sqrt{1+x^4}}\, dx;\quad u = 1 + x^4$

10. (E) $\int_0^1 x^3\sqrt{1+x^4}\, dx;\quad u = 1 + x^4$

11. (E) $\int_0^\pi \sin^2 x \cos x\, dx;\quad u = \sin x$

12. (E) $\int_0^\pi (1 + \sin x)^7 \cos x\, dx;\quad u = \sin x$

13. (E) $\int_{-1}^2 x^2\sqrt{1+x^3}\, dx;\quad u = 1 + x^3$

Section 5.8: Areas of Plane Regions

General Instructions: In each problem, the graphs of the given functions, lines, and other curves divide the plane into a number of regions. Find the area of each such region that is bounded.

1. (E) $f(x) = x^2$, $g(x) = x^3$

2. (E) $f(x) = x^3$, $g(x) = x^4$

3. (M) $f(x) = x^n$, $g(x) = x^{n+1}$ (n is a fixed positive integer)

4. (E) $f(x) = x^2$, $g(x) = 8 - x^2$

5. (M) $f(x) = x^{-101}$, $x = 1$, $x = 2$, the x-axis

6. (M) $x = y^2$, $x = 18 - y^2$

7. (M) $x = y^2$, $y = x^2$

8. (M) $f(x) = x$, $f(x) = 2x$, $f(x) = 3 - x$

9. (E) $f(x) = x^4$, $y = 1$

10. (E) $f(x) = x^4$, $y = 0$, $x = 1$

11. (M) $x = y - y^3$, $x = 0$

12. (M) $y = x\sqrt{1 - x^2}$, $y = 0$

13. (D/N) $y^2 = 4x$, $y = 2x - 4$

14. (M) $x = 6 - y^2$, $x = y$

65

15. (M) $y = 9 - x^2$, $y = 5 - 3x$

Section 5.9: Numerical Integration

General Instructions: Approximate the given definite integrals using Simpson's rule with the indicated number n of subintervals.

1. (D/N) $\int_{1}^{3} \frac{1}{x}\,dx$; $n = 10$

2. (D/A) $\int_{0}^{1} \frac{1}{1 + x^2}\,dx$; $n = 8$

3. (D/A) $\int_{0}^{1} \sqrt{1 + x^3}\,dx$; $n = 10$

4. (D/A) $\int_{1}^{2} \frac{1}{x^2}\,dx$; $n = 10$

5. (D/A) $\int_{0}^{1} x^3\,dx$; $n = 4$

6. (D/A) $\int_{0}^{1} x^4\,dx$; $n = 4$

7. (D/A) $\int_{0}^{1} x^4\,dx$; $n = 10$

8. (D/A) $\int_{0}^{\pi} \frac{\sin x}{x}\,dx$; $n = 10$

Chapter 6 Test Questions

Section 6.2: Volumes by the Method of Cross Sections

1. (D/N) The base of a solid is the circular disk $x^2 + y^2 \leq 1$ in the coordinate plane, and every cross section perpendicular to the x-axis is an isosceles triangle whose height is the same as the length of its base—the latter lies in the disk. Find the volume of the solid.

2. (E) The graph of $x^2 + y^2 = R^2$ is rotated around the x-axis to form a sphere of radius R. Find the volume of the sphere by methods of integral calculus.

3. (D/N) A solid has base B in the coordinate plane. The base B is the region between the x-axis and the graph of $y = x - x^2$ over the interval $[0, 1]$. Every cross section of the solid in a plane perpendicular to the x-axis is a square. Find the volume of the solid.

4. (E) The plane region R is bounded above by the graph of $y = x^{-2}$ and below by the x-axis over the interval $[1, 3]$. Find the volume generated by rotation of R around the x-axis.

5. (E) The region R is bounded by the graph of $y = x^3$, the y-axis, and the horizontal line $y = 1$. Find the volume generated by rotation of R around the y-axis.

6. (E) The region R is bounded by the graph of $y = x^3$, the y-axis, and the horizontal line $y = 1$. Find the volume generated by rotation of R around the x-axis.

7. (M) The region R is bounded by the graphs of $x - 2y = 3$ and $x = y^2$. Set up (but do not bother to evaluate) the integral

that gives the volume of the solid obtained by rotating R around the line $x = -1$.

8. (M) The region R is bounded by the graphs of $x - 2y = 3$ and $x = y^2$. Set up (but do not bother to evaluate) the integral that gives the volume of the solid obtained by rotating R around the line $y = 5$.

9. (M) A solid has its base in the xy-plane; the base is the region bounded by $x = y^2$ and $x = 4$. Each vertical cross section of the region perpendicular to the x-axis is a semicircle with its diameter in the base. Find the volume of the solid.

10. (M) Set up (but do not bother to evaluate) the integral that gives the volume of the following solid: Its base is a circular disk of radius 1 in the xy-plane; cross sections perpendicular to a fixed diameter of the base are equilateral triangles.

11. (E) Use integral calculus to find the volume of a right circular cone of radius R and height H.

12. (M) The plane region R is bounded above by the graph of $y = x - x^3$ and below by the x-axis over the interval $[0, 1]$. Find the volume generated by rotation of R around the x-axis.

13. (M) The region R in the first quadrant is bounded by the coordinate axes and the graph of $y = 4 - x^2$. When it is rotated around the y-axis it generates a solid of volume V. Find V.

14. (D/N) The region R in the first quadrant is bounded above by the graph of $y = \sqrt{\sin x}$ and below by the x-axis, $0 \leq x \leq \pi$. When it is rotated around the x-axis it generates a solid of volume V. Find V.

15. (M) The plane region Q is bounded above by the graph of $x = 16 - y^2$, on the left by the y-axis, and below by the x-axis. When Q is rotated around the x-axis, it produces a solid of volume V. Set up (but do not bother to evaluate) the integral that gives the value of V.

16. (M) The region R is bounded above by the line $y = 1$, on the left by the line $x = 0$, and on the right and below by the graph of $y = x^2$. Find the volume V generated when R is rotated around the horizontal line $y = 2$.

17. (D/N) Suppose that n is a fixed positive integer. Find the volume obtained when the region bounded by $x = 1$, the x-axis, and the graph of $y = x^n$ ($0 \le x \le 1$) is rotated around the y-axis.

18. (M) Find the volume generated when the region bounded by the y-axis, the graph of $xy^2 = 1$, and the horizontal lines $y = 1$ and $y = 2$ is rotated around the y-axis.

Section 6.3: Volume by the Method of Cylindrical Shells

1. (E) The region R is bounded above by the graph of
$$y = \frac{1}{x^2 + 1}$$
and below by the x-axis over the interval $[0, 1]$. Find the volume of the region generated by rotating R around the y-axis.

2. (M) The region R is the first-quadrant region bounded by the coordinate axes and the graph of $y = 2 + 3x - x^3$, $0 \le x \le 2$. Find the volume generated by rotation of R around the y-axis.

3. (M) The region R is bounded below by the x-axis and above by the graph of $y = 2x - x^2$. Find the volume generated by rotation of R around (a) the y-axis; (b) the line $y = -1$.

4. (D/T) The first-quadrant region bounded below by the x-axis and above by the graph of $y = x^3 - 3x^2 + 2x$ is rotated around the y-axis. Find the volume of the solid thereby generated.

5. (M) The region R lies in the first quadrant and is bounded by the graph of

$$y = \frac{1}{(x^2 + 1)^2},$$

the coordinate axes, and the vertical line $x = 2$. Find the volume generated when R is rotated around the y-axis.

6. (D/N) The plane region R is bounded above by the graph of $y = x - x^3$ and below by the x-axis over the interval $[0, 1]$. Find the volume swept out when R is rotated around the y-axis.

7. (M) The plane region R is bounded above by the graph of $y = x - x^3$ and below by the x-axis over the interval $[0, 1]$. Find the volume swept out when R is rotated around the vertical line $x = 2$.

8. (M) The region R in the first quadrant is bounded by the coordinate axes and the graph of $y = 4 - x^2$. When it is rotated around the y-axis it generates a solid of volume V. Find V by the method of cylindrical shells.

9. (M) The plane region Q is bounded above by the graph of $x = 16 - y^2$, on the left by the y-axis, and below by the x-axis. When Q is rotated around the x-axis, it generates a solid of volume V. Set up the integral needed to evaluate V by the

method of cylindrical shells. Do not bother to evaluate the integral.

10. (M) Use the method of cylindrical shells to find the volume obtained when the region between the x-axis and the graph of $y = 1/x$, $1 \leq x \leq 2$, is rotated around the x-axis.

Section 6.4: Arc Length and Surface Area of Revolution

1. (E) Find the arc length of the curve
$$y = \frac{x^4}{16} + \frac{1}{2x^2}, \quad 1 \leq x \leq 2.$$

2. (D/T) Approximate the length of the graph of $y = x^3$ over the interval $[0, 1]$ with the aid of Simpson's rule.

3. (E) Find the length of the graph of
$$y = \frac{x^3}{3} + \frac{1}{4x}, \quad 1 \leq x \leq 2.$$

4. (E) Write the integral that gives the length of the graph of $y = x^4$ from $(0, 0)$ to $(1, 1)$. Do not bother to evaluate the integral.

5. (E) Write the integral that gives the surface area of revolution generated by rotating the graph of $y = x^4$, $0 \leq x \leq 1$, around the y-axis. Do not bother to evaluate the integral.

6. (M) Use calculus to show that the lateral surface area of a right circular cone of base radius R and height H is $\pi R L$, where L is the slant height of the cone.

7. (E) Find the length of the graph of $y = \frac{1}{3}x^{3/2} - x^{1/2}$ from $(1, -2/3)$ to $(4, 2/3)$.

8. (E) Find the length of the part of the graph of
$$y = \frac{x^3}{4} + \frac{1}{3x}$$
over the interval $1 \leq x \leq 2$.

9. (M) The graph of $y = x^3$, $0 \leq x \leq 1$, is rotated around the x-axis. Find the area of the surface thereby generated.

10. (E) Set up (but do not attempt to evaluate) the integral that gives the length of the graph of $y = \sin x$ from $x = 0$ to $x = \pi$.

11. (E) Find the length of the graph of
$$y = \frac{x^3}{12} + \frac{1}{x}$$
over the interval $[1, 2]$.

12. (M) Find the length of the graph of $y = \frac{2}{3}x^{3/2}$ from $(0, 0)$ to $(9, 18)$.

13. (M) Find the area of the surface obtained when the graph of $y = x^2$, $0 \leq x \leq 1$, is rotated around the y-axis.

Section 6.5: Separable Differential Equations

1. (E) Solve: $\frac{dy}{dx} + 2xy = 0$

2. (E) Solve: $\dfrac{dy}{dx} = y^2 \sin x$

3. (M) Solve: $\dfrac{dy}{dx} = 3\sqrt{xy}$

4. (M) Solve: $\dfrac{dy}{dx} = \sqrt[3]{64xy}$

5. (E) Solve: $\dfrac{dy}{dx} = 2x \sec y$

6. (E) Solve: $(1 + x)^2 \dfrac{dy}{dx} = (1 + y)^2$

7. (E) Solve: $\dfrac{dy}{dx} = xy^3$

8. (M) Solve: $\dfrac{dy}{dx} = \dfrac{1 + \sqrt{x}}{1 + \sqrt{y}}$

9. (D/N) Solve: $2y \dfrac{dy}{dx} = \dfrac{x}{\sqrt{x^2 - 16}}$; $y(5) = 2$

10. (D/N) Solve: $\dfrac{dy}{dx} = 2xy^2 + 3x^2 y^2$; $y(1) = -1$

Section 6.6: Force and Work

1. (E) A 100-ft length of steel chain weighing 15 lb/ft is hanging from the top of a tall building. How much work is done in pulling all the chain to the top of the building?

2. (M) A 10-ft long trough filled with water has a semicircular cross section of diameter 4 ft. How much work is done in pumping all the water over the edge of the trough? Assume that water weighs 62.5 lb/ft^3.

3. (D/N) A cylindrical tank of radius R feet and length L feet is lying on its side on horizontal ground. Oil weighing δ pounds per cubic foot is available at ground level and is to be pumped into the tank. Find the work required to do so.

4. (D/N) The graph of $y = x^3$, $0 \le x \le 1$, is rotated around the y-axis to form the surface of a tank. If units on the coordinate axes are in feet, find how much work is done in pumping the tank full of oil weighing 50 lb/ft^3 and available at the level of the x-axis.

5. (M) A spherical tank of radius 100 ft is full of gasoline weighing 40 lb/ft^3. How much work is done in pumping all the gasoline to the level of the top of the tank?

6. (D/N) The graph of $y = x^2$, $0 \le x \le 1$, is rotated around the y-axis to form the surface of a tank. Units on the coordinate axes are in feet. How much work is done in pumping the tank full of oil weighing 50 lb/ft^3 if the oil is initially at the level of the x-axis?

7. (D/N) A tank is in the shape of the surface generated by rotating the graph of $y = x^4$, $0 \le x \le 1$, around the y-axis. The tank is initially full of oil weighing 60 lb/ft^3. How much work is done in pumping all the oil to the level of the top of the tank? (Units on the coordinate axes are in feet.)

8. (D/T) A tank is in the shape of a hemisphere of radius 60 ft and is resting on its flat base (the curved surface is on top). The tank is filled with ethyl alcohol, which weighs 40 lb/ft^3.

How much work is done in pumping all the alcohol to the level of the top of the tank?

Chapter 7 Test Questions

Section 7.1: Exponentials, Logarithms, and Inverse Functions

1. (E) Find the inverse function of $f(x) = 4x - 3$.

2. (E) Find the inverse function of $h(x) = \dfrac{1}{2x + 3}$.

3. (E) Find the inverse function of $g(x) = \dfrac{x}{1 - x}$.

4. (E) Find $f'(x)$ given $f(x) =$
   (a) $\sin(\ln x)$
   (b) $\ln(x^7)$
   (c) $\ln(\cos x)$
   (d) $[\sin(\ln x)]^7$
   (e) $\ln(x^2 + 1)$
   (f) $\sin(x \ln x)$

5. (M) Find $g'(x)$ given $g(x) =$
   (a) $[\ln(\sin x)]^5$
   (b) $\ln(\ln x)$
   (c) $\ln(e^x)$
   (d) $e^{-\cos x}$
   (e) $\ln(\tan x)$
   (f) $\sin(e^{2x})$

6. (M) Find $h'(x)$ given $h(x) =$
   (a) $(1 + \ln x)^7$
   (b) xe^{-x}
   (c) $\dfrac{1}{\ln x}$
   (d) $\sin(e^x)$
   (e) $e^{\sin x}$
   (f) $\ln(x \sin x)$
   (g) e^{e^x}
   (h) $\ln(e^x + e^{-x})$

7. (E) Write an equation of the straight line through the origin tangent to the graph of $y = e^x$.

8. (D/N) Write an equation of the straight line through the origin tangent to the graph of $f(x) = \ln x$.

9. (M) Compute the derivatives of $f(x) = \ln 7x$ and $g(x) = \ln x$. Then state the relationship that must exist between $\ln 7x$ and $\ln x$. Of what theorem is this a consequence?

10. (M) Find $f'(x)$ given $f(x) =$

(a) $\dfrac{e^x}{1 + e^x}$ (b) $\dfrac{7x}{e^x}$

(c) $x^2 \ln x$ (d) $\ln(\sin(e^x))$

(e) $xe^x \ln x$ (f) $\exp(\sin(x^7))$

(Note: $\exp(u) = e^u$.)

11. (D/N) Suppose that L is the shortest line segment from the origin to the graph of $y = \ln x$. Prove that L is normal to the graph at the point where they meet.

12. (M) Given: $f(x) = x^3 + x^2 + x + 1$. Let g be the inverse function of f. Evaluate:
(a) $g'(1)$;   (b) $g'(4)$;   (c) $g'(0)$

Section 7.2: The Natural Logarithm

1. (E) Find $f'(x)$ given $f(x) = x \ln x - x$.

2. (E) Evaluate $\displaystyle\int \dfrac{\cos x}{1 + \sin x}\, dx$.

3. (M) Given: $G(x) = \int_2^x \dfrac{u}{u^2 + 1}\, du$. (a) Find $G'(x)$ by integration, substitution, and subsequent differentiation.
(b) Find $G'(x)$ by using the technique of proof of the fundamental theorem of calculus.

4. (E) Evaluate $\int_0^1 \dfrac{x^3}{1 + x^4}\, dx$.

5. (M) Evaluate $\int_0^{\pi/4} \tan x\, dx$.

6. (M) Find $f'(x)$ given $f(x) =$
    (a) $x \ln(x + 1)$ (b) $\sin(\ln x)$
    (c) $\ln(\sin x)$ (d) $(\ln x)^{17}$
    (e) $\ln x^{17}$ (f) $\ln 17x$
    (g) $\ln(x^2 + 1)$ (h) $x(\sin x) \ln x$

7. (E) Find the indicated antiderivatives and definite integrals.

   (a) $\displaystyle\int \dfrac{1}{x(1 + \ln x)}\, dx$ (b) $\displaystyle\int \dfrac{1}{x}(\ln x)^7\, dx$

   (c) $\displaystyle\int \dfrac{1}{x} \cos(\ln x)\, dx$ (d) $\displaystyle\int \dfrac{1}{\sqrt{x}\,(1 + \sqrt{x})}\, dx$

   (e) $\displaystyle\int_1^2 \dfrac{1}{x(1 + \ln x)}\, dx$ (f) $\displaystyle\int_0^{\pi/2} \dfrac{\cos x}{1 + \sin x}\, dx$

8. (M) Use the linear approximation theorem ("approximation by differentials") to estimate $\ln(1.003)$.

9. (D/T) Sketch the graph of $f(x) = x^2 \ln x$.

10. (D/T) Sketch the graph of $g(x) = (\ln x)^2$.

11. (D/T) Sketch the graph of $h(x) = x(\ln x)^2$.

Section 7.3: The Exponential Function

1. (M) Find the area between the graph of $y = e^x(1 + e^x)^{1/2}$ and the x-axis over the interval $[0, 1]$.

2. (E) Find the average value of e^x on the interval $[-1, 1]$.

3. (E) Find $f'(x)$ given $f(x) =$
    (a) $\ln(1 + e^x)$ (b) $e^{(1 + \ln x)}$
    (c) e^{x^2} (d) $e^{\sin x}$
    (e) x^e (f) $x^2 e^{-x}$
    (g) $\sin(e^x)$ (h) $xe^x \ln x$

4. (M) Find $F'(x)$ given $F(x) = \int_x^{x^2} e^{-u^2} du$.

5. (D/N) Let $G(x) = \int_0^x e^{\cos u} du$. (a) For what values of x is the function G defined? Explain. (b) Find $G'(x)$. [*Warning:* Don't try antidifferentiation.]

6. (M) Evaluate $\lim\limits_{n \to \infty} \dfrac{e^{2/n} + e^{4/n} + e^{6/n} + \cdots + e^{2n/n}}{n}$.

[*Suggestion:* Think about Riemann sums.]

7. (E) Find the indicated antiderivatives and definite integrals.

(a) $\displaystyle\int x \exp(-x^2)\, dx$
(b) $\displaystyle\int \dfrac{1}{2x\sqrt{\ln x}}\, dx$

(c) $\displaystyle\int \dfrac{x}{x^2 - 4}\, dx$
(d) $\displaystyle\int \dfrac{e^x}{1 + e^x}\, dx$

(e) $\displaystyle\int e^x \cos e^x\, dx$
(f) $\displaystyle\int x^2 e^{x^3}\, dx$

(g) $\displaystyle\int_0^{\pi/2} \dfrac{\cos x}{3 - \sin x}\, dx$
(h) $\displaystyle\int_1^9 \dfrac{1}{\sqrt{x}} e^{\sqrt{x}}\, dx$

8. (E) State the *definition* of the number e.

9. (M) Find the most general antiderivative of $f(x) = e^x e^{e^x}$.

10. (M) Find $f'(x)$ given $f(x) =$
 (a) $e^{\sin x}$
 (b) $\cos(x \ln x)$
 (c) $2^{\ln x}$
 (d) $x^2 + 2^x + x^x + 2^2$
 (e) $\ln(x^4 + 1)$
 (f) 10^{-x}
 (g) $(\sin x)^x$
 (h) $e^{-\ln x}$

11. (M) Find dy/dx given $\sin y = e^x$.

12. (D/T) Sketch the graph of $y = x^3 e^{-x}$. Identify and label all extrema, inflection points, asymptotes, and other points of

interest. Make sure that the concave structure is correct and that the graph is large and attractive.

13. (E) Solve the differential equation $e^y\, dx = dy$.

14. (D/T) Without integrating either side, show that for all $u \geq 1$,

$$\int_0^{\ln u} 2x(u - e^x)\, dx = \int_1^u (\ln y)^2\, dy.$$

15. (D/T) Sketch the graph of $f(x) = xe^{-x}$.

16. (D/T) Sketch the graph of $g(x) = x^2 e^{-x}$.

Section 7.4: General Exponential and Logarithmic Functions

1. (M) What is the relationship between $\log_a b$ and $\log_b a$? (Assume that a and b are positive real numbers other than 1.)

2. (M) Find $f'(x)$ given $f(x) =$
   (a) $x^{\ln x}$
   (b) $x^{\sin x}$
   (c) $\log_{10} x$
   (d) $(\sin x)^x$

3. (E) Find dy/dx given $e^{xy} = y + \cos 2x$.

4. (E) Find the area between the graph of $y = 2^x$ and the x-axis over the interval $[0, 1]$.

5. (M) The region R is bounded above by the graph of $y = 2^x$ and below by the x-axis over the interval $[0, 1]$. Find the volume generated by rotation of R around the x-axis.

6. (E) Set up the integral that gives the length of the graph of $y = 2^x$ from $(0,0)$ to $(3,8)$. Do not bother to evaluate the integral.

7. (M) Find $f'(x)$ given $f(x) = $
   (a) 77^{x^3}
   (b) $10^{\sin x}$
   (c) $2^{\ln x}$
   (d) $\log_x 2$
   (e) $\log_2(\ln x)$
   (f) $\ln 2^x$

8. (M) Find the indicated antiderivatives and definite integrals:

   (a) $\displaystyle\int 6^x\, dx$
   (b) $\displaystyle\int \frac{1}{x} 10^{\ln x}\, dx$
   (c) $\displaystyle\int_0^1 x \cdot 2^{-x^2}\, dx$
   (d) $\displaystyle\int_1^3 5^{-x}\, dx$

Section 7.5: Natural Growth and Decay

1. (E) The half-life of radioactive cobalt is 5.27 years. How long will it require for a million grams of this substance to decay until only one gram remains?

2. (D/N) A certain differentiable function $y = y(x)$ satisfies the differential equation $x^2 \dfrac{dy}{dx} = y^2$, and it is also known that $y(x) \to 2$ as $x \to +\infty$. Find the formula for $y(x)$.

3. (M) Carbon-14 has a half-life of approximately 5700 years. Charcoal samples from the Lascaux caves tested in 1959 showed that about 14.7% of the original ^{14}C was still present. Estimate

the age of the samples, and thus determine the probable date of the wonderful paintings found in those caves.

4.   (M) A colony of bacteria grows exponentially, taking two hours to double. At noon there were 10^7 bacteria present.   (a) Set up and solve a differential equation for the number $x(t)$ of bacteria present t hours after noon.   (b) What is the value of t when the colony reaches a population of 10^{10} bacteria?

5.   (M) A bank pays 8% annual interest compounded continuously. Suppose that you deposit a sum P_0 with this bank at time $t = 0$. Derive a formula for the principal $P(t)$ on deposit t years later.

6.   (M) A population of fleas doubles every 10 days. If a dog has exactly 10 such fleas, how long will it take until the dog has 100 fleas?

7.   (E) Solve the differential equation $xy\, dx = dy$.
8.   (E) Solve the differential equation $x^2 y\, dx + dy = 0$.

Chapter 8 Test Questions

Section 8.2: Inverse Trigonometric Functions

1.   (E) Derive the formula for the derivative of $y = \arcsin x$, beginning with the identity $x = \sin y$.

2.   (M) Find dy/dx given $y = \sin^{-1}(\ln x)$.

3.   (D/N) Estimate $\int_0^1 \dfrac{1}{1 + x^2}\, dx$ using inscribed and

circumscribed rectangles and a subdivision of [0, 1] into four equal-length subintervals.

4. (M) Find $F'(x)$ given $F(x) = \int_1^x \arcsin\sqrt{u}\,du$.

5. (M) Find $g'(x)$ given $g(x) =$
  (a) $\sin^{-1}(x^3)$
  (b) $\arctan(\sec x)$
  (c) $\ln(\tan^{-1} x)$
  (d) $\arcsin(1/x)$
  (e) $\tan^{-1}(e^{2x})$
  (f) $\text{arcsec}(e^x)$

6. (E) The region R in the plane is bounded above by the graph of
$$y = \frac{1}{1+x^4}$$
and below by the x-axis over the interval [0, 1]. Find the volume of the solid generated when R is rotated around the y-axis.

7. ((E), except a, which is (M)) Find the indicated antiderivatives and definite integrals.

  (a) $\displaystyle\int \frac{1}{e^{2x}\sqrt{e^{4x}-1}}\,dx$
  (b) $\displaystyle\int \frac{e^x}{1+e^{2x}}\,dx$

  (c) $\displaystyle\int \frac{1}{4+9x^2}\,dx$
  (d) $\displaystyle\int \frac{1}{2+3x^2}\,dx$

  (e) $\displaystyle\int_3^4 \frac{1}{\sqrt{25-x^2}}\,dx$
  (f) $\displaystyle\int_{-1}^1 \frac{1}{1+x^2}\,dx$

Section 8.3: Indeterminate Forms and l'Hôpital's Rule
Section 8.4: Additional Indeterminate Forms

1. (E) Evaluate $\lim\limits_{x \to 0} \dfrac{\tan x}{x}$.

2. (E) Evaluate $\lim\limits_{x \to 0} \dfrac{2x - \sin 2x}{x^3}$.

3. (E) Evaluate $\lim\limits_{x \to 0} x^{(x^{1/3})}$.

4. (E) Evaluate $\lim\limits_{x \to 0^+} \dfrac{x}{\ln x}$.

5. (M) Evaluate $\lim\limits_{x \to 0} \dfrac{x - \sin x}{2e^x - 2 - 2x - x^2}$.

6. (M) Evaluate $\lim\limits_{x \to 0} \dfrac{2 - x^2 - 2\cos x}{x^4}$.

7. (D/N) Evaluate $\lim\limits_{x \to \infty} \left(\dfrac{1}{x} - \dfrac{1}{x \ln x} \right)$.

8. (M) Evaluate $\lim\limits_{x \to 0} \dfrac{1 - \cos 3x}{4x^2}$.

9. (M) Evaluate $\lim\limits_{x \to 0} x \ln(x^2)$.

10. (M) Evaluate $\lim\limits_{x \to \infty} xe^{-x}$.

11. (M) Evaluate $\lim\limits_{x \to 1} \left(\dfrac{1}{x - 1} - \dfrac{1}{\ln x} \right)$.

12. (M) Evaluate $\lim\limits_{x \to 0} \left(\dfrac{1}{1 - \cos x} - \dfrac{10}{x^2} \right)$.

13. (D/N) Evaluate $\lim_{x \to \infty} \left(\frac{x-1}{x}\right)^x$.

14. (M) Evaluate $\lim_{x \to \infty} \frac{(\ln x)^2}{x}$.

15. (D/N) Evaluate $\lim_{x \to \infty} (\ln x)^{1/x}$.

16. (M) Evaluate $\lim_{x \to 0^+} xe^{1/x}$.

17. (M) Evaluate $\lim_{n \to \infty} \left(\frac{n-1}{n+1}\right)^n$.

18. (M) Evaluate $\lim_{n \to \infty} (2^{n+1})^{1/n}$.

Section 8.5: Hyperbolic Functions

1. (D/N) Show as follows that $\sinh^{-1} x = \ln(x + (x^2 + 1)^{1/2})$: First show that the two expressions have the same derivative. This implies that they differ by a constant. Then use some convenient value of x to show that the constant is zero.

2. (D/N) Find the length of the graph of $y = \cosh x$ over the interval $[0, \ln 2]$.

3. (E) Find $f'(x)$ given $f(x) =$
   (a) $\ln(\cosh x)$
   (b) $\cosh(\ln x)$
   (c) $\sinh^{-1}(e^x)$
   (d) $\ln(\sinh^{-1} x)$
   (e) $\cosh(\sinh^{-1} x)$
   (f) $\tanh^{-1}(\sin x)$

4. (E) Evaluate:
   (a) $\int \cosh 2x \, dx$
   (b) $\int \sinh^6 x \cosh x \, dx$

(c) $\displaystyle\int \frac{\cosh x}{\sinh x}\, dx$ (d) $\displaystyle\int \frac{\cosh x}{\sqrt{1 - \sinh^2 x}}\, dx$

(e) $\displaystyle\int x^2 \cosh x^3\, dx$ (f) $\displaystyle\int \frac{\sinh \sqrt{x}}{\sqrt{x}}\, dx$

Chapter 9 Test Questions

Sections 9.2 through 9.7: Techniques of Integration

General Instructions: Evaluate the indicated antiderivatives and definite integrals. Do not use a table of integrals unless otherwise instructed.

1. (M) $\displaystyle\int_0^1 x^2 e^{-x}\, dx$ 2. (M) $\displaystyle\int \frac{x^3}{\sqrt{1 - x^2}}\, dx$

3. (E) $\displaystyle\int \frac{4}{x^2 - 1}\, dx$ 4. (D/N) $\displaystyle\int \sqrt{\frac{1 - x}{1 + x}}\, dx$

5. (M) $\displaystyle\int x^3 \ln x\, dx$ 6. (M) $\displaystyle\int x^3 \sqrt{4 - x^2}\, dx$

7. (D/T) $\displaystyle\int \frac{2x^3 - 12x - 15}{x^4 + 4x^3 + 5x^2}\, dx$ 8. (M) $\displaystyle\int \frac{x}{x^4 + 16}\, dx$

9. (E) $\displaystyle\int \frac{x}{\sqrt{1-x^2}}\, dx$

10. (E) $\displaystyle\int x e^{-x}\, dx$

11. (M) $\displaystyle\int \frac{4x^2}{x^4-1}\, dx$

12. (E) $\displaystyle\int_1^e x^{17} \ln x\, dx$

13. (D/N) $\displaystyle\int \frac{5x^3 + x^2 - 3x - 3}{x^3(x+1)}\, dx$

14. (D/T) $\displaystyle\int \frac{\sqrt{x^2+1}}{x^4}\, dx$

15. (D/N) $\displaystyle\int \sin^3 x\, dx$

16. (M) $\displaystyle\int \sin^2 x \cos^2 x\, dx$

17. (M) $\displaystyle\int x \sec^2 x\, dx$

18. (D/N) $\displaystyle\int \frac{3x+5}{x^4+x^2}\, dx$

19. (M) $\displaystyle\int \tan^3 x\, dx$

20. (M) $\displaystyle\int_{-1}^{0} \frac{1}{\sqrt{3-2x-x^2}}\, dx$

21. (M) $\displaystyle\int \ln(x+4)\, dx$

22. (M) $\displaystyle\int \frac{x^3}{\sqrt{1+x^2}}\, dx$

23. (D/N) $\displaystyle\int \frac{2x^2}{(x^2+4)(x-2)}\, dx$

24. (M) $\displaystyle\int x\sqrt{1-x}\, dx$

25. (E) $\int_1^e x^2 \ln x \, dx$

26. (M) $\int \cos(\ln x) \, dx$

27. (D/N) $\int \tan^3 u \sec^3 u \, du$

28. (D/N) $\int \frac{x^3}{(x^2 + 4)^{3/2}} \, dx$

29. (E) $\int \frac{x^5 + 1}{x^2} \, dx$

30. (M) $\int_1^2 x\sqrt{x - 1} \, dx$

31. (M) $\int \frac{x + 2x^3}{(x^4 + x^2)^3} \, dx$

32. (M) $\int_0^3 \frac{x}{\sqrt{x + 1}} \, dx$

33. (E) $\int_0^3 \frac{x}{\sqrt{x^2 + 1}} \, dx$

34. (E) $\int_0^3 (x^2 + 1)^2 \, dx$

35. (E) $\int_0^3 \sqrt{9 - x^2} \, dx$

36. (E) $\int \arctan x \, dx$

37. (E) $\int_{-1}^2 \frac{2x^3}{\sqrt{1 + x^4}} \, dx$

38. (E) $\int_{-2}^{-\sqrt{2}} \frac{1}{x\sqrt{x^2 - 1}} \, dx$

39. (E) $\displaystyle\int_1^2 \cosh(\ln x)\, dx$

40. (E) $\displaystyle\int \frac{x}{\sqrt{x^2 - 16}}\, dx$

41. (M) $\displaystyle\int_0^{\pi/2} \sin^2 x \cos^4 x\, dx$

42. (M) $\displaystyle\int x \arctan \sqrt{x}\, dx$

43. (M) $\displaystyle\int \sqrt{1 + \cos x}\, dx$

44. (D/N) $\displaystyle\int \frac{1}{1 + e^x}\, dx$

45. (M) $\displaystyle\int_0^{\pi/4} \tan^2 x \sec^4 x\, dx$

46. (M) $\displaystyle\int \frac{1}{\sqrt{4x^2 + 4x + 2}}\, dx$

47. (E) $\displaystyle\int \frac{1}{x^2 + 2x}\, dx$

48. (M) $\displaystyle\int \frac{1}{\sqrt{1 + x^2}}\, dx$

49. (M) $\displaystyle\int \frac{x^2 + x + 1}{x^3 - x}\, dx$

50. (E) $\displaystyle\int_0^{\pi/2} \frac{\cos x}{1 + \sin^2 x}\, dx$

51. (M) $\displaystyle\int \ln(x^2 + 1)\, dx$

52. (E) $\displaystyle\int \frac{x}{\sqrt{9 + x^2}}\, dx$

53. (E) $\displaystyle\int_1^6 x\sqrt{x + 3}\, dx$

54. (D/N) $\displaystyle\int \sqrt{1 + e^x}\, dx$

55. (M) $\displaystyle\int \frac{1}{\sqrt{2x - x^2}}\, dx$

56. (D/N) $\displaystyle\int (\ln x)^4\, dx$

57. (M) $\displaystyle\int \frac{1}{\sqrt{3 + 2x - x^2}}\, dx$

58. (M) $\displaystyle\int \frac{x^3}{1 + x^8}\, dx$

59. (M) $\displaystyle\int \sin^2 3x\, dx$

60. (M) $\displaystyle\int \sec^4 x \tan^3 x\, dx$

61. (M) $\displaystyle\int \frac{3x + 3}{x^3 - 1}\, dx$

62. (D/N) $\displaystyle\int \sqrt{1 + \sqrt{x}}\, dx$

63. (D/N) $\displaystyle\int \frac{3x^3 + 3x^2 + x - 2}{x^4 + x^2}\, dx$

64. (E) $\displaystyle\int \tanh x\, dx$

65. (E) $\displaystyle\int \frac{1}{x^2 + 4x + 13}\, dx$

66. (M) $\displaystyle\int x^3 \ln x\, dx$

67. (M) $\displaystyle\int x(\ln x)^2\, dx$

68. (D/N) $\displaystyle\int e^{-x} \cos x\, dx$

69. (E) $\displaystyle\int_1^2 e^{3x}\, dx$

70. (M) $\displaystyle\int_0^\pi \sin^2 \omega\, d\omega$

71. (M) $\displaystyle\int \frac{1}{x^2 + 4x + 5}\, dx$

72. (D/N) $\displaystyle\int \frac{x}{(x+2)^2}\, dx$

73. (D/T) $\displaystyle\int \frac{x^2 + 5x - 11}{x^3 + x^2 + 4x + 4}\, dx$

74. (M) $\displaystyle\int \frac{\sec^4 x}{\tan^4 x}\, dx$

75. (M) $\displaystyle\int \sin^5 x\, dx$

76. (M) $\displaystyle\int \arcsin x\, dx$

77. (M) $\displaystyle\int \frac{1}{\sqrt{3 + 4x - 4x^2}}\, dx$

78. (M) $\displaystyle\int_1^2 \frac{1}{x[1 + (\ln x)^2]}\, dx$

79. (M) $\displaystyle\int \tan^2 x \sec^3 x\, dx$

80. (M) $\displaystyle\int \sin^4 x\, dx$

81. (M) $\displaystyle\int \tan^3 x \sec^3 x\, dx$

82. (D/T) $\displaystyle\int \frac{1}{1 + 3\sin z + \cos z}\, dz$

83. (E) $\displaystyle\int_0^1 \frac{x^5}{1 + x^2}\, dx$

84. (D/T) $\displaystyle\int \sqrt{x^4 - x^2}\, dx$

85. (D/T) $\displaystyle\int \frac{1}{(x^2 + 1)^2}\, dx$

86. (M) $\displaystyle\int x \arcsin x\, dx$

87. (D/N) $\displaystyle\int \frac{x^3 + 4x^2 + 10x + 3}{x^2 + 3x + 2}\, dx$

88. (M) $\displaystyle\int \frac{1}{3 - 2x - x^2}\, dx$

89. (E) $\displaystyle\int \sqrt[3]{3x}(1 + \sqrt{3x})\, dx$

90. (E) $\displaystyle\int \frac{1}{x \ln x}\, dx$

91. (M) $\displaystyle\int \sin^2 x \cos^3 x\, dx$

92. (E) $\displaystyle\int x^2 e^2\, dx$

93. (E) $\displaystyle\int_0^2 \frac{x}{\sqrt{2x + 5}}\, dx$

94. (M) $\displaystyle\int 3x^2 \arctan x\, dx$

95. (M) $\displaystyle\int 2x(x + 4)^{1/3}\, dx$

96. (D/N) $\displaystyle\int \sin 3x \sin 5x\, dx$

97. (D/T) $\displaystyle\int \frac{1}{\sec x \tan x}\, dx$

98. (D/T) $\displaystyle\int \frac{1}{\sqrt{x} + \sqrt[3]{x}}\, dx$

99. (M) $\displaystyle\int \sqrt{2 - v^2}\, dv$

100. (D/N) $\displaystyle\int \frac{x^2 + 3x + 1}{x^3 + x}\, dx$

101. (D/T) $\displaystyle\int \frac{1}{x}\sqrt{x^2 + 1}\, dx$

102. (M) $\displaystyle\int x \cos 3x\, dx$

103. (D/N) $\int \sqrt{5 - 4x - x^2}\, dx$ 104. (M) $\int x^2 (\ln x)^2\, dx$

105. (M) $\int \dfrac{1}{x^4 + x^2}\, dx$ 106. (M) $\int \sqrt{x^2 - 2x}\, dx$

107. (D/N) $\int x^3 \sqrt{x^2 + 4}\, dx$ 108. (D/T) $\int \sin \sqrt{x}\, dx$

Section 9.8: Improper Integrals

1. (E) Find the area in the first quadrant bounded above by the graph of $f(x) = e^{-x}$ and below by the x-axis.

2. (E) Test for convergence: $\displaystyle\int_{-1}^{\infty} e^{-x}\, dx$.

3. (E) Test for convergence: $\displaystyle\int_{2}^{\infty} \dfrac{1}{x \ln x}\, dx$.

4. (E) Test for convergence: $\displaystyle\int_{0}^{2} \dfrac{x}{\sqrt{4 - x^2}}\, dx$.

5. (M) Evaluate: $\displaystyle\int_{-\infty}^{\infty} \frac{1}{1+x^2}\,dx$.

6. (M) Evaluate: $\displaystyle\int_{1/\pi}^{\infty} \frac{1}{x^2} \sin\frac{1}{x}\,dx$.

7. (M) Find the area between the graph of $f(x) = xe^{-x^2}$ and the x-axis for $x \geq 0$.

8. (M) Evaluate: $\displaystyle\int_{3}^{5} \frac{1}{\sqrt{x^2-9}}\,dx$.

9. (M) Evaluate: $\displaystyle\int_{0}^{\infty} \frac{x}{1+x^4}\,dx$.

10. (M) Find the area between the x-axis and the graph of $y = (x+1)^{-3}$ for $x \geq 2$.

11. (M) Evaluate or prove divergent: $\displaystyle\int_{0}^{\infty} te^{-t}\,dt$.

12. (E) Evaluate or prove divergent: $\displaystyle\int_{0}^{1} \frac{1}{x^{2/3}}\,dx$.

13. (M) Evaluate or prove divergent: $\displaystyle\int_0^\infty \frac{x+1}{x^2+x-1}\,dx$.

14. (E) Evaluate or prove divergent: $\displaystyle\int_0^2 \frac{1}{(x-1)^{4/5}}\,dx$.

15. (D/N) Let R denote the region bounded below by the x-axis and above by the graph of $y = \dfrac{1}{x^2+1}$. Find the volume generated by rotating R around the x-axis.

16. (M) Evaluate or prove divergent: $\displaystyle\int_0^\infty \sin x \, dx$.

Chapter 10 Test Questions

Section 10.3: Area in Polar Coordinates

1. (M) Find the area bounded by one loop of the polar equation $r = 4\cos 2\theta$.

2. (D/N) Sketch the graph of the polar equation $r = -2 + 4\cos\theta$. Then find the area enclosed by the *small* loop.

3. (E) Find the area bounded by the cardioid with polar equation $r = 1 + \sin\theta$.

4. (M) Find the area bounded by one loop of the graph of the polar equation $r = 2\sin 3\theta$.

5. (E) Find the length of the spiral with polar equation $r = e^{-\theta}$ for $\theta \geq 0$.

6. (M) Find the area enclosed by the graph of the polar equation $r = \sin\theta + \cos\theta$.

7. (M) Find the area enclosed by the graph of the polar equation $r = 2 - \sin\theta$.

8. (D/N) Find the area bounded by one loop of the graph of the polar equation $r = \sin\theta \cos\theta$.

9. (D/T) Find the length of the graph of the polar equation $r = \sin\theta \cos\theta$.

10. (D/T) Find the total length of the graph of the polar equation $r = \sin 3\theta$.

11. (M) Find the area enclosed by the graph of the polar equation $r = 4 + 2\sin\theta$.

12. (D/N) Find the area enclosed by one loop of the graph of the polar equation $r^2 = 4\sin 2\theta$.

13. (M) Find the area enclosed by the graph of the polar equation $r = 1 - \sin\theta$.

14. (E) Find the area enclosed by the graph of the polar equation $r = 6\cos\theta$.

15. (M) Find the area enclosed by the graph of the polar equation $r = 4\sin 3\theta$.

16. (M) Sketch the graph of the polar equation $r = 2 - \cos\theta$, then find the area that it encloses.

17. (M) (a) Sketch the graph of the region bounded by the curve $r = \theta$, $\pi \leq \theta \leq \frac{5}{2}\pi$, and the rays $\theta = \pi$ and $\theta = \frac{5}{2}\pi$.
(b) Find the area of the region described in part (a).

18. (D/T) Find the length of the *equiangular spiral* $r = e^\theta$ for $\theta \leq 0$.

19. (M) Find the total area enclosed by the graph of the polar equation $r = 1 + \cos 2\theta$.

20. (M) Sketch the graph of the polar equation $r = \sin^2 \theta$. Then find the total area that the graph encloses.

21. (D/N) Sketch the graph of the polar equation $r = \sin 4\theta$. Then find the total area that the graph encloses.

22. (D/N) Sketch the graph of the polar equation $r = \sin 6\theta$. Then find the total area that the graph encloses.

23. (D/N) Sketch the graph of the polar equation $r = \sin 8\theta$. Then find the total area that the graph encloses.

24. (D/T) Let n be a positive integer. Find the total area enclosed by the graph of the polar equation $r = \sin 2n\theta$,

Section 10.4:   Parametric Curves

Section 10.5:   Integral Computations with Parametric Curves

1. (E) The region bounded by the x-axis and the parametric curve $x = t^3$, $y = 1 - t^6$, $-1 \leq t \leq 1$, is rotated around the x-axis. Find the volume swept out.

2. (E) The region R is bounded by the x-axis and the trajectory of the parametric curve $x = 2\cos t$, $y = \sin t$, $0 \leq t \leq \pi$. Find the volume obtained by rotation of R around the x-axis.

3. (E) Set up the integral that gives the length of the graph of the parametric curve $x = a\cos t$, $y = b\sin t$, $0 \leq t \leq 2\pi$, where a and b are fixed positive constants. Do *not* attempt to evaluate the integral, but simplify it as you would deem appropriate if you had the intention of approximating it by numerical methods.

4. (M) Give the parabola $y = x^2$ a smooth parametrization so that, as the parameter t "goes from $-\infty$ to $+\infty$," each point on the parabola is obtained exactly once.

5. (M) The loop of the folium of Descartes $x^3 + y^3 = 3xy$ has the smooth parametrization
$$x = \frac{3t}{t^3 + 1}, \quad y = \frac{3t^2}{t^3 + 1}, \quad 0 \leq t < +\infty.$$
Write and simplify the integral that gives the area enclosed by this loop.

6. (D/N) The region bounded by the x-axis and the parametrized curve $x = \cos t$, $y = e^t$, $0 \leq t \leq \pi$ is rotated around the x-axis. Find the volume swept out.

Chapter 11 Test Questions

Part 1: Numerical Sequences and Series

1. (E) Test for convergence; if the series converges, find its sum:

    (a) $\sum_{n=1}^{\infty} \dfrac{n^3}{2^n}$

    (b) $\sum_{n=1}^{\infty} \dfrac{10^n}{n!}$

    (c) $\sum_{n=1}^{\infty} \dfrac{5n^2 + 1}{2n^3 - 1}$

    (d) $\sum_{n=1}^{\infty} \dfrac{(-1)^n \pi^{2n}}{(2n)!}$

2. (E) Write a geometric series with first term 2 and sum 5.

3. (E) Test for convergence; if the series converges, find its sum:

    (a) $\sum_{n=1}^{\infty} \dfrac{1}{n! \, 2^n}$

    (b) $\sum_{n=2}^{\infty} \dfrac{\ln n}{n}$

4. (E) Find the sum of the series $\sum_{n=1}^{\infty} \dfrac{1}{n(n+1)}$.

5. (E) Write a geometric series with first term 1 and sum 3.

6. (E) Test for convergence: $\sum_{n=2}^{\infty} \dfrac{3}{4} \cdot \dfrac{8}{9} \cdot \dfrac{15}{16} \cdots \dfrac{n^2 - 1}{n^2}$.

7. (E) Test for convergence. State what convergence test you use.

    (a) $\sum_{n=1}^{\infty} \dfrac{2^n}{n!}$

    (b) $\sum_{n=1}^{\infty} 2^{-1/n}$

    (c) $\sum_{n=1}^{\infty} \dfrac{10}{(n+1)^{3/2}}$

8. (E) Give an example of a series that converges but which does not converge absolutely. Prove that your example has both of the required properties.

9. (M) Let $a_1 = 1$ and, for $n \geq 1$, let $a_{n+1} = 1 - \frac{1}{2} a_n$. Find the limit of the sequence $\{a_n\}$ (or show that the limit does not exist).

10. (M) Test for convergence: $\sum_{n=1}^{\infty} \frac{1}{1 + 2 + 3 + \cdots + n}$. If the series converges, find its sum.

11. ((M) except for f, which is (D/T)) Test for convergence:

    (a) $\sum_{n=1}^{\infty} \frac{n}{10n - 1}$ (b) $\sum_{n=1}^{\infty} \frac{2n}{n^4 + 1}$

    (c) $\sum_{n=2}^{\infty} \frac{\ln n}{n^2}$ (d) $\sum_{n=2}^{\infty} \frac{n}{2n^2 + (\ln n)^2}$

    (e) $\sum_{n=1}^{\infty} \frac{n^n}{n!}$ (f) $\sum_{n=1}^{\infty} (n^{1/n} - 1)$

12. (D/N) Evaluate $\sum_{n=0}^{\infty} \frac{1}{n!(2n + 2)}$.

Part 2: Power Series and Taylor Series

1. (M) Write the Taylor series with center zero for the function $f(x) = \ln(1 + x^2)$. Give the interval of convergence of the series, its interval of absolute convergence, and the interval on which it converges to $f(x)$.

2. (M) How many terms of the Maclaurin series for e^x are needed to be sure that the error in using this finite sum to approximate e^x on the interval $[-1, 1]$ does not exceed 0.001?

3. (E) Find the interval of convergence and the interval of absolute convergence:

   (a) $\sum_{n=1}^{\infty} \frac{(x-1)^n}{n^2 3^n}$

   (b) $\sum_{n=1}^{\infty} \frac{x^n}{n^2}$

   (c) $\sum_{n=1}^{\infty} \frac{2^n (x-1)^n}{n}$

   (d) $\sum_{n=1}^{\infty} \frac{(x-2)^n}{n \cdot 3^n}$

4. (M) Write the Taylor series with center zero for the function $f(x) = \sqrt{x+1}$. Show how to use the resulting series to obtain a good estimate of $\sqrt{2}$.

5. (E) Derive and write the Taylor series with center zero for the function $f(x) = e^{-x}$. Find the interval of convergence of this series.

6. (E) Derive and write the Taylor series with center zero for the function $f(x) = \sin x$. Find the interval of convergence of this series.

7. (D/T) Use Taylor polynomials or Taylor series to estimate

$$\int_0^{0.1} \sin(x^2) \, dx$$

with error not exceeding 0.001. [*Suggestion:* Use the alternating series error estimate.]

8. (D/T) Derive and write the Taylor series with center $c = 0$ for the function $f(x) = \cosh x$. Find the interval of convergence of this series.

9. (D/N) Expand $f(x) = \dfrac{4}{4 + x^2}$ into a power series in powers of x (by any method). Find the interval of convergence of the series.

10. (E) Use power series methods to evaluate $\displaystyle\sum_{n=1}^{\infty} \dfrac{1}{n(n+2)}$.

11. (M) Use power series methods to evaluate $\displaystyle\sum_{n=0}^{\infty} \dfrac{2^n}{n!}$.

12. (M) Use power series methods to evaluate $\displaystyle\sum_{n=1}^{\infty} \dfrac{1}{n \cdot 2^n}$.

13. (M) Write the Taylor series with center 1 for the function $f(x) = x^4$. Find the interval of convergence of the series and the interval on which it converges to $f(x)$.

14. (D/A) Use infinite series methods to approximate the value of the definite integral
$$\int_0^{0.1} \dfrac{1}{x^5 + 1}\, dx.$$
Your answer should have six digits correct or correctly rounded to the right of the decimal point.

15. (D/A) Use infinite series methods to approximate the value of the number $\cos(0.001)$. Your answer should have six digits correct or correctly rounded to the right of the decimal point.

16. (D/A) Use infinite series methods to approximate the value of

$$\int_0^1 \frac{\sin x}{x}\, dx,$$

Your answer should be accurate and should include an error analysis.

17. (M) Evaluate $\displaystyle\sum_{n=1}^{\infty} \frac{17}{n!\, 2^n}$.

18. (D/N) Write the Taylor series with center zero for the function $f(x) = \ln\left(\frac{1+x}{1-x}\right)$. Find the interval of convergence of the series. Can this series be used to approximate $\ln 5$? If so, how; what value of x would you use?

19. (M) Write the Taylor series with center 2 for $g(x) = x^3$.

20. (M) Write the Maclaurin series for $h(x) = \sin x \cos x$.

21. (D/T) One pane of a certain kind of glass transmits half the incident light, absorbs a quarter, and reflects a quarter. Two such panes are used in a double-pane window. What fraction of the incoming light will be transmitted?

22. (D/N) Write the Maclaurin series for $f(x) = \arctan x$. Then find the interval of convergence of the series.

23. (D/N) Use the remainder term of Taylor's formula to obtain an accurate estimate of the maximum error anticipated in approximating $\sin x$ with $x - \frac{1}{6}x^3$ on the interval $[-0.1, 0.1]$.

24. (M) Write the Taylor polynomial with center zero and of degree 5 for the function $f(x) = \sin x$.

25. (D/T) Use a Taylor polynomial to approximate $\cos(0.01)$ with error not exceeding 10^{-7}.

26. (E) Write the Taylor polynomial with center zero and of degree 4 for the function $f(x) = e^{-x}$.

27. (M) Use a Taylor polynomial to approximate $\ln(1.02)$ with error less than 0.001.

28. (D/N) Estimate closely the maximum error expected in approximating $\cos x$ with its 4th degree Taylor polynomial on the interval $[-0.1, 0.1]$.

Find the sums of the series given in Problems 29 through 55.

29. (M) $\dfrac{1}{1} - \dfrac{1}{1+2} + \dfrac{1}{1+2+3} - \dfrac{1}{1+2+3+4} + \cdots$

30. (M) $\dfrac{1}{1^2} + \dfrac{1}{1^2+2^2} + \dfrac{1}{1^2+2^2+3^2} + \dfrac{1}{1^2+2^2+3^2+4^2} + \cdots$

31. (M) $\dfrac{1}{1^2} - \dfrac{1}{1^2+2^2} + \dfrac{1}{1^2+2^2+3^2} - \dfrac{1}{1^2+2^2+3^2+4^2} + \cdots$

32. (M) $\displaystyle\sum_{n=0}^{\infty} \dfrac{1}{(n+2)(n+3)}$ 33. (D/N) $\displaystyle\sum_{n=0}^{\infty} \dfrac{1}{(4n+1)(4n+3)}$

34. (D/N) $\displaystyle\sum_{n=0}^{\infty} \frac{1}{(3n+1)(3n+2)}$ 35. (D/N) $\displaystyle\sum_{n=1}^{\infty} \frac{1}{(4n-3)(4n-2)}$

36. (D/N) $\displaystyle\sum_{n=1}^{\infty} \frac{1}{(2n-1)(2n+1)}$ 37. (D/N) $\displaystyle\sum_{n=1}^{\infty} \frac{1}{n(3n-2)}$

38. (D/T) $\displaystyle\sum_{n=1}^{\infty} \frac{1}{n(n+1)(n+2)}$ 39. (D/T) $\displaystyle\sum_{n=1}^{\infty} \frac{1}{n(n+2)(n+4)}$

40. (E) $\displaystyle\sum_{n=1}^{\infty} \frac{1}{n(n+3)}$ 41. (E) $\displaystyle\sum_{n=1}^{\infty} \frac{(-1)^{n+1}}{n(n+3)}$

42. (D/T) $\displaystyle\sum_{n=1}^{\infty} \frac{-}{n(n+1)(n+3)}$ 43. (D/T) $\displaystyle\sum_{n=1}^{\infty} \frac{(-1)^{n+1}}{n(n+1)(n+3)}$

44. (M) $\displaystyle\sum_{n=2}^{\infty} \frac{n \cdot (-1)^n}{(n-1)(n+1)}$

45. (D/A) $\displaystyle\sum_{n=1}^{\infty} \frac{(-1)^{n+1}}{n(n+1)(n+3)(n+4)}$ 46. (D/A) $\displaystyle\sum_{n=1}^{\infty} \frac{n+1}{n(n+2)(n+3)}$

47. (D/N) $\dfrac{1}{1\cdot 3} - \dfrac{2}{3\cdot 5} + \dfrac{3}{5\cdot 7} - \dfrac{4}{7\cdot 9} + \cdots$

48. (D/T) $\dfrac{1}{1\cdot 2\cdot 3} + \dfrac{2}{3\cdot 4\cdot 5} + \dfrac{3}{5\cdot 6\cdot 7} + \dfrac{4}{7\cdot 8\cdot 9} + \cdots$

49. (D/T) $\dfrac{1}{1\cdot 2\cdot 3} - \dfrac{2}{3\cdot 4\cdot 5} + \dfrac{3}{5\cdot 6\cdot 7} - \dfrac{4}{7\cdot 8\cdot 9} + \cdots$

50. (D/A) $\sum_{n=1}^{\infty} \dfrac{n}{(n+1)(n+2)(n+3)}$

51. (D/A) $\sum_{n=1}^{\infty} \dfrac{n \cdot (-1)^{n+1}}{(n+1)(n+2)(n+3)}$

52. (D/T) $\sum_{n=2}^{\infty} \dfrac{Pn + Q}{(n-1)n(n+1)}$ (P and Q are constants.)

53. (D/N) $\dfrac{1}{1!} + \dfrac{1+2}{2!} + \dfrac{1+2+3}{3!} + \cdots$

54. (M) $\sum_{n=3}^{\infty} \dfrac{n \cdot (-1)^{n+1}}{(n-2)(n+2)}$

55. (M) $\sum_{n=1}^{\infty} \dfrac{1}{n(n+4)}$

Chapter 12 Test Questions

Section 12.1: Vectors in the Plane

1. (E) Use vector methods to prove that the diagonals of a rhombus are mutually perpendicular.

2. (M) Use vector methods to prove that if a quadrilateral has opposite sides parallel, then opposite sides have the same length.

3. (E) Use vector methods—avoiding coordinates wherever possible— to show that the diagonals of a parallelogram bisect each other.

4. (E) Find a unit vector in the plane perpendicular to $3\mathbf{i} - 4\mathbf{j}$.

5. (E) Let $\mathbf{u} = 3\mathbf{i} - 5\mathbf{j}$ and $\mathbf{v} = 2\mathbf{i} + 7\mathbf{j}$. Compute the following:
    (a) $|\mathbf{u}|$
    (b) $2\mathbf{u} - 3\mathbf{v}$
    (c) $\mathbf{u} \cdot \mathbf{v}$
    (d) $\mathbf{u} \cdot \mathbf{u}$
    (e) The component of $\mathbf{u}$ in the direction of $\mathbf{v}$
    (f) $\cos \theta$, where θ is the angle between $\mathbf{u}$ and $\mathbf{v}$
    (g) A unit vector with the same direction as $\mathbf{u}$

6. (E) Let $\mathbf{u} = 3\mathbf{i} + 4\mathbf{j}$. Find all values of c so that $\mathbf{u}$ is perpendicular to $\mathbf{v} = 8\mathbf{i} + c\mathbf{j}$.

7. (D/N) If you have a calculator, find something special about the three plane vectors
$$\mathbf{u} = 9\mathbf{i} + 40\mathbf{j}, \quad \mathbf{v} = 39\mathbf{i} + 80\mathbf{j}, \quad \text{and} \quad \mathbf{w} = 30\mathbf{i} + 40\mathbf{j}.$$
[*Suggestion:* Evaluate $|\mathbf{u}|$.]

Section 12.2: Rectangular Coordinates and Three-Dimensional Vectors

Section 12.3: The Vector Product of Two Vectors

1. (M) Given $\mathbf{u} = \mathbf{i} + 2\mathbf{j} - \mathbf{k}$ and $\mathbf{v} = 2\mathbf{i} - \mathbf{j} + 3\mathbf{k}$, find:
   (a) $\mathbf{u} \cdot \mathbf{v}$
   (b) $|\mathbf{u}|$
   (c) A unit vector in the direction of $\mathbf{u}$
   (d) The component of $\mathbf{v}$ in the direction of $\mathbf{u}$
   (e) The cosine of the angle between $\mathbf{u}$ and $\mathbf{v}$
   (f) $\mathbf{u} \times \mathbf{v}$
   (g) $\mathbf{v} \times \mathbf{u}$
   (h) A unit vector perpendicular to both $\mathbf{u}$ and $\mathbf{v}$
   (i) The area of the parallelogram spanned by $\mathbf{u}$ and $\mathbf{v}$

2. (M) Find the angle between one edge of a *four*-dimensional cube and one of the *longest* diagonals of the cube that meets that edge.

3. (E) Find the angle between the vectors $3\mathbf{i} + 6\mathbf{j} + 2\mathbf{k}$ and $4\mathbf{i} - 2\mathbf{j}$.

4. (E) Find a vector normal to both the vectors $3\mathbf{i} + 6\mathbf{j} + 2\mathbf{k}$ and $4\mathbf{i} - 2\mathbf{j}$.

5. (E) Three sides of a parallelepiped in space coincide with the vectors $\mathbf{i}$, $\mathbf{i} + 4\mathbf{j} + \mathbf{k}$, and $\mathbf{j} + 3\mathbf{k}$. Find the volume of the parallelepiped.

6. (M) Find the angle between one of the *long* diagonals of a cube and one of the edges of the cube that it meets.

7. (E) Use vector methods to find the volume of the tetrahedron three of whose edges coincide with the vectors $\mathbf{i}$, $\mathbf{i} + \mathbf{j}$, and $\mathbf{i} + \mathbf{j} + \mathbf{k}$.

8. (E) Use vector methods to find the volume of the tetrahedron three of whose edges coincide with the vectors $\mathbf{i} + 2\mathbf{j}$, $\mathbf{j} + 3\mathbf{k}$, and $\mathbf{i} - \mathbf{j} - \mathbf{k}$.

9. (M) Let $\mathbf{u} = 4\mathbf{i} - 4\mathbf{j} + 7\mathbf{k}$, $\mathbf{v} = 3\mathbf{j} + 4\mathbf{k}$, and $\mathbf{w} = 2\mathbf{i} + 2\mathbf{j} - \mathbf{k}$.
    (a) Compute $3\mathbf{u} - 2\mathbf{v}$. (b) Compute $\mathbf{u} \cdot \mathbf{v}$.
    (c) Compute the component of $\mathbf{u}$ in the direction of $\mathbf{v}$.
    (d) Compute $\mathbf{u} \times \mathbf{v}$. (e) Compute $\mathbf{u} \cdot (\mathbf{v} \times \mathbf{w})$.
    (f) A parallelogram in space has one pair of sides with the length and direction of $\mathbf{u}$, the other pair with the length and direction of $\mathbf{v}$. Find its area.
    (g) Are the vectors $\mathbf{u}$, $\mathbf{v}$, and $\mathbf{w}$ coplanar (that is, do they lie in parallel planes)? Justify your answer.

10. (E) Construct a unit vector perpendicular to both $2\mathbf{i} - 3\mathbf{j} + 4\mathbf{k}$ and $3\mathbf{i} - \mathbf{j} + 2\mathbf{k}$.

11. (E) Find the area of the triangle with vertices at $(-1, 4, 3)$, $(0, 1, 2)$, and $(-4, -1, 5)$.

12. (M) Suppose that $\mathbf{u}$ and $\mathbf{v}$ are vectors in space such that $\mathbf{u} \times \mathbf{v} = \mathbf{v} \times \mathbf{u}$. What can be said about $\mathbf{u}$ and $\mathbf{v}$? Be *very* specific.

13. (M) Prove that if $\mathbf{a}$ and $\mathbf{b}$ are arbitrary vectors in space, then $\mathbf{a} \times \mathbf{b} = -(\mathbf{b} \times \mathbf{a})$.

14. (E) Give an example of three *nonzero* vectors $\mathbf{a}$, $\mathbf{b}$, and $\mathbf{c}$ such that $\mathbf{a} \times \mathbf{b} = \mathbf{a} \times \mathbf{c}$ but $\mathbf{b} \neq \mathbf{c}$.

15. (E) Find the angle between $\mathbf{i} + \mathbf{j}$ and $\mathbf{i} + \mathbf{j} + \mathbf{k}$.

16. (E) Let $u = 6i - 2j + 3k$ and $v = 3j + 4k$. Compute:
   (a) $u + 2v$
   (b) $|v|$
   (c) $u \times v$
   (d) $v \times u$
   (e) $\cos \theta$, where θ is the angle between u and v

Section 12.4: Lines and Planes in Space

1. (M) Where does the line through $(1, 2, 1)$ and $(3, 1, 1)$ meet the plane containing the three points $(2, -1, 1)$, $(5, 2, 3)$, and $(4, 1, 3)$?

2. (M) Find the point on the plane $6x + 4y + 3z = 12$ closest to the point $(1, 2, 3)$.

3. (M) Find the shortest distance between the parallel planes with equations $6x - 2y + 3z = 12$ and $6x - 2y + 3z = 19$.

4. (E) Write a Cartesian equation for the plane that passes through the origin and is normal to the straight line with equations
$$\frac{x-3}{2} = \frac{y}{3} = \frac{z+1}{6}.$$

5. (E) Find the distance between the skew lines with symmetric equations
$$x - 1 = \frac{y}{2} = \frac{z-3}{6} \quad \text{and} \quad x = -y = \frac{z+1}{2}.$$

6. (E) Find the distance from the point $P(5, 12, -13)$ to the plane with equation $3x + 4y + 5z = 12$.

7. (E) Write a (Cartesian) equation of the plane passing through the origin and the two points $(1, 1, 1)$ and $(1, -1, 3)$.

8. (M) Is there a single plane containing the two lines
$$x - 1 = y - 2 = z - 3 \quad \text{and} \quad 2x = y = 2z - 4?$$
If so, give an equation for the plane. If not, explain carefully why there is no such plane.

9. (M) Find an equation for the plane containing the parallel lines
$$2(x - 1) = y = z + 1 \quad \text{and} \quad 2(x - 2) = y - 5 = z - 1.$$

10. (M) Find the distance between the parallel lines
$$2(x - 1) = y = z + 1 \quad \text{and} \quad 2(x - 2) = y - 5 = z - 1.$$

11. (M) Let $P(x_0, y_0)$, $Q(x_1, y_1)$, and $R(x_2, y_2)$ be three points in the xy-plane. Use the cross product to show that the area of the triangle PQR is
$$\tfrac{1}{2} \left| (x_1 - x_0)(y_2 - y_0) - (x_2 - x_0)(y_1 - y_0) \right|.$$

12. (E) Write the Cartesian coordinate equation of the straight line that contains the two points $P(1, -1, 2)$ and $Q(3, 2, -1)$.

13. (E) Show that the lines with equations
$$x - 1 = 2(y + 1) = 3(z - 2) \quad \text{and}$$
$$x - 3 = 2(y - 1) = 3(z + 1)$$
are parallel.

14. (E) Write a Cartesian equation for the plane containing the two lines with equations
$$x - 1 = 2(y + 1) = 3(z - 2) \quad \text{and}$$
$$x - 3 = 2(y - 1) = 3(z + 1).$$

15. (M) Find the distance between the parallel lines with equations
$$x - 1 = 2(y + 1) = 3(z - 2) \quad \text{and}$$
$$x - 3 = 2(y - 1) = 3(z + 1).$$

16. (M) Find the distance between the two planes whose equations are $2x - y + 2z = 4$ and $2x - y + 2z = 13$.

17. (E) Write symmetric equations of the straight line through the point $(2, 0, -1)$ parallel to the vector $2\mathbf{i} + 2\mathbf{j} + \mathbf{k}$.

18. (E) Write a Cartesian equation of the plane through the origin and the two points $(4, -4, 7)$ and $(0, 3, 4)$.

19. (E) Write an equation of the plane through the point $(1, 2, -1)$ and perpendicular to the line with symmetric equations
$$x - 2 = \frac{y + 1}{2} = \frac{z}{3}.$$

20. (E) Write symmetric equations of the straight line containing the two points $(-1, 3, 7)$ and $(2, -1, -3)$.

21. (M) Use vector methods to find the distance from the point $(-1, 4, 5)$ to the plane with equation $3x - 2y + 4z = 12$.

22. (E) Find the area of the space parallelogram with two adjacent sides coinciding with the vectors $\mathbf{i} - 2\mathbf{k} + 3\mathbf{k}$ and $\mathbf{j} - \mathbf{k}$.

23. (M) Let $\mathbf{u} = 6\mathbf{i} - 2\mathbf{j} + 3\mathbf{k}$, $\mathbf{v} = 3\mathbf{j} + 4\mathbf{k}$, and $\mathbf{w} = \mathbf{i} + 2\mathbf{j} + 2\mathbf{k}$. (a) Write an equation for the plane through the origin parallel both to $\mathbf{u}$ and to $\mathbf{v}$. (b) Find the area of the parallelogram with adjacent sides coinciding with $\mathbf{u}$ and $\mathbf{v}$. (c) Find the component of $\mathbf{u}$ in the direction of $\mathbf{v}$. (d) Find the volume of the parallelepiped with three adjacent sides coinciding with $\mathbf{u}$, $\mathbf{v}$, and $\mathbf{w}$. (e) Write symmetric equations of the straight line through the point $(1, -1, 5)$ parallel to $\mathbf{w}$.

24. (M) Determine whether or not the points $(0, 1, 0)$, $(2, 1, 1)$, $(1, -3, 4)$, and $(4, 2, 3)$ lie in a single plane.

25. (M) Find the distance from the origin to the plane with equation $2x - 3y + 5z = 4$.

26. (M) Write a Cartesian equation for the plane containing the three points $P(0, 1, 2)$, $Q(-1, 2, 0)$, and $R(1, 1, 5)$.

27. (E) Write both symmetric and parametric equations of the straight line through $P(1, -1, 0)$ and parallel to the vector $\mathbf{v} = 2\mathbf{i} - \mathbf{j} + 3\mathbf{k}$.

28. (M) Find the distance from the point $(1, 5, -2)$ to the plane with equation $2x - y + 2z = 11$.

Section 12.5: Curves and Motion in Space

Section 12.6: Curvature and Acceleration

1. (M) A particle moves in space; its position vector at time t is $\mathbf{r}(t) = 6t\mathbf{i} + t^2\mathbf{j} + t^3\mathbf{k}$. Find the tangential and normal components of its acceleration vector at time $t = 1$.

2. (M) A particle moves in space; its position vector at time t is $\mathbf{i} \sin t + \mathbf{j} \cos t + t^2\mathbf{k}$. Find the points at which the tangential component of its acceleration vector is zero. Then find the points at which the normal component of its acceleration vector is zero.

3. (E) A particle moves in space; its path is parametrized by the vector-valued function $\mathbf{r}(t) = 2\mathbf{i} \cos t + 2\mathbf{j} \sin t + t\mathbf{k}$. Find its position, velocity, and acceleration vectors.

4. (E) A particle moves in space; its position vector at time t is $\mathbf{r}(t) = t\mathbf{i} + \mathbf{j}\sin t + \mathbf{k}\cos t$. Find its position, velocity, and acceleration vectors at time $t = 0$. What is its speed at time $t = 0$?

5. (M) Given $R > 0$, show that the trajectory parametrized by the vector-value function $\mathbf{r}(t) = R\mathbf{j}\cos t + R\mathbf{k}\sin t$ is a circle in the yz-plane. Find its curvature and show that its curvature is constant. Write the tangential component a_T and the normal component a_N of its acceleration in terms of t.

6. (M) A particle moves with position vector
$$\mathbf{r}(t) = 5\mathbf{i}\cos t + 5\mathbf{j}\sin t + 12t\mathbf{k}.$$
Find the curvature of its trajectory in terms of t.

7. (M) A particle moves with position vector
$$\mathbf{r}(t) = 5\mathbf{i}\cos t + 5\mathbf{j}\sin t + 12t\mathbf{k}.$$
Resolve its acceleration vector into its tangential and normal components. (It is not necessary to find the unit tangent and principal unit normal vectors.)

8. (M) Given: $\mathbf{r}(t) = 3\mathbf{i}\cos t + 3\mathbf{j}\sin t + 4t\mathbf{k}$, the position vector of a point moving in space. Find the curvature of its trajectory and the tangential and normal components of its acceleration vector at the point $(3, 0, 0)$.

9. (M) Given: $\mathbf{r}(t) = 2t\mathbf{i} + t^2\mathbf{j} + t\mathbf{k}$. Write the symmetric equations of the straight line tangent to the trajectory of $\mathbf{r}$ at the point $(2, 1, 1)$.

10. (D/N) Find the length of the trajectory of $\mathbf{r}(t) = 2t\mathbf{i} + t^2\mathbf{j} + t\mathbf{k}$ from $t = 0$ to $t = 1$.

11. (D/N) Write a Cartesian equation of the plane normal to the trajectory of $\mathbf{r}(t) = e^t\mathbf{i}\sin t + e^t\mathbf{j}\cos t + t^2\mathbf{k}$ at the point $(0, 1, 0)$.

12. (M) Given: $\mathbf{r}(t) = 6t\mathbf{i} + 3t^2\mathbf{j} + 2t^3\mathbf{k}$, the trajectory of a point moving in space. Find the curvature of the trajectory and the tangential and normal components of its acceleration vector at the point $(6, 3, 2)$.

13. (M) Show that the space curve $\mathbf{r}(t) = t\mathbf{i} + \mathbf{j}\sin t + \mathbf{k}\cos t$ has constant curvature by evaluating its curvature for arbitrary t.

14. (M) Write a Cartesian equation of the plane normal at the point $P(1, 1, 1)$ to the "twisted cubic" $x = t$, $y = t^2$, $z = t^3$.

15. (M) Given: $\mathbf{r}(t) = \mathbf{i}\cos 2\pi t + \mathbf{j}\sin 2\pi t + t\mathbf{k}$, a trajectory in space. Find the curvature, the unit tangent vector, and the principal unit normal vector at the point $(1, 0, 1)$.

16. (D/T) Because of Newton's law of gravitation, the acceleration a of gravity at distance $y > R$ from the center of the earth is

$$a = \frac{R^2 g}{y^2}$$

where R is the radius of the earth and g is the gravitational acceleration at the earth's surface. At what value of y will an earth satellite in circular orbit appear to a ground observer to be stationary (because its orbital period is 24 hours)?

17. (D/N) Given: $\mathbf{r}(t) = t\mathbf{i} + 4t^2\mathbf{j} + 2t\mathbf{k}$, the position vector of a particle moving in space. Find its tangential and normal components of acceleration and the curvature of its trajectory at time $t = 0$.

18. (D/N) Write a Cartesian equation for the plane normal to the trajectory $\mathbf{r}(t) = e^t\mathbf{i} + 2t\mathbf{j} + e^{-t}\mathbf{k}$ at the point $(1, 0, 1)$.

19. (M) A particle moves in space; at time t its position is
$$x = t, \quad y = t^2, \quad z = \tfrac{4}{3} t^{3/2}.$$
Find the curvature of its trajectory and the tangential and normal components of its acceleration at time $t = 1$.

20. (D/T) Write a Cartesian equation for the osculating plane for the trajectory
$$x = t, \quad y = t^2, \quad z = \tfrac{4}{3} t^{3/2}$$
at time $t = 1$.

21. (M) Given: $\mathbf{r}(t) = 3\mathbf{i} \cos t + 3\mathbf{j} \sin t + 4t\mathbf{k}$, the position vector of a particle moving in space. Show that it moves at constant speed. Find its acceleration vector $\mathbf{a}(t)$ and its scalar acceleration $a(t)$. Finally show that $a(t) \neq dv/dt$.

22. (M) Given: $\mathbf{r}(t) = \mathbf{i} \sin t + e^t \mathbf{j} + e^t \mathbf{k} \cos t$, the position vector of a particle moving in space. Find its velocity vector $\mathbf{v}(t)$ and its acceleration vector $\mathbf{a}(t)$. Also find the curvature of its trajectory at time $t = 0$.

23. (E) A particle moves along a path in space according to the parametric equations $x = 3t$, $y = 5t$, $z = 16t^2$. Find its acceleration vector.

24. (E) The cross product $\mathbf{B} = \mathbf{T} \times \mathbf{N}$ of the unit tangent vector and the principal unit normal vector is the *unit binormal vector* of a curve. (a) Differentiate $\mathbf{B} \cdot \mathbf{T} = 0$ to show that $\mathbf{T}$ is perpendicular to $d\mathbf{B}/ds$. (b) Differentiate $\mathbf{B} \cdot \mathbf{B} = 1$ to show that $\mathbf{B}$ is perpendicular to $d\mathbf{B}/ds$.

25. (E) The magnitude of the velocity vector $\mathbf{v}$ of a particle moving in space is constant, so that $\mathbf{v} \cdot \mathbf{v} = C$ (a constant scalar). Prove that $\mathbf{v}$ is perpendicular to the acceleration vector $\mathbf{a}$.

26. (M) Find the curvature of the Folium of Descartes with equation $x^3 + y^3 = 3xy$ at the point $(3/2, 3/2)$.

Chapter 13 Test Questions

Section 13.4:   Partial Derivatives
Section 13.5:   Maxima and Minima of Function of Several Variables

1. (M) Find $\dfrac{\partial z}{\partial x}$ and $\dfrac{\partial z}{\partial y}$ given $z = \dfrac{xy}{\sqrt{x^2 + y^2}}$.

2. (E) Find $\dfrac{\partial^2 z}{\partial x^2}$, $\dfrac{\partial^2 z}{\partial y^2}$, and $\dfrac{\partial^2 z}{\partial x \partial y}$ given $z = x^2 e^y$.

3. (M) Given: $F(x, y) = \arctan \dfrac{y}{x}$. Find $\dfrac{\partial z}{\partial x}$ and $\dfrac{\partial z}{\partial y}$.
At what points are either of these partial derivatives discontinuous?

4. (E) Verify that $g_{xy}(x, y) = g_{yx}(x, y)$ given the function $g(x, y) = \cos x \sin y$.

5. (D/N) True or false: If f_x and f_y both exist at the point (a, b), then f is continuous there. Justify your answer.

6. (M) Find $f_x(x, y)$ and $f_y(x, y)$ given $f(x, y) = xy \sin xy$.

7. (E) Verify that $g_{xyz}(x, y, z) = g_{zyx}(x, y, z)$ in the special case $g(x, y, z) = x^2 y^3 z^5$.

8. (E) Given $f(x, y) = x^4 e^{-y}$, compute both first order partial derivatives of f and all four second order partial derivatives.

9. (E) Given $f(x, y) = xye^{xy}$, compute both first order partial derivatives of f and all four second order partial derivatives.

10. (M) The function $z = f(x, y)$ has partial derivatives
$$\frac{\partial z}{\partial x} = 3x^2y - y^2 + y \quad \text{and} \quad \frac{\partial z}{\partial y} = x^3 + x - 2xy - 1.$$
Find a formula for $z = f(x, y)$ itself.

11. (M) The function $h(x, y, z)$ has the following partial derivatives:
$$h_x(x, y, z) = 2xyz - yz^2 + y,$$
$$h_y(x, y, z) = x^2z + x - xz^2, \quad \text{and}$$
$$h_z(x, y, z) = x^2y - 1 - 2xyz.$$
Find a formula for $h(x, y, z)$ itself.

12. (D/N) Suppose that $z = f(x, y)$ is a differentiable function such that
$$\frac{\partial z}{\partial x} = 3x^2 - 3e^x \cos y \quad \text{and} \quad \frac{\partial z}{\partial y} = 3e^x \sin y + 4y^3.$$
Find a formula for $z = f(x, y)$.

13. (M) A box with its base in the xy-plane has its four upper vertices on the surface with equation $z = 48 - 3x^2 - 4y^2$. What is the maximum possible volume of the box?

14. (E) Locate and identify the extrema of
$$z = x^2 - 2xy + y^3 - y.$$

15. (E) Locate and identify the extrema of
$$f(x, y) = x^4 - 4x - y^4 + 4y.$$

16. (E) Write a Cartesian equation for the plane tangent at the point $(1, 2, 5)$ to the graph of $z = x^2 + y^2$.

17. (E) Find the global minimum value of
$$f(x, y) = x^4 - x^2y^2 + y^4.$$

18. (D/N) A house in the form of a box is to have a volume of 10,000 ft³. The walls admit heat at the rate of 5 units per minute per square foot, the roof at 3 units per minute per square foot, and the floor at 1 unit per minute per square foot. What should be the shape of the house to minimize the rate at which heat enters?

19. (M) The sum of three nonnegative numbers is 120. What is the maximum possible value of their product?

20. (E) Locate and identify the extrema of
$$f(x, y) = x^2 - x + y^2 + 2y.$$

21. (M) Find the ellipsoid with equation
$$\frac{x^2}{a^2} + \frac{y^2}{b^2} + \frac{z^2}{c^2} = 1$$
that passes through the point (2, 1, 3) and has minimal volume. (The volume of an ellipsoid with such an equation is $\frac{4}{3}\pi abc$.)

22. (D/N) Find the volume of the largest rectangular solid with sides parallel to the coordinate planes that can be inscribed in the ellipsoid with equation $4x^2 + 9y^2 + 36z^2 = 36$.

23. (D/N) A box in the first octant has three of its faces in the coordinate planes and the vertex opposite the origin in the plane with equation $x + 2y + 3z = 6$. What is the maximum possible volume of such a box?

24. (D/N) A box with no top has a bottom made of material that costs $3/ft² and sides made of material that costs $1/ft². Its volume is 12 ft³. What is the shape of the least expensive such box, and what is its cost?

25. (E) An important differential equation of mathematical physics is $u_{xx} + u_{yy} = ku_t$, where k is a constant and u and v are functions of the space variables x and y as well as functions of time t. Find the value of k such that the function $u(x, y, t) = e^{-3t} \cos x \sin y$ satisfies this equation.

Section 13.6: Increments and Differentials
Section 13.7: The Chain Rule

1. (E) The function $z = z(x, y)$ is defined implicitly by the equation $xy + yz^2 + xz = 3$. Evaluate z_x at $(1, 1, 1)$.

2. (M) (a) Use a calculator to get a good approximation to $(1.1)^2 \ln(1.2)$. (b) Use the differential of the function $f(x, y) = x^2 \ln y$ and its value at $(1, 1)$ to estimate $(1.1)^2 \ln(1.2)$.

3. (M) Leibniz's rule for differentiation under the integral sign implies that if the indicated derivatives are continuous, then

$$\frac{d}{dy} \int_a^b f(x, y)\, dx = \int_a^b \frac{\partial f}{\partial y}\, dx.$$

Verify this formula if (a) $f(x, y) = x^3 y^2$; (b) $f(x, y) = e^{xy}$.

4. (M) Estimate $[(10.01)^2 + (3.99)^2 + (3.02)^2]^{1/3}$ by means of differentials.

5. (E) Use differentials to approximate $(\sqrt{15} + \sqrt{101})^2$.

6. (E) Suppose that f is a differentiable function of two variables and that $w = w(x, y) = f(ay - x, x - ay)$ where a is a constant. Show that $a\frac{\partial w}{\partial x} + \frac{\partial w}{\partial y} = 0$.

7. (M) Suppose that the functions f and g have continuous second-order partial derivatives and that $w = f(u) + g(v)$ where $u = x - at$ and $v = x + at$ for some constant a. Show that $w_{tt} = a^2 w_{xx}$.

8. (E) Use differentials to estimate $\sqrt{(3.01)^2 + (3.99)^2}$.

9. (M) Suppose that f and g are functions that have continuous second-order partial derivatives and that
$$w = w(x, y) = f(x, y) + g(x, y)$$
where $x = u + v$ and $y = u - v$. Express $\dfrac{\partial^2 w}{\partial u^2}$ in terms of f, g, u, and v.

10. (E) Use differentials to estimate $\sqrt{(5.01)^2 + (11.99)^2}$.

11. (E) Use differentials to approximate $\Delta f = f(P) - f(Q)$ if $P = (3, 4)$, $Q = (2.97, 4.04)$, and $f(x, y) = \sqrt{x^2 + y^2}$.

12. (E) Use implicit differentiation to find $\dfrac{\partial z}{\partial x}$ given that z is defined implicitly as a function of x and y by the equation $x^{1/3} + y^{1/3} + z^{1/3} = 1$.

Section 13.8: *Directional Derivatives and the Gradient Vector*

1. (E) Write a Cartesian equation for the plane tangent to the graph of $z = 2x^2 - y^2$ at the point $(2, 1, 7)$.

2. (M) Given: $f(x, y, z) = x^2 y^3 z^6$. In what direction is $f(x, y, z)$ increasing the most rapidly at the point $(1, -1, 1)$? What is its rate of increase in that direction?

3. (M) Let $f(x, y) = x^3 y^2$. (a) What is the largest directional derivative of f at $(1, 1)$? (b) In what direction is the derivative in part (a)? (c) Find the directional derivative of f at $(1, 1)$ in the direction $-\mathbf{i} - \mathbf{j}$. (d) What is the equation of the level curve of f that passes through the point $(1, 1)$? (e) Find the slope of the curve in part (d) at $(1, 1)$. (f) Show that the gradient of f evaluated at $(1, 1)$ is perpendicular to the tangent line to the level curve there.

4. (E) Find a unit vector perpendicular at the point $(1, 1, 2)$ to the surface with equation $z = x^2 + y^2$.

5. (M) Given: $f(x, y, z) = x^2 - 2yz$. What is the direction in which f is increasing the most rapidly at the point $(1, 2, 3)$? What is the directional derivative of f in that direction? What is the directional derivative of f at the point $(1, 2, 3)$ in the direction $2\mathbf{i} + 2\mathbf{j} + \mathbf{k}$?

6. (E) Write a Cartesian equation of the plane tangent at the point $(5, 2, 9)$ to the surface with equation $z = x^2 - 4y^2$.

7. (M) Given: $f(x, y, z) = x^3 - 3xyz + z^4$. In what direction is f increasing the most rapidly at the point $(1, -1, 1)$? What is the rate of increase of f in that direction at that point?

8. (M) Given: $g(x, y, z) = xy - z^2$. In what direction is g increasing the most rapidly at the point $(1, 2, 1)$? What is the rate of increase of g in that direction at that point?

9. (E) Write a Cartesian equation of the plane tangent to the graph of the equation $z = 4x^2 - y^2$ at the point $(1, 1, 3)$.

10. (E) Write a Cartesian equation of the plane tangent at the point $(2, 1, 8)$ to the surface with equation $z = 3x^2 - 4y^2$.

11. (E) Write a Cartesian equation of the plane tangent at the point $(1, 1, 1)$ to the surface with equation $x^2 + 4y^2 + 4z^2 = 9$.

12. (E) Find the points at which a plane parallel to $z = 2x + 2y$ can be tangent to the sphere with equation $x^2 + y^2 + z^2 = 9$.

13. (M) Write an equation of the plane that is simultaneously tangent to the elliptic paraboloid $z = 2x^2 + 3y^2$ and parallel to the plane with equation $4x - 3y - z = 10$.

14. (M) Where does the plane tangent at the point (a, b, c) to the paraboloid $z = x^2 + y^2$ meet the x-axis? Give the answer in terms of a and b; note that $c = a^2 + b^2$.

15. (M) Suppose that f and g are functions of two real variables and have continuous partial derivatives. Prove that
$$\nabla fg = f\nabla g + g\nabla f.$$

Section 13.9: Lagrange Multipliers and Constrained Maximum-Minimum Problems

1. (M) The expression $E = x - y + z$ has a unique maximum value on the surface with equation $z = 1 - x^2 - y^2$. Use the method of Lagrange multipliers to find that maximum and where it occurs.

2. (M) Find a tangent vector to the curve of intersection of the two surfaces $x^2 + 2y^2 + 3z^2 = 36$ and $2x^2 - y^2 + z^2 = 7$ at the point $(1, 2, 3)$.

3. (D/N) Maximize the expression $x^3 + y^3 + 2z^3$ on the intersection of the surfaces $x^2 + y^2 + z^2 = 4$ and $(x - 3)^2 + y^2 + z^2 = 4$.

4. (M) Use the method of Lagrange multipliers to find the extreme values of $3x - 4y + 12z$ on the spherical surface with equation $x^2 + y^2 + z^2 = 1$.

5. (D/N) An aquarium has a slate bottom that costs 8 cents/in.^{2} and glass sides that cost 1 cent/in.^{2} The aquarium is to have volume 1024 in.^{3} Use the method of Lagrange multipliers to find the shape of the least expensive such aquarium.

6. (D/N) Use the method of Lagrange multipliers to find the extreme values of the expression $x^2y^2z^2$ on the spherical surface with equation $x^2 + y^2 + z^2 = 3$ and the points of the surface at which these extrema occur.

7. (M) Use the method of Lagrange multipliers to find the maximum and minimum values of $f(x, y)$ on the curve $x^2y = 4$, $x > 0$, $y > 0$.

8. (D/N) A right circular cylinder is inscribed in a sphere of radius R. Use the method of Lagrange multipliers to find the maximum possible area of its curved surface.

9. (M) Use the method of Lagrange multipliers to find the point or points on the surface $xyz = 4$ closest to the point $(1, 0, 0)$.

10. (M) Use the method of Lagrange multipliers to find the point or points on the graph of $z = 1 + xy$ closest to the origin.

11. (D/N) Use the method of Lagrange multipliers to find the maximum possible volume of a right circular cone inscribed in a sphere of radius R.

12. (D/N) Use the method of Lagrange multipliers to find the maximum possible volume of a cone inscribed in an inverted cone of radius R and height H.

13. (D/T) A wire of length 120 cm is cut into three or fewer pieces, which are then formed into a like number of circles. Use the method of Lagrange multipliers to maximize and minimize the total area of the circles.

14. (D/T) A lump of clay of volume 1000π cm³ is formed into three or fewer spheres. Use the method of Lagrange multipliers to maximize and minimize the total surface area of the spheres.

15. (D/N) Use the method of Lagrange multipliers to find the triangle of maximum area inscribed in a circle of radius R.

16. (M) Find the extreme values of the expression $E = xy + z^2$ on the spherical surface $x^2 + y^2 + z^2 = R^2$.

17. (E) Use the method of Lagrange multipliers to find the length of the longest chord of a sphere of radius R.

18. (M) Use the method of Lagrange multipliers to find the points of the ellipse $x^2 - xy + y^2 = 4$ closest to, and farthest from, the origin.

19. (M) The plane $2y + 4z = 5$ meets the cone $z^2 = 4(x^2 + y^2)$ in a curve. Use the method of Lagrange multipliers to find the point on this curve nearest the origin.

20. (M) Use the method of Lagrange multipliers to find the point or points of the surface $x^2 + y^2 + 3xy + 4z^2 = 9$ nearest the origin.

21. (E) Use the method of Lagrange multipliers to find the point on the ellipse $x^2 + 4y^2 = 4$ closest to $(1, 0)$.

22. (D/T) A triangle is inscribed in a circle. What shape triangle has minimum perimeter (if any)? What shape triangle has maximum perimeter (if any)?

23. (M) Find the global maximum and global minimum values of the expression $E = xy$ on the circular disk $x^2 + y^2 \leq 4$.

24. (M) Use the method of Lagrange multipliers to find the extreme values of the expression $E = x + y - z$ on the spherical surface $x^2 + y^2 + z^2 = 75$.

25. (D/N) A rectangular box has its lower four vertices in the xy-plane and its upper four on the ellipsoidal surface with equation $6x^2 + 3y^2 + 2z^2 = 450$. Use the method of Lagrange multipliers to find the maximum possible volume that such a box can have.

26. (M) Use the method of Lagrange multipliers to find the maximum value of $x + 2y + 2z$ on the spherical surface with equation $x^2 + y^2 + z^2 = 1$.

27. (M) Find the global maximum value and the global minimum value of the expression $x^2 + y^2 - z^2$ on the spherical ball satisfying the inequality $x^2 + y^2 + z^2 \leq 1$.

28. (D/N) Use the method of Lagrange multipliers to find the point on the intersection of $x^2 - xy + y^2 - z^2 = 1$ and $x^2 + y^2 = 1$ that is nearest the origin.

29. (M) Find the global maximum and global minimum of the expression $E = x + y + z$ on the ellipsoid $9x^2 + 4y^2 + z^2 = 36$.

30. (M) Is there a highest point on the surface that has the equation $x^2 - 2xy + y^2 + z^2 + 3xz = 4$? If so, what are its coordinates?

31. (M) Use the method of Lagrange multipliers to find the maximum value of the expression $x - 2y + 2z$ on the spherical surface $x^2 + y^2 + z^2 = 9$.

32. (M) Use the method of Lagrange multipliers to find the maximum value of the expression $x^2 - y^2$ on the spherical surface with equation $x^2 + y^2 + z^2 = 9$.

Section 13.10: The Second Derivative Test for Functions of Two Variables

1. (M) Locate and identify the extrema of
$$f(x, y) = x^4 + 4xy + y^4.$$

2. (M) Locate and classify the critical points of the function
$$f(x, y) = 4xy - x^4 - y^4 + 16.$$

3. (M) Locate and classify the critical points of the function
$$g(x, y) = y^3 - 3x^2y.$$

4. (E) Locate and classify the critical points of the function
$$f(x, y) = x^3 - y^3 + x^2 + y^2.$$

5. (M) Locate and classify the critical points of the function
$$f(x, y) = x^2 - 2xy + y^3 - y.$$

6. (D/N) Locate and classify the critical points of the function $h(x, y) = x^2 - 4x + 4xy + y^2 - 16y.$

7. (M) Locate and classify the critical points of the function
$$f(x, y) = x^4 - 4xy^3 + y^4.$$

8. (E) Locate and classify the critical points of the function
$$h(x, y) = x^2 + 2x + 3y^2 + 4y + 1.$$

9. (M) Locate and classify the critical points of the function $f(x, y) = x^3 - 3xy + y^3$.

10. (M) Locate and classify the critical points of the function $g(x, y) = x^2 + xy$.

11. (M) Locate and classify the critical points of the function $g(x, y) = 2x^2 - 2xy + y^2 + 1$.

12. (M) Locate and classify the critical points of the function $g(x, y) = x^3 - y^3 + 6xy$.

Chapter 14   Test Questions

Section 14.1:   Double Integrals
Section 14.2:   Double Integrals Over More General Regions
Section 14.3:   Area and Volume by Double Integration

1. (M) Evaluate $\int_0^2 \left(\int_{x/2}^1 e^{-y^2} dy \right) dx$ by first reversing the order of integration.

2. (M) Evaluate $\int_0^{\pi/2} \left(\int_y^{\pi/2} \frac{\sin x}{x} dx \right) dy$ by first reversing the order of integration.

3. (D/N) A solid has its base in the xy-plane; the base is the part of the circular disk $x^2 + y^2 \leq 1$ that lies in the first quadrant. The solid has vertical sides and its height at the

point (x, y) is $x + y$. Find the volume of the solid by means of a double integral in Cartesian coordinates.

4. (M) Evaluate $\displaystyle\int_0^1 \int_{\sqrt{y}}^1 \frac{3}{x^3 + 1} \, dx \, dy$.

5. (M) Reverse the order of integration, then evaluate:
$$\int_0^1 \int_y^1 x^2 y \, dx \, dy.$$

6. (D/N) Use a double integral in Cartesian coordinates to find the volume of the tetrahedron in space with vertices at $(2, 0, 0)$, $(0, 1, 0)$, $(0, 0, 4)$, and $(0, 0, 0)$.

7. (M) Correctly reverse the order of integration, then evaluate:
$$\int_0^1 \int_y^1 x e^y \, dx \, dy.$$

8. (M) Correctly reverse the order of integration, then evaluate:
$$\int_0^1 \int_0^x x^2 y^2 \, dy \, dx.$$

9. (M) Correctly reverse the order of integration in the integral
$$\int_0^4 \int_{\sqrt{y}}^{y/2} e^x \cos y \, dx \, dy,$$
but do not bother to evaluate it in either form.

10. (D/N) The triangular region R in the xy-plane has vertices at $(0,0)$, $(1,1)$, and $(0,1)$. Express the double integral

$$\iint_R (y^2 - x^2)\, dA$$

as an iterated integral, then evaluate it.

11. (D/N) The plane region R is bounded by the graphs of $y = x$ and $y = x^2$. Find the volume over R and beneath the graph of $f(x, y) = x + y$.

12. (D/N) Find the volume of the solid between the xy-plane and the graph of $z = xe^y$, $0 \leq x \leq 1$, $0 \leq y \leq 1$.

13. (D/N) First correctly reverse the order of integration, then evaluate the new integral, given

$$\int_0^1 \int_{x^2}^{x^{1/3}} (x + y)\, dy\, dx.$$

14. (D/T) Correctly reverse the order of integration in the integral

$$\int_0^1 \int_{-\sqrt{1-y^2}}^{\sqrt{1-y^2}} x^3 y^3\, dx\, dy.$$

15. (D/T) A solid has its base in the xy-plane, bounded by the graphs of $y = x^2$ and $x = y^2$ for $0 \leq x \leq 1$ and $0 \leq y \leq 1$. Its height at the point (x, y) is xy. Find its volume.

16. (D/T) The integral

$$\int_{-2}^{2} \int_{0}^{4-x^2} y e^x \, dy \, dx$$

can be interpreted as the volume of a solid in space. Describe the solid precisely using sentences (possibly including inequalities, which are mathematical sentences).

17. (D/N) The base of a solid is the region bounded by the graphs of $y = x$ and $y = x^2$ in the xy-plane. It has vertical sides and is bounded above by the surface with equation $z = x - y$. Find its volume.

18. (M) Suppose that f is a function of two variables. Give conditions on f and the plane region R sufficient to guarantee that the integral $\iint_R f$ exists.

Section 14.4: Double Integrals in Polar Coordinates

1. (D/N) The region R in the xy-plane is bounded by the semicircle $x^2 + y^2 = a^2$, $y \geq 0$, and by the straight line segment from $(-a, 0)$ to $(a, 0)$. Find the volume of the solid with base R, vertical sides, and bounded above by the graph of the equation $z = (x^2 + y^2)^{3/2}$.

2. (D/N) Evaluate

$$\int_0^1 \int_0^{\sqrt{2x-x^2}} x \, dy \, dx.$$

3. (D/N) Find the volume of the solid bounded above by the graph of $z = 1 + xy$, with vertical sides, and with base the circular disk $x^2 + y^2 \leq 1$ in the xy-plane.

4. (D/N) Find the volume of the solid bounded below by the xy-plane and above by the graph of $x^2 + y^2 + z = 1$.

5. (D/T) Evaluate

$$\iint_D \frac{1}{x^2 + y^2 + 1} \, dA$$

where D is the circular disk in the plane centered at the origin and with radius $a > 0$.

6. (M) Given: $g(x, y) = \exp(-x^2 - y^2)$; Q is the first quadrant in the xy-plane. Evaluate

$$\iint_Q g(x, y) \, dA.$$

7. (D/N) Evaluate

$$\iint_Q \frac{1}{(x^2 + y^2 + 4)^3} \, dA$$

where Q is the first quadrant of the xy-plane.

8. (M) Correctly convert to a double integral in polar coordinates the iterated Cartesian integral

$$\int_0^1 \int_0^{\sqrt{1-y^2}} \frac{1}{1 + x^2 + y^2} \, dx \, dy,$$

then evaluate the polar double integral.

9. (M) Correctly convert to a double integral in polar coordinates (but do not bother to evaluate)

$$\iint_D \frac{xy}{1 + (x^2 + y^2)^2} \, dA,$$

where D is the disk $x^2 + y^2 \leq 1$.

10. (M) Evaluate

$$\iint_D (x^2 + y^2)^{1/4} \, dA$$

where D is the disk $x^2 + y^2 \leq 1$. [*Suggestion:* Convert to polar coordinates.]

11. (E) Evaluate

$$\iint_Q \frac{1}{(1 + x^2 + y^2)^{3/2}} \, dA$$

where Q is the first quadrant in the xy-plane.

12. (E) The plane region R is the circular disk $x^2 + y^2 \leq 4$. Evaluate

$$\iint_R \exp(x^2 + y^2) \, dA.$$

13. (M) Given: R is the plane region $x^2 + y^2 \leq 1$. Evaluate

$$\iint_R (6 - x + 2y) \, dA.$$

14. (E) Given: R is the plane region $x^2 + y^2 \leq 1$. Correctly convert to a double integral in polar coordinates, then evaluate

$$\iint_R (x^2 + y^2) \, dA.$$

15. (E) Convert into a double integral in Cartesian coordinates:

$$\int_0^\pi \int_0^2 r^2(\cos\theta + \sin\theta)\, dr\, d\theta.$$

Section 14.6: Triple Integrals

Section 14.7: Integration in Cylindrical and Spherical Coordinates

1. (M) Find by a triple integral in spherical coordinates the volume of the solid that is bounded above by the sphere $\rho = 4$ and below by the cone $\phi = \pi/3$.

2. (E) Correctly convert to a triple integral in Cartesian coordinates the cylindrical triple integral

$$\int_0^{2\pi} \int_0^R \int_0^H \frac{r^2}{1+r^2}\, dz\, dr\, d\theta.$$

Don't bother to evaluate it in either form.

3. (D/N) The spherical equation $\rho = a(1 + \cos\phi)$ does not involve θ, and thus its graph is a surface of revolution around the z-axis. (It resembles an inverted apple with the stem at the origin.) Find the volume it encloses by means of a multiple integral in spherical coordinates.

4. (D/N) Find the average distance of points of a solid ball of radius R from its center.

5. (D/T) Find the average distance of points of a solid ball of radius R from a point P on its surface. [Suggestion: Use the ball whose surface has the spherical equation $\rho = 2R\cos\phi$

where $0 \leq \phi \leq \pi/2$ and $0 \leq \theta \leq 2\pi$; choose for P the "south pole" of the ball, which is located at the origin.]

6. (D/N) A sphere of radius 2 has a circular hole of radius 1 drilled through its center (the centerline of the hole lies on a diameter of the sphere). Find the volume of material removed by using a triple integral in cylindrical coordinates.

7. (D/T) A lumberjack cuts a wedge from the trunk of a tree. The tree trunk is cylindrical with radius 2 ft. The lumberjack makes the wedge with two straight cuts: One cut is horizontal and the other is at an angle of 30° from the horizontal. The cuts intersect along a diameter of the trunk. Find the volume of the wedge using a triple integral.

8. (D/T) Find the volume of the solid above the xy-plane inside both the cylinder $r = \cos\theta$ and the ellipsoid $z^2 + 4r^2 = 4$.

9. (D/N) Find the volume of the solid that is bounded above by the paraboloid $z = 4 - x^2 - y^2$ and which lies in the first octant by a triple integral.

10. (D/T) Find the volume of the solid that lies inside both the sphere $x^2 + y^2 + z^2 = 4$ and the cylinder $x^2 + y^2 = 2x$.

Applications of Multiple Integrals

1. (E) Find the centroid of the plane lamina of constant density in the shape of the quarter-circle of radius 4 in the first quadrant.

2. (M) Find the centroid of the uniform plane lamina bounded by the graphs of $y = x^4$ and $y = x^5$ in the first quadrant.

3. (E) Find the moment of inertia of a right circular cone of radius R, height H, uniform density δ, and total mass M about its natural axis of symmetry.

4. (D/N) The uniform space region B is bounded above by the hemisphere $x^2 + y^2 + z^2 = b^2$, $z \geq 0$, and below by the plane $z = 0$ and by the hemisphere $x^2 + y^2 + z^2 = a^2$, $z \geq 0$; of course, $0 < a < b$. Find the centroid of B.

5. (M) Find the mass and center of mass of a planar wire with the shape of $y = x^3$, $1 \leq x \leq 2$, and with density $\delta(x, y) = y$ at the point (x, y). Set up the necessary integrals, but do not bother to evaluate them.

6. (M) Find the centroid of the uniform solid eighth-sphere $x^2 + y^2 + z^2 \leq R^2$, $x \geq 0$, $y \geq 0$, $z \geq 0$.

7. (M) A solid has its base in the xy-plane; the base is the part of the circular disk $x^2 + y^2 \leq 1$ that lies in the first quadrant. The solid has vertical sides, its height at the point (x, y) is $x + y$, and its density at (x, y, z) is xy. Find its mass.

8. (E) A lamina in the xy-plane is a square with vertices at $(1, 1)$, $(1, -1)$, $(-1, -1)$, and $(-1, 1)$, and has constant density 1. Find its moment of inertia about (a) the z-axis; (b) the x-axis.

9. (D/T) A solid of constant density 1 is bounded below by the cone $\phi = \pi/3$ and above by the part of the sphere $\rho = R$ that lies within the cone. Find its moment of inertia about the z-axis.

10. (D/N) The solid hemisphere $x^2 + y^2 + z^2 \leq 1$, $z \geq 0$, has uniform density $\delta > 0$ and mass M. Find its centroid.

11. (E) The cylinder $r = R \sin \theta$, $0 \leq \theta \leq \pi$, $0 \leq z \leq H$ has constant density $\delta > 0$. Find its moment of inertia about the z-axis.

12. (M) Find the centroid of a uniform cone of radius R and height H under the assumption that its base is in the xy-plane and that its axis coincides with part of the nonnegative z-axis. [*Suggestion:* Use cylindrical coordinates.]

13. (M) The region R in the xy-plane is bounded by the graph of the polar equation $r = 1 + \cos \theta$, and its density at the point (x, y) is xy. Set up the integral that gives the total mass M of R.

14. (M) The density of spherical ball $x^2 + y^2 + z^2 \leq R^2$ at the point (x, y, z) at distance ρ from the origin is ρ^2. Set up an integral that gives the total mass M of the ball. It is not necessary to evaluate the integral.

15. (M) A thin rod of linear density δ stretches from $x = -L$ to $x = L$ on the x-axis. A point mass m is located at the point $(0, h)$ on the y-axis. Find the total gravitational force F exerted by the rod on the mass.

16. (D/N) A rectangular block in space consists of those points (x, y, z) for which $0 \leq x \leq 1$, $0 \leq y \leq 1$, and $0 \leq z \leq 1$. Its density at (x, y, z) is $\delta(x, y, z) = xy + z$. Find its mass.

17. (M) The plane lamina bounded by the polar graph $r = \sin \theta$ has area density r at the point (r, θ). Find its mass.

18. (M) Find the moment of inertia about a diameter of a solid uniform sphere of radius R, density δ, and total mass M.

19. (D/N) Find by a multiple integral in cylindrical coordinates the mass of the right circular cylinder $0 \leq r \leq R$, $0 \leq z \leq H$, given its density at (x, y, z) is $x^2 + y^2$.

20. (E) Find the moment of inertia of the cylinder $0 \leq r \leq R$, $0 \leq z \leq H$ of unit density about the z-axis.

21. (M) Find the centroid of a wire in the shape of the semicircular arc $x^2 + y^2 = a^2$, $y \geq 0$, $-a \leq x \leq a$, $z = 0$.

22. (M) Set up an iterated triple integral, complete with correct limits of integration, for the volume V of the first octant pyramid bounded by the plane $x + y + z = 3$ and the three coordinate planes. Do not bother to evaluate the integral.

23. (E) Write an equation in spherical coordinates for the sphere with radius 1 and center $(0, 0, 1)$.

24. (M) A circular ring of radius R and linear density δ lies in the xy-plane. A mass m is at distance h directly above the center of the ring. Find the total gravitational force exerted on m by the ring.

25. (D/T) My volume is $\displaystyle\int_0^{2\pi}\int_0^{1+\cos\theta}(r + r^3)\,dr\,d\theta$. What am I?

26. (D/T) My total mass is $\displaystyle\int_0^{\pi/2}\int_0^{\pi/2}\int_0^1 \rho^4(\sin\phi)^3\,d\rho\,d\phi\,d\theta$. What am I?

27. (D/T) My moment of inertia about the y-axis is
$$\int_{-\pi/2}^{\pi/2} \int_0^{2\cos\theta} r^2 \cos\theta \, dr \, d\theta.$$

What am I?

28. (M) My volume is $\int_0^{2\pi} \int_{\pi/4}^{\pi} \int_0^2 \rho^2 \sin\phi \, d\rho \, d\phi \, d\theta.$ What am I?

29. (M) Find the average distance of points of a circular disk of radius R from its center.

30. (M) Find the average distance of points of a circular disk of radius R from a fixed point on its boundary.

31. (D/T) Find the average distance of points of a square region of edge length a from one of its corner points.

Section 14.8: Surface Area

1. (D/T) Find the area of the part of the hemisphere
$$x^2 + y^2 + z^2 = a^2, \quad z \geq 0$$
that lies within the cylinder with cylindrical equation $r = a\cos\theta$.

2. (D/T) Find the area of the part of the surface $z = x^2 - y^2$ that lies within the cylinder $x^2 + y^2 = 4$.

3. (D/T) Find the area of the part of the paraboloid $z = a^2 - r^2$ that lies above the xy-plane.

4. (M) Use a surface integral to find the curved surface area of a right circular cylinder of radius R and height H.

5. (M) Use a surface integral in cylindrical coordinates to find the curved surface area of a right circular cone of radius R and height H.

6. (M) Use a surface integral in spherical coordinates to find the curved surface area of a right circular cone of radius R and height H.

7. (D/T) Find the surface area of the apple-shaped surface $\rho = 1 + \cos\phi$. [*Suggestion:* You should find that the magnitude of the normal vector at (ϕ, θ) is $8\cos^4\frac{\phi}{2}\sin\frac{\phi}{2}$.]

8. (D/N) Find the area of the part of the surface $2z = x^2$ that lies directly above the triangle in the xy-plane with vertices at $(0, 0)$, $(1, 0)$, and $(1, 1)$.

9. (D/N) Find the area of the surface $z = x + y^2$ that lies directly above the triangle in the xy-plane with vertices at $(0, 0)$, $(1, 0)$, and $(1, 1)$.

10. (D/N) Find the area of the elliptical region that is cut from the plane $2x + 3y + z = 6$ by the cylinder $x^2 + y^2 = 2$.

11. (D/N) Find the area that is cut from the surface $z = x^2 - y^2$ by the cylinder with equation $x^2 + y^2 = 1$.

12. (D/N) Find the area of the part of the sphere $x^2 + y^2 + z^2 = a^2$ that lies within the cylinder $x^2 + y^2 = ay$.

13. (D/N) Describe the surface $\rho = 2a \sin \phi$ and show that its total surface area is $A = 4\pi^2 a^2$.

Chapter 15 Test Questions

Section 15.1: Vector Fields

Section 15.2: Line Integrals

Section 15.3: Independence of Path

1. (E) Find the work done in moving from $(0,0)$ to $(2,4)$ along the parabola $y = x^2$ against the force $\mathbf{F} = x^2 y \mathbf{i} + y \mathbf{j}$.

2. (E) Show that the force field $\mathbf{F} = 2xy^2 \mathbf{i} + 2x^2 y \mathbf{j} + xyz \mathbf{k}$ is not conservative.

3. (M) (a) Show that the force field $\mathbf{F} = 2xy \mathbf{i} + x^2 \mathbf{j}$ is conservative. (b) Construct a function f such that $\mathbf{F} = \nabla f$. (c) Let C be the straight line segment from $(0,0)$ to $(1,1)$ parametrized by $\mathbf{r}(t)$. Evaluate in three different ways the line integral

$$\int_C \mathbf{F} \cdot d\mathbf{r} .$$

4. (M) (a) Show that the force field $\mathbf{F} = (x^2 + y^2) \mathbf{i} + 2xy \mathbf{j}$ is conservative. (b) Construct a function f such that $\mathbf{F} = \nabla f$. (c) Let C be the straight line segment from $(0,0)$ to $(2,2)$, parametrized by $\mathbf{r}(t)$. Evaluate in three different ways the line integral

$$\int_C \mathbf{F} \cdot d\mathbf{r} .$$

Section 15.4: Green's Theorem

Section 15.5: Surface Integrals

Section 15.6: The Divergence Theorem

Section 15.7: Stokes' Theorem

1. (M) Use Green's theorem to transform

$$\int_0^1 \int_0^x x^2 \, dy \, dx$$

into a contour integral. Then evaluate the contour integral directly (by parametrizing the path, etc.).

2. (D/N) Use Green's theorem to evaluate $\oint_C xy \, dx + e^x \, dy$

where C is the curve that goes from $(0, 0)$ to $(2, 0)$ along the x-axis and then returns to $(0, 0)$ along the parabola $y = 2x - x^2$.

3. (D/N) Use Green's theorem to evaluate

$$\oint_C (e^x - y^2) \, dx + (x^3 + \cos y) \, dy$$

where C is the circle $x^2 + y^2 = 1$, oriented counterclockwise.

4. (M) The force $\mathbf{F}$ is given by $\mathbf{F}(x, y) = x^2\mathbf{i} + y^2\mathbf{j}$. The path C is the part of the parabola $y = x^2$ over the interval $[0, 1]$. Find the work done in moving a particle along C from $(1, 1)$ to $(0, 0)$ against this force.

5. (M) The path C is the unit circle $x^2 + y^2 = 1$, oriented counterclockwise. Use Green's theorem to evaluate

$$\oint_C y^2\, dx + x^2\, dy.$$

6. (M) Given: The circular disk D with boundary C whose equation is $x^2 + y^2 = 1$. Use Green's theorem to evaluate

$$\iint_D x^2\, dA$$

7. (E) Construct a function $g(x, y, z)$ such that
$$\nabla g = \langle 3x^2yz + e^y,\ xe^y + x^3z,\ 3z^2 + x^3y \rangle.$$

8. (M) Use Green's theorem to find the area of the ellipse with equation $\left(\dfrac{x}{a}\right)^2 + \left(\dfrac{y}{b}\right)^2 = 1$. [*Suggestion:* This ellipse has the parametrization $\mathbf{r}(t) = a\mathbf{i} \cos t + b\mathbf{j} \sin t,\ 0 \leq t \leq 2\pi$.]

9. (M) Let C be the closed curve $x^2 + y^2 = 1$ in the xy-plane, oriented counterclockwise. Use Green's theorem to evaluate

$$\oint_C (e^x - y^3)\, dx + (x^3 - 4 \sin y)\, dy.$$

10. (M) The region D in the xy-plane is bounded above by the graph of the parabola $y = 1 - x^2$ and below by the x-axis. Use Green's theorem to evaluate

$$\iint_D 2y\, dA.$$

11. (D/N) Use Green's theorem to evaluate the contour integral

$$\oint_C 2xy\, dx + (x^2 - y^2)\, dy.$$

Here, C is the path consisting of the straight line segment from $(0, 0)$ to $(1, 0)$, the straight line segment from $(1, 0)$ to $(1, 1)$, the straight line segment from $(1, 1)$ to $(0, 1)$, and the straight line segment from $(0, 1)$ to $(0, 0)$.

12. (M) Find the work done in moving a particle along the parabola $y = x^2$ from $(0, 0)$ to $(1, 1)$ against the force $\mathbf{F} = \langle x^2, xy^2 \rangle$.

13. (M) Given: C is the path consisting of the straight line segment from $(0, 0)$ to $(1, 0)$, the straight line segment from $(1, 0)$ to $(1, 1)$, the straight line segment from $(1, 1)$ to $(0, 1)$, and the straight line segment from $(0, 1)$ to $(0, 0)$. Use Green's theorem to evaluate the contour integral

$$\oint_C (2^x + e^y)\, dx + (4x^2 - e^y)\, dy.$$

14. (M) Is there a function $g = g(x, y)$ such that
$$\nabla g = \langle e^y - y\cos x, xe^y - \sin x\rangle?$$
If so, find $g(x, y)$. If not, explain why no such function can exist.

15. (M) Find the work done in moving a particle along the semicircle $x^2 + y^2 = 4$, $y \geq 0$, from $(-2, 0)$ to $(2, 0)$ against the force $\mathbf{F}(x, y) = x^2\mathbf{i} - y\mathbf{j}$.

16. (M) Use Green's theorem to transform the integral
$$\int_0^1 \int_0^x y\, dy\, dx$$
into a line integral, then evaluate the line integral.

17. (M) Is $\mathbf{G}(x, y) = \langle e^x - \cos y, e^y - x\sin y\rangle$ the gradient of a scalar potential $\phi(x, y)$? If so, find ϕ. If not, explain why not.

18. (D/N) Find the work done when a particle is moved along the helix $x = \cos t$, $y = \sin t$, $z = 2t$ from $(1, 0, 0)$ to $(1, 0, 4\pi)$ against the force $\mathbf{F}(x, y, z) = -y\mathbf{i} + x\mathbf{j} + z\mathbf{k}$.

19. (M) Evaluate the line integral $\int_C (xy + z^2)\, ds$ where C is the straight line segment from $(0, 0, 0)$ to $(1, 1, 1)$.

20. (D/N) Use Stokes' theorem to evaluate $\iint_S (\nabla \times \mathbf{F}) \cdot \mathbf{n}\, dS$,

where $\mathbf{F}(x, y, z) = 2y\mathbf{i} + 3x\mathbf{j} + e^z\mathbf{k}$; S is the part of the paraboloid $z = x^2 + y^2$ below the plane $z = 4$; $\mathbf{n}$ is the unit normal vector that points generally upward.

21. (D/N) Use Stokes' theorem to evaluate $\iint_S (\nabla \times \mathbf{F}) \cdot \mathbf{n}\, dS$,

where $\mathbf{F}(x, y, z) = yz\mathbf{i} + xz\mathbf{j} + xy\mathbf{k}$; S is the part of the cylinder $x^2 + y^2 = 1$ that lies between the two planes $z = 1$ and $z = 3$; $\mathbf{n}$ is the outer unit normal vector.

22. (D/N) Use Stokes' theorem to evaluate $\oint_C \mathbf{F} \cdot \mathbf{T}\, ds$, where

$\mathbf{F}(x, y, z) = 3y\mathbf{i} - 2x\mathbf{j} + 4x\mathbf{k}$; C is the circle $x^2 + y^2 = 9$, $z = 4$, oriented counterclockwise as viewed from above.

23. (D/N) Use Stokes' theorem to evaluate $\oint_C \mathbf{F} \cdot \mathbf{T}\, ds$, where

$\mathbf{F}(x, y, z) = y\mathbf{i} + z\mathbf{j} + x\mathbf{k}$; C is the boundary of the triangular region with vertices at $(0, 0, 0)$, $(2, 0, 0)$, and $(0, 2, 2)$, oriented counterclockwise as viewed from above.

24. (M) Verify the divergence theorem by computing both sides in its conclusion—the surface integral and the triple integral—for the function $\mathbf{F}(x, y, z) = xy\mathbf{i} + yz\mathbf{j} + xz\mathbf{k}$ and the cube with vertices at $(0, 0, 0)$, $(1, 0, 0)$, $(0, 1, 0)$ $(0, 0, 1)$, $(1, 1, 0)$, $(1, 0, 1)$, $(0, 1, 1)$, and $(1, 1, 1)$. The surface S of this cube is piecewise smooth, so the surface integral will be the sum of six integrals over the six smooth pieces of the surface, but they are easy to parametrize and many of the integrals will be zero.

25. (M) Verify the divergence theorem by computing both sides in its conclusion—the surface integral and the triple integral—for the function $\mathbf{F}(x, y, z) = y\mathbf{i} - x\mathbf{j} + \mathbf{k}$ and the spherical surface with equation $x^2 + y^2 + z^2 = 1$.

26. (M) Verify the divergence theorem by computing both sides in its conclusion—the surface integral and the triple integral—for the function $\mathbf{F}(x, y, z) = z\mathbf{i} + x^2\mathbf{j} + y\mathbf{k}$ and the spherical surface with equation $x^2 + y^2 + z^2 = 1$.

27. (M) Verify Stokes' theorem by evaluating both sides, given that the surface S is the hemisphere $x^2 + y^2 + z^2 = 1$, $z \geq 0$, with generally upward-pointing unit normal vector $\mathbf{n}$, and the vector field $\mathbf{F}(x, y, z) = xz\mathbf{i} + y\mathbf{j} + z^2\mathbf{k}$.

28. (M) Verify the divergence theorem by evaluating both sides, given that the solid B is the solid cylinder bounded by the cylinder $x^2 + y^2 = 1$ on its sides and by the plane $z = 0$ and $z = 2$ on its bottom and top, respectively, and that the vector field is $\mathbf{F}(x, y, z) = xy\mathbf{i} + \mathbf{j} + z^2\mathbf{k}$.

29. (M) Verify Stokes' theorem by computing both sides, given the vector function $\mathbf{F}(x, y, z) = z\mathbf{k}$ and the hemispherical surface $x^2 + y^2 + z^2 = 1$, $z \geq 0$.

30. (M) Use the divergence theorem to evaluate $\iint_S z^2\, dS$ where S is the spherical surface $x^2 + y^2 + z^2 = 1$. [*Suggestion:* The problem here is to recognize z^2 as $\mathbf{F} \cdot \mathbf{n}$ for some vector function $\mathbf{F}$, where $\mathbf{n}$ denotes the outer unit normal vector to S.]

dditional Testing Material

1. (D/N) A motorcyclist must lean her motorcycle at an angle of 45° to negotiate a flat circular track of radius 512 ft at constant speed. What is her speed?

2. (M) Find the points on the graph of $y = x^2$ where the curvature is the greatest and where it is the least. Also find the curvature at all such points.

3. (E) Give the circle with center $(0, 0)$ and radius $r > 0$ any convenient smooth parametrization. Then verify that its radius of curvature ρ is constant, and that in fact $\rho = r$ at each point of the circle.

4. (M) A mass m is fired from a cannon at the origin with initial velocity v_0 and angle of inclination α. The mass m moves in a vertical plane (the xy-plane) close to the surface of the earth, and we ignore air resistance, so its vector acceleration is the constant vector $\mathbf{a} = -g\mathbf{j}$. At time $t = 0$ (seconds) the mass m has vector position $\mathbf{r}_0 = \mathbf{0}$ and its velocity vector then is $\mathbf{v}_0 = v_0\mathbf{i}\cos\alpha + v_0\mathbf{j}\sin\alpha$. Find its position vector $\mathbf{r}(t)$ for time $t \geq 0$ (until the time of its impact), its maximum altitude, and its range (the distance it travels horizontally until impact).

5. (D/T) Suppose that the earth were spinning exactly fast enough so that your weight would be zero if you stood on the equator. How long would a "day" be then? Assume that the earth is a perfect sphere of radius $R = 3964$ mi and that the acceleration of gravity at its surface is $g = 32.16$ ft/s². Give the answer in minutes, rounded to the nearest minute.

6. (M) One smooth parametrization of the ellipse with equation $x^2 + 4y^2 = 4$ is $x = 2\cos t$, $y = \sin t$, $0 \leq t \leq 2\pi$. Use this (or another) parametrization to find the Cartesian coordinates of the points on the ellipse where its curvature is (a) maximal; (b) minimal.

7. (E) Find the point on the graph of $y = e^x$ at which the curvature is the greatest.

8. (E) Find the curvature of the parabola $y = x^2$ at $(0,0)$.

9. (M) Does the graph of $y = \ln x$ have a point at which the curvature is minimal? Maximal? Explain.

10. (M) Find the point on the graph of $y = x^3$ at which the curvature is minimal.

Chapter 1 Answers

Section 1.1

1.
   a. 8
   b. a^3
   c. $(x^2-1)^3$
   d. $(2a-1)^3$

2.
   a. -2
   b. $27a^3-1$
   c. $-x^3+(h+x)^3$

3.
   a. 11
   b. $-\pi$
   c. x^2

4.
   a. $x \neq 1$, $x \neq -1$
   b. $1/2 < x < 1$
   c. $x \leq 6$
   d. $x < 0$ or $x > 2$

5. x may be any real number

6. False; $\sqrt{2}$ is an irrational number

7. False; π is an irrational number

8. $x < -3/2$ or $x > -1$

9. $x < 3/2$

10. $A = 500x - x^2$ $(0 \leq x \leq 500)$

11. $(-\infty, -1) \cup (0, 1)$

12. a. $\mathbb{R}$ b. $\mathbb{R}$ c. $(0, \infty)$ d. $\mathbb{R}$

13. $A(x) = 5x - \dfrac{25}{12}x^2$, $0 < x < \dfrac{12}{5}$

14. $A = \dfrac{3\sqrt{3}r^2}{2}$, $r > 0$

15. $A = \dfrac{\sqrt{3}s^2}{4}$, $s > 0$

16. a. 816 ft   b. 5, 15   c. 20 s

151

Chapter 1 Answers

17. $D = \sqrt{x^4 + x^2 - 6x + 9}$

18. $A = \pi r^2 + \pi(10-r)^2$, $0 < r < 10$

19. No; for any small positive number n, $\frac{n}{2}$ is an even smaller positive number.

Section 1.2

1. $y - 3 = 2(x - 2)$
2. $x = 3$
3. $y - 5 = -2(x - 0)$

4.

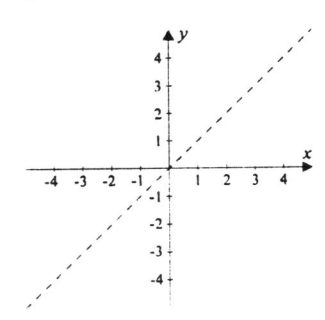

5. $(0, 9)$, $(12, 0)$
6. $y = 3x$
7. the coordinate axes
8. Yes, $m = -2/3$, $m = 3/2$ 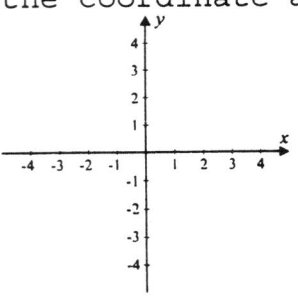

9. $(13/2, 3)$
10. Yes; one has vertices $(0, 0)$, $(12, 16)$, $(-12, 9)$

Section 1.3

1. $(x-2)^2 + (y+3)^2 = 36$
2. 5
3. Center: $(3, -2)$, $r = 4$

Chapter 1 Answers

4.

5. (8, 256)

6. Center $(-2, 3)$, $r = 1$

7. 1/4

8. 20,000 m²

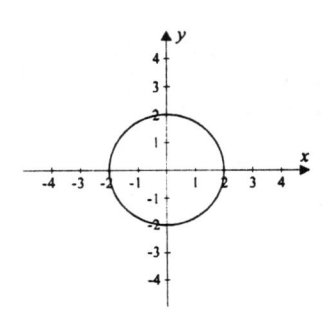

9.

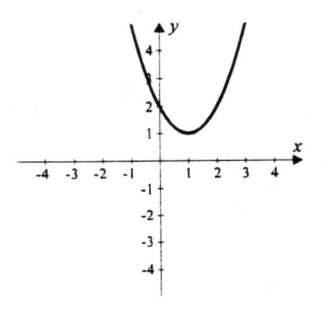

10. $f(-1) = 1$

11. 25

12.

13.

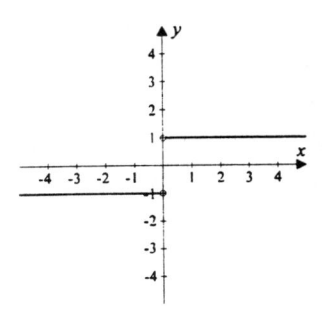

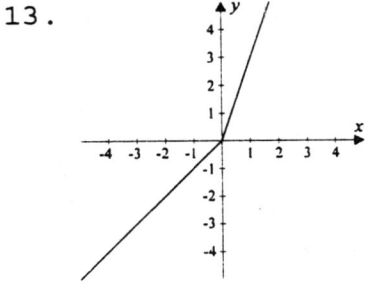

Section 1.4

1. a. $x + \sqrt{x} - 1$, $x \geq 0$ b. $1 + \sqrt{x} - x$, $x \geq 0$ c. $\sqrt{x}(x-1)$, $x \geq 0$
   d. $\dfrac{\sqrt{x}}{x-1}$, $0 \leq x < 1$, $x > 1$

2. a. $\cos x + \sin x$, $\mathbb{R}$ b. $\sin x - \cos x$, $\mathbb{R}$
   c. $(\cos x)(\sin x)$, $\mathbb{R}$ d. $\tan x$, $x \neq$ odd multiples of $\pi/2$

3. Since it crosses the x axis infinitely many times, it cannot be a polynomial of any finite degree.

Chapter 1 Answers

4. For any rational functions f and g, there are polynomials p, q, r and s such that $f = p/q$ and $g = r/s$. Then $f/g = p/q \cdot s/r = ps/qr$. Since ps and qr can both be expanded as polynomials, f/g is a rational function.

5. For any polynomials f and g, same-degree terms of the sum $f + g$ can be collected by the distributive property to make the result a polynomial.

6. If a polynomial is bounded on the interval $x < 0$, then it is a constant function.

7. $f(x) = \sin^2 x$, $g(x) = \cos^2 x$; $f(x) + g(x) = 1$ is a polynomial of degree zero.

8. Proof: Consider any polynomial $p(x) = ax^n + bx^{n-1} + \ldots$, with $n \geq 2$ and a not equal to zero. "..." denotes a string of terms all with degree less than $n - 1$. Then
$p(x) - p(x-1) = ax^n + bx^{n-1} + \ldots - (a(x-1)^n + b(x-1)^{n-1} + \ldots)$
$= ax^n + bx^{n-1} + \ldots - (a(x^n - nx^{n-1} + \ldots) + b(x^{n-1} + \ldots) + \ldots)$
$= anx^{n-1} + \ldots$

Since an does not equal zero, the highest-degree term, and hence the polynomial, has degree $n - 1$.

Chapter 2

Section 2.1

1. $2x$
2. $y = 6(x - 2)$
3. $y = 6x - 9$
4. a. $2z - 5$
   b. $1 - \dfrac{z}{8}$
5. $2(x - 1)$
6. $y = 4$
7. $y = 12x - 16$
8. $2x + 1$
9. $3x^2$
10. $x + 6y = 44$
11. $m = -2$
12. $2x + 3$
13. $2x - 1$
14. $(2, -2)$
15. $x + 4y = 2$

Chapter 2 Answers

16. There are no such lines. Proof: Suppose a line is tangent to the function $y = x^3$ at two distinct points (a, a^3) and (b, b^3). Then two equations of the line are $y = 3a^2(x-a) + a^3$ and $y = 3b^2(x-b) + b^3$. For $x = 0$, $y = -2a^3 = -2b^3$ and hence $a = b$, contrary to the hypothesis.

17. $\dfrac{1}{(x+1)^2}$

18. $y - 9 = 2(x - 5)$
    $y - 9 = 18(x - 5)$

19. $\left(\dfrac{\sqrt{3}}{3}, \dfrac{-2\sqrt{3}}{9}\right), \left(-\dfrac{\sqrt{3}}{3}, \dfrac{2\sqrt{3}}{9}\right)$

20. Suppose a line is tangent to the function $y = x^4$ at two distinct points (a, a^4) and (b, b^4). Then the slope of the line is $4a^3 = 4b^3$ and hence $a = b$, contrary to the hypothesis.

21. $-(x-1)^{-2}$

22. $y = x + \dfrac{3}{4}$

23. $(2, 8), (-2, -8)$

24. $x + 12y = -98$

25. $4x^3$

26. $(3, 27), (-3, -27)$

27. $(1, -2), (-1, 2)$

28. $(4, 64), (-4, -64)$

29. $m = 4, m = 8$

30. $6x^2 - 8x$

31. $y = 2x - 1, y = 10x - 25$

32. $x + y = 2$

33. $(2, -16), (-2, 16)$

34. $\left(\dfrac{a}{2}, 0\right)$

35. $y = -4x + 4$

36. $y = 4x$

37. $\left(\dfrac{2}{3}a, 0\right)$

38. $\left(\dfrac{4}{5}a, 0\right)$

39. $\dfrac{1}{2\sqrt{x}}$

40. 3

41. Suppose a line is tangent to the function $y = x^2$ at two distinct points (a, a^2) and (b, b^2). Then the slope of the line is $2a = 2b$ and hence $a = b$, contrary to the hypothesis.

42. $y = -x + 2, \ y = -\dfrac{1}{9}x - \dfrac{2}{3}$

43. none

Chapter 2 Answers

44. $\dfrac{1}{2}$

45. Proof, by cases: Case 1. The point (a, b) lies on the curve. Then the line through (a, b) tangent to the curve is just the tangent line at (a, b). Case 2. (a, b) does not lie on the curve. Then consider a line through (a, b) and (c, c^3), where c is a solution to the equation $2c^3 - 3ac^2 + b = 0$ (the intermediate value property guarantees at least one solution). c does not equal a, since if it did b would equal a^3 and (a, b) would lie on the curve, which in the present case it does not. But then the equation is equivalent to $\dfrac{(c^3 - b)}{c - a} = 3c^2$, meaning that at (c, c^3) the slope of the line (the left side) and the slope of the curve (the right side) are equal. So the line is a tangent to the curve. Thus there is a line through (a, b) tangent to the curve whether (a, b) lies on the curve or not.

Section 2.2

1. 10
2. 4
3. −1/4
4. 108
5. 1/6
6. 1
7. $\dfrac{1}{2\sqrt{x+5}}$
8. −3/64
9. 5
10. 1/8
11. $6(2x + 3)^2$
12. 4/3

Section 2.3

1. 0
2. −13
3. 3
4. 5
5. −9
6. $y = 1$ for x: $x < 3$
   $y = 2$ for x: $x > 3$
7. −1
8. $\dfrac{1}{2\sqrt{5}}$
9. 1/5

Chapter 2 Answers

Section 2.4

1. Use Intermediate Value Property   2. 36

3. Use Intermediate Value Property

4. Use the intermediate value property of the continuous function $f(x) = 2x^5 - 10x + 5$; note that $f(-2) < 0 < f(-1)$, $f(0) > 0 > f(1)$, and $f(1) < 0 < f(2)$.

5. Use Intermediate Value Property   6.

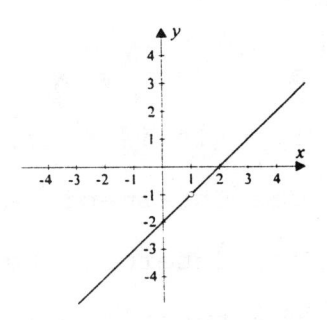

The expression reduces to a linear function except where the denominator equals zero.

7. $f(x) = x + \sqrt{18 - x^2}$ $x: 0 \leq x \leq 3\sqrt{2}$
   $f(x)$ is defined only on a closed interval and continuous on it.

8. One solution

9. One real solution

10. $h'(x) = 4x^3 - 3x^2 + 14x + 3 = 0$. Use Intermediate Value Property

Chapter 2 Answers

11.

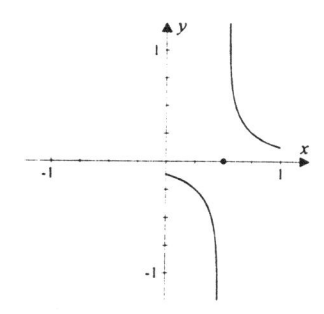

12. It is continuous with the addition of the point (4, 8)

13. a. $f(x) = |x-1|$ b. max = 2, min = 0

    c. It is continuous on a closed interval

14. Use Intermediate Value Property

15. Use Intermediate Value Property

16. The function f is continuous everywhere because $f'(x) = 3x^2$ exists for all x.

17. Yes, right and left limits are both 4

18. No, left limit = 6, right limit = 5

19. Yes, since $j(x)$ is defined and differentiable throughout the interval.

20. $y = 1$ $x: x < 3$
    $y = 1$ $x: x > 3$
    $y = 2$ $x: x = 3$

21. $f(x)$ will be continuous at $x = 2$ when $D = \frac{1}{2}$, discontinuous otherwise. $f(x)$ will be discontinuous at $x = 0$ no matter what C is.

22. Use Intermediate Value Property

Chapter 3

Section 3.1

1. 144   2. —2   3. 200

Chapter 3 Answers

4. $V' = 3x^2$ 5. $A' = 12x$

6. a. 80 liters/min
   b. -80 liters/min

7. a. $-16h - 48$ ft/s
   b. -48 ft/s
   c. 324 ft

8. a. 8   b. $h + 7$ c. 7

Section 3.2

1. a. $60x^4 - 21x^2 + 14x - 14$ b. $\dfrac{1}{(x+3)^2}$
   c. $2(x^5 + x)(5x^4 + 1)$ d. $-x^{-2}$

2. a. $x^3 \cos x + 3x^2 \sin x$ b. $2 \sin x \cos x$
   c. $-(\cot x \csc x)$
   d. $2x \sin x \cos x + \sin^2 x$

3. a. $x^4 + x^3$ b. $-\dfrac{1}{x}$
   c. $2x^8$ d. $x^4 + 7x^2$

4. a. $\ln|x|$ b. $x^4 + 5x^4 \ln|x|$
   c. $\dfrac{2 \ln|x|}{x}$ d. $-\dfrac{1}{\ln|x|} - \dfrac{1-x}{x(\ln|x|)^2}$

5. $y - 32 = 80(x - 2)$ 6. $y + 2 = \dfrac{8}{3}(x - 2)$

7. $\dfrac{x^3}{3} - x$ 8. $x^7 + x,\ x^7 + x + 2,\ x^7 + x + 3$

9. $y - 4 = -4(x + 2)$ 10. $y = -\dfrac{1}{9}x + \dfrac{2}{3}$

11. $-(x-1)^{-2}$ 12. $y - 4 = 3(x - 1)$,
    $y - 4 = 7(x - 1)$

13. $y = 2\sqrt{3}x,\ y = -2\sqrt{3}x$

14. $\dfrac{x^{-2} + \dfrac{1}{x}}{(x-1)^2} + \dfrac{-\dfrac{2}{x^3} - \dfrac{1}{x^2}}{x-1} = \dfrac{2(-x^2 - x + 1)}{x^3(x-1)^2}$

15. $y - 8 = 12(x-2)$

Chapter 3 Answers

Section 3.3

1. a. $10x(x^2 + 1)^4$ b. $\dfrac{1-9x^2}{(x^2+1)^6}$
    c. $19(5x^4+1)(x^5+x)^{18}$
    d. $20x^4(x^4+1)^5(x^5+1)^3 + 20x^3(x^4+1)^4(x^5+1)^4$

2. a. $4x^3 \cos(x^4)$ b. $4 \cos x \sin^3 x$
    c. $3x^5 \cos(x^3) + 3x^2 \sin(x^3)$
    d. $2x \cos(x^2) \sin x + \cos x \sin(x^2)$

3. a. $2\pi \cos(2\pi x)$ b. $100 \cos x \sin^{99} x$
    c. $100 x^{99} \cos(x^{100})$ d. $\dfrac{4(x \sin x)^{1/3}(x \cos x + \sin x)}{3}$

4. a. $2x \cos(x^2)$ b. $7(\sin x)^6 \cdot \cos x$
    c. $10(x^2 + 1)^9 \cdot 2x$ d. $7(x^3 + x^2)^6 \cdot (3x^2 + 2x)$
    e. $3 \cos(3x)$ f. $2x \cos(x^2 + 1)$
    g. $\cos(\sin x) \cdot \cos x$ h. $100(x + 1)^{99} \cdot 1$

5. a. $12x^2(x^3 + 3)^3$
    b. $14x^8 \cos(x^2) \sin^6(x^2) + 7x^6 \sin^7(x^2)$
    c. $7x^6 \cos(x^7)$
    d. $7 \cos x \sin^6 x$
    e. $15 \cos(5x) \sin^2(5x)$
    f. $12x^2 \cos(4x) \sin^2(4x) + 2x \sin^3(4x)$
    g. $7 \cos(7x)$
    h. $8 \cos(8x) \sin(7x) + 7 \cos(7x) \sin(8x) = \dfrac{15 \sin(15x) - \sin x}{2}$

6. a. $-8 \cos x (1 - 2 \sin x)^3$
    b. $133 t^6 \cos(t^7) \sin^{18}(t^7)$
    c. $27 \cos(3z) \sin^9 z \sin^8(3z) + 9 \cos z \sin^8 z \sin^9(3z)$

7. a. $\dfrac{1}{8}(x^3+1)^8$ b. $\dfrac{\sin(x^3)}{3}$
    c. $-\dfrac{1}{4(x^2+1)^2}$ d. $\dfrac{\sin(10x)}{10}$

8. a. $4x(x^2 + 1)$ b. $12x^{11}$
    c. $\dfrac{-4x^3}{(1+x^4)^2}$ d. $3(x + 2)^2$
    e. $10240 x^9$

Chapter 3 Answers

9.
a. $2x \sec(x^2) \tan(x^2)$
b. $3 \sec^2 x \tan^2 x$
c. $-\dfrac{\sec(1/x)\tan(1/x)}{x^2}$
d. $\sec^3 x + \sec x \tan^2 x$

10. Any g for which $g(x) = ax + a - 1$ for some a (Examples: $f(x)$ and the identity function)

11. $g(x) = 1x + 0$, $g(x) = 0x + 0$

12. $y - 8 = 24(x - 3/2)$
    $y + 8 = 24(x + 1/2)$

Section 3.4

1.
a. $\dfrac{5x^{2/3}}{3}$
b. $-\dfrac{2}{x^{3/2}}$
c. $\dfrac{x}{\sqrt{x^2+1}}$
d. $\dfrac{\sqrt{x}}{(x^{3/2}+1)^{1/3}}$

2.
a. $\dfrac{\cos x}{2\sqrt{\sin x}}$
b. $\dfrac{\cos\sqrt{x}}{2\sqrt{x}}$
c. $\dfrac{3x^4 \cos x \sqrt{\sin x + 1}}{2} + 4x^3(1+\sin x)^{3/2}$
d. $\left(1 + \dfrac{1}{2\sqrt{x}}\right)\cos(1+\sqrt{x}+x)$

3.
a. $\dfrac{\sec\sqrt{x}\tan\sqrt{x}}{2\sqrt{x}}$
b. $\dfrac{(\sec x)^{3/2} \sin x}{2}$
c. $7\sec^7 x \tan x$
d. $7x^6 \sec x^7 \tan x^7$
e. $8\sec^2 x \tan^7 x$
f. $8x^7 \sec^2(x^8)$

4. $-\sqrt{1-x^2}$

5. $7x^6 + \pi x^{\pi - 1}$

6.
a. $\dfrac{x}{\sqrt{x^2+1}}$
b. $\dfrac{1}{(1-x^2)^{3/2}}$
c. $\dfrac{\cos x}{2\sqrt{\sin x}}$
d. $\dfrac{\cos(\sqrt{x})}{2\sqrt{x}}$

7. $2x$

Chapter 3 Answers

8. a. $7x^6$ b. $\dfrac{15x^{3/2}}{2}$

   c. $-\dfrac{1}{x^2}$ d. $1 - \dfrac{1}{x^2}$

   e. $\dfrac{1}{(x+1)^2}$ f. $3x^2 - 2x + 1$ g. $-x^{-2}$

9. $f'(x) = \lim\limits_{h \to 0} \dfrac{1}{h}\left[\dfrac{x+h}{g(x+h)} - \dfrac{x}{g(x)}\right]$

   $= \lim\limits_{h \to 0} \dfrac{(x+h)g(x) - xg(x+h)}{hg(x+h)g(x)} = \lim\limits_{h \to 0} \dfrac{x[g(x) - g(x+h)] + hg(x)}{hg(x+h)g(x)}$

   $= \lim\limits_{h \to 0} \left[\dfrac{g(x) - g(x+h)}{h} \cdot \dfrac{x}{g(x+h)g(x)} + \dfrac{1}{g(x+h)}\right]$

   $= \dfrac{-xg'(x)}{[g(x)]^2} + \dfrac{1}{g(x)} = \dfrac{g(x) - xg'(x)}{[g(x)]^2}$

10. a. $7x^6$ b. $-\dfrac{5}{x^6}$

    c. 3 d. 1

    e. $-\dfrac{2}{x^3}$ f. $-7x^6$

11. a. $12x^{11}$ b. $\dfrac{-2x}{(x^2+1)^2}$

12. $y = x^4 - 4x^3 + 4x^2 + 2x$, for example

13. $(1+\sqrt{5}, 6+2\sqrt{5})$ or $(1-\sqrt{5}, 6-2\sqrt{5})$

Section 3.5

1. $f'(x) = 3x^2 + 1$, max = 1, min = −1

2. $f'(x) = 3x^2 - 3 = 0$, min = −2, max = 2

3. $h'(x) = \dfrac{2}{1+x^2}$, min = −1, max = 1/3

4. global maximum = $\left(1, \dfrac{1}{2}\right)$ 5. global maximum = (0, 4)
   global minimum = (0, 0)   global minimum = (2, −16)

6. min = −1, max = 2   7. min = 0, max = 4

8. min = −2, max = 52

Chapter 3 Answers

Section 3.6

1. $A = 2025$
2. $60{,}000$
3. $\sqrt{18}$
4. $\dfrac{2\sqrt{3}}{9}$
5. $45{,}000$
6. 1
7. $w = R,\ h = \sqrt{3}R$
8. $r = \sqrt{\dfrac{1}{2} + \dfrac{1}{2\sqrt{5}}}\,R,\quad h = 2R\left(\dfrac{5-\sqrt{5}}{10}\right)^{1/2}$
 (Must satisfy $r^2 + \left(\dfrac{1}{2}h\right)^2 = R^2$)
9. $\min = 150\sqrt[3]{4},\ \max = 300$
10. $\max = 10\sqrt{2}$
11. $S = 80$
12. 32
13. $\max = 512$
14. $\max = 432,\ \min = 216\sqrt[3]{4}$
15. $180{,}625\ \text{m}^2$ (using all the fence for the square corral)
16. $\dfrac{4\sqrt{3}}{9}\pi R^3$
17. $A = 7{,}200$, width $= 60$, length $= 120$
18. $S = 250$
19. $S = 1{,}152$
20. L^2
21. $x + 7y = 14$
22. $r > \dfrac{1}{2}$
23. $\left(\dfrac{5}{2},\ \sqrt{\dfrac{5}{2}}\right)$
24. $\dfrac{5\sqrt{10}}{3}\ \text{ft}^3$
25. $r = 25$
26. for min, $\dfrac{8}{3}$ and $\dfrac{4}{3}$; for max, 0 and 4
27. $\dfrac{2000\pi}{9\sqrt{3}}$
28. 105 cm wide $\times\ 154$ cm high
29. $12\sqrt{3}$
30. $11 + 22$
31. $(-1,\ 0)$
32. $x = 500$

Chapter 3 Answers

Section 3.7

1. a. $7\cos(7x)$ b. $-10x\sin(5x^2)$
   c. $21\cos(7x)\sin^2(7x)$ d. $-\dfrac{3^{3/2}\sin(3x)}{2\sqrt{\cos 3x}}$

2. a. $2\cos^3 x \sin x - 2\cos x \sin^3 x$
   b. $2\cos 2x \sec 3x + 3\sec 3x \sin 2x \tan 3x$
   c. $\cos x \cos 3x - 3\sin x \sin 3x$
   d. $\sin x \sin(\cos x)$

3. a. $3x^4 \cos x^3 + 2x \sin x^3$
   b. $7\cos^2 x \sin^6 x - \sin^8 x$
   c. $-16x^3 \cos^3 x^4 \sin x^4$
   d. $(3x^2 + 2x + 1)\cos(x^3 + x^2 + x + 1)$

4. a. $(2x+5)\sec(x^2+5x)\tan(x^2+5x)$
   b. $5(2x+5)\sec^5(x^2+5x)\tan(x^2+5x)$
   c. $5\sec 3x \sec^2 5x + 3\sec 3x \tan 3x \tan 5x$
   d. $9x^2 \sec^2 x^3 \tan^2 x^3$

5. a. $\cos x$ b. 0
   c. $\dfrac{\cos x - \sin x}{\sec x + \tan x} - \dfrac{(\cos x + \sin x)(\sec^2 x + \sec x \tan x)}{(\sec x \tan x)^2}$
   $= \dfrac{1 + \cos 2x - \sin 2x - 2(\sin x + \cos x)}{2 + 2\sin x}$
   d. $\dfrac{2\sec^4 \sqrt{x}\, \tan\sqrt{x}}{\sqrt{x}}$

6. $\cos 2x = \cos^2 x - \sin^2 x$

7. $D_x = 2\cos x \sin x$, constant $= 1$

8. a. $-3\cot x \csc^3 x$ b. $-14x \csc^2 7x^2$
   c. $-3\cot 3x \cot 5x \csc 3x - 5\csc 3x \csc^2 5x$
   d. $-12x^3 \cot^2 x^4 \csc^2 x^4$

9. a. $6x^5 \cot 7x - 7x^6 \csc^2 7x$
   b. $\dfrac{-(\cot^2 x \csc x) - \csc^3 x}{2\sqrt{\cot x \csc x}} = \dfrac{-\csc^3 x(3 + 2\cos 2x)}{4\sqrt{\cot x \csc x}}$

Chapter 3 Answers

c. $\dfrac{\cot x(1+\cot x)\csc x}{(\csc x+1)^2} - \dfrac{\csc^2 x}{\csc x+1} = \dfrac{-2\sin\left(\dfrac{x}{2}\right)}{\left(\sin\left(\dfrac{x}{2}\right)+\cos\left(\dfrac{x}{2}\right)\right)^3}$

d. $-8\cot^5 x \csc^8 x - 4\cot^3 x \csc^{10} x$

10. a. $-\tan x$
b. $\dfrac{\cos x - \sin x}{\cos x + \sin x}$
c. $\dfrac{\cos(\ln|x|)}{x}$
d. $\dfrac{\sec^2 x + \sec x \tan x}{\sec x + \tan x} = \sec x$

11. a. $e^{\sin x}\cos x$
b. $e^x \cos e^x$
c. $e^{\tan x}\sec^2 x$
d. $11e^x \sec^{11} e^x \tan e^x$

12. a. $\dfrac{\sin 2x}{2}$
b. $\dfrac{\sin^4 x}{4}$
c. $\dfrac{\sin x^3}{3}$
d. $\dfrac{\sec 2x}{2}$

13. a. $\dfrac{\sec^4 x}{4}$
b. $\sec x$
c. $\dfrac{\sec x^2}{2}$
d. $\dfrac{2(\sin x)^{3/2}}{3}$

14. $\dfrac{\sin \theta}{2}$
max area = 1/2

15. 3/7   16. 1/2   17. $\dfrac{75\sqrt{3}}{4}$

18. $\sin x^3 - \cos x^2$ 19. 49.939

Section 3.8

1. $\dfrac{dy}{dx} = \dfrac{9x^2 y - y^3}{3xy^2 - 3x^3}$; 10/9

2. $\dfrac{dy}{dx} = \dfrac{2xy^2 - x^4}{y^4 - 2x^2 y}$

3. $\dfrac{dy}{dx} = -\dfrac{y^{1/3}}{x^{1/3}}$

4. $\dfrac{dy}{dx} = -\dfrac{y^{2/3}}{x^{2/3}}$;
$\dfrac{d^2 y}{dx^2} = \dfrac{2}{3x^{5/3} y^{1/3}}$

5. $\dfrac{dy}{dx} = -\dfrac{3x^2 + y}{x + 2y}$

6. $y - 2 = -\dfrac{1}{2}(x-1)$

Chapter 3 Answers

7. $(-1, 2)$, $(1, -2)$

8. $(-1, -2)$, $(1, 2)$

9. $y+1 = (x-1)$

10. $(1, 1)$, $(-1, -1)$

11. $(1, 2)$

12. $\dfrac{x - xy^2}{x^2y - 2y^3}$

13. $\dfrac{2x \cos(x^2+y)}{1 - \cos(x^2+y)}$

14. $-3\left(\dfrac{x^2}{y^3} + \dfrac{x^6}{y^7}\right)$

15. $(2^{2/3}, 2^{1/3})$

16. 6 in per sec

17. 1,000 in²/s

18. 330 in²/min

19. 54/33 = 18/11 in/s

20. decreasing at $9\dfrac{1}{2}$ m²/s

21. $\dfrac{590}{\sqrt{145}} \approx 49$ mi/hr

22. $\dfrac{1}{300\pi}$ ft/s

23. 5 ft/s

24. 2/5 ft/s

25. 600 ft/s

26. $12\sqrt{3}$ in²/min

27. 600 cm³/s

28. It is decreasing at $\dfrac{1}{3125\pi}$ ft/s

29. 600/13 mi/h

30. $y' = -\dfrac{5x^4y + y^5}{x^5 + 5xy^4}$, and since by the original equation neither x nor y can equal zero, the numerator, which is equivalent to $y(5x^4 + y^4)$, cannot equal zero.

31. $y - 3 = \dfrac{1}{2}x$ $\quad y + 3 = \dfrac{1}{2}x$ $\quad$ slopes are equal

32. $\pm\dfrac{2}{7}\sqrt{51}$ ft²/min

33. $-\dfrac{18\sqrt{5}}{5}$ ft/s

34. 6,000 km/h

35. $y'' = \dfrac{1}{2x\sqrt{x}}$

Chapter 3 Answers

Section 3.9

1. 1.25992
2. 1.15417
3. 0
4. 1.99526
5. [0,1] (≈ .1613)
6. 0.856675
7. 0.486389
8. −1.35785, 0.714714, 1.25699
9. 0.73909
10. 0.67628
11. 3.99193
12. 4.95968

Chapter 4

Section 4.2

1. 4.00125
2. 9.9995
3. 1.9875
4. 10.1
5. 179/60
6. 82/27 ≈ 3.037
7. 0.999999999996
8. 2.96296
9. 0.00555
10. 2999/300
11. 4.99699
12. 3
13. 1029.12
14. 0.0099998
15. 0.99995
16. 0.51712

Section 4.3

1. Increasing $(-\infty, 0)$, $(1, \infty)$ Decreasing $(0, 1)$
2. Increasing $(-3, 0)$, $(0, \infty)$ Decreasing $(-\infty, -3)$
3. Increasing $(-\infty, -3)$, $(3, \infty)$ Decreasing $(-3, 3)$
4. Increasing $(-\infty, -1)$, $(1, \infty)$ Decreasing $(-1, 1)$
5. Increasing $(0, \infty)$ Decreasing $(-\infty, 0)$
6. Increasing $(-\infty, 0)$, $(2, \infty)$ Decreasing $(0, 1)$, $(1, 2)$
7. Increasing $(0, \infty)$ Decreasing $(-\infty, 0)$
8. Increasing $((4n-1)\pi/2, (4n+1)\pi/2)$
   Decreasing $((4n + 1)\pi/2, (4n + 3)\pi/2)$, n any integer

Chapter 4 Answers

9. Increasing $(n\pi, n\pi + \pi/2)$
   Decreasing $(n\pi + \pi/2, (n + 1)\pi)$

10. Increasing $(-\infty, \infty)$

11. b. $\dfrac{2\sqrt{3}}{3}$ 12. 1 13. $\sqrt[3]{2}$

14. $3\sqrt{3}$ 15. b. $\sqrt{6}$ 16. a. $f' = \dfrac{f(b) - f(a)}{b - a}$
    b. $\sqrt{3}$

17. 1 18. $\sqrt{3}$ 19. $\sin^{-1}(2/\pi) \approx .6901$

20. a. $\dfrac{\sin^5 x}{5} + C$ b. $\dfrac{\sin x^5}{5} + C$

21. 35/27 22. $\dfrac{\sqrt{21}}{3}$ 23. $\sqrt[4]{\dfrac{11}{5}}$

24. $\dfrac{\pi}{2}$

25. Suppose that the function f is differentiable on the interval $[-1, 2]$, that $f(-1) = -1$, and that $f(2) = 5$. Prove that there is a point on the graph of f at which the tangent line is parallel to the straight line with equation $y = 2x$.

26. Let $f(x) = x - \sin x$.
    Since $|\sin x| \le 1$ for all $x \in \mathbb{R}$ and $\sin 1 \approx .84$,
    $x - \sin x > 0$ for all $x \ge 1$,
    $f'(x) = 1 - \cos x > 0$ for $0 < x < 1$
    since $0 < \cos x < 1$ in that interval.
    Therefore $f(x)$ is increasing in $(0, 1)$. But $f(0) = 0$, hence $f(x) > 0$ in $(0, 1)$

27. $f(3) \le -10$ 28. $f(5) > 15$

Section 4.4

1. $\sqrt{2}, \sqrt{2}$ 2. $(1, 1)$ 3. $s = 90$ mph

4. $SA = 300\sqrt[3]{4}$ 5. $x = R$ 6. $-1/4$

7. 2000π in^3 8. max = 1 9. base 30×30 in

Chapter 4 Answers

height 40 in

10. $80^2 = 6,400$ 11. max = 1

12. Let $D = \sum_{i=1}^{n} (x-a_i)^2$. Then $\dfrac{dD}{dx} = \sum_{i=1}^{n} 2(x-a_i) = 0$

$\Rightarrow \sum_{i=1}^{n} (2x) - \sum_{i=1}^{n} 2a_i = 0$

or $2nx = 2\sum_{i=1}^{n} a_i$

or $x = \dfrac{\sum_{i=1}^{n} a_i}{n}$.

Therefore D has a maximum or minimum at $x = (\sum_{i=1}^{n} a_i)/n$.

Now $\dfrac{d^2D}{dx^2} = \sum_{i=1}^{n} 2 = 2n > 0$.

Hence D is minimum for $x = \dfrac{1}{n}\sum_{i=1}^{n} a_i$.

13. $w = 8$ in, $h = 12$ in   14. $h = 24$ in, $w = 16$ in

15. $2\sqrt{15} \times \sqrt{15}$ 16. base = 28 m, $h = 16$

17. 4   18. 3   19. $4(1+2^{2/3})^{3/2}$

20. Let x be the side of the base and y the height of the solid. Then $V = x^2y$. $S = 2x^2 + 4xy = 2x^2 + \dfrac{4V}{x}$.

$\dfrac{dS}{dx} = 4x - \dfrac{4V}{x^2} = 0 \Rightarrow x^3 = V$ or $x = \sqrt[3]{V} \therefore y = \sqrt[3]{V}$, i.e. the solid is a cube. Now $\dfrac{d^2S}{dx^2} = 4 + \dfrac{8V}{x^3} = 4 + 8$ at $x = \sqrt[3]{V} = 12 > 0$

Hence S is minimum at $x = \sqrt[3]{V}$, i.e. when the solid is a cube.

21. $2L$ 22. 18

23. Longest segment is $9/2 = 4.5$

24. 4.2 miles   25. $8\sqrt{2}$ ft^3

Chapter 4 Answers

26. maximum = 2 spheres, $r = \sqrt[3]{\dfrac{3V}{8\pi}}$ 27. 16

28. Let $f(x) = \sqrt{ax} - \dfrac{1}{2}(a + x)$, $x > 0$.

   Then $f'(x) = 0 \Rightarrow \dfrac{\sqrt{a}}{2\sqrt{x}} - \dfrac{1}{2} = 0 \Rightarrow x = a$

   and $f''(x) = -\dfrac{1}{4}\dfrac{\sqrt{a}}{x^{3/2}} < 0$ for $x = a$.

   Hence $f(x)$ has only one maximum at $x = a$ and the maximum value is $f_{max} = \sqrt{a \cdot a} - \dfrac{1}{2}(a + a) = 0$

   For any other value of x, $f(x)$ is negative.

29. 6,000   30. 36 m³   31. $\dfrac{250}{\pi}$ ft × 250 ft

32. One should walk in a straight line from A to a point C on the road which is $\left(4 - \sqrt{\dfrac{3}{5}}\right)$ miles from B and then walk along the road.

33. $\dfrac{64R^3}{81}$ 34. 60 m wide, 120 m long   35. $2\pi R^2$

36. Maximum at $28^3 + 0^2 = 21,952$ 37. Increasing $(0, \infty)$
   Decreasing $(-\infty, 0)$

Section 4.5

1. maximum at $x = 0$
    minimum at $x = 1$
    Increasing for $(-\infty, 0)$, $(1, \infty)$
    Decreasing for $(0, 1)$
    x intercepts: 0, 1.25
    y intercept: 0

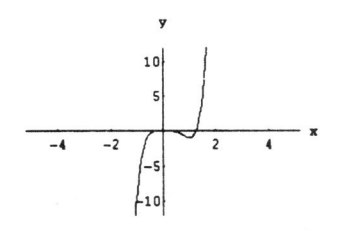

Chapter 4 Answers

2. minimum at $x = -3$
   Increasing for $(-3, 0)$, $(0, \infty)$
   Decreasing for $(-\infty, -3)$
   x intercepts: -4, 0
   y intercept: 0

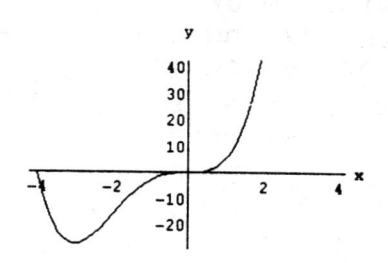

3. maximum at $x = -3$
   minimum at $x = 3$
   Increasing for $(-\infty, -3)$, $(3, \infty)$
   Decreasing for $(-3, 3)$
   x intercepts: $0, \pm 3\sqrt{3}$
   y intercept: 0

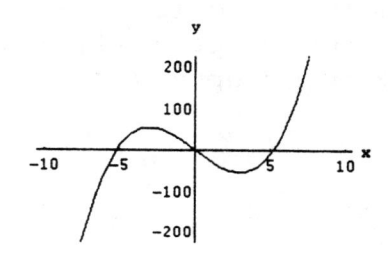

4. maximum at $x = -1$
   minimum at $x = 1$
   Increasing for $(-\infty, -1)$, $(1, \infty)$
   Decreasing for $(-1, 0)$, $(0, 1)$
   x intercepts: $0, \pm \dfrac{\sqrt{15}}{3}$
   y intercept: 0

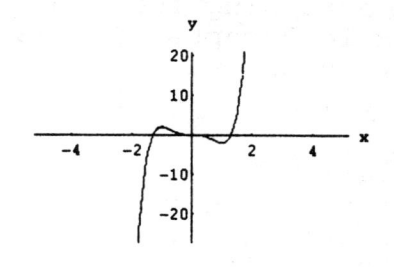

5. maximum at $x = -1$
   minimum at $x = 3$
   Increasing for $(-\infty, -1)$, $(3, \infty)$
   Decreasing for $(-1, 3)$
   x intercepts: $0, \dfrac{3}{2}(1 \pm \sqrt{5})$
   y intercept: 0

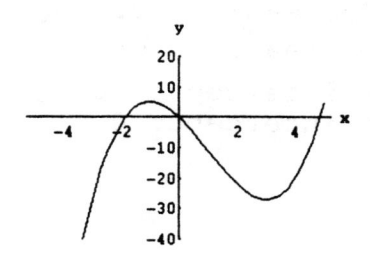

Chapter 4 Answers

6. maximum at $x = -1$
   minimum at $x = 1$
   Increasing for $(-\infty, -1)$, $(1, \infty)$
   Decreasing for $(-1, 1)$
   x intercepts: $0, \pm\sqrt{3}$
   y intercept: 0

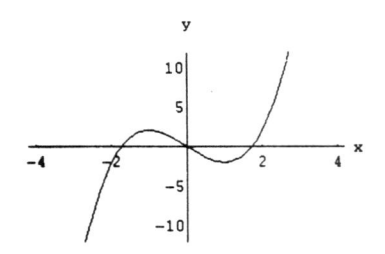

7. maximum at $x = 0$
   minimum at $x = \pm 2$
   Increasing for $(-2, 0)$, $(2, \infty)$
   Decreasing for $(-\infty, -2)$, $(0, 2)$
   x intercepts: $\pm 1, \pm\sqrt{7}$
   y intercept: 7

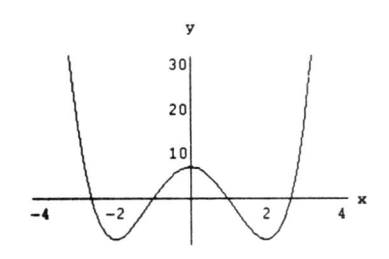

8. minimum at $x = 1$
   Increasing for $(1, \infty)$
   Decreasing for $(-\infty, 0)$, $(0, 1)$
   x intercepts: $0, 4/3$
   y intercept: 0

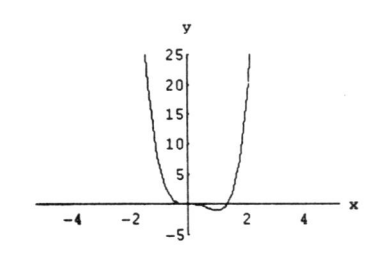

9. maximum at $x = 0$
   minimum at $x = \pm\sqrt{6}$
   Increasing for $(-\sqrt{6}, 0)$, $(\sqrt{6}, \infty)$
   Decreasing for $(-\infty, -\sqrt{6})$, $(0, \sqrt{6})$
   x intercepts: $0, \pm 2\sqrt{3}$
   y intercept: 0

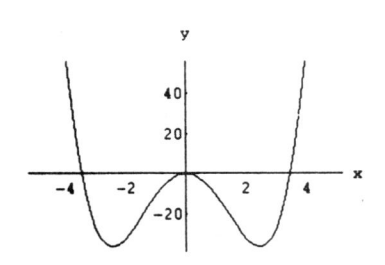

Chapter 4 Answers

10. maximum at $x = 0$
    minimum at $x = \pm 1$
    Increasing for $(-1, 0)$, $(1, \infty)$
    Decreasing for $(-\infty, -1)$, $(0, 1)$
    x intercepts: 0, $\pm\sqrt{2}$
    y intercept: 0

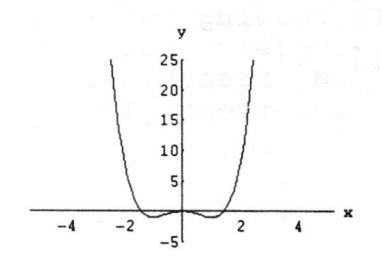

11. minimum at $x = 3$
    Increasing for $(3, \infty)$
    Decreasing for $(-\infty, 0)$, $(0, 3)$
    x intercepts: 0, 4
    y intercept: 0

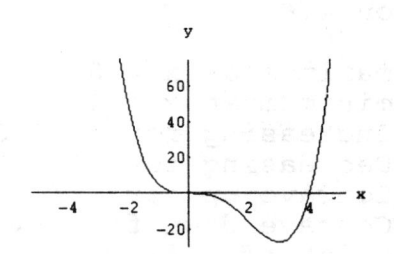

12. maximum at $x = 4$
    minimum at $x = 0$
    Increasing in $(0, 4)$
    Decreasing in $(-\infty, 0)$, $(4, \infty)$
    x intercept: too difficult
    y intercept: -10

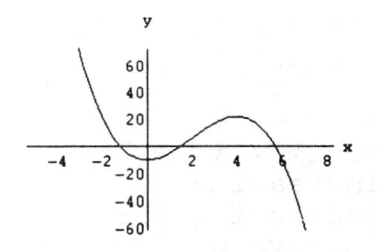

13. maximum at $x = 0$
    minimum at $x = 1$
    Increasing for $(-\infty, 0)$, $(1, \infty)$
    Decreasing for $(0, 1)$
    x intercepts: 0, $3/2$
    y intercept: 0

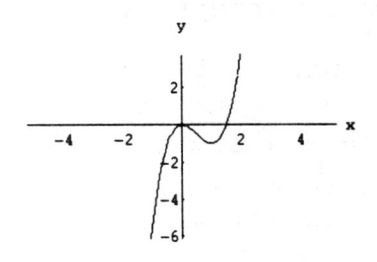

Chapter 4 Answers

14. maximum at $x = 0$
    minima at $x = -1, 1$
    Increasing for $(-1, 0)$, $(1, \infty)$
    Decreasing for $(-\infty, -1)$, $(0, 1)$
    x intercepts: ± 1
    y intercept: 1

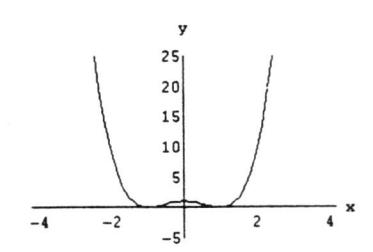

Section 4.6

1. maximum at $x = 0$
   minimum at $x = 1$
   Increasing for $(-\infty, 0)$, $(1, \infty)$
   Decreasing for $(0, 1)$
   Concave up for $(3/4, \infty)$
   Concave down for $(-\infty, 3/4)$
   Point of inflection: $x = 3/4$
   x intercepts: 0, 1.25
   y intercept: 0

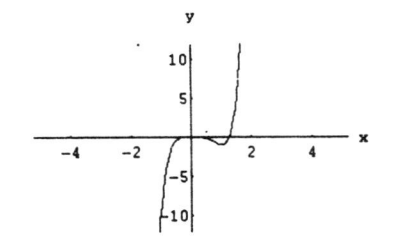

2. minimum at $x = -3$
   Increasing for $(-3, 0)$, $(0, \infty)$
   Decreasing for $(-\infty, -3)$
   Concave up for $(-\infty, -1)$, $(0, \infty)$
   Concave down for $(-1, 0)$
   Points of inflection: $x = -1, 0$
   x intercepts: $-4, 0$
   y intercept: 0

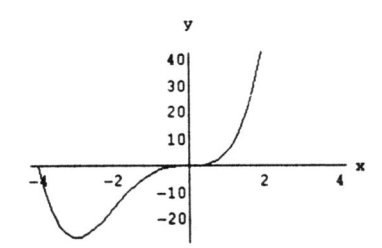

Chapter 4 Answers

3. maximum at $x = -3$
   minimum at $x = 3$
   Increasing for $(-\infty, -3)$, $(3, \infty)$
   Decreasing for $(-3, 3)$
   Concave up for $(0, \infty)$
   Concave down for $(-\infty, 0)$
   Point of inflection: $x = 0$
   x intercepts: $0, \pm 3\sqrt{3}$
   y intercept: 0

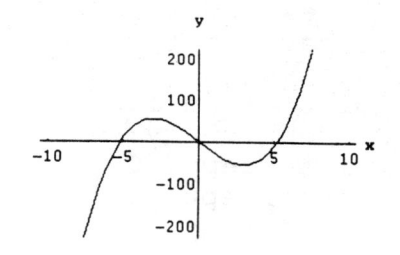

4. maximum at $x = -1$
   minimum at $x = 1$
   Increasing for $(-\infty, -1)$, $(1, \infty)$
   Decreasing for $(-1, 0)$, $(0, 1)$
   Concave up for $\left(-\frac{\sqrt{2}}{2}, 0\right), \left(\frac{\sqrt{2}}{2}, \infty\right)$
   Concave down for $\left(-\infty, -\frac{\sqrt{2}}{2}\right), \left(0, \frac{\sqrt{2}}{2}\right)$
   Points of inflection: $x = 0, \pm \frac{\sqrt{2}}{2}$
   x intercepts: $0, \pm \frac{\sqrt{15}}{3}$
   y intercept: 0

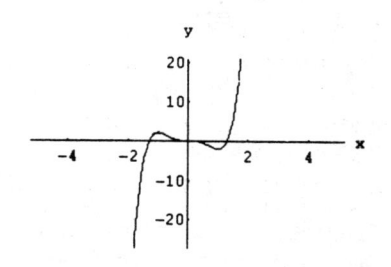

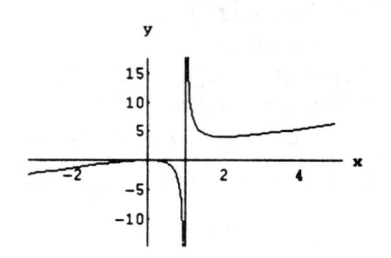

5. maximum at $x = 0$
   minimum at $x = 2$
   Increasing for $(-\infty, 0)$, $(2, \infty)$
   Decreasing for $(0, 1)$, $(1, 2)$
   Concave up for $(1, \infty)$
   Concave down for $(-\infty, 1)$
   Point of inflection: None
   Discontinuity: $x = 1$
   x intercept: 0
   y intercept: 0

Chapter 4 Answers

6. maximum at $x = 0$
   Increasing for $(-\infty, -1)$, $(-1, 0)$
   Decreasing for $(0, 1)$, $(1, \infty)$
   Concave up for $(-\infty, -1)$, $(1, \infty)$
   Concave down for $(-1, 1)$
   Point of inflection: None
   Discontinuity: $x = \pm 1$
   x intercept: 0
   y intercept: 0

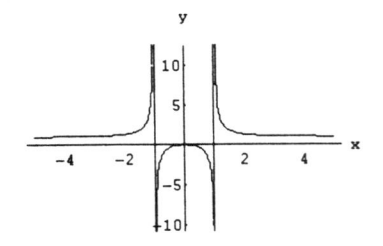

7. Increasing for $(-\infty, \infty)$
   Concave up for $(-\infty, 0)$
   Concave down for $(0, \infty)$
   Point of inflection: $x = 0$
   x intercept: 0
   y intercept: 0

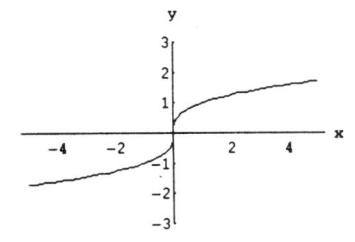

8. minimum at $x = 0$
   Increasing for $(0, \infty)$
   Decreasing for $(-\infty, 0)$
   Concave down for $(-\infty, 0)$, $(0, \infty)$
   x intercept: 0
   y intercept: 0

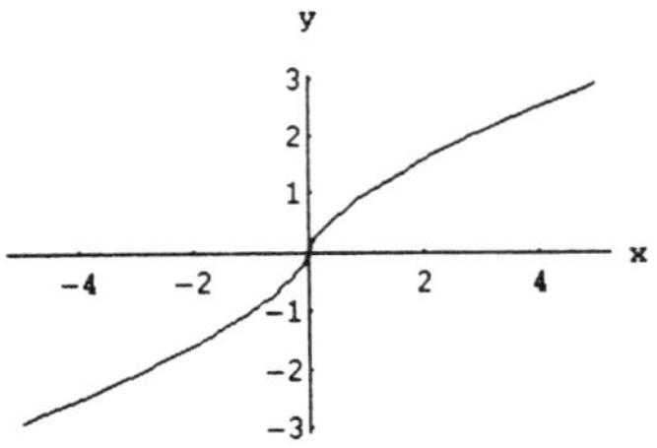

9. maximum at $x = -1$
   minimum at $x = 3$
   Increasing for $(-\infty, -1)$, $(3, \infty)$
   Decreasing for $(-1, 3)$
   Concave up for $(1, \infty)$
   Concave down for $(-\infty, 1)$
   Point of inflection: $x = 1$
   x intercepts: 0, $\frac{3}{2}(1 \pm \sqrt{5})$
   y intercept: 0

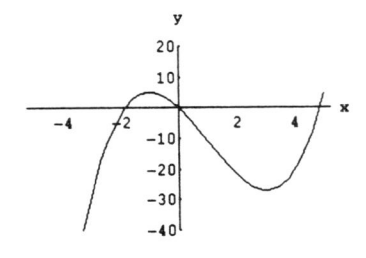

Chapter 4 Answers

10. maximum at $x = -1$
    minimum at $x = 1$
    Increasing for $(-\infty, -1)$, $(1, \infty)$
    Decreasing for $(-1, 1)$
    Concave up for $(0, \infty)$
    Concave down for $(-\infty, 0)$
    Point of inflection: $x = 0$
    x intercepts: $0, \pm\sqrt{3}$
    y intercept: 0

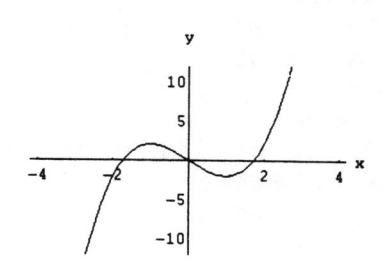

11. maximum at $x = 0$
    minimum at $x = \pm 2$
    Increasing for $(-2, 0)$, $(2, \infty)$
    Decreasing for $(-\infty, -2)$, $(0, 2)$
    Concave up for $\left(\dfrac{2\sqrt{3}}{3}, \infty\right), \left(-\infty, -\dfrac{2\sqrt{3}}{3}\right)$
    Concave down for $\left(-\dfrac{2\sqrt{3}}{3}, \dfrac{2\sqrt{3}}{3}\right)$
    Points of inflection: $x = \pm\dfrac{2\sqrt{3}}{3}$
    x intercepts: $\pm 1, \pm\sqrt{7}$
    y intercept: 7

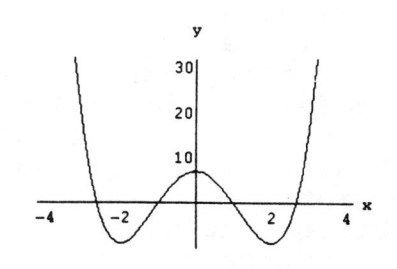

12. minimum at $x = 1$
    Increasing for $(1, \infty)$
    Decreasing for $(-\infty, 0)$, $(0, 1)$
    Concave up for $(-\infty, 0)$, $(2/3, \infty)$
    Concave down for $(0, 2/3)$
    Points of inflection: $x = 0, 2/3$
    x intercepts: $0, 4/3$
    y intercept: 0

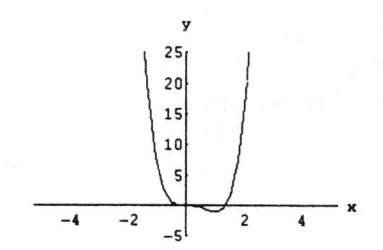

13. minimum at $x = 0$
    Increasing for $(0, \infty)$
    Decreasing for $(-\infty, 0)$
    Concave up for $(-1, 1)$
    Concave down for $(-\infty, -1)$, $(1, \infty)$
    Points of inflection: $x = \pm 1$
    x intercepts: $x = \pm 1$
    y intercept: -1

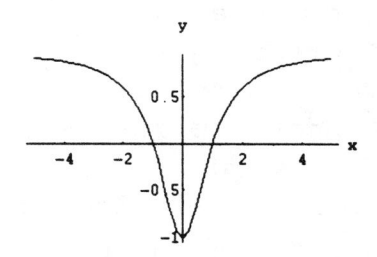

Chapter 4 Answers

14. maximum at $x = 1$
    minimum at $x = -1$
    Increasing for $(-1, 1)$
    Decreasing for $(-\infty, -1)$, $(1, \infty)$
    Concave up for $(-\infty, 0)$
    Concave down for $(0, \infty)$
    Point of inflection: $x = 0$
    x intercept: 0
    y intercept: 0

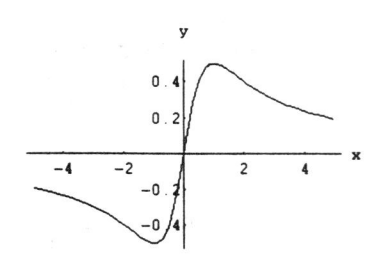

15. maximum at $x = -1$
    minimum at $x = 1$
    Increasing for $(-\infty, -1)$, $(1, \infty)$
    Decreasing for $(-1, 0)$, $(0, 1)$
    Concave up for $(0, \infty)$
    Concave down for $(-\infty, 0)$
    Point of inflection: None
    Discontinuity: $x = 0$
    x intercept: none
    y intercept: none

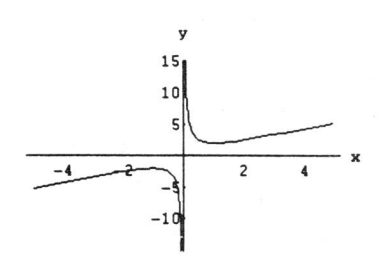

16. no extremum
    Decreasing for $(-\infty, -1)$, $(-1, 1)$, $(1, \infty)$
    Concave up for $(-1, 0)$, $(1, \infty)$
    Concave down for $(-\infty, -1)$, $(0, 1)$
    Point of inflection: $x = 0$
    x intercept: 0
    y intercept: 0
    Discontinuity at $x = \pm 1$

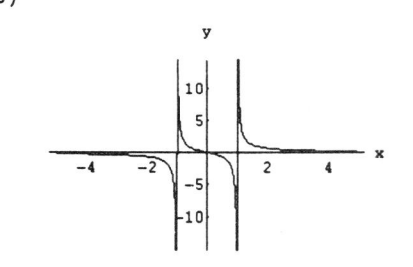

17. maximum at $x = 0$
    minimum at $x = \pm\sqrt{6}$
    Increasing for $(-\sqrt{6}, 0)$, $(\sqrt{6}, \infty)$
    Decreasing for $(-\infty, -\sqrt{6})$, $(0, \sqrt{6})$
    Concave up for $(-\infty, \sqrt{2})$, $(\sqrt{2}, \infty)$
    Concave down for $(-\sqrt{2}, \sqrt{2})$
    Points of inflection: $\pm\sqrt{2}$
    x intercepts: $0, \pm 2\sqrt{3}$
    y intercept: 0

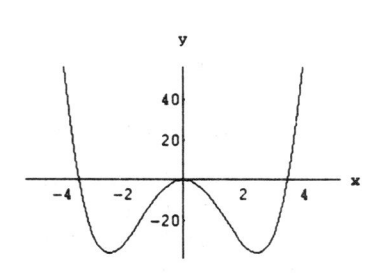

Chapter 4 Answers

18. maximum at $x = 0$
    minimum at $x = \pm 1$
    Increasing for $(-1, 0)$, $(1, \infty)$
    Decreasing for $(-\infty, -1)$, $(0, 1)$
    Concave up for $\left(-\infty, -\frac{\sqrt{3}}{3}\right)$, $\left(\frac{\sqrt{3}}{3}, \infty\right)$
    Concave down for $\left(-\frac{\sqrt{3}}{3}, \frac{\sqrt{3}}{3}\right)$
    Points of inflection: $x = \pm\frac{\sqrt{3}}{3}$
    x intercepts: $0, \pm\sqrt{2}$
    y intercept: 0

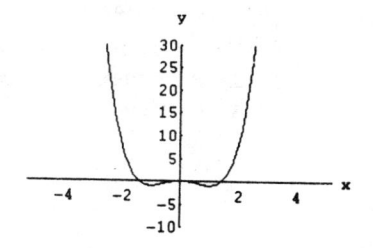

19. maximum at $x = 0$
    minimum at $x = 1$
    Increasing for $(-\infty, 0)$, $(1, \infty)$
    Decreasing for $(0, 1)$
    Concave up for $(1/2, \infty)$
    Concave down for $(-\infty, 1/2)$
    Point of inflection: $x = 1/2$
    x intercepts: $0, 3/2$
    y intercept: 0

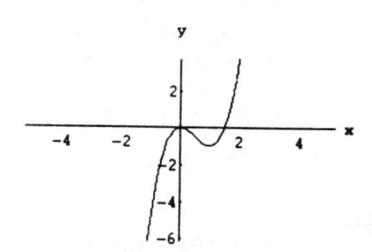

Section 4.7

1. See 4.6 #5
2. See 4.6 #6
3. See 4.6 #7
4. See 4.6 #8
5. See 4.6 #13
6. See 4.6 #14
7. See 4.6 #15
8. See 4.6 #16

9. minimum at $x = \frac{2^{2/3}}{2}$
   Increasing for $\left(\frac{2^{2/3}}{2}, \infty\right)$
   Decreasing for $(-\infty, 0)$, $\left(0, \frac{2^{2/3}}{2}\right)$
   Concave up for $(-\infty, -1)$, $(0, \infty)$
   Concave down for $(-1, 0)$
   Point of inflection: $x = -1$
   Asymptote: $x = 0$
   x intercept: -1
   y intercept: none

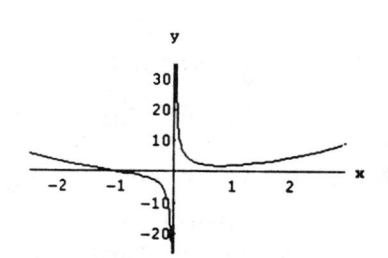

Chapter 4 Answers

10. Decreasing for $(-\infty, 3)$, $(3, \infty)$
    Concave up for $(3, \infty)$
    Concave down for $(-\infty, 3)$
    Asymptotes: $x = 3$, $y = 1$
    x intercept: -3
    y intercept: -1

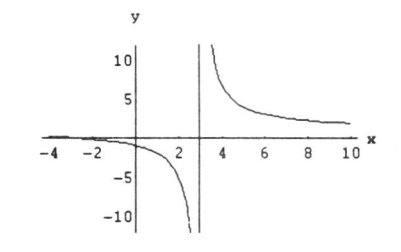

11. Increasing for $(-\infty, -2)$, $(-2, 2)$, $(2, \infty)$
    Concave up for $(-\infty, -2)$, $(0, 2)$
    Concave down for $(-2, 0)$, $(2, \infty)$
    Point of inflection: $x = 0$
    Asymptotes: $x = \pm 2$, $y = 0$
    x intercept: 0
    y intercept: 0

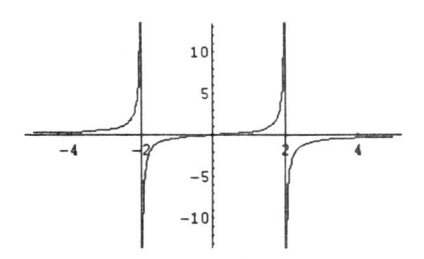

12. minimum at $x = (-4)^{1/3}$
    Increasing for $((-4)^{1/3}, 0)$, $(0, \infty)$
    Decreasing for $(-\infty, (-4)^{1/3})$
    Concave up for $(-\infty, 0)$, $(2, \infty)$
    Concave down for $(0, 2)$
    Point of inflection: $x = 2$
    Asymptote: $x = 0$
    x intercept: 2
    y intercept: none

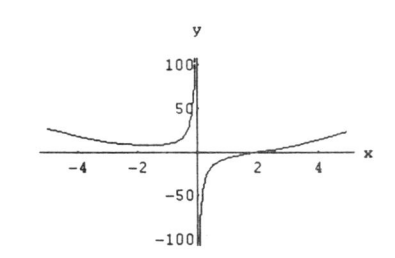

13. maximum at $x = 1 + \sqrt{2}$
    minimum at $x = 1 - \sqrt{2}$
    Increasing for $(1 - \sqrt{2}, 1 + \sqrt{2})$
    Decreasing for $(-\infty, 1 - \sqrt{2})$, $(1 + \sqrt{2}, \infty)$
    Concave up for $(-1, 2 - \sqrt{3})$, $(2 + \sqrt{3}, \infty)$
    Concave down for $(-\infty, -1)$,
        $(2 - \sqrt{3}, 2 + \sqrt{3})$
    Points of inflection: $x = -1$, $2 \pm \sqrt{3}$
    Asymptote: $y = 0$
    x intercept: 1
    y intercept: -4

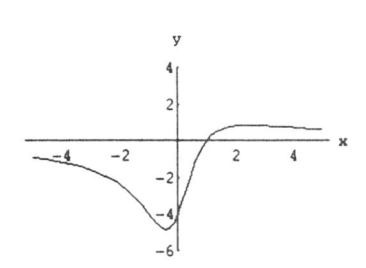

Chapter 4 Answers

14. $x = \pm 1$; $y = 2x$

15. Asymptotes are at $x = 0$, $x = 1$, $y = 0$

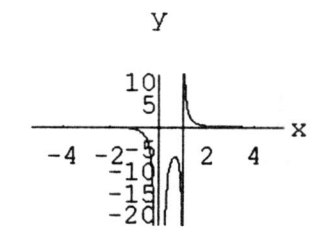

16.

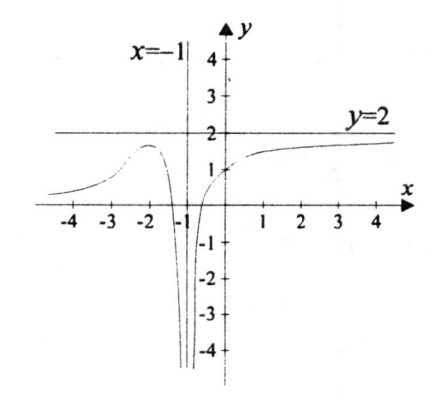

17. Case (i): If $f(x)$ has positive leading coefficient, then $f'(x) > 0$ at the leftmost zero of $f(x)$, $f'(x) < 0$ at the middle zero of $f(x)$, and $f'(x) > 0$ at the rightmost coefficient of $f(x)$. Now apply the intermediate value property of continuous functions to f'.

18.

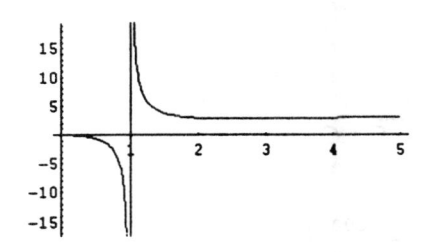

Chapter 4 Answers

19. The graph is concave upward and increasing for $x < 1$, concave downward and increasing for $x > 1$. There are intercepts at $(0, 0)$ and $(2, 0)$. There is a vertical asymptote at $x = 1$ and the line with equation $y = x - 1$ is an oblique asymptote. There are no extrema and no inflection points.

Chapter 5

Section 5.2

1. $-\frac{1}{6}\cos x^6 + C$

2. $\frac{1}{5}\sin^5 x + C$

3. $\sin x^2 + C$

4. $\frac{1}{33}(x^3+1)^{11} + C$

5. $-\frac{1}{4x^4} - \frac{1}{3x^3} + C$

6. $\frac{2}{3}\sin x^{3/2} + C$

7. $-\frac{1}{8}\cos^8 x + C$

8. $\frac{1}{3}x^3 - 2x - \frac{1}{x} + C$

9. $\frac{1}{2}(\cos 2x + \sin 2x) + C$

10. $\frac{1}{48}(x^6-1)^8 + C$

11. $\frac{1}{2}\sin t^2 + C$

12. $\frac{7}{4}u^4 + 7u + C$

13. $\frac{1}{6}(x+1)^6 + C$

14. $\frac{1}{7}\sin 7x + C$

15. $-\frac{1}{2}\cos^2 t + C$

16. $\sin x^3 + C$

17. $-\frac{1}{2}\cot^2 x + C$

18. $2\sqrt{x} + \frac{2}{3}x^{3/2} + C$

19. $2\sqrt{x^2+1} + C$

20. $-\frac{7}{x+1} + C$

21. $\frac{1}{2}x^2 - \frac{4}{x} + C$

22. $\frac{4}{3}\sqrt{x^3+5} + C$

23. $\frac{1}{10}x^{10} - \frac{1}{8}x^8 + C$

24. $\frac{1}{100}\sin^{100} x$

Chapter 5 Answers

25. $\frac{2}{3}(x+1)^{3/2} + C$

26. $\frac{(z^3+1)^{4/3}}{4} + C$

27. $\frac{1}{500}(x^5+7)^{100} + C$

28. $\frac{1}{2}\sin x - \frac{1}{6}\sin 3x + C$

29. $-\frac{(1-x^2)^{3/2}}{3} + C$

30. $-\cos t^2 + C$

31. $-\sin\frac{1}{x} + C$

32. $2\sin\sqrt{x} + C$

33. $y = x^2 + x + 3$

34. $y = \frac{1}{4}(x-2)^4 + 1$

35. $y = \frac{2}{3}x^{3/2} - \frac{16}{3}$

36. $y = 6 - \frac{1}{x}$

37. $y = 2(x+2)^{1/2} - 5$

38. $y = \frac{1}{3}(x^2+9)^{3/2} - \frac{125}{3}$

39. $y = \frac{1}{2}\sin 2x + 1$

40. $y = \sec x + 1$

41. stays in the air 30 seconds
    $v(t) = 960$ ft/s

42. stays in the air $10\sqrt{3}$ seconds
    $v(10\sqrt{3}) = 320\sqrt{3}$ ft/s

43. $h = 64$ ft
    $v = 64$ ft/s

44. $v = 64\sqrt{30}$ ft/s

45. $h = 64$ ft

46. $g = 2{,}000{,}000$ ft/s
    $v = 2000$ ft/s

47. $h = 324$ ft

48. $t = 2\sqrt{15}$ s
    $v = 64\sqrt{15}$ ft/s

49. $v = 768$ ft/s (An unusually powerful crossbow!)
    $h = 9216$ ft

50. $h = 576$ ft

Chapter 5 Answers

51. $h = 996$ ft
    t (back to top of building) $= 3$ s
    t (to ground) $= (3 + \sqrt{249})/2$ s

52. $v = 512$ ft/s
    $t = 32$ s

53. $t = 1/50$ s
    $v = 300$ ft/s

54. $t = 8$ s
    $d = 352$ ft

55. $h = 104{,}000$ ft
    $t = 400$ s

56. $h = 1024$ ft

57. $t = 4\sqrt{33}$ s
    $v = 240\sqrt{33}$ ft/s

58. $v = 60$ ft/s

59. $h = 1000$ ft
    $t = 40$ s

60. $v = 120$ ft/s

61. $t = 88$ s
    $d = 3872$ ft

62. $h = 3$ ft, 0 inches

63. $\dfrac{3008}{135} \approx 22.28$ ft

Section 5.3

1. $21/32 \approx .65625$

2. $A_n = \dfrac{2n^2 - 3n + 1}{2n^2}$; $A = 1$

3. underestimate $= 533/840 \approx .6345238$
   overestimate $= 319/420 \approx .7595238$

4. a. $A(u) = (1/2)mu^2$
   b. $A'(u) = mu$
   c. difference $= 0$

5. a. $\displaystyle\sum_{n=0}^{50} 2n+1$
   b. $\displaystyle\sum_{n=0}^{33} 3n+1$
   c. $\displaystyle\sum_{n=1}^{25} (2n)^2$
   d. $\displaystyle\sum_{n=1}^{20} \dfrac{1}{n^2}$

6. a. 20100   b. 2500   c. 323200   d. 338350

7. underestimate $= 9/4 = 2.25$
   overestimate $= 25/4 = 6.25$

Chapter 5 Answers

8. underestimate = $354/3125 \approx .11328$
   overestimate = $979/3125 \approx .31328$

9. underestimate = $\frac{1}{5}\left(\frac{1}{\sqrt{5}} + \frac{\sqrt{2}}{\sqrt{5}} + \frac{\sqrt{3}}{\sqrt{5}} + \frac{\sqrt{4}}{\sqrt{5}}\right) \approx .5497386$

   overestimate = $\frac{1}{5}\left(\frac{1}{\sqrt{5}} + \frac{\sqrt{2}}{\sqrt{5}} + \frac{\sqrt{3}}{\sqrt{5}} + \frac{\sqrt{4}}{\sqrt{5}} + 1\right) \approx .7497386$

10. underestimate = $\frac{1}{10}\left(\frac{1}{10^{3/2}} + \left(\frac{2}{10}\right)^{3/2} + \ldots + \left(\frac{9}{10}\right)^{3/2}\right) \approx .351169$

    overestimate = $\frac{1}{10}\left(\frac{1}{10^{3/2}} + \left(\frac{2}{10}\right)^{3/2} + \ldots + \left(\frac{9}{10}\right)^{3/2} + 1\right) \approx .451169$

Section 5.4

1. with $x_i^* =$ left-endpoint
   Riemann Sum = $\sum_{i=0}^{4} \frac{1}{5}\left(\frac{5+i}{5}\right)^2 = \frac{51}{25} = 2.04$

2. $f(x) = x^{1/2}$ and limit = $2/3 = \int_0^1 x^{1/2}\, dx$

3. $f(x) = \sin(\pi x)$ and limit = $\frac{2}{\pi} = \int_0^1 \sin(\pi x)\, dx$

4. 8

Section 5.5

1. 64/3   2. 0   3. 2656/315   4. 4
5. 1   6. $4\sqrt{2}/3$ 7. 1/2   8. $-1/12$
9. 2   10. $4 - 2\sqrt{2}$ 11. $\frac{4\sqrt{2} - 2}{9}$ 12. 0

Section 5.6

1. 16   2. $2/\pi$ 3. $4/\pi$ 4. 1/2
5. 1/100   6. 4/3   7. 0   8. 0

185

Chapter 5 Answers

9. $3x^2$
10. $\dfrac{1}{1+x^3}$
11. $3x^3\sqrt{x^{12}+1}$
12. 4π

13. $2x^3$

14. a. $\sqrt{1+x}$

  b. $2x\sqrt{1+x^2}$

15. limit = 0
16. $f(x) = \sin(\pi x)$
  $\int_0^1 f(x)\,dx = \dfrac{2}{\pi}$

Section 5.7

1. $\dfrac{(x^4+1)^{5/2}}{10}+C$
2. $\dfrac{(x^4+1)^{5/2}}{10}+C$

3. $\dfrac{1}{6(1+\cos x)^6}+C$
4. $\dfrac{1}{6(1+\cos x)^6}+C$

5. $\dfrac{1}{6}\tan 6x + C$
6. $\dfrac{1}{7}\sec^7 x + C$

7. $\dfrac{2(x+1)^{3/2}(3x-2)}{15}+C$
8. $\dfrac{1}{8}\sin 8x + C$

9. $\dfrac{\sqrt{2}-1}{2}$
10. $\dfrac{2\sqrt{2}-1}{6}$

11. 0
12. 0
13. 6

Section 5.8

1. 1/12
2. 1/20
3. $\dfrac{1}{(n+1)(n+2)}$
4. 64/3

5. .01
6. 72
7. 1/3
8. 3/4

9. 8/5
10. 1/5
11. 1/4 each
12. 1/3 each

13. 9
14. 125/6
15. 125/6

Chapter 5 Answers

Section 5.9

1. 1.09866 2. 0.785398 3. 1.11145 4. 0.500012
5. 0.25   6. 0.200521 7. 0.200013 8. 1.85184

Chapter 6

Section 6.2

1. $8/3$
2. $4/3 \pi R^3$
3. $1/30$
4. $\dfrac{26\pi}{81}$
5. $\dfrac{3\pi}{5}$
6. $\dfrac{6}{7}\pi$
7. $\int_{-1}^{3} \pi[(2y+3)^2 - (y^2+1)^2] \, dy$
8. $\int_{-1}^{3} 2\pi(5-y)(2y+3-y^2) \, dy$
9. 4π
10. $\int_{-1}^{1} \sqrt{3}(1-x^2) \, dx$
11. $\dfrac{1}{3}\pi R^2 H$
12. $\dfrac{8\pi}{105}$
13. 8π
14. 2π
15. $\int_{0}^{16} \pi(16-x) \, dx$
16. $\dfrac{28\pi}{15}$
17. $\dfrac{2\pi}{2+n}$
18. $\dfrac{7\pi}{24}$

Section 6.3

1. $\pi \ln 2$
2. $\dfrac{56\pi}{5}$
3. a. $\dfrac{8\pi}{3}$ b. $\dfrac{56\pi}{15}$
4. $\dfrac{7\pi}{30}$
5. $\dfrac{4\pi}{5}$
6. $\dfrac{4\pi}{15}$

Chapter 6 Answers

7. $\dfrac{11\pi}{15}$ 8. 8π 9. $\displaystyle\int_0^4 2\pi y(16-y^2)\,dy$

10. $\dfrac{\pi}{2}$

Section 6.4

1. $\dfrac{21}{16}$ 2. ≈ 1.5479 3. $\dfrac{59}{24}$

4. $\displaystyle\int_0^1 \sqrt{1+16x^9}\,dx$ 5. $\displaystyle\int_0^1 2\pi x\sqrt{1+16x^6}\,dx$

6. $S = \displaystyle\int_0^R 2\pi x\sqrt{1+\dfrac{H^2}{R^2}}\,dx$
   $= \dfrac{2\pi L}{R}\displaystyle\int_0^R x\,dx$
   $= \pi R L$

7. $\dfrac{10}{3}$ 8. $\dfrac{23}{12}$ 9. $\dfrac{\pi}{27}[10\sqrt{10}-1]$

10. $\displaystyle\int_0^\pi \sqrt{1+\cos^2 x}\,dx$ 11. $\dfrac{13}{12}$ 12. $\dfrac{2}{3}[10\sqrt{10}-1]$

13. $\dfrac{\pi}{6}[5\sqrt{5}-1]$

Section 6.5

1. $y = Ce^{-x^2}$ 2. $y = \dfrac{1}{C+\cos x}$

3. $\sqrt{y} - x\sqrt{x} = C$ 4. $y^{2/3} - 2x^{4/3} = C$ 5. $\sin y - x^2 = C$

6. $\dfrac{1}{1+y} - \dfrac{1}{1+x} = C$ 7. $\dfrac{1}{y^2} + x^2 = C$ 8. $y + \dfrac{2}{3}y^{3/2} = C + x + \dfrac{2}{3}x^{3/2}$

9. $y = \sqrt{1+\sqrt{x^2-16}}$ 10. $y = \dfrac{1}{1-x^2-x^3}$

Chapter 6 Answers

Section 6.6

1. 75,000 ft·lb   2. $\dfrac{10000}{3}$ ft·lb   3. $R^3 L \pi \delta$ ft·lb

4. $\dfrac{75\pi}{4}$ ft·lb   5. $\dfrac{16\pi}{3} \times 10^9$ ft·lb

6. $\dfrac{70\pi}{3}$ ft·lb

7. 16π ft·lbs

8. $216,000,000\pi$ ft·lbs

Chapter 7

Section 7.1

1. $y = \dfrac{x+3}{4}$ 2. $y = \dfrac{1-3x}{2x}, \; x \neq 0$ 3. $y = \dfrac{x}{1+x}, \; x \neq -1$

4. a. $f'(x) = \dfrac{\cos(\ln x)}{x}$ b. $f'(x) = \dfrac{7}{x}$

   c. $f'(x) = -\tan x$
   d. $f'(x) = \dfrac{7\cos(\ln x) \sin^6(\ln x)}{x}$
   e. $f'(x) = \dfrac{2x}{1+x^2}$ f. $f'(x) = \cos(x \ln x)(1 + \ln x)$

5. a. $g'(x) = 5 \cot x \, (\ln(\sin x))^4$ b. $g'(x) = \dfrac{1}{x \ln x}$

   c. $g'(x) = 1$ d. $g'(x) = \dfrac{\sin x}{e^{\cos x}}$

   e. $g'(x) = \csc x \sec x$ f. $g'(x) = 2e^{2x} \cos(e^{2x})$

6. a. $h'(x) = \dfrac{7(1 + \ln x)^6}{x}$ b. $h'(x) = e^{-x} - \dfrac{x}{e^x}$

   c. $h'(x) = -(\ln x)^{-2} \dfrac{1}{x}$ d. $h'(x) = e^x \cos(e^x)$

   e. $h'(x) = e^{\sin x} \cos x$
   f. $h'(x) = \dfrac{\csc x (x \cos x + \sin x)}{x}$ g. $h'(x) = e^{e^x + x}$

Chapter 7 Answers

7. $y = ex$

8. $y = \dfrac{1}{e}x$

9. $f'(x) = g'(x) = \dfrac{1}{x}, \therefore f(x) = g(x) + C$
   Theorem: Derivative of a constant equals zero.

10. a. $f'(x) = \dfrac{e^x}{(1+e^x)^2}$ b. $f'(x) = \dfrac{7(1-x)}{e^x}$
    c. $f'(x) = x + 2x \ln x$ d. $f'(x) = e^x \cot(e^x)$
    e. $f'(x) = e^x + e^x \ln(x^x) + e^x \ln x = e^x(1 + \ln x + x \ln x)$
    f. $f'(x) = 7x^6 e^{\sin(x^7)} \cos(x^7)$

11. Let (x_1, y_1) be a point on the graph $y = \ln x$. Then D, the square of the distance from the origin, of this point is

$$D = x_1^2 + y_1^2 = x_1^2 + (\ln x_1)^2$$
$$D' = 2x + 2(\ln x_1) \cdot \dfrac{1}{x_1} = 0 \text{ when } D \text{ is extremum.}$$
or $\ln x_1 = -x_1^2$, i.e. $y_1 = -x_1^2$.

Taking the second derivative

$$D'' = 2 + \dfrac{2}{x_1^2} - \dfrac{2(\ln x_1)}{x_1^2} = 2 + \dfrac{2}{x_1^2} - \dfrac{2}{x_1^2}\cdot(-x_1^2) > 0 \quad \text{at } y_1 = -x_1^2$$

Hence D is minimum at $y_1 = -x_1^2$. The equation of the line through the origin and (x_1, y_1) is $y = -x_1 \cdot x$, so its slope is $-x_1$. The slope of the tangent to $y = \ln x$ at (x_1, y_1) is $\dfrac{dy}{dx}\Big|_{(x, y) = (x_1, y_1)} = \dfrac{1}{x_1}$
Hence it is a normal to the curve at $(x_1, -x_1^2)$.

12. a. $g'(1) = 1$ b. $g'(4) = \dfrac{1}{6}$ c. $g'(0) = \dfrac{1}{2}$

Section 7.2

1. $f'(x) = \ln x$ 2. $\ln|1 + \sin x| + C$

3. a. $G(x) = \dfrac{1}{2} \ln(x^2 + 1) - \dfrac{1}{2} \ln 5 \Rightarrow G'(x) = \dfrac{x}{x^2 + 1}$

   b. $\dfrac{d}{dx}\displaystyle\int_c^x f(u) = f(x) \Rightarrow \dfrac{d}{dx}\displaystyle\int_2^x \dfrac{u}{u^2+1}\,du = \dfrac{x}{x^2+1}$

Chapter 7 Answers

4. $\dfrac{\ln 2}{4}$

5. $\ln \sqrt{2}$

6.
   a. $f'(x) = \dfrac{x}{1+x} + \ln(1+x)$
   b. $f'(x) = \dfrac{\cos(\ln x)}{x}$
   c. $f'(x) = \cot x$
   d. $f'(x) = \dfrac{17(\ln x)^{16}}{x}$
   e. $f'(x) = \dfrac{17}{x}$
   f. $f'(x) = \dfrac{1}{x}$
   g. $f'(x) = \dfrac{2x}{1+x^2}$
   h. $f'(x) = x \cos x \ln x + \sin x + \ln x \sin x$

7.
   a. $\ln|1 + \ln x| + C$
   b. $\dfrac{(\ln x)^8}{8} + C$
   c. $\sin(\ln x) + C$
   d. $2\log(1+\sqrt{x}) + C$
   e. $\ln(1 + \ln 2)$
   f. $\ln 2$

8. .003

9.

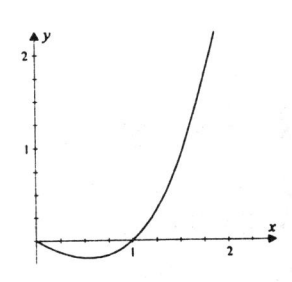

10.

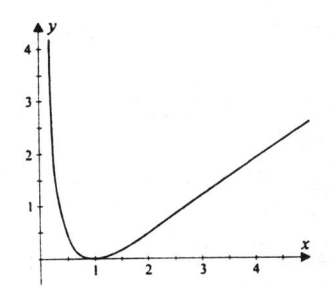

11.

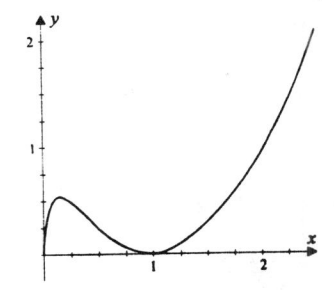

Section 7.3

1. $\dfrac{2}{3}(1+e)^{3/2} - \dfrac{2^{5/2}}{3}$

2. $\dfrac{e^2 - 1}{2e}$

Chapter 7 Answers

3. a. $f'(x) = \dfrac{e^x}{1+e^x}$ b. $f'(x) = \dfrac{e^{1+\ln x}}{x} = e$

   c. $f'(x) = 2xe^{x^2}$ d. $f'(x) = e^{\sin x}\cos x$

   e. $f'(x) = ex^{e-1}$ f. $f'(x) = \dfrac{2x-x^2}{e^x}$

   g. $f'(x) = e^x \cos(e^x)$

   h. $f'(x) = e^x + e^x \ln(x^x) + e^x \ln x = e^x(1+\ln x + x\ln x)$

4. $\dfrac{2x}{e^{x^4}} - e^{-x^2}$

5. a. Since $e^{\cos u}$ is a continuous function of u for all real values of u, $\int_0^b e^{\cos u}\,du$ exists for all b, and therefore $\int_0^x e^{\cos u}\,du$ is defined for all $x \in \mathbb{R}$

   b. $G'(x) = e^{\cos x}$

6. $\dfrac{e^2-1}{2}$

7. a. $-\dfrac{1}{2e^{x^2}} + C$ b. $\sqrt{\ln x} + C$

   c. $\dfrac{1}{2}\ln(x^2-4) + C$ d. $\ln(e^x+1) + C$

   e. $\sin(e^x) + C$ f. $\dfrac{1}{3}e^{x^3}$

   g. $\ln 3 - \ln 2$ h. $2e^3 - 2e$

8. $e = \lim\limits_{n \to \infty}\left(1+\dfrac{1}{n}\right)^n$ 9. $e^{e^x} + C$

10. a. $f'(x) = e^{\sin x}\cos x$ b. $f'(x) = -(1+\ln x)\sin(x \ln x)$

    c. $f'(x) = \dfrac{2^{\ln x}\ln 2}{x}$ d. $f'(x) = 2x + x^x + 2^x \ln 2 + x^x \ln x$

    e. $f'(x) = \dfrac{4x^3}{1+x^4}$ f. $f'(x) = -\dfrac{\ln 10}{10^x}$

    g. $f'(x) = \sin^{x-1} x(x \cos x + \ln(\sin x)\sin x)$

    h. $f'(x) = -\dfrac{1}{x^2}$

Chapter 7 Answers

g. $f'(x) = \sin^{x-1} x (x \cos x + \ln(\sin x) \sin x)$

h. $f'(x) = -\dfrac{1}{x^2}$

11. $\dfrac{dy}{dx} = \dfrac{e^x}{\sqrt{1-e^{2x}}}$

12.

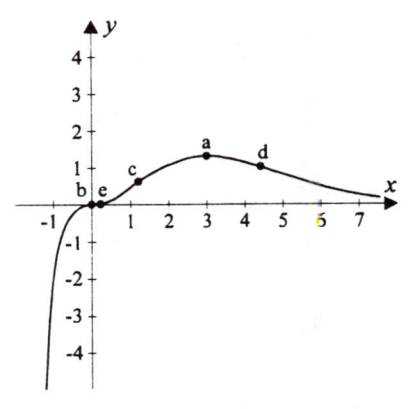

maximum at a
inflection points at b, c, d
maximum curvature at e
asymptote $y = 0$

13. $y(x) = -\ln(C - x)$

14. The derivatives of the left-hand and right-hand expressions are the same: $(\ln u)^2$. Because the left-hand and right-hand expressions agree at $u = 1$, they are therefore equal for all $u \geq 1$.

15.

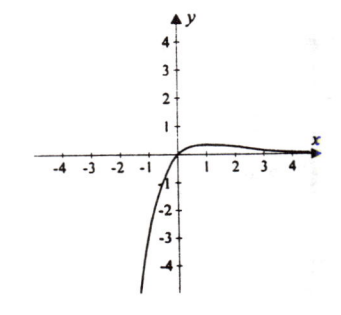

16.

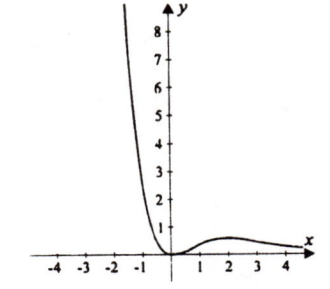

193

Chapter 7 Answers

2.   a. $f'(x) = 2x^{\ln x - 1} \ln x$
       b. $f'(x) = x^{\sin x - 1}(x \cos x \ln x + \sin x)$
       c. $f'(x) = \dfrac{1}{x \ln 10}$
       d. $f'(x) = \sin^{x-1}(x)(x \cos x + \ln(\sin x) \sin x)$

3. $\dfrac{dy}{dx} = \dfrac{2\sin 2x + y e^{xy}}{1 - x e^{xy}}$ 4. $\dfrac{1}{\ln 2}$

5. $\dfrac{3\pi}{2 \ln 2}$ 6. $\int_0^3 \sqrt{1 + (2^x \ln 2)^2}\, dx$

7.   a. $f'(x) = 3 \cdot 77^{x^3} x^2 \ln 77$ b. $(10^{\sin x} \cos x) \ln 10$
       c. $f'(x) = \dfrac{2^{\ln x} \ln 2}{x}$ d. $f'(x) = -\dfrac{\ln 2}{x(\ln x)^2}$
       e. $f'(x) = \dfrac{1}{x \ln 2 \ln x}$ f. $f'(x) = \ln 2$

8.   a. $\dfrac{6^x}{\ln 6} + C$ b. $\dfrac{10^{\ln x}}{\ln 10} + C$
       c. $\dfrac{1}{4 \ln 2}$ d. $\dfrac{24}{125 \ln 5}$ $f'(x) = \dfrac{2^{\ln x} \ln 2}{x}$

Section 7.5

1.   ≈105 years   2. $y(x) = \dfrac{2x}{x+2}$

3.   ≈15,767 years old in 1959. Probable date, 13,808 B.C.

4.   a. $x(t) = 10^7 e^{.3466 t}$ b.   19.9 hours

5. $P(t) = P_0 e^{.08 t}$ 6.   About 33 days

7. $y = C e^{x^2/2}$ 8. $y = C e^{-x^3/3}$

Chapter 8 Answers

Chapter 8

Section 8.2

1. Using implicit differentiation
   $x = \sin y$
   $1 = (\cos y) y'$
   $y' = \dfrac{1}{\cos y}$

   From the drawing
   $\cos y = \sqrt{1-x^2}$, so $y' = \dfrac{1}{\sqrt{1-x^2}}$

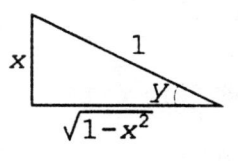

2. $\dfrac{dy}{dx} = \dfrac{1}{\sqrt{1-(\ln x)^2}} \cdot \dfrac{1}{x}$

3. Low estimate:: $\dfrac{2449}{3400} \approx .720294$,
   High Estimate: $\dfrac{1437}{1700} \approx .845294$

4. $F'(x) = \arcsin\sqrt{x}$

5. a. $g'(x) = \dfrac{3x^2}{\sqrt{1-x^6}}$ b. $g'(x) = \dfrac{\sec x \tan x}{1+\sec^2 x}$

   c. $g'(x) = \dfrac{1}{\arctan x \,(1+x^2)}$ d. $g'(x) = -\dfrac{1}{x\sqrt{x^2-1}}$

   e. $g'(x) = \dfrac{2e^{2x}}{1+e^{4x}}$ f. $g'(x) = \dfrac{1}{e^x\sqrt{1-e^{-2x}}}$

6. $\dfrac{\pi^2}{4}$

7. a. $\dfrac{\sqrt{e^{4x}-1}}{2e^{2x}} + C$ b. $\arctan(e^x) + C$

   c. $\dfrac{1}{6}\arctan\left(\dfrac{3x}{2}\right) + C$ d. $\dfrac{\sqrt{6}}{6}\arctan\left(\sqrt{\dfrac{3}{2}}x\right) + C$

   e. $\arcsin\dfrac{4}{5} - \arcsin\dfrac{3}{5}$ f. $\dfrac{\pi}{2}$

Chapter 8 Answers

Sections 8.3 and 8.4

1. 1
2. 4/3
3. 1
4. 0
5. 1/2
6. −1/12
7. 0
8. 9/8
9. 0
10. 0
11. −1/2
12. −∞
13. 1/e
14. 0
15. 1
16. ∞
17. $1/e^2$
18. 2

Section 8.5

1. $\dfrac{d}{dx}\sinh^{-1} x = \dfrac{1}{\sqrt{1+x^2}}$

   $\dfrac{d}{dx}\ln(x+(x^2+1)^{1/2}) = \dfrac{1}{x+(x^2+1)^{1/2}}\left(1+\dfrac{1}{2}(x^2+1)^{-1/2}(2x)\right) = \dfrac{1}{\sqrt{1+x^2}}$

   Hence the two functions differ by a constant.
   We can write $\sinh^{-1} x = \ln(x+(x^2+1)^{1/2}) + C$
   Now, substituting 0 for x in the above equation, we obtain
   $\sinh^{-1}(0) = \ln(0+(0+1)^{1/2}) + C$, or $0 = 0 + C$. ∴ $C = 0$ and the two functions are identical.

2. $\dfrac{3}{4}$

3.
   a. $f'(x) = \tanh x$
   b. $f'(x) = \dfrac{x^2-1}{2x^2}$
   c. $f'(x) = \dfrac{e^x}{\sqrt{1+e^{2x}}}$
   d. $f'(x) = \dfrac{1}{\sqrt{1+x^2}\,\operatorname{arcsinh} x}$
   e. $f'(x) = \dfrac{x}{\sqrt{x^2+1}}$
   f. $f'(x) = \dfrac{\cos x}{1-\sin^2 x} = \sec x$

4.
   a. $\dfrac{\sinh 2x}{2} + C$
   b. $\dfrac{\sinh^7 x}{7} + C$
   c. $\ln|\sinh x| + C$
   d. $\arcsin(\sinh x) + C$
   e. $\dfrac{\sinh^3 x}{3} + C$
   f. $2\cosh\sqrt{x} + C$

Chapter 9 Answers

Chapter 9

Sections 9.2-9.7

1. $2 - \dfrac{5}{e}$

2. $-\dfrac{(x^2+2)\sqrt{1-x^2}}{3} + C$

3. $2\ln|x-1| - 2\ln|x+1| + C$

4. $\arcsin x + \sqrt{1-x^2} + C$

5. $-\dfrac{1}{16}x^4 + \dfrac{x^4 \ln|x|}{4} + C$

6. $\sqrt{4-x^2}\left(\dfrac{x^4}{5} - \dfrac{4x^2}{15} - \dfrac{32}{15}\right) + C$

7. $\ln|x^2+4x+5| - \arctan(2+x) + \dfrac{3}{x} + C$

8. $\dfrac{1}{8}\arctan\left(\dfrac{x^2}{4}\right) + C$

9. $-\sqrt{1-x^2} + C$

10. $-\dfrac{(x+1)}{e^x} + C$

11. $2\arctan x + \ln|x-1| - \ln|x+1| + C$

12. $\dfrac{17}{324}e^{18} + \dfrac{1}{324}$

13. $\dfrac{3}{2x^2} + \ln|x| + 4\ln|x+1| + C$

14. $\sqrt{x^2+1}\left(-\dfrac{1}{3x^3} - \dfrac{1}{3x}\right) + C$

15. $\dfrac{1}{3}\cos^3 x - \cos x + C$

16. $\dfrac{1}{8}x - \dfrac{\sin 4x}{32} + C$

17. $\ln|\cos x| + x\tan x + C$

18. $3\ln|x| - 5\arctan x - \dfrac{5}{x} - \dfrac{3}{2}\ln|1+x^2| + C$

19. $\dfrac{1}{2}\sec^2 x + \ln|\cos x| + C$

20. $\dfrac{\pi}{6}$

21. $(4+x)\ln|x+4| - x + C$

22. $\sqrt{x^2+1}\,\dfrac{(x^2-2)}{3}$

23. $\arctan\left(\dfrac{x}{2}\right) + \ln|x-2| + \dfrac{1}{2}\ln|x^2+4| + C$

24. $\dfrac{2}{5}\sqrt{1-x}\left(x^2 - \dfrac{x}{3} - \dfrac{2}{3}\right) + C$

25. $\dfrac{1}{9} + \dfrac{2}{9}e^3$

Chapter 9 Answers

26. $\frac{x}{2}\cos(\ln|x|) + \frac{x}{2}\sin(\ln|x|) + C$

27. $\frac{1}{5}\sec^5 u - \frac{1}{3}\sec^3 u + C$

28. $\sqrt{x^2+4}\left(1 + \frac{4}{x^2+4}\right) + C$

29. $\frac{1}{4}x^4 - \frac{1}{x} + C$

30. $\frac{16}{15}$

31. $-\frac{1}{4x^4(x^2+1)^2} + C$

32. $8/3$

33. $\sqrt{10} - 1$

34. $348/5$

35. $\frac{9\pi}{4}$

36. $x\arctan x - \frac{1}{2}\ln(x^2+1) + C$

37. $\sqrt{17} - \sqrt{2}$

38. $-\frac{\pi}{12}$

39. $\frac{3}{4} + \frac{\ln 2}{2}$

40. $\sqrt{x^2-16} + C$

41. $\frac{\pi}{32}$

42. $\frac{1}{2}x^2 \arctan\sqrt{x} - \frac{1}{2}\arctan\sqrt{x} - \frac{\sqrt{x}}{2} - \frac{x^{3/2}}{6} + C$

43. $2\sqrt{1+\cos x}\,\tan\frac{x}{2} + C$

44. $x - \ln|e^x + 1| + C$

45. $8/15$

46. $\frac{1}{2}\arcsin(2x+1) + C$

47. $\frac{1}{2}\ln|x| - \frac{1}{2}\ln|x+2| + C$

48. $\operatorname{arcsinh} x + C = \ln|x + \sqrt{x^2+1}| + C$

49. $\frac{3}{2}\ln|x-1| - \ln|x| + \frac{1}{2}\ln|x+1| + C$

50. $\frac{\pi}{4}$

51. $2\arctan x + x\ln|x^2+1| - 2x + C$

Chapter 9 Answers

52. $\sqrt{x^2+9}+C$

53. $232/5$

54. $2\sqrt{e^x+1}-2\operatorname{arctanh}\sqrt{e^x+1}+C$

55. $-\arcsin(1-x)+C$

56. $24x-24x\ln|x|+12x(\ln|x|)^2-4x(\ln|x|)^3+x(\ln|x|)^4+C$

57. $-\arcsin\left(\dfrac{1-x}{2}\right)+C$

58. $-\dfrac{1}{4}\arctan(x^{-4})+C$

59. $\dfrac{1}{2}x-\dfrac{1}{12}\sin 6x+C$

60. $\dfrac{1}{6}\sec^6 x-\dfrac{1}{4}\sec^4 x+C$

61. $\ln|x^2+1|+\ln|x|+5\arctan x+\dfrac{2}{x}+C$

62. $\sqrt{1+\sqrt{x}}\left(\dfrac{4}{5}x+\dfrac{4}{15}\sqrt{x}-\dfrac{8}{15}\right)+C$

63. $\dfrac{2}{x}+\ln|x|+\ln(x^2+1)+5\arctan x+C$

64. $\ln|\cosh x|+C$

65. $\dfrac{1}{3}\arctan\left(\dfrac{x+2}{3}\right)+C$

66. $\dfrac{1}{4}x^4\ln|x|-\dfrac{1}{16}x^4+C$

67. $\dfrac{1}{4}x^2-\dfrac{1}{2}x^2\ln|x|+\dfrac{1}{2}x^2(\ln|x|)^2+C$

68. $\dfrac{\sin x}{2e^x}-\dfrac{\cos x}{2e^x}+C$

69. $\dfrac{e^6}{3}-\dfrac{e^3}{3}$

70. $\dfrac{\pi}{2}$

71. $\arctan(x+2)+C$

72. $\dfrac{2}{x+2}+\ln|x+2|+C$

73. $\dfrac{1}{2}\arctan\left(\dfrac{x}{2}\right)-3\ln|x+1|+2\ln|x^2+4|+C$

74. $-\cot x-\dfrac{1}{3}\cot^3 x+C$

75. $-\cos x+\dfrac{2}{3}\cos^3 x-\dfrac{1}{5}\cos^5 x+C$

76. $\sqrt{1-x^2}+x\arcsin x+C$

77. $-\dfrac{1}{2}\arcsin\left(\dfrac{1-2x}{2}\right)+C$

78. $\arctan(\ln 2)$

79. $\dfrac{1}{5}\sec^4 x\tan x+C$

Chapter 9 Answers

80. $\frac{3}{8}x - \frac{1}{4}\sin 2x + \frac{1}{32}\sin 4x + C$ 81. $\frac{1}{5}\sec^5 x - \frac{1}{3}\sec^3 x + C$

82. $\frac{1}{3}\ln\left|1 + 3\tan\frac{z}{2}\right| + C$ 83. $\frac{\ln 2}{2} - \frac{1}{4}$

84. $\left(x - \frac{1}{x}\right)\frac{\sqrt{x^4 - x^2}}{3} + C$ 85. $\frac{1}{2}\arctan x + \frac{x}{2(x^2 + 1)} + C$

86. $\frac{1}{2}x^2 \arcsin x - \frac{1}{4}\arcsin x + \frac{x}{4}\sqrt{1 - x^2} + C$

87. $x + \frac{1}{2}x^2 - 4\ln|x+1| + 9\ln|x+2| + C$

88. $\frac{1}{4}\ln|x+3| - \frac{1}{4}\ln|x-1| + C$ 89. $\frac{1 \cdot 3^{4/3}}{4}x^{4/3} + \frac{2 \cdot 3^{11/6}}{11}x^{11/6} + C$

90. $\ln|\ln x| + C$ 91. $\frac{1}{3}\sin^3 x - \frac{1}{5}\sin^5 x + C$

92. $\frac{e^2}{3}x^3 + C$ 93. $\frac{5\sqrt{5} - 9}{3}$

94. $x^3 \arctan x - \frac{1}{2}x^2 + \frac{\ln|x^2 + 1|}{2} + C$

95. $(x+4)^{1/3}\left(\frac{6}{7}x^2 + \frac{6}{7}x - \frac{72}{7}\right) + C$ 96. $\frac{\sin 2x}{4} - \frac{\sin 8x}{16} + C$

97. $\cos x + \ln|\csc x - \cot x| + C$

98. $6x^{1/6} - 3x^{1/3} + 2\sqrt{x} - 6\ln|1 + x^{1/6}| + C$

99. $\arcsin\left(\frac{v}{\sqrt{2}}\right) + \frac{v}{2}\sqrt{2 - v^2} + C$ 100. $3\arctan x + \ln|x| + C$

101. $\sqrt{x^2 + 1} + \ln|x| - \ln(1 + \sqrt{1 + x^2}) + C$

102. $\frac{1}{9}\cos 3x + \frac{x}{3}\sin 3x + C$

103. $\left(1 + \frac{x}{2}\right)\sqrt{5 - 4x - x^2} + \frac{9}{2}\arcsin\left(\frac{2+x}{3}\right) + C$

Chapter 9 Answers

104. $\frac{2}{27}x^3 - \frac{2}{9}x^3 \ln|x| + \frac{x^3}{3}(\ln|x|)^2 + C$

105. $-\frac{1}{x} - \arctan x + C$

106. $\left(\frac{x}{2} - \frac{1}{2}\right)\sqrt{x^2 - 2x} - \frac{\ln\left|x - 1 + \sqrt{x^2 - 2x}\right|}{2} + C$

107. $\sqrt{x^2 + 4}\left(\frac{1}{5}x^4 + \frac{4}{15}x^2 - \frac{32}{15}\right) + C$ 108. $2\sin\sqrt{x} - 2\sqrt{x}\cos\sqrt{x} + C$

Section 9.8

1. 1   2. e   3. ∞   4. 2

5. π   6. 2   7. 1/2   8. ln 3

9. π/4   10. 1/18   11. 1   12. 3

13. ∞   14. 10   15. $\frac{\pi^2}{2}$

16. $I = \int_0^\infty \sin x\, dx = \lim_{N\to\infty}\int_0^N \sin x\, dx = \lim_{N\to\infty}(1 - \cos N)$
    since $\lim_{N\to\infty} \cos N$ does not exist, the integral diverges.

Chapter 10

Section 10.3

1. 2   2. $-6\sqrt{3} + 4\pi$

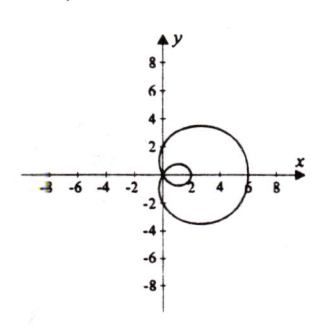

3. $\frac{3\pi}{2}$ 4. $\frac{\pi}{3}$ 5. $\sqrt{2}$ 6. $\frac{\pi}{2}$

Chapter 10 Answers

7. $\dfrac{9\pi}{2}$
8. $\dfrac{\pi}{32}$
9. By numerical integration, 4.84422

10. By numerical integration, 6.6825
11. 18π

12. 2
13. $\dfrac{3}{2}\pi$
14. 9π
15. 4π

16. $\dfrac{9\pi}{2}$

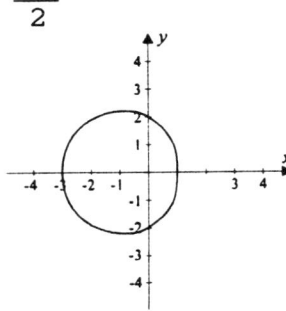

17. $\dfrac{39}{16}\pi^3$

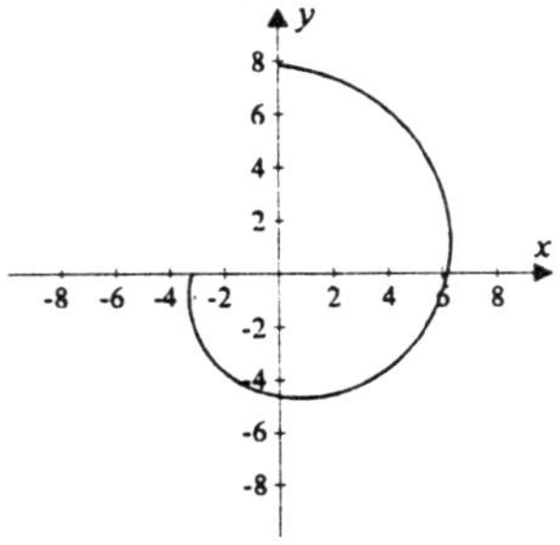

18. $\sqrt{2}$
19. $\dfrac{3\pi}{2}$

20. $\dfrac{3\pi}{8}$ 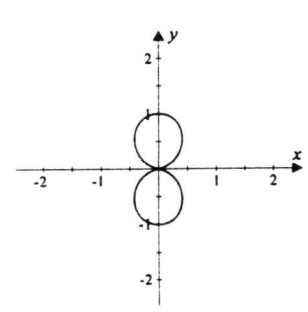
21. $\dfrac{\pi}{2}$

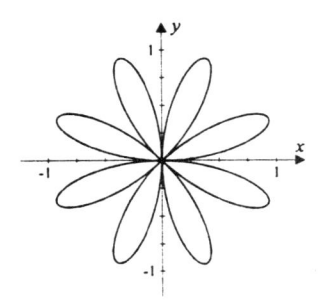

22. $\dfrac{\pi}{2}$
23. $\dfrac{\pi}{2}$
24. $\dfrac{\pi}{2}$

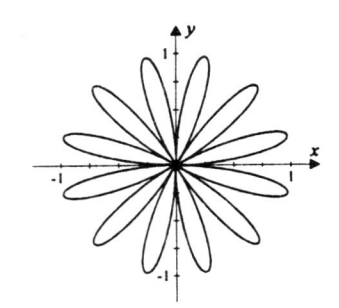

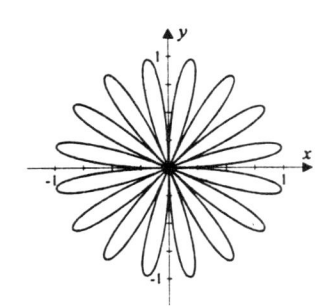

Sections 10.4 and 10.5

1. $\dfrac{16\pi}{15}$ 2. $\dfrac{8\pi}{3}$

3. $\displaystyle\int_0^{2\pi}\sqrt{a^2\sin^2 t + b^2\cos^2 t}\,dt$ 4. $x = t,\ y = t^2$

5. $\dfrac{3}{2}$ 6. $\dfrac{\pi(e^{2\pi}+1)}{5} \approx 337.088$

7. π 8. $8a$

9. $3\pi a^2$ 10. $5a^3\pi$

11. $6a^3\pi^3$ 12. $\dfrac{32a^3}{3}$

13. $16a^2\pi^2$ 14. $\dfrac{e^3-1}{3}$

15. $\dfrac{13\sqrt{13}-8}{27}$ 16. $\displaystyle\int_0^{\pi}\sqrt{2}\,e^t\,dt$

17. $\dfrac{3}{2}$

Chapter 11 Answers

Chapter 11

Part I

1. a. converges, 26   b. converges, e^{10}

   c. diverges   d. converges, -2

2. $\sum_{n=0}^{\infty} 2\left(\frac{3}{5}\right)^n$

3. a. $e^{1/2} - 1$ b. diverges

4. 1

5. $\sum_{n=0}^{\infty} \left(\frac{2}{3}\right)^n$

6. diverges, nth term test

7. a. converges, ratio test

   b. diverges, test for divergence

   c. converges, comparison test with a p-series

8. $\sum_{n=1}^{\infty} \frac{(-1)^n}{n}$

   The Alternating Series Test shows that this series converges. However, $\sum_{n=1}^{\infty} \left|\frac{(-1)^n}{n}\right|$ is the harmonic series, which we know to be divergent.

9. $\lim_{n \to \infty} a_n = \frac{2}{3}$

10. converges, 2

11. a. diverges   b. converges

    c. converges   d. diverges

    e. diverges   f. diverges

Chapter 11 Answers

12. $\frac{1}{2}(e-1)$

Part II

1. $\sum_{n=0}^{\infty} \frac{(-1)^n x^{2n+2}}{n+1}$, $[-1,1]$, $[-1,1]$, $[-1,1]$

2. 6

3. a. $[-2,4]$, $[-2,4]$ b. $[-1,1]$, $[-1,1]$

   c. $\left[\frac{1}{2}, \frac{3}{2}\right)$, $\left(\frac{1}{2}, \frac{3}{2}\right]$ d. $[-1,5)$, $(-1,5)$

4. $1 + \frac{x}{2} + \sum_{n=2}^{\infty} (-1)^{n-1} \frac{1 \cdot 3 \cdot 5 \cdot \ldots \cdot (2n-3)}{2^n n!} x^n$

   $\sqrt{2} \approx 1 + \frac{1}{2} - \frac{1}{2^2 \cdot 2!} + \frac{1 \cdot 3}{2^3 3!}$

5. $\sum_{n=0}^{\infty} \frac{(-1)^n x^n}{n!}$, $(-\infty, \infty)$ 6. $\sum_{n=0}^{\infty} \frac{(-1)^n x^{2n+1}}{(2n+1)!}$, $(-\infty, \infty)$

7. $\approx .00033$ 8. $\sum_{n=0}^{\infty} \frac{x^{2n}}{(2n)!}$ $(-\infty, \infty)$

9. $\sum_{n=0}^{\infty} \frac{(-1)^n x^{2n}}{4^n}$ $(-2, 2)$ 10. $\frac{3}{4}$

11. e^2 12. $\ln 2$

13. $1 + 4(x-1) + 6(x-1)^2 + 4(x-1)^3 + (x-1)^4$, $(-\infty, \infty)$

14. $\approx .0999998$ 15. $\approx .9999995$

16. $\approx .946083$ Error $\leq .0000003$

17. $17(e^{1/2} - 1)$

Chapter 11 Answers

18. $\sum_{n=0}^{\infty} \frac{2x^{2n+1}}{2n+1}$ $(-1, 1)$, yes, set $x = \frac{2}{3}$

19. $8 + 12(x-2) + 6(x-2)^2 + (x-2)^3$

20. $\sum_{n=0}^{\infty} \frac{(-1)^n 4^n x^{2n+1}}{(2n+1)!}$
21. $\frac{4}{15}$

22. $\sum_{n=0}^{\infty} \frac{(-1)^n x^{2n+1}}{2n+1}$ $[-1, 1]$
23. 8.3×10^{-8}

24. $x - \frac{1}{6}x^3 + \frac{1}{120}x^5$
25. $.999500$

26. $1 - x + \frac{x^2}{2} - \frac{x^3}{6} + \frac{x^4}{24}$
27. $.0198$

28. 1.4×10^{-9}
29. $4\ln 2 - 2$

30. $18 - 24\ln 2$
31. $4\pi - 18$

32. $\frac{1}{2}$
33. $\frac{\pi}{8}$

34. $\frac{1}{2}\ln 3 + \frac{1}{18}\pi\sqrt{3}$
35. $\frac{\pi}{8} + \frac{1}{4}\ln 2$

36. $\frac{1}{2}$
37. $\frac{1}{12}\pi\sqrt{3} + \frac{3}{4}\ln 3$

38. $\frac{1}{4}$
39. $\frac{11}{96}$

40. $\frac{11}{18}$
41. $-\frac{5}{9} + \frac{1}{3}\ln 4$

42. $\frac{7}{36}$
43. $-\frac{13}{36} + \frac{2}{3}\ln 2$

44. $\ln 2 - \frac{1}{2}$
45. $\frac{1}{48}$

46. $\frac{17}{36}$
47. $\frac{1}{4}$

Chapter 11 Answers

48. $\dfrac{1}{4}$

49. $-\dfrac{1}{4} + \dfrac{\pi}{4}$

50. $\dfrac{1}{4}$

51. $4\ln 2 - \dfrac{11}{4}$

52. $\dfrac{Q+3P}{4}$

53. $\dfrac{3}{2}e$

54. $\ln 2 - \dfrac{7}{24}$

55. $\dfrac{25}{48}$

Chapter 12

Section 12.1

1. Choose a vertex of the rhombus and let v_1, v_2 be the vectors from this vertex to the two closest vertices. Then $|v_1| = |v_2|$, equal to the length of one of the sides of the rhombus. The diagonals of the rhombus are $v_1 - v_2$ and $v_1 + v_2$. Now, $(v_1 - v_2) \cdot (v_1 + v_2) = v_1 \cdot v_1 - v_2 \cdot v_2 = |v_1|^2 - |v_2|^2 = 0$. Hence v_1 and v_2 are perpendicular.

2. Choose a vertex of the quadrilateral and let v_1, v_2 be the vectors from this vertex to the two closest vertices. v_1 and v_2 represent two of the sides of the quadrilateral and v_1 is not parallel to v_2. The remaining two sides of the quadrilateral are now given by αv_1 and βv_2. Further we have $v_1 + \beta v_2 = \alpha v_1 + v_2$ and therefore $(1-\alpha)v_1 = (1-\beta)v_2$. However since v_1 is not parallel to v_2 this implies $1-\alpha = 0 = 1-\beta$ and therefore $\alpha = 1 = \beta$.

3. Let v and w be the vectors given by the two noncolinear points of the parallelogram and the point of intersection of the diagonals. Then one of the diagonals is given by $v(1+\alpha)$ and the other by $w(1+\beta)$, where α and β are real numbers. However, from #2 we see that $w - v = \beta w - \alpha v$. Therefore $w(1-\beta) = v(1-\alpha)$ and since w is not parallel to v we have $1-\beta = 1-\alpha = 0$. So the diagonals are $2v$ and $2w$, and hence the diagonals bisect each other.

4. $\left(\dfrac{4}{5}, \dfrac{3}{5}\right)$

Chapter 12 Answers

5. a. $\sqrt{34}$ b. $-31\mathbf{j}$ c. -29

    d. 34 e. $-\dfrac{29}{\sqrt{53}}$ f. $-\dfrac{29}{\sqrt{1802}}$

    g. $\dfrac{3}{\sqrt{34}}\mathbf{i} - \dfrac{5}{\sqrt{34}}\mathbf{j}$

6. -6

7. $\mathbf{v} = \mathbf{u} + \mathbf{w}$, i.e. these vectors determine a triangle with whole-number length sides.

Sections 12.2 and 12.3

1. a. -3 b. $\sqrt{6}$ c. $\dfrac{1}{\sqrt{6}}\langle 1, 2, -1\rangle$

    d. $-\dfrac{1}{2}\sqrt{6}$ e. $-\dfrac{3}{2\sqrt{21}}$

    f. $\langle 7, -5, -5\rangle$ g. $\langle -7, 5, 5\rangle$

    h. $\dfrac{1}{\sqrt{99}}\langle 7, -5, -5\rangle$ i. $\sqrt{99}$

2. $60°$ 3. $90°$ 4. $4\mathbf{i} + 8\mathbf{j} - 30\mathbf{k}$

5. 11

6. $54.73561°$ if cube is 3 dimensional; in general, $\cos^{-1}\left(\dfrac{1}{\sqrt{n}}\right)$ where cube is n-dimensional.

7. $1/6$ 8. $4/3$

9. a. $\langle 12, -18, 13\rangle$ b. 16 c. $\dfrac{16}{5}$

    d. $\langle -37, -16, 12\rangle$ e. -118 f. $42.0595 \approx \sqrt{1769}$

    g. no, since $\mathbf{u} \cdot (\mathbf{v} \times \mathbf{w}) \neq 0$.

Chapter 12 Answers

10. $\frac{1}{\sqrt{117}}\langle -2, 8, 7\rangle$
11. $\frac{1}{2}\sqrt{318} \approx 8.91627725$

12. **u** is a scalar multiple of **v**.

13. By right-hand rule, **b** × **a** has opposite direction as **a** × **b**, and since area of parallelogram spanned by **a**, **b** is same as that spanned by **b**, **a**, |**a** × **b**| = |**b** × **a**| but opposite direction, so **a** × **b** = −**b** × **a**.

14. **a** = $\langle 1, 0, 0\rangle$ **b** = $\langle 1, 1, 0\rangle$ **c** = $\langle 0, 1, 0\rangle$

15. ≈35.26439°

16. a. $\langle 6, 4, 11\rangle$ b. 5   c. $\langle -17, -24, 18\rangle$
    d. $\langle 17, 24, -18\rangle$ e. 6/35

Section 12.4

1. $\left(\frac{11}{3}, \frac{2}{3}, 1\right)$ 2. $\left(-\frac{5}{61}, \frac{78}{61}, \frac{150}{61}\right)$ 3. 1

4. $2x + 3y + 6z = 0$ 5. $\sqrt{\frac{4}{125}} \approx .1788854$

6. $\sqrt{\frac{98}{25}} \approx 1.979899$ 7. $2x - y - z = 0$ 8. $-x + z = 2$

9. $-2x + z = -3$ 10. $\sqrt{5} = 2.236068$

11. Area of $\triangle PQR$ = 1/2 Area of parallelogram spanned by **PQ** = $\langle (x_1-x_0), (y_1-y_0)\rangle$ and **PR** = $\langle (x_2-x_0), (y_2-y_0)\rangle$ But Area of parallelogram is |**PW** × **PR**| = $|(x_1-x_0)(y_2-y_0) - (x_2-x_0)(y_1-y_0)|$ yielding result desired.

12. $\frac{x-1}{2} = \frac{y+1}{3} = \frac{z-2}{-3}$ 13. Both have direction vector $\langle 6, 3, 2\rangle$.

14. $-13x + 22y + 6z = -23$ 15. $\sqrt{\frac{689}{49}} \approx 3.7498299$

16. 3   17. $\frac{x-2}{2} = \frac{y}{2} = z+1$

Chapter 12 Answers

18. $-37x - 16y + 12z = 0$

19. $x + 2y + 3z = 2$

20. $\dfrac{x+1}{3} = -\dfrac{y-3}{4} = -\dfrac{z-7}{10}$

21. $\sqrt{\dfrac{9}{29}} \approx .557086$

22. $\sqrt{3} \approx 1.7320508$

23. a. $-17x - 24y + 18z = 0$ b. $\sqrt{1189} \approx 34.481879$

     c. $\dfrac{6}{5}$ d. 29

     e. $x - 1 = \dfrac{y+1}{2} = \dfrac{z-5}{2}$

24. They do not lie in a single plane.

25. $\sqrt{\dfrac{8}{19}} \approx .6488857$

26. $3x + y - z = -1$

27. $\begin{array}{l} x = 1 + 2t \\ y = -1 - t \\ z = 0 + 3t \end{array}$ or $\dfrac{x-1}{2} = \dfrac{y+1}{-1} = \dfrac{z}{3}$

28. 6

Sections 12.5 and 12.6

1. $\mathbf{a}_T = \dfrac{22}{49}\langle 6, 2, 3 \rangle$ $\mathbf{a}_N = \dfrac{6}{49}\langle -22, 9, 38 \rangle$

2. $\mathbf{a}_T = 0 \Leftrightarrow t = 0$ $\mathbf{a}_N \neq 0$ for all $t \in \mathbb{R}$

Chapter 12 Answers

3. $\mathbf{r}(t) = \langle 2\cos t, 2\sin t, t\rangle$
   $\mathbf{v}(t) = \langle -2\sin t, 2\cos t, 1\rangle$
   $\mathbf{a}(t) = \langle -2\cos t, -2\sin t, 0\rangle$

4. $\mathbf{r}(0) = \langle 0, 0, 1\rangle$
   $\mathbf{v}(0) = \langle 1, 1, 0\rangle$
   $\mathbf{a}(0) = \langle 0, 0, -1\rangle$

5. $k = \dfrac{1}{R}$ $a_T = 0$ $a_N = R$

6. $k = \dfrac{5}{169}$

7. $\mathbf{a} = 0\mathbf{T} + \dfrac{60}{13}\mathbf{N} = \dfrac{60}{13}[-\mathbf{i}\sin t + \mathbf{j}\cos t]$

8. $k = \dfrac{3}{25}$ $a_T = 0$ $a_N = 3$

9. $\dfrac{x-2}{2} = \dfrac{y-1}{2} = \dfrac{z-1}{1}$

10. $\dfrac{3}{2} + \dfrac{5}{8}\ln\dfrac{9}{5}$

11. $x + y = 1$

12. $k = \dfrac{\sqrt{2}}{18} \approx .0785674$

    $a_T = \dfrac{18}{\sqrt{3}} \approx 10.392305$

    $a_N = 6\sqrt{2} \approx 8.4852814$

13. $k = \dfrac{1}{2}$

14. $x + 2y + 3z = 6$

15. $k = \dfrac{4\pi^2}{1+4\pi^2} \approx .9752955$

    $\mathbf{T}(1) = \dfrac{1}{\sqrt{1+4\pi^2}}\langle 0, 2\pi, 1\rangle$

    $\mathbf{N}(1) = \langle -1, 0, 0\rangle$

16. $y = \left(\dfrac{144R^2 g}{\pi^2}\right)^{1/3}$

17. $k = \dfrac{8}{5}$ $a_T = 0$ $a_N = 8$

18. $x + 2y - z = 0$

19. $k = \dfrac{1}{9}$ $a_T = 2$ $a_N = 1$

20. $-2x - y + 2z = 1/3$

21. $v = $ speed $= 5$, $\mathbf{a}(t) = \langle -3\cos(t), -3\sin(t), 0\rangle$
    $a(t) = 3 \neq 0 = \dfrac{dv}{dt}$

211

Chapter 12   Answers

22. $\mathbf{v}(t) = \langle \cos(t), e^t, e^t(\cos(t) - \sin(t)) \rangle$
  $\mathbf{a}(t) = \langle -\sin(t), e^t, -2e^t \sin(t) \rangle$
  $k = \dfrac{\sqrt{2}}{3\sqrt{3}} \approx .2721655$

23. $\mathbf{a}(t) = \langle 0, 0, 32 \rangle$

24. a. If $\mathbf{B} \cdot \mathbf{T} = 0$ then $\dfrac{d}{ds}(\mathbf{B} \cdot \mathbf{T}) = 0 \Rightarrow$
   $\dfrac{d\mathbf{B}}{ds} \cdot \mathbf{T} + \mathbf{B} \cdot \dfrac{d\mathbf{T}}{ds} = 0$. But $\mathbf{B} \cdot \dfrac{d\mathbf{T}}{ds} = (\mathbf{T} \times \mathbf{N}) \cdot \dfrac{d\mathbf{T}}{ds}$
   $= \mathbf{T} \cdot \left(\mathbf{N} \times \dfrac{d\mathbf{T}}{ds} \right)$ and $\mathbf{N} \times \dfrac{d\mathbf{T}}{ds} = \mathbf{0} \therefore \dfrac{d\mathbf{B}}{ds} \cdot \mathbf{T} = 0$
   $\Rightarrow \dfrac{d\mathbf{B}}{ds} \perp \mathbf{T}$.

  b. If $\mathbf{B} \cdot \mathbf{B} = 1$ then $\dfrac{d\mathbf{B}}{ds} \cdot \mathbf{B} + \mathbf{B} \cdot \dfrac{d\mathbf{B}}{ds} = 0 \Rightarrow$
   $\dfrac{d\mathbf{B}}{ds} \cdot \mathbf{B} = -\mathbf{B} \cdot \dfrac{d\mathbf{B}}{ds}$. However, $\mathbf{a} \cdot \mathbf{b} = \mathbf{b} \cdot \mathbf{a} \Rightarrow$
   $\dfrac{d\mathbf{B}}{ds} \cdot \mathbf{B} = -\dfrac{d\mathbf{B}}{ds} \cdot \mathbf{B} \therefore \dfrac{d\mathbf{B}}{ds} \cdot \mathbf{B} = 0 \Rightarrow \dfrac{d\mathbf{B}}{ds} \perp \mathbf{B}$.

25. If $\mathbf{v} \cdot \mathbf{v} = c$ then $\dfrac{d}{dt}(\mathbf{v} \cdot \mathbf{v}) = 0 \Rightarrow \dfrac{d\mathbf{v}}{dt} \cdot \mathbf{v} + \mathbf{v} \cdot \dfrac{d\mathbf{v}}{dt} = 0$.
  However, $\mathbf{a} = \dfrac{d\mathbf{v}}{dt}$, hence $\mathbf{a} \cdot \mathbf{v} = -\mathbf{v} \cdot \mathbf{a} = -\mathbf{a} \cdot \mathbf{v} \Rightarrow \mathbf{a} \cdot \mathbf{v} = 0$
  $\therefore \mathbf{a} \perp \mathbf{v}$.

26. $k = 3\sqrt{3}$

Chapter 13

Sections 13.4 and 13.5

1. $\dfrac{\partial z}{\partial x} = \dfrac{y^3}{(x^2+y^2)^{3/2}}$ $\dfrac{\partial z}{\partial y} = \dfrac{x^3}{(x^2+y^2)^{3/2}}$

2. $\dfrac{\partial^2 z}{\partial x^2} = 2e^y$ $\dfrac{\partial^2 z}{\partial y^2} = x^2 e^y$ $\dfrac{\partial^2 z}{\partial x \partial y} = 2x e^y$

3. $\dfrac{\partial z}{\partial x} = \dfrac{-y}{x^2+y^2}$ $\dfrac{\partial z}{\partial y} = \dfrac{x}{x^2+y^2}$

  Discontinuous at $(0, 0)$

Chapter 13 Answers

4. $g(x, y) = \cos x \sin y$

    $\dfrac{\partial g}{\partial x} = -\sin x \sin y;$ $\qquad \dfrac{\partial g}{\partial y} = \cos x \cos y$

    $\dfrac{\partial^2 g}{\partial y \partial x} = -\sin x \cos y;$ $\qquad \dfrac{\partial^2 g}{\partial x \partial y} = -\sin x \cos y \quad$ Hence $g_{xy} = g_{yx}$.

5. False. e.g. $f(x, y) = \dfrac{xy}{x^2 + y^2} \quad (x, y) \neq (0, 0)$
    $= 0 \quad (x, y) = (0, 0)$

    Both partial derivatives exist at (0, 0) and are both equal to 0 but the function is discontinuous at (0, 0).

6. $f_x(x, y) = y \sin(xy) + xy^2 \cos(xy)$
   $f_y(x, y) = x \sin(xy) + x^2 y \cos(xy)$

7. $g_{xyz} = 30xy^2 z^4 = g_{zyx}$

8. $f_x = 4x^3 e^{-y}$ $\qquad f_y = -x^4 e^{-y}$
   $f_{xx} = 12x^2 e^{-y}$ $\qquad f_{yy} = x^4 e^{-y}$
   $f_{xy} = -4x^3 e^{-y}$ $\qquad f_{yx} = -4x^3 e^{-y}$

9. $f_x = ye^{xy} + xy^2 e^{xy};$ $\qquad f_y = xe^{xy} + x^2 e^{xy}$
   $f_{xx} = 2y^2 e^{xy} + xy^3 e^{xy};$ $\qquad f_{yy} = 2x^2 e^{xy} + x^3 y e^{xy}$
   $f_{xy} = e^{xy} + 3xye^{xy} + x^2 y^2 e^{xy} = f_{yx}$

10. $z = x^3 y - y^2 x + xy - y + C$

11. $h(x, y, z) = x^2 yz - xyz^2 + xy - z + C$

12. $z = f(x, y) = x^3 - 3e^x \cos y + y^4 + C$

13. $192\sqrt{3}$ $\qquad$ 14. minimum $(1, 1)$, saddle point at $\left(-\dfrac{1}{3}, -\dfrac{1}{3}\right)$

15. Saddle point at $(1, 1)$. $\qquad$ 16. $2x + 4y - z = 5$ $\qquad$ 17. 0

18. Base is a square of side $10 \cdot 5^{2/3}$
    Height is $4 \cdot 5^{2/3}$

19. $40^3 = 64,000$ $\qquad\qquad$ 20. Minimum at $\left(\dfrac{1}{2}, -1\right)$

Chapter 13 Answers

21. $\dfrac{x^2}{12} + \dfrac{y^2}{3} + \dfrac{z^2}{27} = 1$ 22. $\dfrac{16}{\sqrt{3}}$ 23. 4/3

24. Base is 2 × 2 and height 3. Minimum cost = 36

25. $k = 2/3$

Section 13.6 and 13.7

1. $z_x = -2/3$

2. a. 0.2206 b. 0.2

3. a. $f(x, y) = x^3 y^2$ $\quad \dfrac{\partial f}{\partial y} = 2x^3 y$

   $\dfrac{d}{dy}\int_a^b x^3 y^2 \, dx = \dfrac{b^4 - a^4}{2} y$

   $\int_a^b \dfrac{\partial f}{\partial y} \, dx = \dfrac{(b^4 - a^4)}{2} y$

   b. $f = e^{xy}$

   $\dfrac{d}{dy}\int_a^b f \, dx = \dfrac{be^{by}}{y} - \dfrac{ae^{ay}}{y} - \dfrac{1}{y^2}(e^{by} - e^{ay})$

   $\int_a^b \dfrac{\partial}{\partial y} e^{xy} \, dx = \int_a^b xe^{xy} \, dx = \dfrac{be^{by}}{y} - \dfrac{ae^{ay}}{y} - \dfrac{1}{y^2}(e^{by} - e^{ay})$

4. 5.0032 5. 193.9

6. $w = f(ay-x, x-ay)$ $\qquad$ Let $u = ay-x;\; v = x-ay$

   $\dfrac{\partial w}{\partial x} = \dfrac{\partial f}{\partial u}\dfrac{\partial u}{\partial x} + \dfrac{\partial f}{\partial v}\dfrac{\partial v}{\partial x} = -1\dfrac{\partial f}{\partial u} + 1\dfrac{\partial f}{\partial v}$

   $\dfrac{\partial w}{\partial y} = \dfrac{\partial f}{\partial u}\dfrac{\partial u}{\partial y} + \dfrac{\partial f}{\partial v}\dfrac{\partial v}{\partial y} = a\dfrac{\partial f}{\partial u} - a\dfrac{\partial f}{\partial v}$

   $a\dfrac{\partial w}{\partial x} + \dfrac{\partial w}{\partial y} = 0$

7. $w = f(u) + g(v)$ $\qquad u = x-at,\; v = x+at$
   $w_x = f_u \cdot u_x + g_v \cdot v_x$ $\qquad u_x = 1 \quad v_x = 1$
   $\quad = f_u + g_v$ $\qquad u_t = -a \quad v_t = a$
   $w_{xx} = f_{uu} + g_{vv}$
   $w_t = f_u \cdot (-a) + g_v \cdot a$

Chapter 13 Answers

$$w_{tt} = a^2 f_{uu} + a^2 g_{vv}$$
$$\therefore w_{tt} = a^2 w_{xx}$$

8. 4.99804

9. $\dfrac{\partial^2 w}{\partial u^2} = \dfrac{\partial^2 f}{\partial x^2} + 2\dfrac{\partial^2 f}{\partial x \partial y} + \dfrac{\partial^2 f}{\partial y^2} + \dfrac{\partial^2 g}{\partial x^2} + 2\dfrac{\partial^2 g}{\partial x \partial y} + \dfrac{\partial^2 g}{\partial y^2}$

10. $\dfrac{16893}{1300} \approx 12.9946154$

11. $-.014$

12. $\dfrac{\partial z}{\partial x} = -\left(\dfrac{z}{x}\right)^{2/3}$

Section 13.8

1. $8(x-2) - 2(y-1) - (z-7) = 0$

2. Increasing at a maximum rate in the direction of $-2\mathbf{i} + 3\mathbf{j} - 6\mathbf{k}$, maximum rate is 7.

3.
   a. $3\mathbf{i} + 2\mathbf{j}$; maximum value is $\sqrt{13}$
   b. $\dfrac{(3\mathbf{i} + 2\mathbf{j})}{\sqrt{13}}$
   c. $\dfrac{-5\sqrt{2}}{2}$
   d. $x^3 y^2 = 1$ is the level curve.
   e. slope $= -3/2$
   f. $\nabla f = 3\mathbf{i} + 2\mathbf{j}$. $2\mathbf{i} - 3\mathbf{j}$ is parallel to the tangent at $(1, 1)$. Hence the two are perpendicular.

4. $\dfrac{2}{3}\mathbf{i} + \dfrac{2}{3}\mathbf{j} - \dfrac{1}{3}\mathbf{k}$ or its negative

5. f is increasing most rapidly in the direction
$\dfrac{\mathbf{i}}{\sqrt{14}} - \dfrac{3\mathbf{j}}{\sqrt{14}} - \dfrac{2\mathbf{k}}{\sqrt{14}}$; $2\sqrt{14}$; $\dfrac{4}{3}\mathbf{i} - 4\mathbf{j} - \dfrac{4}{3}\mathbf{k}$

6. $10(x-5) - 16(y-2) - (z-9) = 0$

7. maximum rate $\sqrt{94}$ in the direction

$\dfrac{6}{\sqrt{94}}\mathbf{i} - \dfrac{3}{\sqrt{94}}\mathbf{j} + \dfrac{7}{\sqrt{94}}\mathbf{k}$

8. Increasing most rapidly in the direction $\dfrac{2}{3}\mathbf{i} + \dfrac{1}{3}\mathbf{j} - \dfrac{2}{3}\mathbf{k}$. The maximum rate is 3.

Chapter 13 Answers

9. $8(x-1) - 2(y-1) - (z-3) = 0$

10. $12x - 8y - z = 8$

11. $x + 4y + 4z = 9$

12. $(2, 2, -1), (-2, -2, 1)$

13. $4x - 3y - z = \dfrac{11}{4}$

14. $x = \dfrac{(a^2 + b^2)}{2a}$

15. $\dfrac{\partial}{\partial x}(fg) = \dfrac{\partial f}{\partial x} g + f \dfrac{\partial g}{\partial x}$

$\dfrac{\partial}{\partial y}(fg) = \dfrac{\partial f}{\partial y} g + f \dfrac{\partial g}{\partial y}$

$\nabla(fg) = \left\langle \dfrac{\partial(fg)}{\partial x}, \dfrac{\partial(fg)}{\partial y} \right\rangle = \left\langle \dfrac{\partial f}{\partial x} g, \dfrac{\partial f}{\partial y} g \right\rangle + \left\langle f \dfrac{\partial g}{\partial x}, f \dfrac{\partial g}{\partial y} \right\rangle = f\nabla g + g\nabla f$

Section 13.9

1. Maximum value $3/2$ at $\left(\dfrac{1}{2}, -\dfrac{1}{2}, \dfrac{1}{2}\right)$

2. One tangent vector is $6\mathbf{i} + 3\mathbf{j} - 2\mathbf{k}$

3. $\dfrac{27}{8} + \dfrac{7}{4}\sqrt{7}$

4. $13, -13$

5. base $= (256)^{1/3}$ in², height $= (16{,}384)^{1/3}$ in

6. Minimum: zero, on the three circles:
   $x = 0, \; y^2 + z^2 = 3$
   $y = 0, \; x^2 + z^2 = 3$
   $z = 0, \; x^2 + y^2 = 3$
   Maximum: 1, at all eight points where $x^2 = y^2 = z^2 = 1$.

7. Minimum $= 3$, no Maximum

8. $2\pi R^2$

9. $(2, \sqrt{2}, \sqrt{2}), (2, -\sqrt{2}, -\sqrt{2})$

10. $(0, 0, 1)$

11. $\dfrac{32\pi}{81} R^3$

12. $\dfrac{4\pi R^2 H}{81}$

13. Maximum area $= \dfrac{3600}{\pi}$
    Minimum area $= \dfrac{1200}{\pi}$

Chapter 13 Answers

14. One sphere with radius $\sqrt[3]{750}$ minimizes the area, three spheres with radius $\sqrt[3]{250}$ maximizes area.

15. An equilateral triangle with area $\frac{3\sqrt{3}}{4}R^2$

16. $E_{min} = \frac{R^2}{2}$ $E_{max} = -R^2$ 17. $2R$

18. Closest points $\left(\frac{2}{\sqrt{3}}, -\frac{2}{\sqrt{3}}\right)$, $\left(-\frac{2}{\sqrt{3}}, \frac{2}{\sqrt{3}}\right)$
    Farthest points $(2, 2)$, $(-2, -2)$

19. $\left(0, \frac{1}{2}, 1\right)$ 20. $\left(0, 0, \pm\frac{3}{2}\right)$ 21. $\left(\frac{4}{3}, \pm\frac{\sqrt{5}}{3}\right)$

22. Maximum Perimeter = $3\sqrt{3}R$ (equilateral triangle)

    Minimum Perimeter = $4R$ (trivial case where one side of the triangle is 0)

23. Minimum = -2, Maximum = 2

24. Maximum = 15, Minimum = -15

25. $V_{max} = 500\sqrt{6}$ 26. Maximum = 3

27. Maximum = 1, Minimum = -1

28. $(1, 0, 0)$, $(-1, 0, 0)$, $(0, 1, 0)$, $(0, -1, 0)$

29. $E_{max} = 7$, $E_{min} = -7$ 30. No   31. Maximum = 9

32. Maximum = 9

Section 13.10

1. $(0, 0)$ is a saddle point, Minima at $(-1, 1)$, $(1, -1)$

2. $(0, 0)$ is a saddle point, Maxima at $(1, 1)$, $(-1, -1)$

3. No extrema; $(0, 0)$ is a saddle point

4. Local minimum at $(0, 0)$, local maximum at $(-2/3, 2/3)$

Chapter 13 Answers

5. $(1, 1)$ minimum.
   $\left(-\frac{1}{3}, -\frac{1}{3}\right)$ is a saddle point

6. $\left(\frac{14}{3}, -\frac{4}{3}\right)$ is a saddle point. No extrema.

7. $(0, 0)$ is a saddle point. No extrema.

8. $\left(-1, -\frac{2}{3}\right)$ minimum.

9. $(1, 1)$ is a local minimum, $(0, 0)$ is a saddle point

10. $(0, 0)$ is a saddle point

11. $(0, 0)$ minimum

12. $(0, 0)$ is a saddle point, $(2, -2)$ minimum

Chapter 14

Sections 14.1, 14.2, and 14.3

1. $1 - \frac{1}{e}$ or $1 - e^{-1}$

2. $\int_0^{\pi/2} \left(\int_0^x \frac{\sin x}{x} dy \right) dx = 1$

3. $2/3$

4. $\ln(2)$

5. $\int_0^1 \int_0^x x^2 y \, dy \, dx = 1/10$

6. $4/3$

7. $\int_0^1 \int_0^x x e^y \, dy \, dx = 1/2$

8. $\int_0^1 \int_y^1 x^2 y^2 \, dx \, dy = 1/18$

9. $\int_0^2 \int_{2x}^{x^2} e^x \cos y \, dy \, dx$

10. $\int_0^1 \int_0^y (y^2 - x^2) \, dx \, dy = 1/6$

11. $3/20$

12. $\frac{1}{2} e - \frac{1}{2}$

13. $\int_0^1 \int_{y^3}^{\sqrt{y}} (x+y) \, dx \, dy = \frac{53}{140}$

14. $\int_{-1}^1 \int_0^{\sqrt{1-x^2}} x^3 y^3 \, dy \, dx = 0$

15. $1/12$

Chapter 14 Answers

16. The base of the solid is the area bounded by the x axis and the parabola $y = 4-x^2$ and the height at (x, y) is ye^x. i.e.
$$\left.\begin{array}{l} -2 \le x \le 2 \\ 0 \le y \le 4-x^2 \\ 0 \le z \le ye^x \end{array}\right\}$$

17. 1/60

18. f is continuous on $\mathbb{R}$.

Section 14.4

1. $\frac{1}{5}a^5\pi$

2. $-\frac{1}{3} + \frac{\pi}{4}$

3. π

4. $\frac{\pi}{2}$

5. $\pi \ln(1+a^2)$

6. $\frac{\pi}{4}$

7. $\frac{\pi}{128}$

8. $\int_0^1 \int_0^{\pi/2} \frac{r}{1+r^2} d\theta\, dr = \frac{1}{4} \ln 2\pi$

9. $\int_0^1 \int_0^{2\pi} \frac{r^3 \sin 2\theta}{(1+r^4)} d\theta\, dr$

10. $\frac{4\pi}{5}$

11. $\frac{\pi}{2}$

12. $\pi(e^4 - 1)$

13. 6π

14. $\int_{\theta=0}^{2\pi} \int_{r=0}^{1} r^3 \, dr\, d\theta = \frac{\pi}{2}$

15. $\int_0^2 \int_{-\sqrt{4-y^2}}^{\sqrt{4-y^2}} (x+y) \, dx\, dy$

Sections 14.6 and 14.7

1. $\frac{64\pi}{3}$

2. $\int_0^H \int_{-R}^{R} \int_{-\sqrt{R^2-x^2}}^{\sqrt{R^2-x^2}} \frac{\sqrt{x^2+y^2}}{1+x^2+y^2} \, dy\, dx\, dz$

3. $\frac{8\pi a^3}{3}$

4. $\frac{3}{4}R$

5. $\frac{6R}{5}$

6. $\frac{4}{3}\pi(8 - 3^{3/2})$

219

Chapter 14 Answers

7. $\dfrac{16}{3\sqrt{3}}$

8. $\dfrac{2}{3}\pi - \dfrac{8}{9}$

9. 2π

10. Changing to cylindrical coordinates yields $\dfrac{16}{3}\pi - \dfrac{64}{9}$

Applications of Multiple Integrals

1. $\left(\dfrac{16}{3\pi}, \dfrac{16}{3\pi}\right)$

2. $\left(\dfrac{5}{7}, \dfrac{10}{33}\right)$

3. $\dfrac{3}{10}MR^2$

4. $\left(0, 0, \dfrac{3(b^4-a^4)}{8(b^3-a^3)}\right)$

5. $\bar{x} = \dfrac{\int_1^2 x^4\sqrt{1+9x^4}\,dx}{\int_1^2 x^3\sqrt{1+9x^4}\,dx}$ $\bar{y} = \dfrac{\int_1^2 x^6\sqrt{1+9x^4}\,dx}{\int_1^2 x^3\sqrt{1+9x^4}\,dx}$

6. $\left(\dfrac{3R}{8}, \dfrac{3R}{8}, \dfrac{3R}{8}\right)$

7. $2/15$

8. a. $8/3$ b. $4/3$

9. $\dfrac{1}{12}\pi R^5$

10. $\left(0, 0, \dfrac{3}{8}\right)$

11. $\dfrac{3\pi}{32}R^4 H\delta$

12. $\bar{x} = \bar{y} = 0;\ \bar{z} = \dfrac{1}{4}H$

13. $M = \dfrac{1}{2}\int_{-\pi}^{\pi}\int_0^{1+\cos\theta} r^3 \sin 2\theta\,dr\,d\theta$

14. $M = \int_0^R \int_0^{2\pi} \int_0^{\pi} \rho^4 \sin\phi\,d\phi\,d\theta\,dr$

15. $\dfrac{2Gm\delta L}{h\sqrt{L^2+h^2}}$

16. $3/4$

17. $4/9$

18. $\dfrac{2}{5}MR^2$

19. $\dfrac{\pi H R^4}{2}$

20. $\dfrac{\pi R^4 H}{2}$

Chapter 14   Answers

21. $(0, \dfrac{2a}{\pi}, 0)$

22. $V = \int_0^3 \int_0^{3-x} \int_0^{3-x-y} dz\,dy\,dx$

23. $\rho = 2\cos\phi$

24. $2\pi m G \delta R h (h^2 + R^2)^{-3/2}$

25. A solid with vertical sides, bounded on top by the paraboloid $z = 1+x^2+y^2$ and bounded at the bottom by the x-y plane with $r = 1+\cos\theta$ representing the equation of the base.

26. The portion of a sphere of radius 1 in the first octant whose density at (ρ, θ, ϕ) is given by $(\rho\sin\phi)^2$

27. Circular lamina of radius 1 centered at $(1, 0)$

28. A solid bounded below by a sphere of radius 2 centered at the origin, and on the top by the cone with vertex at the origin whose equation is given by $\phi = \dfrac{\pi}{4}$

29. $\dfrac{2}{3}R$

30. $\dfrac{32R}{9\pi}$

31. $\dfrac{a}{3}[\sqrt{2} - \ln a + \ln(a+a\sqrt{2})]$

Section 14.8

1. $2a^2(\pi - 2)$

2. $\dfrac{\pi}{6}(17^{3/2} - 1)$

3. $\dfrac{\pi}{6}[(4a^2+1)^{3/2} - 1]$

4. $2\pi R h$

5. $\pi R\sqrt{R^2 + H^2}$

6. $\pi R\sqrt{R^2 + H^2}$

7. $\dfrac{32\pi}{5}$

8. $\int_0^1 \int_0^x \sqrt{1+x^2}\,dx\,dy = \dfrac{2\sqrt{2}-1}{3}$

9. $\int_0^1 \int_0^x \sqrt{2+4y^2}\,dx\,dy = \dfrac{3\sinh^{-1}2 + \sqrt{5}+1}{12}$

Chapter 14 Answers

10. $\int_{-\sqrt{2}}^{\sqrt{2}} \int_{-\sqrt{2-x^2}}^{\sqrt{2-x^2}} \sqrt{14}\, dy\, dx = \sqrt{56}\,\pi$

11. $\int_{-1}^{1} \int_{-\sqrt{1-x^2}}^{\sqrt{1-x^2}} \sqrt{1+4x^2+4y^2}\, dy\, dx = \dfrac{\pi(5\sqrt{5}-1)}{6}$

12. $2\pi a^2$

13. A torus of radius a with center on the x-y plane at a distance a from the origin.

Chapter 15

Sections 15.1, 15.2, and 15.3

1. $\dfrac{72}{5}$

2. Since $\dfrac{\partial}{\partial z}(2x^2 y) = 0 \ne xz = \dfrac{\partial}{\partial y}(xyz)$, there is no potential function $\phi(x,y,z)$ such that $\nabla\phi = \mathbf{F}$.

3. a. $\dfrac{\partial}{\partial y}(2xy) = 2x = \dfrac{\partial}{\partial x}(x^2)$ b. $f = x^2 y + C$

    c. 1

4. a. $\dfrac{\partial}{\partial y}(x^2+y^2) = 2y = \dfrac{\partial}{\partial x}(2xy)$ b. $f = \dfrac{x^3}{3} + y^2 x + C$

    c. 32/3

Sections 15.4, 15.5, 15.6, and 15.7

1. $\int_{0}^{1} \int_{0}^{x} x^2\, dy\, dx = \dfrac{1}{2}\oint_C \left(-x^2 y\, dx + \dfrac{x^3}{3}\, dy\right) = \dfrac{1}{4}$
where C is the contour given in the figure.

2. 8/3   3. $\dfrac{3}{4}\pi$ 4. $-2/3$

5. 0   6. $\dfrac{\pi}{4}$

Chapter 15 Answers

7. $g(x, y, z) = x^3yz + xe^y + z^3 + C$

8. πab

9. $\dfrac{3\pi}{2}$

10. $\dfrac{16}{15}$

11. 0

12. $\dfrac{13}{21}$

13. $5 - e$

14. $xe^y - y\sin x + C$

15. $16/3$

16. $1/6$

17. Since $\dfrac{\partial}{\partial y}(e^x - \cos y) \neq \dfrac{\partial}{\partial x}(e^y - x\sin y)$,
    G is not the gradient of a scalar potential.

18. $2\pi + 8\pi^2$

19. $\dfrac{2}{\sqrt{3}}$

20. 4π

21. 0

22. -45π

23. 0

24. $\iint \mathbf{F} \cdot \mathbf{n}\, ds$ over all six surfaces of the cube

$$= \int_0^1\int_0^1 1 \cdot y\, dz\, dy - \int_0^1\int_0^1 1 \cdot 0\, dz\, dy + \int_0^1\int_0^1 1 \cdot z\, dz\, dx$$

$$- \int_0^1\int_0^1 1 \cdot 0\, dz\, dx + \int_0^1\int_0^1 1 \cdot x\, dx\, dy - \int_0^1\int_0^1 1 \cdot 0\, dx\, dy$$

$$= 3/2$$

$$\iiint \text{div}\mathbf{F}\, dV = \int_0^1\int_0^1\int_0^1 (x+y+z)\, dx\, dy\, dz = 3/2$$

25. $\iiint_V \text{div}\mathbf{F}\, dV = \iiint_V 0 \cdot dV = 0$

$\mathbf{F} \cdot \mathbf{n} = z$, and by symmetry, $\iint_S z\, ds = 0$

26. $\iint_\sigma \mathbf{F} \cdot \mathbf{n}\, ds = \iint_\sigma (zx + x^2y + zy)\, ds$ since $\mathbf{n} = x\mathbf{i} + y\mathbf{j} + z\mathbf{k}$

$z = \cos\phi$, $x = \sin\phi\cos\theta$, $y = \sin\phi\sin\theta$

$ds = \sin\phi\, d\theta\, d\phi$, $0 \leq \theta \leq 2\pi$; $0 \leq \phi \leq \pi$

the integral equals $\int_0^\pi 0 \cdot d\phi = 0$.

Chapter 15   Answers

The triple integral equals 0 since div **F** = 0.

27. Curl **F** = $x\mathbf{j}$, **n** = $x\mathbf{i} + y\mathbf{j} + z\mathbf{k}$.

$$\iint_\sigma (\text{Curl } \mathbf{F}) \cdot \mathbf{n}\, ds = \iint_\sigma xy\, ds = \int_0^\pi \int_0^{2\pi} \sin^3\phi \sin\theta \cos\theta\, d\theta\, d\phi = \int_0^\pi 0 \cdot d\phi = 0$$

If C is the unit circle in the x-y plane and
r = $\cos t\, \mathbf{i} + \sin t\, \mathbf{j}$, $\int_C \mathbf{F} \cdot d\mathbf{r} = \int_C \mathbf{F} \cdot \frac{d\mathbf{r}}{dt}\, dt = \int_0^{2\pi} \sin t \cos t\, dt = 0$.

28. **F** = $xy\mathbf{i} + \mathbf{j} + z^2\mathbf{k}$.   div **F** = $y + 2z$

$$\iiint_V \text{div } \mathbf{F}\, dV = \int_0^2 \int_0^1 \int_{-\sqrt{1-y^2}}^{\sqrt{1-y^2}} (y + 2z)\, dx\, dy\, dz = 4\pi$$

$\iint_\sigma \mathbf{F} \cdot \mathbf{n}\, ds = \iint_{\sigma_1} + \iint_{\sigma_2} + \iint_{\sigma_3}$ where σ_1 is the top surface, σ_2 the bottom and σ_3 the side. On σ_1, **n** = **k** and $z = 2$; on σ_2, **n** = **k** and $z = 0$, on σ_3, **n** = $x\mathbf{i} + y\mathbf{j}$ and $x^2 + y^2 = 1$

$\iint_{\sigma_1} z^2\, ds = 4\iint ds = 4\pi$ $\iint_{\sigma_2} z^2\, ds = 0$, where

$\iint_{\sigma_3} y(x^2 + 1)\, ds = 2\int_0^{2\pi} \sin t(1 + \cos^2 t)\, dt = 0$, where

$x = \cos t$, $y = \sin t$ and $ds = 2\sqrt{\left(\frac{dx}{dt}\right)^2 + \left(\frac{dy}{dt}\right)^2}\, dt$

29. Since Curl **F** = 0, $\iint_\sigma (\text{Curl } \mathbf{F}) \cdot \mathbf{n}\, ds = 0$. And since **F** is perpendicular to the tangent vector at every point of the unit circle in the x-y plane, $\int_C \mathbf{F} \cdot d\mathbf{r} = 0$

30. $\iint_S z^2\, ds = \iint_S \mathbf{F} \cdot \mathbf{n}\, ds$ where **n** = $x\mathbf{i} + y\mathbf{j} + z\mathbf{k}$ and **F** = $z\mathbf{k}$. Then by the divergence theorem, $\iint_S z^2\, ds = \iiint_V \text{Div } \mathbf{F}\, dv = \iiint_V 1\, dv = \frac{4}{3}\pi$

Chapter 12 Answers

Additional Testing Material

1. 152.6 ft/s

2. Maximum of 2 at (0, 0), no minimum

3. $\mathbf{f}(t) = \langle r\cos t, r\sin t \rangle$
   $\mathbf{f}'(t) = \langle -r\sin t, r\cos t \rangle$

   $\mathbf{T}(t) = \dfrac{\mathbf{f}'(t)}{|\mathbf{f}'(t)|} = \langle -\sin t, \cos t \rangle$

   $\mathbf{T}'(t) = \langle -\cos t, -\sin t \rangle$

   Curvature $= \dfrac{|\mathbf{T}'(t)|}{|\mathbf{f}'(t)|} = \dfrac{1}{r}$

4. Maximum altitude $\dfrac{v_0^2 \sin^2 \alpha}{2g}$

   Distance $= \dfrac{2v_0^2 \sin\alpha \cos\alpha}{g}$

5. 84 minutes

6. a. Maximum at (2, 0) and (−2, 0)
   b. Minimum at (0, 1) and (0, −1)

7. $\left(-\dfrac{1}{2}\ln 2, \dfrac{1}{\sqrt{2}} \right)$

8. 2

9. Maximum at $\left(\dfrac{-}{\sqrt{2}}, -\dfrac{1}{2}\ln 2 \right)$. No Minimum.

10. (0, 0)

225